The Economics of Poverty

The Economics of Poverty

History, Measurement, and Policy

MARTIN RAVALLION

Georgetown University

OXFORD
UNIVERSITY PRESS

OXFORD
UNIVERSITY PRESS

Oxford University Press is a department of the University of Oxford. It furthers the University's objective of excellence in research, scholarship, and education by publishing worldwide. Oxford is a registered trade mark of Oxford University Press in the UK and in certain other countries

Published in the United States of America by Oxford University Press
198 Madison Avenue, New York, NY 10016, United States of America

Cataloging-in-Publication data is on file at the Library of Congress

9780190212766 (hbk.)
9780190212773 (pbk.)

In 1980 two students at the LSE met
and started talking about the economics of poverty.
For Dominique, with love.

CONTENTS

LIST OF BOXES

LIST OF FIGURES

LIST OF TABLES

PREFACE

The distinguished economic historian Max Hartwell (1972, 3) once wrote that "economics is, in essence, the study of poverty." And the distinguished agricultural economist (and Nobel Laureate) Theodore Schultz (1981, 3) once wrote that "most people in the world are poor. If we knew the economy of being poor, we would know much of the economics that really matters." Alas, these views are not consistent with how most people see economics today. A popular perception is that economics is the study of national income, such as measured by Gross Domestic Product (GDP). While many students of economics today will at some point learn something about why some countries have lower GDP per capita than others, the distribution of income is not commonly seen as the primary focus of economics.

The teaching of economics seems to have become strangely divorced from its applications to real-world problems such as poverty. I say "strangely" for two reasons; first, in my experience, many students are drawn to economics by their hope of understanding such problems, and, second, there are grounds for that hope since economics contains useful insights into important real-world problems such as poverty. I grant that one often finds discussions of the applications of economics to real-world problems in today's textbooks. But it would be fair to say that they are more peripheral than central and often quite superficial.

This book is offered as a corrective. Here the application is taken to be the central motivation for learning economics. The present application is to understanding poverty and the various policy debates about how best to reduce poverty. This is clearly a major issue for developing countries today, but it is also relevant to today's rich world, especially those countries where high and rising inequality is choking off the potential for equitable growth. The application is thus global in relevance. It also has an important historical dimension given that today's rich world was once as poor as today's poor world. How that change happened is an important development question in its own right.

The book aims to span a broad audience, including both economists who are interested in learning about poverty and (as yet) non-economists who are interested in learning about economics as a tool for understanding and fighting poverty. In short, the book aims to be both an introduction to economics—albeit an introduction that is anchored on one important application—and an introduction to the study of poverty and inequality for economists and others who already know some economics but (for the same reason I wrote this book) missed out learning much about poverty and inequality.

You could say I have been working on this book for over thirty years, since I started studying poverty as an economist in the early 1980s. But I only decided to write this book in 2013, when I returned to teaching, at Georgetown University, after twenty-four years at the World Bank. It was plain to me that the existing literature was deficient from the point of view of the needs of two distinct groups of people. The first are current students of economics. The book has served as the textbook for a one-semester undergraduate course in economics, *ECON 156: Poverty*. Although economics was not a strictly enforced prerequisite, virtually all the students had previously done a one-year course in economic principles (macro and micro) and probably half were expecting to move on to intermediate and more advanced economics.

In writing the book, I have also kept in mind the needs of a second group of people. These are more advanced students and professionals, such as researchers and those in government or international organizations. This group already knows some economics, but has had little exposure to its application to understanding poverty and inequality, and is looking for guidance, including for further reading. I have used much of the material in this book as background reading for graduate-level courses at Georgetown University and the Paris School of Economics. And I have taught often on this topic in regular training programs and special lectures for practitioners including staff at the World Bank.

Embracing both audiences calls for a differentiated approach and selectivity on the part of readers. One hundred thirty boxes are inserted into the text along the way to explain the economics to non-economists. (I faced a few hard choices about where to introduce some of the boxes, as there was more than one possibility.) Readers will naturally be selective; trained economists will skip some material plainly designed for non-economists. Some of the boxes are labeled as being somewhat harder, as indicated by an *. Calculus is not required, although some of the boxes assume familiarity with simple linear algebra. Intermediate high-school math should be ample even for the harder boxes.

The boxes try to build up the reader's knowledge of economics, as relevant to poverty, but this does not happen as smoothly as in a conventional economics textbook, since here the text is organized around the topic of poverty not economics per se. I cite many sources and suggestions for further reading along the way to help guide those readers who want to go into greater depth. Ample cross-referencing is provided. For those using this as a textbook, exercises for each chapter are available from http://explore.georgetown.edu/people/mr1185/.

There are many people to thank. I had not planned to write this book prior to joining the faculty of Georgetown University, which proved to be an ideal environment for the purpose, given the combination of scholarship with a deep and longstanding commitment to fighting poverty. The task has benefited from the support of Edmond D. Villani who kindly endowed my chair at Georgetown. As head of the economics department, Francis Vella persuaded me that there was demand for an undergraduate course on poverty. Designing and teaching the Georgetown course led me to write this book. Along the way I have benefited from the feedback of students doing that course, for which this is the sole textbook. All the students of the course had drafts of the book chapters to be discussed in class. I have forgotten some names, but I thank explicitly (in alphabetic order) Taemin Ahn, Tamim Alnuweiri, Brian Bontempo, Kevin Chen, Owen Coffin, Deep Dheri, Isabel Echart, John Flynn, Anna Frenzilli, Geeva Gopalkrishnan, Laura Grannemann, Berk Guler, Will Hilkert, Joshua Lightburn, Atul Menon, Taylor Mielnicki, Clare Murphy, Milan Patel, Neshal Patel, Alexander ("Elizabeth") Rich, Ben Saunders, Morgan Snow, and Matt Walters. Clare was especially good at identifying hard bits that needed work in the draft chapters and Elizabeth and Taylor also read the near-final draft after the course and provided many helpful comments. Cait Brown was the head Teaching Assistant for the first two offerings of ECON 156 and her continual efforts have helped make the book better, especially as a teaching tool. Other students who kindly read much of the book near its completion were Bledi Celiku, Mathew Kline, Naz Koont, and Isabelle van de Walle.

The book draws on research I have done on the economics of poverty spanning thirty years. I have had the benefit of many outstanding research collaborators on the topic, including (in alphabetic order) Arthur Alik Lagrange, Sudhir Anand, Kaushik Basu, Kathleen Beegle, Alok Bhargava, Benu Bidani, Michael Bruno, Shubham Chaudhuri, Shaohua Chen, Gaurav Datt, Lorraine Dearden, Toan Do, Puja Dutta, Chico Ferreira, Emanuela Galasso, Madhur Gautam, Kristen Himelein, Monica Huppi, Jyotsna Jalan, Anton Korinek, Sylvie Lambert, Peter Lanjouw, Michael Lipton, Michael Lokshin, Alice Mesnard, Johan Mistaen, Jose Montalvo, Ren Mu, Rinku Murgai, Menno Pradhan, Prem Sangraula, Binayak Sen, Lyn Squire, Dominique van de Walle, and Quentin Wodon.

An important overall acknowledgment must go to many past colleagues at the World Bank, where I worked for twenty-four years. The interactions (including debates) over many years with Bank colleagues were especially important in helping me link the (often rather abstract) economic foundations of antipoverty policy to the realities of development practice. There are far too many names to mention all here, but (in addition to the Bank co-researchers mentioned above) among past World Bank colleagues who have helped shape my thinking I am especially grateful to Francois Bourguignon, Shanta Devarajan, David Dollar, Gershon Feder, Jeff Hammer, Manny Jimenez, Ravi Kanbur, Beth King, Aart Kraay, Justin Lin, Will Martin, Aaditya Mattoo, Lant Pritchett, Biju Rao, Shlomo Reutlinger, Luis Serven, Nick Stern, Adam Wagstaff, and Mike Walton.

Parts One and Three draw in part on a chapter I wrote, "The Idea of Antipoverty Policy," for the *Handbook of Income Distribution*, edited by Tony Atkinson and Francois Bourguignon (Ravallion 2014a). The chapter had to be very substantially rewritten for the book's broader audience and the book is far more comprehensive, developing the arguments much further in a number of areas—as a result it is five times the length of the chapter. But the debt to the *Handbook* chapter is acknowledged. Since the book benefited from their comments on the chapter, it is fitting I repeat my thanks to those who commented, namely Robert Allen, Tony Atkinson, Pranab Bardhan, Francois Bourguignon, Denis Cogneau, Jean-Yves Duclos, Sam Fleischacker, Pedro Gete, Karla Hoff, Ravi Kanbur, Charles Kenny, Sylvie Lambert, Philipp Lepenies, Peter Lindert, Michael Lipton, Will Martin, Alice Mesnard, Branko Milanovic, Johan Mistaen, Berk Ozler, Thomas Pogge, Gilles Postel-Vinay, Henry Richardson, John Roemer, John Rust, Agnar Sandmo, Amartya Sen, and Dominique van de Walle.

The book also benefited from comments on drafts of various chapters from selected specialists who I approached, namely Harold Alderman, Kaushik Basu, James Boyce, Jaime De Melo, Deon Filmer, Jed Friedman, Garance Genicot, John Hoddinott, Aart Kraay, Michael Lipton, Alice Mesnard, Annamaria Milazzo, Mead Over, Berk Ozler, Thomas Piketty, Steven Radelet, Lyn Squire, Adam Wagstaff, Dominique van de Walle, and Nicolas van de Walle.

I also thank participants at presentations at Georgetown, the World Bank, the International Monetary Fund, the Midwest International Economic Development Conference at the University of Wisconsin–Madison, the University of Technology Sydney, the Paris School of Economics, Oxford University, Sussex University, the London School of Economics, Lancaster University, the Indian Economics Association, the Australasian Meetings of the Econometrics Society, the Canadian Economics Association, the International Association for Research on Income and Wealth, the Society for the Study of Economic Inequality, the 12th Nordic Conference on Development Economics, the 2014 Spring Meeting of Young Economists, Vienna, Centro Studi Luca d'Agliano at the Fondazione Luigi Einaudi, Turin, the World Institute for Development Economics Research, Helsinki and the Australasian Development Economics Workshop at Monash University, Melbourne.

Scott Parris, Economics Editor for Oxford University Press, provided encouragement and comments from the outset and Cathryn Vaulman at OUP ably guided me and the manuscript through the publication process. The book also benefited from the comments of OUP's five anonymous reviewers.

M.R.

ABBREVIATIONS

ADB	Asian Development Bank
AFDC	Aid to Families with Dependent Children
ATET	average treatment effect on the treated
BIG	basic income guarantee
BM	Bourguignon and Morrisson
BMI	body mass index
BMR	basal metabolic rate
BOT	balance of trade
BPL	below poverty line
BPS	Biro Pusat Statistik
BR	Bidani and Ravallion
BRAC	Bangladesh Rural Advancement Committee
BWR	benefit withdrawal rate
CBN	cost of basic needs
CBR	crude birth rate
CCT	conditional cash transfer
CDF	cumulative distribution function
CDR	crude death rate
CGD	Center for Global Development
CGE	computable general equilibrium
COL	cost of living
CPI	consumer price index
CRS	constant returns to scale
DD	difference-in-difference
DFID	Department for International Development, United Kingdom
DHS	Demographic and Health Survey
ECD	early childhood development
EECA	Eastern Europe and Central Asia
EGS	Employment Guarantee Scheme
EITC	earned income tax credit
ELQ	economic ladder question
FAO	Food and Agricultural Organization
FATF	Financial Action Task Force

FEI	food-energy intake
FFE	food for education
FGT	Foster, Greer, and Thorbecke
FHH	female-headed household
FOD	first order dominance
GB	Grameen Bank
GDP	gross domestic product
GIC	growth incidence curve
GLC	generalized Lorenz curve
GTAP	Global Trade Analysis Project
HDI	human development index
HDR	Human Development Report
HIC	high-income country
HT	Harris and Todaro
I2D2	International Income Distribution Database
ICP	International Comparison Program
IFAD	International Fund for Agricultural Development
IFI	international financial institution
IFPRI	International Food Policy Research Institute
IMF	International Monetary Fund
IMR	infant mortality rate
INOPP	inequality of opportunity
ITT	intent to treat
IV	instrumental variable
LAC	Latin America and the Caribbean
LIC	low-income county
LSE	London School of Economics
LSMS	Living Standards Measurement Study
LTP	Lewis turning point
MB	marginal benefit
MC	marginal cost
MDG	Millennium Development Goals
MENA	Middle East and North Africa
MIQ	minimum income question
MLD	mean log deviation
MMU	money metric utility
MPC	marginal propensity to consume
MPI	multidimensional poverty index
MPK	marginal product of capital
MPL	marginal product of labor
MRS	marginal rate of substitution
MTR	marginal tax rate
NGO	nongovernmental organization
NIT	Negative Income Tax
NLMS	National Longitudinal Mortality Study
NPL	New Poor Laws

NREGS	National Rural Employment Guarantee Scheme
NSS	National Sample Survey
OECD	Organization for Economic Cooperation and Development
OLS	ordinary least squares
OPL	Old Poor Laws
OPM	official poverty measure
PA	poverty assessment
PDC	poverty deficit curve
PIC	poverty incidence curve
PIT	poor institutions trap
PMT	proxy means test
PPP	purchasing power parity
PSU	primary sampling unit
PV	present value
RCT	randomized control trial
SDG	Sustainable Development Goals
SNAP	Supplemental Nutrition Assistance Program
SOD	second order dominance
SPM	supplemental poverty measure
SSA	sub-Saharan Africa
SSN	social safety net
SSPL	social subjective poverty line
SUTVA	stable unit treatment value assumption
SWF	social welfare function
TA	Technical assistance
TD	targeting differential
TFP	total factor productivity
TFR	total fertility rate
TOD	third order dominance
UB	unemployment benefits
UK	United Kingdom
US	United States of America
USAID	United States Agency for International Development
WDR	World Development Report
WGI	World Governance Indicators
WHO	World Health Organization
WTO	World Trade Organization

NOTATION

C	Consumption
CI	concentration index
C^F	consumption of food
ES	equivalence scale
$F(y)$	cumulative distribution function
G	Gini index
H	headcount index
K	Capital
L	Labor
$L(p)$	Lorenz curve
m	number of goods
M	mean
n	population size
N	household size
$\underline{N}$	demographics (numbers of people by type)
N^i	number or share of people/workers in sector i
NS	normalized share
p	percentile
P	prices
PG	poverty gap index
q	quantities consumed
r	rate of interest or correlation coefficient
s	savings rate
S	share of spending (or share of transfers)
se	standard error
SPG	squared poverty gap index
TD	targeting differential
u	utility
w	wealth
W	welfare or wage rate
W^i	wage rate in sector i
WI	Watts index
Y	income or output

X characteristics of a person or household

y real income

Z poverty line

Note: When there is any chance of ambiguity a full stop (.) is used to denote the product of two variables.

The Economics of Poverty

Introduction

An economy exists to guide production choices so as to serve peoples' consumption needs. We judge an economy's success by how well it does this. One way to organize the economy is to let a central planner decide what is to be produced and how commodities are to be allocated. In principle this could work well, but it has proved very difficult in practice. The alternative is to rely on a market mechanism, whereby the choices are decentralized and guided by prices. From the late eighteenth century, it started to be understood that free markets could efficiently guide production to serve consumer demands. This way of organizing an economy became dominant over the following two hundred years.

The market mechanism is a clever way of solving the basic problem of tailoring supply to demand without the aid of a central planner. However, even the best functioning market mechanism can hardly be expected to address the needs of poor people well, who (by definition) have little purchasing power over commodities, and the market will naturally tend to channel commodities to those with the buying power. The distribution of that power is plainly very unequal, although more so in some places and times than others. When the market mechanism is combined with an insistence on respecting the initial assignment of property rights (backed up by the government through the legal and judicial system), the outcomes may be judged to be excessively inequitable.

Persistent poverty should not then be a surprise even to the staunchest defenders of free markets. Realizing this, there have been various efforts to try to steer the market economy toward preferred allocations, with less poverty. The idea is to keep the advantages of the market mechanism in tailoring supply to demand but to try to shift its allocations in more equitable ways. This has long been a primary motive for governmental interventions of one sort or another. The means of doing so have involved both efforts to influence the pre-market distribution and to influence how markets operate given that distribution.

The choices that are decentralized in a market economy include those relevant to production and allocation over time as well as at one date. Success in this dynamic allocative task has been uneven over time, and market economies guided by governments have proved vulnerable to periodic shocks, often internally generated. Nonetheless, with varying degrees of success, this mode of economic organization has also delivered overall economic growth—a sizable expansion in the set of commodities available for consumption. But the question remains: whose consumption needs have been served by the growth process?

Looking back over those two hundred years, the number of people living in extreme poverty has not fallen much, but the number represents a much smaller proportion of the world's population. In 1820, roughly 80% of people lived in material conditions that appear to have been reasonably similar to those of the poorest 20% today. Progress has been uneven over time and space. Extreme poverty has become concentrated in what is called today the "developing world." As best as can be determined from the data, the incidence of absolute poverty—as judged by a poverty line aiming to have constant purchasing power—two hundred years ago in what is today's rich world was no lower than in today's poor world. Yet today almost nobody in the rich world lives in "poverty," as defined in today's poor world.

However, while the world has made progress against poverty over the last two centuries, continuing progress is far from assured. High and rising inequality has stalled that progress in some parts of the world, including the United States. And we are seeing generally rising relative poverty in the rich world as a whole over recent decades.

Since the turn of the current century, there have been some encouraging signs of acceleration in progress against extreme poverty in the developing world. Indeed, globally since 2000, we have seen falling numbers of poor people, as judged by a frugal absolute standard, although we also see persistent pockets of poverty in most places. At the same time, we have seen rising numbers of relatively poor people in the developing world and possibly greater vulnerability to risk than ever before. Some long-standing development challenges remain, while new challenges have emerged, especially in assuring equitable growth, which is now a common challenge for both the rich and poor worlds.

We face the choice between two paths going forward. One path has effective policies in place to assure continuing success in reducing poverty globally. That path will come close to eliminating at least the worst forms of poverty that have been with us for millennia within a generation, and it would put a break on rising relative poverty. The other path will see high and rising inequality choking off the gains to poor people from aggregate economic growth, and choking off some of that growth too. On this second path, the number of very poor people in the world will show little decline, and the numbers of the relatively poor will rise markedly. Many challenges are faced in getting us onto the first path, and staying there.

This book aims to provide an accessible synthesis of knowledge relevant to answering three questions that are key to meeting those challenges: How much poverty is there? Why does poverty exist? What can be done to eliminate poverty?

How Much Poverty Is There?

Measuring poverty is one of the oldest topics in applied economics—dating back to a time before the field "economics" was even recognized. The challenges in measuring poverty are not fundamentally different from other issues of economic measurement, which means that the task shares pretty much all of the same conceptual and empirical problems. One difference is that measuring poverty has not just been seen as a task for economists. The interest that the topic attracts among non-economists has brought some important insights, but it has also seen some measurement practices that most economists find questionable. About one-quarter of these pages is devoted to understanding the measurement issues, both conceptual issues and more practical issues.

The best available economic measurements indicate that around 2010, the poorest 20% or so of the world's population—about 1.2 billion people—had a mean consumption of goods and services that was barely 10% of the global mean, and 0.5% of the mean of the top 1% of income receivers. (And that 0.5% is almost certainly an overestimate given the likely biases in the data available.) One might not be so concerned about such large relative disparities in levels of living if the poorest group lived tolerably well. But they do not. The poorest 20% cannot afford what someone in America could buy in 2005 for $1.25 a person per day, or about $1.50 at the time of writing (2014). While many people can (and do) survive on so little, nobody can deny that it is a truly frugal level of living. And a large number of people live just above this line; in addition to the 1.2 billion living below $1.25 a day, the same number again were living between $1.25 and $2.00 a day in 2010. And alongside this extreme, absolute, poverty there is equally striking relative poverty everywhere, including in the developing world as well as in the rich world. Almost three billion people in the world as a whole either live below $1.25 a day or live in what is considered poverty by typical standards of the country they live in.

Underlying these stark numbers, there is a vast loss of human freedom and potential, stemming from the constraints imposed on people by their lack of command over basic commodities. With poverty, schooling is curtailed, health often suffers, and life expectancy is diminished. Low nutritional intakes and poor diets reduce work effort and (for children) bring irreparable losses of ability and productivity in later years. On top of the health and income risks, violence and the fear of violence are everyday facts of life. Poor women are especially vulnerable. And there is a haunting powerlessness to change all this—to reach for a better life—since the lost freedoms associated with poverty often include the ability to influence the non-economic (political and social) processes that bear on those freedoms.

The vast bulk of absolute poverty in the world today is found in developing countries. Possibly more surprising is that (as we will see later) more relative poverty is now found in those countries than in the "rich world." So, applying Hartwell's (1972) definition of economics as the study of poverty, one might argue that the subject must be mainly about the developing world, in marked contrast to what one finds in modern textbooks on economic principles. One could argue that a book such as this would be justified in focusing solely on today's developing world. However, the book strives to take a more global perspective on poverty, drawing on the experience of today's rich world. This is justified on a number of counts. For one thing, there is still a lot of relative poverty in the rich world. For another, the success of today's rich world against absolute poverty contains valuable lessons for today's poor world. Economists and students of economics, including those focusing solely on economic development, can learn much by studying how the body of philosophical and economic thinking that was so deeply rooted in Western Europe, Britain, and North America has evolved since the time that those parts of the world were a lot poorer than they are today.

Why Does Poverty Exist?

One influential school of thought has looked for an answer to this question in the actions taken by poor people themselves. Efforts to blame poverty on the behaviors of poor men and women are long-standing, and survive today. Poverty is attributed to the preferences of poor people—that they are lazy or imprudent or unwilling to take risks—or to past mistakes they have made. In a famous conversation, F. Scott Fitzgerald is claimed to have said that "the rich are different from you and me" to which Ernest Hemingway replied, "Yes, they have more money."[1] Fitzgerald's view can be interpreted as ascribing poverty to differences in the characteristics of people; by contrast, Hemingway's view of the difference implicitly steers us to look more deeply into the constraints that people face in their lives, stemming from how markets and institutions work in distributing incomes.

There can be no surprise that poor people behave differently; the income effect on their decisions is obvious enough. There have been claims of the reverse causation—that poverty is caused by "bad behaviors"—going back centuries. Blaming poor people for poverty has long provided a justification for public inaction against poverty. The implication was drawn that any direct efforts to help poor people are not called for and may even be counterproductive—that such actions simply encourage the same behaviors that create poverty. Some of those who agree that the behaviors of poor men and women are at fault do allow ethical qualifications; for example, that children cannot be blamed for their parent's bad behaviors. Some also recognize that poverty generates costs to non-poor people, such as crime, disease, or the hassles of too many beggars. Such costs may justify antipoverty policies. Indeed, this was essentially the approach of one of the first scholars to outline an antipoverty policy, namely Jean Luis Vives, writing in the early sixteenth century; Vives is also regarded as a founding father of modern psychology.

Economics goes more deeply into understanding how behavior is influenced by economic and (increasingly) social factors that also create poverty. Instead of blaming poor people for their poverty, economics points to the constraints poor men and women face, and how these relate to the deficiencies of prevailing institutions, markets, and governments. Much of this book is devoted to understanding how those constraints are generated and how they might be relaxed. This brings in all areas of economics, from macro to micro, from theory to empirics, from poor countries to rich countries.

What Can Be Done to Eliminate Poverty?

A distinctive feature of economics is its close relationship to policy, and policies related to poverty have been central to that relationship. One of the earliest economists was Kautilya around 300 B.C. in what is now called India. The title of Kautilya's major work

---

[1] It is not certain that this famous exchange ever happened, although it can be considered a simplification of the more likely story, as described in Keyes (2006).

(*Arthashastra* in Sanskrit) can be translated as *The Science of Material Gain*.[2] Kautilya's span of policy advice included policies for addressing the social costs of shocks by providing employment on government-sponsored public works schemes—also interpretable as an early form of Keynesian stabilization. Such social protection policies addressing shocks and crises have had a long history. Their motivation has been in part to assure the stability of the regime—that is clearly what motivated Kautilya's policy advice. Some policies have tried to incentivize better behaviors, by applying conditions to poor relief, such as insisting that recipients work or go to school. In modern times, dating from the nineteenth century, other antipoverty policies have emerged that operate on the constraints facing poor men and women, including making markets and other institutions work better.

It is widely accepted today that eliminating poverty is a legitimate goal of public action, for which governments (in both rich and poor countries) take some responsibility. The ethical motivation for giving priority to poor people can be thought of as combining concerns for two key economic concepts: equity and efficiency. There is an implicit desire to reduce inequality, but not by bringing everyone down to the level of the poorest person, which would increase poverty. Instead, the prioritization given to fighting poverty can be called "maximin"—a view that equity should be addressed by helping the poor (i.e., maximizing the welfare of the most disadvantaged group in society). Some form of the maximin idea is found in many theories of distributive justice.

Views about how best to fight poverty have evolved over many centuries. A long-standing view saw the solution to poverty as changing individual behavior—either by weaning poor people off their bad behaviors, as discussed above, or by encouraging greater generosity by rich people. The modern view put greater weight on the performance of institutions, including the role of governments. The idea of a public responsibility for poverty, beyond protection from severe downside risk, had very little support two hundred years ago, or even one hundred years ago. Today that role is widely (though certainly not universally) accepted. Over time, the domain over which the public responsibility for poverty is defined has stretched progressively from the most local community to the world as a whole. The policy responses in attempting to eliminate poverty include both direct interventions, as are often put under the heading of "social policies," and various economy-wide and global policies—overall policies for economic development that have bearing on the extent of poverty. The term "antipoverty policy" in this book embraces both sets of policies.

The relationship between economic thinking and policymaking has rarely been either as tight or as meritorious as one might have hoped. While knowledge about the realities of poverty has often informed policymaking, misinformation and exaggerated ideological arguments based on little more than anecdotes have also had influence and continue to do so. The story of thinking about poverty is also a story of many economic ideas that came to be widely believed and have much influence on policy, but are either of unknown veracity or demonstrably wrong. If there is hope today that this

---

[2] There are other translations that have been suggested, including "Science of Polity" and "Science of Political Economy." The *Wikipedia* site on the *Arthashastra* provides other examples and references.

has changed for the better, that hope lies in open public debate. By informing such debates in an unbiased way, economics can help fight poverty in the world.

The history of thought provides examples of popular beliefs about poverty that have often persisted and carried policy weight well beyond what their intellectual foundations can support. Examples include that poor men and women are lazy, that they are irrational, that poverty in the world is primarily urban-based, that poor people are invariably bad farmers or entrepreneurs, and (the biggest myth of all) that they are not really poor at all. Better knowledge from (qualitative and quantitative) observations by economists, statisticians, and others has often challenged such beliefs. While false beliefs will not presumably last forever, they can last long enough to serve the benefiting interests well, and it is not often the case that those interests include poor people. The tools of economic analysis can help fight poverty by debunking myths. This rarely guarantees good policies, but it does make for better informed debates, and this has led to better policies at many times in history.

The book's approach to policy is grounded in the normative school of economics that emerged out of moral philosophy, starting in the late eighteenth century. This was developed over a long period to eventually take the form of modern public economics. In the spirit of this approach, the policy analytics here is built on an explicit formulation of social welfare objectives, although it does not define social welfare in the traditional utilitarian way that weights all levels of well-being equally. Reducing "poverty"—by some reasonable definition—is seen here as an ethically defensible goal for public action; indeed, it may be considered the overarching goal in certain domains of policymaking, including in promoting economic development in poor countries.

Some economists have been shy in making ethical judgments about whose interests are to be served by policies (preferring instead to stick to purely positive formulations). However, in truth, economic analysis in practice has rarely been value-free, and has often served specific class interests, though often not the interests of poor people. The history of thought on poverty teaches us that economic thinking has at times provided intellectual rationalizations for policies, or lack of public action, that advance the interests of powerful (typically non-poor) groups. (For example, opponents of antipoverty policies have often been motivated by their concern that such policies would reduce the supply of labor, and so push up wage rates at the expense of profits.) This too is normative analysis (though sometimes that fact is hidden), but with a very different weighting of the interests served by policy.

Road Map

It is not assumed that readers know economics already. Those new to the subject get a lot of help along the way in understanding its concepts and methods. Economics lives through its relevance to real-world problems, and here the problem of global poverty is both the central focus and a vehicle for learning.

The book is in three parts. Part One traces out the history of thought from mercantilist views on the inevitability of poverty through two main stages of "poverty enlightenment," out of which poverty came to be seen as a social bad capable of being greatly reduced and even eliminated.

Part Two looks more closely at measurement and methodological issues. The key concepts are explained, including the various (often ongoing) debates about how best to assess well-being and measure poverty and inequality. Here some of the material is more technical in nature. However, readers who only want to understand the basic elements of prevailing measurement practices can skip the more technical material.

Part Three turns to the main policy debates about how best to fight poverty. After reviewing what we know about the dimensions of poverty and inequality in the world today, readers learn about the theories and evidence concerning the distribution of the benefits from economic growth and the sources of that growth. The discussion then turns to the main economy-wide and sectoral policies, as well as the interventions that are targeted directly at poor people.

The final chapter draws together lessons from all three parts on the challenges to be faced if poverty is finally to be eliminated and rising inequality is to be avoided.

While the book follows a (hopefully) clear logical path through its three parts, it is unrealistic to expect all readers to follow a simple linear progression. Each chapter tries to be reasonably self-contained, although that will depend in part on the reader's prior knowledge. (Those new to economics may need to refer back to referenced boxes in earlier chapters.) For the undergraduate course at Georgetown I do a shorter version of Part Two, skipping chapter 5 after section 5.3 and chapter 6, and I do not cover any of the * boxes. The following table provides a guide for specialized readers.

Type of Specialized Reader	Suggested Reading Strategy
You want an introduction to the economics of poverty. You either know general economics to at least intermediate level or you do not feel the need for a deeper understanding.	Read the text, largely ignoring the boxes.
As above, but you are mainly interested in policy.	As above, but you can skip Part Two.
You want to learn economics but with a focus on the more "micro" side of poverty analysis, especially measurement and evaluation.	Parts One and Two and chapter 10 in Part Three.
As above, but you only want to learn the "macro" side of poverty analysis.	Parts One and Three, although you can skip chapter 10.

PART ONE

HISTORY OF THOUGHT

The poor . . . are like the shadows in a painting: they provide the necessary contrast.
—Philippe Hecquet, 1740, quoted in Roche 1987, 64

Everyone but an idiot knows that the lower classes must be kept poor or they will never be industrious.
—Arthur Young, 1771, quoted in Furniss 1920, 118

May we not outgrow the belief that poverty is necessary?
—Alfred Marshall 1890, 2

This administration today, here and now, declares unconditional war on poverty in America. I urge this Congress and all Americans to join with me in that effort.
—Lyndon B. Johnson's State of the Union Address, January 1964

Our dream is a world free of poverty.
—Motto of the World Bank since 1990

Past writings on poverty have sometimes aimed to excuse poverty rather than explain or eradicate it. The language used to describe poor people has often been biased toward justifying the privileges of those more fortunate. Metaphors and questionable behavioral stereotypes have played a role and have influenced policymaking. However, it is also striking how much mainstream thinking about poverty has changed over the last two hundred years, as exemplified by the sequence of quotes above.

This part of the book tries to describe and understand this transition in views on poverty. The discussion traces out the history of thought from premodern times through two main stages of "poverty enlightenment," out of which poverty came to be seen as a social bad capable of being greatly reduced and even eliminated through public action. This transition in thinking about poverty came alongside significant political and economic reforms in today's rich world; the spread of suffrage was a notable example of the former, and the spread of free-markets exemplified the latter. Chapter 1 focuses on the history up to modern times, which are then the focus of chapter 2. Both chapters start with an overview of the historical record on progress against extreme poverty in the world.

1

Origins of the Idea of a World Free of Poverty

While it cannot be said that past scholarly writings on poverty have always ben- efited poor people, it is notable how formative the topic of poverty has been in many areas of modern scholarship. Early research on poverty, or issues closely related to it, provided starting points for modern psychology (notably in the aforementioned writings of Jean Luis Vives in the early sixteenth century), epidemiology (such as in Dr. John Snow's pioneering investigations of the causes of the cholera epidemics in early nineteenth-century London), household economics (such as Ernst Engel's studies of the differences in spending behavior between poor and non-poor people in Germany in the mid-nineteenth century), social science (such as Charles Booth's careful observational studies of poverty in London in the late nineteenth century), macroeconomics (notably in John Maynard Keynes's efforts to understand the causes of mass unemployment that emerged in the Great Depression of the early 1930s), and, of course, development economics (many examples to follow). Poverty scholars have often played an important role over the last two hundred years in establish- ing the moral and economic case for antipoverty policies and in helping to establish empirical foundations for such policies—and at times debunking some of the myths about poor people that were perpetuated by opponents of such policies. And, as we will see in this book, economists have often had something important to say about such policies.

The interrelationship between scholarship and action is complex, and what emerges in the policy arena depends on many things, including technology, pub- lic awareness, and balances of power. Nonetheless, there is a story to be told about how thinking about poverty has evolved. This helps us understand prevailing debates today. Some of those debates have been going on for ages. But one is also struck by some of the differences in thinking. Recognizing these differences teaches us that the progress of knowledge reinforces and reflects progress more broadly.

This first chapter documents both the similarities and the transitions in thinking about poverty and policy up to the mid-twentieth century. This is not a comprehen- sive history of thought about poverty. Instead, the focus is on thinking about the economics of poverty and implications for antipoverty policy.

1.1 Progress against Absolute Poverty
over the Last Two Hundred Years

There was a great deal of poverty in the world two hundred years ago. Some descriptions of the living conditions for poor people can be found in novels and travel stories written at the time.[1] But just how prevalent was poverty? This requires some statistical detective work.

Gross Domestic Product (GDP) per capita is the most widely used measure of the average income of a population (box 1.1). Based on a great deal of careful data work, and a fair number of guesses, Angus Maddison (1995) estimated world GDP per capita back to 1820. However, GDP tells us nothing about how incomes are distributed within society—the extent of income inequality. The extent of poverty will depend on both aggregate income and its distribution (a relationship that we will come to understand better in Part Two). By combining Maddison's estimate with the data available on the distribution of income, Francois Bourguignon and Christian Morrisson (2002) have estimated that 84% of the world's population in 1820 lived in what they term "extreme poverty."

Box 1.1 Gross Domestic Product

When people talk about a "low-income country" or "economic growth" they are almost always referring to the level or the changes in GDP, typically normalized by population size. GDP is the total market value of the flow of all commodities (goods and services) produced by the specific economy over a given time period, usually one year. Only commodities used for final consumption or investment are included, to avoid double counting; "intermediate products" are left out. Prevailing prices are used for aggregation; a "price" is just the rate at which money can be exchanged for commodities.

GDP has a number of limitations as a measure of economic progress. There are concerns about how well it is measured (notably the things that are typically left out, such as production within the home). There are concerns that (even if measured well) it reveals little about how the benefits of growth are distributed in society or about the attendant environmental costs. Chapter 8 discusses GDP in more detail.

Historical note: Simon Kuznets is credited with inventing the concept of GDP, in a report to the US Congress in the 1930s. He was well aware of the problems in calculating GDP and noted that:

> the clear and unequivocal character of such estimates [of GDP] is deceptive. Theoretical problems arise in defining the area of "nation"; in the choice of stage in the circulation of commodities and services at which

---

[1] A well-known source of examples is Arthur Young's travelogue from rural France in 1787–1789, in which he described (for example) that women and children of tenant farmers did not possess shoes; see Young (1792, 18).

income is to be segregated and measured; in the inclusion, exclusion and basis of evaluation of various commodities and services that are to be added into the national total. Finally, variations among estimates may arise from differences in the types of statistical data used and methods employed. (Kuznets 1933, 5)

Kuznets was awarded the Nobel prize for economics in 1971. In England, James Meade and Richard Stone developed National Accounts to provide breakdowns of GDP during World War II. These tools became widely used across the globe soon after World War II. (Meade and Stone won Nobel prizes in 1977 and 1984 respectively.)

Bourguignon and Morrisson (BM) aimed to assure that their poverty line had constant real value over time. This is difficult given the deficiencies of data, which tend to increase as one goes back in time. BM anchored their poverty line to accord with a previously estimated poverty rate for 1992 using a line of $1 a day at 1985 purchasing power parity, which was a typical line for low-income developing countries at the time.[2] So this is a frugal line. Two hundred years ago, it seems that the vast majority of the world's population was very poor by this standard. By 1992 the proportion had fallen to 24%. We return to discuss the measurement of poverty in Part Two, but for now box 1.2 provides an introduction that will suffice in understanding this calculation.

Box 1.2 How Is Poverty Measured?

Using "income" in measuring poverty does not imply that income is all that is seen to matter to welfare. It has long been recognized in economics that while command over commodities is instrumentally important to a person's welfare, other things matter too. How well these other factors are reflected in a measure of poverty depends on how income is measured, how it is adjusted to allow for different circumstances and how the poverty line is set. Recognizing the limitations of the measures used in practice teaches us that a standard income-based poverty measure will invariably need to be supplemented by other measures, which better pick up the things left out of the poverty measure.

The key ingredient in almost all measures of poverty is a *household survey* that allows calculation of the household's consumption or income. Standard practices in national consumption surveys entail a reasonably comprehensive accounting of all sources of consumption, including allowances for consumption in-kind from own-farm production and gifts. Income surveys are supposed to make a similar accounting of all income sources, though practices vary in the detail and completeness.

continued

---

[2] BM anchored their 1992 figure to the estimate for that year made by Chen and Ravallion (2001).

Box 1.2 (Continued)

Aggregate household consumption or income is almost invariably normalized by an *equivalence scale* to allow for differences in the size and demographic
composition of the household; the simplest such scale is household size. One
also needs to deflate for differences between households in the prices they face,
depending on where they live or at what date they were interviewed.

A poverty line can be defined as the cost of a fixed minimum level of economic welfare needed to not be considered poor in the specific context. This may
be absolute or relative in terms of consumption or income. The absolute line
aims to have a fixed real value over time and space; the relative line rises with the
average consumption or income of the country. The poverty lines used by many
individual countries are absolute over time, but (looked at globally) they are relative between countries, with a tendency to see higher lines in richer countries
(at least above some level of income). It is always good practice to consider more
than one line when measuring poverty.

Lastly, the household survey is used to count how many people live below each
poverty line, and what consumption or income levels they have; are they all living
near the line, or are they spread out with some very much poorer than others?
There are different ways of doing the last step. These days one typically uses the
micro (household-level) data from the survey. But if one has a measure of mean
income and summary statistics on the distribution of income one can make an
estimate of what the poverty measure must be. If there is enough detail in the
summary data, the estimate can be quite accurate for most purposes. (It might
even be more accurate than the micro data by reducing the influence of survey
measurement errors.) That is the method used by Bourguignon and Morrisson
(2002).

The methods used in practice have deficiencies. Intra-household inequalities
are largely ignored. And poverty associated with lack of access to *non-market
goods*, such as healthcare and schooling, is not often well reflected in standard measures. Extra cash in hand may do little to help provide such goods.
Supplementary data are needed for a more complete picture.

Further reading: Part Two takes up these issues in greater depth.

The categories "developed" and "developing world" were clearly much less relevant
around 1800 than today. Of course, there were disparities in average levels of living
across countries, but less so than today—indeed, quite possibly less than one finds
among developing countries today. Average living standards in eighteenth-century
Europe were higher than in Asia or Africa, but the proportionate difference was less
than we see today.[3] Industrial output per capita was higher in India than in the United
States in 1750, though both were low;[4] their divergence came later.

---

[3] See Bairoch (1981), Alam (2006), and Allen (2013). Backward projections have suggested larger
disparities, although these estimates are subject to a number of biases, as discussed in Alam (2006).

[4] See Acemoglu et al. (2005, fig. 10).

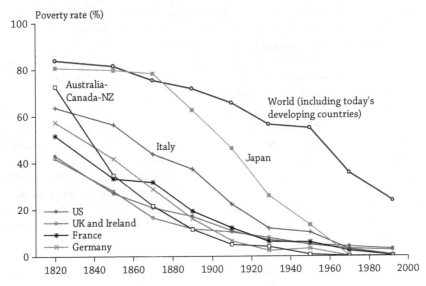

Figure 1.1 Past Poverty Reduction in Today's Rich World.

Using the database of BM and the same poverty line, one can readily calculate what percentage of the population of the countries in their study that are considered rich today lived below their "extreme poverty" line back to 1820. Figure 1.1 gives the results.[5] Such estimates should only be considered as broadly indicative, given the paucity of good data for the nineteenth and early twentieth centuries. But this is the best data we have.

Most of today's rich world started out in the early nineteenth century with poverty rates well below the global average; Japan was an exception. But they were still very poor by today's standards. The BM data suggest that about 40% of the populations of the United Kingdom and United States in 1820 lived in extreme poverty by BM's definition and the proportion was around 50% in Europe.

These calculations suggest that today's rich countries had poverty rates in the early and mid-nineteenth century that are comparable to those found in even relatively poor developing countries today—similar poverty rates to South Asia and sub-Saharan Africa around the end of the twentieth century. The absolute poverty rates in Britain, Europe, and the United States fell dramatically in the nineteenth and early twentieth centuries, though slowing down their rate of progress once quite low poverty rates had been reached. Japan was a late starter but caught up in the twentieth century and maintained a steady rate of decline (in percentage points per annum). Today there is virtually no extreme poverty left in today's rich world, judged by the standards of today's poor countries.[6]

There is much more to say about such numbers and how they are obtained, and Part Two returns to the main issues. However, there are two especially important

---

[5] Ravallion (2014b) presents more detailed results on these calculations and the methods.
[6] See Ravallion and Chen (2013c).

qualifications to figure 1.1 that we should note now. First, the fact that BM tried to keep their poverty line constant in real terms over time makes this an example of an *absolute* poverty measure, as distinct from a *relative* measure in which the poverty line rises with average income. Whether the poverty line is absolute or relative refers to its monetary value, as used to compare with incomes or consumptions in monetary units. It is argued throughout this book, and in some depth in Part Two, that conceptually we should think of the monetary poverty line as corresponding to some fixed level of human "welfare"—it is welfare not income that determines whether one person is better off than another. There can be debates about what constitutes "welfare." But once we agree on a concept, it is ethically compelling to treat everyone the same way. In other words, there is only absolute poverty in terms of welfare. However, this may well require a relative line in terms of incomes. It is plausible that a European or American today needs a higher income to attain the same level of welfare as his or her ancestors two hundred years ago. Relative poverty has certainly not vanished from the rich world!

Second, it should it be presumed that the overall progress against poverty since the early nineteenth century represented a continuation of progress prior to that date. While we do not have comparable estimates to those used above for 1820 onward, one can point to observations from the historical record warning against any presumption that there had been much reduction in poverty prior to 1820. There are a number of observations relevant here.

- The year 1820 was deliberately chosen by Maddison as a turning point in the world economy. There had been very little growth in average income for centuries prior to 1820; indeed, Maddison's (2005) estimates suggest a growth rate of world GDP per capita over the period A.D. 1000–1820 of only 0.05% per annum (implying only a 50% increase over these 820 years).[7]
- There were some inequality-increasing forces at work for two hundred years or more prior to 1820. While (again) data are lacking, historians have painted a picture of the period 1650–1800 as one in which the global spread of colonialism was creating poverty and inequality in the world as a whole.[8] This is not to say that there was little or no poverty or inequality in Africa and the Americas prior to the European arrivals; what little we know suggests otherwise.[9] However, the extent of the European exploitation of their new colonies and the huge cost to the indigenous populations at least initially are undeniable.[10] There was booming production and trade of newly discovered commodities such as sugar and cotton. This created vast new wealth for European and American elites. But, in the main this was not

[7] It is readily verified that $1.0005^{820} = 1.5$.

[8] As in Beaudoin's (2006) history of poverty.

[9] For example, Hernán Cortés described people begging from the rich in present-day Mexico City when he arrived in 1519; see Cortés and Pagden (1986, second letter). Europeans arriving in the Indian subcontinent around 1600 were struck by the extent of poverty and famines (Scammell 1989, 7). The Mexica-Aztec and Inca empires of Central and South America and those of the Mughals in South Asia were based on well-developed hierarchies.

[10] See, e.g., Scammell (1989).

wealth created by trade in free markets with secure property rights—to the contrary this was based on looting, often violent food and land seizures, and slavery, which surely represents the theft of the most fundamental property right of all. In the period of the sugar boom, 1650–1800, 7.5 million individuals were taken from Africa to the Americas to be slaves. (The total number taken from Africa in the Atlantic slave trade is estimated to be 12 million, of which about 10 million survived the journey.[11]) Amerindians were also subjected to coercive labor practices, entailing compulsory work requirements imposed by the new Colonial rulers; the work was obligatory, hard, and the wages were low.[12] Colonial policies put in place inequitable economic and political institutions, with lasting consequences for development in Latin America and elsewehere.[13]

• On top of the economic exploitation, the newly arrived European conquerors introduced deadly new diseases to which locals had little resistance with mass mortality resulting; for example, over the period 1570–1620, the population of Peru halved in size, compared to its pre-conquest level. This is a shocking mortality rate. And poor people living in the colonizing countries were not, it seems, seeing much progress either. Nor does it appear likely that the incidence of poverty had been falling for some time prior to around 1800 in England and much of Europe since real wages had been falling.[14] We cannot be confident, but it is a plausible conjecture that these various forces were creating a rise in global poverty counts and possibly rising poverty incidence (percentage living below the line) for two hundred years or more prior to the early nineteenth century.

It is a conjecture, but a not implausible one, that the pattern (albeit uneven) of declining poverty incidence evident in figure 1.1 was a feature of the last two hundred years, with much less progress against poverty for some significant time prior to the nineteenth century. Historical indicators of health, nutrition, and schooling also reveal how much progress has been made by today's rich countries since the early nineteenth century. Life expectancy at birth in England was around forty years in the early nineteenth century[15]—about the same as in India in the 1950s—while it is around eighty years in England today. US life expectancy has risen from around fifty years in 1900 to nearly eighty years today. Child mortality rates in the United Kingdom and Europe around the turn of the twentieth century were higher than one typically finds in poor countries today.[16]

Around 1800, "the poor" in Europe and North America were essentially those with little or no wealth, who relied for their survival on the supply of unskilled labor. Of course, there was heterogeneity according to employment, wages, and dependency.

[11] See Lovejoy (1989).

[12] With reference to such practices in the Spanish colonies of the Americas, Beaudoin (2006, 39) writes that "their wages were so meager that those remaining in the villages were obliged to send food for those toiling for the Spanish."

[13] See, for example, Acemoglu and Robinson (2012, ch. 1).

[14] See Tucker (1975) and Allen (2007).

[15] See Wrigley et al. (1997).

[16] See Deaton (2013).

More complex forms of poverty were to emerge in modern times. However, in the context of pre-twentieth-century Europe and North America, we can essentially equate poverty with membership of the working class.

1.2 Premodern Ideas about Poverty
Ancient Origins

Until modern times, poverty was not widely seen as a matter for the secular world of laws, taxes, and public spending.[17] The main premodern concept of distributive justice emphasized *meritocracy*—the assignment of rewards according to merit. This had its origins around 350 B.C. in the writings of the Greek philosopher and scientist Aristotle (notably his *Nicomachean Ethics* and *Politics*). Only the most skilled applicant should be chosen for public office.[18] Aristotle's concept of justice was hugely influential. It was clearly appealing to a free and aspiring middle class and gave some hope to poor but free people. The idea posed little challenge to more fundamental inequalities in society.

Ideas of "equal opportunity" and the rights of all to "liberty" were not unknown to Aristotle but were seen as too weak to rule out the benefits of a "natural order" in which subordination, even in the form of slavery, was accepted as just. In a famous passage, Aristotle wrote:

> For that some should rule and others be ruled is a thing not only necessary, but expedient: from the hour of their birth, some men are marked out for subjection, others for rule.... It is clear, then, that some men are by nature free, and others slaves, and that for these latter slavery is both expedient and just. (Aristotle's *Politics*, 350 B.C., bk. 1, pt. 5)

Here Aristotle was making an *instrumental* argument for hierarchies in society—that they served ethically valued ends of social stability and efficiency. If Aristotle had not used slavery as his example, his arguments might have been framed in ways more acceptable to modern ears.[19]

Aristotle knew nothing of Confucius, but around 500 B.C., Confucius identified poverty as one of the "six calamities" that good government should help avoid.[20] (The other five calamities were: early death, sickness, misery, a repulsive appearance, and weakness. There were also five blessings: ample means, long life, health, virtuous character, and an agreeable personal appearance.) However, in common with much Western thinking, chronic poverty associated with wealth inequality was not a concern. Instead, the concern was any threat to the harmonious social order. For

[17] For a fuller account of the history of thinking about distributive justice in Western political philosophy, Fleischacker (2004) is a very good place to start.

[18] This was not to be confused with "corrective justice" (also called "retributive justice"), which was about assigning punishment appropriately to the offense.

[19] See Levin (1997) on Aristotle's views on slavery.

[20] Li (2012) provides an interesting discussion of Confucian thought on poverty.

Confucius, "poverty" would not threaten as long as that order was maintained: "When the people keep their respective places, there will be no poverty; when harmony prevails, there will be no scarcity of people; when there is repose, there will be no rebellions" (Confucius, *Analects*, bk. 16, c. 50, v. 10; quoted in Dawson 1915, 186).

For the bulk of history, governments have played little direct role in reducing poverty, beyond dealing with transient, destabilizing, sources of poverty, such as famines. Private charity has probably been more important historically. Many theologies have extolled charity as a personal virtue, founded on empathy for the plight of others less fortunate.[21] Local religious organizations have long been charged with this beneficence role. This too goes back a long way. Around 50 B.C., the Roman thinker Marcus Tullius Cicero distinguished beneficence (charity) from justice. The former was a matter for personal choice, and not legally demanded of citizens, while justice was a matter for the state. Justice could also constrain beneficence; Cicero was opposed to wealth redistribution. Again, there was little threat to the *status quo* ("natural") order, including the distribution of wealth.

One thousand years after Aristotle, Thomas Aquinas (whose ideas greatly influenced the Roman Catholic Church) was still working with a concept of distributive justice similar to Aristotle in which there was still no suggestion of a responsibility for the state in assuring a minimum standard of living. Aquinas famously allowed that theft might be excused when a person was at risk of dying for lack of food. However, this was an extreme case; Aquinas saw theft as a mortal sin and strongly defended private property rights.

Mercantilism

For some time prior to the late eighteenth century, the dominant school of economic thought saw poverty at home and abroad as a social *good*—possibly unfortunate, but nonetheless essential for the economy of the home country. It may well have been granted that, other things being equal, a society with less poverty is to be preferred, but other things were not seen to be equal. Poverty was deemed essential to incentivize workers and keep their wages low, so as to create a strong, globally competitive, economy. Nor did the idea of what constitutes "economic development" embrace poor people as being necessarily among its intended beneficiaries. There was also widespread doubt about the desirability of, or even the potential for, governmental intervention against poverty. In marked contrast, poverty is widely seen today as a constraint on development rather than a precondition for it. And it is widely (though not universally) agreed today, across both rich and poor countries, that the government has an important role in the fight against poverty.

For much of the sixteenth to eighteenth centuries, when today's rich world was mired in abject poverty, the dominant economic theory of the time was mercantilism. The goal of policy was seen primarily to be increasing the nation's *export surplus*—the balance of trade (BOT), which was equated with the future prosperity and power of the realm. The BOT is zero globally, since global exports must equal global imports; any

---

[21] Singer (2010, ch. 2) discusses further how various religions (Christianity, Islam, Judaism, Confucianism) have valued beneficence.

gain in the BOT for one country must come at the expense of at least one other country. So this economic thinking was not supportive of efforts to reduce poverty globally. Given that development in poor countries was likely to promote the trade balances of those countries, it was seen as potentially detrimental to the home country.

Mercantilists were in favor of government intervention in the economy, but mainly for the purpose of promoting their country's power globally. The main means to maximize the BOT was cheap production inputs, that is, cheap raw materials (for which Colonies proved useful) and cheap, and therefore poor, labor at home. Poverty was seen as an essential precondition for a country's economic development. In mercantilist thinking, poor people were the means to an end. Hunger would encourage work, and lack of it would do the opposite. As Bernard de Mandeville (1732, 286) put it:

> It is manifest, that in a free Nation where Slaves are not allow'd of, the surest Wealth consists in a Multitude of laborious Poor; for besides that they are the never-failing Nursery of Fleets and Armies, without them there could be no Enjoyment, and no Product of any Country could be valuable.[22]

At the core of mercantilist thinking about poverty is how they expected the behavior of workers—most important, their desire to work—would respond to changes in their wages. A seemingly widely held view at the time was that the individual supply curve for unskilled work was negatively sloped. This is what Edgar Furniss (1920, 117) later dubbed "the utility of poverty" (box 1.3). In modern economic terms, this means that the income effect on demand for leisure was assumed to dominate the substitution effect; this is explained in box 1.4. As the Reverend Joseph Townsend (1786) put it: "The poor know little of the motives which stimulate the higher ranks to action— pride, honor and ambition. In general, it is only hunger which can spur and goad them onto labor" (23). And so: "in proportion as you advance the wages of the poor, you diminish the quantity of their work" (29).[23]

Box 1.3 **The Incentive to Work**

The idea of the "utility of poverty" was largely premised on the claim that higher wages would reduce the desire to work (i.e., labor supply). This implies a downward-sloping labor-supply function, as depicted by the bold line in figure B1.3.1. The figure also depicts an upward-sloping labor-supply function, for which a higher wage rate brings forth a higher supply of labor. How can we understand this difference?

---

[22] While de Mandeville was a mercantilist with regard to foreign trade, he was also an early advocate of laissez-faire policies generally and his view on how good social outcomes can emerge from individual self-interest greatly influenced Adam Smith's later ideas about the "invisible hand." See Rosenberg (1963) for further discussion.

[23] Townsend's advocacy of free markets was important in the history of economic thought, with influence on subsequent thinkers (including Malthus and Darwin). See Montagu (1971) and Lepenies (2014).

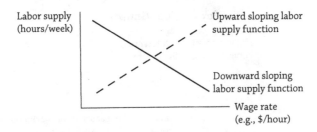

Figure B1.3.1 Alternative Labor-Supply Schedules.

Quite generally, an *incentive effect* exists when some policy or other social or economic change leads people to change their behavior. For example, if you receive a regular transfer payment from the government—a lump-sum payment, meaning that no strings are attached—then this will increase your demand for any "normal good," meaning a good for which demand rises when income rises. It is likely that leisure is such a good. So you will work less. This is called the *income effect*.

If this payment comes with a work requirement—so you have to do some work to get the payment—then this will counteract to at least some extent the work disincentive coming from the income effect on demand for leisure. Specifically, the work requirement will encourage a substitution toward work. In this case the combined effect on labor supply is ambiguous—it could go up or down but we cannot say for sure. Box 1.4 explains this further.

Box 1.4 Income and Substitution Effects

Suppose that the incentive payment discussed in box 1.3 is in the form of an increase in your hourly wage rate. The same reasoning applies. There is both an income effect and a substitution effect. The income effect comes from the higher wage rate, which will allow you to consume more. But that is not all. There will be a substitution effect that makes leisure more expensive, noting that the wage rate is also the price of leisure, since that is what must be given up to work more; if you are free to choose how much you work then taking an extra hour of leisure means that you must give up one hour of work, the price of which is the wage rate.

The trade-off you opt for will depend on your preferences between consumption and leisure. In economics those preferences are often represented by a *utility function*, which traces out a set of "indifference curves." Each such curve gives the locus of all combinations of consumption and leisure that hold utility constant—meaning that the consumer is indifferent between points on this curve. Naturally a higher curve is always preferable. (Note also that the curves cannot intersect.) It is typically assumed that a person choosing how much to

continued

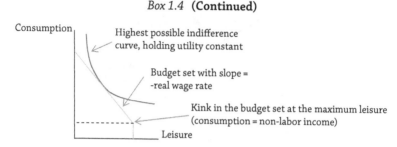

Figure B1.4.1 Consumption–Leisure Choice.

work has smooth convex indifference curves between consumption of goods and leisure time, as represented in the curve in figure B1.4.1. ("Convex" refers to their shape from below, as in a convex lens. By convention, if the shape goes the other way—convex from above—then the function is called "concave.")

The shape of the indifference curve in figure B1.4.1 reflects the substitution possibilities between consumption and leisure, both of which are assumed to exhibit *diminishing returns*, meaning that the extra utility from extra consumption (leisure) falls as consumption (leisure) increases. (For example, if you already have a lot of leisure and little consumption, then you will need a lot of extra leisure to compensate for any less consumption.) The indifference curve will get flatter as you go toward the extremes. The other line in the graph represents the set of all affordable combinations of consumption and leisure. The way the graph is drawn is for an interior solution, meaning that the optimum has both work and leisure. (By contrast, a "corner solution" will have either zero work or zero leisure.)

A higher wage rate will make leisure more expensive. This will induce a substitution away from leisure to consumption. The negatively sloped labor-supply function implicit in the "utility of poverty" idea rests on the assumption that this substitution effect is not strong enough to dominate the income effect of a higher wage rate on the demand for leisure. This is illustrated in figure B1.4.2, where it can be seen that the higher wage rate (with non-labor income unchanged) results in more leisure (and hence less work). But this is not implied by the theory;

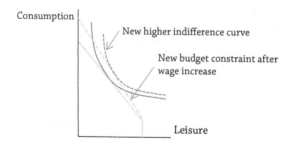

Figure B1.4.2 Effect of a Wage Increase.

one can also imagine an alternative new indifference curve with less leisure. It is not generally considered plausible that the income effect on demand for leisure would dominate among poor men and women. But this is an empirical question.

This is the classic formulation of the labor-supply decision in economics. One questionable feature is that it is assumed that work is only desirable in so far as it increases income and (hence) consumption. If people also gain utility directly from work, then the analysis must be modified accordingly. For example, it has been argued that work has welfare gains in terms of social inclusion—one's capacity to participate fully in society. Unemployment by contrast fosters alienation. Studies of people's own perceptions of their welfare (as discussed further in chapters 3 and 4) typically find that unemployment reduces subjective welfare at given income, casting doubt on the classic model.

Another modification is to allow for self-employment, such as working on one's own farm. Work incentives matter here too, depending on how farming is organized. The self-employed farmer facing a competitive market for his products decides how much work to do and is rewarded by the marginal revenue product of his labor—the output price for his output times the marginal physical product of his own work. In socialist agriculture, by contrast, the land is farmed collectively and output is shared more-or-less equally. The farmworker now gets the average product across all workers in his brigade or commune. This will typically entail diminished incentives for individual work effort, and so lower aggregate farm output. This was realized by countries such as China and Vietnam, which came to abandon socialist agriculture.

Further reading: This topic is covered in most standard introductory economics textbooks (as in, e.g., Bernheim and Whinston 2008). If you want to go more deeply into the topic, a good place to start is Killingsworth (1983).

The idea of a negatively sloped labor-supply curve appears to have been based on little more than casual anecdotes; Furniss (1920, ch. 6) provides many examples from writings of the time, often with references to the attractions of the alehouse when workers got a wage increase. It was plausible that the income effect of higher wages would lead workers to want more leisure. But higher wages also make leisure more expensive—there is bound to be some substitution away from leisure. It is hardly plausible on a priori grounds that the income effect on demand for leisure would dominate for poor workers, although it is sometimes argued that the income effect dominates at high wages, giving a backward bending labor-supply schedule.

Prevalent views of poverty appear to have been in large part attempts to rationalize the privileges of the non-poor or relieve guilty consciences. Workers would simply waste higher wages on leisure and vices. It was not the last time in the history of thought about poverty that self-serving behavioral arguments resting on little or no good evidence would buttress strong economic positions. The underlying economic model of work incentives has also been questioned to the extent that work brings direct welfare gains at given income—by enhancing status and promoting a feeling of social inclusion (box 1.4). Hunger is not then the sole motive for work.

The negatively sloped labor-supply curve is an example of a set of long-standing ideas that saw the behavior of poor men and women as the main cause of their poverty. If not for their lazy appetite for leisure, they might eventually escape poverty by combining higher wages with hard work and savings. Other behavioral explanations have been heard. Another version was that some people were poor because they did not aspire to be anything else—the presumption was that aspirations were intrinsic attributes, rather than psychological rationalizations adopted to deal with the reality facing poor men and women with limited opportunities for themselves and their children.

Those resisting higher wages were no less vocal in their opposition to direct income support for poor working-class people by the government. Their concern is that such antipoverty policies discourage work and so increase wage rates. Box 1.5 discusses the economics of how this could happen in the standard model of a competitive labor market. It is understandable that such an antipoverty policy may be opposed by those who employ labor.

How much of such a second-round effect on the labor market can be expected is a moot point. The income effect on demand for leisure may well be small for poor people. And there may be unemployment with a surplus of laborers desiring work at going wage rates (box 1.5). Then a lower desired labor supply on the part of those receiving transfers is unlikely to make a difference to the wage rates for the type of work they do.

Box 1.5 Why Might an Antipoverty Program Result in a Higher Wage Rate?

Box 1.4 discussed how the supply of labor varies with the wage rate, giving the "supply schedule" for labor. The textbook model of a competitive market also postulates a demand schedule for labor, which gives how the employers' desired amount of labor of a specific type varies with the wage rate. The standard assumption is that demand falls as the wage rate rises. (This is usually justified by a model of the behavior of a profit-maximizing employer; we return to this topic in chapter 8, but for now we can just assume a downward-sloping demand function.)

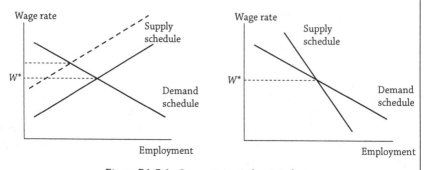

Figure B1.5.1 Competitive Labor Market.

The textbook model of competitive equilibrium assumes that when demand exceeds supply the wage rate will rise, and that it will fall when supply exceeds demand. This is also assumed to happen rapidly such that the equilibrium wage rate is reached virtually instantaneously, equating aggregate demand and supply, at W^* in figure B1.5.1. The figure gives two versions, one with an upward-sloping labor-supply curve (left panel) and one for a downward-sloping curve, as discussed in box 1.3. In both cases, the equilibrium wage is unique. It is also stable in that if there is a perturbation to the wage rate, but nothing happens to the underlying demand and supply schedules, then the competitive market mechanism will return to the old equilibrium.

However, even if it is the case that these policies do reduce work effort and increase wages that does not mean they are a bad idea. Society can still require antipoverty policies as a form of redistribution in favor of the worst off. This recognizes that there will be costs, both to taxpayers and to employers, who may well face higher wages, to the extent that the policy does in fact reduce aggregate labor supply in an economy at or near full employment. But there are extra benefits too given that the "second-round" effect of the policy on wages enhances the gains to poor people, including some who do not actually receive the transfer payment. Advocates of these policies argue that the benefits outweigh the costs. Depending on the weight one attaches to reducing poverty, this is a defensible welfare-economic argument in favor of transfers to poor people, and redistributive policies more generally. There can still be hard choices to make since some policy designs may be more cost-effective than others; that will need to be worked out in the specific circumstances. (Chapter 10 reviews the various policy options found in practice.) The heart of the matter is what weight one attaches to the benefits. Those who point solely to the costs appear to be mainly concerned about the interests of the non-poor, both as taxpayers and employers.

Another long-standing argument against redistributive transfers points instead to the virtues of work. These are seen as moral virtues, not private ones. In other words, these critics are willing to believe that workers themselves would prefer to work less when extra income is received from another source (without conditions attached). But the moral judgment about what is really good for poor men and women is seen to override their revealed preferences. This is an example of the *paternalism* that has often been evident in discussions about poverty measurement and antipoverty policy.

In mercantilist thinking a continual future supply of cheap labor was seen to be crucial for economic development. Large families were encouraged and good work habits were to be instilled from an early age. Like higher current wages, too much schooling would discourage both current and future work effort. Consistently with this model, few sustainable opportunities were expected to be available to any educated children from poor families. In de Mandeville's (1732, 288–311) mind, the only realistic future prospect for the children of laboring (and hence poor) parents was to be laboring and poor. So schooling was seen as socially wasteful:

> To make the Society happy and People easy under the meanest Circumstances, it is requisite that great Numbers of them should be Ignorant

as well as Poor.... Going to School in comparison to Working is Idleness, and the longer Boys continue in this easy sort of Life, the more unfit they'll be when grown up for downright Labour, both as to Strength and Inclination.... There is not a more contented People among us, than those who work the hardest and are the least acquainted with the Pomp and Delicacies of the World.

In this view of economic development, there is little or no prospect of reducing poverty. There was little or no perceived scope for upward mobility of working-class children. They are born poor and stay poor.

Modern progressive ears may be shocked by de Mandeville's views (and similar views still heard occasionally in modern times), but there may well be an element of cruel truth. His claim that a modest amount of extra schooling for working-class children is wasted is consistent with modern economic models of a *poverty trap*, as discussed further in box 1.6. Poor people—by and large the working class—are concentrated at a low level of wealth, below the threshold needed to assure that they can eventually escape poverty. A small increase in their wealth, in the form of extra human capital but not sufficient to get them up to the threshold, will not bring any lasting benefit. In due course, they will fall back into destitution. A large gain in schooling will be needed. And de Mandeville's pessimism on schooling would not surprise many poor children in the developing world today.

It is not hard to find contemporary examples. Katherine Boo's (2012) marvelous book, *Behind the Beautiful Forevers*, describes life in a Mumbai slum. One of the central characters is Sunil, a young scavenger who spends long hours collecting whatever he can find of any value in the trash deposits around Mumbai airport. Sunil is clearly very poor. He is also clearly capable of learning and is aware that with sufficient schooling he might escape his wretched life. But how can he finance sufficient schooling? At one point he spends a few days in a private after-hours school run by a college student who lives in the slum, and after much rote learning he masters the "twinkle-star" song. (In case you have forgotten, the song goes like this: "Twinkle-twinkle little star, how I wonder what you are. Up above the world so high, like a diamond in the sky.") Boo (2012, 68) writes: "He'd sat in on [the English class taught in the slum] for a few days, mastering the English twinkle-star song, before deciding that his time was better spent working for food." By interpretation, the modest amount of schooling that Sunil could afford would be insufficient for him to escape poverty. He is better off addressing his current hunger. That way he will survive, but stay poor.

Box 1.6 Trapped in Poverty?

A *poverty trap* usually refers to a situation in which a household (or firm) has very low wealth and a small increase in its wealth will do nothing to help it permanently escape poverty. Thus, the household is trapped. The only way out is a sufficiently large increase in wealth—such as substantially greater human capital. This needs to be large enough to put the household on a new long-run growth path out of poverty; anything less will mean that the household eventually falls back to its original position.

This type of poverty trap can arise from the existence of *thresholds in wealth*, which are positive minimum levels of wealth needed to experience any future growth. This might arise from physiology, notably the existence of a positive minimum level of nutrition to maintain the body at rest. There are many other ways it can be created. A minimum level of schooling is typically needed to enjoy any future gain in earnings from extra schooling (although there can still be other benefits from even a small amount of schooling). Poor families do not have the current wealth needed to invest enough in their children's schooling and they cannot borrow based on their future earnings gains. A "schooling poverty trap" then arises whereby poverty is perpetuated across generations. Another source of threshold effects is that the feasible production technology may require a positive minimum level of capital.

The existence of high imposed costs of producing more or from taking up new income-earning opportunities can also generate a poverty trap or something quite close to it. Poor people have often been held back by such traps. When an absolute ruler does not have the administrative capability to design efficient tax systems, and has no natural resources to draw on, he may have little choice but to expropriate any extra output from his poor citzens, and in often unpredictable ways that undermine their incentives to produce. Similarly, certain antipoverty programs can impose high marginal tax rates on poor people; the loss of benefits eats up the bulk of the gain in earnings. To give yet another example, when a poor mother considers taking a job offer she must take account of the costs of child care, which may make the net returns to the job very low.

Another usage of the term "poverty trap" is found in the literature on the ways in which group memberships and behaviors can matter to the individual. An example is when living in a poor area impedes personal prospects of escaping poverty, such as due to a lack of role models or lower quality schooling given a lower local tax base. These can be called *geographic poverty traps*.

Membership models also illustrate the idea of a *coordination failure*. If all members of the group could coordinate they can attain their collectively preferred equilibrium. The prospect of coordination failures has motivated planned industrialization efforts in poor countries or lagging regions (as discussed further in chapters 2 and 8). The inability to write enforceable contracts that bind on all members can lead to coordination failures.

There can be poverty without any form of poverty trap. Someone may be comfortably above the threshold yet still considered poor in their society. Sometimes a slow speed of adjustment in response to a shock is confused with a poverty trap.

Poverty traps may well be hard to see in practice even when they exist. They become submerged in social and governmental behaviors that essentially aim to avoid the trap in normal times. With large shocks, however, the trap is exposed. This is a reasonable interpretation of what happens during many

continued

Box 1.6 **(Continued)**

famines, as tragic magnifications of normal market and governmental failures. While famines are dramatic events, they can start quite undramatically. The threat of mass starvation can emerge from seemingly small shocks to a poor economy, or from a steady—even slow—decline in average living standards. And similar, even large, shocks in similar settings can have very different consequences. Market and non-market (including governmental) institutions which may work adequately, though not perfectly, in normal times can easily turn even a moderate aggregate shock into a devastating blow to some poor people.

Historical note and further reading: The term "poverty trap" emerged in the late 1960s (simultaneously in both the developed and developing country literatures) and grew rapidly in usage until the mid-1980s, stabilizing since then. However, while not called a "poverty trap," the idea is found in the writings of the classical economists (especially Malthus 1806). In the 1950s it emerged in formal growth models, including Nelson (1956) and in a section on caveats in Solow's (1956) paper on the theory of economic growth. For overviews of the arguments as to how poverty traps can arise, see Azariadis (2006) and Bowles et al. (2006). Acemoglu and Robinson (2012) describe historical examples of "extractive institutions" that essentially impose such high marginal tax rates on the output of poor people that they have little or no incentive for escaping poverty. Chapter 8 returns to discuss the theory and evidence on poverty traps, while chapter 10 discusses the incentive effects of antipoverty programs. On famines as magnifications of market and governmental failures, see Ravallion (1997b).

1.3 Early Antipoverty Policies

In a setting in which a very high proportion of the population lives in chronic poverty and has little power, it is unsurprising that little serious attention is given to the idea that the state has a redistributive role. That role naturally entails a basic conflict of interest between taxpayers and employers (on the one hand) and poor families (on the other). Public efforts for poor relief can still emerge when the benefits are seen to outweigh the costs. However, the sheer burden of relief—as measured by the required tax rate on the non-poor—will be high when there are large numbers of poor people. And if they have little power to influence policy in their favor, state capacity for redistribution as a means of alleviating chronic poverty will remain weak.

The protection role has been far less contentious even in very poor settings. Indeed, antipoverty policy is an old idea if one thinks of it as state-contingent and temporary redistribution to protect poor people against adverse events—as social protection, as distinct from promotion. (Box 1.7 explains this distinction.) Around 300 B.C., in the *Arthashastra*,[24] the famous Indian academic and advisor to royalty, Kautilya

---

[24] Sanskrit for "The Science of Material Gain," although some scholars prefer the translation, "Science of Politics."

heaped criticism on any king who took actions that impoverished his people or did not respond to shocks.[25] The primary motivation was clearly not the relief of poverty per se but the stability of the kingdom, and the avoidance of being taken over by another king. Kautilya had specific recommendations for famine relief using public works.[26] The goal was not asset creation but to provide extra income to poor men and women in time of need. This is an early reference to an important class of "workfare" programs, which we return to in chapter 10.[27]

Box 1.7 **Protection and Promotion**

A comprehensive antipoverty policy (or set of policies) not only provides a transient (though potentially important) short-term palliative to protect people from negative shocks but also helps families permanently escape poverty. This is the policy's promotion role. Recall the idea of a poverty trap whereby some people are stuck at zero wealth, but they still earn enough to survive. Even when in this trap, higher wages or prices for their outputs increase their welfare, and uninsured shocks to their health (say) have the opposite effect. There is space here for social protection policies providing state-contingent income support. Such policies can exist and be seen as reasonably effective without changing the fact that poor families are stuck in the wealth poverty trap. Chronic poverty can persist with varying degrees of transient poverty.

Further reading: The distinction between the protection and promotion roles of a good antipoverty policy is due to Drèze and Sen (1989). The distinction is developed further, including measures of protection and promotion, in Ravallion et al. (1995). Part Two returns to measurement issues and also the distinction between chronic and transient poverty.

A long-standing view of the role of antipoverty policies was to assure social stability. Working-class families, and probably much of the emerging middle class, were vulnerable to negative shocks—loss of employment, accidents, and sickness. Such shocks could create poverty and hunger, with the potential for poverty traps. They also generated external costs to the non-poor, principally (it seems) the daily discomfort to the urban rich of too many beggars. They could also be politically destabilizing. Limited social protection came to be seen as an essential element of the maintenance of order and hierarchy. Fundamental inequality was thus preserved (in part) by providing a degree of protection from shocks.

It is notable how widespread something like this view has been. It has often been evident in Western thought going back to Ancient Greece and in Eastern thought; for example, Confucianism emphasized the role of good governance in avoiding instability. For example, Chenyang Li (2012, 7) describes the views of the famous Confucian

[25] See Kautilya (n.d., 386–387).
[26] See Kautilya (n.d., 296).
[27] Even earlier, Pericles in Athens around 500 B.C. had implemented large-scale relief work programs to provide work for the poor.

scholar Xunzi (working around 300 B.C.) that "while proper social organization pre-vents chaos and poverty, it also necessitates social hierarchy and hence inequality." There was a presumed inevitability to mass poverty; the challenge was to manage it, to assure a stable regime.

In an early reference to the modern idea of distributive justice, Charles de Montesquieu (1748, 533) makes a passing reference to the idea that the state "owes to every citizen a certain subsistence, a proper nourishment, convenient clothing, and a kind of life not incompatible with health." However, he appears to have in mind a role for the state in protection from shocks and a page later he warns explicitly about incen-tive effects on work, such that "transient assistances are much better than perpetual foundations."

Mainstream thinking has long encouraged a limited role for the state in social pro-tection in the face of risk. In the feudal and slave economies, the employer had a responsibility for insuring workers, who may well have faced subjugation and exploi-tation in return, but were at least protected to some degree. This was not necessarily altruistic in any sense; a slave owner had a purely selfish interest in keeping his prop-erty alive, although that often meant a short and harsh life for the slave spanning his or her productive years. The global slave trade was so large in the seventeenth and eighteenth centuries that replacements were easy to acquire.

With the emergence of a modern capitalist economy, the protection role started to shift to the state. A free labor market exposed workers to the variability of demand across the business cycle and the need to adapt to changing technologies. There was at least an implicit recognition of the limitations of free markets in providing insur-ance against risk. Some degree of state-supported social protection was needed on efficiency grounds and to assure social stability. But this was a role that did not need to challenge the status quo distribution of wealth. That distribution was seen by its defenders, and advocates of social protection, as the outcome of natural processes, which included the competitive market mechanism, and it was not to be tampered with through policy. Persistent poverty was in the natural order of things even though shocks were to be ameliorated to some extent. Indeed, exposure to shocks affecting large numbers of people was seen as a threat to the social order, and various forms of protest emerged even when protest through the ballot box was not yet an option for most people.[28]

The period of the sixteenth to eighteenth centuries saw the emergence of fledgling social policies in Europe, partly in response to rising "pauperism" and vagabondage.[29] There were increasing numbers of dislocated and unemployed workers and beggars in the streets of the major cities. To some eyes the cause was seen to be the moral weaknesses of poor men and women, although deeper explanations could be found in the profound changes there were happening in the organization of production. These included agricultural transformations—such as Britain's enclosure movement of the eighteenth century, which privatized much communal farmland—that increased

---

[28] Piven and Cloward (1993) provide a good history of the protest movements in Europe and North America that have emerged during spells of mass poverty, such as due to recessions, and the policy responses.

[29] On poverty in this period of European history, see Jütte (1994).

average agricultural productivity but also released labor from agriculture, not all of which could be absorbed in the emerging urban-industrial sectors. These changes also came with greater mobility, with implications in turn for family support of the aged.

The idleness of beggars was seen to be a major social problem. Their indolence itself was abhorrent. Writing in the mid-seventeenth century, the influential mercantilist William Petty argued that it would be better to employ idle poor people in some entirely wasteful way—Petty's famous example was a public works project moving the stones of Stonehenge to Tower Hill—than to leave them idle.[30] In practice, the main social policy response was publicly financed workhouses. These had first emerged in the late sixteenth century. The idea was that welfare recipients would need to agree to be incarcerated and obliged to work for their upkeep. The (excellent) *Wikipedia* entry on workhouses describes the work done as follows:

> Many inmates were allocated tasks in the workhouse such as caring for the sick or teaching that were beyond their capabilities, but most were employed on generally pointless work, such as breaking stones or removing the hemp from telegraph wires. . . . Bone-crushing, useful in the creation of fertilizer, was a task most inmates could perform, until a government inquiry into conditions in the Andover workhouse 1845 found that starving paupers were reduced to fighting over the rotting bones they were supposed to be grinding, to suck out the marrow.

What little output that could be produced was not of sufficient value to cover the cost of running the workhouses.[31] That was not the aim, however. The workhouse policy was grounded in the prevailing view that poverty was caused by bad behaviors, which could be controlled and (hopefully) corrected by the workhouses. From the outset, the idea was that the workhouses would be "self-targeting," in that only the most destitute would be willing to be so confined, thus providing (it was believed) a cost-effective means of poverty relief.[32] This idea of self-targeting goes back to at least ancient Rome, where a subsidized foodgrain ration was available to all those willing to stand in a public queue. (Chapter 10 returns to the debates on these policies.)

While hard evidence is lacking, it is clear from the historical record that poverty rates had risen to socially unacceptable levels in the larger cities of Britain and Europe by the early sixteenth century—manifest as a large number of beggars and vagabonds. There was demand for both a framework for thinking about antipoverty policy and concrete suggestions. In an early example of the influence of scholarly thought on antipoverty policy, Juan Luis Vives ([1526] 1999) outlined a rationale for poor relief and a blueprint for action. This was at the invitation of the city of Bruges. Vives's essay was a huge success—it was translated into multiple languages and described by Sidney and Beatrice Webb as the "best-seller of its time."[33]

As the first step, Vives proposed that a census be taken of the poor. Armed with these data, he proposed that all poor but able-bodied men should be given work, both

---

[30] See Petty (1662, 31). On Petty's contributions to economics, see Ullmer (2004).

[31] See Crowther (1981).

[32] See Thane (2000, 115).

[33] See Michielse and van Krieken (1990, 2).

private and public employment. He also advised against allowing immigration, though allowing exceptions for refugees from war. If a person could not earn enough from employment, Vives argued that the state had a role to provide additional cash support to meet basic needs.[34]

Vives's rationale for all this was again protection and not promotion. And it was in no small measure about protecting the interest of rich people. Local relief would help deter outmigration, which threatened to lead to labor shortages and higher wages locally. There was also a role in literally protecting rich people from poor people, with rarely any mention of the need to assure that public institutions protected poor people from crime and violence as well—it was about "policing the poor."[35] Poverty without relief threatened social instability and disease. Providing work for all able-bodied poor men was crucial for national unity and the survival of the state. Protecting the well-off from diseases borne by poor people was also an important part of Vives's rationale.[36] This theme of protecting non-poor people from the external costs of poverty has long been prominent in thinking about policy.[37] So too has the role of rural public-works programs in the lean season as a means of deterring outmigration and so avoiding labor shortages in the peak season.[38]

The Vives proposals built on earlier ideas, but did so within a coherent framework. This was influential in Europe and America. Most famously, something like Vives's proposals became the first of the Old Poor Laws (OPL) in sixteenth-century England, first under Henry VIII and then in more formal legal terms under Elizabeth I.[39] This was a system of publicly provided, locally financed, transfer payments contingent on specific events, notably old age, widowhood, disability, illness, or unemployment. Essentially the central government told local parishes how to deal with their poverty problem, but left them to pay the bill. Confinement to a workhouse, or some other work requirement, was often required, especially when the person seeking relief was deemed to be able-bodied. Aggregate public spending on poverty relief under the OPL reached 2% of England's national income by the late eighteenth century.[40]

The pinnacle of the OPL was the Speenhamland System of 1795 introduced by the justices of Berkshire. There had been a series of poor harvests and the French wars had led to restrictions on food imports. Food prices rose sharply and many food riots ensued. In response, the parish of Speen established what appears to have been the first poverty line to be implemented as an antipoverty policy.[41] The justices of

---

[34] Vives was also concerned about the mentally ill, many of whom were poor, and his thinking on this topic (developed in a later work *On the Mind*) is seen today as a seminal early contribution to psychology.

[35] From the title of the paper by Michielse and van Krieken (1990).

[36] Michielse and van Krieken (1990) discuss further the Vives proposals and their rationale in their historical context.

[37] See the discussion in Piven and Cloward (1993).

[38] See Ravallion (1991b).

[39] The "Old" in OPL refers to the laws up to the reforms of 1834, which we return to. On the history of the English Poor Laws and their influence, see Mencher (1967), Boyer (2002), and Hindle (2004).

[40] See Solar (1995).

[41] Around the same time, Eden (1797) had proposed a "respectability basket" and Davies proposed a "standard of comfort" (Allen 2013).

Berkshire had considered the possibility of imposing a statutory minimum wage rate, but instead decided to implement a targeted transfer program. The scheme guaranteed local working-class residents a basic income set at the cost of three "gallon loaves" of bread per week for a single adult man, with an extra allowance of one and one-half loaves for each dependent (adult wife or children). The monetary value was approximately indexed to the price of bread.[42] Current wages were topped up to assure that the income of the family reached the poverty line; the unemployed received full payment.

The Speenhamland System seems to have been deemed a success, notably in preventing food riots, and so similar schemes were soon introduced elsewhere in the south of England. There were critics though. Two main concerns were raised. First, it was argued that the scheme had undesirable incentive effects—that it encouraged laziness and higher fertility (through earlier marriage). In one respect the critics may well have had a point, given that (taken literally) the system assured a minimum income whether or not one worked. However, the justices were clearly aware of incentives, and payments continued if an unemployed worker found a job.[43] And it was clearly intended to be a low level of basic entitlement, so it is unclear that this would have been any serious disincentive to doing extra work. (Chapter 10 returns to discuss this issue in greater detail.) The second concern of the critics was that workers would end up receiving lower wages and paying higher dwelling rents, given that the difference would be made up by the government. This critique assumed that workers receiving relief could be exploited by their employers or landlords. However, the fact that the scheme was effective in stopping the food riots suggests that workers did gain.

Elsewhere in Europe, relief was still mainly through private charity. Church and private spending on transfers to poor people were clearly low relative to the size of the problem—spending was well under 1% of national income in most countries.[44] In contrast, the disbursements under the OPL in England and Wales were largely financed by local property taxation. There was evidently some displacement of private charity, although the latter continued to exist.[45] But there can be little doubt that the OPL entailed a gain in social protection. By the late seventeenth century almost all parishes of England and Wales were covered and all persons were eligible for relief.

The parishes had the responsibility for implementation, subject to monitoring by central authorities. Being based in the parishes was convenient but never ideal, as many parishes were small and so provided limited scope for pooling risks and exploiting economies of scale (such as in building workhouses).[46] There was undoubtedly considerable horizontal inequity (whereby equally poor people in different

---

[42] The real value in terms of bread declined slightly at high bread prices, from 3 loaves for a single male adult to about 2.8 loaves at 50% above the base-case price; similarly for a family of a husband, wife and two children the poverty line was 6.8 loaves at that price (instead 7.5 loaves at the base price). The justices appear to have allowed for a substitution effect, whereby bread consumption can be lowered at a higher relative price of food without loss of welfare. (These are the author's calculations from the data on the Speenhamland system given at http://www.historyhome.co.uk/peel/poorlaw/speen.htm.) For further discussion of this policy, see Montagu (1971), Block and Somers (2003), and Coppola (2014).

[43] See Coppola (2014).

[44] See Lindert (2013).

[45] On the impact on private charity, see Hindle (2004) and Lindert (2013).

[46] See Marshall (1926).

parishes fared very differently).[47] Nor could these policies be expected to have much impact on the distribution of wealth. However, it is clear that the Poor Laws provided a degree of protection, and it has been argued that they helped break the historical link between harvest failures and mortality.[48]

Until the nineteenth century, the OPL were a long-standing and, by some accounts, successful social protection policy. Peter Solar (1995) argues that they were crucial to England's long-term social stability, including in the late eighteenth century when there was much concern about the possibility of the dramatic instability in France spilling across the English Channel. The OPL were the social policy that made most sense to the elites by helping to assure a relatively docile and sustained working class, and with little threat to the distribution of wealth.

These days the OPL would be called an "un-targeted" policy, and no doubt proposals would be heard to target such a policy better if it was found in a developing country today. However, their universality was important to the long-term success of the OPL, which spanned three hundred years.[49] Broad political support was assured by the fact that anyone could get relief if needed. For example, widowhood was a threat to many of those who would not normally expect to turn to the parish for help.[50] As novels of the time pointed out, even a relatively well-to-do middle-class family could be vulnerable to poverty. This was a favorite theme of the popular nineteenth-century novelist Charles Dickens, who had grown up in a middle-class family but was forced into poverty at the age of twelve when his own father was imprisoned for his unpaid debts.

It has been argued that England's Poor Laws were motivated by the "virtue of charity rather than the virtue of justice," and as such they did not constitute the beginnings of the modern role for public policy in assuring distributive justice.[51] One can conjecture that the motivation for the OPL was at least as much to do with maintaining social stability as charity or justice. However, whatever may have been the motives of policymakers, the OPL constituted a legally enforceable state policy for limited relief from the specified shocks. And parish residents—though not outsiders under the Settlement Laws of the time—had a legal recourse under the OPL, which is why these policies could help assure social stability over some three hundred years.[52] It seems that the OPL came very close to being a premodern example of policies to help assure distributive justice.

Nevertheless, an aspect of the OPL that should not be ignored is that they were clearly intended for protection rather than promotion. This was an early form of organized social insurance intended for a world in which poor and middle-class people faced many uninsured risks associated with uncertain employment, health crises,

[47] Hindle (2004) notes the large geographic differences in pensions, depending on the economic circumstances of the parishes.

[48] See Kelly and Ó Gráda (2010) and Smith (2011).

[49] See Solar (1995).

[50] Widows were listed as eligible for relief from the earliest Poor Laws, and they are mentioned often in the literature; e.g., Hindle's (2004) discussion of parish archival information related to the Poor Laws mentions widows seventy-five times.

[51] See Fleischacker (2004, 51).

[52] See Solar (1995).

harvest failures, and simply bad luck.[53] As long as the financial burden on the local elites was not too large, this was an acceptable social protection policy given that, in its absence, transient poverty came with external costs, such as disease, crime, and social instability.

Protecting the well-off from crime has long been a motivation for both policing and antipoverty policies. The first police force in England, the Thames River Police established in 1800 by Patrick Colquhoun, was established to police workers on the river trade, given widespread looting. Historically, and to this day, less attention was given to protecting poor or otherwise disadvantaged groups from crime and violence, and sometimes even from the police.[54] Inequality is at the heart of the motivation for crime prevention, but it can also be reflected in the socioeconomic incidence of the costs and benefits of that protection.

It has been argued that the OPL had benefits for longer term promotion from poverty by enhanced insurance against risk.[55] By assuring greater social stability, this too would have brought longer term gains. However, it is clear that this was promotion attained *via* protection. Protection was clearly seen as the main aim of the OPL. Critics of the OPL were concerned that they had created dependency, when their only legitimate role was as a short-term palliative.[56]

Instead of focusing on whether the motivation was charity or justice, the more important reason why the OPL (or Kautilya's famine relief policy) did not constitute a comprehensive antipoverty policy is that these policies were unlikely to change the steady-state distribution of the levels of wealth. What these policies were doing was preventing the consumption levels of those either stuck in a wealth poverty trap or settled at some low level of wealth from falling even lower. They provided them a degree of protection, but did little to help them permanently escape poverty. By the economic logic of the mercantilists, the OPL made sense in that they helped assure a relatively docile working class, with little threat to the distribution of wealth and with social protection playing a limited and well-defined role.

By the late eighteenth century, a significant change in thinking was underway.

1.4 The First Poverty Enlightenment

The late eighteenth century was the beginning of a period of economic transformation through industrialization in Britain, Western Europe, and North America. The Industrial Revolution had started in England with the implementation of a number of clever and profitable technical innovations in production. An important early example was James Watt's stationary steam engine with its ability to produce continuous rotary motion, which was to have many applications in manufacturing. This innovation had far reaching implications. For example, it helped facilitate *urban*

---

[53] See Hindle (2004).

[54] See Haugen and Boutros (2014) on the importance to poverty reduction of efforts to protect poor people from violence globally.

[55] See Solar (1995) and Smith (2011).

[56] See, e.g., Townsend (1786). Also see the discussion in Lepenies (2014).

industrialization, since factories no longer needed to be located at fast-flowing water sources (typically in rural areas) to power their water wheels. The mechanization of spinning and weaving for textile production, including steam-powered cotton mills using imported cotton, created a manufacturing boom in English cities such as Manchester.

It was no accident that the Industrial Revolution started in England, where institutions were more encouraging of innovation.[57] England was ahead of the bulk of the rest of Western Europe in re-balancing power between the monarchy and more representative political institutions. A key turning point had been the Glorious Revolution of 1688, which achieved a substantial re-alignment of power between the royalty and parliament, and a new king. In the wake of these political changes, England's patent laws had become relatively well developed by the late eighteenth century. That century also saw the removal of various taxes on manufacturing and cutting back the numerous Royal monopolies in England, making for a more level playing field.

Institutional and policy changes were both a cause and an effect of the Industrial Revolution. Watt's initial invention was clearly driven by his own scientific inquiry, and would probably have happened without a patent.[58] However, England's patent system helped assure the financing that was crucial to make such ideas operational.[59] Naturally there was some political resistance to the new technical innovations, as there were losers as well as gainers at all levels of living. In the case of France, a political revolution was necessary to get an Industrial Revolution started. There were many factors at play in causing the French Revolution, but France's prior backwardness in adopting the new technologies emerging across the English Channel was clearly one factor. A new Constitution in 1789 finally abolished the feudal system in France, and removed the longstanding privileges of Royalty and the aristocracy (such as their ability to avoid taxes).

While there was some resistence, the modernizing institutional reforms and new technologies spread fairly quickly to North America and (in due course) most of Western Europe. Industrialization was well underway in the bulk of today's rich world by the middle of the nineteenth century.[60] Elsewhere, however, the politics were such that the losers from these innovations had the power to prevent their adoption. For example, there was overwhelming resistance to the new policies and technologies from the rulers of Austria-Hungary and Russia, who feared that their power would be undermined.[61]

Distributional conflicts became severe in the lead up to these momentous changes. With poverty and inequality probably rising, there was mounting concern about

[57] Acemoglu and Robinson (2012, Chapter 7) discuss further the likely institutional origins of the Industrial Revolution, and why it started in England.

[58] Scherer (1965, p.182) writes that: "The existence of a patents system seems to have had little or no influence on Watt's invention."

[59] See Scherer (1965). Watt had a great deal of difficulty financing the development of his invention and had to abandon the idea at times to take on wage work. The eventual financing relied heavily on individual benefactors. Scherer suggests that patents were a factor in gaining their support.

[60] The change came later in Japan, after the overthrow of the shogan and the Meiji Restoration of 1968.

[61] See Acemoglu and Robinson (2012, Chapter 8).

prospects for social instability and even rebellion among the working class. There was also frustration among the middle class about the constraints faced on upward mobility. There were clearly some gaping weaknesses in the prevailing mainstream intellectual defenses of the status quo. Inherited inequalities of opportunity and manipulated, noncompetitive, market processes (sometimes facilitated by government) started to be seen as playing an important role in determining the distribution of wealth. This was in marked contrast to defenses of the status quo distribution as a purely natural order given intrinsic differences between people.

The masses started to question long-standing excuses for the deprivations they faced. Of course, there had been sporadic pro-poor protest movements before. For example, there was the (short-lived) "Levellers" movement for suffrage and religious tolerance in mid-seventeenth century England, during the Civil War period.[62] But the late eighteenth century saw both new thinking and more widespread demands for change across Britain, Europe, and America. Popular politics flourished in the cafes and alehouses of London, Paris, and elsewhere in Europe in the late eighteenth century.[63] The historian Crane Brinton (1934, 281) identifies the essential characteristic of the change in thinking in Europe as the transition from the view that "life on this earth is a fleeting transition to eternity, that such life is inevitably one of misery" to "an assertion of the possibility of the harmonious satisfaction here on earth of what are assumed to be normal human appetites." There was a new mass awareness of the scope for economic and political institutions to serve the material needs of all people. Political representation, notably suffrage, was widely seen to be the key. There was a new questioning of established social ranks, famously so in France in the latter part of the eighteenth century. *The Marriage of Figaro* by Pierre Beaumarchais (1778) had Parisian audiences taking side with the servants in laughing at the aristocracy and deeply questioning the latter's privileges.[64] The play is widely seen as a precursor to the French Revolution.

The latter half of the eighteenth century saw a marked upswing in references to poverty in written works. We can see this clearly if the word "poverty" is entered in the *Google Books Ngram Viewer* (the *Viewer* hereinafter).[65] The *Viewer*'s counts are normalized by the total number of words that year. We can call the normalized frequency the "incidence." Figure 1.2 graphs the incidence of the word "poverty" from

---

[62] See Hill (1972).

[63] The Proceedings of the Old Bailey (2012) contains descriptions for London; an example was the "London Corresponding Society," founded in 1792, and dedicated to expanding working-class political representation.

[64] For example, in the fifth act, the servant Figaro asked of the Count who employed him: "What have you done to deserve such advantages? Put yourself to the trouble of being born—nothing more. For the rest—a very ordinary man!" While the play was written in 1778, it was censored by King Louis XVI and did not play until 1784.

[65] This was introduced by Michel et al. (2010). An "n-gram" is just a phrase made up of words ("1-grams"). Michel et al. created a corpus of over 500 billion n-grams (360 billion in English) from over five million books. Naturally the total number of words has increased over time. Michel et al. estimate that there were about one million words in English in 2000, but barely half that number in 1900 (with most of the growth in the last half of the twentieth century). Ravallion (2011c) discusses the use of the *Viewer*, including potential sources of bias.

(a) English

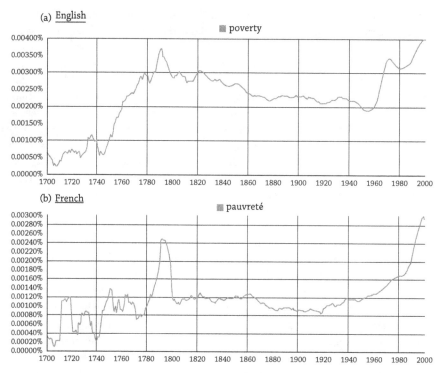

Figure 1.2 References to Poverty in Google Books, 1700–2000. *Source*: Data obtained by the author using the *Google Books Ngram Viewer*.

1700 to 2000 in both English and French.[66] References to poverty peaked around 1790; this was the culmination of a long period of rising attention to poverty in the English language texts, although in French it was a marked spike in attention around the time of the French Revolution.

The three words that best capture the lofty ideals of the period are *"liberté, égalité, fraternité"*—the motto of the French Revolution (and France's national motto from the late nineteenth century). These ideals had lasting impact, but they do not appear to have brought much short-term gain to poor people. There was little sign of any serious new effort to fight chronic poverty, though there was no shortage of effort from France's new leaders to fight its European neighbors, and the ranks of poor men remained a reliable source of foot soldiers for that purpose.[67] The suffrage that emerged was largely confined to *men* with property.

[66] There is more than one word for the idea of poverty in both languages. Another word used for "poverty" (though more in eighteenth- and nineteenth-century English) is "indigence." Adding this (less common) word does not change the basic pattern in figure 1.2. In French, "misère" has often been used similarly to "pauvreté," but misère also has a broader usage embracing psychological/spiritual states of deprivation, not just material; the word is somewhat closer to its common English translation as "misery."

[67] Revolutionary France soon declared war (starting with the Austrian empire in 1792) and the wars continued until Napoleon Bonaparte defeat at Waterloo in 1815.

"Liberty" was understood in a way consistent with modern usage, in that the individual was deemed to have whatever freedoms were consistent with like freedoms for others. "Equality" was not, however, understood as equality of outcomes but in terms of legal rights of *opportunity*—that the law must be the same for everyone and so allow all citizens equal opportunity for public positions and jobs, with the assignment determined by ability (a set of ideas that were formalized in the influential Napoleonic Code of 1804). There was little sign of a perceived role for the state in redistribution of rewards, although some calls for this did start to emerge in the 1790s with the left-wing Jacobin Club and (in particular) François-Noël ("Gracchus") Babeuf.[68] Box 1.8 discusses the distinction between inequality of opportunity and inequality of outcomes, as well as other types of inequality.

Box 1.8 Concepts of "Inequality"

"Inequality" means different things to different people. One difference is between *inequality of outcomes* and *inequality of opportunities*. The former refers to disparities between the levels of a chosen metric of outcomes (consumption, income, or wealth). Some of the inequality in outcomes that we see stems from differences in the efforts made by people; some work harder than others and so earn more. Some of the inequality also stems from differences in the *circumstances*—such as gender, race, inherited wealth, parental circumstances, or natural ability—that have nothing to do with personal efforts. The total inequality in outcomes reflects both sources. In modern usage, inequality of opportunity refers to that part of inequality that is due to different circumstances, and not different efforts. It is often argued that inequality of opportunity is more costly to society and should be avoided; such inequalities are seen as unfair. Inequalities of effort are taken to be of less concern; indeed, there are good reasons (on both ethical and economic grounds) why effort should be rewarded.

There are different concepts of inequality to be aware of. A distinction is made between *relative* and *absolute* inequality. Relative inequality is assessed in terms of the proportionate differences in society—the ratios of incomes (Y^R/Y^P, for two families, one rich and one poor)—while absolute inequality is based on the absolute differences in incomes ($Y^R - Y^P$). When people talk about a "widening gap between the rich and poor," it seems that they often have absolute inequality in mind. Part Two goes further into the distinction between absolute and relative inequality.

continued

---

[68] Fleischacker (2004) gives credit for anticipating the modern concept of distributive justice to Babeuf, though also giving credit to the German philosopher Johann Fichte, a follower of Kant. (A seemingly odd pair: Babeuf is considered a founder of Communism, and was executed in 1797 for his rebellious left-wing ideas, while the anti-Semitic Fichte is considered a key influence on the National Socialist movement in Germany.) However, de Montesquieu appears to have beaten both to the honor.

> ## Box 1.8 (Continued)
>
> Another distinction is between *vertical* and *horizontal* inequality. When we talk about the "inequality," we often mean the vertical (absolute or relative) differences in the gains to the "rich" versus the "poor." However, there can also be horizontal inequalities, meaning that people at the same initial income are affected differently or make different efforts. For example, when a trade reform increases the relative price of food some poor people gain (those who produce more food than they consume) while other equally poor people lose (those who consume more than they produce). Such horizontal inequalities can be very important to assessing a policy change. Part Three returns to the distinction between horizontal and vertical inequality.
>
> Finally, one can make a more evaluative distinction between *good* and *bad* inequality. Good inequalities reflect and reinforce incentives that are needed to foster innovation, entrepreneurship, and growth. Bad inequalities do the opposite by preventing individuals from connecting to markets and limiting the accumulation of human capital and physical capital. A distinction of this sort is often found in both popular and scholarly thought; an example of the latter is John Rawls's (1971) *Theory of Justice* in which inequality (in command over goods, or in liberty or opportunity) is only considered to be justified ("good inequality") if it benefits the poorest group. The discussion returns to Rawls in chapter 2.
>
> *Further reading:* On inequality of opportunity, see Roemer (1998, 2014) and World Bank (2006). On the other concepts above, see Ravallion (2003a, 2014d).

If there was longer term hope for poor people in the new ideas of "*liberté, égalité, fraternité,*" then it was more in "fraternity" than "equality"; as Brinton (1934, 283) explains, "fraternity had meant to the hopeful eighteenth century the outpouring of its favorite virtue, benevolence, upon all human beings, and especially on the downtrodden and the distant—on peasants, Chinamen and South Sea Islanders." Similar views were heard in America where advocates of a strong state role in fighting poverty saw this as an essential element of what it meant to be "a great friendly society."[69]

New philosophical and economic thinking from the mid-eighteenth century had opened the way to this First Poverty Enlightenment in the last few decades of that century.[70] Significant cracks had started to appear in mainstream views on the role of the state in influencing distribution. A key step in philosophical thinking was the rejection of the view that prevailing inequalities were inevitable. The social contract approach that emerged in the seventeenth century (often attributed to Thomas Hobbes) asked a fundamental question: how should we decide what constitutes good government? In modern terms, this is a question of evaluation, and the relevant counterfactual was a "natural state," in the absence of government. Like all counterfactuals,

[69] This is the expression used by Everett in 1827 as quoted in Klebaner (1964, 394).
[70] The identification of the First and Second Poverty Enlightenments is from Ravallion (2011c).

the natural state was unknown and open to debate.[71] Hobbes argued that it would be a state of conflict, of *"all against all."* The question was taken up again in the late eighteenth century by Jean-Jacques Rousseau, who opened up an important new strand of thinking about the distributive role of the state. In his *Discourse on the Origin of Inequality*, Rousseau argued that, while self-interest was a motivation in the natural state, so too was empathy for the situation of others.[72] Human institutions, however, can develop to either support or thwart our natural empathy. Rousseau saw poverty and inequality as stemming in no small measure (though not solely) from bad institutions—social arrangements that created "different privileges, which some men enjoy to the prejudice of others, such as that of being more rich, more honored, more powerful or even in a position to exact obedience." Here Rousseau made a key step in recognizing the role played by institutions, including governments, in influencing distribution.[73] Poverty was not then inevitable.

Prominent philosophical writings called for respect for poor men and women as fellow citizens and questioned paternalism. Immanuel Kant (1785, 62) put forward the idea that every rational human being must be treated "as an end withal, never as means." This was indeed a radical idea, which gave poor people the same moral worth as rich people. Of course there was some measure of respect for poor people even in (say) de Mandeville's earlier writings, but it was a respect for their labor, consistent with the role assigned to them by their birth. They were merely the means to an end. In Kant, by contrast, there was respect for all rational agents and their choices, whatever their economic circumstances. This was an essential step for both political equality and comprehensive antipoverty policy, although both were still a long way off.

Recall that a long-standing view—often attributed to Cicero in Ancient Rome—distinguished justice from beneficence, with only the former entailing a role for the state. Charity was a matter for personal choice and was encouraged and facilitated by most religions. There had been criticism at times that religious organizations were not doing enough to alleviate poverty and that the state should take responsibility; for example, Vives (1526) expressed this view regarding the clergy in the Netherlands. Kant went more deeply, to argue that charity was an inherently unequal relationship between giver and receiver. He questioned the virtue of giving alms that flatter the giver's pride: "Kant sees moral corruption in the private relationships by which well-off people bestow of their bounty to the needy and looks to the state to provide for a more respectful relationship between rich and poor" (Fleischacker 2004, 71). Such philosophical challenges to established thinking about beneficence paved the way for a public debate on the role of the state in fighting poverty and

[71] Rousseau (1754, 11) put the point nicely: "The philosophers, who have inquired into the foundations of society, have all felt the necessity of going back to a state of nature; but not one of them has got there."

[72] Rousseau was writing prior to Darwin. Scientific research on animal behavior has revealed strong social and empathic behaviors (Frans de Waal 2009), suggesting deeper origins for human sociability. It has also been argued that (recently discovered) mirror neurons are the neural foundation of such behavior; see, e.g., Christian Keysers (2011).

[73] Rousseau allowed for the existence of what he termed "natural inequality," which would exist in the counterfactual "natural state." Natural inequality reflected innate differences (health, strength, mental ability).

in distribution more broadly, and an eventual shift of responsibilities from religious organizations to the state.

Economic thinking was also advancing, side-by-side with the new political philosophies. Adam Smith (1776) lambasted the mercantilist view that a country's economic welfare was to be judged by the BOT. This had long been questionable (not least for ignoring corrective adjustments through price changes).[74] Smith argued for a broader conception of welfare based on the population's command over commodities (including basic consumption goods, not just luxury goods, and also including leisure). Thus, Smith opened the way to seeing progress against poverty as a goal for development, rather than a threat to it.[75] Smith was deeply anti-mercantilist in his view that "no society can surely be flourishing and happy, of which the far greater part of the members are poor and miserable" (Smith 1776, bk. 1, ch. 8). Similarly, he saw higher real wages for workers as a good thing, also in contrast to prevailing mercantilist views.

Box 1.9 When Are Free Markets Efficient?

Adam Smith's idea of the "invisible hand" has had a powerful influence on popular economic thinking. Essentially the idea was that the pursuit of individual self-interest could, under certain conditions, be trusted to assure socially beneficial outcomes.

Today economists recognize this as a theorem of welfare economics that sets out the conditions under which a competitive economy will be efficient. "Efficiency" has various meanings in common usage, but to an economist it generally means that no one can be made better off without making someone else worse off. When there is no such inefficiency, we have what is called *Pareto optimality*, named after the late nineteenth-century Italian economist Vilfredo Pareto, who we return to. Establishing this theorem was an important step in the development of economics.

The key conditions for efficient markets are that all agents in the economy:

- maximize their own self-interest (their utility as consumers or their profits as producers)
- have secure property rights (an enforceable command over specific resources)
- know all the prices relevant to their decisions
- take those prices as given (e.g., nobody has monopoly power)
- have access to a complete set of markets with flexible prices that adjust freely to clear all markets (i.e., equating aggregate demand with aggregate supply in each market).

---

[74] See Blaug's (1962, ch. 2) discussion of Smith and the mercantilist doctrines.

[75] See the discussion in Muller (1993, 58). Also see Himmelfarb's (1984a, b) discussion of Smith's views relative to others around the same time.

These can be considered quite strong assumptions and the presumption must be that free markets in the real world are not in general fully efficient. For example, if people do not know prices, they cannot be expected to make good decisions, including beneficial trades across different markets. There can be large welfare gains from better information.

Even with perfect information, the set of markets may well be incomplete. If you think about it, a complete set of markets is a tall order. This requires different markets for commodities in different states of nature (such as the weather) and that there are markets for non-pecuniary externalities whereby one person's choices matter directly to the utility or profits of other agents.

Externalities are a long-standing concern about the efficiency of free markets. To understand this idea, consider a profit-maximizing firm that pollutes the water or air. The firm has two outputs, widgets (say) and pollution, but there is only a market for widgets. Even if the widget market is perfect, the firm will produce too much of both outputs. Creating a market for pollution is hard. But there is an easier solution. By taxing the widget output of that polluting firm we can assure that the firm is induced to produce the lower, socially optimal, amount. The firm does not care any more about pollution than before, but it now behaves as if it cares enough to do the right thing for society by curtailing its widget output. The appropriately guided invisible hand gets us to the best outcome. There is a good case for believing that free markets will undersupply a class of goods known as *public goods*, which we return to (box 1.14).

Even when the economy is efficient in Pareto's sense, there is nothing to guarantee that the allocation it achieves is fair or equitable. That will depend on the initial distribution of endowments prior to entering the market, the preferences of people, and the technologies used in production. Saying that free markets are not in general efficient does not, of course, mean that we should abandon markets. We need to be confident that the alternative allocation mechanism is better! Also, policies (including some that use the market mechanism) can sometimes help make markets more efficient.

Further reading: There are many textbook treatments of this topic, but a good example is Hindriks and Myles (2006). For an interesting example of the gains from better information, see Jensen (2007) on the effects of mobile phone services becoming available to fishermen in the state of Kerala in India.

This was a key time for economic thought. Smith saw the virtue of self-interest, although he did not see it as the sole motive for human behavior.[76] Rather, the behavior of self-interested people could advance their collective welfare in an institutional environment of competitive markets with secure property rights (box 1.9).[77] This was to become a central tenant of economic policy. The required institutions evolved over

[76] See Smith (1759, ch. 1, I.I.1).

[77] Smith built on early views of Aquinas, Grotius, Locke, Hume, and others; see Fleischacker (2004, 34–40).

time in the wake of the new thinking, although the pace of institutional reform was subject to the balance of power among those whose economic interests were affected in the near-term.[78] As has often been the case, sound new economic thinking eventually made for better policies, but the process was inevitably mediated by politics and took longer in some settings than others.

A central policy issue concerned the equity implications of the economic institutions relevant to a competitive and dynamic market economy. Following his friend David Hume, Smith recognized that the institution of secure private property could be in tension with the need to help poor people and the desire for equity more broadly.[79] However, without security of property rights, the risk of expropriation would discourage investment, and costly conflict would be rife. Without legally enforceable contracts innovators and financiers will not trust each other. An institution such as secure property rights was not an end in itself, but means of social advancement, including (ultimately) poverty reduction.[80] By this view, the institution of private property may yield glaring disparities today—for the poor typically have little property to protect, while the rich have ample—but that is the price one has to pay for longer-term advancement. By this view, inequality today was necessary to avoid poverty tomorrow. This view had a lasting influence on thinking about development, but has often been questioned; we return to this topic in chapter 2 and (more fully) in chapter 8.

In formulating his arguments, Smith abandoned many of the orthodoxies of preceding economic thinking, especially those associated with mercantilism. Gone, for example, was the idea of the utility of poverty, with its negatively sloped individual labor-supply function.[81] And (despite some characterizations of Smith's noninterventionist views) he argued in favor of promotional antipoverty policies, such as limited public subsidies to help cover tuition fees for the basic schooling of the "common people."[82] On this and other social issues, Smith was evidently far more progressive than most of his peers.

The changes in popular and scholarly thinking came with implications for other policy debates relevant to income distribution. One such debate, long-standing and continuing today, was on how progressive income taxes should be, and whose incomes should be taxed.[83] (Box 1.10 discusses progressive taxation and other fiscal tools for redistributing incomes.) The milieu gave impetus to arguments for redistributive taxation. Smith had strongly favored exempting subsistence wages, as did others subsequently, including those who favored proportional taxes above the exemption—implying a progressive tax system overall.

---

[78] This idea was to become a theme of the modern political economy of institutions. Part three returns to this topic.

[79] Recognizing this trade-off was a major contribution of Hume and Smith. Thus Fleischaker (2004, 40) writes that "Hume and Smith are thus the first to make the suffering of the poor the problem for the justification of private property."

[80] See Wells's (2010) discussion in the context of Smith's views about slavery.

[81] "Where wages are high, accordingly, we shall always find the workmen more active, diligent, and expeditious, than where they are low" (Smith 1776, 72).

[82] See Rothschild (2001). On Smith's views about tuition subsidies, see Smith (1776, bk. 5, ch. 1, art. 2d).

[83] Musgrave (1985) reviews the history of this and other debates in public finance.

Box 1.10 Fiscal Policy Instruments for Redistributing Incomes

Redistributive policies are found on both the tax and spending sides of the fiscal budget. On the tax side, if the percentage of income paid in taxation rises as individual income rises, then the tax system is said to be "progressive." If the percentage falls as income rises, then it is said to be "regressive." A proportional tax is at a fixed percentage of income no matter what the level of income. A progressive tax will reduce relative inequality of incomes (recalling box 1.8).

The final degree of progressivity in a tax system depends on many things. In the case of income taxes, a key factor is how the base of taxation is defined—what is taxed. As Adam Smith realized, the taxes could be proportional on a component of income that rises as a share of total income thus making the tax progressive overall. In the case of indirect taxation—levied on consumption—a key factor is what exactly is included; for example, it is common for food to be exempted as poorer families tend to spend a higher share of their budget on food, thus reducing the likely regressivity of such taxes. (This is called "Engel's Law," and it is covered further in box 1.16.)

On the public expenditure side, there are some categories of spending that can be explicitly targeted to poor families. This might be through a formal means test whereby a public service if provided to those with an income below some critical level. That is less common in poor countries where "income" is harder to observe; some form of "indicator targeting" or "proxy-means test" is often used instead, whereby only people with certain characteristics correlated with poverty are targeted. For some categories of spending there is a "self-targeting" mechanism, whereby the benefits tend to be concentrated more on poor people without an explicit effort at targeting. This happens when a type of public spending (such as basic healthcare or education services) tends to be used more by poor people, or when the conditionalities applied to participation in a public program (such as work requirements, as in the workhouses) discourage the participation of non-poor people. Chapter 10 discusses these issues in greater detail.

Another policy debate concerned the distribution of the gains from natural resources, notably agricultural land. In a pamphlet (addressed to the government of the new French Republic, but with broader relevance), Thomas Paine (1797) argued that agricultural land was "natural property," to which every person had a legitimate claim. There was, nonetheless, an efficiency case for its private ownership. So instead of being nationalized, agrarian land should be subject to taxation—a "ground rent," the revenue from which should be allocated equally to *all* adults in society, as all have a claim to that property. (He also made provision for an old-age pension.) And this was (explicitly) not to be seen as charity but as a right. Paine's proposal was an antipoverty policy; indeed, it appears to have been the first proposal for a "basic income guarantee"—an idea we return to later in this chapter, and in greater depth in chapter 10.

An important prelude to the eventual emergence of promotional policies came with new thinking on the importance of *schooling*; "illiteracy had become a stigma instead of an ordinary accompaniment of humble life" (Brinton 1934, 279). Condorcet, the late eighteenth-century French philosopher and mathematician, advocated free universal basic education (though warning against the state instructing on moral or political matters, as he greatly valued diversity in views); Condorcet also advocated equal rights for women and all races.[84] However, these were still radical ideas, well ahead of implementation. The classical economists who came to dominate thinking about policy in the nineteenth century also saw education as having the potential to make economic growth more poverty-reducing, notably by attenuating population growth through "moral improvement." But they did not see mass education as having a role in promoting that growth and saw little scope for mass *public* education.[85]

As one would expect, the resistance to mass public education came in large part from those who were threatened by it. There were concerns among the ruling elites that a better educated working class would no longer respect their authority, and the working class had no means of credibly committing to later compensate the ruling class for such a loss of power. This last point is an example of a general class of "commitment problems" that can entail that poor institutions and policies persist.[86] A change in the distribution of political power in the form of electoral democracy would be needed, although this was harder to attain while the masses were both poor and poorly educated. There was also opposition from those employers who relied on child labor and feared a higher wage bill. In some settings (including England) religious organizations also felt threatened, as their own religious schools had been the only hope of schooling for children from poor families. It took a very long time for mass public schooling to become a reality, alongside universal suffrage (or at least universal for men). (Chapter 9 returns to the topic of schooling.)

The First Poverty Enlightenment also marked the birth of empirical research on poverty. If there is one work that can claim to be the pioneering effort in this respect, it is Sir Frederick Eden's (1797) massive three-volume tome, *The State of the Poor*. This was motivated by concerns over the poverty impacts of rising food prices (both from a series of poor harvests and the demands from the Napoleonic wars). While the work had broad scope, including a history of poverty, the most distinctive feature was its empiricism. In contrast to many similarly titled pamphlets and books around this time that relied on crude characterizations of the perceived bad behaviors of poor men and women, Eden was explicitly striving to objectively describe (and in excruciating detail) the "domestic economy" of earnings and expenditures, wage rates and prices, that underpinned the plainly wretched living conditions of selected poor families in England, Scotland, and Wales. Eden did not have the tools of modern economics for studying the welfare impacts of price changes (which we study in chapter 3), although he had the basic intuition right. But this was no mere academic

---

[84] See Stedman Jones (2004).

[85] See Blaug (1962, 216).

[86] See the discussion in Acemoglu et al. (2005, sec. 6) who also point to a number of historical examples.

endeavor. It was explicitly intended to provide a solid empirical foundation for ongoing policy debates, notably on the Poor Laws.[87]

The most important contribution of the First Poverty Enlightenment was in establishing the moral case for the idea of public effort toward eliminating poverty. That moral case developed out of an emerging new respect on the part of the elites for hard-working but poor men and women as people—what can be dubbed "emotional identification."[88] Important new progressive ideas emerged in the writings of Smith, Rousseau, Kant, Fichte, Condorcet, Babeuf, and others. However, we were still a long way from the articulation of a comprehensive antipoverty policy. While the First Poverty Enlightenment brought new thinking relevant to antipoverty policies, it did not mark any dramatic change in the lives of poor people, and they were still being blamed for their poverty. This belief persisted into the nineteenth and twentieth centuries.[89] Except for relief under the Poor Laws in England and Wales, neither private assistance nor public support for poor people showed any marked rise in Europe, from their relatively low levels.[90] The main economic beneficiaries of the First Poverty Enlightenment were probably the existing middle class, who started to aspire to sources of wealth and power they had been excluded from.

1.5 The Transition in Thinking in the Nineteenth and Early Twentieth Centuries
The Industrial Revolution and Poverty

It was widely believed at the time that workers were not sharing much in the new economic opportunities unleashed by the Industrial Revolution.[91] Well beyond the start of the Industrial Revolution, poverty seemed as plentiful as ever. Social novels (such as Dickens's *Oliver Twist* and *Hard Times*, Victor Hugo's *Les Misérables*, and Elizabeth Gaskell's *North and South*) and qualitative observational studies (such as Engels 1845) described the poor health environments and harsh working conditions of Western Europe's new industrial cities in the mid-nineteenth century.

The classical economists following Smith did not share his optimism on the scope for poverty reduction through growth of the emerging industrial sector. They argued that rising demand for unskilled labor in that sector as it expanded would not lead to a sustainable increase in the wage rate, which would eventually return to a low

---

[87] For further discussion of Eden's work and influence, see Stone (1997) and Pyatt and Ward (1997).

[88] This is the term used by de Waal (2009, 116).

[89] See, e.g., Klebaner's (1964) descriptions of views of poverty in nineteenth-century America. Even today one occasionally hears claims that poverty is the fault of poor people; e.g., Palmer (2012, 119) writes that "in orders characterized by well-defined, legally secure, and transferable property rights . . . the lesser affluence of the poor [is] largely a matter of inability or unwillingness to produce wealth or to save."

[90] See Lindert (2013).

[91] Here the focus is on economic thought. Chapter 8 will discuss the evidence on the actual impacts of the Industrial Revolution on poverty, including both the wage workers in the new factories in England and Western Europe and the slaves who were producing the raw materials in the New World.

consumption floor of mere subsistence. The main reason was that any rise in the wage rate above the subsistence level would be undermined by induced growth in the aggregate supply of labor through population growth—higher fertility (associated with early marriage) and/or lower child mortality. The wage rate would return to the subsistence level in due course. The Reverend Thomas Robert Malthus (1806) is famous for this argument, but a version is also found in Smith.[92] The idea that population growth would assure that real wages would stay constant despite technical progress was widely held even to the end of the nineteenth century.[93]

Malthus famously anticipated persistent poverty and famines stemming from his expectation that population growth would outpace the growth of food supply; population would grow as a geometric progression while food supply could only increase arithmetically. While there can be little doubt that the aggregate supply of food is one of the factors determining the sustainable population size, Malthus's dire predictions were not borne out by subsequent history.

To understand why Malthus was (thankfully) proved wrong, we must probe further into the mechanisms linking food supply to fertility and mortality. The Reverend Malthus saw the problem as the "moral weaknesses" of poor men and women. To modern ears this is unconvincing and smacks of paternalism. However, it is credible that higher incomes in preindustrial England would have led to earlier ages at marriage and larger family sizes.[94] One can provide an economic rationale for believing that desired family size would rise with higher income, and it does not require moral judgments. For poor parents in economies without formal social security, children are a form of saving for the future. Also assume that there is little hope for upward mobility; the children of the working class would remain in the working class. So there is little expected return to poor parents from investing more in the "quality" of their children. The unskilled wage rate is then the return to this form of saving (net of maintenance costs). A higher wage would then increase the demand for children and future labor supply. Box 1.11 gives more detail.

Box 1.11 Quality and Quantity of Children

It can be assumed that parents care about consumption today and consumption tomorrow and that they can control fertility. Assume further that their utility function traces out smooth convex indifference curves, similarly to box 1.4 except now the axes are "consumption today" and "future consumption." There is a cost of maintaining children (c per child), and there is a return from their wages when they reach working age but are still dependent on their parents. The equilibrium for parents deciding how many children to have equates the MRS between consumption today and future consumption to the wage rate net of the maintenance cost relative to the latter (MRS = $(w - c)/c$), where w is the child

---

[92] See Smith (1776, bk. 1, ch. 8).
[93] See Sandmo (2014).
[94] This is argued by Wrigley and Schofield (1981).

wage rate. A higher wage rate implies a higher return from saving in the form of children, and hence a higher desired family size. The actual birth rate will adjust to expected mortality.

Further reading: The type of argument sketched above is an application of the approach to "human capital" introduced by Becker (1964) in which parents weigh the expected marginal benefits of schooling against the marginal cost. Under certain conditions, there will be a unique optimal level of investment in schooling for each child.

On formulating the argument this way, some qualifications are evident. The argument may discount too readily the scope for investing more in each child, rather than simply having more children. In Malthus's time, it probably was the case that there was rather little hope of upward mobility for working-class children, but the caveat is more relevant once changes in technology and mass schooling had created opportunities for the advancement of children from initially poor families. Similarly, the classical argument of the income effect on demand for children assumes that there are no other (less costly) savings instruments available. This too would become a more serious critique of the classical argument at a later time when the finance sector had become more inclusive.

These factors would eventually help thwart the Malthusian prediction of doom. But the most important factor was undoubtedly that new technologies would emerge that permitted continually rising farm productivity, at a pace Malthus could never have imagined. Over the subsequent two hundred years, the incidence of extreme poverty would come to fall markedly, although the number of poor people in the world would take a lot longer to decline.

David Ricardo—a friend of Malthus, and the author of the most influential economics text of the first half of the nineteenth century, *Principles of Political Economy and Taxation* (Ricardo 1817)—shared the pessimism of Malthus on the scope for long-run poverty reduction through an expanding economy. However, for Ricardo it was limited natural resources, combined with diminishing returns, which would constrain progress and inevitably bring us to a world of zero growth. Agriculture still accounted for the bulk of economic activity at the time Ricardo was writing, and so agriculture was prominent in his theories. The idea of diminishing returns came out of thinking about farming, though it was to become a key feature of economic theories over the next two hundred years; box 1.12 explains this important idea further.

Box 1.12 Diminishing Returns in Production

Recall box 1.4, where the idea of diminishing returns to consumption and leisure was reflected in the shape of the consumer's indifference curves. Essentially the same idea is found in the economics of production. This is most often

continued

Box 1.12 (Continued)

associated with Ricardo, who got the idea from studying agricultural experiments in England in the early nineteenth century.

Imagine a farm that uses land, rain, the time of a worker, and seeds to produce rice. Suppose you hold constant the size of the plot of land, rainfall, and the number of seeds but you vary the amount of the worker's labor time starting from zero up to twenty-four hours per day. Starting from zero, her extra labor time will, of course, mean extra output as the first seeds are sown. The extra output from applying more labor is called the *marginal product of labor* (MPL). However, after some point, the extra rice obtained by spending more time on the farm will start to fall at given values of other inputs. There will still be more rice from the extra time, but the worker will be spreading herself thin. If the seeds run out, more output from more labor may still be possible (such as by more time weeding), but here too extra time will bring lower and lower gains.

This is illustrated in figure B1.12.1. The curve gives the technically feasible maximum output that is possible from any given labor input, as given by the horizontal axis. The average product (*AP*) at any point is the slope of a straight line starting from the origin (0,0) and forming a tangent to the production function at that point. More generally, the law of diminishing returns says that the marginal product of one input to production—the extra output from increasing the amount of that input holding other inputs *and* the technology constant—will fall as the quantity of that input increases.

The idea of diminishing returns to labor in agriculture had a profound effect on classical economic thinking about population growth, most famously in the ideas of Malthus. When there are diminishing returns to labor, as output rises with a given technology there will inevitably be a point above which the marginal product of labor will fall below its average product. If output is zero at zero labor input, then this will be true immediately. More generally we expect that labor input must be above some critical positive level before any output can be produced, as in the graph in figure B1.12.1. Then the marginal product will exceed the average product at sufficiently low levels of output. (That point is indicated in the graph by the point L^*.)

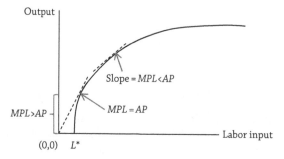

Figure B1.12.1 Output as a Function of Labor Input.

On reflection it is obvious that when the marginal product is less than the average product more labor will mean a lower average product; the extra output from extra labor will be less than average, so the average must fall. Thus, it was argued that agricultural output per worker would tend to fall as the supply of workers rose. This was an essential element of Malthus's views on the adverse effects of population growth on living standards, including poverty.

This came to be known as the law of diminishing returns. While the idea is plausible in many situations, it is not a "law" at all, but rather an assumption that economists make about the nature of the technology used in production. Notice also that Malthus's argument based on diminishing returns to labor assumes that the technology is given. More generally, it has been argued that population growth can help induce technical progress—innovations that allow more to be produced from the same labor input—such that population growth need not result in a higher incidence of poverty. Another argument that can be made is that large populations allow better public goods—especially better infrastructure—which also allow more to be produced from given inputs.

Further reading: Most standard economics textbooks cover this topic. Blaug's (1962) history of economic thought provides a good overview of how these ideas developed in economics. See Boserup (1981) on how population growth has sometimes helped promote technological innovations.

As Ricardo saw it, the main task of economics was to explain how a fixed aggregate output was distributed across the classes—landlords, workers, and capitalists, corresponding to the three factors of production, land, labor, and capital.[95] The working class constituted "the poor," and the main parameter determining their economic welfare was the wage rate, fixed at the subsistence level (as explained above). Technical progress was expected to be labor augmenting—increasing the demand for labor at any given wage rate—but the wage rate would return to the subsistence level in due course, choking off the gains to the poor.

Nor did the most influential classical economists after Smith offer much support for direct public interventions to fight poverty. Indeed, influential classical economists such as Malthus and Ricardo were positively hostile to the idea of antipoverty policy, with incentive arguments figuring prominently. Such policies would (it was claimed) discourage work effort and savings, and create poverty rather than remove it. The seemingly exaggerated claims made about incentive effects among critics of antipoverty policies around this time may well have been little more than the intellectual rationalizations of a political backlash against the First Poverty Enlightenment, notably among the elites in England resisting the new liberal ideas that were spilling over the Channel from France. The economics was hardly decisive. And even Malthus came to a more qualified view in a later edition of his *Essay on the Principle of Population,*

---

[95] This was probably a sensible simplification of the distribution of income at the time, and for much of the nineteenth century, but became less relevant from the late nineteenth century, as greater inequality emerged among workers, who also started to own more capital in the twentieth century.

where he acknowledged that better health and education for working-class families could break the tendency for the working-class population to rise with higher wages.

Debates on the Poor Laws

By the early nineteenth century, a major public debate began about England's Poor Laws (though there had been debates on poverty relief back to at least the late seventeenth century). Recall that relief under the OPL was financed by local taxes on landlords. By 1818 the required tax rate (known as the "poor rate") had risen to six times its level in the mid-eighteenth century.[96] The strongest political push for reform came from the landlords, who had come to dominate the English parliament around this time and were (it seems) no longer worried about impending revolution.[97] The backlash against the Poor Laws invoked incentive arguments, and England's classical economists were widely cited as critics of the OPL, including in America.[98] The distinction between "deserving" and "undeserving" poor emerged around this time and influenced the policy debate.[99]

This was a significant debate in the history of thought on poverty. Indeed, the arguments one hears today in favor of income targeting appear to have arisen in England around this time, although they appear to have then faded from prominence for some time, before returning to the forefront of social policy debates in the 1980s in Europe, North America, and Australia. About the same time, targeting started to be advocated in developing countries. So it is of interest to look more closely at the debates on England's Poor Laws in the 1830s.

Demand for relief under the Poor Laws had risen substantially over the first few decades of the nineteenth century. The labor migration to the cities in response to industrialization had meant that the Parishes were left to finance a rising support bill for children and the elderly. Work could not be found by all those able-bodied workers released from farming, and the unemployed were turning to the state to help them and their families get by. A series of bad harvests and rising unemployment in the wake of the end the Napoleonic wars had also boosted demand for Poor Law relief.

These were not, however, the explanations for the rising relief bill that appear to have gained favor politically. Rather, undesired behavioral responses to the availability of relief were seen to be the reason. In an influential pamphlet, *A Dissertation on the Poor Laws*, Joseph Townsend (1786, 17) wrote that "these laws, so beautiful in theory, promote the evils they mean to remedy, and aggravate the distress they were intended to relieve." This was echoed by many others, including Justice Turnor (1818). Prominent classical economists, including Malthus (1806, chs. 5 and 6) and Ricardo (1817), argued for either abandoning the Poor Laws or at least reforming them to assure better targeting.[100] Prominent observers such as Alexis de Tocqueville (1835) (in a memoir aiming to explain why there were so many paupers in England despite

---

[96] See Piven and Cloward (1993, 21).

[97] See Lindert (2004, ch. 4).

[98] See Klebaner (1964).

[99] See Gans's (1995, ch.1) discussion of labels for poor people.

[100] See the discussion of the views of Malthus and Ricardo on this topic in Sandmo (2014).

the country's affluence) also argued that the Poor Laws were a disincentive to work, such that they helped create the poverty problem they aimed to solve. Assumptions about incentives were the core of these arguments. Public relief from chronic hunger would discourage work, and the fiscal burden on the landholding class would discourage manufacturing growth and innovation in agriculture (Townsend, 1786, sec. 5). Ricardo (1817, 61) predicted (plainly with huge exaggeration) that the cost of the Poor Laws would rise out of control:

> as the legislature benevolently intended, to amend the condition of the poor, but to deteriorate the condition of both rich and the poor; instead of making the poor rich, they are calculated to make the rich poor; and whilst the present laws are in force, it is quite in the natural order of things that the fund for the maintenance of the poor should progressively increase until it has absorbed all the net revenue of the country.

Malthus argued that the Poor Laws encourage early marriage and high fertility (though counter arguments could also have been made that assured old-age support would reduce fertility). Moral hazard appears to have been a concern, whereby assistance to those who took high risks, and lost out, would encourage excessively risky behavior. The Poor Laws came to be seen by many as a cause of poverty rather than its cure. Similar debates were also going on about America's Poor Laws, with calls for reforms to cut their rising cost.[101]

The evidence base could hardly have been strong for the claims that behavioral responses to the laws were an important cause of the poverty they tried to address. The evidence appears to have been largely based on easily manipulated anecdotes and characterizations, with plainly weak claims of attribution; for example, was the claimed high incidence of intemperance a cause or effect of poverty? Nor was there much recognition that nonintervention could be socially costly too—that problems of heterogeneous risk and asymmetric information could entail that the private insurance was unavailable,[102] and that uninsured risk could spill over into production and investment decisions of poor men and women in ways that can impede longer term prospects of escaping poverty. For example, against the concerns that relief would reduce labor supply, it has been argued that the Old Poor Laws had the opposite effect, by providing the security against the risk of unemployment for smallholders considering whether to become laborers instead.[103]

While incentive effects and dependency were a legitimate concern, the economic arguments against England's Old Poor Laws may well have been exaggerated to serve political ends (and it was not the first or last time this happened). The "evidence" was weak and the arguments were somewhat one-sided, with many potential economic benefits ignored.

Significant reforms to the Poor Laws were implemented in 1834 (including repeal of Speenhamland). Spending was slashed, from a peak of about 2.5% of national

---

[101] See Klebaner (1964).

[102] This economic argument for social insurance was not well developed in the literature until much later, notably by Rothschild and Stiglitz (1976).

[103] Solar (1995) makes this argument.

income around 1830 to 1% in 1840—a dramatic cut.[104] Wider use was to be made of workhouses ("poorhouses" in America). These had long existed and had been an element of the Poor Laws for over one hundred years.[105] By the late eighteenth century, 1–2% of the population of London was seeking relief in some eighty workhouses.[106] Their role expanded considerably under the reforms of 1834 to assure better targeting and the new nineteenth-century workhouses in England appear to have been even more unpleasant and punitive places than in the past (described well in *London Lives*). Earnings were paid in kind, as lodging and food (mainly gruel it seems) in the workhouse, and were deliberately meager to assure self-targeting; "all poor people should have the alternative . . . of being starved by a gradual process in the home, or by a quick one out of it" (Dickens 1838, 18).

The policy may well have become better targeted in the sense of excluding the nonpoor, but at the expense of reducing coverage of the poor. As Dickens (1838, 18) also wrote: "The relief was inseparable from the workhouse and the gruel, and that frightened people." Almost immediately, the New Poor Laws became the subject of social criticism. By confining beneficiaries to workhouses, the reformed policy was seen by critics to treat poor people as criminals. The conditions under which inmates were kept became a specific focus of criticism, famously so in the first few chapters of Dickens's (1838) *Oliver Twist*. Common criticisms in the media and literature related to the inhumane treatment of workhouse inmates, including meager rations. There were many anecdotal references to corruption, whereby officials and local suppliers took their take from the stipulated allocations to the workhouses.[107] And the criticisms (which started almost immediately) of the New Poor Laws were not just confined to social critics, but reached deeply into the leading circles of the Conservative Party, including Benjamin Disraeli.[108] The reforms undermined the broad public support that the Old Poor Laws had enjoyed for three hundred years.

A Lost Opportunity in America

Four million people were enslaved in America's southern states just prior to the Civil War (1861–5). The Northern victory secured the survival of the United States and the abolition of slavery. The emancipated slaves needed help immediately, which was implemented by transfers of food, clothing, and fuel, administered by a new government agency, the *Freedmen's Bureau*. This was (explicitly) short-term relief, intended to last for one year. However, there was also a major proposal for promotional poverty reduction near the end of the War. General William T. Sherman issued Special Field

[104] See Lindert (2013, fig. 1).

[105] See Katz (1986) and Jütte (1994) on the history of poorhouses/workhouses in America and Europe, respectively.

[106] See the entry on workhouses in *London Lives, 1690–1800*. Also see in Hindle's (2004, 176) discussion of the use of encouragements to work under the Old Poor Laws, whereby the Church vestry often became a "job-creation service" (176). Workhouses existed elsewhere in Europe including Holland where they were introduced in Amsterdam around 1600 (Beaudoin 2006, 48). Novels such as Dickens (1838) refer to corruption in orphanages and workhouses at the time.

[107] See Fowler (2007).

[108] See Himmelfarb (1984a, b).

Orders whereby previously enslaved African-American families were each to be given 40 acres of land, derived by confiscating 400,000 acres of land along the Atlantic coast of the American South.[109]

It is indicative of prevailing thinking that the idea of such a land reform was not especially radical at the time; there were a number of previous and subsequent examples, under various "homesteading acts." Nor did Sherman see it as a longer-term promotional policy; he was more concerned with the short-term problem he faced of large numbers of refugees seeking help. However, this re-distributive land reform could well have put much of the South on a new path of poverty-reducing growth—"pro-poor growth," which we return to in Chapter 8.

Alas, the promise was never fulfilled, and Sherman's orders were revoked by President Andrew Johnson (the successor to Abraham Lincoln on his assassination). While their freedom was clearly a huge gain, without their own agricultural land, the newly free people were dependent on wage labor, and with a plentiful supply of labor, wages were low. Continuing poverty was reinforced over the coming decades by various state legislative acts and policies ("Jim Crow laws") that greatly constrained the economic and political opportunities for African Americans, including literacy tests for voting and inferior, segregated, schools. While the Union was now firm, the plantation-based economy of the South survived largely intact, and the poverty of African Americans persisted.

Utilitarianism

Social contract theory, as developed by Hobbes and Rousseau, emphasized rights and freedoms. This lost ground in the nineteenth century to a rival school of thought, utilitarianism. This had emerged during the First Poverty Enlightenment in the late eighteenth century, and it also offered qualified support for the idea that the state had a role in determining how incomes should be distributed. But it was explicitly not a rights-based theory. Jeremy Bentham, widely seen as the founding father of utilitarianism, was motivated by practical legalistic and policy reform, and his interventionism led him to reject ideas like "natural rights."[110] Instead, utilitarianism advocated that social choices should be made according to their consequences for individual utilities and that (when some gained utility while some lost) the choices should maximize the sum of utilities across all individuals in the society in question. "Utility" was an inherently subjective concept, often equated with "happiness," but in theory at least more general than happiness. Essentially it is whatever people care about.

This was a significant step in thinking. Recall that Adam Smith had criticized the mercantilists for focusing on the BOT as the objective for assessing social welfare, and advocated instead a focus on the economy's aggregate command over commodities. This was neutral to inequality in consumption or income across society. Utilitarianism

---

[109] Sherman later promised the loan of a mule to each family, and the proposal became famous in the expression "40 acres and a mule." On this period of post-war reconstruction in America see Foner (1988). Also see the discussion in Acemoglu and Robinson (2012, Chapter 12).

[110] Artz (1934, 83) quotes him as describing the *Declaration of the Rights of Man and of the Citizen* as "a hodge-podge of confusion and absurdity."

provided a foundation for thinking about how incomes should be distributed within society. Diminishing marginal utility of income had strong intuitive appeal to the new Benthamite utilitarianism,[111] and it was recognized immediately that this constituted a qualified case against income inequality. This was an instrumental case; equity was not seen as intrinsically desirable but only as a means of raising total utility. The marginal losses to rich donors of any mean-preserving transfer would be outweighed by marginal gains to poor recipients; box 1.13 explains the idea.

Box 1.13 **The Utilitarian Case against Income Inequality**

The utilitarian case against income inequality makes three key assumptions. First, social states are to be assessed by "social welfare" as given by the sum total of the "happiness" or "utility" in society. (This is sometimes called the Benthamite objective.) Social welfare (*SW*) for a population of size *n* can then be written as the sum of individual utilities:

$$SW = \sum_{i=1}^{n} u_i(y_i) = u_1(y_1) + u_2(y_2) + \ldots + u_n(y_n)$$

Here y_i is the income of person i and $u_i(y_i)$ is the (strictly increasing) utility attached by the social evaluator to that level of consumption. Second, everyone derives the same utility from a given income; then $u_i(y_i) = u(y_i)$ for all i. Third, there is diminishing marginal utility of income, meaning that the extra utility from an increase in income is greater the lower the initial income. This is explained by figure B1.13.1. On the vertical axis we have utility, which varies with income, plotted on the horizontal axis. The marginal utility of the income level y_A can be defined as the slope of the tangent on the utility function at that point. The third assumption says that the marginal utility of extra income is lower for anyone with income $y_B > y_A$, that is, that the utility function is concave in income.

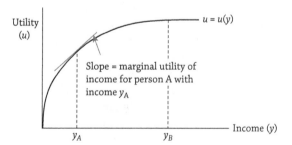

Figure B1.13.1 Utility as a Function of Income.

---

[111] Bentham put it this way: "The excess in happiness of the richer will not be so great as the excess of his wealth" (quoted by Harrison 1987, 57).

If we take money away from the "poor" (at y_A) and give it to the "rich" (y_B) holding mean income constant, then total utility falls. The loss of utility to the poor is greater than the gain in utility for the rich. Similarly, comparing two societies with the same mean income, the one with the lower inequality will have the higher level of social welfare. But notice that a loss of utility to the poorest person can always be justified by a larger utility gain to the richest person. All the utilitarian cares about is the sum of utilities.

The Benthamite objective is an example of a broader class of *social welfare functions*, which summarize the ethical trade-offs made by a policymaker (or independent observer) between people at different levels of welfare. In the Benthamite form above everyone gets equal weight, although with declining marginal utility of income this still implies that income inequality is penalized in assessing social welfare. Against this idea, it is argued by some observers that those with lower welfare should get higher weight.

Further reading: Good expositions on this topic are found in public economics, including Atkinson and Stiglitz (1980, lecture 11), Hindriks and Myles (2006), and Kaplow (2008, pt. 5).

Utilitarianism did not, however, open the floodgates for redistributive interventions. Assuming diminishing marginal utility of income and a common utility function only implied that equality of incomes was optimal if total income was invariant to its distribution. The case was unclear if income redistribution lowered overall output, as Bentham expected. Even aside from incentive effects, merely introducing interpersonal heterogeneity (such that the utility valuation of a given income level varies) upset any claim that income equality maximizes social welfare (though this point did not seem to get the same attention as the growth-equity trade-off).

This new way of thinking permitted certain interventions, including policies that provided limited redistribution of incomes in favor of the poor, but it also framed the case against other interventions that did not raise total utility. There was no case for interventions that did not have an instrumental role in raising someone's utility; if there was something that nobody wanted, then there was no case for providing it.

Over the next two hundred years, utilitarianism came to have a huge influence on economics—it became the "official theory of traditional welfare economics."[112] An appeal of utilitarianism was its ability to draw policy implications from reason and (often casual) empiricism. Bentham and followers, notably John Stuart Mill, had seen government as a necessary evil, and put any actual or contemplated policy effort to the utilitarian test. Some of the literature has (derisively) characterized this as a period of "laissez-faire," although to the eyes of many economists it was a welcome discipline in sound policymaking, to assure maximum social welfare. The real issue was what one meant by "social welfare." The influential rights-based thinkers on policy prior to

---

[112] Sen (2000, 63).

the utilitarians, such as Condorcet, would no doubt have also advocated higher social welfare, but rejected any attempt to equate welfare with "happiness" or "utility."[113]

A long-standing issue for utilitarianism is whether one should judge society's progress by the *total utility* of its population or its *average utility* (the total divided by population size). This matters when population size varies. Adding any person to the population will increase total utility, but average utility will fall if the new life lives below the initial mean utility. The ethical dilemma for those using average utility is plain: if sufficiently poor people die, then average utility rises. But those who favor total utility have their own conundrum: adding people to the population is judged to be a good thing no matter how miserably poor they may be.[114]

One way of getting around this problem is to postulate a more general form of utilitarianism that says that social welfare only increases with a larger population if the extra people have a level of living above a critical minimum, which we can think of as a normative poverty line.[115] Notice, however, that when those living below this line die social welfare is deemed to rise! Indeed, as long as it costs something to the non-poor to lift the poor up to this poverty line it would be better to let them die off. This is ethically unacceptable, of course.

Utilitarianism was probably the most influential example of what philosophers call *consequentialism*. This is the idea that the "ends justify the means"—that actions should be judged by their outcomes, as distinct from deontological ideas about rights and fairness, which judged actions instead by the individual behaviors and social-political processes concerned. Mainstream economic assessments of policies (including redistributive policies) came to adopt consequentialism, and utilitarianism in particular. This is not to say that welfare economics is devoid of concern about the means. Indeed, the economics that emerged over the next one hundred years came to put very high weight on the idea that there was great merit to freedom of exchange and consumer sovereignty. But these were still mostly judged by their outcomes. And there were seeming inconsistencies with how other freedoms were viewed; for example, the freedom of workers to organize themselves in unions to bargain collectively found rather little attention or support from mainstream economists.

By the mid-nineteenth century, it was becoming accepted in prominent progressive circles that the state did have a role in "redressing the inequalities and wrongs of nature" (Mill 1848, 805). Even so, it is clear that poverty was still widely accepted as a normal state of affairs. Poor men and women were still being blamed for their poverty (notably by their excessive reproduction) and there was little role for the state. Even protection was increasingly "targeted" to extreme cases. The best that could be hoped for was that workers would somehow come to see the wisdom of curtailing their desired family sizes. Even among the most progressive utilitarian voices of the time

---

[113] See Rothschild (2001) for further discussion.

[114] This is an example of a class of problems on population ethics that lead to what is called a "repugnant conclusion"; see Parfit (1984).

[115] This was proposed by Blackorby and Donaldson (1984). The social welfare function in box 1.13 then becomes $SW = \sum_{i=1}^{n} u(y_i) - u(\alpha)$, where α is the poverty line. For a recent example of the application of this approach, see Cockburn et al. (2014).

(such as Mill), the closest one came to promotional policies would be to point to a role for (private) education of the working class in reducing population growth.

The Limitations of Charity

It is one thing to identify a moral case for helping poor people but quite another to implement effective action. The emergence of an active role for governments in fighting poverty was premised on a questioning of whether private charity was up to the task. There were concerns that a system of poverty relief based on charity created incentives for begging, which was seen as a major source of externalities from poverty. There were also concerns about uneven coverage of those in need. Private giving is known to be more responsive to the circumstances of specific individuals that the giver knows personally than to the needs of an anonymous mass of unidentified but equally needy people, especially when some distance away. This is thought to be a common feature of the psychology of giving.[116]

Another important limitation of discretionary giving is what economists quaintly call *free riding* (box 1.14). By the mid-nineteenth century, the efficiency of a free-market economy appears to have been widely appreciated. But it was also becoming understood that there was a serious problem of likely under-provision of certain goods, which came to be known as *public goods*. In his *Principles of Political Economy*— clearly the most important economics textbook of the second half of the nineteenth century—Mill (1848, bk. 5, ch. 11) argued that individual incentives may not be strong enough to take an action that is overwhelmingly in the collective interest. Mill gave the example of the need for laws to punish theft and fraud, given that "it is the interest of each that nobody should rob or cheat [but] it is not any one's interest to refrain from robbing and cheating others when all others are permitted to rob and cheat him" (Mill 1848, 583).

The same logic applies to poverty when its relief delivers a collective benefit, but we rely on independent discretionary efforts through private charity. Most people may benefit from less poverty but individual incentives for private action are too weak to do much about the problem, since it is possible to enjoy the benefit without paying a fair share of the cost, or indeed any of the cost. The moral case may well be very strong, and the potential benefits large for all, but action may well be less than optimal unless institutions exist to solve the free-rider problem (as explained in box 1.14). Religious or secular appeals to the virtues of beneficence can be interpreted as efforts to assure a more cooperative outcome for all. However, the temptation to free ride can be great. As a prominent advocate of the moral case for giving observes, "we all see or read appeals to help those living in extreme poverty in the world's poorest countries. And yet most of us reject the call to 'do unto others'" (Singer 2010, 22).

The classic solution to the free-rider problem is to make the action that is vulnerable to free riding mandatory, through legislation or regulation. As Mill (1848, 581) put it, "there are matters in which the interference of law is required, not to overrule the judgments of individuals respecting their own interest, but to give effect

---

[116] See the discussion in Singer (2010, chapter 4).

to that judgment." Thus, Mill recognized that there was an important role for the state in fighting poverty: "I conceive it to be highly desirable that certainty of subsistence should be held out by law to the destitute able bodied, rather than that their relief should depend on voluntary charity" (Mill 1848, 581). However, reasonably comprehensive public efforts against poverty were still a long way off.

Box 1.14 Under-Provision of Public Goods When Their Support Is Discretionary

Suppose that a new labor union is needed to advocate the collective interests of workers. Voluntary contributions (in cash or kind, through work) by workers are the only available means of starting and maintaining the union, but none of the workers know how much value other workers attach to the organization. Thus, we have what is called a "non-cooperative game," in which self-interested players act independently of each other, with each player only knowing her own preferences, but in which all players attach personal value to the public good (in this case the labor union). Some civic-minded workers will no doubt offer to contribute. However, all workers will also realize that they can enjoy the benefits of the union's efforts without contributing much personally. They may announce a willingness to contribute, but it is likely they will understate their true demand, and they may even prefer not to offer to contribute anything. That is an example of free riding. The organization may never get off the ground.

The same idea applies to poverty. Everyone may prefer to live in a world free of poverty. However, free-riding entails that private charity delivers too little poverty reduction.

This is not to say that free riding will always occur. In organized games among real people, cooperation (such as in supplying public goods) appears to emerge more often than the standard economic model would predict. To assess whether there is a role for the state in providing a specific public good we must determine whether private provision is serving the need adequately.

Further reading: Hindriks and Myles (2006) include a good discussion of public goods. A good treatment of the game-theoretic interpretation of the free-rider problem can be found in Binmore (2007). Ostrom (1990) provides an interesting discussion of the ways communities can strive to solve the free-rider problem by the management practices they use for their common-property resources.

Schooling Debates

Children from poor families typically started their working lives at an early age; while the evidence is patchy, it was common prior to the mid-nineteenth century for working-class children in England to start earning from seven years of age, if work was available.[117] The survival of the family demanded that every able-bodied person

---

[117] See Cunningham (1990).

worked. Any skills required would only be those that could be passed on by the family. Idle poor children were abhorrent to the rich; work was seen as the only solution. Child labor was not only condoned but widely seen as desirable; unemployment of poor children was seen as the bigger social problem. The idea of mass public schooling appears to have had little support until the latter part of the nineteenth century. Indeed, echoing de Mandeville's views, a common view was that mass schooling was wasteful, and even dangerous. Even by the middle of the nineteenth century some 40% of children aged five to nine in England and Wales were still not in school.[118]

Nor was the state deemed to have an important role in the schooling that was provided. Prior to the nineteenth century, and well into that century in some countries (including England), almost all schooling received by children from poor families was by religious groups. The system of voluntary schooling in England and elsewhere in Europe was clearly highly stratified and unequal. Schooling by religious groups had a mixed record. In England, the church resisted any public role in provision, yet also left much unmet demand.[119] The debate on mass schooling opportunities continued in England until quite late in the nineteenth century, and the country lagged much of Europe and North America in schooling attainments, despite its wealth.

Poor families did not always see Church schools as being in their interests. Informal private schools were often more promising for those who could afford them. "Backstreet schools" in Austria and Prussia offered more efficient instruction "subordinating religious instruction to the goal of imparting literacy to their pupils" and it appears that these were often favored by poor parents keen on their children's efficient learning and eventual employability.[120] The backstreet schools were seen by poor families to offer a more cost-effective means of acquiring literacy.[121] This echoes observations of the "backstreet schools" found throughout India today, reflecting evident failures of the state-run schooling system.[122]

A change in popular views about schooling for poor families started to be evident in much of Europe and North America from the mid-nineteenth century. The working conditions of children in the factories of the time provided fuel for labor activists, social novels, *and* for the increasingly vocal critics of capitalism, most notably Karl Marx and Friedrich Engels. Prominent calls started to be heard for improving the working conditions of children and for schooling as the better way to address their unemployment. Schooling for poor children came to be seen as key to their self-improvement and mobility. Mass schooling was also seen to have external benefits, such as through reduced crime.

Legislation for compulsory schooling was becoming widespread in Europe and North America by the late nineteenth century.[123] This followed a protracted public

---

[118] This is based on the 1851 census (as reported in Cunningham 1990, table 1); 39% of boys and 44% of girls in this age group were not classified as "scholars" (the alternatives being employment or "at home"). The subsequent spread of literacy was also highly uneven geographically (Stephens 1998).

[119] See Lindert (2004, ch. 5).

[120] Van Horn Melton (1988, 11).

[121] See Van Horn Melton (1988, 11) with reference to Prussia.

[122] See Probe Team (1999).

[123] There were some progressive local initiatives for mass schooling, such as in Massachusetts in the late seventeenth century (Weiner, 1991, ch. 6).

debate.[124] Some argued against almost any intrusion by the state into private decision-making.[125] Others worried that schooling the poor would lead them to hold unrealistic aspirations.[126] From early on the industries that were dependent on child labor lobbied against compulsory schooling. However, over the course of the nineteenth century, industrialists appear to have become more supportive of mass schooling, to assure the more skilled workforce needed for new technologies.[127] This was not simply a matter of schools catering to the needs of new technologies; the debates about schooling were broader and it is not clear that the industrialists had that much influence.[128] Poor parents and local communities were also increasingly vocal in their demands for mass public schooling. It seems that by the latter half of the nineteenth century it had become more realistic for poor working-class parents to aspire for a better life for their children. There were also administrative constraints on enforcement to overcome; it was not until birth registration systems had been developed around the mid-nineteenth century that truancy laws could be properly enforced.[129] While there was overall progress in promoting mass schooling, the pace was uneven and differences in education policies emerged, such as between America and Europe, with the United States doing better at fostering high-quality public education for all, which was to be a key foundation for its equitable growth until the latter part of the twentieth century.[130]

Socialism and the Labor Movement

Widespread poverty, and the elites' indifference to it, is one of the factors that led to the emergence of socialism.[131] (Another was urban industrialization, as it made it easier for workers to organize.) The leading school of socialist thought, Marxism, has seen the root cause of poverty to be capitalism itself. By this view, the profits enjoyed by the capitalist class are simply the other side of the coin to the poverty of workers. And yet those same profits are seen to derive entirely from labor. Indeed, Marx (1867) was keen to attribute all value to labor and built his economics on this foundation, largely borrowing from Ricardo's labor theory of value, but taking it more seriously than Ricardo.[132]

Marxists expect inequality to rise under capitalism, with the capitalist class capturing the bulk of any gains in national income. It is granted that profits will not

---

[124] See Weiner (1991, ch. 6).

[125] In the United States, one occasionally hears arguments that compulsory schooling is unconstitutional, the reference being to the anti-Slavery amendment introduced near the end of the Civil War on the grounds that (it is claimed) compulsory schooling is "involuntary servitude." See, for an example, http://www.4forums.com/political/education-debates/8440-compulsory-education-unconstitutional.html.

[126] See, e.g., Vinovskis (1992).

[127] See Bowles and Gintis (1976), with reference to the United States.

[128] See Vinovskis (1992).

[129] See Weiner (1991, 121).

[130] Also reflecting changes in education policy, as described in Goldin and Katz (2008).

[131] See Landauer (1959).

[132] See the discussion in Blaug (1962, ch. 7).

all be consumed by the capitalists. Their thirst for accumulation would assure that a significant share is reinvested; this made sense in nineteenth-century Europe, when reinvested profit was the main source of funds for supporting industrialization given that workers were too poor to save and financial markets were largely absent. But this reinvestment is seen as the instrument for the continuing exploitation of labor rather than as a means of reducing poverty in the future.

Marx rejected the classical economists' views on how induced population growth would keep the wage rate at a fixed "subsistence" level.[133] Indeed, he rejected any suggestion that poverty is some natural state. But nor did he assume that the wage rate would automatically fall to clear the market. Prevailing social norms were seen to play a role in determining wages, which could vary across social settings and over time. Workers could also organize to secure higher wages. However, without strong labor unions, the presence of surplus labor (the "reserve army of the unemployed") would play a role in constraining the prospects for sustainable wage growth, and so limit the gains to poor families from economic expansion under capitalism.

Marxists have had an ambivalent view of antipoverty policies. The solution to poverty is seen to be Communism, not piecemeal redistributive policies in a capitalist economy (though they have given less attention to establishing the case for why Communism would be any better). Such policies are seen by the hardliners as a mild palliative, and one that might even risk delaying more revolutionary change. Nor is much value attached to the philosophical and economic thinking on poverty that has pointed to a redistributive role for the state; for example, Marx was as disparaging as Bentham about talk of "rights."[134]

Nonetheless, most Marxists have given begrudging support to redistributive policies in a capitalist economy. Some of the demands outlined in the *Communist Manifesto* of Marx and Engels (1848) can be recognized today as quite mainstream antipoverty policies with broad political support, including progressive income taxation and free education in public schools.

The labor theory of value—a key analytic element of Marx's economics—did not have a lasting influence on mainstream economic thought and proved no match intellectually for the competitive general equilibrium model of Léon Walras (1874) that emerged soon after Marx's (1867) major work. Even so, the Walrasian model lacked the appreciation for the historical, social, and political forces shaping economies that one finds in Marx. The idea of the reserve army of the unemployed was to return often, including in development economics (which we return to in chapters 2 and 8). Marx's insistence that human nature is largely a product of social context has had a lasting influence in political philosophy.[135] Instead of seeing poverty as the outcome of individual attributes, one should look to social influences on behavior. Of course, this idea also had pre-Marxian antecedents, notably in Rousseau.

The socialist political organizations and labor movements that emerged in Europe and North America played an important role in progressive social policymaking from the late nineteenth century. There were two aspects of this role. The first was to

---

[133] See Baumol (1983) on Marx's theory of wage determination.

[134] Fleischacker (2004, 97) quotes Marx as calling appeals to "rights" as "ideological nonsense."

[135] See Fleischacker (2004) on this influence of Marxian philosophy on modern theories of distributive justice.

encourage conservatives to take action against poverty and inequality for fear of instability or even revolution. The critiques by the socialist movement prompted pro-poor reforms attempting to soften the harder edges of the inequalities under capitalism. Famously Bismarck in Germany in the 1880s introduced comprehensive social insurance in an attempt to "lure the workers away from the socialists."[136]

Second, political coalitions formed between workers and social reformers to lobby for more comprehensive antipoverty policies in Europe and North America in the late nineteenth century. While the trade unions had taken on social insurance roles for their workers—to help with accidents, sickness, and old age, financed by worker's dues—the coverage was never adequate. It came to be recognized that the state had to provide universal insurance and poverty relief. The political struggle toward that end took many decades, but eventually modern welfare states had emerged across virtually all rich countries by the second half of the twentieth century.

Social Research on Poverty

After Frederick Eden's pioneering work documenting living conditions of poor families in England at the end of the eighteenth century, there seems to have been a hiatus until the mid-nineteenth century, when new research on social problems started to emerge. In public health, this was the time that a link was established between the contamination of drinking water by human waste and cholera, which eventually led to public efforts to assure cleaner piped drinking water (box 1.15). This is an early example of research informing public action to address market failures that perpetuate poverty. Here the policies were not extra cash in hand for poor people but public provisioning.

Box 1.15 **Mapping Cholera Incidence in London**

In an early example of what came to be known as impact evaluation (to be studied in chapter 6), Dr. John Snow mapped the incidence of deaths in a severe and geographically concentrated outbreak of cholera in 1854 London (the world's largest city at the time, and quite possibly its smelliest as well). The map suggested that the incidence of deaths due to cholera was associated with a specific drinking water supplier (the Broad Street pump in Soho) that had been contaminated by a nearby cesspit of accumulated sewerage. Prior to this, the prevailing view was that cholera was an air-borne disease, not water borne.

Within ten years the infrastructure of a modern sewerage system was being developed in London. Snow's research had huge significance for public health globally, with enormous benefit to the world's poor, though still an unrealized benefit for many people today.

Further reading: John Snow is now seen as one of the pioneers of modern epidemiology. Johnson's (2007) book, *The Ghost Map*, describes well the circumstances and impact of Snow's famous map.

---

[136] Landauer (1959, 276).

From the mid-nineteenth century, social research and journalism was helping relatively well-heeled citizens know the living conditions of those less fortunate, which helped promote better informed public debates on antipoverty policy. Famous examples include:

- Friedrich Engels's (1845) description of the harsh working conditions and poor health environments of Manchester in the 1840s.[137]
- Henry Mayhew's (2008) newspaper reports on London's poor in the 1840s.
- Frederic Le Play's budget studies of working-class families in Europe in the mid-nineteenth century.[138]
- Mathew Carey's use of data on budgets and wages of poor families to "startle the complacent into giving alms" in Philadelphia in the 1830s.[139]
- Photograph started to supplement written descriptions of poverty, such as Jacob Riis's (1890) photojournalism describing the slums of New York City in the 1880s.

From the mid-nineteenth century, quantitative data and statistical analysis were also starting to play an important role in improving knowledge of poverty. A pioneer in this regard was the German statistician Ernst Engel (1857), who studied the relationship between household food spending and its total spending. He found what came to be known as *Engel's Law*, namely that the poorer a family is the higher the share of its budget devoted to food, or (equivalently) that the income elasticity of demand for food is less than unity. (See box 1.16 on Engel's Law.)

Box 1.16 The Income Elasticity of Demand and Engel's "Law"

The key to Engel's Law is the concept of the *income elasticity of demand*. This measures the responsiveness of the demand for food (or some other commodity) to a change in income. It can be defined as the ratio of the percentage change in the quantity of food consumed divided by the percentage change in income that brought about the change in food consumption. So if the demand for food rises by 5% as a result of a 10% gain in income, then the elasticity is 0.5.

When the total expenditure of a household rises, we expect its consumption of food to also rise. This means that the income (or total expenditure) elasticity of demand is positive. Studies of demand behavior using household surveys since Engel's first contribution in 1857 have confirmed this and have also typically found that the elasticity is less than unity. This is taken to mean that food is a "necessity," as distinct from goods with an elasticity greater than unity, called "luxuries." Intuitively, we need a minimum amount of food to even stay alive; in that sense food is truly a necessity. The implication is that the share of total spending going to food tends to fall as total spending rises, as illustrated in figure B1.16.1.

continued

---

[137] Though written in German and not published in English until 1887.
[138] See Brooke (1998).
[139] See Klebaner (1964, 384).

Box 1.16 **(Continued)**

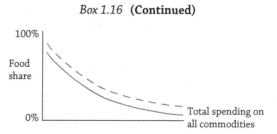

Figure B1.16.1 Theoretical Engel Curve for Food.

Engel's law only concerns one factor determining demand for food, namely income. One also expects the Engel curve to vary with other factors, such as prices and household demographic composition. For example, food demand will also respond to prices, including (of course) food prices. And poor people tend also to be more responsive in their food purchases to food price increase; more precisely, the *price elasticity of demand* for food tends to be higher (more negative) for poorer households. (Analogously to the income elasticity, the price elasticity gives the ratio of the percentage change in the quantity of food consumed divided by the percentage change in food price.) To give another example, as Engel also argued, one expects families with a larger share of children to devote a large share of their budget to food at given total spending, as indicated by the dashed line in the figure.

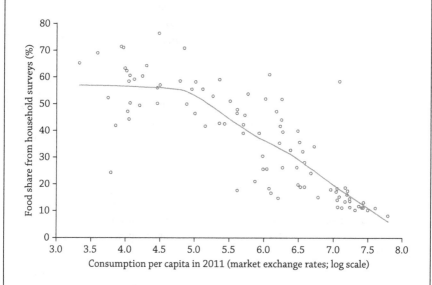

Figure B1.16.2 Empirical Engel Curve for Food across Countries. *Source:* Ravallion and Chen (2015).

Figure B1.16.2 shows what the Engel curve looks like across countries. The horizontal axis uses a log scale, which gives a less congested picture among poorer countries (and it changes the curvature compared to figure B1.16.1). Among poor countries there is little decline in the food share, averaging around 57% of spending. So Engel's Law is rather weak in poor countries (i.e., the income elasticity of demand for food is close to unity). After some point the food share then starts to decline sharply to around 10% for the richest.

Historical note: One hundred years after Engel's first formulation of his "law," Houthakker (1957) found support in survey data across thirty countries using a statistical model giving the log of food spending as a function of log total spending and log household size. Box 1.19 explains this type of model further.

Further reading: Using more advanced analytic methods, there is a good discussion of Engel's approach to studying demand behavior in the classic textbook by Deaton and Muellbauer (1980).

However, after Eden's *The State of the Poor*, the next most important landmarks in modern scientific research on poverty were clearly the studies by Charles Booth and Seebohm Rowntree, documenting the living conditions of England's poor (in London and York, respectively) in the late nineteenth century. These were pioneering measurements using seemingly careful household surveys that revealed to non-poor people how poor people lived. (See box 1.17 on surveys.) Their work attracted much attention. There had been an improvement in the lives of the English working class over the preceding fifty years,[140] though poverty remained. Booth is often credited with the idea of a "poverty line," although there were antecedents, including the Speenhamland line one hundred years earlier. At the time, the English public was shocked that one million Londoners—about one-third of the city's population—lived below his frugal line. And it is a frugal line; by my calculations it was equivalent to 1.5 pounds of good wheat per person per day, which is not very different to lines found in today's developing countries.[141]

[140] This was acknowledged by none other than Friedrich Engels in the 1892 preface to the English edition of his description of the living conditions of the working class in Manchester in 1844.

[141] Marshall (1907) estimates that 21 shillings was equivalent to three-quarters of a bushel of good wheat. At 13.5% moisture by weight a bushel of wheat weights 60 lb according to the Wikipedia entry on "bushel." I assume a household of 4.5 people, which is the lower bound of the range 4.5–5 given by Booth (1993, ch. 4) for the average size of working men's families at the time. Booth's line of 21 shillings per week for a family is thus equivalent to slightly less than 700 gms of wheat per person per day. Of course, this is just the wheat equivalent. A reasonable dietary breakdown would be 400 gms per person for wheat and the remainder for meat, vegetables, and (very minimal) non-food needs. This then is similar to India's national poverty line in 1993, which I have calculated to be equivalent to a daily food bundle per person of 400 gms of coarse rice and wheat, 200 gms of vegetables, pulses, and fruit, plus modest amounts of milk, eggs, edible oil, spices, and tea (World Bank 1997). After buying such a food bundle, one would be left with about $0.30 per day (at 1993 purchasing power parity) for non-food items.

Box 1.17 Household Surveys

The classic household survey collects interview data from a random sample of households. A common sample design entails first taking a random sample of primary sampling units (PSUs), such as villages; the PSUs are selected with probabilities proportional to population size. The second stage takes a random sample of households within the selected villages, typically after doing a listing of all households in the PSU. (More complex sample multilevel designs are sometimes used, although one has to be careful that the design does not unduly reduce the precision of the final estimates; the simple two-stage sampling method is often preferable in practice.)

The survey instrument (or questionnaire) is sometimes designed for a very specific purpose, and sometimes it is a multipurpose instrument, such as the World Bank's Living Standards Measurement Study (LSMS). The latter surveys will include detailed questions on sources of income and on consumption expenditures (including consumption-in-kind, such as from own-farm production). These detailed questions are designed such that it will be possible to aggregate up to obtain a comprehensive measure of income and/or consumption.

The implementing agency will typically produce a statistical abstract summarizing the results from the survey. However, this is often of rather limited analytic and policy interest. Most users today will access the micro data to explore specific questions such as in measuring poverty and inequality, describing the characteristics of poor people, assessing the incidence of participation in antipoverty programs, and modeling behavioral responses.

Further reading: Chapter 3 discusses surveys further, including the main methodological issues that users should be aware of, and provides references to the literature.

Booth's research responded to a demand for clarity and data among legislators. His empirical research into old-age poverty and its geographic variation influenced Britain's introduction of a public pension in 1908 and national insurance in 1911.[142] The research of Booth and Rowntree also stimulated debates about which city or country had more poverty. Around 1900, it was widely believed that about 30% of England's population was poor. This was based on the fact that Rowntree found that 28% of York's population was poor while Booth had found that 31% of London's population was poor. However, as measures of absolute poverty, the two numbers were not comparable, as they used different poverty lines (box 1.18).

---

[142] See Thane (2000, ch. 9) and Himmelfarb (1984a, b).

Box 1.18 "30% of England's Population Is Poor": Early Lessons in Poverty Analysis

Rowntree had found that 28% of York's population was poor, while Booth had found that this was so for 31% of London's population. With no other data, the common belief around 1900 was that 30% of England's population was poor. However, it turns out that Rowntree's line was much higher than Booth's. Here are the calculations made by MacGregor (1910):

% of population living in poverty	York	London
Booth's line	3	31
Rowntree's line	28	50

We see that using either line, the poverty rate was far higher in London. The claim that 30% of England's poor can thus be questioned, as can that the poverty rate was almost as high in York as London.

Later, in the United States, Miller (1964) made a similar observation about the changes in how poverty is measured in the United States. In 1935 the poverty rate by contemporary standards was deemed to be 28%, falling to 10% by 1960. However, the real value of the poverty line had risen over time. Miller calculated that if one used the 1960 line for 1935 the poverty rate then would have been 47%.

Comparisons between countries were also a favorite of the media from an early time. For example, fifteen years after Booth's books appeared, Alfred Marshall was argumentatively claiming that there was even more poverty in Germany than Booth's figures suggested was the case in England; this was in response to Marshall's (1907, 12) perception that "one of the few things which every German knows for certain about England is that there are a million people in London living in extreme poverty on the verge of hunger."

The close observational studies of poverty by Booth and Rowntree were influential in social science research. Robert Hunter (1904) followed their lead in studying poverty in the United States and provided the first estimate of the US poverty rate. Hunter estimated that 10 million people in the United States lived in poverty around 1900, which turns out to be very close to the estimate in figure 1.1, which implies that 10.6 million people in the United States lived in poverty in 1900.[143] Implicitly then, Hunter's poverty lines was quite similar to the "$1 a day" line underlying the estimates in figure 1.1.

---

[143] This is based on a linear interpolation of the estimates for 1890 and 1910, giving 13.9%, and the US population of 76 million from the 1990 census.

The influence of Booth and Rowntree reached further. Village studies in India by Mann and collaborators were influenced by Booth and Rowntree.[144] A long and distinguished tradition of quantitative-economic studies of selected villages followed.[145] Booth's approach influenced the development of quantitative sociology in both Britain and the United States.[146] Peter Townsend's (1979) empirical study of poverty in England some eighty years later clearly owed much to Booth and Rowntree. So too did the Chicago School of Sociology that began studying urban poverty in the United States during the 1930s.

The late nineteenth century also saw the birth of statistical tools that were later to have great value in economics and the social sciences generally, including in research on poverty and antipoverty policies. A case in point is the idea of a *linear regression*, which first emerged in biology, notably in Sir Francis Galton's famous studies of inheritance.[147] Karl Pearson (1896) developed the modern formulation of the regression line and correlation coefficient from the objective of minimizing the error variance. Box 1.19 explains the idea of this statistical tool, which we will hear about often in the rest of this volume. Applications to economic and social behavior followed soon after the emergence of these ideas in biology.[148]

Box 1.19 The Economist's Favorite Statistical Tool: Regression

A regression line is a fitted line relating a dependent variable (*y*) to one or more explanatory variables (*x*). Attention is typically confined to straight lines. The fit is never perfect and some error term (ε) remains. The "best fit" line is typically identified as the one that gives the lowest error variance—the sum of squared errors in using that line to predict the dependent variable. The measured values taken by the error are often called the "residuals." The regression's slope coefficient is denoted β while α is the intercept (when $x = 0$). So the equation of the regression line for *n* observations is:

$$y_i = \alpha + \beta x_i + \varepsilon_i \quad (i = 1, \ldots, n)$$

Galton's original regression had the weight of daughter sweet-pea seeds (the *y* variable) regressed on the weight of the mother seeds (*x* variable). Galton found a positive slope, less than unity, implying what came to be known as "regression to the mean"—the property that intergenerational weight gains tend to be higher for children of lighter parents, so that over time there will be convergence toward the mean. One hundred years later, this property became important in the literature on economic growth (chapter 8).

---

[144] See Thorner (1967).

[145] Including surveys by Rudra and Bardhan (Bardhan 1984a), Bliss and Stern (1982), Walker and Ryan (1990), and Lanjouw and Stern (1998).

[146] On Booth's influence, see the *Wikipedia* entry on "Charles Booth" and the *Archive* maintained by the London School of Economics.

[147] On the invention of regression and correlation, see Stanton (2001).

[148] See Morgan (1990).

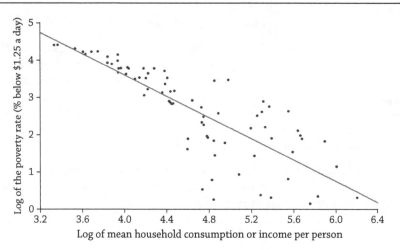

Figure B1.19.1 Log Poverty Rate Plotted against Log Mean Consumption across Countries.

To give an example closer to the topic of this book, figure B1.19.1 plots the natural logarithm of the poverty rate (H) using $1.25 a day as the poverty line against the log of the mean consumption or income (M) across developing countries for which at least 1% of the population is poor by this definition. The figure also graphs the fitted regression line (n = 76):

$$\log H = 9.29 - 1.42 \log M + \hat{e}$$

Here $\hat{e}$ is the regression residual. The slope, $\hat{\beta}$ = −1.42, can be interpreted as saying that a 1% higher mean is on average associated with a 1.4% lower poverty rate.

The overall fit is usually assessed by the squared correlation coefficient (R^2); for these data R^2 = 0.67 (while the correlation coefficient is 0.82). This gives the share of the variance in the dependent variable that is accountable to the explanatory variable; so here we can say that two-thirds of the variance in the log of the poverty rate is represented by the variance in the log mean—the rest being attributable to the variance in the residuals. In assessing the regression, we often also want to know how precisely the slope is estimated. This is given by the standard error of the slope ($se(\hat{\beta})$), which in this case is 0.12. The 95% confidence interval for the slope is the interval bounded below by $\hat{\beta} - 2se(\hat{\beta})$ and above by $\hat{\beta} + 2se(\hat{\beta})$; so we have 0.95 probability that the true value is between −1.66 and −1.18. (The way the standard error is usually calculated assumes that the variance of the error term is constant. We see in the above graph that the variance tends to rise with the mean. On correcting for this the standard error is 0.10.) The t-statistic $t = \hat{\beta}/se(\hat{\beta})$ is used to test the null hypothesis that β = 0.

Fitting a regression line does not, of course, mean that x causes y. Correlation does not imply causality. One reason that the causality in this regression is

continued

Box 1.19 **(Continued)**

questionable is that there will be measurement errors in the surveys, such that if one overestimates the mean, one probably underestimates the poverty measure.

Another concern is that there may be important *omitted variables* in the regression. Practitioners often worry about omitted variables that are correlated with the included ones. Clearly this is a source of bias, in that we do not know how much the estimated coefficient truly reflects the effect of the variable of interest, rather than the correlated omitted variable.

Further reading: For a good introduction to regression analysis, see Wooldridge (2013). Chapter 6 discusses more advanced methods that try to address the problems of inferring causality from data.

New Thinking in the Early Twentieth Century

Near the turn of the century, Alfred Marshall's (1890, 2) *Principles of Economics* was posing the question quoted at the beginning of this chapter. Marshall lamented that the children of poor parents received too little schooling (467), and sketching policies for fighting poverty (esp., 594–599) that were not just intended as short-term moralistic palliatives but were driven by a recognition that persistent poverty was itself a constraint on wealth generation—clearly a very different perspective to the mainstream view in the economics of one hundred years earlier. Marshall (1890, 468) wrote of the "cumulative evil": "The worse fed are the children of one generation, the less they will earn when they grow up and the less will be their power of providing adequately for the material wants of their children; and so onto following generation." Thus: "The inequalities of wealth, and especially the very low earnings of the poorest classes . . . (are) . . . dwarfing activities as well as curtailing the satisfaction of wants" (599).

Marshall's reference here to "dwarfing activities" anticipates a view that is prominent in development thought today whereby certain inequalities are seen as instrumentally important as inhibitors of overall economic progress, notwithstanding their intrinsic relevance in "curtailing the satisfaction of wants." While Marshall was careful to avoid naïve utopianism,[149] his writings reflect a far more positive perspective on social policy, as a means of expanding opportunities for all to share in the potential of a competitive market economy. Here we had a forthright and prominent advocacy of promotional policies such that "children once born into it [poverty] should be helped to rise out of it" (598). He also supported financing such policies through progressive income taxation, arguing that:

> A devotion to public wellbeing on the part of the rich may do much, as enlightenment spreads, to help the tax-gatherer in turning the resources of the rich to high account in the service of the poor, and may remove the worst evils of poverty from the land. (Marshall 1890, 599)

---

[149] See, especially, the comments in Marshall (1907).

Importantly, this new optimism was starting to be shared by poor parents, who raised their demand for the schooling of their children. By the late nineteenth century, it seems that most poor parents in Europe and North America were anticipating that their children would see better economic opportunities than they had. Aspirations were changing. Helped by significant medical and public-health advances that were improving child survival chances and raising life expectancy, investing in their children's schooling was seen as far less risky than it had been early in that century (and before then) when the children of poor working-class children had little real hope of being anything else than working class, and not much chance of being less poor workers than their parents. The demand for mass schooling thus rose along with the supply. Parents were still investing in their children to help secure their future welfare (formal social security systems were not common), but they were investing more in the quality of their children. Fertility rates were falling.

By the turn of the twentieth century, the long-standing model of poverty as being caused by moral failings appears to have receded (though it was never to vanish) in favor of a model that identified shocks and impersonal economic forces interacting with initial inequalities as the main causes of poverty. This change in popular thinking was informed by the new social research on the dimensions and causes of poverty, helped by greater public exposure to that research through the mass media, now reaching a more literate population. There were still efforts made to alter behavior, but they were directed more at the application of new scientific knowledge, notably in curbing disease. The historian Beaudoin (2006, 78) identifies the year 1913, when Albert Schweitzer established his famous hospital in what is now Gabon, as marking the transition between "traditional charity and modern secular relief."

At the same time, new technologies were expanding production possibilities in ways that would in due course transform the lives of people across the globe. In the leading example, the commercialization of the Haber–Bosch process for synthesizing ammonia in 1913 would permit mass production of nitrogen fertilizers, allowing a huge expansion in farm yields. In combination with new pesticides, this technological advance would lead to a fourfold increase in food output per acre over the course of the twentieth century.[150] This would help feed a growing population and so avert Malthusian doom and rising poverty, although the dependence on synthesized nitrogenous fertilizers, and their often highly inefficient usage, would come at a cost to the environment.

The period around the turn of the twentieth century saw popular, progressive, movements in America striving to restrain the market and political power of the various "trusts"—the corporate monopolists that had gained so much power in the latter part of the nineteenth century, leading to market distortions and sharply rising wealth inequality. Action came with the Sherman Act (1890) and a series of reforming Presidents (Theodore Roosevelt, William Taft, Woodrow Wilson). Under Wilson, antitrust legislation and financial-sector regulations were strengthened and the Federal Trade Commission and the Federal Reserve Board were established.

---

[150] See Smil (2011).

After World War I, there was also mounting popular enthusiasm for policy intervention against poverty in the West.[151] The welfare of children growing up in poor circumstances was often a central motivation. Cash transfer programs for widows emerged in the post–World War I period, as did stronger legislation for assuring a minimum school age, restricting child labor, and protecting children from unsafe working environments. In the United States, the first welfare program for poor families with dependent children, the *Mothers' Pension*, had been introduced in Illinois just prior to World War I and expanded to most other states in the twenty-year period after the war. This provided cash transfers to widows and other single mothers with young children, and it was the welfare of children growing up in poverty that was the main motivation.[152]

Economics does not appear to have been especially prominent in thinking about poverty in this period, with other social scientists and statisticians taking the lead. Granted, in the writings of some prominent economists, such as Arthur Pigou (1920, pt. 4, ch. 1), it had become accepted that losses to the "national dividend" could be justified by gains to poor people. However, mainstream thinking in economics was drifting away from its old roots in utilitarian moral philosophy toward a vision of scientific status that eschewed as "unscientific" all interpersonal comparisons of welfare. Naturally, this new direction meant that economists would play less role in normative debates on distributional policy.

If one person can be said to have marked the emergence of this new direction in economics it must surely be Vilfredo Pareto. His (1906) treatise (in Italian), *Manual of Political Economy*, was (in due course) hugely influential, notably in his characterization of optimality in a way that does not require interpersonal comparisons; box 1.20 goes into more detail. Nonetheless, while Pareto strived to avoid all interpersonal comparisons of welfare (thus rejecting the tradition in economics back to Bentham and Smith), Pareto's purely positive empirical studies of income and wealth distribution were to be important to efforts to measure poverty and inequality (box 1.21).

Box 1.20 **Paretian Welfare Economics**

The classical utilitarianism of Bentham and Mill rested on the idea of a cardinal interpersonally comparable utility function. This assigned a number to the utility of each person and those numbers could be added up. Pareto argued that "utility" could not be measured this way and so rejected any idea of cardinal utility and (hence) he also rejected classical utilitarianism. (After all, if utilities are not cardinally comparable between people it is nonsense to talk about adding them up.) Instead, Pareto built his economics on purely ordinal preferences— the ranking of bundles. (A utility function for a specific person could still be allowed, but it was to be seen solely as an analytic device, to represent the ordinal preferences, and for that purpose any function that returned those preferences

---

[151] See Mencher (1967).
[152] See Bortz (1970).

will suffice.) From this starting point, an allocation of commodities was deemed optimal if no person can be made better off (as they themselves assess things, given their preferences) without making someone else worse off.

Pareto showed that one could reach such an optimum through a process of free exchange. Under certain conditions (including those smooth indifference curves in box 1.4) there will be a unique Pareto optimal allocation of goods for any given initial allocation (the "endowments"). Furthermore, under the conditions in box 1.9 (essentially that prices are taken as given and there is a complete set of markets), this optimum can be reached by mutually beneficial exchanges. This was later formalized as the First Fundamental Theorem of welfare economics, namely that competitive market equilibria are Pareto optimal.

This did not get us far in discussing policies on distribution. Once one no longer takes as given the initial assignment of endowments, there are infinitely many Pareto optimal allocations of goods between people. In the eyes of the (many) followers of Paretian economics, no economist could "scientifically" judge one person's welfare relative to another—to say that one person is "better off" than another. Such judgments came to be seen as external to economics (as argued later by Robbins 1935).

This rejection of the cardinal "measurability" of utility can be interpreted as the rejection of all types of data for making welfare comparisons besides the observable commodity demands and supplies of people. From that perspective, it was really an arbitrary a priori restriction on the information that could be brought to bear by an economist on questions of social choice and policy.

Historical note: Vilfredo Pareto's aristocratic origins (born a marquis in Paris, in 1848 to an Italian father and French mother) appear to have had a lasting influence. His rejection of ethical thought led him to ask how economics could be purged of its utilitarian foundations.

Box 1.21 Pareto's "Law"

Pareto also studied the regularities in the upper tail of the distribution of income or wealth. Consider the frequency distribution of wealth in rural Bihar, a state of India, as given in figure B1.21.1.

The figure gives the proportion of the sample ($n = 3,700$) greater than each level of an index of assets. This is called the *survival function*. (This is simply one minus the cumulative distribution function. The insert gives the corresponding histogram.) Naturally the distribution is not perfectly smooth. But if you look at the shape above its peak (the mode), then one can imagine fitting a smooth downward shaped function above the point at which the survival probability starts to fall, which is at an asset index of about 2.5 here.

continued

Box 1.21 **(Continued)**

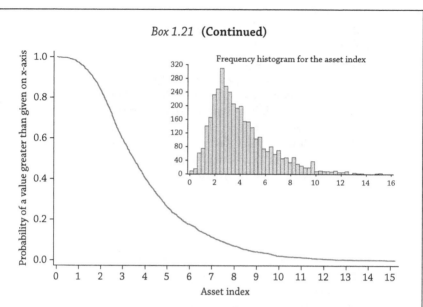

Figure B.1.21.1 Distribution of Wealth in Rural Bihar, India. *Source:* Author's calculations from the data for rural Bihar in 2010 used in Dutta et al. (2014).

On studying the properties of such data (mainly using data for Europe), Pareto concluded that a power function fitted the survival function very well, whereby the proportion of observations with wealth greater than y was $(m/y)^\alpha$, where m is the minimum value of wealth above which the survival function is strictly decreasing and $\alpha > 0$ is a parameter specific to each data set; this parameter came to be known as the Pareto index. For the data in figure B1.21.1, the value of α is about 2. (This is the value implied by the "method of moments" estimator for which $\hat{\alpha} = (\bar{y} - m/n)/(\bar{y} - m)$ in a sample of size n.)

Note on the literature: On the various interpretations that have been given to "Pareto's Law," see Cowell (1977, notes to ch. 4). Pareto's law came to be important in the study of the rising incomes and wealth of the rich in modern times; see the discussion in Atkinson et al. (2011) and Piketty (2014). The data and methods underlying figure B1.21.1 are described in Dutta et al. (2014).

However, in the social sciences more broadly, the incidence of absolute poverty had come to be seen as an important yardstick for measuring social progress. The statistician Arthur Bowley (1915, 213), the inaugural Professor of Statistics at the London School of Economics (LSE), wrote that "there is perhaps, no better test of the progress of a nation than that which shows what proportion are in poverty; and for watching the progress the exact standard selected as critical is not of great importance, if it is kept rigidly unchanged from time to time." In the United States, Allyn Young (1917) argued in favor of focusing measurement attention on the distribution of the levels of income or wealth, rather than the new measures of inequality that were emerging, including the Gini index (which we return to in chapter 5).[153]

The poverty focus gained political momentum in the following decades and markedly so in the wake of the Great Depression. For example, in his second inaugural address, US President Franklin D. Roosevelt (1937) said that "the test of our progress is not whether we add more to the abundance of those who have much; it is whether we provide enough for those who have too little."

Roosevelt introduced a number of new social programs, often bundled under the label "New Deal." These included the Social Security Act, which introduced pensions for the elderly, transfers for families with dependent children, and unemployment benefits. The prior introduction of the federal income tax (under President Taft) provided a progressive method of financing.

From around the turn of the twentieth century, we also started to see the application of statistics to inform public discussion of social issues such as poverty and inequality. A key methodological issue was whether one could rely on sample surveys of households instead of doing a census, and how the sampling was to be done.[154] In the first few decades of the twentieth century, statisticians such as Bowley, Ronald Fisher and Jerzy Neyman had advanced the theory of statistical inference based on random sampling. Starting in 1928, a team at LSE (advised by Bowley) did an ambitious series of surveys of London, focusing on poverty; though influenced by Booth's work thirty years earlier, these new surveys were distinctive in that they relied on formal household sampling methods.[155] However, it took some time before sampling was to become common practice for social and economic surveys.[156] Fisher had developed many of the tools, often as by-products of his own agricultural experiments. His book, *The Design of Experiments* (1935) was the foundation of an experimental method in biology that was much later to become important in evaluating antipoverty programs (as discussed further in chapter 6).

Poverty measurement had emerged as a leading application of social statistics. In due course, sampling methods were to revolutionize the collection of systematic survey data on incomes and/or expenditures for random samples of households by national statistics offices across the world. India was an early leader globally in this field, notably through the Indian Statistical Institute, founded by the eminent statistician P. C. Mahalanobis. This soon led to India's National Sample Surveys (NSS), which started in 1950 and are still used today for measuring poverty in India. As Mahalanobis (1963) put it, "statistics is an applied science and. . . its chief object is to help in solving practical problems. Poverty is the most basic problem of the country, and statistics must help in solving this problem."

---

[153] Young (1917, 478) questioned the fact that the Gini index and other measures of inequality deemed (implicitly or explicitly) zero inequality to be the ideal, arguing that "a dead level of uniformity is neither practical nor desirable."

[154] An early example was the surveys of Russian peasants led by Alexander Chuprov at Moscow University.

[155] On the LSE's social surveys of London, see Abernethy (2013).

[156] On the history of survey sampling methods, see Bethlehem (2009).

By the interwar period, it seems that poverty was no longer being seen in mainstream circles as primarily caused by the bad behavior of poor men and women, but was seen to reflect deeper economic and social problems. If nothing else, the observation of mass involuntary unemployment during the Great Depression made that much clear. And the observations were carried with force to a broad audience through various media of the time.[157] A massive relief effort followed (such as the New Deal in the US), although this primarily aimed at protection rather than promotion.[158]

The Great Depression also stimulated a significant shift in economic thinking about the role of the government in macroeconomic stabilization. This was the Keynesian Revolution. Poverty created by mass unemployment in the Great Depression was an underlying motivation for the Keynesian Revolution in economics. While the primary focus was on stimulating aggregate effective demand so as to restore economic growth, distributional issues were not far under the surface. In Keynes's (1936) *General Theory*, the interpretation of the causes of unemployment predicted that it was lack of aggregate demand that prevented full-employment. This implied that a higher share of national income in the command of poor families would promote growth, until full-employment was reached (box 1.22). That was a significant departure from past thinking, which had emphasized an aggregate growth-equity trade-off.

Box 1.22 Keynes's Argument as to How Inequality Retards Economic Development

John Maynard Keynes did not write much about poverty and inequality, but his economics was geared to understanding what can be an important cause of high poverty rates, mass unemployment, which he attributed to lack of aggregate effective demand in the economy. However, in chapter 24 of his 1936 major work, *The General Theory of Employment, Interest and Money*, Keynes made an argument that explicitly rebuffed the idea of a substantial "growth-equity" trade-off. The idea is simple. Keynes argued that poor families tend to have a higher marginal propensity to consume (MPC) out of income gains than do the rich; and that the MPC declines steadily as income rises. Thus, redistribution from rich to poor would increase aggregate effective demand and so help reduce aggregate unemployment.

Subsequent research on the inter-temporal consumption behavior (such as Friedman's Permanent Income Hypothesis, which we study further in chapter 3) led to a questioning of Keynes's argument, especially when applied to long-run redistribution. It was argued that over the longer term, consumption would

---

[157] The photos and text of Agee and Evans (1941) describing the living conditions and lives of southern tenant farmers in the United States in the mid-1930s was an example.

[158] See Heclo (1986).

match permanent income, and so the aggregate consumption impact of redistribution would vanish. But Keynes was more concerned about the short run. He wrote: "In the long run we are all dead. Economists set themselves too easy, too useless a task if in tempestuous seasons they can only tell us that when the storm is long past the ocean is flat again."

As the Great Depression faded from view, there was a renewal of interest among economists in long-run economic growth. The 1939 paper, "An Essay in Dynamic Theory" by the Roy Harrod marked the beginning of more serious attention to long-run growth; Evsey Domar (1946) had been working along similar lines. The Harrod-Domar model was to have much influence, especially in development policy circles, as it provided the theoretical underpinnings to many post–World War II development plans. The model was overly simple, with its assumptions of a constant capital-output ratio and constant savings rate (as discussed further in chapter 8). Addressing these deficiencies spawned an important economic literature on the theory of growth and distributional change, although progress had to wait until after World War II.

2

New Thinking on Poverty after 1950

The middle of the twentieth century saw a dramatic turning point in progress against extreme poverty globally. Figure 2.1 plots two series for the poverty rate.[1] We see a clear break in trajectories around 1950. An extra 1.5 billion people would have lived in poverty if not for this break.[2] Another observation can be made: the incidence of extreme absolute poverty in the world is lower now than ever before. While there have been calls to end extreme poverty at various times during the last century or so, they are more credible now than ever.

About the same time that the trajectory of poverty incidence was changing, a significant shift in economic and philosophical thinking was underway, with bearing on antipoverty policy.

2.1 The Second Poverty Enlightenment

From about 1960, across the globe—including in the newly free countries of the developing world—there was new optimism among policymakers about the scope for fighting poverty. Evidence for the change in public attention to poverty can be found in the striking rise in the incidence of use of the word "poverty" in the writings of

---

[1] There is a long list of data problems underlying figure 2.1. Bourguignon and Morrisson (BM) (2002) used an early version of the Chen-Ravallion database for their estimates since 1980, but BM had to rely on far fewer and rather scattered estimates of inequality measures from secondary sources for their historical series. Also BM had no choice but to anchor their poverty measures to Gross Domestic Product (GDP) per capita rather than the survey means. Because the survey means are well below GDP per capita, one cannot simply use the Chen-Ravallion poverty line on the BM data set. So BM attempted to make their "extreme poverty" line accord with the $1 a day line at 1985 purchasing power parity of Ravallion et al. (1991) by anchoring their poverty rate to that of Chen and Ravallion (2001) for a common year (1992). In splicing with the Chen-Ravallion series, it is assumed that nobody lives below $1 a day in the developed countries after 1980. This is plausible and is consistent with the author's calculations using the Luxembourg Income Study (LIS) database.

[2] Allowing for a change in the trend rate of poverty reduction (percentage points per year) in 1950, but constraining the estimates to assure continuity in 1950, the trends are –0.26% points per year up to 1950 (with a standard error of 0.03). To assess the extent of the break in 1950, suppose that it had not occurred—that the pre-1950 trajectory had been maintained. We would then have expected to find that 36% (standard error = 3.3%) of the world's population lived below $1 a day in 2005, as compared to the Chen and Ravallion estimate of 14%.

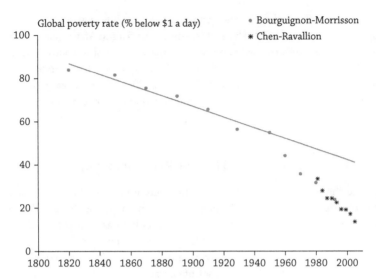

Figure 2.1 Global Poverty Rates, 1820–2005. *Sources:* Author's calculations from the data base used by Bourguignon and Morrisson (2002) (kindly provided by the authors) and from Chen and Ravallion (2010a).

the time, as we saw in figure 1.2. The upturn in attention to poverty started around 1960 in English—a little earlier in French. There was a surge in scholarly interest in income distribution among economists.

By 2000 the incidence of references to "poverty" reached its highest value in three hundred years. And the rise in incidence continued after 2000, up to the latest year (2008) for which the data are available at the time of writing; indeed, with moderate smoothing of the series, 2008 is the year since 1600 when poverty has had most attention in the literature.[3] Comparing figures 1.2 and 2.1, we see that attention to poverty is higher now than ever before while the incidence of extreme poverty is at its lowest point.

Similarly to the First Poverty Enlightenment, the Second was a time of radical questioning and instability. However, unlike the First, it did not come in the wake of rising absolute poverty rates in the rich world. There were demands for new freedoms across the world. There was social ferment and civil unrest in the rich world, and new-found political independence combined with much political and economic upheaval in the poor world. While the 1960s was a famous period in the West, with vocal new

---

[3] The relevant plot up to 2008 and as far back as possible can be found at http://books.google.com/ngrams/graph?content=Poverty%2Bpoverty%2Cpoverty&year_start=1600&year_end=2008&corpus=15&smoothing=4&share=. There are two spikes in 1634 and 1659. Naturally the volume of words in the *Viewer's* database is low in these earlier years, often with only a few books per year. Each of these spikes largely reflects one or two volumes that used the word "poverty" a lot. This is clearly deceptive. With any smoothing parameter greater than three, the peak year becomes the last year in the series, 2008. Also note that the count is case sensitive. The use of capitalized words mid-sentence was more common in English writing of the seventeenth and eighteenth centuries so it is important to include capitalized words when going back that far. But this matters little after 1800 or so.

movements for peace and racial and gender equity, much was also happening in the developing world. In the 1960s alone, thirty-two countries in Africa gained independence, though often with contested borders. China's "Cultural Revolution" started in 1966 and wreaked havoc for ten years. South Asia (Bangladesh and India) and parts of Africa were fighting famines in the 1960s and 1970s, and there was much political instability across the world with numerous independence movements struggling for self-determination.[4]

New Economic Thinking Relevant to Poverty

Similarly to the First Poverty Enlightenment, there was new scholarly thought with bearing on antipoverty policy. In philosophy and economics, the 1960s and 1970s saw renewed questioning of the classical utilitarian paradigm as a basis for public action against poverty and inequality, and in other domains of public policy. Recall that the Benthamite objective of maximizing average utility builds in an aversion to income inequality among people with a given set of characteristics; the key assumption here is diminishing marginal utility of income (as explained in box 1.13). But the utilitarian objective is indifferent to inequality of welfare and silent on individual rights and freedoms. Critics of utilitarianism questioned whether policies that entailed welfare losses to the poorest could ever be justified by sufficiently large gains to the richest. Arguments were being made for the ethical prioritization of helping the poorest first in modern formulations of the principles of justice, which we return to later. The 1970s also saw efforts to generalize the utilitarian schema by embodying an aversion to inequality of utilities. This was done by allowing the marginal social welfare— the increment to social welfare that was deemed to be attached to higher individual utility—to fall with the level of utility. Thus, the representation of the social welfare objective penalized inequality of welfare. In principle, marginal social welfare could then be driven down to a very low level at a sufficiently high level of utility. Once one made the extra step of allowing the possibility that marginal social welfare could go to zero above some point, prioritizing poverty reduction emerged.[5] Whether or not one took that extra step, there was clearly common ground in these different emerging schools of thought about the social welfare objectives of public policy.

For many economists the more contentious step (and it is still contentious) was attaching intrinsic value to "rights" and "freedoms." Dissatisfaction was evident during the Second Poverty Enlightenment with the lack of attention in economics to popular concerns about individual rights and freedoms. Of course, the freedom to

---

[4] In some cases the independence was from Colonial rulers, but in others it was from the post-Colonial nation-states; an example of the latter is Bangladesh, which gained independence from Pakistan in 1971. Even relatively stable India had its share of political upheaval including the "Emergency" in the mid-1970s.

[5] This interpretation is discussed further in Ravallion (1994a), which shows that on introducing inequality aversion into the measure of poverty (as discussed further in chapter 5) and allowing for measurement errors in the data on individual economic welfare, the resulting formulation of the objectives of policy in terms of minimizing poverty can essentially be made as close as one likes to that of maximizing a generalized utilitarian social welfare function.

trade freely was often given high value in economics, but this was an instrumental value—the virtue of competitive exchange was one derived from long-standing (Benthamite or Paretian) formulations of policy objectives. The scope for ethically contestable policies was evident if one did not put certain rights above all else. Motivated by such concerns, more attention in mainstream thinking about poverty was being given to non-utilitarian formulations that put freedom as the central issue, most notably in the writings of the Indian economist, Amartya Sen (1980, 1985a, 1999). The idea that poverty is fundamentally a lack of individual freedom to live the life one wants—a severe deprivation of basic "capabilities" in Sen's terms—and that such freedom has an overriding ethical merit, can be traced back to the Second Poverty Enlightenment (box 2.1).

Box 2.1 Functionings, Capabilities, and Utilities

In the scheme proposed by Amartya Sen, "functionings" are the "beings and doings" of life, such as being safe, able to live to an old age, employed, and being able to participate in social and economic activities more generally. "Capabilities" refers to the set of functionings actually available to a person given his or her circumstances, as determined by the person's own characteristics and environment. Sen proposed that human welfare should be judged by a person's capabilities.

This was proposed as an alternative to the more mainstream "welfarist" approach in economics, which identified people's "utility"—what they maximize in making their choices—as the sole basis for making judgments about relative welfare (such as who is poor and who is not) and about policy (in assessing the benefits and costs of interventions). The capabilities approach aimed to address concerns about the welfarist approach. One such concern was the latter's seemingly excessive emphasis on command over commodities. Another was its lack of explicit attention to rights and freedoms. There were other concerns too, including the possibility that people may make bad choices, or adapt their preferences to their circumstances, and the problems of identifying and measuring "utility" in a way that permitted interpersonal comparisons.

The critique of welfarism that motivated the capabilities approach did not deny that people were rational (maximizing utility), and that social welfare should be judged by individual welfare levels. Rather the important point of departure was in what is meant by "welfare" and (in particular) whether it is determined solely by command over commodities (ignoring other differences between people) and whether it can be equated with the maximand of individual choice.

Further reading: Discussions can be found in many of Sen's writings, but the treatment in Sen (1999, chs. 3 and 4) is especially recommended. Chapter 3 goes into more depth about the debates between "welfarist" and "non-welfarist" schools of thought, and the relevance to poverty.

Underpinning these broader ways of thinking about the objectives of policy one found a new questioning of previous efforts to purge economics of interpersonal comparisons of welfare. Those efforts had their origin in Pareto's characterization of optimality (box 1.20) and drew strength from an influential essay by Lionel Robbins (1935). The period up to around 1950 saw economists striving to avoid interpersonal comparisons, which were seen as unscientific. This left limited scope for normative economic analysis of poverty or income distribution more generally.[6] In due course, the theoretical writings on social choice by Kenneth Arrow (1951) and Sen (1970), led to a reaffirmation of the need for some form of interpersonal comparability in discussing issues such as antipoverty policy.[7] Ethical considerations soon returned to policy analysis by economists. The ethics was still seen as largely external to economics but the subject did not shy away from ethics. Here there was an important contribution for economists in formalizing and interpreting ethical judgments in ways that could (for example) identify precisely when that judgment mattered to the policy inference. For example, what was the critical level of aversion to inequality for which income taxes should be progressive, given their incentive effects? Around the same time, the futility of attempting to infer comparable utilities solely on the basis of observable demand and supply behavior came to be accepted.[8] More information was clearly needed. Efforts to broaden the information base for making interpersonal comparisons of welfare followed two somewhat parallel tracks, one turning to subjective data on self-assessed welfare and one drawing on objective data on attainments of certain basic functionings, such as being adequately nourished for normal social activities. (We return to studying these approaches in more depth in chapter 3.)

An important change in this period was the marked switch of attention from factor distribution to personal distribution. Distribution had been a central issue in classical economics; indeed, in Ricardo's (1817) view it was the defining issue of economics. The Ricardian class-based characterization of distribution (with the working class only supplying labor, the capitalists only deriving income from capital and the landlords from rent) had huge influence in the nineteenth century, especially on the development of socialism, most notably in the class-based analysis of capitalism by Marx. While definitions of class based on a person's qualitative relationship to the means of production have not lost all relevance, they were evidently more salient in the nineteenth century than today. Over time, these models of class-based inequality came to be seen as less empirically relevant for descriptive purposes, notably because of the emergence of an increasingly stratified labor market (simply working for a wage did not mean one was poor), along with a degree of diversification in the ownership of capital, including through new financial institutions such as pension and mutual funds.[9]

---

[6] For an authoritative overview of the history of thought on income distribution, see Sandmo (2014).

[7] Developing arguments first made by Condorcet in 1785, Arrow (1951) established that, under seemingly defensible axioms, a unique social ordering over three or more options that is derived solely from a set of unrestricted individual orderings must be either imposed or dictatorial. Notice, however, that allowing interpersonal comparisons is only one of the possible resolutions of Arrow's dictatorship result (Sen 1970). Also see the discussions in Hammond (1976) and Roemer (1996).

[8] Especially following Pollak and Wales (1979).

[9] These changes were noted at the time, such as in Gordon (1972, ch. 7) and Atkinson (1975, ch. 9).

Along the way, there has been much debate about this change in thinking, and the debate has often been politically charged. Resistance to discussions of interpersonal distribution has been found on both the Right and the Left. On the Right, any talk about "inequality" in the United States is often derided as an effort to promote "class warfare"; by this view, inequality is seen as a dangerous topic, best ignored. On the Far Left, talk about interpersonal distribution is seen as a "neoliberal" effort to create stratifications among the working class that deflect attention from the relationship to the means of production. Representatives of both extremes can still be found, although both appear to be increasingly out-of-touch with reality, and so have moved to the fringes of policy debates.

In keeping with how the increasing complexity of market-based economies leads to greater interest in the interpersonal distributions of income and wealth, the 1970s and 1980s saw new efforts to put *poverty and inequality measurement* on firmer theoretical foundations.[10] There was an explosion of interest in the measurement of poverty and inequality, both in theory and in practice, starting from around 1970.[11] This had largely been at the fringes of mainstream economics, but that is no longer true today.[12]

Other seemingly sacred elements of welfare economics started to be questioned, including whether people are rational, although some of the claims of "irrationality" that emerged from behavioral economics appeared to stem more from limited characterizations of utility functions and/or limited allowances for mistakes. Even the idea that social welfare is always greater when any utility level rises and none falls (the Pareto principle) was being questioned as either a sufficient or a morally compelling basis for policymaking.[13] The Pareto principle was found to be inconsistent with seemingly mild requirements for personal liberty.[14]

With regard to our understanding of the causes of poverty, the 1960s saw a new emphasis on the economic returns to human capital and how choices about investment in schooling weighed the expected future returns against the current costs. (The University of Chicago economists Theodore Schultz (1961) and Gary Becker (1964) were influential in the emerging new economics of education.). There was also a deeper questioning of the efficiency of competitive market allocations. The term "market failure" emerged in the late 1950s and quickly become widely used.[15] Labor and credit markets imperfections, in particular, came to be seen as key to understanding poverty; see box 2.2.

---

[10] Important contributions came from Watts (1968), Atkinson (1970, 1987), Kolm (1976), Sen (1973, 1976a), and Foster, Greer and Thorbecke (1984).

[11] In the *Google Books Ngram Viewer* try entering a set of words such as: poverty line, poverty rate, poverty gap, Gini, Lorenz curve, and household survey. One sees a virtual explosion of rising incidence from about 1960.

[12] For example, the otherwise authoritative 1972 *Penguin Dictionary of Economics* did not include definitions of "poverty" or "inequality" among its 1,700 entries (Bannock et al. 1972). By contrast, the 2008 *New Palgrave Dictionary of Economics* has many references to these topics (Blume and Durlauf 2008), as does the *Oxford Dictionary of Economics* (Black et al., 2012).

[13] As in, e.g., Nath (1969).

[14] See Sen (1970).

[15] The term "market failure" was introduced by Bator (1958).

Box 2.2 Market Failures

A *market failure* (sometimes called "market imperfection") is essentially any situation in which the conditions required for free markets to be efficient do not hold—that Smith's "invisible hand" will not guide the economy to an efficient allocation.

Recall that the efficiency of free markets requires universal price-taking behavior in a complete set of markets all of which clear instantaneously (box 1.9). So market failures can arise due to either noncompetitive features, whereby some agents control prices, or these do not adjust without cost, or market incompleteness. The latter may reflect the absence of markets for externalities or for certain commodities.

An example of a *noncompetitive market* is when there is only one (monopoly) seller of some good. The seller can then set the price, which will exceed what it costs the firm to produce another unit of its output. In other words, price will exceed marginal cost.

We already learned about *externalities* in box 1.9. Recall the example of a factory that pollutes the air without incurring any appropriate charge. The marginal cost of producing the factory's output does not then reflect its full social cost. Prices will not guide us to a social optimum; in particular, there will be too much of this factory's output and (hence) too much pollution.

An example of the *missing market* is when credit is only available to those who have sufficient wealth to put up collateral. Poor families, with too little wealth, will be unable to borrow when they need to. When very poor, certain incentives, such as threats of punishment if one defaults, may carry little weight.

Market failures point to a case for government intervention. If the market failure persists, then it can often be ascribed to government failure.

Further reading: See the note to box 1.9.

The idea that labor markets are competitive, such that wage rates adjust to remove any unemployment, had been in doubt since the Great Depression. In understanding poverty in rich countries in the 1960s, the idea of dual labor markets became prominent.[16] One labor market has high wages and good benefits while the second has low wages and little in the way of benefits. It came to be appreciated that this could be an equilibrium given the existence of high costs of monitoring work effort in certain activities.[17] A high-wage segment emerges in which profit-maximizing firms facing high costs of monitoring choose to pay workers a premium, above market-clearing wages, to incentivize them to do what employers want.[18] (The incentive works given that the worker will face a wage cut if fired.) Other activities with low monitoring costs then form the competitive segment, which is where the working poor are found.

[16] Following, in particular, Doeringer and Piore (1971).
[17] See Bulow and Summers (1986).
[18] Following Shapiro and Stiglitz (1984).

In another strand of the literature of this period, George Akerlof (1970) showed how credit (and other) market failures can arise from asymmetric information, such as when lenders are less well-informed about a project than borrowers, thus constraining the flow of credit. This helped explain the efficiency role of institutions and governments in facilitating better information signals and broader contract choices.[19]

The new economics of information held important implications for understanding persistent poverty. In a perfect credit market even poor parents will be able to take out loans for schooling—to be paid back from children's later earnings. However, if poor parents are more credit constrained than others then we will see an economic gradient in schooling, whereby the children of poor parents get less schooling. This is indeed what we see, almost everywhere. There will be too much child labor and too little schooling in poor families. Poverty will thus persist across generations. Risk market failures can have similar implications; parents will underinvest in their kids' schooling when they cannot insure against the risk of a low economic return from that schooling.

In due course, this new strand of economic thinking pointed to important ways in which inequalities in the initial distribution of wealth can persist and impede overall economic progress. The economics also pointed to scope for promotional antipoverty policies—policies that essentially aim to compensate for credit and risk market failures, such as by compulsory schooling laws and public support for schooling, especially for children from poor families. (Chapters 9 and 10 return to these issues.)

Rawls's Principles of Justice

If there is a single philosophical landmark of the Second Poverty Enlightenment, it must be *Theory of Justice* by the Harvard-based philosopher, John Rawls. This book proposed that the principles of justice should be the social contract agreed among equals in a "veil of ignorance" about where they would find themselves in the real world.[20] Rawls argued that two principles would emerge. First, each person should have equal right to the most extensive set of liberties compatible with the same rights for all. Second, subject to the constraint of liberty, social choices should only permit inequality if it was efficient to do so—that a difference is only allowed if both parties are better off as a result; this is what Rawls called the "difference principle."

Rawls was influenced by past philosophers and economists, including the early formulations of social contract theory (back to Hobbes), and the writings of Kant and Smith.[21] His idea of liberty clearly owed much to the ideas reviewed in chapter 1 from the late eighteenth century. His difference principle was a more radical departure

[19] For example, the idea of asymmetric information gave a new perspective on why share-cropping exists, whereby the tenant pays the owner a fixed share of the farm's output rather than a standard land rent (Stiglitz 1974). Since the work-effort of tenants is unobservable by landowners, an optimal contract strikes a balance between risk sharing and incentives for work. Thus, risk is shared between the two parties.

[20] The veil of ignorance was a thought device to assure that morally irrelevant—inherited or acquired—advantages in the real world did not color judgments about distributive justice.

[21] See Fleischaker (2004).

(though with roots in Smith). It was not the kind of radical egalitarianism that said that equality always trumped efficiency. Indeed, society A, with a great deal of inequality, would be preferred by this moral principle to society B with no inequality if the poorest were better off in society A. Thus, the principle amounts to maximizing the advantages of the worst off group and hence became known as "maximin" (box 2.3).

Box 2.3 **Maximin and Poverty**

Rawls's difference principle was explicitly *not* a proposal to maximize the lowest income, as it is sometimes interpreted, but rather to maximize the welfare of the "worst off group" in society. This can be extended to the idea of "leximin" whereby if the worst off are equally well off in two states then one looks to the next worst off, and so on.

Rawls insisted that some degree of averaging was required in defining the "least advantaged." Rawls wrote, "I assume that it is possible to assign an expectation of well-being to representative individuals holding these positions" (1971, 56). Assigning this expectation is also well advised given that (taken literally) the lowest observed level of living (as measured by consumption) in survey data is likely to contain a transient effect and may well also contain significant measurement error. So Rawls's principle is suggestive of forming some sort of weighed average of the observed consumptions of some stratum of poor people (Ravallion 2014f).

The "worst off" were to be identified by what Rawls called their command over "primary goods." These are all those things needed to assure that one is free to live the life one wants. This is broader than what are often called "basic needs" as it includes social inclusion needs and basic liberties—in short, rights as well as resources.

As Rawls recognized, one will need an index for determining the least advantaged. Possibly because of his evident desire to break all ties with utilitarianism, Rawls avoided using the term "utility function" (or "welfare function"), but this is evidently what he has in mind in his discussions of the *"index problem"* (Rawls 1971, 94)—namely a function that expresses the accepted trade-offs. Rawls agreed that it is also compelling that those trade-offs be consistent with individual preferences over primary goods. However, he argued that we need not be concerned with the preferences of the non-poor under the assumption that their primary goods bundles are bound to dominate those of poor people. Thus, the utility function of the worst off person should be decisive in aggregations across primary goods. "The only index problem that concerns us is that for the least advantaged group" (Rawls 1971, 93).

Whether in fact a sufficiently clear ordering of the primary goods bundles is possible in practice without knowing preferences is an open question. An ordering of the bundles may not require a mathematically precise utility function; a sufficient partial ordering may be possible by only specifying certain generic properties of that function, as discussed in Atkinson and Bourguignon (1982). However, this is ultimately an empirical question.

Notice that Rawls's maximin principle does not imply that we should cease caring about inequality once everyone has risen above some fixed absolute standard. He argues for giving priority to the poorest in a specific society—those who are least advantaged. That is inherently relative. (We return to the distinction between absolute and relative poverty.)

Rawls's maximin principle is sometimes interpreted as an ethical rationale for using absolute poverty measures in monitoring social progress. This is questionable on a number of counts, as elaborated in box 2.3. In fact the Rawlsian approach is more suggestive of a focus on progress in raising the expected level of living of the poorest— the "consumption floor." Chapter 5 returns to this topic.

The Second Poverty Enlightenment had intellectual roots in the First. Rawls saw his difference principle as an interpretation of "fraternity" (as in the French Revolution's motto): "the idea of not wanting to have greater advantages unless this is to the benefit of others who are less well off." This was a natural step (though it took a long time) from the aspirations for fraternity that emerged in the First Poverty Enlightenment. Utilitarianism was seen to be in conflict with fraternity, since it could be used to justify losses to the individual in the name of total utility. There would always be some gain to the richest person that could justify a loss to the poorest. The individual is subordinated to the common good, as measured by the sum of utilities.

Rawls saw his theory as a reinterpretation of Kant. Poor men and women should have the right to veto any scheme that brings gains to the well-off at their expense. Echoing Adam Smith, Rawls saw poverty for some to be unacceptable as the means to others' prosperity. Classical utilitarianism (by contrast) could not guarantee a satisfactory minimum. And only if a satisfactory minimum was assured would the social contract be "stable" in that "the institutions that satisfy it will generate their own support."[22]

The reasoning here is that, as long as the worst off group is happy with the proposed social arrangement, the rest (all doing better than the worst off) would have nothing to complain about.[23] This reasoning is questionable in the real world, since those not in the poorest stratum can be expected to have a different counterfactual in mind when assessing any policy to that of being the worst off. But recall that the social contract is being formed in the absence of information about real-world positions. Rawls argued that maximin would emerge from rational choice behind the veil of ignorance.

Rawls's theory of justice stimulated much debate. John Harsanyi (1975) questioned whether maximin was a more plausible choice for a social contract than maximizing average utility even behind the veil of ignorance unless there was extreme risk aversion. John Roemer (1996, ch. 5) also questioned whether maximin would emerge as the solution. These critiques rested on the assumption that agents behind the veil

---

[22] See Rawls (1967).

[23] This was argued by G. Cohen (1989) among others.

would maximize expected utility, which depends solely on their own consumption (and leisure). Harsanyi argued that when behind the veil of ignorance, we would expect to have an equal chance of being anyone in society, implying that we would choose the utilitarian criterion of total (strictly average) utility rather than maximin. These critiques of Rawls's theory require that subjective probabilities can be assigned to all states behind the veil, which Rawls (1971) questioned.[24] Rawls also argued that Harsanyi assumed that people did not care about risk—that their aversion to risk would lead them to choose maximin when they do not know anything else about the outcomes in society. However, here Rawls was mistaken; the utility functions in Harsanyi's formulation can embody risk aversion.[25]

Other critiques of Rawls emerged. Soon after the publication of *Theory of Justice*, Robert Nozick (1974) published a libertarian critique. Nozick gave primacy to historical property rights above all else.[26] However, it was never clear on ethical grounds why property rights were never to be questioned—to be seen as an end rather than a means.[27]

Some critics took issue with Rawls's concept of primary goods, arguing that this idea does not adequately reflect the freedoms that people have to pursue their goals, recognizing the heterogeneity in the ability of people to transform primary goods into freedoms. This critique led to Sen's conceptualization of welfare in terms of primary "functionings"—"what people are able to be and do (rather than in terms of the means they possess)" (Sen 2000, 74). (Chapter 3 returns to this set of ideas.)

One can defend the key aspects of Rawls's principles of justice without accepting his rationale in terms of a social contract formed behind the veil of ignorance. Peter Hammond (1976) showed that a generalized version of maximin—the leximin rule in Box 2.3—can be derived from a set of axioms, including a requirement that reducing the disparities in welfare between the rich and the poor is socially preferred, other things being equal. Similarly, Marc Fleurbaey and Francois Maniquet (2011, chapter 3) showed that leximin is implied by what they termed the "priority among equals" axiom. Again this requires that more equitable allocations are socially preferred but that this never trumps efficiency in the sense that a situation in which everyone is better off is always preferred. Roemer (2014) argues for a version of maximin but from a different starting point, namely the desire to equalize opportunities. Recall that this was premised on the view that poverty reflected exogenous circumstances, as well as personal efforts (box 1.8). Severe empirical challenges remain in cleanly separating efforts from circumstances, but the conceptual distinction is very important to thinking about antipoverty policy (as has long been recognized in policy debates reviewed below). In striving to equalize opportunities, we would not want to bring everyone down to a common but low level of opportunity. Instead, Roemer

---

[24] Though see the response in Harsanyi (1975).

[25] This was pointed out by Arrow (1973).

[26] Pogge (1989) reviews this and other critiques of Rawls's principles of justice and provides a reinterpretation and (vigorous) defence of Rawls's original arguments.

[27] Contrast this view with those of Adam Smith who also advocated the importance of secure property rights, but for their instrumental importance to social welfare rather than intrinsic merit (chapter 1).

advocates that policy choices stemming from an "equal opportunity ethic" should maximize the welfare assigned to the worst off group, defined by a vector of exogenous
"circumstances"—those things that cannot be traced back to the choices made by the
individual.[28]

Rawls opened the way to new non-utilitarian thinking on poverty and antipoverty
policy. This marked a return to the themes that emerged in the First Poverty
Enlightenment, although these now found more complete and rigorous formulations.
Reducing poverty came to be seen as a legitimate moral goal for society, in what
came to be called "sufficientarianism" in philosophy.[29] Importantly, the model of what
caused poverty had also changed. Rather than being blamed solely on the bad behaviors of poor people, poverty came to be seen as stemming in no small measure from
circumstances beyond their control, given the interaction between unequal circumstances of birth (on the one hand) and market-governmental failures (on the other).
Poverty was fundamentally unacceptable because of the loss of individual freedom
it entailed—freedom to pursue opportunities for personal fulfilment. And the judgments of what constituted "poverty" were framed in terms of lost opportunities, which
depended on personal characteristics as well as "income."

This perspective gave both measurement and policy a deeper ethical foundation
than was possible in classical utilitarianism. It was still granted that there was an
important role for individual responsibility—that poverty did sometimes stem from
bad choices. But this had ceased to be the dominant model. Careful opportunity-based
formulations emerged in the writings of both philosophers,[30] and economists.[31]

So far the discussion has focused on the new philosophical and economic thinking
of the Second Poverty Enlightenment. No less important to policymaking were the
new data, the new empirical research on those data, and the more popular writings
and social movements around this time. We now turn to these.

A change in popular attention to poverty was underway across the rich world.
This is evident in the marked increase in references to phrases such as "antipoverty,"
"poverty alleviation," and "redistribution" in the *Google Books Ngram Viewer*. The
industrialized world saw a boom in social spending in the second half of the twentieth century.[32] One rich country was especially prominent in the new debates about
poverty and policy.

The Rediscovery of Poverty in America

A process of structural change had been underway in the US economy since 1940.
This entailed large displacements of unskilled labor, notably through the moderniza-
tion of agriculture in the South. The latter had started during World War II, which

---

[28] This assumes that a unique vector exists, dominated by all others. Given that choices ("efforts")
vary, Roemer proposes to maximize the average welfare level of the worst off group, averaged across
levels of effort.

[29] Recent discussions can be found in Freiman (2012) and Shields (2012).

[30] Such as J. Cohen (1989), Arneson (1989), Van Parijs (1992), and Widerquist (2013).

[31] Including Sen (1985a), Roemer (1998), and Fleurbaey (2008).

[32] See Lindert (2004).

had simultaneously called for more labor in the defense industry (and hence less available for farming) alongside rising demand for food.[33] A major structural change was underway. Over a twenty-year period, some 20 million people who had previously depended on relatively unskilled labor in farming (as either tenant farmers or wage laborers) moved to the cities in search of work, which many found, but many did not. And employment prospects were racially differentiated, with appreciably higher unemployment rates emerging among African Americans in the country's major cities.

A share of the country's dispersed southern rural poverty was transformed into geographically concentrated northern urban poverty. The bulk of the poor still lived elsewhere.[34] But the concentration of new urban poverty in the inner cities was an important new feature of the US poverty map. Inner-city poverty was also the outcome of economic forces. A strong income effect on demand for new housing and land area encouraged higher income households to move to the suburbs, where they could obtain a larger quantity of housing at a lower unit price of land. Higher transport costs (with higher income households tending to have a higher value of time) mitigated this effect, but not enough to outweigh the income effect on demand for housing.[35] It has been argued that these economic forces were encouraged by public policies, such as suburban mortgage subsidies favoring whites.[36]

The outcome was rising economic differentiation of America's cities in the post–World War II period, with dense concentrations of poverty emerging in the inner urban areas of the country's major cities. This came to be seen as a process that perpetuated urban poverty. Lower local tax bases in the inner cities meant that locally financed inner-city services suffered, and this included schooling, which is heavily dependent on local financing in the United States.[37] The urbanization of poverty was also associated with social and demographic changes; the cities did not have the institutions for community support and risk sharing found in the established rural communities that many migrants came from. Traditional families also started to change, with rising incidence of single-parent families.[38] Whether the overall poverty rate increased in this process of the urbanization of US poverty is unclear; living conditions were poor in the rural South and there were winners and losers in the process of structural change. Even so, it is clear that there was a dramatic change in America's profile of poverty over this period.

In the context of the rising overall living standards of post–World War II America, knowledge about the living conditions of the country's poor clearly shamed many Americans. The rediscovery of poverty in the midst of overall affluence was stimulated by important social commentaries. Two stand out. The first is John Kenneth Galbraith's (1958) *The Affluent Society* and the second is Michael Harrington's (1962)

[33] For further discussion of these changes and their influence on antipoverty policy in the United States in the 1960s, see Piven and Cloward (1993, ch. 7).

[34] See Jargowsky (1997).

[35] On the economics of this residential differentiation the classic treatment is Muth (1969, ch. 2).

[36] See Rothstein (2012).

[37] Economic models incorporating these features were later developed, including Bénabou (1993). For an overview of poverty incorporating such neighborhood effects, see Durlauf (2006).

[38] See Piven and Cloward (1993, ch. 8).

The Other America. Galbraith was an economist and Harrington was a political scientist and activist. Both books were bestsellers at the time.[39] The success of Harrington's book was clearly a surprise; the first print run was 2,500 copies, but by the mid-1990s it had sold 1.3 million copies.

Knowledge had made this new awareness of poverty possible. The First Poverty Enlightenment lacked the theories and data that we take for granted today in trying to understand poverty and so inform public action. Nor was there much sign yet of the theories and movements that could claim to represent the interests of poor people. That had changed by the 1950s. Authors like Harrington and Galbraith could formulate accessible arguments grounded on a body of theory and data, the latter stemming from sample surveys and analytic work in measuring living standards and setting poverty lines. Many people were shocked in the early 1960s when the official calculations indicated that almost one-in-five Americans lived in poverty.

While the type of quantification initiated by Booth and Rowntree seventy years earlier had played a role in these developments, credibly reported qualitative observations in the media and popular books were hugely influential, including on policymaking at the highest levels. Many people were influenced by Harrington's efforts to "describe the faces behind the statistics" (17):

> Tens of millions of Americans are, at this very moment, maimed in body and spirit, existing at levels beneath those necessary for human decency. If these people are not starving, they are hungry, and sometimes fat with hunger, for that is what cheap foods do. They are without adequate housing and education and medical care. . . . The millions who are poor in the United States tend to become increasingly invisible. Here is a great mass of people, yet it takes an effort of the intellect and will even to see them. . . . The other America, the America of poverty, is hidden today in a way that it never was before. Its millions are socially invisible to the rest of us.

This was research aimed squarely at promoting change through knowledge. In an introduction to a 1993 reprint of *The Other America*, Howe (1993, p. xii) describes its central premise: "that if only people knew the reality they would respond with indignation, that if people became aware of 'the invisible poor' they would act to eliminate this national scandal."

Galbraith and Harrington described a new "minority poverty" in America. A long period of poverty reduction had meant that poor people were now a minority, albeit a sizable one. While overall economic growth had allowed many of the "old poor" to move into the new middle class, others were left behind or thrown into poverty from which they could not escape. Widely held views about upward mobility and equality of opportunity in America also came into question based on empirical studies showing how much parental income and schooling affects the life chances of children.[40]

---

[39] References to both books in the *Viewer* skyrocketed from the 1960s; the graph can be found at http://ngrams.googlelabs.com/graph?content=The+Affluent+Society%2CThe+Other+America&year_start=1800&year_end=2000&corpus=0&smoothing=3. In Britain *The Poor and the Poorest*, by Brian Abel-Smith and Peter Townsend (1966) was also influential.

[40] See Duncan et al. (1972) and Bowles and Gintis (1976).

There were differences between Galbraith and Harrington in their understanding of the new poverty in America. Galbraith identified two reasons why so many of the old poor were unable to participate in the new opportunities. The first was physical or mental disability—what Galbraith called "case poverty"—while the second was that some were trapped in geographic pockets of poverty (his "insular poverty"). While not rejecting these categories, Harrington argued that this was incomplete in that many of the minority poor had been negatively impacted by the same economic expansion that had benefited so many others. Significant economic change had created their poverty, reinforced by discrimination (including in public policies and the legal system), and they were unable to recover. Here Harrington is making an important point—that even pro-poor overall progress comes with losers as well as winners. And his descriptions of many of the minority poor sound a lot like the outcomes of a model of wealth dynamics whereby large negative shocks create persistent poverty, and recovery to get back on track is no small thing. (Recall box 1.6 on poverty traps. Chapter 8 discusses these models in greater depth.)

The writings of social commentators such as Harrington and Galbraith helped stimulate demands for public action against poverty. So too did concerns about social instability—that the inner cities were erupting in discontent, as exemplified by the riots in a number of major US cities in the late 1960s.[41] However, the demands for better antipoverty policies were also coming from poor people themselves, reflecting both the economic changes that had led to a geographic concentration of poverty among African Americans in inner cities. The bulk of America's poverty was elsewhere, but it had a new voice in the inner cities. Poor people had come to play an important role in the political processes that led to new policies. Community-based organizations emerged in poor areas across America's cities. This reflected the economic changes that had been underway since 1940, which had led poor people to be more concentrated spatially in the country's large northern cities and thus more capable of organizing themselves to protest and to vote.[42] As in most areas of policy, the response to economic realities was mediated through evolving political processes, partly rooted in those same realities. This is exemplified by the remarkable policy response to the rediscovery of poverty in America.

America Declares War on Poverty

In the wake of expanding public awareness, mass protests, and political debates, a vigorous federal political response to poverty in America came in the 1960s.[43] The policies included greatly expanded eligibility for Aid to Families with Dependent Children (AFDC)—a program of transfers to poor single mothers that dated back to the New

---

[41] Katz (1986) and Piven and Cloward (1993) emphasize the political motivation for the new antipoverty policies that emerged in America around this time. Also see the discussion in Piven and Cloward (1979, ch. 5).

[42] On the role played by political factors (both protests and through the ballot box) in the surge of antipoverty policies in the 1960s, see Piven and Cloward (1993).

[43] On the history and political context of the War on Poverty, see Sundquist (1968) and Piven and Cloward (1993).

Deal in the 1930s. Importantly, the response also included many new social programs, popularly known as the Johnson administration's *War on Poverty*. This was a set of legislated programs introduced in 1964–65 covering nutrition (Food Stamps), health (Medicare and Medicaid), education, housing, training, and various community-based programs. The new initiatives included *Head Start*, a pre-school program to help assure that children from poor families were not disadvantaged when starting school.

These direct interventions against poverty were part of a broader set of *Great Society* programs that included many important promotional policies for reducing poverty. An example is the *Elementary and Secondary Education Act* of 1965 which boosted federal aid to public education, including programs targeted to schools in poor areas. The new effort was framed in plainly promotional terms: "Our chief weapons . . . will be better schools, and better health, and better homes, and better training, and better job opportunities to help more Americans, especially young Americans, escape from squalor and misery and unemployment rolls" (Lyndon B. Johnson's State of the Union Address, January 1964).

While poverty reduction was the explicit overall goal, the new programs had an empowerment objective, namely to reach African Americans in the ghettos of the northern cities and to better integrate them into urban government. Thus, there was an urban bias in program allocations, and especially a ghetto bias; rural poverty received relatively less attention. This bias can be interpreted as a response to the social disorder that had emerged in the 1960s. But it also had explicit promotional motives, namely to help assure that currently underprivileged and excluded groups would have better access to public services in the future.[44] This was aiming to be a comprehensive antipoverty policy, combining promotion and protection (box 1.7).

With this extra objective in mind, many of the new programs also had a new delivery system, bypassing the existing layers of government by relying on new agents at community level. This was framed in terms of the ideas of citizen participation and local initiative; these ideas were to re-emerge in the community-based antipoverty policies that came to prominence from the 1990s in the developing world.[45] The use of a new administrative arrangement reflected the fact that state and local governments (especially in the South) had come to be seen as obstacles to pro-poor policies and civil rights legislation. The political structures of the time were not seen as a reliable means of empowering the urban poor to assure a sustained escape from poverty.

There has been some debate about why we saw this new antipoverty policy in the United States in the 1960s. The rise in public spending on antipoverty programs was not, it seems, prompted by a mass shift in American public opinion.[46] However, electoral outcomes in the United States also depend on voter registration. The urbanization of African Americans had increased their registration rates and voting power for influencing civil rights and antipoverty policies.[47] Social instability, most evident

[44] See Piven and Cloward (1993, ch. 9).

[45] See Mansuri and Rao (2012) for a review of these efforts at community-based development.

[46] Heclo (1986) refers to US polls indicating that the public was evenly divided on whether welfare spending should increase.

[47] This also came with a significant change in the Democratic Party, which had been attracting a majority of black voters since around 1940, at the expense of the Republican Party.

in inner-city rioting and rising crime in the 1960s, was also of widespread concern, including to whites. This too helped motivate action by government. There was also a degree of paternalism in the policies, as evidenced by the heavy reliance on transfers in kind rather than cash. In-kind transfers appear to have been more politically acceptable.

But this was not just about politics. The policy response was also intellectually grounded in the evidence, ideas, and debates of the period. There was an undeniable shift in policy thinking, with rising influence of liberal social commentators and social scientists from about 1960. From early on, the policy effort was framed in non-utilitarian and non-welfarist terms, especially emphasizing rights and opportunities; for example, the main piece of legislation was called the Economic Opportunity Act and the agency created to oversee federal spending on the new policies was called the *Office of Economic Opportunity* (OEO). The intellectual shifts of the time encouraged an active effort by federal authorities to challenge the many local laws and policies that worked against the interests of poor people, including racial discrimination and denying welfare benefits to those perceived to be undeserving.[48] There was also greater federal government support for nongovernmental organizations that informed poor men and women of their legal rights and entitlements.

The debates about these new social policies continued through the subsequent decades. From early on, the new administrative arrangements drew opposition from many state and local governments who were being largely left out of the process. There were accusations of corruption. Echoing similar debates going back two hundred years or more, some prominent critics argued that these programs would create poverty by discouraging work and saving, while others (more supportive in principle) felt that the programs were underfunded and uncoordinated. Undoubtedly mistakes were made. Some of the original programs were modified or abandoned, but a number continue today (including Food Stamps and Head Start).

An important innovation of the Second Poverty Enlightenment was the new effort put into learning about the effectiveness of antipoverty policies. The policy effort also came with an evaluative effort from an early stage, including various randomized experiments of pilot antipoverty programs. In the United States, knowledge support to the *War on Poverty* was provided by (among other efforts) a new national institute created in 1966, *The Institute for Research on Poverty* at the University of Wisconsin–Madison, which was charged with studying the causes of poverty in the United States and evaluating antipoverty programs using both experimental and non-experimental methods. Similar efforts emerged in many other countries. (Chapter 6 returns to these methods.)

The initiators of the War on Poverty in the United States were mostly not economists, but economists were involved in the debates and policymaking efforts of this period; this was also the case in the United Kingdom and Europe around the same time. Some prominent contributions by economists were closer to the welfarist-utilitarian tradition, which they were clearly more comfortable with than talk of "rights." The proposals were also motivated by a desire to close loop holes and remove

[48] See Piven and Cloward (1993, ch. 9).

defects in the developing welfare state. Important concerns included the disincentives to work due to high implicit marginal tax rates on poor people associated with sharply means-tested benefits. Indeed, some of the schemes imposed 100% marginal tax rates on recipients; in other words, the welfare benefits were withdrawn by $10 for each extra $10 of income from other sources.[49] Friedman (1962) made a radical proposal for a Negative Income Tax (NIT) to replace other welfare programs. A NIT could, on paper at least, claim to eliminate poverty by assuring that no income (at least as recorded in the tax system) fell below a certain level. This was to be financed by income taxes, configured such that no income fell below the stipulated level. A similar proposal for a guaranteed income was made for the United Kingdom by Meade (1972). America's Earned Income Tax Credit (EITC), introduced in 1975, contained some elements of the NIT idea. EITC provides a tax credit (negative tax) for working families with incomes below a stipulated level. This is phased out as income rises up to that level. The size of the negative tax depends on the number of children (as well as income). Many other countries have since introduced similar policies.[50] (We return to these and other forms of targeted policies in chapter 10).

2.2 Debates and Backlashes

The backlash against the policies of the War on Poverty gained strength politically from the late 1970s. Political support from middle-income voters may have been weakened somewhat by the highly targeted nature of most of the programs. However, it does not appear that there was any significant erosion of overall public support for the antipoverty programs in the United States. Instead, the balance of political power had changed, with business interests becoming better organized politically to fight these programs, on the grounds that they were reducing profits by holding up wages.[51] Ronald Reagan's election to the presidency in 1980 marked the turning point. Restrictions on program eligibility, administrative efforts to withhold benefits from those eligible, and lower spending levels on antipoverty programs followed.[52]

Concerns about adverse incentive effects loomed large in the rationales given, such as claims that welfare benefits to single mothers encouraged families to break up.[53] Repeated claims were heard that the welfare state is creating poverty, echoing Townsend (1786). However, as in the nineteenth century debates on the Poor Laws, rather little credible supportive evidence was presented, and evidence to the contrary could be cited.[54] Metaphors (often with racial connotations) were exploited politically by opponents of antipoverty policies; metaphors and empirically dubious behavioral

---

[49] Moffitt (2002) provides a history of welfare programs in the United States, focusing on these aspects.

[50] Including Austria, Belgium, Canada, Denmark, Finland, France, Holland, New Zealand, Sweden, and the United Kingeom.

[51] See the discussion in Piven and Cloward (1993, ch. 11).

[52] For example, while 81% of the unemployed were receiving unemployment allowances in 1975 the share was reduced to 26% by 1987 (Piven and Cloward 1993, 360).

[53] An influential attack against welfare programs came from Murray's (1984) *Losing Ground*.

[54] See Ellwood and Summers (1986). Also see the commentary on the debate by Blank (1995).

characterizations have often influenced policymaking.[55] Yet the realities of life for those struggling on social assistance in the United States were very different to the rhetoric of welfare critics. In his book, *Living on the Edge*, Mark Rank (1994, 1) quotes a fifty-one-year-old divorced mother living on welfare: "as far as my own situation is concerned, it's pretty rough living this way. I can't see anybody that would ever settle for something like this just for the mere fact of getting a free ride, because it's not worth it."

Of course, this is an anecdote. But it is consistent with careful research by economists. Hilary Hoynes' (1997) empirical investigation of the incidence of female headship in the United States cast doubt on the many claims that the benefits provided to single mothers played an important role.[56] The fact that the majority of the direct beneficiaries of US antipoverty programs such as AFDC were children and teenagers also casts doubt on claims made about large incentive effects on work effort and savings.[57] Indeed, if there was any work disincentive for children we would surely judge it a good thing—that it would reduce child labor and lengthen schooling, and so reduce the chance of poverty being passed onto the next generation. Work disincentives for mothers may well also bring benefits in early childhood development.

Nor was it plausible that the welfare state was creating poverty in the United States. It would require an implausibly high work effort for poor families to make up for their welfare receipts by working more, at least at the minimum wage (box 2.4). So it is implausible that there would be less poverty without the transfers. The EITC is designed to maintain incentives to gain extra income from work, that is, the implicit marginal tax rate (MTR) facing beneficiaries is well below 100%. However, the designs of some other US programs in some states have implied high MTRs, with the likelihood of adverse incentive effects, and even poverty traps.[58]

Box 2.4 **How Hard More Would Poor People Need to Work to Replace Public Transfers?**

The Congressional Budget Office (2012) estimates that the poorest quintile of US families in 2009 in terms of household income (adjusted for family size) received $7,600 in market income on average, and $22,900 in transfers from the government. To argue that the average family in the poorest quintile would have a higher income without the transfers by working harder you have to believe that

---

[55] Examples include the references to "deadbeat dads" and "welfare queens" by political opponents of antipoverty policies in the United States. See Cammett (2014) for further discussion of the role of metaphors in debates on US poverty law. Also see the papers in Katz (1993).

[56] Hoynes replicated the correlation between female headship and the generosity of welfare benefits found in cross-sectional data, but found that this was not robust to allowing for heterogeneity in the propensity to form female-headed households due to other factors. Her study used panel data (chapter 3).

[57] See the more polemical but still persuasive arguments in Albelda et al. (1996).

[58] For further discussion, see Moffitt (2002).

this family could make up that $22,900 by extra work. If all the $7,600 came from work, then that would require four times more work than the family has now. At the federal minimum wage rate of $7.25 per hour in 2009, making up the $22,900 would require an extra sixty-three hours of work per week (for a fifty-week year). If the family had just one earner who brought in the family's market income from working at the minimum wage rate, then that earner would need to work eighty-four hours per week to break even. Suppose instead that a second adult goes to work to make up for the transfers. Then extra costs of travel-to-work and childcare will probably be incurred. Allowing $4 a day for transport cost and $10 a day for childcare, the net hourly wage rate for an eight-hour day for the second earner would be $5.50 per hour and making up the $22,900 would require that the second earner does eighty-three hours of market work per week.

Those who claim that poverty would be less without these public transfers appear to be saying that poor families could find two full-time jobs at the minimum wage in the absence of the transfers.

The original War on Poverty initiatives had a long-term influence, and many of the specific programs of that period survived well beyond it.[59] Per capita public spending on welfare programs in the U.S. has trended upwards.[60] Of course, the debates continued. Cuts to social spending were made at times (depending on which party was in power). Work incentives often figured prominently in the policy debates, with calls for either lower marginal tax rates or work requirements (or both). As the historian Michael Katz (1987) put it, after declaring a *"War on Poverty,"* America started to declare a *"War on Welfare."*[61]

The biggest change came with the *Personal Responsibility and Work Opportunity Reconciliation Act*, signed into law by the Democratic President William Clinton in 1996. AFDC was replaced by *Temporary Assistance for Needy Families*, under which financial assistance was limited to five years in a lifetime, and recipients had to get work within two years.[62] Echoing England's New Poor Laws in the 1830s, welfare receipt now came with work requirements. Although far less draconian than the workhouses, the rationales were similar: to incentivize behavioral change by poor people. The modern policy discussions in the United States talked more about the claimed promotional gains from work experience, the moral virtues of work, and the benefits to local communities, although it is not clear that these arguments were much more than a politically appealing rationale for getting people off the welfare

[59] Califano (1999) points out that thirty years later, eleven of the original twelve programs from 1964/65 were still funded.

[60] See Moffitt (2015) for time series evidence on this point.

[61] The latter term is due to Katz (1986, 1987); also see Piven and Cloward (1993) and Albelda et al. (1996).

[62] There are differences across US states in the details of implementation.

rolls to cut transfers to the poor.[63] Similarly to England's 1834 reforms, there was a large reduction in the number of people receiving help in the United States in the years following the 1996 reforms.[64]

Poverty and Inequality in America

January 8, 2014, marked the 50th anniversary of the Johnson administration's declaration of a War on Poverty. Past debates on whether the War of Poverty had succeeded resurfaced in the U.S. media. A common claim heard is that (to paraphrase): "Since poverty remains the war was lost, and so the policies were misconceived," and one still hears this type of claim today. The basis for this claim is the fact that the official poverty rate in the United States is still around 15% (the official figure for 2012), having been 19% when the War on Poverty was declared. Figure 2.2 gives the official poverty rates from the US Census Bureau back to 1973, the earliest year reported. (The figure also gives the rates for 125% and 150% of the official line; the series show strong co-movement.) Unofficial estimates of a longer series indicate that the US poverty rate had been falling for some years prior to the beginning of the War on Poverty, thanks in large part it seems to a pro-poor process of economic growth.[65] Box 2.5 describes the official poverty lines used in the United States.

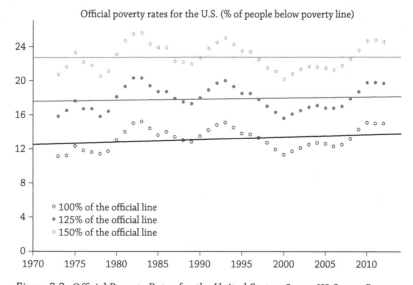

Figure 2.2 Official Poverty Rates for the United States. *Source:* US Census Bureau.

[63] For example, with reference to the claims made that taking women off AFDC would enhance community life, Piven and Cloward (1993,394) remark that "No social analyst explained convincingly why these women would contribute more to their communities by taking jobs flipping hamburgers." Also see the discussion in Katz (1987).

[64] See Lichter and Jayakody (2002).

[65] For evidence on this point, see Iceland (2003).

Supporters of the War on Poverty point out that the poverty rate fell over the decade after the War on Poverty was declared.[66] Some observers looked at the evidence and argued that it was the War on Welfare that stalled progress against poverty, rather than the policies of the War on Poverty.[67] Declining real value of the monthly payments made through AFDC in the 1980s and 1990s helped put a halt to the progress that had been made against poverty in America. Also notable is that this came with a marked shift in the demographic profile of US poverty, favoring the elderly. The incidence of poverty continued to fall among the elderly in the United States after 1980, albeit at a slower rate. Peter Lindert (2013) attributes this difference to a bias in US social spending in favor of the elderly over the young, in common with other rich countries.

Box 2.5 America's Official Poverty Line and Comparisons with Other Countries

The US government uses an absolute line, originally developed in 1965 by Mollie Orshansky (1965), an economist working for the Social Security Administration. Poverty was defined as making less than three times the cost of a minimally adequate diet; the factor of three came from a 1955 study suggested that food expenditure accounted for one-third of a typical family's budget. Since the late 1960s there has only been an annual price index adjustment; no adjustment has been made to reflect rising standards for defining "poverty." Currently the threshold is set at $24,069 for a family of four ($16 per person per day).

Figure B2.5.1 shows how national poverty lines vary across countries (in $ per person per day at 2005 purchasing power parity; $n = 95$). For the poorest twenty or so countries, the average line is $1.25 a day. At around $13 per person per day in 2005 (for a family of four with two children—about $16 a day in 2014), the official poverty line in the United States is roughly ten times higher than one finds in the poorest countries. (Although the implicit poverty line in Hunter's famous 1904 study of poverty in the United States appears to be quite close to the lines found in poor countries today, in that both suggest a headcount of around 10 million poor in 1900.) However, the US line is low when compared to other similarly rich countries today. At roughly the same average income, Luxembourg has a line of $43 a day. A better comparison is with the average value among the rich countries, which is around $30 a day, roughly double the US line. In fact the US line is the average line for countries with only about one-third of the mean consumption level of the United States. (This is calculated

continued

---

[66] For further discussion of US progress against poverty in this period, see Meyer and Sullivan (2012) and Iceland (2013).While income poverty rates crept back up after 1980, consumption-based measures continued to fall. On the choice between these measures, see Slesnick (2001).

[67] See Albelda et al. (1996).

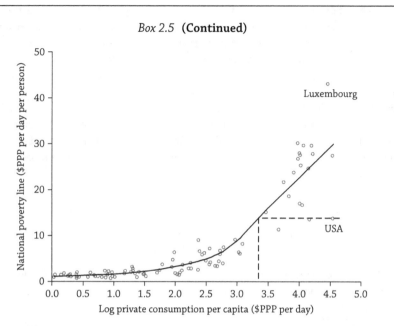

Figure B2.5.1 Poverty Lines across Countries of the World in 2005 Prices. *Source:* Author's calculations from the data set compiled in Ravallion (2012b).

by inverting the line of best fit in figure B2.5.1, to find the consumption per person corresponding to the US line, as indicated by the dashed lines.) Studies of data on the incomes that different families deem to be necessary to make ends meet also suggest that the official poverty line in the United States is below the level above which people tend to think they are not poor (de Vos and Garner, 1991). (This is an example of the "social subjective poverty line" studied further in chapter 4.)

Further reading: See Fisher (1992) and Johnson and Smeeding (2012), which also discussed the supplementary measures that have been introduced in recent years. Chapter 4 returns to the debates on the US official poverty line. On poverty lines across the world, see Ravallion (2012b).

It is clear is that there has been remarkably little progress against income poverty since the 1970s. (Indeed, income groups other than the upper 10% have seen little progress; one estimate suggests that average real income of the poorest 90% in the United States has seen negligible growth since the 1970s.[68]) However, there is just not much one can really infer with any confidence from the historical time series alone about the effectiveness of antipoverty policies in the United States. More relevant poverty statistics than the official poverty rate of 15% in 2012 are given by the new

[68] See Papadimitriou et al. (2014, fig. 8), based in part on top income shares from Alvaredo et al. (2014).

series produced by the Census Bureau that provides poverty rates calculated with and without government transfers. The calculations indicate that the poverty rate in the United States would have been about twice as high if not for the transfers—the very same policies that the critics say have failed.[69] Put in this perspective—relative to the counterfactual of the absence of these antipoverty policies—the War on Poverty looks like a huge success. This suggests that existing programs need to expand if the poverty rate is to fall.

These calculations are instructive, although attribution problems remain in saying just how much poverty reduction was achieved. Simply subtracting public transfers received from total income assumes that recipients would have worked no harder in the absence of the transfers, which is implausible given the likely incentive effect (as introduced in box 1.4). It is unclear how much difference this would make to the calculations, but the issue should not be ignored. (We return to this topic in chapter 10.)

From the late 1970s, America's economic growth started to bypass the country's poor and also its middle class. Indeed, the bulk of the income gains accrued to the rich. Figure 2.3 plots the income shares of the top 1% in the United States back to 1913.[70] As can be seen from figure 2.3, "high-end inequality" rose sharply; the share of household income held by the richest 1% of American households has more than

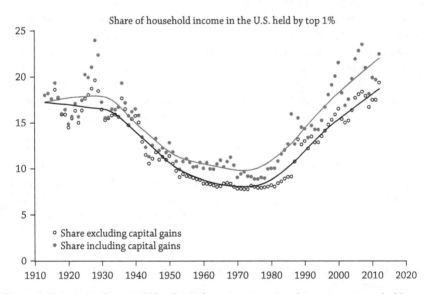

Share of household income in the U.S. held by top 1%

Figure 2.3 Income Share Held by the Richest One Percent of American Households.
Source: Alvaredo et al. (2014); author's estimates of a nearest neighbor smoothed scatter plot.

[69] See Fox et al. (2013).

[70] These estimates use a method devised by Piketty and Saez (2003) based on income tax records. Since the income tax system was only introduced in 1913 this is the earliest year for which the estimates are available.

doubled since 1980. This was enough to assure that the majority of the income gains since then accrued to the top 1%.[71]

Why have we seen so little gain to America's poor and middle class, while the rich have done so much better? Three main reasons can be identified from the literature.[72] The first is the change in education policy in the 1970s. The Dutch economist Jan Tinbergen (1975) identified the "race between education and technology" as a key factor in how inequality evolves. If the schooling system produces enough graduates to keep pace with the extra demand stemming from new technologies, then the skill premium will not rise. Rising earnings inequality in America has stemmed from rising demand for skilled labor, relative to the supply.[73] As economists Claudia Goldin and Lawrence Katz (2008) demonstrate, the United States was doing well in this race for a long period up to around 1980, but ceased doing so after education policy changes in the 1970s. This too has a distributional dimension. The share of college graduates coming from poorer families has fallen over time and they are far less likely to attend America's selective colleges.[74]

The second cause is the re-emergence of high rates of return to wealth relative to the growth rate of national income, as demonstrated by the economist Thomas Piketty (2014). Because rich people hold most of the wealth, high returns are fuelling higher inequality. Strikingly, the estimates of the income and wealth shares of the very rich in the United States made by Piketty and others suggest that high-end inequality in that country has returned to its level of the period prior to World War I.[75] Piketty focuses on non-human wealth. No less important is the change in the structure of returns to *human capital*, notably the rise in salaries at the high end and changes in the work available at the low end. While the rising high-end earnings reflect, in some degree, the first factor of higher skill premiums, it does not seem believable that the soaring salaries earned by the CEOs of large American corporations reflect returns to "skill" in competitive labor markets. At the other end of the wage distribution, the manufacturing jobs with decent benefits were being replaced by low-wage service-sector jobs with few benefits and little or no security.

A third (and related) set of causes relates to public policies. On the one hand, US policies for de-regulation of the financial sector and cutting taxes on high incomes have created a share of the rise in high-end inequality. Overall tax cuts on the rich left less money for public programs and public goods that would (directly or indirectly) benefit poor people, and also helped fuel deficits that further constrained public

---

[71] Piketty (2014) calculates that the top 1% of income recipients captured 60% of the income gains in the thirty years following 1977.

[72] A fourth factor is the rise in assortative mating in the United States, whereby high (low) income persons tend to marry high (low) income persons. However, a careful empirical analysis by Decancq et al. (2015) does not suggest that this is a quantitatively important contributing factor to the rise in household earnings inequality.

[73] See Autor (2014).

[74] See Greenstone et al. (2013).

[75] This includes America's so-called "Gilded Age" of the last few decades of the nineteenth century, as satirized by Mark Twain and Charles Warner in their novel about corruption and greed in Washington, DC.

spending that would have helped reduce poverty.[76] On the other hand, policies have failed to deliver sufficient redistribution of the gains to both skilled workers and the owners of capital associated with rising pretax inequality. The composition of taxation has shifted over time from the progressive income tax to regressive taxes. And, since 1980, America's poor have seen a declining share of federal transfer payments.[77]

While many of the increasingly affluent middle-class Americans in the 1960s were shocked to learn about extreme poverty in their midst, many middle-class Americans in the new millennium have been shocked by the signs of the rising extreme affluence of a small elite, alongside their own economic stagnation. The contemporary equivalent of Harrington's *Other America* is Piketty's *Capital in the 21st Century* (to be discussed further in chapter 8). They are very different books in many ways, though both were surprise bestsellers,[78] and both opened up much-needed public debates on redistributive policy.

Culture of Poverty?

The claims from the eighteenth century that the "bad" or "immoral" behavior by poor men and women caused their poverty continued to resurface at times and are still heard today. In attempting to explain America's poverty amidst affluence, the ideas of a "culture of poverty" and an "underclass" that emerged in the 1960s were much debated. Echoing the debates of prior times reviewed above, critics saw these ideas as ignoring more deep-rooted "structural" inequalities.[79] In some, more sophisticated, versions of the "underclass" idea, such as in sociologist William Julius Wilson's (1987) *The Truly Disadvantaged*, a "culture of poverty" was seen to stem from structural inequalities and so part of their explanation; echoing Harrington, Wilson emphasized macroeconomic factors, including structural changes in the economy, urban structural changes, and aggregate unemployment rates. America's black "underclass" was now being explained by social and economic forces. (Chapter 8 returns to discuss in more depth this class of "membership models" of poverty.)

While the debate continues on whether there is space for policy intervention aimed at changing culture,[80] looking back over two hundred years it is clear that there has been a significant shift in thinking about poverty, from primarily blaming poor people to identifying deeper factors beyond their control, but amenable to public action. This new view does not deny personal responsibility, or the scope for mistakes or seemingly irrational behaviors.[81] In due course, new evidence also emerged suggesting that the

---

[76] For further discussion of the role played by politics in rising high-end inequality in America, see Hacker and Pierson (2010).

[77] See Wolf (2014).

[78] And similarly successful in terms of copies sold, though at the time of writing Piketty's book looked like it would overtake Harrington's.

[79] See Gans (1995) and O'Connor (2002).

[80] See, e.g., Steinberg's (2011) comments on Small et al. (2010).

[81] Behavioral explanations of poverty have drawn some support from experiments suggesting that people do not always behave rationally, although the experiments are often open to other interpretations, notably about the nature of the optimizing behavior (Saint-Paul 2011).

stresses of poverty diminish cognitive ability, again clouding cause and effect.[82] But the key point to emerge was that "bad choices" was a dangerously incomplete explanation of poverty. As David Shipler (2005, 6) nicely puts it with reference to America's working poor: "Each person's life is the mixed product of bad choices and bad fortunes, of roads not taken and roads cut off by the accident of birth or circumstances."

Relative and Subjective Poverty

As poverty came to be seen as a social-bad that society should try to eliminate, the best way to measure poverty became a key discussion point. As noted at the beginning of this chapter (box 1.2), there are two ways of thinking about poverty, absolute and relative. Under absolute poverty, the poor are defined as those who fall below a threshold of income or consumption that is fixed in real terms across all the subgroups being compared. Instead, relative poverty allows that minimum to vary across those groups, typically rising with the group's average income. Proponents of the former approach argue that we should ignore borders between countries in assessing poverty; two people with the same command over commodities should be treated the same way even when one lives in a rich country while the other lives in a poor one. Advocates of relative measures point to the relative deprivation experienced by a poor person living in a rich country (say) and also to the higher (socially specific) costs incurred in being able to participate in economic and social life in a rich country compared to a poor one.[83] The case for relative lines rests on the view that poverty must be seen as absolute in the space of welfare, whether defined in terms of utility or capabilities; as Sen (1983, 163) put it, "an absolute approach in the space of capabilities translates into a relative approach in the space of commodities."

Prior to the Second Poverty Enlightenment, it seems that poverty was mainly seen in absolute terms. This changed radically in much of the rich world in the 1960s.[84] Of course, there were antecedents to the idea of relative poverty that emerged. Famously, Adam Smith held a conception of poverty that was socially specific; in a famous passage in the *Wealth of Nations* (1776, bk. 5, ch. 2, art. 4) Smith pointed to the social role of a linen shirt in eighteenth-century Europe, whereby "a creditable day-labourer would be ashamed to appear in public without a linen shirt."[85] Smith wanted the poverty line to be relevant to its context. To some degree that is what we see across countries (as we saw in box 2.5). However, while one might accept Smith's view that the poverty standard for a specific setting should reflect prevailing norms, it is not clear that the line should be adjusted over time. Recall that Bowley (1915) had been

---

[82] See Mani et al. (2013).

[83] Relative deprivation here means that a person's welfare depends directly on his or her consumption or income judged relative to the average for some reference group, such as fellow residents of a country or neighborhood.

[84] Doron (1990, 30) describes this change in the 1960s: "The reformers of the period, and certainly the radicals among them, rejected the absolute approach, which contents itself with guaranteeing a minimum of subsistence. . . . The needs of men are not stable and absolute but relative and related to the circumstances of the society in a particular period of time."

[85] See Smith (1776, bk. 5, ch. 2, art. 4).

adamant on this point: the line should have fixed real value over time, making it absolute, even if it is relative between countries. Logically, however, a line that is fixed in real terms cannot remain relevant to prevailing living standards indefinitely in growing economies.

From the time of the Second Poverty Enlightenment, it came to be more widely accepted that poverty was relative, and (hence) socially specific, and that this applied both across countries and over time in a growing economy. The challenge was how to implement this idea. The period also saw efforts to anchor poverty measures to public assistance thresholds.[86] This led to concerns that the poverty count was then subject to political manipulation; a political party that came to power opposed to poor relief might lower the poverty rate by cutting benefit levels.

The Second Poverty Enlightenment saw a new concept of relative poverty in both America and Western Europe. The economist Victor Fuchs (1967) appears to have been the first to propose that the poverty line should be set at 50% of the current (group-specific) median income. The line had an elasticity of unity with respect to the average income. When the line is set at a fixed percentage of the mean (or median) we can call it a "strongly relative measure."

It was understood that this new measure, when applied over time as well as space, was really about relative distribution. An immediate implication of the strongly relative lines is that when all income levels rise by the same proportion the measure of poverty remains unchanged. Economic growth that does not change relative inequality will leave the poverty measure unchanged. Such relative poverty could in principle be eliminated; there is no theoretical reason why the distribution of income could not be such that nobody lived below half the mean. Whether that could be attained in practice was another matter.

This new idea of strongly relative poverty had more influence in Western Europe than in America, and little influence in the developing world. The official line in the United States is an absolute line over time (with fixed real value; see box 2.5), as are almost all lines in developing countries. However, as Fuchs (1967) notes, the US poverty line in the 1930s was probably substantially lower in real terms than the 1960s.[87] There has been a positive gradient in the US line, over a long period of time. Indeed, it may well have increased by a factor of ten or more over the course of the twentieth century.[88] Similarly we are seeing rising real poverty lines in rapidly developing countries such as China and India.[89]

In due course, the most widely used definition of poverty in Western Europe followed Fuchs's suggestion, with national poverty lines often set at a constant proportion of the current median. Eurostat (2005) has produced such poverty measures, as has the influential Luxembourg Income Study (LIS), which started in the mid-1980s

[86] An early example was Abel-Smith and Townsend (1966) describing poverty in Britain.

[87] See Fuchs (1967), who based this claim on a necessarily rough calculation, asserting that if the 1960s standard in the United States was applied to the 1930s, then two-thirds of the US population would have been deemed poor as compared to President Roosevelt's estimate that "one third of the nation" was so in the 1930s.

[88] This is suggested by a comparison of Hunter's (1904) poverty line with the official line.

[89] See Ravallion (2012b).

and uses poverty lines set at 40–60% of the median in its summary statistics at country level.[90] The debate about absolute versus relative poverty continues today. This is an important debate. We examine its more technical aspects in Part Two, but it is worth reviewing the debate here.

Critics of relative lines have been concerned about seemingly unequal treatment of people at similar levels of real income at different dates or different countries. The advocates of relative lines for rich countries would not presumably have been comfortable in applying the same idea in comparing poverty measures between the majority population and minorities within one country; indeed, the Second Poverty Enlightenment started to see a breakdown of past discriminatory practices in this respect. There were clearly (though rarely explicit) moral bounds to relativism. However, a welfarist case for relativism still exists if a higher level of personal real income is needed to attain the same level of welfare in a richer country.

The more problematic issue is why the poverty line should be *strongly* relative, that is, proportional to the mean or median. If we consider more closely the most common arguments made in favor of relativism, neither is obviously compelling in this respect. Two arguments can be identified. The first concerns social inclusion. A linen shirt in eighteenth-century Europe is an example of what can be termed a "social inclusion need." The idea of such needs has been influential in social policy discussions in Western Europe and Scandinavia since the 1980s though the idea of social inclusion goes back a long way, including to Adam Smith.[91] The existence of social inclusion needs has been the primary justification given for the Western European relative poverty lines.[92] However, while we can readily agree that social inclusion is an essential element for avoiding poverty that does not justify strongly relative poverty lines. The cost of that shirt will be roughly the same for the poorest person as for the richest. More generally, the cost of social inclusion cannot be expected to go to zero in the limit, as mean income goes to zero, as implied by strongly relative lines. That would almost certainly understate the costs of social inclusion in poor countries.

The second argument made for the strongly relative measures is that they allow for *relative deprivation*—that people care about their income relative to that of a relevant reference group. The sociologist Garry Runciman (1966) was an influential advocate of this view. In economics, James Duesenberry (1949) provided an innovative model of consumption behavior (well ahead of its time) based on the idea of relative deprivation, whereby a person's welfare depended on own-income relative to the mean in the country of residence.[93] When applied to poverty measurement, this implies that a welfare-consistent poverty line would need to be a rising function of the mean—the

---

[90] For a critical review of the methods used by LIS in their data compilations, see Ravallion (2014c).

[91] See the discussion in Spicker (2007, ch. 8). An influential contribution to the recent attention to social inclusion was Silver (1994).

[92] See Spicker (2007, ch. 8), who goes further to argue that "social exclusion" came to be synonymous with "poverty" for the European Commission by the turn of the twenty-first century; Spicker argues that exclusion was a more politically acceptable term for at least one EC member.

[93] Duesenberry's model was developed to resolve an empirical puzzle: Kuznets (1946) had shown that over the longer term aggregate consumption in the United States was roughly proportional to aggregate income—implying a constant average propensity to consume (APC)—yet cross-sectional

higher monetary line in a richer country will be needed to compensate for the welfare cost of feeling relatively deprived.

However, on closer scrutiny, this is not convincing as an explanation for strongly relative poverty lines. As long as we think that poverty is absolute in the space of welfare (or capabilities) one can only derive these strongly relative poverty measures if welfare *only* depends on relative income (own income relative to the median). In other words, one needs to assume that welfare does not depend on own-income at given relative income. This must surely be considered a very strong assumption.

None of this denies the welfare-relevance of social inclusion needs or relative deprivation. The case is now stronger than ever for incorporating relativist concerns in poverty measurement. Rather the issue is how best to do that. To allow for a (positive) minimum cost of social inclusion, one requires what have been dubbed "weakly relative measures."[94] These have the feature that the poverty line will not rise proportionately to the mean, but with an elasticity less than unity for all finite mean incomes.[95] (Chapter 4 discusses the various poverty lines further.) This is consistent with the historical experiences of countries that have seen rising real incomes over a long period, including the United States.[96] Consistently with the national lines found across countries (such as in box 2.5), one can devise global poverty measures using a schedule of weakly relative lines that contain the absolute lines (typical of poor countries) and relative lines (typical of rich ones) as the limiting cases.[97]

Another strand of the new literature on poverty measurement emphasized the scope for calibrating welfare and poverty measures to subjective questions in surveys. These could take the form of asking an individual how they would rank themselves on a scale from "poor" to "rich" say,[98] or a more general question on satisfaction with life or happiness. Alternatively, the survey questions asked what income level they believed to correspond to specific subjective welfare levels.[99] A special case was the "minimum income question," which derived the monetary poverty line as the fixed point in the regression function relating personal subjective minima to actual incomes. In other words, the line was drawn such that people with an income below it tended to think their income was inadequate for meeting their needs, while those above the line

---

studies at one date suggested that the APC fell as income rose (as was assumed by Keynes). Duesenberry argued that the APC depended on relative income, which changed little over the longer term, yet in a single cross-section one will observe a declining APC as income rises.

[94] See Ravallion and Chen (2011) . A weakly relative line was proposed earlier by Foster (1998). This was given by the weighted geometric mean of an absolute and a strongly relative line. While this is also weakly relative, it has a constant elasticity, whereas the elasticity rises from zero to unity in the Ravallion and Chen (2011) proposal—consistently with the data on national lines in box 2.5.

[95] It can be argued that a globally relevant schedule of poverty lines should also have this property, and global measures following this approach are available in Ravallion and Chen (2013).

[96] See, e.g., the discussion of the evolution of the US poverty lines in Schultz (1965).

[97] See Ravallion and Chen (2011). The Ravallion-Chen poverty lines have three parameters: an absolute minimum income level, a minimum social inclusion cost, and a relativist gradient; chapter 4 will discuss these lines in greater detail.

[98] These came to be known as Cantril ladders following Hadley Cantril (1965).

[99] Following Van Praag (1968).

tended to think their own income was adequate. Alternatively, the poverty line could be identified as the fixed point of adequacy across multiple dimensions of welfare.[100] Part Two goes into greater detail on these measures.

The Basic-Income Movement

From the 1970s we started to see arguments being made in support of the idea of a "basic-income guarantee" (BIG). The idea is that the government provides a fixed cash transfer to every adult, whether poor or not. This has been called many things including a "poll transfer," "guaranteed income," "citizenship income," and an "unmodified social dividend." We heard already about an early advocate of something like this policy, namely Paine (1797), although the idea had long been in tension with ideas about the intrinsic merit of work (such as Petty's 1662, recommendation to employ the idle poor, even if their output had no value). The BIG idea gained momentum in the 1990s.[101]

The BIG idea has spanned both rich and poor countries, and the political spectrum from Left to Right. While the advocates have primarily been found in rich countries, variations have been found in developing countries.[102] The arguments made in support have taken a number of forms. BIG has variously been seen as a "right of citizenship," or a foundation for economic freedom—to relax the material constraint on peoples' choices in life—to assure that "the life options of (society's) members need no longer be constrained by the obligation to earn a living."[103] The Belgian philosopher Philippe Van Parijs (1992, 1995) argues for "basic income capitalism"—combining the power of private ownership of the means of production and free markets to expand output, with a substantial basic income for all.

Others have pointed instead to the fact that a BIG can be an administratively easy way of assuring that poverty is eliminated, and inequality attenuated, and with modest distortionary effect on the economy as a whole. There are no substitution effects of the transfers themselves since there is no action that anyone can take to change their transfer receipts. However, there will be income effects on demand for leisure. Opponents of the BIG idea echo the long-standing concerns that the welfare state will undermine work incentives and increase wages at the expense of profits. How much effect a BIG will have on labor supply is unclear, noting also that the transfer may help get around other constraints on work opportunities, such as in self-employment or migration, which are limited by credit constraints. On balance, work may even increase. (An example is discussed in chapter 10.) Supporters also point out that there is no stigma associated with a BIG, given that there is no purposive targeting to poor people. It can also be expected that, provided there is a universal unique identity number for all citizens, a BIG will be less vulnerable to corruption.

---

[100] Following Pradhan and Ravallion (2000). For a critical survey of the various approaches found in this literature, see Ravallion (2014e).

[101] See, e.g., Rhys-Williams (1943), Friedman (1962), Van Parijs (1995), and Raventós (2007).

[102] See, e.g., Bardhan (2011).

[103] Van Parijs (1992, 466).

While the BIG idea has had supporters across the political spectrum, it has not yet been implemented anywhere to my knowledge at national level.[104] Its close cousin the EITC has, however, been implemented in many countries (the United States in 1975; other examples are found in the United Kingdom, Canada, Sweden, and elsewhere). These are typically designed to avoid imposing high marginal tax rates on poor people, so as not to discourage work effort. Chapter 10 returns to these policies.

2.3 Poverty in the Developing World

Development challenges were prominent in the aftermath of World War II, including in the reconstruction of war-damaged Europe. But even bigger challenges were found elsewhere in the form of extreme and deeply rooted poverty. From the outset, the governments of the many newly independent states in the post–World War II period appear to have been genuinely committed to longer term poverty reduction.[105] But there was much debate about how to achieve that.

Planning for Rapid Industrialization

The economies of the newly independent countries were based mainly on agriculture, but that is not what policymakers in those countries saw in the rich world, where the non-farm sector dominated. That is consistent with the pattern we find across countries today, as indicated in figure 2.4.[106] The share of agriculture falls from an average of about 40% for the poorest twenty countries in terms of income per capita to just 1% for the richest twenty. This pattern is a key element of what is often called *structural transformation*.[107]

The pattern in figure 2.4 is readily explicable. Food is a necessity for human life, so it is natural that economic activity starts with agriculture. However, by the same logic, as the economy grows, the share of output accountable to the (primarily rural) agrarian economy tends to fall. This too is to be expected. With overall growth, we will tend to see a falling share of income devoted to food; this is the economy-wide version of Engel's Law (box 1.16). Since aggregate supply will come into balance with demand in a closed economy, we can thus expect agriculture to represent a falling share of output

---

[104] At the time of writing, a referendum is planned in Switzerland in 2016 to vote on whether a basic income scheme should be implemented. There is also a basic-income movement in the United Kingdom; see http://basicincome.org.uk/. Two towns in Manitoba in Canada introduced a basic-income scheme for five years in the 1970s, which one can read about here: http://basicincome.org.uk/interview/2013/08/health-forget-mincome-poverty/.

[105] In the context of India, see Chakravarty's (1987) discussion of economic planning in the 1950s and 1960s. Also see the interesting (and sometimes entertaining) discussion in Bhagwati (1993, ch. 2).

[106] The gross national income figures are lagged by ten years to reduce the possibility of spurious negative correlation due to the fact that GDP is an element of the denominator in constructing the share variable.

[107] With the greater global coverage of national accounts data, structural transformation was much researched in the 1960s, 1970s, and 1980s, but has received less attention since then. See the review of the body of work in Syrquin (1988). Also see the discussion in Lin (2012).

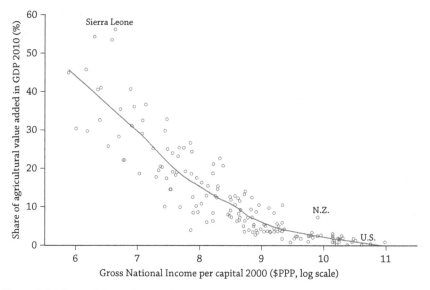

Figure 2.4 Share of Agriculture in GDP across Countries. *Source:* Author's calculations from World Development Indicators (World Bank 2013).

as the economy grows. Nonetheless, there is a variance in the sector composition at given mean income (figure 2.4). For example, New Zealand (as indicated in figure 2.4) has an unusually high share of its income from agriculture, for a country at its average income; much of the country's farm output is exported.

But how were policymakers in the newly independent states to achieve structural transformation? They held out little hope that the private sector could get there on its own. Coordination failures among private agents were seen to be a serious obstacle. An influential paper by Paul Rosenstein-Rodan (1943) pointed to the complementarities between the investments made by different firms in an underdeveloped economy. Given the linkages in economic activity, if all firms invested, then they would all do well, but no individual firm has the incentive to invest when others do not. Thus, development stalls—a form of a poverty trap (box 1.6). There is scope here for beneficial governmental intervention, but this can take many forms. A "government-light" approach supports well-informed negotiation and contract enforcement among the firms that need to coordinate their actions. A "government-heavy" route entails central planning to control, or even take-over, private decision-making. This came to be known as the "big push"—the idea that a large initial investment across multiple sectors would be essential for development.

Policymakers in many of the newly independent states initially opted for the government-heavy approach. There were a number of reasons. Some were encouraged by the apparent economic success of the Soviet Union. The colonial experience had also led many to be suspicious of "free market" arguments. For example, openness to external trade was expected to mainly serve the interests of rich countries. There was an underlying skepticism about how quickly or appropriately economic agents would respond to price signals even in a closed economy. Traditional farmers were thought to be inefficient, with little hope for changing that. There was also pessimism about the scope for rapid labor absorption from the fledgling manufacturing sector, which was often seen to face increasing returns to scale at least initially.[108]

Thus, the early emphasis was on the use of central planning to promote relatively capital-intensive industrialization in a closed economy. But there were dissenters from the outset, and they had some good reasons.

The Planners' Critics

There were concerns about the "government-heavy" approach from the outset. Instead of a big push across all sectors, some observers thought it would be more effective to identify a leading sector in the specific setting, which would stimulate activity elsewhere.[109] Finding the key leading sector posed a further challenge, however. Some observers questioned the priorities chosen by the planners, especially the emphasis given to developing the capital goods sector, as in India's Second Plan (1956–61).[110] They pointed out that capital was scarce in poor countries, but labor was abundant, so surely a market-driven and (in all likelihood) labor-intensive industrialization process made more sense.

It was also argued that the planners gave too little attention to Adam Smith's warning that food supply would constrain urban growth in a closed economy. Some argued that poor people were financing the industrialization push, which typically depended on extracting a surplus from agriculture, which provided most of their incomes. Moreover, the demands of rapid industrialization displaced other policies; for example, rural infrastructure (electrification and roads) took a back seat to the needs of fledgling industries.

A further problem is that poor countries often lacked the administrative capabilities needed to make a success of central planning. In economies with large informal sectors, the early enthusiasm for creating formal regulations and controls to coordinate, or (even more ambitiously) take over, private firms was out of step with the ability for effective implementation and enforcement. Bringing politicians' aspirations in line with administrative capabilities has been a long-standing challenge.

The set of ideas held by many of the post–World War II planners in the newly independent states came to be known as the "structuralist approach," following the Oxford economist Ian Little (1982), who had studied this approach in India. Little's most famous student at Oxford was undoubtedly Manmohan Singh, who went on to be the Finance Minister of India in the early 1990s (and Prime Minister, 2004–14); Singh set about dismantling many of the policies Little had criticized and launched a new growth trajectory for India.

---

[108] See, e.g., Clark ([1940] 1957).

[109] Hirschman (1958) was an early advocate of this approach. Also see the discussion in Ray (1998, ch. 5).

[110] This was directly influenced by a two-sector growth model in Mahalanobis (1953). An important critique of the Second Plan was by Vakil and Brahmanand (1956). For a broader critique of planning see Lal (2000).

The Aid Industry and Development Economics Are Born

Growth economics taught the planners that a high investment rate was crucial to reaching their growth targets.[111] Being a poor country meant that the investments required for those targets could not be financed solely from domestic savings. The global private financial markets of today were not yet available. Foreign aid was seen as the answer.

The post–World War II period saw the emergence of large-scale international development aid programs, initially focusing on rebuilding Europe but turning global soon after. In 1944, the UN Monetary and Financial Conference at Bretton Woods, New Hampshire, led to the creation of the International Bank for Reconstruction and Development (the World Bank) and the International Monetary Fund (IMF). Numerous bilateral aid programs also emerged. (Chapter 9 discusses development aid in greater depth).

The new aid industry needed knowledge, and the emergence of development economics in the 1950s was the main response. An influential paper by Arthur Lewis (1954) articulated a model of economic development with firmly classical roots. The stylized economy had a dualistic structure, with a fledgling "modern," primarily urban, sector and a poorer traditional, primarily rural, sector with a large amount of surplus labor for much of the year. Development proceeded by the modern sector reinvesting its profits and so expanding to absorb labor from the traditional sector. Chapter 8 returns to this influential model and its implications for poverty and inequality.[112]

By the 1970s, development economics had become firmly established as a field.[113] It was becoming more widely presumed that the developing world's poor were no less economically rational than others, and so the economics that had largely emerged in Europe and North America (built on the assumption of individual rationality) could be adapted to the realities of the developing world. By this view, people are essentially the same; it is the resources and institutions that differ. Schultz (1964, 649) argued that farmers in developing countries are efficient, but poor:[114] "poor people

---

[111] Section 8.1 reviews the growth theories in greater depth.

[112] Subsequent contributions in the 1960s and 1970s to the understanding of economic growth in dual economies included Jorgenson (1961), Ranis and Fei (1961), Fei and Ranis (1964), Harris and Todaro (1970), and Fields (1975). Ranis (2004) reviews the influence of the Lewis model and the related debates, such as about the opportunity cost of rural labor absorbed into the modern sector. The Lewis model and its successors are studied further in chapter 8.

[113] For example, the *Journal of Development Economics* was launched in 1974. The first volume included an authoritative 40 page review of the literature on distribution and development (Cline, 1975).

[114] Schultz's views were a marked departure from thinking at the time, and there was much debate in the following years; for an overview, see Abler and Sukhatme (2006). Some recent thinking emphasizes the possibility of feedback effects from poverty to the decision-making process; see, e.g., Duflo (2006). Using field experiments, modern behavioral economics suggests at most a small "development gap" in the extent of economic rationality (Cappelen et al. 2014), although sample selection processes (such as relying on university students as the subjects of the experiments) cast doubt on the broader validity of these findings.

are no less concerned about improving their lot and that of their children than those of us who have incomparably greater advantages. Nor are they any less competent in obtaining the maximum benefit from their limited resources." This view did not rule out abundant inefficiency in underdeveloped economies. But they were institutionalized inefficiencies, not the failings of poor people to optimize given those institutions.

Bringing Inequality in from the Cold

Given that the first thing most economists learnt about a "developing country" was its low GDP per capita, it is possibly not surprising that the new subject of development economics focused so much on how to assure rising GDP per capita. To provide analytic back-up to thinking about policy, the 1950s saw renewed interest in the economics of growth, with important theoretical advances (including the Solow-Swan model discussed further in chapter 8). However, concerns about income inequality were initially downplayed as second-order matters to economic growth in the fifteen years or so after World War II. And any concerns about non-income dimensions of welfare were subsumed within a set of things that economic growth would take care of in due course.

The existence of a great deal of extreme poverty and high inequality within developing countries started to attract substantial mainstream scholarly attention from the time of the Second Poverty Enlightenment. Some early assessments were still not encouraging on the scope for either rapid or equitable growth in the developing world.[115] Industrialization and urbanization eventually came to be widely seen as at best a mixed blessing for the developing world's poor.[116] Many people went even further in concluding that GDP growth would do little to help poor people—ignoring the fact that the type of growth promoted by the early development policies did little to support agriculture, where the poor were concentrated, and nor did they support labor-intensive non-farm development.

The Western public's attention to rising numbers of poor in the "Third World" also surged during the Second Poverty Enlightenment, as did foreign aid (a topic of chapter 9). Among economists, Dudley Seers (1969) was an influential early advocate of greater focus on distribution, and poverty in particular. In his foreword to an overview by the World Bank of twenty-five years of development, the Bank's first Chief Economist, Hollis Chenery (1977, p. v), explained the change of view as follows:

> The difficulty of attempting social change and growth simultaneously in the conditions of the 1950s . . . led to an emphasis on increased GNP as a measure of success in development. This . . . has now been replaced by a more complex

---

[115] For example, Ahluwalia et al. (1979, 299) argued that "not only have the poorest countries grown relatively slowly, but growth processes are such that within most developing countries, the incomes of the poor increase much less than the average."

[116] An influential example was Markandaya's (1955) best-selling social novel, *Nectar in a Sieve*, which represented non-farm economic growth—when a factory is built near the village of the novel's central characters, a poor rural family—as being far more a source of threats to livelihoods than a route out of poverty.

statement of social objectives, which recognizes that economic growth is
a necessary but not sufficient condition for social progress and that more
direct attention should be given to the welfare of the poorest groups.

While low GDP per capita was the first piece of quantitative data available to the
new development economists, what they saw on the ground in developing countries
was abject poverty. The emphasis on economic growth could be justified if it was
sure to reduce that poverty. But this was not assured. There was much debate as to
whether economic growth would reliably reduce poverty.[117] In due course, a consensus emerged that "growth is necessary but not sufficient for poverty reduction" (as in
the above quote from Chenery). Indeed, this became something of a mantra in mainstream development circles from the 1990s (including the World Bank). Strictly, it was
never correct. Since income and wealth can always be redistributed (even in poor countries, where inequality is often high), economic growth is logically neither necessary
nor sufficient for poverty reduction. What was really meant is that growth creates a
potential for poverty reduction provided it comes with the conditions (including policies) needed to assure that poor men and women can participate in, and contribute to,
that growth. We return to these issues at length in Part Three.

From the 1980s, many economists were active in giving greater emphasis to the
challenges of global poverty reduction, with emphasis on poor countries, where those
challenges were obvious and severe by any absolute standard. The World Bank's
(1990a) World Development Report (WDR), entitled *Poverty*, was influential in development policy circles, and soon after a "world free of poverty" became the Bank's
overarching goal (in no small measure as a response to that report and the subsequent efforts by Bank staff to operationalize its messages). A large body of empirical
research on poverty followed in the 1990s, helped by a number of texts that provided
useful expositions for practitioners of relevant theory and methods.[118]

The period saw a broadening of the range of policies under consideration, especially
in the developing world. Indeed, by the 1990s, it seems that nothing in the policy arena
was off-limits in discussing impacts on poverty. This brought a new danger too, since
without a clear assignment of policy instruments to goals, there was a risk of policy
paralysis; if every policy must do well in attaining every goal, then all policies may be
deemed to fail, yet if each one does well against just one or a few goals, and does little
damage elsewhere in the list of goals, then the whole package may perform very well.
Thankfully, economic analysis, and a measure of good sense, could often be trusted to
guide effective policy action, recognizing the trade-offs.

By the late twentieth century, there had been a complete reversal in policy thinking
about poverty, from the view two hundred years earlier. Instead of seeing poverty as
necessary for development, eliminating poverty came to be seen as the main goal of
development.

---

[117] Compare, e.g., Adelman and Morris (1973) with Ahluwalia (1976); the former argued that
growth would initially be poverty (as well as inequality) increasing in poor countries while the latter
agreed that growth would tend to increase inequality but not so much that poverty incidence would
not fall with growth.

[118] Examples include Ravallion (1994b), Sadoulet and de Janvry (1995), Deaton (1997), and Grosh
and Glewwe (2000).

Rebalancing Development Thinking

Underlying the evolution in development thinking summarized above, one can identify four efforts to rebalance growth-centric development thinking. These efforts all emerged in the 1970s and 1980s, with lasting impact today.

The first was the new emphasis given to *agriculture and rural development*. Many observers argued that public support for agriculture was wasteful given how poor farmers were, stemming from their low farm yields. However, others came to argue that low farm productivity was caused by market and other institutional failures— lack of knowledge, lack of access to credit and insurance, and possibly land-market failures too. Credit and risk market failures became an active research agenda in development economics.[119] The implication was that policies that addressed those failures or compensate for them could have large benefits. And those benefits favored poor people, given that the vast majority of the world's poor lived in rural areas. Chronic poverty and low productivity came to be seen as jointly determined by the constraints facing poor people.

From a more economy-wide perspective, a number of development economists also stressed the importance of agricultural productivity growth to the success of industrialization in largely closed and capital-constrained economies. Industrialization required a larger and well-fed industrial workforce, drawn out of farming.[120] So farm productivity simply had to rise if we were to see a pro-poor process of industrial development.

A speech in Nairobi in 1973 by then President of the World Bank, Robert McNamara, signaled the rebalancing in mainstream with regard to agriculture and rural development. A volume by economist Michael Lipton (1977) was influential in pointing to the significant urban biases in thinking at the time. Both efficiency and equity arguments were made for greater emphasis on smallholder development and redistributive land reforms, based on the empirical observation that agricultural productivity (output per acre) tended to be higher on smaller farms.[121] Research in this period also exposed the extent to which poor farmers were exploited by government policies, such as through the monopsony power of marketing boards in Africa.[122] The 1970s and 1980s saw many contributions by economists, including on smallholder decision-making, tenure systems, technology diffusion, and agricultural pricing and trade.[123]

A second rebalancing also started in the early 1970s, with greater attention in development thinking on the *"informal sector"*—a concept that came to play a central

---

[119] A good overview of the literature up to the early 1990s can be found in Besley (1995b).

[120] Note that Lewis (1954) had recognized the importance of agricultural growth, although his basic theoretical model did not. An important theoretical paper by Ranis and Fei (1961) had stressed the need for agricultural growth in an extended version of the Lewis model. However, broader awareness of the importance of this point did not appear to emerge for another ten years.

[121] This was demonstrated by Berry and Cline (1979) and largely reaffirmed in careful surveys of the evidence by Binswanger et al., (1995) and Lipton (2009).

[122] The volume by Bates (1981) was influential.

[123] The volume edited by Reynolds (1975) included a number of contributions.

role in the operations of the International Labour Organization.[124] Definitions varied, but informality most often meant that individual agents are largely beyond the reach of government for the purposes of taxation or regulation.[125] Policy discussions have often exhibited urban-bias in thinking about the informal sector. Logically, the sector was that part of the economy outside the formal modern sector. Given the obvious sectoral interlinkages, the only defensible definition of the sector was essentially equivalent to Lewis's (1954) "traditional sector": the large numbers of people in both urban informal activities *and* traditional agriculture who would rather have a modern-sector job but cannot find one. There are too few such jobs available for them at the current stage of economic development. High rates of urban unemployment were symptomatic. Indeed, by an economic model that came to be prominent— that of Harris and Todaro (1970)—high rates of urban unemployment can arise in equilibrium, given the rigidities in the formal labor market (which we return to in chapter 8).

A continuing challenge for policy is what to do about the informal sector. Here views differed radically. Some policymakers focused on the need to expand the formal sector, others focused on the labor-market rigidities, while others focused on the needs of those in the informal sector, and so were drawn to policies such as providing credit to informal enterprises or enhancing farm productivity. The policy debate was further clouded by the realization that many of those in the informal sector were there by preference.

The third rebalancing concerned gender. Women had occasionally been referred to explicitly in the major texts of development economics. For example, Lewis acknowledged women explicitly as a part of the labor surplus that was to be absorbed by the growing capitalist sector, arguing that "one of the surest ways of increasing the national income is therefore to create new sources of employment for women outside the home" (Lewis 1954, 404). Over time, development economics became somewhat more conscious of gender issues. However, the deeper change in thinking was that gender equity came to be seen by economists as more than just something relevant to GDP growth. The gender dimensions of poverty were becoming more prominent in development policy debates from the 1970s. The first of the UN's series of World Conferences on Women was held in Mexico City in 1975. The fourth of these conferences, in Beijing in 1995, is widely considered to have been a turning point, notably through its *Platform for Action*, which was adopted unanimously by 189 countries.[126] Gender equity became prominent in mainstream writings on development economics, such as World Bank (2001b), and it was the topic (rather belatedly) of the 2010 WDR (World Bank 2011), which pointed to the successes in reducing some key gender inequalities, including basic schooling.

[124] The term "informal sector" was introduced in 1972, in a report in the ILO's first mission to Africa (ILO 1972). See Bangasser (2000) on the history.

[125] Implicit taxation of the agricultural sector as a whole is still possible through government actions that change the terms of trade facing farmers, such as the prices they receive for their marketed outputs.

[126] See http://www.unwomen.org/en/how-we-work/intergovernmental-support/world-conferences-on-women#sthash.V2avhhFt.dpuf.

Here too there were debates. For example, the debates on abortion in the United States spilled over into developing countries through the Mexico City Policy (also known as the "global gag rule") introduced in the United States in 1984 under the Republican administration of President Reagan, but rescinded by subsequent Democratic Presidents Clinton and Obama. Under this policy, the US Agency for International Development (USAID) is barred from funding NGOs in developing countries that use any of their resources (whether from USAID or not) from providing family planning advice or information regarding abortion.

Today, gender equity is in the mainstream of development-policy thinking, with broad acceptance of the (instrumental and intrinsic) value of equal opportunities for schooling and independent economic opportunities.

The fourth rebalancing came in the 1980s and 1990s with a new emphasis given to *human development*. Of course, it can hardly be maintained that the prior idea of development was in any sense "inhuman."[127] It was not disputed that human development indicators (generally focusing on attainments in basic health and education) tend to be higher in countries with higher GDP per capita. It was also agreed that there was an economic return to schooling, as emphasized by the recognition of the economic role of "human capital." Schooling for children from poor families was no longer seen as a waste of public resources, but rather as an essential precondition for growth. Mainstream development economists had come to see human development as crucial for progress against poverty (as well as GDP per capita). An early example was the World Bank's (1980) WDR entitled *Poverty and Human Development*. The emphasis most East Asian countries have long given to broadly shared investments in human development also came to be recognized by the late 1980s as a crucial element to their success, even though the role played by some other elements of the East Asian policy package remained contentious.[128]

The rebalancing was not just in the recognition of the instrumental value of human development to GDP but concerned its intrinsic value, combined with a recognition that policies to promote human development made for better societies at given GDP per capita. Some countries did much better in various indicators of human development than suggested by their GDP. In the most researched example, Sri Lanka's long-standing emphasis on basic health and education services had brought a large dividend in longevity and other human development indicators relative to countries at a similar level of average income.[129] Building on this theme, the series of *Human Development Reports* by the *United Nations Development Programme* started in 1990 and have consistently argued for public action to promote basic health, education, and social protection in developing countries, rather than focusing solely on growth in GDP.

Initially this fourth rebalancing was framed (mainly by economists) in terms of "basic needs."[130] The idea here was that a list of basic needs could be identified (e.g., schooling, healthcare, safe water) and these should be set as development priorities.

---

[127] As Rist (1997) and others noted.

[128] For further discussion, see World Bank (1993), Fishlow and Gwin (1994), and Rodrik (1994).

[129] See Sen (1981b).

[130] Notably in Streeten et al. (1981).

This approach was much debated. One concern is that it lacked a clear identification of the ends which these needs were intended to serve. Sen's (1980, 1985a) concept of "capabilities" was soon seen to better define the ends for the new human development school (box 2.1).[131] This was presented by its advocates as a philosophically superior formulation to "basic needs," which were represented as more operational and pragmatic than conceptual.[132]

There were concerns about the appearance of paternalism in having external agents (in donor countries or international agencies) identifying poor peoples' "basic needs," rather than letting poor people do that for themselves.[133] This concern carries weight, not least in developing countries. Sen's capabilities approach, or something like it, was again seen as preferable. Defenders of the basic needs approach could always draw on some form of limited consultation with poor men and women in identifying basic needs. ("Participatory Poverty Assessments" emerged, in part to fill this role.) Nor could one always sustain the view that poor men and women know best what is in their interests. The risk of being paternalistic needs to be balanced against the risk of "free-choice-fetishism."[134]

A less paternalistic—and to most eyes, more agreeable—approach was to focus instead on assuring the freedom of each person to define and satisfy their own basic needs, as they see fit. Since economic freedom is clearly a crucial precondition (though rarely sufficient) for such self-fulfillment, this approach is quite consistent with a focus on reducing income poverty. A poverty line can be derived as the cost of a bundle of basic needs (as discussed further in chapter 4). However, one is deemed to be poor if one cannot afford that bundle, rather than if one fails to attain one or more of its elements. The role of the bundle of basic needs is then to help anchor the poverty line.

Debates on the Poverty Focus

Not all economists were comfortable with these new ways of thinking about the goals of development. Most Western-trained economists came from the welfarist tradition, with its origins in utilitarianism. They were often comfortable in assuming that preferences were pretty much common to all people and could be presented by a continuous and smooth function of one's consumptions, which depended on income and prices via markets. Economists were less comfortable with, or at least less familiar with, the rights-based school of moral philosophy that also emerged in the late eighteenth century (section 1.3), but had been largely eclipsed by utilitarianism and (later) Paretian welfare economics (box 1.20).

One concern was with violations of the Pareto principle. If one interprets that principle as saying that social welfare must always increase if *anyone* experiences a welfare gain, then a poverty measure cannot qualify as a (negative) social welfare function.

[131] For further discussion of these issues from various philosophical perspectives, see Sen (1985a), Wiggins (1987, essay 1), Alkire (2002), and Reader (2006).

[132] This critique may well have been exaggerated; philosophers such as Wiggins (1987) and Reader (2006) have illuminated the deep philosophical roots of the basic needs idea.

[133] See, e.g., Alkire (2002).

[134] Reader (2006, 344).

In practice, a standard poverty measure is likely to be incomplete even if poverty reduction is the sole objective—one will need other information such as on command over non-market goods and intra-household welfare (as discussed further in Part Two).

However, we can still sensibly demand that any poverty measure should at least satisfy a weaker version of the Pareto principle, namely that social welfare cannot fall if anyone experiences a welfare gain and must rise if any poor person gains. This principle carries weight for measuring poverty, as we will see in Part Two.

Another thing that economists trained in the welfarist tradition were uncomfortable with was the degree of arbitrariness found in specifying "basic needs" or "poverty lines" in practice. For example, Nicholas Stern (1989, 645) asked in his survey of development economics: "What needs are basic and more worryingly what levels are held to be essential minima?" That may be a hard question, but (of course) that does not mean we must avoid it. There will clearly be some judgment to make in setting a poverty line, although the need for judgment is hardly unique to discussions about poverty and human development.

The analytic preference among most economists for continuous and smooth functions did not fit easily with the idea of a "poverty line" (although there is clearly greater acceptance today than in, say, the 1980s). Nor were discontinuities in utility at certain levels of consumption especially evident empirically, although that is hardly a damaging observation once the deep problems of identifying utility from demand behavior are properly acknowledged. (Chapter 3 returns to the problems of identifying individual welfare from observable behavior in markets.)

However, if one accepts that poverty exists, then there must be at least one poverty line. The philosopher Soran Reader (2006) drew the analogue with night and day; nobody would deny that they exist, but saying at what precise time one turns into the other is a judgment call. It does not get us far for the fans of continuity to protest that "midnight is really just a dark sort of day."[135]

Along with smooth welfare functions typically comes an assumption of unbounded substitutability; some gain in command over one valued thing can always be found that would justify the loss of something else of value. This is often applied by economists to social choices, in keeping with the utilitarian tradition. But (as has long been recognized) this can leave many troubling implications. Do we accept a constraint on liberal freedoms because it will help promote economic growth? Do we accept that any gain to the richest person can justify a loss to the poorest? Do we accept that "Bites of chocolate, if sufficiently numerous, can morally have more weight than a single premature death"?[136] Any economic advice that ignores the distinct possibility that most people will answer "no" to these questions risks falling on deaf ears.

We do not need to abandon the favored assumption of a continuous utility function to advance targets for society. Indeed, such targets have long played a role in focusing attention and motivating action in all areas of policy. Saying that the poverty line is (say) $2 a day per person in China does not beg for a demonstration that there is some jump in individual welfare on attaining $2. Rather it asserts a social value of public effort to assure that people in China should reach at least $2 a day. Like all moral

---

[135] Paraphrasing a point made by Reader (2006, 349).

[136] Arneson (2005, 25).

judgments it is contestable. And to mobilize public action it is important that there is sufficient agreement about the poverty line in the country concerned.[137] The ownership of a national poverty line in the country concerned is of first-order importance to developing a consensus on efforts to eliminate poverty.

When such a poverty target is reached we may or may not stop work; in the context of a growing developing country it is more likely that a new target will be set for the future. (The Government of China has recently doubled its official poverty line, from about $0.80 to $1.90 a day, to better reflect rising living standards.) When there is nobody left in the world living below (say) $1.25 a day, one can expect that calls for lifting the living standards of the poorest will still be heard, even though they then live above $1.25 a day. The idea of a "poverty line" or a "basic income" can be interpreted as a target that is deemed to be relevant to a specific context.

How much these (sometimes esoteric) debates about the philosophical foundations mattered to development policy came to be seen as a moot point by some observers, keen to focus instead on action. It can be readily agreed that health and education matter to peoples' welfare at given current consumptions of commodities (if only because they matter to future consumption). Economic growth may not have been necessary for human development, but it certainly made it more feasible, if only by generating a larger tax base. Nor could it be credibly argued that income poverty was unimportant to human development. The importance to human development of combining income-poverty reduction with better access to basic services came to be widely appreciated.

Better Data

We have seen huge advances in our knowledge about poverty in the world, anchored firmly to observations and data. For most of the developing world, poverty was "majority poverty"—in marked contrast to Galbraith's characterization of "minority poverty." Travel and visual media made it visible to those in the West, though, of course, it was already very visible to almost everyone in the developing world. And poverty data were playing an important role in the post-Independence policy debates in some poor countries, including India, notably through its National Sample Surveys. As was the case with the poverty research by Booth and Rowntree in late nineteenth-century England, around 1990 many people were shocked to learn that there were about one billion people in the world living on less than $1 per day, at purchasing power parity.[138]

Since 1990 there has been a massive expansion in survey data collection and availability, and refinements to the methodology.[139] The efforts of country statistics offices—often with support from international agencies such as the UNDP, the

[137] One way of setting a poverty line forces this point, by asking at what income level people in the country concerned tend to say they are not poor; these are the "subjective poverty lines" discussed further in chapter 4.

[138] See World Bank (1990a) and Ravallion et al. (1991).

[139] For example, the original estimates of global absolute poverty measures by Ravallion et al. (1991) used data for twenty-two countries, with one survey per country, while the latest estimates

World Bank, and the International Comparison Program—to collect household survey data and price data have provided the empirical foundation for domestic and international efforts to fight poverty since the 1980s. From the mid-1980s, the *Demographic and Health Surveys* (DHS) supported by USAID (and other donors) started to provide high-quality nationally representative survey data on the non-income dimensions of welfare, as relevant to assessing attainments of certain basic needs.

Public access to socioeconomic data is crucial. Such access was rare prior to the 1990s.[140] But this has gradually improved, with help from efforts such as the World Bank's Living Standards Measurement Study (LSMS), which facilitates the collection of household-level survey data in developing countries, the Luxembourg Income Study (LIS), which facilitated access to harmonized micro data, though mostly for rich countries, and the DHS.

Globalization and Poverty

The word "globalization" is used in many ways but it typically refers to the movement of factors of production, commodities, and ideas across national borders. Over the last two hundred years there have been two main periods of expanding global trade, namely from the mid-nineteenth century to World War I and after World War II, but with unevenness over time and across countries within both periods. And in both periods, globalization was much debated.

There is broad agreement today that liberalizing restrictions on international migration is good for both global equity and efficiency. Migration tends to go from places where labor is abundant to those where it is scarce. From a global perspective the loss of output in the former (sending) country is likely to be less than the gain in the receiving country. The studies to date suggest large global efficiency gains from relaxing restrictions on migration.[141] And the gains can be expected to attenuate wage disparities, and so help put a break on global inequality. Global poverty could fall substantially. The opponents to freer migration tend (naturally) to come from those who benefit from restrictions on migration, mainly in the rich world. There are still substantial unexploited opportunities for more equitable global expansion through international labor market integration.

However, this is not where the bulk of the globalization debate is centered. That has concerned whether other (non-labor) dimensions of globalization have helped or hurt progress against poverty. Distributional concerns have long been prominent in the many debates about the merits of greater openness to external trade and ideas.

---

in Chen and Ravallion (2010a) are based on survey data for 125 countries with more than six surveys per country.

[140] Indonesia's Central Bureau of Statistics was ahead of the curve here, with outside researchers being able to obtain the micro data for its SUSENAS from the early 1980s. India's National Sample Survey became public access in the mid-1990s. I would guess that about half the surveys for developing countries are now public access (subject to application processes), and the proportion is increasing.

[141] See Hamilton and Whalley (1984); an update by Moses and Letnes (2004) suggests that the potential global efficiency gains have risen over time since the Hamilton and Whalley study. Also see in Rosenzweig's (2010) estimates of inter-country wage disparities adjusted for schooling differences.

This was apparent in the globalization debates of the late twentieth century, continuing today. As Sen (2001) argued, the real concern of the so-called "anti-globalization" protestors is surely not globalization per se, for these protests are among the most globalized events in the modern world; rather, their concerns seem to stem in large part from the continuing deprivations and rising disparities in levels of living that they see in the current period of globalization.

Critics of globalization have been genuinely concerned about the seemingly entrenched poverty that they see in the world today. There exist widespread perceptions that poverty and inequality are high and rising. For example, the web site of the International Forum on Globalization confidently claims that "globalization policies have contributed to increased poverty, increased inequality between and within nations."[142] Others have argued the opposite. At around the same time an article in the *Economist* magazine wrote that "growth really does help the poor: in fact it raises their incomes by about as much as it raises the incomes of everybody else ... globalization raises incomes, and the poor participate fully."[143] Another commentator wrote (with remarkable confidence) that "evidence suggests that no one has lost out to globalization in an absolute sense. . . . Growth is sufficient. Period."[144]

How can we understand such conflicting views? It can be granted that, despite the progress made, the available data on poverty and inequality are still far from ideal, though neither side of this debate has paid much attention to the data problems. There are also potentially important differences in the types of data used. The "pro-globalization" side has tended to prefer "hard" quantitative data while the other side has drawn more eclectically on various types of evidence, both systematic and anecdotal or subjective. Differences in the data used no doubt account in part for the differing positions taken. However, since both sides have had access to essentially the same data, it does not seem plausible that such large and persistent differences in the claims made about what is happening to inequality in the world stem entirely from one side's ignorance of the facts.

One reason why such different views persist is that it is difficult to separate out the effects of globalization from the many other factors impinging on how the distribution of income is evolving in the world. The processes of global economic integration are so pervasive that it is hard to say what the world would be like without them. These difficulties of attribution provide ample fuel for debate, though they also leave one suspicious of the confident claims made by both sides. However, the policy issues are not typically about whether there should be globalization but what else is needed to make it work for the common good, including poverty reduction.[145]

Conflicting assessments can also stem from hidden contextual factors. Diverse impacts of the same growth-promoting policies on inequality can be expected given the differences between countries in initial conditions. Similarly, policy reforms can

---

[142] See http://www.ifg.org/store.htm.

[143] *The Economist*, May 27, 2000, 94.

[144] Bhalla (2002, 206).

[145] Basu (2003, 898) puts it this way: "In reality, globalization is a bit like gravity. We may discuss endlessly whether it is good or bad but the question of not having it does not seriously arise."

shift the distribution of income in different directions in different countries.[146] Yet both sides make generalizations about distributional impacts without specifying the context. In a given country setting, there may well be much less to disagree about.

There is another reason for the continuing debate about the facts: the two sides in this debate do not share the same *values* about what constitutes a just distribution of the gains from globalization. The empirical facts in contention do not stem solely from objective data on incomes, prices, and so on, but also depend on value judgments made in measurement—judgments that one may or may not accept. It can hardly be surprising that different people hold different normative views about inequality. And it is well understood in economics that those views carry weight for how one defines and measures inequality, though recognizing that it is ethics not economics that determines what trade-offs one accepts between the welfare levels of different people. What is more notable in the present context is that important differences in values have become embedded in the methodological details underlying statements about what is happening to inequality in the world. The differences are rarely brought to the surface and argued out properly in this debate.

It appears now that, by and large, the reasons for conflicting views are not to be found in the data used but rather in the concepts and measures used for interpreting those data.[147] Part Two looks more closely at the measurement issues. Part Three returns to the policy issues.

New Millennium, New Hope, New Challenges

By the turn of the twenty-first century, a new optimism on the scope for global poverty reduction had emerged, grounded in the better data and analytic tools available. National poverty elimination targets and strategies for reaching those targets were developed in many countries, both rich and poor. In 2010 the European Union adopted its Europe 2020 poverty reduction target to reduce by 25% the numbers of Europeans living below national poverty lines. Globally, the Millennium Development Goals (MDGs) were developed in the 1990s and ratified in 2000 at the UN's Millennium Assembly, which was the largest meeting of world leaders up to that date. The first MDG included halving the developing world's 1990 "$1 a day" poverty rate by 2015. Other goals related to reducing hunger, universal primary education, gender equity, reducing child mortality, improving maternal health, combatting diseases, assuring environmental sustainability, and global partnerships.

The MDGs were an important part of an effort to mobilize action against poverty by all parties involved. By setting agreed goals it was hoped that rich countries would be more generous in their aid budgets and would focus their aid more on poverty. Goals that aim to mobilize action cannot be either too ambitious or too easy. There is a judgment call here, and the choices made would inevitably be questioned by some observers.[148] However, a substantial increase in aid flows did come in the wake of

---

[146] For further discussion, see Ravallion (2001b).

[147] See Ravallion (2004).

[148] For example, Pritchett and Kenny (2013) dubbed them "low-bar targets" and favor more ambitious targets.

the MDGs, and the new programs gave greater emphasis to the social sectors (health, education, and social protection) and to sub-Saharan Africa.[149] Causality is hard to establish with confidence, but it appears likely that the MDGs helped in their purpose of encouraging rich countries to be more generous and to focus on poverty. As expected, changing the institutions and policies of some aid recipients would be a bigger challenge. Chapter 9 returns to this topic.

While many factors were involved besides the MDGs and their impact on aid, there has been considerable progress against extreme absolute poverty since the turn of the new millennium. Using the $1.25-a-day poverty line in 2005 prices, the first MDG was attained in 2010, a full five years ahead of the date set for reaching the goal.[150] And, for the first time, the progress we are seeing against absolute poverty has spanned all regions of the developing world since the new millennium began. As Steven Radelet (2015) puts it, we seem to have experienced a "breakthrough from the bottom." Continuing that success against extreme poverty could lift one billion people out of extreme poverty by 2030.[151]

However, some other measures suggest a less positive picture.[152] Progress has been uneven across countries, though that can hardly be a surprise. In the aggregate, there has been slower progress against absolute poverty using higher poverty lines, such as $2 a day, reflecting a marked "bunching up" just above the $1.25 a day line. There has also been less progress against poverty when judged by relative lines that are typical of the country concerned (rather than using a common line across countries). Chapter 7 will look more closely at the evidence on these points.

There are also concerns that the world's poorest are being left behind. For example, at the launch of the 2011 *Millennium Goals Report* (UN 2011), the UN Secretary-General Ban Ki-moon said that "the poorest of the world are being left behind. We need to reach out and lift them into our lifeboat."

Similarly, a press release by the International Food Policy Research Institute (IFPRI) carried the headline: "The world's poorest people not being reached."[153] Standard poverty measures may not be picking up well what is happening for the poorest; chapter 5 will return to this point.

There are also differences in the views taken on what has been happening to "inequality," with some people saying it is rising while others say it is falling. By probing further into how inequality is conceptualized and measured, Part Two of this book will offer some clues as to why people might hold different views even with the same primary data.

It is becoming widely agreed that the specter of rising inequality in many countries assuages the hope for continuing progress against poverty. High inequality has come to be seen as a threat to both sustained growth and poverty reduction. Old excuses for inequality—that it is simply the price to be paid for overall progress—have come to be seen as questionable or just plain wrong. This was old news to some, but from the turn

[149] See Kenny and Sumner (2011).
[150] See Chen and Ravallion (2013).
[151] As argued by Ravallion (2013).
[152] See Ravallion and Chen (2013b) on the following points.
[153] The press release was for an IFPRI report Ahmed et al. (2007).

of the century a new mainstream view was emerging that saw unequal opportunities in life as a key constraint on development, as exemplified by the World Bank's (2006) report *Equity and Development*.[154]

This was an important change in thinking, which now poses a huge challenge for policymaking. The traditional separation created between "policies for growth" and "policies for equity" has come to be seriously questioned since the 1990s. Citizens and policymakers are asking about the distributional impacts of the policy reforms that have promised higher economic growth. The new millennium has also seen a significant change in the set of development policies, which have now come to embrace a range of direct interventions, variously called "antipoverty programs," "social safety nets," and "social assistance." Part Three will look more closely at both the various debates about policy as they relate to poverty and inequality.

Some of the debates of two hundred years ago live on today. For example, at the time of writing the US Congress had just implemented substantial cuts to the Supplementary Nutrition Assistance Program ("Food Stamps"). During the relevant House of Representatives Committee Meeting, a congressman was quoted as saying that "while it was a Christian duty to care for the poor and hungry, it was not the government's duty."[155] One often heard such claims two hundred years ago. The difference today is that the vast majority of people in the world clearly do not agree.

The desire to end poverty is stronger than ever today. In 2013 the World Bank's (then new) President Jim Yong Kim announced a goal for bringing the "$1.25 a day" poverty rate down to 3% by 2030.[156] In September 2015, a UN Summit—a high-level plenary meeting of the General Assembly—agreed on a set of Sustainable Development Goals (SDGs) for the period after 2015. This comprises 169 desired goals, with eradicating extreme poverty (judged by $1.25 a day) by 2030 as the first.[157] Nobody today can seriously doubt that progress against poverty over the coming decades will be seen as a crucial yardstick for assessing both national and global progress.

This completes the review of the history of thought on poverty. While there is continuing debate on the causes of poverty and on policy prescriptions, modern writings are invariably premised on a belief that poverty is something that can be greatly reduced with the right economic and social policies and, indeed, eliminated. By this view, poverty is in no small measure a global public responsibility, and governments and the economy are to be judged (in part at least) by the progress that is made against poverty. Part Three is devoted to the broad set of policies relevant to progress against poverty and inequality. But first we need to learn more about how these concepts are defined and measured.

---

[154] See Bourguignon (2014) for an interesting retrospective view on this report.

[155] See Fifield (2013).

[156] This was based on the arguments made in Ravallion (2013).

[157] The process of setting goals by high-level committees representing many national and sectoral interests makes a long list very likely. The full list can be found here: https://sustainabledevelopment.un.org/focussdgs.html

PART TWO

MEASURES AND METHODS

One of the themes of Part One was the role that knowledge has played in policy debates and in mobilizing public action against poverty across the globe. Statistics on poverty and inequality have long been newsworthy and policy relevant. However, relatively few people understand how those statistics are arrived at. This part of the book is devoted to the measures and methods used in the analysis of poverty and inequality. Some of the issues have been touched on in Part One, but here the discussion will go more deeply into the "why" and "how" of measurement. We are typically interested in measuring poverty for one or both of the following reasons:

- *Monitoring progress and setting goals:* Poverty and inequality measures are often used in broad descriptions of how a country is doing. They are important elements of a "dashboard" of social indicators for monitoring.
- *Targeting and evaluating policies:* Policymakers often assign benefits based on differences in poverty measures between groups or differences in readily observed proxies for poverty. (That does not require that the observed proxies are the *causes* of the underlying welfare differences, although causal inferences often come into play when we try to *evaluate* policies).

Chapter 3 looks more closely at how "welfare" is measured. Here the key concepts are explained, including the various (ongoing) debates. Chapters 4 and 5 turn to the problem of how to aggregate the survey-based information one obtains on a chosen indicator of economic welfare into a summary statistic on poverty and/or inequality. Again, key concepts are explained, as are the debates. The task of constructing a poverty measure can be thought of as two steps: how to set a poverty line (chapter 4) and how to form an aggregate measure and study its properties (chapter 5). Chapter 6 reviews the issues that arise in assessing the poverty impacts of policies, and the main methods found in practice.

3

Measuring Welfare

While money can't buy happiness, it certainly lets you choose your
own form of misery.

—Groucho Marx

At the foundation of most measures of poverty and inequality is a concept of individual welfare. In economics, "welfare" (or "well-being," which is used interchangeably here) is generally equated with "utility"—a subjective assessment of all the things a person cares about. Economists have often tried to infer what those things are from behavior, and one aspect of behavior in particular: what people choose to buy and sell in markets. However, it is now recognized that this provides rather limited data for that task. Other information has been sought such as self-perceptions of welfare and observable attainments, such as being well-nourished. A broader concept of welfare has also been sought, allowing for external evaluations of a person's welfare that may or may not accord with their utility, defined as whatever people maximize.

Differences over how one thinks about welfare can matter greatly to the descriptive and normative claims made about poverty. The chapter begins with a review of the main conceptual issues in defining and measuring welfare. It then turns to the main issues to be aware of in empirical implementations and the various measures found in practice. As we will see, each of the methods has both strengths and weaknesses.

3.1 Concepts of Welfare

Approaches to welfare measurement differ in terms of the importance attached to the individual's own judgments about his or her well-being. They also differ in terms of the factors they try to include within a single measure. It is very widely agreed that individual welfare depends in part on household command over commodities, but it is also widely agreed that it depends on other things as well. The debates are mainly about what other factors are relevant and how they should be weighted. There are also differences in how one thinks about the concepts of poverty as "absolute" or "relative" (recalling the discussion in chapter 2). To understand the difference between the measures found in practice and judge their relative merits one needs to understand their conceptual foundations.

Welfarism

The standard economic approach to monitoring social progress overall and assessing policies aims to rely solely on the individual welfare levels in the relevant population. Social states are judged by (and only by) individual welfare levels. (This is sometimes called "individualistic.") This approach has its roots in classical utilitarianism (section 1.5), although it is more general, as we will see.

But what do we mean by "welfare levels"? One specific definition of welfarism says that we should strive to base welfare comparisons and public policy decisions solely on the individual utilities, defined as what people maximize in their own choices. It is clearly a big step to equate the personal objective that guides one's choices—the utility function that represents the set of indifference curves, such as in boxes 1.4 and 3.1—with one's "welfare" or "well-being" (interchangeable terms for the present purpose).

An important message of this version of welfarism is that, in assessing individual well-being, one should avoid making judgments that are inconsistent with the preferences that guide people's own choices. So this version of welfarism is fundamentally opposed to *paternalism*—any presumption that someone else knows what is good for you even if you do not agree. Each person is presumed to be a rational actor maximizing his or her utility. This approach will include all those commodities that people chose to consume in assessing their welfare. But it does not stop there. "Utility" in economics is whatever people care about. To say that this only includes market commodities is an unjustified specialization.[1] As long as markets exist and are deemed to be competitive, prevailing prices can be used for aggregating the commodities consumed and in deflating for differences in the cost-of-living to derive the welfare metric. However, this is a partial welfare metric to the extent that people also care about non-market goods.

The utility-based approach draws on a model of rational consumer choice. The essence of the approach is the idea of a *utility function* (recall boxes 1.4 and 1.9). This serves two distinct roles in utility-based welfarism. First, it is a convenient representation of the consumer's preferences over her affordable consumption bundles. The consumer is presumed to be able to order those bundles from the best to the worst and pick the best among the feasible options. In this first role, the utility function is nothing more than an analytically convenient way of representing the consumer's preferences. Box 3.1 summarizes the standard model.

Box 3.1 Consumer Choice

Each person is assumed to have a preference ordering over her budget set, defined as the set of all feasible consumption bundles (which can be taken to include leisure). To keep things simple, suppose that there are two goods, food and clothing, consumed in the amounts Q_F and Q_C with prices P_F and P_C ("F" for

---

[1] As we will see, some critiques of welfarism have been based on that overly narrow specialization; while relevant in some cases these critiques lack more general validity.

food and "C" for clothing). Total spending on the two goods is denoted Y, and this is held constant in this thought experiment. The affordable sets of bundles (Q_F, Q_C) are those for which:

$$P_F Q_F + P_C Q_C \leq Y.$$

The consumer is able to rank the affordable combinations, (Q_F, Q_C), satisfying this equation. Assuming that more of either good is better (often called the "non-satiation" assumption), we only need to consider the budget allocations that exactly absorb the available budget (since if one is at an interior point where $P_F Q_F + P_C Q_C < Y$, then it is possible to afford more of one good with no less of the other). The consumer is assumed to be rational, meaning that she picks her preferred bundle. And the economy is competitive, in that the consumer cannot alter the prices faced.

It is convenient and generally uncontentious to assume that the preference ordering can be represented by a continuous utility function, $U(Q_F, Q_C)$, which is maximized subject to the budget constraint (and the time constraint if we added a third dimension of leisure). The utility function is normally assumed to trace out strictly convex indifference curves (Box 1.4). (Recall that the indifference curve gives the locus of all the combinations of the two choice variables that attain a given level of utility.) The slope of the indifference curve is called the *marginal rate of substitution* (MRS), which is defined as the increment to consumption of one good that is needed to compensate for one less unit of another good, while keeping utility constant. The quantities of food and clothing that maximize utility are denoted Q_F^* and Q_C^*. These will clearly depend on the prices, P_F and P_C, and of course income, Y.

We can now characterize the consumer's equilibrium. The key feature will be that there is no reallocation of the fixed budget between food and clothing that would make the consumer better off. Consider figure B3.1.1, which shows the budget constraint and two indifference curves. (The origin may be at positive values to allow for biological minima.) The dashed curve is clearly not the highest level of utility the consumer can reach, which is the solid curve. The consumer is indifferent between (say) A and B (even though only B exhausts the budget) but prefers the point C to both. At this point the MRS equals the relative price of food.

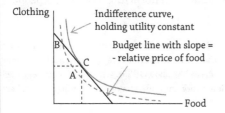

Clothing — Indifference curve, holding utility constant

Budget line with slope = - relative price of food

Figure B3.1.1 Consumer Choice.

Critics of this model have pointed to situations where personal choices do not appear to be rational. There is a risk here that what is seen to be "irrational" may well reflect an overly narrow view of what people care about. For example, if we ignore the fact that people (including poor people) have concerns about their relative position in society, as well as their absolute level of living, we may misunderstand their behavior, such as when they spend their scarce resources on celebrations. To give another example, people may derive utility today from knowing that they will be less poor in the future, and this may influence inter-temporal decision-making.[2]

In the second role, the utility function is assumed to provide sufficient information for assessing whether a person is better off over time, or after a policy change, or in determining one person's welfare relative to another. This latter role has proved to be contentious. One critique questions whether personal preferences should be given this status in assessing welfare. Some observers have questioned whether the choices are morally sound. For example, it is sometimes argued that the decision to buy some luxury good is not ethically defensible when people (including children) are dying from poverty-related causes in the world.[3]

Another objection is that "utility" is not something we observe. That is true, but we can still use the idea to motivate welfare comparisons in more familiar monetary terms—in the "income space." However, we must then be confident that our measure based on the observables is calibrated to be consistent with our concept of utility. When it is a monetary measure and it is consistent with utility it is called a *money-metric of utility* (or sometimes *equivalent income*). This can be readily defined in theory, by finding the income equivalent to utility at fixed reference prices and personal characteristics. (We return to this concept in chapter 4.)

Arguably the bigger problem is *heterogeneity* across people in their welfare-relevant non-market characteristics. People differ in the utility they can be expected to derive from a given consumption bundle. Some people have characteristics—being elderly, or disabled, or living in a cold climate, or living in a place where public services are poor—whereby they need more of certain market goods to attain the same level of utility. Given this heterogeneity, an interpersonally comparable utility index cannot be inferred by looking only at objectively measurable demand and supply behavior. We may well be able to find a utility function consistent with that behavior, but it will not be unique; there can be many such functions, varying with personal characteristics. So the idea that one can infer utilities of heterogeneous individuals from looking solely at their demand and supply behavior is easily ruled out (as explained further in box 3.2). Given that heterogeneity in how command over commodities translates into welfare, we will inevitably need to broaden the information base for assessing welfare, beyond observed behavior in markets. This calls for information relevant to people's

---

[2] This is especially evident in the idea of "rational expectations" in economics as the mean forecast given current information. It can be readily shown that such expectations are only rational for a rather special formulation of the underlying utility function; see Ravallion (1986). What are sometimes called "irrational expectations" may well be perfectly rational once one understands what the decision makers concerned care about.

[3] See, e.g., Singer (2010).

welfare that economists have not traditionally favored, such as data on capabilities and also subjective well-being data. We return to these types of data.

Box 3.2 **The Challenge of Inferring Utility from Behavior in Markets**

A fundamental premise of economics is that the observed commodity demands and labor supplies of households are utility maximizing. The basic model assumes a utility function that depends on the quantities consumed of all goods and services and the leisure time left after working. (See box 3.1.) Recall that this function represents consumer preferences in that the utility function ranks commodity bundles identically with how the consumer ranks them. This utility function is then maximized subject to the budget constraint, which says that the total expenditure on commodities plus the imputed value of leisure time (time taken for leisure times the market wage rate) cannot exceed "full income" given by the value of the time endowment plus all other income (including profits from own enterprises).

If demands and supplies are consistent with this model, then we can in general solve backwards from the observed demands and supplies of a given individual to recover a utility function that is consistent with the choices made. When we come to compare people in different households, with different sizes and demographic compositions, and differences in other characteristics (such as health and disability), we must allow the possibility that these differences matter to both the observed demands and to the level of utility attained given those demands. However, we cannot expect that the ways those differences influence utility at given demands (and supplies) will be properly reflected in the observed demand and supply behavior. In general there will be multitude utility functions (reflecting the heterogeneous characteristics) that can support the observed behavior as an optimum. Thus, we say that the utility function is "unidentified" from observed demands and supplies alone when people differ in their welfare-relevant characteristics.

Further reading: These issues are discussed further in Pollak and Wales (1979) and Browning (1992).

The upshot of these observations is that there is a deep problem in implementing the welfarist agenda that we should rely on the utility derived from consumer choice in deciding whether one person is better off than another. The problem stems from likely heterogeneity in the utility obtained from given choices. It is a "deep" problem because more data on people's actual choices will not make the problem go away. For all practical purposes, we will need to make external judgments in deciding whether one person is better off than another. Again, this is not to say we should ignore the data on choices, but rather to say that we should not kid ourselves that this is sufficient information.

In practice, policymakers, evaluators, and most applied economists today are willing to admit explicit interpersonal comparisons of utility between people or households with different characteristics when discussing policies, although typically these judgments are largely coming from outside economics. (Those economists who are not willing to admit such information are likely to be left out of informing the many important policy debates that require interpersonal comparisons.) It is generally understood that in thinking about policy, one can make interpersonal comparisons of welfare yet respect personal preferences when relevant. And it is clear that the information that can be brought to bear in making interpersonal comparisons goes beyond observable behavior in markets. A large literature has emerged on both the theory and measurement of the social welfare implications of some long-standing policy issues, built on such welfarist foundations.[4]

What are the alternatives to welfarism? What arguments are made for and against them? Can these alternative approaches help in identifying a reliable metric of welfare?

Extensions and Alternatives to Welfarism

Poverty assessments are sometimes based on certain elementary achievements—specific forms of deprivation, such as being able to afford to be adequately nourished. One might count how many people do not attain specific nutritional requirements for good health and normal activities. Or one might identify a list of other specific deprivations related to (say) housing conditions, water and sanitation, and ownership of consumer durables.[5] No special role is assigned to consumer preferences in these approaches.

Two concerns arise. First, there is a nagging worry about the arbitrariness in deciding what dimensions matter and (when necessary) how one should value one type of commodity (such as food) against another (clothing say). Second, there is a concern that these approaches can be overly paternalistic: experts are essentially saying that "we know better than you about what is good for you." By ignoring preferences one may well decide that people are worse off after some policy change (say) even if the people concerned do not agree. For example, one can imagine relative price changes due to (say) an external trade reform that are unambiguously utility-increasing yet entail substitution effects that result in lower caloric intakes in the neighborhood of nutritional norms. A utility-based assessment will say there has been a gain while an observer concerned only with nutritional intakes will not.

There is scope for an intermediate position. Even if we do not think people always make the best decisions for themselves, we need not accept that someone else knows better. That would need to be justified in the specific circumstances. Nor does an acceptance of the need for normative judgments in assessing welfare open the door to

---

[4] Normative public finance has been a fruitful field for such work; important early expositions included Atkinson and Stiglitz (1980) and Newbery and Stern (1987). The measurement of social welfare within a welfarist framework advanced rapidly in the 1980s; important contributions included King (1983) and Jorgenson and Slesnick (1984).

[5] See, e.g., Alkire and Santos (2010). Chapter 5 returns to this example.

unbounded paternalism. It is one thing to say that the set of things we can conceivably infer about welfare from behavior alone cannot be sufficient for deciding who is poor and who is not, or in assessing policies, and quite another to argue that preferences have no role. There are situations in which we can say something about the revealed preferences of individuals, which are respected within a structure that still recognizes the need for external judgments about who is better off.

This echoes the ideas of Rawls (1971), as discussed in chapter 2. We need some index to identify the least advantaged group, based on primary commodities. It might be enough to simply know that "more is better," although more likely there will be trade-offs involved, requiring an assumption about preferences. Rawls recognized this, but argued that we need focus only on the preferences of the least advantaged group. It is still not an easy task to identify such preferences given heterogeneity, as discussed above. And there can be a problem of circularity: we might agree with Rawls that it is the preferences of the poor that matter, but we may well have to make an assumption about preferences before we can figure out who is poor. However, there are ways of addressing this problem, as we will see in chapter 4.

Once one recognizes the deficiencies in available data, observations on specific deprivations can have an important role within a broadly welfarist approach. We return to this point in section 3.3.

Capabilities

An alternative to both the traditional utility-based approach and the specific-deprivations approach has been proposed by Amartya Sen.[6] Sen rejects "utility" as the sole metric of welfare; he also rejects the non-welfarist formulations, such as those that focus solely on specific commodity deprivations or income alone. Recalling box 2.1, Sen argues instead that "well-being" is really to do with *being* well, which is about being able to live long, being well-nourished, being healthy, being literate, and so on; as Sen (1987, 25) puts it, the "value of the living standard lies in the living, and not in the possessing of commodities." In Sen's view, what is valued *intrinsically* are people's capabilities to function. "Poverty" is a lack of capability.

There has been much discussion of Sen's proposal over the last twenty-five years.[7] It has come to be seen by many observers as the main competing theoretical foundation to the welfarist approach in economics. However, it is possible to interpret the capabilities approach in a way that is consistent with welfarism once one allows for heterogeneous preferences over commodities.[8] This only requires that one thinks of capabilities as the direct generators of utility. A person's utility is determined solely by her attainable functionings, which depend in turn on income,

---

[6] See, *inter alia*, Sen (1980, 1985a, 1987, 1992).

[7] There was an early debate between Sen (1979) and Ng (1981). Also see Sen (1987) and the comments therein by Kanbur and Muellbauer. For a thoughtful defense of welfarism against Sen's critique, see Kaplow (2008, pt. 5).

[8] Utility can be viewed as one of the welfare-relevant functionings—the attainment of personal satisfaction through choice. This interpretation is found in Sen (1992, ch. 3). But it is not common among advocates of the capabilities approach.

the prices faced, and her characteristics. Box 3.3 discusses further this interpretation of the capabilities approach. Some might still reject the view that welfare can be equated with the maximand of personal choice.

Box 3.3 A Welfarist Interpretation of Capabilities

In the standard economic model, welfare depends on the consumption of commodities but preferences over commodities may vary between people. Without loss of generality, we can think of this as a common utility function that depends on personal characteristics as well commodities consumed.

An encompassing way of thinking about welfare is to define it as a common function of capabilities—the attainable functionings of that person. We can write this as follows:

$$Utility = U(Functionings).$$

It is assumed that the function U does not vary across people. (When using only a partial set of observed functionings in practice, this assumption need not hold). Functionings depend in turn on commodities consumed and personal characteristics:

$$Functionings = f(Commodities\ consumed, characteristics).$$

Substituting this equation into the first we are back to a more familiar form for economists:

$$Utility = u(Commodities\ consumed,\ characteristics).$$

Through economic and social interactions (including via markets), the attainable functionings of a person and hence the utility derived, will depend on incomes, prices, and characteristics. Capabilities are enhanced by higher income but are not solely determined by income. There will exist (in general) a money metric of capability-dependent-welfare.

There is a critique one sometimes hears of income-based poverty measures on the grounds that welfare, including capabilities as an interpretation of welfare, depends on more than income. This misses the mark.[9] The capabilities approach points to the inadequacy of basing welfare assessments on income alone, but so too does the welfarist approach. Although measurement practices may well be deficient, the use of a monetary metric does not in principle imply that only income matters. Suppose that we agree that welfare is only about capabilities. We can still use an income-based

---

[9] For example, Iceland (2013, 47) criticizes income-poverty measures on the grounds that they "overlook the core problem associated with poverty—that of capability deprivation."

measure of the incidence of poverty to measure "capability-poverty" as long as capabilities depend at least in part on income.[10] It is reasonable to assume that more income allows one to do more things—to expand the feasible set of functionings. Then all we need to do is set the poverty line such that a person at that income level will attain the critical level of capability-welfare that is needed to not be considered poor by the capabilities approach. So the issue is not the use of income-based poverty measures—which can in principle be constructed to be perfectly consistent with the capabilities approach—but whether the poverty lines properly reflect the cost of a given level of welfare at prevailing prices. (We return to these issues in chapter 4.)

Another questionable argument one hears is that "capabilities" are observable but "utility" is not. This too misses the point. The comparison to make is not between capabilities and utility but capabilities and consumptions, which are no harder to measure. In making comparisons of people with different capabilities we will sometimes (possibly quite often) need to decide how we weight one functioning relative to another. That requires a utility function. By either approach, welfare depends on consumptions and personal characteristics (box 3.3). That is not then a difference.

Social Effects on Welfare

Yet another issue underlying differences in how people think about welfare relates to the role played by "social needs." Economists have traditionally taken the view that a person's welfare depends solely on her personal command over commodities (and personal and household characteristics). There is no explicit role for social context in assessing poverty. The alternative view is that people have social needs that depend on context—that poverty can stem from *social exclusion*. This can entail explicit exclusion from certain activities (such as being employed), but it typically means more than that—it can also arise from relative deprivation (being poor relative to others in the society one lives in) or a perceived lack of opportunity for future progress.

There has been much debate about absolute versus relative poverty. It is sometimes argued that, while absolute poverty entails objective deprivation in nutrition and health, relative poverty is only "in the mind"—a subjective, psychological state such as envy. This view has come to be seriously questioned by the evidence of biological responses to relative poverty, notably through heightened stress, as indicated by cortisol levels.[11] For example, one study found significantly higher cortisol levels thirty minutes after awakening among British civil servants with lower socioeconomic status.[12] Enhanced cortisol levels are found when subjects are placed under evaluative threat, meaning that they could be judged negatively by others.[13]

---

[10] More precisely we require that the welfare derived from capabilities is a continuously increasing function of income as well as other variables determining capabilities.

[11] Cortisol is a hormone produced in the adrenal cortex and released at higher levels when a person is under stress.

[12] See Kunz-Ebrect et al. (2004).

[13] See the meta-study by Dickerson and Kemeny (2004).

Social effects on welfare can be encompassed within both the welfarist and capabilities approach to measuring poverty. A simple but attractive formulation by Anthony Atkinson and Francois Bourguignon (2001) is to say that one is not poor if one is capable of attaining both absolute "survival needs" and minimum "social inclusion needs" for participating in social and economic activity.

The idea of *relative deprivation* also has relevance for how we think about welfare and measure poverty. Whether starting from a welfarist or non-welfarist position, many people would agree that relative position often matters to people's welfare. The welfarist will say that one's personal utility is lower at given "own-income" when one lives in a place where all others have a higher income than in a place where everyone has a lower income—one experiences a disutility of relative deprivation in the former case. (The non-welfarist will probably point instead to one's diminished capability for participating in social and economic life in the former setting.) The weight attached to relative position can often be crucial to the conclusions one draws about poverty. box 3.4 illustrates this point with some simple numerical examples.

Box 3.4 Which Distribution Has More Poverty?

Consider two income distributions (think of the units as dollars per day or per hour):

$$A : (1, 1, 1) \qquad B : (2, 3, 10).$$

We can all agree B is more unequal. But everyone in B has a higher income than in A. If we think of income as the "primary good," then Rawls's difference principle (chapter 2) will prefer B to A; the inequality has benefited the poor. Income poverty is lower in B, but inequality is higher.

However, as we also saw in chapter 2, Rawls and Sen have emphasized that primary goods are not only commodities, but are broader, potentially including not being relatively deprived. Suppose instead that welfare is own income normalized by the mean. The normalized distributions of welfare are then:

$$(1, 1, 1) \qquad (0.4, 0.6, 2).$$

"A" now has both lower inequality and lower welfare poverty for all poverty lines less than 1.

More generally, suppose that the welfare of person i is:

$$\alpha y_i + (1 - \alpha)(y_i/\bar{y}) \quad 1 \geq \alpha \geq 0.$$

Here y_i is i's own income while $\bar{y}$ is the mean income of the group. The welfarist assessment of which distribution has more poverty is now seen to depend on the value taken by the preference parameter α. It is readily verified that the poorest person is better off in B if (and only if) $\alpha > 0.375$. That is an empirical question, though hardly an easy question.

Arguably the most important contribution of the capabilities approach was the explicit recognition it gave to the fact that households vary in their capacity to convert commodities into well-being. This was implicit in the mainstream welfarist approach, but in practice that approach was too often simplified to the point of ignoring heterogeneity in relevant non-income factors in welfare. That mistake is harder to make when one thinks about welfare in the space of capabilities. However, as we see later in this chapter and in chapter 5, some approaches found in practice that have claimed to be motivated by "capabilities" are seriously oversimplified in other respects.

Opportunities

The idea of "opportunities" has motivated another alternative to welfarism. The idea of inequality of opportunity (INOP) has a long history. As we learned in chapter 1, the surge of attention to inequality in the latter part of the eighteenth century was far more about inequality of opportunity than of outcomes. Since then, advocates of efforts to promote equality of opportunity have been found on both the Left and Right. Roemer (1998) argues that we need only worry about inequalities that stem from circumstances beyond an individual's control—those things that are not traceable to the individual's own choices (box 1.8). The classic example of a circumstance is parental education. Suppose that the son of well-educated parents mistakenly underinvests in schooling and grows up poor. An opportunities approach may deem him to be well off based on his parents' schooling even though his income is low.

According to the supporters of the INOP approach, inequality of outcomes is fine as long as it reflects personal efforts. Efforts are taken to be choice variables that depend on circumstances. This approach implies that the welfare metric for assessing inequality and poverty should be the component of income or consumption that is attributable to circumstances. This is often retrieved by regressing income on circumstances.[14]

There is a continuing debate on the merits of this view. People make mistakes and chance also plays a role.[15] The opportunities approach typically treats mistakes the same way as well-considered choices. While the ethical status of mistakes is reasonably clear in the opportunities approach, many observers will be willing to help those for whom past mistaken choices have caused current deprivations. It is surely unimaginable that any civilized society would do nothing about extreme, possibly life-threatening, deprivations on the grounds that they are traceable to some mistaken choices by the persons concerned or their bad luck. Inequalities stemming from choices or luck can hardly be banned from public redress.

The INOP approach in practice rests on a regression model of income on circumstances, which is then used to measure INOP.[16] It is acknowledged that income also depends on effort, but it is argued that this is chosen by people themselves and is then a function of their circumstances. Thus, the regression of income on circumstances

---

[14] See, e.g., Bourguignon et al. (2007), Barros et al. (2009), and Ferreira and Gignoux (2011). Also see the discussion in Roemer (2014). Section 3.3 discusses this approach further.

[15] See the discussion in Kanbur and Wagstaff (2015).

[16] Examples can be found in Barros et al. (2009), Ferreira and Gignoux (2011), and Roemer (2014).

used in the INOP literature can be given a "reduced form" interpretation.[17] However, it should be noted that this predicted value is not in general a utility-consistent welfarist approach, which would instead use as the welfare metric a monetary equivalent of the maximum utility attainable when effort is chosen optimally, given circumstances. This is explained in box 3.5. The implication is that the INOP approach can deem someone to be better off (worse off) when they do not agree. There are also problems in operationalizing the idea of a welfare metric that depends solely on circumstances. We return to these problems in section 3.3.

Box 3.5 Measuring INOP When Effort Matters to Welfare

Utility can be taken to be a function of income and effort, with the former entering positively and the latter negatively:

$$Utility = U(Income, Effort).$$

Income in turn depends on effort and circumstances:

$$Income = F(Effort, Circumstances).$$

Then the chosen level of effort (denoted with a *) depends on circumstances:

$$Effort^* = E(Circumstances).$$

This is the level of effort that maximizes utility. If we substitute the last equation into the second equation for income, then we have an equation for income as a function of circumstances. When written as a regression model the predicted value of income based on circumstances has been widely used in the INOP literature.

The person's welfare is the maximum level of utility they can derive, which depends on their circumstances as follows:

$$Utility = U[F(Effort^*, Circumstances), Effort^*].$$

We can see here that circumstances matter to welfare in two ways, namely through income, but also independently of income, given that greater effort gives disutility. (We can always express this level of welfare in monetary units, giving an exact money-metric of utility.) So the predicted value of income based on circumstances cannot be a valid monetary measure of welfare. And the difference arises precisely because utility depends on effort, as argued in the INOP literature.

Further reading: See Ravallion (2015a) for further discussion of this problem in how INOP is measured in practice.

---

[17] The term "reduced form" comes from simultaneous equation models in which one (endogenous) variable $Y1$ is a function of another endogenous variable ($Y2$), which is in turn a function of exogenous variables (X). On substituting out $Y2$, we obtain the reduced form for $Y1$ as a function of X.

A Less Ambitious Goal

This tour of the conceptual issues in thinking about welfare must make one skeptical of ever coming up with an ideal fully comprehensive and yet operational measure of "welfare," embracing everything that matters. It might well be preferable to set more modest goal of measuring "economic welfare" and defining poverty in that more narrow dimension. It is unlikely to capture everything that matters to a person's happiness (say). But that would be asking too much of any single measure. As long as we agree that a lack of personal command over commodities is an important dimension of social progress, we are on safe ground in measuring poverty and inequality that way. However, as we will see, even this less ambitious task still poses challenges for the analyst.

3.2 Using Household Surveys for Welfare Measurement

Household surveys are the single most important source of data for making poverty comparisons; indeed, they are the only data source that can tell us directly about the *distribution* of living standards in a society, such as how many households do not attain a given consumption level. Box 1.17 introduced the basic idea. Here we go into more depth, pointing to the care that must go into setting up and interpreting such data. This section surveys the main issues one should be aware of. Box 3.6 summarizes the key concepts from statistics used here.

Box 3.6 **Some Key Statistical Concepts about Sample Surveys**

Sample surveys are used to reduce the cost of estimating parameters of interest for the relevant *population*, which is the set of people you are interested in making inferences about. The analyst should have a clear idea of what the relevant population is for the context in which she is working.

A sample survey collects data on a subset (sample) of people in the population, for the purpose of drawing reliable conclusions about some key features of interest about that population. Those features are the statistics one is interested in. The sample is drawn from a *sample frame*, which may take the form of a listing of the population. (If you survey the entire population, then you are doing a census.)

In using a sample survey to estimate population parameters, one is typically concerned with obtaining statistically unbiased estimates, meaning that in sufficiently large samples the survey-based estimate will converge on the true population parameter. One is typically also keen to assure that the sample estimates are reasonably precise, meaning that their standard error is low relative to the parameter estimate.

An important concept is *statistical independence*. Two events are said to be statistically independent (or simply "independent") if the probability of one event

continued

Box 3.6 **(Continued)**

occurring is not altered either way by the fact that the other event has happened. We can extend the same idea to any two variables, which can be said to be independent if the probability distribution of one variable does not depend on the values taken by the other variable. (The probability distribution, or simply "distribution," of a variable gives the probability of the variable taking each possible value.)

Two samples are independent if the fact of being selected for one of them has no bearing on the probability of being selected for the other. Independence in the selection of samples is assured by randomization. There are many ways of doing this, but the simplest is to assign a number to each potential sample point in the sample frame and draw a subset of those numbers randomly, using a random number generator. Software for drawing random samples is readily available both within existing statistical software packages (such as Stata, SPSS, or SAS) and stand-alone products (such as the *Research Randomizer*).

Randomization is an important example of a sampling method. A simple random sample is just what it sounds like: one lists everyone in the sample frame and draws a single random sample, containing those who will then be approached to be interviewed. A more complex form of sampling involves *stratification*. Here you break the population up into well-defined subgroups (strata) and then do simple random sampling within each stratum, but at different rates. The idea is that you oversample certain types of people, such as those living in households who participated in a public program being studied.

In calculating summary statistics from the sample, one typically wants a good estimate for the population from which the sample was drawn. This requires that one weights each observation from the sample according to how many people it represents in the population. In effect, the weights allow one to convert the actual sample (however complex its design) into a sample random sample. (The inverse of the sampling rate is called the expansion factor, giving the number of people in the population represented by that sample point.) These weights are important data in their own right and should always be available to users for anything but a simple random sample (in which all sample points can be equally weighted). The weights are needed to obtain unbiased estimates of the descriptive statistics for the population. (In estimating a regression model the case for weighting is less obvious; box 5.12 returns to this case.)

Drawing a simple random sample for a large geographic area can add to the cost of the survey, since one may well end up with a very scattered sample. And if one does not have an up-to-date census, it may not be feasible to draw a simple random sample. *Cluster sampling* (also called two-stage sampling) can then help. By this method, one first randomly samples clusters of households, such as villages or city blocks; these can be called the primary sampling units (PSUs). PSUs are picked with probability proportional to their size, as usually based on the latest Census. One then samples households randomly within the selected clusters, after doing a complete listing of the households in each sampled cluster. If cluster sampling has been used, it is often important to know how this was done; for example, if only one cluster was picked in each of the regions then the regional poverty map may be quite misleading. And one should be wary of having too many stages to the sampling since the precision of estimation for population parameters may fall considerably.

Units within the same cluster cannot be considered to be independent, as they may well share some common attribute (such as associated with living in the same village). An important difference between stratification and clustering is that the former typically increases the precision of your estimates from the sample while the latter reduces that precision. The estimates of the sampling variance need to be adjusted (upward) for clustering. The extent of the adjustment depends on how strongly correlated the outcomes of interest are within the clusters (often called the "intra-cluster correlation"). When one is estimating a regression model (box 1.19) the thing to focus on is the intra-cluster correlation of the regression's error term.

One of the key design choices for a sample survey is how many households to interview in each PSU versus how many PSUs to sample. If one wants to estimate average values for the PSUs, then one clearly needs adequate samples at the PSU level. However, for a given aggregate sample size, larger samples at the PSU level reduce precision in estimating population characteristics. The choice depends on how much variance there is within PSUs and the purposes of the surveys—notably whether the study calls for estimates at the PSU level.

Errors are expected in small samples, even when random. While you cannot expect to get it exactly right in a small sample, as the sample size increases you should be getting closer to the truth. If not, then something must be wrong in the estimation method. For example, your sample might not in fact have been drawn randomly, so it is not representative of the population. When using a sample survey to measure poverty, a large-sample bias occurs if rich people refuse to participate in the survey—they are just too busy, or are never home, or maybe your interviewers cannot get past their guard dogs! So you overestimate the poverty rate. This type of problem is sometimes called *survey response bias*. While sampling error arises because you do not have a large sample, this form of non-sampling error does not go away as your sample size increases.

Even if everyone who is sampled randomly is available to be interviewed, *measurement error* is still a concern in surveys (and censuses). For example, some people (probably more the rich than the poor) may be making wild guesses at key components of their income or consumption. Large samples help average-out some types of errors but not all. For example, if (as is often claimed) rich people deliberately understate their incomes in a survey, then this will persist in large samples.

continued

Box 3.6 **(Continued)**

When analyzing survey data, one often uses the idea of *statistical significance*. This takes account of both the size of the statistic and its sample *standard error*, measuring the precision of the estimate. If an estimate is said to be "significant at the 5% level," what is usually meant is that there is only a 5% chance that the true value is in fact zero.

Further reading: The classic treatment of sampling is found in Kish (1965). More recent introductions to the topic can be found in Iarossi (2006) and Bryman (2012). A comprehensive overview of survey methods can be found in Bethlehem (2009).

The household surveys found in practice can be classified along four dimensions:

1. *The sample frame:* The survey may represent a country's population, or some more narrowly defined subset, such as residents of a region. The appropriateness of a survey's sample frame naturally depends on the inferences one wants to draw from it.

2. *The unit of observation:* This can be the household itself or the individuals within the household or both. A "household" is usually defined as a group of people eating and living together. Household structures can sometimes be complex, such as in societies where polygamy is practiced or where communal living in compounds is common (such as in rural areas of the Sahel region of Africa), making it difficult to distinguish one household from another.[18] Most household surveys include some data on individuals within the household, though this rarely includes their consumptions, which are typically aggregated to the household level; examples include India's *National Sample Surveys* (NSS), Indonesia's *National Socio-Economic Surveys* (SUSENAS), and the World Bank's LSMS surveys. An example of a survey which collected individual food consumption data is the survey of rural households in the Philippines that was done by the *International Food Policy Research Institute* (IFPRI) in the 1980s.[19] When there are multi-cell households (associated with different wives) complex surveys are required.[20]

3. *The number of observations over time:* A single cross-section, based on one or two interviews within a short period, is the most common. In a panel (also called longitudinal) survey members of the same household are resurveyed over an extended

---

[18] See Scott (1980a), UN (1989), and Rosenhouse (1990).

[19] See Bouis and Haddad (1992).

[20] De Vreyer et al. (2008) have developed a survey method for multi-cell households and applied this in Senegal. Also see the application to studying intergenerational inequality in Lambert et al. (2014).

period. Such surveys are harder to implement and more costly, but have some advantages (box 3.7).

4. *The principal living standard indicator collected:* The most common indicators of poverty used in practice are based on household consumption expenditure or household income. Some surveys collect both (such as Indonesia's SUSENAS and the World Bank's LSMS), but others specialize (e.g., India's NSS does not include all income sources, while most of the household surveys available for Latin America do not include consumption). Not having both income by source and expenditure by type can be a serious limitation for certain purposes, including assessing the poverty impacts of changes in prices. (We return to this application.)

Box 3.7 Panel Data and Its Applications

Most surveys entail interviewing members of one household over a short period of time (a few days or possibly in just one visit). This is a single cross-sectional survey—by far the most common form. By contrast, in a panel survey, two or more rounds of survey data are collected on the same household. There is often a reasonably long period (a year is common) between successive interviews.

With such data one can better understand *poverty dynamics*—the transitions into and out of poverty. Consider the table B3.7.1 classifying the population into four groups, labeled (in italics).

Table B3.7.1 **Poverty Dynamics**

Poor in Both Years	*Escaped Poverty(i.e., poor in the first year, but not in second)*	Poor in First Year (sum of row)
Fell into Poverty(i.e., not poor in the first year, but poor in second)	*Not Poor in Either Year*	Not poor in first year (sum of row)
Poor in second year (sum of column)	Not poor in second year (sum of column)	Population (sum of all four cells)

With two cross-sectional surveys one can put numbers in the row and column totals, but one has no idea about the inner four boxes (in italics). The poverty counts may even be the same in the two dates, yet that is consistent with both complete persistence (the same people are poor in both years) and complete "churning" (all those who were poor in the first year escaped poverty, while all who were not poor in the first year fell into poverty in the second). More likely

continued

Box 3.7 (Continued)

the truth is somewhere between the two. Only with panel data can one complete the table, filling in the inner four boxes.

Another application is in studying *mobility*—the movements of people up or down the income or other ladder. For example, one might study the intergenerational correlation of incomes or schooling (such as when one asks how many children of illiterate parents became literate). This type of question is clearly important to measuring and understanding inequality of opportunity in society. When studying income mobility, there are various measures that have been proposed, including the correlation coefficient between incomes at date 1 and those at date 2 and the rank correlation coefficient. Not all these measures require panel data; for example, one can ask about the respondent's parents in a cross-sectional survey.

While panel data have advantages, they are more costly to collect since one must find the same households. In any changing population, a panel survey cannot be representative at all dates; typically it is only so for the first survey round. There can also be biases due to *attrition*, whereby some nonrandom subsample drops out of the panel. This would be the case if attrition is due to households with a higher propensity to migrate for work. And time-varying measurement errors can be a concern; at least some of those "off-diagonal" elements in the array above (those who moved in or out of poverty) will be measurement errors. (For example, if a household's income was underestimated in period 1 this might be corrected in period 2.)

Three well-known examples of panel data sets are the University of Michigan's Panel Study of Income Dynamics in the United States, the Village Level Surveys by the International Crops Research Institute for the Semi-Arid Tropics in India, and the Russia Longitudinal Monitoring Study run by the University of North Carolina over the last twenty years. Very few surveys collect individual consumption data on a longitudinal basis (an exception is the aforementioned IFPRI survey for the Philippines). A modified version of the classic panel has been used in some LSMS surveys, whereby half of each year's sample is resurveyed the following year. This cuts the cost of forming a panel data set, while retaining some of the advantages.

There are some examples of panel data sets that have been constructed from existing data sets, rather than being designed as longitudinal surveys from the outset. One example is for China, where the samples for the cross-sectional urban and rural surveys done by the National Bureau of Statistics are not rotated every year. It is thus possible to construct panels for some periods (Chen and Ravallion 1996).

A second example is the study by Chetty et al. (2014) of intergenerational income mobility in the United States. Chetty et al. use income tax records to link children to their parents (who had typically filed for them as dependents prior to leaving home). They find that measures of income mobility have been quite stable since the 1970s. For example, they estimate that the probability of a child born into the bottom quintile of incomes rising to be in the top quintile as an adult was 0.08 for those born in 1971 versus 0.09 for those born in 1986. This seems puzzling given the rise in income inequality although (as Chetty et al. note) a large amount of that rise has been at the very top of the distribution in the United States.

Further reading: See Ashenfelter et al. (1986) on the arguments for and against collecting panel data. On using panel data to study poverty dynamics (in the context of testing the performance of a safety net), see Ravallion et al. (1995). On the measurement of mobility, see Fields (2001, chs. 6 and 7). On the implications of measurement error in panel data, see Glewwe (2012).

The most common survey used in poverty analysis is a single cross-section for a nationally representative sample, with the household as the unit of observation (though with some information obtained from specific individuals), and it includes either consumption or income data. The following are the main problems to be aware of when interpreting household consumption or income data from such a household survey.[21]

Survey Design

Even very large samples may give biased estimates for poverty measurement if the survey is not random, or if the data extracted from it have not been corrected for possible biases, such as due to sample stratification (box 3.6). A random sample requires that each person in the population or each subgroup in a stratified sample has an equal chance of being selected. This guarantees *statistical independence*—the assumption that underlies most of the results used routinely in making statistical inferences about population parameters from sample surveys. (See box 3.6 on statistical independence.)

Poor people may not be properly represented in sample surveys; for example, they may be harder to interview because they live in remote areas or are itinerant. Indeed, a *household* survey may miss one distinct subgroup of the poor: those who are homeless. Also, some of the surveys that have been used to measure poverty were not designed for this purpose, in that their sample frame was not intended to span the entire population. Examples include labor force surveys, for which the sample frame is typically restricted to the "economically active population," which precludes certain subgroups of the poor. Key questions to ask about any survey are: Does the sample frame span the entire population? Is

[21] There are a number of other issues in survey design which I will not cover here, including questionnaire design and field organization. See Iarossi (2006), Bethlehem (2009), and Bryman (2012) for useful overviews of these issues. Also see UN (1989). The classic LSMS questionnaire design is described in Grootaert (1986) and Ainsworth and van der Gaag (1988).

there likely to be a response bias, in that the likelihood of cooperating with the interviewer is not random (box 3.6)?

Naturally selective response—whereby some types of households are less likely to participate in surveys—can be a serious concern when measuring poverty or inequality. The expectation is that it tends to be the relatively well-off who are less inclined to participate. Then we will overestimate the poverty rate unless the bias can be corrected; the implications for measuring inequality are theoretically ambiguous.[22] We shall return to this issue below.

A question for survey design is whether those who agree to participate should be paid. Practice is uneven in this respect with some surveys making payments (often modest) and others not. The use of new technologies for doing surveys (such as mobile phones) has also brought up this issue. Response rates tend to be lower than for household surveys, so it may seem attractive to find some form of compensation, such as by giving free phone time to those who agree to participate. However, there is a risk that such practices will actually make matters worse; yes, the overall response rate will rise, but the sample may well be even more biased, with less representation by the rich. This is explained further in box 3.8. We shall return to the problems of selective response—whereby some types of households are less likely to participate in surveys—when we consider measurement errors further below.

Box 3.8 The Economics of Survey Participation

Survey participation is a matter of individual choice; nobody is obliged to comply with the statistician's randomized assignment. There is some perceived benefit from compliance—the satisfaction of doing one's civic duty—but there is a cost as well. That cost can be expected to rise with income. For example, the opportunity cost of the time required to comply rises with income (due to higher wage rate), while the time itself is roughly independent of income. The potential survey respondent must weigh the perceived benefits against the cost.

It seems reasonable to expect that the marginal cost (MC) of survey participation rises with participation (as measured by the time spent doing the survey); the longer you spend doing the survey, the more it starts to eat into other valued activities. We can also assume that higher income implies a higher MC of participation. The latter property can be rationalized in terms of the foregone income of time spent doing a survey, which will be higher for those with higher wage rates.

---

[22] Notice that selective compliance is not the same as making income transfers between the rich and poor, which must change inequality measure. With selective compliance one is moving shares of the population, which creates the ambiguity. This is explained in more technical terms in Korinek et al. (2006).

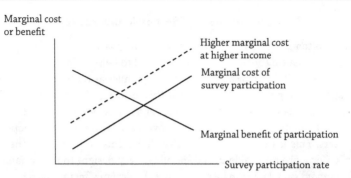

Figure B3.8.1 The Choice to Participate in a Survey.

It is reasonable to assume that the marginal benefit (MB) of participation is not affected by participation, or at least does not rise with participation. Let us also assume that the MB does not rise with income.

Under these conditions, there is an optimal level of individual participation, equating MB with MC, as illustrated in figure B3.8.1. As income rises the desired participation falls. The rich will be less likely to comply than the poor.

A fixed fee paid to those who agree to participate will increase the probability of participation, but it can also increase the likelihood of a bias whereby the response rate falls with income. This happens if the fee is a stronger incentive for the poor to participate. So compensating survey participants may increase your sample size but reduce your ability to draw valid inferences about the distribution of income in the population from that sample.

Further reading: A more complete discussion of this topic can be found in Korinek et al. (2006). In a more elaborate model of survey participation, Korinek et al. (2006) show that under certain conditions one can get an inverted U relationship, whereby the poorest and the rich are less likely to want to participate in the survey than middle-income groups.

There are various methods of sampling that can help achieve a more cost-effective survey than would be possible with simple random sampling (box 3.6). Stratified random sampling—whereby different subgroups of the population have different (but known) chances of being selected but all have an equal chance in any given subgroup—can increase the precision in poverty measurement obtainable with a given number of interviews; for example, one can oversample certain regions where the poor are thought to be concentrated. Cluster sampling, by contrast, reduces precision, since the surveyed households within a given cluster cannot be considered independent (boxes 3.6 and 3.9).

---

* Box 3.9 The Design Effect on Standard Errors

One is often interested in having a sufficiently large sample for each PSU, such as for measuring geographic variables used to help explain poverty or even poverty rates by PSU. This calls for adequate samples at the second stage of the two-stage sampling design (box 3.6). But this leads to a further problem. For a given aggregate sample size, larger samples at the local level increase the standard error of the overall estimate of the poverty measures or other population parameters. This is called the design effect (*DE*). This is the ratio of the actual variance (for a given variable in the specific survey design) to the variance in a simple random sample. It can be shown that the design effect is given by

$$DE = 1 + \rho(B - 1),$$

where ρ is the correlation coefficient within the PSU and B is the sample size drawn in each PSU. Study designs can thus face a trade-off between the need for precision in estimating the population parameters of interest and the ability to measure the things one is interested in at PSU level.

Further reading: The classic treatment of this topic is Kish (1965, ch. 5).

The choices made in questionnaire design can matter to the measures obtained from a given sample. Qualitative research methods and pilot testing can improve survey design, to assure that the subject, phrasing, and sequencing of questions can address the hypotheses to be tested. Focus groups can be a useful qualitative tool in the design stage of a survey, such as in formulating relevant questions. Pilot testing is essential for any draft questionnaire.

One general point should be clear: one should be aware of any significant changes in survey design across the domain of the poverty comparison, such as differences in the sample frame or questionnaire. Changes in the wording of a question, or changes in the location of the same question in a survey instrument, can change the results.[23]

Goods Coverage and Valuation

The coverage of goods and income sources in the survey should be comprehensive, covering both food and non-food goods when measuring consumption, and all income sources when measuring income. Consumption should cover all monetary expenditures on goods and services consumed plus the monetary value of all consumption from income in kind, such as food produced on the family farm, or hunted and gathered from common property resources, and the imputed rent for owner-occupied housing.[24] Similarly, the income definition should include income received in kind

---

[23] See, e.g., Kilic and Sohnesen (2014), who cite other relevant evidence.

[24] For further discussion of consumption and income definitions in household surveys, see UN (1989). On measuring consumption, also see Deaton and Zaidi (2002).

although practices vary. Local market prices often provide a good guide for valuation of own-farm production or owner-occupied housing. The valuation of noncash benefits from public services is often difficult, though potentially important. For transfers in kind of market goods, prevailing prices are generally considered to be satisfactory for valuation. Non-market goods (such as free use of a public health clinic or school) present a more serious problem, and there is no widely preferred method. A separate monitoring of the use of public services by poor people will be needed.

A common problem facing the welfare analyst using a household survey is that the survey may not be properly integrated, in that categories do not match in relevant ways across different segments of the survey. For example, to evaluate the welfare effects of a change in food staple prices in a food-producing country, it is not enough to know the budget shares of consumption at the household level—one must also know household food production. Whether a household gains or losses from a change in the price of food depends on consumption net of production; if you consume more than you produce of some good, then you will be worse off when the price of that good rises. However, it is quite common that household surveys in rural areas either do not include data on farm production, or they do not use the same commodity categorization in the consumption and production schedules. This can make those surveys virtually useless for analyzing certain policy problems such as trade reforms. (Chapter 9 discusses trade policies further.)

Variability and the Time Period of Measurement

It has long been recognized that the existence of variation over time in incomes and/or prices has implications for the definition and measurement of "real income." Income observed over a relatively short period of time may be deceptive about economic welfare. John Hicks (1939, 176) defined a person's "income" as "what he can consume during the week and still expect to be as well off at the end of the week as he was at the beginning."

It is sometimes argued that what we really need to measure is "wealth." A common economic definition is the discounted present value of all future incomes, although this is making some rather strong assumptions (box 3.10). Finding a unique definition of wealth that can be considered realistic and comprehensive has proved difficult in practice.

Box 3.10 **Wealth as the Present Value of Future Income**

The present value (PV) of a person's current and future incomes is a common economic definition of "wealth." To obtain the PV, we cannot simply add up all current and future incomes, since this would treat $1 in the future as equivalent to $1 in your hand today, which cannot be right. We need to discount future incomes. The present value of income over the two periods is given by:

$$W = Y_1 + \frac{Y_2}{1+r},$$

continued

Box 3.10 (Continued)

where Y_1 and Y_2 denote incomes realized at date 1 ("today") and 2, respectively, and r is the rate of interest, which is the rate at which future income is discounted to obtain the PV. Hence, r is also called the "discount rate," although this term often refers to the personal discount rate, which is also called the rate of time preference, rather than a market rate of interest. To understand this formula (some version of which often appears in economics and finance) note that if you had the sum $Y_2/(1 + r)$ at date 1 and invested it for one year you would have Y_2 at date 2. We can readily generalize this formula to any longer time period. Defining that stream as the sequence of incomes $Y_1, Y_2, \ldots, Y_{T-1}, Y_T$ from now (date 1) to T years in the future:

$$W = Y_1 + \frac{Y_2}{1 + r} + \frac{Y_3}{(1 + r)^2} + \ldots, \frac{Y_T}{(1 + r)^T} = \sum_{t=1}^{T} \frac{Y_t}{(1 + r)^t}.$$

If the stream of income is constant Y (called an "annuity") then this simplifies to:

$$W = \frac{Y}{r} \left[1 - \frac{1}{(1 + r)^T} \right].$$

All this is clearly making some strong assumptions including perfect foresight with no uncertainty. (This can be relaxed to perfect stochastic foresight, allowing for unpredictable errors—sometimes called "rational expectations.") The method also runs into a problem when some markets are missing for some components of wealth.

There is also a practical problem in implementing this definition: we cannot obtain future incomes from a household survey today. However, we can ask about current consumption. Under certain conditions, consumption depends on wealth, not current income. Box 3.11 goes further into this topic.

The existence of income variability over time is one reason some analysts prefer current consumption to current income as the indicator of economic welfare. Real incomes of the poor can vary over time in predictable ways (as well as unpredictable ones). This is particularly true in underdeveloped rural economies depending on rain-fed agriculture. Under certain conditions, consumption will then reveal *permanent income*, as given by the return to long-term wealth. This is an implication of Milton Friedman's (1957) Permanent Income Hypothesis (box 3.11).

However, even when those conditions do not hold, such as when credit markets work poorly, there are often ways in which people can smooth their consumption in response to changes in their incomes or the prices they face, such as by drawing on savings or turning to their friends and family.

Box 3.11 Inter-Temporal Consumption Choice and the Permanent Income Hypothesis

Consider the static consumer choice problem discussed in boxes 1.4 and 3.1, but now replace "clothing" by "consumption at date 1" and replace "food" by "consumption at date 2." Utility depends on both, and we assume convex indifference curves reflecting the scope for substitution, similarly to box 3.1.

A pioneering model of inter-temporal consumption behavior was provided by Friedman (1957) and is called the Permanent Income Hypothesis (PIH). This was developed as an alternative to the simplest Keynesian model, which assumed that current consumption depended on current income. (Other alternatives were the relative-income hypothesis of Duesenberry [1949] and the life-cycle model of Ando and Modigliani [1963].) Friedman postulated that both income and consumption in any period had both permanent and transient components; we can write these as:

$$Y = Y^P + Y^T,$$
$$C = C^P + C^T$$

for income (Y) and consumption (C), respectively. "Permanent income" $\left(Y^P\right)$ is taken to be determined by long-run wealth over some time horizon; for a sufficiently distant horizon, we can simply set $Y^P = rW$. Transient income $\left(Y^T\right)$ fluctuates over time, and Friedman assumed that Y^T had zero mean and was uncorrelated with the other variables in his model. The key element of the PIH is that permanent consumption is directly proportional to permanent income: $C^P = kY^P$. Friedman postulated that the coefficient k depends on factors such as the rate of interest and preferences.

The idea that current consumption reveals wealth is attractive, but it does require some strong assumptions. In particular, it assumes that the consumer has perfect foresight and access to a perfect credit market. Yet people (and no less poor people) grapple with uncertainty about the future and are exposed to uninsured risks. And markets are incomplete, meaning that not all income-generating components of wealth have prices attached to them, to enable straightforward aggregation.

While the strong implications of the PIH (such as $C^P = kY^P$) have not received much empirical support, a number of studies have found that consumption responds more to permanent income than transient income. There is normally some degree of consumption smoothing, even for poor people.

Further reading: For a good discussion of consumption in an inter-temporal context, see Deaton (1992). (Deaton won the 2015 Nobel prize in economics.)

This observation has two distinct implications for welfare measurement: (1) current consumption is almost certainly a better indicator than current income of the *current* standard of living, and (2) while current consumption is unlikely to be ideal, it is a better indicator of *long-term* well-being than current income, as consumption will reveal at least some information about incomes at other dates, in the past and future.

While there is a strong case for preferring consumption over income in measuring welfare, it should not be forgotten that a number of factors can make current consumption a noisy welfare indicator. Even with ideal smoothing, consumption will still (as a rule) vary over the life cycle. Thus, two households with different lifetime wealth—one "young," the other "old"—may happen to have the same consumption at the survey date. This may be less of a problem in traditional societies where the extended family is still the norm, though that is rapidly changing.

There are other sources of noise in the relationship between current consumption and long-term standard of living. Different households may face different constraints on their opportunities for consumption smoothing. It is generally thought that the poor are far more constrained in their borrowing options than the non-poor.

There is also evidence that poor people tend to be less well-insured (box 3.12). While consumption smoothing and risk-sharing arrangements clearly do exist, how well they perform from the point of view of poor people is a moot point.[25] The literature on risk and insurance in poor rural economies suggests three stylized facts: (1) income risk is pervasive; (2) household behavior is geared in part to protecting consumptions from such risk; (3) the mechanisms of doing so are both private and social, the latter comprising various informal risk-sharing arrangements among two or more households.

Box 3.12 **How Well Are the Poor Insured? Evidence from Rural China**

Are all rural households equally vulnerable to uninsured risks? One study addressed this question using a six-year household panel data set for rural China. This was not planned as a panel, but the sample design entailed long periods in which there was little sample rotation (box 3.7). The study used this constructed panel data set to test for systematic wealth effects on the extent of consumption insurance against income risk. Motivated by the theory of risk-sharing, the tests entailed estimating the effects of income changes on consumption, with current income treated as endogenous, after controlling for aggregate shocks through interacted village–time dummies. The study also tested for insurance against covariate risk at village level. To test for wealth effects, the study stratified the sample on the basis of household wealth per capita, and whether or not the household resides in a poor area. The method avoided the problems identified in past tests for risk-sharing, which were biased in favor of showing that there was insurance even when there was none.

The full insurance model was convincingly rejected. The lower a household's wealth, the stronger the rejection, in that the implied marginal propensity to

---

[25] Relevant empirical work for developing countries includes Bhargava and Ravallion (1993), Townsend (1994), Ravallion and Chaudhuri (1997), Jalan and Ravallion (1999), and Dercon and Krishnan (2000).

consume out of current income is higher for poorer households. While there are clearly arrangements for consumption insurance in these villages of southern China, they work considerably less well for the asset-poor households.

Such results strengthen the case, on both equity and efficiency grounds, for public action to provide better insurance in underdeveloped rural economies. The specific form that such action should take in given circumstances is still, however, an open question. The results of this study also suggest that, unless credit and insurance options for poor families can be improved, one should not be surprised to see persistent inequality, and an inequitable growth process, in this setting.

Further reading: The study referred to is by Jalan and Ravallion (1999), which gives full details. On the sources of bias in past methods of testing for insurance, see Ravallion and Chaudhuri (1997).

Advocates of using income data in preference to consumption often point to constraints on inter-temporal choice and risk sharing. However, such constraints do not justify believing that current income is a better welfare metric than consumption. We need not presume that markets are perfect to expect that consumption will be smoothed to some extent in the face of income fluctuations. Households can save and they do have foresight.

Another argument sometimes made for preferring current income measures is that they better reflect what is called "potential consumption." But this too is questionable. First, we can question whether potential consumption is a valid welfare indicator. A poor farmer may get a bumper harvest once in twenty years, but he can hardly be judged to be no longer poor, even in that fortunate year. Second, even if we accept that potential consumption is what we are after, income is hardly a good measure; we would surely want to know liquid wealth, and here too actual consumption may well be more revealing.

A further argument made for using current income to measure economic welfare arises when assessing the distributional implications of taxes or transfers. For current income, there is a straightforward accounting identity whereby we can add transfers and subtract taxes. That is not so for consumption, given that there could well be a savings response. We would need to figure out the likely response. However, this practical advantage of income is not as great as it may seem at first given that income in the absence of the taxes or transfers will not in general equal income minus the net transfer (gross transfer minus taxes paid). For example, households can respond through their labor supply (recall box 1.4) or private transfers may respond. Either way (whether using income or consumption), we may end up having to model behavior to properly assess the incidence and targeting of public spending.

Some of these issues have implications for survey design. Since many of the rural poor face marked seasonality, income over a whole year will better reflect living standards for agricultural households than over one quarter say. However, interviewee recall is imperfect, and can rarely be relied upon to span the frequency of income variation. Thus, consumption will often be a better guide, as discussed above. Careful survey design can also enhance precision in estimating consumption. Better estimates can generally be obtained by adapting the period of recall to the frequency at which the type of good is purchased; recall for one week may be fine for food, while a three-month period is probably more appropriate for clothing, say. With panel data one can enhance precision in estimating typical living standards by averaging the multiple consumption or income observations over time.[26]

Measurement Errors in Surveys

Systematic errors in the incomes or expenditures reported in surveys have important implications for measures of poverty and inequality based on those surveys.[27] Classical measurement error in the reported incomes of sampled households leads to overestimation of standard inequality measures.[28]

Two types of measurement error are identified by survey statisticians. The first is "item nonresponse." This can occur when some of the sampled households who agree to participate refuse to answer specific questions, such as on certain components of their incomes, which can be sensitive. Missing values are also likely for dwelling rents when the responded owns the dwelling; even when surveys ask for an imputed rent, this is often unknown. Various imputation/matching methods address item nonresponse by exploiting the questions that are in fact answered, although this does not appear to be done as often as it should be in practice. Box 3.13 explains how this can be done in more detail.

---

* Box 3.13 **Regression as a Tool for Dealing with Missing Data**

The essential idea here is to statistically model the observed responses to the question for which data are missing and use that model to predict the missing responses. That can be done using a regression model; recall from box 1.19 that this gives the predicted value of a dependent variable (Y) as a linear function of one or more explanatory variables (X). The dependent variable is the response when it was given and the predictor variables are things that were answered by a larger sample, including those who did not respond.

Suppose we have a full sample of N households but only a subset of $M(< N)$ of them responded to the income questions. Let the set of income responders be IR. We have K variables that everyone responded to. Then we can imagine running a linear regression on the M observations with complete data:

$$Y_i = \alpha + \beta_1 X_{1i} + \beta_2 X_{2i} + \ldots + + \beta_K X_{Ki} + \varepsilon_i \text{ for all } i \text{ in the set } IR.$$

---

[26] See, e.g., Ashenfelter et al. (1986), Ravallion (1988a), Lanjouw and Stern (1991), Chaudhuri and Ravallion (1994).

[27] There is a large literature but some important contributions include Van Praag et al. (1983), Chakravarty and Eichhorn (1994), Cowell and Victoria-Feser (1996), and Chesher and Schluter (2002).

[28] A classical measurement error has zero-mean and is uncorrelated with the true value of that variable. In some applications of the concept, it is also uncorrelated with other relevant variables. For further discussion in the context of inequality measurement, see Chakravarty and Eichhorn (1994).

Here Y_i is the income response, X_{ki} is the kth explanatory variable, $k = 1, \ldots, K < M - 1$ and ε_i is the error term, which can include errors in the reported incomes. For example, when the missing data are the dwelling rentals (invariably missing for owner-occupiers), then the X's should include all the dwelling and location characteristics available in the survey. Such a regression for imputing rents is often called a "hedonic regression." The parameters $\alpha, \beta_1, \beta_2, \ldots, \beta_K$ are fixed numbers across the sample. The values of these parameters can be estimated by the method of Ordinary Least Squares (OLS), which chooses the estimates to give the best possible fit to the data—specifically to minimize the sum of the squared errors. We can then use the predicted values for the rest of the sample, not in the set IR, using the data we have on the X's for those observations (and the estimated parameters based on the above model) in forming the predicted values.

An alternative to a regression is to use matching methods. These do not require a (potentially restrictive) parametric regression model of the missing variable. Instead, for each missing value one finds the most similar observation for which a response was recorded, where "similar" is defined by the predicted probability of responding (often called the "propensity score," following Rosenbaum and Rubin 1983).

Further reading: On regression models in general, see Wooldridge (2013). See Little and Rubin (1987) for more on imputation methods. The use of matching methods in this context is an instance of their general application to problems of missing data, which includes the problem of impact evaluation; we return to this topic in chapter 6.

Such methods are not an option for the second type of measurement error, namely "unit nonresponse." Typically there is some proportion of sampled households that does not participate in a survey, either because they explicitly refuse to do so or nobody is at home (box 3.6). Some surveys make efforts to avoid unit non-response, using "call-backs" to non-responding households and fees paid to those who agree to be interviewed (though recall box 3.8).[29] Nonetheless, the problem is practically unavoidable and non-response rates of 10% or higher are common; indeed, there are national surveys for which 30% of those sampled did not comply.[30]

Under certain conditions, one can correct survey data for selective compliance after the data are collected. Anton Korinek et al. (2007) propose a method for addressing this source of bias. The idea is to use the geographic distribution of survey response rates (the proportion of the original random sample for that area that agreed to be interviewed) to infer how the probability of agreeing to be interviewed varies with

---

[29] On reducing bias using call-backs, see Deming (1953), Van Praag et al. (1983) and Groves (2006).

[30] Scott and Steele (2004) report non-response rates for eight countries, which are as high as 26%. Holt and Elliot (1991) quote a range of 15%–30% for surveys in the United Kingdom. Philipson (1997) reports a mean non-response rate of 21% for surveys by the National Opinion Research Center in the United States.

income and other covariates. Under certain conditions one can infer those probabilities, allowing for the fact that the measured incomes are biased by selective noncompliance.[31] Once one has the estimated probabilities one can re-weight the data to correct for the problem. Korinek et al. find that the probability of being interviewed falls steadily as income rises, from 95% or higher for the poorest decile to only 50% for the richest. Thus, the observations one has on rich households need to be weighted up relative to those for poor ones. The key condition for this method to work is that one has at least someone from each income level who agrees to be interviewed.[32] Box 3.14 gives a simple example of the idea.

---

* Box 3.14   Correcting for Selective Compliance in the Simple 2 x 2 Case

Statistics offices often try to correct for selective compliance (whereby certain types of people do not respond to surveys) while doing the survey. There are limits to how effectively this can be done. It is sometimes possible to correct for survey bias *ex post*, using the available data on response rates and the (potentially biased) survey statistics.

To illustrate, consider the case of two income groups and two areas, A and B with known overall survey response rates of P_A and P_B. In other words $P_A\%$ of those who were randomly sampled in area A were actually interviewed. There are two income groups, "poor" and "non-poor." Survey-based estimates are made of the proportion of people who are poor or mean income (or other stats).

Two key assumptions are made. First, it is assumed that all the poor have the same response rate (P^P) and all the non-poor have the same response rate (P^N) and that $P^P > P^N$. This is a simple *behavioral model of compliance*. Second, it is assumed that the probability of compliance does not vary between groups A and B independently of income.

That is enough to correct for the bias due to selective compliance in the sample survey. Consider first the data we have on the data on the response rates, P_A, P_B. These are the weighted means of the response rates for the poor and non-poor, with weights given by the true (but unobserved) poverty rates in areas A and B, denoted H_A and H_B, respectively. Thus we have:

$$H_A P^P + (1 - H_A)\, P^N = P_A$$
$$H_B P^P + (1 - H_B)\, P^N = P_B.$$

Next consider the estimated poverty rates in A and B, denoted $\hat{H}_A$ and $\hat{H}_B$. These are determined by the survey response rates of the poor and non-poor, as well as the true poverty rates; more precisely we have the following formulae for the observed (but potentially biased) poverty rates:

$$\frac{H_A P^P}{H_A P^P + (1 - H_A) P^N} = \hat{H}_A$$

---

[31] See Korinek et al. (2007).

[32] This is called the "common support" assumption.

$$\frac{H_B P^P}{H_B P^P + (1 - H_B)P^N} = \hat{H}_B.$$

We have four (nonlinear) equations in four unknowns. That does not guarantee that a solution exists, but it does for all practical purposes in this case. We then solve these four equations for P^P, P^N, H_A, and H_B as functions of the data on P_A, P_B, $\hat{H}_A$, and $\hat{H}_B$. In the special case in which there is no survey bias—that poor and non-poor are equally likely to respond $\left(P^P = P^N\right)$—we have $\hat{H}_A = H_A$ and $\hat{H}_A = H_A$.

For example, suppose that the estimated poverty rates are 55% and 31% and survey response rates are 66% and 58% for A and B, respectively. Then $P^P = 0.9$, $P^N = 0.5$, and the true (unbiased) poverty rates are $H_A = 40\%$ and $H_B = 20\%$. We can apply the same idea to other statistics, such as means.

Note on the literature: This simple 2 x 2 example is purely for expository purposes. Of course, in reality we have many income groups and areas. A more general estimation method is found in Korinek et al. (2007).

These errors are of special concern in the context of measuring poverty and inequality, which depends on responses to questions pertaining to incomes and expenditures and those questions can sometimes be sensitive. Some analysts have argued that misreporting of incomes in household surveys justifies scaling up the income distribution so that its mean equals GDP per capita or Private Consumption per capita in the National Accounts System (NAS).[33] We can call this the *uniform rescaling method.* This method ignores the fact that what is called "Private Consumption" in the NAS includes components of institutional consumption, as well as personal consumption, which could introduce a systematic overstatement of household welfare levels. The mismatch in what is being measured is even worse if the scaling up is to GDP per capita itself, rather than only to per capita consumption from the NAS, since GDP includes many things that are not attributable to current household incomes or expenditures. The extent of the gap between the two data sources depends on the economy. In economies with substantial subsistence agriculture and other forms of production for own consumption, it is unlikely that the national accounts system provides a more accurate portrayal of real consumption than the surveys. For example, the latter will typically include information on consumption from own production at the household level.

Income underreporting or selective compliance in surveys is a real concern in measuring poverty and inequality. However, it is unlikely that the proportionate error is constant, leaving relative inequality unchanged.[34] If richer households tend to underreport more than middle-income or poorer households, then the uniform rescaling

[33] See, for instance, Bhalla (2002) and Sala-i-Martin (2006). The series of poverty measures back to 1820 used in chapter 1 from Bourguignon and Morrisson (2002) also uses this method. However, in this case the authors had no choice, since the historical survey data were mostly long lost.
[34] See, e.g., Banerjee and Piketty (2005) and Korinek et al. (2006).

method will "over-correct" at the bottom of the distribution, leading to an underestimation of poverty incidence. It appears likely that richer households are also less likely to participate in surveys.[35] As noted, this has theoretically ambiguous implications for inequality. Evidence for the United States indicates that selective compliance entails a non-negligible underestimation of overall inequality.[36] Poverty measures are overestimated, but this bias is small in a neighborhood of the US poverty line. By contrast, assuming instead that the response rate is a constant (independent of income) substantially underestimates the poverty rate and does nothing to correct the bias in the inequality measure.

The likelihood that underreporting and selective compliance lead to an underestimation of "top incomes" in surveys has led to interest in the use of supplementary data from income tax records.[37] The methods typically employ Pareto's Law for fitting the upper tail (recall box 1.21). (The figures on the income shares of the top 1% in the United States in figure 2.4 were estimated this way.) This method also has its pros and cons. Underreporting and compliance problems are undoubtedly less severe in countries (typically rich countries) where the income tax system is well developed, but the problems remain elsewhere. The measures obtained this way need not accord well with the types of real income measures preferred when using sample survey data; in particular, the income concept in the tax records need not accord with the concept that is preferred for measuring poverty or inequality and it is often difficult to identify households from income tax records, so it is not possible to adjust for differences in family size or composition. Most important in this context, the method is better suited to correcting the upper end of the distribution in countries with well-developed income tax systems. It is less relevant for measuring poverty.

Interpersonal Comparisons of Welfare

Household size and demographic composition vary across households, as do prices. These factors generate differences in well-being at given household expenditures. There are various approaches to normalize for these differences based on demand analysis, including equivalence scales, cost-of-living indices, and equivalent income measures.[38] The basic idea of these methods of welfare measurement is to use demand patterns to reveal consumer preferences over market goods.[39] The consumer is assumed to maximize utility, and a utility metric is derived that is consistent with observed demand behavior, relating consumption to prices, incomes, household size, and demographic composition. The resulting measure of household utility will

[35] This is consistent with the findings of Korinek et al. (2007).

[36] See Korinek et al. (2006).

[37] See, e.g., Atkinson, Piketty, and Saez (2011) and Piketty (2014).

[38] There are a number of good expositions of these topics, including Deaton and Muellbauer (1980). Empirical examples can be found in, inter alia, King (1983), Apps and Savage (1989), Jorgenson and Slesnick (1989), De Borger (1989), and Ravallion and van de Walle (1991a).

[39] Though there are measures based on the distance function, or "quantity metric utility," which do not assume that markets exist; see Deaton and Muellbauer (1980) for discussion and references. However, data on preferences are still required.

typically vary positively with total household expenditures, and negatively with household size and the prices faced.

The most general formulation of this approach is the concept of "equivalent income," defined as the minimum total expenditure required for a consumer to achieve his or her actual utility level when evaluated at predetermined reference prices and demographics fixed over all households.[40] This gives an exact monetary measure of utility; indeed, it is sometimes called *money-metric utility* (MMU). Quite generally, equivalent income can be thought of as money expenditures (including the value of own production) normalized by the two *deflators*: a suitable price index (if prices vary over the domain of the poverty comparison) and an equivalence scale (since household size and composition vary). These deflators are discussed further in the next section.

There are a number of concerns that one should be aware of in all such behavioral welfare measures. A serious problem arises when access to non-market goods (environmental characteristics, public services, demographic characteristics) varies across households, as discussed in section 3.1. Consumptions of market goods only reveal preferences *conditional* on these non-market goods; they do not, in general, reveal *unconditional* preferences over both market and non-market goods. (For example, if you live in a place where there is a good quality and free public health clinic you will spend less on private health care.) A revealed set of conditional preferences over market goods may be consistent with infinitely many utility functions representing preferences over all goods (box 3.2). It is then a big step to assume that a particular utility function which can be found to support observed consumption behavior as an optimum is also the one which should be used in measuring welfare.

Household surveys of consumptions and expenditures are the most basic and widely used data for implementing consumption-based welfare indicators. A separate community survey—done at the same time as the interviews, and often by the same interviewers in the enumeration areas chosen for the survey—can provide useful supplementary data on the local prices of a range of goods and on the provision of local public services. By having the community-level data matched to the household level data one can greatly improve the accuracy and coverage of household welfare assessments.

The recall of interviewees on public services and the prices implicit in their reported quantities consumed and expenditures on various goods can also be used for these purposes. However, there are a number of issues to be aware of. Knowledge about local public services depends on usage. This can be an unreliable indicator of actual availability. Estimates of prices (often called "unit values") can be retrieved from the survey data by dividing expenditures by quantities at the level of each commodity type. This can be useful extra data, but it needs to be handled with care since richer households will tend to purchase higher quality goods within each category. Nor can prices for non-food goods be obtained this way as the data rarely allow meaningful comparisons, so only expenditures are typically obtained in surveys.

[40] See, e.g., King (1983). Blackorby and Donaldson (1987) discuss the relationship between such an equivalent income and the "welfare ratio" defined by the ratio of nominal expenditure to the poverty line, defined in turn as the minimum expenditure needed to attain the (fixed) reference welfare level.

3.3 Alternative Measures in Theory and Practice

The most common measure of individual welfare for the purpose of measuring poverty and inequality is household consumption or income normalized for differences
in household size and possibly composition, and also deflated to allow for differences
in the prices faced. This provides a valuable indicator of economic welfare—indeed, it
is clearly the best indicator currently available. However, as the above discussion has
emphasized, it also has some limitations in both theory and practice that users should
be aware of. Thankfully, other indicators are often also available that can provide useful extra information relevant to assessing individual welfare and measuring poverty
and inequality.

Real Consumption per Equivalent Single Adult

Real consumption per equivalent adult is given by total nominal expenditure on all
goods and services (including the value of consumption from own production), divided
by the two deflators identified above: a cost-of-living index (measuring differences
in the prices faced) and an equivalence scale (for differences in household size and
composition). We can write this as Y/Z, where Y is total household consumption (or
income) and Z is the combined equivalence scale and price deflator. The deflator can
be interpreted as the cost to that household of a reference level of economic welfare.
When the latter is deemed to be the level above which the household is not considered
poor, then Z is a poverty line. We return to discuss poverty lines in greater depth in
chapter 4. For now we focus on equivalence scales and price indices in general, whether
for setting a poverty line or for welfare comparisons more generally.

There is a sizable literature on these deflators.[41] From the point of view of making
sound poverty comparisons, a key point about price indices is that only under rather
special conditions is it true that a single index is appropriate for both the poor and
non-poor. In general, the index will depend on the reference standard of living chosen.
If there are no differences in *relative* prices, then one need only adjust for inflation,
though, of course, one still wants a good price index for doing so. Another case in
which only the rate of inflation matters is when there are differences in relative prices,
but the budget shares are the same across income levels.[42] This property rarely holds
empirically; recall Engel's Law (box 1.16). Boxes 3.15 and 3.16 review price indices in
greater depth.

For example, poverty comparisons for India have generally used the Consumer
Price Index for Agricultural Laborers, which is weighted more heavily in favor of
the basic wage goods consumed by the poor than (say) the Consumer Price Index.
However, this is still a Laspeyres Index in that the weights do not change over time.
There are generally better indices than this, as discussed further in box 3.16. This can
be important when there are differences in relative prices within the domain of the
poverty comparisons being made.

---

[41] On both, see Deaton and Muellbauer (1980). For more detail on price indices, also see Diewert's
(1980) survey. Also see Browning's (1992) survey of the literature on equivalence scales.

[42] This is an implication of what are termed "homothetic" preferences.

Box 3.15 **Price Indices**

The usual form of a price index is a number giving a measure of the cost of living at a specific date and place expressed as a percentage of the comparable cost for some reference date and place. For example, if the Consumer Price Index (CPI) for 2015 takes the value 125 relative to the base year 2010, then it is telling us that the overall level of prices is deemed to be 25% higher in 2015 than in 2010.

Table B3.15.1 **Example of Laspeyres Index**

Items in the Basket	Quantity in the Basket	Price in Base Year (2010)	Price in Current Year (2015)
Rice	10 kg	1.2	1.5
Shoes	1 pair	4	5
Cost of the basket		16	20

The simplest (and still common) price index is a relative measure of the cost of a fixed basket of goods in one year/place compared to another. This is called the *Laspeyres Index*. Consider the example in table B3.15.1.

To calculate the price index, one divides the cost of the basket in 2015 by its cost in 2010 giving 20/16 = 1.25. This says that prices have risen by 25% over the period.

It can be seen that there are two elements to a price index: prices of goods and the weights on those goods. The prices are usually obtained by a special-purpose price survey, which asks for market prices of specific goods, such as "coarse quality rice." It is important that the product standards are reasonably specific, to assure that one is comparing similar qualities of goods. The weights are usually based on a consumer budget survey. The CPI is typically weighted to accord with consumption patterns of middle-income families in the specific setting. This may not be appropriate for measuring poverty. (For example, middle-income families will probably have a lower budget share devoted to food than do poor families.)

Further reading: Box 3.16 goes into greater depth about price indices for those who want to learn more. A specific form of price index is the purchasing power parity (PPP) exchange rate (often normalized by the official exchange rate). This is widely used for making international comparisons of real incomes. We return to this index in chapter 7.

*Box 3.16 **More on Price Indices**

The Laspeyres Index uses weights fixed at the initial date, while the Paasche Index uses the weights for the final (typically current) date. However, the preferred consumption bundle will typically vary according to relative prices (box 3.1). Thus, the fixed-weight indices introduce a bias in measuring the cost of a reference level of utility. The bundle needs to be adjusted to allow for substitution.

There are various indices that have been proposed in the literature to allow for substitution. One such index is the Fisher Index, given by the geometric mean of the Laspeyres and Paasche indices. Another is the Törnqvist Index. The log of the Törnqvist for place or date i relative to base 0 is given by:

$$\ln T_{i0} = \sum_{j=1}^{n} \left(\frac{S_{ij} + S_{0j}}{2} \right) \ln \left(\frac{P_{ij}}{P_{0j}} \right).$$

Here there are n goods, indexed $j = 1, 2, \ldots, n$. The budget share of good j at date/place i is denoted S_{ij}, while P_{ij} is the corresponding price. The corresponding values for the base location or date are labeled "0." This is a bilateral index, in that it compares each date or place to a fixed reference. In making joint space-time comparisons the base becomes a specific date and place.

One problem that can arise is that the comparisons may not be *transitive*, meaning that the index of place C relative to the base A will not in general be the product of the index of place C relative to base B and the index of place B relative to base A. To assure transitivity one needs a multilateral index, such as the method used by the World Bank in constructing PPP exchange rates, which compares prices in each country with an artificial average country. By this method one makes bilateral comparisons between all possible pairs of countries and then one calculates the Nth root of the product of all the indices.

Another problem is that prices may well be missing for some goods and/or places. As noted in the text, the lack of spatial indices is especially worrying in developing countries. The best statistics offices collect spatial price data. But this is not yet the norm. "Short-cut" methods have been proposed such as by using the geographic differences in the food Engel curves to identify latent differences in price relatives; see, for example, Almås (2012). There are many other reasons why Engel curves may shift geographically besides cost-of-living differences, so it is unclear how reliable this method is. In what appears to be the only test of the Engel curve method to date Gibson et al. (2014) found that it performed poorly in a situation in which geographic price relatives were data (for Vietnam). (We return to the problems of using the food share as a welfare metric later in this section.)

Sometimes the prices for the stipulated goods (as described in the detailed product standards used in a good price survey) are missing, because that good is not sold locally; this is common in poor areas where only a narrow range of relatively low-quality goods are sold in local markets. It is tempting for the surveyor to replace the missing price with that of another somewhat similar good but of lower quality that is sold locally. This creates a potential bias in that lower quality goods, with correspondingly lower prices, are used in poorer places, leading the price index to underestimate the true cost of living in poor places. This has been a problem with past rounds of the International Comparison Program (ICP), although the 2005 ICP round made a special effort to avoid using such potentially biased price imputations.

Further reading: There is a good discussion of this topic in Deaton and Muellbauer (1980). The Törnqvist Index is analyzed by Diewert (1976), who shows that this is the correct index whenever the log of the consumer's cost function (the minimum cost of a given utility level at the prevailing prices) is a quadratic function of the log of prices and utility.

While it is well recognized that one should adjust for changes in the cost of living over time, the existence of geographic differences in prices is less commonly dealt with in poverty comparisons. However, such variability can be large, especially in developing countries, where transport costs are often high and there are other impediments to market integration spatially. This has obvious implications for poverty comparisons between regions or urban and rural areas (say). Failure to account for spatial differences in the cost of living can also lead to pronounced biases in aggregate poverty measures.[43] Spatial price variability can also help greatly in identifying demand parameters, as needed for estimating behaviorally consistent welfare measures (including cost-of-living indices). The main problem to be aware of is the possible heterogeneity of the goods encompassed by the usual categories in available spatial price data. This is particularly important for goods such as "housing," but even a good such as "rice" varies in quality.[44]

Households also differ in size and composition, and so a simple comparison of aggregate household consumption could be quite misleading about the well-being of individual members of a given household.[45] Most analysts now recognize this problem and use some form of normalization. For a household of any given size and demographic composition (such as one male adult, one female adult, and two children), an equivalence scale measures the number of adult males (typically) which that household is deemed to be equivalent to. (Boxes 3.17 and 3.18 go further into scales.) The key question is: "equivalent" in what sense? Ideally we would like to be confident that when total household consumption (or income) is normalized by the scale we use we

[43] For example, Bidani and Ravallion (1993) show that ignoring spatial price variability leads to a sizable overestimation of aggregate poverty measures for Indonesia.

[44] For examples of approaches to constructing spatial price indices in a developing country, see Ravallion and van de Walle (1991b) and Bidani and Ravallion (1993).

[45] Compare, e.g., Visaria's (1980) results (from various Asian surveys), when households are ranked by total expenditures with those using expenditure per person.

get a monetary measure of interpersonally comparable welfare. In other words, we want the scale to assure that two people with the same equivalent income are equally well off. Achieving this ideal in practice is another matter. This goes back to the same problem we learned about in box 3.2 concerning the difficulty in inferring welfare from observed behavior. In practice we are almost certainly going to have to make value judgments that do not draw solely on observed behavior but seem reasonable.

Box 3.17 The Speenhamland Equivalence Scale of 1795

Recall the Speenhamland poverty lines in England's Poor Laws (chapter 1). The line was only partially indexed to the price of bread. At the normal price of bread a single male adult was assured a minimum income that would enable the purchase of three loaves of bread per week. For each dependent (wife and children) he was to be assured an extra one and one-half loaves. This is a simple example of an equivalence scale. Following the Speenhamland scheme, to measure consumption (or income) per equivalent single adult we would divide it by the number of single male adults plus half the number of women and children.

Today most equivalence scales do not make a difference between the weight on an adult man and that for a woman. But children are often given lower weight than adults, on the presumption that they have lower consumption needs. Sometimes an allowance is also made for economies of scale in consumption, whereby two people (say) can live more cheaply together than apart. Collectively consumed commodities such as housing (until it gets too crowded) allow such economies of scale.

Further reading: Box 3.18 goes into greater depth on equivalence scales for readers who want to learn more.

---

* Box 3.18 A More Complete Treatment of Equivalence Scales

We can let $ES(\underline{N}, \pi)$ denote the equivalence scale, giving the number of single adults (say) deemed to be equivalent to a household with demographic characteristics represented by a vector $\underline{N}$ and a vector of scale parameters π. (Here a "vector" is just a list of things.) The demographics vector is denoted $\underline{N}$ with an underscore, while household size is simply N. The scale is taken to be normalized such that $ES(\underline{1}, \pi) = 1$, where $\underline{1}$ is the demographic vector for a household of a single male adult (i.e., $\underline{N} = (1, 0.0....0)$), although other normalizations have been used, such as two adults. An example is:

$$ES(\underline{N}, \pi) = (N_m + \alpha N_f + \beta N_c)^\theta, \tag{1}$$

where $\underline{N} = (N_m, N_f, N_c)$ in which N_m, N_f, and N_c are the numbers of male adults, female adults, and children, respectively, and $\pi = (\alpha, \beta, \theta)$ all of which are bounded below by 0 and above by 1. Here θ represents the economies of scale in consumption. For the Speenhamland lines, $\alpha = \beta = 0.5$ and $\theta = 1$. A popular special case is to set $\alpha = \beta = 1$, giving n^θ as the scale. In testing scale sensitivity, the parameters π are allowed to take multiple values, indexed by the subscript i. Also let y denote total household consumption or income. The scale is then used to normalize household consumption or income giving $Y/ES(\underline{N}, \pi)$ as the household welfare metric for measuring poverty, interpreted as the economic welfare of each household member.

A conceptually attractive rationale for setting equivalence scales is to postulate that $Y/ES(\underline{N}, \pi)$ should be a MMU, meaning that the normalized ("real") income depends only on the utility level. The MMU is obtained by evaluating the consumer's cost function (giving the minimum cost per person of reaching utility per person of U) at fixed reference demographics—and fixed prices, ignored here—for only then will it be a stable and strictly increasing function of utility.

To see what this involves more clearly, we can postulate that the consumer's cost function can be written in the form:

$$C = \varphi(U).ES(\underline{N}, \pi)/N, \qquad (2)$$

for any strictly increasing function φ, common to all individuals. To obtain the corresponding MMU we need to fix the demographics at fixed reference levels giving:

$$Y^e = \varphi(U).ES(\underline{N}^r, \pi)/N^r, \qquad (3)$$

where $\underline{N}^r$ is a fixed reference vector of demographic characteristics. Thus, Y^e is a stable strictly increasing function of utility, that is, it is an MMU. When U is the actual level of utility attained by the household U_i, the value of C is then the actual total expenditure, Y_i. On making these substitutions into equation (2) and rearranging we have the equivalent income function:

$$Y_i^e \equiv \frac{Y}{ES(\underline{N}_i, \pi)} . \frac{ES(\underline{N}^r, \pi)}{N^r} \text{ for all } i. \qquad (4)$$

Notice that, for the reference household, equivalent income is simply income per person, and this holds whatever parameters are chosen for the scale.

Further reading: There is a comprehensive discussion of equivalence scales in Deaton and Muellbauer (1980). The above approach is a slightly more general version of the formulation found in Deaton and Zaidi (2002).

The measurement choice made can matter to the lessons drawn, including our assessments of who is poor. Consider the relationship between poverty and family size. We can define the *household-size elasticity* of the welfare indicator as the percentage decrease in that indicator resulting from a given percentage increase in household size. That elasticity will often be a matter of the judgment made by the researcher or policymaker. In general, there is a critical value of this elasticity of the welfare indicator above which large families are deemed poorer, but below which it is smaller families that are deemed to be poorer.[46] So if we are considering the possibility of implementing an antipoverty policy that favors larger families (with more children), it matters what value this elasticity takes in our empirical measure. If we simply divide household consumption by household size (an elasticity of −1), then we will almost always find that larger families tend to be poorer. If (at the other extreme) we do not divide by household size, and just use total household consumption as the welfare indicator, then we will almost certainly come to the opposite conclusion. And somewhere between the two extremes there will be no correlation between poverty and household size.[47]

In the practice of assigning equivalence scales, the answer is typically based on observed consumption behavior from surveys. In essence, one looks at how household consumptions of various goods during some survey period tend to vary with household size and composition (as well as prices and total expenditures) over the cross-section of households surveyed. For example, by one common method, a demand model is constructed in which the budget share devoted to food consumption of each household is regressed on the log of total consumption per person and the numbers of persons in various demographic categories living in the household.[48] The food share is then interpreted as an inverse welfare indicator. By fixing some reference welfare level and, hence (it is assumed) food share, one can use the regression equation to calculate the difference in consumption which would be needed to exactly compensate one household for its different composition to that of another household.[49] In practice, such methods tend to assign an adult male equivalence less than one to adult females and children.

There are a number of problems with this practice. The example discussed above, based on an estimated Engel curve, assumes that different households with the same food share are equally well-off; this is difficult to justify within the welfarist paradigm.[50] (And if one is happy with that assumption, then one need not bother with estimating equivalence scales for welfare and poverty measurement—the food share itself is sufficient information.) As already noted, the welfare interpretation of observed food consumption behavior is also clouded by the fact that there will

---

[46] Recall the concept of an elasticity from box 1.16. There it was the income elasticity of demand. Here we are talking about the elasticity of the welfare indicator with respect to household size; if the indicator falls by 20% when household size increases by 25%, then the elasticity is −0.8. In the context of measuring poverty, see Lanjouw and Ravallion (1995).

[47] For further discussion of this point, see Lanjouw and Ravallion (1995).

[48] This is known as the Leser-Working form of the Engel curve; see Deaton and Muellbauer (1980).

[49] See, e.g., Lazear and Michael (1980), van der Gaag and Smolensky (1982), and Deaton and Muellbauer (1980). An alternative method is to base the estimate of child costs on the empirical effect of demographic variables on demands for "adult goods" (such as visiting a cinema); this is called the Rothbarth method; see, e.g., Deaton and Muellbauer (1980). This is thought to be more applicable in rich economies, where (as a rule) the distinction between "adult goods" and "child goods" is clearer. An application of the method to a developing country can be found in Bargain et al. (2014).

[50] For further discussion of the limitations of this approach, see Nicholson (1976), Deaton and Muellbauer (1980), and Lanjouw and Ravallion (1995).

often be multiple utility functions (indeed, infinitely many) which generate the same behavior. Relevant parameters of well-being will not then be identifiable from that behavior. Another issue is that child costs can also be financed by parents drawing on their savings rather than by reducing their current consumption, so that the effect on consumption may occur at a later date than the survey (the children may even have grown up).[51] Purely static observations of consumption and household demographics can thus be a misleading guide in forming equivalence scales.

The welfare interpretation of equivalence scales constructed from consumption behavior also depends on the view one takes about how consumption allocations are made *within* the household. The interpretation of the empirical evidence on which equivalence scales are based may be quite different if the data are assumed to be generated by an adult male dictatorship (at one extreme) rather than the maximization of a function of the well-being of all household members. Consider a model of bargaining within the household, in which intrahousehold allocations reflect the outside options of household members.[52] The equivalence scale derived from consumption behavior can then be taken to embody two distinct aspects of distribution within the household: real differences in "needs" between certain age and gender groups (possibly also associated with economies of scale in household consumption), and inequalities in outside options or "bargaining power." While the analyst and policymaker would rightly want to incorporate the first into household welfare comparisons, one would be loath to incorporate the second, as this would perpetuate and even reinforce an existing welfare inequality.

The potential policy implications of this measurement problem can be illustrated with a simple example, using the hypothetical data given in table 3.1. There are five persons, living in two households. Household A has one adult male, one adult female and two children, while B comprises a single adult male. The three poorest persons are in household A. To make the example sharper, I shall assume that this is also true when consumptions are normalized for differences in needs. The government can make a transfer to the household which is deemed to be the poorest, but it cannot observe distribution *within* any household; all the government knows is aggregate household consumption, and household composition.

Table 3.1 **Consumptions within Two Hypothetical Households**

Household	Individual Consumptions of				Household Consumptions	
	Male adult	Female adult	First child	Second child	Per person	Per equivalent male adult
A	40	20	10	10	20	40
B	30	—	—	—	30	30

[51] For an analysis of the implications of inter-temporal consumption behavior for the estimation of equivalence scales, see Pashardes (1991).

[52] For a survey of such models, see McElroy (1990). Also see Schultz (1990) and Thomas (1990).

Which of the two households, A and B, should be first to receive help? As long as at least some of it benefits women and children, the answer is clearly household "A." But to know this, you would have to know individual consumptions. In terms of household consumption per person (which is known), the answer is also A. Using this equivalence scale, which gives the same weight to all persons, at least some of the benefits will go to the three poorest persons. However, consider instead a household scale that assigns 0.5 for an adult female, and 0.25 for each child. There are thus two equivalent adult males in household A, which then has a consumption per equivalent adult male which is more than that of household B. B will receive help first, and none of it is likely to go to the poorest 60% of the population.

Of course, this is only an example, and one based on (possibly) quite extreme inequality within household A. The example, however, is adequate to demonstrate two key points: First, while observable consumption behaviors are important data, assumptions about unobservables will be required. Second, seemingly innocuous assumptions made when making inter-household comparisons of well-being in empirical work can have considerable bearing on policy choices.

Setting equivalence scales remains one of the most difficult steps in applied welfare measurement. And the choices made can matter to the policy conclusions, especially when one is talking about social policies that favor some demographic groups over others. Consider household size. The demographic profile of the poor can have implications for, *inter alia*, population policy and the targeting of transfers, such as family allowances. But whether one deems larger and younger households to be poorer than others can depend crucially on untestable assumptions made in welfare measurement. In developed countries, even poor families consume commodities with economies of scale in consumption; two can live less than twice as expensively as one.[53] In poor countries, such commodities play little part in the budgets of the poor—their consumption bundle is dominated by goods such as food and clothing for which few scale economies exist. For this reason, the developing country literature on poverty has tended to simply divide household consumption or income by household size. As a first-order approximation this is defensible, though it almost certainly understates the extent of the scale economies in consumption even for the poor. However, that is not the only consideration. Welfare measurement may also be influenced by the purpose for which a measure is used. For example, recognizing the likelihood, but unobservability, of larger intra-household inequalities in larger households, a policymaker may want to put higher weight on household size than implied by scale economies in consumption alone.

In view of the difficulties in choosing an indicator, one should know how much the choice matters. We need to test the sensitivity of measures to the assumptions made. However, testing the sensitivity of poverty measures to changes in the parameters of a welfare measure is not a straightforward matter. To understand the problem better, suppose that we want to know how the measure of poverty changes when we change the scale parameter holding other things constant. There are many examples of such tests in the literature. One recent example provided estimates of aggregate poverty

---

[53] See Lazear and Michael (1980), Nelson (1988), and Lanjouw and Ravallion (1995).

rates for the developing world allowing for scale economies in consumption and differences in expenditure needs between adults and children.[54] The study compared their measures to those based on a "per capita" scale.[55] The differences are substantial. For the developing world as a whole, the poverty rate in 2000 falls from 31% to 3%–13% depending on the scale used.

It is far from clear how to interpret such comparisons. The essential problem is that we are missing a conceptual basis for making consistent welfare comparisons across different scale parameters. To understand the sensitivity test, it should first be noted there must be a fixed point or "pivot" to anchor the comparisons. This is the specific type of household for which the choice of scale parameters does not matter. The results one gets on the sensitivity test depend crucially on what pivot one happens to choose. Mechanically recalculating the distribution of the real income per equivalent person using different scale parameters and then applying the same "per capita" poverty line only makes sense if a single adult is deemed to be the pivot. But this is an arbitrary choice and also a rather extreme case in the distribution of household types in terms of their demographics. And the choice of pivoting point can make a large difference to the degree of sensitivity one finds to differences in the scale parameters; box 3.19 goes into more detail and gives examples.

---

* Box 3.19 **Pitfalls in Testing the Sensitivity of Poverty Measures to Equivalence Scales**

Recall box 3.18 on equivalence scales. The reference is arbitrary in the MMU function and practice has varied greatly. Deaton and Zaidi (2002) recommend modal demographics and an example of that method can be found in Citro and Michael (1995) using US data. Lanjouw and Ravallion (1995) use instead the mean demographics in their data for Pakistan in 1994, implying a reference household size of 7.4. A strand of the literature has instead used a single (male) adult as the reference, setting $\underline{N}^r = \underline{1}$. Examples are found in Coulter et al. (1992), Duclos and Mercader-Prats (1999), and Batana et al. (2013).

Three remarks can be made. First, the term $ES(\underline{N}^r, \pi_i)/N^r$ in the MMU function (equation 4 in box 3.18) creates the "pivot" in the comparisons across scales; for the reference household the money metric of welfare is always income per person, independently of the scale parameters. But where should this pivot be? In testing the sensitivity of scales one can be concerned about pivoting the comparisons around either extreme in the range of household sizes. For one thing, the extremes tend to be unusual; a household of just one (male) adult is untypical, not least in developing countries, where average household size is around 5. For another, when an allowance is made for scale economies and lower child costs, larger households will tend to have lower scales and higher imputed equivalent

continued

---

[54] See Batana et al. (2013).
[55] Their specific comparison was with Chen and Ravallion (2010a).

*Box 3.19 (Continued)

incomes. Setting the reference at either extreme will arguably exaggerate sensitivity (giving a larger reduction in poverty relative to the per capita scale when the single adult is the reference and a larger increase when the largest household is chosen.)

Second, there is no reason why the choice of the pivot needs to coincide with the scale normalization. While setting $ES(\underline{1}, \pi) = 1$ is common (though not universal) practice, that does not make $\underline{N}^r = \underline{1}$ any more or less compelling as an option for the reference. Recall that the MMU function takes the general form of equation 3 in box 3.18. Any function satisfying equation 3 is a valid MMU for the assumed cost function (in equation 2 of box 3.18).

Third, the choice of reference cannot be decided by relying on some prior poverty line for a given scale. For example, the $1.25 a day line proposed by Ravallion et al. (2009) is a per capita line. Naturally, it is also the line for a single adult. But that does not mean that the single adult should be the reference in sensitivity tests. One might equally well chose 5 as the reference for the tests and observe that $6.25 a day is the total income poverty line for that household from the per capita scale. The fact that the $1.25 line has been used as the per capita line merely says that $ES(\underline{N}, \pi_i) = N$; it does not constitute any logical case for setting $\underline{N}^r = \underline{1}$.

These points matter because the choice of the reference makes a difference quantitatively. The choice of reference demographics is immaterial at a fixed π, since $ES(\underline{N}^r, \pi)/N^r$ is then simply a multiplicative constant (and the poverty line is similarly scaled). However, the choice can matter greatly when testing sensitivity to changes in π. Two examples serve to illustrate just how much this choice matters.

For the first, suppose that there are three households with incomes per capita, 1, 2, and 3, and household sizes 5, 4, and 3 (respectively). The per capita poverty line is taken to be 2, giving a poverty rate of 2/3. If one switches to the "square-root scale" (income normalized by the square root of household size) and keeps the poverty line at 2, then poverty vanishes! If instead the references are 4, 5, or 6, then the poverty rate would return to 2/3. If the reference is set at 7 or more then everyone is deemed poor. We can get anything from zero poverty to 100% in switching to this scale!

Second, consider the result reported by Batana et al. (2013) that the global poverty rate falls from 31% to 3% when one switches from the per capita scale to a square-root scale while fixing the poverty line at $1.25 a day, based on Ravallion et al. (2009). However, it would arguably be more consistent with how the $1.25 line was set to interpret it as the per capita line for a household with the demographics typical of people living in a neighborhood of the poverty line. Suppose that Batana et al. had set the reference at 5—a seemingly reasonable guess for average household size around the per capita poverty line. Then they would have had to apply a poverty line of $2.80 to their distributions of income using the square root scale $(Y/N^{0.5})$, rather than \$1.25. Such a large difference in poverty lines would have greatly attenuated their claimed sensitivity to the change in scales. Indeed, without differences in household size the gap would vanish.

Further reading: See Ravallion (2015b) for further discussion.

Without a defensible conceptual basis for setting the pivoting point, one can get any answer one likes to the question of how sensitive poverty measures are to changes in the parameters of the welfare function. So it is not clear that any useful inference can be drawn.

In looking for a seemingly defensible basis for setting the reference, one possibility is to apply the same logic that has made it compelling to measure poverty using parameters (such as those of the price index and allowances for non-food goods) that accord reasonably well with the circumstances of poor people. The idea here is that one should not use atypical parameters in assessing their welfare. That is a value judgment, but it is seemingly acceptable, and indeed widely accepted in practice. The single adult reference is very unlikely to qualify by this reasoning.

Predicted Welfare Based on Circumstances

Some researchers have replaced the household welfare indicator derived from a survey (after adjusting for cost-of-living differences when relevant) by its predicted value based on a regression of that indicator against a number of covariates, typically observed in the same survey. (By definition, actual, observed consumption equals predicted consumption plus an error term.) Box 3.13 already introduced a version of this idea in the context of dealing with missing data.

One possible interpretation of the predicted value based on reliably measured covariates is that it purges the survey-based welfare indicator of measurement error. The worry is that the predicted value also purges the welfare indicator of potentially important unobserved determinants of welfare—things that are not contained in the survey but are real factors relevant to why one household's measured welfare is higher than another's and are not adequately proxied by the covariates.

In one recently popular application of this approach, the covariates are deliberately chosen to represent the "circumstances" of a person or household that is deemed to be beyond the control of that person or household. This is motivated by the approach to measuring "inequality of opportunity" proposed by Roemer (1998) (which we heard about in section 3.1 and in box 1.8).[56] More generally, by this interpretation the predicted values contain postulated factors that are deemed (on a priori grounds) to be

---

[56] Roemer (1998) has been the leading exponent of the "circumstances-effort" distinction in measuring inequality of opportunity; also see the discussion of approaches to measurement in Roemer (2014). Empirical examples are found in Bourguignon et al. (2007), Barros et al. (2009), and Ferreira and Gignoux (2011).

more welfare relevant than the excluded variables. When measuring INOP, the aim is to isolate that share of the variance in measured welfare that is attributable to circumstances, such that the remaining variance is due to effort, and is (by this reasoning) ethically benign.

The more conceptual concerns that have been raised about this approach were noted in section 3.1. Putting these concerns aside, let us agree that we only attach welfare significance to those attributes that a person is not responsible for—her circumstances. The issue is then whether we can be reasonably confident that we have in fact isolated the share of inequality due to circumstances. One immediate concern is that the observed list of circumstances used in practice is clearly only partial, and contingent on the variables collected in surveys. Comparing two different surveys for the same country, one survey might suggest that 30% of the variance is due to circumstances while the other suggests 60% simply because the latter survey had more variables that could be used to account for differing circumstances. Yet the interpretation is very different; in the former case one concludes that 70% of the observed inequality is benign (being due to effort and so not of ethical concern) while the other survey says it is only 40%. Those circumstances that are observed are probably correlated with those that are not, casting doubt on the interpretation of the regression coefficients.

Another, possibly more worrying, concern is present. The observed circumstances may well be correlated with latent aspects of effort, including the ways in which efforts intervene in how circumstances translate into outcomes. This clouds the welfare interpretation. Box 1.19 noted the problem of omitted variables in regression analysis; here the problem arises from how latent effort interacts with circumstances to determine outcomes. If we are going to believe that these predicted values really do measure the amount of income or schooling (say) that is accountable to circumstances but not effort, then we must assume that effort is statistically ignorable—uncorrelated with circumstances. We can relax this somewhat by allowing effort to depend in part on circumstances. However, we will still be in trouble as long as there is any component of effort that is not causally determined by observed circumstances but is still correlated with them. The scope for interaction effects between effort and circumstances adds to this concern.

At the heart of the matter here is the challenge of credibly separating what is due to circumstances and what is due to effort. Those who blame poor men and women for their poverty will readily identify behaviors that they think caused poverty. "Laziness" is the favorite example given. By the opportunities approach, poor but lazy people should not be rewarded by policy. However, circumstances rarely dictate outcomes beyond any doubt. Rather, there are efforts that can be made to make up for disadvantageous initial circumstances. Those who think that poor people are often lazy will need to be convinced that the circumstances that are identified empirically are not just picking up these latent behaviors (either on their own, or interacting with circumstances). This will be a challenge if it is believed that laziness is at least in part passed down from parents to children. That will be evident in a positive correlation between own education and parental education. The son or daughter still has the freedom to choose to work harder than the parents did, and some with poorly educated parents will undoubtedly do so. However, the correlation between latent effort and parental education will remain. Ruling out this correlation is key to believing that the predicted values based on observed circumstances provide credible welfare indicators in the opportunities approach.

Food Share

Recall box 1.16 on Engel's Law that the budget share devoted to food tends to decrease with total real consumption expenditure. This observation has often been invoked to justify using the food budget share as an inverse indicator of living standards.

However, there are also a number of concerns with using the food share as a welfare indicator. The relationship between the food budget share and total consumption per person (let alone welfare) will generally differ across households. There are numerous sources of such heterogeneity, including differences in relative prices, access to certain goods (entertainment and eating out is much easier in urban areas), demographic differences, the type of work done (notably how much energy is expended), differences in the climate (the food share may have to fall in places with cold climates), and differences in preferences. These differences cast doubt on the validity of the food share as an indicator of real consumption, including as a basis for setting price indices (box 3.16). It is clearly problematic to conclude that the geographic differences in food spending at given total spending solely reflect differences in price levels, as needed for setting cost-of-living indices. Also, the income elasticity of demand for food can be very close to unity for poor households, in which case the food share can be a quite volatile indicator. (Recall box 1.16 on the income elasticity of demand.)

This is not to say that careful analysis of budget shares (including food shares) is of no use for welfare analysis. The identification problems in deriving welfare metrics solely from demand behavior (as noted in box 3.2) loom large when making interpersonal comparisons of different types of households. So one approach is to do the demand analysis and derive the corresponding welfare metrics for specific types of households. Interpersonal comparisons between these types will then need to be based on external information, such as attainments of certain functionings (notably health and nutrition) or observations about self-assessed welfare. With care in its use, budget data can still throw useful light on aspects of living standards.

Nutritional Indicators

As both terms are commonly understood, under-nutrition is a distinct concept to poverty. The difference is in the definition of the individual welfare indicator being used—nutrient intakes (notably food energy but also micronutrients) versus a broader concept of consumption, which embodies other attributes of food besides their nutritional value, and non-food consumption. Thus, in a somewhat mechanical sense, one can view under-nutrition as "food-energy poverty," and measure it in quite a similar way.[57]

---

[57] On the meaning and measurement of "nutritional status," see the useful overview in Behrman (1990).

There are arguments for and against using nutrient intakes as an indicator of well-being. As with the food share, a practical advantage in countries with high rates of inflation, or inadequate price data, is that distributional data on food-energy intakes do not need to be adjusted for inflation.[58] However, against this, nutrition only captures one aspect of well-being. Even in low-income countries, food staple consumption will have a high weight in any demand-consistent welfare indicator, but it will never have a weight of one.

Again it may be argued that consumption behavior is an incomplete guide for welfare measurement; the weight people attach to nutrient intakes may be considered "too low for their own good." However, while one can sometimes question welfarist arguments that assume that people are always the best judge of their own welfare, one should be equally suspicious of any measure of living standards that ignores consumer behavior (section 3.1).

Given the obvious uncertainties on this issue, the only sensible solution seems to be to monitor selected non-welfarist indicators, such as under-nutrition, side by side with welfarist ones. Only if the two types of measures disagree on the poverty comparison need one delve further into the issue. When one has to do so, a convincing non-welfarist assessment should identify plausible reasons why revealed preference is inconsistent with well-being. Are there reasons why consumption behavior is misguided, such as due to the intrahousehold inequalities discussed above in the context of equivalence scales? Is it an issue of imperfect information (with possible implications for education policies)? Or is it a more fundamental problem, such as irrationality (due, e.g., to cognitive dissonance) or incapacity for rational choice (such as due to simply being too young to know what is good for you, and not having someone else make a sound choice).

The above comments also apply to anthropometric measures, such as the weight-for-age or weight-for-height of children. These measures avoid the uncertainties in setting individual nutritional requirements, although similar uncertainties are found in setting anthropometric standards. Such indicators also have the advantage that they can reveal living conditions *within* the household. However, there is one further point about these measures: by some accounts (including some nutritionists) the use of child anthropometric measures to indicate nutritional need is questionable when broader concepts of well-being are invoked. For example, it has been found that seemingly satisfactory physical growth rates in children are sometimes maintained at low food-energy intake levels by not playing.[59] That is clearly a serious food-related deprivation for any child. Again, one should be wary of overly narrow conceptualizations of the meaning of individual "welfare" when making poverty comparisons.

Qualitative and Mixed Methods

Qualitative data might come as text (reporting what was said, or the researcher's direct observations), or in some form of categorical data (e.g., wealth rankings). Qualitative

---

[58] This does not mean that food-energy intakes are unaffected by inflation or changes in relative prices; but these are not things we need to worry about in *measuring* changes in under-nutrition.

[59] See Beaton (1983).

methods are diverse (with new ones appearing regularly), but they are generally sub-jective and context-specific.[60] Examples can be found in the *Participatory Poverty Assessments* (PPAs) that became popular at the World Bank in the 1990s.

To some extent the differences between qualitative and quantitative methods reflect the differences in the type of data sought. For example, sample surveys of (largely independent) individuals would clearly be of limited use for studying the social relations between people. Qualitative studies using small purposively selected samples may be very effective in revealing locally public facts about a village, say, but should clearly not be relied on for measuring poverty or inequality. There is an emerging gray area between "pure" qualitative and quantitative methods, within which one finds var-ious mixed methods that combine qualitative and quantitative research tools in often creative ways.[61]

There are also differences in philosophical foundations. The notion of "cause and effect" is a cornerstone of the quantitative tradition in poverty analysis, as manifest in innumerable efforts to quantify the welfare and poverty impacts of policies and socio-economic changes, as discussed further in Part Three.[62] This difference too is blurred in practice, and it is common to find attempts to attribute causality in qualitative work on poverty. The problems in doing so do not appear to be inherently different between the two types of methods. To identify a causal effect convincingly, qualitative work has to take on board the same standards of inferential rigor that are applied to quantitative work.[63] Otherwise the advance made in knowledge may be illusory.

Another difference sometimes mentioned concerns the objectives of social science research. Some qualitative work aims to help empower those who directly partici-pate, while there is no such tradition in quantitative work. Quantitative methods have nonetheless served a not dissimilar advocacy role at times. Indeed, as we saw in Part One, since their inception, household surveys have been used to help mobi-lize public opinion to help fight poverty. This leaves open the important question as to whether there might be a trade-off between the quality of analysis and any pre-scriptive, empowerment role it might assume; the existence of such a trade-off is sometimes evident from quantitative analyses that try to serve an advocacy role.

These observations suggest that the divide between these two schools of thought is not as deep as some debates between methodological advocates might lead one to think. The best current practice is sensibly eclectic, often using a combination of meth-ods. Nonetheless, there are some important differences to note. It has often been observed that there are discrepancies between objective survey-based assessments of poverty and perceptions on the ground based on qualitative research. This hap-pens in both self-assessments as well as assessments by trained observers in the field.

[60] Chung (2000) describes the various methods found in practice.

[61] Tashakkori and Teddlie (1998) and Shaffer (2013) give examples. Examples in development country settings can be found in Rao (1997), Hentschel (1999), Kozel and Parker (2000), and Rawlings (2000).

[62] This is in keeping with the positivist roots of the quantitative tradition in economics. By con-trast, the main (constructivist/naturalist) philosophical founders of qualitative methods often reject this notion of causation.

[63] As discussed in Holland (1986), for example. Chapter 6 returns to this topic.

To give an example of the former, while about 30% of Russian adults in a national sample survey placed themselves on the lowest two rungs of a subjective welfare ladder, only about half of these were also among the 30% of adults living in households with incomes below the poverty line.[64] People who think they are "poor" are not classified as such in conventional poverty statistics and vice versa. To give an example of the latter, one study used subjective assessments of poverty in a north Indian village, based on the observations of resident investigators over one year.[65] This involved classifying households into seven groups (very poor, poor, modest, secure, prosperous, rich, very rich) on the basis of observations and discussions with villagers over that year. The researchers found that being a landless agricultural laborer in their surveyed village is virtually a sufficient condition for being deemed "apparently poor" by their more anthropological method; 99% of such households are deemed poor by this characteristic, though this is only so for 54% when their measure of permanent income is used, based on averaging current incomes over four interviews spanning twenty-five years. It is clear that the investigators' perception of poverty is much more strongly linked to landlessness than income data suggest. One cannot rule out the possibility that the investigator holds an overly stylized characterization of poverty. For example, the poor in village India are widely assumed to be landless and underemployed. But this may be exaggerated.

Qualitative data can contain clues about peoples' welfare that cannot be found in standard quantitative sources.[66] Although economists (and some other social scientists) have traditionally shunned subjective data, there have been important exceptions. An early example is the Income Evaluation Question (IEQ).[67] The IEQ asks respondents what income they considered "very bad," "bad," "not good," "not bad," "good," "very good." The answers to the IEQ have been used by van Praag and others since to identify a utility function. A version of this method is based on the Minimum Income Question (MIQ). This asks what income is needed to "make ends meet." We will return to the application of this method in setting poverty lines in chapter 4.

A more open-ended approach has emerged which abandons the income-based metrics entirely and uses instead self-rated welfare as the welfare indicator. In a common version, people are asked to place themselves on a ladder—sometimes referred to as a Cantril ladder[68]—according to their "happiness" or "satisfaction with life as a whole."[69] This is probably too broad a concept for measuring poverty or "economic welfare"; when one says that someone is "poor" one typically does not mean that they are unhappy.

A better starting point for subjective poverty measurement is to define the rungs of the Cantril ladder along a dimension from "poor" to "rich." Examples can be found in

---

[64] See Ravallion and Lokshin (2002).

[65] See Lanjouw and Stern (1991).

[66] Shaffer (2013) surveys past efforts to use qualitative data to help validate standard metrics of welfare and poverty.

[67] See van Praag (1968).

[68] Following Cantril (1965).

[69] This has spawned a large literature in psychology, and a budding literature in economics. For a survey of the psychological literature, see Diener et al. (1999). Oswald (1997) discusses recent work in economics.

the public opinion research done by the Social Weather Station in the Philippines and the Eurobarometer.[70] The Social Weather Station asks a sample of adults whether they are "poor," "borderline," or "non-poor." The Eurobarometer asks a similar question but uses a ladder from one to seven, and identifies those who place themselves on the lowest two rungs as the poor. A number of researchers have studied the "economic welfare question" in which respondents place themselves on a ladder (nine steps is common) where on the bottom stand the poorest people, and on the highest step stand the rich.[71] This can be used to try to better understand the factors influencing individual welfare, including the discrepancies between subjective perceptions of well-being and the "objective" indicators traditionally favored by economists.

Qualitative work has also been used in a form of triangulation in making interpersonal comparisons of welfare, whereby participants and/or facilitators do welfare rankings of others. This can be thought of as a means of validating self-assessments. This has also motivated researchers to rely on observed covariates from survey data, aiming to isolate robust, systematic, covariates of self-rated welfare.[72] In principle, it is possible to also triangulate welfare assessments using focus groups formed from random samples within the primary sampling units.

While it is clearly not a feasible method for national level poverty comparisons over time (say), qualitative data can bring useful new information to the task. Economists have tended to eschew subjective and/or open-ended questions about people's well-being; oddly, while they generally think that people are the best judges of their own welfare, economists resist asking people directly how they feel. We will consider examples in the next subsection.

Self-Assessed Welfare

Widely used measures of subjective welfare (also called "subjective well-being") ask respondents to rate their "economic welfare," "satisfaction with life," or "happiness" on an ordinal scale. These measures have found enumerable applications in the psychological and social sciences and have recently become popular in economics.[73]

One of the most frequently asked questions with these data is whether money buys happiness, as economists routinely assume. At a given date, people with higher incomes tend to report that they are happier—in the sense that a higher proportion put themselves in the "very happy" group (say)—and they also tend to report higher subjective welfare in other dimensions. However, in a famous early study, Richard Easterlin (1974) argued that average happiness did not rise with economic growth in a number of countries.[74] This has come to be known as the Easterlin paradox. Easterlin

---

[70] See Mangahas (1995) and Riffault (1991), respectively.

[71] See, e.g., Ravallion and Lokshin (2002).

[72] See Ravallion and Lokshin (2002) for an example, using panel data for Russia.

[73] Reviews of the relevant economics literature can be found in Frey and Stutzer (2002), Di Tella and MacCulloch (2006), and Dolan et al. (2008). The psychological literature on subjective welfare is reviewed in Diener et al. (1999) and Furnham and Argyle (1998). An alternative approach is to ask what level of income is needed to attain a given position on a ladder, such as not being "poor." This is the "Leyden method" devised by van Praag (1968).

[74] Also see Easterlin (1995).

attributed this to relative deprivation effects on welfare, whereby happiness depends on own-income relative to the mean. Betsy Stevenson and Justin Wolfers (2008) revisited this issue and argued that the income effect on average happiness is robust across countries, within countries, and over time. The United States is a notable exception in the Stevenson and Wolfers study; for the United States it seems that there is support for the Easterlin paradox.

There are a number of concerns about the veracity of the findings from this literature. There is no commonly agreed meaning to "happiness" or "satisfaction with life." Common practice is to postulate that there is some underlying continuous variable that represents happiness and generates the categorical responses to the survey questions. A regression model is then used to infer a difference in means for this continuous variable. However, it is not widely appreciated that we can always transform that continuous variable in a way that changes its spread and so reverses the inferred rankings of average happiness.[75] No robust claim can be made that the underlying continuous distribution of happiness has a higher mean for one group than another without further restrictions on the nature of the utility function that gives the cardinal representation of happiness. And one can find no discussion of what those restrictions might be in the literature to date. So these claims about the differences in mean happiness are essentially arbitrary, with no scientific basis. All one can really know is whether one group reports more frequently than another group that it is "happy" or "very happy." For some purposes that may be enough, but the huge number of regressions for happiness and satisfaction with life found in the literature have questionable foundations.[76]

Arguably this problem is less worrying when using survey responses on perceived economic welfare, such as the economic ladder question (ELQ) in which, instead of asking about "happiness," the respondent is asked to place themselves on a ladder from "poor" to "rich."[77] Here the latent variable can be interpreted as the respondent's wealth or some other defensible money-metric of utility, with appropriate normalizations for household size and prices. While the distribution of happiness is essentially unknowable, we can more readily imagine plausible a priori restrictions on a variable such as being rich or poor that would potentially allow robust comparisons of the means based on the observed (categorical) survey responses. For example, it is much more plausible that wealth is log-normally distributed than normally distributed.

Even then, another problem looms. Different people may well have different ideas about what it means to be "poor" or "rich" (or "happy" or "satisfied" with one's life),

---

[75] This is intuitively obvious, although the point has been ignored by the (huge) literature running regressions that try to infer differences in mean happiness. A formal demonstration of the non-robustness of such comparisons can be found in Bond and Lang (2014), who discuss applications, including the Easterlin paradox.

[76] This includes the more sophisticated nonlinear estimation methods (ordered probit and ordered logit) that postulate a latent continuous variable generating the ordinal responses. For further discussion, see Bond and Lang (2014).

[77] For example, Ravallion et al. (2015) use the following version of the ladder question: "Imagine a 6-step ladder where on the bottom, the first step, stand the poorest people, and the highest step, the sixth, stand the rich. On which step are you today?"

leading them to interpret survey questions on subjective welfare differently.[78] For example, the Young Lives Project (2009) reports the comment of a six-year-old in rural Vietnam, named Duy, as saying that "We are nearly rich as we have a new cupboard, but we haven't got a washing machine." Duy clearly has a different idea of what it means to be "rich" than those in Vietnam more familiar with the living conditions of the truly rich. Survey respondents can be expected to interpret subjective questions relative to their personal frame-of-reference, which will depend on latent aspects of their own knowledge and experience. As Sen argues, why should a "grumbling rich" be judged poorer than the "contented peasant."[79]

Two applications of subjective data illustrate the problem. The first is their application in the interpersonal comparisons of welfare required for poverty measurement. Measures of "subjective poverty" are becoming common.[80] These measures tell us what proportion of survey respondents place themselves on the bottom rung (or possibly second lowest rung) of a welfare ladder from "poor" to "rich." But if the rungs of the welfare ladder are not understood the same way by different respondents, it is unclear what meaning can be attached to such measures.

The second application relates to the many studies of the covariates of subjective welfare.[81] This is another example of the idea of using predicted values that we heard about already in the context of operationalizing the idea of INOP. In now standard practice, a regression is run of the survey responses against individual and household characteristics, such as age, gender, marital status, income, education, employment status, and household demographics.[82] Such regressions offer the prospect of identifying various welfare effects and trade-offs of interest (including to policymakers) under seemingly weaker identifying assumptions than required by widely used methods that rely solely on objective circumstances, such as income or consumption. We can agree in principle that a person's economic welfare does not only depend on the household's current consumption or income, but is also influenced by the size and demographic composition of the family and characteristics such as education and employment. "Prices" are missing for these other attributes. Subjective data offer a solution for identifying the trade-offs and constricting a composite index based on the regression.

---

[78] While this discussion focuses on heterogeneity in scales, there are other concerns with survey design. For example, Conti and Pudney (2011) find that minor re-designs in questions on satisfaction of life/work led to large changes in answers, particularly for women, finding that distortions in responses influence findings with respect to correlates of women's job satisfaction. For an overview of the concerns about inferring welfare effects from subjective data, see Ravallion (2012a).

[79] See Sen (1983, 160).

[80] Examples include Mangahas (1995), Ravallion and Lokshin (2002), Carletto and Zezza (2006), and Posel and Rogan (2013).

[81] Examples include van de Stadt et al. (1985), Clark and Oswald (1994, 1996), Kapteyn et al. (1998), Oswald (1997), Winkelmann and Winkelmann (1998), Pradhan and Ravallion (2000), Ravallion and Lokshin (2001, 2002, 2010), Senik (2004), Luttmer (2005), Ferrer-i-Carbonell (2005), Bishop et al. (2006), Kingdon and Knight (2006, 2007), Fafchamps and Shilpi (2009), Knight and Gunatilaka (2010, 2012), and Posel and Rogan (2013).

[82] In some cases this is a linear regression although more often it is an "ordered probit," which allows the thresholds in the welfare space at which ordinal answers switch to be unevenly spaced, though constant across individuals.

The empirical literature on self-assessed welfare has called into question some standard economic models and their policy implications. An example is the finding from a number of papers that unemployment lowers subjective welfare at given income.[83] This is not what the standard economic model of work-leisure choice would suggest (as summarized in box 1.4), since unemployment at given income implies greater leisure, which is assumed to yield utility. The welfare cost of unemployment is seen to occur entirely through the loss of income. However, there may well be an independent disutility of unemployment that is missing from the standard model, possibly associated with the quantity constraints on choice that involuntary unemployment entails or stemming from the social status generated by employment. There is also evidence that the unemployment generates psychological distress.[84]

These are plausible conjectures, although there are other possibilities. Recall that it is unclear that robust claim can be made about the difference in average continuous happiness of one group relative to another (in this case the employed versus unemployed) based solely on ordinal responses to survey questions.[85] If one way of giving a continuous (cardinal) representation of "happiness" suggests that the unemployed are less happy, then, in general, there will exist another representation (with a different spread of values) that suggests the opposite. And there is no obvious basis for saying that one is right and the other is wrong.

Another concern is that the significant effect of unemployment in regressions for subjective welfare may well reflect latent personality traits that jointly influence both the probability of becoming unemployed and self-assessed welfare. These different interpretations of why we find that unemployment is a significant (negative) predictor of subjective well-being clearly have rather different implications of policy. If one thinks that the unemployed have lower utility at given income, then one would think rather differently about policies like unemployment compensation and income taxation.[86] However, that is less obvious if instead the effect is associated with latent psychological factors that one would probably not consider welfare relevant.

There is evidence from psychological research that intrinsic, inter-temporarily stable, personality traits systematically influence reported well-being. A meta-analysis of research in psychology identified 137 personality traits correlated with subjective well-being, grouped under five commonly used headings in psychology: "extraversion," "agreeableness," "conscientiousness," "neuroticism" or "emotional stability," and "openness to experience."[87] These psychological traits are not normally measured in standard socioeconomic surveys, as used in modeling subjective welfare. But, as we will see, their presence is of concern in using such data to assess the welfare effects of (say) unemployment.

[83] See, e.g., Clark and Oswald (1994), Theodossiou (1998), Winkelmann and Winkelmann (1998), and Ravallion and Lokshin (2001).

[84] For example, in a study of mental health in the United States, Mossakowski (2009) finds that unemployment spells for young adults are associated with higher levels of depressive symptoms.

[85] This is an instance of the more general problem discussed in Bond and Lang (2014).

[86] For example, Mirrlees (2014) points to the correlation between unemployment and subjective welfare to motivate an analysis of optimal taxation when work gives utility. Chapter 9 returns to this point.

[87] See De Nerve and Cooper (1999).

Turning to the literature in psychology, what personality traits matter? Of the 137 personality traits identified in the aforementioned meta study, the strongest correlates with subjective well-being within the five categories mentioned above are[88]: *extraversion*: "social competence"; *agreeableness*: "collective self-esteem," "fear of intimacy" (negative), "interpersonal locus of control," "social emotionality," "social interest," "social tempo," "trust"; *conscientiousness*: "desire for control," "inhibition" (negative), "plasticity"; *neuroticism*: "distress" (negative), "emotional stability," "rebellious-distrustful" (negative), "repressive defensiveness" (negative), "social anxiety" (negative), "tension" (negative); *openness to experience*: "self-confidence," "self-respect." These are sources of heterogeneity that one would want to control for in making interpersonal comparisons of welfare for most purposes; the fact that a person is inhibited, rebellious, or unconfident, would not normally constitute a case for favorable tax treatment, for example. If these psychological factors happened to be uncorrelated with the other variables of interest, then we would not need to control for them when measuring the welfare effect of unemployment, say. Explanatory power will be lower, but the latent psychological factors will not bias the results. However, it is plausible that a number of the personality traits that raise self-rated welfare are also positively correlated with income and negatively correlated with unemployment. The above list of personality traits thought to promote a feeling of well-being overlaps considerably with the desirable things human resource managers are told to look for when interviewing job candidates.[89] This makes sense, since there is evidence that happy workers are more productive in various ways.[90] For example, there is a large literature in psychology suggesting that various personality traits influence worker absenteeism.[91] Some of these traits overlap noticeably with those thought to influence subjective well-being, such as extraversion, conscientiousness, and emotional stability.[92] One can also conjecture that certain personality traits simultaneously promote happiness, but make survey respondents disinclined to say they are sick. The implication is clear. The statistically strong effect found of unemployment, for example, in regressions for subjective welfare could just be picking up these omitted personality traits.

Similar biases can arise in the estimated effects of other factors, such as income, health, and family size. For example, subjective welfare data suggest larger economies of scale in consumption than the aforementioned methods using objective data. However, the demographic effects found in cross-sectional studies (notably of household size, at given income per capita) have not been found to be robust.[93] The extent of the scale economy of household size in individual subjective welfare suggested by a number of papers in the literature may well reflect latent personality effects on the demographic characteristics of the respondent's household. The cross-sectional

---

[88] I chose personality traits with a weighted mean correlation coefficient (across samples) of 0.30 or higher; the correlation is positive unless noted otherwise.

[89] See, e.g., Darity and Goldsmith (1996).

[90] Frank (1985) reviews the evidence.

[91] Examples include Judge et al. (1997) and Salgado (1997).

[92] See De Neve and Cooper (1999).

[93] See, e.g., Ravallion and Lokshin's (2002) study for Russia using panel data.

results on this issue may well be seriously biased by a latent tendency for intrinsically happier people to have larger families.

Another concern relates to latent differences in how subjective questions are interpreted by those being interviewed. The regression estimator assumes that the thresholds—the values of the underlying welfare metric at which ordinal responses on the stipulated scales change—are constant parameters, the same for all respondents. "Scale heterogeneity" can be defined as any situation in which this assumption does not hold (i.e., that the thresholds are idiosyncratic). If there is such heterogeneity and it is correlated with the covariates in subjective welfare regressions, then biased inferences about the underlying welfare function will be drawn from the regressions found in the literature. This concern arises in addition to more familiar concerns about the possible endogeneity of regressors, which create correlations with the error term in the underlying continuous variable for subjective welfare; see the earlier discussion in this section on predicted welfare metrics.

Concerns about such systematic measurement errors in subjective questions have prompted some observers to warn against their use as dependent variables. Marianne Bertrand and Sendhil Mullainathan (2001, 70) conclude that "subjective variables cannot reasonably be used as dependent variables, given that the measurement error likely correlates in a very causal way with the explanatory variables." This dismisses a great many past and potential applications using subjective welfare questions.

But is such a negative assessment really warranted? It would be fair to say that the potential problem of systematic scale heterogeneity has received little more than passing attention in the extensive empirical literature making subjective welfare comparisons. One (otherwise thorough) survey of the findings of a large number of papers running regressions for subjective welfare did not even mention the potential for bias due to systematic differences in scales (though it did note concerns about the possible endogeneity of some regressors).[94] A seemingly widely held view is reflected in the authoritative survey paper by Bruno Frey and Alois Stutzer (2002), which notes the scope for scale heterogeneity in self-reported welfare responses but claims that this does not invalidate regression models for such data. That claim is hard to defend on a priori grounds given the aforementioned concerns about bias. It would seem premature to either ignore the problem (following the advice of Frey and Stutzer) *or* to abandon subjective poverty/welfare regressions knowing only that there is a *potential* for bias (following Bertrand and Mullainathan).

A recent strand of research has tried to throw light on the robustness of subjective welfare regressions to these various problems. One study used panel data for Russia to try to remove the effect of latent individual personality traits, which were interpreted as additive effects in their model.[95] (On panel data, recall box 3.7; chapter 8 will go into more depth into this use of panel data.) The study found that past cross-sectional studies have greatly overestimated the welfare loss from unemployment, which is probably

[94] The survey referred to is by Dolan et al. (2008). Some papers run linear regressions for the ordinal responses on subjective welfare rather than a nonlinear model (of which the Ordered Probit is the most popular option). The assumption of constant scales is explicit in the Ordered Probit, but the problem is clearly still present in the linear models.

[95] See Ravallion and Lokshin (2001).

picking up latent personality traits. Nonetheless, the researchers still find that there is a welfare loss from becoming unemployed controlling for the loss of income.

Asking survey respondents to place vignettes describing hypothetical households or situations on the same scale has been used to address concerns about scale heterogeneity in a few studies of subjective data on health status, political efficacy, and job satisfaction.[96] Following this approach, there has been interest in the potential for using vignettes to study frame-of-reference effects on subjective welfare and offered various tests for confounding effects of scale heterogeneity using data.[97]

The studies to date using vignettes have found considerable scale heterogeneity— so much so that standard subjective poverty measures cannot be trusted.[98] Box 3.20 discusses the findings further. However, on a more positive note, subjective welfare regressions that ignore scale heterogeneity still give quite similar results to those that address it. Thus, these findings suggest that scale heterogeneity is a serious concern in using raw subjective welfare and subjective poverty data. Nonetheless, it seems that one can learn something useful from using such data as dependent variables in situations in which there is no option but to assume constant scales. Thus, subjective data may be more valuable for studying the trade-offs between dimensions of welfare (especially when this includes non-market goods) than as direct welfare measures. We will return to the use of subjective data in setting poverty lines in the next chapter.

Box 3.20 **Do You Think You Are as Poor as This Family?**

Survey respondents in Tajikistan, Guatemala, and Tanzania were posed the following question: "Imagine a 6-step ladder where on the bottom, the first step, stand the poorest people, and the highest step, the sixth, stand the rich. On which step are you today?" They were then given vignettes of four stylized families. Respondents were asked to put each of these families on the same six rung scale. They were then asked again about their own welfare. The following are the vignettes for the poorest family.

Tajikistan: "Family A can only afford to eat meat on very special occasions. During the winter months, they are able to partially heat only one room of their home. They cannot afford for children to complete their secondary education because the children must work to help support the family. When the children are able to attend school, they must go in old clothing and worn shoes. There is not enough

continued

---

[96] King et al. (2004) and King and Wand (2007) designed vignettes to establish common points on the heterogeneous reference scales regarding political efficacy in China and Mexico. Kristensen and Johansson (2008) used vignettes in anchoring subjective scales for job satisfaction. Kapteyn et al. (2008) use vignettes to compare life satisfaction between respondents in the United States and the Netherlands. Bago d'Uva et al. (2008) used them for correcting self-assessed health data for reporting bias.

[97] See Beegle et al. (2012), who used data for Tajikistan. Ravallion et al. (2015) extended the analysis further using vignettes for Guatemala and Tanzania.

[98] See Beegle et al. (2012) and Ravallion et al. (2015).

Box 3.20 **(Continued)**

warm clothing for the family during cold months. The family does not own any farmland, only their household vegetable plot."

Guatemala: "Family Castillo lives in an adobe house with one room and no latrine. The house does not have electricity or running water. The family eats beans and tortillas, but is never able to afford meat, eggs."

Tanzania: "Joseph's/Josephine's family has 6 people—3 adults and 3 children— living in a mud house with the river as the main source of water. One of the children is in primary school. None of the adults are literate. The family has no land and supports itself by engaging in casual agricultural labor for a large landowner. They have one small meal a day and very rarely eat *matooke*, meat or fish. The family has no furniture and sleeps on the floor."

The study found that 14% of the Tajikistan respondents implicitly felt that they were no better off than the household described above (i.e., they put that household at or above the rung on which they put themselves). By contrast, only 7.5% put themselves on the lowest rung. So there is considerable heterogeneity in scales among the poor. For the Guatemala sample, 32% of survey respondents were no better off than the poorest vignette above. This is closer to the poverty rate of 25% based solely on the subjective welfare responses. In Tanzania 25% of the sample put their own welfare at or below that of the family above.

Further reading: Ravallion et al. (2013).

3.4 Three Principles

This chapter has emphasized that assessments of individual welfare for the purposes of measuring poverty require value judgments and that the data are invariably defi- cient in important respects. Recognizing this, three principles should, in my view, guide the measurement choices made in practice.

Principle 1: Strive to Be Absolutist in the Space of Welfare

A guiding principle is that assessments of poverty should always be absolute in the space of individual welfare. This can be seen as the foundation for any eco- nomic approach to measuring poverty. By this definition, the measurement of poverty must be consistent with a reasonably well-defined concept of individual welfare. The issue is more to do with what we mean by "welfare." There are different concep- tual approaches, although one can often find a common ground between the main schools of thought. Capabilities are arguably absolute but they are also multidimen- sional and, when trade-offs are relevant, a utility function defined on functionings is needed for evaluation. At some level of analysis, there remains an important role for consumption of privately provided goods and services as one determinant of welfare. The limitations of private consumption as the sole welfare indicator are also quite well recognized. For example, it is widely agreed that access to publicly provided goods should also be considered.

At the heart of the matter in implementing Principle 1 is the information that is brought to bear on the problem of making interpersonal comparisons of welfare for the purpose of measuring poverty. An approach that respects preferences over commodities will generally prefer a measure of *total* consumption, typically obtained by aggregating over quantities consumed using their (possibly household-specific) prices. However, there are multiple utility functions (varying with individual characteristics) that can yield the same consumption bundles at the budget-constrained maxima of those functions. The capabilities approach draws on a broader set of information related to what people can and cannot do, as the direct generators of welfare. But here too there are multiple indices consistent with that idea. Value judgments may still be needed.

In principle, one can think of an encompassing welfarist approach that is capable of allowing for a potentially wide range of factors when making interpersonal comparisons of welfare, beyond command over market goods. In theory, one can also postulate a money-metric of this broad welfare concept—this can be defined as the income that a person would need at certain fixed reference characteristics to attain her actual level of welfare, as determined by her actual income and her characteristics. External judgments will invariably be called for in implementation. The idea of capabilities can be seen as an extra source of welfare-relevant information, beyond what can be learnt from looking solely at consumption of commodities. This can help in identifying a welfare metric among the options consistent with observed consumption patterns.

Principle 2: Avoid Paternalism

This requires the analyst to respect poor people's revealed preferences. When prices exist, there is a compelling case for using them to weight observed consumptions of commodities in forming an aggregate index of welfare, though sometimes the observed prices may need adjustment to properly reflect the opportunity costs of consumption. Claims of irrationality on the part of poor people (or anyone else) are hard to prove. The claims one hears may well reflect an overly simplified idea of what people care about, or fail to recognize that people make mistakes at times, or the claims fail to allow for temporary costs of adjustment. Granted choices are not always well-informed, but nor do outsiders hold perfect information. (Chapter 10 discusses information interventions.) The burden of proof is on the paternalist. If a person chooses freely to spend some of a meager income on something that is not found on some external observer's favored list, then respect for that person demands we question that list. My prior is that the person concerned is in a better position than anyone else to know what she needs. If existing markets work reasonably well (notably that people can buy as much or as little as they want), then market prices should be used for valuation, when they exist. Absent any constraints on the quantities chosen (beyond the budget constraint), the rational consumer will equate her own valuations with relative prices.

This makes it compelling to base poverty and inequality measures on a reasonably comprehensive measure of aggregate expenditure on commodities, with an appropriate normalization for differences in prices and household size and (possibly) composition. Non-welfarist approaches typically offer little practical guidance on how multiple dimensions of welfare should be aggregated, and indeed market prices are often ignored, even when they are available.[99] This is hazardous, as it can create inconsistencies between the external observer's assessment of how the welfare of poor people has changed and what those people themselves would say. In my view, practitioners (in market economies) need to have a good reason *not* to use market prices in valuation; they may not be perfect for aggregation purposes (due to constraints on choice), but they should not be ignored.

Principle 3: Recognize Data Limitations

We have seen that revealed preferences over market goods do not provide sufficient information for making welfare comparisons between people with different characteristics. We need to draw on other data, and here the idea of capabilities has much appeal as an intermediate space between utility and commodities. Sometimes information on capabilities can usefully guide the calibration of the poverty measure, such as when it is anchored to attaining nutritional needs for normal activity levels. There will often be situations in which other information is needed, external to the poverty measure. This will often include data on access to key non-market goods, such as access to public services, and indicators of intra-household inequalities, which are unlikely to be captured in a household survey (as discussed further in the next section).

Principle 3 is not an afterthought, but is key, though it is sometimes forgotten in standard approaches to measuring poverty. We should always be aware of the limitations of the metric being used and be cautious about relying on a single indicator. A great deal can be learnt about living standards from a sufficiently comprehensive measure of the consumption of commodities. But there will be relevant aspects of well-being that are not reflected in that measure. This points to the need to supplement poverty measures based on distributions of household consumption with other indicators which (though possibly quite crude on their own) do have a better chance of picking up the omitted variables such as access to public services and intra-household inequalities.

---

[99] See, e.g., the measure of poverty in Alkire and Foster (2011) and the comments in Ravallion (2011b). Composite indices are discussed further in chapter 5.

4

Poverty Lines

Poverty lines have both descriptive and normative roles. The former is about making poverty comparisons over time and space. The latter is in formulating antipoverty policies. Even before there were poverty measures for descriptive purposes, there were attempts to define what constitutes a reasonable minimum income level to not be considered poor in specific settings for the purposes of policy. Indeed, the basic idea of such a "poverty line" is one of the oldest concepts in applied economics, going back to at least the eighteenth century, such as in the Speenhamland antipoverty policy (see chapter 1).

The economic interpretation of a poverty line is as the cost of attaining a given level of economic welfare or "standard of living" in different places or different dates. The dependence of cost-of-living (COL) indices and equivalence scales on the choice of the fixed reference standard is well understood (as we learned in chapter 3). The key thing about a poverty line is that the reference is for the minimum level of economic welfare needed to not be considered "poor." That can be determined either objectively—meaning that it is set by an observer, based on data—or subjectively, meaning that it is based on what people themselves think about what constitutes poverty in the society in question. We consider objective lines in section 4.2, and turn to subjective lines in 4.3. But first we review past debates about the idea of a poverty line.

4.1 Debates about Poverty Lines

Today almost everyone has heard of the idea of a "poverty line" and has some personal concept of what standard of living it implies. Poverty lines exist, but views differ on what it means to live at the poverty line.

One thing is agreed almost everywhere today: poverty lines are not "survival lines." It is undeniable that there exist levels of consumptions of various goods (food, clothing, and shelter) below which survival beyond short periods is threatened. However, in most societies, including some of the poorest, the notion of what constitutes "poverty" goes beyond the attainment of the absolute minimum needed for survival. The reference standard of living for defining the poverty line is almost never the lowest level of living in society.

One school of thought rejects the use of poverty lines altogether, arguing that a person with an observed standard of living ever so slightly below some "poverty line" cannot be appreciably worse off than someone slightly above it. Yet one does not have to believe that there is a jump (a discontinuity in mathematical terms) in any observable welfare indicator to justify such a line. Recall from chapter 3 that there is no escaping the need for external ethical judgments in making welfare comparisons. It is entirely defensible for an external observer to judge that there is a qualitative difference in welfare at one or more critical levels in a specific society. Poverty lines can be seen as normative social judgments, with no less validity than (say) one's inequality aversion.

It seems that almost everyone has a concept of "poverty," even if they do not see some discontinuity. Surveys invariably find that there is a unique level of income above which people in the specific society and time tend to think they are not "poor" but below which they are. This point is called the "social subjective poverty line" and it is an important concept that we will return to in section 4.3 of this chapter.

Setting an explicit poverty line can also help focus public attention and action on the situation of poor people. As we learned in chapter 1, the various poverty lines that emerged in England, the United States, and elsewhere around the turn of the twentieth century (in the work of Rowntree, Booth, Hunter, and others) helped many well-off people comprehend just how little some people had to live on, and this helped mobilize action to reduce poverty. Similarly, in modern times, anyone can fairly readily comprehend just how frugal the material level of living is of someone with less than $1 per day at their disposal. This sharply focuses attention on material deprivation. Even before it was feasible to count how many people were living below some poverty line, setting a line was seen to be a useful step in formulating concrete antipoverty policies, such as exemplified by the Speenhamland system in 1795.

Some observers have also worried about the judgments that are required in setting poverty lines.[1] Yet in this respect poverty lines are not fundamentally different to many other ideas in applied economics. Indeed, the choice of a reference bundle of goods for setting a poverty line is no more inherently arbitrary a judgment than that of setting the reference bundle of goods for the Consumer Price Index (CPI). Yet very few of those who reject the idea of a poverty line as being "arbitrary" would also reject the use of a CPI on the same grounds. More generally, in both theory and application, all measurement of welfare (including COL indices) calls for a judgment on the reference household characteristics and prices to essentially anchor the "ruler" for measurement. This can be called the "referencing problem."[2]

Another issue often debated is the extent to which poverty lines should respect the *revealed preferences* of poor people themselves. We already confronted this issue in the discussion of welfare measurement in chapter 3. On the presumption that poor families know best how to spend their scarce resources, we should focus on the aggregate resource constraints they face. In practice this means that we focus on their total income or expenditure rather than how much they spend on (say) calories. The same issue is confronted in discussing poverty lines. If poor people know best, then we would want the composition of the poverty bundle used to construct the line to accord

---

[1] For example, an undergraduate textbook on economics notes (with reference to poverty lines): "Critics argue that defining bundles of necessities is a hopeless task" (Case et al. 2012, 375).

[2] See Ravallion (2012c).

with their spending behavior. This approach rules out what can be termed *paternalistic poverty lines*. An example of the latter would be a line that added up the cost of a list of normative "basic needs" to obtain some line Z without regard to whether people with an expenditure of around Z in that same setting would split their budget similarly.

This issue becomes important when there are changes in prices. A paternalistic line does not guarantee that when people at the poverty line gain (loss) from those price changes the poverty count will fall (rise). This is because the paternalistic line does not put weight on the prices that are consistent with the weights chosen by poor families themselves.

The following discussion will focus on the main alternative methods of setting poverty lines found in practice. It is worth noting at the outset that a number of the methods reviewed here have in common the idea of anchoring the monetary poverty line to an explicit non-monetary indicator of welfare. Box 4.1 explains the commonly used regression method. In various ways, the methods are trying to introduce information on some welfare indicator into the problem of making poverty comparisons.

---

*Box 4.1 **Using a Welfare Regression to Identify the Poverty Line**

A number of the methods reviewed in this chapter can be represented in the following generic form. We have a *welfare indicator* W_i for household or person i which depends on (say) log household income, Y_i, as well as other welfare-relevant characteristics, X_{ki} $(k = 1, \ldots, K)$. Let us write this as a simple linear regression model:

$$W_i = \alpha + \beta \ln(Y_i) + \gamma_1 X_{1i} + \ldots + \gamma_K X_{Ki} + \varepsilon_i \ (i = 1, \ldots, N).$$

Here the parameter β is taken to be positive and the error term ε_i is assumed to have the usual property of zero mean given the values taken by the regressors. The literature on measuring welfare has provided a number of interpretations of W_i. It might denote the food share, nutritional status, or subjective welfare.

We now ask: How should we deflate money income to be a valid metric of expected welfare, denoted $E(W_i)$? The answer is clear: we find poverty lines that assure a fixed level of the welfare indicator. These are found by setting W_i in the above equation to a fixed reference level, $\bar{W}^z$, and then solving the following equation for the poverty line Z_i:

$$\bar{W}^z = \alpha + \beta \ln(Z_i) + \gamma_1 X_{1i} + \ldots + \gamma_K X_{Ki}.$$

The solution is:

$$\ln(Z_i) = [\bar{W}^z - \alpha - \gamma_1 X_{1i} - \ldots - \gamma_K X_{Ki}]/\beta.$$

continued

*Box 4.1 (Continued)

Now we see that deflating money income by these poverty lines will assure that we have an exact money metric of the expected value of the welfare indicator, $E(W_i)$, noting that:

$$\ln(Y_i/Z_i) = [E(W_i) - \bar{W}^z]/\beta.$$

Since $\bar{W}^z$ is a constant and assuming that $\beta > 0$ we see that $\ln(Y_i/Z_i)$ is nothing more than a rescaled version of expected welfare.

This still leaves begging the question of how $\bar{W}^z$ is set. That will still require a judgment call, although it is often easier to make that call in the "W space" than the "Y space." For example, we might look at the stipulated nutritional requirements for good health and normal activities, or we might focus on some obvious point on a subjective scale, such as "my consumption is adequate." Robustness to other choices should always be tested.

4.2 Objective Poverty Lines

A theme of this chapter's treatment of poverty lines is to view them as deflators to allow for differences in the costs of attaining a reference standard of living. The COL will typically vary across certain subgroups, such as large and small households, or those living in urban versus rural areas. Any welfare comparisons, including poverty or inequality measures, will clearly need to normalize measured nominal consumptions or incomes for these COL differences to obtain real values.[3] This is widely understood in applied economics. The distinctive thing about poverty measurement is that the normalization is anchored to a reference level of living that is needed to not be considered "poor" in a specific context. Of course, any deflator for COL differences must have some (implicit or explicit) reference, so poverty measurement is not conceptually different in this respect. What differs in practice is the type of data that are often used in deciding what that "poverty reference" should be.

Basic Needs Poverty Lines

A common approach in defining a poverty line is to start by identifying certain basic consumption needs, deemed relevant to the domain of the poverty comparison—the basic needs bundle. The most important basic need is clearly the food expenditure necessary to attain the food-energy intake required to support normal activity levels. This is then augmented by an allowance for non-food goods.

---

[3] This gives what Blackorby and Donaldson (1980, 1987) dub a "welfare ratio."

This method can be given an economic interpretation. At a theoretical level, one can think of the problem of setting a welfarist poverty line as entailing two steps. First, a reference utility level is determined, which can be thought of as the poverty line in utility space. Second, one determines the cost of reaching that utility level in a specific context, such as "rural areas of country X." In the space of nominal consumption, the poverty line is then the point on the consumer's cost function—giving the minimum expenditure needed to attain any given utility level—corresponding to that reference utility.[4] The basic needs bundle is one that attains the poverty level of utility at prevailing prices. In economic terms, this bundle must be found on the demand functions holding utility constant, as explained in box 4.2.

Box 4.2 An Economic Interpretation of the Poverty Bundle

Recall box 3.1. We can readily see how the amounts of food and clothing that are consumed vary as we move along the same indifference curve, only changing relative prices, as in figure B4.2.1.

Consider two poverty bundles, A and B, which attain the same level of utility—the reference level of utility needed to not be considered poor—but at a different relative price of food. Bundle A $\left(Q_F^{*A}, Q_C^{*A}\right)$ can be thought of as pertaining to rural areas where food is relatively cheap, while B is for urban areas. As is plain now, one poverty bundle cannot be right if relative prices differ. As long as there is substitutability (as in the indifference curve in figure B4.2.1), the poverty bundles must vary with prices.

The poverty line is the cost of the appropriate bundle. For A this is:

$$Z^A = \sum_{j=1}^{m} P_j Q_j^{*A}.$$

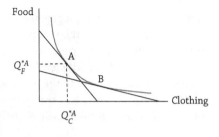

Food

Q_F^{*A}

A

B

Clothing

Q_C^{*A}

Figure B4.2.1 Poverty Bundles with Changing Relative Prices.

continued

---

[4] In more formal terms, let $c(p, x, u)$ denote the minimum cost of the utility level u for a household with characteristics x when facing prices p; then $z = c\left(p, x, u_z\right)$ is the monetary poverty line corresponding to fixed utility poverty line u_z.

Box 4.2 (Continued)

(We can write a similar equation for B.) Here the notation allows for any number of goods m goods (since the math liberates us from the constraint of a two-dimensional graph.) The Q_j^*s are called the *utility-compensated demands*. These are the quantities demanded at the poverty level of utility when facing the prices $P_1, P_2, \ldots, P_m$. (They are called "utility-compensated" because they give the consumer's demand at a given level of utility.)

When the poverty line is the above price-weighted aggregate of the utility-compensated demands, corresponding to the poverty level of utility, the line is automatically the minimum expenditure to attain that level of utility. Furthermore, if a person has an actual expenditure less than Z, then they have a level of attained utility less than the poverty level of utility.

Historical note: One of the many contributions of John Hicks to economics was the idea of the "utility-compensated demand function," found in his 1939 volume *Value and Capital*. This is sometimes called the Hicksian demand function.

However, this does not get us very far in solving the problem of setting poverty lines, but merely translates it from one space (consumption) into another (utility). For many of the purposes of measurement, the welfarist framework does not include a sufficiently well-defined notion of what poverty means. As discussed in chapter 3 (section 3.1), non-welfarist approaches to drawing poverty lines can be interpreted as attempts to expand the information base used in measuring poverty to include indicators of capabilities—the attainments of specific valued functionings, such as being adequately nourished to support normal activity levels.

Food-energy requirements for normal activity levels have been widely used in setting poverty lines. Requirements vary across individuals and over time for a given individual.[5] Nutritionists have estimated food-energy requirements for maintaining body weight at rest, processing food, and sustaining various activity levels.[6]

In using these estimates in calculating a poverty line, a normative judgment must be made about activity levels. Actual activity levels may reflect poverty. It is plausible that the poorest are underweight and that their activity levels are constrained by this fact. In such a setting, incorporating existing differences in activity levels (and, indeed, weights) into subgroup poverty lines will clearly lead to a bias in the poverty comparison, in that the poverty lines need not be clearly anchored to a reasonable conception of what would constitute a fixed standard of living over the domain of that comparison.

Having set food-energy requirements how can we find a monetary poverty line? One approach is to simply ask: what is the total expenditure (or income) of people

---

[5] For further discussion of the implications of variability in requirements for measuring undernutrition and poverty, see Osmani (1987), Kakwani (1989), and Dasgupta and Ray (1990).

[6] The classic source is WHO (1985). FAO (2001) provides an update with more detail on, *inter alia*, age-specific requirements and allowances for different activity levels.

whose average caloric intakes meet their requirements? This is the *food-energy intake* method. A second approach (and the main rival to the first method in practice) finds instead a combination of foods that attains the food-energy requirements, as well as other nutritional needs, and calculates the cost of that bundle, to give a food poverty line. This is then augmented for non-food needs. This is the *cost-of-basic needs* (CBN) method.

One approach to determining the bundle is to minimize the cost of achieving the food-energy requirements at given prices. A potential problem in practice is that this method can yield a composition of the diet that is alien to existing food habits, which are often well defined by traditions going back centuries. The minimum cost of the stipulated number of calories may be a good deal less than the expenditure level at which the poor typically attain that calorie level. Attaining adequate nutrition is neither the sole motive for human behavior, even for most of the poor; nor is it the sole motive in food consumption.

A better approach is to constrain the choice of the bundle in a way that is consistent with prevailing local food tastes. A simple numerical approach proceeds by first making a guess of the poverty rate—the percentage living below the poverty line. Let's say we guess initially that the poverty rate is 30%. The bundle of goods can then be chosen to accord with the consumption pattern of (say) people living between the 25th and 35th percentiles (or a tighter interval if the sample size permits), as estimated from a household expenditure survey. The actual consumptions of this group are then scaled up or down (keeping all relativities within the bundle the same) until they achieve the stipulated food-energy and other nutritional requirements. Prices and tastes may vary within a country; a traditional food staple in one region may be alien in another. To deal with this we can use the average consumption bundle in each region of those living between the 25th and 35th percentiles nationally. Again, this is scaled up or down to reach the nutritional norms.

Having set the food bundle, its cost should ideally be estimated separately for each of the subgroups in the poverty profile. In practice the main concern is with the variation in food prices between regions and (particularly) between urban and rural areas. It is has become fairly common for statistical agencies to monitor prices in both urban and rural areas, and using such data the food poverty line can be constructed. Armed with prices we can then calculate the food poverty line in each region, augment this with an allowance for non-food needs (using the methods discussed below) and calculate the poverty rate. If this turns out to be reasonably close to the first guess of 20% then one can stop. The job is done. However, if the initial guess is much higher or lower one can repeat the exercise at the new poverty line. Based on my experience, the method converges fairly quickly.[7]

Another approach found in practice is to rely on a local "Expert Group" to set the basic needs bundle, for both food and non-food. An example of this approach in practice is the method used to set Russia's official poverty lines, which are described in box 4.3.

---

[7] I developed this method for use in World Bank poverty assessments in the early 1990s. It has been used many times since then by me or World Bank colleagues and I have never heard of it failing to converge fairly quickly.

Box 4.3 **Russia's Poverty Lines**

Russia's official poverty lines are based on region-specific poverty baskets determined by local governments following the guidelines of an inter-ministry expert group, which also reviews the draft consumer baskets submitted by the local governments and provides recommendations to the federal government, which makes the final decision on the composition of the regional baskets. The expert group evaluates the nutritional composition of every regional basket as well as the composition of the non-food components.

Food baskets are defined based on nutritional requirements for calories, proteins, fats, and carbohydrates for various demographic groups. The baskets vary across sixteen geographical zones of Russia, to account for differences in caloric requirements by climatic zones and for regional differences in food consumption patterns. (The caloric requirements for adult males, for example, range from 3,030 kcal per day for the colder northern regions to 2,638 kcal per day for the warmer zones.) Norms for the consumption of proteins and carbohydrates can also vary substantially across zones. The final food poverty bundles comprise thirty-four items, which differ between zones. For example, northern zones include deer meat while the southern zones include larger shares of (relatively cheaper) fruits and vegetables. Food bundles for the zones with a predominantly Muslim population do not include pork.

Three zones for non-food goods and three zones for services/utility baskets are defined according to climatic conditions in Russia. The basket for non-food goods provides detailed quantities for six groups. These groups are similar to those used in the construction of the food basket, except that separate baskets for non-food goods are defined for elderly men and women. The service basket consists of consumption norms for seven main utilities. While the food and non-food baskets are defined at the individual level, the service baskets are defined on a per capita basis.

The non-food bundles consist of a number of personal items and some consumer durables. The non-food goods include specific items of clothing, footwear, pens, and notebooks. Goods for the household's collective use are also included, comprising furniture (table, chair, chest of drawers, mirror, etc.), appliances (TV, refrigerator, clocks), kitchen items (plates, pots and pans, silverware), as well as towels, sheets, blankets, and pillows. Every item in the non-food bundle has an approximate usage time that varies for different age-gender groups

The services bundle includes allowances for housing, heating, electricity, hot and cold water, gas, and transportation. (There is no allowance for health or education since by law, at least, these are free in Russia.) The norms for heating and electricity vary by zones, with larger allowances in cooler places.

Price information on the items in the poverty baskets is collected quarterly by the Russian Central Statistical Agency in 203 cities and towns of Russia for 196 food and non-food items and services. The poverty lines for every geographic zone are calculated by multiplying the quantities of the items in the baskets by the corresponding prices in an appropriate city or town within the zone.

Further reading: Russia's poverty lines were established under guidelines developed by the Ministry of Labor and Social Development (MLSD 2000). For further detail, see Ravallion and Lokshin (2006).

Instead of identifying a complete set of both food and non-food goods comprising the poverty bundle (as in the case of Russia), a more common approach in practice is to set a food bundle, and then add an allowance for non-food spending consistent with the spending patterns of those who have attained the food poverty line. These are sometimes called *Engel curve methods*. By one version of this method, one first estimates the cost for each subgroup of a food bundle which achieves the stipulated food-energy intake level, and then divides this by the share of food in total expenditure of some group of households deemed likely to be poor, such as the poorest 20% in each subgroup.

A variation on this method is that proposed for the United States by Mollie Orshansky (1965), which we already heard about in chapter 2 (box 2.5). Having set the food poverty bundle to minimize the cost of attaining the predetermined nutritional needs Orshansky then deflated this by the average food share (of poor and non-poor) to derive the total poverty line. This became the basis of the official poverty line for the United States, which remains the official line at the time of writing (in 2014). However, there has been much dissatisfaction with this line. This is hardly surprising; indeed, it is a credit to the Orshansky method that it has survived so long. Calls have been heard for updating the method to be more relevant to current standards of living and consumption patterns. There have also been calls to embrace a broader definition of income, allowing for benefits from the government. Box 4.4 summarizes the debate and proposed recent revisions.

Box 4.4 **Dissatisfaction with the Official Poverty Line for the United States and a New Measure**

Recall box 2.5. Critics of the official poverty line for the United States have pointed to a number of concerns. Fox et al. (2013, 2) summarize the issues well:

The official poverty measure (OPM) understates the extent of poverty by using thresholds that are outdated and may not adjust appropriately for the needs of different types of individuals and households, in particular, families with children and the elderly. At the same time, it overstates the extent of poverty, and understates the role of government policies, by failing to take into account several important types of government benefits . . . which are not counted in cash income. Because of these (and other failings), official poverty statistics do not depict an accurate picture of poverty or the role of government policies in combating poverty.

continued

Box 4.4 **(Continued)**

The US Census Bureau has produced a new measure that attempts to address these concerns; the new measure is called the *supplemental poverty measure* (SPM). This gives a higher overall threshold, but the income aggregate is more comprehensive, including benefits received in kind (rather than cash). The net effect turns out to imply only a slightly higher overall poverty rate, which rises to 16.0% in 2012 using the SPM, from 15.1% using the OPM. The child poverty rate is lower using the SPM, with 18.0% of children deemed to live in poverty, as compared to 22.3% using the OPM. However, the incidence of poverty rises for the elderly (14.8% as compared to 9.1%) (Short 2013).

The new measure introduces a degree of relativism into US poverty measurement, which has traditionally followed an absolute approach, whereby the line is only updated for inflation. The new measures were influenced by Citro and Michael (1995) who recommended that US poverty lines should be anchored to the current median of expenditures on food, clothing, and shelter. This would clearly generate poverty lines with a positive elasticity to the mean, but the elasticity will be less than unity given that these goods tend to be necessities. However, one concern with this approach is that it is unclear why concerns about relative poverty would apply only to necessities; one might expect social inclusion needs that go beyond necessities in a country such as the United States.

An important change is that the new methodology allows a seemingly straightforward accounting of the impact of public antipoverty programs. Without those programs, the poverty rate for 2012 would rise from 16.0% to 30.5% (Fox et al. 2013). A 14% point reduction in the poverty rate is attributed to direct interventions.

The new poverty numbers also suggest that the incidence of poverty in the United States would have risen far more in the absence of the public programs. However, the claimed poverty impact of the US programs ignores behavioral responses—the incentive effects that we heard about in box 1.4, and that have been much discussed back to at least the eighteenth century and continuing today. The calculations reported in Fox et al. subtract from the new income aggregates all receipts from the public programs and then recalculate the poverty measures. However, while we have often heard exaggerated claims about incentive effects of antipoverty programs (as noted in chapter 1), it is hard to believe that they are entirely absent. There is bound to be some displacement, such as through labor supply, at least at times and in places of low unemployment for poor men and women.

The revisions to the US poverty line are welcome, but still rather limited in capturing relative poverty, and more research is clearly needed on the impacts of public programs. Chapter 10 returns to this topic.

Further reading: Critiques of the official poverty line are found in Citro and Michael (1995) and Blank (2008). On the SPM, see Short (2011).

The Orshansky poverty line for the United States is an example of an Engel curve method in which the non-food component of the poverty line is set based on food spending behavior. Orshansky assumed a food share of one-third, so she multiplied the food poverty line by three to get the total line. Such methods do not assure that the resulting poverty lines have constant real value across the domain of the poverty comparisons being made (over space or time). Differences in the purchasing power of the resulting lines (combining food and non-food components) can emerge simply because of differences in average real consumption or income across subgroups or dates; those with a higher mean will tend to have a lower food share, which will thus lead one to use a higher poverty line. Again, an inconsistency can arise whereby a given standard of living is deemed to constitute poverty in one place but not another. With no better information, it is probably better to use a fixed food share.

There are refinements to the type of method used by Orshansky, as embodied in the official US poverty lines. With a little extra effort, one can calibrate the non-food allowance to a regression model of food demand behavior. The essential idea here is to look at how much is spent on non-food goods either by households who are just capable of reaching their nutritional requirements, but choose not to do so, or by those whose actual food spending equals the food poverty line.[8] The former allowance for non-food needs is arguably a lower bound to what should be considered reasonable; the logic here is that anything that someone who can afford to reach the food poverty line gives up for non-food goods must be considered a basic non-food good, though there may be other basic non-food goods. Of course, quite large sums might be spent by some households on non-food goods, even though their nutritional requirements are not being adequately met. One would not necessarily want to identify all such households as "poor." There will also be some variation in spending patterns at any given budget level, such as due to measurement errors or random differences in tastes. Given this heterogeneity, a more reasonable approach is to ask: what is the average value of non-food spending by a household who is either just capable of reaching the food line with their total expenditure, or whose food spending matches the food poverty line? These methods can often be implemented quite easily with readily available data. Box 4.5 describes the method in greater detail.

Box 4.5 Setting the Non-Food Poverty Line Based on the Food Demand Function

Let $C^F(C)$ denote the mean level of food spending (C^F) by a household with total spending C. This relationship is assumed to have the shape of the bold curved line in figure B4.5.1. Suppose that we have set the food poverty line, which we denote Z^F. A seemingly reasonable lower bound to the allowance for non-food needs is the spending on non-food goods by those whose total spending is just enough to cover their basic food needs, but who choose instead

continued

---

[8] Ravallion (1994b) outlined this approach, which has been widely used in developing countries.

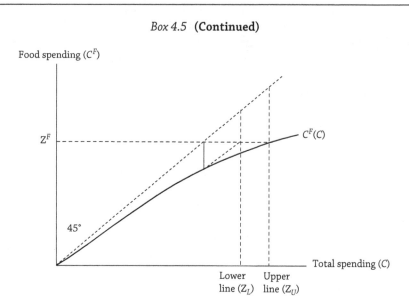

Figure B4.5.1 says: *Box 4.5* **(Continued)** at top; axes: Food spending (C^F), Total spending (C); curve $C^F(C)$; line Z^F; 45°; Lower line (Z_L), Upper line (Z_U).

Figure B4.5.1 Setting the Non-Food Component of the Poverty Line Based on Food Demand.

to divert some money to non-food needs. This is $Z^F - C^F\left(Z^F\right)$. We can then find the total poverty line by adding Z^F to this allowance for non-food needs, giving the total poverty line $Z_L = 2Z^F - C^F\left(Z^F\right)$.

Clearly this is a minimal allowance for non-food needs in that it only includes the non-food spending that displaces the stipulated basic needs for food. A more generous allowance is to look instead at the non-food spending of those whose actual food spending equals Z^F. This level of non-food spending is obtained by inverting $C^F(Z^F)$ at the point where $C = Z^F$, as in the graph above to obtain Z_U.

The fact that the upper line (Z_U.) accords with spending behavior at the poverty line is an appealing feature, assuming that people know best how to spend their income. Against this advantage, the Engel curve is likely to shift with tastes and relative prices. And there is nothing to guarantee that those shifts will be consistent with assuring the same level of welfare is attained at the different poverty lines.

Explicit consideration of the normative functionings that should be met for someone to not be considered poor can also help in setting the non-food component (recalling the discussion of the capabilities approach in chapter 3). Indeed, something like this idea is often implicit in practice. (Although "functioning" are not mentioned explicitly, such a concept appears to be implicit in the Russian poverty lines described in box 4.3.) Conceptually, one might justify the use of a higher real poverty line in urban areas than in rural areas by an appeal to the view that the capabilities to do various things (such as participating fully in the society) should be considered in measuring living standards (and hence treated as fixed in a comparison of absolute poverty). On the other hand, the commodities needed to achieve these capabilities are relative, and so vary from place to place. To see what bearing this argument might have on the setting of poverty lines, let us assume that we are concerned with two main functionings: the first is that of being adequately nourished to maintain health, while the second is that of participating fully in the society in which one lives. Both require food, to maintain a healthy weight, and to maintain the necessary activities for participating in society. This food requirement is not particularly difficult to measure, and the real food consumption level needed to reach it is unlikely to vary much between (say) urban and rural areas.

However, that is not true of the non-food component of the poverty line, and here it could plausibly be argued that achieving the same absolute living standard requires a more generous non-food commodity bundle in urban areas. For example, achieving the same capability for participating with dignity in urban society may well require that more is spent on clothes, housing, and transport than is the case in a village. This argument would generally lead one to prefer the food-share method, where the allowance for food varies little, while that for non-food varies according to the typical food share of the poor. (In the food-energy method, by contrast, even the allowance for food will tend to be a good deal higher in urban areas.) However, if we extend the list of basic capabilities somewhat, then it ceases to be clear that we would want a more generous poverty line in urban areas. For example, if we include the capability of obtaining the help of a doctor when sick, then the cost of doing so may well be very much higher in rural areas, given the far lower density of doctors there. There is a good case for setting a higher consumption poverty line in a geographic area that is deprived in access to public goods, although this is rarely done in practice.[9]

Updating Poverty Lines over Time

There are two methods found in the practice of updating poverty lines over time. In the first, the method used in the base date is simply repeated at the next date. In the second method, the old line is updated for inflation over the period using the best available price index (as in America's OPM method described in box 4.4). For some of the methods found in practice there is only one option, such as for the strongly relative lines. For the absolute lines, we have been looking at in this section using the Engel curve method the choice between these methods can be important to the results.

Putting aside data problems, if the data aim is to make strictly absolute poverty comparisons over time, then the second method is generally considered preferable. The reason is that repeating the calculations used in the base date may well introduce some differences in the real value of the poverty line associated with shifts in the Engel curve, such as shifts due to changes in relative prices or tastes.

---

[9] In the (many) developing countries where "urban bias" is severe (Lipton 1977), this should lead one to set a higher poverty line in rural areas.

There are two important caveats. First, CPIs are not always reliable for this purpose. One problem is that the standard CPI is often anchored to middle-income or urban spending patterns, which often means that it gives too low a weight on food for the purposes of updating poverty measures. It is better to use the CPI by components, especially when one has a separate food and non-food CPI. This re-weights the index to accord with spending patterns at the poverty line. In some (thankfully rare) cases the CPI data are contaminated by political manipulation.[10] A further problem is that the CPI might not adequately reflect changes in the economy. When goods that were previously provided publically without charge (or subsidized) become private goods, such as due to public-sector reforms, the prices facing consumers can rise substantially. These changes may not be reflected in the CPI.

Second, for the basic-needs lines that use the method of setting the upper poverty line discussed in box 4.5, there is an a priori argument that can be made in favor of updating over time by repeating the method used in the first date. Jean Lanjouw and Peter Lanjouw (2001) show that this updating method assures that the resulting poverty measures are robust to changes in the internal composition of the food bundles stemming from changes in the survey instrument. This robustness result is striking and makes for a compelling case for using the upper bound Engel curve method when survey comparability is a concern.

Revealed Preference Tests of Poverty Lines

Recall that an absolute poverty line in the welfare space requires a monetary line for each subgroup in the population that is the cost of a common (interpersonally comparable) level of welfare. Suppose we follow the economic approach of defining "welfare" by a utility function defined on commodities. An income poverty line is interpreted as the money metric of the minimum critical level of utility needed to not be poor, giving "utility consistency."

There are then some testable implications of the utility consistency of poverty lines, drawing on Paul Samuelson's (1938) theory of revealed preference (box 4.6). The theory can be readily used to derive testable necessary conditions for utility consistency across those groups that are deemed to share common consumption needs—a common utility function defined on commodities. All that this test requires is the set of "poverty bundles" and their prices. However, poverty lines may well reflect differing consumption needs as well as differing prices. Then the information base for testing poverty lines must be expanded; it is not sufficient to just know quantities and prices. Self-assessments of subjective economic welfare—as discussed further below—offer a promising route for testing consistency across different needs groups.

One study applied these ideas to an assessment of Russia's official poverty lines (box 4.3).[11] Russia's striking climatic differences across regions suggest that the same

---

[10] A famous example is Argentina since 2007; see *The Economist* (2013). The bias introduced in the official CPI makes a big difference to the poverty rate for Argentina; while the government's estimate of the poverty rate for the urban population is 5%, the Catholic University of Argentina calculates that the poverty rate is 27%, once one corrects for the bias in the CPI.

[11] See Ravallion and Lokshin (2006).

consumption bundle is unlikely to yield the same utility even if relative prices do not vary. (Large regions of Russia have average annual temperatures well below freezing, while other regions have moderate northern European climates.) By implication, poverty lines should have higher value (assessed by a quantity index) in colder climates. That is what was found in the data. However, the study also found violations of revealed preference criteria that cannot be easily ascribed to the sources of needs heterogeneity invoked explicitly in setting the poverty bundles. Nor do the differences across needs groups accord with self-rated perceptions of economic welfare. The researchers conclude that there are latent utility inconsistencies in Russia's official poverty lines and they speculate on their origin.

Box 4.6 Applying Samuelson's Theory of Revealed Preferences to Poverty Bundles

Consider, two groups, A and B (urban and rural areas, say), each with a poverty line, which is the cost in each group of bundles of goods specific to each group. Utility consistency requires that these two bundles yield the same utility. If needs are identical in A and B, then there is a straightforward revealed preference test. This requires that the poverty line for A is no greater than the cost of B's bundle for a member of group A, for otherwise the bundle in B is affordable when A was chosen, implying that A is preferred. But then the two bundles cannot yield the same utility (judged by the common preferences). Similarly, the group B poverty line cannot be greater than the cost in that group of the bundle for A. If this test fails, then we can reject consistency though passing the test does not assure consistency for all possible utility functions. For example, suppose again that there are just two goods, food and clothing. Four "poverty bundles" are proposed as indicated in figure B4.6.1. Utility consistency is rejected for bundles A and B; but the test is inconclusive for C or D.

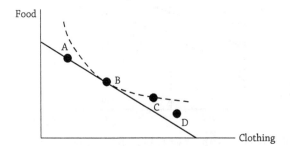

Figure B4.6.1 Revealed Preferences.

Historical note: Paul Samuelson published his clever paper on revealed preference when he was twenty-three years of age, while a student at Harvard University. He went on to be one of the most influential economists of the twentieth century.

The Food-Energy Intake Method

This method proceeds by first fixing a food-energy intake (FEI) cut-off in calories, and then finding the consumption expenditure or income level at which a person typically attains that FEI.[12] This can be estimated from a regression of calorie intake against consumption expenditures or income.[13] In essence, one is defining the poverty line as the total consumption expenditure at which one can *expect* a person to be adequately nourished in the specific society under consideration. If the average level of FEI at a given consumption expenditure is strictly increasing in consumption, and the food-energy requirement is a single (fixed) point, then this definition will yield a unique poverty line. Notice that the method automatically includes an allowance for non-food consumption, as long as one locates the *total* consumption expenditure at which a person typically attains the caloric requirement.

When the aim is to measure absolute poverty using a line with constant real value, the FEI method runs into a serious problem. The relationship between FEI and consumption expenditure (or income) is unlikely to be the same across regions/sectors/dates, but will shift according to differences in affluence, tastes, activity levels, relative prices, publicly provided goods, or other variables. This is illustrated in figure 4.1, which illustrates how the method can be used to set separate urban and rural poverty lines. The curved lines represent the mean FEI at each level of nominal "income" (or consumption per person). Food-energy expenditures tend to be higher in rural areas at given income. And there is nothing in this methodology to guarantee that these differences are the ones which would be considered relevant to poverty comparisons. For example, agricultural work tends to be more strenuous than most urban activities, and thus entails higher food-energy requirements to maintain body weight.[14] If one used a higher food-energy requirement in rural areas, one could address this problem.

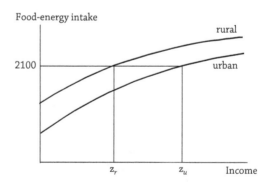

Figure 4.1 Anchoring the Poverty Lines to Food-Energy Requirements.

[12] See Osmani (1982) and Greer and Thorbecke (1986a, b) for expositions of this method. Other examples can be found in Dandekar and Rath (1971) and Paul (1989). The method has also been used by a number of governments, including Indonesia (which we return to).

[13] On the specification of such regressions, and the econometric problems that need to be considered, see Bouis and Haddad (1992).

[14] See, e.g., the estimates of caloric requirements for various activities given in WHO (1985).

There are other reasons for the shift in the "calorie-income" relationship in figure 4.1. The relative price of food tends to be higher in urban areas. Nominal food prices are typically higher to compensate for transport costs from rural areas. Also, many non-food goods are cheaper in urban areas—indeed, many such goods are often not available in the countryside. Tastes appear also to change with urbanization, in favor of non-food goods. Probably most worrying is the fact that richer households will tend to buy more expensive calories; using this method of setting poverty lines will mean that one sets a higher line in richer areas—it becomes more like relative lines than absolute lines.

As a result, one can end up making inconsistent poverty comparisons whereby individuals, who one would deem to have the same standard of living in terms of their total real consumption, are being treated differently. Indeed, comparisons of absolute poverty across regions, sectors, or dates using the FEI method may be misleading for many purposes, as explained in box 4.7.

---

*Box 4.7 Pitfalls of the FEI Method of Setting Poverty Lines

Consider two households, one with higher real consumption than the other. Which will be deemed "poorer" relative to poverty lines constructed by the FEI method? The answer is not obvious, and there can be no presumption that the poorer household will be correctly identified. To see why, let real expenditure of household i be y_i for which $y_2 > y_1$, and let $P_i^k = c_i^F / k_i$ denote the average price paid for a calorie, where c_i^F is real food expenditure by i, and k_i is the food-energy (caloric) intake, normalized by the stipulated requirement. Then $y_i = P_i^F k_i + c_i^{NF}$ where c_i^{NF} is real non-food spending. Assume that food spending increases with total spending, and that the average price of a calorie (food expenditure divided by FEI) does also $\left(P_2^k > P_1^k \right)$. Then the richer person buys more expensive sources of food energy, such as imported food-grains, or by eating in restaurants. Furthermore (for the purpose of this example), suppose that FEIs are the same for both households ($k_1 = k_2$) and that both are undernourished, that is, food-energy requirement exceeds intake ($k_i < 1$). Then the poverty gap (the deficit from the poverty line, as derived by the FEI method) must always be higher for the less poor household. To see this, note that the poverty line implied by the FEI method is $Z_i = P_i^F + c_i^{NF}$ (since $k = 1$ at the calorific requirement). Then $Z_i - y_i = P_i^F (1 - k_i)$ which is greater for the better off household. Thus, under these conditions, the poverty line will not only be higher for the better off household, but the poverty gap *falls* as the standard of living falls. The same result can also be obtained if FEI is higher for the better off household, provided that the elasticity of intake with respect to expenditure is sufficiently low; the necessary and sufficient condition is that the elasticity of FEI does not exceed the product of the income elasticity of the calorie price times the proportionate shortfall of intake from requirement.

Further reading: For further discussion of the FEI method, see Ravallion (1994b, 2012c) and Ravallion and Bidani (1994).

The problems with the FEI method of setting poverty lines were identified in a study for Indonesia.[15] Indonesia's Central Bureau of Statistics (Biro Pusat Statistik: BPS) uses a version of this method for constructing its poverty lines. It proceeds by first fixing an FEI cut-off in calories, and then finding the consumption expenditure at which a person typically attains that FEI. One then counts the number of people with expenditure less than this amount. Thus, one is estimating the number of people whose total consumption expenditures would be insufficient to attain the predetermined FEI, *given* the prevailing relationship between FEI and total consumption across the population. The method is applied separately to each sector (urban/rural) and each date. The BPS method (or variations on it) has been used in poverty studies for other countries. The Indonesian practice is not unusual.

This method has been found to generate differentials in the poverty lines between urban and rural areas that are far in excess of the COL differential.[16] The differentials over time tend also to exceed the rate of inflation. As is typically the case in developing countries, the relationship between food-energy consumption and total expenditures is very different between urban and rural areas, with higher calorific intakes at any given consumption expenditure level in rural areas. For example, as already noted, this could simply reflect a tendency for households in more affluent areas to buy more expensive calories. Differences in relative prices (food being relatively cheaper in rural areas) and tastes may also be important. For the same reasons, the relationship between calorie intake and income or consumption appears also to be shifting over time, with progressively lower FEIs at any given real expenditure level.

The difference in the food-energy and income relationship between urban and rural areas of Indonesia was so large that, at any given food-energy requirement level, the urban poverty line exceeds the rural poverty line by a magnitude which is sufficient to cause a rank reversal in the estimated headcount index of poverty between the two sectors.[17]

Clearly one wants the poverty lines used to properly reflect differences in the COL across the sectors or dates being compared. However, as discussed above, the food-energy method is quite unlikely to generate poverty lines which are constant in terms of real consumption or income across the sectors/dates being compared given that the relationship between FEI and consumption or income is not going to be the same across sectors/dates. In fact, the poverty lines generated by this method appear to behave more like relative lines; indeed, the BPS lines have been found to have an elasticity with respect to the mean that is close to unity.[18] We turn next to consider such relative lines.

Relative Poverty Lines

A difference between the literatures for developing and developed countries is that absolute poverty considerations have dominated the former, while relative poverty

[15] See Ravallion and Bidani (1994).
[16] See Ravallion and Bidani (1994).
[17] Similar findings were obtained for Bangladesh by Ravallion and Sen (1996) and Wodon (1997).
[18] See Ravallion and Bidani (1994).

has been more important in the latter.[19] Much of the developed country literature has taken the view that poverty is entirely "relative."[20] The position one takes on this issue is salient to some important development debates. In particular, as we will see in chapter 8, the extent of relativism one builds into poverty measurement matters greatly to the long-standing policy debates about economic growth and poverty.

We have seen earlier that some of the methods used to set "absolute lines" are implicitly introducing relative considerations. The lines we consider now make this explicit. The most common practice in doing so is to use some proportion of the arithmetic mean or median of the distribution of consumption or income as the poverty line; for example, many studies have used a poverty line which is set at about 50% of the national median.[21] Such poverty lines are known as "strongly" relative lines.[22] One should not be surprised to find that such lines yield quite different poverty comparisons to fixed (absolute) lines.[23] For example, the official absolute line for the United States gives a poverty rate of 15% in 2010 while if the line had been set at 50% of the median, the rate would have been 20%.[24]

Is there a compelling case for using poverty lines set at a constant proportion of the mean? Poverty measures are discussed in greater detail in chapter 5, but for now we need only note that almost all measures of poverty have the property that if one doubles (say) all incomes *and* the poverty line then the poverty measure is unchanged. So if the poverty line is set at a constant proportion of the mean, then the measure depends solely on the relative distribution of income. It might be argued that this is still a good measure of "relative poverty," to the extent that what one is really trying to capture in this concept is the amount of *inequality* in the distribution. We should, however, then ask whether or not a ranking of distributions in terms of a strongly relative measure will preserve their ranking in terms of an appropriate measure of inequality. However, as we will see in chapter 5, this is not the case in general. The details of this argument must be modified somewhat if the relative poverty line is set at a constant proportion of the median, rather than the mean.[25] The outcome will then depend on how the ratio of the median to the mean changes with increases in the mean (depending in turn on how the skewness in the distribution evolves). Nothing

[19] There are exceptions; for example, an absolute poverty line has historically been used by the US government, though see box 4.4.

[20] See, e.g., Townsend (1985), commenting on Sen (1983); also see Sen's (1985b) reply.

[21] Following Fuchs (1967); see the discussion in chapter 2. An alternative, though less common, approach is to define the poor as those who consume low amounts of certain commodities, relative to the "norm" in a particular society, as assessed by (say) the modal consumption; on this approach, see Townsend (1979) and Desai and Shah (1988).

[22] Following Ravallion and Chen (2011).

[23] See Atkinson (1991), who shows how poverty comparisons across countries in Europe are affected by this choice; there is substantial re-ranking when one compares poverty measures based on a constant proportion of each country's mean income with those obtained using the same proportion applied to a constant mean across *all* countries. For a comparison of absolute and relative poverty lines for a developing country, see Sahota (1990).

[24] These are the estimates reported in Iceland (2013).

[25] As in Fuchs (1967). This has been the practice in a number of studies, particularly for developed countries; see, e.g., the work of Smeeding et al. (1990) using the Luxembourg Income Study. For an example in a developing country, see Sahota (1990).

more can be said in general, though one certainly cannot rule out the possibility that the poverty measure may turn out to be an *increasing* function of the mean. Again, it is unclear what significance one should attach to such a measure.

Critics of strongly relative measures in which the poverty line is a *constant* proportion of the mean (or median) point out that if all incomes increase by the same proportion then the measure of poverty will be unchanged. The critics argue that this is a deceptive property. It is hard to imagine that a poor person whose income has increased by (say) 100% is not less poor. Yet that is what such measures will tell us.

Seemingly perverse poverty trends have been found using strongly relative measures. For example, one study found that relative poverty measures for Ireland were rising despite higher absolute real incomes for most of the poor.[26] Another study found that relative poverty measures for New Zealand were deceptive in showing falling poverty despite lower absolute levels of living for the poor.[27] The UNDP (2005, 334) writes, "It is clear that when economic conditions change rapidly, relative poverty measures do not always present a complete picture of the ways that economic change affects people's lives."

Starting from the position that our poverty comparisons must be absolute in the space of welfare (chapter 3, section 3.1) provides conceptual guidance on what a relative line in the income space would look like. We can suppose that a person's welfare depends on both their own income and their relative income, defined as the ratio of their own income to the income of the country they live in. We can call this the "relative-income hypothesis." We can then see why the income poverty line needed to attain a fixed level of welfare will rise with the mean; the monetary line will need to be higher to compensate for the greater relative deprivation implied by living in a richer country. However, only in the extreme case in which welfare depends on relative income alone—and not on own income at given relative income—will we get a poverty line that is a constant proportion of the mean. As long as people care about their own income, as well as relative income, the poverty line will rise with mean income but not proportionately. Box 4.8 explains this further.

Box 4.8 **The Welfarist Interpretation of a Relative Poverty Line**

The welfarist interpretation of a relative poverty line argues that poverty should be seen as absolute in the space of "welfare," rather than in the consumption or income space, and that welfare depends (positively) on both own income and relative income—own income relative to mean income in the country of residence. It follows that for a poverty line to be a money-metric of welfare it must be an increasing function of mean income.

To see this more clearly, suppose that welfare depends on "own income," Y, and "relative income," Y/M, where M is the mean for the country of residence. Under this specific form of the relative-income hypothesis, welfare is

---

[26] See UNDP (2005, box 3), based on Nolan et al. (2005).
[27] See Easton (2002).

$$W = W(Y, Y/M).$$

This is taken to be smoothly non-decreasing in both Y and Y/M. The poverty line in the income space is denoted Z and is defined implicitly by:

$$\bar{W} = W(Z,\ Z/M),$$

where $\bar{W}$ is the fixed poverty line in the welfare space.

The solution for Z is then a smoothly non-decreasing function of M. However, only in a rather special case will it be directly proportional to the mean with the same slope everywhere, as assumed in the literature on relative poverty. It is plain that the special case is when welfare does not depend on own income, so it can be written as:

$$W = V(Y/M).$$

Here V is some strictly increasing function. Again fixing welfare at $\bar{W}$ and solving for the poverty line we now have:

$$Z = k.M.$$

Here $k = V^{-1}(\bar{W})$ is the constant of proportionality in the strongly relative poverty measure.

There is another point to note: Even if we assume that people do not care about their own income at given relative income, the value of k is unlikely to be constant but will vary with other welfare-relevant factors such as the extent of inequality and how equitably public services are allocated.

The upshot of this analysis is that we can give relative poverty lines a welfarist interpretation. However, the resulting lines are not going to look like those used in the literature on the strongly relative poverty except in the seemingly unlikely limiting case in which people do not care about their own income independent of their relative income.

Further reading: For further discussion, see Ravallion (2008c, 2012b).

Recall that another justification for relative lines is found in the idea of "*social inclusion*" (chapter 3). However, this argument is also questionable. Consider the classic example of a social inclusion need found in Adam Smith's description of the role of a linen shirt in eighteenth-century Europe (chapter 1).[28] Since a socially acceptable linen shirt cannot cost any less for the poorest person (let alone cost zero in the limit), it

---

[28] In more recent times, a number of studies have also pointed to the social roles played by clothing, festivals, celebrations, and communal feasts; see, e.g., Rao (2001), Banerjee and Duflo (2008), and Milanovic (2008).

simply cannot be that the relative line is a constant proportion of the mean. The analogous commodity to a linen shirt in middle- and high-income countries today may well be a cell phone, but the point remains: it is plausible that ideas about what "poverty" means in terms of real income change as economies develop, but it is not plausible that the poverty line is a constant proportion of mean income.

How then do poverty lines vary across countries? A survey of poverty lines across ninety-five countries, both developing and industrialized, reveals that the elasticity of the poverty line with respect to mean consumption is increasing in the mean. (The results are given in box 2.5.) At the mean point of the country means the elasticity is 0.66. However, among low-income countries, the elasticity is very much lower, at about zero. Among the highly industrialized countries the elasticity is close to unity.

In short, this cross-country comparison suggests that real poverty lines tend to increase with growth, but slowly for the poorest countries. Notions of absolute poverty—whereby the poverty line does not vary with overall living standards—appear to be relevant to low income countries, while "relative poverty" is more relevant to high-income countries. Furthermore, the proportionality assumption often made in the developed country literature appears to be quite reasonable for the advanced industrialized countries, though the measure obtained is very difficult to interpret in terms of conventional concepts of inequality and poverty. The use of a constant proportion of the mean is also hard to defend conceptually (box 4.8).

A new concept of "weakly relative poverty" has emerged in recent times that contains these two extremes of absolute poverty and (strongly) relative poverty as special cases. Consistently with how national poverty lines vary across countries (as in box 2.5), the key feature of these weakly relative lines is that the elasticity of the poverty line to the mean rises from zero in the poorest countries to unity in the richest (though never reaching unity). Chapter 2 (section 2.1) had introduced this idea, and box 4.9 goes into greater detail. When used to measure poverty globally, one can interpret these lines as indicating the extent of poverty when judged by the standards typical of each country, given its average consumption level.

Box 4.9 **Absolute, Weakly Relative, and Strongly Relative Poverty Lines**

Figure B4.9.1 plots the poverty line (for a country, say, but it could be sub-national) against mean income. Both are in real units (deflated for COL differences). The absolute line is fixed. The strongly relative line is directly proportional to the mean, so it is zero at zero mean income and rises linearly. The weakly relative line of Ravallion and Chen (2011) is also marked. This is the absolute line up to some critical income level, but then rises with the mean after that. Notice that the relative component of the weakly relative line does not go to zero at zero income. Thus, it can allow for a positive minimum cost of social inclusion in the poorest countries.

To understand the properties of a strongly relative line, note first that we can write a poverty measure in the following generic form (later boxes will also make use of this equation):

$$P = P\left(M/Z, L\right),$$

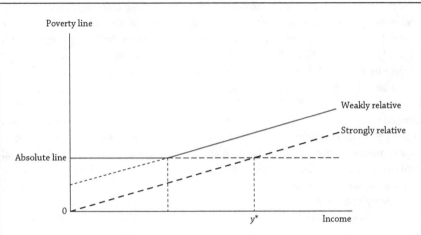

Figure B4.9.1 Relative Poverty Lines.

where Z is the poverty line, M is the mean of the distribution on which poverty is measured, and L is the Lorenz curve of that distribution (one can think of this as a vector of parameters of the Lorenz curve), which summarizes all relevant information about relative inequalities. A *strongly relative poverty line* is set at a constant proportion of the mean, $Z = k.M$, where k is some constant, such as 0.5, as often used in many European studies. The measure of poverty becomes $P(k, L)$, and depends *solely* on the Lorenz curve. If all incomes increase by the same proportion, then $P(k, L)$ would remain totally unchanged; there would be no change in relative inequalities and so $P(k, L)$ would not change. And the poverty line would simply increase by the same proportion.

Further reading: See Ravallion (2012b).

Consistency versus Specificity

For many of the purposes in making a poverty comparison—such as deciding what region or country should receive aid—the most important thing is that the poverty line yields a welfare-consistent comparison, in that the measured poverty of any person depends only on their standard of living, and not in which subgroup (such as region or ethnic group) they happen to belong. Consistency requires that the poverty line is the monetary equivalent of a fixed level of welfare. This is hard to be sure of empirically, but it is clear from the above discussion that many popular methods of setting poverty lines can rather easily fail this test. (Recall box 4.7 on the FEI method.) There are variations on these methods that are more likely to yield consistent poverty comparisons and are typically feasible with the available data. However, no method will ever be uncontentious, given the existence of immeasurable determinants of well-being. Recognizing that a certain amount of arbitrariness is unavoidable in defining any poverty line in practice, one should be particularly careful about how the choices made affect the ordinal poverty comparisons, for these are generally what matter most to the policy implications. Chapter 5 will return to this point.

Internal welfare consistency can be at odds with another seemingly sensible principle: poverty lines must be considered socially relevant in the specific context. If a proposed poverty line is widely seen as too frugal by the standards of society, then it will surely be rejected. Nor will a line that is too generous be easily accepted. We should not then be surprised that richer countries tend to use an implicitly higher reference welfare level for defining poverty. This point has long been recognized. For example, Tibor Scitovsky (1978, 116) noted that, among developed countries in the 1960s, richer countries tended to have higher poverty lines and he explained this as follows: "in the advanced countries, the poverty norm has long ago ceased to reflect a physiological minimum necessary for survival and has become instead a 'minimum social standard of decency,' the life-style that a particular society considers the minimum qualification for membership."

Scitovsky's observation does not apply only to the rich countries today, but in fact applies to all except the poorest countries. As is clear from the preceding discussion of the main methods used to set absolute lines, there are many free parameters that can be brought into the analysis to influence the line obtained. The stipulated food-energy requirements are similar across countries, but the food bundles that yield a given nutritional intake can vary enormously (such as in the share of calories from coarse starchy staples rather than more processed foodgrains, and the share from meat and fish). The non-food components also vary, either explicitly or implicitly (through shifts in the food demand functions). There are relativist gradients in both the food and non-food components of the national poverty lines for developing countries, though the elasticity with respect to mean consumption is higher for the non-food component.[29]

The judgments made in setting the various parameters of a poverty line are likely to reflect prevailing notions of what poverty means in each country. And those norms clearly go well beyond the "physiological minimum necessary for survival." The basal metabolic rate implies a positive lower bound to the cost of nutritional requirements (for all positive food prices). The cost of the (food and non-food) goods required for social needs must also be bounded below. The poverty lines found in many poor countries are certainly frugal. Consider, for example, the average daily food bundle consumed by someone living in a neighborhood of India's national poverty.[30] The daily food bundle per person comprised 400 grams of coarse rice and wheat, 200 grams of vegetables, pulses, edible seeds and fruit, plus modest amounts of milk, eggs, edible oil, spices, and tea. After buying such a food bundle, one would have been left with about $0.30 per day (at 1993 purchasing power parity) for non-food items.

Such a frugal line is clearly too low to be acceptable in middle-income (and certainly in rich) countries, where higher overall living standards naturally mean that higher standards are used for identifying the poor. Consider instead the daily food bundle used by one study for constructing Indonesia's poverty line for 1990.[31] This comprised 300 grams of rice, 100 grams of tubers and similar amounts of vegetables, fruits and spices as in the India example; but it also included fish and meat (about 140 grams in

---

[29] See Ravallion et al. (2009).

[30] These are the author's calculations, as reported in World Bank (1997). The official poverty line for India in 1993 was used.

[31] The study referred to is Bidani and Ravallion (1993).

all per day), and the overall diet was more varied and probably preferable by the tastes of most consumers.[32] This bundle would in turn be considered too frugal for defining poverty standards in many richer countries.

The position one takes on this issue depends in part on the purpose of the poverty measures. If they are intended to be purely descriptive one might opt for specificity—choosing a line that is considered appropriate in each setting, with no claims of comparability across settings. If instead one is using the poverty measures to inform policymaking, welfare consistency will often trump the merits of specificity.

However, welfare consistency only implies a constant real poverty line if we postulate that welfare depends solely on one's own consumption. As soon as we allow for social effects on welfare, such as due to perceptions of relative deprivation in richer countries or the costs of assuring social inclusion, the welfare-consistent poverty line will rise with average income. It seems unlikely that it would rise in direct proportion to average income, but it will demonstrate some gradient.

Are the weakly relative poverty lines described in box 4.9 necessarily welfare-consistent? They will be if the gradient in poverty lines across countries only reflects relative deprivation (in a welfarist model) or costs of social inclusion (in a capabilities-based model). However, that cannot be known since there is another possibility: richer countries may use higher reference levels of welfare in determining their poverty lines. One can think of this as a model of social norms determining national lines. National poverty lines with constant purchasing power can be thought of as providing a lower bound to the extent of global poverty; this lower bound is relevant if one assumes that the national lines only vary according to social norms. The weakly relative lines fitted to national lines can be interpreted as providing an upper bound, in which the national lines are assumed to reflect the costs of attaining a common level of welfare. The truth is no doubt somewhere between the two bounds.

4.3 Subjective Poverty Lines

We have seen that different countries tend to use different poverty lines, and richer countries tend to have higher lines. The same is true of individuals. One approach to setting poverty lines explicitly recognizes that poverty lines are inherently subjective judgments people make about what constitutes a socially acceptable minimum standard of living in a particular society. The challenge is how to go from this observation to derive a single poverty line.

One approach has been based on survey responses to the following *Minimum Income Question* (MIQ):[33] "What income level do you personally consider to be absolutely minimal? That is to say that with less you could not make ends meet." The answers found in survey responses tend to be an increasing function of actual income. This is a key assumption for this approach to setting poverty lines. Furthermore, the studies that have included this question have tended to find a relationship as depicted

---

[32] Vegetarians would presumably need to be compensated for the meat and fish by similarly protein-rich foods and would then prefer this version of the Indonesian bundle over the Indian bundle described above.

[33] This is paraphrased from Kapteyn et al. (1988).

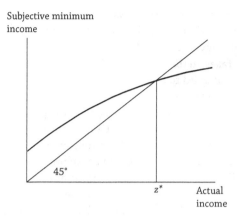

Figure 4.2 The Social Subjective Poverty Line.

in figure 4.2. The point Z^* in the figure can be called the *social subjective poverty line* (SSPL)This is an obvious candidate for a poverty line; people with income above z^* tend to feel that their income is adequate, while those below Z^* tend to feel that it is not. Thus the SSPL can claim to reflect the collective understandings of what constitutes "poverty" in the specific setting, rather than using a concept imposed from outside that setting. This approach, or variations on it, has been applied in a number of European countries.[34]

There are likely to be other factors besides income that influence the answers to the MIQ. We can think of those answers as a function of income Y and a list of other variables, given by the vector X (similarly to box 4.1). Then Z^* will also be a function of X. It is readily verified that any variable in X that shifts the curved line upward (downward) in figure 4.2 will increase (decrease) Z^*. Thus we can see, for example, how the social subjective poverty line varies with household size, demographics, or location.

Judgments are called for in deciding what variables to include in the X vector, or at least in deciding which ones should be allowed to shift the SSPL. This is a difficult but poorly understood issue. Should this include all the observable covariates of subjective welfare, or only those things that one would deem relevant to poverty lines on a priori grounds? The problem is that there are predictors of subjective welfare that are not normally considered welfare-relevant for tasks such as setting poverty lines or formulating antipoverty policies. Consider, for example, the common finding in the literature for developed economies that unemployment reduces subjective welfare at a given level of income.[35] If one included this variable in the vector X, then one would conclude that the unemployed should have a higher poverty line than the employed, *ceteris paribus*. Most other approaches to setting a poverty line would not have this feature, and objections would surely be raised; indeed, the standard economic model in which utility depends on the commodities consumed and leisure predicts

---

[34] See, e.g., Hagenaars (1987).

[35] Examples include Clark and Oswald (1994), Winkelmann and Winkelmann (1998), and Ravallion and Lokshin (2001).

that the unemployed would be better off at given income. (They would prefer not to be unemployed but in this model that would only be for the added income and hence consumption that employment allows.) As noted in chapter 3, this standard economic model may well be incomplete, as it misses important psychic costs of unemployment. Those who argue that a welfare-consistent poverty line should not be any higher for the unemployed are implicitly arguing that their concept of "welfare" should not allow for such psychic costs. This would surely be unacceptable to those who equate "welfare" with utility or happiness.

One can postulate that only a subset of the X variables that have predictive power for survey responses on subjective minimum income should be used as shift variables for the SSPL. Those variables that are left out of the SSPL might be set at sample average values, say. In this respect the SSPL approach shares common features with all the other approaches described above, namely that external value judgments about interpersonal comparisons of welfare are required. This is unavoidable. However, the SSPL approach does allow for non-market goods, and their weights (the missing prices) are determined by the data. Thus, the method narrows the range of choices for which external value judgments are required. Of course, one must still accept that subjective questions about welfare provide a sufficiently credible signal for making such choices, after one has statistically isolated that signal from the noise that also comes with such data.

In applying the MIQ in many developing countries, one will also find that "income" is not a well-defined concept, particularly (but not only) in rural areas. It is not at all clear whether one could get sensible answers to the MIQ. In work with Menno Pradhan, I proposed a method for estimating the SSPL based on qualitative data on consumption adequacy, as given by responses to appropriate survey questions.[36] Instead of asking respondents what the precise minimum consumption is that they need, one simply asks whether their current consumptions are adequate. This provides a multidimensional extension to the one-dimensional MIQ. The SSPL is the level of total spending above which respondents say (on average) that their expenditures are adequate for their needs. For empirical implementation, the probability that a sampled household will respond that its actual consumption of each type of commodity is adequate can be modeled as a nonlinear regression, called a "probit." Under certain technical conditions, a unique solution for the subjective poverty line can then be obtained from the estimated parameters of the probit regressions for consumption adequacy.

There have been some estimates of SSPLs.[37] Interestingly, the estimates to date suggest that the overall poverty rate based on the SSPL is roughly similar to that implied by objective poverty lines.[38] It may well be that the choice of parameters in

[36] See Pradhan and Ravallion (2000).

[37] I focus on application to developing countries. The applications to date include Pradhan and Ravallion (2000) using data for Jamaica and Nepal; Ferrer-i-Carbonell and Van Praag (2001), for Russia; Taddesse and Shimeles (2005), for Ethiopia; Gustafsson et al. (2004), for urban China; Lokshin et al. (2006), for Madagascar; Bishop et al. (2006), for urban China; and Carletto and Zezza (2006), for Albania.

[38] An exception to this finding is reported for the United States by de Vos and Garner (1991), where the SSPL is well above the prevailing (absolute) line, though the US line has not been updated in real

the "objective" absolute lines already approximated the expected SSPL in the specific context. However, the *structure* of the poverty profile has turned out to be different in some respects. While objective poverty lines for developing countries often imply that larger households are poorer, this is not typically the case in cross-sectional studies using the subjective approach, which tends to suggest greater economies of scale in consumption than normally assumed. For example, in using the economic ladder question (chapter 3) to test the welfare consistency of prevailing objective poverty lines for Russia, striking differences were revealed in the properties of the equivalence scale.[39] The objective poverty lines had an elasticity of 0.8 to household size, while the subjective indicator called instead for an elasticity half this size.[40]

Subjective data have thrown new light on the debate on whether poverty is absolute or relative. One finds little credible support for the idea of a relative poverty line set at a constant proportion of the current mean income. Poverty lines calibrated to subjective welfare tend to rise with mean income but with an elasticity less than unity, suggesting that they are more like the "weakly relative poverty lines" as defined by Ravallion and Chen (2011).[41]

A number of papers have reported evidence of effects on subjective welfare that can be interpreted as indicative of "relative deprivation," meaning that self-assessed well-being tends to fall as social comparators become better off, at given "own income."[42] One study reports regressions for subjective welfare in the United States that imply a particularly strong relativism, whereby own income does not matter to subjective well-being independently of income relative to the mean in the area of residence.[43] The bulk of the evidence has been for relatively rich countries. The work that has been done for developing countries has been less supportive. The tests for relative deprivation effects in self-reported happiness have found rather little support for the idea and even evidence of *positive* external effects of higher "neighbors' income," rather than the negative effect predicted by the theory of relative deprivation.[44]

terms since the 1960s; a more current absolute line for the United States would probably be closer to the SSPL.

[39] See Ravallion and Lokshin (2002).

[40] Similarly, see Pradhan and Ravallion (2000), using data for Jamaica and Nepal; Bishop and Luo (2006), using data for urban China; and Rojas (2007), using data for Mexico. For a more general discussion of economies of scale in consumption in developing countries, see Lanjouw and Ravallion (1995).

[41] Hagenaars and Van Praag (1985) estimated an elasticity of 0.51 for eight European countries. For the United States, Kilpatrick (1973) estimated an elasticity of about 0.6 for subjective poverty lines, and De Vos and Garner (1991) found an own-income elasticity of the US subjective poverty line of 0.43.

[42] See Oswald (1997), Frank (1997), Frey and Stutzer (2002) and Clark et al. (2008). Reviewing the evidence, Frey and Stutzer assert that "there is little doubt that people compare themselves to other people and do not use absolute judgments" (2002, 412). This would seem to be overstated.

[43] See Luttmer (2005).

[44] See Senik (2004), Kingdon and Knight (2007), and Ravallion and Lokshin (2010) using data for Russia, South Africa, and Malawi, respectively.

5

Poverty and Inequality Measures

To recap the story so far in Part Two: We have learned about how "economic welfare" is measured. Household command over commodities is key, although it is unlikely to be sufficient information. In calibrating welfare metrics and setting poverty lines, economists have turned to two main sources of that extra information. The first source is data on attainments of certain basic functionings, such as being adequately nourished for good health and normal activities. The second is information on self-assessments of welfare, for estimating social subjective poverty lines. While there is bound to be some arbitrariness to any poverty line (as there is in other aspects of economic and social measurement), following Bowley and others, monitoring progress in reducing the number of people living below some fixed line is a justifiable approach to measuring social progress.

Applying the various tools reviewed in chapters 3 and 4, we end up with a distribution of the measures of individual economic welfare in the relevant population. Typically, this will be a measure of total household consumption or income normalized by the household-specific poverty line, interpreted as a deflator for differences in needs (associated with differences in the size or composition of the household or in the prices faced). This chapter turns to the task of aggregating the information on the distribution of the chosen measure of economic welfare into one or more summary statistics on poverty or inequality.

Poverty and inequality measures have both descriptive and normative roles. The latter has proved to be more contentious, and it is worth reviewing the issues. So the chapter begins with a discussion of the various normative foundations that have been proposed for measurement, linking back to the discussion in Part One. This will make clear that in thinking about measuring poverty it makes sense to start with a discussion of how we measure inequality. The chapter then discusses the main measures of poverty found in practice. The chapter also reviews the various tools of analysis that have been developed. These include decompositions that can be done of an aggregate poverty measure and tests for assessing the robustness of ordinal poverty comparisons—when we only need to know whether there is greater poverty in one place or at one date than another, or with and without a policy change—to the assumptions made about poverty lines and measures. One important lesson from that discussion will be the importance of considering a range of poverty lines. This leads naturally to a discussion of the size of the "middle class," taken up later in the chapter. Measures of poverty and inequality are hardly far removed from policymaking, but there are measures that have been developed in the literature that are "hard wired" to assessing the performance of specific policies. A prominent example is the set of measures of "targeting performance," which are reviewed later in this chapter.

All of the measures described in this chapter can be calculated from your own primary data set using standard statistical packages, such as Stata, Eviews, SAS, and SPSS. Specially designed, user-friendly software products are now also available to calculate the various measures and tests in this chapter; good examples are *DAD* and the poverty module of *ADePT*.[1]

5.1 Normative Foundations

Recall that in classical utilitarianism (as formulated by Bentham and Mill, as discussed in chapter 1) the yardstick for social progress and policy evaluation is the arithmetic sum of utilities. This still penalizes income inequality, assuming diminishing marginal utility of income (box 1.13). In fact, we can quite generally think of a measure of income inequality as the loss of aggregate social welfare associated with that inequality.

For expository purposes, consider the following highly stylized case. Everyone has the same utility function, which depends solely on each person's own real income. To sharpen the analysis further, suppose that this common utility function is simply the log of income. Suppose also that we can attain any distribution of a fixed total income we like by transfers. (This ignores incentive effects, which we heard about in Part One and we will return to in Part Three.) Since everyone is taken to have the same utility function, the utilitarian social welfare objective is maximized when everyone has the same income.

In this stylized set-up, any inequality of income entails a loss of social welfare. The aggregate social welfare is the maximum social welfare less the loss attributable to inequality. And the implied measure of inequality is one of those we will consider in detail later (in box 5.4), namely the *Mean-Log Deviation* (MLD). Thus, we have a clear (albeit highly simplified) ethical foundation for how we should go about measuring inequality in practice. In a similar fashion, an important paper by Anthony Atkinson (1970) showed how one can derive a broad class of normatively grounded inequality measures for a more general utility function for which the log of income is a special case.

One objection that can be raised is that lower levels of welfare should get higher weight; we do not just care about income inequality in society, we also care about inequality of individual welfare levels. Another way of thinking about this is that we want our measure of inequality to reflect our ethical aversion to poverty. But how should we incorporate an aversion to inequality of welfare? The literature has not helped much in addressing this question. In principle one way of answering the question is to postulate a generalized version of the utilitarian schema. Instead of insisting that social welfare equally weights individual welfare levels, we can postulate

---

[1] There are also useful guidebooks on using standard software programs; see Duclos and Araar (2006) (using DAD), Haughton and Khandker (2009) (using Stata), and Foster et al. (2013) (using ADePT).

a *social welfare function* (SWF) that puts decreasing weight on higher levels. (We will give an example in the next section.)

Following this approach, if we insist on the strong form of the Pareto principle (as discussed in chapter 1), then we would demand that all weights are positive. But one can relax this to allow a weaker requirement that all weights are non-negative. This allows the possibility that the weight goes to zero above some point—that there is some level of individual welfare above which we put negligible social value to further gains. A poverty measure can be given a normative interpretation along these lines.[2]

Alternatively, we can follow Rawls's (1971) (non-utilitarian) proposal that our principles of justice should focus first on the poorest stratum and (consistently with the priority given to liberty) we should make social choices that do most to raise the welfare of those in that stratum. This is the "maximin" SWF (box 2.3). A poverty measure is sometimes thought of as a way of implementing this normative approach. However, there are two qualifications. First, a conventional poverty measure does not attach any explicit weight to the typical welfare level of the poorest and may even be unaffected by changes in that level. Second, notice that Rawls clearly has in mind a relative measure, in that it is specific to the context. The idea is not that we stop as soon as everyone is above some (possibly quite austere) poverty line. Rather, once that point is reached, we then move on to consider the next most disadvantaged group. At each step, we still need to identify the most disadvantaged.

Yet a further ethical motivation for poverty measures can be devised by considering inequality of opportunity. We can think of this as combining concerns for equity and efficiency. There is an equity motivation in reducing inequality of opportunity in society—to assure a more level playing field. But it comes with an efficiency consideration, namely that we do not want to reduce inequality by bringing everyone down to the level of the poorest person. Thus, we are drawn again toward some form of "maximin"—a view that policy should maximize the welfare of the most disadvantaged group in society.[3]

5.2 Measuring Inequality

Most people have a reasonably clear idea about the difference between "poverty" and "inequality." As these terms are normally defined, poverty is about *absolute levels of living*—how many people cannot afford certain pre-determined consumption needs. "Poverty" can be said to exist in a given society when one or more persons do not attain a level of economic well-being deemed to constitute a reasonable minimum by the standards of that society. Inequality is about the *disparities in levels of living*; for example, how much more is held by rich people than poor people. This section reviews the strengths and weaknesses of some common measures of inequality.

In applied work, economists typically measure inequality by looking at the *ratios* of individual incomes to the overall mean. By this approach, the measure of inequality is unchanged if all incomes increase at the same proportionate rate. (As noted in

[2] On this approach, see Ravallion (1994a).
[3] This is argued by Roemer (1998, 2014).

box 1.8, that is not the only defensible concept of inequality; we return to this point.) A useful graphical tool for measuring inequality is the *Lorenz curve*, giving the share of total income held by the poorest p percentage of the population, ranked by household income per capita (or per equivalent single adult). Box 5.1 goes into further detail on the Lorenz curve.

Box 5.1 The Lorenz Curve, Gini Index and Distribution Function

The Lorenz curve gives (on the vertical axis) the share of total income held by (on the horizontal axis) the poorest p percentage of the population, when ranked by income (figure B5.1.1). The curve is rising throughout, with increasing slope, as shown by the bold curved line in figure B5.1.1. The 45 degree line represents perfect equality; everyone has the mean real income, $\bar{y}$. (It is now assumed that nominal income or consumption has been normalized by a price index and equivalence scale to give "real income" denoted by the lower case y.) Intuitively, the more the Lorenz curve bends out the more inequality. If the richest person has all of the income, then the Lorenz curve is the entire area below the diagonal.

The Gini index is twice the gray-shaded area in figure B5.1.1. This is equal to half the average absolute difference between all pairs of incomes in the population, expressed as a proportion of the mean. The index lies within the interval [0,1]. When everyone has the mean income and this is positive, then the Gini index is at its lower bound of 0. When the richest person has all the income, the Gini index approaches its upper bound of 1 as the population size rises.

The Lorenz curve is related to the *cumulative distribution function* (CDF), $p = F(y)$, giving the proportion of the population with income no greater than y. The slope of the CDF is called the density function, giving the proportion of the population with income y. If we invert the CDF (flipping the axes) we obtain the *quantile function* $y(p)$. (For example, $y(0.5)$ is the median.) Then the slope of the Lorenz curve at point p gives the quantile function normalized by the mean $y(p)/\bar{y}$, where $\bar{y}$ is the mean.

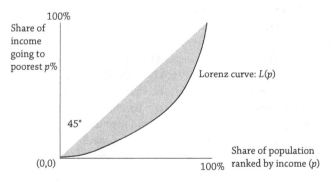

Figure B5.1.1 Lorenz Curve.

Historical note: Max Lorenz was an American economist who developed the idea of the Lorenz curve (as it came to be known) in 1905, at the age of twenty-nine, while studying for his PhD at the University of Wisconsin–Madison. Corrado Gini was an Italian statistician who developed his famous index of inequality in 1912. Gini's paper was published in Italian. Hugh Dalton (1920) drew the attention of English-speaking readers to Gini's measure and its relationship to the Lorenz curve.

A simple inequality measure is the gap between the richest and poorest person. But that is surely too simple, as it ignores everyone else. We would do better to take an average of all the gaps. If we divide the average gap between all pairs of incomes by twice the mean, then we will have an index that lies between 0 (everyone has the mean, so there is no inequality) and an extreme upper limit of unity (the richest person has all the income in a population of infinite size). This is the most famous inequality index, the *Gini index*.[4] The Gini index also has a simple relationship with the Lorenz curve (boxes 5.1 and 5.2).

The Gini index is one of a number of measures that have been proposed that satisfy what is often called the *transfer axiom* (also called the transfer principle) as explained in box 5.3, which also discusses other desirable properties of a measure of inequality. The transfer axiom can be a powerful property for assessing whether inequality has increased or not without specifying what specific measure of inequality is being used. If Lorenz curve A lies entirely above that for B (only touching each other at the two limits) then inequality is unambiguously lower for A than B for any measure satisfying the transfer axiom, including the Gini index.[5]

---

*Box 5.2 **More on the Gini Index***

We have a distribution of real income, $y_1, y_2, \ldots, y_n$, with mean $\bar{y}$. The absolute gap between the income of person i and that of person j is $|y_i - y_j|$. Imagine forming the *mean absolute gap* (Δ) over all the n^2 pairs of incomes. One would obtain:

$$\Delta = \frac{1}{n^2} \sum_{i=1}^{n} \sum_{j=1}^{n} |y_i - y_j|.$$

(Notice that the double Σ is needed because we calculate the absolute gaps between all pairs of incomes.) The Gini index, designated G, is then obtained

continued

---

[4] For example, the US Census Bureau estimates that the Gini index for 2009 is 0.469. Mean annual household income per capita is $28,051 (averaged over 2008–2012). So the implied mean income gap between people is $26,312.

[5] See Atkinson (1970) for a proof of this claim.

*Box 5.2 (Continued)

by simply normalizing Δ to assure that its maximum value, when the richest person has all of the income $(n\bar{y})$, does not exceed unity. It is readily verified that this requires that $G = \Delta/(2\bar{y})$. When the richest person has all of the income, the upper bound of the index is $1 - (1/n)$. This reaches unity in the limit, as n goes to infinity.

Further reading: A now classic treatment of the Gini index is found in Sen (1973). A more technical exposition is found in Sen (1976b). Also see the update to Sen (1973) by Foster and Sen (1997).

Box 5.3 **Desirable Properties of an Inequality Measure**

The *transfer axiom* says that if one transfers a given sum of money from person A to a poorer (richer) person B without changing their ranking then inequality must fall (rise); clearly, the Lorenz curve will shift upward (downward) at least somewhere. This axiom makes a lot of sense, and it has been widely accepted. Most of the inequality measures found in practice (including the Gini index described in box 5.2) satisfy this axiom, although there are some that do not, including the variance of the log of income and the ratio of the mean to the median.

Consider the following change in distribution. Initially, in state A, the income levels (in dollars a day, say) in a society of five people are:

A: (0, 10, 10, 10, 10);

$3 is transferred from one of those with $10 to the poorest person, creating the distribution:

B: (3, 7, 10, 10, 10).

The change satisfies the transfer axiom. This is reasonable, but we should acknowledge that objections can be raised:

- The number of pairs of people with the same income has fallen in going from state A (three such pairs) to B (two).
- Those who keep $10 may well feel the loss to one of their own more than the gain to the distant and distinct poor person with zero income.
- The number of people who may feel relatively deprived (poorer than someone else) has risen, from one to two.

Another widely accepted axiom is called *anonymity* (also called *symmetry*). Essentially this says that it does not matter who has which income level. There are no names attached to the incomes in the lists above. If we swapped the incomes of the poorest person in A with one of those with $10 we will obtain:

$$C: (10, 10, 10, 10, 0).$$

Under anonymity, the measures of inequality for A and C are identical. This too can be questioned: in the real world, the person who previously had $10 will no doubt raise an objection! Telling people that inequality has not changed may not be persuasive when there has been considerable churning of incomes, with both gains and losses.

A third axiom is called *scale invariance*. This says that multiplying all incomes by a constant does not change the inequality measure. So the following distribution has the same inequality as A:

$$D: (0, 20, 20, 20, 20).$$

This too can be questioned, given that the absolute gap between the richest and poorest person has doubled. People's judgments about inequality appear often to be inconsistent with scale independence.

A fourth axiom is *replication invariance* (also called population invariance), which says that the measure of inequality is unchanged when we duplicate the population, or pool identical populations. For example, the following distribution has the same inequality as A:

$$E: (0, 10, 10, 10, 10, 0, 10, 10, 10, 10).$$

Another axiom is called *decomposability*. This says that the total inequality can be written as the sum of the inequality between groups plus inequality within groups. Suppose we partition A into two groups:

$$A1: (0, 10) \text{ and } A2 (10, 10, 10).$$

Then group A1 has high inequality (the maximum income difference), while A2 has no inequality. Intuitively, the amount of inequality between the two groups (comparing the difference in their means) is somewhere between the amounts of inequality within each group.

An objection to decomposability is that in this set up, group memberships only have salience via the incomes of those in the groups. The groups have no special identity. However, it appears to be the case at times that group identities (such as by race or gender) matter more than this decomposition would suggest. Claims that group identities do not matter to inequality because the between group component of an inequality decomposition is small may not fit well with perceptions on the ground.

Further reading: An important early paper on inequality measurement was Atkinson (1970). A formal treatment of the axioms of inequality measurement can be found in Cowell (2000). The discussion of the transfer axiom above draws on Kolm (1998) while that on group identities draws on Kanbur (2006). Also see Foster et al. (2013, ch. 2).

The Gini index does not have all the properties that one might hope for in a measure of inequality. If we measure "global inequality" similarly to how we measured global poverty, then we would ignore all country borders, pooling all residents, and measure the inequality among them as if it were one country. This overall measure will naturally depend on the inequality between countries as well as that within them. Thus, its evolution over time will depend on growth rates in poor countries relative to rich ones (roughly speaking), as well as the things happening within countries—economic changes and policies—that affect inequality. However, if we are comparing country performance at regional or global levels then, we will want to isolate the within-country component of inequality. While there are many inequality measures and one can always calculate the average inequality index for a group of countries, only for a subset of inequality measures will that average accord with the within-country component of total inequality—implying a clean separation of the part we are interested in from the total inequality. Such an exact decomposition is known to be impossible for the popular Gini index (boxes 5.1 and 5.2).[6] The MLD offers a practical solution. This is given by the (appropriately weighted) mean across sampled households of the log of the ratio of the overall mean income to individual income; see box 5.4 for more detail.

---

*Box 5.4 **The Mean Log Deviation: A Simple and Elegant but Not Much Used Measure of Inequality**

The Gini index has long been the most popular measure of inequality, but it is not the best by some criteria. Consider instead the MLD. For a distribution of consumption or income $y_1, y_2, \ldots, y_n$ (all elements of which are assumed to be positive) with mean $\bar{y}$, the MLD is simply:

$$MLD = \frac{1}{n} \sum_{i=1}^{n} \ln \left(\frac{\bar{y}}{y_i} \right).$$

Like the Gini index, this measure satisfies the transfer axiom (box 5.3). However, unlike the Gini index, MLD is exactly decomposable by population subgroups. To see how, suppose now that these n individuals are assigned to N mutually exclusive groups (countries, say). Let y_{ij} denote the consumption of person i in group j containing n_j people. Then we can rewrite MLD as:

$$MLD = \ln \bar{y} - \sum_{j=1}^{N} s_j \sum_{i=1}^{n_j} \ln y_{ij},$$

---

[6] The exception is when the distributions of the different countries, or subgroups, being compared do not overlap, which is unlikely in general.

where s_j is the population share of group j. We can go further and write this as:

$$MLD = MLD^W + MLD^B,$$

where:

$$MLD^W = \sum_{j=1}^{N} s_j \left(\ln \bar{y}_j - \sum_{i=1}^{n_j} \ln y_{ij} \right), \text{ and}$$

$$MLD^B = \ln \bar{y} - \sum_{j=1}^{N} s_j \ln \bar{y}_j$$

are the within-country and between-country components, respectively, and $\bar{y}_j$ is the mean for group j. So total inequality is the population-weighted sum of inequality within groups and inequality between them.

MLD also lends itself to implementing the distinction between "vertical" and "horizontal" inequality noted in box 1.8. Chapter 9 will return to this point.

Further reading: MLD is one of the "generalized entropy measures" proposed by Theil (1967). Bourguignon (1979) shows that (under mild restrictions on the properties of the inequality index) MLD is the only measure satisfying the transfer axiom that is decomposable with population weights.

Following the discussion in section 5.1, we can think of the inequality measure as the loss of social welfare due to inequality. Thus, we can ask what SWF underlies each index, and see if that is ethically appealing. The SWF corresponding to the Gini index weights incomes by their rank in the distribution, with highest weight on the lowest income (box 5.5). This SWF is questionable. It is not clear what ethical justification can be given to using the rank in the distribution as the weight for incomes. A utilitarian would presumably also object that the implicit utility function does not exhibit diminishing marginal utility of income. (The weights are how the Gini index comes to satisfy the transfer axiom.) The MLD is more appealing in this respect as it is the inequality measure corresponding to the utilitarian SWF when utility is log income (box 5.5). However, we can also object to the equal weighting of welfare levels in the utilitarian objective on the grounds that this does not adequately reflect our aversion to poverty (section 5.1). This can be dealt with by a hybrid measure, combining Gini-type weights with declining marginal utility. Thus, one can generalize the MLD to incorporate the Gini-type SWF in which utilities are weighted by ranks. This simultaneously addresses both the deficiency of the Gini index (that its implicit SWF does not reflect diminishing marginal utility of income) and of the MLD (that it does not give higher weight to lower utilities). Box 5.5 goes into more detail on this measure of inequality.

*Box 5.5 Inequality and Social Welfare

Recall from section 5.1 that inequality measures can be thought of as the loss of social welfare due to inequality at a given mean income. If we order the incomes from lowest to highest, $y_1 \geq y_2 \geq, \ldots, \geq y_n$, then the SWF corresponding to the Gini index is given by:

$$\frac{2}{n^2} \sum_{i=1}^{n} iy_i = \left(\frac{1}{n} + 1 - G\right) \bar{y} \cong (1 - G)\bar{y} \text{ for large } n.$$

Here we see that the "Gini SWF" has incomes that are rank-weighted with the highest weight on the poorest person. (Note that $\sum iy_i = y_1 + 2y_2 + \ldots + ny_n$). If you take \$1 from person j and give it to person k (and nothing else changes), then the Gini index will rise if (and only if) $k > j$. The Gini index times the mean can be interpreted as the social welfare loss from inequality. While the Gini-SWF gives higher weight to lower levels of welfare, it measures the latter simply by income. Thus, it does not incorporate the utilitarian idea of diminishing marginal utility of income.

We can easily see the implicit SWF in the MLD if we rewrite the first equation in box 5.4 as:

$$\frac{1}{n} \sum_{i=1}^{n} \ln y_i = \ln \bar{y} - MLD.$$

On the left-hand side, we have the mean utility for a common utility function of the form $\ln y_i$. The log transformation embodies diminishing marginal utility of income (box 1.13). This is the SWF implicit in using the MLD as the measure of inequality. On the right-hand side, we have the log of the mean, which is the maximum of the mean utility when a fixed total income is redistributed, less MLD. Thus, we can interpret MLD as the loss of social welfare due to inequality, assuming that incomes can be redistributed without altering total income. (This verifies the claim made in section 5.1.)

A more general utility function is proposed in Atkinson (1970), taking the form $y^{1-\varepsilon}/(1 - \varepsilon)$ for $\varepsilon \neq 1$ and $\ln y$ for $\varepsilon = 1$. A higher value of the parameter ε implies that a greater penalty is attached to income inequality. This generates the corresponding class of Atkinson inequality measures.

While MLD (and the more general Atkinson function) incorporates diminishing marginal utility of income, it weights utilities equally. A simple way of responding to this concern is to adopt the Gini-type SWF with rank-weights (box 5.2) while maintaining the assumption that utility is log income (rather than the level of income, as in the Gini index). So the new SWF would be $\sum_{i=1}^{n} i \ln y_i$, where incomes are ordered from the richest ($i = 1$) to the poorest ($i = n$). The new version of the MLD would take the form:

$$MLD^* = \frac{2}{n(n + 1)} \sum_{i=1}^{n} i \ln \left(\frac{\bar{y}}{y_i}\right).$$

(Note that $\sum_{i=1}^{n} i = \frac{n(n+1)}{2}$.) One drawback is that this modified index loses the neat decomposability property of MLD (box 5.4).

Another possible candidate for a measure of "inequality" is the strongly relative poverty measure, in which the poverty line is set at a constant proportion of the mean (as discussed in chapter 4). This makes our aversion to poverty very clear. However, one should be careful as this measure does not respect the transfer axiom. One can construct examples whereby distribution A Lorenz dominates B—so that A has less inequality than B for any well-behaved measure of inequality—and yet the strongly relative measure is higher for the A distribution.[7] The strongly relative poverty measure could indicate higher poverty in A than B, even though inequality and absolute poverty are unambiguously lower in A than B. And such examples are also possible when the transfers are only made among the poor. Thus, the strongly relative poverty measure is not only independent of the mean, it need not be consistent with reasonable normative judgments about relative poverty.

So far in this section, we have only discussed relative inequality, whereby if all incomes are multiplied by a constant the measure is unchanged. By this approach, inequality depends on the ratios of incomes in the population. "Absolute inequality" depends instead on the *absolute differences* in levels of living, rather than relative differences, as captured by the ratios to the mean. Standard practice is to measure inequality using a relative measure, consistently with the scale invariance axiom (box 5.3). However, one can equally well measure inequality in terms of the absolute differences, not normalized by the mean.[8] To understand this distinction, consider an economy with just two household incomes: $1,000 and $10,000. If both incomes double in size then relative inequality will remain the same; the richer household is still 10 times richer. But the absolute difference in their incomes has doubled, from $9,000 to $18,000. Relative inequality is unchanged but absolute inequality has risen sharply.

The choice between absolute and relative inequality measures comes down to whether one accepts the scale invariance axiom for inequality measurement (box 5.3). Recall that this says that multiplying all incomes by a constant leaves the measure of inequality unchanged. However, it should not be forgotten that this is an axiom. We do not have to accept it. You can prefer to say that *adding* an equal amount to all incomes does not change inequality. (This is sometimes called translation invariance.) If one keeps the mean constant (at some reference value, such as the base year) when

---

[7] This is shown in Ravallion (1994b) by exploiting the analytic properties of the Lorenz curve (following Gastwirth 1971).

[8] In one of the earliest papers on measuring inequality, Dalton (1920) discussed both absolute and relative measures. Kolm (1976) noted the distinction (as discussed later). But the distinction largely vanished from the subsequent literature until it re-emerged in the context of the globalization debate (Ravallion 2003a, 2004).

calculating the Gini indices over time, then it becomes an absolute Gini index, as distinct from the relative index in box 5.2.

This is no mere academic debate. Perceptions on the ground that "inequality is rising" appear often to be referring to an absolute concept of inequality, as reflected in commonly heard statements such as "the rising gap between the rich and the poor." And the distinction matters to how one views distributional policies. Serge Kolm (1976) gives the following example. May 1968 saw mass protests by students and workers in France, which eventually led to the Grenelle agreement for a 13% increase in all salaries. However, many of the protesters felt cheated, for in their view this agreement would increase income inequality.[9] As we will discuss further in chapter 8, whether one thinks about inequality as absolute or relative matters greatly to the long-standing policy debates about the distribution of the gains from economic growth.

It is not that one concept is "right" and one "wrong." They simply reflect different value judgments about what constitutes higher "inequality." And it appears that many people think about inequality in absolute terms. Yoram Amiel and Frank Cowell (1992, 1999) did some simple but clever experiments to identify which concept of inequality is held by people. They found that 40% of the university students they surveyed (in the United Kingdom and Israel) think about inequality in absolute rather than relative terms.[10] In 2014, I fielded a subset of the types of questions used by Amiel and Cowell to my class of undergraduates (using a confidential computer-based questionnaire tool); these were students doing a course based on this textbook although the survey was done before we got to the lecture dealing with the axioms of inequality measurement. From the 130 responses, the class was roughly evenly split between those who thought about inequality in relative terms versus those who thought about it in absolute terms. Interestingly, the "absolutists" were a clear majority when the stylized incomes were "low" but the "relativists" became the majority when the incomes were "high." However, almost all agreed with both the anonymity and transfer axioms.[11]

5.3 Measuring Poverty

Suppose we now have a measure of individual welfare that has been estimated for each household in a sample. Sometimes we may have a sequence of values of this measure over time for each household. This *time profile* is used in distinguishing transient from chronic poverty (section 5.4).[12] But for now we imagine just one value for each household. How do we aggregate this information into a measure of poverty for each of the distributions being compared? The literature has identified numerous axioms for a desirable measure of poverty. Box 5.6 reviews the main ones.

[9] For this reason, Kolm calls the absolute measure the "Leftist measure" while the relative measure is "Rightist." I leave it to the reader to judge how closely this distinction matches peoples' politics.

[10] Harrison and Seidl (1994) report similar findings for a large sample of German university students.

[11] More so it seems than the students surveyed by Harrison and Seidl (1994).

[12] A time profile of welfare measures is also postulated in constructing measures that allow for selective premature mortality (Kanbur and Mukerjee 2007); we return to this point.

Box 5.6 Desirable Properties of a Poverty Measure

The most widely agreed property is called the *focus axiom*. This says that the measure of poverty should be unaffected by any changes in the incomes (or consumptions) of those who are not deemed to be poor (and stay so after the changes). A concern raised about this axiom is that it assumes that we know with certainty who is poor and who is not.

Another property that is considered desirable is called the *monotonicity axiom*. This says that, holding all else constant, the measure of poverty must rise if a poor person experiences a drop in her income. This is appealing, but (as we will see) it is not satisfied by the most common measure of poverty. An extension of the last axiom is called *subgroup monotonicity*. This says that if we partition the population into two groups, each with a fixed size, and poverty increases in one group while remaining unchanged in the other then aggregate poverty must rise. This also seems reasonable; it would certainly be odd to find that after successfully reducing poverty in (say) rural areas, without any loss to poor people in urban areas, and no change in the urban–rural composition of the population, that poverty in the country as a whole has risen. Subgroup monotonicity is satisfied for all *additive measures*, meaning that aggregate poverty is the arithmetic sum of the individual levels of poverty in the population.

A number of other axioms have been proposed that are similar to inequality measurement (see the discussion in box 5.3). In the context of poverty measures, *scale invariance* means that the measure is unchanged when all incomes *and* the poverty line increase by the same proportion. (The measure is then said to be homogeneous of degree zero.) *Replication invariance* requires that the measure is unchanged when we replicate the current population, or pool identical populations. The *transfer axiom* for poverty measures says that the measure falls whenever a given sum of money is transferred from a poor person to someone who is even poorer (without changing their ranking).

Note on the literature: In some of the literature, measures that satisfy scale invariance are referred to as "relative poverty measures," as distinct from "absolute poverty measures," which satisfy instead a translation invariance property, in that they are invariant to adding the same absolute amount to all incomes and the poverty line. This is essentially the same distinction we heard about with regard to inequality measures (section 5.2). I shall not use this terminology here as there is a risk of confusion with the distinction between absolute and relative poverty lines (chapter 4).

Further reading: A seminal early contribution was made by Sen (1976a). Blackorby and Donaldson (1980) discuss a number of issues, including the scale invariance axiom. See Foster and Shorrocks (1991) on subgroup monotonicity. Zheng (1993) lists other axioms. Also see Foster et al. (2013, ch. 2) for an overview of the various axioms that have been proposed in the literature.

Poverty Measures

There is now a large literature on poverty measures.[13] I will focus solely on additive measures. This is not unduly restrictive, and this class of measures is known to have desirable properties (box 5.6).[14] Rather than discuss all of the measures that have been used or proposed, I shall focus on a few representative additive measures and discuss the pros and cons of each. Box 5.7 provides a glossary.

Box 5.7   Glossary of Measures of Poverty

Headcount index (H)	The proportion of the population living in households with income per person (or per equivalent single adult) less than or equal to the poverty line. Suppose q people are poor by this definition in a population of size n. Then the headcount index, H, is simply the proportion of the population deemed poor: $H = q/n$. This satisfies the focus and scale invariance axioms but none of the other axioms in box 5.6.
Poverty gap index (PG)	Mean distance below the poverty line as a proportion of the line where the mean is taken over the whole population, counting those above the line as having zero gap. To see how this measure is defined, let consumptions be arranged in ascending order; the poorest has $Y1$, the next poorest $Y2$, etc., with the least poor having Yq, which is (by definition) no greater than the poverty line Z. Now define the *proportionate poverty gap* of person i as $(Z - Y_i)/Z = 1 - Y_i/Z$ if the person is poor ($Y_i < Z$); if the person is not poor, then the gap is set to zero. PG is then the mean proportionate poverty gap, so defined. This fails the transfer axiom in box 5.6.
Income gap ratio (I)	Mean distance below the poverty line as a proportion of the line, among the poor alone. This fails the monotonicity and transfer axioms in box 5.6.

---

[13] For useful surveys, see Foster (1984), Atkinson (1987), and Hagenaars (1987).

[14] See Atkinson (1987) and Foster and Shorrocks (1991). The latter's requirement of subgroup monotonicity (what they call "subgroup consistency") essentially requires additive measures. The Sen (1976a) index does not qualify.

Squared poverty gap index (SPG)	As for PG except that the proportionate poverty gaps are weighted by themselves. Thus, to calculate SPG one takes the mean of the squared proportionate poverty gaps, $(1 - Y_i/Z)^2$ for the poor, and zero otherwise. This measure satisfies all the axioms in box 5.6.
The Watts index (W)	Mean proportionate gap, measured as the log of the poverty line less the log of income, counting the non-poor as having zero gap. This satisfies all the axioms in box 5.6. It also satisfies a number of other axioms found in the literature (Zheng 1993).

The simplest (and most common) measure is the *headcount index* of poverty, given by the proportion of the population for whom the measure of economic welfare Y is no greater than the poverty line Z. This is simply one point on the CDF, namely $F(Z)$, where F is the proportion of the population with income or consumption below Z (or, more precisely, living in households with income per capita less than or equal to Z).

While H has been by far the most popular index, it is not the best. H is easily understood and communicated and for certain sorts of poverty comparisons, such as assessing overall progress in reducing poverty, it may be quite adequate (though preferably always calculated for at least two poverty lines). However, for some purposes, including analyses of the impacts on the poor of specific policies, the H has a serious drawback. To see why, suppose that a poor person suddenly becomes very much poorer. What will happen to H? Nothing. The index is totally insensitive to differences in the depth of poverty among the poor.

This can be important when looking at progress against poverty over time, or the impacts of policies on poverty. Each panel in figure 5.1 gives two CDFs. In each case the upper one is (say) before a policy change and the lower one is after that change.

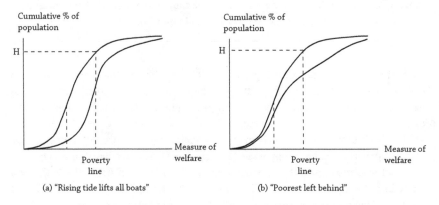

Figure 5.1 Stylized Representations of Poverty Reduction.

The impact on H is similar, but the distribution of the gains among the poor is very different, with much larger gains (as measured by the horizontal differences) among those below the poverty line in case (a).

Box 5.8 Different Ways of Defining the Poverty Gap Index

In box 5.7, PG is defined as the mean of the proportionate poverty gaps in the population, where the gap is set to zero for the non-poor. Another way of defining PG is as $PG = I.H$, where I is the "income gap ratio" and is defined by $I = 1 - M^z/Z$, where M^z denotes the mean consumption of the poor. Note, however, that the income gap ratio is not a very good poverty measure. To see why, suppose that someone just below the poverty line is made sufficiently better off to escape poverty. The mean of the remaining poor will fall, and so the income gap ratio will increase. And yet one of the poor has become better off, and none is worse off; one would be loath to say that there is not less poverty, and yet that is what the income gap ratio would suggest. This problem does not arise if the income gap ratio is multiplied by the head count index to yield PG; under the same circumstances, that measure will register a decrease in poverty.

PG also has an interpretation as an indicator of the potential for eliminating poverty by targeting transfers to the poor. The *minimum* cost of eliminating poverty using targeted transfers is simply the sum of all the poverty gaps in a population; every poverty gap is filled up to the poverty line. The cost would be $(Z - M^z).q$ (recall that q are poor). Clearly this assumes that the policymaker has a lot of information; one should not be surprised to find that a very "pro-poor" government would need to spend far more than this in the name of poverty reduction. At the other extreme, one can consider the *maximum* cost of eliminating poverty, assuming that the policymaker knows nothing about who is poor and who is not. Then the policymaker would have to give Z to everyone to be sure that none is poor; the cost is $Z.n$. The ratio of the minimum cost of eliminating poverty with perfect targeting to the maximum cost with no targeting is simply PG. Thus, this poverty measure is also an indicator of the *potential* saving to the poverty alleviation budget from targeting. Of course, realizing that potential in practice is a different matter, as we will see in chapter 10.

A better measure for capturing gains below the line is the *poverty gap index* (*PG*), which is simply the mean of the proportionate poverty gaps in the population (box 5.7). Box 5.8 discusses various ways of defining PG, to help understand its properties.

A drawback of the PG is that it may not convincingly capture differences in the *severity* of poverty among the poor. For example, consider two distributions of consumption for four persons; the A distribution is (1,2,3,4) and the B is (2,2,2,4). For a poverty line $Z = 3$ (so that $H = 0.75$ in both cases), A and B have the same value of $PG = 0.25$. However, the poorest person in A has only half the consumption of the poorest in B. One can think of B as being generated from A by a transfer from the least poor person to the poorest. The poverty gap will be unaffected. In other words, this measure does not satisfy the transfer axiom.

There are a number of poverty measures in the literature that penalize inequality among the poor and so satisfy the transfer axiom (box 5.6).[15] In applied work the bulk of attention has focused on additive measures, meaning that aggregate poverty is equal to the population-weighted sum of poverty levels in the various subgroups of society. There are conceptual and practical advantages to such additivity in the construction of poverty profiles and in testing hypotheses about poverty comparisons; the discussion will return to some of these issues.

The earliest additive measure that penalizes inequality among the poor was proposed by Watts (1968). This is the mean proportionate poverty gap (log of the ratio of poverty line to income), counting the non-poor as having no gap. (Box 5.9 describes the Watts index in more detail.) This index has many desirable features, although it has not been used much and was little known until the mid-1990s.[16] The measure is especially attractive when we come to discuss the incidence of the benefits of economic growth later in this chapter and in chapter 8.

The Watts index is a member of a large class of additive distribution-sensitive measures.[17] A recent example is the squared poverty gap (*SPG*) introduced by James Foster, Joel Greer, and Erik Thorbecke (1984). This is similar to *PG* with the (important) difference that the individual proportionate poverty gaps are weighted by those gaps, giving the squared proportionate gap.[18] A proportionate poverty gap of (say) 10% of the poverty line is given a weight of 10% while one of 50% is given a weight of 50% (notice that, in the case of *PG*, they are weighted equally). Again we take the mean of these squared proportionate gaps across the population (counting the gap as zero for the non-poor).

Box 5.9 The Watts Index: An Old Measure Nobody Paid Much Attention to Turns Out to Be the Best!

The Watts index was the first poverty measure to penalize inequality among the poor, and it is arguably the best. The index satisfies all the desirable axioms for a poverty measure described in box 5.6, plus other properties that have had advocates in the literature. We can define the Watts proportionate poverty gap of

continued

---

[15] One of the earliest such measures that attempted to do this was proposed by Sen (1976a, 1981a). However, this did not satisfy the transfer axiom, as was pointed out by Thon (1979), although Shorrocks (1995) showed that a simple re-normalization of the Sen index did satisfy the transfer axiom and also assured continuity (so there was no jump in the index when someone crossed the poverty line).

[16] Zheng (1993) rediscovered the Watts index and demonstrated its desirable properties in more formal terms.

[17] As characterized in formal terms by Atkinson (1987).

[18] That is in fact how the authors came up with the index (based on communication with Erik Thorbecke).

Box 5.9 (Continued)

person i as $\ln(Z/Yi)$ if the person is poor ($Y_i < Z$); if the person is not poor, then the gap is zero, of course. Note that this is not the same as the proportionate poverty gap ($1 - Y_i/Z$), which is why we shall call $\ln(Z/Yi)$ the Watts proportionate poverty gap. Now take the mean of these proportionate poverty gaps in the population. If incomes are ordered such that $Y_i \le Z$ if an only if $i < q$, then the Watts index is:

$$W = \frac{1}{n} \sum_{i=1}^{q} \ln(Z/Y_i).$$

(Notice that the headcount index is $H = q/n$.) If all the incomes of poor people grow at a rate g, then W/g is approximately the average time it takes to exit poverty at the growth rate g (Morduch 1998). If all the incomes in the population grow at the same rate (so that the Lorenz curve remains unchanged), then the elasticity of the Watts index to the mean is $-H/W$.

Note on the literature: The Watts index did not start to be acknowledged in the literature on the theory of poverty measurement for about twenty-five years after Watts's (1968) paper. Zheng (1993) drew attention to the many desirable features of the index. It also became important in the later literature on "pro-poor growth," which we return to in section 5.6.

One drawback of the distribution-sensitive measures is that they are not as easy to interpret as PG or (especially) H.[19] For poverty comparisons, however, the key point is that a ranking of dates, places, or policies in terms of SPG should reflect well their ranking in terms of the severity of poverty. It is the ability of the measure to order distributions in a better way than the alternatives that makes it useful, rather than the precise numbers obtained.

On comparing the above formulae for H, PG, and SPG, a common structure is evident. This suggests a generic class of measures in which the proportionate poverty gaps are raised to the power α, which is a non-negative parameter. This is the Foster-Greer-Thorbecke (FGT) class of poverty measures, for which we can use the generic symbol P_α. When $\alpha = 0$, we get the measure $P_0 = H$; when $\alpha = 1$, we get $P_1 = PG$; while $\alpha = 2$ gives us $P_2 = SPG$. For all $\alpha > 0$, the individual poverty measure in the FGT index is strictly decreasing in the living standard of the poor (the lower your standard of living, the poorer you are deemed to be). Furthermore, for $\alpha > 1$, it also has the property that if the increase in your measured poverty due to a fall in standard of living will be deemed greater, the poorer you are.[20] The FGT measure is then said

---

[19] The measure can be thought of as the sum of two components: an amount due to the poverty gap and an amount due to inequality among the poor. More precisely, let CVp^2 denote the squared coefficient of variation of consumption among the poor. Then $SPG = I.PG + (1 - I)(H - PG)CV_p{}^2$.

[20] For a complete axiomatic characterization of the FGT class of poverty measures, see Foster and Shorrocks (1991, proposition 7).

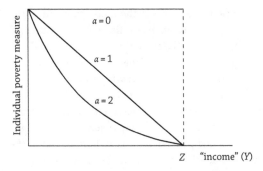

Figure 5.2 Individual Poverty Measures for Various Values of the Inequality-Aversion Parameter (α) in the FGT Index.

to penalize inequality among the poor whenever $\alpha > 1$. One can say that the index is "strictly convex" in incomes ("weakly convex" for $\alpha = 1$). In the limit, as α goes to infinity the index becomes the lowest level of income observed in the data.

Figure 5.2 shows how the relationship between individual poverty and the economic-welfare metric varies across the different values of α. The higher the value of α, the more sensitive the measure is to the well-being of the poorest person; as α approaches infinity it collapses to a measure which only reflects the poverty of the poorest person. Figure 5.1 also illustrates another conceptual attraction of *SPG*, namely, that the individual poverty measure hits zero *smoothly* at the poverty line; thus there is negligible difference in the weight the measure attaches to someone just above the poverty line versus someone just below it.[21] Given the aforementioned concerns about introducing discontinuities in the individual poverty measure and the uncertainties in measuring living standards discussed above, this is a desirable property.[22]

Does it really matter which of these measures one uses? Intuitively, the answer depends on whether, and how, relative inequalities in the society have changed. If all consumption levels (poor and non-poor) have changed by the same proportion— sometimes called a "distribution neutral" growth or contraction—then all of these poverty measures will yield the same ranking in the poverty comparison, and the ranking in terms of absolute poverty will depend solely on the direction of change in the mean of the distribution.

However, the differences between these measures can become quite pronounced otherwise. Consider, for example, two policies: *Policy A* entails a small redistribution *from* people around the mode of the distribution, which is also where the poverty line happens to be located, *to* the poorest households. (This is actually a fair character-ization of how a reduction in the prices of domestically produced food staples would affect the distribution of welfare in some Asian countries.) *Policy B* entails the opposite

[21] This relates to a long-standing issue of whether poverty is best viewed as a discrete or continuous phenomenon. For further discussion, see Atkinson (1987). This measurement issue has been found to be important in the context of analyzing the effects of risk on poverty (Ravallion, 1988a) and in characterizing optimal poverty reduction schemes (Bourguignon and Fields 1990; Ravallion 1991b).

[22] It is not shared by some other distributionally sensitive poverty measures, including Sen (1976a).

change—the poorest lose, while those at the mode gain. (An increase in food staple prices in the above example.) A moment's reflection will confirm that the headcount index H will prefer policy B; $H_A > H_B$, since changes in H depend solely on which direction people are crossing the poverty line. However, a measure such as SPG will indicate the opposite ranking, $SPG_A < SPG_B$, since it will respond relatively more to the gains among the poorest than among the not-so-poor.

The need to examine higher order poverty measures, such as PG and SPG, also depends on whether or not the poverty comparison in terms of the headcount index has considered more than one poverty line, as recommended in the previous section. If only one poverty line is used, then it should be considered imperative, in my view, to check the higher order measures. But values of H for one or two extra poverty lines can often provide an adequate substitute. If, for a given poverty line, the higher order measure gives a different result to the headcount index, then this will also hold for an alternative headcount index based on a sufficiently low poverty line.

There is another concern about the standard poverty measures discussed above. As we will learn in chapter 7, there is selective mortality in that poorer people are less likely to survive. When a poor person dies, standard measures will show a decline in poverty. (This is obvious for the headcount index, but it also holds for the higher order measures reviewed above.) Similarly, higher fertility rates for poor families will tend to increase the poverty rate in a purely mechanical way. This is an instance of a generic problem in welfare economics when one uses any form of average welfare (such as per capita income or per capita utility) in assessing social progress with varying populations: the demise of anyone below the average will increase the average. That is not ethically acceptable. Given this problem, we need supplementary measures on mortality, in case this is why we are seeing falling poverty measures.

The standard measures of poverty can also be modified to better reflect our judgments on this matter. Ravi Kanbur and Diganta Mukerjee (2007) propose an intriguing solution based on the idea of a *normative lifetime, L,* such that poverty is measured using the time profile of incomes for all those born L years ago, whether they are still alive today. An income must be imputed for the years not living; a seemingly natural assumption to make is that all those now dead have a lower imputed income than when they were alive. (Newly rich vampires are ruled out!) Having established this time profile the measurement problem proceeds similarly to before. For example, one can derive a modified version of the FGT index.[23]

The Consumption Floor

This refers to the typical level of living of the poorest in a given society. We can think of this as the lower bound of permanent consumption (recalling box 3.11). Human physiology makes it likely that consumption levels below some critical (positive) value are unlikely to be sustainable for more than a fairly short time period. This is the *biological floor.* Social and political factors may also come into play to influence the level of the consumption floor, which can thus rise above the biological floor in a specific society.

[23] Kanbur and Mukerjee (2007) show how this is done and address a number of implementation issues in making this approach operational.

The idea of the consumption floor has been around since at least the time of the first economists. Early ideas of the "subsistence wage" can be interpreted as the wage rate required to assure that the consumption floor is reached for a typical family. The classical economists identified the consumption floor as the point at which the population is constant; any temporary increase (decrease) in consumption in a neighborhood of the floor would induce population growth (contraction). The idea of a floor has been a key feature of development models for dualistic economies, such as in the original model of Lewis (1954), which we return to in chapter 8. The idea of a consumption floor has often been built into demand models, famously in Engel's Law (box 1.16). It has sometimes been incorporated in modern economic models of the growth process, which we also return to in chapter 8.[24] And the idea of a consumption floor is found in discussions of the problem of determining the optimal population size.[25] When living close to the consumption floor, the prospects for investment and sustained growth will naturally be limited.

This is quite a different concept to a poverty line, which is not typically intended to be a biological floor, in the sense that nobody lives below that level for any sustained period of time. Naturally, any poverty line aims instead to reflect what "poverty" means in a specific society, on the understanding that (potentially many) people live below that level. The poverty line is invariably above the biological floor.

Indeed, the idea that we should judge progress in part at least by success in raising the floor is missing from virtually all standard poverty measures. Raising the floor automatically reduces, *ceteris paribus*, any measure of poverty satisfying the monotonicity axiom (box 5.6). However, none of the standard axioms of poverty measurement attach any explicit value to the level of the floor. This appears to be due in large part to the difficulties in identifying the floor.[26]

Nor does the fact that an overall poverty measure is falling tell us that the poorest are doing better—that society's consumption floor is rising. The floor may stay put, even though fewer people living at or near it. This is illustrated in figure 5.3. The decline in the poverty rate is similar but in panel (a) the level of living of the poorest is unchanged.

As we saw in chapter 2, an important school of modern political philosophy has argued that we should judge a society's progress by its ability to enhance the welfare of the poorest, following the principles of justice proposed by Rawls (1971). This has been proposed as a principle for judging development success. For example, in what came to be known as his "talisman," Mahatma Gandhi (1958, 65) wrote that "recall the face of the poorest and weakest person you have seen and ask if the step you contemplate is going to be any use to them." Watkins (2013, 1) refers explicitly to the Gandhi's talisman and argues that "as a guide to international cooperation on development, that's tough to top."

Quantifying the consumption floor is not easy, however. With a sound sampling design and large enough sample, we can be confident about an estimate of the overall mean, but it is far from clear how reliably we could estimate the consumption floor.

---

[24] See, e.g., Azariadis (1996), Ben-David (1998), and Kraay and Raddatz (2007).

[25] See Dasgupta (1993, ch. 13).

[26] See, e.g., Freiman's (2012) comments on Rawls's maximin principle.

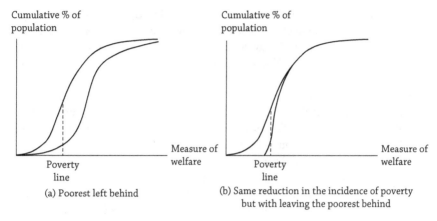

Figure 5.3 Same Reduction in the Poverty Count but Different Implications for the Poorest.

If we were to know the true consumption and any other relevant aspects of welfare, we could estimate the floor directly from a sufficiently large sample. However, we must recognize the existence of measurement errors (chapter 3). There are also likely to be transient effects in the data, whereby observed consumption in a survey falls temporarily below the floor (such as due to illness), but recovers soon after the survey is done. Given the measurement errors, there is a non-negligible chance that anyone within some stratum of low observed consumption levels is in fact at the floor.

We can postulate a probability that a person with a given observed consumption is in fact living at the floor. These probabilities are not data, of course. But there are some defensible assumptions we can make in lieu of the missing data. It is reasonable to assume that the probability of being the poorest person is highest for the person who *appears* to be worst off in our data. It is also reasonable to assume that the probability declines as the person's observed measure of welfare rises. Beyond some point there can be no chance that person is the worst off. Box 5.10 explains this idea in more detail and proposes a specific functional form, based on a member of the class of Beta distributions in statistics, which establishes a useful link with FGT class of poverty measures. Thus, we can readily apply existing poverty measures to the task of implementing a Rawlsian approach to assessing social progress, although the focus switches to ratios of FGT measures.

Box 5.10 **An Approach to Estimating the Expected Value of the Consumption Floor**

Let the consumption floor be denoted, y^{min}. This is the lowest level of permanent consumption in a population. However, it is not observed given transient effects and measurement errors. Our data comprise n *observed* consumptions, y.

We can treat the consumption floor as a random variable, meaning that it has a probability distribution given the data. The task is to estimate the mean of that distribution based on the observed consumptions. We can write this as:

$$E(y^{\min} | y) = \sum \phi(y_i) y_i.$$

Here the probability that person i, with the observed y_i, is in fact the worst off person is $\phi(y_i)$. For example, if we are certain that the person with the lowest observed y also has the lowest permanent consumption, then this formula returns that value. More generally we cannot be sure that the person with the lowest y is in fact the worst off person (as discussed in the text). However, it may be reasonable to trust our data sufficiently to believe that she has the highest probability of being the worst off. The probability then falls as observed consumption rises, until it reaches zero at some level z.

A specific functional form satisfying these assumptions is:

$$\varphi(y_i) = k(1 - y_i/z)^\alpha \text{ for } y_i \leq z$$
$$= 0 \text{ for } y_i > z$$

Here there are three parameters, k, α, and z, all positive constants. The k parameter assures that the probabilities add up to unity, which requires that $k = 1/(nP_\alpha)$, where P_α is the FGT measure (with y's rank-ordered starting from the lowest):

$$P_\alpha = \frac{1}{n} \sum_{i=1}^{q} (1 - y_i/z)^\alpha.$$

However, in contrast to the FGT poverty measure, now the parameter α determines how fast the chance of being the poorest person falls as y increases rather than the degree of aversion to inequality among the poor, as in the FGT index. Rather than draw this, we can use figure 5.1 and redefine the vertical axis as the probability of being the poorest person. The third parameter, z, is not a standard poverty line; rather it is the point above which we no longer think there is any chance that a person is the worst off.

We can then derive the following formula for the expected value of the consumption floor:

$$E(y^{\min} | y) = z(1 - P_{\alpha+1}/P_\alpha).$$

For example, if we assume that the probability of being the worst off person falls linearly with y up to z, then the expected value of the floor is $z(1 - SPG/PG)$. Note that $\alpha = 0$ can be ruled out; the probability must fall as y increases. To put the point another way, if one uses $\alpha = 0$, then every consumption below z is equally likely to be the lowest, so $z(1 - PG/H)$ is the mean consumption of the poor.

continued

---

*Box 5.10 **(Continued)**

With falling poverty measures over time, the expected value of the consumption floor will only rise if the proportionate rate of decline in the $P_{\alpha+1}$ measure exceeds that for P_α. Intuitively, a rising floor requires faster progress against the more distribution-sensitive FGT measure.

Further reading: Ravallion (2014 f) goes into more detail and provides an application to data for the developing world. We review the results in chapter 7.

Estimation Issues

Two distinct types of data are encountered in practice: household-level (sometimes called "unit record") data and tabulated grouped data derived from the household-level data. Unit record data are typically only available in a machine-readable form, while grouped data are often found in governmental statistical publications. Quite different problems are encountered in estimating poverty measures on these two types of data.

All of the additive poverty measures above can be readily and accurately calculated as the means of the corresponding individual poverty measures when one has access to unit record data. The main points to be aware of are:

(1) It should not be presumed that estimates of poverty measures from unit record data are more accurate than those from grouped data, since the latter can "average out" errors in the unit record data, such as negative consumption figures, which might otherwise add a sizable bias to estimates of the severity of poverty.

(2) Most large household surveys use stratified samples, whereby the chance of being selected in the sample is not uniform over the population. This is often done to assure adequate sample sizes in certain regions. Estimates of population parameters from a stratified sample are unbiased, if weighted by the appropriate inverse sampling rates (box 3.6). Provided your data set includes the sampling rate for each household or area, it is easy to do so.[27]

(3) One should be clear on whether one wants to estimate poverty among households or poverty among people. For example, suppose one ranked households by consumption per person, but measured poverty in terms of the proportion of households who are below the poverty line. Household size tends to be negatively correlated with consumption per person, so your calculation will tend to underestimate the number of persons who are living in poor households (though it will not necessarily underestimate the number of poor persons; that also depends on the distribution within the household, which is typically unknown).

The most defensible position on this last issue is to recognize that poverty is experienced by individuals, and not by households per se, and so it is poverty among persons that we are trying to measure. Although we may not know anything about distribution

---

[27] For further discussion, see, e.g., Levy and Lemeshow (1991).

within the household, that does not mean that we should only measure poverty among households. A common practice is to assume an equal distribution within households when constructing the estimated distribution of individual consumptions. This may well lead one to underestimate poverty among persons, and the magnitude need not be negligible.[28] However, it is not clear what would be a better assumption. Further research using individual consumption data, when available, may be able to throw light on best practice when such data are not available.

Sometimes in practice one only has grouped data, such as income shares of households ranked in deciles, or income frequency distributions. (And even household-level data can be interpreted as grouped individual data.) Poverty lines rarely occur at the boundaries of the grouped data. So we must find some way of interpolating between those boundaries. Linear interpolation is the easiest method, but it can be quite inaccurate, particularly when the poverty line is far from the mode of the distribution (such as when it is found in the typically quite nonlinear lower region of the CDF.[29]) Quadratic interpolation is usually feasible with the same data, and is generally more accurate, though one must be wary of the possibility that the probability density (slope of the frequency distribution) implied by this method does not become negative. Another method of interpolation which can be very accurate, and is also useful in certain policy simulations, involves estimation of a parameterized Lorenz curve. This is a precise mathematical model of the Lorenz curve, and a number of specifications have been proposed in the literature. The accuracy depends greatly on the particular specification used, and some tend to dominate others on many data sets.[30]

Hypothesis Testing

Testing hypotheses about differences in poverty between two situations is not difficult for additive poverty measures when the poverty line is treated as fixed (i.e., measured without error). Recall that additive measures can be calculated as the sample mean of an appropriately defined individual poverty measure. For random samples, the standard error can then also be readily calculated.[31] This allows us to test hypotheses about poverty, such as whether it is significantly higher in one subgroup than in another.

---

[28] See, e.g., Haddad and Kanbur (1990).

[29] For example, I have come across one estimate of the headcount index for a country (which can remain unnamed) that was obtained by linear interpolation in the lowest class interval of the grouped distribution; the estimate was 9.5%. However, when one re-estimated with a model of the Lorenz curve (based on a Beta specification; see below) that took account of the nonlinearity, one obtained a figure of 0.5%! This is an extreme case, though large errors are likely from linear interpolation at the lower end of any grouped distribution.

[30] Two specifications that have been found to work well in practice are the generalized quadratic model and the Beta model; see Villasenor and Arnold (1989) and Kakwani (1980a), respectively. Formulae for poverty measures as functions of the Lorenz curve parameters and the mean of the distribution are found in Datt and Ravallion (1992).

[31] The key result from statistics being used here is called the Central Limit Theorem. Let a sample mean M of any variable be calculated from a random sample of size N and let μ denote the true value

For the headcount index, the standard error can be calculated the same way as for any population proportion.[32] These methods can be extended to other additive poverty measures. Nanak Kakwani (1990) has derived formulae for the standard errors of a number of other additive measures, including the FGT measures.[33]

Summary

Where does this tour of the extensive literature on poverty measurement leave us? The additive and smooth distribution sensitive poverty measures that have been proposed (such as the Watts index and *SPG*) have considerable theoretical appeal. Nonetheless, the "lower order" measures—the headcount and poverty gap indices—are sure to remain popular if only because they are much easier to interpret. As a rule, the headcount index also tends to be less sensitive to some common forms of measurement error at the bottom of the observed distribution. It is important to know whether a poverty comparison is sensitive to the choice of poverty measure, and not just because of the uncertainties involved in that choice; differences in rankings by different measures can also tell us something about the precise way in which the distribution of living standards has changed. Section 5.5 will describe some analytical tools that can help assess sensitivity to the choice of poverty measure.

5.4 Decompositions of Poverty Measures

Decompositions can be useful tools in poverty analysis. The discussion here will first discuss how a single aggregate poverty number can be decomposed to form a poverty profile. It will then look at two useful ways of decomposing changes in poverty over time.

Poverty Profiles

A "poverty profile" is simply a special case of a poverty comparison, showing how poverty varies across subgroups of society, such as region of residence or sector

of the mean. Then it can be shown that $(M - \mu)N$ approaches a normal distribution with mean zero as N increases.

[32] Like any population share, H has a binomial distribution in random samples, approaching a normal distribution as sample size increases. Thus the standard errors—the standard deviation of the sample distribution of the headcount index—is given by $\sqrt{[H. (1 - H) /N]}$ for a sample of size N. For all but very small sample sizes (less than 5), a useful rule-of-thumb is that the approximation involved in using the normal distribution will be accurate as long as the absolute value of $\sqrt{\{(1 - H) /H\}} - \sqrt{\{H/ (1 - H)\}}$ does not exceed 0.3N (Box et al. 1978).

[33] The standard error of the FGT measure (P_α) is $\sqrt{\left[\left(P_{2\alpha} - P_\alpha{}^2\right) /N\right]}$, which yields the aforementioned standard error for the headcount index as the special case when $\alpha = 0$. This formula does not take account of survey design; typically there will be a degree of clustering in survey design that will raise standard errors of those in simple random samples; and there will be a degree of stratification that will lower them. Also one will often need to weight the observations, such as by household size. For formulae for the standard errors that deal with these common features of data, see Howes and Lanjouw (1997). Also see Preston (1992).

of employment. A poverty profile can be useful in assessing how to target public resources, and it can provide clues as to how the sectoral or regional pattern of economic change is likely to affect aggregate poverty.[34]

A "poverty map" is an example. In everyday life, we experience poverty and inequality through local geographic experiences. The costs to poor and non-poor people alike can also be quite localized, such as welfare losses from perceptions of relative deprivation, or the heightened instance of crime often associated with high-inequality areas. Additionally, when implementing antipoverty policies, one often wants to target poor areas.

For all these reasons, the level of *geographic disaggregation* that is possible using a household sample survey can be inadequate—the sampling design may not be representative at local level. To address this problem, various methods of small-area estimation have been developed that exploit the existence of common variables in both the census data and the sample survey to make predictions of poverty and inequality measures at a finer geographic level. The key is to build a regression model of the welfare indicator (as used for measuring poverty or inequality) as a function of variables that are observed in the sample survey as well as in the Population Census. (Box 5.11 goes into more detail on such regression models.) One can then use this model to predict the poverty rate at a finer level than is possible from the sample survey. Naturally there are limits to how far one can go reliably with this method, but one can certainly get a finer picture than is possible with the original sample. The challenge is to derive good estimates of the standard errors of the estimated small-area poverty measures, recognizing that there may be idiosyncratic unobserved factors that make an area have a high poverty rate.[35]

Box 5.11 Regression Models of Poverty and Their Applications

Recall box 1.19 on regression. A common form of the regression model for poverty in a sample of N households is as follows:

$$\ln(Y_i/Z_i) = \alpha + \beta_1 X_{1i} + \beta_2 X_{2i} + \ldots + +\beta_K X_{Ki} + \varepsilon_i \ (i = 1, \ldots, N).$$

Here Y_i is consumption for household i, Z_i is the poverty line for that household, X_{ki} is the kth explanatory variable, $k = 1, \ldots, K < N - 1$ and ε_i is the error term to allow for omitted variables and errors in measuring the dependent variable $\ln(Y_i/Z_i)$. The parameters $\alpha, \beta_1, \beta_2, \ldots, \beta_K$ are typically estimated by the method of Ordinary Least Squares (OLS), which chooses the estimates to minimize the sum of the squared predicted errors. Then the parameter

continued

---

[34] See Kanbur (1987a) for an insightful discussion of the uses of poverty profiles in policy analysis.

[35] Elbers et al. (2003) provide a method for constructing poverty maps and their standard errors that has been widely used. On the performance of these methods in practice, see Christiaensen et al. (2012).

Box 5.11 (Continued)

estimates, $\hat{\alpha}, \hat{\beta}_1, \ldots, \hat{\beta}_K$, assure that the error term has zero mean. The predicted value of $\ln(Y_i/Z_i)$ is then $\hat{\alpha} + \hat{\beta}_1 X_{1i} + \ldots + \hat{\beta}_K X_{Ki}$.

When using such a model to calibrate a proxy-means test or in poverty mapping the X's are the variables that are observed in both the survey that includes $\ln(Y_i/Z_i)$ and in another survey or census that does not. It is assumed (often implicitly) that the values reported for the X's for a given household at a given date are the same in the two surveys; this can be called the *survey-invariance assumption*. The only test of this assumption to date was not encouraging (Kilic and Sohnesen 2014), though more evidence is needed.

In some applications, the parameters are interpreted as *causal effects* of the explanatory variables. An important assumption for a casual interpretation is that the X's are *exogeneous*, essentially meaning that they are uncorrelated with the error term ε_i. Then the method gives unbiased estimates of the parameters (meaning that they converge on the true values in sufficiently large samples) (It is typically also assumed that the error terms are independent between observations and have constant variance.) The dependent variable for consumption relative to the poverty line is typically logged to help assure that the error term is normally distributed, as is assumed by standard statistical tests.

Another maintained assumption in writing the regression model in the form above is that the parameters are constant across the population. If the parameters vary across the strata used in the sampling, then OLS will not give an unbiased estimate of the mean parameters for the population as a whole. This has motivated some researchers to use a *weighted regression*, similarly to the idea of using inverse sampling weights in calculating summary statistics from a stratified sample (box 3.6). However, regression parameters are not quite the same thing, and the weighted regression estimator will not deliver an unbiased estimate of the true value of the parameters even in large samples. Under the maintained assumption that the parameters are constant, weighted regression is not needed, but nor is it necessarily better when parameters vary. It is better to deal directly with the expected parameter heterogeneity in formulating the model.

For example, suppose that the sampling rate is higher in urban areas and that the parameters of interest also differ between urban and rural areas. Then one should include interaction effects with an urban dummy variable (taking the value unity in urban areas and zero in rural) in the regression, or estimate the model separately for urban and rural areas (equivalent to including a full set of interaction effects). The population estimate of the parameters should then be obtained by weighting the strata-specific estimates by the population proportions. (That is not in general what a weighted regression estimator gives you!)

Further reading: Among many good introductions to econometrics, see Wooldridge (2013). On the arguments for and against weighted regression, see Deaton (1997) and Solon et al. (2013).

Essentially the same method can be used to calibrate a *proxy-means test* (PMT), which aims to predict economic welfare from short surveys that include previously validated predictors of welfare from a longer survey. We will return to PMT in chapter 10.

Additive poverty measures greatly facilitate such poverty comparisons. (Indeed, to my knowledge, policy applications have relied solely on additive measures.) Suppose the population can be divided into K mutually exclusive subgroups. The poverty profile is simply the list of poverty measures across the K groups. Aggregate poverty can then be written as the population weighted mean of the subgroup poverty measures (recalling that we restrict attention to additive measures). One can also define "clusters" of subgroups, as one disaggregates further and further, the poverty profile at each step adds up to that of the previous step, using population weights.

In addition to the computational convenience of additive poverty measures in forming poverty profiles, additivity guarantees "subgroup monotonicity" (box 5.6) in that when poverty increases (decreases) in any subgroup of the population, aggregate poverty will also increase (decrease).[36] This property is intuitively appealing for any poverty profile. Indeed, an evaluation of the effects on aggregate poverty of targeted poverty alleviation scheme—whereby the benefits are concentrated in certain subgroups—may be quite misleading unless the poverty measure used has this property; the measure of aggregate poverty may show an increase even if poverty fell in the target group, and there were no changes elsewhere. Subgroup monotonicity can thus be viewed as a desirable property in evaluating antipoverty policies.[37]

One possible objection to additivity is that it attaches no weight to one aspect of a poverty profile: the differences between subgroups in the extent of poverty. Consider two equal-sized groups with initial poverty indices 0.70 and 0.20, respectively. Aggregate poverty is 0.45 according to any (population weighted) additive measure. One is to choose between two policies X and Y. Under policy X, the poverty profile changes to 0.70 and 0.10, while under policy Y, the profile becomes 0.60 and 0.20. By any additive poverty measure, one should be indifferent between X and Y; both yield an aggregate poverty index of 0.40. Yet, in contrast to X, the gains under policy Y have gone to the poorer rural sector.

Should we prefer policy Y? The answer is "yes," if one is concerned about inequalities between groups *independently* of absolute living standards. Provided that the underlying poverty profile is measured well, then policies X and Y *are* equivalent in their impacts on living standards of the poor. The gains to the urban poor under policy X were the same in magnitude and accrued to people at the same level of living as those to the rural poor under policy Y. So any ranking of these policies must assign independent weight to factors beyond the impacts on living standards. The difficulty is in identifying what sort of factors should be considered relevant to forming such judgments, and how they should be traded-off against living standards. It may well be that one ends up preferring a distribution in which small gains are made by rural poor

---

[36] Indeed (given certain assumptions of a technical nature), subgroup monotonicity implies, and is implied by, the class of additive measures; see Foster and Shorrocks (1991).

[37] There are otherwise attractive measures which can fail to satisfy this condition, such as the Sen (1976a), Kakwani (1980b), and Blackorby-Donaldson (1980) indices.

households to one in which large gains occur to the urban poor at identical levels of living. That would seem hard to defend.

The conclusion could be quite different if there are reasons to believe that the distribution of measured living standards is faulty, and (in this example) has led to an overestimation of well-being in the rural sector. This might be due to the (common) fact that survey-based consumption measures exclude urban bias in the distribution of benefits from public goods; more speculatively, considerations of individual envy across sectors could have a similar implication. But these are more straightforward problems conceptually, and need not lead one to reject additivity as a desirable property.

There are two main ways of presenting a poverty profile. The first ("type A") gives the incidence of poverty or other poverty measure(s) for each subgroup defined in terms of some characteristic, such as place of residence. The second ("type B") gives the incidence of characteristics among subgroups defined in terms of their poverty status, such as being deemed poor or not. The type A profile is not always a feasible option, notably in situations where the population cannot be classified into mutually exclusive groups. For example, data on the consumption of various commodities by different income groups cannot be presented in such a form, though it can be presented in a type B poverty profile. But in many circumstances the poverty profile can be presented in either form. Box 5.12 discusses this choice further.

Box 5.12 Alternative Representations of a Poverty Profile

Consider the hypothetical data in the left-hand panel of the following table. There are 1,000 people in two regions, north and south. From a household survey, we can estimate the numbers of poor and non-poor people in each region, as given in the table. The two types of poverty profile are given in the right-hand panel. They clearly give a different impression, though of course they are measuring different things.

Table B5.12.1 **Alternative Representations of a Poverty Profile for Hypothetical Data**

	Numbers of Persons		Poverty Profile	
Region	Poor	Non-poor	Type A: % of Region's Population Who Are Poor	Type B: % of Total Poor in Each Region
"South"	100	100	50	33
"North"	200	600	25	67

Suppose that one is using the poverty profile to select a target region for a poverty alleviation scheme. The scheme allocates a small sum of money to all residents in the chosen target region. This is an example of what is sometimes called "indicator targeting" (examples of which will be given in chapter 10). It is imperfect targeting because (as is invariably the case) the policymaker does not know who has which standard of living even when a distribution of living standards can be constructed from a household sample survey; rather the policymaker relies on an imperfect indicator of living standards, in this case region of residence.

A moment's reflection will confirm that more of that money will go to the poor, if the "south" is chosen as the target region for the data in table 5.1. The type A profile is the right guide for targeting when one is aiming to have greatest impact on the poverty gap. This is an example of a quite general principle: when making lump-sum transfers to different subgroups of a population with the aim of minimizing the aggregate value of the FGT poverty measure P_α, the next unit of money should go to the subgroup with the highest value of $P_{\alpha-1}$.

Further reading: Kanbur (1987a) discusses the use of poverty profiles in targeting an antipoverty budget. Also see the discussion in Besley and Kanbur (1993). Chapter 10 looks more closely at specific targeted policies.

Poverty profiles have traditionally taken the form of a tabulation of poverty rates by different groups of households, defined by a set of characteristics (demographic, educational, or geographic). This is a rather limited statistical tool for representing the poverty data. An obvious concern arises when the attributes are correlated. For example, in developing countries we invariably find that poverty rates are higher in rural areas (as we will see in chapter 7) and for household heads with less schooling. But we also tend to find less schooling in rural areas. So is it schooling or rural residence that best predicts the poverty rate? This question can be addressed by using instead a multivariate poverty profile, in the form of a regression model in which a potentially large set of variables is identified as potential explanatory factors for an individual's economic welfare relative to the poverty line, and one lets them "fight it out" statistically to determine how much each variable matters, controlling for the other variables. This is a regression model of poverty, as explained more fully in box 5.11.

Changes in Parameters versus Changes in Quantities

If we think of an individual's economic welfare as a function of certain quantities (e.g., "assets") and the returns to those quantities, then it is natural to ask how much of an observed change in a measure of poverty is due to one versus the other. For example, did poverty fall because people acquired more schooling or because the rate of return to their schooling rose?

This type of question is familiar in economics in the form of the Blinder-Oaxaca decomposition, explained in box 5.13. This has been widely used in studying wage differentials, whereby the difference between the average wages of men and women (say) is apportioned between differences in their characteristics (education, experience, etc.) and structural differences in the returns to those characteristics, as would arise from discrimination.

Box 5.13 **The Blinder-Oaxaca Decomposition**

Recall the regression model in box 5.11, but rewrite it in the more compact form:

$$\ln(Y_i/Z_i) = \beta X_i + \varepsilon_i.$$

β and X are now lists of parameters and variables, respectively. (These lists are called "vectors.") The list of parameters is arranged in a row, while the list of variables is a column and their product βX_i is simply $\beta_1 X_{1i} + \beta_2 X_{2i} + \ldots + +\beta_K X_{Ki}$. (To make it even more compact, one of the X's can be thought of as a list of "1's" so that the corresponding β is the intercept α.)

Now imagine we have two groups, A and B, such as the ethnic majority and the ethnic minority, and the parameters can be different between them. So we have two equations:

$$\ln(Y_i/Z_i) = \beta^A X_i + \varepsilon_i^A \text{ for group A and}$$

$$\ln(Y_i/Z_i) = \beta^B X_i + \varepsilon_i^B \text{ for group B.}$$

(The error terms have zero mean given the X's, as in box 1.19.) Let $E_A(.)$ be the mean of the term in parentheses for group A and similarly for $E_B(.)$. The difference in means between A and B is due in part to differences in the parameters ("returns") and in part due to differences in characteristics. The Blinder-Oaxaca decomposition apportions the difference in the means as follows:

$$E_A[\ln(Y/Z)] - E_B[\ln(Y/Z)] = \beta^A E_A(X) - \beta^B E_B(X) = R + C + I.$$

Here:

$$R = (\beta^A - \beta^B)E_B(X)$$
$$C = \beta^B[E_A(X) - E_B(X)]$$
$$I = (\beta^A - \beta^B)[E_A(X) - E_B(X)].$$

R is the component attributed to differences in returns; it gives the gain (or loss) to group B if it had A's parameters but keeping its own characteristics. C is due to the difference in mean characteristics evaluated using B's parameters; this is the gain (or loss) to group B if it had the characteristics of group A but keeping its own parameters. The term I is the interaction effect between differences in means and differences in parameters. Notice that if you add up C and I you also have a component attributable to differences in characteristics but evaluated at A's parameters. Or if you add the R and I you have a term attributable to differences in returns, but now evaluated using A's characteristics.

Further reading: This widely-used decomposition was devised independently by Blinder (1973) and Oaxaca (1973).

However, there are potentially many applications relevant to understanding poverty; here are two examples. The first example used the method to determine how much of the difference in living standards between geographic areas and urban/rural sectors of Bangladesh can be attributed to differences in the mobile non-geographic characteristics of households, versus geographic differences in the returns to those characteristics, interpretable as the underlying structural differences in living standards by location or sector.[38] Using survey data for Bangladesh, the study found significant and sizable geographic effects on living standards after controlling for a wide range of non-geographic characteristics of households, as would typically be observable to policymakers. The geographic structure of living standards is reasonably stable over time, consistent with observed migration patterns, and robust to testable sources of bias.

The second example used the method to help understand ethnic inequality in Vietnam.[39] The ethnic minorities in Vietnam (similarly to China) tend to have lower living standards than the majority population. The minorities tend also to be more prominent in remote areas. The study used the decomposition method to quantify the relative importance of poor economic characteristics versus low returns to characteristics in explaining the relative disadvantage of the minority groups. The researchers found that the ethnic inequality is due in no small measure to differences in returns to productive characteristics. In particular, the minority groups tend to have lower returns to schooling, which is often associated with their location.

Growth and Redistribution Components

How much of an observed change in poverty can be attributed to changes in the *distribution* of living standards, as distinct from *growth* in average living standards? The usual inequality measures, such as the Gini index, can be misleading in this context. One certainly cannot conclude that a reduction in inequality (by any measure satisfying the transfer principle in box 5.3) will reduce poverty. And even when a specific reduction (increase) in inequality does imply a reduction (increase) in poverty, the change in the inequality measure can be a poor guide to the quantitative impact on poverty. Inequality measures can be quite uninformative about how changes in distribution have affected the poor.

One can readily quantify the relative importance of growth versus redistribution. The change in poverty is decomposed as the sum of a growth component (the change in poverty that would have been observed if the Lorenz curve had not shifted), a redistribution component (the change that would have been observed if the mean had not shifted), and a residual (the interaction between growth and redistribution effects). Box 5.14 provides details.

[38] See Ravallion and Wodon (1999).
[39] See van de Walle and Gunewardena (2001).

* Box 5.14 **Decomposing the Change in Poverty into Growth and Redistribution Components**

Let $P(M/Z, L)$ denotes measured poverty when the distribution of living standards has the mean M and Lorenz curve L and the poverty line is Z. The latter is constant so we can set $Z = 1$ to simplify notation. The change in poverty between dates 1 and 2 (say) can then be decomposed as follows:

$$P_2 - P_1 = P(M_2, L_2) - P(M_1, L_1) = G + R + I.$$

Here G denotes the growth component, R is the redistribution component, and I is an interaction effect between growth and redistribution. The growth and redistribution components are defined by:

$$G = P(M_2, L_r) - P(M_1, L_r) \text{ and}$$
$$R = P(M_r, L_2) - P(M_r, L_1).$$

Here the subscript "r" denotes a fixed reference value, such as the initial value. The growth component is the change in the poverty measure due to the actual change in the mean but holding the Lorenz curve constant at the reference value. The redistribution component is the change attributed to the actual shift in the Lorenz curve holding the mean constant at the reference value.

The interaction effect (I) arises from the fact that the effect on the poverty measure of a change in the mean (Lorenz curve) depends on the Lorenz curve (mean). We can write this in two ways:

$$I = [P(M_2, L_2) - P(M_2, L_r)] + [P(M_r, L_1) - P(M_r, L_2)] + [P(M_1, L_r) - P(M_1, L_1)]$$

$$= [P(M_2, L_2) - P(M_r, L_2)] + [P(M_r, L_1) - P(M_1, L_1)] + [P(M_1, L_r) - P(M_2, L_1)]$$

The first way of writing I is the sum of the three changes in the poverty measure due to changes in the Lorenz curve holding the mean constant, while in the second way it is the sum of the changes due to difference in the mean holding the Lorenz curve constant. The interaction effect is of interest in its own right, as it tells us whether the growth effect (redistribution effect) varies according to the extent of inequality (level of the mean).

Here is an example. The data are for Brazil in the 1980s, when both poverty and inequality were rising.

Table B5.14.1 **Poverty Measures for Brazil in the 1980s**

	1981	1988
Headcount index (%)	26.5	26.5
Poverty gap index (x100)	10.1	10.7
Squared poverty gap index (x100)	5.0	5.6
Gini index	0.58	0.62

Here are the decomposition results, using the initial year as the reference:

Table B5.14.2 **Decompositions Based on Table B5.14.1**

	Growth (G)	Redistribution (R)	Interaction Effect (I)
Headcount index (%)	−4.5	4.5	0.0
Poverty gap index (x100)	−2.3	3.2	−0.2
Squared poverty gap index (x100)	−1.4	2.3	−0.3

While there was no change in the headcount index, this reflects two equal and opposite effects: a decline attributed to growth and an increase attributed to rising inequality. The "higher order" measures put more weight on the redistribution component. (Chapter 8 will discuss the case of Brazil further and also discuss the country's more recent success in reducing poverty and inequality.)

Further reading: Datt and Ravallion (1992) give further details on this decomposition method. The same basic idea can also be applied to human development indicators (Lambert et al. 2010).

The Sectoral Decomposition of a Change in Poverty

When analyzing the sources of observed reductions in aggregate poverty and exploiting the additivity property of poverty measures one can make use of another simple decomposition formula. The idea here is to throw light on the relative importance of changes within sectors versus changes in the distribution of the population between them, such as due to migration. For example, we may want to know how much of a decline in aggregate poverty over time is due to progress against poverty within urban areas versus rural areas, and how much is attributable to population urbanization. We can answer this easily on exploiting the additivity of poverty measures. Box 5.15 provides details.

---

* Box 5.15 **Sectoral Decomposition of a Change in Poverty**

Let P_{it} denote the additive measure for sector i with population share n_{it} at date t, where there are m such sectors, and $t = 1, 2$. The aggregate measures for dates 1 and 2 are P_2 and P_1. Then we can write:

$$P_2 - P_1 = \sum (P_{i2} - P_{i1})\, n_{i1} \text{ (Intrasectoral effect)}$$

$$+ \sum (n_{i2} - n_{i1})\, P_{i1} \text{ (Population shift effect)}$$

$$+ \sum (P_{i2} - P_{i1})(n_{i2} - n_{i1}) \text{ (Interaction effect)}$$

continued

Box 5.15 **(Continued)**

where the summations are done over $i = 1, \ldots, m$. The "intrasectoral effects" tell us the contribution of poverty changes within sectors (such as urban and rural areas), controlling for their base period population shares, while the "population shift effects" tell us how much of the poverty in the first date was reduced by the various changes in population shares of sectors between then and the second date (such as through population urbanization). The interaction effects arise from any correlation between sectoral gains and population shifts; a negative interaction effect tells us that people tended to switch to the sectors where poverty was falling although the causality is unclear.

The table gives an example for China. The table gives the total change in each of three measures and its decomposition into rural, urban and population shift effects. The figures in parentheses give the % breakdown. Of the almost 45% point reduction in the headcount index over this 20 years period, over 72% is attributable to the reduction in poverty within rural areas,23% to population urbanization and 5% to urban poverty reduction. (Chapter 8 discusses China's success against poverty in more detail.)

Table B5.15.1 **Decompositions of Changes in Poverty Measures over Time for China**

	Poverty Measures for China (% point change 1981–2001)		
	Headcount Index	Poverty Gap Index	Squared Poverty Gap Index
Within rural	−32.5	−10.4	−4.5
	(72)	(74)	(75)
Within urban	−2.1	−0.3	−0.1
	(5)	(2)	(1)
Population shift	−10.3	−3.3	−1.4
	(23)	(24)	(24)
Total change	−44.9	−14.0	−6.0
	(100)	(100)	(100)

Source: Author's calculations from the data set compiled by Ravallion and Chen (2007).

Further reading: This decomposition is from Ravallion and Huppi (1991).

Transient versus Chronic Poverty

So far we have focused on poverty measures that are essentially "static" in that they reflect living standards in some period of time, usually defined by the available surveys. Some of the poverty observed this way is likely to be transient, in that it is due to temporary shortfalls. This is common in underdeveloped rural economies, where incomes are dependent on climatic conditions and imperfect credit and insurance arrangements leave farm households exposed to income risk. Transient poverty is likely to be common in economies undergoing structural changes with diverse impacts at the household level, such as spells of unemployment that some can cope with more easily than others. Divorce or widowhood can also result in transient poverty, although these demographic shocks can also have long-term effects.[40]

There are three main reasons why we want to know how much of observed poverty is transient. First, in assessing overall progress against poverty we may not be indifferent to whether it is transient or not. Consider two countries in which half of the population is poor at each of two dates, but in one country it is exactly the same households who are poor over time, while in the other it is none of the same households. Few observers will view these two extremes the same way. Yet that is what a conventional poverty measure, such as the proportion of the population living below the poverty line at one time, does.

Second, distinct policies are called for in addressing transient poverty. Increasing the human and physical assets of poor people, or the returns to those assets, is thought to be more appropriate against chronic poverty. Insurance and income-stabilization schemes are more important policies when poverty is transient. (We return to policies in Part Three.) Knowing how much the currently observed level of poverty is transient may thus inform policy choices.

Third, the existence of transient poverty can influence policy choices. The policies chosen will depend in part on the information available. A long-standing policy issue is how much transfers and public services should be targeted. Variability over time will clearly make current consumption a noisy indicator of longer term welfare, and so weaken the case for efforts to target the long-term poor based on static data.

So how can we isolate how much of the poverty that is observed at one date is transient? We need panel data, which track the same households over time and measure consumption or income in each time period (box 3.7). With such date we can identify the time profile of consumption. We can then define *transient poverty* as the poverty that can be attributed to inter-temporal variability in consumption. In other words, if the consumption of a household does not change over time, then we can say that there is no transient component to poverty. The poverty that is found based instead on average consumption over time can be called *chronic poverty*. A household whose mean consumption is above the poverty line cannot be chronically poor by this definition although it can experience transient poverty.

Following this approach we can measure transient poverty by the contribution to the mean level of poverty observed over time of the inter-temporal variability in consumption (or income). By this approach, one does not identify transient poverty as

[40] For example, see van de Walle (2013) on the effects of widowhood on children in Mali.

simply crossing the poverty line. Transient poverty is positive for someone who is always poor, but whose consumption varies, for example, due to uninsured income risk. However, the poverty focus does mean that consumption fluctuations entirely above the poverty line are ignored. The effect of variability below the line is determined by the weights built into the poverty measure, as discussed earlier in this chapter. Box 5.16 goes into greater detail.

---

*Box 5.16 Chronic versus Transient Poverty

When we have panel data, we can measure a stream of consumptions over time for each household. Let $(y_{i1}, y_{i2}, \ldots, y_{iD})$ be household i's (positive) consumption stream over D dates, where y_{it} is consumption of i at date t. We can take consumption to be normalized by the poverty line so that $y_{it} = 1$ at the poverty line. Next let $P = P(y_{i1}, y_{i2}, \ldots, y_{iD})$ be the corresponding poverty measure for household i.

Quite generally, P reflects both the level of mean consumption over time and how consumption varies around the time mean $(\bar{y}_i)$. We can define the chronic poverty component as:

$$C_i, = P(\bar{y}_i, \bar{y}_i, \ldots, \bar{y}_i).$$

We can then define the transient component as the remainder:

$$T_i = P(y_{i1}, y_{i2}, \ldots, y_{iD}) - P(\bar{y}_i, \bar{y}_i, \ldots, \bar{y}_i).$$

So the inter-temporal poverty measure is the sum of the chronic and transient components. Corresponding to each of the household-specific poverty measures there is an aggregate poverty measure across all households, which we denote by dropping the subscripts i.

It is reasonable to impose a number of conditions on the aggregate poverty measure. First, it is assumed that the measure is both inter-temporally and inter-personally *additive*. As we saw earlier in this chapter, it is common to restrict attention to inter-personally additive measures, whereby aggregate poverty is a population-weighted mean of an individual poverty measure. This implies that if poverty increases in any one subgroup and does not fall in any other, aggregate poverty must increase. We apply the same restriction to the inter-temporal poverty measure, so that aggregate poverty for a given household is the expected value over time of a date-specific individual measure, denoted by p_{it}. A possible objection to this assumption is that the extent of household poverty at one date may depend on expenditures at a prior date (e.g., acquiring a bicycle now may make one less poor in the future). This objection is less persuasive if the measure of consumption in a given period includes the imputed value of all commodities consumed in that period, even those purchased previously.

The second set of assumptions concerns the properties of the dated individual poverty measure, which we can take to be a function of consumption at that date, that is, $p_{it} = p(y_{it})$. A simple example is $p_{it} = 1$ if $y_{it} < 1$ and $p_{it} = 0$ otherwise. The inter-temporal poverty measure is then the proportion of dates for which household i falls below the poverty line and the aggregate poverty index is the inter-temporal mean of the headcount index. While this is a simple example, it does not provide a very satisfactory measure of poverty, since the measure tells us nothing about how far below the line the household falls (box 5.6).

We can assume instead that the measure: (1) penalizes losses to the poor and only the poor, in that p is strictly decreasing up to the poverty line, and zero thereafter; (2) penalizes (or at least does not reward) inequality increases among the poor, so p is at least weakly convex in y; and (3) is continuous at the poverty line. There appears to be broad agreement on the desirability of these properties. When combined with (1), continuity precludes the possibility of consumption changes for the least poor (in a neighborhood of the poverty line) being given a higher weight than those among the poorest. An example is the *SPG* measure for which $p_{it} = (1 - y_{it})^2$ if $y_{it} < 1$ and $p_{it} = 0$ otherwise.

Further reading: This approach was introduced in Ravallion (1988a) and applied there to data for India. Jalan and Ravallion (1998a) provide an application to data for China. Rodgers and Rodgers (1993) use the same approach and discuss its advantages over alternatives in the literature including those based on the number and length of spells of poverty.

For example, a study using a six-year panel data set for rural China found that consumption variability accounts for a large share of observed poverty and is likely to constrain efforts to reach the long-term poor using data on current consumptions.[41] Indeed, they find that half of the mean squared poverty gap and over one-third of the mean poverty gap is transient, in that it is directly attributable to year-to-year fluctuations in consumption.

5.5 The Robustness of Poverty Comparisons

An important reason for measuring poverty is to make an *ordinal poverty comparison*—an assessment of which of two situations has more poverty. Has poverty increased? Is it higher in one place than another? Is there more poverty with some policy change? However, at a number of points so far we have seen that there is pervasive uncertainty about possibly crucial aspects of a poverty comparison. There are likely to be errors in our living standards data, unknown differences in needs between households at similar consumption levels, uncertainty and arbitrariness about both the poverty line and precise poverty measure. Given these problems, how robust are our poverty comparisons? Would they alter if we made alternative assumptions?

Good practice in any of the approaches to setting a poverty line discussed above is to consider at least two possible lines. The lower one might be interpretable as

[41] See Jalan and Ravallion (1998a).

an "ultra-poverty line," such that persons with consumption expenditures below that point behave in a way which suggests that they face a serious health risk of under-nutrition.[42] Higher lines are sometimes called "vulnerability" lines, although this is a deceptive label, since there is no explicit recognition of the risk element that is implied by that word. (Section 5.7 returns to this point in the context of defining the "middle class.") But whatever one calls the various lines it is important to know whether the poverty comparison is robust to the choice.

Indeed, there is a good case for considering lines that span quite a wide range of the distribution of consumption or income. A strand of research in poverty analy-sis by economists has shown how we can answer questions about the robustness of qualitative rankings in terms of poverty.[43] I shall give an elementary exposition of the approach, again oriented to the needs of the analyst trying to make a reasonably robust poverty comparison. The analysis is easier for a single dimension of well-being, but I will also give an introduction to multidimensional dominance.

Taking the idea of multiple lines further, imagine the curve that is traced out as one plots the headcount index on the vertical axis and the poverty line on the horizontal axis, allowing the latter to vary from zero to the maximum consumption. This is simply the CDF, which can be thought of as the *poverty incidence curve* $F(z)$. Each point on the curve gives the proportion of the population consuming less than the amount given on the horizontal axis; see figure 5.4, panel (a). The slope of the poverty incidence curve is the density of the data at the poverty line (the probability of having an income equal to the poverty line).

On calculating the area under this curve up to each point, one traces out the *poverty deficit curve* $D(Z)$ (figure 5.4, panel (b)). Each point on this curve is simply the value of the *PG* index times the poverty line Z. If one again calculates the area under the poverty deficit curve at each point, then one obtains a new curve, which can be termed the *poverty severity curve* $S(Z)$ (figure 5.4, panel (c)); each point on this curve is directly proportional to the FGT measure *SPG*.[44]

Suppose we do not know the poverty line z, but we are sure that it does not exceed Z^{max}. Nor do we know the poverty measure, but we can know some of its properties, including the aforementioned additivity property.[45] Then it can be shown that poverty will unambiguously fall between two dates if the poverty incidence curve (the CDF) for the latter date lies nowhere above that for the former date, up to Z^{max}. This is called the *First Order Dominance* (FOD) *condition*.

Figure 5.4, panel (a), illustrates FOD. When we plot the CDF (cumulative percent-ages of the population below various consumption levels) in states A and B, we find

[42] This approach follows Lipton (1983, 1988).

[43] On the use of dominance conditions in ranking distributions in terms of measures of inequality, see Atkinson (1970); on rankings in terms of poverty, see Atkinson (1987) and Foster and Shorrocks (1988a,b).

[44] Ravallion (1994b, appendix 2) gives more formal definitions of $F(z)$, $D(z)$, and $S(z)$, and it proves the main results in this subsection can be proved.

[45] More precisely, attention is restricted to poverty measures which are additive, or any measure which can be written as a monotonic transformation of an additive measure. All the FGT measures qualify. Atkinson (1987, 1989, ch. 2) characterizes the set of admissible poverty measures and gives other examples from the literature.

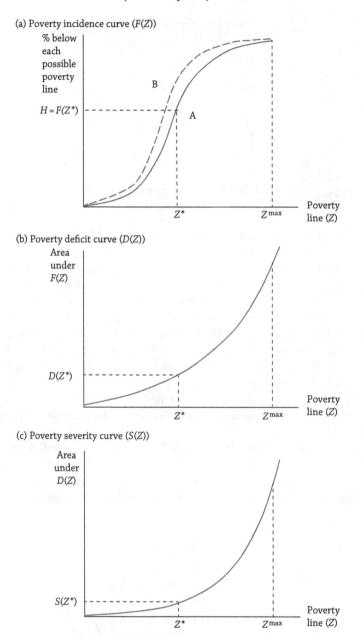

Figure 5.4 The Construction of the Three Poverty Curves. (a) Poverty incidence curve ($F(Z)$) (b) Poverty deficit curve ($D(Z)$) (c) Poverty severity curve ($S(Z)$).

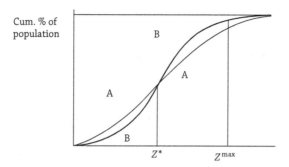

Figure 5.5 Intersecting Poverty Incidence Curves.

that the curve for A is everywhere below that for B. Poverty is lower in state A than in B, no matter what the poverty line or measure.

If the curves intersect as in figure 5.5 (and they may intersect more than once), then the ranking is ambiguous. Some poverty lines and some poverty measures will rank the distributions differently to others. We need more information. One can restrict the range of poverty lines, or one can impose more structure on the poverty measure.

If one excludes the headcount index and restricts attention to additive measures which do reflect the depth of poverty such as *PG* and *SPG* (i.e., measures which are strictly decreasing and at least weakly convex in incomes of the poor), then we can use a *Second Order Dominance* (SOD) *condition*. A fall in poverty then requires that the poverty deficit curve, given by the area under the CDF, is nowhere lower for the earlier date at all points up to the maximum poverty line, and at least somewhere higher. This is illustrated in figure 5.6.

SOD over the entire distribution is equivalent to another idea, called generalized Lorenz curve dominance. The *generalized Lorenz curve* (GLC) is simply the ordinary Lorenz curve (box 5.1) scaled up by the mean; thus it plots (on the vertical axis) the cumulative value of the welfare indicator (normalized by the population size) for the

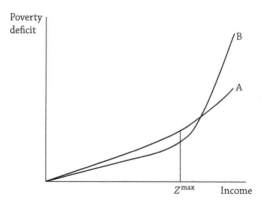

Figure 5.6 Poverty Deficit Curves That Intersect above the Maximum Poverty Line.

poorest p percent of the population ranked by that indicator (on the horizontal axis).[46] If the GLC of distribution A is everywhere above that of B, then the area under A's CDF must be everywhere lower than B's. Notice that the highest point on the GLC is the mean; thus a necessary condition for poverty to fall for all possible poverty lines and all measures reflecting the depth of poverty is that the mean has not fallen. By similar reasoning, another necessary condition is that the lowest level of living has not fallen (the lowest point on the GLC—just before it hits zero—is the lowest level of living). If Z^{max} is the highest income, then it is immaterial whether one tests SOD using the poverty deficit curve or the generalized Lorenz curve, though for lower values of Z^{max} it is better to use the poverty deficit curve.

When SOD is inconclusive, one can further restrict the range of admissible poverty measures. If one is content to rely solely on distribution sensitive measures such as *SPG* (but now excluding H and PG), then a *Third Order Dominance* (TOD) *condition* can be tested; an unambiguous poverty comparison for all poverty lines then requires that the poverty severity curve is everywhere higher in one of the two situations being compared. If necessary, one can go on to test higher order dominance, though the interpretation of the (increasingly) restricted class of measures becomes less clear.[47] To illustrate the three dominance tests, box 5.17 gives a simple example.

Box 5.17 An Exercise in Dominance Testing

Consider an initial state in which three persons have consumptions in amounts (1, 2, 3). Any final state in which one or more of these persons has a higher consumption, and none has a lower consumption, will imply a lower poverty incidence curve (strictly lower and no higher anywhere), and hence no higher poverty for any poverty line or poverty measure; examples of such final states are (2, 2, 3) or (1, 2, 4).

Consider instead the final state (2, 2, 2). The poverty incidence curves now cross each other: some poverty lines and some poverty measures will judge this final state to be an improvement, while others will judge it to be worse than the initial state. (Compare the headcount indices for $z = 1.9$ and $z = 2.1$.) However, the poverty deficit curves do not cross each other; for the initial state, the poverty deficit curve is (1, 3, 6) (corresponding to consumptions 1, 2, and 3), while it is (0, 3, 6) for the final state (2, 2, 2). Thus, poverty will have fallen (or at least not increased) for all poverty lines and all measures which are decreasing in consumptions of the poor, such as PG and SPG. (There is an unambiguous fall in poverty for all such measures as long as the poverty line is two or less.)

continued

---

[46] On the generalized Lorenz curve, see Shorrocks (1983) and Lambert (2001). Also see Thistle (1989) (who defines the GLC somewhat differently, but the difference is not crucial here). On the relationship between the GLC and the poverty deficit curve, see Atkinson and Bourguignon (1989) and Foster and Shorrocks (1988b).

[47] Among the FGT class, the fourth order dominance test restricts attention to $P\alpha$ measures for values of $\alpha = 3$ or higher. See Kakwani (1980b) for an interpretation of such measures.

Box 5.17 (Continued)

But what if the final state has consumptions (1.5, 1.5, 2)? The table B5.17.1 gives the poverty incidence, deficit and severity curves. Even if we confine attention to distribution sensitive poverty measures, some poverty lines will rank the states differently to others. But note that the intersection point of the poverty severity curves is above 2; any poverty line less than this point will indicate that poverty has fallen for all distribution sensitive measures, such as *SPG*. (Fourth order dominance holds for all points, implying that FGT measures for $\alpha = 3$ or higher, and the Watts measure will show a fall in poverty for all possible poverty lines.)

Table B5.17.1 **Poverty Incidence, Depth, and Severity Curves for Three People with Initial Consumptions (1,2,3) and Final Consumptions (1.5,1.5,2)**

Consumption (Z)	Poverty Incidence Curve (F(Z))		Poverty Deficit Curve (D(Z))		Poverty Severity Curve (S(Z))	
	Initial	Final	Initial	Final	Initial	Final
1	1/3	0	1/3	0	1/3	0
1.5	1/3	2/3	2/3	2/3	1	2/3
2	2/3	1	4/3	5/3	7/3	7/3
3	1	1	7/3	8/3	14/3	15/3

When two frequency distributions are quite close, we may also want to assess whether the difference between them is statistically significant. For FOD, this can be done quite easily using the Kolmogorov-Smirnov test, based on the largest vertical distance between the two CDFs.[48] Statistical inference is more difficult for higher order dominance, and more advanced methods are needed.[49]

Similar ideas can be applied in circumstances in which poverty lines vary across households or individuals in an unknown way. For example, errors in measuring the standard of living can entail that we should be using different poverty lines for different individuals. Unknown differences in "needs" at given consumption levels could also mean that the true poverty lines vary. There may be considerable, unknown, interpersonal variation in nutritional requirements. Errors in accounting for differences between households in their demographic composition or the prices they face may also entail some underlying variation in the appropriate poverty lines.[50]

[48] Expositions on this simple test, and tabulations of critical values, are readily available; see, e.g., Daniel (1990, ch. 8).

[49] For further discussion, see Bishop et al. (1989) and Howes and Lanjouw (1991).

[50] For a general discussion of multivariate dominance tests under various assumptions about how multiple dimensions interact in determining welfare, see Atkinson and Bourguignon (1982). In the

Poverty comparisons are clearly more difficult when the poverty line has an unknown distribution, but even then unambiguous conclusions may be possible if one is willing to make some assumptions. Provided that the distribution of poverty lines is the same for the two (or more) situations being compared and is independent of the distribution of living standards, FOD of one distribution over another implies an unambiguous poverty ranking. This holds no matter what the underlying distribution of poverty lines.[51]

Another case of interest is when one knows the distribution of needs (such as family size) as well as consumption, but one does not know precisely how these two variables interact to determine welfare. For two dimensions of welfare, such as aggregate consumption and family size, one can derive bi-variate dominance tests which are more or less stringent depending on the assumptions one is willing to make about the way in which differences in needs interact with consumption in determining well-being; the precise tests depend on (among other things) whether the marginal social valuation of consumption is higher or lower in larger families. In a special case wherein the marginal valuation of consumption is independent of family size and the marginal distribution of size is fixed, the problem collapses back to the standard dominance tests above.

Let us suppose first that we know nothing about how needs interact with consumption in determining poverty. For additive poverty measures and a fixed distribution of the population across different needs, all of the above dominance tests can be applied separately to each of the groups identified as having different needs. Thus, one can test for FOD among (say) rural households, separately from urban households, or large families separately from small families. If we find that FOD holds for each group separately, then we can conclude that FOD also holds for the aggregate, no matter what the difference in needs is between the groups. If FOD fails, then, by restricting attention to measures of the depth and severity of poverty, one can then test for SOD for each needs group separately, or TOD, if necessary.

These will often be quite stringent tests. Weaker tests can be invoked if one is willing to rank needs groups in terms of the marginal welfare attached to an increment of consumption. Suppose one can, and let group 1 have the highest marginal social valuation of consumption (i.e., the steepest individual poverty measure). Let us also assume that this ranking is the same at all possible consumption levels (so group 1 always has the highest marginal valuation of consumption).[52] When ranking distributions in terms of poverty measures we will also need to assume that the poverty measure, as a function of consumption, is not discontinuous at the poverty line.[53] This precludes the headcount index, but few other measures; the condition holds for *PG* and *SPG* as illustrated in figure 5.4. Under these conditions one can apply simple *partial dominance tests*, where the test is done cumulatively by the ranked needs groups starting

specific context of inequality comparisons when needs differ, see Atkinson and Bourguignon (1987) and Bourguignon (1989). The discussion in Atkinson (1992) is in the context of poverty measures.

[51] For further discussion in the context of measuring under-nutrition when nutrient requirements vary in some unknown way, see Kakwani (1989) and Ravallion (1992a).

[52] This follows Atkinson and Bourguignon (1987).

[53] See Atkinson (1987).

from group 1, rather than separately for each group.[54] Thus, dominance is tested on the CDF for group 1 in the two situations compared, then for the population weighted sum of groups 1 and 2, then for 1, 2, and 3, and so on. This makes dominance more likely. For example, although poverty may increase in some needs groups, aggregate poverty may be found to have fallen as a result of some policy change.

However, these tests have to be modified further when the distribution of needs also changes, such as when the proportion of the population living in urban areas has increased over the period of the poverty comparison, as is typically the case in inter-temporal poverty comparisons for developing countries. It is theoretically possible that FOD may hold separately for each of urban and rural areas, and yet not hold in the aggregate for all possible distributions of needs between the two sectors and all possible ways in which consumption and needs interact to determine well-being. More general tests can be devised for such situations.[55]

5.6 Pro-Poor Growth and Growth Incidence

The question often arises as to how the gains from aggregate economic growth (or the losses from contraction) are distributed across households according to their initial incomes or expenditures. The analytic tools described above can be easily modified to address this question.

We can readily calculate the *growth elasticity of poverty*, defined as the ratio of the proportionate change in the poverty measure to the rate of growth in the mean over the same period.[56] With multiple observations it is common practice to estimate the regression coefficient of either the poverty measure on the mean (as in box 1.19) or the proportionate rate of change in poverty on the rate of growth. Such a regression coefficient can be interpreted as an estimate of the average elasticity.[57] If all the growth accrues to the non-poor, then the elasticity will be zero. If all income levels grow at the same rate (leaving inequality unchanged), then the elasticity will automatically be negative.[58] But, even then, how large it is (in absolute value) will depend on many things, including the initial level of inequality. We return to this issue in chapter 8.

This elasticity can be a useful summary statistic, but it can be instructive to look further at how growth rates vary across the whole distribution. When we compare two CDFs over time (as in figure 5.4, panel (a)), the vertical differences between the two

[54] See Atkinson and Bourguignon (1987) for details.

[55] A formal treatment of this topic can be found in Atkinson and Bourguignon (1982).

[56] So if the rate of growth in the mean is 2% per annum and the headcount index is falling at 3% per annum (that is percent not percentage points), then the elasticity is –1.5.

[57] Strictly they are weighted averages. For example, suppose we have two observations over time for each country. It can be shown that if there is no common trend in the log poverty measure (though there can be an idiosyncratic "country fixed-effect"), then the estimate based on the regression coefficient of the growth rate of the poverty measure on the growth rate of the mean across countries is a weighted average of the country-specific elasticities, with weights given by the shares of the sum of squared growth rates in the mean. In other words, countries with higher growth rates (either positive or negative) get higher weight.

[58] Analytic formulae for the elasticity can then be derived for specific poverty measures; see Kakwani (1993).

curves give the differences in the poverty rates at that poverty line while the horizontal differences give the average income gain or loss at the initial percentile. We could instead invert the curves to obtain the quantile functions so that the vertical differences give the income gains. But we can go a step further and calculate the growth rate over time for any given percentile of the distribution, $g(p)$. We first calculate the quantile function at the first date, then the quantile function at the second date, and then we calculate the growth rate for each percentile. This is called the *growth incidence curve* (GIC) showing how the growth rate for a given quantile varies across quantiles ranked by income.[59] For example, the point on the GIC corresponding to the 50th percentile is the growth rate of the median (not to be confused with the average growth rate of the poorest 50%). If the growth rate is positive everywhere, then clearly we have FOD over all possible poverty lines. Box 5.18 gives an example.

Box 5.18 **Growth Incidence Curve for China**

We have all heard about China's high growth rate in mean income. But how did that vary across the distribution? Figure B5.18.1 gives the GIC over the period 1990–2005. There is FOD. Thus, absolute poverty has fallen no matter where one draws the poverty line or what poverty measure one uses within a broad class. The curve is increasing, with lower growth rates for poorer percentiles. The annualized percentage increase in income per capita is estimated to have been 4.5% for the poorest percentile, rising to 9.5% for the richest.

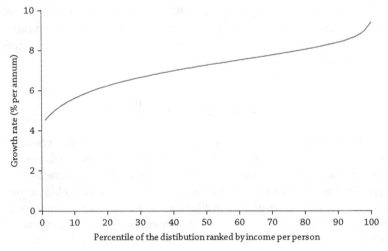

Figure B5.18.1 Growth Incidence Curve for China.

---

[59] Ravallion and Chen (2003) introduced the GIC based on calculating growth rates on the quantile functions. This gives the growth rate of each percentile (or even finer if one wants). In some of the literature one finds instead average growth rates being calculated for larger fractiles, such as deciles, based on the comparison of the fractile means. This averaging is unnecessary.

The area under the growth incidence curve tells us something quite useful. If one calculates this area up to the initial value of the headcount index of poverty, then one has the mean growth rate for those who were initially poor. Furthermore, it can be shown that this gives the change in the Watts index of poverty, motivating Ravallion and Chen (2003) to dub this area as the *rate of pro-poor growth*. This is the right way to measure growth over any period if one wants the measure to be consistent with progress in reducing the Watts index of (absolute or relative) poverty. Notice, however, that a positive rate of pro-poor growth by this measure does not mean that poor people have an above average growth rate; inequality can still be rising even though Watts poverty is falling.

These tools can also be applied in measuring another idea, "*shared prosperity*." In 2013 the World Bank announced that one of its two development goals is "sharing prosperity"—an idea that the new president at the time, Jim Yong Kim, was keen on.[60] The Bank plans to measure success in this goal by the growth rate in the mean for the poorest 40% of the population.[61] This has the appeal of simplicity, but that comes with a cost. A concern with this measure is that it does not tell us anything at all about how much rising prosperity is shared among the poorest 40%, or how the losses from economic contraction are being spread. For example, the mean of the poorest 40% could rise without any gain to the poorest.

Using the ideas discussed in this section, we can now see a simple corrective: Instead of measuring the growth rate of the mean for the poorest 40% we should measure the mean growth rate of the poorest 40%. This subtle difference in wording makes a big difference in the properties of the measure. With this change, the measure now reflects any changes in the distribution of income among the poorest 40%. If inequality falls (rises) among the poorest 40%, then the mean growth rate will be higher (lower) than the growth rate of the mean. And there is virtually no extra cost in monitoring. The mean growth rate of the poorest 40% is easy to calculate from the quantile functions for the two dates (the inverses of the CDFs).

5.7 Measuring the "Middle Class"

Prior to the availability of national survey data on incomes or consumptions, it was common practice to define "class" in purely qualitative terms, such as in the ideas of the "working class" and "capitalist class." When one talked about income distribution one typically meant the factor distribution, giving income shares going to workers, versus capitalists and landowners. Arguably this practice also made more sense in less diversified economies than today. (As we noted, being "poor" and "working class" were virtually synonymous up to the mid-nineteenth century in England and other industrializing countries. That is no longer true.) Since the 1960s it has been more common

---

[60] The other is to eliminate absolute poverty: the specific target for this is to bring the headcount index of the developing world for $1.25 a day down to 3% by 2030; this was noted in chapter 2, and further discussion can be found in Ravallion (2013).

[61] This was the measure favored in 2012 by the Bank's new Chief Economist, Kaushik Basu, though Basu's writings favored focusing on the poorest 20%, giving what he dubbed "quintile income" (Basu 2011, ch. 8).

to use quantitative data on distributions of income, consumption, or (less often) wealth; this reflects both the availability of such data and the greater heterogeneity in living standards that emerged within the old class categories. (The factor-distribution of income still plays a role in understanding how inter-personal distribution evolves, and we return to this topic in chapter 8.)

The idea of the "middle class" is popular and there are a number of reasons why it has been studied widely by sociologists and economists. Even when development policy discussions give highest weight to outcomes for the poorest, standard assessments of social welfare outcomes are rarely indifferent to those who are not so poor. So there is a case for looking above standard poverty lines in assessing social progress. It has also been argued that there is an instrumental importance of the middle class to the pace of progress for poor people. This is suggested by a strand of the literature pointing to the role the middle class can play in promoting economic growth, such as through fostering entrepreneurship, shifting the composition of consumer demand, and making it more politically feasible to attain policy reforms and institutional changes conducive to growth; chapter 8 will review the main arguments from that literature.

The prospects for reversing past progress also depend on the distribution of past gains, in so far as this determines how many people might be vulnerable to even small income losses. Consider figure 5.7, which plots three hypothetical CDFs, giving the proportion of the population living below each income level. The initial distribution is marked "A." If all incomes increase by a similar proportion, then the distribution shifts to "B." There will be a fall in poverty across all possible poverty lines and a wide range of measures.[62] Alternatively (and there are other alternatives), the gains may be larger at lower poverty lines, with little or no reduction in poverty at high lines, as in distribution "C." Poverty is also unambiguously lower for C than for A, but C has a bigger bulge in the middle of the distribution, in that the density is appreciably higher at the median than for B and this holds in a wide interval around the median.

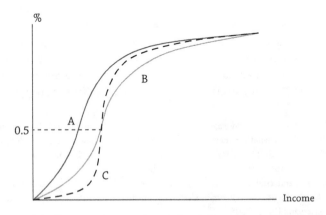

Figure 5.7 B and C Have Less Poverty than A, but B Has a Larger "Middle-Income Bulge".

---

[62] See Atkinson (1987).

In terms of the prospects of falling below low poverty lines, distribution C has more people vulnerable to an aggregate economic contraction than B. So it is important to know whether the developing world has moved toward something more like C than B.

Absolute and Relative Approaches

There is a large literature on defining and measuring the "middle class," mostly in the context of developed countries where the main issue has been the (claimed) decline in the middle class in the United States (and some other Western countries) over recent decades. Similarly to poverty measurement, there is both an absolute and relative approach. Starting with the latter, being "middle class" has been defined as having an income within some interval that includes the median and the interval has often been symmetric in the income space around the median. The lower and upper bounds have been set in diverse and ad hoc ways. Much of the literature has focused on the interval from 75% to 125% of the median.[63]

In contrast to this relative definition (with real-income bounds specific to each country), other authors have defined the middle class in purely absolute terms, with common real-income bounds across countries. However, the definitions have varied. One study defined being middle class as the set of people living between the mean incomes of Brazil and Italy,[64] while another study identified the middle class as those living between $2 and $10 a day, at 1993 PPP.[65] The latter two studies do not even use overlapping intervals; nobody is likely to be "middle class" by *both* definitions.[66] Yet another study used instead a lower bound of $2 a day and an upper bound of $13 a day, both at PPP for 2005.[67]

The differences we see in the measures used in this literature appear to be largely a matter of whether one is after a definition appropriate to rich countries or poor ones. People living below $10 a day would clearly not be considered "middle class" in most developed countries; indeed, they would be living well below the US poverty line, which was $13 a day in 2005.[68] Yet it is likely that many people in developing countries living below the US poverty line or Brazil's mean would be deemed "middle class."

Consider the two most populous countries. The closest concept to "middle class" in China is "Xiaokang"; eventually achieving the "Xiaokang society" is the goal of China's pro-market reforms, instigated in 1979 under Deng Xiaoping's leadership. The Government of China's National Bureau of Statistics set a minimum income for Xiaokang in 1991;[69] when converted to 2005 PPP dollars, Xiaokang requires $2.24 per

---

[63] Following an influential early paper by Thurow (1987). For example, this is Pressman's (2007) definition in his study of whether there has been a decline in the middle class for eleven developed countries, including the United States. Birdsall et al. (2000) defined the middle class as those with incomes between 75% and 125% of the median in each country.

[64] See Milanovic and Yitzhaki (2002). Also see Bussolo et al. (2008) (and their results reported in World Bank 2007a) who use the Milanovic-Yitzhaki definition in identifying a "global middle class."

[65] See Banerjee and Duflo (2008).

[66] Brazil's GDP per capita in 2005 was over $20 per day (using either the 1993 or 2005 PPPs).

[67] See Ravallion (2010a).

[68] I have used the line for a family of four from the website of the Department of Health and Human Services (2008).

[69] The source (in Chinese) is http://baike.baidu.com/view/14275.htm.

day in rural areas and \$3.47 a day in urban areas; I estimate that over 500 million Chinese were Xiaokang by 2005 (using PovcalNet), which (as we will see) far exceeds the number living above the US poverty line. It is clear that many people who would be deemed "poor" in the United States are thought of as Xiaokang in China.

This is true in India too. It is often claimed that 300 million people are now "middle class" in India; see, for example, the *Wikipedia* entry on the "Standard of Living in India" (although I have had little success in tracking down the origin of that number). The surveys done by the National Council of Applied Economic Research (NCAER) are often used in defining India's middle class; based on that source, one study for India gives a range of definitions implying that 100–250 million people are middle class around 2000.[70] From the most recent NCAER survey, one study for India deems 25 million households (about 120 million people) to be middle class in 2007–08.[71] As we will see, all these estimates far exceed the likely number of people in India who are not poor by US standards.

One can also question the relevance of other definitions found in the literature. It seems implausible that a definition of the middle class relevant to developing countries would be centered on the median, which might more reasonably be deemed a lower bound. Indeed, the median consumption in the developing world in 2005 was \$2 a day.

Consistently with the idea of measuring global poverty by international standards anchored to poverty lines in developing countries, one way to define the "middle class" aims to reflect ideas of what it means to be middle class in poor countries, not rich ones.[72] The *developing world's middle class* can be defined as those who live above the median poverty line of developing countries of but are still poor by US standards; by contrast, the *Western middle class* can be thought of as those not poor by US standards. For the lower bound, Ravallion uses the median among seventy national poverty lines for developing countries, drawn from in-country poverty measurement studies by the World Bank and national governments.[73] Each of the national lines in this sample is designed to attain recommended food-energy requirements with (socially specific) allowances for basic non-food needs. The median of these national lines is \$2.00 per day at 2005 PPP. The upper bound was set at the US poverty line of \$13 a day in 2005 prices.

Vulnerability and the Middle Class

All these definitions of the "middle class" miss something important: the dynamics. I expect that those who see themselves as middle class tend to be on a more positive trajectory over time—they are upwardly mobile (or aspiring to be), which influences many aspects of their attitudes and behavior, including to inequality.[74] And they have a little more of a buffer against shocks and crises.

---

[70] See Sridharan (2004).

[71] See Shukla (2008).

[72] The following definition is due to Ravallion (2010a).

[73] The data are found in Ravallion et al. (2009).

[74] See Ravallion and Lokshin (2000).

As the financial crisis emanating from the US housing and finance markets spilled over to the developing world in 2008–09, many people were naturally asking whether there will be a reversal of the recent progress against poverty. That will depend in part on the distribution of the impacts of the crisis, and it should not be presumed that the poorest will be affected most; ironically, the same things that have kept many people poor in the first place—geographic isolation and poor connectivity with national and global markets—will help protect them from this type of crisis. But the concern is very real: there are now many people in the developing world who are no longer poor by the (frugal) standards of the past, but are in no believable sense members of the "middle class," even by standards relevant to countries such as China and India today.

Another way of defining the middle class is to explicitly recognize the existence of such downside risk—"vulnerability." There are people who are not considered "poor" in a specific society but face a non-negligible chance of falling into poverty. They can be said to be vulnerable to poverty. The middle class is identified as those who are reasonably safe from falling into poverty. By this approach, there are people who are not considered "poor" in a specific society but face a non-negligible chance of falling into poverty. They can be said to be vulnerable to poverty. The middle class can then be identified as those who are reasonably safe from falling into poverty.[75] Using panel data one can calculate the probabilities of falling into poverty among the non-poor (recall box 3.7 on panel data).[76] By setting some critical value of the probability (a matter of judgment) one can find the level of consumption or income above which the probability of becoming poor within some period is low enough to be considered "middle class." For example, one study found that if one aims to assure that the middle class in Vietnam have at most a 3% chance of becoming poor within two years, then one would have to set the vulnerability line at 30% above the county's current official national line.[77] The same study showed that absolute poverty is falling in Vietnam, and that the proposition in the middle class is rising, but that the opposite is true of the United States.

We have seen that many ways have been used to define the middle class. The recent approaches that build in explicitly the risk of falling into poverty are an advance over the earlier approaches of setting either absolute or relative income cutoff points for determining the middle class. These new approaches capture the idea of the "comfort" of not being too vulnerable to down-side risk, which seems to be a distinctive element in the popular concept of the "middle class" across the globe.

5.8   Poverty and Inequality of Opportunity

We have noted that individual welfare may well depend on relative position in society as well as absolute levels of living. A welfare-consistent measure of poverty—absolute in the space of welfare—will then have a relative aspect in the space of income or

---

[75] See Lopez-Calva and Ortiz-Juarez (2014) and Dang and Lanjouw (2014).

[76] One does not strictly require panel data. Dang and Lanjouw (2014) show how one can simulate the relevant probabilities using models based on two or more cross-sectional surveys.

[77] See Dang and Lanjouw (2014).

consumption. The precise form this takes depends on exactly how relative position is deemed to alter welfare. The "relative income hypothesis" is one possibility, and this leads us to relative poverty lines (though the implied lines will not be directly proportional to mean income as long as "own income" also matters to welfare). Such a measure will build in a trade-off between inequality and absolute poverty.

There is another way that such a trade-off has been introduced into measurement, namely through the idea of an "opportunity index" reflecting both absolute opportunity and the inequality of opportunity. We already came across inequality of opportunities as a concept in Part One and chapter 3. How can we implement this idea empirically?

The approach that has emerged in recent literature focuses on those determinants of welfare that a person cannot reasonably be considered personally responsible for, namely, her circumstances (as discussed in chapter 3, section 3.1). "Poverty" is thus seen as being ethically salient and compelling for policy to the extent that it is due to circumstances but not effort.[78] As was also noted in chapter 3, this ethical judgment can be questioned.

Being poor can be interpreted as an opportunity forgone. So the poverty rate is interpretable as an inverse metric of opportunity. However, it does not reflect the inequality in those opportunities. It has been argued that the average opportunities attained in a society should be discounted for inequality of opportunity. A simple way of thinking about this is in the form of the following measure of opportunities discounted for inequality:

Opportunity index = (1 – Poverty rate)
  x (1 – Inequality of the poverty rate across types of people)

Consistently with the circumstances-effort distinction one might want to measure the poverty rate based on the distribution of predicted welfares based on observed circumstances (chapter 3, section 3.3). However, the more notable difference here is that an inequality index is introduced to reflect the disparities in the poverty rate (interpreted as disparities in opportunities attained) across types of households defined in terms of their circumstances. For example, if this inequality index is measured by the sum of absolute deviations between the type-specific poverty rates and the overall rate then (after normalization to situate the index between zero and unity), we have a version of the World Bank's *human opportunity index*.[79]

This formulation introduces an explicit trade-off between poverty and inequality. Of course, inequality of opportunity will undoubtedly also be directly poverty increasing. But here the argument is that in judging development progress we should be willing to have a higher poverty rate if there is a sufficiently lower inequality of opportunity. The opportunity index so defined need not rank distributions in the same way as a poverty index.

---

[78] Following a distinction introduced by Roemer (1998).
[79] Based on Barros et al. (2009). Also see the discussion of this class of indices in Roemer (2014).

5.9 Targeting and Incidence Measures

Most rich countries today have extensive welfare systems for which poverty reduction is an important objective and most developing countries are embarking on new social policies with explicit antipoverty objectives. (Chapter 10 discusses these policies in more detail. Here the focus is on methods.) So it is natural to look for a way of measuring targeting performance. Related measures are also used in assessing *benefit incidence*—the correspondence empirically between the benefits received from public programs and consumption or income levels.

In principle, one might choose to measure targeting performance by a program's impact on poverty relative to an explicit counterfactual, such as an untargeted allocation of the same budget.[80] Then the interpretation for poverty is unambiguous. That is not, however, the approach that has dominated the literature and practice. This discussion focuses on the targeting measures commonly found in practice, and on which much of our current knowledge about "what works and what doesn't" is based. Definitions of the measures can be found in box 5.19.[81]

Targeting Measures

Measures based on the *concentration curve*—giving the cumulative share of transfers going to the poorest $p\%$ of the population ranked by (say) household income per person—have been prominent in the literature on targeting and incidence of the benefits of public programs. The first three measures in box 5.19 are based on the concentration curve. The popularity of S is evident in the fact that meta-studies have found that this was the most readily available measure in their many primary sources.[82] The measure's popularity may well stem from its ease of interpretation.

Against this advantage, the measure has some obvious drawbacks. For one thing, it tells us nothing about how transfers are distributed among the poor; two programs can have the same share of transfers going to the poor, but in one case the gains are heavily concentrated among the poorest, while in the other case they only reach those just below the poverty line. Another concern is that this measure does not directly reflect the overall size of the transfer program, which will clearly matter to impacts on poverty.[83]

---

[80] As in Ravallion and Chao (1989).

[81] Box 5.19 does not cover all the measures found in the literature. For a more comprehensive (though more technical) discussion of these and other measures, including their analytic properties, see the excellent volume by Lambert (2001).

[82] See Grosh (1994, 1995) and Coady, Grosh, and Hoddinott (2004a, b) who provide the shares going to the poorest 10%, 20%, and 40% for eighty-five of the antipoverty programs in their study (though with missing data in some cases).

[83] The literature on targeting has pointed to the possibility that the share going to the poor can vary with the scale of a program, through the political economy of program capture; chapter 9 discusses this issue further.

Box 5.19 The Concentration Curve and Measures of Targeting

Figure B5.19.1 shows the concentration curve, $C(p)$. On the vertical axis, we have the cumulative share of transfers, while on the horizontal axis we have the proportion of the population ranked by (say) household income per person. If the transfers are uniform—in that each person receives the same amount—then the concentration curve is simply the 45 degree diagonal line. Intuitively, the further the actual curve is from the diagonal the better targeted are the transfers made by a given program.

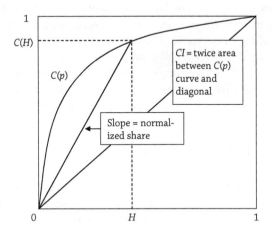

Figure B5.19.1 Concentration Curve.

Table B5.19.1 **A Glossary of Measures of Targeting**

Share going to the poor (S)	Share of transfers going to those who are initially deemed poor (or other reference group based on income). This is simply $S = C(H)$, where C is the concentration curve and H is the poverty rate.
Normalized share	Share going to the poor divided by proportion who are poor.
Concentration index (CI)	Area between the concentration curve and the diagonal (along which everyone receives the same amount). CI is bounded above by 1 (at which point the poorest person receives all payments) and below by –1 (the richest person receives all).
Coverage rate	Program participation rate for the poor.
Targeting differential	Difference between the coverage rate and the participation rate for the non-poor.
Proportion of Type 1 errors	Proportion of (ineligible) non-poor who are assigned the program.
Proportion of Type 2 errors	Proportion of the poor who fail to receive the program.

In their comparison of the targeting performance of various antipoverty programs across the world, David Coady et al. (2004a, b) prefer to use the normalized share (NS), as obtained by dividing S by the poverty rate, H (box 5.19), arguing that this is more comparable than the ordinary share (S) because it measures performance relative to a "common reference outcome . . . that would result from neutral (as opposed to progressive or regressive) targeting" (69).[84] By "neutral targeting" they mean a uniform transfer. If the transfer is uniform then clearly $NS = 1$. However, finding a value of NS "close" to unity does not imply that the allocation is "close" to being uniform. There are many ways one could get a value for NS near unity, with rather different interpretations. Similarly to S, the NS measure is insensitive to how transfers are distributed among the poor. The poor can receive $H\%$ of the transfers, but different people among the poor receive very different amounts; for example, the money could all go to either the poorest person or the least poor person; either way $NS = 1$. NS also approaches unity as H approaches 100%, no matter how the money is distributed. When the reference outcome is this ambiguous, the usefulness of the measure becomes theoretically questionable.

The *concentration index* (CI) is widely used in studies of fiscal incidence. This can be thought of as a "generalized S" in that, instead of focusing on one point on the concentration curve, CI measures the area between the curve and the diagonal (along which the transfer is uniform); in box 5.19 CI is just twice the area marked A.[85] This measure has the attraction that it reflects distribution among the poor, and (indeed) over the whole range of incomes. A disadvantage is that it is not as easy to interpret as S or NS. The same CI can entail very different allocations of transfers. And, as with the previous measures, it tells us nothing directly about the scale of the transfers.

Although these measures are all based on the concentration curve, they can give quite different results. Of course, S and NS will always be in the same ratio to each other when the same value of H is used for all programs. However, these two measures can rank programs differently when H varies, as happens in the case study presented later, and would presumably do so in many applications. To illustrate, consider a transfer scheme operating in two cities and giving all participants the same amount. In city A all the transfers go to the poorest 20% and the overall poverty rate is 50% while in city B the transfers go to the poorest 40% and the poverty rate is 10%. A far higher share of the transfers goes to the poor in A ($S = 100\%$ versus 25% in B). City A also has the higher concentration index ($CI = 0.8$ in A versus 0.6 in B). By contrast, it is in city B where the scheme is deemed to be better targeted according to the normalized share ($NS = 2.5$ for B versus 2 for A). More generally, the concentration curve for program A could lie everywhere above that for program B and yet NS is higher for B, given its lower H.

---

[84] Coady et al. (2004a, b) used $H = 40\%$ when it was available, which was the case for about half the programs in their study, and the next lowest available number (20% or 10%) when the value for $H = 40\%$ was not available. In the earlier comparative study of targeting performance by Grosh (1994), the value of H was set at 40% in all programs studied, in which case the first two measures will (of course) rank identically.

[85] To assure that all measures go in the same direction, I multiply the usual definition of CI by -1.

A rather different measure is the "targeting differential," *TD*, which is the difference between the program's participation rate for the poor—which one can call the coverage rate—and that for the non-poor (box 5.19).[86] Alternatively, one can normalize the targeting differential by the mean transfer over all recipients; let's call this *TD**. (When the transfer is uniform, *TD* = *TD**.) However, it turns out later that the choice between *TD* and *TD** makes very little difference in the case study. Since *TD* is easier to interpret the present discussion shall focus on this measure.

To interpret the targeting differential, note that when only the poor get help from the program and all of them are covered, *TD* = 1, which is the measure's upper bound; when only the non-poor get the program and all of them do, *TD* = −1, its lower bound. (In the "two cities" example above, *TD* = 0.67 for city B and 0.4 for A.) This measure is easy to interpret, and it automatically reflects both leakage to the non-poor and coverage of the poor.

It has become common to also refer to the incidence of "Type 1" and "Type 2" errors in the context of targeting. A Type 1 error can be defined as incorrectly classifying a person as poor, while a Type 2 error is incorrectly classifying a person as not poor. A Type 1 error entails a leakage of transfers to the non-poor, while a Type 2 error implies lower coverage of the poor. In measuring the proportions of Type 1 and Type 2 errors one can normalize by the populations of the non-poor and poor (respectively).[87] Standard targeting measures depend on the incidence of both types of errors. For the measures based on the concentration curve it should not be presumed that they will be largely unaffected by Type 2 errors; indeed, all these measures can be thought of as functions of the proportions of these two types of targeting errors.[88] That is also true of the targeting differential, for which the relationship is particularly clear: *TD* is simply one minus the total proportions of Type 1 and Type 2 errors.[89] So this particular measure automatically gives equal weight to both types of errors. However, for the measures based on the concentration curve it is an empirical question what weights are attached to these two errors of targeting.

A further distinction is between the "vertical" and "horizontal" dimensions of targeting. The former refers to the differences in gains between people at different levels of pre-reform income (or some other relevant metric); how much goes to the poor versus the non-poor? This has been the main focus of the literature on measuring the targeting performance of programs. However, policymakers and citizens can also be

---

[86] This measure was proposed by Ravallion (2000). Also see Galasso and Ravallion (2005) on the properties of this measure and the discussion in Stifel and Alderman (2005).

[87] One might prefer to normalize by population size; similar formulae for this case are easily derived, but the essential point remains.

[88] Consider, e.g., the share, *S*. It is readily verified that $S = 1 - T1(1 - H)/P$, where *P* is the overall program participation rate and *T1* is the proportion of (ineligible) non-poor who are assigned the program. Alternatively, where *T1** is the proportion of participants who are Type 1 errors. But one can equally well write *S* as a function of Type 2 errors, namely $S = (1 - T2)H/P$ (or $S = (H/P) - T2*$), where *T2* is the proportion of the poor who fail to receive the program. Nor is *P* likely to be independent of *T1* and *T2*; e.g., higher coverage of the poor (lower *T2*) may tend to come with larger programs. Thus, *S* can be taken to depend on *both T1* and *T2*.

[89] More precisely, $TD = 1 - (T1 + T2)$ using the notation from the previous footnote.

concerned about the horizontal differences in treatment—the differences in the benefits received by people at the same pre-reform level of income and (associated with such differences) the extent of "re-ranking," whereby the program alters the initial, pre-reform, ranking of households. Clearly Type 2 errors reflect such horizontal differences, but we can go further and isolate a component that is attributed solely to the horizontal differences. While the technical exposition would take us beyond the scope of this book, a clever decomposition along these lines has been developed by Bibi and Duclos (2007).

Despite their popularity in analytic work and policy discussions on antipoverty programs, there has been little or no research into the performance of these measures in providing useful indicators for either the poverty impacts of social programs or their cost-effectiveness in reducing poverty. At the same time, the literature on the economics of targeting has repeatedly warned against assuming that a better targeted program—as judged by any of these measures—will have greater impact on poverty. (Chapter 10 returns to this issue.)

In the only comparative study to date of these measures of targeting performance, it was found that none of them reveal much about the success of a large cash transfer program in China (the *Dibao* program which we will return to in chapter 10) in achieving its objective of eliminating extreme urban poverty.[90] The cities of China that are better at targeting this program, as assessed by these measures, are generally *not* the ones where the scheme came closest to attaining its objective. More encouragingly, the study found that the targeting differential does have a statistically significant positive correlation with the program's poverty impacts. But even the *TD* is far from being a perfect indicator of poverty impacts.

None of these targeting measures appear to be reliable indicators of a program's cost-effectiveness (i.e., poverty impact at given program spending). The one exception is that the share going to the poor is a statistically significant predictor of cost-effectiveness in reducing the poverty gap index. But, even then, about 60% of the variance in the cost-effectiveness ratio is left unexplained. All the other measures perform poorly, or even perversely, as indicators of cost-effectiveness.

These findings echo some of the warnings in the literature against relying on standard measures of targeting performance for informing policy choices concerning antipoverty programs. The findings of the aforementioned comparative study of different measures of targeting also cast doubt on the generalizations found in the literature about what type of program "works best," and so should be scaled up, based on cross-program comparisons of targeting measures.[91] The external validity of these programmatic comparisons is highly questionable when the targeting measures have such a poor fit with poverty impacts. It is also unlikely that past findings on the socioeconomic factors influencing targeting performance at country level are robust to seemingly arbitrary differences in the measures used.

One question is left begging: Why have the literature's warnings carried so little weight in practice? Possibly the more "theoretical" objections to these targeting measures have fallen on deaf ears for lack of clear evidence on how the measures

---

[90] See Ravallion (2009d).
[91] See Ravallion (2009d).

perform in practice. The results of case studies such as the one previously described will then help. One can also conjecture that the preference for targeting measures that put a high weight on avoiding leakage to the non-poor stems from fiscal pressures, given that reducing leakage helps cut public spending, while expanding coverage does the opposite. While one does not doubt that such thinking has had influence at times, it is surely misguided. For if the problem was to minimize public spending (unconditionally), then why would governments bother with such programs in the first place? Evidently there is a demand for these policies, as part of a comprehensive antipoverty strategy. A more credible characterization of the policy problem would then give positive weight to both avoiding leakage and expanding coverage of the poor.

From that perspective, measures of targeting performance that penalize both errors of targeting make more sense—again echoing recommendations found in the literature.[92] However, that conclusion would still miss the point. Analysts and policymakers might be better advised to focus on the estimable outcome measures most directly relevant to their policy problem. Impacts on poverty can be assessed with the same data and under the same assumptions as required by prevailing measures of targeting performance.[93]

Behavioral Effects

As we first heard in chapter 1, targeted antipoverty policies are likely to lead to changes in the behavior of beneficiaries as well as non-beneficiaries. Past discussions of all such policies have fallen into two main camps. According to one camp, the incentive effects of targeted policies are so large that the policies end up creating poverty by discouraging the efforts of poor people to escape poverty by their own means. (As we saw in chapter 1, concerns about incentives were prominent in the early nineteenth-century debates on England's Poor Laws, which provided targeted relief to the poor. Similar concerns are still heard today.) By contrast, the second camp has largely ignored incentive effects or down-played their importance. In practice, the measures of targeting and benefit incidence described above have typically used income net of transfers/taxes as the indicator of economic welfare in the absence of the policies being studied. With the availability of new micro data sets there has been a huge expansion in studies of tax and benefit incidence. It has become routine in such studies to ignore incentive effects, and this is true in countries at all levels of development.[94]

Consider what is clearly the most common method of assessing benefit incidence, by which one studies how mean transfer receipts (or tax payments) vary by class intervals of households ranked by their "net income," defined as observed total income minus transfers received and/or taxes paid. Various targeting measures are

---

[92] See especially Cornia and Stewart (1995).

[93] See Ravallion (2009d).

[94] The examples, of which there are many, include Kakwani (1986), Atkinson and Sutherland (1989), Sahn and Younger (2003), Bourguignon et al. (2003), Ben-Shalom et al. (2012), and Lustig et al. (2014). Reviews of studies of benefit incidence in developing countries can be found in van de Walle (1998a) and Demery (2003).

then calculated (as reviewed above). This method (or some variation on it) is what Bourguignon and Da Silva (2003, 9) term the *"accounting method,"* implicitly recognizing that behavioral responses are being ignored. The method has the attraction of simplicity, in that the calculations are straightforward. However, net income (so calculated) need not accord well with income in the absence of intervention given behavioral responses. The potential for bias in assessments of benefit incidence is plain.

Reviews of past literature using the accounting method have warned that incentive effects are being ignored.[95] Nonetheless, it has been claimed that the method provides a "reasonable approximation" and a "satisfactory short-cut for the study of a policy's distributional impact."[96] It has never been especially clear what such confidence is based on. The main defense of the method is what can be dubbed the *fixed-income assumption.* This says that people have little ability to influence their income and so incentive effects are minimal. In supporting this view, applications in developed countries have pointed to the relative inflexibility of working hours to justify non-behavioral incidence analysis.[97]

However, it is unclear that this is plausible even in rich countries, especially given that part-time work has become more common, and the assumption is hardly plausible in developing countries with large informal sectors. While the best examples in the literature are explicit about their assumptions, non-behavioral benefit incidence analyses continue in applied work, and often uncritically. It would be hard to exaggerate the policy influence that these empirical studies have had across the world.[98]

One way to better inform these policy discussions is to study behavioral responses directly, such as by looking for labor-supply effects.[99] This is certainly of interest, although (especially in a developing country setting) one would need to allow for other sources of such effects in addition to labor supply. (Labor-force participation— sometimes called the extensive margin of the labor-supply response—is clearly also relevant, but so too is self-employment, household formation, migration, and transfer behavior.) However, this approach does not tell us directly about benefit incidence, which is arguably the main thing of interest to policymakers.

Another approach focuses instead on the problem of estimating the mean *benefit withdrawal rate* (BWR), given by the average rate at which transfer receipts respond to differences in household income—the marginal tax rate. This can also be interpreted as a measure of targeting performance, telling us how much transfer receipts decline with higher pre-transfer income. Focusing on the BWR also allows us to draw on simulation results from the literature on optimal income taxation in which the marginal tax rate is the key policy parameter of interest.

---

[95] See, e.g., van de Walle (1998).

[96] Lustig et al. (2014, 290) and Sahn and Younger (2003, 29), respectively.

[97] See, e.g., Kakwani (1986, 117) in the context of Australia.

[98] Coady et al. (2004a, b) and Grosh et al. (2008) survey existing programs in developing countries. Virtually all of the work covered by these meta studies has ignored incentive effects.

[99] Examples of this approach (spanning various approaches) include Atkinson (1995, ch. 7), Sahn and Alderman (1995), Bingley and Walker (1997), Lemieux and Milligan (2008), Skoufias and Di Maro (2008), and Fan (2010).

As is recognized in the literature, the BWR is a key parameter for any social policy.[100] Yet while incentive effects have motivated the calculations of BWRs, they have often been ignored in the estimation methods found in practice, in common with the benefit incidence literature more broadly. Past methods have either calculated conditional means of actual transfers/taxes at each level of net income or calculated the transfers/taxes implied by the formal rules. Yet behavioral responses are clearly relevant to estimating the BWR by either method. So too are measurement errors in the statistical methods, such as due to misreporting of incomes. What is identified as "imperfect targeting" in social programs could simply reflect such errors.[101]

Although appreciated in theory, the implications of latent incentive effects and income measurement errors for assessments of the performance of social spending has had too little attention in practice, especially in applications to developing countries.[102] One side ignores incentive effects and the other side almost certainly exaggerates them (as was plainly the case in the debates over England's Poor Law reforms in the early nineteenth century, as discussed in chapter 1). Neither position is satisfactory and more evidence is needed.

5.10 Mashup Indices

It is often said that "poverty is multidimensional," by which it is meant that it is not only about command over commodities. As we have learned in this chapter and chapters 3 and 4, the fact that one measures poverty in the space of real income does not mean that real income is all that matters to welfare. That is also a matter of how one sets the poverty line, interpreted as a money metric of welfare, which can be quite broadly defined in principle. However, as the discussion in the last two chapters has also emphasized, measurement practice is typically limited in some key respects, notably in the ability to credibly capture access to non-market goods, intra-household inequalities, and differences in welfare-relevant characteristics that cannot be identified from observed behavior.

There is also a danger in being too "multidimensional," in the form of a long list of essentially ad hoc dimensions. While a clean mapping of policies to objectives may be illusive, it is clear that some policies are better for some objectives. Insisting that all policies serve all goals runs the risk of turning poverty measurement into a "counsel of despair: the problem of poverty is too big, too complicated and too awkward to deal

---

[100] See, e.g., Moffitt (2002), Holt and Romich (2007), and Maag et al. (2012).

[101] For further analysis of this point, see Ravallion (2008b).

[102] One possible approach that that can be implemented with essentially the same data as prevailing methods is proposed by Ravallion and Chen (2013a). Their key assumption is that incentive effects and classical measurement errors only impact certain income components but that these still have predictive power for isolating exogenous variation in total income net of transfers/taxes. They provide an empirical application for a large cash transfer program in China and find a sizable bias in the benefit incidence picture that is implied by either the formal administrative rules or the usual statistical practice of calculating conditional means at different net incomes.

with."[103] As Harold Watts (1968) pointed out in the context of the Johnson administration's War on Poverty, if every program is required to address every dimension in
some long list there is a possibility that every program will be deemed a failure, even
when the whole package is a success.

The temptation to form a single (unidimensional) composite index from a list
of multiple dimensions has been strong. In practice, many indicators are used to
track development progress. The World Bank's annual *World Development Indicators*
presents hundreds of such indicators. The UN Millennium Development Goals are
defined using a long list of indicators. Some widely used development indicators
are already composite indices. Examples are GDP, total consumption expenditure, or
the Human Development Index (which we return to). New composite indices appear
regularly.

For some of the composite indices in use, economics provides some useful clues on
how the index should be constructed. When markets exist and work reasonably well,
prices provide a defensible basis for aggregating quantities, as is common practice.
This is not so for another type of composite index that is becoming popular. For these
indices neither the menu of the primary series to be aggregated nor the aggregation
function is predetermined from theory and practice; instead, both are moving parts—
key decision variables that the analyst is essentially free to choose. Borrowing from
Web jargon, these can be called *mashup indices*. These indices typically aggregate across
multiple deprivations using pre-assigned weights; we can call this *deprivation aggregation*. Prices are avoided in this approach, even when they are available. Box 5.20 goes
further into this difference.

---

*Box 5.20 Aggregation with and without Prices

One can distinguish two approaches to forming an aggregate poverty index.
The first is to use prices (actual or imputed) to form a composite index for
aggregate consumption, to be compared to a poverty line defined in the same
space. Ideally this is not just consumption of market goods and services, but
should include imputed values for non-market commodities. For market goods,
either their market prices or appropriate shadow prices can be used. For non-
market goods, the missing "prices" will need to be assigned on a priori grounds
or estimated. In practice, most poverty measures require imputations for missing
prices, so this approach is a natural extension of prevailing practices. In principle we can broaden this approach to allow for non-commodity dimensions of
welfare. The space defined by all primary dimensions of welfare (including commodities) can be called the "attainment space" (though the term "achievements"
is also used in the literature), and the aggregation can be called *attainment aggregation*. The weights on attainments can be called "prices," understood to include
imputed prices.

---

[103] Spicker (2007, 8).

A simple example of a poverty measure using attainment-aggregation is the headcount index:

$$P^A \equiv F_y(z), \tag{1}$$

where F_y is the CDF for aggregate consumption y and z is the poverty line in that space. To keep things simple for expository purposes (including graphing), suppose that there are two attainments in amounts x_1 and x_2, with prices p_1 and p_2, so $y = p_1 x_1 + p_2 x_2$.

The second approach measures poverty in each of the dimensions separately and then aggregates the dimension-specific "deprivations" into a composite index. This is deprivation aggregation. To see more clearly how this second approach works, consider again the two continuous attainments, x_1 and x_2, with distribution functions F_1 and F_2, respectively. Poverty lines, denoted z_1 and z_2, are defined in each space and the weights on deprivations are w_1 and w_2 ($w_1 + w_2 = 1$). Then a simple example of a poverty measure using deprivation-aggregation is the weighted incidence of poverty across the two dimensions:

$$P^D \equiv w_1 F_1(z_1) + w_2 F_2(z_2). \tag{2}$$

This is only one possible way of aggregating deprivations. Alternatively, one can focus on the joint distribution and ask what proportion of the population is poor in at least one of the two dimensions. Letting F_{12} denote the joint distribution function, the poverty measure is then $F_1(z_1) + F_2(z_2) - F_{12}(z_1, z_2)$. Alternatively, one might ask what proportion is poor in both dimensions, that is, $F_{12}(z_1, z_2)$. One can introduce an extra parameter, such that a household is deemed to be poor if its weighted deprivation exceeds a critical value. However, all these measures are some weighted aggregation of deprivations, and (implicitly) a nonlinear function of the cutoffs z_1 and z_2. This discussion will focus on the analytically convenient form in (2), though this simplification does not appear to come at much loss.

It is evident that these two approaches will not, in general, give the same measure, even when the poverty lines are consistent in that $z = p_1 z_1 + p_2 z_2$. This is clear from figure B5.20.1. Attainment aggregation identifies as poor all those people whose consumption of the two goods is within the triangle with vertices, z/p_1, 0, and z/p_2; instead, the deprivation approach identifies some subset of those with $x_1 < z_1$ or $x_2 < z_2$ (the two unbounded rectangles of width z_1 and z_2 in figure B5.20.1). Without knowing the weights and data one cannot say which will give the larger count of who is poor. If deprivation-aggregation measure focuses on those who are poor in *both* dimensions ($x_1 < z_1$ and $x_2 < z_2$), then the "deprivation poor" will never outnumber the "attainment poor" $\left(y < p_1 z_1 + p_2 z_2\right)$. However, that need not hold for other deprivation measures, including equation (2). For example, if the deprivation poor are defined as those who are poor in *either* dimension ($x_1 < z_1$ or $x_2 < z_2$), then they will never be fewer in number than the attainment poor.

continued

*Box 5.20 **(Continued)**

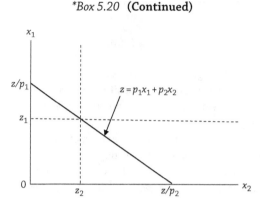

Figure B5.20.1 Attainment Aggregation versus Deprivation Aggregation.

Notice that the case for deprivation aggregation cannot rest solely on the deficiencies of market prices as a means of valuation. Even if p_1 and p_2 were the true shadow prices, there can be no presumption that $P^D = P^A$; this would be a fluke. Furthermore, suppose that for some z_1 and z_2, the weights in the deprivation-aggregation measure were chosen to deliver an MRS between attainments of p_1/p_2. Then for any (non-uniform) distributions, the two measures would deviate for any changes in z_1 or z_2, as this would change the densities determining the MRS in the deprivation-aggregation measure.

Further reading: See Ravallion (2011b) and the more general treatment in Ravallion (2012a).

In the deprivation-aggregation approach, the weights on deprivations are taken to be known and explicit, while the weights on the underlying attainments (such as how much one has of some commodity) are implicit. The papers in this literature provide some elegant mathematical formulations of their measures, but provide little guidance on where the weights attached to deprivations come from. In practice, the weights on deprivations are set by the analyst, with no obvious reason to suppose that they would be accepted by those one is trying to help by measuring poverty: policymakers and, of course, poor people.

The literature has also been close to silent about the trade-offs between the attainments that are built into such indices. Interest in those trade-offs does not rest on any view that the poverty measure should be seen as some policy maximand. Rather the interest stems from the need to understand the properties of the index. The trade-off is given by the marginal rate of substitution (MRS), which is simply the marginal weight on one attainment relative to that on another. While the weights on deprivations are explicit, neither the marginal weights on attainments nor the implied MRSs have received much attention in the literature on these indices.

Probably the most famous mashup index is the *Human Development Index* (HDI), published each year in the *Human Development Report* (HDR).This is a composite of life expectancy, schooling, and log real GDP per capita. In a similar spirit, the Multidimensional Poverty Index (MPI), created for the 2010 edition of the HDR, aggregates household-level deprivations in health, education, and income; box 5.21 summarizes these two indices.[104]

Box 5.21 Two Mashup Indices

The three core dimensions of the *Human Development Index* (HDI) are life expectancy, schooling, and gross national income per capita. Two variables are used to measure education: mean years of schooling and the expected years of schooling, given by the years of schooling that a child can expect to receive given current enrollment rates. The three core dimensions of the HDI are then put on a common (0, 1) scale. The HDI is then obtained by taking the equally weighted geometric mean of these rescaled variables. Box 5.22 looks more closely at this index.

The *Multidimensional Poverty Index* (MPI) is composed of two variables for *health* (malnutrition and child mortality), two for *education* (years of schooling and school enrollment), and six for deprivation in *living standards* (namely cooking with wood, charcoal, or dung; no conventional toilet; lack of safe drinking water; no electricity; dirt, sand, or dung flooring and not owning at least one of a radio, TV, telephone, bike, or car). Poverty is measured separately in each of these ten dimensions. The equally weighted measures for each of these three main headings are then weighted equally to form the MPI. A household is identified as being poor if it is deprived across at least 30% of the weighted indicators.

Further reading: The HDI is described in UNDP (2010) and the index is given for 170 countries. The MPI was developed by Alkire and Santos (2010) (implementing a theoretical approach in Alkire and Foster 2011). UNDP (2010) provide the MPI for more than 100 countries.

The trade-offs built into any composite index used for assessing social progress are crucial to assessing that index and its implications for development policy. Surprisingly, however, the trade-offs between attainments embodied in indices such as those in box 5.21 are rarely given much attention—the HDRs do not appear to have ever quantified the trade-offs incorporated in the HDI. Given that these indices aggregate "income" and "non-income" dimensions of welfare they imply monetary valuation for the latter. For example, if one creates a composite index of income (Y) and life expectancy (LE) of the form $\alpha Y + \beta LE$, then one is implicitly attaching a monetary value of β/α to an extra expected year of life. In other words, the income gain needed

---

[104] These are the two mashup indices that have received the most attention in the literature on poverty and human development. Other examples include the *Ease of Doing Business Index* (Djankov et al. 2002) and the *Pillars of Prosperity Index* (Besley and Persson 2011, ch. 8).

to compensate for one year less *LE* is β/α—the MRS holding the composite index constant. When one calculates the trade-offs implied by the HDI they imply far lower valuations of life in poor countries than rich ones—so much so that one must surely question the ethical foundations of the index.[105] Box 5.22 goes into further detail.

We know that governments in rich countries implicitly put a higher monetary value on saving lives (such as through public spending on healthcare or safety) than do those in poor countries. But do we want to build that fact into an index such as the HDI? We might well demand instead that all lives be valued equally no matter where one lives.[106] By that standard the HDI is hard to defend.

Mashup indices such as the HDI have raised public awareness about important development issues. But it is clear that these indices need closer scrutiny. This is not to say that mashup indices have no value in monitoring social and economic progress. GDP is a composite index, using prices as weights on its components (box 1.1). But GDP is not a mashup index, since there is a theoretical basis for the aggregation. As argued in chapters 3 and 4, when prices are known, a good case must be made for not using them, or for modifying them to better reflect the social opportunity costs of consumption. Prices should not be ignored. When prices are not known, then the composite index must come with explicit warnings about what trade-offs across the underlying dimensions are being imposed. Users need to be properly informed. Alas, that has not typically been the case.

Box 5.22 Trade-Offs Built into the HDI

The HDI aggregates country-level attainments in life expectancy, schooling, and income per capita (box 5.21). Each year's rankings by the HDI are keenly watched in both rich and poor countries. The twentieth *Human Development Report* introduced a new version of the HDI. The main change is that the authors relax the HDI's past assumption of perfect substitutability between its three components. However, most users will probably not realize that the new HDI has also greatly reduced its implicit weight on longevity in poor countries, relative to rich ones. This is illustrated in figure B5.22.1.

Consider, for example, Zimbabwe, with a 2010 HDI of 0.14 on a (0,1) scale, which is the lowest HDI of any country; the next lowest is the Democratic Republic of the Congo (DRC) with 0.24. Given Zimbabwe's low income, the new HDI gives a marginal weight on life expectancy for 2010 of only 0.0017 per year. Yet Zimbabwe's life expectancy in 2010 of 47 years is the fourth lowest in the world.

---

[105] Ravallion (2012c) elaborates this argument. The MPI also implies trade-offs between material aspects of living standards and other dimensions, though they are harder to calculate than for the HDI; for further discussion, see Ravallion (2011b).

[106] That is not far-fetched. For example, in 2013 the website of the Bill and Melinda Gates foundation says on its landing page that "all lives have equal value."

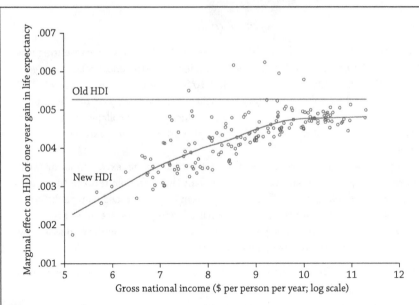

Figure B5.22.1 The HDI's Implicit Weight on Life Expectancy. *Source:* Author's calculations from data in UNDP (2010).

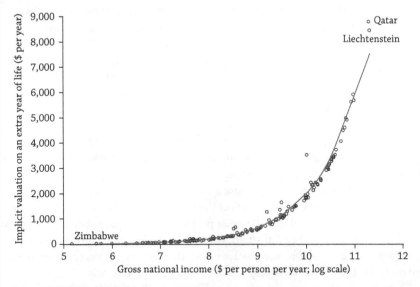

Figure B5.22.2 The HDI's Implicit Monetary Valuation of an Extra Year of Life. *Source:* Author's calculations from data in UNDP (2010).

Given that the HDI also includes average income, we can calculate the weight on life expectancy relative to income (i.e., the MRS which is the implicit monetary value of life). The implied value of life varies from very low levels in poor

continued

Box 5.22 **(Continued)**

countries—the lowest value of $0.51 per year is for Zimbabwe, representing less than 0.3% of this country's (very low) mean income—to almost $9,000 per year in the richest countries, which is around 10% of their incomes. Figure B5.22.2 gives the HDI's implicit monetary valuations for an extra year of life. A poor country experiencing falling life expectancy due to (say) a collapse in its health-care system could still see its HDI improve with even a low rate of economic growth.

By contrast, the new HDI's valuations of the gains from extra schooling seem unreasonably high—many times greater than the economic returns to schooling. These troubling trade-offs could have been largely avoided using a different aggregation function for the HDI, while still allowing imperfect substitution.

While some difficult value judgments are faced in constructing and assessing the HDI, making its assumed trade-offs more explicit would be a welcome step.

Further reading: On the HDI, see UNDP (2010). On the implicit trade-offs embodied in the HDI, see Ravallion (2012c).

Aggregation across deprivations cannot in general yield poverty measures that would be acceptable to poor people. The mashup index obtained this way will not in general be consistent with the choices made by someone living at the poverty line. Deprivation aggregation essentially ignores all implications for welfare measurement of consumer choice in a market economy. While those implications need not be decisive in welfare measurement, it is clearly worrying if the implicit trade-off between any two market goods built into a poverty measure differs markedly from the trade-off facing someone at the poverty line. When calibrated correctly, an attainment-aggregation measure using prices guarantees that poor people would accept the trade-offs built into the poverty measure. But there is no obvious calibration method for which this holds using deprivation aggregation. For example, everyone may agree that they are better off in situation A than B (such as before and after a change in prices or some other welfare shock), yet a measure using deprivation aggregation can show higher poverty in A, given that it does not reflect the trade-offs that consumers have chosen. Similarly, the approach will identify some people as poor because they are lacking in one or more things that they can afford, but have no interest in acquiring, such as due to differences in demographics or relative prices. Poverty comparisons between people and over time (which are never easy) could be especially problematic.

These observations may not carry much weight with advocates of deprivation-aggregation, since they reject prices as weights.[107] What are their arguments? Three (related) critiques of using prices for aggregation can be identified in the literature. In the first, it is argued that the attainment approach entails a "loss of information on dimension-specific shortfalls."[108] It is true that attainment aggregation does not use

[107] See Tsui (2002), Bourguignon and Chakravarty (2003), and Alkire and Foster (2011).
[108] Alkire and Foster (2007, 7).

the information on how far an attainment falls short of the stipulated poverty line in that dimension. However, such dimension-specific poverty lines are not typically data, but must be assigned. One can equally well defend attainment aggregation on the grounds that it does not require this extra task.

Second, critics of using prices to aggregate in the attainment space argue that this practice avoids the problem of measuring "multidimensional poverty" by turning it into a more familiar "one-dimensional" poverty measure.[109] However, as is plain from the above discussion, both approaches collapse the multiple dimensions into one; they just do it in different spaces. The real issue is *how* one does this aggregation, and whether one accepts theoretical restrictions implied by consistency with consumer welfare. So this critique brings us back to the point already discussed.

Third, advocates of deprivation-aggregation criticize attainment aggregation on the grounds that prices are missing or deemed unreliable.[110] This is the more important issue, which deserves closer scrutiny. Of course, by either approach, weights must be assigned, and switching the space in which they are assigned cannot on its own address any of the concerns about using market prices as weights. One can agree that market prices do not accord with shadow prices in general without preferring to aggregate in the deprivation space, which rejects the use of *all* prices; this holds across dimensions of poverty that relate directly to market goods as well as non-market goods. It is one thing to recognize that not all goods are market goods, or that there are market distortions, and quite another to ignore market prices when they are data.

It has been argued that setting even initially arbitrary weights on deprivations should be viewed as the start of a public debate on what weights are appropriate.[111] Public opinion might be considered an important clue to setting weights on deprivations, or shadow prices on attainments. Setting the weights in some initially ad hoc way might then be thought of as the first step in an "iterative public debate" about what the weights should be.

Stimulating such a debate could well be a valuable contribution. However, there is little sign as yet that this has led to new weights in past mashup indices. Consider again the HDI (boxes 5.21 and 5.22). Its weights were set twenty years ago, with equal weight to the (scaled) sub-indices for health, education, and GDP. Equality of the weights was, of course, an arbitrary judgment, and it might have been hoped that the weights would evolve in the light of the subsequent public debate. But that did not happen. The weights on the three components of the HDI (health, education, and income) have not changed in twenty years, and it is hard to believe that the HDI got it right first go.

Setting initial weights and revising them in the light of subsequent debate would also point to the need to know the trade-offs in the most relevant space for understanding what the weights really mean. Arguably, the fact that multidimensional poverty indices have assigned weights in the deprivation space rather than the attainment space (as discussed in box 5.20) does not make it easy for the debate to proceed on a well-informed basis. I would conjecture that most people will find it easier to

---

[109] See, e.g., Bourguignon and Chakravarty (2003) and Alkire and Foster (2007).

[110] See Tsui (2002), Bourguignon and Chakravarty (2003), and Alkire and Foster (2007).

[111] See Alkire and Foster (2007).

attach a monetary value (or market-good equivalent) to a non-market good than to assess what trade-off is acceptable between the corresponding two poverty measures. If the welfare dimension for which prices are missing is (say) health status, it is surely easier for people to judge how much money they would pay for better health than what trade-off they would accept between poverty in income space and poverty in health space. Indeed, given the opaqueness about the trade-offs in the primary attainment dimensions built into an index such as the MPI, it can be argued that users (including policymakers) may end up tacitly accepting, and acting upon, trade-offs that they would find objectionable when revealed. This can hardly be helpful in advancing open public debate about the weights. The weights need to be transparent. Here again it is far from clear that the deprivation space is superior to the attainment space for this purpose.

To conclude, I would suggest that users should ask the following questions about any new composite index:

What is the index measuring? The fact that the target concept is unobserved does not mean we cannot define it and postulate what properties we would like its measure to have. Yet this is not common in the industry of composite indices. The frequent lack of conceptual clarity about what exactly one is trying to measure makes it hard to judge the practical choices made about what pre-existing indicators get used in the composite.

What trade-offs are embedded in the index? We need to know the trade-offs built into the index if it is to be properly assessed and used. At one level the weights in most composite indices are explicit. Common practice is to identify a set of component variables, group these in some way, and attach equal weight to these groups. But little or no attention is given to what the implied trade-offs are in the space of the primary dimensions being aggregated and whether those weights are defensible. Nor do the implied trade-offs appear to have been taken into account in choosing the aggregation functions for most composite indices of development.

How robust are the rankings? Theory never delivers a complete specification for measurement, so judgments are required about one or more parameters. There is also statistical imprecision about parameter estimates. For these reasons it is widely recommended scientific practice to test the robustness of the derived rankings. But users of mashup indices are rarely told much about the uncertainties that exist about the series chosen, the quality of the data, and their weights. Few rigorous robustness tests are provided. Very few of the websites for mashup indices make it easy for users to properly assess the sensitivity of these indices to changing weights. Yet it would be relatively easy to program the required flexibility into the websites so that users could customize the index with their preferred weights and see what difference it makes.

How should the index be used by policymakers? Given the real constraints that countries face, it is not credible that any one of these indices is a sufficient statistic for country performance. We might well rank the countries very differently if we took account of their stage of economic development.

Policymakers might be better advised to use the component measures most appropriate to each policy instrument rather than the mashup index. While many things affect your personal health, you would not want your doctor to base your checkup on a mashup index. Similarly, a mashup index of all those dials on your car's dashboard may fail to reveal that you are about to run out of fuel.

Arguably, mashup indices exist because theory (and not just economic theory) has given too little attention to the full range of measurement problems faced in assessing development outcomes. Theory needs to catch up.

Thankfully, progress in development does not need to wait for that to happen. A mashup index is not essential for many of the purposes of evidence-based policymaking. Indeed, it may even distort policymaking by encouraging policymakers to focus on readily observed proxies rather than the deeper characteristics of the economy and society that ultimately matter to development outcomes.

6

Impact Evaluation

We saw a few times in chapters 1 and 2 that knowledge about poor people has often informed private and public action against poverty. Since the time of the Second Poverty Enlightenment, there has been an expansion of analytic effort by economists and others to improve knowledge about the effectiveness of both specific antipoverty policies and the distributional implications of a broader range of policies. (The need for knowledge goes beyond the public sector. Given the magnitude of private charity, it is no less important to know about the performance of various charities and NGOs.)

However, learning about the effectiveness of what is done to reduce poverty is not easy, and mistakes are made, both rejecting good efforts and accepting bad ones. This chapter reviews the problems encountered in learning about policy effectiveness.[1] The discussion here will focus on the methods; many examples of real-world applications will be found in Part Three.

The chapter starts with a discussion of why we need evaluation to help fill pressing gaps in our knowledge. The discussion then turns to the evaluation problem and how it is addressed in practice. Next, some broader issues about learning from evaluations are examined, and what other methods might be needed as a complement to standard methods in practice. Finally, the chapter discusses the ethical concerns about evaluation.

6.1 Knowledge Gaps

To help inform antipoverty policymaking, researchers should ideally be filling the gaps between what we know about the effectiveness of policies and what policymakers need to know. Many such gaps persist. Why? One answer is that it is simply very hard, or just very costly, to credibly fill the gaps. But there is more to it than that. Like many other market failures, imperfect information plays a role. Here the problem is that development practitioners cannot easily assess the quality and expected benefits of an evaluation to weigh against the costs. Short-cut non-rigorous methods promise quick results at low cost, though rarely are users well informed of the inferential dangers. This constitutes what can be termed a *knowledge market failure*. (Recall box 1.9 on market failures more generally.)

---

[1] The discussion here will be brief, but a fuller (though more technical) review of the topic can be found in Ravallion (2008a).

One cause of knowledge market failures is the externalities that are present in evaluations. The benefits of an evaluation are rarely confined to that specific project but rather spillover to future projects, which benefit from the results of the prior evaluations. (For example, the team doing a project in one country today will have probably learned from evaluations of past projects including those in other countries.) Current project managers cannot be expected to take proper account of these external benefits when deciding how much to spend on the evaluation of their own project. There are clearly larger externalities for some types of evaluations, such as those that are more innovative—the first of their kind.

Publication biases can also come into play in creating knowledge market failures, whereby it is often easier to publish findings of a positive impact or those that resonate well with current beliefs. It is plain that this can distort public knowledge about what works and what does not.[2] For example, one study found evidence that there has been a publication bias toward studies finding a negative impact of higher minimum wage rates on employment.[3]

Furthermore, errors can occur in the literature, and it can take time to correct them. In recognition of its originality, the first paper on a topic will probably get published prominently, in one of the "top journals." Subsequent papers will tend to be relegated to lesser journals or may even have a hard time getting published. Citations will tend to favor the top journals. But the first paper may not have got it right. Or it may be valid in the specific context but have limited validity in different circumstances. When the topic concerns the impact of a policy, or an issue that is very relevant to that impact, policy knowledge will tend to be skewed accordingly.

Methodological preferences on the part of evaluators can reinforce these problems. Here the main concern in practice relates to the uses of *social experiments*, whereby some units are randomly assigned a treatment while other randomly chosen units are retained as controls. This can be a powerful tool for estimating the mean impact for those assigned to participate in the program (as we will discuss later). However, randomization is clearly only feasible for a nonrandom subset of policies and settings, so we lose our ability to make inferences about a broad range of policies if we rely solely on randomized experiments. For example, it is rarely feasible to randomize the location of medium- to large-scale infrastructure projects and sectoral and economy-wide reforms, which are core activities in almost any poor country's development strategy. Indeed, the very idea of randomized assignment is antithetical to the goals of many development programs, which typically aim to reach certain types of people or

---

[2] Basu (2014, 462) nicely elaborates this point. With reference to the question of whether medicine (M) improves school participation (P), Basu shows that in a deliberately stylized situation in which there is no true impact of M on P: "With 10,000 experiments it is close to certainty that someone will find a firm link between M and P. Hence, the finding of such a link shows nothing but the laws of probability being intact. Yet, thanks to the propensity of journals to publish the presence rather than the absence of 'causal' links, we get an illusion of knowledge and discovery where there are none." While we all have our anecdotes, it remains, however, that there is little solid evidence on the extent of this bias.

[3] See Card and Krueger (1995). The evidence for this was that with more data the precision of the estimated impacts in the published literature did not increase as one would expect without the publication bias.

places. Governments will (hopefully) be able to do far better in reaching poor people than a random assignment. Randomization also tends to be better suited to relatively simple programs, with clearly identified participants and nonparticipants, with little scope for the costs and benefits of participation to spill over into the group of nonparticipants.

6.2 Threats to the Internal Validity of an Evaluation

An important set of issues in evaluation relate to the *internal validity* of an evaluation, which refers to whether valid inferences are drawn for the study population. This section reviews the main threats to internal validity in practice.

Evaluation is in no small measure a problem of *missing data*. To understand why, imagine that for each individual there are two possible values of the outcome variable, namely the value under treatment and its value under the counterfactual.[4] (Thinking of antipoverty policies as "treatments" is unfortunate, but the word has stuck.) The *causal impact* at the individual level is the difference between the two. However, this concept of causal impact is purely theoretical; impact at the individual level is unobservable, since an individual cannot be in two different states of nature at the same instant.

All an impact evaluation can hope to do is to identify certain summary statistics about the distribution of the causal impacts. The summary statistic that gets the bulk of attention is the mean impact for those treated. When not all assigned units take up the treatment, we can distinguish the mean impact on the units that are given the opportunity to take up that intervention—called the *intent-to-treat* (ITT) parameter—from the average impact for those who actually take up the offer, which is called the *average treatment effect on the treated* (ATET).

To fix ideas it is helpful to start with a naïve estimate of the program's average impact, which is to compare the means of the relevant outcome indicators between participants and nonparticipants. Why might this be deceptive?

Endogenous Interventions

In drawing inferences about impact from data a great deal of effort typically goes into dealing with the possibility that the policy is endogenously placed, meaning that its placement is correlated with latent determinants of outcomes.

To first illustrate this problem in a more macro context, suppose that we want to learn about the effectiveness of a policy that increased the economy's openness to external trade. We might use a regression (as in box 1.19) in which the dependent variable is GDP per capita and the regressors include a measure of past trade reform to promote openness. We clearly cannot conclude from a significant regression coefficient on (say) past trade reform that a specific trade reform will promote growth;

---

[4] This is the approach to causality outlined in Holland (1986), following Rubin (1974), which has become the standard.

possibly the correlation we see between growth and trade reform reflects a higher propensity to reform in economies with better GDP growth prospects for some other reason. And even if we do not face this problem, we cannot draw a lesson for any one specific country from the average impact across all countries, as identified by the regression.

Similarly, at the micro level, suppose that one regresses log household consumption (say) on participation in an antipoverty program (with controls for, say, household size and composition, and location). Further, suppose that one finds that the regression coefficient on participation is small and not significantly different from zero. Do we conclude that the policy has failed? That would be questionable if the program has been targeted to poor people, creating a negative correlation between log consumption and placement. We may well find that the program has increased participants' consumption once we control for its placement.

This is the problem of *endogenous program placement*, which has long been recognized in economics.[5] Essentially the problem is that one of the regressors in the basic regression model (box 1.19) is correlated with the error term, violating the key assumption for valid causal inferences from that regression. Anyone concerned with identifying policy impacts using quantitative data must take this problem seriously.

In evaluating assigned programs, an obvious problem with this naïve estimate is that there could well be a difference between these two groups in the distribution of outcomes in the absence of the intervention. The difference in mean outcomes in the absence of the intervention is often called *selection bias*. As a result the naïve estimator will be biased for almost any imaginable parameter of interest, including mean impact. There are two sources of this bias. First, there can be a bias due to differences in *observable* characteristics. Second, there can be a bias due to differences in *unobservables*.[6] This source of bias arises when, for given values of the observable factors, there is a systematic relationship between program participation and outcomes in the absence of the program. In other words, there are unobserved variables that influence both the outcomes and program participation. In all evaluations, it is useful to have a good idea early on of how exactly participants were selected, or why they chose to participate.

Note that there is nothing to guarantee that these two sources of bias will work in the same direction. For example, the selection on observables in a targeted antipoverty program is almost always based on observable covariates of poverty. The selection process on unobservables need not, however, go in the same direction. Sometimes it will and sometimes not. To give an example of the latter, suppose that those with latent political connections manage to get themselves selected for the program. Then the two sources of bias could well go in opposite directions. If one only eliminates the selection bias based on observables, then the total bias may then be even greater than in a naïve estimator comparing the means with no adjustment for bias.

---

[5] While there are antecedents in the broader literature, an important contribution is raising awareness of this issue in development contexts was made by Pitt et al. (1995).

[6] The term "selection bias" is sometimes confined solely to the latter component though other authors use that term to denote the total bias. For further discussion, see Heckman et al. (1998).

So it is important to think about all sources of bias and their likely direction. Indeed, it is not impossible that the efforts made to reduce selection on unobservables are actually steering one further from the truth!

Spillover Effects

The comparison group of nonparticipants may well incur costs, or receive benefits, from the treatment. If there are hidden impacts for nonparticipants, then comparing the outcomes of treated units with those for the nonparticipants will clearly bias the results. This holds with randomized evaluations as well as other (non-experimental) evaluations. Spillover effects can stem from the fact that both groups trade in common markets or from the behavior of intervening agents (governmental/NGO).

Spillover effects may well be quite common in antipoverty programs. To give an example, consider an aid-financed poor-area development project. A plausible source of interference in this setting is through local public-spending responses to the external aid, whereby the local government cuts its own development spending in the villages targeted for external aid, and the spending is diverted in part at least to the nonparticipants used to form the comparison group.[7] Indeed, it would be quite rational for the local government to respond this way. Even though the spending allocations of that government may not be of intrinsic interest, it is a good idea to know about them, so as to test for such spillover effects.

Misspecification of the Impact Dynamics

In designing an impact evaluation one typically needs to make a prior assumption about the time period in which the impacts (both positive and negative) are expected.[8] One needs to be confident that the impact will actually occur between the baseline and endline of the data collected. Yet the theory of how the intervention has impact may not offer much guidance on the timing of that impact. And if one gets the timing wrong, then potentially large biases in the impact estimates can arise; for example, there may be longer lags in the impact than assumed by the data collection.

Behavioral Responses to an Evaluation

In collecting the data for an evaluation, it is often the case that people know they are being observed and that this alters their behavior in some way. This is an instance of a class of problems—often called "Hawthorne effects"—in which the fact of participation in an experiment on its own leads to different outcomes.[9] For example, the fact of being observed in the workplace may change a worker's productivity independently of

---

[7] This specific example is studied in Chen et al. (2009). Chapter 10 returns to this topic.

[8] See King and Behrman (2009) for a useful discussion of this point. Studies of impact dynamics include Behrman et al. (2004) and Tjernström et al. (2013).

[9] For a taxonomy of the various ways this can happen, see Friedman (2014b).

the intervention.[10] To know whether there is a behavioral response to being observed one needs to compare impacts to those with stealth.

In some evaluations, the data are generated in a way that makes Hawthorne effects unlikely. For example, if one is using multipurpose survey data that includes questions on program participation, then one would be less worried about Hawthorne effects than if it is a study done specifically for assessing the intervention in question. Nonetheless, Hawthorne effects may well be more common than is thought.

6.3   Evaluation Methods in Practice

As we have seen, a policy will have impacts at the individual level but identifying those impacts is rarely feasible in practice. Evaluations in practice aim instead to measure some key summary statistics for the distribution of the (unobservable) individual level casual impacts of a policy. The summary statistic that gets most attention is the mean impact of the policy.

There are various methods that are used in estimating the mean impact of assigned programs (including antipoverty programs), as summarized in box 6.1. The following paragraphs offer some general comments on the main methods found in practice. The choice of method depends on many factors, including the type of program (whether a pilot or at full-scale) and the resources available for data collection.

Box 6.1 **Methods of Impact Evaluation: A Summary**

- *Social experiments.* Here the selection into the treatment and comparison groups is entirely random in some well-defined set of people. In the context of evaluating proposed social programs, these are called randomized control trials (RCTs). Then in large samples, and without spillover effects from the treatment to the controls (as discussed in section 6.2), the difference in mean outcomes reveals the true average impact. In one-off experiments on small samples ($n < 100$ say), there is no guarantee that randomization will work well in representing the population—the sample may turn out to be unbalanced relative to relevant characteristics. When feasible, stratification according to likely baseline covariates of impact can increase precision of the impact estimate (i.e., reducing its variance). For example, in evaluating a training

continued

---

[10] This example is from the origin of the term "Hawthorne effect." The story is told that the Western Electric Company's Hawthorne Plant in Chicago in the 1920s found that the productivity of workers improved with better lighting, but that it also improved when the lights were dimmed! An analysis of the original data (long thought to have been lost) by Levitt and List (2011) suggests that this was greatly exaggerated. However, there are numerous valid examples of behavioral responses to being observed; see the summary in Friedman (2014a).

Box 6.1 **(Continued)**

program one might split the sample into age and education groups and then use simple randomization within these groups. Adaptive randomization methods adjust the assignment to treatment or control along the way to improve covariate balance.

- *Matching.* Here one tries to pick an ideal comparison group from a (typically) larger survey. The comparison group is matched to the treatment group on the basis of a set of observed characteristics, or using the "propensity score" given by the predicted probability of participation given observed characteristics. (These scores are from a regression of participation on the observed variables likely to influence participation. The same regression is a useful test for whether a randomized assignment has worked well; if it has, then the regressors should have no explanatory power.) Of course, this only addresses the first source of selection bias (section 6.2), based on observables. The identification and measurement of the relevant covariates of program placement and their balancing between treatment and comparison groups are crucial to the credibility of these methods.
- *Double difference (or "difference in difference") methods.* Here one compares a treatment and comparison group (first difference), before and after a program (second difference). An example is found in the study by Card and Krueger (1995) on the effects of raising the minimum wage rate, as estimated by comparing employment changes in places that saw such an increase with those that did not. (Chapter 9 will discuss this topic further.) This assumes that the selection bias is constant over time. Controlling for observable differences between units in the baseline that influence the trajectories can help reduce bias.
- *Discontinuity designs:* Sometimes one can infer impacts from the differences in mean outcomes between units on either side of a critical cut-off point determining program eligibility. Examples include a proxy-means test that sets a maximum score for eligibility and programs that confine eligibility within geographic boundaries. The impact estimator is the difference in mean outcomes either side of the discontinuity. One can allow for a degree of fuzziness in the application of eligibility tests. The key identifying assumption is that the discontinuity is in outcomes under treatment not outcomes under the counterfactual. The plausibility of this assumption must be judged in each application.
- *Instrumental variables methods.* An instrumental variable is something that is correlated with participation, but not with outcomes given participation (i.e., the way it influences outcomes is entirely through participation). If such a variable exists (and there is no guarantee that it does in the specific application), then it can be used to identify a source of exogenous variation in outcomes attributable to the program, recognizing that its placement is not random but purposive. The IVs are first used to predict program participation, then one

> sees how the outcome indicator varies with the predicted values, conditional on other characteristics. Box 6.4 goes into greater detail.
>
> *Further reading:* To introduce the methods of impact evaluation, Ravallion (2001a) tells the fictional story of Ms Speedy Analyst as she tries to unravel the mystery of the vanishing benefits. Ravallion (2008b) surveys the theory and methods of impact evaluation relevant to assessing antipoverty programs. For a more general treatment using advanced methods see Lee (2005).

Social Experiments

A classic method of estimating mean impact is a social experiment, whereby access to the program is randomly assigned, with a randomly chosen control group used to identify the counterfactual. In large samples, this tool is well suited to estimating the average impact of the treatment. For this purpose, the key feature of an experiment is that in sufficiently large samples there will be negligible difference in mean counterfactual outcomes between the treated and untreated units. In practice, social experiments take the form of RCTs (Box 6.1), and the sample sizes are not often large. Then it is important to test for equality of the means of variables unaffected by the intervention (including pre-intervention outcomes) between the treatment and control sample (called a "balancing test").

There will be no selection bias in a perfect experiment since, in the absence of the intervention, everything will be the same on average between the treatment and control samples, including the specific outcomes of interest. "Perfect" is demanding, however. It requires (among other things) that all those units that are randomly assigned the treatment from the relevant population take it up, and none of those who were randomized out take it up.

In practice, experiments are rarely perfect and internal validity is rarely assured. Doing one-off experiments with relatively small samples does not guarantee a reliable estimate of even the mean impact; one can draw a bad sample. For this reason, it is always important to test that treatment and control groups are balanced in terms of relevant covariates even when both samples were drawn randomly. Of course, this test can only be done based on the observable data. So even for a well-run experiment with perfect compliance, unless the sample size is large, there can be undetectable biases.

In practice, there is rarely perfect compliance with the randomized assignment. Some of those offered the treatment choose not to take it up. Then a non-experimental correction will be needed. We return to this point in due course.

Another concern in practice is that it is often unclear what inferences can be drawn for the relevant population given that some unknown, and non-random, process has determined the larger sample of people from whom the random samples of treatment and control units are to be drawn. To make the RCT feasible, one may have to rely on some friendly local NGO that agreed to the experiment. Or we rely on a set of people who apply to a program. We do not know how these larger samples were drawn, and so we lose our ability to make claims about the relevant population as a whole even though we have drawn random samples from the larger sample. Again we end up back in the world of non-experimental methods of evaluation.

Non-Experimental Methods

Various non-experimental methods exist that can also identify mean impact. All of them try to address endogenous program placement, though they are also confined to the observable data in doing so, and they require further assumptions to deliver a valid estimate of mean impact. The specific assumptions differ between methods, but for the most part they come down to the choice between one of two options:

- The first option assumes that there are sufficient control variables such that placement of the program can be treated as effectively random given those controls. Naturally, this puts a lot of onus on the data. In times gone by, when evaluative research relied on pre-existing data sets, this was a highly problematic assumption. With richer multipurpose data sets, often designed specifically for the evaluation, the assumption is less contentious (since the researcher can collect the necessary data) but the assumption can still be questioned. In more technical jargon, this assumption says that placement is *conditionally exogenous*—independent of outcome conditional on the observable data.
- The second (alternative) approach requires a form of conditional independence, but this time it is that there exists another variable that is correlated with placement but independent of the outcomes of interest given placement. In other words, this *instrumental variable* (IV) is assumed to only alter outcomes via treatment. This is called the *exclusion restriction* (since the IV is being excluded from the regression for outcomes).

The choice between these approaches depends in no small measure on the specifics of the program being evaluated and the data available. The rest of this section looks more closely at some popular non-experimental methods.

Difference-in-Difference (DD) Estimators

This is a very intuitive method: one compares the change over time in outcomes in the treatment group with that for the comparison group of nonparticipants. The changes are measured between the baseline and endline dates. The key assumption is that the selection bias is constant over time. (This is sometimes called the "parallel trends assumption.") That assumption does not always hold. For example, infrastructure improvements may well be attracted to places with rising productivity, leading the standard DD method to overestimate the economic returns to new development projects. The opposite bias is also possible. Poor-area development programs are often targeted to places that lack infrastructure and other conditions conducive to economic growth. It is a good idea to control for differences in initial conditions in using the DD method. In doing so, one is making a conditional exogeneity assumption (the first option above), namely that the changes in placement are exogenous to the changes in outcomes given the control variables.

Another issue that can arise in practice is that one sometimes does not know at the time the baseline survey is implemented who will participate in the program. One must make an informed guess in designing the sampling for the baseline survey; knowledge of the program design and setting can provide clues. Types of observation units with characteristics making them more likely to participate will often have to be over-sampled, to help assure adequate coverage of the population treatment group and to provide a sufficiently large pool of similar comparators to draw upon.

Fixed Effects Regressions

In an impact evaluation, this is really another way of doing a DD method, but the method has wider applicability and so it is worth considering more closely. It is often the case that there is a natural clustering of observations in terms of real income (or some other outcome variable) in a regression being used to estimate the income gains from a policy. Call these the "effects." These might be "good" and "bad" geographic areas in a single cross-sectional data set or households with inherently different real incomes in a panel data set (with multiple observations for each household). In trying to draw valid inferences from the regression, this clustering is not worrying on its own right if these effects are uncorrelated with the variables of interest (although when it reflects the sample design one needs to allow for this in the estimation to assure that the standard errors of regression coefficients are correct). However, if the effects are correlated with the policy, then we clearly have a problem—maybe the presumed policy impact is really just due to the fact that the placement of the policy depends on which of the clustered groups the observation belongs. The fixed effects regression addresses this problem, by explicitly including the effects in the model. Box 6.2 gives further detail. The key assumption being made here is that the problem of endogenous program placement is fully captured by the fixed effects in the regression error term. (This is another version of the conditional exogeneity assumption above.) However, box 6.3 also provides a warning about these (popular) methods when one considers the patterns of measurement error in the data.

Box 6.2 **Fixed Effects Regressions**

Recall that a regression is a line of best fit relating one or more explanatory variables to a specific dependent variable (box 1.19). With data on N cross-sectional units over T time periods, the *fixed effects regression* takes the form:

$$Y_{it} = \beta X_{it} + \eta_i + \varepsilon_{it} \ (i = 1, \ldots, N; \ t = 1, \ldots, T).$$

Here Y_{it} is the dependent variable, X_{it} is a list of explanatory variables, and $\eta_i + \varepsilon_{it}$ is the composite error term. This has two components, namely the "innovation

continued

Box 6.2 (Continued)

error" ε_{it} and η_i, which is often called the "fixed effect" (referring to the fact that it is fixed over time; the term "individual effect" is also used). This is the intercept (when $X_{it} = 0$) for each cross-sectional unit. The innovation error term has a mean of zero, but this is not true of the fixed effect, which embodies all the time-invariant unobserved factors not picked up by the explanatory variables. Also, unlike the innovation error term, the fixed effect can be correlated with the explanatory variables. If we did not have the time series observations, this would present a severe problem for estimating the key parameters of interest, the β's, since we would lose our ability to distinguish what is due to the X's and what is due to the η_i's. The neat thing is that by combining the time series and cross-sectional data we can solve this problem. The simplest way to see this is if we take the first difference over time, giving:

$$\Delta Y_{it} = \beta \Delta X_{it} + \Delta \varepsilon_{it}.$$

Here $\Delta Y_{it} = Y_{it} - Y_{it-1}$ and similarly for ΔX_{it}. Now we have removed the troubling η_i's. Alternatively, we can include a complete set of N country-level fixed effects; these are essentially country-specific intercepts. We do not need to actually include these intercepts, since we can take the differences of all variables from their time-means to get rid of the problem. (Strictly the first-difference method will only give the same results as the country-fixed effects method when $T = 2$. For $T > 2$ the differencing creates a potential problem of a correlation over time in the differenced error terms.) This can come at a cost, however, when there are significant time-varying measurement errors in the data. The differenced variable ΔX_{it} will have a higher share of its variance that is due to measurement error, which will make it harder to detect its true impact on the dependent variable.

Further reading: There is a good discussion of fixed-effects regressions and related estimation methods in Wooldridge (2002, ch. 10). We will return to discuss some of the concerns about these methods in box 6.3.

Box 6.3 Perils in Fixed-Effects Regressions

In box 6.2 we saw that by differencing the data (or taking deviations from time means) we can get rid of the troubling fixed effects. This can come at a cost, however, when there are significant time-varying measurement errors in the data. The differenced variable ΔX_{it} will have a higher share of its variance that is due to measurement error, which will make it harder to detect its true impact on the dependent variable. It is not possible to say in general whether the "fixed effects cure" is worse than the disease—whether we end up closer to the truth; this is often called an "attenuation bias," reflecting the tendency for the regression coefficient on a mismeasured variable to be biased toward zero. (Intuitively, when there is lots of measurement error the true relationship becomes blurred, and one is more likely to incorrectly conclude that there is in fact no relationship.) That depends on the application one has. The simulations by Hauk and Wacziarg (2009) suggest that the attenuation bias can be large in fixed-effects growth regressions (where the Y_{it} is a growth rate—the change in log income per capita—so that ΔY_{it} is the change in the growth rate).

Another window on the problem is by considering two variables that measure something quite similar, and we know must be highly correlated, but which both contain time-varying measurement errors. An example is the mean consumption of a country from household surveys and the private consumption component of domestic absorption in the national accounts for the same country at (as close as possible) the same date. These are not exactly the same thing, but they should be highly correlated. That is exactly what we see when we compare the levels of these two variables. Their growth rates tend also to co-move quite strongly, though not as correlated as the levels. However, when we compare the changes in the growth rates, the relationship becomes very weak, with less than 10% of an increase in the log of consumption per capita from the national accounts being reflected in the survey means. This is clearly not because there is no real relationship. Rather it is because the signal-to-noise ratio deteriorates enormously when we measure the changes in the changes.

The point is not that fixed-effects regressions should be abandoned. Rather it is that there is a trade-off to consider. There are situations in which the omitted-variable bias in the ordinary "levels regression" is likely to be the main concern, trumping worries about measurement error, and pointing to the usefulness of a fixed-effects specification. But there will be other situations in which the reverse is true.

Note on the literature: For further discussion of fixed-effects regression, see Deaton (1997, ch. 2) and Wooldridge (2013, ch. 14). Further details on the example comparing survey means and national accounts consumption are available from the author.

Instrumental Variables Estimators

The standard IV method shares some of the weaknesses of other non-experimental methods. As with an OLS regression, the validity of causal inferences typically rests on ad hoc assumptions about the outcome regression, including its functional form. The propensity score matching method (box 6.1) makes fewer assumptions of this sort. However, when a valid IV is available, the real strength of that method is its robustness to the existence of unobserved variables that jointly influence program placement and outcomes. Box 6.4 explains this method more fully.

*Box 6.4 **Instrumental Variables**

An instrumental variable (IV) is a variable that is not already in the regression as an explanatory variable, is correlated with the endogenous explanatory variable, but is uncorrelated with the error term of that regression. One can think of the estimation as requiring two stages (hence, it is sometimes called "Two-Stage Least Squares" although the two can be collapsed into one stage in the computations). The IV is first used to predict the endogenous variable. Then one sees how the dependent variable varies with the predicted values, conditional on the IV, and other variables used for controls.

To see more clearly how the method works, let the regression of interest for the dependent variable Y_i be:

$$Y_i = \beta D_i + \varepsilon_i. \tag{1}$$

Here D_i is the endogenous variable. (We can readily include other control variables, treated as exogenous, but they are left out to keep the notation simple.). We have an IV, Z_i, such that:

$$D_i = \gamma Z_i + u_i. \tag{2}$$

Substituting (2) into (1) we get the "reduced form" model:

$$Y_i = \beta(\gamma Z_i + u_i) + \varepsilon_i = \pi Z_i + v_i. \tag{3}$$

If we run ordinary least squares (OLS) on (2) and (3) and take the ratio of their coefficients, then we get the IV estimator: $\hat{\beta}_{IVE} = \hat{\pi}_{OLS}/\hat{\gamma}_{OLS}$ (in obvious notation). Alternatively, we can run the OLS regression of Y on the predicted value of D:

$$Y_i = \beta(\hat{\gamma} Z_i) + v_i. \tag{4}$$

(The usual OLS standard error you get will not be right, given that the regressor was estimated already, but statistical packages do the correction needed.)

This looks easy, but there are some pitfalls. It is often easy to find variables that are not in the regression of interest and are correlated with the endogenous variable. The harder task is usually to justify that this variable should not already be in the model (i.e., to justify the "exclusion restriction"). In other words, the variable Z cannot also appear as an independent variable on the right-hand side of equation (1).

Consider, for example, the data in box 1.19. As was noted there, measurement error in the surveys may create a spurious negative correlation. To address this concern, one could use private consumption from the national accounts as the IV for the survey mean, on the assumption that the measurement errors are independent. (Consumption in the national accounts is typically estimated as a residual at the commodity level rather than being estimated from surveys, so the assumption seems defensible. One caveat is that common measurement errors from the PPP exchange rates will still be present.) This gives:

$$\log H = 10.60 - 1.70 \log M + \hat{e}.$$

The regression coefficient is actually higher than in box 1.19, though so is its standard error, which rises to 0.17. However, this could be questioned if we think that there is some reason why higher national accounts consumption is associated with lower inequality, so that the IV slope coefficient becomes more negative than the true value. However, there is no obvious reason why this would happen.

Further reading: For further discussion of IV estimation, see Wooldridge (2013, ch. 15).

The IV method has become very popular in applied economics. However, the advantages of the method rest on the validity of its assumptions, and large biases can arise if they do not hold. The best work using this method gives close scrutiny to those assumptions. Testing the exclusion restriction is difficult, however. In the happy circumstance of having more than one valid IV, then one can do an "over-identification test" to see whether all but one of the IVs is a significant predictor of outcomes given program placement. However, one must still have at least one IV and so the exclusion restriction is fundamentally untestable within the confines of the data available. Nonetheless, appeals to theoretical arguments or other evidence (external to the data used for the evaluation) can often leave one reasonably confident in accepting, or rejecting, a postulated exclusion restriction in the specific context.

In practice, the IV method sometimes gives seemingly implausible impact estimates (either too small or too large). One might suspect that a violation of the exclusion restriction is the reason. For example, it is sometimes the case that one has a strong prior that OLS will overestimate program impact, given an a priori belief that placement is positively correlated with latent factors that have a positive effect on outcomes (i.e., that placement is positively correlated with the error term). If one thinks one has a valid IV but finds that the IV estimate is even larger than the OLS estimate, then one should worry that this is because the exclusion restriction is not valid. In effect, the predicted value of program placement based on the IV is picking up the omitted factors that influence outcomes. The IV estimate is even more biased![11]

On a priori grounds one cannot say which, if either, of the conditional independence assumptions described above is more credible. That needs to be judged in

---

[11] If it is possible to rule out certain values for Y on a priori grounds, then this can allow us to establish plausible bounds to the impact estimates, following an approach introduced by Manski (1990). Another approach to setting bounds is found in Altonji et al. (2005). For further discussion of these methods in the present context, see Ravallion (2008a).

each application.[12] Ultimately, prior judgments based on other external information (including economic theory) must determine whether the assumptions made by any evaluation method (including experiments) are to be believed.

6.4 The External Validity of an Evaluation

So far we have focused on the main methods of evaluation found in practice and the main issue has been internal validity. This is important, but there are a number of other threats to the validity of an evaluation. This section focuses on how we can learn from an evaluation in one context about other contexts, including scaling up to the population as a whole. That is the problem of *external validity*. This tends to get less attention than internal validity.

One reason that knowledge gaps persist is that, in practice, the standard evaluation methods reviewed above sometimes fall short in addressing the questions of greatest interest to policymakers (as discussed in section 6.1). The following points are illustrative of the other things policymakers often want to know besides internal validity:

- Impact evaluations in economics have typically used the "do-nothing" counterfactual. In other words, the control group gets nothing.[13] This is rarely (in my experience) of much interest to policymakers, who will more likely want to know impact relative to the next best policy option. Governments will rarely want to do nothing instead of the program in question. Evaluations need to consider carefully what is the most policy-relevant counterfactual in each case.
- Policymakers will want to know what might be expected if the program is scaled up or applied to a different setting (such as a different region of the country). They will also want to know average impact in the real-world setting in which the program is not in fact randomly assigned, recognizing that the same program cannot be expected to have the same impact for everyone. Thus, the real-world program can be expected to attract those who are likely to benefit, rather than some random sample of the population. This is the problem of external validity, which we return to later.
- Policymakers often want to know more than average impact, which may be seen as rather limited information. What types of people tend to gain, and what types loose? Policymakers may also want to know what proportion of the participants benefit. They naturally want to know costs, as well as benefits. The bulk of evaluation attention often goes into figuring out the benefits. While this is undeniably

---

[12] There have been some attempts to test one method against another in the context of a randomized evaluation in which one assumes to be correct for mean impact; see the review in Ravallion (2008b). One then sees how well various non-experimental methods perform; examples include Lalonde (1986), Dehejia and Wahba (1999), Glazerman et al. (2003), and McKenzie et al. (2010). These are useful contributions to knowledge, although doubts remain given that the researcher already claims to know the correct answer, and must make numerous choices in executing the non-experimental method; see, for example, Smith and Todd (2001) (commenting on Dehejia and Wahba 1999).

[13] In the impact evaluations done for full-scale programs, the leave-out counterfactual is typically "business-as-usual," whereby the control population receives the standard package of services.

important, it is no less important than the costs in deciding whether to implement the policy at scale.

- Policymakers will also want to know how a program might be designed differently to enhance impact. Many evaluations in practice are "black boxes"—they reveal very little about the underlying processes at work, and so provide little useful information for thinking about alternative designs for the program.

None of these are especially easy questions, and they will often call for innovative data and methods. The rest of this section will go further into the main external validity issues in practice.

Heterogeneity in Impacts

Inferences for other settings, or scaling up in the same setting, based on the results of an impact evaluation can be way off the mark when there is heterogeneity of impacts, as is to be expected as a rule. This can stem from heterogeneity of participants or from contextual factors. For example, an intervention run by an NGO might be totally different when applied at scale by government officials facing different incentives. To give another example, in a poor setting with many possible points of intervention, the first thing one does may achieve a high return regardless of what it is that is done. However, this can clearly be deceptive if one is trying to learn about program performance in an environment of comprehensive policy adoption. The converse holds too: it can be hazardous drawing lessons for policy in poor (including intervention-poor) settings from rich ones.

When the heterogeneity is in observables, we can imagine replicating evaluations across different types of participants and settings so as to map out all the possibilities.[14] However, this is unlikely to be a viable research strategy. The dimensionality of the problem could well be too large to make this feasible; nor are individual researchers likely to be willing to do near endless replications of the same method for the same program, which are unlikely to have good prospects for publication.

A social experiment randomly mixes low-impact people (for whom the program brings little benefit) with high-impact people. The scaled-up program will tend to have higher representation from the high-impact types, who will naturally be attracted to it; this is an instance of what James Heckman and Jeffrey Smith (1995) dubbed *randomization bias*. Given this purposive selection, the national program is fundamentally different to the RCT, which may well contain rather little useful information for scaling up. This is an instance of a more general point made by Robert Moffitt (2006) that many things can change—inputs and even the program itself—when a pilot is scaled up.

To learn about the effectiveness of the full range of interventions for fighting poverty, we would need a very different approach. We would need to randomly choose which projects or policies get evaluated, and then pick the best available method, whether it uses randomization or not. And then everything should get published, as long as it meets purely technical standards. Papers about failed policies should have

---

[14] This is proposed by Banerjee (2007) who advocates RCTs for this purpose.

no less chance of publication to successes. That approach would have a better chance of delivering reliable knowledge about what works and what does not. Absent such an approach, the scope for bias in our knowledge is plain.

Portfolio Effects

We are often interested in assessing the impact of a set of interventions—the *development portfolio*. This may comprise various things that are (ostensibly) financed by the domestic resources of developing countries. Or it might be a set of externally financed projects spanning multiple countries—a portfolio held by a donor country or international organization, such as the World Bank.

The bulk of the new evaluative work is assessing the impact of specific projects, one at a time. Each such project is only one component of the portfolio. (And each project may itself have multiple elements.) Evaluators worry mainly about whether they are drawing valid conclusions about the impact of that project in its specific setting, including its policy environment. The fact that each project happens to be in some development portfolio gets surprisingly little attention.

So an important question is begging: How useful will all this evaluative effort be for assessing development portfolios? When you think about it, assessing a development portfolio by evaluating its components one-by-one and adding up the results requires some assumptions that are hard to accept. For one thing, it assumes that there are negligible *interaction effects* among the components. Yet the success of an education or health project (say) may depend crucially on whether infrastructure or public sector reform projects (say) within the same portfolio have also worked.[15] Indeed, the bundling of (often multisectoral) components in one portfolio is often justified by claimed interaction effects. But evaluating each bit separately and adding up the results will not (in general) give us an unbiased estimate of the portfolio's impact. If the components interact positively (more of one yields higher impact of the other), then we will overestimate the portfolio's impact; negative interactions yield the opposite bias (see box 6.5).

Box 6.5 **The Bias in Assessing the Impact of a Portfolio One Component at a Time**

To keep things simple, suppose that the portfolio has two projects, labeled 1 and 2, in amounts x_1 and x_2 (both nonnegative). Together the two projects yield a measured outcome:

$$y = \alpha + \beta_1 x_1 + \beta_2 x_2 + \beta_3 x_1 x_2 + \varepsilon.$$

---

[15] To give a more specific example, the health gains from impact of nutrition supplementation are known to depend on how safe the health environment is, which depends on water and sanitation infrastructure. (We will return to this example in section 9.4.)

Here we assume that $E(\varepsilon \,|x_1, x_2) = 0$ (where $E(.)$ denotes the mean—the mathematical expectation—of the term in parentheses). The projects are said to interact positively (negatively) if $\beta_3 > (<) \, 0$.

The impact of the portfolio (relative to the standard counterfactual: $x_1 = 0$, $x_2 = 0$) is:

$$\Delta \equiv E(y \,|x_1, x_2) - E(y \,|x_1 = 0, x_2 = 0) = \beta_1 x_1 + \beta_2 x_2 + \beta_3 x_1 x_2.$$

This is recognizable as a standard design for evaluating any two-pronged intervention, whereby one group gets project 1, the other gets 2, and a third gets both. Under standard conditions, the interaction effect is identified, and so is the overall impact of the portfolio.

Now imagine that two evaluations are done separately, one for each project. The first is assumed to assess project 1 conditional on the existence of project 2. The derived conditional impact of project 1 is then:

$$\Delta_1 \equiv E(y \,|x_1, x_2) - E(y \,|x_1 = 0, x_2) = \beta_1 x_1 + \beta_3 x_1 x_2.$$

Similarly, the impact of project 2 is assessed given that project 1 exists:

$$\Delta_2 \equiv E(y \,|x_1, x_2) - E(y \,|x_1, x_2 = 0) = \beta_2 x_2 + \beta_3 x_1 x_2.$$

We then try to figure out the impact of the portfolio by adding up the measured impacts from these two separate evaluations, to obtain:

$$\Delta_1 + \Delta_2 = \Delta + \beta_3 x_1 x_2.$$

It can be seen that $\Delta_1 + \Delta_2$ over- (under-) estimates the overall impact of the portfolio (Δ) if there is a positive (negative) interaction effect; only if there is no interaction will we get the right answer.

We appear to be building up our knowledge in a worryingly selective way that is unlikely to address well the existing, policy-relevant, knowledge gaps. What do we need to do? There are two sorts of things we need to do to address this problem, though both are likely to meet resistance. The first requires some central planning in terms of what gets evaluated. Nobody much likes central planning, but we often need some form of it in public goods provision, and knowledge is a public good. A degree of planning, with judicious use of incentives, could create a compensating mechanism to assure that decentralized decision-making about evaluation can better address policy-relevant knowledge gaps.

Second, we need to think creatively about how best to go about evaluating the portfolio as a whole, allowing for interaction effects among its components, as well as among economic agents. This is not going to be easy. Standard tools of impact evaluation may have to be complemented by other tools, such as structural modeling and cross-country and cross-jurisdictional comparative work. We will need to look at public finance issues such as fungibility and flypaper effects (which we return to). And we will almost certainly be looking at general equilibrium effects—big time in some cases!—which can readily overturn the partial equilibrium picture that emerges from standard impact evaluations. There is scope for more eclectic approaches, combining multiple methods, spanning both "macro" and "micro" tools for economic analysis. The tools needed may not be the favored ones by today's evaluators. But the principle of evaluation is the same, including the key idea of assessing impact against an explicit counterfactual.

If we are serious about assessing development impact, then we will have to be more interventionist about what gets evaluated and more pragmatic and eclectic in how that is done.

General Equilibrium Effects

Partial equilibrium assumptions (taking prices as given) may be fine for a pilot antipoverty program, but general equilibrium effects (sometimes called "feedback" or "macro" effects) can be important when it is scaled up nationally. (Box 6.6 further explains the difference between partial equilibrium and general equilibrium analysis.) For example, an estimate of the impact on schooling of a tuition subsidy based on an RCT may be deceptive when scaled up, given that the structure of returns to schooling will alter.[16] To give another example, a small pilot wage subsidy program may be unlikely to have much impact on the market wage rate, but that will change when the program is scaled up.

Box 6.6 **General Equilibrium Analysis**

Every market has a supply and demand side. Institutionally, we can think of the supply of goods as being done by firms maximizing their profits and the demand by consumers, maximizing their utilities, though consumers also supply labor to firms, and firms also have demands for goods. In partial equilibrium analysis one only considers one market at a time, or sometimes just one side of the market. Other prices are fixed. Partial equilibrium analysis of some of the policies relevant to poverty and inequality can be deceptive. In studying a small targeted antipoverty program, it is reasonable to take prices as given. But if the program is large enough, then the redistribution of income involved can be expected to alter prices, and this clearly matters to the overall impact

---

[16] See, for example, Heckman et al. (1998) who demonstrate that partial equilibrium analysis can greatly overestimate the impact of a tuition subsidy once relative wages adjust. In further work, Lee (2005) finds a much smaller difference between the general and partial equilibrium effects of a tuition subsidy in a slightly different model.

on the distribution of real income. Economy-wide policy reforms, such as trade liberalizations, are likely to impact many markets (chapter 9).

In a general equilibrium analysis one considers all markets for both goods and factors of production. In the case of the competitive general equilibrium model, all prices are assumed to be flexible, such that all markets clear, meaning that there is no excess of aggregate supply over aggregate demand for any good or factor unless its price has been driven down to zero. The model is solved for the market clearing prices subject to all relevant accounting identities, such as household budget constraints. In general, the demand and supply of each good depends not only on the price of that good but on all other prices, thus creating a potentially complex set of cross-market interaction effects. When it exists, the set of equilibrium prices, clearing all markets, will depend on all the exogenous non-price variables that affect the demands and/or supplies of all goods and factors.

The benchmark model has a complete set of markets, including for commodities in different states of nature, such as different dates and places, or under different realizations of the various uncertainties. In applications, however, it is realistic to allow for missing markets and/or fixity of certain prices (often called "sticky prices"). The latter usually applies to factor markets, and the most common example is when one or more wage rates are sticky downwards, thus generating unemployment of labor; this is sometimes called a Keynesian model. How that unemployment is allocated (the "rationing regime") is then relevant to the model's solution.

Historical note: The first rigorous formulation of the competitive general equilibrium model was Walras (1874), and the solution is still known as the Walrasian equilibrium. One of the early mathematical challenges in modern economic theory was to prove the existence of a unique Walrasian equilibrium. The first such proof was provided by Wald (1951). The application of these ideas to policy evaluation was stimulated by the development of Computable General Equilibrium (CGE) models, for which a key step was the method of numerical solution proposed by Scarf and Hansen (1973).

Further reading: The now classic advanced treatment of competitive equilibrium theory is Arrow and Hahn (1971). Most economics textbooks cover the topic; see, for example, Varian (2014) and, for a more advanced treatment, Varian (1978). On CGE models, see Ginsburgh and Keyzer (1997), which uses some advanced methods but covers a usefully broad ground, including CGE models with sticky prices.

In economy-wide policies (the subject of chapter 9), general equilibrium effects are likely. When some countries get the economy-wide program but some do not, cross-country comparative work can reveal impacts; these tools are discussed further in chapter 8. That identification task is often difficult, because there are typically latent factors at the country level that simultaneously influence outcomes and whether a country adopts the policy in question. And even when the identification strategy is accepted, carrying the generalized lessons from cross-country regressions to inform policymaking in any one country can be problematic.

There are a number of promising examples of how simulation tools for economy-wide policies such as Computable General Equilibrium (CGE) models can be combined with household-level survey data to assess impacts on poverty and inequality; this approach is discussed further in chapter 9, section 9.8. These simulation methods make it far easier to attribute impacts to the policy change, although this advantage comes at the cost of the need to make many more assumptions about how the economy works.

Structural Models

Without estimating a full-blown general equilibrium model, much can often be learned by studying some key aspects of the (market and non-market) interrelationships between economic players that are missed by partial equilibrium analysis. This is often called "structural modeling."[17]

Structural models make more assumptions about how an economy works than the standard evaluation tools reviewed in section 6.3. As far as possible, one would like to see those assumptions anchored to past knowledge built up from rigorous *ex post* evaluations. For example, by combining a randomized evaluation design with a structural model of the relevant choices made by participants and nonparticipants, and exploiting the randomized assignment for identification, one can greatly expand the set of policy-relevant questions about the design of a program that a conventional evaluation can answer.[18]

In structural models, an important role is played by economic theory in understanding why a program may or may not have impact. However, the theoretical models can often be questioned. The models used may make assumptions that are considered unrealistic in the specific setting. For example, the models that have been used in the literature on evaluating training and other programs in developed countries assume that selection is a matter of individual choice among those eligible. This does not sit easily with what we know about many antipoverty programs in developing countries, in which the choices made by politicians and administrators appear to be at least as important to the selection process as the choices made by those eligible to participate. We often need a richer theoretical characterization of the selection problem to assure relevance.[19]

[17] For a useful overview of *ex ante* methods, see Bourguignon and Ferreira (2003). A more advanced treatment of the range of tools available for structural modeling can be found in Heckman and Leamer (2007, chs. 70–72).

[18] Examples using the impact evaluation of a large antipoverty program in Mexico can be found in de Janvry and Sadoulet (2006), Todd and Wolpin (2006) and Attanasio et al. (2012). Chapter 10 returns to this program.

[19] An example of one effort in this direction can be found in the Galasso and Ravallion (2005) model of a decentralized antipoverty program; their model focuses on the public-choice problem facing the central government and the local collective action problem facing communities, with individual

6.5 The Ethical Validity of an Evaluation

Economists have given more thought to the (internal and external) validity of the conclusions drawn from impact evaluations than to the ethical validity of how the evaluations were done. This is not an issue for all evaluations. Sometimes an impact evaluation is built into an existing program such that nothing changes about how the program works. The evaluation takes as given the way the program assigns its benefits. So if the program is deemed to be ethically acceptable, then this can be presumed to also hold for the method of evaluation. (I leave aside ethical issues in how evaluations are reported and publication biases.) We can dub these *ethically benign evaluations*.

Another type of evaluation deliberately alters the program's (known or likely) assignment mechanism—who gets the program and who does not—for the purposes of the evaluation. Then the ethical acceptability of the intervention does not imply that the evaluation is ethically acceptable. Call these *ethically contestable evaluations*. The main examples in practice are RCTs. Scaled-up programs almost never use randomized assignment, so the RCT has a different assignment mechanism, and this may be contested ethically even when the full program is fine.

A recent debate about the ethical validity of RCTs illustrates the main issues. In a *New York Times* blog post Casey Mulligan (2014) essentially dismisses RCTs as ethically unacceptable on the grounds that some of those to which a program is assigned for the purpose of evaluation—the treatment group—will almost certainly not need it, or benefit little, while some in the control group will.[20] In a response, Jessica Goldberg (2014) defends the ethical validity of RCTs against Mulligan's critique. On the one hand, she argues that randomization can be defended as ethically fair given limited resources, while (on the other hand) even if one still objects, the gains from new knowledge can outweigh the objections.

Let us look more closely at this debate. It is surely a rather extreme position (not often associated with economists) to say that good ends can never justify bad means. It is ethically defensible to judge processes in part by their outcomes; indeed, there is a long tradition of doing so in moral philosophy, with utilitarianism as the leading example (chapter 1). It is not inherently "unethical" to do an RCT that knowingly withholds a treatment from some people in genuine need, and gives it to some people who are not, as long as this is deemed to be justified by the expected welfare benefits from new knowledge. Ethics has been much discussed in medical research. In that context, the *principle of equipoise* requires that there should be no decisive prior case for believing that the treatment has impact.[21] One can modify this to require that the treatment has an expected impact sufficient to justify its cost.[22] By this reasoning, only if we are sufficiently ignorant about the likely gains relative to the costs should we evaluate further.

---

participation choices treated as a trivial sub-problem. Such models can also point to instrumental variables for identifying impacts and studying their heterogeneity.

[20] As an example, Mulligan endorses Sachs's arguments as to why the Millennium Villages project was not set up as an RCT.

[21] See Freedman (1987).

[22] This is proposed by McKenzie (2013).

It has often been argued that whenever rationing is required—when there is not enough money to cover everyone—randomized assignment is a fair solution.[23] This can be accepted when information is very poor, or allocative processes are skewed against those in need. In some development applications we may know very little *ex ante* about how best to assign participation to maximize impact. But when alternative allocations are feasible (and if randomization is possible, then that condition is evidently met) and one does have information about who is likely to benefit, then surely it is fairer to use that information, and not randomize, at least unconditionally.

Conditional randomization can sometimes help relieve ethical concerns. The idea here is that one first selects eligible types of participants based on prior knowledge about likely gains, and only then randomly assigns the intervention, given that not all can be covered. For example, if one is evaluating a training program or a program that requires skills for maximum impact one would reasonably assume (backed up by some evidence) that prior education and/or experience will enhance impact and design the evaluation accordingly. This has ethical advantages over simple randomization when there are priors about likely impacts.

But there is a catch. The set of things observable to the evaluator is typically only a subset of what is observable on the ground (such information asymmetry is, after all, the reason for randomizing in the first place). At local level, there will typically be more information—revealing that the program is being assigned to some who do not need it and withheld from some who do. The RCT may be ethically unacceptable at (say) the village level. But then whose information should decide the matter? It may be seen as quite lame for the evaluator to plead, "I did not know" when others do in fact know very well who is in need and who is not.

It is sometimes argued that *encouragement designs* avoid ethical concerns.[24] The idea here is that nobody is prevented accessing the primary service of interest (such as schooling) but the experiment instead randomizes access to some form of incentive or information. This may help relieve ethical concerns for some observers, but it clearly does not remove them—it merely displaces them from the primary service of interest to a secondary space. Ethical validity still looms as a concern when any "encouragement" is being deliberately withheld from some people who would benefit and given to some who would not.

While ethical validity is a legitimate concern in its own right, it also holds implications for other aspects of evaluation validity. It is known that the fact that an RCT invariably uses a different assignment mechanism to the scaled-up program can generate a bias in the inferences for scaling up drawn from the RCT, given heterogeneity in impact. Here we have another concern: heterogeneity in the ethical acceptability of RCTs. That will vary from one setting to another. One can get away with an RCT more easily with NGOs than governments, and with small interventions, preferably in out-of-the-way places. (By contrast, imagine a government trying to justify why some of its underserved rural citizens were randomly chosen to not get new roads or grid connections on the grounds that this will allow it to figure out the benefits to those

---

[23] See, for example, Goldberg (2014).

[24] Again, see Goldberg (2014) for example.

that do get them.) As already noted, an exclusive reliance on randomization for identifying impacts will create a bias in our knowledge in favor of the settings and types of interventions for which randomization is feasible; we will know nothing about a wide range of development interventions for which randomization is not an option. Given that evaluations are supposed to fill our knowledge gaps, this must be a concern even for those who think that consequences trump concerns about processes.

There may well be design changes to many evaluations that could assure their ethical validity, such as judged by review boards. One might randomly withhold the option of treatment for some period of time, after which it would become available, but this would need to be known by all in advance, and one might reasonably argue that some form of compensation would be justified by the delay. Adaptive randomizations are getting serious attention in biomedical research; for example, one might adapt the assignment to treatment of new arrivals along the way, in the light of evidence collected on covariates of impact.[25]

A final observation: There can also be ethically troubling internal inconsistencies between the behavioral assumptions that policymakers adopt in how they rationalize an intervention and how that intervention is being evaluated. In assessing the poverty impacts of social programs, a widespread practice is to use consumption expenditure or income as the measure of household economic welfare (with normalizations for prices and household demographics). Yet the programs being assessed sometimes assume that people themselves do not care solely about their consumption or income. Box 6.7 provides an example. Thus, there can be an inconsistency between the rationale for the policy and how it is evaluated (whether experimental or not). Furthermore, removing this inconsistency may well alter the evaluation results.

Box 6.7 An Example of Inconsistent Judgments about Welfare

Workfare programs impose work requirements on welfare recipients. The work is not typically enjoyable and may well be unpleasant. Indeed, the fact that the work involved is unpleasant is one reason why workfare programs have long been used to fight poverty, in both rich and poor countries. The policymaker (implicitly or explicitly) agrees that the work is unpleasant and would almost certainly not consider doing it. As Hirway and Terhal (1994, 21) put it, "as the labour involved in these works is not attractive, to say the least, for those who can avoid participation, there is a kind of built-in check on entitlement to relief."

Yet the evaluation methods found in practice attach no welfare penalty to doing this work. Two people with the same real income are deemed to be equally poor even if one of them derives all that consumption from hard grinding toil while the other enjoys leisure time or some relatively pleasant form of work.

continued

---

[25] The US Food and Drug Administration (2010) has issued guidelines for adaptive evaluations.

Box 6.7 **(Continued)**

This is a troubling inconsistency between the outcome measure used for evaluation and the policymaker's rationale for the intervention. How can the policymaker justify ignoring the fact that the work is unpleasant when assessing the welfare gains from the program?

This is clearly troubling within a welfarist approach which says "welfare" should only be assessed by whatever people maximize (Chapter 3), even ignoring the identification problems involved in inferring utility from observed behavior (box 3.2). Most evaluations in practice are essentially non-welfarist. But that does not justify a situation in which the policymaker's rationale for the intervention is inconsistent with how it is being evaluated. If we judge that people are worse off doing this work, such that only the poor will participate, then surely we cannot ignore the welfare loss from this work in assessing the program?

Further reading: Alik Lagrange and Ravallion (2015) provide an example of this inconsistency in evaluations of a large antipoverty program in India. They show how the inconsistency can be eliminated, and that doing so implies that the program is more effective in reaching poor people than is thought, but also does less to reduce their poverty than is thought.

This completes our review of measures and methods. Of course, there is much more one could say about the details, but this has at least given a broad sketch. Using the tools of Part Two, the rest of this book is devoted to describing the dimensions of poverty and inequality in the world and to understanding why we see more progress against poverty in some countries than in others, and the related policy debates. While our knowledge remains imperfect, the discussion in Part Three will try to distill some lessons about interventions against poverty from the literature.

PART THREE

POVERTY AND POLICY

To recap the story so far: Part One focused on the history of thought on poverty and how we came to think that fighting poverty is a legitimate goal for public action. Part Two discussed the measurement of welfare and poverty and the methods available to assess the welfare and poverty impacts of policies. Building on these foundations, this third part turns to the many policy debates about how best to fight poverty and reduce inequality.

Chapter 7 gives an overview of poverty and inequality in the world. This chapter uses many of the ideas from Part Two, along with a great many empirical studies using data from across the globe, to measure and describe poverty in the world today. This provides an empirical foundation for the rest of Part Three.

Chapter 8 reviews the debates on growth, poverty, and inequality. The discussion draws on both economic theory and extensive empirical evidence from both multi-country comparative studies and more in-depth case country studies.

Chapter 9 reviews past and ongoing debates on the main categories of economy-wide and sectoral policies, including the priority given to urban versus rural development, mass schooling, labor, industry and trade policies, information campaigns, and development aid.

Chapter 10 turns to both the economic arguments for targeted policies and the evidence on how successful they have been (to the extent that we can tell from the research so far). The discussion covers the main forms of targeted transfers (in cash or kind) as well as other forms of targeted antipoverty policies.

7

Dimensions of Poverty and Inequality

We can now apply the concepts and analytic tools described in Part Two to provide an overview of what we know about poverty and inequality in the world. The discussion is non-technical but it will still take note of methodological issues that have bearing on the results. The chapter begins with inequality in the world. The chapter then turns to poverty. The latter half of the chapter turns to the non-income dimensions of welfare.

One overall caveat should be noted. The description here will be highly aggregated, mostly taking the country as the unit of observation. That level of aggregation is appropriate for this volume. However, many of the costs of poverty and inequality are quite localized at sub-national level. And the local picture can differ substantially from that at the country level.[1]

7.1 Global Inequality

Large Income Disparities in the World

Figure 7.1 gives mean household income per capita for the world in 2008 by ventile (each ventile has 5% of the world's population of 6.7 billion in 2008). Each bar is mean income for that ventile ranked by income per person. The mean income of the poorest 25% is almost exactly $1.00 per day, while that of the top 5% is $94. Of course, there are disparities within each ventile. For example, the mean for the top 1% is $176 per day—176 times greater than the mean for the poorest 25%. Imagine an extra bar on the right in figure 7.1, twice the height of the bar for the richest 5%. While the data are not as good, it is very likely that the disparities are even greater for wealth. Such disparities suggest that there is a *potential* for supporting public goods, including redistribution as a means of fighting poverty, by taxing the rich, or charitable giving by the rich.[2]

Looking back over two hundred years, figure 7.2 gives the estimates of the Mean Log Deviation (MLD) across all people of the world over 1820–1992 from Bourguignon and Morrisson (2002); recall that this was also used in figure 1.1. The figure gives the

---

[1] For example, Washington, DC (where the author lives) has a Gini index of income inequality of about 0.60; this is well above the national index for the United States of 0.45, and it is higher than that for almost all countries in the world.

[2] Singer (2010) argues for greater charitable giving as a means of fighting global poverty.

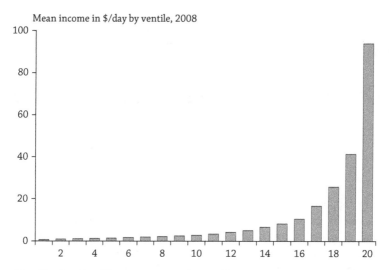

Figure 7.1 The Parade of Incomes across the World. *Note:* Currency conversions use Purchasing Power Parity exchange rates. *Source:* Author's calculations from data in Lakner and Milanovic (2013).

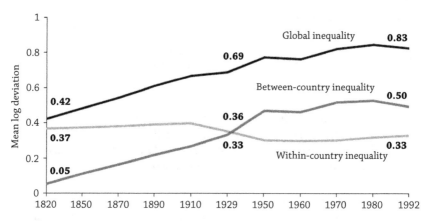

Figure 7.2 Bourguignon-Morrisson Series for Global Inequality. *Source:* Bourguignon and Morrisson (2002).

"between" and "within-country" components.[3] The fall in the incidence of extreme poverty evident in figure 1.1 came with an increase in global inequality. However, this was due to rising inequality *between* countries. There is a sign that the rise in inequality both globally and between (but not within) countries was attenuated from around 1980.

The concept of "global inequality" in figure 7.2 can be thought of as pooling all persons in the world and calculating the inequality among them, ignoring all country

---

[3] Recall from box 5.4 that the MLD is exactly additively decomposable, unlike the Gini index.

borders. This is one of three concepts of inequality found in the literature and popular discussions.[4] The other two concepts can be termed "inter-country inequality" and "international inequality." The former concept treats each country equally, no matter what its size. This is the concept of inequality that is found in most discussions of economic convergence in the world (i.e., whether poorer countries are growing faster than richer countries). (We return to this idea in chapter 8.) By contrast, international inequality weights countries by their populations, corresponding to the "between-country" component of the global MLD in figure 7.2. It is important to be clear which of these concepts one is using since the distinction matters to the answer one gives to the question as to whether "inequality" is rising or not in the world as a whole over the second half of the twentieth century. International inequality has been showing a falling overall trend while inter-country inequality has tended to rise.[5]

In measuring global inequality it also matters whether one allows for the fact that prices for those goods that are not internationally traded tend to be lower in poorer countries where wage rates are lower. PPP exchange rates allow for this tendency. Box 7.1 goes into more detail on PPPs. Using PPP rates the global Gini index is around 0.65 while it rises to 0.80 using official exchange rates.[6]

Box 7.1 Purchasing Power Parity Exchange Rates

PPP rates are based on surveys of the prices actually paid for a great many goods and services in each country. PPP rates are calculated from the price surveys done by the International Comparison Program (ICP). The 2005 ICP collected primary data on the prices for 600–1,000 (depending on the region) goods and services grouped under 155 "basic headings" deemed to be comparable across 146 countries. The prices were obtained from a large sample of outlets in each country. The price surveys were done by the government statistics offices in each country, under the supervision of regional authorities. At the time of writing the latest ICP survey round was for 2011.

While there have been improvements over the various ICP rounds, the PPPs still have some limitations that users should be aware of. The ICP price surveys for some counties were largely confined to urban areas. Based on ICP sampling information, Chen and Ravallion (2010a) treat the 2005 consumption PPPs as urban PPPs for a number of countries, using the urban–rural poverty lines at country level for these countries to correct the PPP. (Section 7.2 returns to urban and rural poverty comparisons for China and elsewhere.)

continued

---

[4] The distinction between these three concepts is due to Milanovic (2005b).

[5] See Milanovic (2005b). Note, however, that China has a large weight in the results for international inequality; if one repeats the calculations dropping China, then there is little or overall trend in international inequality over the period 1950–2000 as a whole, and an increase emerges in the last twenty years of that period (Milanovic 2005b).

[6] See Milanovic (2005b). These are his estimates for 2002.

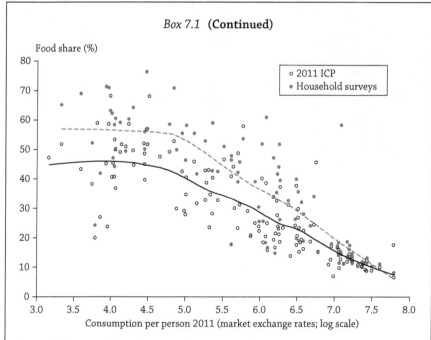

Figure B7.1.1 Food Engel Curves from National Accounts versus Surveys.
Source: Ravallion and Chen (2015).

A further concern is that the weights attached to different commodities in the PPP rate may not be appropriate for measuring poverty. The ICP tends to use lower food shares than implied by household surveys in poor countries. Figure B7.1.1 compares the Engel curves from household surveys with the food shares in the household consumption PPPs from the latest ICP round, for 2011. There is a large difference, around 11% points for the poorest quarter of countries. Given that there were large upward shifts in the relative prices of food over the period 2008–10, especially in poor countries, PPP comparisons between 2011 and 2005 understate the increase in consumer prices facing poor people.

Users should also be aware of the methodological differences between rounds of the ICP. For example, the fact that the 2005 ICP used much more detailed quality standards for recording prices in the surveys makes its comparability with the prior rounds (1993 and 1996) questionable. Thus, the most common practice in past research on economic growth, global inequality, and poverty is to do the PPP conversion at one date (the base date of the ICP) and then use national deflators (such as the Consumer Price Index or the implicit GDP deflator) for inter-temporal comparisons within countries.

Changes in the data and methods used by new ICP rounds have at times implied some puzzling changes for specific countries. New and (hopefully) better data often bring surprises. However, in the case of the ICP, researchers have been handicapped in understanding the changes because the primary survey data on prices have not been publically available (though we would normally hope that prices are public knowledge in all market economies). Public access to these data is needed to better understand revisions to PPPs, and to construct PPPs more appropriate to poverty measurement.

Further reading: World Bank (2008a, b) describes the methods and results of the 2005 ICP. For broader commentaries on the various methodological issues, see Deaton and Heston (2010) and Ravallion (2010a). On some of the puzzles in the 2011 ICP, see Ravallion (2014g).

Inequality in the Developing World

Most rich countries have experienced an overall rise in inequality since the 1970s.[7] The increase dates from the 1980s for some countries (the United States, United Kingdom, and the Netherlands) and the 1990s for others (Canada, the Nordic countries, and Germany). Italy has seen little overall increase over this period. France, which has seen falling inequality since 1970, is an exception, though there has been little change (in either direction) since 2000.[8]

Has the developing world also experienced rising inequality? Figure 7.3 plots total MLD for the developing world as a whole and the between-country component. These calculations have been made across essentially the same set of developing countries

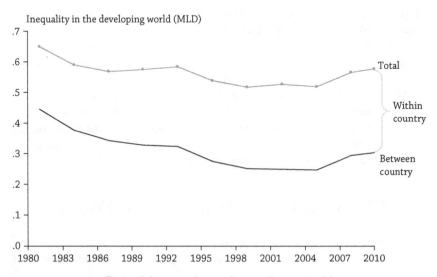

Figure 7.3 Inequality in the Developing World.

[7] Morelli et al. (2014) provide estimates of the Gini index for ten such countries.
[8] See Morelli et al. (2014).

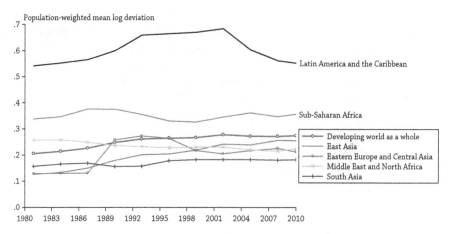

Figure 7.4 Evolution of Average Inequality within Countries.

used above for measuring poverty and (when relevant) using the same methods as for
the poverty measures described above.

We see that there has been a trend decrease in total inequality in the developing
world, though with ups and downs, and an increase over 2005–10. However, that pattern has largely been due to inequality *between* countries. Over the period as a whole,
we see that the between-country component has fallen while the within-country component has risen. The latter accounted for less than one-third of inequality in the
developing world as a whole in 1981, but almost half in 2008. However, this pattern has reversed since 2002, with inequality rising between countries but falling on
average within.

Figure 7.4 plots the within-country component by region. Latin America and the
Caribbean (LAC) have persistently had the highest average inequality,[9] though falling
noticeably since around 2000. Over 90% of LAC's inequality is within countries. SSA is
the region with the second highest average inequality, but with no clear trend. South
Asia has generally been a region of low inequality, though rising since the early 1990s.
East Asia started out as the region with the lowest inequality within countries, but
has seen a steady rise in inequality (side by side with a trend reduction in inequality
between countries). EECA saw a sharp rise in average inequality in the 1990s (coming
with the transition to a market economy) but has seen generally falling inequality since
then. MENA has seen steadily falling average inequality.

7.2   Poverty Measures for the Developing World

In discussing poverty in the developing world, much attention is given to the headcount index for the World Bank's "$1 a day" poverty line, the latest update of which

---

[9] While we have preferred to use consumption-based distributions, incomes are more commonly
used in Latin America. Incomes tend to show higher inequality than consumption for the same economy. This accounts for some, but almost certainly not all, of the gap between LAC's measures and
other regions.

(at the time of writing) is $1.25 a day at 2005 PPP; box 7.2 explains this line further. While this is important information, we also need to look both below and above this line, as chapter 5 emphasized.

Box 7.2 Why $1.25 a Day?

No single poverty line should ever be taken too seriously, and one should always check the poverty measures for multiple lines, above and below (recalling chapter 5). However, as we have seen in the history of thinking on poverty (Part One), the bulk of public attention has focused on one line. We can think of this as the "benchmark" line. (Given the media attention, "headline" might be a better word.)

Since its inception, the "$1 a day" line has been anchored to the national lines found in the poorest countries on the grounds that anything lower would be too frugal to be taken seriously. And there was a pedagogic value in that most people in the world know how little someone can buy with $1. Numerically, this line has also identified roughly the poorest billion people in the world. Of course, it is a deliberately frugal line. Some say it is too frugal. That is why we need multiple lines.

The original "$1 a day" line was based on a sample of national lines for twenty-two countries (Ravallion et al. 1991). Ravallion, Chen, and Sangraula (RCS) (2009) compiled a more up-to-date and much larger set of national lines for developing countries from the World Bank's country-specific *Poverty Assessments* and the *Poverty Reduction Strategy Papers* done by the governments of the countries concerned. (These data were used in box 2.5, supplemented with lines for rich countries.) While the original set of national lines was drawn from sources for the 1980s, the RCS lines are all post-1990. RCS converted the national lines to a common currency using the consumption PPPs from the 2005 ICP (World Bank 2008a, b). The same PPPs were then used to convert the international line back to local currencies at the survey dates.

RCS considered various ways of calculating the average line for the poorest countries, including (1) the "eyeballing method," whereby the line was a simple average of the national lines for the poorest fifteen to twenty countries; (2) an "intercept method," whereby the line was the predicted value of the national line in the poorest country in the sample; and (3) and econometric method in which a piecewise linear regression function was estimated with a parametric "switch point" after which the regression function takes on a positive slope. All three methods pointed to $1.25 a day for 2005. Each country-level observation of a national poverty line in poor countries was treated equally, which is consistent with the aim of identifying a typical national line for such countries.

Adjusting this line consistently with the new PPPs for 2011, the equivalent line in PPP dollars for India (say) is about $2.00 a day in 2011 prices. (This is calculated by converting the $1.25 a day line for 2005 to Indian rupees and then

continued

Box 7.2 **(Continued)**

converting to 2011 local prices using the CPI for India, and finally converting back to 2011 dollars using the 2011 PPP.) This line gives a poverty measure for India very close to the measure using $1.25 a day at 2005 PPP. Notice that it is not correct to simply update the $1.25 line for 2005 for inflation in the United States. This will understate the poverty line in terms of purchasing power in most developing countries given that they have had higher rates of inflation than the United States.

Naturally, middle-income developing countries tend to have higher lines than low-income countries. Region-specific versions of the $1.25 day line have also been proposed; for example, for Asia the Asian Development Bank (ADB 2014) used $1.51 a day—which is calculated essentially the same way as the $1.25 line but only for Asian countries. The average line for all developing countries in the RCS data set is $2.50 a day. Chen and Ravallion (2010a) give estimates of global poverty incidence for multiple lines from $1.00 a day to the US line of about $13 a day in 05.

As this book went to press, the World Bank updated the $1.25 a day line to 2011 prices. On adjusting only for inflation in the same low-income countries used to set the $1.25 line, the Bank's new line in 2011 prices is $1.90 a day.

Further reading: See Ravallion et al. (2009) on the $1.25 a day line. For a critique of the "$1 a day" poverty measures, see Reddy and Pogge (2010) and the reply by Ravallion (2010d).

Data and Measurement

The $1.25 a day international line is a frugal line indeed, being set at the average line found among the twenty or so poorest countries (box 7.2). Virtually all those living in poverty judged by this line are found in the developing world. Naturally, richer countries have higher lines. We saw this in box 2.5. The average line found in the developing world is $2 a day at 2005 PPP. The highest poverty line is for Luxembourg, at $43 a day, over thirty times the $1.25 a day line. Granted this is an extreme value. But even the US poverty line is over ten times the $1.25 a day line.

After converting the international poverty line of $1.25 at PPP to local currency in 2005 prices, the lines are then converted to the prices prevailing at each survey date for each of the surveys employed, using the best available country-specific Consumer Price Index (CPI). The weights in this index may or may not accord well with budget shares at the poverty line. In periods of relative price shifts, this will bias comparisons of the incidence of poverty over time, depending on the extent of the substitution possibilities for people at the poverty line. Given the steep rise in food prices around 2008, extra effort was made to assure that the price indices adequately reflected those increases at country level.

The roughly 900 surveys used (spanning 125 countries) were mostly done by governmental statistics offices as part of their routine operations. Following past practice, poverty is assessed using household per capita expenditure on consumption or household income per capita as measured from the national sample surveys. When there is a choice, consumption is used in preference to income, on the grounds that consumption is likely to be the better measure of current welfare on both theoretical and practical grounds (chapter 3).

Taking the most recent survey for each country, 2.1 million households were interviewed in the surveys used for 2008. In the aggregate, 90% of the population of the developing world is represented by surveys within two years of 2008.[10] However, survey coverage varies by region and over time. The coverage rate in 2008 varies from 47% of the population of the Middle East and North Africa (MENA) to 98% of the population of South Asia. Naturally, the further back one goes, the fewer the number of surveys—reflecting the expansion in household survey data collection for developing countries since the 1980s. And coverage deteriorates in the last year or two of the series, given the lags in survey processing.[11]

The measures of consumption (or income, when consumption is unavailable) in the primary survey data set are reasonably comprehensive, including both cash spending and imputed values for consumption from own production. But even the best consumption data need not adequately reflect certain "non-market" dimensions of welfare, such as access to certain public services, or intra-household inequalities. For these reasons, standard poverty measures need to be supplemented by other data, such as on infant and child mortality, to obtain a more complete picture of living standards. (This is taken up again later in this chapter.)

Absolute Poverty Measures

Putting all these elements together, figure 7.5 shows how the headcount index has varied over 1981–2010. Results are given for both $1.25 a day and $2.00 a day; as noted above, the former line is representative of the national lines found in the poorest twenty or so countries while the $2 line is the overall mean line across developing countries.[12]

Over this period of thirty years, we see that the percentage of the population of the developing world living below $1.25 per day was more than halved, falling from 53%

[10] Some countries have graduated from the set of developing countries; the same definition is used over time to avoid bias. The definition used here is anchored to 2005.

[11] Chen and Ravallion (2013) provide more detail on the points made in the paragraph.

[12] Recall that these are in 2005 PPP. As noted in box 7.2, using the newly released 2011 PPPs and the same set of low-income countries used to set the $1.25 line, the corresponding line is about $1.90. At the time of writing, the World Bank has not yet released its revised global poverty estimates using the 2011 PPPs. My own calculations suggest that the aggregate poverty counts, global trends over time, and broad regional patterns are affected little by changing from $1.25 a day in 2005 prices to $1.90 a day at 2011 PPP. While the new PPPs imply a number of changes in the poverty measures for specific countries, the main results reported here appear likely to be reasonably robust.

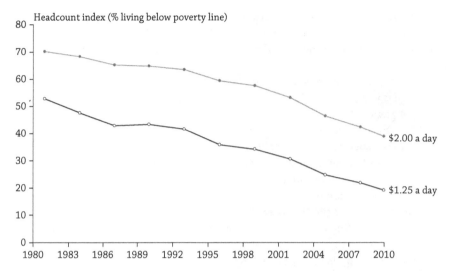

Figure 7.5 Headcount Indices for the Developing World. *Note:* Poverty lines in 2005 PPP. *Source:* PovcalNet (http://iresearch.worldbank.org/PovcalNet/index.htm?1).

to 19%. The trend rate of decline in the $1.25 poverty rate is 1% point per year.[13] The number of poor fell from 1.96 billion to 1.1 billion. The first Millennium Development Goal (MDG) of halving the 1990 "$1 a day" poverty rate by 2015 was achieved five years ahead of time.

China's success against absolute poverty has clearly played a major role in this over-all progress. Excluding China, the $1.25 a day poverty rate falls from 41% to 22% over 1981–2010, with a rate of decline that is half the trend including China.[14] Strikingly, the number of people outside China living below $1.25 a day is no lower in 2008 than in 1981. However, the count of the $1.25 a day poor *outside* China rose then fell, with a marked decline since 1999, from 1.3 to 1.0 billion in 2010.

There has been only slightly less progress in absolute terms for the $2 per day line than for the $1.25 line (though less in proportionate terms). The poverty rate by this higher standard has fallen from 70% in 1981 to 39% in 2010. The trend is also about 1% per year; excluding China, the trend is only 0.4% per year.[15] Clearly, in proportion-ate terms, the rate of progress has been lower for the higher poverty line. Over the period as a whole, the number of people living under $2 per day fell from 2.6 billion to 2.3 billion in 2010.

The number of people living *between* $1.25 and $2 a day has doubled over 1981–2010, from about 600 million to 1.2 billion. Most of drop in the number of people who are poor by the $1.25 per day standard represents people who are still poor by the

[13] Regressing the poverty rate on time the estimated trend is –1.1% per year with a standard error of 0.05%, with $R^2 = 0.98$.

[14] The regression estimate of the trend falls to –0.53% per year (standard error of 0.05%; $R^2 = 0.94$).

[15] The regression coefficient on time is –0.97 (standard error = 0.09); excluding China, the regres-sion coefficient is –0.44 (standard error = 0.07%).

standards of middle-income developing countries, and certainly by the standards of what poverty means in rich countries. This marked "bunching up" of people just above the $1.25 line suggests that the poverty rate according to that line could rise sharply with aggregate economic contraction. The discussion will return to this point.

As one would expect, there is much less progress at very high poverty lines. For example, over 90% of the population of the developing world lives below the US poverty line (about $13 per person per day in 2005 prices). The proportion of the developing world's population living in poverty by US standards has fallen from 97% in 1990 to 93% in 2010.[16]

Figure 7.6 gives graphs for the poverty gap indices discussed in chapter 5; we focus here on the *PG* index, but the figure also gives *SPG*. The *PG* index for $1.25 per day fell from 21.3% to 6.2% over the period 1981–2010. (For $2 a day, *PG* fell from 36.7% to 15.6%.) The aggregate poverty gap for 2010 is $166 billion per year for $1.25 a day, rising to $669 billion for $2 per day.

While the precise counts are naturally sensitive to the choice of the poverty line, a decline in the incidence of absolute poverty since 1980 is indicated over a wide range of lines and measures. This can be seen from figure 7.7, which plots the cumulative distribution function (CDF). (Recall the dominance results summarized in chapter 5.) The figure gives the poverty rate up to a poverty line of $13 per person per day, which is the official line for the United States in 2005 (for a family of four). To avoid cluttering figure 7.7 gives four CDFs at nine-year intervals.

The claim that poverty fell between either 1981, 1990 or 1999 and 2008 is robust; this also holds for a broad class of additive poverty measures including all those that penalize inequality among the poor (chapter 5). However, the claim that poverty fell over time from 1981 to 1990 to 1999 is not robust for poverty lines above $5 a day.

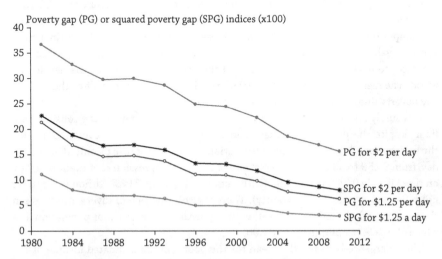

Figure 7.6 Poverty Gap Indices for the Developing World. *Note:* Poverty lines in 2005 PPP. *Source:* PovcalNet (http://iresearch.worldbank.org/PovcalNet/index.htm?1).

[16] Using *PovcalNet*.

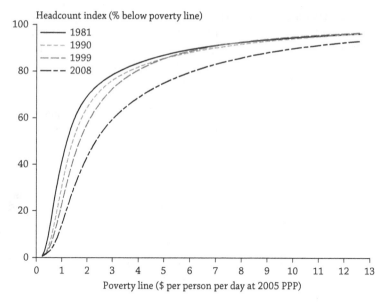

Figure 7.7 Cumulative Distribution Functions up to US Poverty Line. *Source:* Chen and Ravallion (2013).

Estimates of the Consumption Floor

Recall from chapter 5 that we need to take account for measurement error and transient effects in estimating the consumption floor. Employing the method outlined in chapter 5 (box 5.10) let us assume that there is no chance of being the poorest person if one's consumption (or income when consumption is not available) is above $1.25 a day and that the probability of being the poorest person declines linearly with observed consumption up to that point. Then we can use the result in box 5.10 to estimate the expected value of the consumption floor. Figure 7.8 gives the estimates, as well as the mean consumptions of both the poor and the overall population of the developing world. The mean level of the floor is $0.67 per day—slightly over half of the $1.25 a day poverty line. It has proved to be very stable over time.

It is surely striking how little progress has been made in raising the consumption floor despite the progress that has been made against absolute poverty. Over this thirty-year period, the estimated consumption of the poorest rose by only 10 cents per day, from $0.59 to $0.68. The growth rate of the floor (regression coefficient of its log on time) is only 0.34% per annum (with a standard error of 0.08%, although this does not reflect all sources of uncertainty). There is also some sign of divergence between the poor as a whole and the poorest, with a growth rate for the poor population as a whole of 0.46% per annum (s.e. = 0.06).[17]

The divergence between the mean for the poor and the estimated income of the poorest is minor compared to the expanding gap between both and the overall mean of household consumption per person (figure 7.8), which grew at an annual (per capita)

---

[17] And the divergence is statistically significant; t – test = 4.39; prob. = 0.14%.

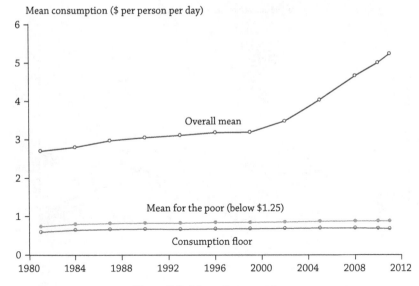

Figure 7.8 Mean Consumptions.

rate of 2.1% over this period (s.e. = 0.24%) and the rate of growth roughly doubled from the turn of the century.

Recall that the consumption floor is not defined here as the biological minimum for survival, but rather the lower bound to the actual distribution of permanent consumptions. These results suggest that, so far, the developing world has not had much success in raising the consumption floor above the biological floor. The estimated mean floor of $0.67 is remarkably close to Lindgren's (2015) (independent) estimate of the "physical minimum line," which aims to measure the cost in international dollars of a "barebones basket" of food items that assure at least 2100 calories per person per day. The estimates in Figure 7.8 can thus be interpreted as telling us that the consumption floor has only risen slightly above the biological floor.

Poorest Left Behind?

In principle one could imagine that progress against overall poverty could be attained in large part by lifting people near the poverty line out of poverty, with little gain to the ultra-poor. One often hears claims to that effect. Indeed, as noted in chapter 2, there is a popular view that the world's poorest are being "left behind."

To be concrete, let us define *ultra-poverty* as those living within $0.20 a day of the consumption floor. Figure 7.9 gives the percentage and headcount of the number of ultra-poor by this definition.[18] We see that there was substantial progress in reducing the proportion of the population living in ultra-poverty by this definition. Indeed,

---

[18] Ravallion (2014f) gives estimates for a range of possible definitions of "ultra-poverty" and all are consistent with the picture here.

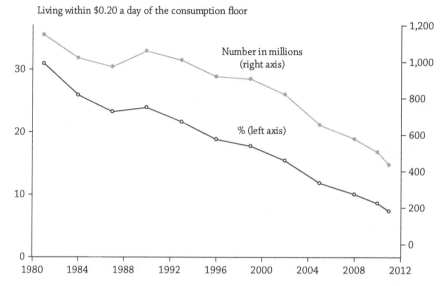

Figure 7.9 Numbers and Percentage of the Population of the Developing World Living near the Consumption Floor. *Source:* Ravallion (2014f).

progress in lifting people out of ultra-poverty comes with roughly equal progress in reducing the number of people living under $1.25 a day.

In principle, the progress against ultra-poverty could have simply swelled the ranks of the "poor but not ultra-poor." Clearly the data are more suggestive that it is the poor but not ultra-poor who are the ones who have been left behind—the bulk of the reduction in overall poverty rates (for $1.25 a day or $2.00) has been for the ultra-poor.

So the data are not consistent with the idea that the ultra-poor are left behind. One is more tempted to dub figure 7.9 a "breakthrough from the bottom."[19] However, one must also keep figure 7.8 in mind. The consumption floor has risen very little over this thirty-year period, and in that sense it is meaningful to say that "the poorest of the world are being left behind" (recalling the quote from Ban Ki-moon in chapter 2). Thankfully there are far fewer people living near the consumption floor today than thirty years ago, but it remains that over 400 million people live within a small margin of that floor and must be considered highly vulnerable to downside risk.

Differing Fortunes across Regions

Not all regions of the developing world have shared equally in the progress that has been made against poverty. Indeed, there has been a marked re-ranking. Figure 7.10 plots the $1.25 a day poverty rate for the three regions that account for the bulk of the poor, East Asia, South Asia, and sub-Saharan Africa (SSA). (These three account for

---

[19] This is the phrase used by Radelet (2015) in describing the progress that has been made against absolute poverty.

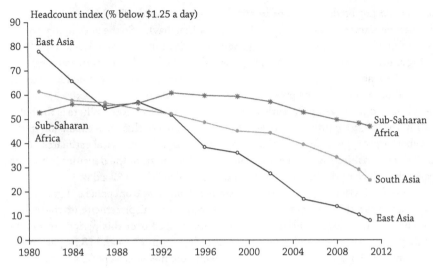

Figure 7.10 Differing Fortunes for Poor People in Three Regions. *Source:* PovcalNet.

96% of those living below $1.25 a day in 2008.) We see a marked reversal of fortunes. Looking back to 1981, East Asia had the highest incidence of poverty, with 77% living below $1.25 per day. South Asia had the next highest poverty rate and SSA had the lowest of the three regions. By the early 1990s, SSA had swapped places with East Asia, and by 2008 East Asia's poverty rate had fallen to 14%, while SSA's was 48%. However, there is good news here in that the poverty rate in SSA has been falling since around 2000.

The Developing World's Bulging Middle Class

So far we have focused on the bottom tail—those living below $1.25 or $2 a day.[20] Let us now see what has been happening above these lines. Like "poverty," the term "middle class" is defined differently in different countries at different levels of economic development. Recall the discussion in chapter 5 of the various ways of defining and measuring the size of the "middle class." Some observers have applied a rich-world concept of what it means to be middle class to the developing world. If one said that to be "middle class" one had to live above the US poverty line than (as was noted above) that would apply to barely one person in twenty in the developing world, and that proportion has changed little in the last few decades. Such a definition is of questionable relevance to the developing world.

The developing world's "middle class" is defined here as those who live above the average poverty line of developing countries ($2 a day in 2005) but are still poor by US standards ($13 a day). Within this group, the "upper middle class" are defined as those

[20] This is the definition proposed by Ravallion (2010b); chapter 5 discusses this definition and alternatives in the literature.

who would not be deemed poor in any developing country. The highest line among developing countries appears to be $9 a day (for Uruguay).[21] So the developing world's "upper middle class" are those living above $9 a day but less than $13 a day. Those living above $13 a day can be thought of as the middle class by Western standards.

In 1990, about one person in three in the developing world was middle class by this definition; by 2005 the proportion had risen to one-in-two.[22] An extra 1.2 billion people joined the developing world's middle class over 1990–2005. Where is the bulge within the ($2, $13) interval? To get a finer breakdown of this huge expansion in the number of people who live between $2 and $13 a day, the empirical estimates of the CDF's and densities for are given in figure 7.11. We see from the densities in the top panel that much of the bulge emerged in the few dollars above $2 a day.

While a reduction in poverty is indicated for all lines (bottom panel of figure 7.11), it is clear that this has not been a simple rightward displacement of the densities. Indeed, the mode has remained almost unchanged over this period, at around $1.00 per day. The mean and median have increased, from $3.14 and $3.94 per day for 1990 and 2005, respectively, for the mean, while the medians were $1.47 and $2.13. Instead of a simple rightward displacement, we have seen a marked "bunching up" due to a shift in densities from just below the $2 a day line to just above it, with the bulk of the gain in the interval $2 to $6 a day.

It is clear that only a very small share of the expansion in the developing world's middle class was due to its "upper middle class," defined as those living above the

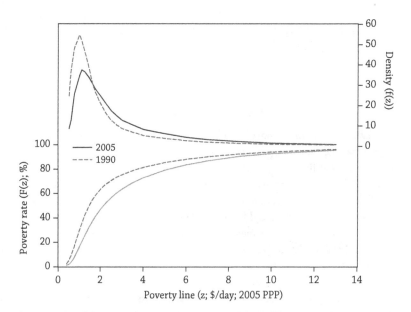

Figure 7.11 Distributions for the Developing World as a Whole in 1990 and 2005.
Source: Ravallion (2010b).

<hr>

[21] See Ravallion et al. (2009).
[22] See Ravallion (2010b).

highest poverty line found among developing countries, but still below the US line. Over 1990–2005, the proportion of the developing world's population living between $9 and $13 per day rose from 3.1% to 4.3%, or from 139 million to 233 million. Of the extra 1.2 billion people who joined the middle class, only 95 million made it to this upper stratum.

Figure 7.12 shows the extent to which the poverty rate has fallen according to different poverty lines up to the US line. It can be seen that the reduction in the poverty rate peaks at about $1.50 a day (almost exactly the 1990 median). The impact on the poverty rate falls below 5% points at poverty lines of about $6 a day or higher. The shift in the density functions reflects in part the overall positive growth in the mean as well as distributional changes.

A natural way of assessing the contribution of distributional changes to the "bulging middle" is to construct a counterfactual for the second date in which the Lorenz curve does not change relative to the base date, but the overall growth rate is the same as that observed in the data. (This follows the decomposition of changes in poverty measures into "growth" and "redistribution" components discussed in box 5.14.) Figure 7.12 also gives the poverty impacts when the distribution moves horizontally according to the proportionate increase in the mean between 1990 and 2005, that is, all 1990 income levels are scaled up by the same growth rate, leaving relative distribution at its 1990 level.

Comparing the two curves in figure 7.12, it is evident that the actual changes in relative distribution had substantial impacts on poverty, as judged by developing country standards. Under the counterfactual, we would have seen lower poverty impacts at low poverty lines and higher impacts at high lines. When assessed relative to this

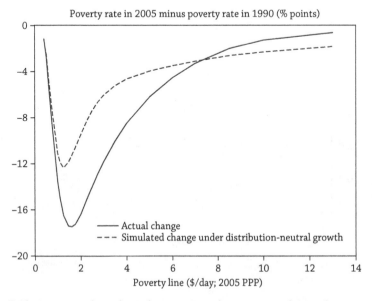

Figure 7.12 Assessing the Bulge Relative to Distribution-Neutral Growth.
Source: Ravallion (2010b).

counterfactual, the bulge now starts below the 2005 median and persists until a turning point at about $8 per day. If we define the bulge as more than a 2 percentage point gap between the actual and counterfactual distributions, then it spans the interval $1.00–$5.00 per day, containing 63% of the developing world's population. (The region $1.25–$5.00 contains 53% of the population.) If instead we define the bulge as more than a 6 percentage point gap, then the region narrows to about $1.50–$3.00 a day (or about 0.6 median to 1.4 median); 30% of the population is in this interval.

Focusing on the $2 a day line, the actual growth process implied a 25.8% (proportionate) reduction in the poverty rate over 1990–2005.[23] The implied growth elasticity of poverty reduction with respect to the survey mean is –1.0. (Recall section 5.6 on this elasticity.) By contrast, the counterfactual growth process yields a 15.0% drop in the $2 a day poverty rate and an elasticity of –0.6. The elasticity varies markedly with the poverty line. Figure 7.13 gives the elasticity of the poverty rate in 2005 with respect to the mean holding relative distribution constant across the full range of poverty lines. The elasticity rises sharply at low lines, from about 1.0 at $2 a day to 3.0 at around $1.00 a day.

Figure 7.13 also gives the elasticities that would have been obtained in 2005 if the growth process over 1990–2005 had been distribution-neutral for the developing world as a whole. The distributional shifts have raised the elasticity across all lines, but only noticeably so over about $2 a day. The overall growth process in the developing world has clearly been more pro-poor than implied by distribution-neutral growth.

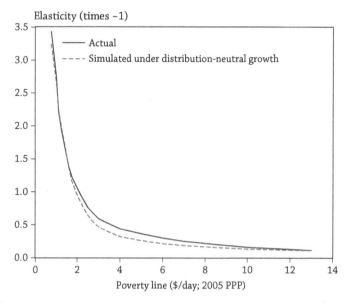

Figure 7.13 Elasticities of the Poverty Rate to Distribution-Neutral Growth.
Source: Author's calculations.

[23] See Ravallion (2010b).

The "bulging middle" can thus be seen as an implication of a pattern of aggregate economic growth in the developing world as a whole that has favored poor people. The high growth rates of China and India have played an important role in producing the middle-income bulge in the developing world as a whole; indeed, China alone accounts for half of the 1.2 billion new entrants to the middle class over 1990–2005.[24] However, while China and India have naturally carried a large weight in the aggregate outcomes, the expansion in the middle class is evident for about 70% of developing countries.

There is a markedly bimodal distribution across countries in the relative size of the middle class; this is evident in the density functions in figure 7.14. Taking a share of 40% as the cutoff point, thirty countries are in the lower mode and sixty-nine are in the upper one for the most recent survey; the corresponding counts for the earliest surveys are forty-two and fifty-seven. Over time, there has been a shift of density toward the upper mode, away from the lower one.

Two distinct types of countries are now found within the developing world, according to whether they have a large middle class or a small one, with sub-Saharan Africa now prominent in the latter group.

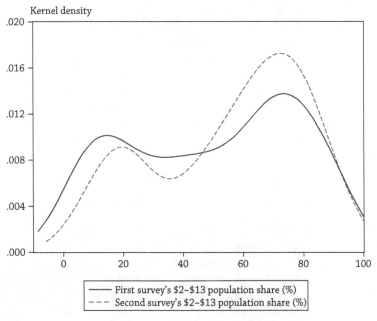

Figure 7.14 Densities of Middle-Class Population Shares. *Note:* Non-parametric density functions fitted using an Epanechnikov kernel. *Source:* Ravallion (2010b). *Source:* Author's calculations.

[24] See Ravallion (2010b).

7.3 Poverty Measures for Urban and Rural Areas

In rich countries there is typically not much difference in the incidence of poverty between urban and rural areas. In the United States, for example, the official poverty rate in 2012 is 18% outside metropolitan areas as compared to 15% within those areas, though rising to 20% in inner-city areas.[25] Using the new partially relative measures (box 4.4), the 2012 poverty rate is lower in rural areas; it is 14% outside metropolitan areas versus 16% within them, and 21% in the inner-city areas.

The urban–rural dimensions of poverty are much more salient in the developing world where the population is becoming more urban over time, reflecting migration, urban sprawl, and the growth of rural villages and towns. Population urbanization figures prominently in the questions asked about poverty by policymakers and the development community at large. How much of poverty is found in rural versus urban areas? How quickly is the problem of poverty shifting to urban areas? Not so long ago, good data for addressing such questions were scarce. That has changed. Even fifteen years ago, we did not have access to anything like the number of reasonably well-designed and executed household surveys from developing countries that we have today—thanks in large part to the efforts of national statistics agencies throughout the world, and the support of the donor community and international development agencies. While many data problems remain, there has been an undeniable advance in our knowledge about poverty in the world.

In the last section we studied poverty measures based on international poverty lines of $1.25 and $2 a day, converted to local currencies using PPP rates. PPP's do not provide a cost-of-living (COL) differential between urban and rural areas and, as was noted in box 7.1, the price surveys are often "urban biased." Box 7.3 discusses an example, for China. To do a breakdown between urban and rural areas, urban and rural PPPs can be calculated based on the national PPP and the differential between the urban and rural poverty lines at country level. The best available data on the COL differences facing poor people is the World Bank's country-specific *Poverty Assessments* (PAs). These are core reports within the Bank's program of analytic work at the country level.[26]

Box 7.3 **Urban Bias in the ICP's PPP for China**

Prior to the release of the 2005 ICP (box 7.1), the global income and poverty calculations for China rested on an estimate of the country's PPP for 1993 that was not based on a 1993 price survey, since China had not participated in the 1993 ICP, but rather was an updated version of an older (1986) PPP for China. China's estimated level of poverty in 2004 was thus rooted in a PPP rate that was almost twenty years old, and even then was not drawn from the ICP.

---

[25] See Short (2013).

[26] Each report describes the extent of poverty and its causes in that country. To give an indication of the scale of a typical PA, the average cost is about $250,000. When one considers that the PAs have now been done for over one hundred countries, one can see that this has been a large investment in knowledge about the world's poor.

In this light, the estimates in World Bank (2008b) of China's PPP rate for 2005, based on the ICP price survey for that year, are undeniably important new data. The results for China's first participation in the ICP attracted considerable attention, as they suggest that China's economy in 2005 was 40% smaller than we thought. For example, one observer at the time claimed that the new PPP for China adds 300 million to the count of that country's poor. Some observers have gone further to claim that the new PPP casts doubt on the extent of China's, and (hence) the world's, progress over time against poverty.

All this begs for a more careful scrutiny of China's 2005 PPP and its implications for the extent of poverty in the country and how much progress it has made against poverty. Chen and Ravallion (2010b) focus solely on the implications of the 2005 consumption PPP released by the World Bank (2008b). Their analysis combines the results of the 2005 ICP with a new compilation of national poverty lines for developing countries and tabulations of the distribution of consumption and income in China provided by the National Bureau of Statistics (NBS), based on their household surveys.

A careful scrutiny of the PPP for China does not suggest that its implications for the extent of poverty in that country (by international standards) are anywhere near as dramatic as some casual observers have suggested. On a priori grounds, it was plain that the 300 million count for the increase in the number of China's poor was a gross exaggeration because it ignored the fact that the 2005 ICP price survey is not representative of the cost of living in rural China, where prices (particularly for the goods such as food for which the poor have a high budget share) are appreciably lower than in urban areas. Instead of an extra 300 million people deemed to be poor by the standards of what "poverty" means in low-income countries, Chen and Ravallion calculate that the figure is closer to 130 million for poverty measured in terms of consumption.

Of course, there can be no denying that this is a large upward adjustment in our assessment of China's poverty. Given that China had never agreed to participate in the International Comparison Program prior to 2005, it is possibly not too surprising that the prior estimates of China's PPP rate from non-ICP sources were so far off the mark. This reaffirms the importance of global participation in the ICP.

However, even if Chen and Ravallion had not done their calculations, it should have been obvious enough that the new PPP rate alone could not entail the sort of downward revision to China's rate of progress against poverty over time that some observers claimed. That is because the real growth rates are unaffected by the change in the PPP, and it is China's high growth rates that have driven poverty reduction. Given that the same growth rate can have different implications for the change in the poverty count depending on the initial level of poverty, one may well find an even greater progress. That is indeed what Chen and Ravallion find when they estimate China's poverty measures over time by the new international poverty line of $1.25 a day at 2005 PPP.

By estimating everything from the primary data, one can assure a relatively high degree of internal consistency (compared to other compilations of distributional data). But, of course, there are comparability problems one cannot resolve. One such concern is that different countries have different definitions of "urban" and "rural." Another concern is that the urban–rural COL differential may vary by income, so the differential provided in PAs for middle-income countries may not be right for the international line. Another data concern is that the non-food component of the poverty line is typically set according to food demand behavior in urban and rural areas separately. Somewhat different methods are found in practice, depending on the data available. And even with exactly the same method, food demand behavior can differ between urban and rural areas in ways that have rather little bearing on comparisons of living standards (as discussed in chapter 3).

There is little that can be done about these data problems. While the precise estimates obtained will (of course) depend on the measurement assumptions, there is no obvious reason to expect a systematic bias one way or the other.

On average, one finds that the urban poverty line is about 30% higher than the rural line. There is also a tendency for poorer countries to have higher ratios of the urban line to the rural line. This is to be expected given that transport infrastructure and internal market integration tend to improve as countries become less poor.

Even allowing for the higher COL facing the poor in urban areas, one finds that the "$1.25 a day" rural poverty rate is higher than the urban rate. In 2008, the rural poverty rate of 31% is more than double the urban rate (table 7.1). About three-quarters of the developing world's poor still live in rural areas.

We also see that poverty is becoming more urban over time. The share of the $1.25 a day poor living in urban areas rose from 18% in 1990 to 25% in 2008 (while the urban share of the population as a whole rose from 37% to 46% over the same period). But even so, it will be many decades before a majority of the poor live in urban areas. While current UN population forecasts imply that 60% of the developing world's population will live in urban areas by 2030, it is expected that this will be true of less than 40% of the poor by 2030.[27]

The poor are urbanizing faster than the population as a whole, reflecting a lower-than-average pace of urban poverty reduction (table 7.1). One's concern about this finding must be relieved by the fact that there has been more rapid progress against rural poverty. Over 1990–2008, the count of $1.25 a day poor in urban areas fell by only 10 million, from 320 to 310 million. However, the number of rural poor fell by over 500 million (from 1,464 million in 1990 to 926 million in 2008).

There are marked regional differences in a number of these respects. Almost half of Latin America's poor live in urban areas, although this is still lower than the urban sector's share of the total population (table 7.1). By contrast, less than 20% of East Asia's poor live in urban areas. There are also exceptions at the regional level to the overall pattern of poverty's urbanization; indeed, there are signs of a ruralization of poverty in Eastern Europe and Central Asia, although the poverty rates for that region are low overall.

---

[27] Based on the results of Ravallion et al. (2007).

Table 7.1 **Poverty Rates for Urban and Rural Areas**

	Urban Share of Population (%)		Urban Share of the Poor (%)		Poverty Rate (% living below $1.25 a day)					
					1990			2008		
	1990	2008	1990	2008	Rural	Urban	Total	Rural	Urban	Total
East Asia and Pacific	29.4	46.3	13.1	16.4	67.5	24.5	54.9	20.1	4.6	12.9
Europe and Central Asia	63.0	63.9	39.5	24.7	2.2	0.9	1.4	1.5	0.3	0.7
Latin America and Caribbean	70.3	78.1	45.6	44.6	21.0	7.4	11.5	13.1	3.0	5.2
Middle East and North Africa	51.7	58.2	17.9	22.0	9.1	1.9	5.4	4.1	0.8	2.2
South Asia	25.0	29.9	20.9	24.8	50.5	40.1	47.9	39.0	30.2	36.3
Sub-Saharan Africa	27.9	35.2	22.6	30.1	55.1	41.5	51.3	48.4	38.3	44.9
Total	36.8	45.5	17.9	25.1	52.5	20.5	40.3	30.8	13.2	21.5

Source: Author's calculations with the assistance of Shaohua Chen and Prem Sangraula.

7.4 Global Measures of Poverty

The last two sections have focused on absolute poverty in the developing world. When we think about the world as a whole, including the rich world, it becomes compelling to switch to relative poverty, as discussed in Part Two.

Dissatisfaction with Standard Poverty Measures

While ideas on many things seem to be converging globally, there is one important topic where two distinct views of the world still coexist, with rather little communication between them. That topic is poverty. The rich world of "high-income countries" has, by and large, maintained a highly relative idea of what poverty means, emphasizing the distribution of relative incomes in the place of residence. The developing world has instead viewed poverty as absolute, meaning that two people with the same command over commodities are treated the same way irrespective of where they live. The following discussion provides a global perspective, incorporating relative poverty.

There are reasons for dissatisfaction with the standard measures of absolute poverty. The idea of what poverty means is changing in the developing world. For example, in 2011 China doubled its national line from 90 cents a day to $1.80 (at 2005 purchasing power parity). Having quadrupled its mean income in thirty years or so, it is hardly surprising that China has revised upward its real poverty line. Other countries—including Colombia, India, Mexico, Peru, and Vietnam—have also done so recently.

At the root of this emerging dissatisfaction in the developing world with standard measures based on low "subsistence" lines is the fact that they do not take account of the concerns people everywhere face about relative deprivation, shame, and social exclusion, as discussed in chapter 3. It has long been recognized that, for such reasons, an absolute line in the welfare space requires a varying relative line in terms of consumption.[28] Absolute measures in the consumption or income space ignore such "social effects" and assume instead that it does not matter where one lives, once one knows a person's own level of consumption. That assumption is difficult to defend. Absolute income lines may not then correspond to a common level of welfare across countries. To the extent that "poverty" means a low level of welfare and welfare depends on relative consumption as well as own consumption, higher monetary poverty lines will be needed in richer countries to reach the same absolute level of welfare.

In characterizing "global poverty," might the world as a whole turn instead to the relative poverty measures popular in Western Europe and at the OECD?[29] Recall that these use strongly relative set at a constant proportion (typically around half) of the current mean or median (chapter 4).[30] Until recently, this approach has attracted very little interest outside Western Europe.[31] However, as discussed in chapter 4, these measures of relative poverty have a feature that leads one to question their relevance to developing countries. In particular, they ignore the fact that the costs of avoiding relative deprivation and social exclusion cannot fall to zero, but must have a positive minimum. The relevance of strongly relative measures for capturing what poverty means in developing countries is questionable.

So it seems that if we are to take a truly global perspective on poverty we need a new way of measuring it. This section applies the idea of a "weakly relative" poverty measure, as explained in chapter 4. This helps shed new light on a number of questions. If we take seriously the idea that people living in rich countries need higher expenditures to maintain a given standard of living, then is it still true that the incidence of poverty is lower in rich countries? How important is relative poverty in today's developing world, and how has this changed? How does this compare to high-income countries (HICs)? And what are the implications for development policy of a higher weight on relative poverty?

A Globally Relevant Measure of Poverty

We can do better in measuring global poverty than either of the methods favored in the "two worlds," while still taking seriously the idea of social effects on welfare. This requires that we modify the usual concept of relative poverty to make it relevant to

---

[28] See, e.g., the discussion in Sen (1983, 1985b).

[29] Examples of relative lines include Atkinson (1998), Eurostat (2005), Nolan (2007), and OECD (2008, ch. 5).

[30] For example, the European Union (Eurostat) poverty lines are set at 60% of the national median equivalized income.

[31] Garroway and de Laiglesia (2012) provide such relative measures for developing countries.

poor countries as well as rich ones, as discussed in chapter 4. Weakly relative measures aim to capture the costs of social inclusion in a consistent way across countries. (Recall box 4.9.) By this approach, a person is counted as poor if she is either absolutely poor or relatively poor, where the latter concept aims to allow for relative deprivation and the costs of social inclusion, in addition to assuring that absolute needs are met.[32] The resulting measures are called "weakly relative"—to distinguish them from past strongly relative measures in which the poverty line is set a constant proportion of the mean. Unlike the strongly relative measures, these new measures fall when all incomes increase by the same proportion; this is an immediate implication of requiring that the cost of social inclusion has a positive lower bound. So the new measures essentially put a higher weight on growth in the mean than did the old relative measures. The new measures also put a higher weight on income inequality, relative to growth in the mean, than an absolute measure.[33]

In operationalizing the idea, I will use an absolute line of $1.25 a day at 2005 prices, while the relative line rises with the country and year-specific survey mean above $1.25 a day, at a gradient of 1:2. The schedule of weakly relative lines is:

$$Z_{it} = \$1.25 + 0.5 \max(M_{it} - \$1.25, \ 0),$$

where M_{it} denotes the survey mean for country i at date t. This schedule of poverty provides an excellent fit with cross-country data on national poverty lines. Indeed, its parameters are very close to those implied by an econometric estimate of the piecewise linear schedule (flat initially then rising linearly above some point, with both that point and the slope treated as parameters to be estimated).[34]

Figure 7.15 gives the average poverty lines over time both globally and for HICs and the developing world separately.[35] For the world as a whole, the average line in 2008 is $5.88 per day, up from $4.45 in 1990. The lines are, of course, markedly higher in HICs, given their higher average consumption levels. At $23 a day, the average line for HICs in 2008 is eight times higher than for developing countries.

The elasticity of the poverty line to the mean for HICs turns out to be very close to unity—the limiting case corresponding to the strongly relative lines. Indeed, the mean (and median) elasticity for HICs is 0.97 (compared to a mean of 0.67 for developing countries). So for the HICs, this is pretty close to the more familiar strongly relative lines, implying that they largely depend on relative distribution.

---

[32] This builds on an approach proposed by Atkinson and Bourguignon (2001), but with the key difference that the Ravallion-Chen measure allows the cost of social inclusion to have a positive lower bound.

[33] To illustrate this last point, suppose that, from the perspective of fighting absolute poverty, the government is indifferent between letting inequality rise by some amount and an increase in the mean in the amount ΔM. Fixing ΔM, we can then ask how much less inequality would be accepted if the government switched to our new poverty measure, letting the poverty line adjust to the new mean. Chen and Ravallion (2013) show that only about one-third of the increase in inequality that was acceptable when using an absolute measure would be tolerated if the country switched to our new measure, all else held constant.

[34] See Chen and Ravallion (2013) for details.

[35] Note also that these average lines are purely for descriptive purposes; they have no analytic role, since poverty lines are calculated at country-year level.

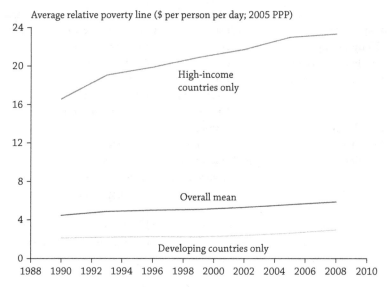

Figure 7.15 Average Relative Poverty Lines. *Source:* Author's calculations from the data compiled by Ravallion (2012b).

These differences matter most to developing countries. The average value of the corresponding strongly relative lines (set at half the mean) for the poorest fifteen countries is $0.64 a day, only half of the $1.25 a day line. The poverty line for the country with the lowest mean would be only $0.38 per day, an almost unimaginably low level of living. Similarly, one study proposed a global relative line set at 50% of the median.[36] This gives lines that are well below the poverty lines typical of even low-income countries, and certainly middle-income countries.[37] While strongly relative lines might make sense in very rich countries, they cannot plausibly capture the social inclusion needs of the world's poorest—or even their basic survival needs.

Interpreting the Global Relative Poverty Measures: Two Bounds

There are two ways to interpret these weakly relative poverty measures. The first interpretation is the simplest: it says that to not be considered "poor" one must be neither absolutely poor (by the international $1.25 a day standard) nor poor by the standards that are typical of the specific country of residence and time. The qualification "typical of the specific country" recognizes that one is using a predicted line, based on a model. Even if one used the actual lines when one had them one would end up using the predicted values almost everywhere.[38]

[36] See Garroway and de Laiglesia (2012).

[37] This is plain from a graph in Garroway and de Laiglesia (2012), although they do not comment on this point.

[38] For example, Chen and Ravallion (2013) estimate poverty measures for each of ten years for 120 countries. They only have national lines at one date for about seventy-five countries. That means that 94% of the data on the "true" date-specific national lines are missing.

By the second interpretation, one is estimating a globally relevant line that is absolute in the space of welfare, but relative in the space of commodities. If we believe that welfare depends on both "own-income" and income to the country and date-specific mean income, then an absolute line in terms of welfare must be a relative line in terms of mean income (chapter 4). Similarly, if we believe that there are costs of social inclusion that vary with the average income of the country and time one lives in, then a truly absolute approach to poverty as low welfare requires relative lines.

However, there is an important caveat to this second interpretation. Welfare *standards* for defining poverty may well differ between rich and poor societies, and evolve over time in growing economies. This can result in higher monetary poverty lines in richer countries even without social effects on individual welfare; rather, it is the reference level of welfare—the underlying level of welfare that is deemed necessary to not be considered "poor"—that rises with mean income. And we cannot distinguish empirically between differences in poverty lines arising from differing social norms from differences due to social effects on welfare.

This clouds the welfare interpretation of all relative poverty lines whether weakly or strongly relative. Social effects on welfare are no doubt at play, but so too are differences in underlying welfare norms. Relative poverty lines make sense if one thinks that the fact that richer countries have higher lines largely reflects social effects on welfare. One would be less inclined to accept relative lines if one thought that the differences stem largely from social norms. While rich countries are free to use higher reference welfare levels for defining poverty that does not mean we should do so in making global poverty comparisons, which should presumably apply a common *welfare* norm on ethical grounds. For this reason, it can be argued that both absolute poverty measures and their weakly relative measures need to be considered, and that they can be interpreted as the lower and upper bounds to an unobserved schedule of poverty lines that accord with a common level of welfare globally.

Truly Global Poverty Measures

We now observe how much poverty there is in the world based on the schedule of weakly relative lines outlined above.

The absolute ($1.25 a day) poverty rate in HICs is assumed to be zero. Calculations from the survey data suggest that this is plausible, although we must acknowledge that there are limitations to how well one can expect to measure such extreme poverty using standard household surveys; for example, it is hard to sample homeless people.

For this purpose, the calculations summarized here use almost 1,000 household surveys for almost 150 countries, 21 of which are HICs.[39] For the latest year, the surveys are representative of about 90% of the population, and that proportion is about the same for the developing world as for HICs. The survey data go back to the late 1970s, but (naturally) coverage is poorer the further back one goes. Here we start the clock in 1990.[40] For developing countries, the database is available at the website PovcalNet. For the HICs, the database is the Luxembourg Income Study (LIS).

---

[39] For further details on the data, see Ravallion and Chen (2013).

[40] A consistent methodology is used, following Chen and Ravallion (2010a, 2013).

All relevant exchange rate conversions are at purchasing power parity (PPP) using the 2005 PPP rates for household consumption from the ICP.[41]

There are differences between the underlying surveys that one cannot correct for. An example is the fact that we are constrained to use income from the surveys for HICs while we use consumption data for about two-thirds of the developing countries (including imputed values for consumption from own-farm product). Household disposable income is used from the LIS data files. This will typically have a higher mean than consumption. However, for relative poverty comparisons, the more important difference is that incomes tend to have higher inequality. There tends to be greater inter-temporal variability in incomes than in consumption, which can be smoothed to some extent. (Progressive income tax systems in HICs will help smooth disposable incomes, but we can still expect them to be more variable over time than consumption.) I expect that this difference will lead one to overstate relative poverty incidence in HICs, when compared to the situation if one had consumption surveys for HICs.

Figure 7.16 shows how the various measures discussed above have been changing, at three yearly intervals from 1990 to 2008; table 7.2 gives the precise numbers and the counts of people living in poverty. The "truly global" poverty rate combines absolute poverty (as judged by poverty lines found in the poorest countries) with social inclusion needs (as judged by poverty lines typical of the country one lives in). And it represents all countries, whether rich or poor.

We see in figure 7.16 that the global poverty rate has been falling steadily from 50% in 1990 to 44% in 2008. But underlying this, we see sharply falling absolute poverty rates for the developing world, and rising (weakly) relative poverty rates in

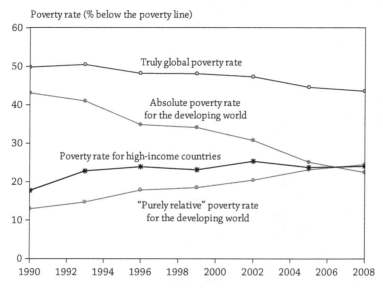

Figure 7.16 Global Poverty Rates and the Differences between Rich and Poor Countries. *Source:* Author's calculations.

[41] See World Bank (2008a, b).

Table 7.2 **Global Poverty Measures, 1990–2008**

	1990	1993	1996	1999	2002	2005	2008
Poverty rate (% of population who are poor either absolutely or relatively)							
Global total	49.8	50.5	48.2	48.1	47.3	44.6	43.6
For those in high-income countries	17.7	22.8	23.9	23.1	25.3	23.7	24.0
For those in the developing world	56.0	55.7	52.7	52.6	51.2	48.2	46.9
Of whom absolutely poor	43.1	41.0	34.8	34.1	30.8	25.1	22.4
Of whom relatively poor only	13.0	14.7	17.9	18.5	20.4	23.1	24.4
Number of poor (millions)							
Global total	2,626.5	2,786.5	2,778.9	2,887.7	2,949.0	2,883.4	2,912.1
For those in high-income countries	143.5	188.9	201.8	199.0	222.4	212.4	219.2
For those in the developing world	2,483.0	2,597.6	2,577.1	2,688.7	2,726.6	2,671.0	2,692.9
Of whom absolutely poor	1,908.6	1,910.3	1,704.0	1,743.4	1,639.3	1,389.6	1,289.0
Of whom relatively poor only	574.4	687.3	873.1	945.3	1,087.3	1,281.4	1,403.9
Poverty gap index (%)							
Global total	17.9	18.0	17.1	17.1	17.1	15.6	15.2
For those in high-income countries	5.8	7.7	8.4	7.7	10.0	8.0	8.3
For those in the developing world	20.3	19.9	18.7	18.8	18.3	16.9	16.3

Source: Authors' calculations.

both worlds, though less steeply for HICs. There are also clear signs of convergence in the overall poverty rates between the two worlds; in 1990, the overall poverty rate (absolute plus relative) was three times higher in the developing world, but this had fallen to double by 2008.

Possibly the most striking finding is that weakly relative poverty is now overwhelmingly a problem of the developing world. Despite the fact that the average line in developing countries is only one-eighth of that for HICs, the proportion of the population who is relatively poor is about the same at 24% in both sets of countries in 2008 (table 7.2). (If we had consumption data for HICs, then we would expect lower poverty measures, so this would strengthen our conclusion that relative poverty is higher in developing countries.)

In terms of the poverty counts, nine out of ten people who are poor by the typical standards of the country they live in but not absolutely poor are now found in developing countries. The developing world contained 92% of the poor, and 86% of the purely relatively poor (its share of the world's total population, given that the purely relative poverty rates are about the same).

The composition of global poverty counts has changed markedly since 1990. Figure 7.17 gives the pie charts for 1990 and 2008. The developing world's share of relative poverty has been rising fairly steadily. In 1990, 1.9 billion people comprised the absolutely poor (living below $1.25 a day) in the developing world, while 0.6 billion were the developing world's relatively poor; the remainder comprised about 140 million relatively poor in the HICs. By 2008, the total number of poor had risen to 2.9 billion.

But we can see from figure 7.17 that the composition had shifted dramatically. The number of absolutely poor had fallen to 1.3 billion, while the number of relatively poor had risen to 1.6 billion, 1.4 billion of which lived in the developing world. The proportion of the population of the developing world today who are relatively poor but not absolutely poor is almost certainly higher than that found in HICs.

Table 7.2 also gives the poverty gap indices (see chapter 5, section 5.2). Here too we see signs of convergence of poverty rates between the two groups of countries, with the ratio of the PG index for HICs to that for developing countries falling from 3.5 to 2.0 between 1990 and 2008. The income gap ratio (the ratio of the PG index to the poverty rate) has in fact fully converged between the two worlds, at 0.35 in 2008 (up from 0.33 in HICs in 1990, and down slightly from 0.36 in developing countries). The mean income of the poor is the same proportion of the weakly relative poverty line in the two worlds.[42]

Differences in Weakly Relative Poverty among Developing Countries

So far we have focused on developing countries as a whole. Figure 7.18 gives the geographic breakdown of the poverty rates for 1990 and 2008. In 2008, sub-Saharan Africa was the region with the highest absolute poverty rate (48%) and the highest

---

[42] Recall that the income gap ratio is the difference between the poverty line and the mean consumption or income of those living below the line, expressed as a proportion of the line.

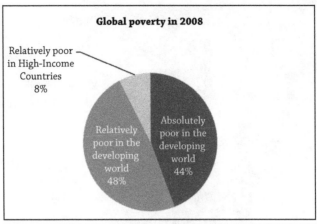

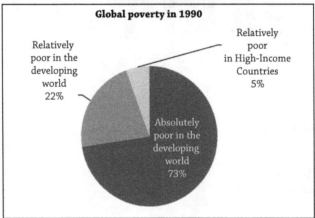

Figure 7.17 Shares of Global Poverty 1990 and 2008.

overall (absolute and relative) rate (61%) while Latin America was the region with the highest "relative only" rate. Four regions (Latin America, Middle East and North Africa, East Asia, Eastern Europe and Central Asia) had a higher "relative only" rate in 2008 than the HICs.

The incidence of weakly relative poverty rose in all regions over 1990–2008, while the incidence of absolute poverty fell. The relative poverty rate in HICs was higher in 2008 than in 1990, but has fluctuated around about 24% since the mid-1990s, with no trend in either direction (figure 7.16). East Asia is the only region that has seen a decline in the total number of people who are either absolutely poor or relatively poor, which fell from 1,047 million in 1990 to 840 million in 2008 (figure 7.19). However, this was almost solely due to China, where the number of poor people has fallen by over 200 million since 1990. In the rest of East Asia and other regions, the decline in the incidence of poverty has not been sufficient to reduce the counts of the number of poor. South Asia saw the largest increase in the count of poor people. This was entirely due to an increase in the number of relatively poor; indeed, the number of absolutely poor fell over this period (from 617 to 571 million). In HICs, the count of the poor has fluctuated around 200 million since the mid-1990s.

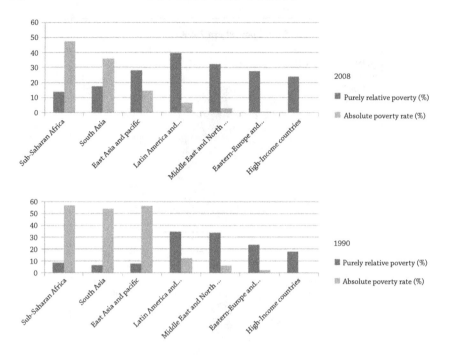

Figure 7.18 Poverty Rates across Regions of the World.

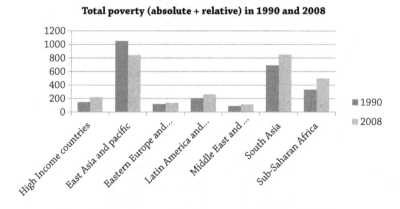

Figure 7.19 Counts of Total Poverty for 1990 and 2008.

It is of interest to see how much co-movement there is over time and across regions of the developing world between the various measures of poverty and inequality we have studied. This can be tested by studying the changes over time. Table 7.3 gives the correlation coefficients among the changes in poverty and inequality measures. We see a significant correlation (at 5% level) between changes in total inequality and changes in the (weakly) relative poverty measure discussed above. The correlation is also positive for absolute poverty, but not significant. So there are no signs here

Table 7.3 **Correlation Matrix for the Changes in Poverty and Inequality Measures**

	Total inequality (MLD)	Inequality between countries	Inequality within countries	Absolute poverty	Relative poverty
Total inequality (MLD)	1.000	0.635	0.746	0.140	0.256
Inequality between countries	0.635	1.000	−0.041	0.179	0.085
Inequality within countries	0.746	−0.041	1.000	0.027	0.258
Absolute poverty rate	0.140	0.179	0.027	1.000	0.866
Relative poverty rate	0.256	0.085	0.258	0.866	1.000

Note: n = 60 (regions and years pooled); correlation coefficients over 0.25 (in absolute value) are significant at the 5% level; 0.32 is the critical value for 1%.

Source: Author's calculations.

of a "poverty-inequality trade-off" whereby higher inequality is to be anticipated as the "price" to be paid for faster poverty reduction.[43] Such a trade-off has often been assumed in development policy thinking, but the evidence is weak.[44]

Concluding Comments on Relative Poverty

It is no surprise that richer countries use higher poverty lines. The issue is why. To the extent that this difference can be attributed to the extra cost of attaining the same level of welfare in rich countries (given the existence of social effects on welfare due to concerns about social exclusion and relative deprivation) a welfare-consistent global measure should respect these differences. However, in doing so, it does not seem plausible that the line could be directly proportional to the mean (or median), as is standard practice in Western Europe and OECD countries. This might well be defended as a reasonable approximation in rich countries, but it almost certainly understates social inclusion needs in poor countries. An alternative approach is called for that bridges the absolute and (strongly) relative measures found in past practice in the "two worlds." To not be judged "poor" a global citizen must be neither poor by the standards of the poorest countries nor poor by the standards of the country and time she lives in.

The estimates of global poverty measures discussed above indicate that about one-quarter of the population of HICs is poor. This is still only about half of the incidence of total poverty in the developing world, although that difference is almost entirely due to the presence of absolute poverty in the developing world. What is more striking is that the incidence of purely relative poverty is now higher in the developing world than in the rich world.

[43] This echoes the findings of Ravallion (2005c) using country-level data over time (including China).
[44] See Ravallion (2005c); chapter 8 returns to this point.

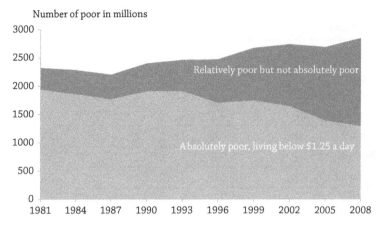

Figure 7.20 Declining Numbers of Absolutely Poor along with Rising Numbers of Relatively Poor.

The world's success against extreme poverty is undeniable, although we should not forget that over one billion people still live below $1.25 a day. And one should not be surprised that this success has come with rising numbers of relatively poor people. A great many more people can now afford the frugal consumption bundles underlying the poverty lines found in low-income countries, but they are not yet reaching the more generous allowances for social inclusion typical of the countries in which they live. We have seen falling numbers of absolutely poor people in the world alongside rising numbers of relatively poor (figure 7.20).

Strikingly, the incidence of relative poverty in the developing world now exceeds that found in HICs. While very few people living in rich countries are poor by the standards of the world's poorest countries, when one adopts a concept of poverty that tries to allow for social exclusion and relative deprivation consistently with the structure of national poverty lines one also finds that relative poverty—as well as absolute poverty—is overwhelmingly found in the developing world.

7.5 Poverty and the Non-Income Dimensions of Welfare

Alongside the progress that has been made against absolute poverty globally, the world has seen substantial progress in key non-income dimensions of welfare. Over 1990–2012 the infant mortality rate (the number of infants dying before reaching one year of age per 1,000 live births) in the world as a whole fell from sixty-three to thirty-five (World Bank 2013). The mortality rate for children under five fell from ninety (per 1,000 births) to forty-eight over the same period. And overall life expectancy at birth rose from sixty-six to seventy-one years.[45] Maternal mortality rates have also

---

[45] The latter figure is for 2011, the latest available estimate at the time of writing (World Bank 2013).

been falling globally since 1980.[46] This is undeniable progress, but these aggregates hide some large disparities both in progress over time and across the world at a given point in time. The infant mortality rate (IMR) for "low-income countries" (as classified by the World Bank) is ten times higher today than found in "high-income countries"; the IMRs for 2012 are fifty-six and five, respectively.[47] Among the main regions of the developing world, sub-Saharan Africa does worst today on most of the health-sensitive indicators (such as IMR and life expectancy), although here too there have been improvements since 2000, as we saw for the poverty measures (Figure 7.10).[48]

Many aspects of individual welfare have gender dimensions, with women and girls often disadvantaged. Girls appear to have a short-term biological advantage in early life, but this fades quickly. By the time of the schooling years, the inequality is evident.[49] However, there is good news here too, as we are seeing progress in reducing these disparities. The gender gap in primary school enrollment rates is closing or gone in many developing countries, although large gaps remain at higher levels of education.[50]

Attainments in many of these dimensions of basic health and education tend to be higher in higher income countries and sustained economic growth tends to be accompanied by improvements in these indicators. However, like income poverty, there is no guarantee that growth will necessarily lead to better outcomes for human development; that depends crucially on how the benefits of that growth are allocated within society (both across people and across types of commodities).[51] Chapters 8 and 9 will return to these issues.

There are large disparities *within* poor countries, although these disparities are hidden from view in these aggregate statistics. A statistic such as *life expectancy at birth*—the expected number of years that a newborn child will live given prevailing mortality patterns—can only be calculated for a group of people, by knowing their empirical mortality rates by age. Thus, it is not meaningful to measure the life expectancy of a specific individual and so study the inter-personal distribution of life expectancy in a similar way to how we study poverty and inequality based on survey data on consumptions or incomes.[52] Nonetheless, it is of much interest to compare life expectancy or mortality rates between different groups of people, and (in the present context) the groups we are interested in are defined by their income or wealth.

This section reviews evidence on the disparities between poor and non-poor people in non-income dimensions of welfare.[53]

---

[46] See Hogan et al. (2010).

[47] These income classifications are rather arbitrary and almost certainly outdated, but they suffice for the present purpose.

[48] See World Bank (2013).

[49] On the schooling disparities by gender, see Hill and King (1998) and World Bank (2001b). Recent data suggesting progress toward reducing these disparities can be found in World Bank (2011).

[50] See World Bank (2011, esp. fig. 3, p. 10).

[51] For further discussion, see Anand and Ravallion (1993).

[52] On this and other differences, see the discussion in Sen (1993).

[53] Lipton and Ravallion (1995) reviewed literature for developing countries up to the mid-1990s. Here the discussion will focus on results since then.

The Economic Gradients in Schooling and Learning

Poor people tend to get less schooling, and poverty can impair learning ability at school. This is an important factor perpetuating poverty. This section reviews the evidence supporting these claims.

There is now a large literature documenting these socioeconomic gradients in both rich and poor countries. The rich world has been well served by the Luxembourg Income Study (renamed "LIS" in 2011), which has facilitated the creation of, and access to, "harmonized" data files at unit-record level on household incomes, employment, and other characteristics for multiple countries.[54] LIS and other data sources for rich countries have allowed researchers to describe socioeconomic gradients in health and education. For example, a compilation of results from studies for ten rich countries indicates positive correlations between children's cognitive skills and their own and their parents' educational attainments.[55]

The International Income Distribution Database (I2D2) maintained at the World Bank aims to be a globally harmonized collection of about six hundred nationally representative household surveys.[56] One study of these data provides a useful description of a number of the non-income aspects of the lives of the income poor, as measured by the $1.25 a day poverty line—approximately the poorest quintile.[57] Those in the world living below $1.25 a day tend to have less schooling; for poor women the mean years of schooling is 5.7, as compared to 8.6 years for the "non-poor" by this definition. For men the corresponding figures are 6.7 years and 9.0 years. Notice that the schooling gap between men and women is greater for the poor.[58]

The Demographic and Health Surveys (DHSs) have been an important source of data on socioeconomic differentials in a number of non-income dimensions of welfare including schooling. DHSs do not include consumption or income data. However, a *wealth index* of the assets and consumer durables identified in the survey roster is often used as the wealth proxy, and this seems to work well.[59] It is not clear how well the DHS wealth index reflects actual wealth or the most widely used indicator of living standards, namely aggregate expenditure on consumption (including imputed values for consumption in kind). Nor is it clear how comparable values of the DHS wealth index are across countries or over time. However, the index has now been widely used, and the user community appears to be generally satisfied with the results.[60] Over two

---

[54] For an overview and assessment of LIS from the perspective of poverty and inequality analysis, see Ravallion (2014c).

[55] See Ermisch et al. (2012).

[56] At the time of writing I2D2 was not publicly available, but this will hopefully change soon.

[57] See Olinto et al. (2013).

[58] We will return to discuss other findings from the Olinto et al. study.

[59] This was developed by Gwatkin et al. (2000, 2007), following a methodology outlined in Filmer and Pritchett (1999). Details on the methodology can be found at http://devdata.worldbank.org/hnpstats/pvd.asp. The estimates for various demographic and health variables are also available at that site, and (for a broader set of variables) at http://www1.worldbank.org/prem/poverty/health/.

[60] Filmer and Scott (2012) compare socioeconomic gradients using asset indices with consumption per person for countries where this is feasible and find similar results on the overall gradients by the two methods. However, there are differences in the rankings of households.

hundred DHS surveys are now available for over sixty countries, and most now have the wealth index already calculated.

The DHSs indicate that children from poorer families get less schooling. Deon Filmer at the World Bank has long been mining these data and has produced some useful public-access data tools. Figure 7.21 uses one such tool to provide school completion rates across countries from the DHS for the richest and poorest quintiles (labeled 5 and 1, respectively) based on this asset index.[61] Among countries where 50% of those aged fifteen to nineteen had completed grade 6, the mean completion rate was 76% for the richest quintile of families but only 24% among the poorest.[62]

It is of interest to note how the socioeconomic schooling gap varies with the mean. Naturally the gap vanishes as the mean goes toward unity (figure 7.21). But what about countries with relatively low levels of schooling? It is sometimes argued that generalized education expansion will tend to increase inequality when starting from very low schooling rates. Again it depends on whether one is concerned about absolute inequality or relative inequality, as is seen in figure 7.22 where we see from panel (a) that the mean ratio of the grade 6 completion rate for the richest quintile to the poorest declines as the overall school completion rate rises, but from panel (b) we see that the absolute gap shows an inverted U, with the gap rising first then falling, and with a turning point at a mean completion rate of 55%. About two-thirds of the observations

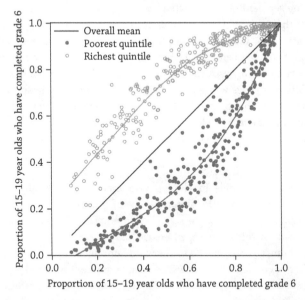

Figure 7.21 Grade 6 School Completion Rates for the Richest and Poorest Quintiles across Developing Countries. *Source:* Estimates from World Bank site: "Educational Attainment and Enrollment around the World."

[61] See Filmer (2014).

[62] These were estimated using a cubic function of the mean fitted to the data in figure 7.22. The standard errors were about 1% in both cases.

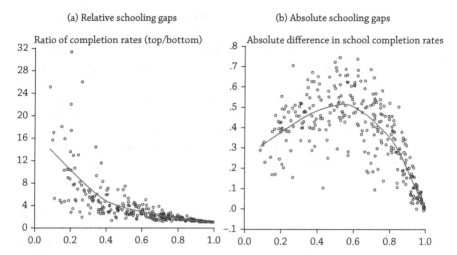

Figure 7.22 Relative and Absolute Schooling Gaps between the Richest and Poorest Quintiles across Developing Countries. *Source:* Author's calculations from the data underlying figure 7.21. Horizontal axis as in figure 7.21.

are in the falling segment of the inverted U. We will return to consider the economic implications of this inverted-U relationship in chapters 9 and 10.

The implications for inequality in labor earnings depend, of course, on how earnings vary with schooling. In empirical labor economics, it is typically assumed that the log of labor earnings is linear in the amount of schooling, in which case the relative inequality in labor earnings will also follow the inverted-U relationship as education expands. This suggests that to avoid putting upward pressure on inequality when education expands in countries with low initial levels of schooling one will need to either target the gains in schooling to children from poor families or (if only a generalized increase is possible) implement potentially large expansions in overall schooling, so as to get over the "hump" in panel (b).

Socioeconomic differentials in child development are especially important in understanding the intergenerational persistence of poverty. The differences are evident in performance at tests for pre-school children. The *Peabody Picture Vocabulary Test* is widely used for this purpose, whereby children are shown pictures and asked to identify which image corresponds to the word announced by the test giver. Studies across a number of countries have revealed sizable differences in test results in early childhood between rich and poor families. These differences clearly reflect the greater amount of time and resources that well-off parents can devote to their children than poor parents. One study for the United States finds that wealthy parents will have spent an average of 1,300 more hours per child in a range of "enrichment activities" such as talking to parents, music lessons, travel, and summer camp during the first six years.[63]

---

[63] See Phillips (2011).

Wealth differentials in ability at early age have been found for a number of Latin American countries (Chile, Colombia, Ecuador, Nicaragua, and Peru).[64] Across these countries, and splitting each into urban and rural areas, the differences in Peabody test scores between children three to six years of age in the poorest 25% of families according to a wealth index and those in the richest 25% range from 0.5 to 1.2 standard deviations and are all statistically significant. Between the poorest 10% and richest 10% the differences are in the range 1.0–1.6 standard deviations. A Blinder-Oaxaca decomposition (box 5.13) indicates that 75%–86% of the difference in test scores is accountable to wealth differences. Other evidence consistent with this conclusion has come from Cambodia and Mozambique, suggesting that the forces at work are not just confined to middle- or high-income countries. Young children from poor families in both countries suffer sizable cognitive delays that increase with age.[65]

The literature has identified a number of risk factors in early childhood development, most of which are likely to be linked directly or indirectly to poverty. A child's readiness for school, learning ability, and performance at school are known to depend on prior conditions related to family circumstances affecting cognitive ability, social-emotional competence, and sensory-motor development.[66] Poor nutritional status— as indicated by stunting and iron and iodine deficiencies—is recognized as a key risk factor in child development, along with inadequate cognitive stimulation. Talking to young children helps stimulate language skills from an early age, fostering later success in learning. There is evidence for the United States that the socioeconomic gradient in language proficiency emerges even before eighteen months of age.[67]

Even when poor parents are fully informed about the longer term benefits of investing their time and other resources in their children from an early age, they will face trade-offs. The pressures on time are great when both parents need to work long hours. Time spent with children may mean less food for them, which also matters to their development.

There are likely to be important feedback effects whereby poverty in childhood has negative effects on productivity and (hence) incomes. The availability of long-period panel data has revealed that the ability differences in childhood persisted into the earning years in the United States.[68] There is also some evidence for developing countries of adverse long-term effects on adult earnings of stunting in the first few years of life.[69] Chronic under-nutrition in childhood not only reduces schooling but also leads to a higher likelihood of being poor as an adult. We return to these topics in chapter 8 when we discuss poverty traps and other sources of persistent poverty, and in chapter 10 when we discuss targeted interventions.

[64] See Schady et al. (2014).

[65] See Naudeau et al. (2011).

[66] See Walker et al. (2007).

[67] This was found by Fernald et al. (2013), using observational longitudinal studies of infants.

[68] See Heckman (2008). Knudsen et al. (2006) argue that the ability of policy to reach poor children will be key to the productivity of the US future workforce.

[69] See Hoddinott et al. (2011), Hoddinott, Behrman et al. (2013) and Hoddinott, Alderman et al. (2013).

The Economic Gradient in Health and Nutrition

We have known since the 1970s that there is a strong correlation between a country's average real income and indicators of health and nutrition and health.[70] The correlation is even stronger once one allows for the nonlinearities, whereby the higher income brings larger gains in average health status in poorer countries. (Chapter 9 will return to comment on the policy implications of this correlation.)

Within countries, poor people tend also to be less (mentally and physically) healthy and more vulnerable to illness and so face lower survival prospects. Children with poor parents tend to receive less healthcare. There is also a large literature documenting these socioeconomic gradients. Much of the work has used cross-sectional surveys, such as in LIS or most of the surveys in the LSMS. Longitudinal observations have been less common, but have provided valuable insights. (Recall box 3.7 on panel data.) For example, much has been learned about the socioeconomic gradients in health from the longitudinal Whitehall Studies in Britain starting in the 1960s.[71] These followed male London-based Civil Servants over long periods. A number of socioeconomic differences in health behaviors and mortality and disease rates were evident.

It appears likely that the socioeconomic gradients in the health and education tend to be larger in poorer countries. A number of new data sources have emerged since the mid-1990s, reflecting the huge expansion in household survey availability (as noted in chapter 2). The attraction of many of these surveys is that they are multipurpose, meaning that they cover many attributes of household and individual circumstances, including welfare-relevant indicators. And with access to the micro data (rather than tabulations in some grouped form) one can look at the joint distribution of multiple welfare indicators.

DHSs have been an important source of data on socioeconomic differentials in health and nutrition. These surveys generally include detailed modules on the health and nutritional status of women and children. The standard measures are based on weight, height, and age; the latter is invariably self-reported for adults and parentally reported for children, while weight and height are typically measured by the investigator in the field. In measuring the nutritional status of children, two widely used measures are *weight-for-height* ("wasting") and *height-for-age* ("stunting"). Wasting is usually indicated by a child being two standard deviations below the median weight given height of a reference population. Stunting is indicated by a child being two standard deviations below the median height for age of the reference population. (The reference population is typically based on child growth curves established in the 1970s for healthy well-nourished children in the United States.) The timing of under-nutrition is key to its welfare consequences, especially for longer term living standards. A loss of body growth (muscular mass and body fat as well as height) in the first few years is not typically regained.[72]

---

[70] Early demonstrations of this correlation across countries were Preston (1975) and Isenman (1980).

[71] The Whitehall II study began in 1985, based at University College London; on the findings, see the study's website: http://www.ucl.ac.uk/whitehallII/research/findings.

[72] See Stein et al. (2010).

A widely used index of adult nutritional status from the DHS is the *body-mass index* (BMI),[73] given by weight in kilograms divided by height in meters squared. This is a rough measure of the shape of the human body. The BMI cutoff for identifying underweight adults is usually set at 18.5.

The DHSs indicate general improvements in a range of nutritional and health indicators (stunting, wasting, infant and child mortality, and HIV prevalence) for the developing world as a whole since 1990, and that the poorest 40% (based on the wealth index) have seen similar rates of progress to the population as a whole.[74] This is also true of key interventions for improving health, including immunization. However, that is not true of all countries; indeed, a number of countries have seen little or no progress, with the poor lagging. And health indicators and intervention coverage rates for the poor have deteriorated in some countries.[75]

Income elasticities of demand for food and (hence) nutrition have been found to be quite low in some studies.[76] However, this can be deceptive about nutritional status. In settings with widespread nutritional inadequacies, a low income elasticity of demand is perfectly consistent with a high elasticity of *nutritional adequacy*, since even small gains in nutritional intakes can make a big difference.[77] Nor is it a simple one-way relationship; when poverty causes poor nutrition this leads those affected to cut back on their activity levels, and so reducing their future incomes in a self-reinforcing cycle of poverty and under-nutrition.[78]

There are large differences across developing countries in the incidence of underweight and stunted children even if we control for income as best we can. This was shown in a study by Adam Wagstaff at the World Bank who estimated children's health statistics across countries from the DHSs but with the important twist that the estimates were done at a given (low) income level, which was set at $1 a day.[79] The percentage of underweight children varied considerably; for example, at the low end of the distribution the rate was 13% in Brazil, as compared to 58% in India (in the mid-1990s in both cases). The study found these differences to be negatively correlated with public health spending per capita. This is consistent with other findings that cross-country differences in public health spending matter more for the poor than for others.[80] The well-off are better able to protect their children's nutrition and health status from weak public provisioning and poor health environments, although they are still vulnerable to these things.

The Young Lives Project has provided a new source of data on the living conditions of children in a selected set of developing countries. (Readers will recall the six-year-old Duy in Vietnam, from chapter 3, who was in the Young Lives Project.) One study used these data to study the relationship between poverty and childhood under-nutrition

[73] This also called the Quetelet index.
[74] For evidence on this point, see Wagstaff et al. (2014).
[75] See Wagstaff et al. (2014).
[76] See, e.g., Behrman and Deolalikar (1987).
[77] See Ravallion (1990a).
[78] Bhargava (2008) reports evidence on this feedback effect from poverty to the allocation of time using data from Rwanda.
[79] See Wagstaff (2003).
[80] See Bidani and Ravallion (1997).

in four countries, Ethiopia, India (although only one state, namely Andhra Pradesh), Peru, and Vietnam.[81] Anthropometric measures of stunting and wasting were correlated with measures of poverty, primarily based on a mashup index of wealth, with controls for other sources of heterogeneity in the data. The study found that poorer families had consistently and significantly worse anthropometric outcomes for their children. They also found that the impact of poverty on stunting, which is a good indicator of long-term under-nutrition, tended to be greater the younger the children.

Nutrition is not simply a matter of incomes and prices. One contingent factor is the local health environment. Nutrition absorption is mediated by health-affected capacity to ingest, absorb, and use energy. Absorption rates can be quite low for people facing persistent fecal-oral contamination where they live; this is called *environmental enteropathy*.[82] Poor families across the globe tend to live in poorer places, with less access to basic services. Of those living below $1.25 a day, 80% do not have access to proper sanitation, as compared to 39% of those living above $1.25 a day.[83] And almost three-quarters (74%) of the poor by this definition do not have piped water at home, as compared to 44% of the "non-poor." Over half (51%) of those living below $1.25 a day do not have electricity at home, while this is only true of 13% of those living above $1.25 a day. Figure 7.23 summarizes the results.

A key aspect of the local environment relevant to health is exposure to air pollution. An especially damaging form of such pollution is a high concentration of fine particle matter in the air. This is produced by a variety of activities, including the exhausts of trucks and passenger vehicles, brick kilns, coal-burning power plants, waste disposal by open fires, and the debris produced by construction sites. High concentrations of fine particle matter result in permanently impaired lung functioning, and are also believed to retard brain development in children. Poor people tend to spend more time outdoors, and are far less able to afford air purifiers. Thus the health costs of

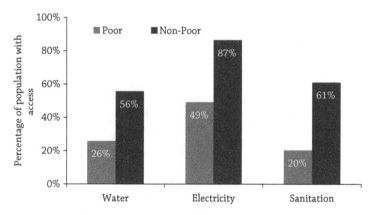

Figure 7.23 Access to Basic Services. *Source:* Olinto et at. (2013).

[81] See Petrou and Kupek (2010).

[82] For reviews of the evidence on enteropathy, see Humphrey (2009) and Korpe and Petri (2012).

[83] See Olinto et al. (2013).

air pollution are likely to be higher for the poor. There is supportive evidence for that hypothesis in research for Delhi India, which has one of the highest concentrations globally of fine particle matter in the air.[84]

These socioeconomic differences in exposure to air pollution are likely to be strongest in urban areas, especially in high-growth settings with weak environmental regulations. Another source of air pollution found in rural (as well as urban) areas of developing countries is the use of traditional biomass fuels for cooking and kerosene lamps. These generate indoor air pollution that is a recognized health hazard, with health costs that are disproportionately borne by women and children.[85] Again, this is more likely to affect poor families, since more wealthy households can afford cleaner fuels, including natural gas and electricity.

Obesity

While under-nutrition is still common among the world's poorest, over-nutrition is now a concern in rich countries. Obesity has become a major concern in America. There has been a steep rise in average weight in the United States since around 1980, due to rising caloric intakes rather than reduced energy expenditures.[86] As a result, about one in three adults in the US population are now classified as "obese."[87] This is not confined to the United States; the incidence of obesity appears to be rising globally, including in a number of middle-income developing countries. Indeed, the most complete assessment to date indicates that, while the incidence of overweight and obese adults is still lower in the developing world, it is increasing at a higher proportionate rate there than in the rich world.[88] Obesity has already become a major concern for public health, since overweight people have a higher incidence of a number of life-threatening diseases, and treatment comes at a large cost.[89]

The most common indicator for obesity is a BMI over 30, while "overweight" is identified by a BMI over 25. BMI is a rather crude indicator for this purpose. An important limitation is that it makes no distinction between weight in the form of fat and that in the form of muscle. While BMI has been widely used, there is some evidence that waist-to-height is a better predictor of disease risk. However, since most of the literature has used the BMI cutoffs these will also be used here.

The first explanation for obesity one typically hears is to blame overweight people for simply eating too much relative to their physical activity levels. However, as the *Economist* magazine (2014a, 81) puts it in its review of the documentary film *Fed Up*, "It is too simplistic to blame obesity merely on lack of willpower. That would let both food companies and politicians off the hook." This refers to how certain food companies have deliberately made their products more calorific and addictive (sugar

---

[84] See Foster and Kumar (2011). Also see the discussion in Boyce (2015).

[85] See Dasgupta et al (2006), using data for Bangladesh. Also see Duflo et al. (2008) for a review of the evidence on the health effects of indoor air pollution.

[86] See Cutler et al. (2003).

[87] See Ogden et al. (2012).

[88] See Ng et al. (2014).

[89] See Wang et al. (2011).

content is a key culprit according to *Fed Up*[90]) and how little government regulations (especially in the United States) have done to deal with this problem.

If one probes into past explanations for rising obesity incidence one finds things that are also relevant to progress against poverty. Among the factors that have been identified as causes is that new technologies have reduced energy expenditures at work. Of course, this does not explain why energy intakes or activity levels outside work did not adapt. And, while it is true that work has tended to become less physically demanding, the economic transformation away from manual work in the countries where obesity is of greatest concern seems to have preceded the rise in obesity rates by a long a time period.

It has been argued that access to healthy foods is a problem in the United States, especially for poor families.[91] Against this, it has been estimated by the Economic Research Service of the United States Department of Agriculture that only a small proportion (possibly 5%) of the population live in "food deserts"—too far from afford-able nutritious foods;[92] since this is a far smaller proportion than the obesity rate it is clearly not the whole story.

However, there is evidence that proximity to outlets for less healthy food matters. One study found that greater proximity to fast-food restaurants in the United States is associated with higher incidence of obesity.[93]

The relationship between obesity and poverty generally differs between poor and rich countries. While there is little data, the descriptions found in the social novels of the time suggest that obesity was positively correlated with wealth when today's rich countries were relatively poor.[94] The same pattern is evident in the data for today's poor countries. A review of the evidence from over three hundred published studies suggested a tendency for the literature using data from less developed countries (identified by those with a low to medium Human Development Index) to find a positive socioeconomic gradient in the incidence of obesity for both men and women.[95] For women in Nigeria, for example, the overall obesity rate in the 2008 DHS is 6%, but it is 13% for the richest wealth quintile, and only 2% for the poorest quintile. This is consistent with the results of numerous DHSs for sub-Saharan Africa, which collect anthropometric data for adult women.[96] Using the DHS wealth index, both average height and BMI rise with wealth, with only a sign of reversal in slope at the highest wealth levels.

By contrast, there is a tendency for a negative socioeconomic gradient in women's obesity incidence (whereby poorer women are more likely to be overweight) in

---

[90] *Fed Up* points to how much sugar is used in prepared foods in the United States, and not just conventional "sweets." Insulin helps the body store sugar as fat. Sugar also works a lot like a drug, with not dissimilar addictive neurochemical effects. There is also evidence that it impedes signals to the body that one has eaten enough.

[91] See, e.g., Brownell and Horgen (2004).

[92] See Ver Ploeg et al. (2009).

[93] See Currie et al. (2010).

[94] See, e.g., Dickens (1838) in which well-off local officials are invariably portrayed as overweight, in what appears to be a stereotype.

[95] See McLaren (2007).

[96] See Garenne (2011, fig.10).

developed countries.[97] This was less evident for men in the studies reviewed; indeed, for men living in developed countries there appears to be little or no overall socio-economic gradient in obesity incidence. For men in the United States, the data do not suggest that obesity incidence is higher for poorer people, but there is a rela-tionship for women; better educated and higher income women are less likely to be overweight.[98] Average obesity rates tend to have a racial differential as well in the United States, with the highest rates recorded for African American women.

One finds higher obesity rates in poorer states of the United States. I find that the correlation coefficient across states between the obesity rate in 2012 and the official poverty rate (2010–12) is 0.44, which is significant at the 1% level.[99] The correlation is even higher (r = 0.75) if one controls for the differences across states in the incidence of "high incomes," which can be done by adding a regression control for the ratio of the mean to the median.[100] Figure 7.24 shows the relationship between obesity incidence and poverty with and without this control variable. (Notice how much the data point for Washington, DC, shifts up when one controls for the mean relative to the median; this reflects the high inequality in DC.)

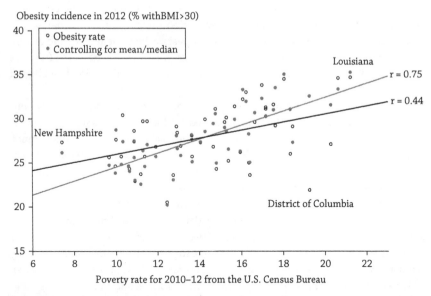

Figure 7.24 Relationship between Obesity Incidence and Poverty across States of the United States. *Source:* Author's calculations from the data sources in text.

[97] See McLaren (2007).

[98] See Ogden et al. (2010).

[99] For this calculation, I used the self-reported obesity rates by state as compiled by the Center for Disease Control while for the poverty rate I used the three-year average poverty rate for 2010–12 from the US Census Bureau.

[100] I used the calculations of the mean and median household income per person reported in Korinek et al. (2006) from the Current Population Survey for 2004.

This does not, of course, establish causality. Poverty incidence may well be picking up some other causative factor. For example, poverty incidence is also higher among African Americans, who also have higher obesity rates. The correlation reflects higher average obesity rates among poorer people in the United States, but the source of those differences is unclear.

It is possibly striking that the relationship between obesity and poverty looks so different between rich and poor countries. However, there may well be more consistency than appears at first sight. Recall that in Africa we start to see an attenuation of BMI at relative high wealth levels.[101] It may well be that we are looking at a roughly globally consistent pattern of an inverted U relationship between BMI and wealth. This would be interesting to test.

Economic arguments have been made about the causes of rising obesity. Some have blamed large (often multinational) food companies, which have developed high-volume food production and distribution systems that make unhealthy foods relatively cheap and accessible, backed up by ample spending on advertising (often aimed at children) by these companies.

Relative prices appear to have also played a role. It has been argued that technological changes in America since the 1970s have reduced the time price of eating.[102] Prior to those changes, almost all meals were prepared at home from the raw ingredients. New technologies such as deep freezers, better preservatives, artificial flavors, vacuum seals, and microwaves have allowed large-scale food manufacturing at central locations exploiting economies of scale. As a result of these changes, the full price of food (including time in preparation and cleaning up) fell, which stimulated higher demand.

Furthermore, the relative price of healthy foods may well rise with economic development to the extent that fresh unprocessed produce is not as easily traded internationally and so its price is more dependent on the local prices of non-traded inputs, including land and labor. While some healthy foods are internationally traded, there is a component that is not, and so a reasonable composite bundle of healthy foods may well be more expensive in richer countries given that real wages are higher.

How might such price effects explain the correlation with poverty in rich countries? The need for both adults to work in the wage-labor market will make the poor and middle-income families more sensitive to the lower time price of processed foods. Poor people may be expected to be especially sensitive to price differences between healthy and unhealthy diets, and so will consume a higher share of these unhealthy foods when they have easy access. This is only a hypothesis at this stage, but it may merit testing.

To the extent that rising obesity reflects changes in relative prices associated with technological changes it comes hand in hand with welfare gains for well-informed and rational consumers. One should then be cautious about the policy implications, such as taxing certain foods.[103] However, legitimate policy concerns remain when information on the health costs of the foods consumed is imperfect or habit-forming unhealthy food diets persist even for well-informed consumers. Public information campaigns

---

[101] See Garenne (2011).

[102] See Cutler et al. (2003).

[103] See Lakdawalla et al. (2005) on this point.

in rich countries have tried to teach people about the nutritional contents of food and drink (calorific values or "exercise prices," such as how many miles of walking are needed to burn the calories in a sugar-laden soft drink) and the health costs of being overweight. We discuss this type of policy further in chapter 9.

Socioeconomic Differences in Mortality

Socioeconomic gradients in health status have been found in micro-data for numerous settings.[104] One expects this to be reflected in mortality rates, but here data are a bigger constraint. While data are readily available for overall death rates, that is not the case for death rates conditional on income or other socioeconomic variables. An exception is for the United States, where the National Longitudinal Mortality Study (NLMS) surveyed over one million adults from multiple waves of the Current Populations Surveys, thus allowing mortality data to be linked to socioeconomic data. The data reveal death rates for the poor that are two-to-three times higher than for upper income households for most age-gender groups.[105] One study found that the life expectancy of the poorest quintile was 25% lower than for the richest quintile.[106]

The NLMS has an unusually large sample size. The surveys routinely used to measure poverty across the globe typically have adequate sample sizes for that purpose, but cannot provide reliable estimates of relatively low-frequency events such as adult deaths. Censuses can help as a source of mortality data (if the appropriate questions are asked), but they typically do not include the data needed for measuring poverty. Thus, we generally do not get data on deaths and living standards for the same sampled households.

One way to address this data problem is by using the DHS wealth index. The differences in death rates for children indicate that on average the poorest quintile in developing countries has an infant mortality rate that is 17% higher than average, though this rises to 35% if one focuses on low- and middle-income countries only. Using this method, death rates by age group have been estimated for the poorest 20% of the population of the developing world.[107] This uses a method in which the country is the unit of observation for income and death rates. This method has the drawback that differences *within* countries are ignored; the differentials are driven entirely by between-country differences in average incomes (though states were used for China and India). By this method, deaths in the poorest 20% account for 35% of all deaths at age group zero to four years, falling to 32% for ages five to twenty-nine, 27% for thirty to forty-four, 23% for forty-five to fifty-nine and 20% for sixty plus. These death rates for children age zero to four in the poorest quintile are 80% above the mean, while they

---

[104] Evidence of this point can be found in Watkins and van de Walle (1985), Marmot et al. (1991), Pappas et al. (1993), Sorlie et al. (1995), Wilkinson (1996), Mackenbach et al. (1997), Gwatkin et al. (2000), Wagstaff (2000), Case et al. (2002), and World Bank (2006).

[105] See Sorlie et al. (1995). Earlier estimates by Pappas et al. (1993) for 1986 suggested even larger differentials (though it is not clear why). Naturally the mortality differentials narrow considerably among the elderly (Sorlie et al. 1995). Evidence for Western Europe can be found in Mackenbach et al. (1997).

[106] See Rogot et al. (1992).

[107] See Gwatkin (2000).

are 60% above the mean for people five to twenty-nine years old, 20% above the mean for those aged thirty to forty-four but the differential largely vanishes at higher ages.

Given the aforementioned concerns about the DHS wealth index, it is of interest to also see what can be learnt from surveys for which more familiar consumption or income measures are available for adequate sample sizes. Using nine such surveys for developing countries, one study estimates the infant and under-five mortality rates grouped into quintiles according to household income or expenditure per person.[108] Using the poorest quintile, the mortality rates of children in poor families are 10%–80% higher than the mean mortality rates (depending on the country).

The demographic surveillance system implemented in Matlab thana in Bangladesh by the International Center for Diarrhoeal Disease Research has been an important source of data on socioeconomic inequalities in health within a developing country. One study reports death rates among those with no education that are about double those found for people with five or more years of formal education.[109] Another study found significant real income effects on mortality arising from higher prices for food staples in Matlab thana.[110]

Recognizing the aforementioned data problems in studying the socioeconomic differences in social indicators, Bidani and Ravallion (BR) (1997) developed an indirect econometric method using cross-country (or cross-regional) aggregates. An econometric-decomposition method on cross-country data is used to estimate the differences in various social indicators between the poor and non-poor; hereinafter this is termed the BR method. In essence, the regression coefficient of the social indicator on the poverty rate across countries estimates the difference between the mean social indicator for the poor and that for the non-poor. However, unlike the DHS-based estimates (based on the poorest 20% in each country), this time the concept of poverty is absolute, in that it is intended to be fixed across countries.

This method indicates sizable socioeconomic differences in mortality rates. Using data for the 1980s and '90s, BR find that those living under $2 a day can expect to live nine years less than those living above $2 a day and that their children are 50% more likely to die before their first birthday. Thus the incidence of poverty is seen as an important determinant of aggregate health outcomes. The differences between countries in public spending on health and in schooling also matter, but more so for the mortality rates of the poor than the non-poor. Using the same method, another study estimates that the crude death rate (CDR) for the world's poor in the mid-1990s was 22.6 per 1,000 people with a standard error of 2.5; the CDR for the non-poor was 8.1 (standard error of 0.5).[111]

When using a common international poverty line, it is not surprising that the BR method suggests a lower gap in the death rates between the poor and non-poor in regions with a high incidence of poverty, such as sub-Saharan Africa. Indeed, one study finds that one cannot reject the null hypothesis that the CDR is the same for

---

[108] See Wagstaff (2000).

[109] See Hurt et al. (2004).

[110] See Ravallion (1987a).

[111] See Ravallion (2005b). All standard errors are corrected for heteroscedasticity using White's method.

the poor as the non-poor in SSA.[112] Measurement errors could well be part of the reason, whereby mortality (especially of infants) may well be underestimated for the poor. Another explanation lies in the fact that SSA has a higher absolute poverty rate than average for the developing world (as we saw earlier in this chapter). So a lower death rate differential is to be expected, assuming that the death rate declines monotonically with income. Nor can one rule out the possibility of bias. One reason to suspect underestimation of the death-rate differential using the BR method is attenuation bias due to greater noise in the poverty data for SSA. There are other possible factors. It might be conjectured that the HIV/AIDS epidemic in Africa may has weakened the correlation between the death rate and poverty. At the early stages of the epidemic, it appears that HIV/AIDS incidence was higher among non-poor groups (at least as indicated by education and living in urban areas). However, there is evidence that this has changed over time, as better educated (and hence less poor) groups were better able to protect themselves from the disease.[113]

Poverty appears also to an important factor in explaining the unusually high infant mortality rate found in the United States, as compared to similarly rich countries. The United States has an IMR more typical of countries with much lower GDP per capita.[114] One study looked at the sources of this mortality gap relative to Austria and Finland.[115] Echoing the aforementioned findings for developing countries, the study found that the bulk of the gap was attributable to the socioeconomic gradients in mortality rates. Little or no difference in mortality rates between the United States, Austria and Finland was evident amongst similarly the advantaged socioeconomic groups.

The relationship between survival and income is very unlikely to be linear. Under certain restrictions on the properties of the distribution of personal constitutions and the household production function for health one can derive a relationship between survival chance and consumption that will exhibit declining marginal gains as consumption rises above some point.[116] At high levels of income, nutrition, and healthcare, further reductions in already low death rates are not easily attainable, nor strongly linked to further income gains. There is supportive evidence for such a nonlinear relationship between survival chances and incomes. The aforementioned Matlab data from rural Bangladesh have also revealed a sharp nonlinearity in the relationship between mortality risk and nutritional status; there is not a large difference in mortality rates among mildly malnourished and adequately nourished children, but

---

[112] See Ravallion (2005b). South Africa is an outlier, with a high CDR relative to its poverty rate (the death rate is 20% while the poverty rate is 7.1%). The correlation between the CDR and the poverty rate is stronger if one drops South Africa, but it is still not statistically significant. Dropping South Africa, the estimated CDR for the poor in Africa is 20.3 (standard error of 2.7) while that for the non-poor is 16.2 (standard error of 1.7).

[113] See de Walque (2004). There is evidence of lower usage rates for condoms among the poor; the aforementioned analyses of the DHS data indicate a condom usage rate of 18% for the poorest quintile, versus 27% on average (http://devdata.worldbank.org/hnpstats/pvd.asp.). Against this effect, access to multiple sex partners probably rises with income (at least among males).

[114] Chen et al. (2015) point out that the IMR in the US is similar to Croatia, even though GDP per capita is three times higher in the US.

[115] See Chen et al. (2015).

[116] See Ravallion (1987a, ch. 2).

the risk of death rises sharply among those who are severely malnourished.[117] One widely cited study finds that the income slope of mortality is greater at the low end of the income range.[118] However, the causal interpretation of such evidence is unclear; low income may be proxying for other variables such as low education and poor health services.[119]

Shocks to aggregate income can also be life-threatening in poor countries. One study looked at the effects of changes in national income on infant mortality rates in developing countries.[120] The researchers found that negative shocks to national income resulted in a higher IMR, with stronger effects for girls than boys.

Socioeconomic Differences in Fertility

The overall Crude Birth Rate (CBR) for low- and middle-income countries in 2011 is 21 births per year per 1,000 people.[121] (For low-income countries alone, it is 33; for high-income countries, it is 12.) Fertility rates (births per woman, in 2012) range from 1.1 in Macao China to 7.6 in Niger (the rate is 1.9 in the United States). Fertility rates have tended to fall with rising average incomes, though this could be reflecting other factors such as maternal education.[122]

Poor families, judged by consumption or income per person, tend to have higher birth rates. These are country averages and we want to look more deeply into the socioeconomic differences within countries. The same analyses of the DHS data summarized above provide estimates of the differentials in fertility rates according to the DHS wealth index.[123] Averaged over forty-five developing economies, the total fertility rate is estimated to be 6.2 for the poorest quintile as compared to 3.3 for the richest quintile, with a population average of 5.7. However, to study the birth-rate differentials between the poor and non-poor it is simpler to use instead the overall age-specific fertility rate calculated as the number of births per 1,000 women aged fifteen to forty-nine.[124] The overall birth rate per capita of women fifteen to forty-nine is 154.0 for the poorest quintile versus 113.4 for the population as a whole. This implies that the birth rate of poor families is 40% above the mean, under the assumption that the population share of women fifteen to forty-nine is the same for the poor as the population as a whole. (That assumption may not hold in reality, but it is probably not far wrong.)

---

[117] See Watkins and van de Walle (1985) for a review of the evidence on this point.

[118] See Preston (1975).

[119] See Anand and Ravallion (1993).

[120] See Baird et al. (2011). Chapter 8 (box 8.18) discusses this study in greater detail.

[121] See World Bank (2013).

[122] See Schultz (2006).

[123] See http://www1.worldbank.org/prem/poverty/health/data/index.htm.

[124] To derive the birth-rate differential from the differential in the total fertility rate (TFR) between the poor and the population as a whole one would need to assume that the age distribution of poor women is the same as that for the population as a whole, which seems unlikely to hold. If instead one bases the calculations of the birth-rate differential on the general fertility rate, then one can get away with a weaker assumption that the overall population share of women aged fifteen to forty-nine is the same for the poor versus non-poor. (Note that the TFR is obtained by aggregating the age-specific fertility rates by year for women fifteen to forty-nine years.)

There are regional differences. The implied ratios of the birth rate for the poor to the overall mean birth rate are 1.8 for East Asia, 1.3 for EECA, 1.9 for Latin America, 1.3 for the Middle East and North Africa, and 1.2 for both South Asia and sub-Saharan Africa. Using the BR method, one finds that the implied birth rate for the poor is 61.3 (standard error of 3.4) per 1,000 people versus 15.9 (standard error of 0.9) for the non-poor.[125] However, there is a marked clustering of low birth rates and low poverty rates in the countries of Eastern Europe and Central Asia (EECA). Excluding EECA the birth rate for the poor is 55.5 (3.1) versus 20.4 (1.0) for the non-poor; the birth rate for the poor is thus double the mean rate.

The demographic differential implied by the BR method is also lower for Africa. Focusing only on the observations for SSA, the birth rate for the poor is 46.9 (standard error of 5.1) versus 31.4 (2.7) for the non-poor, implying that the birth rate for the poor is 20% higher than the mean rate, which is similar to the differential implied by the DHS. As for the death rate differential, the higher poverty rate in SSA is a plausible explanation for the lower birth rate differential, although the aforementioned attenuation bias cannot be ruled out.

How should we interpret these socioeconomic differentials in fertility? Such observations have led some observers to blame poor men and women for their poverty on the grounds that they reproduce too much. We saw in chapter 1 that this argument was often made by the influential classical economists from around the turn of the nineteenth century. However, when we think about the choice problem facing poor families, it can be argued that the causation goes in the other direction—that poverty is the cause of a high birth rate not the effect. Poor parents may well have less control over their family size, given that contraception is often costly. Let us assume, however, that they can control family size. The desired number of births will be the sum of desired family size and the expected number of infant deaths. Both these variables can be expected to depend (directly or indirectly) on the family's wealth. First, consider desired family size. In poorer countries formal social security systems tend to be weak or absent, such that children are desirable for support beyond one's earning years or if there is an accident or health shock. This will be even more important for poor parents within poor countries, for they will lack the wealth to support or insure themselves. Second, we have seen that, across the globe, the children of poor parents are less likely to survive. To assure that they attain their desired family size, child deaths have to be replaced. So an implication of higher mortality for poor families is higher fertility. On both counts, poverty and the conditions that create it emerge as a cause of a high birth rate rather than a consequence.

The relationship between fertility and income will also depend on the source of income. As Paul Schultz (2006) has argued, some sources of income will tend to increase fertility while other sources will have the opposite effect. Schultz argues that higher returns to non-human assets will tend to increase desired family size, while higher wages for women will reduce desired fertility by increasing the opportunity cost of having children.

---

[125] See Ravallion (2005b).

Family Size and Composition

It has long been observed that larger households tend to have a higher incidence of poverty, as measured by household consumption or income per person. This is confirmed by the results of a study using six hundred household surveys spanning the developing world.[126] The researchers found that poor families tended to have more children; for the poor, 34% of family members were twelve years or younger, as compared to 20% for the non-poor. The same study found that the "$1.25 a day" poverty rate was 32% among children (twelve years or younger), rising to 52% if one focused on low-income countries. Figure 7.25 shows the age composition of the developing world's absolutely poor, compared to the non-poor.

This relationship is sensitive to changes in measurement assumptions. The biggest issue is the equivalence scale used in comparing households of different size and demographic composition (chapter 3). The claim that large households tend to be poorer is not robust to changes in measurement assumptions.[127] The more one allows for economies of scale in consumption the less likely one will find that larger households are poorer, as discussed in chapter 3. Children are also found to be more likely to be poor than adults when using the "per capita" scale, given that child/adult ratios are larger in poor households. However, this too is a questionable basis for claiming that children are poorer given the likely sensitivity to the scale used. More convincing evidence is found in the indications that child stunting in Pakistan is more likely in larger households.[128]

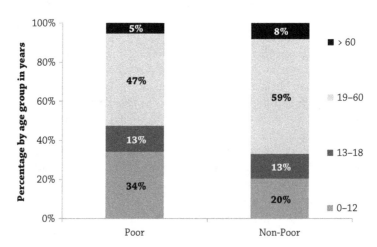

Figure 7.25 Age Profiles for the Developing World's Poor Compared to the Non-Poor. *Source:* Olinto et al. (2013).

[126] See Olinto et al. (2013).
[127] As demonstrated by Lanjouw and Ravallion (1995).
[128] See Lanjouw and Ravallion (1995).

Female-Headship and Poverty

The concept of a "household head" has been widely used in household surveys to create an internal structure to the household roster, even if the designated headship carries little real meaning.[129] In practice, headship is self-assessed by survey respondents and the concept is unlikely to be defined the same way everywhere.[130]

The headship concept has, nonetheless, been prominent in the literature and policy discussions related to poverty. Beliefs that female-headed households (FHHs) tend to be poorer and that the incidence of female-headship was rising have led to concerns that poverty would self-perpetuate. By this view, the disadvantages faced by single mothers would not only entail higher poverty today, but would make it more likely that the children in those families would be poor as adults. To some observers, female-heads in poor families, and single mothers in particular, were seen as further examples of how "bad behaviors" were the root cause of poverty.

The empirical foundation for believing that FHHs tend to be poorer is far from firm, however. It holds in official poverty data for the United States.[131] Some studies for developing countries have also found that FHHs are poorer by standard measures, but it is not clear that this is true in the majority of cases.[132] The evidence also warns against regional generalizations; for example, FHHs are more likely to be poor in East, Middle, and Southern Africa but not Western Africa.[133] Whether the incidence of FHHs is rising over time is also unclear, although there is evidence from DHSs that this is so in Africa since 1990.[134]

There is also a (poorly recognized) measurement issue that clouds poverty comparisons between male- and female-headed households. Because FHHs are likely to be smaller, one can expect sensitivity of this aspect of the poverty profile to the allowance one makes for scale economies in consumption. Simply dividing by household size (or the number of equivalent adults) is likely to understate the extent to which FHHs are in fact poorer.[135] The reliance on household aggregate consumption or income as the welfare indicator has also been a serious limitation (which we return to below). Using individual welfare indicators there is evidence for Africa that women fare better in FHHs.[136]

Another issue is heterogeneity within this group of households. It has become recognized that FHHs are a diverse group, warning against generalizations.[137] The reason

---

[129] Some surveys have even abandoned the concept, identifying a reference person instead with no assumption of headship.

[130] See Rosenhouse (1990).

[131] FHH's have a poverty rate almost double the average rate; 29% of those living in an FHH live below the official US poverty line in 2012, as compared to 15% nationally and 7.5% for married-couple families (Short 2013).

[132] Reviews of the evidence can be found in Buvinic and Gupta (1997), Lampietti and Stalker (2000), and Quisumbing et al (2001).

[133] See Milazzo and van de Walle (2015).

[134] See Milazzo and van de Walle (2015).

[135] An example (for Mali) is found in van de Walle (2013).

[136] See Milazzo and van de Walle (2015).

[137] See Chant (1997) and Milazzo and van de Walle (2015).

for being a FHH is important. It is clearly very different when this stems from the loss of the main (male) breadwinner due to illness or accident versus his temporary migration to obtain higher earnings to be shared with the family.

A study of the reasons for rising female headship using DHSs for Africa over 1990–2013 found that the most important factors explaining this trend were rising age at first marriage and higher education levels.[138] Both factors increased the incidence of FHH's and including them in the regression made the trend term largely vanish. The same study found that a number of other factors influence the level of FHH incidence, such as HIV prevalence (positively), the share of Muslims (negatively), and civil wars (positively), but these factors did not account for the rising trend. This suggests that the rising incidence of FHHs in Africa may well be a sign of women's empowerment stemming from later marriage and more schooling.

Missing Women

While there are gender dimensions to all the non-income aspects of welfare discussed above, a prominent issue in the literature is that of "missing women." This refers to a discrepancy between the actual counts of women in a specific population with what one would have expected based on the "counterfactual" demographic breakdowns found in rich countries. For example, in the United States and United Kingdom the sex ratio at birth is 1.05 (105 males to every 100 females), while in China and India it is around 1.20.

Sen (1990) drew attention to the sizable number of missing women and argued that this was probably due to selective abortion (though this is less likely among the poor) and parental allocations favoring boys.[139] Sen's total count of missing women was 100 million, although a subsequent calculation put the count at 60 million.[140]

The underlying causes of son preference are not well understood, but a prime contender is that sons are believed to provide more reliable old age security for parents. In China, for example, the tradition has been that sons look after elderly parents, while daughters move to their husband's family. Gender differences in labor market outcomes (reflecting in part at least discrimination) undoubtedly also play a role. In India, wedding costs (including a dowry—a still common practice even though it was outlawed in the 1960s) also generate a preference for sons. Additionally, in most societies, the family name and wealth are passed on through men.

It has been widely believed that the bias against girls is largely confined to Asia (China and India being prominent in the literature) and to the pre-natal period or the first few years of life. This form of gender bias is thought to be far less evident in sub-Saharan Africa.[141] One study has questioned this prevailing view.[142] By a careful accounting of the flows of missing women by age and cause of death, judging excess

---

[138] See Milazzo and van de Walle (2015).

[139] Visaria (1969) had earlier argued that ratios of males to females above 1.05 found in the Indian censuses were due to unusually high female mortality rates relative to male rates.

[140] See Coale (1991).

[141] See, e.g., Klasen (1996).

[142] See Anderson and Ray (2010).

mortality against rich-country gender ratios, the researchers confirmed that there are missing female children but also find evidence of excess deaths among *adult* women in Africa and Asia. The incidence of excess mortality turns out to be higher in sub-Saharan Africa than in South Asia. In sub-Saharan Africa, the most common causes are HIV infection and maternal mortality. In India cardiovascular diseases and "injuries" are important causes, in addition to maternal mortality. In China, major causes are cardiovascular and respiratory diseases, as well as injuries. The same study found evidence of excess mortality among adult women in the United States in 1900.[143]

There have been two follow-up studies. In the first, by the World Bank, the findings of the aforementioned study were confirmed.[144] A subsequent study questioned the data used by the earlier work (especially for Africa) and the choice of reference standard, arguing that rich country demographics are inappropriate given the difference in health/disease environment compared to developing countries.[145]

These conflicting studies have been based on aggregate country level data, typically from the Population Census of each country. It is of interest to see what can be learnt from micro data, notably the DHS. One of the few studies to date used the 2008 DHS for India and Nigeria and finds evidence that the preference for sons influences adult women's health and mortality; women who happen to initially give birth to girls tend to reduce their subsequent interval between births in the hope of having a son, with adverse health consequences.[146] Another study found evidence that married women in Senegal insure against potential widowhood by trying to have sons using similar strategies with potentially similar consequences.[147]

There are indications that son preference is fading in China, where the gender imbalance has been large, with 121 boys born for each 100 girls in 2004. This appears to have been the peak. In 2013 the number had fallen to 118, and the downward trend is expected to continue. It appears that as China develops the reasons for son preference are becoming less relevant.

The Feminization of Poverty

We saw earlier in this chapter that absolute poverty rates are falling in the developing world, and there are signs of acceleration since 2000. Are we seeing similar economic progress for poor women as for men? While it is not something that is easily quantified, there can be little doubt that women across the globe are pushing back against traditional roles and norms. Girls are getting better educated. For example, primary-school completion rates for girls in low- and middle-income countries rose over the same period, from 75% to 88% of girls in the relevant age groups. Many are taking a more active role in the economic life outside the home than their mothers and many are taking greater control of their bodies and lives.

[143] See Anderson and Ray (2010).

[144] See World Bank (2011).

[145] See Klasen and Vollmer (2013).

[146] See Milazzo (2013). The genders are balanced in number at birth in the aggregate. Assuming that there is in fact son preference this implies that Milazzo can treat the gender of the first born as exogenous in her regressions.

[147] See Lambert and Rossi (2014).

While there has been progress for women and girls, it has been slow and uneven in much of the developing world, and with frequent setbacks. Since 2000, the female labor force participation rate in developing countries has actually fallen slightly; in 2011, 50% of women over fifteen in low- and middle-income countries were in the labor force, as compared to 52% in 2000.[148] (Although slow progress on this front partly reflects the aforementioned gains in schooling.) It remains the case throughout the world that women face greater obstacles to escaping poverty than do men.

The way that poverty is conventionally measured probably hides its gender dimensions. As explained in chapter 3, the standard assumption is that there is an equal distribution within the household. The only way that poverty rates would then differ between men and women is that the gender breakdown differs according to consumption or income per person (or per equivalent single adult). There are ways that this can happen, by the departure of adult men from poor families, either through selective mortality or migration/dissolution. However, it remains that the standard measures are unlikely to reflect well the gender dimensions of poverty. This is a deep data problem, since it would add greatly to the cost of standard surveys to capture intra-household distribution, and it is not even clear that this is technically feasible. This has not stopped some observers, as box 7.4 explains.

Box 7.4 Counts of Poor Women

One often hears that 70% of the world's poor are women. This was reported in the 1995 *Human Development Report* (UNDP 1995). Soon after that report came out, Hilary Clinton, and the (then) President of the World Bank, James Wolfensohn, quoted the 70% figure in their speeches. It has been repeated many times since. For example, it appears in the 2006 *Encyclopedia of World Poverty* (Muhutdinova 2006). The figure is still being quoted twenty years after it appeared. For example, it was quoted by Carly Fiorina (former chief executive of Hewlett-Packard) in a 2014 TV broadcast (Greenberg 2014).

The origin of this number remains a mystery. Soon after the UNDP report appeared, I tried to figure out the source, including asking the report's statistician, but no source was identified. Blog posts by *Oxfam*'s Duncan Green (2010) and *Politifact*'s Jon Greenberg (2014) ask where the figure came from, and report that they could not find its source either. The figure is still being quoted as the truth twenty years later, but it has no known basis in fact!

There have been other efforts to count poor women. A 1992 IFAD report, *The State of World Rural Poverty*, gives estimates of the number of rural women living in poverty by country (Jazairy et al. 1992). That has to be estimated, since it is not data from any standard household survey. The IFAD report does not say how the numbers were estimated, but it does say what variables were used and one can easily figure out the formula (as I did in my review of the report; see Ravallion

---

[148] See World Bank (2013).

1994c). The IFAD numbers for poor women by country are exactly equal to half the number of people living in poor households *plus* one-quarter of those living in female-headed households, whether poor or not. The rationale for the latter step is a mystery. The IFAD calculation tells us that 60% of the world's poor are women. At least we can figure out where the IFAD number comes from, even if we do not believe it.

Another approach is to use incomes from survey data but only consider single-person households. *The World's Women* report for 2010 presents such estimates, mainly for Europe (United Nations 2010, box 8.4). Using a relative line set at 60% of median income, poverty rates are higher for women in twenty-four out of twenty-eight countries. Using a lower poverty line, at 40% of the median, the pattern reverses, with higher poverty rates among men for most countries.

However, standard income-based poverty measures are not the most obvious place to look for welfare disadvantages experienced by women. There are four hypotheses that can be identified concerning the feminization of poverty. First, it is likely that poor women typically work longer hours than do men, notably when account is taken of domestic labor and child care (within the household). The pressure of poverty to increase female labor force participation does not typically come with reduced work at home. Second, poor women typically face fewer opportunities for independently escaping poverty. Their domestic commitments and cultural taboos often prevent them from taking up new opportunities as readily as can men. Third, in some cultures widows face effective barriers against employment or remarriage, and are treated as second-class citizens within the home. This leads to high risks of poverty. Fourth, women and girls are more vulnerable to shocks and violence. The threat of sexual violence looms large for many women across the globe; we return to look at this issue more closely in the next subsection.

The extent of disadvantage suffered by female-headed households depends crucially on why they are female headed. A number of studies in Africa have found that households headed by widows are especially impoverished relative to others.[149] One study demonstrated that widow-headed households in India were unusually poor in terms of consumption per person.[150] Using the 2006 consumption data for Mali, another study found that female and especially widow-headed households have significantly lower living standards than others in both rural and urban areas.[151] Importantly, this study found that the adverse welfare effects of widowhood persist even after widows are remarried and absorbed into male-headed households. However, Africa is a diverse set of countries in terms of its family structures and institutions, and with much diversity within some countries as well; this diversity warns against generalizations.

---

[149] See Appleton (1996) and Horrell and Krishnan (2007).
[150] See Drèze and Srinivasan (1997).
[151] See van de Walle (2013).

Some recent studies have found support for the hypothesis that women are more vulnerable to shocks. In a study for India, adverse rainfall shocks were found to reduce girls' survival chances to school age relative to that of boys.[152] A cross-country study of the effects of changes in national income on infant mortality rates found that GDP gains have similar effects on the IMRs of boys and girls, but girls are more vulnerable to contractions.[153] The results indicate that a 6% contraction in GDP per capita increases the IMR for girls by 7.4 deaths per 1,000 births, which is about three times the average effect. (Chapter 8 will discuss this study in more detail.)

While there have been a number of studies of risk sharing using micro data, the bulk of the literature focuses on how well the household as a whole is able to cope with risk. In one of the few exceptions, one study was able to take advantage of panel data for Ethiopia on adult nutritional status as measured by BMI.[154] The researchers found that poorer people are less able to smooth their consumption in the face of income risk, and that this holds within households as well as between them. Furthermore, women in poor households are the most exposed to uninsured risk. These results are all the more striking when one realizes that their data come from a setting in which chronic under-nutrition is common, even relative to other poor countries let alone relative to the norms for rich countries. The aforementioned study of widows in Mali is also suggestive of considerable exposure to shocks. In this case the shock is the loss of a husband.[155] And those shocks are passed onto the next generation through worse schooling outcomes of children. Thus, widowhood in this context is a mechanism for the intergenerational transmission of poverty.

Violence and Poverty

Civil wars tend to be more common in poorer countries. The causality undoubtedly goes in both directions: the loss of life and destruction of civil wars holds back progress against poverty, but poverty can also encourage civil war; low wages, for example, imply a lower opportunity cost of war.[156]

This type of violence gets a lot of media attention. However, even in normal times, with no such large-scale conflict, there is ever-present violence: intimidation, theft, extortion, abuse, beating, torture, enslavement, rape, murder, or some combination of these. The victims can be individuals, whole families, enterprises (such as small businesses harassed by entrepreneurial predators), or entire communities. Mostly it is illegal, but even so it is commonplace. So too is the often debilitating fear of violence. Gary Haugen has called this the "hidden terror of poverty."[157]

---

[152] See Rose (1999).

[153] See Baird, Friedman and Schady (2011).

[154] See Dercon and Krishnan (2000).

[155] See van de Walle (2013).

[156] On the developmental costs of civil wars, see Collier et al. (2003). On the determinants of civil wars, see the review in Blattman and Miguel (2009) and the analysis in Besley and Persson (2011, ch. 4), which makes the point about the opportunity cost. Besley and Persson also argue that the threat of *external* conflict can help strengthen weak states.

[157] Haugen and Boutros (2014, 16).

Qualitative work has often identified safety as an important concern of poor people, especially when they live in poor areas.[158] With reference to urban slums in sub-Saharan Africa, it has been observed that "to outsiders these slums can seem vaguely scary, but most outsiders have no idea how scary these slums feel to the insiders—the people who actually live there."[159] It is not obviously safer in poor rural villages. Village studies have described the many forms that violence takes (and not necessarily physical), where those empowered to enforce the law can sometimes be the biggest threat to poor people.[160]

The well-off also have greater ability to protect themselves from crime and violence. Indeed, it may well be that, globally, poor people are disproportionately the victims of many forms of violence. It is a plausible hypothesis that the scale of the problem of violence is greater when the public justice institutions are least developed or effective, which tends as a rule to be in poor places. Discrimination against disadvantaged minorities by the legal system has been a common concern, and not just in developing countries. For example, it has been argued that failures of the legal system to treat violence against blacks the same way as whites is a causative factor in America's high murder rate.[161] A discriminatory, or even more deeply failed, public legal system fosters parallel private arrangements. Private resources are needed to assure protection (including through bribes), and so poor people are typically the least well protected—they cannot afford safety and justice even when the formal laws claim to provide them to all.

Thus, we can expect that poverty and powerlessness often go hand in hand. As Singer (2010, 6) puts it: "extreme poverty is not only a condition of unsatisfied material needs. It is often accompanied by a degrading state of powerlessness." While this is a plausible conjecture, is there supportive evidence? In one of the few studies to address this question, longitudinal survey data for Russia included questions on people's perceptions of their own power or self-efficacy, and the answers could be compared with both objective and subjective data on the economic welfare of the same respondents. A strong association was evident in the data, whereby perceptions of powerlessness tend to be greatest among the poorest.[162] The same study also found a notable gender difference, with women reporting less power than men. This remained true with regression controls for personal and household incomes and other likely objective covariates of powerlessness.

As was noted in the last subsection, violence against women at normal times, within the home or community, is an important non-income dimension of the feminization of poverty. The form of this violence that has received the most attention

---

[158] See, e.g., Narayan and Petesch (2002), UN Habitat (2003), and Pradhan and Ravallion (2003). The latter paper shows that Brazilian survey respondent's expressed desire to improve public safety rises with own-income, but at given income, living in a poor area increases the concern about public safety.

[159] Haugen and Boutros (2014, 30).

[160] See, e.g., Hartmann and Boyce (1983) in an excellent book entitled *A Quiet Violence*.

[161] This is comes out clearly in Leovy's (2014) account of the murder of a young black man in South Los Angeles.

[162] See Lokshin and Ravallion (2005) for details.

is sexual, although that is not the only form; wife beating and other forms of intimidation are known to be common. Domestic violence is even socially accepted to some degree, though clearly underreported in official crime data.[163] In some DHS surveys, respondents are asked whether wife beating is justified under specific circumstances (notably when she argues with her husband, refuses to have sex, or burns the food). On average, 29% of the female respondents in the forty countries where the question was asked said that wife beating was justified.[164] In 2006, sixty countries had laws against domestic violence, though such laws are less common in developing countries.[165] Reporting and enforcement are another matter even in rich countries. Fear, shame, and stigma often mean that the abuse remains unreported. And even when it is reported, police are often unwilling to act when the crime is committed against poor people.

Sexual violence is primarily against women.[166] The empirical evidence on this topic is not as strong as for the other non-income dimensions of poverty discussed earlier in this chapter. Sexual violence tends to be more hidden from formal statistical observation, especially in places where legal institutions are weak. Well-documented field observations have provided insights on the common forms of violence and the deficiencies in the legal system across the world.[167]

A large share of sexual violence is within the household. Official statistics and even surveys are of questionable reliability in this context, with underreporting likely. Even so, the WHO's survey-based estimates indicate that a remarkably high 35% of adult women have experienced sexual and/or physical violence. Such violence is found in countries at all levels of development, but its reported incidence tends to be higher in poorer countries. Figure 7.26 gives the WHO's estimates of the prevalence of sexual violence against women by region. The incidence rates are highest in the poorest two regions (Africa and South and East Asia) but they are still high in developed countries.

Evidence on socioeconomic gradients in sexual violence within countries has been found using DHS data, since some of these surveys included questions to women on their experiences of sexual violence. Leland Ackerson and S.V. Subramanian (2008) study the socioeconomic gradients in the life-time incidence of intimate-partner sexual violence using India's 1999 DHS (called the National Family Health Survey).[168] The sample is large—90,000 ever-married women aged fifteen to forty-nine—although non-sampling errors may well be severe. For example, better educated respondents may be less inclined to admit to the existence of domestic violence, given that they are likely to be more aware of how it might be judged by the interviewer.

---

[163] Specially designed surveys have been more revealing; see, e.g., Jejeebhoy (1998) on this form of violence in two states of rural India. Men are also subjected to domestic violence, though far less often; World Bank (2011) cites survey evidence for some developed countries.

[164] See World Bank (2011, 83).

[165] See World Bank (2011, 83).

[166] For example, in a national survey, 2% of men in the United States reported being raped sometime in the lives; the proportion was 15% for women in the United States (Tjaden and Thoennes 2000).

[167] See, e.g., Haugen and Boutros (2014).

[168] I have not seen similar studies for other countries.

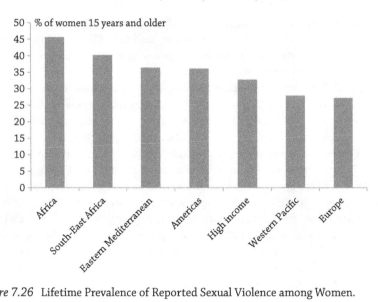

Figure 7.26 Lifetime Prevalence of Reported Sexual Violence among Women.
Source: WHO (2013b).

The study's findings are suggestive of a quite strong association between poverty and vulnerability to intimate-partner sexual violence. Twenty-six percent of Indian women in the poorest wealth quintile reported such sexual violence. The incidence fell as wealth rose, to 6% for the richest quintile. Such descriptive statistics do not tell us about causality. There are a number of reasons why poverty could play a causal role. As noted, money helps buy protection, both in the form of private goods and through improved access to public legal protection. When poverty forces both parents to work, this leaves children unsupervised and hence more vulnerable. Poverty sometimes forces women into occupations that have greater risk of sexual abuse, including being a sex worker. Criminals target poor women and children for enslavement in forced prostitution or labor, since they are more easily attracted with promises of a better life for them and their families, and they have less power to draw on the legal system for help.[169]

A woman's education emerges as another factor in the incidence of sexual abuse. In the Ackerson and Subramanian study, 21% of those women with no formal education reported intimate-partner sexual abuse, with the incidence falling steadily with education, to 2% for those with thirteen years or more schooling. Furthermore, the wife's education is also an important predictor when one uses regression to control for other factors, including poverty. This is suggestive that education empowers women to resist, which may be especially important when dealing with the risk of the partner's sexual violence. (Although there have also been many cases of young educated women in public places in India's cities being targeted by rapists.) The husband's education shows a similar gradient in predicting sexual violence against women in the Ackerson

---

[169] See Haugen and Boutros (2014, ch. 2).

and Subramanian study although this is attenuated when one controls for household wealth and wife's education. Better educated men tend to live in less poor households with better educated wives, and the latter factors appear to account for the correlation between sexual violence and husband's education.

There is another dimension to poor people's exposure to violence, stemming from the biases in legal systems. If you do not have the normal degree of protection in a given society, then you face greater risk of having any wealth gain being illegally appropriated by others, thus dulling the incentive for escaping poverty. In his memoir of growing up poor in northeastern Alabama, the distinguished journalist Rick Bragg (1997, 297) puts the point well: "It is a common condition of being poor. . . you are always afraid that the good things in your life are temporary, that someone can take them away, because you have no power beyond your own brute strength to stop them."

Developing more effective legal institutions and processes that work for all citizens is likely to be crucial for reducing violence generally, and especially the violence facing poor people across the world. A policy agenda for reducing violence by fostering better and more inclusive legal institutions can be seen as an investment in longer term economic progress. We return to this issue in chapter 9, when we come to discuss institutional development.

Growth, Inequality, and Poverty

> Growth really does help the poor: in fact it raises their incomes
> by about as much as it raises the incomes of everybody else....
> In short, globalization raises incomes, and the poor participate
> fully.
>
> —*The Economist*, May 27, 2000, 94

> There is plenty of evidence that current patterns of growth and
> globalization are widening income disparities and hence acting as
> a break on poverty reduction.
>
> —Justin Forsyth, Oxfam Policy Director, Letter to *The*
> *Economist*, June 20, 2000, 6

> One cannot predict with any confidence that economic growth will
> translate into reductions in poverty.
>
> —Jeff Shantz 2006

> It is in the nature of "development" not only to make an over-
> abundance of goods available to consumers but also to produce
> inequality and exclusion. All the texts on "development" are unan-
> imous in concluding that the gap between North and South (but
> also between rich and poor in each) is continually widening.
>
> —Gilbert Rist 2008, 255

As these quotes suggest, there is much debate on whether economic growth and globalization facilitate or impede progress against poverty and inequality. A long-standing
and widely held view is that economic growth in a capitalist economy is bound to be
inequitable. We saw in Part One that the classical and Marxist economists of the nineteenth century saw little scope for equitable economic growth in a capitalist economy.
This pessimistic assessment persists, including in development circles (as exemplified by the quote above from the anthropologist Gilbert Rist). Economic thinking in
the twentieth century has provided a more qualified view. Famously, Simon Kuznets
(1955) argued that rising inequality is likely as underdeveloped capitalist economies
start to grow, but that inequality will fall once some higher income level is reached.
Yet inequality has been rising in much of the rich world. Thomas Piketty (2014) argues
that this is to be expected in a developed capitalist economy. What reasoning is behind
these views and does the evidence support their claims?

The continuing debates about how much poor people benefit from aggregate economic growth have been informed by various economic theories about growth and

distributional change. This chapter begins with a discussion on these theories before reviewing the evidence. The chapter concludes with case studies for China, India, and Brazil.

8.1 Theories of Economic Growth and Distributional Change
Some Basic Concepts

Following common usage, "economic growth" means higher GDP per capita and the "rate of growth" is the annual percentage increase in GDP per capita. Recall from box 1.1 that GDP is an aggregate of the production of all the goods and services— or at least the ones that are traditionally acknowledged as goods and services, which essentially means that we can attach market prices to their quantities and add them up to get GDP. Although widely used, GDP has a number of limitations, as summarized in box 8.1.

Box 8.1 **Limitations of GDP as a Measure of Progress**

Recall how GDP is defined (box 1.1): it is the total market value of the goods and services produced by the economy over a year. There have been four main criticisms of GDP as a measure of progress.

1. *GDP is not measured well in practice:* There are mainly concerns about what is left out. GDP does not include imputed values for domestic labor time or leisure. (Thus, GDP falls if someone leaves the wage-labor market to take up the same work at home.) There are also issues of implementation, which are especially relevant to countries with large informal sectors and weak statistical capacity. The data have improved greatly since Kuznets's first estimates. For most rich countries, the National Accounts from which GDP is derived accord with international guidelines provided by the Statistics Division of the United Nations, in cooperation with a number of other international organizations. However, the application of these standards in poor (and some middle-income) countries is uneven. The latest guidelines are for 2008, about two-thirds of Africa's population lives in countries that have not yet implemented the previous (1993) guidelines (Devarajan 2011).
2. *GDP does not take account of the environmental consequences of growth:* GDP does not allow properly for the exhaustible natural resources used up in production and applies market prices that do not always reflect opportunity costs. Then maximizing GDP comes at too great a cost to the environment.
3. *GDP can be a poor measure of the average economic welfare of a population:* Here there are concerns that not all of GDP is consumed by households. A share constitutes the profits of firms and banks; these profits can be expected to eventually benefit households, but that will take time. Another share comprises taxes collected by governments. GDP also includes incomes that accrue

to foreigners. In principle, household surveys can provide a better measure of average household living standards than the national accounts, although recall the concerns raised in chapter 3.

4. *GDP says nothing about how incomes are distributed:* At the extremes, imagine two societies with the same GDP per capita, but in one it is virtually all accounted for by the consumption of the super-rich, while in the other it is fairly equally distributed. GDP makes no distinction between the two, yet they would be very different places to live in!

Further reading: Jerven (2013) points to concerns about the quality of national accounts data for Africa. An early formulation of the environmental critique is Mishan (1967); Mishan was one of the few serious economists expressing this concern (and apparently he had a hard time getting his book published). Dasgupta and Heal (1979) provided an authoritative treatment of the economics of exhaustible resources. Much of the rest of this book pertains to the fourth critique. Fleurbaey (2009) reviews the various alternatives to GDP that have been proposed.

It is a convenient simplification to treat GDP as a composite output, which is produced by combining homogeneous labor with stocks of homogeneous capital and land. Furthermore, it is assumed that GDP is produced under constant returns to scale, with diminishing marginal products of all factors of production. This is the *aggregate production function*. Box 8.2 explains the concept further. This is a foundation of most of macroeconomic theory, and also the bulk of the empirical work on the determinants of the rate of aggregate economic growth (which will be reviewed later in this chapter).There was much debate about the idea since it first gained prominence in the 1950s; especially contentious was the assumption of homogeneous aggregate "capital" as a factor of production.[1] Defenders of the idea of an aggregate production function argued that it is an innocuous and analytically useful simplifying assumption.

Box 8.2 The Production Function

Total output Y is taken to be a function of the inputs of capital (K) and labor (L), namely $Y = F(K, L)$. These inputs are heterogeneous in reality; for example, the "K" stands for all the machines and other non-labor inputs (many of which are previously produced goods) and the "L" includes various types of labor (skilled and unskilled). But to keep things simple, K and L are treated as homogeneous. Sometimes the production function is written as $Y = A.F(K, L)$

continued

---

[1] For an overview of this debate, see Cline (1975). There is an insightful, though technically demanding, discussion of the debate in Bliss (1975, ch. 8).

Box 8.2 **(Continued)**

where A is a positive number, called *total factor productivity* (TFP); this refers to an increase in output that is not attributable to higher K or L.

The extra output that is possible by an investment that increases the capital stock K by one unit (holding A and L constant) is called the *marginal product of capital* (MPK). Similarly there is a marginal product of labor (MPL). The typical production function exhibits declining MPK, meaning that a given increment to the capital stock produces less and less as the amount of that capital stock increases. (Recall box 1.12 on Ricardo's idea of diminishing returns.) Similarly, the MPL falls as L rises.

It is normally assumed that K and L can be substituted, as reflected in the curvature of the *isoquant*, which gives all the technically feasible combinations of K and L that can attain given Y (analogously to the indifference curves in boxes 1.4 and 3.1). The slope of the isoquant is the MRS, the ratio of MPL to MPK. (This is sometimes called the marginal *technical* rate of substitution, to distinguish it from the MRS of the utility function.) The *elasticity of substitution* is defined as the proportionate change in K/L divided by the proportionate change in the MRS. This measures the curvature of the isoquant—how much substitution is technically feasible.

An example of a production function is $Y = K^\alpha L^\beta$ where α and β are positive parameters. This is the Cobb-Douglas function. This form is popular but rather special, notably in how much substitutability is allows for between K and L; specifically the Cobb-Douglas MRS is directly proportional to K/L so the elasticity of substitution is unity.

Suppose that K and L increase by a factor λ ($\lambda = 1.2$ when each input increases by 20%, say). If Y also increases by λ, then we have what is called *constant returns to scale* (CRS). (If Y increases by $\lambda > 1$, then we have "increasing returns to scale," while if $\lambda > 1$, it is "decreasing returns to scale.") Under CRS the parameters of the Cobb-Douglas function must have $\alpha + \beta = 1$ and output per worker (y) can be written as a smooth function of capital per worker (k). Write this form of the production function as $y = f(k)$, as in figure B8.2.1.

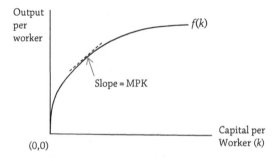

Figure B8.2.1 Output per Worker as a Function of Capital per Worker.

Now consider the choice of k by a profit-maximizing firm that is unable to influence the rate of interest, r, it faces on its borrowing. Suppose first that MPK > r. Then the firm would clearly want to invest more, since each extra unit of capital "pays for itself" by covering the interest payment needed to finance it. So capital per worker will increase, which will bring down MPK until it reaches r, when the incentive to invest will vanish. Conversely, if MPK < r, then one would want to disinvest, increasing MPK. Thus, the profit-maximizing level of capital k^* satisfies the equilibrium condition that MPK = r.

If we now consider multiple firms, or multiple economies, we can readily see that aggregate output will be maximized when all marginal products come into parity. For if MPK is greater for firm (or economy) A than B, then there will be an aggregate gain from reallocating capital from B to A, which will lower the MPK in A and raise it in B (given diminishing marginal products). The same holds for labor.

Further reading: Most economics textbooks cover this topic. A good introduction to the standard approach can be found in Weil (2005). More advanced treatments can be found in Barro and Sala-i-Martin (1995) and Acemoglu (2009).

To help understand the dynamics of aggregate poverty measures, the chapter will use some basic ideas from the study of economic dynamics. The most important concept is that of a stable, steady-state equilibrium—a point at which there is no inherent dynamic for further change and a small shock will return the economy to that same point. Box 8.3 summarizes this concept and the main ideas on dynamics we will need later in this chapter.

Box 8.3 Concepts for Studying Economic Dynamics

Consider a person who owns a production process for future wealth and has access to a perfect credit market, meaning that she can finance her desired capital stock for that production process at a rate of interest r, taken as given. She consumes a share s of her wealth at any date. If she did not consume anything at date t she would have a wealth at date $t + 1$ that comprised her surplus from the own production activity (denoted π) plus the return from investing her wealth (rw_t).

The *recursion diagram* maps from current wealth to future wealth, as illustrated in figure B8.3.1. Note that π also depends on the rate of interest, as this determines the opportunity cost of the capital used in her production process, but we do not need to make that explicit here. We can write:

$$\pi = f(k^*) - rk^*,$$

continued

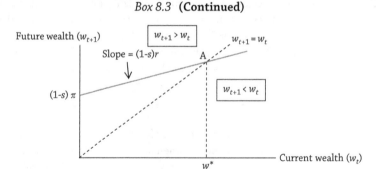

Box 8.3 **(Continued)**

Figure B8.3.1 A Linear Recursion Diagram for Wealth Dynamics.

where k^* is the optimal capital stock, which yields an output of $f(k^*)$. If the latter is the standard production function described in box 8.2 and she maximizes profit, then she will equate the marginal product of capital with the interest rate $MPK = r$.

Allowing for consumption, her wealth at $t + 1$ is then given by:

$$w_{t+1} = (1 - s)(\pi + rw_t).$$

This is the equation for the recursion diagram in figure B8.3.1. The bold line is the simple linear recursion diagram implied by this model. The 45 degree line separates the space into two regions, one in which wealth is rising (above the line) and one in which it is falling (below the line). A *steady-state equilibrium* is a situation in which wealth is constant over time. The steady-state equilibrium is at point A, corresponding to the level of wealth w^*. Notice that an upward (downward) shift in the recursion diagram entails an increase (decrease) in the steady-state level of wealth.

The point A is called a *stable equilibrium*. To see what this means consider someone at point A who receives a transient (short-lived) wealth gain, which puts the person at some point to the right on the bold line. Now the person will be in a region at which wealth is declining over time. Thus, the person will eventually return to point A. Similarly, a transient negative wealth loss will put the person in the region in which wealth is rising, and so she will head back to point A in due course. However, as we will see, there are other possibilities for the recursion diagram, with multiple equilibria and not all stable.

Further reading: As for box 8.2.

Building on these concepts, the rest of this section provides an overview of the main theoretical arguments that have been made in the past about the distribution of the gains and losses associated with aggregate economic expansions. Section 8.2 turns to the evidence.

Past Debates on Whether Poor People Benefit from Economic Growth

Not only were the classical economists largely pessimistic about the scope for poverty-reducing growth, they also questioned whether sustained economic growth was even possible. Of course, there can be temporary growth, as the economy moves toward its "steady state"—a situation in which the economic aggregates are unchanging (box 8.3). And this may well entail higher growth in initially poorer countries—the process of economic convergence, which we will return to. However, by this view, the economy will fall eventually into a state of zero growth. As we saw in chapter 1, the leading classical economist of his time, David Ricardo, held this view, pointing to the inherent fixity of natural resources and the "law" of diminishing returns (box 1.12). By this logic, redistribution would be the only way to reduce poverty. This view is not widely held in modern times, though it still has its exponents; for example, Rist (2008, 254) writes that "development can occur only through the constant tapping of resources that are by no means inexhaustible; so, far from fulfilling the promise of abundance, economic growth can lead only to general scarcity."

Modern-day thinking has emphasized the scope for technical progress to expand the production of goods and services from given inputs. The issue is then how much poor people can be expected to share in this expanding output. This chapter will review the theories and evidence on this issue.

The measurement choices discussed in Part Two matter greatly to how one assesses the distribution of the benefits of economic growth. The value judgments made in measuring inequality carry considerable weight for the position one takes on whether growth tends to be inequality increasing or not. Finding that the share of income going to the poor does not change on average with growth does not mean that "growth raises the incomes (of the poor) by about as much as it raises the incomes of everybody else" as claimed by *The Economist* magazine (in the quote at the beginning of this chapter).[2] Given existing inequality, the absolute income gains to the rich from distribution-neutral growth will be greater than the gains to the poor. For example, for the richest decile in India, the income gain from aggregate growth will be about four times higher than the gain to the poorest quintile; it will be fifteen to twenty times higher in Brazil or South Africa.[3] This distinction between absolute and relative inequality may help us understand the long-standing debate on growth and equity. Different sides in the debate may well hold different ideas about what "inequality" means. For example, when non-economists such as Rist (2008) and others talks about the widening gap between rich and poor they may well have in mind absolute inequality, not relative inequality. The common economic definition in terms of relativities is not beyond question; if one does not accept the scale independence axiom, then one can justifiably reject relative measures in favor of absolute ones (satisfying translation invariance; recall boxes 5.3 and 5.5).

The same point can be made about how one measures poverty—namely whether one judges that the measure of poverty is unchanged if all incomes and the poverty

---

[2] *The Economist* was referring to the working paper version of Dollar and Kraay (2002) (which was careful in noting that it was studying proportionate changes).

[3] See Ravallion (2003a).

line increase by the same proportion (scale invariance), or whether that only holds for a common absolute increase (translation invariance; see box 5.6).

A more contentious issue is whether one thinks about poverty as absolute (a fixed real poverty line) or relative (a line rising with average income), as discussed in chapters 4 and 5. Those who say that globalization is good for the world's poor tend to be undisguised "absolutists." Intuitively, the more "relative" is your poverty measure, the less impact economic growth will have on its value. By contrast, many critics of globalization appear to think of poverty in more relative terms. At one extreme, the "strongly relative" measures discussed in chapter 4 (in which the poverty line is proportional to mean income) will behave a lot like a measure of inequality. This method can show rising poverty even when the levels of living of the poor have in fact risen. As argued in chapter 4, that is surely an extreme position that would seem hard to defend. While we can agree that relative deprivation matters, it appears to be very unlikely that individual welfare depends *only* on one's relative position. Absolute levels of living also matter.

However, the explicit acceptance of poverty among economists and non-economists alike over some two hundred years or more was not the product of such a relativist view. While Adam Smith is often cited as supporting the idea that poverty is relative, it is unlikely that he would subscribe to strongly relative measures. Recall from chapter 3 that Smith pointed to the social role of a linen shirt in eighteenth-century Europe. However, this merely suggests that Smith would have wanted a poverty line to be relevant to the society in which poverty is being estimated.

Growth was not expected to be inequality-neutral. Most classical and Marxist economists saw little hope that even a growing capitalist economy would deliver rapid poverty reduction, or even any poverty reduction. While Smith was optimistic about the potential for a progressive, poverty-reducing, market economy, later prominent classical economists, such as Malthus and Ricardo, were more pessimistic on the prospects for higher real wages and (hence) less poverty. This suggests that they anticipated rising inequality from a growing capitalist economy.

In the absence of technological progress, the idea of diminishing returns to labor led the classical economists to expect that growth in the labor force would (at least after some point) lead to lower output per worker. It was understood that technical progress might well counteract diminishing returns at least for some period of time, by allowing more to be produced from given inputs. This depended on the nature of the technical progress. In principle this could either increase the demand for labor or decrease it, but the more common classical view was that it would tend to be labor augmenting—on balance increasing the demand for labor and thus putting upward pressure on the real wage rate, bringing down the incidence of poverty and probably lowering income inequality as well. However, working against this force, the classical economists anticipated a demographic response to rising wages such that the "moral weaknesses" of poor men and women would entail a higher rate of population growth, thus weakening the impact of growth on poverty (as noted in chapter 1).

The socialist movement that emerged toward the middle of the nineteenth century shared the same pessimistic view on the prospects for poverty reduction, but took it to be a damning criticism of capitalism. The thirst for profits to finance capital accumulation, combined with the large "reserve army" of unemployed, was seen as the constraint on rising real wage rates, rather than population growth.

There is ample scope for debate on both the classical and Marxist arguments. The classical perspective is that the poor could be expected to gain from growth provided that they showed "moral restraint," keeping birth rates low such that the aggregate effect entails that real wage gains from labor-augmenting technical progress can persist. Another (more modern) interpretation of their position is to argue that technical progress would be poverty-reducing provided that it came hand in hand with the right *social policies*—complementary policies for education, healthcare, and social protection. And if the rate of population growth is restrained, then the reserve army must inevitably get depleted, with real wages eventually rising.

A further argument as to why economic growth fueled by technical progress would be poverty reducing was found in a famous paper on the theory of savings, by Frank Ramsey (1928). The well-known part of this paper laid out a model of optimal savings; box 8.4 provides details on the Ramsey model of savings.

Box 8.4 Ramsey's Model of Savings

Ramsey provided a dynamic model of the choice between consumption today and consumption tomorrow. He imagined a planner who maximized an intertemporal sum of time-specific utilities derived from consumption and leisure, with a production function for output that depended on capital and labor inputs. Ramsey then derived a relatively simple rule for optimal savings, which can be represented (in a highly simplified form) in figure B8.4.1. We have consumption at two dates, and an indifference curve representing preferences between consumption today and consumption tomorrow. As before, the slope of this curve is the marginal rate of substitution (MRS). To this we add a "transformation curve," which gives the maximum feasible consumption "tomorrow" at each possible level of consumption today, taking account of production possibilities.

In each period, output is either consumed or saved, and savings equals investment. Investment today raises the capital stock and hence output tomorrow. Extra consumption today means less consumption tomorrow, so the curve is

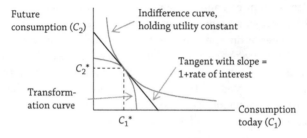

Figure B8.4.1 Inter-Temporal Consumption Choice.

continued

Box 8.4 **(Continued)**

downward sloping. The shape of the curve reflects the shape of the production function, which gives output per worker at any date as a smooth function of capital per worker, with diminishing marginal product of capital, as in box 8.2. Because of a declining MPK, the transformation curve must bend down, as in the graph. To see why, suppose that one consumes very little today (C_1 close to zero). Then there will be more for tomorrow, but the MPK tomorrow will be relatively low, given that there is so much capital available. So extra consumption today when C_1 is close to zero will come with only a small drop in consumption tomorrow. It is evident that the optimum consumptions are $\left(C_1^*, C_2^*\right)$ in figure B8.4.1, at which the MRS between consumption levels over time equals the MRT.

Historical note: Frank Ramsey was a mathematician and economist at Cambridge University, England, and a protégée of Arthur Pigou and John Maynard Keynes. He wrote two seminal papers on economics, one on optimal taxation and one on optimal savings. He died at twenty-six after complications from surgery.

In the last section of Ramsey's paper there is a model of poverty. It is based on the idea that there was a distribution of time preference rates (discount rates) in society. (Recall from box 3.10 that the time preference rate is the personal rate at which the future is discounted.) Ramsey treated the discount rate as an exogenous preference parameter. He identified the poor as those with a discount rate greater than the equilibrium rate of interest. Ramsey concluded that "equilibrium would be attained by a division of society into two classes, the thrifty enjoying bliss and the improvident at the subsistence level."[4] One implication of Ramsey's model is that, by putting upward pressure on the rate of interest, an exogenous increase in the steady-state level of output will reduce the incidence of poverty, as shown in box 8.5. Unlike the classical model, technical progress will benefit poor people in the Ramsey model of poverty.

Box 8.5 **Ramsey's Model of Poverty**

In the last section of Ramsey's famous paper, "A Mathematical Theory of Savings," he sketched a model of poverty. In Ramsey's view, different people have different rates of time preference—their personal rates of discount. (Recall box 3.10 on discounting.) Those people with a discount rate less than the rate of interest accumulate capital until they reach their maximum conceivable utility, their "bliss point," denoted Y_1. Those with a discount rate greater than the rate of interest would de-accumulate over time and eventually reach the lowest possible consumption—some meager "survival" level denoted Y_0. (Note that $Y_1 > Y_0$.)

[4] Ramsey (1928, 559).

The "poverty rate" in this model can be thought of as the proportion of the population with a discount rate greater than the rate of interest. Denote this by $H(r)$ and note that H must be a decreasing function of r for any given distribution of time preference rates in the population.

Ramsey did not go into the implications of his model. But it is easy to see that an exogenous increase in the steady-state level of output will increase the equilibrium rate of interest and thus reduce the poverty rate. Figure B8.5.1 shows this. The curved bold line on the right panel is the locus of the combinations of interest rates and output levels equating the rate of interest (r) to the marginal product of capital (MPK). (See box 8.2 for further explanation of why $r = MPK$ in equilibrium.) The straight positively sloped line in the right panel is all the combinations of r and Y that satisfy the adding up condition that $Y = H(r)Y_0 + (1 - H(r))Y_1$. One solves the model by finding the rate of interest and level of capital stock (and hence output) that satisfy this adding-up condition while assuring that $r = MPK$.

With technical progress aggregate output increases at a given rate of interest, shifting out the curve in the right panel of figure B8.5.1, and thus lowering the poverty rate.

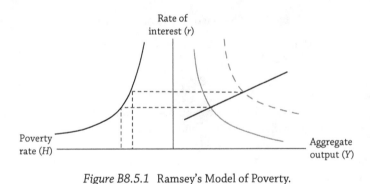

Rate of
interest (r)

Poverty
rate (H)

Aggregate
output (Y)

Figure B8.5.1 Ramsey's Model of Poverty.

Versions of this type of model of the causes of poverty are longstanding. The general feature is that the distribution of income is assumed to reflect the operation of competitive market forces given an underlying distribution of innate characteristics of people—their preferences, talents, and aptitudes. The occupational structure of society and the distribution of income emerge through a sorting process, based on how characteristics are rewarded by free markets given individual efforts and initiatives.[5] For example (as in the Ramsey model), some people end up poor because they have high discount rates. Another example postulates that people differ in their risk preferences, such that some of those willing to take risk end up rich, while those more averse to risk stay poor.

[5] This is the essence of what came to be known as the Roy model, following Roy (1951). For a modern discussion of this influential model, see Heckman and Taber (2008).

As we saw in chapter 1, alternative models had started to emerge in the First Poverty Enlightenment. These models took a very different perspective. Instead of explaining poverty in terms of how innate differences between people are rewarded by the market economy, they saw individuals as fundamentally the same (or with only minor differences) and pointed instead to how institutions (including not-so-free markets) worked. In these new models, poverty could be seen as the cause, rather than the effect, of the differences found between people in their preferences and behaviors. We will return to discuss various examples.

The post–World War II period naturally saw greater emphasis among policymakers on assuring the conditions for long-run economic growth. Post-Independence policies in most developing countries also strove for economic growth, facilitated by government planning in relatively closed economies, although capabilities for effective implementation were often weak. Planning documents were influenced by the Harrod-Domar equation (box 8.6). This equation was prominent in growth economics up to around 1960 but was then eclipsed by more complete models of growth. The equation continued to be influential in developing planning, including in setting foreign-aid requirements, as discussed further in chapter 9.

Box 8.6 The Harrod-Domar Equation

The Harrod-Domar equation gives the rate of growth in GDP per capita as:

$$g = \frac{s}{c},$$

where s is the savings rate (the share of output that is saved) and c is the capital-output ratio ($c = K/Y$ where K is the capital stock and Y is output).

Where does the Harrod-Domar equation come from? The simplest way of deriving the equation is as follows. Aggregate investment in period t (I_t) is just the change in the capital stock. Write this as:

$$K_t = K_{t-1} + I_{t-1}.$$

(We can easily add an allowance for depreciation here.) The economy is taken to be in macroeconomic balance, which requires that aggregate investment equals aggregate savings. So we can rewrite this as:

$$K_t = K_{t-1} + S_{t-1}.$$

We have $K_t = cY_t$, $K_{t-1} = cY_{t-1}$. The value of c is also taken to be exogenously fixed, giving what is called a "fixed-coefficient technology." And $S_{t-1} = sY_{t-1}$, where the savings rate s is also assumed to be fixed exogenously. Substituting these into the above equation we have:

$$cY_t = cY_{t-1} + sY_{t-1}.$$

On rearranging this last equation it is easy to see that we get the Harrod-Domar equation:

$$g_t \equiv \frac{Y_t - Y_{t-1}}{Y_{t-1}} = \frac{s}{c}.$$

This is not a causal model, however. Indeed, it is virtually an identity. The assumptions of a constant c and s were seen by subsequent economists as especially worrying, and these assumptions were relaxed in subsequent developments to growth theory.

Historical note: The Harrod-Domar equation faded from view in modern economics, but a version of it in the form $c = s/g$, resurfaced seventy-five years later in Piketty (2014, 166) who dubbed it the "Second Fundamental Law of Capitalism." (Piketty's first law is the identity that the share of output attributed to capital is simply the rate of return to capital times the ratio of capital to output.) However, the earlier cautions about causal interpretation remain. The discussion returns to Piketty (2014).

The Harrod-Domar equation was interpreted by poor countries as saying that they were too poor to save, which kept their growth rates low, so they stayed poor—the essence of a macro-poverty trap. The private sector could not be relied on to deliver the saving and investment needed for long-run growth. The only solution (it was argued) was for the government to intervene to assure that there was sufficient saving and investment by drawing on external development assistance to boost the rate of investment (section 8.5 returns to this issue).

The Harrod-Domar model was over-interpreted in early development thinking. There is no theory of savings in the model; the saving rate is exogenous, as is the fixed-coefficient technology. Nor was it clear why the government was capable of saving and investing more than the private sector. There were concerns that the politics would end up with bloated government consumption, in either capitalist or socialist economic systems.[6]

Development in a Segmented Economy

Recall from chapter 7 that we see very different levels of living across the countries of the world. Underlying the large "between-country" component of global inequality (such as evident in figure 7.12) one finds large disparities in the wage rates for similar labor, and this remains true when one controls for education.[7] This implies between-country differences in the marginal products of labor such that there are reallocations of labor between countries that will increase global output, and they will also

---

[6] As argued by Wallerstein (1971).

[7] See Rosenzweig (2010), who estimates the "skill prices" across countries and shows that the pattern is consistent with migration flows.

reduce global inequality. These unexploited opportunities for equitable growth persist in large part because of restrictions on the migration of labor between countries. Essentially, those who benefit from the existing disparities have the power to restrict entry.

There are not dissimilar processes at work within countries, though rarely do they entail internal passports and visas.[8] Within a developing economy, we see different segments or sectors with different average levels of living—most notably between urban and rural areas. Over time we also see a process of *structural transformation* to varying degrees across countries. Recall from chapter 2 that, in a closed economy, the fact that food is a necessity means that the composition of demand shifts away from agricultural outputs toward manufacturing goods and services as the economy develops. Today's rich countries went through such a transformation in the past, and today's developing countries are also doing so.

Socialist economies sometimes achieved high rates of economic growth through forced structural transformation in initially segmented economies: a planned re-allocation of factors of production across sectors, notably between agriculture and industry (such as in the Soviet Union) was technically difficult, had uneven success and was often manipulated for political ends. There were welfare costs of forced re-allocation of labor and the narrow economic gains would eventually vanish, and the socialist planning system provided only weak incentives for technical innovation within sectors (as was evident in the Soviet Union by the 1970s).

The literature on comparative development has instead stressed the success of Western Europe, Scandinavia and North America in developing the institutions and the infrastructure to foster a combination of technical innovation with structural transformation with little economic planning. Free internal trade in factors of production and goods in a system with secure property rights and supportive public infrastructure have clearly been the more important factors than planning in the long-term economic development of today's rich world.[9] The case for structural transformation needs to be qualified when the country is not closed, but open to external trade. Then we may find a degree of country-specialization according to endowments (such as cultivatable land). This will influence the pattern of sectoral change as the economy grows. For example, a middle- or even high-income country may still depend heavily of farming because it has an abundance of fertile land, leading it to export its food surplus to buy manufactured goods from a poorer economy without such good land.[10] However, while this qualification is important, the models of growth in a segmented economy that we consider now assume a closed economy.

As we heard in Chapter 2, early policy-oriented discussions were pessimistic on the prospects of domestic economic growth bringing much benefit to poor, primarily rural, people in the near term. It was widely believed that growth in low-income countries was bound to be inequitable at least initially. Progress against poverty would be slow, although the expectation was that eventually poverty incidence would start to fall rapidly.

---

[8] China is an exception, which we return to later in this chapter.

[9] See, for example, Morris and Adelman (1988) and Acemoglu and Robinson (2012).

[10] Recall the example of New Zealand in figure 2.4.

The classical reason for this pessimism was seemingly widespread *underemployment of labor* in the rural economy and the urban informal sector. In developed economies, or the formal sector of developing economies, "unemployment" is defined as a situation in which one's usual status is looking for work rather than being employed. That is not the relevant definition for most of the world's poor, who cannot afford to be idle. For them the relevant concept is underemployment, which can be interpreted as the time-rate of unemployment (i.e., the proportion of time in the workforce spent wanting more work but not finding it). A common characterization of life in rural areas of a developing country and in the urban informal sector is that most people are doing at least some work, but that they are rarely fully employed beyond peak seasons in agriculture (such as the harvest time). This is the labor surplus. It appears that this was also a common feature of the today's rich world when it was poor, and it is still common in today's developing world.

Building on this characterization, Lewis (1954) proposed an important and influential model of economic development in a segmented labor-surplus economy. The model postulates the existence of a fledgling capitalist sector, which is primarily industrial, but it could also include commercial farming. The modern capitalist sector is an island in the midst of a traditional, primarily farming, sector where most people are found and live on a meager subsistence income determined by the average product of farming. The main source of growth is the expansion of the modern sector. The constraints on that expansion are the capital and natural resources available to the sector. (Skilled labor may also be a constraint, although Lewis thought this would only be temporary.) Expansion occurs through the reinvestment of the profits from the capitalist sector and that expansion draws labor from the traditional sector but without lowering its output while the labor surplus remains. When that surplus is finally absorbed the economy reaches its *"Lewis turning point"* (LTP). Box 8.7 explains the model further.

Box 8.7 **The Lewis Model of Economic Development**

Let N^u denote the share of the (fixed) workforce in the urban economy, with $1 - N^u$ in the rural economy. There is a fixed "subsistence" rural wage, denoted W^r. (There need not be a rural labor market; the rural "wage" may simply be the average product in agriculture, which is shared.) The economy starts at $N^u = 0$ and develops by modern sector enlargement, which generates rising demand for unskilled workers—an upward shift in the marginal product of labor (MPL^u) in the modern sector. Under profit maximization, the capitalist will hire N^u workers such that the marginal product of the last worker is the modern-sector wage rate W^u. Rural labor is absorbed by the modern sector with (it is assumed) little or no opportunity cost. The rural wage increases once the rural labor surplus is absorbed, at the Lewis turning point (LTP).

Figure B8.7.1 illustrates the model. Looking from left to right the horizontal axis gives the share of the labor force working in the modern sector (from right to left it gives the share in the traditional sector). The bold line that is initially

continued

Box 8.7 (Continued)

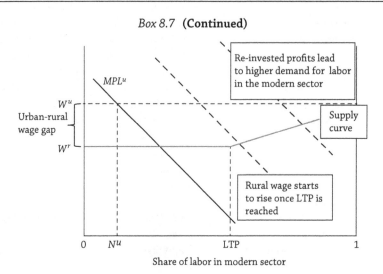

Figure B8.7.1 The Lewis Model of Economic Development.

flat then bends upward shows the supply curve for labor to the modern sector. Only after the LTP does the rural wage rate respond to the progressive upward shift in the MPL^u curve, as indicated by the dashed negatively sloped lines.

In the figure, the modern-sector wage rate is set above the subsistence wage. (Lewis discussed various reasons for such a differential.) This creates a problem. While agricultural output does not fall as labor is absorbed from that sector (up to the LTP), the workers who have moved to the industrial sector will presumably demand more food at their higher wage rate, putting upward pressure on food prices in a closed economy, and so lowering the real wage in terms of food. Rising farm productivity can offset this effect (as Lewis noted), but it is not clear where this would be coming from.

Historical note: Arthur Lewis was born in Saint Lucia in 1915. He studied economics at the London School of Economics before joining the faculty of the University of Manchester, where he developed his model of economic development in the 1950s. In 1979 he won the Nobel Prize in economics.

Note on the literature: Ray (1998, ch. 10) has a good discussion of the Lewis model. In the subsequent literature, Ranis and Fei (1961) and Fei and Ranis (1964) drew attention to the need for an appropriated balanced combination of agricultural and industrial productivity growth.

How will poverty measures evolve with development in this model? One relevant factor is the size of the wage gap between urban and rural sectors. As Lewis noted, a migrating worker need not expect to keep 100% of his wage; he is likely to have commitments to send money home to his kin and he may also be compelled to find work for others in his kin group. This implicit tax may well slow the pace of migration and (hence) development. Indeed, modern-sector employers will undoubtedly be aware of the prospect for nepotism among migrants trying to employ their kin.[11] These "network effects" are known to be important in determining migration patterns, including the types of workers who migrate.[12]

However, it is safe to assume that there is some net gain to the migrant and family. If the poverty line is above the product of the modern-sector wage rate and the number of workers per capita, but below the incomes of the capitalists, then the growth process in the labor-surplus period will not reduce the headcount index of poverty. But it will do so if the poverty line is between the rural and urban wage rates (appropriately adjusted for labor-force participation). This occurs entirely from the gains to the newly recruited modern-sector workers.

Looking instead at the poverty gap (or other higher order measures) the outcome is unclear. Given the labor surplus, the rural wage rate would not rise for some time, until the surplus is absorbed; the extent of rural underemployment essentially chokes off the "trickle-down" benefits of economic growth through higher rural wages, although remittances and network effects can still bring benefits to the rural poor. But there are also potential losses to the poor. With no change in aggregate farm output, upward pressure on food prices in a closed economy can be expected if there is a real wage gap (box 8.7). This will entail falling command over food in the rural sector and thus a greater depth of poverty (as reflected in the poverty gap). When the LTP is reached, rural wages will start to rise, reducing the depth of poverty and (after some point) its incidence as well. (This effect may be dampened somewhat by the subsequent export of capital.)

Income inequality, on the other hand, can be expected to rise initially, as the fledgling capitalist sector expands. There are two sources of rising inequality. The first is the rising share of profits in national income while the second is any real-wage gap between traditional and modern sectors. Once the economy passes the LTP, rural wages start to rise, attenuating inequality. Thus, we may see an inverted-U relationship between inequality and mean income.

Once the LTP is reached, this becomes the standard model of a competitive labor market (box 1.5), with marginal products of labor equalized between the sectors. There can be no reallocation of labor that would increase aggregate output given the current technologies. The only explicit source of inequality in the model will also have vanished, since the wage differential will go to zero. Then any poverty measure (with the standard properties discussed in chapter 5) must also reach its minimum value for any given set of technologies available for production.

The Lewis model has been hugely influential. Its relevance can be questioned in some settings, notably when the economy has passed its LTP, or never really had a labor surplus because the wage rate had fallen to a level that cleared the market. (Although the labor-surplus assumption of the Lewis model is not essential; we can instead imagine abundant labor with a low market-clearing wage rate.) The assumption that labor can be withdrawn from the rural economy without any loss of output

---

[11] See Hoff and Sen (2006) for further discussion and analysis of this potential impediment to development.

[12] See, e.g., McKenzie and Rapoport (2010).

requires either zero marginal product of labor or that with one less worker on the family farm the other members will work harder (substitute away from leisure) to make up the difference, leaving total labor supply unchanged.[13] In today's developing world, these conditions appear to be less relevant in some settings than others. As we will see, it may well be the case that sustained economic growth has meant that some (large) developing countries today are near or even passed their LTP.

Another important foundation for the view that inequality would rise initially as poor countries developed was provided by Kuznets (1955) and came to be known as the *inverted-U hypothesis*, whereby inequality first increases with growth in a poor country but falls after some critical income level is reached.[14] We have seen that this is also suggested by the Lewis model, although Kuznets also allowed for inequality within each of the urban and rural sectors, though with high inequality in the former. The first few people who move to urban areas see large gains (as both workers and capitalists), driving up the initially low level of inequality. As the urban economy expands competition drives down this premium, and eventually inequality starts to fall. The Kuznets hypothesis is discussed further in box 8.8. The hypothesis is often invoked in development policy discussions. A popular view is that it justifies the expectation that growth will inevitably be inequality increasing in poor countries, but (more optimistically) that it will eventually start to decline; "just be patient" the story goes. But a turning point is not assured (box 8.8).

Box 8.8 The Kuznets Hypothesis

The Kuznets Hypothesis postulates that the level of income inequality first increases as an initially very poor country starts to develop economically, but after some time inequality reaches its peak, and then starts to fall, as in figure B8.8.1. Inequality reaches its maximum at y^*.

In rationalizing this relationship Kuznets considered a dualistic economy comprising a low-mean, low-inequality rural sector and a high-mean, high-inequality urban sector, and growth occurred through the migration of workers from the former to the latter. (Kuznets also considered a different explanation

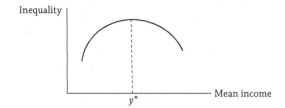

Figure B8.8.1 Stylized Kuznets Curve.

---

[13] See Rosenzweig (1988) for further analysis of these conditions.

[14] Elaborations of this model include Robinson (1976), Fields (1980), and Anand and Kanbur (1993).

based on savings behavior.) In one possible formulation of the migration process, a representative "slice" of the rural distribution is transformed into a representative slice of the urban distribution, preserving distributions within each sector. It is easy to see what this implies for distributional dynamics. Assume that everyone is initially in the rural sector. When the first subgroup of the rural sector moves into the urban sector under the Kuznets process inequality will appear that was not there before, namely that between a typical urban resident and a typical rural resident. Inequality will increase. Consider the last subgroup to leave the rural sector. Inequality between sectors will vanish. But urban inequality will remain. Only if the between-sector effect dominates will there be a turning point. Otherwise inequality will keep increasing.

Historical note: The Russian-American economist Simon Kuznets was a pioneer of empirical economics. (We already noted his contributions to national income accounting in box 1.1.) More formal versions of a model of development that can generate an inverted-U were provided by Robinson (1976) and (for a range of inequality indices) Anand and Kanbur (1993). (In the Robinson formulation using only the variance of log incomes as the inequality index one does not need higher inequality in the urban sector for the inverted-U; a higher mean suffices.)

It is easy to see that if poverty is initially higher in the rural sector then aggregate poverty must fall under the Kuznets process of migration described above.[15] So the Kuznets argument can also be interpreted as a model of how poverty is reduced through *urbanization*; similarly to the Lewis model, the expanding modern sector of the economy would reduce poverty directly by absorbing rural labor. The incidence of absolute poverty would fall even though relative inequality was rising at least initially.

These models treat labor as homogeneous, but that is not so in reality. Workers in the traditional sector with characteristics and skills that better match the needs of the expanding modern-sector workforce will naturally be better placed to get the new, better paid jobs. Depending on the type of work demanded by the modern sector, initial inequalities in human development can thus interact with the modern-sector growth process to influence the pace of poverty reduction. (We will return to this point in the case study for India, where the inequalities in human development are large.)

The evolution over time of the inequalities in schooling discussed in chapter 7 (section 7.4) also has bearing on how earnings inequality changes. A long-standing assumption in labor economics is that the log of labor earnings is approximately linear in schooling.[16] Recall that the absolute gap in primary school completion rates

---

[15] This holds for all additive poverty measures, as described in chapter 5.

[16] This is known as the Mincer earnings function, following Mincer (1958), who rationalized this relationship using an economic model of the returns to schooling. That model has since been very

between the top and bottom quintiles shows an inverted-U relationship (figure 7.21, panel b). Thus, we can expect the relative inequality in labor earnings to also follow an inverted-U.

Alongside the urban–rural dimension of inequality, evidence started to emerge in the 1960s about how the regional dimension of inequality evolved with economic development. Lewis had once said that "development must be inegalitarian because it does not start in every part of the economy at the same time."[17] Here again we must be careful to distinguish absolute regional disparities from relative ones; the absolute gaps between rich and poor regions can rise while relative regional inequality falls.[18] Empirical investigations of the regional patterns of growth have been broadly consistent with Lewis's intuition: regional relative inequalities tend to rise in the early stages of economic development (as exemplified by the historical evidence available for many of today's rich countries), but inequality-decreasing processes of regional convergence start to emerge during more mature growth.[19]

Recall that "urban bias" was common in early development thinking in the decades following World War II (chapter 2). This was reinforced by the prevailing economic models. For a surprisingly long time, the theories of development did not allow for the possibility that a dynamic agricultural sector might drive poverty reduction; the sole driver of poverty reduction (albeit with rising inequality at least initially) was seen to be modern-sector enlargement. It was well understood from the outset that rural areas were poorer (in terms of incidence as well as sheer numbers of poor people), but the solution to their poverty was seen to be labor absorption from an expanding urban economy. However, a serious challenge to this view came with observations on the role played by agriculture in the early stages of the development of countries such as Japan and Taiwan.[20] An early stage of labor-augmenting technical change in agriculture was identified among successful countries (including in industrialization). Expanding the use of irrigation, fertilizers, and higher yielding crops boosted both yields and the demand for agricultural labor. From around 1980 a significant shift in development thinking and policymaking toward what has been dubbed *"traditional-sector enrichment"* was evident in the literature.[21] Chapter 9 will return to the policy debates on traditional-sector enrichment versus modern-sector enlargement as routes to poverty reduction.

A second inadequacy of the prevailing economic models up to the 1970s was that they ignored a seemingly important feature of developing economies: urban unemployment and (hence) *urban poverty*. In Part One of this book, we came across examples of how changes in the agricultural economy have at times displaced rural labor but without all of the displaced workers being able to find jobs in the urban economy.[22]

widely used in labor economics. For an overview of the large body of research instigated by Mincer's paper, see Heckman et al. (2003).

[17] Lewis (1976, 26).

[18] Recall the distinction between absolute and relative inequality discussed in chapter 5.

[19] An important early contribution on the evidence was made by Williamson (1965).

[20] See Ishikawa (1978, 1981) and Booth and Sundrum (1984).

[21] See Fields (1980).

[22] For example, we saw in chapter 1 that this was an important cause of the rise in urban poverty in England and Europe in the sixteenth century and in chapter 2 we heard about a similar process in the post–World War II US economy.

Lewis (1954) assumed that the modern-sector wage rate was set exogenously higher than the fixed subsistence wage in rural areas. He gave various reasons for such a differential including a trade union for manufacturing workers. This wage gap points to another concern about the model. Even though there is a rural labor surplus there is "full employment" in the (narrow) sense that all those "outsiders" who cannot get into the emerging modern sector form the residual rural workforce. However, there is a geographic dimension to the dualism here. Given transport costs to input and output markets, the modern sector will almost certainly be concentrated in urban areas. So there is a sense in which the Lewis model is not in equilibrium: all the rural workers will want to move to urban areas.

The Harris-Todaro Model

Well-intentioned policies can sometimes have unintended consequences. An example is when the Kenyan government in 1964 tried to reduce urban unemployment by providing extra government jobs in the capital city, Nairobi. There was an unexpected outcome: the chance of getting one of these new jobs attracted new workers from rural areas to Nairobi. Indeed, so many rural workers came that the urban unemployment rate actually rose. Harris and Todaro (1970) provided an economic model to help understand what went wrong with this policy, and this important model came to be widely used in development economics.

The Harris and Todaro (HT) model helped address some of the aforementioned concerns about early development models. The key feature of the model is that the wage rate in the high-wage, urban economy is fixed above the market-clearing level creating urban unemployment. Rural workers are attracted to the cities by the higher wages, but not all find work. The equilibrium is reached when workers no longer want to move, which requires that the rural wage rate has parity with the expected wage rate in the urban economy, allowing for the chance of unemployment. Box 8.9 explains the model further. A key feature of this model is that there is excessive migration from rural to urban areas, relative to the free mobility equilibrium with flexible wage rates. The Kenyan government's policy backfired because the extra work in urban areas attracted more rural workers, increasing Nairobi's unemployment rate.

Box 8.9 **The Harris-Todaro Model**

The urban manufacturing-sector wage rate is exogenously fixed above the market clearing level, such as due to a minimum wage law. No such institutions exist in rural areas (or are not enforceable), so the agricultural wage rate (W^r where the "r" is for rural) is flexible. If rural workers expect an earnings gain from moving to cities they will do so; otherwise not. A *free mobility equilibrium* is when nobody has an incentive to migrate. If you do not get an urban formal-sector job at the prevailing wage W^f, you end up stuck in the cities at a very

continued

Box 8.9 (Continued)

low standard of living, which we can think of as the urban informal sector wage rate, W^i. The expected wage rate for a rural migrant is a weighted average of W^f and W^i with weights given by the probabilities of getting each wage rate. Those probabilities are assumed to be equal to the average employment rates. So the expected urban wage rate is:

$$W^{ue} = \left(\frac{N^f}{N^f + N^i} \right) W^f + \left(\frac{N^i}{N^f + N^i} \right) W^i.$$

Here N^f, N^i are the proportions of the workforce that are in the urban formal and informal sectors, respectively. So the weights on the two urban wage rates are the respective shares of the urban workforce. Note that $N^f + N^i + N^r = 1$, where N^r is the proportion in the rural sector.

An equilibrium condition equates the rural wage rate with the expected wage rate in the urban economy, as given above. In the original HT model, the urban unemployed have zero income (although this can be relaxed). Then a migration equilibrium requires that $W^r = W^{ue}$.

Figure B8.9.1 illustrates the model for the special case in which $W^i = 0$ (as assumed by HT). The share of the workforce in urban areas is measured on the horizontal axis. (So the rural share can be read from right to left.) There are two MPL curves drawn, one for the urban formal sector and one for rural work. Notice that equilibrium requires that the area $(1 - N^r)W^r$ must equal the area $N^f W^f$. Notice also that the full-employment allocation of labor between sectors (which would drive the rural wage down to $W^{r\,min}$) is not consistent with equilibrium under free mobility, since it leaves an incentive for rural workers to move to the cities. The first rural worker to do so will have a very high chance of getting one of the high-wage urban jobs. The equilibrating factor is urban unemployment. The last worker to move will be indifferent between the rural wage and the expected wage in urban areas.

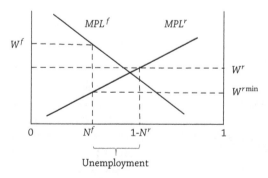

Figure B8.9.1 Equilibrium in the HT Model.

Further reading: There is a good discussion of the HT model in Ray (1998, ch. 10). Fields (1987) provides an overview of the critiques of the HT model and how they can or might be addressed. The HT model's stronger assumptions were relaxed in subsequent work. Sah and Stiglitz (1992, ch. 13) provide a more general formulation of the HT model in which the migration equilibrium requires the equalization of *expected utility* rather than expected wages. Suppose that the utility enjoyed by an urban resident (whether in a formal or informal sector job) is $U^u(W)$ at wage W, while the corresponding utility function for a rural worker is $U^r(W)$. A free mobility equilibrium now requires:

$$U^r(W^r) = \frac{N^f}{1 - N^r} U^u(W^f) + \frac{N^i}{1 - N^r} U^u(W^i).$$

This formulation can allow for greater urban amenity value as an additional attractor for rural migrants. El-Gamal (1994) provides a more complex dynamic version of the HT model, incorporating a learning process on the part of migrants.

The idea of labor market dualism (whereby the same workers had different wages depending on their sector of employment) was not new at the time the HT model was proposed, but the problem was now seen to rest squarely in the urban economy. The "poor" in this model can be interpreted as the urban unemployed and some share of the rural sector (depending on the distribution of non-labor assets). Labor-augmenting technical progress in the urban economy will now increase urban employment, thus reducing the poverty rate. Such technical progress may or may not reduce urban unemployment, since it may attract rural workers.[23] If rural workers are attracted, then the technical progress will raise the rural wage rate, giving another benefit to the rural poor.

However, higher agricultural productivity in the form of an exogenous increase in the marginal product of labor in the farm sector (at any given level of agricultural employment) will unambiguously reduce urban unemployment and reduce the gap between the urban and rural wage rates. In this model low farm productivity is a cause of high inequality and poverty.

The HT model treats the urban informal sector as a residual sector for those waiting for a formal sector job. Here Harris and Todaro were motivated by the urban labor markets they saw in Africa. The relevance is less clear to labor markets elsewhere. It has been argued that in some settings it is more realistic to view the informal sector

---

[23] I say "may" here because it is in fact theoretically ambiguous whether an exogenous increase in the MPL for the modern (urban) sector will reduce rural employment; the extra urban employment may come entirely from the urban unemployed. Using the calculus it can be shown that (for the model in box 8.9) as long as the (absolute) wage elasticity of demand for rural labor is not greater than $(1 - N^r) N^u / N^r$, then rural employment will fall and the rural wage rate will rise.

as an unregulated micro-entrepreneurial sector, with workers free to choose between it and the more secure formal sector.[24]

The HT model provided a foundation for thinking about development policy in the presence of dualistic labor markets, in which workers in the better off (urban) sector are protected by a binding minimum wage rate (and possibly other benefits and regulations). A number of potential policy responses can have perverse effects. Indeed, the HT model was motivated by the puzzle of why a policy of trying to reduce the urban unemployment rate by creating new government jobs in the cities had actually increased the unemployment rate (box 8.9). In section 8.5, we will discuss another policy response that may well have undesirable effects, namely restricting migration into urban areas.[25]

Labor-Market Frictions

The HT model assumes that the urban wage rate is exogenously fixed above the market-clearing level. This can be thought of as an institutional feature of the (stylized) economy. We can relax this assumption while still allowing for urban unemployment. One way is to introduce search costs into the model, which can generate frictional unemployment as a steady-state equilibrium of the dynamic process of matching workers with jobs.[26] The urban unemployed are then seen as waiting to find an urban job, which they may never find.[27] This perspective suggests policy implications, such as providing better information to market participants so as to improve the matching of workers and vacancies.

There is also a related set of concerns about the HT assumption of competitive (price and wage taking) firms in the urban economy. One could introduce an explicit labor union in the HT model, which has bargaining power over the urban wage rate. Alternatively, the non-competitive feature could well be on the labor demand side. It is known that if the labor market is characterized by monopsony power then a minimum wage rate will have the opposite effect to that found in the HT model: by forcing the monopsonist to behave more like a competitive firm it will increase urban employment at least up to some point (beyond which the employment reducing effect will come into play).[28] Nor did the basic HT model have an explicit urban

[24] Maloney (2004) argues for this interpretation based on evidence for several Latin American countries. Albrecht et al. (2009) provide a formal model consistent with this interpretation and discuss some policy implications.

[25] Another feature of the HT model is that it can be an example of a transfer paradox. Suppose that a small tax is levied on the urban wage and used to make a corresponding transfer to rural workers. Ravallion (1984) shows that (once equilibrium is restored) rural workers will end up worse off than before if the wage elasticity of demand for labor is higher in the urban manufacturing sector than in agriculture.

[26] Recall box 8.3 on the concept of a steady-state equilibrium.

[27] Dynamic models of the labor market with this feature are discussed in Pissarides (2000). An influential model was provided by Mortensen and Pissarides (1994). There is a useful overview of these models in Royal Swedish Academy of Science (2010) (prepared as background to the Nobel Prize awarded to Peter Diamond, Dale Mortensen, and Christopher Pissarides for their work on this topic).

[28] Monopsony power is said to exist if a single firm or set of colluding firms have the market power to set the wage below its competitive level.

informal sector; rather oddly, the urban unemployed appear to live on nothing. Also there was no difference between urban and rural areas in other (non-labor) respects; yet rural workers may well be attracted to urban areas even without an expected wage gain; this too could be relaxed. (Box 8.9 points to how some of these criticisms have been dealt with in the literature.)

There can also be unemployment in the rural labor market, although this takes a different form. Development models have treaded the rural economy in rather different ways. In the HT model unemployment is only found in the urban labor market while Lewis had made a very different assumption, namely, that there was a labor surplus in rural areas, with the wage rate essentially fixed at a subsistence level. As economists learned more about developing economies, they realized that there was rural unemployment, especially in the lean season for agriculture, and that this was associated with poverty.[29] This is still true in rural areas; for example, in rural India in 2010, 15% of the poorest households (in terms of consumption per person) reported a spell of unemployment in the previous week, falling to 5% for the richest.[30]

New models appeared in the literature that could explain the existence of unemployment in rural areas despite the absence of any institutional impediments to falling wages (such as binding minimum wage rates or trade unions). The most important example is the *efficiency wage hypothesis*. This assumes that output depends on both the quality and quantity of the labor inputs, with quality determined by the individual consumption levels of workers.[31] By the usual version of the model labor input is assumed to be weighted by an "efficiency index," which depends positively on the wage rate.[32] There have been a number of interpretations of this index. One of them is that a lower wage rate means that workers will be less well-nourished and so be less productive. Other interpretations point to the possibility that a lower wage encourages higher labor turnover, shirking on the job, or simply reduces the morale of workers, again making them less productive. Given its efficiency index, each firm chooses a wage (and, hence, quality of workers) to maximize profits, taking account of the efficiency cost of a lower wage rate. If the firm's chosen wage exceeds the supply price of labor, then the firm will resist wage cutting and the wage rate will stay above its market-clearing level. There will be unemployment.

Another potentially important modification to standard models is in what they assume about price adjustment out of equilibrium. The standard assumption of competitive market adjustment is that prices and wages adjust rapidly to reach the new equilibrium. (Recall box 1.5.) But that is a strong assumption. Consider a shock to food prices (such as we saw globally in 2008). The standard assumption can lead one to expect that poor net consumers of food (spending more on food than their revenue from food production) will be protected to at least some degree from such price shocks.[33] That is hard to reconcile with what we see on the ground. However, what

---

[29] For an overview of this literature, see Lipton and Ravallion (1995).

[30] See Alik Lagrange and Ravallion (2014), using nationally representative survey data for rural India in 2009–10. "Unemployment" was defined as an adult household member reporting at least one half day of unemployment in the previous week.

[31] See Leibenstein (1957) and Bliss and Stern (1978).

[32] See Mirrlees (1975) and Stiglitz (1976).

[33] See, e.g., Jacoby (2013), using data for India.

the models are missing is that, in practice, there are frictions, such as the search and transaction costs noted above in the context of the urban labor market. This applies to other markets too, evident as lags in price and wage adjustment. An implication of these frictions is that inflationary shocks (typically coming through the goods markets) can bring welfare losses. For example, in a study for Bangladesh, it was shown that a rise in nominal food prices had large and adverse short-term effects on the rural poor due to the stickiness of wage adjustment.[34] The protection afforded by competitive labor-market corrections did come eventually, but the adverse welfare effects on poor people were large over a year or two.[35]

The HT model is an important example of how the living conditions of the rural poor can be linked to those of the urban poor. In the HT model such a "horizontal linkage" is assured by the migration equilibrium condition, whereby the agricultural wage rate comes into parity with the expected wage rate in the urban economy. Another important source of linkage is through remittances from urban workers who have migrated to their families back in rural areas. Trade in common markets (for basic needs) also create such linkages. Furthermore, there are reasons to suspect that these linkages are stronger for poor people than for the rich. The elites in the two sectors may well have weaker connections in some respects, especially due to migration and remittances. Indeed, there may well be very few people in rural areas living at similar levels to the urban elites. One can think of this as a ladder in which the lower rungs are firm but the top rungs are weak or nonexistent. Thus, we can also expect that growth favoring the poor in one sector can have distributional effects on the other sector. We will return at times to such distributional linkages between urban and rural sectors.

As we have seen in this discussion, the *urbanization process* has long played a key role in development theory. A common feature of these various models is that population urbanization (given that poverty is initially concentrated in the rural sector) is poverty reducing. Yet at the same time there may well be too much migration and, even if that is not the case, the process may well be associated with rising urban poverty. This has led to some important development policy debates, which we take up in chapter 9.

Modern Growth Economics

The modern theory of economic growth emerged in the 1950s in two papers, by Robert Solow (1956) and Trevor Swan (1956). The prevailing Harrod-Domar model was seen as too rigid, with its exogenously fixed savings rate and fixed output per unit of capital. The contribution of the Solow-Swan model was to introduce the scope for substituting

[34] See Ravallion (1990c).

[35] Advocates of the competitive market model often acknowledged that there may be lags in wage adjustment but argue that they only apply in the "very short term" (Jacoby 2013, 3). However, without a specification of the dynamics of market adjustment out of equilibrium it is not clear what this means. One is reminded of Keynes's comment (box 1.22) that "economists set themselves too easy, too useless a task if in tempestuous seasons they can only tell us that when the storm is long past the ocean is flat again."

capital for labor in production. This feature was introduced by postulating a smooth aggregate production function, giving GDP as a smooth function of labor and capital inputs. But the model shared another weakness of the Harrod-Domar model, namely that the savings rate was taken to be exogenous. In fact the essential ingredients for a model with endogenous savings had already been in place, following Ramsey's (1928) paper on optimal savings (box 8.4). With some extensions (adding in population growth and/or capital depreciation), we could have had a more general Solow-Swan model thirty years earlier.[36] But history put some important distractions in the way, notably Ramsey's untimely death, the Great Depression, and World War II!

Box 8.10 The Solow-Swan Model

The model assumes that output is produced from homogeneous labor and capital under CRS (box 8.2). The labor force is taken to grow at an exogenous rate. There is one representative agent. The economy need not be in its steady-state equilibrium. Capital will accumulate over time if the investment rate exceeds the rate of depreciation of capital. Conversely, the capital stock will fall if depreciation exceeds the rate of investment. A fixed share of output in any period, $s.f(k)$, is invested and capital depreciates at the constant rate δ. The increment to capital per worker in any time period t is then the difference between the amount invested and depreciation:

$$k_{t+1} - k_t = s.f(k_t) - \delta k_t.$$

Each economy has a unique steady-state level of capital per worker, and (hence) output. Figure B8.10.1 illustrates these features. When the investment rate exceeds the depreciation rate, the capital stock will grow toward its steady-state value k^* yielding steady-state output per worker y^*. (Notice that the equilibrium at (k^*, y^*) is stable; see box 8.2.) Conversely, when the depreciation rate exceeds the investment rate, the capital stock will contract until the steady-state level of capital is reached.

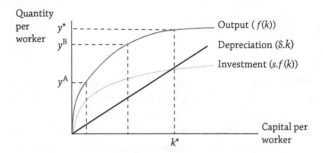

Figure B8.10.1 Equilibrium in the Solow-Swan Model.

continued

---

[36] As pointed out by Newbery (1990).

Box 8.10 **(Continued)**

This model implies higher growth rates in poorer countries, conditional on their steady-state income. Consider two growing countries (A and B) with the same steady-state level of capital and output per worker. Hence, we say *conditional* convergence, as we control for the steady-state levels. One country (A) is poorer than the other, but both expand toward their (common) steady state, with growth falling to zero when they reach that point. Given diminishing MPK the poorer country, with lower capital per worker, will grow faster; its investment rate is the same but its higher MPK yields a higher output gain.

The question is left begging as to why investment rates and (hence) steady-state levels of income differ.

Historical note: Robert Solow developed his model of economic growth at the age of thirty, at MIT, where he spent most of his career. (Solow won the Nobel Prize in 1987 for his work on the theory of growth.) The basic ideas of the model are also found in the independent paper by Swan (1956). Trevor Swan spent most of his career at the Australian National University.

Further reading: As for box 8.2.

An important implication of the Solow-Swan model for debates about poverty lies in the idea of a process of *convergence* in mean incomes across countries with different starting points but with similar and unique long-run mean incomes. The model was interpreted by some observers as implying that there was an automatic self-correcting process whereby a high initial level of poverty would eventually be reduced by economic growth. By this argument, countries starting out with a low mean income (and hence high absolute poverty rate) would tend to have a higher marginal product of capital (given that they had so much less capital per worker and that there are diminishing returns), which would entail a higher rate of economic growth than for a growing high-income country with a similar rate of investment (box 8.10). And so the initially poorer country would eventually catch up. Strictly this was a process of dynamic transition, not a model for explaining differences in the steady-state level of income. However, with suitable controls for the latter, a body of empirical work confirmed the prediction of conditional convergence.[37]

Since the Solow-Swan model is an aggregate model, with no heterogeneity, it was a questionable foundation for arguing that poverty would be self-correcting. There was no inequality in this model. It would take another fifteen years to see inequality of wealth appearing explicitly in the Solow-type model.[38] With no market failures, inequality-reducing dynamic forces could be identified in this extended growth model. In due course it would also come to be understood that market failures—such as those

[37] Following an important early contribution by Barro and Sala-i-Martin (1992).
[38] This was done by Stiglitz (1969).

due to asymmetric information in the credit market (as discussed in chapter 2)—had important implications for distributional dynamics, including the possibility that inequality and poverty could persist.

As Solow was well aware, a modified version of this model can readily yield a poverty trap (though Solow did not use that term, which emerged later in the literature). The original (1956) paper outlined one possible trap, arising from assumed nonlinearities in how population growth rates depend on mean income, with population growth falling at low incomes but rising with higher incomes, then tapering off at higher incomes. The model would then have multiple steady-state solutions, including a "low-level attractor," meaning a stable but low level of mean income. A country that finds itself in such an equilibrium will need a large gain in capital per worker to escape the trap, and move to a path of sustainably positive growth. (We return to consider various sources of poverty traps.)

The mid-1950s also saw a renewal of interest in so-called "Malthusian" arguments about how an economy could be trapped in poverty.[39] Here the mechanism was through endogenous population growth. At low levels of capital per worker, income would be so low, and the death rate so high, that (it was assumed) population growth rates would be very low (or even negative). At somewhat higher capital per worker higher population growth rates would be seen, though tapering off and possibly with declining population at high income levels. The model was completed by the rising investment function, such as in box 8.10. This set-up generated a poverty trap—a stable low level of capital per worker. It also implied the existence of a higher level steady state which was unstable; with a sufficient boost to capital per worker the economy would move onto a continuing growth path. This type of model was not, however, empirically well-grounded (even from what we knew at the time in the 1950s). In particular, the characterization of population growth ignored the high fertility rates in poor countries, which entailed that population growth rates tended to be higher the poorer the country. Allowing for this, the poverty trap was no longer implied.

Just as the Great Depression (understandably) saw a displacement of interest in issues of long-run growth (in favor of a focus on stabilization and understanding crises) research on long-run economic growth lost favor during the crises-prone 1970s and 1980s. The mid-1980s saw a renewal of interest in long-run growth, and (similarly to the 1950s) the new work had clear roots in former economic thought. Greater attention was given to the sources of *technical progress*—how to produce more from given inputs of labor, capital and land. The role and special nature of technology had long been recognized. Alfred Marshall (1890) recognized knowledge and organization as inputs to production, but inputs (like capital goods) that were themselves produced. The Solow-Swan model implied that we would not see sustained growth unless technology continually improved. However, the productivity of a specific firm may well depend on the overall capital–labor ratio in the economy as a whole—interpretable as endogenous technology.[40] Later this became a key feature of a series

---

[39] Notably in Nelson (1956) and Solow (1956).

[40] See Frankel (1962) and Aghion and Howitt (1998).

of so-called "AK model" of endogenous growth.[41] Important contributions in the late 1980s built on the idea that new knowledge was produced in a process of "learning-by-doing."[42] The new models of endogenous growth postulated the existence of an externality or spillover effect, whereby the overall productivity of a firm's own capital and labor inputs depending on the actions by other firms, including their expenditures on research and development.[43] This line of thinking recognized a big difference between knowledge of new technologies and ordinary capital goods, which tend to be highly excludable, in that one firm's use of (say) a machine precludes others using that same machine. That is less clear for knowledge, since it can be hard to prevent others using the same idea. This non-rival nature of ideas creates an economic problem, in that individual firms may face too little incentive to invest in new knowledge. To show how technological innovation can still happen, Paul Romer (1990) postulated a model of what is called "monopolistic competition," whereby firms could enjoy extra rents to compensate for their sunk costs of developing new technologies and new products. Thus, technology and (hence) productivity growth became endogenous, and we could start to talk about how the policy and institutional environment might foster, or impede, that growth. By the same token, bad policies, including weak institutions for enforcing property rights, could impede economic advancement.

Scholars still debate just how much policy reforms can bring about a sustainably higher growth rate. Some pointed to the fact that we have seen lasting reforms in the industrialized countries—new openness to trade, better investment climates, more schooling—but not any higher long-run growth rate.[44] (The experience of many developing countries since the 1990s appears to provide a counterexample, however.) In a modified version of the Romer (1990) model incorporating decreasing returns to new knowledge, Charles Jones (1995) shows that, although growth in this modified model is still generated endogenously through research and development, this does not matter to the model's long-run growth rate. Indeed, in Jones's model the long-run growth rate depends on little more than the rate of population growth.[45]

Institutions and Growth

In trying to understand the large and persistent cross-country differences in real incomes, a number of economists and political scientists have pointed to the differences found in *institutions*, defined as the set of prevailing man-made constraints on human interaction, including trade.[46] A strand of the modern literature on long-run growth has emphasized the role played by a number of institutional factors—closed politically regimes, weak state capacities for efficiently raising revenue, poorly enforced property rights, governmental restrictions on labor mobility—in retarding

[41] The "AK" label came from the way the production function is often assumed, in which output was given by $AK^\alpha L^{1-\alpha}$ (the Cobb-Douglas form with CRS; recall box 8.2).

[42] Arrow (1962) was influential here.

[43] Important contributions included Romer (1986, 1990) and Lucas (1988). An earlier paper by Frankel (1962) had been influential.

[44] This is pointed out by Jones (1995).

[45] Aghion and Howitt (1998, ch. 12) provide an interesting commentary on this debate, though more advanced analytic methods are called for.

[46] This is essentially the definition of institutions proposed by North (1990).

the scope for sustained economic growth.[47] Some of the literature points to the possibility of *threshold effects*. Once a certain level of state capacity and institutional development is reached, innovation, domestic market expansion, diversification, and structural transformation become feasible, and these reinforce further institutional development in a progressive cycle. Reaching that threshold has been crucial for the economic success of Western Europe and North America.[48]

In their book *Why Nations Fail* Daron Acemoglu and James Robinson (2012) argue that "inclusive political institutions"—essentially, reasonably democratic governments, as distinct from "extractive" regimes only serving the interests of the ruling elite—are a crucial precondition for sustained economic growth.[49] Acemoglu and Robinson point to many examples in world history that can be interpreted consistently with their theory. There is also a persistence to instituions. Economic institutions unfavorable to investment and growth can still serve the interests of local elites, and so be hard to change when those elites are powerful. Politics is thus seen as being at the root of understanding failed states.[50]

The degree of security provided by the state for individual property rights has long been seen as a key factor. Since at least Adam Smith it has been argued that insecure property rights discourage investment, given the risk that the owner will not be able to reap the benefits of his investment. Insecurity of property rights, often associated with unpredictable and unaccountable expropriations of private wealth by powerful predatory rulers, has come to be seen as a serious institutional impediment to longer-term economic development.

As Smith also recognized, sound economic institutions are themselves created. Weak states in terms of their administrative capacity foster inefficient economies and thus perpetuate poverty. A key factor here is how governments raise their revenues. They do so in ways that are more costly to growth—creating insecure property rights—when they lack the administrative capacity for more efficient forms of taxation. Timothy Besley and Torsten Persson (2011) provide an economic analysis of how state capacities develop endogenously as investments by governments. When a government faces little external threat or has ample natural resources it will rationally choose to invest little in administrative capacity, fostering low investment and growth over the longer term.

How do poverty and inequality fit into this story? Economically dysfunctional institutions that do little more than serve the interests of a ruling elite clearly help perpetuate poverty, and probably increase inequality. Better (in the sense of "pro-market") institutions alone offer some hope for poor people, but it must be judged a rather limited hope based on experience. The favored institutions tend in practice

---

[47] An overview of the literature on the role of institutions in promoting long-run growth can be found in Acemoglu et al. (2005, sec. 2). The modern economic analysis of the origins of state capacity owes much to Besley and Persson (2010, 2011).

[48] Arguments along these lines can be found in North and Thomas (1973), North (1990) and Morris and Adelman (1988).

[49] *Why Nations Fail* is an ambitious book, so it is not surprising that it has received both praise and criticism. The review by Green (2012) provides links to other reviews.

[50] Sections 8.4 and 9.10 discuss Acemoglu and Robinson (2012) further in the context of a case study of China and aid policies respectively.

to perform less well for poorer people. Legal enforcement, including of property rights, is typically less reliable for the poor. (Indeed, in economies where property rights of the well-off were quite well protected, some poor people suffered the theft of the most fundamental property right of all, namely ownership of their own bodies, through enslavement.) This distributional aspect does not get sufficient attention in thinking about the role of pro-market institutions. As a working hypothesis, we can expect that in countries where institutions are less inclusive of the rights and needs of poor people we will see less equitable growth processes, with slower progress against poverty. Section 8.3 reviews some research testing this hypothesis. Chapter 9 returns to the topic of institutions in the context of policies for fighting poverty.

Factor Distribution and Growth

It will be recalled that the principle concern of classical economics was the factor distribution of income—how income is divided between labor and capital (which we can take to include land) (chapter 1). From the time of the Second Poverty Enlightenment, attention turned to inter-personal distribution. And, as we saw in chapter 3, poverty and inequality are defined and measured in terms of the latter distribution, so this change of emphasis makes sense in the present context. However, factor distribution can have an important bearing on inter-personal distribution, so it should not be ignored.

How will factor distribution change with growth in a capitalist economy? The models in the classical and Marxist tradition suggested that distribution would shift against labor. For example, Nicholas Kaldor (1955) derived the share of profits in output as a function of: (1) the differential rate of savings for capitalists and workers; (2) the "capital-output ratio" (the ratio of investment to the increment in output) and (3) the exogenous growth rate of output. This model was interpreted as indicating that, *ceteris paribus*, a higher growth would shift the shares of output toward profits away from labor, again suggesting an inequitable process. However, this could be mitigated by changes in the other two factors.

The properties of the production function also have bearing on how factor distribution evolves with economic growth. Rising capital per worker will naturally put upward pressure on capital's share of income. But there will be an offsetting decline in the marginal product of capital relative to that for labor (given diminishing marginal products, as explained in box 8.2). Which of these two effects dominates depends on whether the elasticity of substitution is below unity; if it is then we can expect rising capital per worker to come with a *rise* in the income share going to labor.

A renewed interest in long-run income distribution came with a much-read, and much-debated, book by Piketty (2014), *Capital in the Twenty-First Century*.[51] To understand the argument of this book one must first be clear on what is meant by "capital." Piketty's capital is not the "K" in a standard production function (box 8.2). Rather, it is non-human wealth—a diverse composite of all marketable assets; this includes physical capital but also financial capital and real property, but it excludes

---

[51] By January 2015, the book had sold 1.5 million copies in multiple languages.

human capital. This level of aggregation may mask important differences between types of assets. Some components of wealth are not productive in the sense in which physical capital (k in the production function) is productive. For example, the steep rise in housing prices seen in many rich countries since 2000 will push up the value of Piketty's "capital," but this will not raise output as normally measured; the rise in house prices may be a short-term effect of financial and monetary policies rather than a sustainable long-term trend.

The gap between the rate of return to this concept of capital and the rate of growth in GDP plays an important role in Piketty's analysis. Some of the annual return (r) to Piketty capital is consumed, leaving a share s to be reinvested. Then income from capital grows at the rate $s.r$.[52] If this is greater than the rate of growth in mean income (g), then the capitalists' share of total income will rise. Since ownership of capital tends to be very unequally distributed, overall income inequality will also rise. Thus, we can expect to see rising income inequality whenever the growth rate of income per capita is sufficiently low relative to the rate of return to capital.[53]

Piketty presents an ambitious compilation of evidence from diverse sources spanning two hundred years to argue that the rate of return to his broad concept of capital has historically exceeded g (and by a wide margin) such that the income share of capital has been rising, putting upward pressure on overall inequality in the rich world. He also argues that we have been seeing such a rise in inequality in the United States, Britain, and France.[54] (We already saw this for the United States in chapter 2.) The middle half of the twentieth century until around 1980 was (Piketty argues) the exception to this trend whereby the rate of return on non-human wealth (after tax and losses) fell below the growth rate, thus attenuating the higher inequalities of the past. Wars, high taxes on inheritance and incomes, nationalizations, and the Great Depression kept down the rate of return on capital and (hence) inequality. However, according to Piketty, this was an aberration.

Looking forward, Piketty argues that inequality will continue to rise as the growth rates of advanced capitalist economies fall. That is only one possible scenario. There are two forces that can act to slow the rise in inequality or even prevent it. The first is that one can expect higher rates of capital accumulation to bring down the rate of return on capital. This is what the idea of diminishing returns tells us (box 1.12). Piketty accepts this idea and points to evidence suggesting that diminishing returns have been setting in over recent times. However, he contends that this effect will not be strong enough to stall the rise in income inequality. Empirically, he argues that over the long run the capital-income ratio has co-moved with capital's share of income, despite some tendency for the rate of return on capital to fall as capital accumulates.

---

[52] If the rate of interest on a bank deposit is r% per annum and that income flow is fully reinvested, then the capital stock will grow at r% per annum as will the annual income from capital.

[53] The word "sufficiently" is needed to allow for consumption from capital income.

[54] Such an ambitious data effort will inevitably involve many assumptions, some of which might be questioned. For example, in one such critique, Giles (2014) questioned Piketty's claim that wealth inequality was rising in Britain. This critique rested on combining tax-based estimates with more recent survey-based estimates, which are likely to underestimate wealth at the high-end (as discussed in chapter 2). A consistent series based on tax-records supports Piketty's interpretation of the evidence.

The key issue here is how much substitutability there is between capital and labor in production, as measured by the elasticity of substitution (box 8.2). For example, imagine if capital and labor are perfectly substitutable; then having more capital would not make any difference to output (i.e., the returns to capital would not fall). As capital per worker rises one expects the rate of return to capital to fall. Piketty argues that the elasticity of substitution exceeds unity, so that there is enough substitutability that the rate of return to capital will not fall much as the capital stock rises. Some critics have argued otherwise.[55] Piketty points to evidence of sufficiently high elasticity of substitution for his argument to be right in the rich world, although it is less clear for the developing world. Piketty's evidence is mainly based on the long-term co-movement he finds between the capital-income ratio and the share of capital. However, note (again) that Piketty's "capital" is the heterogeneous; while we can expect substitutability between machines—industrial capital—and labor, that is not so clear for real property, some important components of which (notably housing) are not productive. The long-term co-movement that Piketty finds between the capital-income ratio and the income share of capital may well reflect other forces operating on the non-productive components of Piketty capital such as real property booms.[56]

The second potentially offsetting force is if lower growth rates lead capitalists to save less. Even if $r > g$, as long as s falls enough, capital's income share will not rise. To the extent that owners of capital start to consume more from their income (and so reinvest less) once the economy as a whole is expanding less rapidly, the rise in capital's share of national income will be attenuated. Without a better understanding of savings behavior we cannot say whether or not this adjustment will take place. Will the owners of capital feel compelled to let their capital keep growing indefinitely in the far less dynamic but rich economy of the future? Would the rich advocate less economic growth to boost their income share? The motives of capitalists are puzzling in Piketty's model, and by assuming that the savings rate is constant, Piketty rules out this potential correction mechanism.[57]

One might also anticipate a political economy response that would restore many of the conditions that kept down the rate of return on capital in the period 1920–80. However, there is also the potential for social instability and distortionary political responses that could also undermine growth prospects.

If one considers what has been happening to the incidence of poverty there is an important difference between the old period (roughly pre–World War I) of rising inequality in America and the new one (since around 1980): in the former period, poverty was falling but that has not been the case in the current period. From a Rawlsian perspective, the rise in inequality in America prior to World War I can be judged more morally defensible to that in the current period.

---

[55] For example, Hassett (2014) argues that returns to capital will fall more quickly than Piketty thinks, given limited substitution possibilities.

[56] Stiglitz (2014) discusses these issues further. One point Stiglitz makes is that the recent rise in the value of Piketty capital reflects the real property boom since the 1980s stemming from financial market deregulation in the United States.

[57] Krusell and Smith (2014) criticize this aspect of Piketty's analysis, arguing that it implies economically implausible savings behavior. Also see Ray's (2014) review of Piketty (2014).

How Inequality and Poverty Can Retard Growth

The tradition in development economics up until around 2000 viewed changes in distribution as the outcomes of the growth process. More recently, arguments have been made suggesting the reverse causation, whereby the initial distribution is seen an underlying determinant of growth and subsequent distributional changes.

Recall from chapter 1 that a strand of thought back to the mercantilists has essentially argued that a more unequal initial distribution of income ensured a higher long-run mean income for any given initial mean. The precise form of this argument evolved over time and there were differences among exponents. Some believed that growth would, in due course, help reduce poverty while others thought this unlikely. Incentives always played a role in the arguments, though rarely with much evidence beyond anecdotes. Mercantilists worried about adverse effects of higher wages on work effort and export competitiveness. Later arguments suggested that inadequate aggregate savings constrained growth. By this view, in a fully employed (closed) economy, capital accumulation is constrained by a low aggregate domestic savings, and rich people can naturally afford to save more than can poor people. Thus—the argument went—efforts to redistribute income in favor of the poor risked retarding growth and (hence) had ambiguous implications for poverty reduction.

The twentieth century saw a number of new ideas challenging such "utility of poverty" arguments. As we learned in chapter 1, there was an early hint of this challenge in Marshall (1890). Similarly, in the 1920s and 1930s, Gunnar Myrdal believed that "an equalization in favor of the low-income strata was also a productive investment in the quality of people and their productivity" (Myrdal 1988, 154). But there was little immediate take-up of these ideas.

It appears to have been long understood that rich people saved a greater share of income than poor people, who were often assumed to save nothing.[58] It would then have been only a small step to the conclusion that a higher poverty rate at a given mean income would yield lower aggregate savings and (hence) a lower growth rate in any economy for which aggregate savings constrained growth. But that conclusion was never drawn to my knowledge. It was, however, understood at least back to the 1930s that the same property of the savings function implied a growth–equity trade-off, whereby higher inequality would generate higher savings and (hence) higher growth. Recall that Keynes (1936, ch. 24) questioned the existence of such a trade-off in an economy in which lack of aggregate effective demand was the constraining factor preventing economic growth (box 1.22).

In the 1990s, we started to see some serious questioning of the instrumental case for poverty and inequality even in a fully employed economy. By this view, poor and/or unequal societies stifled investment, invention, and reform.[59] These ideas opened up a new window on the potential role of antipoverty policies in economic development.

One argument as to why poverty could self-perpetuate (in the absence of effective policies) relates to the idea that (1) poverty fosters a high rate of population growth

---

[58] As in the models of Kalecki (1942) and Kaldor (1955).

[59] Voitchovsky (2009) provides a survey of the arguments and evidence on how the initial level of inequality influences the subsequent growth rate.

which (2) entails lower economic growth. The latter step in the argument can be rationalized in terms of standard models of economic growth, such as the Solow-Swan model discussed above. A higher rate of growth of the labor force dilutes the capital stock. A higher rate of population growth acts in a similar way to a higher rate of depreciation in lowering the steady state level of capital per worker and (hence) mean income (box 8.10).[60] Step (1) requires that we also consider distribution. The modern version of this argument emphasizes the role played by inequality. An undeniably important dimension of inequality in the world is that people living in poorer families tend to be less healthy and to die sooner (chapter 7). This and other factors—including a dependence on children for old-age support and inequalities in maternal education—play a key role in generating another socioeconomic gradient: fertility rates tend to be higher in poor families. On balance, the natural rate of population growth tends also to be higher for the poor. Thus, we can expect lower rates of progress against poverty in countries with higher population growth rates, and there is some supportive evidence.[61]

These arguments have been seen to support claims about what is sometimes called the "demographic dividend" from policies that reduce fertility in developing countries. By this view, lower fertility rates promote lower dependency rates, i.e., more workers for the number of dependent children. This is expected to bring an immediate gain in household consumption per person and a longer-term gain through the enhanced quality of the workforce, notably through the greater investments that parents can afford to make in the quality of their children, notably their schooling. However, we should be cautious about the policy implications drawn from such arguments if the policies used to reduce fertility come with welfare costs to parents, as has sometimes been the case.[62]

An important strand of the late twentieth-century literature pointed to the implications of borrowing constraints associated with asymmetric information and the inability to write binding enforceable contracts. Credit market failure leaves unexploited opportunities for investment in physical and human capital and there are assumed to be a diminishing marginal product of capital. (This idea can be extended to also embrace technical innovation, assuming that everyone gets new ideas, but that the poor are more constrained in responding.) In such a model we expect that wealth-poor and credit-constrained people will have a higher marginal product of extra capital than better-off households. However, the credit constraints entail that the poor cannot realize their potential. Then higher current inequality of wealth implies lower (or at least no higher) future mean wealth at a given value of current mean wealth.

This argument can be formalized with a simple dynamic model of personal wealth incorporating a borrowing constraint. "Wealth" is used here in a broad sense, including

---

[60] Evidence of an adverse effect of population growth on the growth rate of GDP per capita can be found in Kelley and Schmidt (1995, 2001) and Williamson (2001).

[61] Evidence can be found in Eastwood and Lipton (1999, 2001), who regressed changes over time in poverty measures for a cross-section of countries on the fertility rate (with various controls) and found an adverse demographic effect on poverty. Using time series data for India, Datt and Ravallion (1998a) find evidence that higher rates of population growth were poverty increasing.

[62] On the adverse welfare consequences of the coercive efforts sometimes made to encourage poor women in developing countries to have fewer children see Hartmann (1987).

human capital—education, health, and nutrition—as well as physical capital. The key feature of the model is that mean future wealth in a growing economy will depend on the initial level of inequality; a mean-preserving increase in wealth inequality will entail lower mean wealth in the future (i.e., a lower growth rate). The intuition is that the more wealth-poor people, the more credit constrained people, and hence the greater the number of unexploited investment opportunities, which means less growth. Box 8.11 explains the idea in more formal terms.

Box 8.11 **Growth and Inequality in a Credit-Constrained Economy**

There is some initial distribution of wealth in the economy. The level of wealth for an individual at date t is w_t. A fixed share of the person's current wealth is used to augment current consumption, leaving the remainder for the next period. Each person has a production function yielding an output in the amount $f(k)$ from the person's own capital stock k. (Recall box 8.2.) Given the interest rate there is a desired capital stock equating the MPK with the interest rate. Let k^* denote the individual's desired capital stock.

Because lenders are imperfectly informed about borrowers the lenders only allow a person to borrow up to λ times her wealth. There are two wealth strata. First, there are those with wealth less than $w^{**} = k^*/(\lambda + 1)$. (Notice that $w < k^*/(\lambda + 1)$ implies that current wealth plus maximum borrowing is less than desired capital stock.) Someone in this group has a desire to invest but is constrained such that her MPK exceeds the interest rate, given the borrowing constraint.

Those in the second group—with wealth above w^{**}—are free to implement their desired investments. For this group the borrowing constraint no longer binds, that is, someone in this group is able to invest her unconstrained optimal amount equating the MPK with the prevailing interest rate. If the MPK is greater than the interest rate, then more will be invested, bringing down the MPK, and the opposite holds if the MPK is less than the interest rate.

Now consider the dynamics of wealth for each person. (It may help to review boxes 8.2 and 8.3.) The recursion diagram takes the form of the bold line in figure B8.11.1. For the first group, with initial wealth up to w^{**}, the curvature in the recursion diagram reflects the person's own production function. Because of the credit constraint, a person with wealth less than w^{**} depends on her own production function, which has diminishing returns. For those in the richer group, with wealth above w^{**}, the own-production function is no longer a constraint, since they are free to implement their personally preferred investments.

The unique stable equilibrium is at the wealth w^*. There is also a "destitution equilibrium" at zero wealth. However, it is not stable; any small gain in wealth will put the destitute onto a growth path toward their own long-run equilibrium at w^*. In this model there can be a large long-term gain from even a small transfer to the destitute (at zero wealth), as it will nudge them out of their low-level equilibrium.

continued

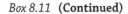

Box 8.11 (Continued)

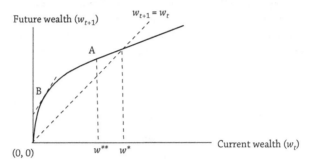

Figure B8.11.1 Nonlinear Recursion Diagram Due to a Credit Constraint.

There will also be aggregate gains from certain inequality-reducing redistributions of wealth. Consider two people, at points A and B, both of whom are investing and seeing growth as they move toward their steady-state level of wealth at w^*. Now imagine a redistribution of wealth from richer A to poorer B, for whom the credit constraint is binding. The MPK is lower for A than B, so it is clear that aggregate output rises; the absolute loss of output for A will be less than the gain to B. Thus, the mean value of future wealth at given mean current wealth will depend on the extent of inequality in the initial distribution; the higher the inequality the lower the growth rate. There will also be such aggregate gains from redistributions from those who are not credit-constrained toward those who are. However, there will be no such gains from redistributions among those who are not constrained (i.e., wealth greater than w^{**}).

There is another observation one can make about this model. Plainly, a larger density of people near the zero wealth equilibrium will entail lower subsequent growth for a given initial mean. It is assumed that the poverty line does not exceed $k^*/(\lambda + 1)$ and let H_t^* denote the poverty rate (headcount index) at this maximum poverty line. Now consider the growth effect of a mean-preserving increase in the poverty rate. I assume that H_t^* increases and that no individual with wealth less than $k^*/(\lambda + 1)$ becomes better off. If this holds, then we can say that poverty is unambiguously higher. Then the simple fact of a credit constraint implies that unambiguously higher current poverty incidence—defined by any poverty line up to the minimum level of initial wealth needed to not be liquidity constrained in investment—yields lower growth at a given level of mean current wealth.

Note on the literature: The above model is due to Banerjee and Duflo (2003, sec. 3.2), though with antecedents in the literature (as noted by Banerjee and Duflo), including Aghion and Bolton (1997) and Piketty (1997). Banerjee and Duflo make the point about inequality. Ravallion (2014a) demonstrates the last point about poverty.

Other sources of economic inefficiencies can create inequalities as well. This can happen if a relatively privileged subgroup is able to restrict entry and thus set their wage rate or output price profit above the market clearing level. Recall the HT model (box 8.9). Microeconomic foundations for the type of wage inequality postulated in that model are provided by the "insider-outsider" model of a labor market in which the insiders (with jobs) negotiate their wages with a view to keeping themselves employed, while the unemployed are essentially disenfranchised, with little or no influence unless there is an exogenous boost to demand.[63] When such non-competitive features are present in the labor market, we will find higher inequality and mean income almost certainly falls. In the HT model, the gaps between the urban wage rates and other wages are sources of inequality that lower total output. The greater the gap the lower the share of the population that get the high-wage jobs and (hence) the higher the poverty rate.

Labor-market failures in the form of persistent unemployment can also have lasting adverse consequences for both equity and efficiency; this happens when there is duration dependence in unemployment, whereby the longer a person is unemployed the less likely he or she will find a job. There are a number of ways this can happen. Human capital is developed in part by working; thus longer spells of unemployment create a de-skilling that makes it harder to get a job. Another way this can happen is that unemployment is associated with psychological distress and depression.[64] This psychological scarring may make it harder to get a job.

One channel whereby high inequality can impede growth is via the security of rights over property and contract enforcement. One study found that high inequality (measured in terms of income, land, and ethnic polarization) is associated with poorer enforcement of rights at country level.[65] Furthermore, the study found the adverse impact of inequality on growth is attenuated once one controls for rights enforcement.

Inequality is also thought to promote crime, which can be expected to reduce an economy's overall output. In a narrow sense, the wealthy have the most to lose from theft, and the poor have most to gain from it. This has motivated arguments that areas with higher inequality tend to have higher crime rates.[66] There is supportive evidence for this correlation.[67]

Another class of models is based on the idea that high inequality restricts efficiency-enhancing cooperation, such that key public goods are underprovided, or

---

[63] Blanchard and Summers (1986) provided an influential early model with these features. A large literature has since studied the potential for hysteresis in unemployment whereby the economy's "natural rate of unemployment" (the rate that is consistent with a constant rate of inflation) at any date depends positively on past levels of unemployment. For a review in the context of dynamic macroeconomic models, see O'Shaughnessy (2011).

[64] See Mossakowski's (2009) study of the psychological effects of unemployment on young people in the United States.

[65] See Keefer and Knack (2002).

[66] As argued in an influential paper by Ehrlich (1973).

[67] See Ehrlich (1973), Witt et al. (1999), Fajnzylber et al. (2002), Demombynes and Ozler (2005), and Imrohoroglu et al. (2006).

desirable economic and political reforms are blocked.[68] Raghuram Rajan (2009a) provides an interesting analysis of how the two main types of economic reforms that are seen as key to poverty reduction, namely making markets more competitive and expanding access to education, can be blocked in a democracy in which three classes— the rich oligopolists who benefit from market distortions, an educated middle class, and the uneducated poor supplying unskilled labor—strive to preserve their rents. The model helps us understand India's slow progress toward mass literacy.[69]

It has also been argued that inequality impedes the provision of public goods. Public safety is an example. Income gains may do more to raise concern for public safety among the poor than the rich (which is clearly possible even if it is the rich who care most about public safety). There is presumably only so much public safety one can possibly want, so diminishing income effects must eventually set in. The concern for public safety will then be concave in income, implying that aggregate concern is lower when inequality is higher. Income gains do more to raise concern for public safety among the poor than the rich. The lower aggregate concern about public safety can then be expected to translate into less public action and higher crime rates in more unequal communities.[70]

A new interpretation of the impacts of *colonialism* has identified adverse longer term effects of initial (pre-European) conditions of high inequality via policies and institutions adopted by the colonial powers.[71] The essence of this argument is that the geographic patterns of colonialism (notably between North and South America) reinforced or implanted greater initial inequality and population heterogeneity into in some colonies than others. One colonial origin of inequality was the creation of European enclaves in the colonies that were greatly advantaged over the natives. There were also important geographic differences in the extent of inequality prior to the arrival of Europeans; the empires of the Aztecs and Incas were densely populated (relative to North America) and were already relatively well developed and controlled by powerful elites. In the context of these initial conditions in Central and South America, it has been argued that the European colonizers saw little reason to create institutions such as secure property rights that were conducive to longer term economic growth.[72] The more profitable strategy for the southern colonizers was to exploit the local land and labor as much as possible, with little regard for property rights. By contrast, the Europeans settlers in North America had a stronger incentive to establish sound institutions to serve their own interests, such as fee-simple ownership rights for land.[73] This was also more conducive to developing promotional

---

[68] Arguments along these lines include Bardhan et al. (2000), Banerjee and Iyer (2005), Acemoglu and Robinson (2006), Rajan (2009a, b), and Stiglitz (2012).

[69] See Weiner (1991).

[70] Pradhan and Ravallion (2003) outline this hypothesis and find support for it using survey data for Brazil.

[71] Engerman and Sokoloff (2006) provide a good overview of the arguments. North (1990) was an influential early contribution. The evidence assembled by Acemoglu et al (2005) is broadly consistent with the arguments about the colonial origins of the current disparities in real incomes globally. The modern arguments echo Adam Smith's views on the endogeneity of institutions (chapter 1).

[72] See, e.g., Acemoglu et al. (2005) and Acemoglu and Robinson (2012).

[73] See North (1990).

antipoverty policies (such as mass schooling) that were favorable to both long-term growth and poverty reduction.[74]

Sorting out the causality between inequality and institutions is never going to be easy. While arguments can be made suggesting that high initial inequality impedes the development of institutions conducing to longer term development, there is undoubt-edly a feedback effect, whereby weaker institutions foster higher inequality, such as protecting rents enjoyed by the rich or not protecting the poor against exploi-tation. There is evidence from panel data for developing countries that, while the causality clearly goes both ways, the influence of inequality on institutions is the stronger factor in accounting for the correlation between inequality and institutional development.[75]

But is it initial inequality that matters, or something else, such as poverty, the size of the middle class or the extent of polarization? Inequality is not the same thing as poverty; inequality can be reduced without a lower poverty measure by redistributing income among the non-poor, and poverty can be reduced without lower inequality. (Similarly, efforts to help the middle class may do little to relieve current poverty.) In fact there is another implication of credit market failures that has received less attention until recently. While the literature has emphasized that higher inequality in a credit-constrained economy implies lower growth that is also true of higher current wealth poverty for a given mean wealth.[76]

This implies an aggregate efficiency cost of a high incidence of poverty. But note that the theoretical prediction concerns the level of poverty at a *given* initial mean wealth. Without controlling for the initial mean, the sign of the effect of higher pov-erty on growth is ambiguous. Two opposing effects can be identified. The first is the usual conditional convergence property described above, whereby countries with a lower initial mean (and hence higher initial poverty) tend to have higher subsequent growth in a growth model (box 8.10). Working against this, there is an adverse distri-butional effect of higher poverty, which shifts the steady-state level of income in the economy. Which effect dominates is an empirical question, which we will return to in section 8.3.

Credit-market imperfections are not the only argument suggesting that poverty can persist. Economic history has pointed to the ways in which coercive (non-market) labor institutions, such as slavery and serfdom, not only impoverish people today, but stifle incentives to innovate, with implications for how much poverty persists.[77] This can also happen if because of the existence of a subsistence consumption require-ment; then higher poverty incidence—defined as failure to meet the subsistence requirement—implies lower growth.[78] Another example can be found in theories that

---

[74] For example, the state of Massachusetts in the United States introduced mass schooling policies in the late seventeenth century that were a century or more ahead of most European countries (Weiner 1991, ch. 6).

[75] See Chong and Gladstein (2007).

[76] Ravallion (2001b) argued that poverty retards growth when there are credit market failures.

[77] This argument is made by Acemoglu and Robinson (2012) who point to supportive historical evidence.

[78] See Lopez and Servén (2009) for an economic model with this feature.

postulate impatience for consumption (high time preference rates associated with low life expectancy) and hence low savings and investment rates by poor people.[79] While the literature has focused on initial inequality, it can also be argued that a higher initial incidence of poverty means a higher proportion of impatient consumers and hence lower growth.

Yet another example is found by considering how work productivity is likely to be affected by past nutritional and health status. Only when past nutritional intake is high enough, above basal metabolic rate (BMR), will it be possible to do any work, although diminishing returns to work will presumably set in later.[80]

Impacts of poverty on the nutrition of young children in poor families are of special concern. Poor nutrition in the early years of life is likely to retard child growth, cognitive and learning ability, schooling attainments, and (in all likelihood) earnings in adulthood.[81] Chronic under-nutrition in children can stem from either low nutritional intake or low nutritional absorption due to constant fecal-oral contamination.[82] This can mean that direct nutritional supplementation does little or nothing to improve children's nutritional status (measured by stunting) until the health environment improves.[83] This type of argument can be broadened to include other aspects of child development that have lasting impacts on learning ability and earnings as an adult.[84] And the handicap of poverty can emerge in the pre-natal period. Maternal and pre-natal conditions are now also thought to matter to child development and (hence) economic outcomes later in life.[85] For example, food deprivation experienced while in the womb has been found to have a negative effect on a number of dimensions of adult health.[86] By implication, having a larger share of the population who grew up in poverty (including living in poor health environments) will have a lasting negative impact on an economy's aggregate output. Economic disadvantaged can then be passed on across generations. This is not inevitable; for example, better maternal knowledge about infant health can help compensate.[87]

In another strand of thought on how poverty can perpetuate, it is argued that poverty reduces cognitive ability.[88] Given physical limitations to that human cognitive capacity, the concerns generated by poverty crowd out thinking about other things relevant to personal economic advancement. In a survey of the literature on

---

[79] See, e.g., Azariadis (2006).

[80] See the model in Dasgupta and Ray (1986).

[81] See Glewwe and Jacoby (1995), Alderman et al. (2006), Benton (2010), and Currie (2011).

[82] This is known as environmental enteropathy (see, e.g., Korpe and Petri 2012).

[83] Kinsey (2013) identifies this as one possible reason why the incidence of chronic under-nutrition has not fallen in his panel data for Zimbabwe.

[84] See Cunha and Heckman (2007).

[85] See Currie (2011), Dasgupta (2011), and Aizer and Currie (2014).

[86] Strong support for this claim came from the Dutch Hunger Winter during World War II. A blockade by German forces near the end of World War II greatly reduced food supply to 4.5 million Dutch people; 22,000 died during the famine. For an overview of the lessons learnt about the link between intrauterine nutrition and adult health, see Schulz (2010).

[87] See the discussion in Aizer and Currie (2014).

[88] Mani et al. (2013) present supportive evidence from both experimental and observational studies.

the psychological effects of poverty, Johannes Haushofer and Ernst Fehr (2014, 862) conclude that:

> The evidence indicates that poverty causes stress and negative affective states which in turn may lead to short-sighted and risk-averse decision-making, possibly by limiting attention and favoring habitual behaviors at the expense of goal-directed ones. Together, these relationships may constitute a feedback loop that contributes to the perpetuation of poverty.

What we see here is a complete reversal in the causation postulated by the long-standing model of poverty being caused by "bad behaviors." The behaviors that have more often been seen as causes of poverty may instead be its effects.[89]

There are also theoretical arguments involving market and institutional development, although this is not a topic that has received as much attention in this literature. While past theories have often taken credit-market failures to be exogenous, poverty may well be a deeper causative factor in financial development (as well as an outcome of the lack of financial development). For example, given a fixed cost of lending (both for each loan and for setting up the lending institution), liquidity constraints can emerge as the norm in very poor societies.

The economic and political institutions of a society have played a role in thinking about how the initial distribution of wealth influences long-run growth. Weak institutions, such as poor rule of law or missing markets, can influence the distribution of wealth and power, but also be influenced by it. And weak institutions can be expected to matter more in poor and unequal societies, for they will often have a harder time developing better institutions. Inequalities and institutions interact in jointly influencing an economy's long-run level of average income.

We have seen that a number of arguments can be made as to how high initial inequality and/or high poverty can lower the steady-state level of mean income. Then the higher speed of convergence in the mean toward its steady-state value associated with a country starting out poor would be offset to some extent by a lower steady-state level of mean income. Thus, poverty measures need not converge despite the mean-income convergence property of the Solow-Swan model.[90]

Poverty Traps

The arguments reviewed above point to a number of sources of persistence in poverty, including across generations. Persistence is sometimes confused with a poverty trap (box 1.6). The idea of a poverty trap refers to a situation in which there are multiple equilibria, some preferable to others. Persistence, on the other hand, can occur even when there is a unique equilibrium; it is just that the process of adjustment toward that equilibrium is slow.

In development economics it has been argued that the combination of interdependence among households and/or firms with coordination failures can mean that the

---

[89] See, e.g., Johannes and Fehr (2014).
[90] See Ravallion (2012d).

economy gets stuck in an inferior equilibrium, which is the trap. This is an example of a *coordination game* (box 8.12). It will be recalled from chapter 2 that the scope for coordination failures was one of the early arguments for industrial policies and development assistance. Coordination failures can also lead to recessions and even mass unemployment.[91]

Box 8.12 The Coordination Game

A *Nash equilibrium* is a situation in which no player in a game has any personal incentive to change his play given what all other players do. In other words, each player can do no better given the choices made by others. A *coordination game* has more than one such equilibrium and one player is better off in one of the equilibria, with no other player worse off (in which case we say the equilibria can be Pareto ranked).

For example, imagine a village with a privately-owned river and a farmer. In the status quo the river flows freely, and the farmer relies solely on rainfall to grow his crops. But there is development potential. The river owner could build a dam at a cost of \$100. If the farmer chooses to build an irrigation canal, also costing \$100, from the dam to his farmland, then he can grow an extra crop worth \$400 and pay a water charge to the dam owner of (say) \$200. If both players make their investments, they make profits of \$100 each.

Table B8.12.1 gives the joint payoffs (Y_F, Y_R), where Y_F is the payoff for the farmer and Y_R is the payoff for the river owner. The status quo is a Nash equilibrium, which will persist unless the players can coordinate their actions to reach the preferred equilibrium with both investments.

Table B8.12.1 **Joint Payoffs in a Stylized Coordination Game**

		River owner	
(Y_F, Y_R)		Build dam	Do not build dam
Farmer	Build irrigation canal	(100,100)	(–100,0)
	Do not build canal	(0,–100)	(0,0)

Historical note: The Nash equilibrium is named after the American economist-mathematician John Nash (the subject of the 2001 movie *A Beautiful Mind*). Nash (1951) noted the scope for multiple equilibria.

Further reading: Schelling (1960) discusses various forms of coordination failure and how they can be avoided. The macroeconomic implications of coordination failures are studied in Cooper (1999). Basu (2011) uses the coordination game to help understand social phenomena such as ethnic/racial polarization.

---

[91] See Cooper (1999).

An important class of dynamic poverty traps arises from the existence of *threshold effects* in production or consumption. To understand these models, recall that one of the less desirable features of the standard economic model of growth in the present context is that it does not allow for threshold effects (as noted in box 8.2), which some observers have identified as potential causes of poverty. Here a "threshold" essentially means that at low initial levels of wealth future wealth will be even lower, and possibly even zero. Box 8.13 explains the idea more fully. Such models predict that a large exogenous income gain may be needed to attain a permanently higher income and that seemingly similar aggregate shocks can have dissimilar outcomes.[92]

Box 8.13 **Threshold Effects in Production**

The standard representation of the production function in box 8.2 assumes that something can be produced from almost nothing; that the production function starts at the origin and that diminishing returns set in immediately. This does not seem plausible. So let us now add in the idea of a *threshold capital stock* needed to produce any output, that is, $f(k) = 0$ for all $k \leq k^{min}(>0)$. The bold curved line in figure B8.13.1 illustrates the production function with the threshold.

Unless one has sufficient capital (given by k^{min}), nothing can be produced. Once the threshold is reached, output emerges in the next time period. However, we assume that diminishing returns start to set in immediately. In more technical terms we say that the production function $f(k)$ is strictly positive, strictly increasing, and strictly concave for all $k > k^{min}$. (The "concave" refers to the shape of the curve when looking at it from below.) If the threshold has not been reached, then there will be no demand for capital since it will not allow any output to be produced.

Alternatively one can smooth out the kink by imagining an "S" shaped function (as indicated by the curved dashed line in figure B8.13.1). This is sometimes

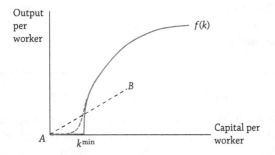

Figure B8.13.1 Threshold Effect on Production.

continued

---

[92] Growth models with such features are discussed further in Day (1992) and Azariades (1996, 2006).

Box 8.13 **(Continued)**

called a "low-level non-convexity," borrowing an idea from set theory: a set is said to be "convex" if all the points on a straight line joining any two points in the set are also contained in that set. As can be seen in figure B8.13.1, a straight line joining the origin at A with (say) point B contains points that are outside the set of production possibilities. Thus, one can see why it is called a *low-level non-convexity*.

There is more than one interpretation of such a threshold effect on wealth dynamics; the following are some examples:

- A persuasive argument for its existence based on the fact of a positive BMR; maintaining the human body at rest requires a minimum food-energy intake before any physical work can be done. Physiology generates the threshold.[93]
- Threshold effects can also arise from the existence of a lumpy "threshold good" in consumption or production.[94] Try getting an earnings bump from just one day of schooling! There is clearly some critical minimum, such as attaining a certified level.
- When a person is close to the lowest possible utility, punishment incentives do not bite much. Thus, a poor person may have a hard time convincing lenders (and others) that she is trustworthy.[95] The credit market failure may thus stem from poverty itself.

The existence of such a threshold effect can create a poverty trap. We can readily see how by introducing a threshold effect into the type of model outlined in box 8.11. The analytics are explained in more detail in box 8.14. One implication is that it is no longer true in general that higher inequality will impede growth in a credit-constrained economy. Then there will exist increases in inequality embracing the lower end of the wealth distribution (below k^{min}) that can increase the growth rate of wealth. Thus, the type of model illustrated by box 8.14 has ambiguous implications for how much an exogenous reduction in inequality will promote overall growth. That depends crucially on precisely *where* in the distribution the reduction in inequality occurs.

Box 8.14 **A Dynamic Poverty Trap**

Let us now modify the model in box 8.11 to allow a (positive) minimum level of k below which no future output is possible, as illustrated in the recursion diagram in figure B8.14. Above this critical level, positive future wealth can be generated but diminishing returns to capital start to set in (box 8.2).

---

[93] See Dasgupta (1993) for an elaboration of this point.

[94] See Galor and Zeira (1993) on the implications of threshold effects in production on the growth process. See Just and Michelson (2007) on the implications of lumpiness in consumption.

[95] See Banerjee and Newman (1994) for this argument.

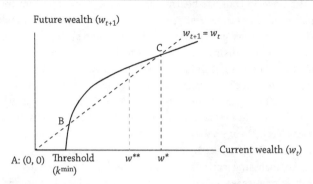

Figure B8.14.1 Wealth Dynamics with a Threshold Effect on Production.

Some people have zero wealth (or even negative net wealth allowing for liabilities, but we can lump them all into the "zero wealth" category). Even those with zero wealth can still earn a current labor income, consumed fully in each period. Future wealth is zero at low levels of current wealth $(w_t < k^{min})$. For levels of initial wealth greater than k^{min} but less than $k^*/(\lambda + 1)$, diminishing returns set in as in box 8.11. (Future wealth is then said to be a strictly concave function of current wealth.) Also similarly to box 8.11, at higher wealth $(w_t > w^{**} = k^*/(\lambda + 1))$, the recursion diagram becomes linear, since then the borrowing constraint no longer binds, so that the shape of the own-production function no longer matters to the dynamics. The modified version of the recursion diagram is given in figure B8.14.1.

There are potentially three equilibria for each person. Two of these, namely points A and C in figure B8.14, are *stable* while the middle one, at point B, is *unstable* in that shocks will move those at B toward A or C. (Recall box 8.3.) To see why, imagine someone at point B. Any small wealth gain will put her in a region of accumulation (current wealth lower than future wealth) and so the person will progress toward point C. Similarly, a small contraction will put her on a path to point A. Repeat the same thought experiment and you will see that points A and C are stable equilibria.

Note that, in contrast to the model in box 8.11, the growth impact of higher inequality is now ambiguous. In particular redistribution from those below k^{min} to those in the interval (k^{min}, w^{**}) will increase expected future wealth at given mean current wealth. The existence of the threshold effect makes the relationship between total output and the distribution of income more complex; some inequality increasing redistributions will reduce output, while others will increase it.

Further reading: See the note to box 1.6. On the economics of poverty traps and the many ways they can arise, see Azariadis (1996, 2006), Dasgupta (1997), and Bowles et al. (2006).

The idea of a poverty trap has bearing on how we think about antipoverty poli-cies. Such policies are sometimes represented in a rather static way, in which it is all about filling income poverty gaps using transfers of some sort. Dynamic processes of wealth accumulation, and disinvestment, play little or no role. However, an impor-tant economic foundation for thinking about antipoverty policy is provided by an understanding of *economic dynamics* at the micro (individual or household) level.

In the long run, after repeated small shocks, an economy characterized by a poverty trap (box 8.14) will settle in a state that can be thought of as having two main classes of people. One class has little or no wealth, given that its members are caught in a *wealth poverty trap* (at point A in box 8.14). There can be many reasons in practice why peo-ple are so trapped, including lack of any marketable skills, social exclusion, geographic isolation, debilitating disease, or environmental degradation. The second class com-prises people who have settled at their respective steady-state levels of wealth (w^*) (point C in box 8.14). There can still be inequality within each class. There can be ine-quality of labor earnings among the poorer class, and there can be wealth inequality among those at their various steady-state levels of wealth even when not caught in a poverty trap. The "poor" can be identified as two groups of people, namely those caught in a poverty trap and those not trapped, that is, those for whom their steady-state level of wealth turns out to be very low, even though they are not caught in a poverty trap.

Some country or place may well be in the fortunate situation of not having anyone in either of these groups. For example, the poverty trap may be there, but institu-tions in that country in normal times are able to make sure that nobody falls into the trap. The trap may only become empirically relevant in macro crises, when those institutions come under significant stress. (Although it would clearly be hazardous to say that the trap is not a concern, or to conclude from empirical observations at nor-mal times that it does not exist.) Similarly, there may be nobody who is judged poor in their stable equilibria. Poverty can be eliminated. What we are studying here are policies that come into play precisely because, based on the (quantitative and qualita-tive) data available, there are good reasons to believe that there is a serious problem of poverty (i.e., that there are people in one or both of these two groups).

The poverty-trap models reviewed above rely on features of the dynamics of wealth accumulation at the individual level—notably the existence of a low-level non-convexity, such as due to thresholds (box 8.2). Another class of models in the literature is based instead on how group memberships matter to your personal prospects. These can be called *membership models*.[96] They have similar outcomes to dynamic poverty traps; the key difference is that now the persistence of poverty emerges from exter-nal effects of group membership, such as living in a poor area and/or a poor ethnic association.

Historically, the development of membership models reflected the efforts by economists and other social scientists to understand the concentrations of urban pov-erty that had emerged in the US post–World War II (chapter 2). Spending per student on schools and (hence) school quality is heavily dependent on neighborhood wealth

---

[96] This is the term used by Durlauf (2006), who provides a good overview of the relevant literature.

in the United States due to the heavy reliance on local property taxes for financing.[97] Thus, poverty can self-perpetuate; children from poor families, concentrated in poor areas, are less likely to receive well-funded schooling and so less likely to enjoy the full returns to schooling later in life.[98] There are also external effects of neighborhood characteristics, such that children growing up in poor areas are disadvantaged.[99]

Local school funding in the United States is an example of a broader class of causes of poverty stemming from how group (also called network) memberships influence the costs and benefits of acquiring skills or other assets that provide a route out of poverty. Because of the heavy reliance on local property taxation to finance schools in the United States, children growing up in poor neighborhoods are less likely to acquire the human capital needed to advance. Sociologists have also emphasized how the lack of role models can limit the life chances of children growing up in poor neighborhoods.[100] The network effects get built into expectations about future prospects, further inhibiting progress out of poverty.[101]

The existence of *geographic externalities* in economic development can have similar implications.[102] (Later in this chapter we will study the example of geographic poverty traps in rural China.) In these models, living in a poor area makes it less likely one will escape poverty in the future, because living in a poorly endowed area lowers the productivity of personal investments. This is a causal effect of location on poverty, not simply a geographic concentration of people with similar characteristics. If the external effect is strong enough, then a poverty trap can be present. This can also happen when there are network effects on migration (as noted earlier in this chapter). Migrants face an implicit tax for supporting their kin back home. When employers are wary that members of a network (such as a kin group) will favor each other in access to jobs and other opportunities the network members will have a hard time finding work, and may take costly actions to hide their network linkage.[103]

Another form of poverty trap can emerge with weak law enforcement, and weak state capacities generally, such that poverty and corruption reinforce each other in a vicious cycle. In her vivid description of life in a Mumbai slum Boo (2012, 62) recounts that "as every slum dweller knew, there were three main ways out of poverty: finding an entrepreneurial niche... politics and corruption... and education." This is in large

---

[97] The federal government covers about 14% of school funding, with 44% and 42% coming from state and local governments (Reich 2014). The heavy reliance on local financing, in combination with residential segregation, generates high inequalities in funding per student in the United States, such that "the vast majority of OECD countries either invest equally into every student or disproportionately more into disadvantaged students. The U.S. is one of the few countries doing the opposite" (Schleicher, quoted by Porter 2013).

[98] A model with these features can be found in Bénabou (1993). Also see Fernandez and Rogerson (1997), who examine the role played by town-planning regulations (residential "zoning").

[99] Borjas (1995) provided an influential empirical demonstration of this point for the United States. As Borjas points out, residential segregation by ethnicity makes it hard to distinguish external ethnic effects from geographic factors.

[100] See, e.g., Wilson (1987).

[101] See, e.g., the model in Kim and Loury (2014).

[102] See Jalan and Ravallion (2002).

[103] See Hoff and Sen (2006).

part a choice between legal and illegal entrepreneurship. Under certain conditions, one can find a *predation trap*.[104] This is a stable equilibrium in which predatory behavior is endemic and profits from productive enterprise are low. Box 8.15 explains how this can arise.

Box 8.15 The Predation Trap

Predatory entrepreneurship entails various forms of extortion and demands for protection money by gangs, rebels, middlemen, and corrupt politicians. Budding entrepreneurs can choose to be either predators or producers with mobility between the two groups. Predators prey on producers, extracting rents.

How can a "predation trap" come to exist? Similarly to the earliest development models (section 8.1), suppose that there is a traditional sector and a modern sector. Entrepreneurs can choose freely either to be producers or predators. Producers in the traditional sector are competitive and earn no profit. Producers in the modern sector earn profits from production processes that exhibit increasing returns to scale, meaning that if all production inputs increase by (say) 10%, then output will increase by more than 10%. As firms modernize they earn profits that in turn increase aggregate demand for the modern-sector output, which increases profits for all producers in that sector. In the absence of predation, the whole economy will eventually be in the modern sector.

Now introduce predators. Figure B8.15.1 gives the profit curves for predators and modern producers, both plotted against the share of the entrepreneurs who choose to be modern-sector producers. The levels of these profit curves are determined by the size of the economy, and the powers of the state to enforce the law. Profits for modern producers increase with the number of such producers, while profits for predators fall with their number. Predators crowd each other out.

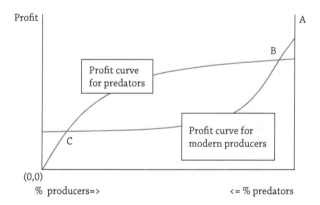

Figure B8.15.1 Multiple Equilibria in a Model with Predation.

---

[104] This is the term used by Mehlum et al. (2003).

This congestion lowers their individual profits and more so as the number of predators increases. This is not much of a problem for the first few predators, since for them extra predators do not crowd out their profits much. However, when all are predators and none are producers, there is no possible profit from predation; thus the profit curve for predators passes through the (0,0) point in figure B8.15.1. The fewer the number of predators, the more modern producers gain (individually) from an increase in their number. The natural assumption is that if profits for modern producers are greater than (less than) for predators, then the share of producers rises (falls).

We can see that there are three equilibria in figure B.8.15.1, identified as the points at which profits are equal between being a predator or being a modern-sector producer. Points A and C are stable, but point B is not. (You can see that a small shift to the right from point B will entail that the share of producers rises, until A is reached; by contrast a shift to the left will send the economy toward point C.) Point C is the predation trap—a stable low-level equilibrium in which predators abound.

There are essentially two ways of getting out of a predation trap. The first is if the economy expands sufficiently for some other reason, pushing up the profit curve for producers enough to eliminate the predation trap. Alternatively, legal enforcement could lower the profit curve for the predators.

Further reading: This box is a simplified version of the model in Mehlum et al. (2003), which adopted some key features of the model of industrialization by Murphy et al. (1989). Another model with a predation trap is provided by Nunn (2007), which he uses to explain African underdevelopment given prior colonial exploitation.

We have seen that economists have established how a poverty trap can emerge as an economically stable equilibrium. Social and political stability is another matter. The latter types of instability can arise in many ways, defying simple generalizations about their economic causes. However, it is plausible that a large mass of people caught in poverty traps can threaten social stability, especially so if their labor earnings and (hence) consumptions are very low, either in steady state, or as a result of some severe shock, and in the latter case the threat to stability may well be even greater.[105] Arguably the riots in US cities in the 1960s were the result of the geographic poverty traps that had emerged. The Johnson administration's War on Poverty was in part a political response to that instability,[106] although it also reflected the new thinking about the causes of poverty at the time, as discussed in chapter 2.

Motivated by the idea of a poverty trap, we can think of two broad types of antipoverty policies. There can be policies that provide short-term palliatives, possibly

---

[105] In *Politics*, Aristotle (350 B.C., unnumbered) put the point nicely: "It is a bad thing that many from being rich should become poor; for men of ruined fortunes are sure to stir up revolutions."

[106] As argued by Piven and Cloward (1993).

to maintain social stability by assuring that current incomes do not fall below some crucial level, even though poor people remain poor, either because they are caught in a wealth poverty trap or because they have a low steady-state level of wealth. These are purely *protection policies*. And there are *promotion policies* that allow poor people to attain the higher level of wealth needed to escape poverty. For those caught in a poverty trap, this will require a sufficiently large wealth gain to put them on a path to eventually reaching their own (higher and stable) steady-state level of wealth. For those not caught in a trap, but still poor, promotion will require some combination of higher wealth and higher returns to their wealth. Chapters 9 and 10 will discuss how past policies have performed in both protection and promotion.

8.2 Evidence on Growth and Distributional Changes

Having reviewed the various theoretical arguments, we now turn to the empirical evidence in this section and section 8.3. That evidence has come from a wide range of sources, including time series observations of specific economies, cross-country comparisons and micro-level panel data. These quantitative data can be powerful tools for many purposes. However, we must also be aware of their limitations. Unlike the "hard sciences," quantitative economic data (either "macro" or "micro") can rarely provide a definitive test of any theory. There is always a risk that the thing one is looking for simply cannot be identified in the type of data available. Box 8.16 gives two examples relevant to this context. There is still much one can learn from data, but it is almost always a challenging task.

Box 8.16 **Just Because You Can't See It Does Not Mean It Is Not There**

Suppose we wanted to test whether there is the type of labor market equilibrium implied by the HT model in which workers move between urban and rural areas according to the expected difference in earnings. (Recall box 8.9 on the HT model.) We might look for evidence of migration taking place. But then if we are in equilibrium, there will be no migration. Yet it would clearly be wrong to dismiss the HT model. One could look for data on wage disparities and unemployment rates, but a natural generalization of the HT model would allow for differences in the non-wage amenities between urban and rural areas; there are important unobservable factors to consider. Possibly the more conclusive evidence lies in qualitative data: looking for institutional impediments or other frictions to wage adjustment in the formal sector, or looking for evidence of significant impediments to mobility.

To give another example, suppose we are looking for evidence of a poverty trap. Again the trap may well be there but not be easily detected in the quantitative economic data one can find in normal circumstances when the economy has settled into its equilibrium. It may even be that those who are

---

trapped in destitution are simply unobservable by standard methods, in that they are homeless (and thus not amenable to a standard household survey). The existence of the trap would also provide strong incentives for protecting people from large negative shocks. These arrangements may work adequately in normal times, but fail in crises or famines. Yet the potential for the trap is there all the time, and greatly influences the economy. We would need a large shock to really see what is happening, but shocks occur infrequently.

The Industrial Revolution Did (Eventually) Benefit Wage Workers

The question of whether workers benefited from the Industrial Revolution has long been debated by economists and economic historians. The focus in the literature has largely been on wage workers in the home country. Rising demand for labor in the wake of the Industrial Revolution would hopefully push up the wage rate. Alas, there could be no such gain for most of the workers in the New World who were producing the imported raw materials for the new factories in England and Western Europe since those workers were enslaved.[107] Indeed, the higher plantation output needed to supply the raw materials for the Industrial Revolution required more slaves and/or higher slave productivity—that is, they were compelled to work even harder.[108] (There is little to suggests that their rations improved much.) The textile manufacturing boom made slavery more profitable, and slave-based production expanded rapidly in the New World, including North America. So this dimension of global poverty was unlikely to be relieved by the Industrial Revolution in the near term, and in all likelihood it got worse.

Regarding the wage workers at home, there appears to have been a consensus at the time (including on the part of both the nineteenth-century classical economists and the socialist critics of capitalism, following Engels 1845) that Britain's Industrial Revolution that started around 1760 brought little or no gain to the working class or even led to their impoverishment (as section 1.5 discussed). With the benefit of hindsight, and better data and analysis, it appears that the Industrial Revolution was in fact poverty reducing through rising real wage rates. But there was a long lag before wages responded. Just how long depends on the position one takes in a debate on price indices and other data issues.[109] Either way the pessimists appear to have been right for at

---

[107] On the role of slavery in the history of cotton see Beckert (2014, Chapter 5).

[108] While other factors were no doubt involved, it is notable that the Atlantic slave trade saw a sharp rise in the number of embarked slaves in the wake of the Industrial Revolution; see the *Voyagers* database at http://www.slavevoyages.org/tast/database/search.faces. Baptist (2014) documents the rise in productivity per slave in the cotton plantations of America's south in the first half of the nineteenth century.

[109] Hartwell (1961) questioned the prevailing view for over one hundred years that the Industrial Revolution had made the English working class worse off. Hartwell drew on various quantitative sources, including evidence that, although nominal wages had changed little, the prices of agricultural and manufactured goods had fallen. There was much debate at the time about Hartwell's claims,

least a few decades after the technical innovations.[110] Real wages in Britain did start to rise in the nineteenth century despite continuing population growth. And there is evidence that the gains in real wages for the working class from the mid-nineteenth century came hand in hand with improved nutritional status.[111]

Why did we see a seemingly long lag in the real wage rate response in the home country to the Industrial Revolution? Recall that the classical economists saw induced population growth as the reason why any initial upward pressure on the real wage rate would be counteracted by rising labor supply. This link could be broken if families chose instead to invest in higher quality children rather than more children when their wages rose. This required that parents perceive the potential for upward mobility of their children and have access to affordable decent schooling. These conditions started to materialize later in the nineteenth century, after real wages started to rise. Along with rising female labor-force participation rates, the higher wage meant a higher opportunity cost of having children.[112] Fertility started to decline in England and most of Europe in the last quarter of the nineteenth century.[113] So it seems we need to look elsewhere for an explanation.

A better explanation can be found in the Lewis model (box 8.7) in which a surplus of labor in the rural economy keeps wages at a low level until that surplus is absorbed by the economy's modern (urban) sector, as this expands due to technical progress. By this interpretation, it took many decades to absorb enough of the labor surplus in rural areas (as the economy transformed from primarily agrarian to primarily industrial) to bring about rising real wages—to reach the LTP (box 8.7).

This explanation also points to a conceptual confusion about the gains from the Industrial Revolution. There are likely to have been gains to poor people even if real wages in industry did not rise. Those gains come from the difference between earnings in industry and those in agriculture, from which the bulk of the new industrial workforce had been drawn. Wages in manufacturing were higher on average and less variable over time than labor earnings in traditional agriculture. (There were also likely to have been gains in non-income dimensions of life, including greater opportunities for social and political interaction.) Box 8.7 shows the existence of such a wage differential is often built into the Lewis model. The historical record also indicates that industrial workers themselves saw (pecuniary and non-pecuniary) gains.[114] This account appears to stand in marked contrast to the prevailing historical record.

including a famous debate with Hobsbawn. In later research, Feinstein (1998) found only a small gain (less than 15%) in the real value of average labor earnings for the English working class between 1780 and 1850. Clark's (2005) series of builders' real wage rates in England suggests higher wages from about 1800, while Allen (2007, 2009) argues that the increase started closer to 1830.

[110] Also see Williamson (1985) and O'Rourke and Williamson (1997).

[111] See the Fogel et al. (1983) series on mean height of working-class boys in London, which tracks quite closely Tucker's (1975) series on real wages of London artisans. However, Cinnirella (2008) puts the turning point (after which mean height rose) much later, around the mid-nineteenth century.

[112] The female labor force participation rate is the proportion of working-age women who have a job remunerated in cash or kind. This typically includes wage work and self-employment but excludes domestic labor in the home.

[113] See Rothenbacher (2002).

[114] Griffin (2013) provides a great many autobiographical accounts consistent with this view.

However, the more positive assessments can be reconciled with the popular picture of the poverty and squalor of working-class life in the industrial towns of England and elsewhere in the nineteenth century. The two accounts reflect different counterfactuals. Educated, middle-class observers saw poverty and squalor relative to their own living conditions, and that is perfectly believable. Yet industrial workers themselves saw many advantages relative to the (often disguised) unemployment and other deprivations faced in rural areas and the pre-industrial cities. The potential for confusion by not properly distinguishing these two counterfactuals echoes in development debates today.

In one important respect it can be credibly argued that industrial workers were worse off than agricultural workers in the first half of the nineteenth century, namely in their health environment. The industrial cities were rife with diseases associated with the geographic concentration of poverty.[115] The health innovations of the latter half of the nineteenth century (such as in water and sanitation) were key to the subsequent improvement in the overall living standards of all classes.

There is another side to the story of how technical progress helped reduce poverty in Western Europe. The technical progress relevant to poor people also concerned innovations that reduced the costs of living. Falling food prices in Europe during the latter half of the nineteenth century reflected the invention of refrigeration and lower freight transport costs.[116]

Evidence on Distribution Post-Kuznets

The empirical foundations for the expectation that relative inequality would inevitably rise in growing developing countries were not particularly secure over the long period of time in which the Kuznets Hypothesis (box 8.8) was influential in development thinking. Kuznets drew mainly on data for some currently developed countries in the first half of the twentieth century. In fact Kuznets warned that the evidence was scarce for his idea; he wrote: "In concluding this paper, I am acutely conscious of the meagerness of reliable information presented. The paper is perhaps 5 per cent empirical information and 95 per cent speculation, some of it possibly tainted by wishful thinking" (Kuznets 1955, 26).

Dissatisfaction with the data available continued, and the attendant data controversies fueled much debate. A prominent, and influential, example was the debate in the 1970s on how equitably the gains from economic growth in Brazil had been distributed. Such debates fueled calls for better data for measuring poverty and inequality.[117] Better evidence emerged much later. Indeed, there has been a huge growth in the availability of distributional data from household surveys since around 1980. Numerous papers tested for the inverted-U in cross-sectional data and found evidence of such a relationship. However, the cross-sectional relationship can be misleading about how

---

[115] Engels (1845) and others documented these urban–rural differences.

[116] See Williamson (1998).

[117] Contributions in the Brazil debate included Fishlow (1972), Fields (1977), and Ahluwalia et al. (1979).

inequality evolves over time in any one country.[118] As better evidence accumulated, it turns out that very few low-income countries have developed over time in a manner consistent with the Kuznets Hypothesis.[119] Studies of the few initially poor countries that have seen a sustained long-term rise in inequality have not pointed to the Kuznets process of migration as being a key factor.[120] Nor is it likely that falling inequality in the United States and other rich countries in the first half of the twentieth century was due to a Kuznets process.[121]

Instead we have learned that growth in developing countries tends to be distribution-neutral on average, meaning that changes in inequality are roughly orthogonal to growth rates in the mean.[122] This is not to deny that there is evidence of rising relative inequality within many countries, including China and India (which we return to in section 8.5).

Rising inequality in the United States has dampened the gains to poor people from economic growth. The (absolute) poverty rate in the United States has been remarkably persistent, at around 15%.[123] However, if one goes back further in time, one finds that economic growth had been associated with falling absolute poverty rates in the United States.[124] The break when America's poverty rate stopped falling with economic growth was around in the mid-1970s. The growth process became far less pro-poor; indeed, on recalling figure 2.4, it can reasonably be said that the country's growth process has been decidedly "pro-rich."

The point here is that rising inequality is not correlated with growth rates; indeed, among growing economies, inequality tends to fall about as often as it rises.[125] Mechanically, distribution-neutral growth implies that the changes in any standard measure of either absolute or weakly relative poverty will be negatively correlated with growth rates in the mean. Thus, it is no surprise that we also find that measures of absolute poverty tend to fall with economic growth.[126]

Higher growth rates in poor countries have clearly been the main proximate cause of the higher rates of poverty reduction in the developing world seen since the turn of the present century. Since then, growth takeoffs for low-income and middle-income countries have become more common, lasted longer, and the take-offs have been grounded in better macroeconomic policy regimes.[127] What we are seeing is broadly consistent with the conditional-convergence predictions of modern growth theory (box 8.10). And the developing countries that have enjoyed higher rates of economic

[118] Papanek (1978) made this point.

[119] As shown by Bruno et al. (1998) and Fields (2001).

[120] See, e.g., Ravallion and Chen (2007) on China, which we return to later.

[121] See Piketty (2006).

[122] See Ravallion (1995, 2001b), Dollar and Kraay (2002), Ferreira and Ravallion (2009), and Dollar et al. (2013).

[123] Using the "*Supplementary Poverty Lines*" (box 4.4); the figure is slightly lower using the old official method; see Fox et al. (2013).

[124] See Iceland (2013, fig. 13). Also see the analysis in Iceland (2003).

[125] For evidence on this point, see Ravallion and Chen (1997), Ravallion (2001b), and Ferreira and Ravallion (2009).

[126] Ferreira and Ravallion (2009) review the evidence on this point.

[127] See Bluedorn et al. (2013).

Table 8.1 **Correlation Coefficients between Growth Rates and Changes over Time in Poverty and Inequality Measures**

	Total inequality (MLD)	Inequality between countries	Inequality within countries	Absolute poverty	Log absolute poverty	Relative poverty	Log relative poverty
Log mean consumption or income	0.116	0.067	0.092	–0.668	–0.750	–0.581	–0.525

Note: n = 60 (pooling regions and reference years, as in chapter 7); correlation coefficients over 0.32 (in absolute value) are significant at the 1% level.

growth have seen faster progress against absolute poverty. To provide a consistent overall comparison across the main measures of poverty and inequality used in chapter 7, table 8.1   provides correlation coefficients (essentially adding the change in the log mean to table 3.3.) We see significant negative correlations with the poverty measures, but not with inequality.

Economic growth has generally meant a lower absolute poverty rate, but over time it has also meant that in many developing countries relative poverty considerations have become more important. The evidence of rising numbers of relatively poor in the developing world presented in chapter 7 can thus be seen as the other side of the coin to falling numbers of absolutely poor people. By contrast, rising relative poverty in high-income countries has come mainly from changes in relative distribution, associated with rising inequality.

The emergence of concerns about relative poverty in the developing world also has implications for the emphasis given to economic growth versus redistribution in fighting poverty. Without lower inequality, future progress against relative poverty in the developing world will undoubtedly be slower than that against absolute poverty.

The relationship between poverty reduction and economic growth is potentially complex, as it depends on initial distribution (including poverty) with important interaction effects between growth and distribution in how they impact on poverty.[128] However, here we are focusing on a purely statistical aspect of the difference between absolute and relative measures. Intuitively, one expects that growth in the mean will be less effective in reducing relative poverty, given that the poverty line rises with the mean above a critical level.

This is confirmed by figure 8.1, which plots the proportionate rates of poverty reduction against the growth rates in the mean.[129] The overall elasticity of absolute poverty reduction to growth in the mean is around –2. The weakly relative poverty is also responsive to growth, but less so, with an elasticity of –0.4—one-fifth of that for absolute poverty. And the elasticity will decline with growth, since the relative poverty line will rise as the mean rises.

[128] For a fuller discussion, see Ravallion (2012d).

[129] The growth rates are annualized log differences expressed in percentages. The data points are region-year aggregates.

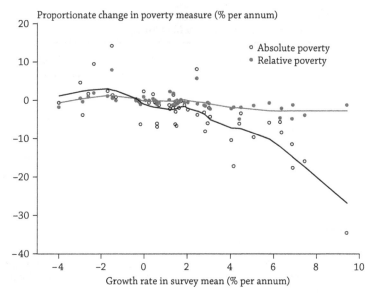

Figure 8.1 Growth and Poverty Reduction in the Developing World. *Source:* Author's calculations. Each data point is a region-year combination spanning 1981–2010.

Policy efforts to fight relative poverty will almost certainly need to give greater consideration to how best to reduce inequality than has been the case in the past, when the main focus has been on absolute poverty. This topic is taken up further in chapters 9 and 10.

Growth and Non-Income Dimensions of Welfare

Recall from chapter 3 that poverty measures are almost invariably based on household aggregates, and so they cannot be considered adequate for reflecting distribution within the household. They are also based on consumption of market goods, and so need not reflect well differences in public provisioning. It is important to also look at relevant other measures, of which child under-nutrition is undeniably important.

The incidence of child under-nutrition tends also to decline with economic growth. A study of the effects of economic growth on both poverty measures (using the $1.25 a day line) and measures of child wasting found that at high levels of either, growth is associated with gains, and with a similar elasticity between the poverty measure and the child wasting measure.[130] However, the same study also found that once relatively low levels of wasting are reached, growth becomes much less effective, suggesting that more targeted interventions will then be called for. Chapter 10 returns to discuss some of the interventions available.

An undeniably important dimension of inequality relevant to growth and poverty reduction is that people living in poorer families tend to be less healthy and to die

---

[130] See Block et al. (2012).

sooner; chapter 7 reviewed evidence on this point. This and other factors (including inequalities in women's education and access to family planning services) play
a key role in generating another socioeconomic gradient: fertility rates tend to be
higher in poor families (chapter 7). On balance, the natural rate of population growth
tends also to be higher for the poor. This is one reason why one tends to find lower
rates of progress against poverty in countries with higher population growth rates.
Cross-country regressions suggest that higher fertility rates are associated with less
progress against poverty.[131] Time series evidence for India has pointed to the same
conclusion.[132] There is also evidence of an adverse effect of population growth on GDP
growth.[133]

How the gains from growth are used by a country is also important to the outcomes for poor people.[134] Recall from chapter 7 that we find large differences across
countries in the incidence of undernourished children even if we control for income
as best we can. These differences partly reflect differences in public health provisioning and the efficacy of that provisioning, and these things will depend in part on the
overall economic resources of a country and how those resources are deployed. Recall
that differences in indicators of child health and nutrition have been found to be negatively correlated with public health spending per capita.[135] This is not surprising,
as one would expect that better off parents can more easily protect their children's
nutrition and health status from weak public provisioning and poor health environments. To the extent that the benefits of aggregate economic growth are channeled
through the fiscal system into better public healthcare, better social outcomes are to
be expected. Political scientists have also argued that sustained growth shifts "policy
sentiment" in favor of poor people.[136]

Growth and Types of Inequality

A common empirical finding in the literature is that changes in *relative* inequality have
virtually zero correlation with rates of economic growth. However, this may carry little
weight for those who are concerned instead about absolute inequality, which tends
to rise with growth, and fall with contraction.[137] Figure 8.2 shows the relationship
between changes in both relative and absolute inequality and growth rates for about
one hundred countries. Each point is constructed from two household surveys for a

---

[131] See Eastwood and Lipton (1999, 2001).

[132] Using time series data for India, van de Walle (1985) and Datt and Ravallion (1998a) found
evidence that higher rates of population growth were poverty increasing.

[133] See Kelley and Schmidt (1995, 2001) and Williamson (2001).

[134] See Sen (1981b) and Anand and Ravallion (1993).

[135] See Bidani and Ravallion (1997) and Wagstaff (2003).

[136] See Durr (1993).

[137] On essentially the same data used by Dollar and Kraay (2002), Ravallion (2003a) finds a strong
positive correlation—a correlation coefficient of 0.64—between annualized changes in the absolute
Gini index (in which absolute differences in incomes are not scaled by the mean) and annualized rates
of growth in mean household income or consumption, estimated from the same surveys. Yet the same
data indicate virtually zero correlation ($r = -0.06$) with relative inequality, as measured by the ordinary
Gini index.

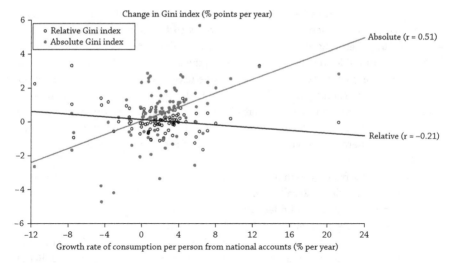

Figure 8.2 The Concept of Inequality Matters to Assessing Whether Inequality Rises in Growing Developing Economies. *Note:* Absolute Gini indices scaled by mean between initial and final years. *Source:* Author's calculations on updating the data set used by Ravallion (2003a).

given country. The median date of the first survey is 1989 while that for the second survey is 2008. We see that higher growth rates (measured here by the growth rate of real private consumption per capita from the national accounts for the same time period) are associated with somewhat lower relative inequality measures but higher absolute measures.

It may well be that past and ongoing debates about the distribution of the gains from growth in the developing world rest in no small measure on this (rarely discussed) conceptual difference in how inequality is defined. Unlike those who see inequality as relative, those who view it in absolute terms will expect to see a trade-off between reducing inequality and reducing poverty. That does not mean that any policy that is good for one is necessarily bad for the other, or that it is impossible to have both; the correlation is just that—a correlation. However, it does help us understand why some growth-promoting and poverty-reducing policy reforms come in for serious criticism and may even be blocked by a non-negligible number of observers concerned about widening gaps in living standards between the rich and the poor. How policymakers deal with that critique may matter greatly to progress against poverty.

A further source of confusion stems from lack of clarity about whether one is talking about inequality between countries or between people (wherever they live). Some of the claims about rising "inequality" have been based on the fact that, looking back over the last thirty years or so prior to the 1990s, initially poorer countries have tended to experience lower subsequent growth rates.[138] But, of course, countries vary enormously in population size. If one takes account of this, then the picture of rising

---

[138] See, e.g., Pritchett (1997).

inequality changes dramatically. Total inequality between people in the world can be thought of as having two components: the amount of inequality *between* countries and the amount *within* countries. Since one naturally weights by population when calculating overall inequality, the between-country component is also population weighted. Given the population weighting, the between-country component has tended to fall, even though poorer countries have not tended to have higher growth rates.[139] The two largest countries are naturally prominent in this finding. China and (more recently) India have enjoyed high growth rates and this has been a major contributing factor to lowering overall inequality in the world.

There is also evidence of relative inequality convergence, whereby relative inequality tends to increase in low inequality countries, and decrease in high inequality countries.[140] The evidence suggests that countries are converging toward a Gini index of around 40%–41%,[141] although the precise number may well be sensitive to measurement assumptions (as discussed in Part Two). However, the process of inequality convergence is clearly not rapid. Consider two countries with Gini indices of 30% and 60%; the past pattern indicates that in fifteen years they can be expected to reach 35% and 51%.

Such inequality convergence is consistent with growth theory in the tradition of the Solow-Swan model; under certain conditions, a fully competitive market economy contains dynamic forces for moderating wealth inequality (even when the poor save less than the rich).[142] The evidence we see of inequality convergence can also be explained by how economic policy convergence in the world during the 1990s interacted with pre-reform differences in the extent of inequality.[143] To see why, suppose that reforming developing countries fall into two categories: those for which pre-reform controls on the economy benefited the rich, keeping inequality artificially high (arguably the case in much of Latin America up to the 1980s), and those in which the controls had the opposite effect, keeping inequality low (as in Eastern Europe and Central Asia prior to the 1990s). Then economic policy reforms can entail sizable redistribution between the poor and the rich, but in opposite directions in the two groups of countries.

There has been much debate about the role of globalization. By one view, it benefits the rich countries at the expense of poor ones. The colonial experience of many of today's developing countries was often seen as being consistent with this view of globalization. However, the evidence does not support this as a generalization. Indeed, it appears that the periods of global trade openness fostered a degree of economic convergence across countries. Williamson (1998) argues that the prior period, 1870–1914, fostered economic expansion and convergence within the "Atlantic economy" (Western Europe and North and South America).

[139] See Ravallion (2013).

[140] See Bénabou (1996), Ravallion (2003b), and Gallup (2012).

[141] See Ravallion (2003b).

[142] As demonstrated by Stiglitz (1969) and Bénabou (1996). Also see the discussion in Bertola (2000).

[143] This is argued by Ravallion (2003b).

Urbanization and Poverty

We have seen a long-run process of urbanization. Starting in the early nineteenth century, there has been a substantial increase in the share of the world's population living in urban areas, from around 10% in 1800 to over 50% today. (The point at which the population was more urban than rural is believed to be 2007.) What has this meant for poverty? The precise mechanisms linking urbanization to poverty are many and have been much studied by development economists. We have seen earlier in this chapter that, since it began, development economics has viewed the process of modern-sector enlargement as a key dynamic for poverty reduction. Most modern-sector activities tend to be concentrated in urban areas, so we can then expect a correlation between rates of urbanization and rates of poverty reduction, although we should not then conclude that urbanization has a causal role; modern-sector enlargement through technical progress is the common factor jointly influencing both urbanization and poverty.

There are a number of possible causal factors linking urban economic growth to poverty reduction. On the one hand, such growth often provides new opportunities to rural out-migrants. Some of the latter may well escape poverty in the process, though others may see little or no gain, and some of the rural migrants to urban areas may well end up worse off. On average, there is likely to be a gain, otherwise migration will presumably cease. There can also be important second-round impacts of urbanization on the living standards of those who remain in rural areas, through higher remittances from urban areas and the fact that there are fewer people competing for the available employment in rural areas.

However, the overall gain to poor people, and falling national poverty rate, may well come with little or no progress against *urban* poverty; indeed, we saw that this has been the case for the bulk of the developing world in chapter 7. The common presumption is that, as long as the urbanization process is reducing poverty nationally, we should not worry about rising urban poverty incidence. Of course, those living in urban areas may have a different view.

We find a positive correlation across countries between GDP per capita and the share of the population living in urban areas.[144] What about the relationship between urbanization and poverty? We must first be clear about how we define and measure poverty. We saw in chapter 7 that the incidence of absolute poverty tends to be higher in the rural areas of developing countries. For relative poverty it is less clear given that average living standards are higher in urban areas; inequality also tends to be higher. These factors may entail that poor people in urban areas feel more relatively deprived. This can be acknowledged, while agreeing that absolute living standards are lower in rural areas and that the poorest should be our first concern.

Across countries, the overall (urban plus rural) poverty rate tends to be lower when the share of the population living in urban areas is higher, as shown in figure 8.3. Furthermore, higher growth rates in the urban population share are associated with

---

[144] See, e.g., Bloom et al. (2008, fig. 1).

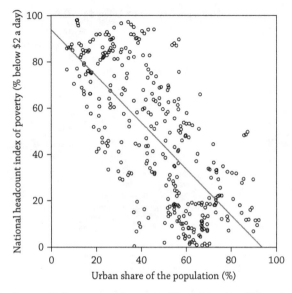

Figure 8.3 Headcount Indices across Countries Plotted against Urban Population Shares. *Source:* Author's calculations from the data set of Ravallion et al. (2007). Countries and dates are pooled.

faster rates of poverty reduction.[145] This correlation is attributable to the common effect of overall economic growth.

The evidence suggests that population urbanization has done more to reduce rural poverty than urban poverty.[146] Urbanization in the developing world appears to be having a compositional effect on the urban population, which slows urban poverty reduction, even though poverty is falling in rural areas and for the population as a whole. Chapter 9 will return to the policy debates on urbanization and poverty.

Progress against Absolute Poverty

Around 1950 there was a turning point in the trajectory of global extreme poverty, as seen in chapter 2, with the figure reproduced as figure 8.4. The post–World War II damaged economies were rebuilding and the newly independent economies of the developing world were striving for rapid economic growth, and with some success. For example, although India's post-Independence growth rates were hardly impressive by today's standards they were well above the trend of the pre-Independence period.[147]

---

[145] This is demonstrated in Ravallion et al. (2007).

[146] See Ravallion et al. (2007).

[147] GDP per capita grew at only 0.1% per annum in the period 1900–1947, as compared to 1.8% in the 1950s, and 1.2% over the 1960s and 1970s (Drèze and Sen 2013, table 1.1, p. 4),

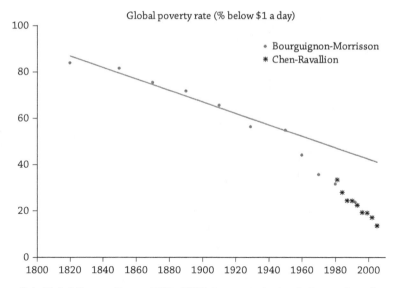

Figure 8.4 Global Poverty Rates, 1820–2005. *Sources:* Author's calculations from the database used by Bourguignon and Morrisson (2002) (provided by the authors) and from Chen and Ravallion (2010a).

China's enormous progress against absolute poverty since around 1980 was an important factor in the developing world's overall success against poverty.[148] This came alongside rising inequality. So China's experience since around 1980 might superficially be seen as testimony to the idea that the country has been in the rising segment of the Kuznets inverted-U. See box 8.8 on the Kuznets Hypothesis and box 8.17 on China.

Box 8.17 **China's Spectacular Progress against Absolute Poverty since 1980**

Figure B8.17.1 shows the headcount index for China starting from 1981, when modern household surveys began in China. We see that China experienced a steeper rate of decline in poverty incidence than average for developing countries. The poverty rate in 1981 was 84%, but had fallen to 13% in 2008. The long-run trend (the slope of the regression line in figure B8.17.1) was a decline of 2.4% points per year (with a standard error of 0.14% points; $R^2 = 0.97$; $n = 12$). At this pace, nobody would be left living under $1.25 by 2014; more precisely, the projection of the regression line hits zero at 2013.5, with a 95% confidence interval of (2011.3, 2015.7). However, a nonlinearity may well set in before then, slowing the pace of progress at low poverty rates. Growth rates will start to fall after some point (as predicted by the conditional convergence), and the last few percent are much harder to reach with either overall economic growth or direct interventions.

---

[148] See Chen and Ravallion (2010a, 2013).

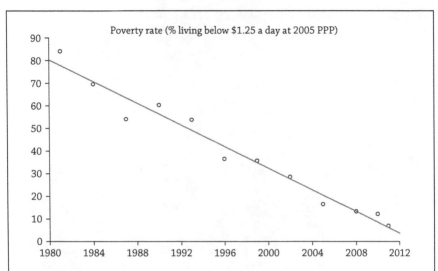

Figure B8.17.1 Poverty Rate in China since 1980. *Source:* Author's calculations from the data set developed by Ravallion and Chen (2013a).

However, here too, the model just does not fit the facts. For one thing, inequality is lower in urban China than in rural China. For another, decompositions of the actual changes in poverty do not suggest that the Kuznets process of growth through modern-sector enlargement was the main driver of growth and poverty reduction in China.[149] One must look elsewhere, notably to the initial agrarian reforms—including the massive land reform under which the land of the collectives was assigned to individual farmers—and market liberalization more broadly, for an explanation of China's rapid poverty reduction in the 1980s. Manufacturing growth came to play an important role later, though that success was premised in part on favorable initial conditions, notably the Communist legacy of investments in human development, including in rural areas. Unlike many developing countries, there was a large literate rural population to draw on as the workforce for China's labor-intensive modern-sector enlargement.

By the turn of the twentieth century there was enough evidence to be confident that higher growth rates tended to yield more rapid rates of absolute poverty reduction.[150] The huge expansion in the availability of household surveys allowed researchers to track how various indicators of household welfare moved during aggregate economic expansions and contractions. As a rule, measures of absolute poverty tend to fall with positive growth and rise with contraction. Also, the expected rate of poverty reduction is zero at zero growth.[151] This is what one would expect given that economic growth tends to be distribution-neutral on average.

[149] See Ravallion and Chen (2007).
[150] See Ravallion (1995, 2001b, 2007), Fields (2001), Dollar and Kraay (2002), Kraay (2006), and World Bank (1990b, 2001a). Also see the review of the arguments and evidence on this point in Ferreira and Ravallion (2009).
[151] This was demonstrated by Ravallion (2001b).

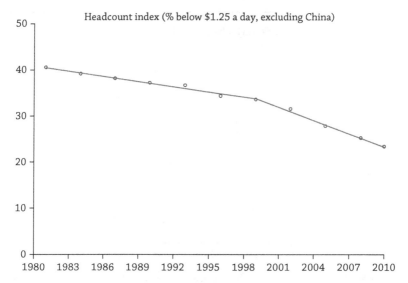

Figure 8.5 Poverty Rates for the Developing World outside China. *Source:* Ravallion (2013).

A more poverty-reducing process of global economic growth emerged in the developing world after 2000, and not just because of China's growth. The trend rate of decline in the "$1.25 a day" poverty rate for the developing world outside China rose from a miserably low 0.4 percentage points per year over 1980–2000 to a very respectable 1.0 percentage points per year after that, as can be seen from figure 8.5.[152]

To help understand the extent of this shift in trajectories, imagine if the pre-2000 trajectory had continued. Then 30% of the population of the developing world outside China would have lived below $1.25 a day in 2012 instead of 23% percent, representing an extra 280 million people who would otherwise have lived below $1.25 a day. If the developing world can maintain this post-2000 trajectory without a rise in overall inequality then one billion people will be lifted out of extreme poverty by sometime around 2030.[153]

The future trajectory for poverty reduction in the developing world depends in part on when the economic forces of convergence toward the steady-state level of mean income start to come into play. Without an increase in the steady-state ("long-run") level of mean income, growth rates will inevitably start to fall as one gets closer to that level. This has prompted fears of a "middle-income trap."[154] However, others argue that there is still ample scope for increasing the steady-state level of mean income, including through better policies.

[152] The difference in trends is significant $(t = 10.01, p < 0.00005)$.

[153] See Ravallion (2013) on how this can be done. World Bank (2014b) present some simulations that suggest this will take longer. (Also see Yoshida et al. 2014). However, it should be noted that those simulations require all countries to grow at the same rate, which is very unlikely. The calculations in Ravallion (2013) relate instead to the growth rate for the developing world as a whole. Note also that unchanging inequality in the world as a whole does not imply that all countries have the same growth rate.

[154] It is not clear that the idea of a middle-income trap is distinguishable from mean convergence; see the discussion in Pritchett and Summers (2014).

Inequality as an Impediment to Pro-Poor Growth

The term "pro-poor growth" is used in two different ways in the literature.[155] The first definition refers to a growth process in which poverty falls more than it would have if all incomes had grown at the same rate. This definition focuses on the distributional shifts during the growth process; roughly speaking, for growth to be deemed "pro-poor" inequality must fall, in that incomes of the poor grow at a higher rate than those of the non-poor. A concern with this definition is that rising inequality during a period of overall economic expansion may come with large absolute gains to the poor yet this is not deemed to be "pro-poor growth." Indeed, that is what we have seen in China; by this first definition China's huge success in reducing poverty has not stemmed from pro-poor growth. The second definition focuses instead on poverty in a growing economy: the extent to which growth is pro-poor depends on how much a chosen measure of poverty changes (as discussed in chapter 5). Naturally, this will depend in part on what happens to distribution, but only in part—it will also depend on what happens to average living standards. I will use this second definition, although I will note some situations in which the first definition would say something very different.

Given that economic growth in the developing world has tended to be distribution neutral on average, pro-poor growth by the first definition has not been the norm; roughly half the time growth has come with rising inequality. Growth has typically been "pro-poor" by the second definition. But the more interesting question is: How much impact did growth have on poverty? Did poverty fall a lot or a little? As we have also seen, the answer depends in part on what happens to inequality—whether growth was pro-poor by the first definition.

However, even if inequality does not change, for a given rate of growth, progress against poverty is faster in some countries and in some time periods than others. A key factor in explaining these differences is the initial level of inequality. The literature has shown that the poverty impact of a given rate of growth depends in part on the initial level of inequality.[156] This is intuitive; if the poor have a low share of the pie and inequality does not fall, then they will tend to have a low share in the increments to the size of the pie due to growth. A simple characterization of this dependence is found in the following formula:[157]

Proportionate rate of change in the absolute poverty rate
= β (1-Gini index of inequality) × Rate of growth in mean income

[155] The first definition was proposed by Baulch and McCullock (2000) and Kakwani and Pernia (2000). The second is due to Ravallion and Chen (2003).

[156] See Ravallion (1997a, 2007, 2012d), World Bank (2006), Bourguignon (2003), and Humberto Lopez and Luis Servén (2006).

[157] Ravallion (1997a, 2007) found this relationship in household survey data over time for developing countries. Ravallion (2007) found that the fit could be improved slightly by using the squared value of 1-Gini index in the distributional correction, but this is ignored here. Ravallion (1997a) did not find that the elasticity of poverty to growth varied systematically with the mean, although if incomes are log-normally distributed, then such a variation is implied theoretically (Bourguignon 2003; Lopez and Servén 2006).

Here β is a (negative) constant. The term β times 1-Gini index of inequality in the equation above can be interpreted as the *growth elasticity of poverty reduction* (i.e., the proportionate rate of poverty reduction divided by the rate of growth). The formula says that the proportionate rate of progress against poverty is directly proportional to the growth rate in the overall mean, where the coefficient of proportionality goes to zero when the inequality index is at its highest value of unity, but the coefficient reaches its maximum when inequality is zero.

Figure 8.6 shows the relationship between the rate of poverty reduction and the distribution-corrected rate of growth in the mean using data for about ninety developing countries.[158] The estimated value of β is found to be about −4.5 (with a standard error of 0.66). Of course, there is also a variance around the line of best fit in figure 8.6, due to changes in distribution over time and measurement errors. To help capture this, one can add a regression control for the changes in the Gini index between the same two surveys. Then the value of β falls slightly, to −3.6 (standard error of 0.56). Figure 8.6 also gives the relationship when one controls for changes in inequality.

In probing more deeply into the ways in which inequality matters to pro-poor growth two specific sources of inequality have been studied by economists. The first relates to inequality in agricultural land holdings in rural economies. The more unequal the distribution of cultivable land, the less one expects gains in overall agricultural productivity to reduce poverty; when poor farm households have less land

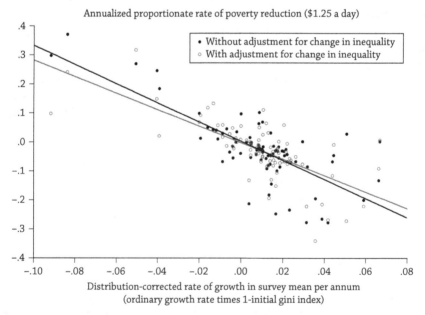

Figure 8.6 Absolute Poverty Reduction and the Distribution-Corrected Rate of Growth. *Source:* Author's calculations based on the data and model described in Ravallion (2012d).

[158] This is an updated version of the data set described in Ravallion (2012b).

they will gain less from the higher farm productivity.[159] The initial distribution of agricultural landholdings has also been seen to play a role in the qualitative aspects of the growth process, especially the extent of labor absorption. Smallholders tend to have a higher demand for labor (both own-labor and hired labor) per hectare than large land owners.[160] Thus, agriculture is more labor absorbing and (hence) poverty reducing when the inequality of land is relatively low. For example, in Taiwan, the initial conditions for more pro-poor growth in a market-based economy were laid by a radical redistributive land reform, which led to productive and dynamic owner-farmed smallholdings.[161]

The second source of income inequality emphasized in the literature on pro-poor growth is *human capital*. Here too the argument is intuitive. In a setting in which poor people are also poorly schooled (or unhealthy), they will be less well equipped to participate in new economic opportunities. This is thought to be especially important for new opportunities coming from the non-farm economy, where skill demands tend to be higher than in agriculture. We will return to this topic in section 8.4 when comparing progress against poverty in China and India.

Economic Crises and Poverty

Vulnerability to shocks and crises has long been a fact of life for poor people everywhere. Technological innovations often have losers as well as gainers. A famous example is the introduction of the potato to the mass consumption bundle in Europe during the early seventeenth century. This was an important innovation that lowered the cost of a nutritionally adequate diet for poor people. Yet the potato blight that hit Europe in the 1840s brought a severe famine; in Ireland, where the population had become heavily dependent on potatoes as the main food staple, one million people died from starvation and related diseases during the Potato Famine of 1845–52. So, while poor people benefited from the potato innovation, they also bore the (huge) cost of the accompanying downside risk. Policy failures did not help, however. Powerful free-trade advocates insisted that food could be exported from famine-afflicted Ireland, and that happened.[162] In fact, food exports during famines are not uncommon; the negative income effect of the shock can readily curtail effective demand in the affected economy.[163] But insisting on free trade in such circumstances is not good economics. Even accepting the economic arguments about the gains from free trade in normal times, these did not rule out temporary export taxes or quantitative restrictions on food export on welfare grounds when famine threatened, especially when other, more reliable, forms of social protection were not up to the task.[164] (Chapter 10 returns to this issue.)

---

[159] This may well be mitigated by indirect effects via the market for agricultural labor; in the case of India, Datt and Ravallion (1998a) find evidence of this indirect channel via the labor market.

[160] See Booth and Sundrum (1984) and Lipton (2009).

[161] See Fei et al. (1979).

[162] See Woodham-Smith (1962).

[163] For further discussion and references to the literature, see Ravallion (1997b).

[164] See Do et al. (2014).

We saw in chapter 7 that the developing world has developed a "middle-class bulge," where "middle class" is defined as not being poor by the average poverty line of developing countries ($2 a day) but still poor by Western standard (judged by the US line of $13 a day). And the bulge is at the low end of this range. This more dense middle of the distribution is an implication of a pattern of aggregate economic growth in the developing world as a whole that has favored very poor people. This success against extreme poverty has come with continuing vulnerability to aggregate economic contraction, with one-in-six people in the developing world now living between $2 and $3 per day.

The generalizations one often hears that the poor will bear the brunt of crises should be viewed with caution. Many factors will influence the outcomes, including both initial conditions and policies, in both the macro and micro domains. Inequality itself is one of the initial conditions that matter. We have seen that high initial inequality tends to mean lower gains to the poor from an expanding economy. By the same token, under otherwise identical conditions, the poor in high inequality countries are often more protected from economic contractions.[165]

The impacts of an economic contraction will rarely be confined to the poorest, and not all of the poor need be affected. Indeed, some will be protected by the same things that have kept them poor in the first place—geographic isolation and poor connectivity with national and global markets. Research on Indonesia's severe economy-wide crisis of 1998 found sharp but geographically uneven increases in poverty, reflecting both the geographic unevenness in the economic contraction and the differing initial conditions at the local level.[166] Proportionate impacts on poverty were greater in initially better off and less unequal districts. Another study of the same crisis found that most households were impacted, but that it was the urban poor who suffered most; the ability of poor rural households to produce food mitigated the worst effects of high inflation.[167] By contrast, the rural poor bore a heavier burden of the shock in Thailand around the same time, in part because of their greater integration with the urban economy.[168]

Such research findings lead one to expect that, at any given level of living, some people will lose more than others and some may even gain. Thus, it can be deceptive to focus solely on an aggregate measure of income poverty, for which the impact might be modest and yet there are large welfare changes under the surface. For example, while the 1998 financial crisis in Russia saw only a modest 2% point increase in the poverty rate, longitudinal data (tracking the same households before and after the crisis) revealed substantial losses and gains.[169]

While acknowledging these caveats, it remains that the bulk of the evidence does suggest that poverty rates rise during macroeconomic crises. For example, the many

[165] See Ravallion (1997a, 2001b).
[166] See Ravallion and Lokshin (2007).
[167] See Friedman and Levinsohn (2002).
[168] See Bresciani et al. (2002).
[169] See Lokshin and Ravallion (2000).

negative macroeconomic shocks (defined as GDP contractions of 4% or more) experienced by the countries of Latin America—the region of the developing world with the highest inequality—in the 1980s and 1990s were *all* associated with higher absolute poverty rates.[170]

Across the developing world as a whole, crises (defined as spells of negative growth) have been distribution-neutral on average, with inequality rising about as often as it falls.[171] Thus, the main reason absolute poverty rates tend to rise in crises is simply that mean income has fallen. But (again) this is a generalization across countries; there are certainly many countries in which crises have been associated with rising inequality.

Even if not identified as a "crisis," *macroeconomic instability* in the form of high inflation rates has proven costly to poor people. We already noted that wage stickiness can generate significant short-term welfare effects from shocks to goods prices. In a multi-country study it was found that poor people are more likely than others to identify inflation as a "top national concern."[172] The same study found evidence that objective welfare indicators, including poverty measures, deteriorated with inflation. We will return to cite other evidence in the case studies on Brazil, China, and India, in section 8.4. The fact that inflation can hurt the poor in the short term needs to be considered in macroeconomic policy decisions.

The welfare losses from crises and macroeconomic instability can last a lot longer than the shock itself. The poorest can be particularly vulnerable to even small shocks. Productive activity is simply not feasible at low levels of nutrition; this threshold effect means that a negative shock of sufficient size can push a poor household past its tipping point and so put it on a path to destitution, while the same household bounces back in due course from even a slightly smaller shock. (This is an example of a dynamic poverty trap; see box 8.14.)

Exposure to crises during the body's periods of growth can also entail long-term costs. Comparing adult heights of women in sub-Saharan Africa using DHS's for thirty-three countries, one finds a pattern consistent with the hypothesis that when periods of (positive) economic growth coincide with the growth spurts of adolescent girls at around age ten then their nutrition improves resulting in taller adults, while economic contractions at age ten are followed by shorter adults.[173]

This evidence for sub-Saharan Africa also points to the potential for longer term reversals in human development. Strikingly, the average height of African women was actually falling from the late 1960s—coinciding with falling average incomes until the mid-1990s.[174]

---

[170] See Lustig (2000).

[171] See Ravallion and Chen (2009).

[172] See Easterly and Fischer (2001, 160).

[173] See Garenne (2011), who compares the average BMI of cohort c (such as those born in 1970) with national income per capita at $c + 10$ (i.e., 1980). Garenne shows such a pattern in aggregate time series data (aggregating across the thirty-three countries) and summarizes his country-level analysis of spells of expansion and contraction that appears to be consistent with the aggregate time series data.

[174] See Garenne (2011).

   Research on specific past crises has also found signs of lasting impacts. A study of
the impacts of the East Asia crisis found that about half of Indonesia's poverty count
in 2002 was attributed to the 1998 crisis even though macroeconomic recovery had
been achieved well before 2002.[175] Many of the things poor families have to do to help
protect their current living conditions have lasting consequences. Debts often rise; key
productive assets (such as livestock or land) are sold. And kids are taken out of school
to save money and add to the family's current earnings. And these adjustments are
often difficult to reverse.
   Macroeconomic shocks are also life-threatening in poor countries. An ambitious
study by Sarah Baird, Jed Friedman, and Norbert Schady spanning 1.7 million births
in fifty-nine developing countries, attempted to identify the effects of changes in
national income on infant mortality rates.[176] Box 8.18 discusses the study's methodology in more detail as it illustrates a number of points. The key finding is that
negative shocks to national income resulted in higher IMR. In their basic specification,
a 1% drop in GDP per capita resulted in a 0.2–0.4 increase in the number of deaths
per 1,000 live births. Female IMR was also found to be more sensitive to shocks than
male IMR.

Box 8.18 Macroeconomic Shocks and Infant Mortality

   Recall that a regression is a line of best fit relating one or more explanatory
variables to a specific dependent variable (box 1.19). Also recall the discussion
of fixed effects regressions in box 6.2. Baird et al. (2011) used the micro data
from 123 Demographic and Health Surveys spanning fifty-nine countries. The
survey years ranged from 1986 to 2004. The surveys included 760,000 women
and 1.7 million births. They then collated these with country-level data from
the National Accounts on GDP per capita at purchasing power parity. The DHS
obtained birth and death histories. (Recall that chapter 7 used these data in
studying the non-income dimensions of poverty.)
   In testing for an effect of income shocks on IMR their basic regression
specification took the form:

$$D_{ict} = \alpha_c + \beta \ln Y_{ct} + f_c(t) + \varepsilon_{ict}.$$

   On the LHS we have a dummy variable taking the value 1 if child i in country c
in year t died in the first year of life, and zero of the child survived. The first thing
we see on the RHS is a country-specific intercept, called a "country fixed effect."
Then we have the term for the effect of national income (GDP per capita, logged).
After that we have a country-specific time trend, which is just some function of
time. Finally we have the innovation error term.

---

[175] See Ravallion and Lokshin (2007).
[176] See Baird et al. (2011).

The impacts of a crisis and other shocks (such as droughts) on children are understandably of great concern, given both the current welfare losses and the importance of early childhood development to longer term livings standards (as discussed in chapter 4).[177] For example, when poor families are compelled to cut short their kids' schooling in response to a shock this creates a lasting impact on poverty since school dropouts tend to earn less as adults. This impact will also vary, depending on the extent of the shock and initial conditions. Declining wages make child labor less attractive, and schooling more so, but (at the same time) lower parental incomes increase the value of the extra money that children can bring to the family budget if they work.

The balance of these forces will vary from place to place. In low-income countries schooling tends to decline in a macroeconomic or agro-climatic crisis while in middle- and high-income countries schooling rates increase.[178] Impacts on the nutrition of young children in poor families are also of special concern. A number of research findings suggest that poor nutrition in the early years of life retards child growth, cognitive and learning ability, schooling attainments, and (in all likelihood) earnings in adulthood.[179]

While there are persuasive ethical arguments for focusing the social policy response on the poorest among those who are vulnerable, there are also instrumental arguments for such a focus, related to the longer term implications of the crisis. The expectation is that it will be the children of the poorest families who are most likely to be taken out of school and see a decline in their nutritional and health status. Thus, the shock can create more persistent poverty across generations unless short-term assistance is directed to the poorest among those whose livelihoods are under threat.

8.3 Evidence on Distributional Impediments to Growth

Motivated by the new theoretical models of endogenous growth, the period from the late 1980s saw greatly enhanced attention to long-run growth empirics.[180] The key tool is the *growth regression* (box 8.19), which entails regressing country's annualized growth rates over some period of time on their initial mean incomes and a set of control variables typically representing the initial conditions observed at the beginning of that period. As explained in box 8.19, the virtually universal functional form for these growth regressions assumes that each country has just one steady-state equilibrium. Thus, this empirical tool essentially rules out the idea of multiple equilibria. Thus, it was never an appropriate tool for testing for the more complex forms of dynamics implied by poverty traps.

---

[177] A useful review of the arguments and evidence on how shocks affect early childhood development can be found in Friedman and Sturdy (2011).

[178] See Ferreira and Schady (2008).

[179] See, e.g., Alderman et al. (2006), Ferreira and Schady (2008), and Heckman (2008).

[180] The first of this new wave of empirical studies of the determinants of the rate of economic growth appears to have been Kormendi and Meguire (1985).

Box 8.19 Cross-Country Growth Regressions

A typical growth regression has the form:

$$g_{it} = \alpha + \beta Y_{it-\tau} + \gamma X_{it} + \varepsilon_{it}.$$

On the LHS we have the growth rate for mean income of country i (typically GDP per capita) over a time period of length τ years, from $t - \tau$ to t. This growth rate is typically measured as the annualized log difference, $g_{it} \equiv \ln(Y_{it}/Y_{it-\tau})/\tau$, where Y_{it} is mean income at date t. On the RHS we have the initial mean income (often also entering in log form) and a set of control variables, X_{it}, which can include initial conditions ($X_{it-\tau}$) as well shocks during the period. If the estimated value of β is negative, then we have what is called "conditional convergence," whereby initially poorer countries tend to see higher rates of growth at given $X_{it-\tau}$. (Recall from see box 8.10 that this is an implication of growth theory.) Finally on the RHS we have an error term, ε_{it}, which collects all the unobserved variables and measurement errors. As in all regressions, the assumptions made about the properties of this error term determine the appropriate estimation method, and the potential biases in the results obtained for the key parameters of interest, α, β and γ. (Note that γ is really a list of parameters, corresponding to the variables in X.) The standard assumption is that ε_{it} has a mean of zero given the values taken by $Y_{it-\tau}$ and $X_{it-\tau}$. This can be written in the form $E(\varepsilon_{it} \,|\, Y_{it-\tau}, X_{it-\tau}) = 0$, where the E denotes the mathematical expectation (the mean) of the term in parentheses.

Notice that the above specification implies a unique steady-state equilibrium for the level of mean income for each country at each date, which we can denote Y_{it}^{*}. To derive that equilibrium we set $g_{it} = 0$ (since the change in income is zero when in the steady state). Then from the above equation we can see that the expected value of the steady-state level of mean income for country i is simply:

$$E(Y_{it}^{*}) = \frac{\alpha + \gamma X_{it}}{-\beta}.$$

Thus, we can think of the X_{it} as controls for the steady-state income level. Notice that as long as $\beta < 0$ any variable in X that is found to result in a higher growth rate (the relevant element of the list of parameters in γ is positive) will also result in a higher steady-state level of mean income.

Note on the literature: There is a good discussion in Barro and Sala-i-Martin (1995, ch. 12).

There is a huge literature on growth empirics using the cross-country growth regression with specifications mainly differing according to the set of variables included in the controls (X). Box 8.20 summarizes the results of a (valiant) attempt to identify a robust set of predictors. The robustness of the results from these regressions has been a serious concern in virtually all areas of their application. A specific variable that is a statistically significant predictor of the growth rate in one study may cease to be so in another, once one changes the specification of other variables in the model. This kind of sensitivity is not too surprising given the correlations often found among the X's, so that if one study leaves out some crucial X that happens to be quite highly correlated with some variable of special interest the coefficient on the latter variable will naturally change. Additionally, the potential for multiple equilibria in the real world can mean that the same set of X's (even when the list of observed X's is close to complete) can yield different steady-state solutions. This can seriously confound the identification of the effects of interest.

Box 8.20 Searching for Robust Predictors of the Rate of Growth

Among the many variables that have been used as predictors of the rate of growth, a few authors have asked: what are the most robust predictors? Examples include Fernandez et al. (2001) and Sala-I-Martin et al. (2004). This discussion will focus on the latter paper.

Sala-I-Martin et al. took a weighted average of OLS coefficients across multiple models. Their dependent variable was the growth of GDP per capita at purchasing power parities between 1960 and 1996.The three most robust predictors were the relative price of investment (usually taken as a measure of the extent of policy distortions), the primary school enrollment rate, and the initial level of real GDP per capita. Here is their list of the eighteen most robust predictors (with explanations when called for):

1. East Asian dummy: a dummy variable taking the value 1 for the countries of East Asia and 0 otherwise.
2. The enrollment rate in primary education in 1960.
3. Investment price: The average investment price level between 1960 and 1964 on purchasing power parity basis from Penn World Tables.
4. GDP 1960 (log): Logarithm of GDP per capita in 1960.
5. Fraction of tropical area: The share of the country's land area within geographical tropics.
6. Population density coastal (within 100 km of the coastline) in 1965.
7. Malaria prevalence in 1966.
8. Life expectancy in 1960.
9. Fraction of the population that is Confucian.
10. African dummy: a dummy variable taking the value 1 for the countries of sub-Saharan Africa and 0 otherwise.
11. Latin American dummy: a dummy variable taking the value 1 for the countries of Latin America and 0 otherwise.
12. Fraction of GDP in mining.
13. Dummy variable for former Spanish colonies.

continued

Box 8.20 **(Continued)**

14. Years open: Number of years that the economy has been open between 1950 and 1994.
15. Fraction Muslim: Fraction of population Muslim in 1960.
16. Fraction Buddhist: Fraction of population Buddhist in 1960.
17. Ethno-linguistic fractionalization: Average of five different indices of fractionalization which is the probability of two random people in a country not speaking the same language.
18. Government consumption share: Share of government consumption in GDP for 1961.

Policy lessons? Many variables on this list have little or no policy relevance. For that purpose we want to know what it is about being a former Spanish colony (say) that is bad for growth. (Acemoglu and Robinson, 2012 ch.1, point to some more policy relevant answers, including weak enforcement of property rights in those colonies.) Also worrying from a country-policy perspective is that being a robust positive predictor of growth based on cross-country comparisons does not permit us to claim that an exogenous increase in the value of that variable (due to a policy) will increase the rate of growth in any one specific country. Suppose that the variable X can either take the value of 1 or 0 (switching on and off the policy). The impact in any one country is the difference between the growth rate when $X = 1$ and that when $X = 0$ for that country. However, we cannot possibly observe the same country with $X = 1$ and $X = 0$ at the same time. So we cannot know the causal impact of X at that level. All a regression can identify is the mean impact. (This point applies to all regressions, not just growth regressions.)

Macro Evidence That Inequality Impedes Growth

There are many qualitative accounts of how extractive political institutions serving the interests of ruling elites have held back the economic progress of poor people.[181] By expropriating their property or output these institutions undermine incentives to escape poverty. These are essentially inequalities of power that impede growth. In extreme cases they constitute poverty traps.

A strand of the empirical literature on economic growth has tried to provide quantitative evidence by testing for measures of inequality as initial conditions in growth regressions. The results have generally supported the view that higher initial inequality impedes growth.[182] And the effect is quantitatively large and statistically significant. One study found that a one percentage point increase in the Gini index

---

[181] Acemoglu and Robinson (2012) provide many examples.
[182] See Alesina and Rodrik (1994), Rodrik (1994), Persson and Tabellini (1994), Birdsall et al. (1995), Clarke (1995), Perotti (1996), Deininger and Squire (1998), Knowles (2005), Voitchovsky (2005), Hertzer and Vollmer (2012), and Berg et al. (2012).

results in a decrease in long-run mean income of 0.013%; when normalized by standard deviations, this is about half the growth impact of the investment share.[183] Another study found that more unequal countries tend to have less sustained spells of growth, and this effect is also quite large; a one percentage point higher Gini index is associated with a decline in the length of the growth spell of 11%–15%.[184] A follow-up study looked at the effects of governmental redistribution, using the difference between the Gini index of inequality before and after governmental taxes and transfers.[185] The study found that governments of countries with higher initial inequality tend to redistribute more, but that lower post-tax inequality yields higher growth rates and more prolonged spells of growth at any given level of governmental redistributive effort. Furthermore, such effort appears to be generally benign with regard to its impact on growth; it appears to take quite high levels of redistribution before an adverse impact emerges.

Not all the evidence suggests that inequality is harmful to growth.[186] The main reason why some studies have been less supportive appears to be that they have relied on identifying the effects of changes in inequality on changes in growth rates. This addresses the problem of time-invariant latent heterogeneity in growth rates by including country-level fixed effects in growth rates. However, this approach appears to have little power for detecting the true relationships given that the changes over time in growth rates will almost certainly have a low signal-to-noise ratio (box 6.3). Simulation studies have found that the coefficients on growth determinants are heavily biased toward zero in fixed-effects growth regressions.[187]

There is also evidence that inequality has different effects on growth in the short-term compared to the long-term. In the short-term, higher inequality stimulates growth, but this effect is wiped out by adverse longer-term effects of higher inequality.[188]

There are a number of remaining issues in this literature. The bulk of the literature has used consumption or income inequality measures (as discussed in Part Two). Theoretical arguments based on borrowing constraints point to the importance of *wealth inequality*, not income inequality. There is evidence of adverse effects of wealth inequality in growth.[189]

The aspect of initial distribution that has received almost all the attention in the empirical literature is inequality, as typically measured by the Gini index of (relative) inequality. The popularity of the Gini index appears to owe more to its availability in secondary data compilations on income and consumption inequality measures than

---

[183] See Herzer and Vollmer (2012).

[184] See Berg et al. (2012).

[185] See Ostry et al. (2014).

[186] See Li and Zou (1998), Barro (2000), and Forbes (2000).

[187] See Hauk and Wacziarg (2009).

[188] See Halter et al. (2014), who interpret the short-term effects as "economic" (such as through higher savings rates) while the long-term effects are related to the political economy, such as through the provision of public goods.

[189] See Rodrik (1994), Birdsall and Londono (1997), and Deininger and Olinto (2000), all using cross-country data, and Ravallion (1998a) using regional data for China.

to any intrinsic relevance to the economic arguments.[190] However, the significance of the Gini index in past studies may well reflect an omitted variable bias, given that one expects that inequality will be highly correlated with poverty at a given mean.[191]

There are also issues about the relevant control variables when studying the effect of initial distribution on growth. The specification choices in past work to test for effects of initial distribution have lacked clear justification in terms of the theories predicting such effects. Consider three popular predictors of growth, namely *human development*, the *investment share*, and *financial development*. On the first, basic schooling and health attainments (often significant in growth regressions) are one of the channels linking initial distribution to growth.[192] Turning to the second, one of the most robust predictors of growth rates is the share of investment in GDP;[193] one of the main channels through which distribution affects growth is via aggregate investment. Indeed, this is one of the channels identified in the theoretical literature.

Finally, consider private credit (as a share of GDP), which has been used as a measure of "financial sector development" in explaining growth and poverty reduction.[194] The correlations are suggestive in that countries with more developed and more competitive financial sectors tend to see higher subsequent growth rates. However, there may well be deeper causative factors at work. The theories discussed above based on borrowing constraints suggest that the aggregate flow of credit in the economy depends on the initial distribution. Deeper political and economic inequalities, as well as problems of asymmetric information, inhibit financial sector development.[195]

In each of these three examples, inequality also matters to the control variables, as well as directly, given those variables. Nor is it clear why the specific direct effect identified in these papers is of interest. In testing for whether inequality matters, as suggested by theory, we are probably more interested in knowing the total effect.

While the theories and evidence reviewed above point to inequality and/or poverty as the relevant parameters of the initial distribution, yet another strand of the literature has pointed to various reasons for why the size of a country's *middle class* can matter to the fortunes of those not (yet) so lucky to be middle class. It has been argued that a larger middle class promotes economic growth, such as by fostering entrepreneurship, shifting the composition of consumer demand, and making it more

---

[190] The compilation of Gini indices from secondary sources (and not using consistent assumptions) in Deininger and Squire (1996) led to almost all the tests in the literature since that paper was published.

[191] An "omitted variable bias" arises in a regression when some relevant variable is excluded from the model that is correlated with the included variables. In this case, although the poverty rate is relevant on theoretical grounds, it is omitted from standard tests, but is clearly correlated with the inequality index at a given mean.

[192] Indeed, that is the link in the original papers of Loury (1981) and Galor and Zeria (1993). More recently, Gutiérrez and Tanaka (2009) show how high initial inequality in a developing country can yield a political-economy equilibrium in which there is little or no public investment in basic schooling; the poorest families send their kids to work, and the richest turn to private schooling.

[193] See, e.g., Levine and Renelt (1992).

[194] For example, see Beck et al. (2000, 2007).

[195] See, for example, the historical analysis of the differing trajectories of the United States and Mexico in the nineteenth century in Acemoglu and Robinson (2012).

politically feasible to attain policy reforms and institutional changes conducive to growth.[196] This has been an issue in India, where it was argued back to the 1970s that "inequality" constrained the growth of the manufacturing sector by limiting the size of the domestic market for consumer goods.[197] Here too it can be argued that it was not inequality that was the culprit but the relatively small middle class, or the extent of absolute poverty that generated the domestic demand constraint in a relatively closed economy. The argument has been heard less in the more open economies of today. However, the Indian middle class has been influential in promoting reform.[198] Using cross-country regressions, one study finds that a larger income share controlled by the middle three quintiles is a significant predictor of rates of economic growth.[199]

So we have three main contenders for the distributional parameter most relevant to growth: inequality, poverty, and the size of the middle class. The fact that very few encompassing tests are found in the literature, and that these different measures of distribution are not independent, leaves one in doubt about what aspect of distribution really matters. As already noted, when the initial value of mean income is included in a growth regression alongside initial inequality, but initial poverty is an excluded but relevant variable, the inequality measure may pick up the effect of poverty rather than inequality per se. Similarly, the main way the middle class expands in a developing country is almost certainly through poverty reduction, so it is unclear whether it is a high incidence of poverty or a small middle class that impedes growth. Furthermore, a relative concept of the "middle class," such as the income share of middle quintiles, is probably correlated with a relative inequality measure, clouding the interpretation.

Possibly the strongest evidence to date to support the view that it is poverty not inequality that impedes growth in developing countries comes from the observation that we see convergence in average living standards among developing countries and greater progress against poverty in faster growing economies yet we do not see poverty convergence; the poorest countries are not enjoying higher proportionate rates of poverty reduction.[200] This paradox can be resolved by arguing that a high initial incidence of poverty, at a given initial mean, impedes subsequent growth (consistently with a number of the theories outlined above). This is consistent with data for almost one hundred developing countries, which reveal an adverse effect on consumption growth of high initial poverty incidence at a given initial mean.[201] High poverty at a given initial mean appears to matter more than inequality, or measures of the middle class or of polarization. Also, starting with a high incidence of poverty limits progress against poverty at any given growth rate. For many poor countries, the growth advantage of

---

[196] Analyses of the role of the middle class in promoting entrepreneurship and growth include Acemoglu and Zilibotti (1997) and Doepke and Zilibotti (2005). Middle-class demand for higher quality goods plays a role in the model of Murphy et al. (1989). Birdsall et al. (2000) conjecture that support from the middle class is crucial to policy reform.

[197] See, e.g., the discussion in Bardhan (1984b, ch. 4).

[198] See, e.g., Sridharan (2004).

[199] See Easterly (2001).

[200] See Ravallion (2012d).

[201] See Ravallion (2012d).

starting out with a low mean is lost due to their high poverty rates. That does not, however, imply that any antipoverty policy will promote growth as this depends on many factors (as discussed in chapters 9 and 10).

Evidence from Micro Studies

The arguments summarized above as to why poverty can bring lasting efficiency costs do not require the existence of a poverty trap. However, when a poverty trap is present the cost of poverty can rise greatly. So it is important to ask whether such traps have economic significance.

On a priori grounds, it is highly plausible that threshold effects exist. Biology alone makes this plausible; unless one can support the nutritional needs of the body at rest it will be impossible to do any work. Whether this is of economic significance in practice (even in poor economies) is another matter. Simple arithmetic suggests that human caloric requirements can be covered with seemingly modest spending on food staples.[202] However, this is not conclusive. Environmental enteropathy can generate quite low nutrition absorption rates given the persistent fecal-oral contamination in the environments in which many people live. In effect, the implicit price of an absorbed calorie capable of fueling work effort is higher, possibly far higher, than the nominal price. Furthermore, we have also learned that work productivity depends on the *personal history* of nutrition and health.[203] Someone who is stunted due to a long history of under-nutrition—low intakes and/or low absorption—can be in current nutritional balance (able to afford current food-energy requirements) but have such low productivity that a poverty trap emerges. It may not be a strict threshold, but a smoother, S-shaped function, as in box 8.13.

Other sources of *threshold effects* are also plausible on a priori grounds, such as the fact that a minimum level of schooling is essential before schooling can be a viable route out of poverty (recalling from chapter 1 the story of Sunil, the boy from the Mumbai slum, in Boo, 2011). One can also interpret the aforementioned arguments on how poverty reduces cognitive functions as stemming from biological threshold effects—that a minimum level of time not worrying about the financial and other stresses created by poverty is needed to escape poverty.

In testing for threshold effects, a strand of the literature has looked for lumpiness in non-human capital requirements. The results have been mixed. One study found evidence of nonlinear wealth effects on new business start-ups in Tunisia, but did not find signs of threshold effects.[204] Nor do data on Mexican microenterprises reveal any sign of non-convexities in production at low levels.[205] By contrast, however, one of the few studies using wealth data found compelling evidence of the nonconvexity in asset data for rural Kenya and Madagascar.[206]

---

[202] See Deaton's (2006) review of Fogel (2004). Subramanian and Deaton (1996) calculate that nutritional requirements can be met with a small fraction of the daily wage rate, using data for India. Similar reasoning leads Swamy (1997) to question the nutrition-based efficiency wage hypothesis.

[203] See Dasgupta (2011).

[204] See Mesnard and Ravallion (2006).

[205] See McKenzie and Woodruff (2006).

[206] See Barrett et al. (2006). Also see the discussion in Carter and Barrett (2006).

It can also be difficult to detect theoretically plausible threshold effects on dynamics in standard micro-data sets.[207] For one thing, depending on the frequency of the observations over time in the data, the existence of the unstable "middle" equilibrium (such as point B in the figure in box 8.14) can generate *sample attrition*—the destitute simply drop out of the data (including by becoming homeless) and they are clearly not a random subsample so bias can be expected.[208] For another, there will be high social returns to informal risk-sharing arrangements to prevent most people falling into the trap. The trap is still there, but may only be evident in extreme situations when those social relationships break down. It has been argued that this is a plausible interpretation of what happens in *famines*.[209]

A testable implication of the models based on credit-market failures is that individual wealth should be an increasing concave function of its own past value. In principle, this can be tested on suitable micro panel data, though most data sets have only consumption or income, not wealth. This also requires a more complex form of dynamic specification than found in the standard cross-country growth regressions discussed above; crucially we require specification that allows the possibility of multiple equilibria and a reasonably long time series in the panel data is needed. In one of the few studies to estimate such a model, supportive evidence on concavity was found in panel data on incomes for Hungary and Russia.[210] This was confirmed by another study for China.[211] Similar findings have also been reported using data for Ethiopia and Pakistan.[212] These studies do not find the threshold properties in the empirical income dynamics that would be needed for a poverty trap. However, using similar methods, but arguably a better identification strategy, evidence has been found of a low, unstable, equilibrium in the income dynamics for a long panel of households in rural India.[213]

Micro-empirical support for the claim that there are efficiency costs of poor nutrition and healthcare for children in poor families has come from a number of studies. In a recent example, an impact evaluation of a conditional cash transfer (CCT) scheme in Nicaragua found that the transfers to poor families improved the cognitive outcomes of children through higher intakes of nutrition-rich foods and better healthcare, and these gains persisted two years after the program ended.[214] This echoes a number of findings on the benefits to disadvantaged children of efforts to compensate for family poverty.[215] (Chapter 10 will discuss CCT schemes further.)

Compared to the bulk of pre-twentieth-century thinking (as discussed in chapter 1), we are more optimistic today about the prospects of eliminating absolute

---

[207] For further discussion, see Day (1992).

[208] For further discussion of the econometrics of this problem in testing for poverty traps, see Lokshin and Ravallion (2004).

[209] See Ravallion (1997b).

[210] See Lokshin and Ravallion (2004), who provide a model and estimation method that addresses a number of concerns about potential biases.

[211] See Jalan and Ravallion (2004).

[212] See Naschold (2013).

[213] See Dercon and Outes (2013).

[214] See Macours et al. (2012).

[215] For reviews of this literature, see Currie (2001, 2012)

poverty through an expanding economy. But we are also cognizant of the condition-alities in the impact of growth on poverty. Under the right conditions, economic growth can be a powerful force against poverty. Those conditions pertain in large part to aspects of both the initial distribution and how it evolves. The focus of much antipoverty policy has shifted over time toward efforts to assure that the conditions are in place that will allow poor men and women to contribute to an expanding overall economy, and so escape poverty for themselves and their children, permanently.

8.4 Pro-Poor Growth? Case Studies of China, Brazil, and India

The types of broad-brush cross-country comparisons in the last two sections can be instructive, but they need to be complemented by a more in-depth examination of specific countries. Here we will apply the ideas learned about in this chapter to three of the world's largest countries: China, Brazil, and India.[216] All three have made progress against poverty in recent decades, but with some interesting differences.

China

We saw in box 8.17 how much progress China has made against absolute poverty since the pro-market reforms started in the late 1970s. What is less well understood is exactly how this happened.

From 1978, China undertook a series of agrarian reforms, starting with the Household Responsibility System and supported by reforms to free up markets for farm outputs and inputs.[217] The scale of the reforms is nothing short of amazing. The collectives were dismantled and virtually all of the farmland of the world's most populous country was allocated to the farmers. The allocation appears to have been relatively equitable, at least within communes. Each farm household was then respon-sible for supplying a contracted output quota to the state, but was free to keep (and sell) everything in excess of the quota. This system had much better incentives for individual production, since each farmer kept the marginal product of his labor. These reforms to incentives and associated steps toward freeing up markets for farm out-puts were clearly the main reason for the dramatic reduction in poverty in China in the early 1980s.

The sectoral pattern of growth has been important. Growth in the rural economy accounts for the majority of China's success since 1980.[218] Looking back over the period since 1981, rural economic growth in China has had a far higher poverty impact than has urban economic growth. Similarly growth in agriculture did more to reduce poverty than growth in either the manufacturing or services sectors. Indeed, judged by the impact on poverty nationally, China's primary-sector growth has had about

---

[216] This section draws on Ravallion (2011a), which contains a fuller set of references to the literature.

[217] See Fan (1991) and Lin (1992). On the history of China's economic policies, see Brandt and Rawski (2008).

[218] See Ravallion and Chen (2007).

four times the impact of growth in either the secondary or tertiary sectors. Box 8.21 explains how these conclusions were derived.

---

*Box 8.21 **Testing Whether the Pattern of Growth Matters**

By decomposing the overall growth rate into its components, we can test whether the "pattern of growth" matters to poverty reduction. Consider first GDP per capita Y_t, which we can divide into n sources as $Y_t = \sum_{i=1}^{n} Y_{it}$. Now take the differences over time. Let $\Delta Y_t \equiv Y_t - Y_{t-1}$ denote the change over time. We can write the growth rate of GDP as the share-weighted sum of the growth rates across the n sources, that is, $\Delta \ln Y_t = \sum_{i=1}^{n} s_{it-1} \Delta \ln Y_{it}$, where $s_{it} = Y_{it}/Y_t$ is the share of GDP due to the i's source. (This uses the approximation $\Delta Y_t/Y_{t-1} \cong \Delta \ln Y_t$.) Suppose we now estimate a regression equation of the following form:

$$\Delta \ln P_t = \pi_0 + \sum_{i=1}^{n} \pi_i s_{it-1} \Delta \ln Y_{it} + \varepsilon_t.$$

The dependent variable, $\Delta \ln P_t = \ln(P_t/P_{t-1})$, is the proportionate rate of poverty reduction, where P_t is the poverty measure for date t, and ε_t is a standard regression error term (box 1.19). In the special case in which $\pi_i = \pi$ for $i = 1, .., n$, the above equation collapses to a simple regression of the rate of poverty reduction on the rate of GDP growth ($\Delta \ln Y_t$). Thus, testing the null hypothesis $H_0 : \pi_i = \pi$ for all i tells us whether the composition of growth (such as its sectoral or geographic pattern) matters. Here are the estimates of the π coefficients for China:

Table B8.21.1 **Regressions for the Proportionate Rate of Poverty Reduction**

Growth rate	(1)	(2)	(3)
GDP per capita	−2.60 (−2.16)	n.a.	n.a.
Primary GDP (share-weighted)	n.a.	−8.07 (−3.97)	−7.85 (−4.09)
Secondary GDP (share-weighted)	n.a.	−1.75 (−1.21)	n.a.
Tertiary GDP (share-weighted)	n.a.	−3.08 (−1.24)	n.a.
Secondary + tertiary GDP (share-weighted)	n.a.	n.a.	−2.25 (−2.20)
R^2	0.21	0.43	0.42

Note: t-statistics in parentheses below each regression coefficient; recall from box 1.19 that $t = \hat{\pi}/se(\hat{\pi})$ is used to test the null hypothesis that $\pi = 0$; an absolute value of t of 2 or higher can be considered statistically significant.

continued

Box 8.21 **(Continued)**

The sectors are primary (mainly agriculture), secondary (mainly manufacturing), and tertiary (mainly services). Column (1) gives the regression imposing $\pi_i = \pi$ for $i = 1, 2, 3$; then it is just the overall GDP growth rate that matters. However, when we relax this restriction, we see in column (2) that growth in the primary sector had much more impact than either of the other sectors. One cannot reject the null hypothesis that $\pi_2 = \pi_3$, and imposing this restriction we get column (3). Growth in the primary sector has about four times the impact on poverty as growth in the other two sectors combined.

This analysis has to be modified when the income sources are for people (each with one source only) and people can change their source during the process of growth. This is the case if one is studying the urban–rural composition of growth. The analysis is similar, but with the differences that we end up with another factor in the regression, namely the population growth rate of urban areas. As noted in the text, this regression analysis implies that rural economic growth has been far more important to overall poverty reduction in China than either urban growth or population urbanization.

Further reading: These regression tests were proposed by Ravallion and Datt (1996), which gives results for India. The methods are described further in Ravallion and Chen (2007), which gives more detailed results for China. Also see the province-level analysis in Montalvo and Ravallion (2010).

The historical legacy of China's low level of inequality at the outset of the reform period helped assure that the poor could contribute to, and benefit from the growth-promoting reforms. Low inequality tends to mean that the poor not only have a larger share of the pie but also a larger share of the increases in the size of the pie.[219] Importantly, China's initially low income inequality came with relatively low inequality in key physical and human assets. Low inequality in access to farmland in rural areas in the wake of the agrarian reforms appears to have been particularly important in ensuring that China's agricultural growth was pro-poor. On breaking up the farming collectives, it was possible to assure that land within communes was fairly equally allocated across households. There was no guarantee that this would happen, as the more powerful households in the prior regime may well have been able to capture more, or better land. This is likely to have happened in some communes, but it was clearly not the rule. Thus, we had in effect a major redistributive land reform around 1980, at the outset of China's sustained surge in overall economic growth, continuing today. However, marked inter-commune inequality remained, given that household mobility was restricted; we return to those restrictions. With a relatively equal allocation of land—through administratively assigned land-use rights rather than ownership—the agricultural growth unleashed by the rural economic reforms of the early 1980s was better able to help assure rapid poverty reduction in the rural areas. This also helped

---

[219] For evidence on this point, see Ravallion (1997a, 2007).

provide a more secure foundation for the necessary subsequent increase in labor supply from rural areas, which was a crucial complement to investments in physical capital in the rapidly expanding non-farm economy.

Relatively low inequality in access to basic health and education also helped China attain more pro-poor (poverty-reducing) growth. For example the (gross) primary enrollment rate in China around 1980 was well over 100% of the relevant age group, the adult literacy rate (proportion of people fifteen years and older who can read and write) was 66% in 1981 (and rose to 93% in 2007), and the infant mortality rate was well under 50%, with life expectancy at birth being sixty-five years. These are good social indicators by developing-country standards even today—similar in fact to India's, though twenty-five years later, and better than India's at the time when India's economic reforms started in earnest. China's achievements in basic health and education largely pre-date its economic reforms.[220] So while socialism proved to be a generally inefficient way to organize production, it left a positive legacy of relatively low inequality in health and schooling at the outset of China's reform period. This has undoubtedly helped in assuring that the subsequent farm and (especially) non-farm growth was poverty reducing. The favorable initial conditions in terms of inequality (in various dimensions) combined with the early emphasis on agriculture and rural development assured a rapid pace of poverty reduction in China during the first half of the 1980s (box 8.17).

While the initial agrarian reforms were crucial, an important factor in China's success against poverty is the fact that overall development policies have fostered labor absorption by non-farm sectors, which is seen to play a role independently of other factors such as agricultural growth and external trade flows.[221] This echoes long-standing arguments on the importance of exploiting the comparative advantage of low-income countries in labor-intensive production.[222] Poverty incidence tended to be lower in provinces and dates where the manufacturing sector was relatively labor-intensive (relative to the rest of the economy).[223] This can be interpreted as the effect of a "development strategy" that favors comparative advantage in labor-intensive manufacturing.

China's initial conditions at the outset of the reform process were especially conducive to rapid poverty reduction through a labor-absorbing manufacturing sector growth. This strategy requires sufficiently high levels of basic schooling attainments; even relatively unskilled manufacturing jobs require basic literacy and numeracy skills. Here China's initial conditions were good, with a high level of literacy around the time reforms began, including in rural areas where abundant labor could be drawn upon.

Chinese governments exercise an unusual degree of control over the urbanization process through the registration (*hukou*) system. This is essentially an internal passport, whereby those with rural registration who migrate to the cities do not have the same rights as urban-registered citizens unless they can obtain urban registration.

---

[220] See Drèze and Sen (1995), Chaudhuri and Ravallion (2006), and Heckman and Yi (2014) for further discussion.

[221] See Lin and Liu (2008).

[222] See, e.g., World Bank (1990b) and Schiff and Valdes (1992).

[223] See Lin and Liu (2008).

Not having local *hukou* matters to the family's welfare (including access to schooling and healthcare), and so rural migrants to the cities often leave their families behind in their village. Because of the long-standing restrictions on migration, large differences in living standards are still found between China's cities and its rural areas.

Why does the registration system exist? The *hukou* system was devised in the 1950s (not long after the Communist Party came to power) to control the expansion of the urban population, with attendant concerns about urban slums and unemployment, and to allow municipal governments to limit social spending on education, healthcare, and housing, by assuring that only those with local *hukou* can benefit. The policy is a way of protecting the higher wages and other benefits enjoyed by those with urban *hukou*.

Might the *hukou* system be defended as an attempt to limit the excess urbanization associated with free mobility given urban labor market regulations, as in the Harris-Todaro model (box 8.9)? This is quite a difficult question. It can be granted that the free mobility equilibrium will generate challenging new urban problems. But restrictions on migration are a questionable policy response. One relevant issue concerns the workings of urban labor markets, which are in part determined by policy choices. If urban labor markets are already distorted by fixity of the wage rate for the (high-wage) urban *hukou* jobs, then restricting migration will probably make matters worse, by further widening the gap between the marginal products of labor in the different sectors.[224] So the policy may well come with an efficiency cost. From an equity point of view, there will be both gainers and losers among the poor, where the poor are identified as those (in urban or rural areas) who cannot get the protected formal-sector jobs and associated benefits in the urban areas. The *ex post* earnings of those rural workers who would otherwise be unemployed in the cities may well be higher if they are collectively prevented from migrating. However, non-migrant rural workers will see lower wage rates than under free mobility, since more people will compete for the available rural work. One cannot, in general, predict dominance at even the second or third order in ranking the free mobility and restricted mobility distributions in such a situation (using the ideas from chapter 5).

There are also potentially important equity concerns within the cities, with a "two-class" system emerging whereby urban workers with rural *hukou* have lower wages and receive less benefits from the government. There are both horizontal and vertical aspects to the resulting inequality. Rural migrants are typically poorer than the permanent urban residents (a vertical inequality). And otherwise identical urban workers receive different net benefits depending on their *hukou*. The injustice of the *hukou* system is becoming well recognized in China and there is pressure for reform.

The *hukou* system is not the only impediment to poor rural people migrating in China. As is the case almost everywhere, there are many uninsured risks associated with migration, given the prospects of unemployment in the cities and also the risks of crime and violence. In China's case there is another risk of migration, namely the prospect of losing the family's agricultural land through administrative reallocation within

---

[224] In terms of the figure in box 8.9 the new wage rate in rural areas will be driven down to W^{rmin}. While urban unemployment is eliminated, the gap between the marginal products of labor in the two sectors will have widened.

the origin village. Recall that, although China took the bold step from 1978 of privatizing the agricultural land that had previously been farmed collectively, it did not take the next step of creating a private market in that land, such that individual farmers had assured ownership rights, and the land could not be administratively reassigned. China's central government resisted creating a free market in agricultural land-use rights for fear of a rural proletariat of landless laborers emerging. Interestingly, neighboring Vietnam did undertake this second reform starting in 1993, after following China in privatizing land allocation (in 1988). Similarly to China, there had been concerns about taking this step. A study of Vietnam's reforms found that there were probably some losers from these pro-market agrarian reforms, but on balance they were poverty reducing.[225] (We return to the contrast between China and Vietnam in agrarian land policies in chapter 9.)

China's rapid economic growth has been accompanied by a steep rise in inequality since the mid-1980s.[226] The trend rate of increase in the Gini index was 7 percentage points per decade.[227] If this trend continues, then China will reach the level of inequality found in the world's high-inequality countries (such as Brazil) by around 2025, although (as discussed below) there are reasons to expect the rise in inequality in China to slow down and even stop in the near future. While a trend increase in inequality is evident, the increase is not found in all sub-periods: inequality fell in the early 1980s, in the mid-1990s, and again in 2004.[228] Favorable initial conditions meant that China's growth could bring rapid gains to the poor, but rising inequality then started to reduce the gains.

The upward pressure on inequality over most of the reform period has come from a number of sources, including the freeing up of labor markets and an associated rise in the returns to schooling. Some of this was good inequality, at least initially, as it came with the creation of new economic opportunities. But other inequalities have been less benign in that they have generated inequality of opportunity. In this respect, the new inequalities in health and schooling (especially at secondary and tertiary levels, where there can be a heavy burden on parents for financing) have created concerns for future growth and distributional change.[229] The large geographic disparities in living standards are symptomatic of deeper biases in public resource availability, which also contribute to unequal opportunities, depending on where one lives.

While basic schooling was widespread in China at the outset of the reform period around 1980, some significant inequalities in educational attainment remain in China, and these have become an increasingly important source of unequal opportunities. A junior high school education and, in some instances, a senior high school education has become a *de facto* prerequisite for accessing non-farm work, particularly in urban areas where even unskilled wages still typically exceed labor earnings in farming.

The pattern of growth has also influenced the evolution of inequality in China, reflecting both good inequalities—as resource flows respond to new opportunities— and bad ones, such as when some poorly endowed areas are caught in *geographic*

---

[225] See Ravallion and van de Walle (2008).

[226] Knight (2013) provides a useful overview of research on rising inequality in China.

[227] See Ravallion (2011a).

[228] See Ravallion and Chen (2007).

[229] For further discussion, see Chaudhuri and Ravallion (2006) and Heckman and Yi (2014).

poverty traps (section 8.1). Box 8.22 discusses geographic poverty traps further. Rural and, in particular, agricultural growth tended to bring inequality down in China, and lack of growth in these sectors in some periods has done the opposite.[230] Rural economic growth reduced inequality within *both* urban and rural areas, as well as between them. The spillover effect from rural economic growth to urban areas reflects the horizontal links between poor people in the two sectors described in section 8.1.

Box 8.22 Geographic Poverty Traps in Rural China

A geographic poverty trap can be defined as any situation in which the characteristics of a household's area of residence—its "geographic capital"—entail that the household's consumption cannot rise over time, while an otherwise identical household living in a better endowed area enjoys a rising standard of living. This can arise when there are *geographic externalities* that influence growth rates at the farm household level, through effects on the marginal product of own capital. Living in a poor place entails that the marginal product of your capital is lower than it would otherwise be. Thus, those living in poor areas have less incentive to invest and you will be less likely to see rising living standards in the future. One can think of this as a common factor that limits the opportunities for advancement among people living in the same poorly endowed place.

Geographic poverty traps may well be very common, but they are hard to detect empirically. We find persistently poor areas in many countries, but it is not easy to say whether this is just a geographic concentration of people with poor individual endowments, with no interdependence, or a true geographic poverty trap. Using a relatively long panel data set for rural China, Jalan and Ravallion (2002) used an econometric method that, under certain (testable) conditions, allowed them to identify geographic effects on the micro growth process at the farm household level. Their estimation method is robust to the possibility that significant coefficients on geographic variables in their growth regressions could be picking up the effects of omitted household characteristics.

The study found that the aspects of geographic capital relevant to household consumption growth embrace both private and publicly provided goods and services. Private investments in agriculture, for example, entail external benefits within an area, as do "mixed" goods (involving both private and public provisioning) such as healthcare. Publicly provided goods, such as rural roads, generate non-negligible gains in living standards.

The study found that there were decreasing returns to private capital, which created a convergence force within areas, but that the external effect of geographic capital created overall divergence in the growth process. In other words, given the wealth of an area, households with more private capital saw lower

---

[230] See Ravallion and Chen (2007).

growth rates, while at given household wealth, households living in richer areas (higher wealth per capita) saw higher subsequent growth.

The prospects for growth in poor areas depend on the ability of governments and community organizations to overcome the tendency for underinvestment that such geographic externalities are likely to generate. In further research on the same data set for China, it was found that the level and composition of local economic activity affected private returns to local human and physical infrastructure endowments. This suggests that rural underdevelopment can arise from underinvestment in certain externality-generating activities, of which agricultural development emerges as the most important.

Further reading: Jalan and Ravallion (2002) describe the method and results in detail; Ravallion (2005a) extends the analysis of Jalan and Ravallion to allow for inter-sectoral externalities. The estimation method employs the non-stationary fixed effects estimation method of Holtz-Eakin, Newey, and Rosen (1988). The geographic poverty trap described above is an example of the class of membership models discussed in section 8.1.

Was rising inequality simply the price that China had to pay for growth and (hence) poverty reduction? That is a difficult question, but it should not be presumed that such a trade-off exists. The answer depends crucially on the source of inequality; when it comes in the form of higher inequality of opportunity it is likely to entail a cost to aggregate growth prospects. China's experience actually offers surprisingly little support for the view that there is an aggregate trade-off. There are a number of empirical findings that lead one to question that view. First, while it is true that inequality tended to rise over time, the periods of more rapid growth did not bring more rapid increases in inequality; indeed, the periods of falling inequality (1981–85 and 1995–98) had the *highest* growth in average household income. Second, the sub-periods of highest growth in the primary sector (1983–84, 1987–88, and 1994–96) did not typically come with lower growth in other sectors. Finally, the provinces with more rapid rural income growth did not experience a steeper increase in inequality; if anything it was the opposite.[231] An analysis of provincial panel data suggests that, as far as poverty is concerned, there was little or no trade-off between the sectoral pattern of growth and the overall level of growth.[232]

Looking forward it will be harder for China to maintain its past progress against poverty without addressing the problem of rising inequality. We can expect that the historically high levels of inequality found in China today will inhibit future prospects for poverty reduction. High inequality is a double handicap; depending on its source— especially how much comes from inequality of opportunity—it means lower growth and a lesser share for the poor in the gains from that growth. At the outset of China's transition period to a market economy, levels of poverty were so high that inequality

---

[231] See Ravallion and Chen (2007).
[232] See Montalvo and Ravallion (2010).

was not an important concern. That has changed. Inequality has become an important policy concern in China.

There are some forces at work today that will probably put a brake on rising inequality in China. Probably most importantly, the country appears to be approaching (or even reached) its own "Lewis turning point." (Recall box 8.7 on the Lewis model.) As more and more labor is absorbed from rural areas by the expanding modern sector, a point will be reached after which we see rising rural wages, once the labor surplus has vanished. Just how soon a LTP will be reached is unclear. Since the mid-2000s there have been reports of shortages of migrant labor in some of the key export-oriented coastal areas, which has led some observers to suggest that the turning point has been reached. However, rising wages for migrant labor in the coastal areas does not imply that the "inland" rural labor surplus has been fully absorbed;[233] another possible explanation is a tightening of the *hukou* system in some coastal areas. On taking account of the expected labor-force growth, the turning point is expected to be around 2020–25.[234] The consequent rise in real wage rates for relatively unskilled labor, combined with the expected increase in the supply of skilled labor (due to the large expansion in university education since the early 2000s), will put downward pressure on overall earnings inequality.

A number of policy changes have also helped attenuate rising inequality. From the mid-1990s, there were reductions in the implicit tax on farmers that was created by the procurement system in the late 1970s—whereby farmers were obliged to sell a share of their output to the state at prices below market prices. A progressive relaxation of the *hukou* system is also expected, which will probably put downward pressure on inequality. There were also new redistributive social protection programs from the late 1990s, which chapter 10 returns to. Such policies can be expected to play a more important role in the future.

A slow-down in China's economic growth rates should not be surprising since much of the economic growth since the reforms began in the late 1970s has been "catch-up growth," by undoing the failures of the prior economic regime. Sectoral re-allocation from the rural (agricultural) to urban (industrial) sectors has clearly been an important source of growth (even though it has not been the main factor in overall poverty reduction). The scope for such re-allocations is getting more limited. Some observers go further to argue that China's current political system is a constraint on its economic development. This is an instance of the more general argument made by Acemoglu and Robinson (2012) that inclusive political institutions are required for sustained economic growth (section 8.1). The more concrete manifestations in the case of China are that property rights are not well protected and the Communist Party still exercises considerable control over the economy. Thus, Acemoglu and Robinson (2012, p.437) claim that "Chinese growth, as it has unfolded so far, is just another example of growth under extractive political institutions, unlikely to translate into sustained economic development."

This is too pessimistic an assessment. The development attained by China over the last 30 years is impressive to anyone, and it is likely to be sustained, even with

---

[233] See Knight et al. (2011).
[234] See Das and N'Diaye (2013).

lower growth. Firmer property rights laws would probably help, although not all innovations in the past have required especially secure property rights. And an outward shift in production possibilities leading to a higher long-term mean income can occur by adapting technologies developed elsewhere.

There will nonetheless be mounting pressures for liberalizing political reform in China. The rapidly expanding middle class, stemming from the success against absolute poverty, is unlikely to tolerate unnecessary constraints on its freedoms indefinitely. How the tension between rising demands for reform and the Communist Party's desire to retain power will resolve itself remains unclear.

Even with lower growth rates, there is potential for reducing relative poverty and inequality in China through redistributive policies. A simple way of quantifying that potential is to ask how much one would need to tax the "non-poor" in China to eliminate poverty.[235] There would be (understandable) resistance to taxing the middle class to finance transfers to the poor. So let us suppose (for the sake of this illustrative calculation) that a linear progressive income tax could be levied on all those in China living above (say) the US poverty line, and that the revenue generated was used to finance redistribution in favor of the poorest, sufficient to bring everyone up to the international poverty line of $1.25 a day (say). The necessary marginal rate of taxation can be readily calculated.[236] The calculations do not allow for behavioral responses to the taxes and transfers (such as through work effort); such responses could well entail that the tax rate will need to be higher than this figure, though how much so is unclear. (Chapter 10 returns to the topic of behavioral responses to redistributive policies.) The answer is a tax rate of 36% in 2005; that is, those Chinese living above the US poverty line would need to pay a tax of roughly one-third of the difference between their income and the US poverty line.[237] (The average tax rate would start at zero for those at the US poverty line, and then rise as income rises above that line). Later we will see how this compares to Brazil and India. However, the more important point here is that if one repeats this calculation for 1981, it is clear that such a policy would have been impossible at the outset of China's reform period: the required marginal tax rate then would have been far greater than 100%. In other words, the poverty gap was so large then, and the country so poor, that redistribution was not a realistic option.

Brazil

While Brazil is famous for many things (not least football), in the context of this book the country's high level of inequality makes it stand out. Recall from chapter 7 that

[235] Of course, this is a rather stylized and hypothetical question. It is not claimed that such a policy is politically or economically feasible. But at least it gives us a way of measuring the capacity for reducing poverty through redistribution, given the distribution of income in China.

[236] Consider two poverty lines, z_U and z_L with $z_U > z_L$. The marginal tax rate τ on incomes above z_U (yielding a tax in amount $\max[\tau(y - z_U), 0]$ on income y) needed to generate the revenue to bring everyone up to the lower poverty line can be readily derived as $\tau = PG(z_L)z_L/[\bar{y} - (1 - PG(z_U))z_U]$, where $PG(.)$ is the poverty gap index and $\bar{y}$ is the overall mean. For further discussion of this measure of the capacity for redistribution, see Ravallion (2009d).

[237] For China in 2005, $PG(1.25) = 4.0\%$ and $PG(13) = 73.8\%$, while $\bar{y} = \$3.55$ per day at 2005 PPP.

Latin America and the Caribbean is the region of the developing world that has had highest average inequality of incomes. Within LAC, Brazil has a level of inequality well above the regional average by most measures.[238]

The other side of the coin to this high inequality is that Brazil clearly has a larger capacity for using redistribution to address its poverty problem than countries with lower inequality. Consider again the marginal tax rate on the non-poor (by US standards) needed to fill all the poverty gaps (by the $1.25 a day standard). We saw that in China that would require a marginal tax rate of 36% on incomes above the US poverty line. By contrast, in Brazil in 2005, it would only require a marginal tax rate of 0.7%![239] Even for the $2 a day line, the necessary marginal rate would only be 4%. (Using $3 a day, which is close to Brazil's national poverty line, the tax rate rises to about 12%.) Of course, realizing this potential in practice is another matter, and we will see later the policies Brazil adopted.

Like China, Brazil has seen major economy-wide changes since the 1970s though in Brazil's case the macroeconomic management of its market economy has historically been a greater challenge than for China. The period of economic stagnation in the 1980s and early 1990s in Brazil was marked by hyperinflation, as a result of accumulated fiscal deficits and an accommodating monetary policy. This was a period of Latin American macroeconomic populism, with persistent budget deficits, high inflation, trade distortions, extensive government ownership of productive enterprises in certain sectors, and an inefficient social security system that did not reach the poor. Through a combination of the de-indexation of labor contracts and an exchange-rate-based stabilization policy (known as the Real Plan), the government finally managed to control inflation in 1994. This also marked the conclusion of a process of trade liberalization which began in 1988 with tariff reductions and the removal of quantitative restrictions.

In many ways, the new policy regime from the mid-1990s conformed to the "Washington Consensus" on the merits of macroeconomic stability, fiscal prudence, trade reform, and privatization of some state-owned enterprises.[240] (We return to the Washington Consensus in the next chapter.) However, one important difference from the Washington Consensus was that the new policies were accompanied by significant reforms to social security and assistance transfers, which also became better targeted over time.[241]

Economy-wide reforms from the mid-1980s allowed modest growth, but the impact on poverty was disappointing. Brazil's higher inequality was a key factor. For example, Brazil's Gini index of income inequality, at a little under 0.60 in the mid-1990s, was twice that in China in the early 1980s when its reform process began. Brazil's higher inequality meant that, with no change in inequality, the country

---

[238] In figure 7.11, we see that the LAC average value for the MLD in 2010 is 0.55; the corresponding figure for Brazil is 0.64.

[239] Recalling the earlier notation, for Brazil in 2005, $PG(1.25) = 1.6\%$ and $PG(13) = 52.3\%$, while $\bar{y} = \$9.16$ per day at 2005 PPP.

[240] For further discussion, see Ferreira et al. (2010) and, on trade policies, Ferreira et al. (forthcoming).

[241] See Barros and others (2006), Ferreira et al. (2008), and Ferreira et al. (2010).

needed even higher growth than China's to attain the same rate of poverty reduction. Underlying this high income inequality one finds inequality in human resource development, notably schooling attainments, which have a marked income gradient in Brazil. These inequalities limited the ability of the poor to participate in, and to benefit from, aggregate growth.

However, there is a very important difference between Brazil in its reform period (after the mid-1990s, say) and China (and also India, which we turn to next). Brazil saw a reduction in inequality over time, including inequality between regions and between urban and rural areas.[242] As we saw earlier, this was the key factor that allowed Brazil to reduce poverty despite modest growth.

Similarly to China, the pattern of Brazil's growth mattered to the outcomes for the poor. While it was growth in the agricultural sector that had the dominant role in reducing poverty in China, in Brazil it was in the services sector, which was consistently more pro-poor than growth in either agriculture or industry. There was a lower growth rate in the services sector after 1994, which had a (small) negative effect on the rate of poverty reduction. So the reform pattern of growth was not pro-poor.

However, this change in the pattern of growth in Brazil was more than compensated for by slightly positive overall growth after 1994. In fact the bulk of Brazil's poverty reduction in the period since the mid-1980s took place *after* 1994. Using regression decomposition methods, World Bank economist Francisco Ferreira and colleagues find that an important factor bringing down the poverty measures from 1994 onward was the substantial reduction in inflation rates (under the Real Plan).[243]

Social policies also helped. In attempting to realize that potential for reducing poverty through redistribution, an important role has been played in Brazil by various cash transfer programs. These included both noncontributory, unconditional transfers as well as CCTs, targeted to poor families, which have played an important role from the late 1990s onward. (Chapter 10 discusses these programs further.) CCTs have emerged in a number of developing countries in recent times, following early examples such as the *Food-for-Education* (FFE) program in Bangladesh and the *PROGRESA* program (renamed *Oportunidades* and then *Prospera*) in Mexico.

The expansion and reforms to the federal government's social assistance spending, including on *Bolsa Familia* helped reduce inequality and poverty.[244] Indeed in the absence of these transfers, and given the generally poor performance in terms of economic growth, it has been estimated that the headcount index in Brazil would have been about 5 percentage points higher in 2004.[245]

---

[242] See Ferreira et al. (2008).

[243] See Ferreira et al. (2010).

[244] Unlike Mexico's CCT, the PROGRESA (later renamed *Oportunidades*), Brazil did not invest heavily on evaluations of impacts of *Bolsa Familia*, so it is difficult to infer any impacts. Ferreira et al. (2010) rely on time series data. Soares and others (2006) use instead inequality decomposition methods calibrated to household survey data. They find that, although the size of the average transfer was low, the excellent targeting meant that *Bolsa Familia* alone could account for one-fifth of the decline in inequality in Brazil after the program's introduction.

[245] See Ferreira et al. (2010).

The poverty impacts of social assistance spending, inflation, and other changes in the policy environment entailed distributional effects on poverty (given that they are still found after one controls for the growth effect). In addition to the pure growth effect, the sectoral pattern of growth embodied a pro-poor distributional effect.

But the dominant distributional effects were from macroeconomic stabilization and social spending. The cumulative total effect on poverty of these two elements of the policy package was far larger in magnitude than the effects of changes in the level and composition of economic growth.[246] Looking forward, we can expect that the higher levels of schooling for the children of poor families (such as promoted by the CCT programs) will help promote more pro-poor growth.

Two main lessons emerge from the Brazilian experience. First, reforms to make social policies more pro-poor can play an important role in sustaining poverty reduction, even during a period of economic stagnation. Second, sensible macroeconomic and trade policies need not hurt the poor and, in the specific case of taming hyperinflation, are likely to make a significant contribution in the fight against poverty, even when that is not the primary objective. As a new economic and political crisis unfolds in Brazil at the time of writing in 2015, these lessons will hopefully not be forgotten.

India

There has been much debate about whether economic growth has helped reduce poverty in India. The sectoral pattern of growth has been an issue. One concern has been whether the agricultural growth process stimulated by the Green Revolution of the 1960s brought gains to the rural poor. Some scholars argued that the new agricultural growth process had largely by-passed the rural poor, while others pointed to farm-output growth as the key to rural poverty reduction.[247] Better data and richer models helped to inform this debate. One study found that higher farm productivity (output per unit area) brought both absolute and relative gains to India's rural poor, with a large share of the gains coming through higher real wages due to higher farm productivity.[248] Despite the many past debates on the social and environmental impacts of the Green Revolution, the potential for technological innovation to promote higher farm productivity and hence to reduce poverty and under-nutrition is now well recognized.[249]

There has also been a debate about how much urban economic growth has benefited the poor. India's heavily protected industrialization strategy in the decades following Independence served the interests of the country's politically influential capitalist class.[250] However, India's post-Independence planners were also hopeful that this development strategy would bring lasting longer term gains to both the urban and rural poor through the absorption of surplus labor in rural areas, along the lines of the Lewis model (box 8.7).

---

[246] See Ferreira et al. (2010).

[247] For an overview of this debate and references, see Datt and Ravallion (1998a).

[248] See Datt and Ravallion (1998a).

[249] An important contribution was made by Lipton and Longhurst (1989). For a recent overview of these debates, see Pritchard et al. (2014).

[250] See Bardhan (1984b, ch. 6).

Most observers of the Indian economy have not shared the planners' optimism in this respect. Recall from chapter 2 that the Second Plan had emphasized the need for rapid, relatively capital-intensive, industrialization in a closed economy. This was debated at the time, with some scholars arguing that the Plan put too little emphasis on exploiting India's comparative advantage in labor-intensive production, and that the plan was too pessimistic on the prospects for labor-absorption through agricultural and rural development.[251] It was also argued that the latter is key to attaining India's long-standing hope for a pro-poor process of industrialization.[252] This debate continues.

While there had been some steps toward economic reform in the 1980s, India's reforms only started in earnest in 1991, in the wake of a balance of payments crisis. A series of reforms supported the private sector and promoted a more open economy, with some efforts at restructuring the public sector.[253] Significant steps were taken in trade and industrial policy, though (unlike in China) agriculture has been neglected. Policy reforms in other areas (lower industrial protection and exchange rate depreciation) have brought indirect benefits to agriculture, notably through improved terms of trade, higher demand for farm products through the urban income effect, and some growth in agricultural exports. However, at the same time, the reform period saw a decline in public investment in key areas for agriculture, notably rural infrastructure.

The evidence from India's *National Sample Surveys* suggests that economic growth has been poverty reducing, including in the reform period. However, a number of factors appear to have dampened the impact on poverty. The rise in inequality is one factor, as noted by a number of observers.[254] Underlying this rise in inequality—and dulling the impact of growth on poverty—one finds signs of geographic and sectoral divergence in India's growth process.[255] One aspect of this is the urban–rural composition of growth. As in China (and most developing countries) absolute poverty measures are higher in the rural sector, though the urban–rural gap is not as large as that found in China. The ratio of mean consumption in the urban areas of India to its rural areas is about 1.3, which is about half the ratio found in China.[256] India has also seen divergence over time between urban mean consumption and the rural mean, which has contributed to rising overall inequality. Additionally, inequality has risen within both urban and rural areas since the early 1990s.[257]

Like China, past research has pointed to the importance of rural economic growth to national poverty reduction in India. Historically, rural economic growth has been

---

[251] See the critique of the Second Plan in Vakil and Brahmanand (1956).

[252] An important contribution was made by Eswaren and Kotwal (1994) emphasizing the role played by agricultural growth in assuring that industrial sector growth benefited poor people.

[253] For an overview of the reforms, see Ahluwalia (2002).

[254] See Ravallion (2000) and Sen and Himanshu (2004).

[255] See Datt and Ravallion (2002, 2011). This appears to precede the reform period starting in 1991. Bandyopadhyay (2004) finds evidence of "twin peaks" in India's growth process over 1965–1997, whereby the divergence is between two "convergence clubs," one with low income (50 percent of the national mean) and one with high income (125 percent).

[256] See Ravallion and Chen (2007) and Datt and Ravallion (2011).

[257] See Datt and Ravallion (2011). This is only true within urban areas if one corrects for changes in survey design.

the more important factor in overall poverty reduction. Similarly to China, rural economic growth had pro-poor distributional effects in urban areas. Until the 1990s
urban economic growth (while it did help reduce urban poverty) brought little gain
to the rural poor, and came a poor second to the rural sector in terms of its impact on
poverty nationally.

There are encouraging signs that the process of economic growth is changing in
India, making urban economic growth more pro-poor.[258] There is also evidence of
stronger linkages from urban economic growth to rural poverty reduction emerging
since the early 1990s, alongside a more economically diversified rural economy. Since
2000 we have also seen a tightening of rural casual labor markets, with rising real wage
rates, and also a narrowing of the urban–rural wage gap.[259] Two factors appear to be
in play here. First, high returns to skills have encouraged more students to stay on
at school, thus reducing the supply of unskilled labor, especially in rural areas. There
has also been a decline in the labor-force participation of rural women. Second, there
has been a construction boom across India, especially in (rural and urban) infrastructure, which had been neglected for a long period. The combination of lower supply of
unskilled labor and rising demand for that labor in construction, transport, and services has clearly been an important driving force in higher casual wages, in both farm
and non-farm sectors. It appears that (like China) India may well have reached its LTP.
However, this may depend on the construction boom continuing.

A striking difference with China is found in the relative importance of different
sectors to poverty reduction. In common with most (growing) developing economies,
India's trend rate of growth has been higher in the modern industrial and services
sectors—both of which tend to be urban based—than in the agricultural sector.
However, the importance of agricultural growth to China's success against poverty
stands in marked contrast to India, where the services sector has been the more powerful force. In this respect India has more in common with Brazil. The most likely
explanation for this difference lies in the initial distribution of assets, with access
to agricultural land and human development being much more equitably distributed
in China than India. (Recall that China's advantage in land distribution reflected
the historical opportunity created by the de-collectivization of agriculture and the
introduction of the Household Responsibility System.)

Similarly to both China and Brazil, periods of high inflation hurt India's poor.[260]
We know more about the transmission mechanism in India, in which short-term
stickiness in the wages for relatively unskilled labor played an important role.[261]

Performance has differed markedly between states of India, particularly in the
extent to which non-farm economic growth has reduced poverty. This is linked in
turn to differences in initial conditions, most notably in human development.[262]

---

[258] See Datt and Ravallion (2011). Updates to this study using more recent data suggest that the
process of more pro-poor urban economic growth has continued.

[259] See Hnatkovska and Lahiri (2013) for evidence on this point. They also show that the narrowing
of the wage gap persists when one controls for education and occupation.

[260] For evidence on this point, see Datt and Ravallion (1998a) and Ravallion and Datt (2002).

[261] See Datt and Ravallion (1998a).

[262] See Datt and Ravallion (2002) and Ravallion and Datt (2002).

Inequalities in human development have undoubtedly retarded poverty reduction in all three countries, but the problem is surely greatest in India. As already noted India's schooling inequalities were clearly larger than those of China at the beginning of their reform periods. India had still not attained a 100% primary enrollment rate by 1990, although China had reached that level ten or more years earlier. Almost 80% of adults (fifteen years and older) in China were literate in 1990, as compared to slightly less than half in India. And in the early 1980s, when China was embarking on its economic reforms, two-thirds of adults were literate—still appreciably higher than in India when its main reform period started ten years later.[263]

Gender inequalities at the outset of the reform period also stand out in India. The (absolute and proportionate) differences between male and female enrollment and literacy rates were higher for India.[264] Only about one in three adult women (and only one-half of adolescent girls) were able to read and write at the time India embarked on its current reform period. By contrast, when China embarked on its reforms ten years earlier, over half of adult women and 70% of adolescent women were literate.[265] Over time, the gender gaps in education and literacy have been narrowing in India, although large gaps persist, especially when one reaches secondary and tertiary levels of schooling.

India also lags in its health attainments. India's infant mortality rate in 1990 was 80 deaths per 1,000 live births, more than twice that of China in 1990, and there was also an eight-year difference in life expectancy (sixty years in India as compared to sixty-eight years in China).

Subnational differences in these and other inequalities also reveal their importance to poverty reduction. Across the states of India, the differences in the impacts of non-farm economic growth on poverty reflect inequalities in a number of dimensions; low farm productivity, low rural living standards relative to urban areas, and poor basic education all inhibited the prospects of the poor participating in the growth of the non-farm sector.[266] Interstate differences in initial levels of schooling appear to have been the dominant factor in explaining the subsequent impacts of non-farm economic growth on poverty. Recall that in the Lewis model (and subsequent models) labor is homogeneous and in principle anyone in the traditional sector could get the modern-sector work that becomes available as that sector expands. In reality, labor is heterogeneous and some rural workers are better placed than others to take advantage of non-farm economic growth. Those with relatively little schooling and few assets, or little access to credit, were less well positioned to take advantage of the new opportunities unleashed by modern-sector enlargement. Sub-nationally, India's disparities in

[263] For a good discussion of these and other differences between China and India in human development attainments at the outset of their respective reform periods, see Drèze and Sen (1995, ch. 4).

[264] For a discussion of the reasons for this gender gap in India, including its historical roots in Brahminical tradition as well as more current biases in the schooling system and parental behavior, see Drèze and Sen (1995, ch. 6).

[265] The adolescent literacy rates are from Drèze and Sen (1995, table 4.2).

[266] See Ravallion and Datt (2002).

literacy rates are driven more by the differences in female literacy, which has greater explanatory power for the rate of poverty reduction.[267]

The potential for using income redistribution to address India's poverty problem is more limited than in China or (especially) Brazil. Repeating the hypothetical tax rate calculation made above for China and Brazil, it would be impossible to raise enough revenue from a tax on Indian incomes above the US poverty line to fill India's poverty gap relative to the $1.25 a day line; the required marginal tax rate would exceed 100%.[268] Indeed even at a 100% marginal tax rate, the revenue could fill only 20% of India's aggregate poverty gap.

India has had a long history of direct interventions, often aimed at fighting poverty, notably through food subsidies, farm-input subsidies, subsidized credit schemes, and workfare schemes. There are a number of reasons for caution in making an assessment of the poverty impacts of such programs, including political economy considerations.[269] But few careful observers would contend that India's record in using these policies to fight poverty is anything but mixed. By conventional assessments of who is "poor," these interventions have probably reduced poverty somewhat, but they have not been well-targeted and there have been persistent problems of corruption. There has been much debate as to whether India should take up the types of conditional cash transfer schemes that have been popular elsewhere. The new national identity cards (known as the *Aadhaar*) being rolled out in India will, in due course, help greatly with the administrative control of such programs.[270] However, it will be crucial to combine this type of incentive scheme for promoting investment in the human capital of poor children with "supply-side" efforts in delivering better health and education services. Some observers have favored unconditional cash transfers to poor families. Chapter 10 will discuss these policy options further.

[267] See Datt and Ravallion (1998b).

[268] Recalling the earlier notation, the value of $PG(13)$ is 86.7% in India. With a value of $PG(1.25)$ of 10.51% and mean consumption of $1.76, the required marginal tax rate would be almost 500%!

[269] See Ravallion (2009b) in the context of an antipoverty program in China, though the points made are reasonably generic. On the political economy of targeting, see Gelbach and Pritchett (2000).

[270] At the time of writing, about half of India's population has been covered by the Unique Identification Program though progress has tended to be slower in the poorer states. For further discussion, see Gelb and Raghavan (2014).

9

Economy-Wide and Sectoral Policies

A distinction is often made between two ways that policies can matter to poverty and inequality. First, policies can influence how markets work to generate incomes; and, second, policies can influence how the outcomes from market processes are distributed. It has been argued by some that governments should avoid the first role. The argument is that free markets will be efficient—that the pie will be larger, allowing more scope for "post-market" redistribution. Against this view, it is plain that the various conditions for markets to be efficient in the absence of intervention do not hold in reality (recall box 1.9) and that the deviations from efficiency have important implications for equity. For example, poorer people are more likely to be the ones locked out of access to credit and other inputs needed for productive investments.

The separation between these two roles for policies—one for efficiency and one for equity—is hard to maintain as a realistic characterization of the policy problem. One of the implications of imperfect information and imperfect (including incomplete) markets is that we cannot insist on a clean separation between policies aimed at promoting "efficiency" and those intended for promoting "equity." It may sometimes help as an expository tool to classify policies according to their main aims. But it is not defensible to think of antipoverty policies as *only* including a set of direct interventions targeted to the poor, or to ignore the distributional impacts of economy-wide and sectoral policies for promoting growth or efficiency more broadly on the grounds that direct interventions will be able to compensate any losers.

Antipoverty policymaking cannot be shy about influencing the outcomes of market processes, and rely solely on "post-market" redistribution. The interactions between market failures and inequality (as discussed in the last chapter) point to the scope for redistributive interventions on efficiency grounds as well as for equity. For example, transfers targeted to poor people will not only directly reduce poverty but will also help families get around the constraints they face, such as in keeping their children in school. These policies are the topic of chapter 10. However, not all antipoverty policies are explicitly targeted to poor people. These can be interpreted as policies that try to address market and other institutional or governmental failures that help perpetuate poverty. This chapter reviews past and ongoing debates on such "un-targeted policies," sometimes called "sectoral policies."

55585858588588858888588888588888858888888588888888888

9.1 Urban versus Rural

Let us briefly take stock of the observations in previous chapters about the urban and rural dimensions of poverty. We saw in chapter 7 that the bulk of absolute poverty in the world is still found in rural areas. Not only do the majority of poor people still live there, but poverty rates in developing countries tend to be higher in rural areas. We also learned in chapter 8 that urbanization has generally been seen by development theorists as a positive factor in national growth and poverty reduction. We also saw that the evidence is broadly consistent with the view that higher rates of urbanization are associated with higher rates of poverty reduction.

Why do we see these urban–rural disparities in living standards? There are two competing models.[1] In one model, people sort themselves out through unrestricted migration. Then location has no causal role in creating the differences in poverty rates that we see geographically; with free mobility people with the same characteristics will have the same welfare level no matter where they live. The alternative model points instead to frictions in location choice (including costs of moving) and search costs that can generate persistent geographic differences in living standards—differences that are not fully accountable to the mobile non-geographic characteristics of individuals.

It is not easy to distinguish these models empirically. The main problem is that we cannot easily distinguish unobserved individual factors (e.g., a high latent skill in urban-type jobs) from impediments to mobility (such as due to credit-market failures or uninsured risks). However, from what we know there appears to be some truth in both models. There is clearly some degree of sorting consistent with the first model.[2] There are also urban–rural differences in living standards that appear to be hard to explain without the second model. For example, as we noted in chapter 5, a study for Bangladesh found that the urban–rural differences in living standards persisted when one controls for differences in observable non-geographic characteristics.[3] Similarly, the urban–rural wage differentials found in India persist when one controls for observable worker characteristics.[4] In both these cases, the unexplained differences may well reflect a selective process of migration (although in the Indian case rather little of the urban–rural gap appears to be due to migration). In chapter 8 we also learned about geographic poverty traps, and pointed to supportive evidence for rural China where micro panel data allowed tests that are robust to latent individual characteristics (box 8.22). While these are only scattered studies, in thinking about policy it is clear that we should not presume that poor areas are only poor because households with observable attributes that foster poverty chose to be geographically concentrated.

[1] The differences between these two models are elaborated further in Ravallion (1998b), which discusses how the difference can be distinguished empirically.

[2] Young (2013) reports evidence from DHS's consistent with such sorting although Young's findings do not rule out the second model.

[3] See Ravallion and Wodon (1999).

[4] See Hnatkovska and Lahiri (2013).

Urban–Rural Prioritization for Development

Historians of poverty have described how in ancient and medieval times, cities and city-states flourished by exploiting their rural hinterlands as the source of both food and manual labor, especially for construction. Both food and labor were often obtained from rural areas by forced procurement. Urban elites often ate well while the peasants who produced the food were left hungry.[5]

Over the centuries, various forms of taxation of agriculture have been used to support urban elites. The taxation was often implicit, such as through public food procurement and agricultural trade policies that exploited poor farmers by keeping the prices they received below market prices. In much of Africa, for example, the pricing policies of marketing boards (left over from Colonial times) greatly reduced the incentives for farmers to use productivity-enhancing inputs (such as fertilizers) or invest in their land.[6] At times in history, the level of (explicit or implicit) taxation was often so high as to constitute a poverty trap—destroying farmers' incentives to expand production by cultivating more land or adopting new technologies. Hence some form of coercion by government was often required to assure that enough food was produced.

Nor did the emerging capitalist class in the newly industrializing economies (whether Western Europe or North America two hundred years ago or today's developing world) have much incentive to reduce urban bias. The new (mainly urban) industrial sector relied on drawing its labor force from the rural economy. The capitalists had no obvious incentive to promote rural productivity growth, since it would push up wages, and they used their political influence accordingly.[7]

There are some inherent tensions, however, which were seeds of change. The fundamental tension was that absorbing rural labor to build the cities and staff the factories left less labor to grow and process the food. The practice of appropriating food directly reduced the incentives for farmers to grow that food and came to be seen as unacceptable in modern thinking. Over time the coercive practices gave way to market forces although some key tensions remained. Agricultural productivity would need to rise to avoid the economy falling into a Malthusian trap. While economists such as Lewis (1954) saw modern-sector enlargement as the main driving force for growth in a labor-surplus economy, Lewis also recognized the need for agricultural growth, and this was emphasized in the subsequent elaborations and extensions to his model.[8] (Recall box 8.7.) In due course, technical progress in agriculture came to be seen by many economists as a key prior condition for industrial development.

The urban-rural prioritization in development is still debated. Economists such as Michael Lipton (1977) identified urban bias in public pricing and spending policies as an important cause of poverty. Counterarguments have long been made, however, pointing to the urban economy as the engine of overall growth, which (it is claimed)

---

[5] This is described by the historian Beaudoin (2006, ch. 1).

[6] See Bates (1981).

[7] This was recognized by Lewis (1954).

[8] Lewis (1954, 433) wrote that "industrial and agrarian revolutions always go together, and . . . economies in which agriculture is stagnant do not show industrial development." Also see the more formal treatment of the need for balanced growth in Ranis and Fei (1961).

will eventually trickle down to the rural poor.[9] This section reviews the arguments and evidence on this important debate.

Given that poverty measures tend to be higher in rural areas, might there be a case for believing that a pro-rural bias is justified on distributional grounds? One side of the debate on the role played by the rural sector in poverty reduction essentially treats agriculture as an unproductive traditional sector, which will soon be swept away by modernizing development. The main role for agriculture in the early stages of development was to be a source of government revenue to support urbanization and industrialization. This can take the form of explicit taxation of agricultural outputs or inputs (notably land) or pricing policies, including foodgrain procurement pricing (as in the case of China and Vietnam where farmers have often been obliged to sell grain to the government at below-market prices). In the very early stages of development, there are not many options to agriculture as a source of public revenues, although that excuse seems rather lame in most real-world cases; typically there are options, both on the revenue and spending sides of the government budget.

This side of the debate has generally acknowledged that there is more poverty in rural areas, but it is argued that the only real hope for the rural poor is to find jobs in the urban or peri-urban non-farm economy. Greater labor absorption from the urban economy has long been seen as the key to poverty reduction. This policy logic drew support from development theories such as the Lewis model. Some of those on this side of the debate have also gone so far as to argue against any policies that restrict migration from rural to urban areas, and some have even argued against direct interventions to relieve rural poverty on the grounds that they will slow progress against poverty through urbanization or other dynamic forces in economic geography.[10]

The other side of the debate has argued that the rural economy could also be an important source of growth, and that growth in the rural economy is more likely to be poverty reducing.[11] As discussed in chapter 2 (section 2.3), various constraints facing poor farmers in access to knowledge and inputs can generate higher economic returns to policy support for smallholder agriculture that helps relax those constraints. Evidence in support of this view has come from recent impact evaluations.[12] This side has also pointed to the problems of urban slums and argued that there is too much urbanization; recall that in the Harris-Todaro model (box 8.9) the distortion in urban labor markets will create excessive urbanization. This will also occur when the agricultural sector is unproductive, in the sense of a low marginal product of farm labor, which will encourage urbanization, but this could well come with rising poverty. The optimal taxation of urban and rural sectors is influenced by migration in the presence of the minimum wage rate in the urban labor market.[13] Tax policies should then

---

[9] There has been much debate about this aspect of the history of the Industrial Revolution; see the discussion of this debate in Boserup (1985).

[10] See, e.g., World Bank (2009).

[11] See, e.g., Lipton and Ravallion (1995).

[12] See e.g. Duflo et al. (2008) and Beaman et al. (2014).

[13] See Sah and Stiglitz (1992, ch. 13), who provide a more general formulation of the HT model, whereby the key equilibrium condition is equality of the expected utility in urban areas of a potential migrant from rural areas with her actual utility in rural areas (box 8.9).

reduce migration, such as by lower taxation of the rural surplus, relative to what is implied without the distortions in urban labor markets. However, that does not justify other policies that have tried to reduce urban poverty by discouraging rural migrants, by harassing slum dwellers or by more benign neglect, such as doing little to improve amenities in urban slums. The analysis must also take account of the welfare losses to urban slum dwellers.

We have already learned how externalities can sometimes lead to coordination failures generating persistent poverty (chapter 8). The hypothesis that there are externalities through knowledge spillovers has been built into theoretical models of economic growth. In the context of rural development in poor countries, similar ideas have motivated policy arguments that getting one activity going locally stimulates others, in a "virtuous cycle" of growth; John Mellor (1976) provided an influential statement of this hypothesis, and a number of studies have found seemingly strong effects of agricultural growth on rural nonfarm development.[14] Recall from the China case study in chapter 8 that externalities have been identified as a factor in the unbalanced growth process.

The debate continues today. There is some truth on both sides. One thing is clear enough: the appropriate balance of fiscal (tax and spending) policies between the urban and rural sectors will be contingent on specifics of the setting, and can thus be expected to vary from country to country and also over time within one country. A key contingent factor is how well urban labor markets work. If those markets are competitive then the case for believing that there is excess urbanization is weak. As in the HT model, the limiting case in which the urban wage rate is at its competitive level (in parity with the rural wage, allowing for cost-of-living differences and worker heterogeneity) implies that free mobility of labor will assure the highest mean income and lowest poverty measure that can be reached for the given technologies in production. However, excess migration is likely when urban labor markets are distorted, yielding high involuntary unemployment in urban areas. That appears to be the case more often than not.

Growth, Poverty, and Urbanization

Countries that have urbanized faster have seen higher growth, but we should not conclude that the urbanization was the cause of the growth, or that "pro-urban" policies are good for growth. Indeed, empirically, the case is weak for believing that policies that favor the urban economy will necessarily help promote economic growth. This is the conclusion of David Bloom and colleagues in their study of the relationship between urbanization and economic growth.[15] They used the tool of growth regressions (box 8.19), whereby rates of economic growth were regressed on the initial share of the population living in urban areas, in addition to the initial mean income and other control variables deemed to determine long-run income. The researchers found that, once they control for initial mean income and other factors, the initial share of

---

[14] See, e.g., Haggblade et al. (1989), Hazell and Haggblade (1993), and Ravallion (2005a).
[15] See Bloom et al. (2008).

a country's population living in urban areas is not a statistically significant predictor of the subsequent rate of economic growth. This is not suggestive that there is an independent role for policies that promote population urbanization.

As we learned in chapter 8, growth is not all that matters to poverty reduction. We have seen that higher growth rates tend to come with a faster pace of poverty reduction (though how much so depends crucially on aspects of distribution in both income and non-income dimensions). However, we have also learned that the sectoral pattern of growth matters. Some sectors matter more to poverty reduction than is evident in their immediate contribution to overall growth. To illustrate this point, let us consider the recent development paths of the two most populous countries in the world, China and India.

We have seen that China has made enormous progress against extreme absolute poverty (box 8.17). It is clear that an important role was played by the geographic and sectoral pattern of growth. Like most developing countries, living standards tend to be lower in rural areas of China, but (as noted already) the country's disparities between rural and urban areas are particularly large. Around 1980, shortly after the market-oriented reform process began, the chance of being poor was about ten times higher in China's rural areas than in its urban areas.[16] Thus, it was very important that the reforms were started in the rural economy.

Growth in the rural economy has accounted for the majority of China's success against poverty since 1980.[17] Looking back over the period since 1981, one finds that rural economic growth in China has had a far higher poverty impact than urban economic growth. Similarly, growth in the primary sector (mainly agriculture) has done more to reduce poverty than growth in either the secondary (mainly manufacturing) or tertiary (mainly services) sectors. Indeed, judged by the impact on poverty nationally, China's primary-sector growth has had about four times the impact of growth than either the secondary or tertiary sectors.[18] The provincial data for China suggest that virtually all of the growth impacts on poverty worked through the primary sector.[19]

However, despite the country's success in reducing absolute poverty, it can also be argued that China could have had an even faster pace of progress against poverty. Both mean income and long-run growth rates have also been lower in rural areas, yielding economic divergence between China's cities and their rural hinterland. This has been particularly strong since the mid-1990s. Similarly, while there was rapid agricultural growth in some periods, including the early 1980s, the sector's growth rate has since tended to decline. One expects agriculture's share of national output to fall with

---

[16] See Ravallion and Chen (2007).

[17] See Ravallion and Chen (2007).

[18] See Ravallion and Chen (2007). These results are based on regressions of the proportionate rate of poverty reduction over time on the growth rates by sector, weighted by their shares of output. If the composition of growth did not matter, then the coefficients on the share-weighted growth rates would be equal across different sectors. Instead one finds large and significant differences. For details, see Ravallion and Chen (2007), who use national time series data, and Montalvo and Ravallion (2010), who use provincial panel data.

[19] See Montalvo and Ravallion (2010).

sustained economic growth in any developing country, but in China the relatively poor performance of the farm sector (both relative to other sectors, and compared to the first half of the 1980s) has constrained the pace of poverty reduction that was possible with China's (high) aggregate growth. The indications of strong externalities on rural development in China generated by the agricultural sector also point to the possibility of aggregate inefficiencies stemming from policy biases in favor of other sectors.[20] To help assess the role of the sectoral imbalance in the growth process, imagine that the same aggregate growth rate was balanced across sectors. Such balanced growth would have taken half the time—ten years rather than twenty years—to bring the headcount index down to 10%.[21]

The sequence in China was roughly right: initial attention in the reform period from 1978 was given to the rural sector, and agrarian reforms to restore farmer incentives (in land allocation and prices) were crucial to assuring a sustainably pro-poor development path.[22] This sequencing in the reform process appears to have been important in other countries of East Asia.[23] However, rather few developing countries outside East Asia appear to have got the sequence right; China's experience contains an important lesson for Africa today.[24]

Consider instead India. We have already reviewed past and ongoing debates about how much India's poor have gained from economic growth (section 8.4). Higher farm productivity has generally been poverty reducing, despite the high inequality in access to land. The transmission effect through the labor market has helped here.[25] The longer term rigidity of real wages implied by classical arguments (as reviewed in chapter 1) has not been borne out by India's experience. Urban economic growth has not helped as much as was hoped by India's early planners in the 1950s, although there are encouraging signs that a more pro-poor nonfarm growth process has emerged since the 1990s (section 8.4). However, delivering better health and education services to poor people than at present will be crucial to the potential for future urban economic growth to make a serious dent on poverty in India. At the time in the early 1990s that India embarked on its current reform path its attainments in basic health and education were well short of China's at the time (over ten years earlier) that China embarked on its reforms. India has long faced a "human development handicap" in assuring pro-poor growth from its non-farm sectors. In terms of the sectoral composition of growth, what is also notable in comparison to China is the importance of India's services sector. As discussed in section 8.4, this can be attributed to the fact that access to agricultural land is much less equitably distributed in India.

[20] See Ravallion (2005a).

[21] See Ravallion and Chen (2007).

[22] Given that the rest of the economy was growing rapidly, China could delay reforms to its State-Owned Enterprises (SOEs). Indeed, it was not until the late 1990s (twenty years after the agrarian reforms began) that China started reforming its SOEs. Some observers have suggested that this should have happened sooner.

[23] For example, Vietnam followed a similar sequence from the late 1980s; for further discussion, see Ravallion and van de Walle (2008). Earlier literature on this topic is discussed in Lipton and Ravallion (1995).

[24] Those lessons are discussed further in Ravallion (2009a).

[25] This is demonstrated by Datt and Ravallion (1998a).

In development thinking across the world, "urban bias" came to be recognized as bad for growth and poverty reduction.[26] There were efforts to re-prioritize development policy in the 1970s and 1980s. World Bank President Robert McNamara's (1973) "Nairobi speech" signaled such an effort from the international development institutions (chapter 2). However, the temptation to industrialize rapidly—"run before you have walked"—has remained strong for governments. Combined with huge inequities in access to finance and human development, the subsequent growth paths have been disappointing, both in terms of growth and (especially) poverty reduction.

There is no denying that new urban problems can emerge in poor and rapidly urbanizing countries. As we have seen, the pace of urbanization will be excessive if it is driven by regulation in urban labor markets whereby a high-wage segment of insiders is able to keep the wage rate above the market-clearing level. The consequent urban unemployment will drive a wedge between the marginal product of labor in the rural sector and that in the high-wage urban sector (as in the Harris-Todaro model reviewed in box 8.9.). If this is the only distortion (though that is a big "if"), then total output will be lower than without it and inequality and poverty will be higher. And there will be too much migration from rural to urban areas. We see something akin to this in much of sub-Saharan Africa.

However, as we saw in chapter 8, the experiences of countries over time are generally consistent with the view that a rising share of the population living in urban areas plays a positive role in overall poverty reduction. The notable exception is in sub-Saharan Africa where the urbanization process has not been poverty reducing in the aggregate.[27] Interestingly, it was experiences in this region of the world that motivated the Harris-Todaro model. The less pro-poor urbanization process in Africa might well reflect greater regulation of urban labor markets in that region, although agricultural policies may well have played a role as well. The region has seen very little overall growth in agricultural productivity (much less than other regions of the developing world).[28] The low productivity of labor in farming has generated a process of urbanization in Africa that has not been as pro-poor as elsewhere.

Past research also points to the potential importance of *urban* policies to rural poverty reduction. Some policies matter more to the urban economy, such as minimum wage rates for formal sector work. (Section 9.5 will discuss minimum wage rates further.) However, many of the things that matter to the pace of urbanization and the gains it brings to the poor (including the rural poor) depend on actions by urban governments, including service provision, transport, land-use regulations, land titling, and legal protection. But urban governments are typically answerable to only their urban constituents. A city government, on its own, will probably devote too few resources to actions that yield external benefits to its rural hinterland. Indeed, some incumbent urban residents may expect to be worse off from policies that help rural migrants. It is not then surprising that past urban policies have often ignored the needs of migrants and have even burdened them with extra costs (both pecuniary and non-pecuniary).

---

[26] Lipton (1968, 1977) drew early attention to these biases in development policymaking.

[27] This is shown by Ravallion et al. (2007).

[28] See World Bank (2007b).

The Role of Agriculture and Rural Development

Policies to promote agricultural and rural development will continue to play a crucial role in fighting poverty. There are two aspects of that role. The first is that rural economic development is directly pro-poor, given that so many of the world's poor are still dependent on the rural economy. The second role is in helping to create the initial conditions for more pro-poor *urban* economic development through the absorption of rural labor into expanding non-farm sectors. An undernourished, unhealthy, illiterate, and vulnerable rural population will not be well equipped to contribute to, as well as benefit from, modern-sector enlargement over time. This second role has often been missing in past debates.

9.2 Land Policies

Land is the main non-human asset of poor people globally. The security of land rights is crucial to their economic welfare. Tenure security is traditionally defined in terms of formal, individual, titles of private ownership. There have been many efforts (often supported by external development assistance) to foster individual ownership through land titling, with expected benefits to the government in efforts to tax land value and also expected gains in both efficiency (promoting land investment through greater tenure security and access to credit) and equity (notably in promoting women's empowerment).[29] However, it has also come to be understood that long-established social institutions play an important role in how land is allocated and used. The benefits from efforts to foster individual ownership titles are known to be uncertain when individual titling is introduced in an indigenous (customary) system of tenure, which is probably why the evidence that such efforts have their expected benefits appears to be mixed.[30]

Managing land-use changes in growing and urbanizing economies poses a special set of challenges, the outcomes of which have mattered greatly to the lives of poor people across the globe. Land-use rights are sometimes ill-defined in terms of formal laws and administrative processes (though, as noted, they may be well defined in local customary law). At the same time, local governments often have power over land use and can easily extract a share of the change in the value of land when it changes from agricultural to non-farm uses. The appropriation of agricultural land for large-scale infrastructure projects (such as dams) for urban expansion—infrastructure, urban housing, and new enterprises—and for mining enterprises has pitted locally powerful governments and agencies against rural people in developing economies across the globe. Poor farmers living in close proximity to expanding urban areas or in mineral-rich areas are especially vulnerable. Disputes over land have also been common in

---

[29] On the productivity gains from titling, see Feder and Noronha (1987), Barrows and Roth (1990), Besley (1995a), and Deininger (2003).

[30] Ensminger (1997) discusses the conflict between private property rights and customary norms and institutions in Kenya. Deininger (2003) reviews the evidence. A recent example of a study pointing to success of land titling in raising productivity is Holden et al. (2009); an example finding little or no impact is Jacoby and Minten (2007).

post-conflict settings. Land conflicts have attracted media and scholarly attention throughout the developing world.[31]

Success in addressing these challenges requires central governmental efforts to secure and protect the legal rights of rural people and assure fair compensation for land acquisition. This is not going to be easy since central government officials and judiciary may also come to share in the rents generated by land-use changes. The mobilization of local residents to stand up for their (formal or customary) rights may well be crucial in developing a countervailing power to local elites. Externally, aid donors have become more sensitive to these issues and have required appropriate assurances from recipient governments as a condition for financing projects that entail land acquisition and displacement. At the global level, guidance for the management of natural resources in post-conflict situations has been provided by the UN *Peacebuilding Commission* created in 2005 and in subsequent UN reports and guidelines.

Land policies and their implications for poverty have been much debated in the context of countries in transition from socialist command economies to market-based economies. Agricultural productivity in both China and Vietnam increased appreciably on switching from socialist agriculture back to the family-farm model. Incentives for production were greatly enhanced when farmers received something closer to the marginal product of their labor (rather than average product, as in the socialist model for collective farming; recall box 1.4). This policy change was both efficient and pro-poor.

The bigger challenge was what to do about agricultural land rights. Vietnam took the step of introducing the essential ingredients of a market in land-use rights through various land laws in the 1990s.[32] These reforms were much debated, with concerns that a destitute rural proletariat would emerge, as poor farmers sold their land, and would soon add to the ranks of the urban poor. Similar concerns in China were compelling enough to stall such reforms. Dominique van de Walle and I studied closely these reforms in Vietnam and compared them to China.[33] We found that Vietnam's land law reforms were on balance poverty reducing. Vietnam's more radical approach of allowing voluntary exchange played an important role in the evolution of land allocation but did not have the dire consequences predicted by those who favored the Chinese model of administrative land allocation. Starting from a relatively equitable allocation of land, relatively free exchange in Vietnam's case did not end in peril and poverty for the rural population, although (as in any major policy reform) there are both losers and gainers. Also, Vietnam's experience suggests that the efficiency gains do not happen overnight and may well take many years to be realized. But gains can be expected, including gains for the poor.

The absence of a free market in land (or land-use rights) can also leave farmers exposed to administrative reassignment of their land without adequate compensation. This has been a serious problem for poor families living near China's rapidly expanding

[31] Boone (2014) describes numerous examples in Africa. The volume edited by Unruh and Williams (2013) describes land disputes in seventeen post-conflict countries across the world.

[32] The 1993 Land Law introduced official land titles and permitted land transactions for the first time since communist rule began. Land remained the property of the state, but usage rights could be legally transferred, exchanged, mortgaged, and inherited. A further (much debated) Resolution in 1998 removed restrictions on the size of landholdings and on the hiring of agricultural labor.

[33] See Ravallion and van de Walle (2008).

cities. A large gap exists between the price local authorities at the urban fringe can get for the land in non-farm uses and the compensation paid to farmers. (The local revenue so generated goes to may uses, and it is clear that not all of them are in the public interest.) The lack of an agricultural land market is also likely to bring down the cost of acquiring land for urban expansion, which encourages a more low-density form of urbanization with higher transport costs and more pollution.[34]

Land has also played an important role in direct interventions against poverty, as discussed further in Chapter 10.

9.3   Healthcare Policies

Ill-health and its treatment are concerns for poor people and many others.[35] It was noted in chapter 7 that health outcomes at country level tend to improve as average income increases. While it is plausible that higher incomes lead to better health outcomes, it is an oversimplification to say that economic growth is all that matters. For one thing, the causality undoubtedly goes both ways; higher average income allows for better health, which in turn raises productivity and future incomes. (Recall from chapter 8 that better schooling and health has often been found to both enhance overall growth prospects and to help assure that growth is poverty reducing.) For another, there is a large variance in health outcomes at a given average income. The relationship between health and income is mediated by other factors, including healthcare policies.[36]

Indeed, the cross-country health–income correlation may well be spurious, in that it may reflect other omitted variables correlated with average incomes, such as the incidence of absolute poverty, human capital, and access to key social services. Poor people tend to have worse health outcomes (as we saw in chapter 7). And (as we learned in chapter 8), higher average income tends to mean fewer poor people. The gain in average health outcomes with economic growth can be modest if that growth by-passes poor people. Higher average income also generates more resources for better health services overall, including through governmental provision financed by taxation. Controlling for such factors, average incomes on its own may matter far less than is suggested by the simple correlation.

There is evidence in support of this view: Sudhir Anand and I found that when we control for governmental health spending and the incidence of poverty in cross-country regressions, the formerly strong relationship between a country's income-per-person and its health outcomes becomes much weaker.[37] This is not to say that economic growth is irrelevant to better health outcomes, but rather that growth must come with less poverty and better health services, especially for poor people, if it is to bring significant gains in overall health outcomes. The issue is how the income

---

[34] For further discussion, see The Economist (2015).

[35] In qualitative work, poor people often refer to health issues; see, e.g., Narayan and Petesch (2002).

[36] Sen (1981b) was influential in pointing to this variance and the specific example of Sri Lanka. Further analysis of this case was provided by Anand and Ravallion (1993).

[37] See Anand and Ravallion (1993). Also see the further analysis in Bidani and Ravallion (1993).

gains are distributed and how the gains are spent, recognizing that capacities for both private and public spending are required to achieve better overall health. There are a number of relatively low cost and effective ways of improving healthcare.[38] Countries such as (at various times) China, Costa Rica, Cuba, Malaysia, South Korea, and Sri Lanka have demonstrated how this can be done even at a low average income.[39]

A similar argument holds true for nutrition. In unhealthy environments, using extra income solely for extra calories may do little for nutritional status. The health environment needs to improve. But one person cannot do that on her own; it will typically require governmental effort in key areas such as water and sanitation (which we return to in the next section). When the public sector has failed, extra income for poor people may do rather little to assure better nutrition.

The role of the public sector in healthcare *delivery* has been much debated. Public financing plays a significant role almost everywhere, but national healthcare systems differ in the extent to which the government is directly involved in the delivery of services. Increasingly this is seen to be the role of the private sector, which is widely thought to be a more efficient provider, although there is also evidence of inefficiencies in private provisioning.[40] This takes us beyond the scope of this book.

However, one issue in the *financing* of healthcare (whether public or private in terms of delivery) is very relevant here, namely to what extent poor users pay for their services. It is common in both rich and poor countries for health facilities and insurers to charge a fee to all users, including poor people. This has been a subject of much debate since "user fees" started to become popular in the 1980s. Critics argue that such fees discourage usage, especially by poor people, who can be discouraged by even a seemingly modest fee. They also point to the externalities that are common in health, especially related to infectious diseases; when there is an external benefit to a person's healthcare there is a case for subsidizing the price. Defenders of user fees claim that there will be excessive usage of healthcare if the users do not pay the full price, and that the revenues generated by user fees help support a better quality of care. A number of policy advisors (including the World Bank) have argued that user fees are a necessary evil to finance health and other services—that the positive effect of the higher service quality that fees allow outweighs the negative effect on demand. There can be no doubt that the extent to which the revenues from user fees are passed back to the facilities matters to the outcomes for healthcare. However, there have been concerns among critics of user fees that the revenues generated do not feedback to better services, but are spent on other things.

The basic economic model of consumer demand (as summarized in box 3.1) does not offer any strong predictions about whether poor people will be more responsive to price increases than others. Box 9.1 explains this point further. Thus, it is an empirical question.

[38] Examples include nutrition supplementation for young children, teaching basic hygiene practices such as boiling drinking water, eliminating open defecation, oral rehydration therapy, promoting reproductive healthcare, and breast feeding.

[39] Mehrotra and Jolly (1997) provide an overview of this topic and a number of case studies.

[40] This widely held view does not appear to stand up well as a generalization; see the review of over one hundred past studies for developing countries in Basu et al. (2012). Inefficiency appears to be common to both delivery modes.

Box 9.1 **Do Poor People Respond Differently to Price Changes?**

Recall box 3.1. Now imagine we have two types of consumers, "poor" and "rich." They have the same preferences (though this is not essential), but different incomes. Both face the same prices. For concreteness let the goods now be called "healthcare" and "food." The price of healthcare increases (a higher user-fee). Nothing else changes.

Let y^R and y^P denote incomes of the rich and poor, and p_0 and p_1 are the initial and final prices of healthcare, respectively, with $p_0 < p_1$. The maximum affordable level of healthcare is income divided by the price of care (in other words when nothing else is consumed). Thus, we have that:

$$\frac{y^R - y^P}{p_0} > \frac{y^R - y^P}{p_1} \text{ which implies that } \frac{y^R}{p_0} - \frac{y^R}{p_1} > \frac{y^P}{p_0} - \frac{y^P}{p_1}.$$

Thus, we see that the maximum attainable level of healthcare must fall more for the rich than the poor when price rises. However, the *chosen* level of healthcare may well fall more for the poor.

Figure B9.1.1 shows this. The bold lines are the initial budget lines and indifference curves and the dashed lines are those after the price increase. In this case, the rich person's healthcare consumption changes little (only her food consumption falls). But the poor person, who already has less healthcare, now chooses even less than before the price increase; she prefers to maintain her food consumption.

But notice that it is only one possibility. The reader can readily verify that one can even draw a different set of indifference curves that give the opposite result: with a larger decline in healthcare usage for the rich. The fact that most readers probably do not think that this is plausible reflects an implicit assumption about preferences, namely that the indifference curves look something like those in the graph. That is why we say it is an empirical question.

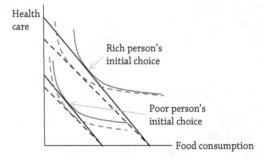

Figure B9.1.1 Effects of Higher User Charges for Healthcare on Poor and Rich Consumers.

Studies of food demand have indicated greater price responsiveness for poor consumers.[41] In the context of demand for healthcare, an important early study for the World Bank by Paul Gertler and Jacques van de Gaag, using LSMS survey data for Cote d'Ivoire and Peru, demonstrated that poor families were so much more price responsive that user fees reduce their health outcomes.[42] Since then, other evidence has indicated that poor families can be very price responsive. For example, even a modest fee was found to bring a large drop in take-up of deworming drugs in Kenya.[43] Conversely, removing user fees improved the nutritional status (weight-for-age) of poor children in South Africa, though more so for boys than girls.[44] It has been suggested that poor people tend to be especially sensitive to the prices charged for preventative care, which is a type of healthcare that is often associated with large externalities.[45]

In the light of the new research, the bigger concern for policymakers today is that poor people do not get the preventative healthcare that they need, rather than that they will overuse subsidized care.[46] At the same time, there are continuing concerns about overuse of some medications when they are heavily subsidized.[47]

Since 2000 there has been more attention to the policy challenges in assuring that poor people pay little or nothing for good quality preventative healthcare (i.e., how to achieve a well-targeted price subsidy for that care).[48] This brings us to the topic of the economics of targeting, to be taken up in chapter 10.

9.4 Water, Sanitation, and Hygiene

Recall how in the 1850s Dr. John Snow's early epidemiological investigations in London revealed that cholera was more likely a water-borne disease than air-borne, as had been commonly believed (box 1.15). Severe diarrhea is one of the symptoms of infection by cholera, although diarrhea is also a symptom of gastrointestinal infection stemming from bacterial, viral, and parasitic organisms. While the infection can be spread via contaminated food or water or from personal contact, Snow's research pointed clearly to the importance for public health of separating waste disposal from drinking water. This research finding was the foundation for both better health knowledge and public investments in water and sanitation. As it tended to be poor people (though not exclusively) who were most exposed to disease, this also emerged as an important instrument of antipoverty policy.

---

[41] An early contribution was Timmer (1981).

[42] See Gertler and van de Gaag (1990). For recent discussions of the policy issues, see Meessen et al. (2006) and Dupas (2014).

[43] See Kremer and Miguel (2007).

[44] See Tanaka (2014).

[45] See, e.g., Dupas (2014).

[46] See the review of evidence from RCTs in Dupas (2014).

[47] See, e.g., the evidence on malaria treatments in Cohen et al. (2015).

[48] In some cases, the price subsidy has come with aid to cover transport and other costs. See, e.g., the discussion of the Cambodia Health Funds in Meessen et al. (2006).

Diarrhea is still common in the world and children are its main victims. It is estimated to have been associated with 700,000 deaths of children under five annually in 2011—about 10% of child deaths under the age of five.[49] Over two-thirds of these deaths occurred in the first two years of life. This is not only a concern at the time of illness; diarrhea is believed to be a cause of poor child growth.[50]

There are well-researched actions that can prevent and treat diarrhea, and also pneumonia (which accounts for a further 1.3 million child deaths in 2011).[51] Breastfeeding of infants reduces the onset and severity of both diarrhea and pneumonia. There are also effective vaccines against common causes of both diseases. Oral rehydration salts have proven effective for treating diarrhea. And interventions to improve water, sanitation, and hygiene have been identified. Following sound standardized protocols for identification and treatment at community level can also help greatly.

High diarrhea incidence among children is typically a symptom of a generally poor health environment, with poor infrastructure for water and sanitation as a common feature. The health gains from improving that infrastructure can be huge. Half or more of the dramatic drop in child mortality in urban areas of the United States during the late nineteenth and early twentieth centuries has been attributed to broad access to clean water, in the form of treatment technologies for drinking water and sewerage.[52] While all children are vulnerable to a poor health environment, it is plausible that those from poor families tend to be the most vulnerable.

Public programs have expanded access to piped water in developing countries. However, this does not seem to be having the same sort of impact that it had in the United States over one hundred years ago. Evaluations have suggested that improving water supply on its own is unlikely to bring much benefit; reviews of multiple evaluations have argued that more effective interventions focus on protecting or treating water at the source or point of use, and on sanitation and hygiene practices.[53]

Support for this broader approach has also come from the arguments and evidence on the existence of enteropathy, whereby a poor health environment—including poor water and sanitation—is now seen as important cause of chronic under-nutrition. The regular ingestion of fecal bacteria by children living in poor health environments (in particular, where open defecation is common) is known to reduce nutrient absorption and thus results in higher rates of stunting (even if diarrhea is not also present).[54] Thus, poor basic infrastructure can perpetuate poverty via chronic under-nutrition.

---

[49] See Fischer et al. (2013).

[50] Humphrey (2009) reviews the epidemiological evidence on this point.

[51] See WHO (2013a) and Bhutta et al. (2013).

[52] See Cutler and Miller (2005). The analysis relied on a difference-in-difference estimation method discussed in chapter 6, exploiting the variation in the timing of technology adoption across cities of the United States.

[53] See Waddington et al. (2009) and Zwane and Kremer (2007).

[54] See Humphrey (2009) for a review of the biomedical evidence. Spears (2013) reports cross-country regressions suggesting that India's unusually high rate of child stunting is mainly due to the country's high incidence of open defecation. He finds that the correlation across countries persists with controls for GDP per capita. Sears does not control for differences in the distribution of income; it might be expected that one would also need to control for the incidence of poverty to identify the

This illustrates the point made in chapter 6 that interventions can sometimes inter-act powerfully with each other, such that one on its own can be ineffective. This fact can be hidden from view in standard "one-at-a-time" evaluations. Access to piped water interacts with private health inputs to health, such as hygienic water storage, boiling water, oral re-hydration therapy, medical treatment, sanitation, and nutrition. With the right combination of public and private inputs, diarrheal disease is almost entirely preventable. However, behavior and inequalities in income and education play an important role. Public inputs such as access to a piped water network can either dis-place parentally chosen private inputs or be complementary to them. Even when there are child-health benefits (factoring in parental spending effects) the gains could well by-pass children in poor families, when allowing for parental responses to poverty.

For example, if piped water increases the marginal health benefit for parents of spending more on their children's health, and such spending is a normal good, then the health gains from piped water will tend to rise with income. This is not implausible on a priori grounds. Piped water in rural areas of developing countries is safer than many alternative sources, but it is often the case that it needs to be boiled or filtered and stored properly to be safe to drink. This can be a burden for a poor family. A poor, or poorly educated, mother may not know or understand the additional precautions needed or may reasonably think that there are better uses of the time and money needed to provide this complementary input to piped water.

There is evidence that the provision of private inputs to child health depends on socioeconomic characteristics of the child's family. It is estimated that about 80% of the poorest quintile (in terms of a composite wealth index) of families in rural India in the 1990s did not use oral rehydration therapy when a child had diarrhea, as compared to 50% in the richest quintile.[55] Similarly, about half of those in the poorest quintile did not seek medical treatment, as compared to one-quarter in the richest. There is also evidence suggesting that parental education, notably of the mother, matters to child health outcomes,[56] though whether it is formal education as such, or knowledge gained by education or some other means (such as interacting with others) is a moot point. For example, one study found strong effects, in both coefficient size and statis-tical significance, on child morbidity in Kenya of the parental scores on cognitive tests; the maternal score was a much stronger predictor than the paternal score.[57]

The upshot of all this is that being connected to a piped water network may well be of limited relevance to poor people from an epidemiological standpoint. Income poverty and lack of education and knowledge constrain the potential health gains from water infrastructure improvements. The incidence of health gains need not favor children from poor families even when facility placement is pro-poor.

There is evidence to support this argument. A study of the child-health gains from access to piped water in India found strong interaction effects with poverty and maternal education, using careful propensity score matching to balance the observable

effect of open defecation (probably correlated with poverty) on child height (similarly to Anand and Ravallion 1993 and Bidani and Ravallion 1997).

[55] See Gwatkin et al. (2000).

[56] Strauss and Thomas (1998) provide a survey.

[57] See Bhargava (1999).

covariates of villages with piped water versus those without (box 6.3). Indeed, the study found that the health gains from piped water largely by-pass children in poor families, particularly when the mother is poorly educated. Such findings point to the importance of combining water infrastructure investments with effective public action to promote health knowledge and income poverty reduction.

Sanitation and hygiene programs have become widespread in the developing world. A typical program entails a roving trained sanitation promoter visiting villages to publicize the benefits of better water and sanitation practices, including the use of latrines, and often in combination with a subsidy for latrine construction. Social shaming has been part of these interventions, which strive to harness the power of social pressure and peer monitoring to assure behavioral change. One such intervention is the Open-Defecation Free project in India where about half the population defecates in the open.[58] A randomized trial in Orissa, India, of one such intervention combining subsidies with shaming found significant impacts on latrine usage including for the relatively poor.[59] In another RCT in Maharashtra, a similar intervention was found to significantly reduce the incidence of child stunting (low height-for-age).[60]

9.5 Schooling Policies

It is probably not easy for most readers of this book to fully comprehend just how socially and economically disabling it is to be illiterate. Illiteracy limits most employment opportunities beyond traditional subsistence farming, and even then it limits one's ability to find ways of increasing the productivity of agriculture.[61] It also impedes physical and social mobility, and renders a person more vulnerable to subordination to the will of others and exploitation in all domains of economic life. As we saw in the last section, education (especially maternal education) assures greater benefits to poor people from basic infrastructure.

Like health, education outcomes tend to improve with economic growth. However, also like schooling, both the distribution of the income gains and sectoral policies matter. Growing developing countries have tended to see improvements in education outcomes. But that does not mean that growth is all that matters. A study of the gains in average education in Morocco and Vietnam found that a far more important factor than the extent of economic growth per se was the *structure* of how growth and distributional changes affected schooling. In other words, *how* the aggregate income gains were spent in society appears to have mattered far more than how much income gain there was.[62] Public policies have clearly played a role in such structural changes.

As we saw in chapter 7, children from poor families tend to get less schooling and are less likely to be literate. This economic gradient in education persists to this day

---

[58] See Spears (2013).

[59] See Pattanayak et al. (2009).

[60] See Hammer and Spears (2013).

[61] This was a theme of the research over many decades of Theodore Schultz; see, e.g., Schultz (1981).

[62] See Lambert et al. (2010).

almost everywhere and has long been seen to perpetuate poverty across generations.[63] Efforts to assure that poor families participate fully in the gains in schooling in countries with relatively low levels of schooling may be needed to avoid rising income inequality. Policies that can promote the schooling of poor children can thus be seen as an important social policy idea that could improve both equity and efficiency, and credibly allow people to escape poverty, permanently.

Why Do Children from Poor Families Get Less Schooling?

There are those who blame parents; by this view, poverty persists because poor parents do not see the value of schooling. As a generalization, this does not appear to be valid. Poor parents typically understand the benefits of schooling because they can see for themselves the better lives it allows. Attitudinal surveys such as those done by the Probe Team (1999) for states of India with low schooling attainments indicate that there is ample aspiration among even poor parents for schooling their children. Where public schools are of poor quality, parents turn instead to private schools and tutors.

While it does not appear plausible that parental attitudes are an important reason for education inequality in poor countries today, it remains true that the aspiration for schooling is often stronger for boys than for girls. But here too the problem goes deeper than the attitudes of individual parents. The gender bias in schooling choices may reflect discrimination against women in the labor market, lowering expected returns to girls' schooling. There are also externalities involved (recalling box 1.9). In many countries, when a girl marries she leaves the parental home, and even village, to settle in the husband's home, and so the girl's parents may not expect much longer term personal gain from investing in the girl's schooling—the benefits from such investment are largely external to the parents actually making the decision.

There is also an important, but often neglected, social element. For example, for India the Probe Team (1999, 24) noted that:

> when asked why their daughters never went to school, some parents simply say "girls don't go to school in our community." In other words, they are following what they see as a social norm. Some go on to say that if other parents sent their daughters to school, they would send their daughters to school too.

Individuals parents may well aspire to schooling their girls but this will require solving a difficult collective action problem. We can readily understand the problem when girls tend to be badly treated at school, especially so when few of them are attending school. There is a (non-pecuniary) "harassment cost" incurred by girls attending school and this is likely to be higher (per girl) when there are fewer other girls at school. When they are a small minority, girls are more likely to be picked on and harassed (on the way to school or at school), making school unpleasant and even dangerous. Sexual violence against girls in school—including by teachers as well as other students—is alarmingly common, and not just in the developing world.[64] Parents know that the harassment

---

[63] Economic models of the intergenerational transmission of inequality by this means have been proposed by Becker and Tomes (1979) and Loury (1981).

[64] See WHO (2002, ch. 6).

occurs but also that there is safety in numbers. Box 9.2 explains how the social norm that few girls go to school can be a stable "bad equilibrium." Switching to the "good equilibrium" may require a significant incentive, as discussed further in chapter 10.

Physical accessibility to schools has historically been a constraining factor for many poor families, although this is becoming less relevant today in most countries given the efforts made to build schools. For example, by 1993, 94% of the rural population of India lived within one kilometer of a primary school though this fell to 57% for middle (upper primary) schools.[65] The evidence does not suggest that proximity is a major factor in the schooling gap between rich and poor.[66]

Box 9.2 An Economic Interpretation of Social Norms against Girls' Schooling

To understand social norms in economic terms, we can assume that individual parents weigh up the benefits and costs of sending each girl to school. The expected benefit varies. To simplify the analysis we can suppose that the benefit is uniformly distributed, meaning that all benefit levels are equally likely. There is also a "harassment cost" incurred by girls attending school when very few other girls attend and parents know this cost.

Dynamics also play a role. Suppose that the expected cost of a girl attending school depends on last year's school enrollment rate for school-age girls (S_{t-1}). The cost is prohibitively high when no girls attend school, but falls the higher is last year's enrollment rate of girls. At first the cost does not fall much at all, but once some critical level (S^*) of the girls' schooling rate is reached it starts to fall rapidly, reaching zero when most are in school. (See the figure on the right-side of Figure B9.2.1.) When no girls are in school the cost is certain to exceed

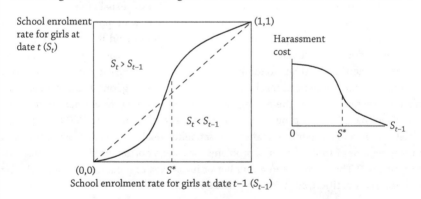

Figure B9.2.1 Multiple Equilibria in Girls' Schooling.

continued

---

[65] See Probe Team (1999).
[66] See the simulations by Filmer (2007).

Box 9.2 **(Continued)**

the expected benefit, while when all girls are in school the expected cost is certain to be less than the benefit. A plausible assumption is that the school enrollment rate of girls rises (falls) when the expected benefit net of cost is positive (negative).

Using the tools described in chapter 8, it is now clear that there can be two stable steady-state equilibria for this model, one with no girls in school and one with all of them in school, as illustrated in figure B9.2.1. The relationship between the enrollment rate this year and that last year is initially convex from below given that the cost only falls slowly at first, but it is concave after some point. There is also a middle-level steady-state solution but this is unstable.

Getting out of the bad equilibrium at (0,0) can be difficult. Hiring more female teachers can help, although it may be hard to find them locally given that so few girls go to school. A subsidy for schooling girls can help; we return to this in discussing Conditional Cash Transfers in chapter 10.

This is another example of a coordination failure. If all parents got together and agreed to send all their girls to school, then the preferred equilibrium would be reached.

However, there are important qualifications. First, even when physical distance is not a constraining factor, there can be social barriers that impede access. For example, in India, caste differentiation of areas within a single village can create such barriers. Girls are often less geographically mobile such that even modest distances can be an obstacle. Girls' schooling is often inhibited by factors such as the lack of designated girls' toilets in schools, few female teachers, and the fear of sexual violence.

Second, physical access matters little if the school is of poor quality, such as when teachers do not even turn up for the work they are paid to do. For India, the Probe Team documented the strikingly low level of actual teaching activity among teachers at the time of their unannounced spot checks on visiting sampled schools; only one-quarter of the head teachers were actually teaching; one-third were absent. Effective teaching time in the aggregate amounted to only 6 hours per student per year. There have been improvements in some areas of India since 2000, such as in infrastructure and teacher attendance, but schooling quality remains a major problem in many regions of India.[67] Similar problems have been documented now in a number of countries.[68] There have been a number of initiatives to enhance school quality by promoting competition, such as with private schools, although there are concerns that private schools may respond to competition by focusing their efforts on kids from wealthier families, exacerbating the economic gradient in human capital. A trade-off is likely.

Out-of-pocket costs of schooling can be a serious burden for poor families everywhere, and on top of these costs there are the forgone labor earnings. The inability of

---

[67] See Probe Team (2011).
[68] See World Bank (2004b).

poor families to finance their children's schooling has long been recognized as a key factor in the economic gradient in education, and in how unequal initial wealth distributions persist and generate efficiency costs. This is of continuing relevance in today's developing world, and in the rich world too (albeit at different levels of schooling).

Mass Schooling as a Policy Response

The long-standing policy response has been to mandate that schooling is compulsory for all up to some age. Such policies are a modern idea, advocated at times, but little known prior to the nineteenth century (chapter 1). Past and ongoing policy debates over mass education have raised many issues, but a fundamental one is whether compulsory schooling is even in the interest of poor families, for it was typically their children who were un-schooled. Opponents of compulsory schooling point to the costs (primarily their forgone earnings) to poor families of sending their children to school. While making schooling compulsory could break the poverty trap, a short-term trade-off was to be expected due to the costs imposed on poor families. Advocates argue, in effect, that the longer term benefits from breaking out of a poverty trap outweigh these costs.

The history of the emergence of compulsory schooling in today's rich world is instructive. After much debate, compulsory schooling, with a significant state role in both public provision and support for private schooling, emerged in virtually all industrialized countries by the early twentieth century. In England, the Elementary Education Act of 1870 was a breakthrough in establishing a secular public sector institutional framework, including democratic school boards. Implementation was uneven geographically, and there was a continuing struggle for control of schools between the democratically elected local bodies and religious organizations.[69] It was not until the 1880 Act of the same name that education was compulsory in England for children aged five to ten. This happened in France about the same time. In the United States, thirty-four states had compulsory schooling laws by 1900, thirty of which required attendance until at least age fourteen. Japan in the Meiji period (1868–1912) was not far behind the West in promoting mass education, which was virtually universal by the end of the period. Mass public education (though with tertiary education left largely to the private sector) was given high priority throughout developing East Asia, with educational attainments far surpassing most developing countries, and some developed countries.

The payoffs from mass public education have been huge. Economists Claudia Goldin and Lawrence Katz identify equitable, broad-based, education as a key factor in the US record of relatively equitable and rapid growth in the period 1940–80.[70] The ability of the schooling system to support a relatively rapid increase in education attainments in the United States in this period (though slowing down greatly after 1980) meant that the supply of skilled workers kept up with the extra demand stemming from new technologies, thus attenuating the inequality-increasing effects of technical progress favoring demand for relatively skilled labor. The fact that American

---

[69] See Stephens (1998).

[70] See Goldin and Katz (2008).

educational expansion was so broad-based in this period was key. A more elitist schooling system would have entailed a more unequal distribution of the gains from growth.
Goldin and Katz argue that rising earnings inequality in the United States since
1980 stems in large part from the fact that the education system has not allowed the
supply of the types of skilled labor required for the new technologies of the time to
keep up with the demand; as soon as the United States education system's output of
college graduates stopped growing in the 1980s the premium earned by skilled labor
over unskilled labor started rising. And, given credit-market failures, children from
poor families face a greater handicap than others in this race between education and
technology.

Broad-based education has also been identified as a key factor in East Asia's relatively equitable growth. Using a regression of GDP per capita growth rates over
1960–85 on primary and secondary education attainments in 1960—with controls
for initial GDP per capita, population growth, and the share of investment in GDP—
an influential report by the World Bank (1993) identified primary education as the
most important single factor, accounting for somewhere between 58% (Japan) and
87% (Thailand) of GDP growth. Such calculations can be sensitive to model specification; the education variables could well be correlated with other omitted factors.
However, it is striking that primary education is found to account for a greater share
of the variance in growth rates than private (non-human) investment.

The importance of mass education has long been acknowledged in India; indeed, a
directive principle of state policy in the 1949 Constitution was free compulsory education to the age of fourteen.[71] However, implementation lagged greatly, with large
inter-state differences, and often poor quality schooling, such as indicated by low
levels of teacher activity.[72]

The state of India that has made the most progress in mass public education over
the longer term is Kerala.[73] Expanding literacy to the whole population was a high priority of the state government from the 1950s. But even by the 1951 census, almost
half of the state's population over five years of age was literate, as compared to only
20% in India as a whole. This appears to have reflected a history of prior successes
in schooling provided by Christian missionaries in Kerala back to the early nineteenth century. But considerable progress was made over the thirty years after 1951 in
expanding literacy to the whole population; by the 1990s, 90% of Kerala's population
was literate (as compared to about 50% for India as a whole).

These inter-state differences in educational attainments in India have been found
to interact strongly with India's growth process in determining the impact of that
growth on poverty. This was found in one study comparing rates of poverty reduction
across the states of India.[74] While the responsiveness of poverty measures to gains in
farm yields did not vary significantly across states, those for non-farm output varied considerably. The non-farm growth process in India tended to be significantly

[71] A Right to Education Act was passed by India's parliament in 2009, essentially ratifying the
Constitution.

[72] See the studies by the Probe Team (1999, 2011).

[73] Kerala is a famous example, but there are others including Himachal Pradesh; see the discussion
in the Probe Team (1999, ch. 9).

[74] See Ravallion and Datt (2002).

more poverty reducing in states with initially higher literacy rates, and inter-state differences in literacy rates were the dominant factor.[75] For example, Kerala's afore-mentioned success in mass schooling has generated a far more pro-poor process of non-farm economic growth than found in other states.

Banning Child Labor

A more controversial policy response is to ban child labor. The rationale is in part to avoid the potentially adverse consequences to the current well-being of children of hard labor at an early age. Such bans have also been proposed and legislated as a pro-motional antipoverty policy on the presumption that a ban will encourage schooling and so reduce future poverty. It is sometimes acknowledged that there is a trade-off in the short term—that an effective ban on child labor reduces the labor earnings of poor families. But it is argued that the ban will help break the education-induced poverty trap. The (often implicit) assumption is that any time spent working would otherwise be devoted to schooling. This assumption is questionable and there is evidence to the contrary.[76]

Child labor appears to become less common as economies develop. At the early stage of a country's development, child labor is abundant, while fertility is high and mean output is low. With economic growth stemming from technical progress, the returns to schooling rise, making child labor less attractive, and also lowering fertility. One study modeled an interesting version of a poverty trap with these features.[77] In this model, the economy eventually converges to a new equilibrium in which child labor has vanished. An effective ban on child labor will speed up the transition to this new equilibrium.

In economies with large informal sectors, the enforcement of bans on child labor is difficult. Legislation to set a minimum working age was introduced in some countries in the late nineteenth century, although it is unclear how much this helped reduce the incidence of child labor; one study indicates little effect.[78] Compulsory schooling may well be a better way of implementing a ban on child labor than an actual ban.[79] Chapter 10 will turn to targeted interventions for promoting schooling of the poor in which incentives play a key role.

9.6 Public Information Campaigns

Ignorance has long been identified as a cause of poverty. Formal schooling is an impor-tant instrument for changing public knowledge, but there have also been many efforts to intervene more selectively in the form of an *information campaign*. Examples include

[75] Among those factors identified by Ravallion and Datt (2002).
[76] See Ravallion and Wodon (2000a) using data for Bangladesh, and the observations made by the Probe Team (1999) in India.
[77] See Hazan and Berdugo (2002).
[78] See Moehling (1999).
[79] On this argument, see Basu (1999).

campaigns to teach people to boil their water when contamination is suspected or to teach women to exclusively breastfeed for the first six months after a birth.

There has been recent interest in the scope for using information-based interventions. It has been argued that lack of information might be a decisive factor inhibiting successful action by poor people to get the services to which they are entitled. The promise of information interventions to improve local governance is summarized by Ghazala Mansuri and Vijayendra Rao (2012, 79): "The rectification of information failures ... has the potential to improve the ability of citizens to mobilize themselves to hold states and markets more accountable. With better information, citizens become more aware and better able to make more informed electoral decisions, which results in greater electoral accountability."

There is support for the idea that better information is associated with better program performance. For example, US antipoverty programs appear to have worked better in places with greater access to radios.[80] Also in the United States, a customized information package on college options increased college application and admission rates for low-income families.[81] Information campaigns have also shown promise in developing countries. A study for India found that a community-based information campaign led to short-term gains in schooling outcomes.[82] In Uganda, there were significant impacts of information through a newspaper campaign on school outcomes in Uganda.[83] Even without a campaign, there is evidence that state governments in India are more responsive in their relief efforts to negative agricultural shocks when the mass media is more active.[84]

Some other evaluations of specific information interventions have been less encouraging. Another study for India was less encouraging on the scope for using such interventions to improve the monitoring of education service providers.[85] In rich countries facing concerns about rising obesity incidence there have been efforts to post information on the "calorie prices" of food.[86] A recent review of both experimental and non-experimental evaluations found mixed evidence for impacts.[87] In another study for India, it was found an entertaining fictional movie to teach people their rights under the National Rural Employment Guarantee Scheme in Bihar had rather mixed results; box 9.3 discusses this example further. A comprehensive review of relevant field experiments has been fairly encouraging of the scope for using information campaigns for promoting democracy and better governance, although the evidence of economic gains from community-based information campaigns appears to be more mixed.[88]

[80] See Strömberg (2004).

[81] See Hoxby and Turner (2013).

[82] See Pandey et al. (2009).

[83] See Reinikka and Svenson (2005).

[84] See Besley and Burgess (2003).

[85] See Banerjee et al. (2010).

[86] For example, US legislation in 2010 requires restaurant chains with twenty or more outlets to post calorie counts.

[87] See Swartz et al. (2011).

[88] See Moehler (2010).

Box 9.3 **Using a Movie to Teach Poor People Their Rights under the Law**

India's ambitious National Rural Employment Guarantee Act of 2005 created a justiciable "right to work" for all rural households implemented through the National Rural Employment Guarantee Scheme (NREGS). This could well be the largest antipoverty program ever; according to the administrative data, over 50 million households in India participated in 2010.

The scheme promises one hundred days of work per year to all rural households whose adults are willing to do unskilled manual labor at the notified minimum wage. Work is to be made available within fifteen days to anyone who asks for it, failing which the state government is liable to pay an unemployment allowance. Open village meetings (*Gram Sabhas*) are supposed to identify suitable projects and local government institutions (*Gram Panchayats*) are given a central role in planning and implementation.

In their study of this program in one of India's poorest states, Bihar, Dutta et al. (2014) began with an extensive, state-wide, survey of rural households' knowledge about NREGS in the context of a multi-purpose survey of 3,000 randomly chosen households, with separate interviews of adult men and women in each household. For those who had heard of the scheme, the study asked twelve questions about the scheme's rules and processes. The results revealed that public awareness is low. Men gave the right answer for only four of the twelve questions on average, while the average score for women was two and a half.

To assess whether poor awareness is a causative factor in determining the program's low participation rate Dutta et al. did an RCT for an information intervention in the form of a high-quality and entertaining fictional movie, which aims to inform people of their rights under the Act. After showing the movie in forty randomly chosen villages (with 110 retained as controls), the study did a second round of surveys, returning to the same villages and households, and with the same twelve questions.

The study found that the information intervention was successful in enhancing knowledge of entitlements and processes under NREGS. The test scores improved significantly, validating the intervention. But it did not result in better program performance on average. There were earnings gains for illiterate individuals who were already NREGS participants, but no gains (alas) for those who want help but are not getting work from the scheme. Strikingly, perceptions of local conditions and processes related to the scheme became significantly more positive for those who had access to the movie.

The results suggest that the movie created a form of collective delusion in the villages—a belief that this important public service works better than it really does. Keep in mind however that this is a setting in which genuine empowerment of poor men and women may not be in reach without a more responsive supply-side in public-service delivery.

continued

Box 9.3 **(Continued)**

The authors conclude that complementary actions are needed on the supply-side to assure that the scheme's potential is realized. Dutta et al. go further into the scheme's supply-side problems, and outline some reforms to the scheme that could assure that well-informed poor people can get the services they are entitled to under this ambitious program.

Mixed results of this sort might not be surprising. Three observations can be made. First, public information about a program may well reduce participation, as some people decide that the program is not for them.[89] Second, incomplete information is only one of the possible reasons why poor people do not access services.[90] Third, mixed results might also stem from unevenness in the quality of the information intervention itself.

At the heart of this problem is the question of why the information of poor people is so imperfect in the first place. There is something troubling about a policy stance aimed at the "rectification of information failures" if in fact those failures are endogenous. Knowledge can hardly be exogenous to the forces that create and perpetuate poverty. Knowledge has at times been deliberately withheld from poor people by those who control their lives, and benefit from doing so. Even government officials charged with implementing antipoverty programs have been found at times to resist efforts to properly explain the rights and regulations to actual or potential participants, as doing so comes at a cost to them, including reducing their own power.[91]

What one considers one's "rights" in poor Indian villages may well depend more on what local officials and elites say than the rather abstract central dictates in official legislation. In such a setting poor men and women may not know their rights because there is no point knowing them when the reality of their lives does not admit those rights in practice. The same village leaders who are supposed to provide access to services have an important say in many other aspects of life, and a poor person would naturally think twice about making some demand on local officials after hearing an information campaign. Such a campaign alone will not be sufficient for people to be willing and able to take action to get what they are due. The same factors that create poverty will make information about one's legal rights largely irrelevant to one's agency in accessing services. Learning one's rights is not the same thing as being empowered to demand those rights or ensuring they are granted.

An information campaign can also distort beliefs, similarly to propaganda. Imagine you are a poor disempowered person in a village somewhere in rural India. How would you interpret an outsider's information campaign credibly describing legal rights you

---

[89] See, e.g., Hertel-Fernandez and Wenger (2013) with regard to an information campaign for a US program.

[90] For further discussion, see Keefer and Khemani (2005) and Cappelen et al. (2010).

[91] For example, Piven and Cloward (1993, ch. 7) describe how welfare officials in the United States have at times resisted explaining to poor men and women about their rights under the law—including their eligibility for relief—arguing that the poor should just trust the officials.

are supposed to have but do not have in practice? You may see it as a convincing representation of a better village in which people like you, but not you, have a say in local affairs, with clear rights and access to services. You would like to live in such a village. You may even start to think this is in fact your village—suppressing evidence to the contrary.[92] Or it may be seen as a vision of the same village you do live in, but in which you are just an isolated exception. Whether you are convinced of either interpretation will no doubt depend on how your friends and neighbors react. If the campaign is effective enough (including large enough) it can have a bandwagon effect—a version of what Irving Janis (1972) dubbed a "groupthink."[93]

There is a literature spanning a number of disciplines pointing to the possibility for erroneous beliefs to emerge and be maintained for some time.[94] One of the few empirical studies found that an erroneous propaganda message can influence beliefs; in the application studied the beliefs concerned water privatization in Argentina.[95] In the context of the study summarized in box 9.3, the movie used to inform poor men and women of their rights appears to have created a groupthink—a distortion to widely held beliefs. This is evident in the fact that perceptions of program efficacy and of conditions in the village as a whole became more positive, but this did not translate into better outcomes at the individual level for most people.

There is an important role for public information and there have been some success stories. But there have been failures too. The context is key. If the supply-side already works well, then an information campaign could make a huge difference to the performance of an antipoverty program. But otherwise, simply learning about rights may do little or nothing to help.

9.7 Price Interventions

We now turn to a class of policies that aim to help poor people by influencing the market prices relevant to their welfare. Two markets have been prominent in such policies, the labor market (where the wage rate is the price of labor time) and the rental market for housing.

---

[92] In psychology this is known as the theory of cognitive dissonance, following Festinger (1957). On the economic implications of cognitive dissonance, see Akerlof and Dickens (1982). Ravallion (1986) discusses how this can help explain otherwise puzzling features of inter-temporal market behavior involving expectations.

[93] Janis defined a groupthink as a psychological drive for consensus in a group, a drive that suppresses contrary information and dissent. Janis used this idea to help explain aspects of American foreign policy in the 1960s. However, it has long been recognized that the idea has broader applications. Bandwagon effects have been studied in various contexts, including public opinion formation; see, e.g., Nadeau et al. (1993). Bandwagon effects stimulated by new poll results are a well-known phenomenon in elections; for further discussion, see Marsh (1985).

[94] Bénabou (2013) provides an economic model of how such erroneous beliefs held by groups of people can emerge and persist for some time among individually rational agents. Bénabou also points to arguments about the relevance of such behavior in diverse settings. Also see the interesting discussion in Bénabou and Tirole (2006, 705) of "the nearly universal human tendency to want to believe that people generally get what they deserve."

[95] See Di Tella et al. (2010).

Minimum Wages

Minimum wage rates appeared in the late nineteenth century, with the first such law being introduced in New Zealand in 1894. There has been much debate on this policy, especially in the United States where the minimum wage rate has not been indexed for inflation and only revised irregularly.[96] Advocates of the effort to restore the real value of the minimum wage in the United States argue that this will help reduce poverty among working families, and help reduce overall inequality. Critics have long pointed to concerns about the possible negative effects on employment of minimum wage rates, especially for young workers.

A simple and influential economic argument postulates a negatively sloped labor demand function (equating the marginal revenue product to the wage rate facing profit-maximizing firms) and thus predicts a higher binding minimum wage rate will increase unemployment. Those who keep their jobs will be better off but those who lose their jobs, or cannot get a job, are worse off. The key assumption made here is that the labor market is competitive, meaning that both sides of the market take the wage rate as given and that the market clears.

Against this view, it has been argued that these are strong economic assumptions, which do not accord well with how labor markets work in reality. The minimum wage rate may not be enforceable everywhere in the economy, and the existence of uncovered (informal) sectors clouds the implications; we saw this already in the discussion of the Harris-Todaro model (box 8.9). But even with full enforcement, unlike the competitive labor market model, firms need not initially be operating efficiently, but may be induced to become more efficient when the minimum wage rises. There are many ways that a firm can adapt to higher wages, notably through managerial efforts to enhance productivity.[97] Another argument is that many firms have a degree of market power ("monopsony power"). Firms still equate marginal revenue with the marginal cost of employment and the extra worker, but now the marginal cost takes account of the effect on the wage rate. Assuming that the firm faces a rising (positively sloped) supply curve for labor, the firm will hire fewer workers than an otherwise identical competitive firm and it will pay less than the competitive wage rate. Hiring yields a rent to the employer. A binding minimum wage rate that is set at the competitive level will reduce this rent and so increase employment.[98]

The argument that a minimum wage rate will decrease employment came to be questioned following an important study by economists David Card and Alan Krueger (1995). The authors reviewed previous work and came to the conclusion that past

---

[96] At the time of writing (mid-2015) the Federal minimum wage rate is $7.25 an hour and has not increased in nominal terms since 2009. Indeed, the real value of the minimum wage rate in the United States has been on a trend decline since around 1970 and has also fallen as a percentage of average hourly earnings (Elwell and Levine 2013). In April 2014, the US Senate debated but did not pass legislation to increase the federal minimum wage rate to $10.10 per hour, which would have restored it to a value close to its real value in 1968 of $10.57.

[97] For more detailed discussions of how this can happen, see Kaufmann (2010) and Schmitt (2013).

[98] Similar outcomes from a minimum wage are possible in models with labor-market frictions due to search costs, and models in which higher wages induce greater work effort. For a review of this literature see Holmlund (2014).

increases in the minimum wage rate in the United States had not in fact resulted in lower employment. They also presented results of a new study of the effect of a rise in 1992 in the minimum wage rate in fast-food restaurants in New Jersey. Card and Krueger compared the changes in employment between New Jersey restaurants and those in neighboring Pennsylvania, which did not have a rise in the minimum wage rate. (Here Card and Krueger were using the idea of a difference-in-difference estimator from the theory of program evaluation; see box 6.3.) Against the expectations of most economists at the time, but consistently with the non-competitive model sketched above, the higher minimum wage rate actually increased employment. There was a subsequent debate over the Card-Krueger findings, and there have been a number of follow-up studies.[99]

A limitation of the Card-Krueger study is that it relates to just one place, warning against generalizing across the American states. One follow-up study essentially replicated the Card-Kruger study by comparing employment across over three hundred pairs of neighboring US counties with differing minimum wage rates.[100] The same study also addressed a concern with the Card-Krueger study, namely that the states being compared may be on different prior employment trajectories. The researchers found that higher minimum wages increased worker's earnings but had little or no average effect on their employment.[101] A reasonable summary of the state of knowledge at present would probably be that adjusting the minimum wage rate to ensure at least constant real value would have little or no adverse effect on employment.

Of course, the distributional impacts of the minimum wage are not just about its employment effects, although these have received the bulk of the attention. The expectation is that a higher minimum wage rate will reduce both earnings-poverty and earnings-inequality by pulling up labor earnings at the low end. The gains will be larger for the lowest paid workers, so that there will also be a reduction in inequality among low-wage earners. One study found that the falling real minimum wage rate in the United States accounted for about one-quarter of the rise in overall earnings inequality.[102] Focusing instead on the dispersion in wages at the low end—specifically the ratio of the mean earnings of the poorest decile to the overall median—another study found that the falling real value of the minimum wage accounted for 70% or more of the increase in this aspect of earnings inequality in the 1980s.[103]

The implications for poverty and inequality in terms of family incomes are less clear since minimum wage workers are not found solely among low-income families, some of whom do not include wage workers. Nonetheless, earnings from relatively unskilled labor can be expected to account for a larger share of the incomes of the poor than that of the non-poor, so it is expected that overall poverty and inequality will also fall with a rise in the minimum wage rate. There are also likely to be income losses, notably for those owning firms that use minimum-wage labor intensively. These losses will not

---

[99] See, in particular, the comments by Newmark and Wascher (2000) and the reply by Card and Krueger (2000). Recent reviews of the evidence include Bazen (2007) and Schmitt (2013).

[100] See Dube et al. (2010).

[101] See Dube et al. (2010).

[102] See Dinardo et al. (1996).

[103] See Lee (1999).

plausibly be concentrated among the poor or even middle-income groups, but will be well up the income ladder. On taking account of where in the distribution of family income one finds low-wage workers, moderate increases in the minimum wage rate are likely to reduce poverty.[104]

There have also been concerns that a minimum wage rate discourages on-the-job training for affected workers and so helps perpetuate poverty. The argument is that such workers will not be able to take a wage cut while in training, which will discourage the employer from supporting it. Again this assumes a competitive labor market. In the non-competitive case, training can make the minimum-wage worker more productive and so help the monopsonist win back some of that lost rent due to the minimum wage rate.[105] The evidence for the United States and United Kingdom appears to be more consistent with the latter model in that there is no sign that affected workers get less training, and even some indication that they get more.[106]

As already noted, for the minimum wage rate to play a role against poverty it has to be enforceable, and that depends on the extent of formalization in the labor market, public administrative capacity, and the quality of the legal system. The enforcement of minimum wage legislation has been famously weak in many developing countries with large informal sectors (including traditional farming). For example, it has been found that three-quarters of India's casual labor was paid less than the country's (state-level) statutory minimum wage rates.[107] Chapter 10 discusses one policy that has been used in India to try to essentially enforce a minimum wage rate by the government acting as an employer. As we will see, this brings new costs and new benefits too, both of which need to be properly considered.

Rent Controls

The idea here is simply to freeze rents for private sector housing or control their rate of increase in line with other prices. Rent controls appeared in Europe and North America during both world wars, but have lingered. Once in place, beneficiaries naturally resist removing the controls. In the United States, the post–World War II period saw suburban housing construction booms such that rent controls faded from relevance. That was not so much the case in Europe, where rent controls from even World War I still persisted in some countries until the turn of the present century.

The need for rent controls in war time, to assure that everyone has affordable housing, is rarely disputed. But there has been much debate about their merit in normal times. Advocates argue that rent controls assure that housing is affordable for poor families. Critics question whether rent controls in practice have been

[104] See Gramlich (1976) and Card and Kruger (1995, ch. 9).

[105] For further discussion on the incentives for training in non-competitive labor markets, see Acemoglu and Pischke (2003) and Pischke (2004).

[106] See Card and Kruger (1995, ch. 5) and Booth and Bryan (2007) for the United States and United Kingdom, respectively.

[107] See Murgai and Ravallion (2005) using data for 2004–05.

an effective policy instrument for reducing poverty and inequality.[108] Direct income support through transfers or the tax system (using negative taxes for those at low incomes) appears to be a more promising route. (Chapter 10 returns to these policies.) It is argued that direct income support can be better targeted to poor people and is less paternalistic about what people choose to spend their incomes on.

There are also broader costs to rent control. The traditional economic analysis assumed that the housing market is perfectly competitive; this requires that consumers can buy as much housing service as they like at the prevailing price, with zero transaction costs, and housing producers can supply all they want at that price, and both consumers and producers take the market price as given. The main concern is then that by imposing a maximum rent, below the market-clearing rate for the housing unit, there will be excess demand (more housing will be demanded than supplied at the controlled price). There are concerns about how the available supply is allocated; for example, landlords with a taste for discrimination will have the power to exercise that taste. "Insiders" will benefit, but those entering the market will have a harder time finding housing, especially if they are in socially excluded minority groups vulnerable to discrimination. Concerns are also raised that rent controls discourage maintenance and investment by owners, helping to create urban slums. At the rent-controlled price of housing the owner will prefer to reduce the services provided by the housing unit.[109] Owners of rent controlled properties will also have an incentive to sell for owner-occupation, further reducing the supply of rental accommodation.

Analogously to the debate on minimum wage rates, the debate on rent controls has also questioned the assumption of a competitive housing market. Transaction and search costs can be high, information is imperfect (including on the part of landlords, who cannot easily distinguish good tenants from bad ones) as are capital markets. Also, the heterogeneity of housing and diversity in consumers' tastes can mean that the market is very thin for a specific housing unit, rendering the assumption of perfect competition implausible. The literature has developed a number of models with imperfect competition which have the feature that the owner can exploit the tenant by charging a rent above the marginal cost of provision.[110] As long as the market imperfection cannot be remedied directly, a moderate rent control can make the market more efficient, although (similarly to the argument about minimum wages) if the rent control forces the price too low, then this efficiency gain will be lost. These models of the housing market incorporating search costs and imperfect competition can also explain one of the paradoxes of cities throughout the world whereby homelessness co-exists with housing vacancies.

[108] In a review of past studies of the costs and benefits of rent control, Turner and Malpezzi (2003, 35) conclude that "rent control can be a very inefficient redistributive mechanism."

[109] Note that the rent control applies to the rental for a housing unit, which is price times a quantity of housing services, not a price per se. So the owner tries to find the combination of price and quality that satisfies the rent control constraint. For further discussion, see Frankena (1975) and Arnott (1995).

[110] Arnott (1995) provides a useful overview of this literature. For a discussion of rent controls in a model with imperfect competition, see Arnott and Igarashi (2000).

9.8 Trade Policies

Saying that growth typically reduces poverty does not, of course, mean that any growth-promoting policy will do so or that all poor people will benefit. That depends on the distribution—horizontally as well as vertically (box 1.8)—of the gains and losses from that policy. There may be vertical inequalities—between people at different levels of mean income—generated in the process that mitigate the gains to poor people from growth. And there can be horizontal inequities, whereby people at the same initial levels of income fare very differently; some poor people may well lose from a policy that is poverty reducing in the aggregate.

Whose Gains from Trade?

Economists are in broad agreement on the potential for aggregate economic gains from greater integration of sub-national and national economic activity. The classic argument supporting that view is that integration through trade in goods and mobility of factors of production bring the marginal products of those factors into closer parity between countries, thus bringing us closer to the "first-best" solution in which (given diminishing returns) global output is maximized when marginal products are equalized. (Recall box 1.12 on diminishing returns, and box 8.2 on marginal products of factors of production.)

Yet policies promoting integration have been much debated and have generated a lot of opposition. These debates are in part about the distribution of the gains from integration. Critics of integration often claim that the gains are reaped mainly by the rich. Some have gone further to argue that the poor are hurt. As we will see, this is not a plausible generalization, though it may well hold in specific cases. It should not be presumed that there is necessarily a "growth-equity trade-off." The factor of production for which global integration is least developed is in the labor market. The huge differences in wage rates for similar work across the globe cannot be good for the efficiency of the global economy, but nor is it likely to be good for equity. Greater integration of global labor markets though migration is likely to be poverty and inequality reducing globally, although there will undoubtedly be some losers, including among relatively poor people in rich countries.

The traditional model of international trade assumes a world of perfect competition in all goods and factor markets (including full employment). All prices and wages are taken as given and they adjust flexibly to clear all markets. In the basic "101" model there are two goods and two factors of production, skilled and unskilled labor. There is free mobility of labor between industries and regions. There is no specialization; all goods produced in each country are in equilibrium. Imports are perfect substitutes for the home-produced goods.

In this model, patterns of trade between countries depend on their initial endowments of the factors of production—giving rise to *comparative advantage* whereby each country has certain goods that it is relatively better at producing, given the country's endowments. For poor countries, their comparative advantage is in goods that use unskilled labor intensively, given that such labor is their abundant factor of production. With openness to trade, poor countries will tend to export labor-intensive goods and import goods that use their scarce factor intensively, namely capital. In a competitive economy with mobile factors of production this will tend to increase the wages of the abundant factor (unskilled labor) in poor countries (box 9.4).

* Box 9.4 The Stolper-Samuelson Theorem

In understanding the distributional impacts of trade reforms, an important question is how changes in output prices (such as due to trade reforms) affect the prices of the primary factors of production. Suppose that there are two goods, food and clothing, and two inputs to production, labor and land. Perfect competition drives profits down to zero in both sectors. Let w denote the wage rate for labor and r denote the land rental rate—the "factor prices." Perfect factor mobility is assumed, so factor prices are common across sectors. The prices of food and clothing are p_F and p_C, respectively. Zero profits imply that.

$$p_F = \alpha_{FL}w + \alpha_{FE}r$$

$$p_C = \alpha_{CL}w + \alpha_{CE}r.$$

Here the α's are the ratios of input use to output. So α_{FL} is labor use per unit output in food production, α_{FE} is the land used per unit output (E is for "earth"), and similarly for α_{CL} and α_{CE}. To simplify, the α's are assumed to be fixed (giving what is called a "fixed coefficient technology"). Naturally land is used more intensively in producing food, while labor is used more intensively in the production of clothing. So we can reasonably assume that.

$$\frac{\alpha_{FE}}{\alpha_{FL}} > \frac{\alpha_{CE}}{\alpha_{CL}}.$$

On rearranging these two equations, we can plot the corresponding two equations for the wage rate as a function of the rental rate on land.

$$w = \frac{p_F}{\alpha_{FL}} - \left(\frac{\alpha_{FE}}{\alpha_{FL}}\right)r$$

$$w = \frac{p_C}{\alpha_{CL}} - \left(\frac{\alpha_{CE}}{\alpha_{CL}}\right)r.$$

The first equation is the wage-rent locus for food, the second is that for clothing. Figure B9.4.1 plots these two equations. The point of intersection gives the equilibrium wage rate and land rental rates for given output prices, and given α's for the technologies.

Suppose now that there is an increase in the price of food (such as due to lower tariffs on food imports), as shown by the shift to the dashed line. The equilibrium wage rate will fall, and the equilibrium rental rate will rise. This is an example of

continued

* Box 9.4 (Continued)

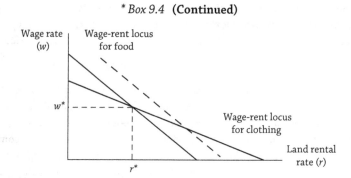

Figure B9.4.1 General Equilibrium in the Stolper-Samuelson Model.

a more general result: an increase (decrease) in the price of a good raises the real return to the factor of production that is used intensively in the production of that good.

Further reading: This is a simple general equilibrium model (as discussed in box 6.3). The relationship between factor prices and output prices in this specific model was derived in an influential paper by Stolper and Samuelson (1941). It can also be derived under weaker assumptions (Jones and Scheinkman 1977). Davis and Mishra (2007) provide a good overview of the Stolper-Samuelson theorem and the subsequent theoretical and empirical literature.

Thus, the simple version of the theory predicts that openness to trade (such as by reducing tariff and non-tariff barriers) helps reduce poverty and inequality in developing countries. But the assumptions of this model can be questioned. If existing political and economic institutions are not conducive to competitive markets then the outcomes for poor people can be very different.[111] More realistic models (with multiple goods and factors of production and frictions, such as in labor mobility) suggest more complex distributional impacts, which can differ among similarly poor countries. Conflicts over trade policy are to be expected, although the support for freer trade of a specific group (such as workers) can vary, including over time.[112]

The traditional competitive model of trade among countries with different endowments has had much influence, including on policymakers. The policy implications need not hold if the assumptions are not valid. There are market imperfections in reality, associated with imperfect competition, externalities, and missing markets. (Recall boxes 1.9 and 2.2.) Traditional trade theory is also highly aggregated. In reality, there are some goods that are not internationally tradable. Also there are non-competing

---

[111] In what is surely the worst example of adverse impacts on poor people of foreign trade, the opening of Africa to the Atlantic trade in colonial times prompted local elites to capture and sell people as slaves so as to buy imported guns and luxury goods.

[112] This is a theme of Rogowski (1989), which provides historical examples.

goods: goods that are only produced elsewhere. Also some of those noncompeting goods are required for the domestic production of other goods. Imported goods are rarely perfect substitutes for home goods; there is considerable heterogeneity in the quality of goods. Countries specialize. There are other important sources of heterogeneity. Firms differ in their productivity and openness favors more productive ones. There is also heterogeneity in net-trading positions at given income. Popular discussions of economic change have often pointed to the heterogeneity in impacts, although economic analyses have tended to focus more on the average gains (including average gains at a given income level).[113]

The Globalization Debate

Globalization has long been debated, but here we focus on the debate that emerged in the 1990s and continues today. The focus here will be on the implications of trade openness for the extent of poverty and inequality.

The many qualifications to the standard "101" trade model in economics discussed above cloud predictions on the distributional impacts of trade openness. For example, some of the most labor-intensive goods are services, which are not typically tradable internationally. (Exceptions include some quite skill-intensive services.) Furthermore, impediments to free mobility of labor may mean that the wage gains are captured within the firms/industries that benefit from openness. Geographic differences emerge in the gains from trade. The heterogeneity can also cloud the picture. Firms making the high-quality exports gain from liberalizing trade reforms, as do their more skilled workers. So the question is open: Is the prediction from trade theory 101 that openness reduces poverty and inequality in developing countries borne out by the evidence?

One hears claims for and against. On one side of the debate, a book by the International Forum of Globalization (2001) asks "Does globalization help the poor?" and answers with a confident "no." To give an example on the other side, a book by Surjit Bhalla (2002) asks "Who has gained from globalization?" and answers "the poor." However, while the assertions have often been confident, it is rare for either side of this debate to provide the sort of analysis that would be needed to credibly allow attribution of the claimed changes in poverty and inequality to "globalization." We are not given any evidence that would allow one to identify the role played by greater openness to external trade (as one aspect of globalization) in the distributional changes observed, versus other factors such as rising agricultural productivity, demographic factors, changes in the distribution and returns to education, and internal policy reforms.

More careful analytic work has attempted to identify the causal effects of greater trade openness on aggregate growth and/or inequality, with controls for at least some of the other factors that are likely to matter. A number of attempts to throw empirical light on the welfare effects of trade liberalization have been made using aggregate

---

[113] Recall that Harrington (1962, ch. 2) emphasized this point in describing the new "minority poverty."

cross-country data sets, whereby levels of measured inequality or changes over time in measured inequality and/or poverty are combined with data on trade openness and other control variables.[114]

The 1990s and 2000s saw many estimates of cross-country growth regressions. (Recall boxes 8.17 and 8.18.) Some of the X's have included policy-relevant variables and variables describing the types of institutions found in each country. A number of studies in this literature have found support for the view that trade openness—typically measured by trade volume as a share of GDP—promotes economic growth. A meta-study of all the cross-country growth regressions with an average of seven regressors (chosen from sixty-seven candidates drawn from the literature) found that trade volume is a significant factor in two-thirds of the regressions, though it is not among their subset of eighteen robust predictors of economic growth (box 8.20).

It is unclear that trade volume can be treated as exogenous in these cross-country regressions; higher trade volume may be a response to growth rather than a cause. The policy implications are also unclear since trade volume is not a policy variable.[115] The policy debate is typically about *trade-policy reforms*—actions by governments to reduce their restrictions on trade and related fiscal policies. A study spanning the second half of the twentieth century found that liberalizing trade reforms added 1.5 percentage points to growth rates on average, with investment rates rising appreciably.[116] Trade liberalization increased aggregate trade volume. However, there can be marked differences in these effects across countries.

As noted in chapter 2, developing countries tended to have highly restricted trade regimes in their post-Independence periods. These policies are likely to have retarded economic growth. Sequences of partial reforms since the early 1980s have made their economies more open. Developing countries are also affected by the trade restrictions and related policies of rich countries. Subsidies to agricultural producers in the rich world have been widely criticized for the harm they do to poorer producers in the rest of the world.[117]

What do we know about the distributional effects of trade expansion? A number of studies have combined survey-based measures of income inequality at country-level with data on trade and other control variables to assess the distributional impacts of trade openness.[118] The evidence is mixed. One study found little or no effect of trade volume on inequality.[119] Yet other studies using different specifications for their tests have reported adverse effects.[120] A comprehensive study using panel data for 114 countries found a significant poverty-reducing effect of various measures of

---

[114] Examples include Bourguignon and Morrisson (1990), Edwards (1997), Li et al. (1998), Barro (2000), Lundberg and Squire (2003), and Dollar and Kray (2004).

[115] For further discussion, see Rodrik (1994) and Rodriguez and Rodrik (2001).

[116] See Wacziarg and Welch (2008).

[117] A good overview of the arguments and evidence can be found in Anderson and Winters (2008). There are some difficult analytic and measurement problems in quantifying these costs; see, e.g., Venables (2008).

[118] As reviewed by Winters et al. (2004).

[119] See Dollar and Kraay (2004).

[120] Lundberg and Squire (2003) find evidence that higher trade volume tends to increase inequality.

globalization, both economic (such as trade openness) and social (information flows through the Internet and open media).[121]

There can be gainers and losers at all levels of living even when a standard measure of inequality or poverty is unchanged. There are many sources of heterogeneity, yielding horizontal impacts of reform. For example, geographic disparities in access to human and physical infrastructure affect prospects for participating in the opportunities created by greater openness to external trade. Differences in household demographic composition influence consumption behavior and hence the welfare impact of the relative price changes due to trade openness.

We know very little about the horizontal impacts of reform; the bulk of the literature has focused instead on vertical impacts (such as differences between the rich and the poor). An important source of horizontal impacts for policies that entail changes in relative prices (including trade reforms) is that people differ in their net-trading positions in the relevant markets. Your net-trading position for a given commodity is the difference between how much of it you produce and how much you consume. Box 9.5 summarizes the economics.

Box 9.5 **The Welfare Gain from Price Changes**

Recall boxes 3.1 and 9.1. There the consumer does not produce either good. That is hardly realistic. Indeed, globally a great many poor people in the world produce food, say. Let us modify the analysis for this case. Suppose that X_F^s of food is produced (the superscript "s" is for "supplied"). This provides revenue of $p_F X_F^s$. Of course, there are costs too. Suppose that producing X_F^s of food costs $c(X_F^s)$, where c is some increasing function (meaning that producing more costs more). The budget constraint can now be written as follows:

$$p_F X_F^d + p_C X_C^d \leq p_F X_F^s - c(X_F^s) + Y.$$

Here we use a superscript "d" to distinguish food demand. On the left-hand side of this equation we have total spending on food and clothing while on the right-hand side we have total income, including income from other sources (Y).

Now consider a rise in the price of food keeping the price of clothing unchanged. Expenditure rises by X_F^d for each one-unit increment in the price of food, but total income rises as well, by X_F^s. Intuitively the consumer-producer is better-off (worse-off) as a result of this increase in the price of food if the rise in expenditure is less-than (greater-than) the rise in total income (i.e., if $X_F^d < (>)X_F^s$). If you are a net supplier of food you gain from the increase in the price of food, while you lose if you are a net demander.

This obvious principle generalizes to any number of commodities consumed and/or produced. Suppose that n goods are consumed and/or produced and the

continued

---

[121] See Bergh and Nilsson (2014).

*Box 9.5 **(Continued)***

price of good i changes by the amount Δp_i. We can then measure a household-specific monetary value of the change in welfare as the following weighted sum of all the price changes, with weights given by the household's "excess supply" $(X_i^s - X_i^d)$ for each good:

$$(X_1^s - X_1^d)\Delta p_1 + (X_2^s - X_2^d)\Delta p_2 + \ldots + (X_n^s - X_n^d)\Delta p_n = \sum_{i=1}^{n} (X_i^s - X_i^d)\Delta p_i.$$

For example, this is how Ivanic et al. (2011) estimated the impact of the 2010–11 surge in food and other prices on global poverty. They first use their data from household surveys to measure poverty before the increase in food and other prices. They then calculated the new distribution. The difference in the measure of poverty is then the estimated impact of the surge in food prices. Despite the fact that many poor people are food producers in the world, Ivanic et al. found that poverty rates rose in the world on balance.

Boxes 9.6 and 9.7 summarize two case studies of this heterogeneity in the welfare impacts of liberalizing trade reform, for China and Morocco, respectively. The results indicate a sizable, and at least partly explicable, variance in impacts across households with different characteristics—differences that influenced their net trading positions in the relevant markets. Substantial horizontal impacts are evident in these trade reforms, warning against simply thinking about the vertical impacts. The horizontal impacts have implications for the political economy of reform. For example, in the Morocco case study, average gains tended to be lower for the gainers, but there were many more of them. Even when the average gain was positive, this aspect of the distribution of gains and losses could stall policy reform; the large number of (small) gainers will have less incentive and capability to organize than will the small number of people incurring large losses. Knowledge about horizontal impacts can also inform the design of compensatory social protection policies (as discussed further in chapter 10).

Box 9.6 **Distributional Impacts of China's Accession to the World Trade Organization**

An aggregate inequality or poverty measure need not change with trade reform even though there are both gainers and losers at all levels of living. Geographic disparities in access to human and physical infrastructure affect prospects for participating in the opportunities created by greater openness to external trade. Differences in the demographic composition of families influence consumption behavior and hence the welfare impact of the shifts in relative prices is often associated with trade openness.

China's accession to the World Trade Organization (WTO) entailed a sizable reduction in tariffs, quantitative restrictions, and export subsidies, with implications for the domestic structure of prices and wages and thus for household welfare and its distribution.

In measuring the welfare impacts of this trade reform, Chen and Ravallion (2004b) combined results from a CGE model with a large and detailed household survey. The CGE model simulated the complete set of price and wage changes induced by the trade reform. The specific CGE model used to derive the price changes in response to WTO accession in China was developed by Ianchovichina and Martin (2004). This is a competitive market-clearing model from the Global Trade Analysis Project (GTAP). Hertel (1997) contains a useful compendium of papers describing the standard GTAP model with applications.

The welfare impacts are derived from a household model that incorporated own-production activities. Thus, they could measure the expected impacts across the distribution of initial levels of living, but also look at how the impacts vary by other household characteristics, including location and demographic characteristics. Thus, one can provide a reasonably detailed "map" of the predicted welfare impacts by location and socioeconomic characteristics, with implications for social protection policy.

Before China's official WTO accession in 2001, the economy had already started to adapt to the expected change. The study found an overall gain of about 1.5% in mean income, all in the period leading up to WTO accession. Inequality was affected only negligibly, and poverty fell—again mostly in the pre-reform period.

However, there were both winners and losers, including among the poor. The generally positive gains among urban households tend to fall slightly (as a proportion of income) as income rises. The generally negative impacts for rural households reach quite high levels among the very poorest. Farm income is predicted to fall due to the drop in the wholesale prices of most farm products plus higher prices for education and healthcare. About three-quarters of rural households are predicted to lose real income in the post-reform period. This is true for only one in ten urban households. Impacts also differed widely across regions. One spatially contiguous region stands out as losing the most from the reform: namely the northeast provinces of Heilongjiang, Jilin, Inner Mongolia, and Liaoning. Both the absolute and proportionate impacts are highest in this region—indeed, more than 90% of farmers in Heilongjiang and Jilin are predicted to experience a net loss in income. There were also some systematic demographic correlates of these welfare impacts, as discussed in Chen and Ravallion (2004a).

Box 9.7 **Distributional Impacts of a Proposed Trade Reform in Morocco**

The Government of Morocco has long considered de-protection through substantial cuts in tariffs on imported cereals. There were concerns about the impact
of these reforms on poverty and inequality. Working with the World Bank, a CGE
analysis was done of the impacts of this trade reform. This prior study had not
looked at the impacts at household level, even though a suitable survey was available. To assess the social impacts of the proposed reform Ravallion and Lokshin
(2008) used the prior general equilibrium analysis to simulate the household
level welfare impacts using the methods in box 9.6.

In the aggregate, they found only a small short-term impact of de-protection
on the poverty rate. (The impact was considered "short term" because it only
factored in the impacts of changes in prices; longer term positive impacts on
agricultural productivity are not allowed for.)

Urban households tended to gain, including poor ones, but there were adverse
impacts on rural poverty. In value terms, the losses to the net producers of cereals outweighed the gains to the net consumers among the poor, such that, on
balance, rural poverty incidence rose. There was a sizable, and at least partly
explicable, variance in impacts across households. Impacts were larger in some
provinces than others. Mean welfare losses for rural households in some areas of
the country were 10% or more of consumption, with even larger welfare losses
among the poor in a few specific regions. Also, the average losses tended to be
larger than the average gains, but the former were spread over fewer people.

Ravallion and Lokshin showed that the overall change in inequality, measured by MLD (box 5.4) can be exactly decomposed into (1) a *vertical component*
that depends on how mean impacts of the reform vary with pre-reform income,
and (2) a *horizontal component*, which depends on the deviations in impacts
from their conditional means. They found that full de-protection generated a
small upward increase in overall inequality, measured by MLD. However, this
was the net effect of a (small) drop in vertical inequality and (larger) increase
in horizontal inequality. It was the latter that dominated.

So, where does all this leave us? The anti-trade policies with respect to quotas, tariffs, and exchange-rates of the post-Independence developing countries were never
likely to bring much benefit to poor people, the bulk of whom produced tradable
goods from primarily non-tradable inputs. While this remains a plausible generalization, there is likely to be considerable heterogeneity across countries in such effects,
and one might be skeptical of basing policy advice for any specific country on generalizations from either economic theory or cross-country regressions.[122] For example,
some studies have found evidence that higher trade volume is inequality increasing
in poor countries but that the reverse holds at higher mean income.[123] The macro

---

[122] For further discussion, see Ravallion (2006).
[123] This was found by Ravallion (2001b) and Milanovic (2005a).

perspective, focusing on impacts on an aggregate measure of poverty or inequality, hides potentially important horizontal impacts, with implications for other areas of policy, notably social protection efforts that may well be needed to complement the growth-promoting reforms.

Trade policies have also played a role in social protection, though this too has been much debated. Governments of food-exporting but famine-affected areas have often implemented food export bans in the hope of protecting vulnerable citizens. Classical economists were influential in arguing against such policies in favor of free trade. For example, in his book *The Conquest of Famine*, Wallace Aykroyd (1974) describes how the Governor of Bombay in the early nineteenth century quoted Smith's *The Wealth of Nations* in defending his policy stance against any form of trade intervention during the famines that afflicted the region. Various Famine Commissions set up by the British Raj argued against the trade interventions that were being called upon to help protect vulnerable populations. Smith and other classical economists had considerable influence on British policy responses to the severe famines in Ireland in the mid-nineteenth century.[124] In modern time, free trade has been advocated as a means of stabilizing domestic food consumption in the presence of output shocks.[125] Others have been less supportive. Real income declines in the famine affected areas can generate food exports while people starve.[126] Regulated trade through taxes or even export bans may then be preferable ways of helping vulnerable groups to the feasible alternatives.[127]

Critics of trade interventions for the purpose of protection from external price shocks have pointed out that such a policy can exacerbate the problem of price volatility.[128] However, in the absence of better options for aggregate inter-temporal smoothing, the optimal non-trade protection policy would entail transfers between net food producers and net consumers, to co-insure. And this too would exacerbate the volatility.[129] So one cannot simply argue that the external trade intervention is an inferior form of social protection; any such protection would have a similar feature. Trade interventions will probably entail some price distortions, which must be evaluated against the distortions generated by alternative schemes. There are situations in which trade insulation can dominate feasible options for protecting vulnerable citizens.[130]

The key point is to avoid sweeping generalizations about policies. To take another example consider active industrial policies—the effort to encourage selected promising sectors or firms using tariffs, subsidies, or tax breaks.[131] Advocates point

[124] See Woodham-Smith (1962).

[125] See World Bank (1986).

[126] See Sen (1981a) and Ravallion (1987b). The analysis of the time series data for famines in British India in Ravallion (1987b) indicated that the aggregate income effects were not strong enough to undermine the consumption-stabilizing effects of unrestricted trade.

[127] See Ravallion (1997b).

[128] See, e.g., Martin and Anderson (2012).

[129] As shown by Do et al. (2014).

[130] This point is illustrated in a formal model by Do and Ravallion (2014).

[131] A good review of this class of policies and the debate surrounding them can be found in Harrison and Rodríguez-Clare (2010). Supportive discussions can be found in Rodrik (2004) and Lin (2012); a more critical perspective can be found in Pack and Saggi (2006).

to the successes of some East Asian countries with these policies, though sometimes downplaying the failures of other countries with similar policies. Instead of debating for or against such policies in the abstract, the focus should be on understanding under what conditions these, or other interventions, work.

9.9 Development Aid

There are different views on the relevance of national borders to antipoverty policies. Classical utilitarian arguments for redistributive policy did not typically extend beyond national borders and nor did some rights-based ideas. For example, John Rawls (1999) argued that rich countries have no moral obligation to help poor countries as long as the latter are reasonably well governed. Other philosophers, such as Peter Singer (2010), argue instead that national borders, distance, or characteristics such as race are not morally relevant to the case for helping disadvantaged people who we can help.

The ethical case for supporting greater global equity has two distinct aspects. First, there is empathy for the plight of those less fortunate, wherever they happen to have been born. Second, there is a case for compensation for actions (or inactions) by rich countries that impose costs on poor ones. Here are three examples:

- Global warming: The bulk of the stock of greenhouse gasses in the atmosphere is due to today's rich world, although the future costs of global warming will be borne by much of the poor world, notable those living closer to the equator and in the densely populated delta regions.
- Trade restrictions: The restrictions on trade and mobility (notably of labor) that rich countries impose on processes of global integration bring costs to poorer countries.
- Money laundering: Looting of poor country assets by rich elites in those countries is facilitated by failures of rich countries to properly control international money laundering.

It is unclear to what extent the large aid flows from rich countries to poorer ones that emerged in the post–World War II period reflected either empathy or compensation. There were other reasons for that aid, including perceived external costs to rich countries from the actual or potential instability that was threatened by global poverty, including the perceived threat of communism spreading further. Whatever the motive, the flow of development aid has been substantial. This section reviews the debates and evidence on the poverty impact of development aid.

External Development Assistance

It has been estimated that total foreign aid since 1960 amounts to $4.7 trillion in 2013 prices.[132] Aid flows have been rising over time. Many people have naturally been

---

[132] This is reported in Barder (2013) using data from the OECD.

drawn to ask how much all that money has contributed to promoting poverty reduction, which is now an explicit objective of much (multilateral and bilateral) aid. The range of answers one can find to this question spanning fifty years is remarkable. There are strongly held opinions both for and against the notion that foreign aid is a good thing even for recipient countries, with assessments ranging from extremely positive about the role of aid to quite negative. On the positive side, Bill and Melinda Gates (2014) write that "foreign aid is ... a phenomenal investment. Foreign aid doesn't just save lives; it also lays the groundwork for lasting, long-term economic progress." Contrast this with Angus Deaton's (2013, 272) assessment that "giving more aid than we currently give—at least if it were given as it is given now—would make things worse, not better." Making sense of the debates is a challenge.

While $4.7 trillion sounds enormous, it needs to be put in perspective. In the aggregate, the flow of external development assistance only accounts for about 1% of the national income of developing countries today.[133] Also, with greater mobility of capital across borders, private financial flows have overtaken official development aid as a source of finance for investment in most developing countries.[134] Private financial flows are assumed to be motivated solely by profit, although this is changing somewhat with the emergence of "impact investing," which emphasizes social or environmental benefits, as well as profits.

If there is a role for governmental development aid, it must be that it serves different goals to private investment finance. Since the 1990s, aid has become firmly linked to the goals of fighting poverty and promoting human development. This was the explicit focus of the United Nations' Millennium Development Goals (MDGs) that emerged in the mid-1990s and were ratified in 2000 by the Millennium Assembly. (Indeed, the first MDG was to halve the developing world's 1990 "$1 a day" poverty rate by 2015.) Arguing that aid was aimed at poverty reduction appears to have helped stimulate donors into providing more aid. Donors have recognized that aid has distinct goals to the private financial flows to developing countries. Aid can be directed at relaxing pressing constraints on development that the private sector cannot easily address, notably in providing complementary public inputs such as spreading technical knowledge, supporting more capable public administrations, and helping to supply public goods. It has also been argued that a well-designed aid program can help break poverty traps (section 8.1) so as to put a poor economy on a better longer term development path.[135]

Some superficial observations may lead one to conclude that aid has helped greatly. As we saw in chapter 7 there was a marked acceleration in progress against absolute poverty after 2000, although this was not generally true when one looks at other MDGs.[136] The UN's secretariat claims that the MDGs themselves helped in this progress.[137] That may well be, but there is little obvious basis for that claim.

[133] This is the "rough estimate" made by Temple (2010, 4431).

[134] See the series on capital flows to emerging markets since the mid-1990s in the Economist (2014d).

[135] See, e.g., Sachs (2005b) and Temple (2010).

[136] See Friedman (2013).

[137] In the preface to United Nations (2011), Ban Ki-Moon writes that "the MDGs have helped to lift millions of people out of poverty, save lives and ensure that children attend school."

Other factors changed from around 2000, including private investment flows to developing countries and the fact that macroeconomic policy frameworks have become more conducive to sustained growth.[138]

Aid has mattered more in some countries than others. It is skewed toward poor and (in terms of population) small countries. The fact of being a country (even if very few people live there) appears to attract a positive minimum amount of aid.[139] So the countries of sub-Saharan Africa tend to obtain a larger share of income in the form of aid, and in very poor countries aid can account for as much as one-third of national income.[140] In these cases, the aid money can make a huge difference. Assuming that the distribution of aid is uniform within countries (for lack of any better option), one study estimated that about 40% of all development aid goes to the poorest 10% of the world's population, and 65% goes to the poorest 20%.[141] These figures would be even more impressive if not for the "small country bias" in development aid allocations; per capita aid allocations tend to be lower in more populous countries.

The economic rationale for favoring poor and small countries has never been made very clear, but one possible rationale is that these countries are less "credit worthy," meaning that they face higher interest rates or are more rationed for loans from other sources. This is certainly possible (small countries, for example, tend to be more exposed to risk, such as from natural disasters). Another possible argument is that poor countries have less capacity for domestic redistribution in attempting to fight poverty. I do not know of any tests of the credit-worthiness argument, but there is evidence in support of the second argument.[142]

Aid and Poverty Reduction

There has been much research on how much benefit has come to poor countries from aid. There are both "macro" and "micro" strands. The former has primarily concerned the effect of development aid on the rate of economic growth of the recipient country. The micro strand has mainly been concerned with the impacts of specific aid-financed development projects (a topic that is also taken up in chapter 10, though without focusing on aid-financed interventions alone).

In dangerously simple calculations in the 1960s and 1970s, planning and finance ministries in developing countries would set a target growth rate, reverse the Harrod-Domar equation (box 8.6) and solve for the rate of investment needed to attain it given the prevailing capital-output ratio, deduct the expected domestic savings rate

---

[138] See Lim (2012) and Bluedorn et al. (2013).

[139] Thus, aid per capita or as a percentage of national income tends to fall with population size; see Temple (2010, fig. 4).

[140] See Temple (2010).

[141] See Bourguignon et al. (2009). This seems to contradict a claim in Deaton (2013, 277): "That half of the world's poor people received only a fortieth of the development aid," which Deaton suggests is "one of the odder inequality measures in the world." However, the two claims can be reconciled once one notes that the "half of the world's poor" referred to by Deaton are those living in China and India; those two countries receive relatively little aid relative to their populations. The other half of the world's poor received a lot of external aid.

[142] See Ravallion (2010b).

(typically low in poor countries) and come up with a financing gap that would hopefully be met by external development assistance. That assistance was thus seen as pure external investment. An alternative approach to determining external aid requirements focused instead on foreign exchange requirements to bridge the gap between expected import demands and export earnings.[143]

The problem is that these arguments are divorced from the realities of how aid is delivered, which is between governments not through a market mechanism. Thus, the social benefits to recipient countries must depend on government behavior.[144] Politicians on both sides of the aid relationship may well have preferences that do not accord with welfare objectives in recipient countries, including the goal of poverty reduction. Thus, the development impact of aid is in no small measure an issue of political economy.

Bilateral (from one country to another) aid accounts for about three-quarters of all aid—the rest goes through multilateral organizations such as the World Bank and the various regional development banks. The aid policies of many bilateral donors have come under much criticism. Country preferences for aid often reflect historical ties and foreign policy considerations rather than genuine need or efficacy. And there can be no doubt that the strategic and foreign-policy priorities of the governments of the larger rich countries have often influenced both bilateral and multilateral aid allocations and aid-project implementation. Simulations by economists Paul Collier and David Dollar suggest that an allocation of current development aid that was aimed at minimizing aggregate poverty would deviate greatly from the allocation in the 1990s.[145] More of the poverty-minimizing allocation would go to countries with severe poverty but reasonably good policies; three-quarters of the world's poor were estimated to live in such countries. According to their calculations the poverty-minimizing allocation of aid would almost double the total impact of aid on the number of poor in the world.

Another reason why aid (especially bilateral aid) has not had more impact on poverty is that it has often been tied to recipient countries buying goods and services produced by the donor country. One study reports estimates indicating that this practice reduces the real value of aid by 15%–30%.[146] Development projects by bilateral donors are not always well coordinated with that of other donors. And the "pet projects" of development ministries (possibly serving the interests of a local lobby in the donor country) need not make a lot of sense in the context of agreed strategies for poverty reduction in the recipient country. Given the litany of criticisms, it is

---

[143] Different constraints may be dominant at different stages of development, as postulated in the "two-gap" model of Chenery and Strout (1966), which became widely used in development aid agencies, including the World Bank.

[144] The aid literature and practice has taken this point on board in part through the process of determining the constraints on the "absorptive capacity" for external capital of recipient countries, which was seen to depend on the availability of required skills (especially for aid administration). However, these arguments were often missing any consideration of the political economy of how governments behave in response to external aid.

[145] See Collier and Dollar (2002).

[146] See Temple (2010, 4431).

understandable that many observers feel that a reallocation of aid from bilateral form to multilateral would enhance its impact.

No less important to its performance are the responses of the recipient government. There must be a strong prior that project aid is fungible. External development assistance is said to be "fungible" when the recipient government can essentially treat the aid as generalized budget support, and spend it how the government sees fit. Even when the aid is seemingly tied to a specific project it can still be fungible, given that the choice of what project to seek aid for is in large part the choice of the recipient country. Box 9.8 explains fungibility in more detail.

Box 9.8 Fungibility and Flypaper Effects

Consider a country "Labas" with two projects it would like to do, one of which has a low social return and the other has a high return. The government of Labas can only afford to fund one of the two domestically. Let us assume that without external aid it will fund the one with higher social returns. Now suppose an external aid donor is available, and it is looking for good projects to fund in poor countries to please its own domestic political constituency. The government of Labas will naturally choose the project that is most attractive to the aid donor, which we can take to be the one with high social returns. And it will then use its domestic resources to fund the project with low returns—a perfectly rational response. The net gain from the aid is not the high return project (which the aid donor thinks it is funding), but rather the low return project. This is called fungibility.

One implication is immediate: The "results based" aid donor (whether bilateral or multilateral) who ignores fungibility will invariably be drawn to monitor and evaluate the project that the government of Labas put up for funding. The donor will thus evaluate the wrong project from the point of view of assessing the impact of its aid. It will probably overestimate the impact of that aid. (And this holds even if the aid donor can get agreement to use a randomized assignment for the evaluation; this is one of the sources of bias in evaluation that chapter 6 discussed.)

Given its importance, there has not been as much empirical research on fungibility as one would hope. In a study using data for the 1970s and 1980s for about forty countries, Feyzioglu et al. (1998) found evidence of fungibility whereby government spending in a number of sectors (agriculture, energy, education) fell with extra concessional lending to those sectors.

A "flypaper effect" is said to exist when the project aid sticks to a sector, even though there is fungibility within that sector. For example, van de Walle and Mu (2007) studied the impacts of aid-financed rural road development in Vietnam. The aid was fungible, but it did not leak much out of the transport ministry. So the evaluation could safely be focused on that ministry rather than all government spending.

The calculation described above of aid requirements using the Harrod-Domar equation is naïve given that governments are presumably already making inter-temporal decisions about how much should be consumed now versus invested for the future. It may well be no less naïve to presume that these governments conform to the Ramsey (1928) formulation of the maximization of the forward looking sum of utilities (box 8.5; Ramsey did not have a discount rate but this can be incorporated). The point remains that one can expect the recipient government to want at least some of the aid to be consumed rather than invested, and the scope for fungibility makes that feasible. Finding that aid is consumed is not a bad thing per se. Government consumption includes many things that matter to poverty reduction, such as immunizing children or helping them stay in school. That is an empirical issue—to see what governments spend aid on, as distinct from what they ask to be given the aid for.

Some observers have argued that aid props up bad governments and thus does more to perpetuate poverty than eliminate it.[147] This is the "aid curse," drawing an analogy with the resource curse, whereby natural resource discoveries can undermine the longer term development of other sectors. The extent of this aid curse depends crucially on the social preferences of political leaders in recipient countries. Figure 9.1 illustrates one possibility.

There are two income groups, the poor with income Y_P and that of the non-poor (Y_{NP}), where the latter includes the political leader. (I have collapsed this into just two dimensions so that I can use a graph, but there can be many more income groups.) The leader's preferences trace out strictly convex iso-welfare contours. The constraint on feasible income combinations is also indicated in the diagram; this gives the maximum attainable Y_P for any given Y_{NP}. Finally let (Y_P^*, Y_{NP}^*) denote the political leader's (unique) optimum in the absence of the aid. Now imagine that an external donor comes along and makes aid available in the form of an income transfer to the poor in the amount A per poor person. Targeting is assumed to be perfect, so this is not a problem. The leader now chooses a new optimum (Y_P^{**}, Y_{NP}^{**}). Without any further

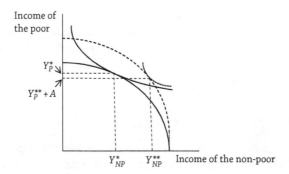

Figure 9.1 An Example in Which the Leader's Social Preferences Entail That the Poor Are Worse Off with External Aid Even When It Is Targeted to the Poor.

[147] Versions of this argument can be found in van de Walle (2001), Moss et al. (2006), Moyo (2009), and Deaton (2013, ch. 7) among others.

restrictions on the leader's social preferences we cannot rule out the possibility that the poor will end up worse off after the aid, that is, it is possible that $Y_p^{**} + A < Y_p^*$. This is illustrated in figure 9.1 in which the dashed curved lines are post-aid.

Given that we do not know much about those preferences, we can see why there is so much debate on the issue of aid and poverty. Some observers point to leaders who do not favor the poor, and so can subvert aid directed at poverty reduction. Other observers take a more positive view of the preferences of leaders, or are more optimistic on the scope for constraining those preferences. But figure 9.1 is only one possibility; under different social preferences the poor can gain, and it is even possible that the gain would exceed the amount of aid. The aid curse can be avoided even if the political leadership in the recipient country does not agree with the aid agency's poverty reduction goal. There are social preferences that give higher (indeed far higher) weight on gains to the non-poor than to the poor but still imply that aid directed at poor people will benefit them.[148] (There will still be a displacement of domestic resources away from the poor in response to the aid, but not so much as to create the aid curse.) Without knowing more about the leader's social preferences, we cannot say whether the aid will benefit poor people.

It is now plain that there is lots of scope for debate. The "Mobutu story" does happen but it is only one possibility. There have been some studies of the attitudes of elites to poor people. No clear picture seems to emerge, although what we know from this literature warns against any generalization that the type of social preferences in figure 9.1 is common in practice.[149] While the aid curse is theoretically possible, its empirical relevance remains unclear. More research on the social preferences implicit in the domestic policies of aid receiving governments would help.[150] And that evidence needs to take a broader perspective than simply focusing on how well "targeted" the aid projects are to poor people.

There is another reason to question the generality of the aid curse idea. Aid-supported policy reforms can also operate on the constraint set facing political leaders with given social preferences (not necessarily agreeing with the poverty focus of aid donors). Some of the domestic policy reforms that aid tries to encourage—which the discussion returns to below—can be thought of as ways of assuring that economic institutions in recipient countries better serve the interests of poor people—that higher Y_P is attainable at given Y_{NP}. Thus, local leaders will rationally choose more pro-poor allocations of domestic resources even without a change in their preferences. Aid will in turn yield greater net gains to poor people.

Aid and Growth

None of this means that development aid is ineffective. But it does point to the need for evidence. The obvious place to look is to see if overall development outcomes have

[148] A simple example that assures that the poor will always gain from the aid is that the leader maximizes a weighted sum of the utilities of the poor and non-poor and $Y_P + Y_{NP}$ is fixed.

[149] See, e.g., Reis and Moore (2005).

[150] An example is found in Ravallion (1988b), studying a large antipoverty program in Indonesia.

improved in the wake of external development assistance. Here the bulk of the literature has focused on whether aid has promoted economic growth. This is an imbalance in the literature, given that much development aid (indeed, the bulk of it I would expect) is not striving to promote growth as such, but rather to promote other development goals, including poverty reduction and human development. In defense it might be argued that growth is all that matters to attaining these other goals, but that is questionable as we have seen in this chapter. The impacts of overall growth on poverty are contingent on a number of factors, notably related to initial inequalities (in income and non-income dimensions), which are also targeted by development aid. And human development depends crucially on the effective delivery of better public services for health, schooling, and social protection—all of which are also the focus of much development aid. Furthermore, these and other objectives of aid are clearly more to do with the impact of aid on government consumption than on (public or private) investment.

Another defense is that growth is easily measured. This strand of the literature appears largely to have been a spin-off from the literature on growth empirics (boxes 8.19 and 8.20). There have been many papers looking at this particular spin-off.[151] The marginal cost of adding aid as a regressor in growth regressions was clearly low. But this may be nothing more than the streetlight effect—the old parable about the drunk man who looks for his wallet under the street lamp, but not because that is where he lost it but rather that this is where the light is best.[152]

That said, what have we learned about the growth impacts of aid? (What did the drunk find?) The first attempt to test whether development aid promotes economic growth in recipient countries came to a strikingly negative conclusion: in the study's (relatively small) sample of developing countries, higher levels of aid were associated with lower rates of domestic saving.[153] However, this study's findings could well reflect the endogeneity of development aid; countries with lower savings rates will attract more aid to make up for the gap in their investment needs. A follow-up study tried to identify the causal effect of aid on savings using an instrumental variable (IV) (box 6.4).[154] The study used the investment rate as the IV for aid and found that the conclusion of the first study was reversed: aid promoted higher savings. However, the investment rate is a questionable IV.[155] Both the investment rate and the savings rate will depend on the rate of interest (albeit in opposite directions), which is not included in the estimated regression for savings. This creates a correlation between the investment rate and the error term.

A number of other efforts followed over the next thirty years, armed with bigger and better data sets and various arguments about how best to identify the impact of aid on growth. Much of the more recent literature has instead used historical strategic

[151] Doucouliagos and Paldam (2008) provide an overview and references to almost seventy papers on this topic.

[152] Development economists are not alone in being vulnerable to the streetlight effect; Freedman (2010) argues that this is a common problem in scientific research.

[153] See Griffin and Enos (1970).

[154] See Over (1975).

[155] As Over (1975) noted.

links between aid donors and recipients ("friends of United States," "friends of OPEC," and "friends of France"), population size and the ten-year lag of aid as IVs.[156] Some of these IV's are easier to accept than others on a priori grounds. For example, it is believable that former colonial relationships between the aid donor and recipient would influence the amount of aid provided but would have little or no independent effect on the domestic economy (i.e., that colonial history was deemed to only matter via aid). Population size and lagged aid are more questionable. On the former, the size of the domestic market can matter to economic outcomes. And the stickiness (lack of change) in aid over time may well mean that lagged aid is contaminated by similar endogeneity concerns to current aid. The first study using these IVs found that aid promoted higher investment in the recipient countries, although this was not robust to dropping some countries with high aid/GDP ratios (although it is not entirely clear why these should be dropped).[157] However, using similar IVs, a later study found little or no sign of a positive impact of development aid on growth.[158] The governance responses to aid may well be part of the reason; there is evidence that governance-dependent industries grow less rapidly with extra external aid.[159]

The rules applied by aid agencies in assigning aid have been used by one study in trying to identify the impact of aid on economic growth.[160] Since the late 1980s, the World Bank has used an arbitrary income threshold as one factor in allocating its concessional lending. If crossing this threshold has no real significance for growth independently of its effect on the aid received, then this aspect of how eligibility is determined provides a valid IV for aid. Using this approach, it has been found that a one percentage point increase in the ratio of aid to income adds about 0.35 percentage points to the growth rate.[161] However, here too, the identifying assumption can be questioned. The existence of latent domestic policy responses to aid eligibility may well entail that what we attribute to aid is actually due to those policy responses. This is another example in which the IV goes wrong; in this case aid eligibility can have an effect on national income independently of the amount of aid received. (This will be clearer when we turn to aid and domestic policies below.)

It is unlikely that aid has a common effect across all countries. Country policies differ in ways that alter the impact of aid. One study claimed supportive evidence that the impact of aid is greater in countries with good policies (such as a budget surplus, low inflation, and trade openness).[162] In other words, the study found evidence of an interaction effect between domestic policies and the growth impact of aid. A series of subsequent papers questioned the robustness of these findings.[163] The sensitivity of results from cross-country regressions to changes in data and model specification is evident.

A study by economists at the Center for Global Development (CGD) in Washington, DC, did a careful job in replicating and explaining past findings in the literature found

---

[156] Following Boone (1996).

[157] See Boone (1996).

[158] See Rajan and Subramanian (2008).

[159] See Rajan and Subramanian (2007).

[160] See Galiani et al. (2014).

[161] See Galiani et al. (2014) for details on this calculation.

[162] See Burnside and Dollar (2000).

[163] See, in particular, Hansen and Tarp (2001) and Easterly et al. (2004).

signs of more positive impacts when one allows for lags in the impact of aid and also for diminishing returns.[164] The study questioned all past IVs and chose instead to treat aid as exogenous, after controlling for country fixed effects. Since the least questionable IVs in past work (notably colonial history) do not change over time this assumption of aid exogeneity is not as questionable as it might appear at first. The key assumption the authors need is that aid is predetermined with respect to future shocks to growth, which seems a reasonable assumption on a priori grounds. Under that assumption, the findings of growth impacts of aid are compelling, although the impacts are lower than other studies have suggested.[165]

A review of recent studies of the growth impact of aid by Channing Arndt, Sam Jones, and Finn Tarp concludes that a fair degree of consensus has emerged: "In rough terms, these studies suggest that receipt of foreign aid equal to 10 per cent of GDP over a sustained period is expected to boost growth by approximately one percentage point on average."[166] Far from an "aid curse" it appears that the bulk of the evidence suggests that a sustained aid commitment to poor countries has been good for their overall economic growth, on average.

As was noted in the discussion of growth regressions (boxes 8.17 and 8.18), the types of regressions used to test for an impact of aid on growth are misspecified if one believes that there are in fact multiple steady-state equilibria. And the potential for multiple equilibria and (hence) poverty traps has been prominent in the arguments for development aid. Here the idea is that aid can help move a country from a low-level equilibrium to a higher one—a large change in mean income. Models such as Richard Nelson (1956) were taken to indicate that developing countries would need large inflows of external assistance to escape poverty. Jeffrey Sachs (2005a, b) invoked the poverty traps idea to argue that a large expansion of development aid is called for to ensure a permanently higher average income in currently poor countries. Critics have questioned this argument on the grounds that we have seen positive growth in poor countries.[167] However, this is not strictly inconsistent with the existence of multiple equilibria and poverty traps. Very little of the cross-country growth literature has taken seriously the implications of poverty traps for their econometric specifications.

The above discussion has focused solely on the impact of aid on average income. The impact on poverty will, of course, also depend on its impact on relative distribution within countries. On this the more macro literature has been largely silent. Clues, however, are found in a strand of the literature that has looked at the impact of aid on social indicators such as infant mortality rates. This is of intrinsic interest, but it is also of interest as a clue to distributional impacts. One study found no significant impacts of aid on the change over time in infant mortality, life expectancy, or the primary enrollment rate; indeed, the only significant impact found was on government consumption.[168] Other subsequent studies have similar findings.[169]

---

[164] See Clemens et al. (2011).

[165] For example, the Clemens et al. (2011) estimate of the growth impact of extra aid is about half that implied by the IV estimate of Galiani et al. (2014).

[166] Arndt et al. (2014, 2).

[167] See, e.g., Easterly (2006).

[168] See Boone (1996).

[169] See the review in Temple (2010).

Another limitation of the discussion so far is that we have talked about aid as some sort of homogeneous entity—something like budget support. In practice, the bulk of development aid takes the form of project aid.

Asking how much development aid promoted development through the specific projects that claimed to be externally financed is not a very promising approach, since we cannot have much confidence that the aid actually financed those projects and not something else; indeed, there must be a reasonable presumption that the aid did finance something else, though possibly within the same ministry, giving what is quaintly called a "flypaper effect" (box 9.7).

The existence of fungibility does not in any way diminish the interest in studying the impacts of specific projects, and chapter 10 returns to that issue in the context of direct interventions for fighting poverty. But that is a different task than assessing the gains from development aid. And the existence of fungibility points to the need to evaluate a broad range of what governments do—not just those things that the aid donor is supposedly funding. (Alas, that is almost certainly not the case; while I have not seen evidence, a disproportionate amount of evaluative effort would appear to go to the externally funded development projects.)

The likelihood of fungibility must, however, cast doubt on claims about the positive benefits of aid drawing on evaluations of only the (supposedly) aid-financed projects (box 9.8).

It has been argued that a few of the claimed successes in development aid have brought such large benefits that we need not be so concerned about average impacts. An aid specialist at CGD, Owen Barder (2013), points to the Green Revolution in India and the elimination of smallpox across the globe. Let us look more closely at each of these. While there is no doubt that both are examples of huge successes in development, the issue here is how much that success can be attributed to development assistance.

The bulk of the gains to poor farmers from the Green Revolution came from technology adaptation and diffusion, which was driven in large part by domestic governmental efforts in India.[170] There was assistance from donors, especially technical assistance (TA) (which we return to below). However, the historical record on this success story does not say much about the role of aid as a financial input. Aid actually helped get the green revolution going in a rather perverse way. India's dependence on food aid and the uncertainties about the latter in the 1960s contributed to the enthusiasm in India for adopting the new seed technologies, supported in part by external aid. Their success eventually entailed displacement of food aid.

On smallpox, Barder points to the volume by Ruth Levine and colleagues at CGD that which documents this and other examples of success stories in global health.[171] These too were huge successes. But, again, the case is still far from proven that development aid was instrumental or even necessary. Barder makes a striking calculation. He divides total aid (the $4.7 trillion mentioned above) by the number of lives saved by eradicating smallpox, which is deemed to be 60 million, so $78,300 per death averted.

[170] See Lipton and Longhurst (1989) and Pritchard et al. (2014).
[171] See Levine et al. (2004).

Using the (seemingly highly conservative) thresholds established by the UK's National Health Service this would be judged a cost-effective intervention.

The problem with this calculation is that we cannot attribute the eradication of smallpox entirely to foreign aid. Indeed, Barder acknowledges that the eradication of smallpox was mainly financed by the affected countries. He still claims that "the effort succeeded because of the contribution of foreign aid" but immediately adds the qualifier "though I acknowledge that no one can say for certain what would have happened in the absence of aid." So we really cannot say what the cost was per death averted by development aid. It may well be that the true figure would be judged cost-effective by any reasonable standard, but we really do not know since, as with the Green Revolution, a lot of the work was done by the countries themselves. An accounting of costs of smallpox eradication indicates that about two-thirds of the cost was provided by the endemic countries, with the rest coming from aid.[172] As we noted already, we do not know how much of that one-third was actually a net addition to resources available for this purpose.

But maybe all this misses the point. The contribution of development aid to development successes such as eradicating smallpox could be hard to identify by conventional statistical methods (including growth regressions). Yet there can be little doubt that the leadership of the World Health Organization from the mid-1960s in the effort was crucial (and it also led to the Expanded Program on Immunization that remains active). While we cannot say how much the access to external financial resources on its own contributed directly, and we can have little hope of credibly identifying the effect, the (economic and political) complementarity between TA and financial aid must be acknowledged. Even if the aid that was deemed to be devoted to (say) smallpox eradication was fungible, the fact that it was available may well have made a huge difference to the political feasibility, implementation, and sustainability of the domestic effort. The aid just made it easier for that effort to materialize and (in combination with the technical assistance) succeed. But the heavy lifting was ultimately up to poor countries themselves.

We began this section with two quotes giving radically different assessments of the case for expanding current development aid, one from Bill and Melinda Gates and one from Angus Deaton. This discussion has confirmed what many readers probably suspected, namely that the truth is somewhere between the two. There is little convincing evidence to support Deaton's claim that more aid makes matters worse in poor countries. But nor can it justify the kind of confidence reflected in the Gates quote.

9.10 Policies, Aid, and Institutions

We have seen that the development aid received by a country does not depend only on how poor it is. Historically there have been foreign policy motives of donor countries, and these still play some role today. But there are other economic factors influencing

---

[172] See Levine et al. (2004).

aid allocations. Increasingly, aid is being used to reward country efforts to implement "good policies," side by side with the traditional role of aid as help for poor countries.

To better understand what is going on here, it is very useful to have an economic model in mind. We can think of the amount of aid per capita received by a country as a decreasing function of income per capita and an increasing function of certain aid *eligibility criteria* based on observable aspects of policy effort and other factors, such as access to private capital. As we have also seen in the last section, a number of studies suggest that aid generally promotes economic growth, so we can also assume that a country's level of income is an increasing function of its aid receipts. But income also depends on domestic policies, independently of the aid received. My "policy wish list" (shared I am sure by many) would include universal access to good quality health care, education, social protection, and infrastucture, financed by an equitable system of domestic taxes, plus a legal system which protected property and other rights for all residents, and a regulatory environment and information system that protected the public interest while still assuring reasonably easy entry for new firms and for workers looking to change their jobs. To keep things simple we can imagine an index of such good policies, which is chosen by each country. Combining these assumptions we can then see how aid and income are jointly determined in an equilibrium for which aid matches income, which is consistent with the aid received. Better policies will shift the equilibrium, resulting in more aid and higher income. Governments weigh up the political as well as economic benefits and costs of implementing better policies. Aid can then incentivize socially preferred public choices. Box 9.9 explains this model further.

Box 9.9 **The Joint Determination of Aid, Income, and Domestic Policy**

It can be assumed that each recipient government knows that its aid allocation (A) is a decreasing function of both its income (Y, which may be the distribution of income, but we treat it as one variable here for simplicity) and an increasing function of the donor-imposed eligibility criteria (E):

$$A = A(Y, E).$$

Income depends in turn on both A and domestic policies, represented by an index P:

$$Y = Y(A, P).$$

We now have a simple model for determining A and Y, as illustrated in figure B9.9.1. The equilibrium solutions for both variables are functions of E and P. Let the solution for Y be $Y^* = Y^*(E, P)$, where the $*$ indicates that it is the equilibrium value of Y. Better policies increase Y directly, but also indirectly, via higher aid. The dashed line in figure B9.9.1 shows the effect of a better policy, which both attracts more aid and raises the country's income.

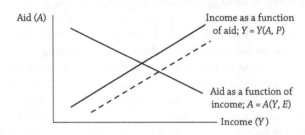

Figure B9.9.1 Joint Determination of Aid and National Income.

Given this model, each aid-receiving country now chooses its domestic policies. For concreteness suppose that the country maximizes Y net of the costs of implementing its policies. The marginal benefit (MB) is equated with marginal cost (MC) of better policies. It is reasonable to assume that there are diminishing returns to better policies, and that better policies enhance the marginal benefit of aid eligibility, that is, the increment to income from being aid eligible is greater when policies are better. Furthermore, the MC is assumed to rise (or at least not fall) as policies improve—it gets harder once the low-lying fruit are picked. The policy choice is illustrated in figure B9.9.2, where P^* is the government's optimal policy.

Under these assumptions, aid eligibility encourages better domestic policy choices, since it increases the marginal benefit from those policies, as illustrated in figure B9.9.2. As we saw already, the better policies in turn raise income, and this happens independently of the actual amount of aid received.

An implication of this model for policy evaluation is that the eligibility criteria are not valid IVs for aid when running a regression of income on aid unless one can control fully for policies. Yet not all of the policy choices are likely to be data in the regressions used to assess the impact of aid on income. (Indeed, many policies are missing in standard regression tests in the literature.) Furthermore, since the eligibility for aid promotes better policies we can expect the IV estimate of that regression to overestimate the true impact of aid, since it confuses better domestic policy responses with aid.

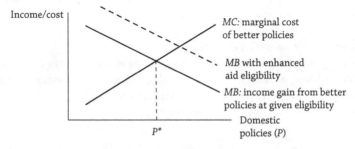

Figure B9.9.2 Domestic Policies in Equilibrium.

However, it would be naïve to imagine that aid recipients do not know that something like this model is at work. And it would be unrealistic to presume that all aspects of domestic policy are observable by aid donors. Domestic policy choices will take account of both the aid-income model and the information available to all the parties. Being eligible for aid according the donor's criteria can be expected to influence the recipient's income in two ways. First, there will be a direct effect on income. Second, there will be an indirect effect via the policy choices made by the recipient (including in those aspects unobserved by the donor). Box 9.9 identifies conditions under which the indirect effect is such that aid eligibility enhances policies and so raises income, in addition to the direct effect.

Policy Advice and Economics

The debt crises of the 1980s brought a wave of structural adjustment programs supported by the International Financial Institutions (IFIs), aiming to restore macroeconomic balances and implement policy reforms aimed at promoting economic growth. The set of policies advocated by the IFIs came to be known as the "Washington Consensus," which we already heard about in chapter 8. Box 9.10 describes the policies.

Box 9.10 **The "Washington Consensus"**

The set of policies normally identified include the following:

1. Fiscal discipline by containing fiscal deficits.
2. Cutting generalized subsidies in favor of services like primary education, primary healthcare, and infrastructure investment that were expected to assure pro-poor growth.
3. Tax reforms such as a broader tax base and avoiding high marginal income tax rates.
4. Assuring that interest rates are market determined.
5. Assuring that the exchange rate is competitive.
6. Liberalizing trade, such as by eliminating quantitative restrictions and only allowing low and relatively uniform tariffs.
7. Liberalizing foreign direct investment.
8. Privatizing state-owned enterprises.
9. Getting rid of regulations that restrict entry or competition (with exceptions allowed on safety, environmental, or consumer protection grounds) and prudential oversight of financial institutions.
10. Assuring legal security for property rights.

Further reading: The term "Washington Consensus" was coined by Williamson (1989) who discusses the concept further.

The "structural adjustment programs" of the IFIs implemented in the 1980s in the wake of the debt crises had aimed to implement something like this Washington Consensus in participating developing countries in the context of substantial fiscal adjustments. Prior to these reforms most developing countries had macroeconomic imbalances, overvalued exchange rates, rationing regimes for foreign exchange, extensive price controls, and subsidies (on many goods and on agricultural inputs, especially fertilizers). There was ample scope for liberalizing reforms that would promote macroeconomic stability and growth. Adjustment lending tied to reforms made it politically easier to implement them.

The critics of adjustment efforts argued that they were externally imposed and ill-conceived agendas for reform.[173] In the 1980s it was often claimed that these programs increased poverty and inequality and one still hears such claims.[174] The claims were rarely based on good evidence and, by and large, they did not stand up well to more careful empirical scrutiny.[175] It became clear that the lack of rapid success in promoting growth (such as in the reforming countries of sub-Saharan Africa) was more often due to the lack of sustained reform rather than to a failure of reforms to promote growth.[176]

However, some of the criticisms were valid. Early reform efforts focused more on short-term goals associated with macroeconomic imbalances than longer term development goals. The early Bank and Fund programs paid too little explicit attention to the implications for income distribution and human development.

And there was a serious perception problem: the Washington Consensus looked far too much like a consensus formed among an elite group in one rich country, making the policies an easy target for critics. From a marketing point of view, the label "Washington Consensus" was unfortunate.

Given that the World Bank had produced *Redistribution with Growth* some ten years earlier (Chenery et al. 1974), it is perhaps surprising that its own adjustment programs in the early and mid-1980s did not give more attention to the impacts on poor people. A change in thinking within the IFIs was underway by the late 1980s, and add-on programs to "compensate the losers from adjustment" were becoming common. "Social protection" emerged as a growing form of development assistance. This gave donors and the IFIs a response to the critics of their adjustment programs, although it was questioned whether recipient governments should be borrowing to finance such programs, rather than relying on domestic taxation. However, an important change was underway in that it was becoming widely recognized that poverty and inequality mitigation has to be designed into economy-wide reform programs from the outset.

By the time the "Washington Consensus" was being heralded by observers around 1990 it was being seriously questioned, including in Washington! The problem was not with the specifics of the Washington Consensus but with what was left out of it, most notably the explicit focus on the welfare goals—especially poverty reduction, but

---

[173] See, e.g., Cornia et al. (1987), Spicker (2007), and Broad and Cavanagh (2009).

[174] For example, Spicker (2007, 127) asserts that these programs generally increased inequality and poverty.

[175] See, e.g., World Bank (1994) and Jayarajah et al. (1996).

[176] See World Bank (1994) and Sahn et al. (1997).

also human development more broadly—that must ultimately justify all development policies.

In thinking about the social impacts of adjustment, many economists had a "benchmark model" in mind that invoked the Stolper-Samuelson theorem (box 9.4). It was assumed that the traded-goods sector of the economy was more labor-intensive than the non-traded goods sector, on the grounds that comparative advantage of developing countries was in labor-intensive products. The model predicted that poor people would tend to gain as workers from the relative price shifts associated with adjustment programs. However, there are a number of mitigating factors that cloud the gains to poor people and can also entail that adjustment increases poverty, at least in the near term; box 9.11 goes into more detail.

Box 9.11 Poverty and Structural Adjustment

The benchmark economic model underlying the arguments made about the impacts on poverty of structural adjustment programs rested on the observation that there were two types of goods: *traded* and *non-traded*. Domestic market conditions only affect the price of non-traded goods. Adjustment will reduce domestic demand for both traded and non-traded goods. Producers of traded goods can sell to foreigners instead, but producers of non-traded goods will initially suffer unemployment and reduced incomes. To restore full employment, the price of the non-traded goods must fall, relative to the traded goods; this is called a real devaluation.

How will this affect poor people? Assume that the poor are net suppliers of labor, and fairly mobile across sectors. Then the economic theory tells us that the real wage in terms of non-traded goods will rise during the adjustment if (and only if) the traded goods sector is more labor-intensive than the non-traded goods sector (box 9.4). Policy discussions often assume this (on the grounds that LDCs' comparative advantage lies in labor-intensive products), and therefore predict that the poor will gain as employees from the relative price shifts associated with adjustment.

This is a simple yet powerful argument. But there are some caveats to consider. First, some non-tradables in developing countries are relatively labor-intensive, such as parts of the construction sector and informal sub-sectors of many other industries. Then the employment effects of real devaluation are more ambiguous than the benchmark model predicts.

Second, the benchmark model assumed that relative prices adjust rapidly and factors of production are mobile across sectors (box 9.4). In reality, some prices adjust sluggishly and there are impediments to labor mobility. Significant unemployment may persist in some sectors. So we also need to know whether the poor are concentrated in the sectors with less flexible prices. A common characterization of developing countries is that the rural sector tends to have flexible prices, while the modern sector has more rigid prices. Given that poverty tends to be concentrated in the rural sector (chapter 7), the positive impacts of adjustment via wages and employment may be felt quite quickly in the rural sector.

Third, the welfare outcomes for the poor will also depend on patterns of consumption and price changes. The direction of the change in welfare for a worker will depend on the magnitude of the real-wage response relative to the share of income devoted to traded goods. A key category of goods for the poor is food. It is often assumed that these goods are tradable (although there are exceptions, including most roots and tubers). Then food prices rise during adjustment. Policy discussions often assumed that the rural poor are net producers of these goods. However, the poor are quite heterogeneous with respect to their trading position in food markets, and many are net consumers. Poor net-consumers of food staples in rural areas also rely heavily on agricultural labor markets and can be expected to benefit from employment effects; provided that the wage response is large enough they will gain. This process can be painfully slow; a study for Bangladesh found that the dynamic response of wages to rice price increases consistent with time series evidence is not fast enough to avoid sizable short-term welfare losses.

The fourth caveat is that the welfare impacts of adjustment also depend on how public expenditures are cut. If the poor initially benefit little from public spending, then they can lose little from cuts. However, although often poorly targeted, public expenditures in many developing countries do benefit the poor. Unless adjustment is to be associated with a short-term increase in poverty, public expenditure cuts will have to spare such programs.

Further reading: Early contributions to the economic analysis of the distributional impacts of adjustment were Knight (1976), Addison and Demery (1985), and Kanbur (1987b). On the caveats discussed here, see Lipton and Ravallion (1995). The Bangladesh study is found in Ravallion (1990b).

Here again we should be wary of simple theoretical arguments about the welfare impacts of such policies. Even if the benchmark model is right for average impacts, there will be heterogeneity, with potential policy implications (as noted already in the context of trade-policy reforms). A benchmark economic model can offer a useful first step to thinking about the likely impacts, but evidence will typically be needed to resolve the issue, and the simple generalizations one often hears on both sides of these debates are often too simple to be credible. Thankfully substantial progress has been made since the 1970s in collecting relevant household level data for informing these debates and (from the mid-1980s) adjustment lending programs started to include resources for collecting such data and monitoring welfare impacts.

Conditions for Effective Aid

Attaching conditions to aid—such as how much can be spent on imports versus augmenting foreign-currency reserves, and what exactly the aid is spent on

domestically—presupposes that the donor is better informed and/or better motivated (such as having more pro-poor or less myopic perferences) than the recipient
government. Economic models of aid conditionality have been developed treating
the recipient government as the "agent" of the donor (the "principle"), given different preferences.[177] However, donors appear at times to overstate their comparative
advantage in deciding what a poor country needs.

There is a deeper concern. In *Dissent on Development*, Peter Bauer (1971, 98) put
the challenge to aid donors this way "if . . . the conditions for development are not
present then aid—which in these circumstances will be the only source of external
capital—will be necessarily unproductive and therefore ineffective." Bauer poses a
serious challenge: if country circumstances (including policies and governance) are not
already conducive to aid being effective then it will fail, but if they are conducive then
the aid will not be needed. By this view, if there is any role for development aid and
development institutions, then it is to lead private flows, and soon become redundant.
If there is one thing that simply has to work as a pre-condition for any form of aid to
work, it is government itself. So one can see a likely point of agreement here between
Bauer (1971) and Rawls (1999) in the view that establishing the conditions for good
government is the strongest (both authors may well prefer "only") justification for
global redistribution.

Without necessarily going quite so far, the view that country institutions and policies are key to aid effectiveness was long taken as self-evident in the corridors of
institutions such as the World Bank, although there was not always agreement about
what "better" meant. Ideally, one would hope that an institution such as the Bank
would consistently argue for pro-poor policies in its client countries, even when these
are not politically feasible at present. At times the World Bank has made efforts to
combine aid with conditions on pro-poor policy improvements, or to be more selective in terms of what countries get aid. However, too often it seems that the Bank's
"country strategy" essentially mirrors that of the government. When the government
pays little attention to poverty, the Bank often falls into line. This is not surprising; too much friction with the government threatens the volume of lending to the
country—essentially the Bank's "bottom line." Ideally, the strategies of aid donors and
international development banks like the World Bank should be poverty focused even
when the government does not care about poverty. This does not mean that external
policy advice should ignore the specifics of each country. The Washington Consensus
was often criticized for its "one-size-fits-all" approach.[178] There is more than one
model for economic development, as China's success with a more interventionist
policy regime illustrates.

An influential formulation of the problem in terms of "binding constraints" specific to each country was provided by Ricardo Hausmann and colleagues.[179] The idea is

---

[177] See Azam and Laffont (2003) and Jack (2008).

[178] Jokes were heard about Bank-Fund reports on country *X* that simply replaced the country name
(and apparently in at least one case the old name was retained—this was before the computerized "find
and replace" option).

[179] See, in particular, Hausmann et al. (2008).

to assess for each country what exactly is restraining economic growth and to target policy reforms accordingly. One or more constraints may emerge that are "binding," such that reforms in other areas of policy will not succeed until these constraints are relieved. This offers the promise of more effective aid and policy advice. While greater effort by the aid donors to tailor their policy advice to country circumstances has become evident since the 1980s, it would be fair to say that country-policy advice still tends to be far less heterogeneous than country circumstances.

While the "one-size-does-not-fit-all" critique has validity, another set of critiques of the Washington Consensus focus instead on what is seen to be missing. Politics seems to stand out; indeed, it is not even mentioned in the Washington Consensus (Box 9.10), yet it can be argued that a country's economic institutions and policies are determined in part at least by its political institutions. For example, recall from chapter 8 that Acemoglu and Robinson (2012) argue that the "inclusiveness" of political institutions—the pinicle being an electoral democracy with universal suffrage, but with varying degrees of inclusiveness in practice—determines how inclusive economic institutions are, which is seen as the key to assuring sustained economic growth. This would suggest that aid should be conditioned on measures of the inclusiveness of political institutions. The counter argument is that there are multiple political routes to reducing poverty. Countries without especially inclusive political institutions but with sufficiently strong (centralized) states have in some circumstances generated ample economic reform and growth.[180] A country can enjoy long-term growth, without generating technological innovation within its borders, by importing technologies developed elsewhere. And we have seen great success against poverty in some countries that do not have very inclusive political institutions, with China since the late 1970s as surely the star example; if one had applied political conditionality China would clearly not have qualified for aid when it was much poorer than today.

The most important thing missing from the Washington Consensus is that its economic foundations give too little attention to country-specific impediments to progress, and to one set of impediments in particular: prior inequities in key dimensions relevant to each country. These may be inequalities of power in some cases, or access to capital or social services in others, or in how minority groups are being treated. These inequalities constrain the scope for market-friendly, growth-promoting reforms, and for assuring that poor people also enjoyed the freedoms unleashed by those reforms. Aid should then focus on working with governments and civil society groups to support policies that directly redressed those specific inequities.

---

[180] See, for example, Sachs (2012), reviewing Acemoglu and Robinson (2012). The latter book does discuss (at some length in Chapter 5) how "extractive" political regimes can generate economic growth. However, Acemoglu and Robinson argue that inclusive political institutions are crucial for technical innovation—essentially re-affirming the longstanding view that secures property rights are the key to innovation (section 1.5). But here too there are important exceptions in history, such as China's (highly inventive) Song dynasty. Also note that sustained growth in initially poor countries can occur without innovation in those countries, but instead arises from technological diffusion, which has been fostered by some quite authoritarian regimes.

Capital Flight and Odious Debt

When assets leave a country it is called *capital flight*. This can be legal, but there is also illegal capital flight. For example, some of the lending to a country might be looted and end up in private foreign bank accounts. The country must still pay back the loans, which then constitute an *odious debt*.

The magnitude of illegal capital flight is naturally hard to measure. Economists James Boyce and Léonce Ndikumana have made an estimate for sub-Saharan Africa that suggests that roughly half the money borrowed by the region's governments has flowed back out as capital flight.[181] Box 9.12 explains the method used to measure capital flight.

Box 9.12 The Detective Work Needed to Estimate Capital Flight

The Balance of Payments (BoP) is a series of accounts for which the bottom line is the net change in a country's foreign currencies. A surplus (deficit) implies a net inflow (outflow) of foreign currencies.

When we compare the officially recorded inflows and outflows of foreign currencies in the various accounts with the net change in the stock of reserves, we get the first clue to how much capital flight has occurred. This is essentially a residual, after netting out the recorded flows. It contains measurement errors in the various accounts as well as actual capital flight. There is, of course, much uncertainty about such estimates of capital flight.

A number of refinements to this method have been proposed to try to improve the estimates. One refinement is to use the independent assessment of the stock of a country's debt done by the World Bank's *Global Development Finance* database, and considered more accurate than the cumulative sum of borrowing in the BoP. Boyce and Ndikumana make these and other adjustments to allow for mis-invoicing of exports and imports and unrecorded remittances.

Further reading: The residual method was developed by the World Bank (1985). Boyce and Ndikumana (2001) and Ndikumana and Boyce (2011, ch. 2) implement the refinement described earlier.

Some types of lending are probably more vulnerable to this form of looting than others. Lending for large-scale infrastructure projects such as dams is often identified as an important contributor to odious debt.[182] Given the extra monitoring of grant and concessional lending by aid donors, non-concessional borrowing may well be even more prone to such looting, whereby some share of the money is privately appropriated by those with the political power to do so.

It is tempting to put estimates of capital outflow from developing countries side by side with aid inflows, suggesting that it is a revolving door. When legal and

---

[181] See Ndikumana and Boyce (2011). For details on the methodology, see Boyce and Ndikumana (2001).

[182] See, e.g., Leslie (2014).

administrative institutions are weak, there is certainly a risk that the public and private aid flows into a country will switch into private flows out of it. However, illegal capital flight includes looted domestic resources stemming from private financial inflows. We do not know how much development aid has been re-diverted in the past, or how much of extra aid is likely to be so diverted. All we know is that the data, albeit imperfect, suggest massive illegal capital flight.

On balance, Africa turns out to be a net creditor to the rest of the world, with foreign assets exceeding its debts. A large share of those assets is held by the rich, while the poor are left with the liabilities incurred to make those assets possible. On top of the forgone public investments, indebted poor countries are left with greatly restricted fiscal space for fighting poverty well into the future. Thus, "the revolving door between foreign borrowing and capital flight has left the African people paying debt service on loans from which they did not benefit" (Ndikumana and Boyce 2011, 87). The obvious injustice of this situation prompted global campaigns for debt relief in the 1990s and responses from the creditors in the late 1990s, providing substantial relief in the form of debt cancellation for a number of the most highly indebted poor countries. Critics of such debt forgiveness argue that it creates a problem of moral hazard, encouraging excessive borrowing.

More could be done to recover stolen assets, which would help discourage future theft. Tighter controls by rich countries on international money-laundering could help. But here the performance is uneven. The Financial Action Task Force (FATF) has established standards for customer due diligence and record-keeping procedures, and the OECD reports on the progress of its member countries in compliance. The top performer is Belgium, which is deemed fully compliant with five of the eight FATF recommendations, "largely compliant" with two of them and noncompliant with one.[183] At the other end of the distribution, one of the lagging countries is Australia, which is deemed "partially compliant" with two, and noncompliant with the rest. Yet Australia currently strives to be one of the most generous donors of aid globally (as a share of GDP).

This is another way in which aid donors can alter the constraint set facing political leaders in a pro-poor way. By limiting the opportunities for non-poor people in aid-receiving countries to hide their resources abroad, the international community essentially shifts the constraint set in figure 9.1 in a pro-poor way, to assure that local leaders adopt more pro-poor allocations without any change in their social preferences.

Poverty and Poor Institutions

Across the world as a whole there is a striking correlation between the level of economic development, such as measured by GDP per capita, and various measures of what can be termed "good institutions"—the basic infrastructure needed to support a reasonably efficient market economy. There are many dimensions to such institutions, including better "rule of law," more politically stable, and more capable states,

---

[183] This refers to an assessment by the OECD of its members' compliance with the standards set by the FATF.

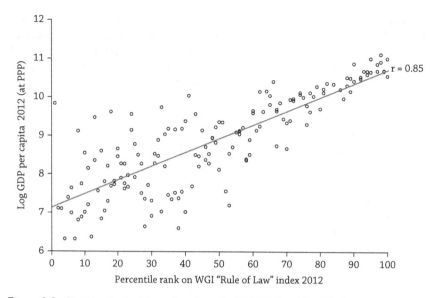

Figure 9.2 GDP Per Capita Plotted against the WGI "Rule of Law" Index. *Source:* Author's calculations from the estimates in *Worldwide Governance Indicators* and the World Development Indicators.

such as measured by tax revenues as a share of GDP. (These tend to co-move together, reflecting underlying complementarities.[184])

Figure 9.2 is indicative.[185] The figure gives log GDP per capita country by percentiles in the World Governance Indicator (WGI) for "Rule of Law" (WGI-RL), which aims to reflect how much confidence citizens have in the rules of society and how much they follow those rules. This is created by aggregating various components measuring property rights, contract enforcement, policing and the courts, and the incidence of crime and violence.

There is a strong correlation in figure 9.2, although the high GDP variance among the poor performers in terms of law and order is notable; the correlation is driven more by the good performers than the poor ones. Indeed, if you focus on the lower half of the countries in terms of WGI-RL, then the correlation coefficient drops from 0.85 on the full sample to 0.38, though this is still statistically significant at the 1% level.

The capacity and performance of public administrations tend also to be weaker in poorer countries. An innovative study mailed ten letters to nonexistent business addresses in each of 159 countries and measured how long it took (if at all) for the letters to be returned to the American sender.[186] This is a simple and intuitive

[184] See Besley and Persson (2011) for further discussion of these complementarities, notably between legal and fiscal dimensions of good institutions.

[185] A number of researchers have pointed to similar correlations between indicators of "good institutions" and average income including Kaufmann and Kraay (2002), Acemoglu et al. (2005), and Besley and Persson (2011).

[186] The study is documented in Chong et al. (2014).

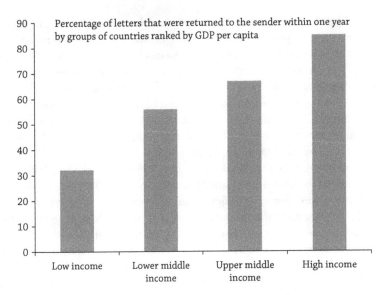

Figure 9.3 Return to Sender, Address Unknown. *Source:* Chong et al. (2014).

indicator of the capacity of different states to deliver a basic service—in this case to return mail to the sender when it could not be delivered. In all, 60% of the letters were returned to the sender, but there was a big difference between rich and poor countries, as shown in figure 9.3.

Do the correlations evident in figures 9.2 and 9.3 reflect a causal effect of better institutions? As Hume and Smith argued (chapter 1), it is plausible that an environment in which law and order is largely absent retards innovation and investment, and hence limits economic growth. If this poor institutional environment persists over time, then the country is very likely to end up at a lower average income. And the cost is not only in terms of lower average income. Violence, in many forms, is common in poor countries (as discussed in chapter 7). The proximate cause is the lack of legal enforcement, and that lack is especially evident when the victims of violence are poor.

By one interpretation of evidence such as figure 9.2, better institutions for defining and protecting legal rights directly help countries prosper and people live better, especially safer, lives. It was tempting to treat the infrastructure of laws and their enforcement mechanisms as being largely pre-determined to economic outcomes. The relatively good institutions found in high-income countries were developed and refined over a long period, indeed centuries. They did not develop after some spurt of economic growth. If one compares the WGI index for Rule of Law in 2012 (as used in figure 9.2) with its value in 1996 (the earliest available estimate) one finds a correlation coefficient of 0.91 (n = 199); this suggests considerable persistence over these sixteen years.[187]

[187] There are comparability problems in the WGI data over time (as summarized on the WGI website and the technical papers referred to). It is not clear that these problems would lead one

Motivated by these arguments, some researchers have tried to quantify the long-run economic costs of poor institutions. They do this by running a regression of growth rates of GDP per capita on an index of the quality of institutions, with controls for other factors (including the initial level of GDP).[188] However, counterarguments could be made suggesting that the causality goes in the opposite direction, to at least some extent. The infrastructure of good institutions is costly and so more affordable for richer countries. And some of the initial advantages of history and geography that promoted better institutions probably also fostered sustained growth. The two were jointly determined by other factors, creating a false positive correlation.

In attempting to isolate the causal impact of good institutions one might look for an IV that matters to the quality of institutions but not to GDP through some other route. If this IV exists, then it identifies a source of exogenous variation in outcomes attributable to better institutions—recognizing that the existence of seemingly good institutions in richer countries is not random. Finding a valid IV in this case is not easy, given that most things one would expect to influence institutional quality could well also have an independent effect on outcomes at any given level of institutional quality. While it is not so difficult to find one or more variables that are correlated with better institutions it is far harder to establish that the only way they matter to economic development is via better institutions. (Recall box 6.4 on IV estimation.)

For example, an influential study by Acemoglu and colleagues of the economic gains from better institutions used the historical mortality rates of European settlers in the colonies as the IV for current institutions (measured by the risk of expropriation of private property) in explaining differences across countries in GDP per capita.[189] The researchers showed convincingly that institutions are rated to be lower quality in countries with higher mortality rates. However, the concern remains that past mortality rates may well be correlated with features of the health environment that are persistent over time and so also matter to the evolution of GDP.[190] Then this IV is not valid for identifying the causal effect of institutions on GDP; the significance of predicted institutions (predicted from settler morality) could simply be the causal effect of a better health environment rather than a causal effect on GDP of better institutions for property rights enforcement.

There are also some examples in this literature of the discontinuity designs for assessing impacts that we heard about in chapter 6 (box 6.1). A striking example is found in the Acemoglu and Robinson (2012) book *Why Nations Fail*. The authors compare the two sides of the city of Nogales, one side in the United States and the other side in Mexico, with residents of the former side enjoying better living conditions across a wide range of criteria. Acemoglu and Robinson argue that the differences cannot be attributed to geography or climate (the same on both sides of the border) or

---

to overestimate the degree of persistence; at least some of the changes observed over time reflect measurement errors.

[188] See, e.g., Knack and Keefer (1995) and Clague et al. (1997).

[189] See Acemoglu et al. (2001).

[190] Acemoglu et al. (2001) note this possibility and defend their identification strategy. However, they cannot rule out the existence of latent aspects of the health environment relevant to settler mortality rates that also independently influence GDP.

culture (essentially the same people founded the city). Rather they attribute the difference to the better institutions of the United States. Of course, this is just one city. There are some other examples, such as the differing fortunes of North and South Korea, and East and West Germany prior to the fall of the Berlin Wall. A more statistically powerful demonstration would require more examples of places spanning borders this way, though naturally there are not that many to point to. But even so, the few examples we have are telling. Sorting out the causality will never be easy, and it undoubtedly runs both ways. But even if we cannot be very confident about the empirics, it is clear enough that many poor countries tend be poor in part at least because of persistently poor institutions. Some thought to the dynamics of institutional development points to clues as to why some countries seem to get stuck with bad institutions, and it also provides a warning for the efforts of the development community to try to improve policies and institutions in poor countries. We take up these issues next.

Understanding Persistently Poor Institutions

Since the 1980s, a number of economists and political scientists have put forward various arguments as to why bad institutions can persist, often drawing on historical examples from across the world.[191] If there is one economic argument that stands out it must surely be the idea of "limited commitment." As Acemoglu and colleagues point out it is not adequate to simply say that bad institutions persist because they serve the interests of politically powerful people, who risk losing that power under better institutions. We also need to have a situation in which the potential beneficiaries of the better institutions have no credible means of compensating those in power.[192] The latter condition is called limited commitment. In a world of limited commitment powerful beneficiaries of the status quo will rationally try to block collectively beneficial reforms.

If we now add to this idea the (plausible) assumption that poor people are the least able to muster the compensation required then we can also understand why institutions that are conducive to persistent poverty can be left unreformed without external assistance. Indeed, it is the reforms most helpful to poor people that will get least attention.

This idea also has an important implication for economies that are well endowed with natural resources, namely that we can expect a political "resource curse," given that there will be higher potential rents to be captured by political elites. With access to the higher rents, the elites will be even less willing to support institutional reforms.

In probably the worst-case scenario, the state itself becomes the predator in some form of the predation trap, a version of which was described in box 8.15. This will leave little or no incentive for creating even basic legal protections, since the state itself is the entity to be protected against. The legal system will not protect the poor,

---

[191] See, for example, North (1990), Acemoglu et al. (2005), Engerman and Sokoloff (2006), and Acemoglu and Robinson (2000, 2012).

[192] See Acemoglu et al. (2005).

or possibly almost anyone else for that matter.[193] How long such extreme cases can survive is unclear. For example, with success the elite controlling the state may expand to the point where the internal cooperation among the elite starts to breakdown.

The type of threshold effect we heard about in chapter 8 can also exist with respect to institutions. By further consideration of the dynamics of institutional development we can see clearly how an economy can get stuck with persistently poor institutions. To see this sharply, let us make the following assumptions:

- Policies—both domestic and external, and embracing both technical and financial assistance—can help develop political, legal, and administrative institutions that are good for longer term development including eliminating poverty. Domestic policies and external assistance can help promote well-defined property rights, a higher quality of fiscal management, more efficient revenue mobilization, greater transparency and accountability in the public sector and a better quality of public administration generally; in short, more capable states.[194] These things take time.
- Little or no domestic or external effort to improve things (beyond emergency relief) will be forthcoming if the country's institutions are too dysfunctional to start off with. There is some threshold that must be reached to have hope of developing better institutions.[195]
- External assistance and domestic efforts will start to stabilize and even decline when institutions are sufficiently well developed.

Putting these elements together we have a simple model of multiple equilibria in institutional development in which we can find a *poor institutions trap*—a PIT. Figure 9.4 explains how a developing country can get into a PIT, despite otherwise

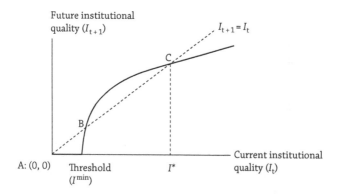

Figure 9.4 The PIT: A Poor-Institutions Trap.

[193] For an insightful economic analysis of the case and less extreme versions in which legal capacity can emerge in equilibrium, see Besley and Persson (2011, ch. 3).

[194] These are the aspects of institutions that are emphasized by the World Bank's *Country Policy and Institutional Assessments* (CPIA).

[195] Following the last footnote, one can think of this as a very low score in the World Bank's CPIA, which would essentially kill aid.

good initial conditions, favorable to development. On the vertical axis we have "future institutional quality" while on the horizontal axis we have "today's institutional quality." We see the threshold labeled I^{min}. Once that is reached, external assistance combines with complementary efforts by citizens and governments to generate better institutions. After some time, when institutional quality is reasonably high, the effort moves to other places and tasks where it is needed more.

We can identify three steady-state equilibria. Point A is the PIT—the worst case in which persistently bad institutions prevail. Point C is where the country needs to be. Between these two equilibria, we have point B. This is clearly better than A, but alas it is dynamically unstable.

Three implications of this simple model are notable. First, two observationally similar economies at one point in time may well have very different levels of institutional development and (hence) economic trajectories. Standard regression tools (such as reviewed in box 8.19) will not then be valid for studying economic growth and institutional development, since there will be no unique mapping from the observable data and the expected value of long-run income.

Second, getting out of the PIT will not be possible with a small positive incentive for reform; then the country will just bounce back into the PIT in due course. Escaping the PIT will require a more substantial gain in institutional quality (to get past point B) than simply reversing the (possibly small) shock that landed the country in a PIT.

The third implication concerns how such an economy might respond to shocks. With a big enough shock even an economy at point C could end up in a PIT. Indeed, this is one explanation for African underdevelopment. The shock of colonial exploitation and slavery so impaired domestic institutions and productive capacity that it essentially eliminated the equilibrium at point C, leaving Africa stuck in a PIT.[196] By this interpretation, aid and domestic efforts at institutional development are trying to restore the point C equilibrium—essentially to undo the damage of colonialism.

Consider instead even a small positive shock to institutions in a country at its point B. This will put the country on a virtuous cycle, progressing toward point C. But a negative shock will create a vicious cycle—a downward spiral all the way into the PIT, at point A.

This last point has a further implication for development aid. Today some poor countries—often called "fragile states"—are at their middle point B, while others are at A. For example, I am willing to conjecture that Madagascar was at its own "point B" prior to the coup in 2009. In the wake of the coup, development assistance contracted markedly (by about half), tourism slumped, and an already poor country got poorer. Unlike much of the developing world, Madagascar made very little progress against absolute poverty for many years after the coup, and by some measures things have got worse. It took five years to restore constitutional governance.

The international community's decision to pull out in response to the coup in Madagascar was no doubt seen as providing an incentive for a rapid rebound to democracy, and a favorable continuing trajectory of development. But when viewed in terms of the model outlined above, the impact may well have been much larger

---

[196] A complete economic model of this explanation can be found in Nunn (2007).

than expected, by forcing the country into a PIT. We do not know for sure if that is the case, but nor do the donors. And there are big risks to poor people in decisions made in ignorance. At a minimum, we should try to better understand the dynamics of institutional development—to see whether the PIT model sketched above is realistic. That is not an easy research question, but it reflects an important knowledge gap in our understanding of development.

If my characterization of the dynamics is roughly right, then the lesson for aid donors is clear: by all means be willing to reward positive political shocks, but be careful about punishing negative ones. Given the instability, this response may well help put longer term institutional development in the country back even further. A more prudent approach may well be to maintain the baseline of assistance, stay engaged on the planned development path and remind all of the benefits of doing so. This path should include support for better political institutions. But aid donors should be wary of cutting aid in poor and fragile economies when there is a negative political shock. That stick the donors are wielding may well hurt far more than they think!

The PIT model also warns against thinking that even modest levels of development aid will help. The type of institutional change needed to get out of the PIT could well be huge, and if the effort falls short the dynamics will eventually see the country back in its PIT. In assessing aid it may well be inadequate and even deceptive to look at the returns to small increments—running regressions or do RCTs. A longer term historical view will be needed. And patience.

We have seen that there are many ways in which poor institutions can be a persistent feature of poor countries. The pattern in figure 9.2 is not surprising. We cannot expect that good institutions will emerge spontaneously. Change will not be easy, quick, or guaranteed. We should be encouraged that history teaches us that institutions have emerged in due course to provide the fiscal and legal support required for a successful market economy, although even then constant vigilance is needed, especially in assuring that the institutions are inclusive.

Targeted Interventions

We now turn to a class of antipoverty policies that strive to target poor people as the direct beneficiaries. As we saw in Part One, there has been much debate about these policies. Some see them as an essential policy instrument for both protection and promotion. Others claim that such policies are wasteful and ineffective—at best short-term palliatives to make up for the real causes of poverty. (To some observers the real causes are the bad behaviors of poor people, while to others the real causes are deeper structural deficiencies or governmental failures.)

The policies we shall study now are typically triggered by signals provided by people. The signals might be events (e.g., illness) or circumstances, such as reported low income, or attributes associated with low income. The policy rationale has emphasized the desire to assure some form of income security. The protection motive has long dominated, but (as we will see) promotional objectives have gained prominence in the rationales for these interventions.

The next section provides an overview of the coverage of these policies. The chapter then turns to some generic economic issues—information, incentives, and policy design before reviewing the main types of targeted interventions found today.

10.1 An Overview of Coverage

The new millennium has seen a significant change in the set of development policies, which have now come to embrace a range of direct interventions, variously called "antipoverty programs," "social safety nets," and "social assistance." The common feature is that they use direct income transfers to poor families. This was rare (in the developing world) prior to the mid-1990s. Since 2000 or so, many more developing countries have been implementing such programs, mainly in the form of (conditional and unconditional) transfers and workfare schemes.[1] Today, somewhere around one billion people in developing countries currently receive social assistance.[2] It appears to be the case that every developing country has at least one such program. The monitoring data are not ideal, but one estimate indicates that the proportion of the population

---

[1] See World Bank (2014a).

[2] Barrientos (2013) estimates that 0.75–71 billion people in developing countries were receiving social assistance sometime around 2010. The figure has undoubtedly risen since then.

of developing countries receiving help from these programs is growing rapidly, at around 9% per annum (3.5% points per annum).[3]

But is any of this reaching the poorest? Many programs aim (implicitly or explicitly) to raise the consumption floor above its biological level; indeed, this aim is captured in the phrase "safety net." While not all social safety net (SSN) policies in developing countries explicitly aim to raise the floor, some prominent programs in practice can be interpreted that way, including the two largest programs to date in terms of population coverage, namely the *Dibao* program in China and the *National Rural Employment Guarantee Scheme* in India (both of which we return to below).

The fact that SSN coverage is expanding so much in the developing world raises the hope that the lower bound of the distribution of consumption is rising above its historical level (i.e., that the consumption floor is rising). However, as we saw in chapter 7, that does not appear to be the case (figure 7.4).

One of the cruel ironies of antipoverty policy is that the governments of poorer countries are less effective in reaching their poor through direct interventions. As economies become more developed, the tax base for redistributive policies expands.[4] At the same time poor people tend to become easier to reach—geographic concentrations become more obvious, for example—and the administrative capabilities for reaching them are greater. The transition from a predominantly informal to a predominantly formal economy makes a big difference, on both the financing side and in terms of the policy options, including through more effective enforcement of formal rules.

So it is not too surprising that the best available evidence suggests that only about one-third of those families in the poorest quintile are receiving anything from safety-net policies. And the performance tends to be worse in poorer countries. These observations are based on data compiled by the World Bank on the coverage of safety-net programs across the developing world, using household surveys that identified direct beneficiaries of these for each of over one hundred countries spanning 1998–2012. Comparing regional averages one finds that the coverage of the poorest quintile is weaker in the two poorest regions, sub-Saharan Africa (SSA) and South Asia. In SSA, only 20% of the poorest 20% of the population (ranked by income or consumption per person) receive anything from the SSN. By contrast, in Latin America the proportion is 53%.[5] Figure 10.1 gives the data at country level.

Taking a simple average across countries, the data indicate that only about half (48%) of the poorest quintile receive anything from the public SSN; on weighting by population the share falls to 36%. However, there is huge variation, spanning the range from virtually zero to virtually 100% coverage. Some of this is undoubtedly measurement error. But there is clearly a strong and positive income gradient across countries

---

[3] See Ravallion (2014f). This is based on the twenty-five countries with more than one observation in the compilation of survey-based estimates of SSN coverage in the World Bank's ASPIRE database. The observations span 2000–2010.

[4] Some suggestive calculations on how the tax burden of redistribution changes with the level of economic development can be found in Ravallion (2010b).

[5] See World Bank (2014). For South Asia the overall coverage rate is 25%, for MENA it is 28%, for East Asia it is 48%, while for EECA it is 50%.

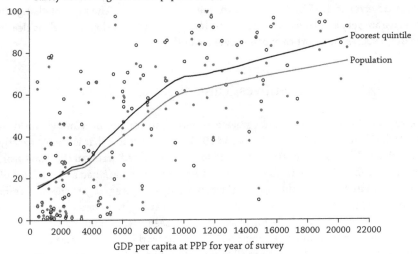

Figure 10.1 The Share of the Poorest 20% Receiving Help from the Social Safety Net in Developing Countries. *Source:* Safety-net spending includes social insurance and social assistance, including workfare programs. Social safety-net coverage rates for poorest quintile (poorest 20% ranked by household income per person) from the World Bank's ASPIRE site: http://datatopics.worldbank.org/aspire/indicator_glance. The data are available for 109 countries; the latest available year is used when more than one survey is available. GDP from World Development Indicators.

in safety-net coverage. The average elasticity of SSN coverage of the poor to GDP is about 0.9.[6]

It is also notable that the coverage rate for the poor tends to exceed that for the population as a whole. The average difference between the two coverage rates is not large, although it tends to rise with GDP per capita.[7] Richer countries tend to be markedly better at covering their poor, although the bulk of this is explained by differences in the overall coverage rate.

None of this means that poor countries are powerless to help their poor through direct interventions. Indeed, there are signs that they are doing better in this respect. The World Bank's database indicates that safety-net coverage is increasing over time. Unfortunately, there are only twenty-five countries with more than one observation. Comparing the latest and earliest surveys for those countries, I calculate that the overall coverage rate (for the population as a whole) is increasing at 3.5% points per year

[6] The regression coefficient of the log of coverage rate for the poor on the log of GDP per capita is 0.91 with a standard error is 0.13. The corresponding elasticity for the population as a whole is 0.80 (s.e. = 0.11). If one controls for the overall coverage rate of the population there is no longer any statistically significant effect of GDP on the coverage rate of the poorest quintile.

[7] Regressing the log of the ratio of coverage rate for the poor to the overall coverage rate on the log of GDP per capita gives a regression coefficient of 0.16, with a standard error of 0.04.

(standard error of 1.1% points). Unfortunately, the coverage rate for the poor is not increasing at quite the same pace; for them the rate of increase is 3.0% points per year (standard error of 1.0%). This is not just due to GDP growth. The rates of change in coverage are very similar when one controls for growth. The developing world is clearly making a successful effort to expand coverage of this class of policies.

10.2 Incentives, Targeting, and Leakage

We saw in chapter 7 that the aggregate poverty gap for the developing world in 2010 relative to the $1.25 a day line was $166 billion per year.[8] That is almost exactly the estimated size of the postharvest food loss in the United States in the same year, which is estimated by the US Department of Agriculture to have had a retail value of $162 billion in 2010.[9] In other words, the developing world's aggregate shortfall from the (frugal) line of $1.25 a day was the same as America's food loss due to wastage and other factors. Such calculations have at times been used to motivate claims that it should be easy to eliminate extreme poverty in the world. To paraphrase the type of claim made: "If we could just divert all that wasted food in America to poor people in the developing world the problem of poverty would vanish."

This is a striking calculation, but to an economist it is questionable claim for a number of reasons. Of course, a higher poverty line would give a larger gap; recall that the total gap rises fourfold if we simply switch to a poverty line of $2 a day. However, there are a number of other economic reasons why the cost of eliminating poverty could well be far greater than the poverty gap suggests. Those reasons are the topic of this section.

Information and Incentives

The stage of development influences the types of policies needed. For example, recall the concerns about rising inequality in rich countries. What should be the policy response? One solution that has been proposed is a progressive *global* tax on wealth (excluding human capital), to try to bridge the gap between its rate of return and the overall growth rate of income.[10] Such a tax is probably technically feasible in most rich countries today (although there may well be political opposition from the wealthy) but most countries in the developing world do not yet have the required administrative capabilities. The tax would not have global coverage.[11] Poor places tend as a rule to

---

[8] These are PPP dollars.

[9] Food loss refers to the total amount of edible food postharvest that was available for human consumption but was not in fact consumed. There are many reasons for the loss, including loss in cooking, shrinkage, deterioration due to mold, and plate waste. The estimated food loss is from Buzby et al. (2014).

[10] See Piketty (2014).

[11] To avoid the tax, mobile capital would flow to the developing world, promoting greater investment and growth. That might be welcome, but it is clearly not reducing the rate of return on capital in the rich world. There are other ways of lowering the rate of return on capital, as this will depend

have weaker administrative capabilities, which tends to mean less reliable information for deciding who should receive help. This naturally influences the types of policies found in practice. Self-targeting mechanisms (such as using work requirements, as in the workhouses we heard about in chapter 1) and indicator-based targeting (such as programs focused on poor communities) tend to be more popular in developing countries (including when the rich countries of today were developing), notably when there is a large informal sector. By contrast, income tax system and transfer payments that require formalization dominate in rich countries. The information constraint stemming from a large informal sector not only influences the types of policies, it also constrains the ability to finance antipoverty policies through taxation. Poorer countries thus have fewer public resources available for addressing their poverty.

New information technologies also increase transfer effectiveness by allowing better validation of applicant information and lowering transaction costs. The example of identity card in India was noted in chapter 9. When properly implemented, this can avoid the scope for corruption such as through multiple payments to the same person or fictitious "ghost applicants." When the banking system is sufficiently well developed, automated teller machines and short messaging services through cell phones can reduce the costs of making transfers, including private transfers.[12] However, these conditions do not hold yet in most of the developing world.

The information constraints are obvious enough, given that informalization essentially means that one has little systematic data on actual or potential beneficiaries. A less obvious but no less important incentive constraint stems from the fact that the informal sector is a feasible option for anyone in the formal sector (though the converse is less true). Thus, a social policy that can apply only to a formal-sector worker (given that formality is required for administration) will have an added efficiency cost through the scope for substituting informal for formal activities.[13]

Incentive effects have long figured in the debates about targeted direct interventions across all settings. A perfectly targeted set of transfers to poor families in the imaginary world of complete information—meaning that the transfers exactly fill the poverty gaps and so bring everyone up to the desired minimum income—would impose a 100% *marginal tax rate* (MTR) on recipients and is likely to destroy incentives to work among the poor, as discussed in box 10.1 (Here the MTR is just minus one times the BWR from chapter 5.) This is very unlikely to be optimal from the point of view of poverty reduction given labor-supply responses. Yet the tax-benefit systems of some countries have been found to entail high MTRs, approaching or even exceeding 100%.[14] Social policy reforms since around 2000 have aimed to reduce MTRs, to encourage welfare recipients to take up work opportunities when available without too much loss of benefits. Such policies are often labeled "making work pay policies." Examples include the EITC in the United States, which tops up incomes when they fall below a certain level and is

on many other things in the economy, including tax rates on corporate profits and the level of the statutory minimum wage rate.

[12] See, e.g., Gibson et al. (2014) and Jack et al. (2013).

[13] Similarly, informal-sector firms can evade taxation by resorting to cash (Gordon and Li 2009).

[14] See OECD (1997), which found MTRs around 100% in the tax-benefit systems in some countries, including Australia and the United Kingdom.

Box 10.1 Incentive Effects of a Perfectly Targeted Cash Transfer Scheme

First, we need some simple concepts from statistics. Recall from box 5.1 that the cumulative distribution function (CDF) gives the proportion (p) of the population living below a given income (y). The CDF is written $p = F(y)$. Assuming that incomes have been normalized appropriately for differences in prices and household characteristics, the headcount index of poverty is $H = F(z)$, where z is the poverty line. The inverse of the CDF is called the *quantile function*, which we can write as $y = y(p)$. Figure B10.1.1 gives a stylized quantile function.

Suppose that a perfectly targeted cash transfer scheme is implemented that exactly fills the gaps between z and $y(p)$, which is the area above the bold curve ($y(p)$) but below the poverty line up to point A. Consider the p_0th poorest person initially living below the poverty line with an income of $y(p_0)$. Under perfect targeting, that person gets a transfer payment in the amount $z - y(p_0)$. Suppose now that this person receives an offer of a job earning extra income, though still not enough to reach the poverty line in the absence of the cash transfer scheme. If the person takes this job and doing so entails no forgone income from other activities, then her pre-transfer income will rise by the full amount of the earnings from that job. But then she will find that her transfer payment falls by exactly the same amount, so that she ends up back at the poverty line post-transfers. She will be working harder but with no higher income. The marginal tax on her extra earnings will be 100%. Since there is no income incentive to take on the extra work, and it comes with reduced leisure time, she will not accept the job offer. This is yet another example of a poverty trap, but this time it was created by the antipoverty program.

This assumes that work is undesirable. As noted in box 1.4, while that is the standard assumption made by economists, it is not obviously true. Paid work can give social status. Indeed, the evidence from regressions for subjective welfare suggests that people's self-reported welfare tends to fall when they become

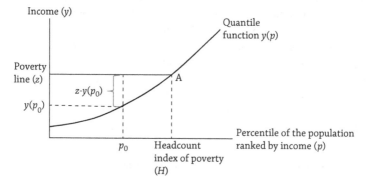

Figure B10.1.1 Perfect Targeting without Information Constraints or Incentive Effects.

unemployed even when there is no loss of income, although there are a number of concerns about the robustness of these findings (chapter 3). If this also held for extra work effort, then there will be no work disincentive of a 100% MTR.

Even when the design entails a 100% MTR on recipients, the actual rates in practice can be far lower, either because of imperfect implementation of the formal rules or because of how other tax-transfer programs interact with the program in question to determine the final incidence.

now an important source of extra income for poor people.[15] The *Working Families Tax Credit* in the United Kingdom is a similar policy.

There has been research on the labor-supply effects of transfer programs, especially in the United States. The topic attracted much attention from economists in the 1970s and again in the 1990s—two periods when major policy reforms were being implemented or debated (chapter 2). The responses that have been studied include both hours of work (the intensive margin) and labor-force participation (the extensive margin of the labor-supply response). The assumption is that the greater the labor-supply response, the larger the efficiency cost of the policy since that cost is taken to stem from the policy-induced changes in behavior. Those changes are often called the "distortions," on the presumption that the situation in the absence of policy intervention is efficient. That, of course, is questionable. It is plausible that the economy is not working fully efficiently in the absence of intervention, which means that there is scope for improvement. One should then be careful about the label "distortionary."

In developed country settings, responses on the intensive margin appear to be typically small, reflecting the relative fixity of hours of work in formal jobs. More responsiveness can be expected at the extensive margin. This is less plausible for transfers to poor people in poor countries, where one is unlikely to see much response at the extensive margin. Poor men and women cannot be expected to stop working in response to a transfer that covers (say) 20% of their consumption, although responses at the intensive margin are likely.

The bulk of the evidence for developed countries does not support the view that there are large work disincentives associated with targeted antipoverty programs; indeed, some studies have been hard pressed to find anything more than a small response.[16] From what we know about labor-supply responses, it is evident that poor people gain significantly from transfers in a country such as the United States.[17]

---

[15] The Congressional Budget Office (2012) estimates that federal transfers (including the EITC as well as food stamps and Medicaid) accounted for 75% of the total income of the poorest quintile in 2009.

[16] For useful overviews, see Moffitt (1992, 2002). Also see the discussion in Grosh et al. (2008), which spans both developed and developing countries.

[17] See Saez (2006) for further discussion and references. The labor supply of married women in the United States is thought to be more responsive than that of men, although there is evidence that they are converging to be similarly unresponsive (Blau and Khan 2007).

Of course, the extent of the labor-supply response depends on program design. There can be little doubt that very high MTRs have a disincentive effect on labor supply, although the designers and/or implementers of safety-net programs are aware of this fact and higher MTRs can generally be avoided. From the research to date, the bottom line on this much debated policy issue is that the long-standing critiques of antipoverty programs (going back to Townsend, Ricardo, and Malthus, as discussed in chapter 1) as creating most of the poverty they relieve by discouraging work are greatly exaggerated.

The behavioral responses also need to be seen in the context of a welfare-economic formulation of the policy problem. The existence of an incentive effect does not, of course, rule out any antipoverty policy, as long as we expect sufficient gains through improved distribution. The policymaker faces an efficiency-equity trade-off.[18] As a result, there will be limits to the extent to which redistributive taxes and transfers can be used to reduce poverty, even when that is the sole objective.

One hundred and forty years after the heated debates over the reforms to England's Poor Laws (section 1.5), a rigorous formulation of the problem of redistributive policy with imperfect information and incentive effects was finally available in the form of the optimal tax model of James Mirrlees (1971). The government observes income, but not the effort or skill that went into deriving that income (though this is known to the individuals concerned). So welfare is unobserved even when preferences are known. People are presumed to care about income net of taxes (positively) and work effort (negatively). The policy problem is then to derive an income tax schedule that maximizes social welfare. The key policy parameter is the MTR on income. Higher taxes on the rich allow for more redistribution to the poor, but there are limits to this redistribution, since the taxes discourage work effort, which reduces the revenue available for the antipoverty policy. The policy problem is to balance these forces, so as to come up with the socially optimal tax schedule. Mirrlees assesses alternative tax schedules against a utilitarian social welfare objective. Box 10.2 discusses the model further.

Box 10.2 **The Equity-Efficiency Trade-Off in Income Redistribution**

We saw in chapter 1 that a long-standing problem for antipoverty policy is the trade-off between equity and efficiency when information is imperfect. Mirrlees (1971) provides the first rigorous formulation of this problem. The original paper is technically difficult, but it is worth understanding the basic framework of the Mirrlees model. (The fact that the paper is so difficult reflects in large part the fact that the policy problem is so difficult once one takes incentives seriously.)

---

[18] This is sometimes called a "distortion-distribution" trade-off, though "distortion" is a loaded word, as noted.

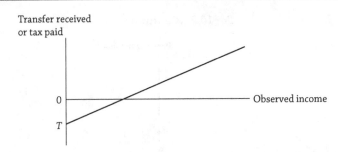

Figure B10.2.1 Simple Linear Income Tax Schedule with Negative Tax for the Poor.

The problem is to find an optimal income tax schedule, where "optimal" is defined by maximizing total utility. Figure B10.2.1 gives an example of an income tax schedule. There is a transfer in the amount T to the poorest person. This falls as income rises and becomes a tax after some point, and the tax burden rises with income. (It is drawn as a linear tax function, but it can be nonlinear.)

The key contribution of the Mirrlees formulation is that it captures the trade-off between the equity and efficiency implications of higher tax rates on incomes in the real world situation in which neither the effort people make to derive their incomes nor their skills (income per unit effort) are observable by the policymaker, although each person knows his or her own effort and skill. The policymaker must rely on taxing the income each person derives from her effort given her skill.

Mirrlees made a number of simplifying assumptions to facilitate the analysis. (Some of these assumptions were relaxed in the subsequent literature.) Each individual maximizes utility, which depends on consumption (income net of tax) and leisure (the proportion of the day not working), as in box 1.4. There is only one type of labor and one consumption good and there is no inter-temporal choice to be made. Everyone has the same preferences and there is no migration. There is an exogenous distribution of skill, interpreted as the personal economic gain from work. The "rich" are taken to be those with high skill. Taxes are levied on observed income.

Mirrlees showed that the optimal marginal tax rates were less than 100% and positive almost everywhere, although the optimal tax schedule is not necessarily progressive (box 1.10). Extracting revenue from the rich for redistribution to the poor is constrained by the fact that the rich can hide the fact that they are rich, given that their skill and work effort are unobserved. So there is an incentive constraint that the highest skill person must still be no worse off than if she was to represent herself to the tax authority as in fact less skilled than she really is. And notice that being "worse off" here is not just about post-tax income, given that there is a disutility of work.

The incentive constraint limits the economically feasible redistribution. To illustrate, consider figure B10.2.2. In the left panel, we see indifference curves

continued

556POVERTY AND POLICY

Box 10.2 **(Continued)**

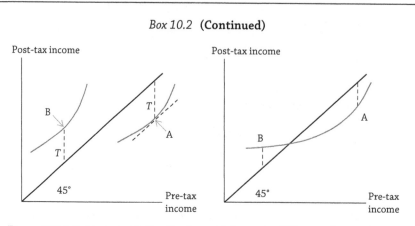

Figure B10.2.2 Limits to Redistribution with Incentive Effects and Imperfect Information.

for post- and pre-tax income. These are implied by the consumption-leisure indifference curve in box 1.4, but now they are drawn in the space of post-tax and pre-tax incomes. Higher post-tax income is naturally preferred, but higher pre-tax income at given post-tax income implies greater work effort, which gives disutility. Thus, the indifference curves are now positively sloped, though it is still true that "up is better." Now consider the tax T levied on the income of the rich person at point A and transferred to the poor person at B in the left panel of figure B10.2.2. At point B, we see the indifference curve for the rich person (as drawn) is higher than at point A. (The indifference curve for the poor person is not drawn and will be different, since the wage rate is different, which means a different disutility of pre-tax income, even when the underlying preferences over consumption and leisure are the same.) So this redistribution is not incentive compatible; the rich person will choose to work less and thus cut her tax bill to be at point B rather than A. The lower redistribution in the right panel is the maximum feasible tax, whereby the rich person is indifferent between A and B.

In the special case of the linear tax schedule in figure B10.2.1, the optimal tax rate (the slope of the bold line) for any given distribution of skills depends on two things: (1) how much the policymaker cares about poverty and inequality—specifically how much the marginal social valuation of extra income rises as income falls; and (2) how responsive work effort is to higher net wages (holding utility constant).

A seemingly striking feature of the optimal tax schedule characterized mathematically by Mirrlees—a feature that surprised many people when the paper appeared—is that the MTR goes to zero at the top of the skill distribution. This is not too surprising when one realizes that maximizing the revenue extracted from the richest person would imply a zero MTR. (This is clear in figure B10.2.2, noting that the slope of the tangent is the marginal tax rate. Revenue is maximized when the tangent is parallel to the 45 degree line, implying zero MTR.) However, this does not constitute a case against high MTRs on the rich (as some observers

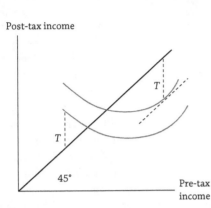

Figure B10.2.3 More Redistribution Is Feasible When Some Work Is Desirable.

have suggested) when tax rates apply to groups of people not specific individuals. As Mirrlees (1976, 340) puts it "calculations suggest to me that these end results are of little practical value . . . it is usually true that zero is a bad approximation to the marginal tax rate even within most of the top and bottom percentiles."

Again it should be noted that the assumption that work is undesirable at given consumption is key here. Suppose instead that some work (though not too much) gives pleasure to the rich person in the left panel of figure B10.2.2. The indifference map now looks like figure B10.2.3, with a downward sloping segment at low levels of work effort. Now the larger redistribution is incentive compatible.

Historical note: The Scottish economist James Mirrlees was educated at Edinburgh and Cambridge Universities and spent most of his career at Oxford University, where he developed his approach to characterizing optimal taxation with asymmetric information. Mirrlees was awarded a Nobel Prize for this work in 1996.

Further reading: While the original Mirrlees paper is technically demanding, there is a more accessible exposition in the classic text by Atkinson and Stiglitz (1980, ch. 13). Dixit and Sandmo (1977) discuss the linear tax version. A useful overview of the Mirrlees model and its (considerable) influence in economics can be found in Boadway (1998). Also see the more recent comprehensive treatment of optimal taxation in Kaplow (2008). The possibility that work gives pleasure is considered in Mirrlees (2014), which points out that this can also make 100% MTR's optimal.

The aspect of this problem that makes it so difficult (both in the real world and analytically) is that the information constraint comes with an incentive constraint on the extent of redistribution, given that one cannot tax the "rich" beyond the point at which they would be better off to hide the fact that they are rich. When this constraint is met the solution is said to be *incentive compatible*. The Mirrlees objective function was utilitarian, but this framework can also be adapted to a poverty reduction objective. Simulations suggest that marginal tax rates around 60%–70% would be called for in an optimal antipoverty policy using transfers allowing for incentive effects on labor supply.[19]

While labor-supply responses are clearly part of the story, there are other effects of antipoverty programs that we know less about, such as impacts on child development, and behavioral responses through savings, migration, and private transfers. For example, the evidence that time spent talking with children at an early age is important for their cognitive development (as discussed in chapter 7) raises the question as to whether it is socially optimal for poor parents with young children to be working long hours. The argument that lower time prices of prepared food have encouraged obesity must also make one wonder about the social costs of high labor-force participation rates in poor families, which would presumably encourage diets to shift in favor of less healthy prepared foods to save time in domestic production. Maybe poor families work too hard, suggesting that any displaced labor supply due to an antipoverty program is a good thing. That must be considered a conjecture at this stage, but it does point to the need for a more comprehensive understanding of behavioral responses.

The BIG Idea

At the opposite extreme to perfect targeting one can imagine a *basic income guarantee* (BIG). As discussed in chapter 1, this provides a fixed transfer payment to every adult, whether poor or not.[20] So there is no explicit targeting. Since there is nothing anyone can do to change their transfer receipts, the only incentive effect of the BIG transfer is the income effect on demand for leisure, which will lead people to work less unless they derive utility from their work. A complete assessment of the implications for efficiency and equity of a BIG (or any set of transfers) must also take account of the method of financing. The administrative cost would probably be low, though certainly not zero given that some form of personal registration system would probably be needed to avoid "double dipping" and to assure that larger households receive proportionately more.

Proposals in developed countries have typically allowed for financing through a progressive income tax,[21] in which case the idea becomes formally similar to the Negative Income Tax (NIT),[22] though the mode of administration may differ and in the NIT version the transfer comes *ex post*, while the basic income is intended by its advocates to be paid *ex ante*. Box 10.3 discusses a combined basic income financed by a proportional tax on income. However, notice that progressive income taxes require a lot of information, so one cannot argue that a BIG financed this way avoids the aforementioned information and incentive issues.

A BIG can probably be devised as a feasible budget-neutral way of integrating social benefits and income taxation.[23] There have also been detailed proposals for some developing countries, including South Africa.[24] A BIG could be costly, although that

[19] See by Kanbur et al. (1994). Also see Kanbur and Tuomala (2011) on alternative characterizations of the policy objective.

[20] Recent discussions of the BIG idea include Raventós (2007), Bardhan (2011), and Widerquist (2013).

[21] Such as proposed by Meade (1972).

[22] As advocated by Friedman (1962).

[23] This is demonstrated by Atkinson and Sutherland (1989) for Britain.

[24] See the papers in Standing and Samson (2003).

Box 10.3 A Basic Income Financed by a Proportional Income Tax

Figure B10.3.1 shows various quantile functions. (Recall from box 5.1 that the quantile function is the inverse of the CDF.) A BIG is introduced, giving a transfer b to everyone, financed by a proportional tax at the rate t on all incomes. The scheme is configured such that the net benefits are greatest for the poorest but remain positive up to the income level z, after which there is a net loss.

Three observations can be made: First, notice that if z is the poverty line, then the scheme has no effect on the headcount index, but will reduce all other measures discussed in chapter 5. Second, notice that, although the information problem of identifying poor people no longer arises for the basic income scheme, this advantage is lost once the scheme is financed this way. If one still wants to assure that only the poor receive a net gain, then the information/incentives problem returns. Third, there will be an NIT that can achieve the same final distribution of income as any tax-financed BIG. In the above example, those with an income below z incur negative taxes while those above z pay positive taxes.

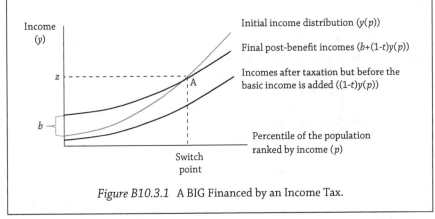

Figure B10.3.1 A BIG Financed by an Income Tax.

---

depends on the benefit level and method of financing. There may well be ample scope for financing by cutting current subsidies favoring the non-poor.[25] This type of scheme would appear to dominate many policies found in practice today; for example, it would clearly yield a better incidence than subsidies on the consumption of normal goods, which is a type of policy still found in a number of countries.

As yet there have been very few examples of universal uniform cash transfer schemes in practice. However, there is a long tradition of using uniform (untargeted) state-contingent transfers. What this means is that the transfer is more or less uniform for people who fall into certain categories defined by some event ("state") such as being elderly or unemployed. Given that a BIG is likely to have at least some state-contingent aspect (such as being an adult and resident of a specific place), there is a conceptual common ground with state-contingent transfers, of which there are many examples, as discussed in section 10.2.

---

[25] As Bardhan (2011) argues is the case for India.

Targeting

The bulk of the direct interventions found in practice fall somewhere between the extremes of "perfect targeting" and "no targeting." In countries where means testing is a feasible option (mostly rich countries) the benefit level can be progressively phased out as income rises above some level, below which some guaranteed support is provided. This can be done relatively easily through the income tax system.

The ideal rate of benefit withdrawal depends on the strength of the expected labor-supply response. As already discussed, such incentives can never be ignored in social policy, although (as we saw in chapter 1) history also teaches us that concerns about incentives are often invoked, with little or no evidence, to serve the needs of political opponents to such policies. (It also seems that incentives get far more attention in discussing programs intended to help poor people than other programs.) With better data and analytic tools, it can be hoped that future policy debates will be better informed about actual behavioral responses than in past debates.

The early emphasis of social policymaking in the period following World War II was for broad inclusion. Antipoverty policy was a tool for *social solidarity*, and targeting was not seen as important—indeed, it would have threatened the very aims of social policy in this period. That changed in many countries by the last two decades of the twentieth century. Efforts to improve the cost-effectiveness of direct interventions in both the rich world and developing countries called for better targeting.

This has been a recurrent debate. We saw in chapter 1 that this was an issue in the debates over England's Poor Laws in the early nineteenth century. The reforms in the 1830s called for better targeting, motivated in large part by the fiscal burden on the landholding class. Similarly, calls for better targeting in the West came in the wake of the 1979 oil crisis, and in many developing countries facing debt crises in the 1980s.

The political support for greater targeting comes from two distinct groups, with very different motives. On one hand, some want existing public resources to have greater impact on poverty; their aim was to help poor people. The other side is keen to cut the total cost of public support for poverty, to reduce its fiscal burden, including the tax burden on the rich; their aim is in large part to help non-poor people. The coalition of these different interests has pushed for greater effort at targeting antipoverty programs.

The recent emphasis on targeting in many countries (both rich and poor) has typically defined targeting as avoiding "leakage" of benefits to the non-poor, implicitly downplaying concerns about coverage of the poor.[26] Readily measurable proxies for poverty are widely used for such targeting in settings in which income means testing of benefits is not an option. Efficiency considerations point to the need for using indicators that are not easily manipulated by actual or potential beneficiaries, although this is rarely very clear in practice. Geographic proxies have been common, as has gender of the recipient, family size, and housing conditions.[27] These targeting methods

---

[26] As pointed out by Cornia and Stewart (1995).

[27] Grosh et al. (2008) provides a useful overview of the targeting methods found in practice in developing countries, with details on many examples.

can be thought of as a *proxy means test* (as discussed in chapter 5; recall box 5.11) in which transfers are allocated on the basis of a score for each household that can be interpreted as predicted real income or consumption, based on readily observed indicators. Depending on how it is designed, this type of scheme can have better incentive effects than perfect means testing and can have a higher impact on poverty for a given outlay than a poll transfer. The main alternative targeting method uses communities themselves to decide who is in need. Such *community-based targeting* exploits local information that is not normally available for the proxy means test (PMT), but it does so at the risk of capture by local elites.[28]

Targeting performance in practice is often determined in large part by the *local political economy*. Leakage of benefits to the non-poor may sometimes be essential for the political sustainability of an antipoverty program. In programs with relatively large start-up costs, early capture by the non-poor may well be the only politically feasible option (especially when the start-up costs must be financed domestically). This can be dubbed "early capture" by the non-poor. In the (relatively few) studies that looked for early capture it was found to be present.[29]

When budget cuts are called for, economists often advise governments to target their spending better. Yet this may run up against political-economy constraints in practice that limit the welfare losses to the non-poor from spending cuts. It may be especially difficult to protect the poor from public spending cuts in countries in which the poor are already the main beneficiaries of that spending. The outcome is unclear on a priori grounds and will depend on the specifics of the setting. A study of a major social program in Argentina, the *Trabajar Program*, illustrated how cuts can come with worse targeting performance; in the *Trabajar* case the allocation to the poor fell faster than that to the non-poor when aggregate spending on the program was cut.[30]

An issue that has received less attention is the specification of the target group. When transfers are unproductive, the ethical case is strong for targeting the poorest. However, when there are productivity effects, such as arising from the existence of credit-market failures (chapter 8), the poorest are not necessarily the people with higher returns to transfers. For example, one study for Mexico found that transfers to poor farmers increased their agricultural investments, with longer term income gains.[31] However, the gains were found to be lower among those farmers with the smallest holdings, who are presumably the poorest. If the policy had focused solely on those farmers, it would have had less impact on poverty. This is only one study, and further research is needed on both the productivity effects of transfers and the implications for targeting.

---

[28] Discussions of community-based targeting can be found in Alderman (2002), Galasso and Ravallion (2005), Mansuri and Rao (2012), and Alatas et al. (2012). The latter paper compares this form of targeting with PMT for a cash transfer program in Indonesia. The study finds that PMT does somewhat better at reaching the poor but community-based targeting better accords with local perceptions of poverty and is better accepted by local residents.

[29] See Lanjouw and Ravallion (1999), Ravallion (1999b), and Dutta et al. (2014).

[30] See by Ravallion (1999b).

[31] See de Janvrey et al. (2001).

Leakage

Critics of antipoverty programs have long pointed to any signs of benefits going to ineligible people. There might be non-poor citizens pretending to be poor (recalling box 10.2) or corrupt local officials taking their cut. Tightening up administrative processes can sometimes help. So too can the use of new technologies, such as smart cards with biometric information. Some leakage is hard to avoid, however, and the costs of reducing it to zero may well be prohibitive. As noted above, some leakage may even help in assuring a broader base of political support for the program. Furthermore, efforts to eliminate leakage can run against the overall aims of the program. Box 10.4 illustrates this point. As in all aspects of program design, one must consider both the costs and benefits of reducing leakage in the specific context.

Box 10.4 Some Ways of Fighting Corruption on Antipoverty Programs Can Backfire

Suppose that local officials have the power to determine how many people participate in the program. We can think of a workfare program, which provides a level of employment, denoted E, which cannot exceed the demand for work on the scheme, denoted D. However, the local officials have the power to prevent some of those who want work on the scheme from getting it. The local corrupt official maximizes his personal profit given the (exogenous) demand for work on the scheme. The official's problem is then to choose E to maximize:

$$R(E) - C(E) \text{ subject to } E \leq D.$$

Here $R(E)$ is the official's own revenue from corruption at employment E and $C(E)$ is the cost of corruption. The marginal benefit (MB) is the slope of the revenue function $R(E)$ while the marginal cost (MC) is the slope of $C(E)$. It is assumed that the MC increases with employment; the official needs to trust more people and runs a greater risk of getting caught as employment expands. The official's marginal benefit can be assumed to be constant, although this can be weakened to allow it to fall with employment. The profit-maximizing level of employment provided by the official sets MC = MB, as illustrated by E^* in figure B10.4.1. There will be unmet demand in equilibrium if $E^* < D$, as illustrated.

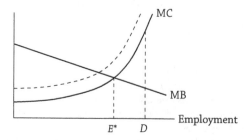

Figure B10.4.1 Optimal Level of Rationing Given a Rising Marginal Cost of Corruption.

Now suppose the central government (or some higher level of government to the local official) decides to crack down on corruption by raising the marginal cost of corruption facing the local official. For example, the penalty for getting caught might rise, or extra surveillance might be used to increase the probability of getting caught. This is illustrated by the upward shift in the MC function in figure B10.4.1. The level of employment provided by the official will contract. There will be less corruption but also less work will be provided by the scheme.

A better solution to corruption in this case may well be to make the model outlined above irrelevant to the behavior of local officials. That requires that they do not have the power to enforce rationing in the first place; that the demand constraint becomes binding on their behavior. This is the idea of an *Employment Guarantee Scheme* (EGS). This will require that there is adequate funding to assure that all who want work can get it at the scheme's wage rate. It will also require that those who want work under the scheme are aware that the law entitles them to that work (or an unemployment allowance if the work cannot be provided) and are able to act on that awareness. This will require adequate administrative and legal processes for addressing grievances and for punishing local officials who do not comply with the law. Ultimately, when the demand constraint is not binding on local officials this too can be taken to reflect in no small measure the administrative capabilities of the state. The discussion returns to the EGS idea.

A strand of the literature has focused on how local institutions have influenced targeting performance and impacts on poverty. A study of the *Food-for-Education* program in Bangladesh found that a number of village-level characteristics were significant predictors of the extent to which the program was effective in reaching poor people within the village. Weaker program outcomes for poor people were evident in more unequal villages.[32] In neighboring West Bengal, however, one study did not find that similar factors had much influence on the pro-poor targeting of publically supplied credit and farm inputs, although such factors did influence employment generation for poor people.[33] In a study for Brazil, it was found that local political institutions matter to the performance of a conditional cash transfer program, with much larger impacts in reducing school dropout rates in municipalities where the mayor faces re-election.[34]

These findings point to the need for caution in forming generalizations across diverse settings. They also suggest that the problem of poor-area targeting may be more complex than simply reaching poor places and also involves aspects of local institutions if one is to maximize the aggregate impact on poverty. These contingent factors can be subtle, however, and feasibility in practice is another matter.

Some delivery mechanisms are more costly than others. Delivering aid to poor people in the commodity form, such as food, is likely to be more expensive than delivering as cash. The extra delivery costs are a form of leakage. This needs to be weighed up

---

[32] See Galasso and Ravallion (2005).
[33] See Bardhan and Mookherjee (2006).
[34] See De Janvry et al. (2011).

against the possible benefits of payments in kind. Various arguments are made in favor of in-kind payments, including that these are automatically indexed for inflation (while nominal cash transfers need to be adjusted), that in some settings local markets for the goods concerned do not work well, and that payment in kind yields a preferred distribution of benefits and (in particular) that payment in the form of food differentially benefits mothers and children. The effects on market prices of transfers can also depend on the mode of delivery. Payments in cash to poor people will tend to increase demand for food and so increase local prices of non-traded foods (with adverse effects for poor consumers), while payments in the form of food will have the opposite effect (with adverse effects for poor producers). One should be wary of generalizations in favor of one mode of delivery, as the balance of costs and benefits is likely to depend on the setting, such as how well food markets work, and the degree of spatial integration of local markets.

There is evidence that in-kind transfers of food do encourage greater consumption of the goods in question, as one would expect.[35] Whether one considers that a good thing or not depends crucially one whether we think that recipients are spending too little on those goods. That is often unclear, and there is a risk of making paternalistic judgments that ignore the preferences and knowledge of poor people and the constraints that influence their economic decisions.

There are also *measurement errors* in the income data used for assessing targeting performance. This is rarely acknowledged explicitly in policy discussions, but can have important implications for leakage. In assessing the targeting performance of antipoverty programs, common practice is to include a question on program participation in a survey that also asks about incomes. Armed with such data, one then measures the proportion of participants who are poor and the program's coverage of the poor to quantify the errors of exclusion and inclusion. These calculations have influenced numerous program assessments in practice. However, the concept of "poverty" underlying a program's objectives often appears to be broader than the way "income" is normally defined and measured from surveys (i.e., there are other welfare-relevant variables in deciding eligibility besides current income). While the program's administrators can typically list this broader set of variables, they are often vague about the precise weights attached to them. The problem for the evaluator is that the program's apparent "mis-targeting" could simply reflect the fact that the survey-based measure of income is not a sufficient statistic for deciding who is "poor." The policymaker has a different objective to that assumed by the evaluator.

This concern should be taken more seriously in practice. It is possible to test how robust assessments of targeting performance are to this source of welfare measurement errors.[36] This can be done by calibrating a broader welfare metric to the observed program assignment and the qualitatively known program objectives, under the counterfactual of perfect targeting. Instead of imposing a prior judgment about how "welfare" is to be measured one can derive the measure that best explains the observed assignment of the program. In other words, the weights on the various determinants of welfare are chosen to be as consistent as possible with the policy choices

---

[35] See Cunha (2014), based on a RCT of Mexico's food assistance program.

[36] The method described below is found in Ravallion (2008b).

actually made. If we find that the program is still poorly targeted, then this cannot be easily attributed to the possibility that the policymaker has a different concept of welfare.

For example, China's *Minimum Livelihood Guarantee Scheme* (popularly known as *Dibao*) is a cash transfer program.[37] The program is known to be quite well targeted, but mis-targeting is evident in the available survey data. Some of this mis-targeting is due to discrepancies between survey incomes and the latent welfare metric used in targeting the program. There is also evidence of substantial leakage to those who should not be eligible, and incomplete coverage of those who should be, even when income and other relevant household characteristics are weighted optimally from the point of view of predicting program participation.[38]

The debate on targeting continues. One thing can be agreed: better targeting is not the objective of the policy design problem, but only one potential instrument. And it is not necessarily the best instrument given the (sometimes hidden) costs and the political economy response to targeting, whereby finely targeted programs can undermine the political support for social policies.[39] My own assessment is that it is not difficult in most settings today to avoid substantial leakage of benefits to the non-poor. The bigger challenge is to assure high coverage of the poor. This points to the appeal of combining universal eligibility—nobody is excluded—with a sensible degree of targeting, such that benefits are greater for poorer people. There will be some disincentive, but as long as the MTR does not go over 70% (say) this should not be of concern.

10.3 Targeted Transfers

State-Contingent Transfers Financed by Taxation

We start with a class of transfers that are not normally considered to be "targeted," in that they do not involve an explicit effort at means testing or some other form of low-income targeting. What they target instead is an event, and hence they are called *state-contingent transfers*. However, it is plain that these events are seen to be associated with some form of (temporary or permanent) deprivation. Those who experience the event are typically poorer (before or after) in some relevant dimension (e.g., when the main breadwinner loses her job, or a farmer's crop fails). Thus, there is often a degree of implicit targeting of poor people.

Recall from chapter 1 that the essential idea of England's Old Poor Laws was state-contingent transfers financed by taxation. There was little effort at income targeting prior to the nineteenth century; the 1834 reforms aimed to target benefits to those in greatest need, notably through work requirements. The idea of untargeted state-contingent transfers (as in the Old Poor Laws) re-emerged in twentieth-century Britain in the form of the *Beveridge Report*,[40] which outlined detailed proposals for

---

[37] For an overview of this program, see Ravallion (2014h). We return to the program below.

[38] For further details, see Ravallion (2008b).

[39] For further discussion, see van de Walle (1998b), De Donder and Hindriks (1998), and Gelbach and Pritchett (2000).

[40] See Beveridge (1942).

social insurance, whereby all those of working age would be obliged to pay a national insurance contribution to finance state contingent transfers to the unemployed, the sick, elderly, or widowed. (See box 10.5 on social insurance.) However, unlike the Old Poor Laws, this was to be a national scheme, rather than implemented locally. Two other elements completed the social protection policy. First, family allowances were proposed, to cover the costs of dependent children (after the first child). Second, an income top-up was proposed for those falling below absolute standards taking account of all income sources.[41] While the aim of these proposals was squarely to eliminate poverty, Beveridge was opposed to means testing—universal provision at a flat rate was seen to avoid the costs of targeting and to encourage social cohesion.[42] The past, deliberately stigmatizing, approach typified by the workhouses was to be abandoned. The hardships and vulnerabilities of life in Britain in the immediate post–World War II period may well have helped assure the popularity of Beveridge's plan.[43] With the implementation of the Beveridge plan in the form of the National Assistance Act, the last workhouse closed in 1948.

Box 10.5 Social Insurance and Social Assistance

As normally understood, "social insurance" is public provision of untargeted transfers to cover adverse events, such as illness, disability, accidents at work, old age, or unemployment. This is a growing component of public spending in many countries and is a large share of spending in most rich countries. Participation is typically compulsory, and access to social insurance is often tied to past contributions. The case for public provisioning is typically based on market failures and/or mistakes made by people in their past choices. The market failures come from asymmetric information, in that people are better informed about how much risk they are exposed to than are potential insurers. The market will provide too little insurance. Under certain conditions, the private insurance market may not even exist (Rothschild and Stiglitz 1976). Thus, the government needs to step in. Efforts to assure social solidarity—that all members of society exist in bonds of mutual responsibility—have been influential in arguments for broad-based social insurance in Western Europe and (especially) Scandinavia.

"Social assistance" usually refers to targeted transfer programs (notably in the United States). These are typically means tested, and often with conditions attached, such as time limits and work requirements. It should not be presumed that social assistance is necessarily more "pro-poor." The explicit targeting may mean that a higher share of the transfers goes to poor people, but it can also entail weak political support for the program. The targeting can also come with hidden costs of stigma or in complying with the conditions. It is an empirical question whether better targeting delivers a greater impact on poverty.

---

[41] This came to be known as the "Supplementary Benefit" and became more important in practice than Beveridge envisaged; see the discussion in Meade (1972).

[42] There is an interesting discussion of Beveridge's arguments in Thane (2000, esp., ch. 19).

[43] See Thane (2000, 369).

Similar efforts were underway elsewhere soon after World War II. In France, the long-standing ideas of social inclusion and social solidarity (going back to the First Poverty Enlightenment, as discussed in chapter 1) came to influence social policy through an effort to attain broad coverage of social insurance. Again, the idea was not to "target the poor" but rather to assure universal coverage at some reasonable minimum level of living, including access to employment opportunities and key social services for health, education, and social protection. As in Britain, this was something that everyone was seen to need and this was key to broad political support. The set of policies that emerged by the 1970s were termed the *"minimum income for inclusion."* America's Social Security System also grew out of prior social policy thinking and relief efforts (notably in response to the Great Depression), but a fairly comprehensive set of state-contingent transfers, financed by taxation did not emerge until after World War II.

All rich countries today now have a set of direct interventions using both cash and in-kind transfers financed by taxation. Significant public resources are devoted to these schemes and there is a large literature.[44] Poverty reduction is typically an explicit aim, though not the only aim; social objectives of insurance for all and social inclusion/community solidarity are also emphasized in the literature and policy discussion, especially in Europe.

There is continuing debate about these policies.[45] Similarly to the 1834 reforms to the Old Poor Laws, calls for finer targeting were becoming common from around 1980, in attempting to reduce the fiscal cost of social insurance. In due course, the more finely targeted policies that emerged came to be questioned, notably when they entailed high MTRs (in combination with other policies, including the income tax schedule), with the aforementioned risks of creating a poverty trap. "Making work pay" reforms emerged in the 1990s, such as EITC, to try to bring down MTRs facing poor workers.

Unemployment benefits (UB) have been a much debated example of this class of policies. Critics argue that this form of state-contingent transfer leads people to stop working. An appeal is often made to the standard economic model of consumption-leisure choice (box 1.4). Identifying the welfare effect of unemployment has not been easy, however. As noted in chapter 3, a number of studies of self-assessed welfare have suggested that unemployment entails a loss of welfare at given income. As also noted, there are potential biases in the latter studies. In one study (for Russia) that attempted to address these concerns, a bias was identified, but not sufficient to reverse the claim that unemployment entails a loss of welfare at given income.[46] The study's results imply that a large UB would be needed to attract a worker out of work; indeed, if we consider a worker choosing between staying employed (which is assumed to be the only source of income for the household) and being unemployed and receiving unemployment benefits, the UB would have to be four times higher than the wage to attract the worker out of work. However, while becoming unemployed entails a large welfare loss, that loss is not fully restored when an unemployed person

---

[44] A good recent overview can be found in Marx et al. (2014).
[45] America's Social Security System was decried as "socialism" in some quarters, and still is.
[46] See Ravallion and Lokshin (2001).

gets a job, except via the income gain. This implies a long-term welfare loss from even transient unemployment at given income. It also suggests that high UBs do not attract people out of work, but that they may well discourage a return to work. Further research of this sort is needed.

While uniform but state-contingent transfers are common in the rich world and in EECA, they are not common in developing countries. It seems that developing countries have largely skipped this stage in the history of social policy. However, it is not entirely clear why this is the case or that it is a good idea from the point of view of sound policymaking. To explain why uniform state-contingent transfers of the social insurance type are not used, it is sometimes claimed that such policies are unsuitable to poor economies; they would be too costly, and targeting is called for. While the fiscal burden of social policies must never be ignored, it is notable that the Old Poor Laws were invented in what was clearly a poor economy by today's standards. For some three hundred years the Old Poor Laws provided a degree of social protection and stability at seemingly modest cost.[47]

One example of a state-contingent transfer in a developing country is South Africa's old-age pension. This is paid to all women over sixty and men over sixty-five. There is supposed to be a means test but in practice it appears that this is not implemented and virtually everyone who is eligible by age gets the transfer. And it is a sizable sum—about double the median African income.[48] With some degree of income pooling within households, the simple economics of work–leisure choice (as summarized in box 1.4) would imply that this transfer reduced work. One study found evidence in a cross-sectional survey that the scheme did just that.[49] However, using longitudinal data (to allow for household fixed effects, as discussed in box 6.2) another study found the opposite.[50] The pension appears to have helped families get around credit constraints on outmigration by younger adult family members (often leaving the pension recipient to look after the children).

There have often been calls for "better targeting" of the types of state-contingent transfers reviewed above, in an effort to either cut the fiscal cost of uniform state-contingent transfers or to assure a greater impact on poverty for the same public expenditure (or both). As we will see, while better targeting may help in both respects, finely targeted policies have costs that are often hidden but must be considered in any proper evaluation of the policy options.

Unconditional Subsidies and Transfers

Subsidies on the consumption of normal goods (meaning that they have a positive income elasticity of demand) are clearly not going to be well targeted. Their incidence will be automatically skewed toward the non-poor, who will have higher demand for the subsidized goods. Efforts have been made in many countries to replace such generalized subsidies with some form of more targeted subsidy or cash transfer program,

[47] See Solar (1995).
[48] See Ardington et al. (2009).
[49] See Bertrand et al. (2003).
[50] See Ardington et al. (2009).

although such reforms often meet stiff resistance from those who lose. For example, Yemen cut its subsidies on fuel in 2014, but had to reinstate them soon after in the face of mass protests.

Subsidies on essential goods with some form of pro-poor targeting have been common. As soon as one subsidizes a market good one creates an opportunity for profit from the gap between its market price and the subsidized price, and it can be no surprise that non-poor people try to seize that opportunity. For example, India has a system of food rations at subsidized prices allocated according to whether a household had received a "Below Poverty Line (BPL)" card. Survey data for 2004–05 indicate that those in India's poorest wealth quintile are the least likely to have some form of ration card, to allow access to subsidized goods, and that the richest quintile are the most likely.[51] One study used the BPL card allocation as a counterfactual for assessing the distribution of the benefits of NREGS in the state of Bihar; another counterfactual considered by the same study is a BIG.[52] These two counterfactuals attained almost exactly the same level of poverty as the gross disbursements under NREGS. So, overall, the BPL cards were no better targeted than a BIG.[53]

One policy issue is whether the transfers should be in cash or in kind. Food has clearly been the most common form of in-kind payment. An example is the *Supplemental Nutrition Assistance Program* (SNAP) in the United States, popularly known as "food stamps" (after the original mode of delivery using stamp books, which have been replaced by electronic benefit transfer cards, like debit cards). SNAP is targeted to income and asset-poor families and can only be legally spent on food and beverages from authorized retailers (with some restrictions on what can be purchased, notably excluding alcoholic beverages and hot foods).

Advocates of in-kind transfers argue that this will assure a better distribution within the household, favoring women and children. Critics argue that this is paternalistic—that it would be better to make a direct cash transfer and let the family decide its priorities—and unnecessarily costly, since public resources are required for monitoring and enforcement. (Some retailers are willing to exchange cash for food stamps, discounting their face value and pocketing the difference.) The emphasis on targeting women in poor families also runs the risk of burdening women with even more work and responsibility—exacerbating the existing gender inequity.[54]

Unconditional cash or in-kind transfers targeted to poor people are found in many countries today, but have been more common in developed countries. An exception is China. Direct redistributive interventions have not been prominent in China's efforts to reduce poverty. Enterprise-based social security remained the norm, despite the dramatic changes in the economy, including the emergence of open unemployment and rising labor mobility. However, this is changing. The *Dibao* program has been the Government of China's main response to the new challenges of social protection in the more market-based economy. This program aims to guarantee a minimum income

---

[51] See Ajwad (2006).

[52] See Murgai et al. (2015).

[53] At the time of writing, the Government of India is embarking on significant reforms to its allocation system for these food rations, which will hopefully assure more pro-poor outcomes.

[54] On this argument, see Chant (2008).

in urban areas by filling the gap between actual income and a *"Dibao* line" set locally. On paper this suggests a poverty trap, with 100% marginal tax rates on poor people (as discussed in box 10.1). One study of the incentive effects of the program concluded that the marginal tax rate in practice is far lower—closer to 10%. Local officials have sufficient discretion to be able to actively smooth *Dibao* payments to lower the tax rate in practice.[55] This illustrates a more general point that the way a program works in practice can differ greatly from its formal design.[56]

While in theory a program such as *Dibao* would eliminate poverty, the practice appears to fall well short of that goal, due largely to imperfect coverage of the target group and horizontal inequity between municipalities, whereby the poor living in poor areas fare worse in accessing the program.[57] Looking forward the challenges presented are in reforming the program and expanding coverage.

As discussed in chapter 8, credit-market failures have long been identified as a reason why poverty persists. Poor people are often credit constrained, which is one of the reasons they are poor. And it is likely that they are more credit constrained than those financing the transfers. Then targeted cash transfers will have productive effects by supporting investment in physical or human capital by poor people. Compensating for the market failures can then be good for *both* equity and efficiency.

This argument is fine in theory, but what is the evidence? There have been a number of studies of this aspect of transfers, consistent with the view that transfers can help alleviate credit constraints.[58] One study looked at the longer term impacts for children who had been helped by the *Mothers' Pension* in the United States in the fifteen years or so after World War I. Boys whose mothers had received help from the program grew up better schooled and lived a longer life with a higher average income than comparators drawn from those applicants who had been rejected.[59] In today's developing world, there have been a few studies suggestive of longer term impacts from cash transfers in Africa.[60] Two studies of the *Malawi Social Cash Transfer Scheme* found positive effects of the transfers on investment in farm tools and livestock.[61] Similar findings were obtained in a study of the impacts of Zambia's *Child Grant Program*,[62] and Ethiopia's *Productive Safety Net Programme*.[63] However, not all studies have found such effects. A study of the *Livelihood Empowerment against Poverty Program* in Ghana did not reveal much impact on productive impacts, although the unpredictable nature of the transfer payments may have been a factor.[64]

An important source of heterogeneity in the longer-term impacts of transfers to poor people is literacy, which conveys many advantages, including the ability to learn and adapt, which are important to the success of entrepreneurial initiatives.

[55] See Ravallion and Chen (2013b).
[56] As Moffitt (2002) points out in the context of welfare programs in the United States.
[57] See Ravallion (2009c, d).
[58] Alderman and Yemtsov (2014) provide a useful review.
[59] See Aizer et al. (2014).
[60] See Goldstein (2014) for further discussion of the longer-term impacts of cash transfers.
[61] See Boone et al. (2013) and Covarrubias et al. (2013).
[62] See Seidenfeld et al. (2013).
[63] See Hoddinott et al. (2012).
[64] See Handa et al. (2013).

The combination of transfers (assets and cash) targeted to the poorest with efforts to promote human development—especially (ordinary and financial) literacy and specific skill training—has been emphasized as a strategy for poverty reduction by the Bangladesh Rural Advancement Committee (BRAC).[65] An important component of BRAC activities since 2002 has provided transfers to the "ultra-poor" who are often left out of micro-credit schemes (discussed further later in this section). Evaluations of the Bangladesh program have suggested that there are economic gains to the participants over time, mainly through the opportunities created for diversification out of casual labor in agriculture.[66] A study spanning six countries (Ethiopia, Ghana, Honduras, India, Pakistan, and Peru) found evidence of sustained economic gains from BRAC programs three years after the initial asset transfer, and one year after the disbursements finished.[67] In most cases, the cost of the BRAC program was less than the present value of the extra earnings over time.

Insurance benefits can also be expected since risk markets are imperfect. Given income variability over time, the set of recipients over the longer term will be greater than at any one date. This has been documented for the United States by exploiting the long panel data sets available.[68] These indicate that two-thirds of adult Americans will at some point in their lives live in a household that receives benefits from targeted transfers, such as food stamps or Medicaid.[69] By contrast, the participation rate at any one date is no more than 10% or so. Similarly, it has been argued that the popularity of the *Employment Guarantee Scheme* in Maharashtra stemmed in part from the fact that many people who would not normally participate faced downside risk and could turn to the program if needed. We study this class of programs in more detail in the next section. Before doing so, we turn to a class of targeted interventions aiming to incentivize the creation of human wealth for poor families.

Targeted Incentives for Investing in Human Capital

We saw in chapter 7 that children from poor families tend to get less schooling and worse healthcare. This is common across the globe. We learned in chapter 8 that this is also one of the mechanisms perpetuating poverty across generations. The implications for inequality are less clear. As was also noted in chapter 8—based on the data in figure 7.21 and an economic model of the returns to schooling—a generalized expansion in education is likely to increase inequality initially in countries with low initial levels of schooling. This will probably reverse later, and the majority of developing countries today are likely to be in the region in which education expansion will tend

---

[65] This is the world's largest NGO in terms of staff, with over 100,000 employees across 14 countries. It was founded in 1972 as a modest relief and rehabilitation project for refugees returning to Bangladesh after the Liberation War.

[66] See Emran et al. (2014) and Bandiera et al. (2013).

[67] See Banerjee et al. (2015).

[68] See Rank and Hirschl (2002).

[69] Also see Rank's (2005) interesting discussion of this aspect of various welfare programs in the United States.

to lower income inequality.[70] In the poorest countries, however, there may well be a case for targeting the gains in schooling to the poor, for both reducing poverty and its persistence, and for attenuating rising inequality.

We also learned about economy-wide policies for promoting schooling in chapter 9. While the costs of schooling (including forgone earnings of children) figured in the nineteenth-century debates about the idea of compulsory education, there was not much discussion of the obvious policy response: a bursary for children from poor families. Smith (1776) and Mill (1859) advocated such a policy. Marshall (1890, 594) took a less sympathetic attitude and proposed instead penalizing poor parents (a public policy of "*paternal discipline*") who neglected to send their children to school or to care for their health. Educational institutions have for a long time provided relief on tuition fees and other costs to selected students, often based on some sort of means test. England's 1870 *Elementary Education Act* recommended tuition subsidies for children from poor families.[71] However, implementation of public policies providing any form of schooling incentive for poor parents had to wait until the middle of the twentieth century, after which it started to become common practice to build in incentives for children from poor families to stay in school. Britain's 1942 *Beveridge Report* recommended a universal child allowance paid up to the age of sixteen if the child stayed in school.[72] Australia had a school bursary program from the 1960s that essentially paid parents from poor families to keep their children in school beyond the school leaving age as long as the children passed a special exam. It is common today for various forms of education subsidies (scholarships, tuition subsidies, subsidized loans) to be means tested. Essentially, education for poor families is subsidized while the well-off cover the full cost or more of their children's schooling.

In the development literature in the 1990s, targeted bursaries came to be known as *conditional cash transfers* (CCTs). The idea of making antipoverty policies conditional on behavioral change goes back a long way (recall the arguments for public works as a relief policy found in ancient Rome and in Kautilya's *Science of Material Gain*, as discussed in chapter 1). Most targeted interventions against poverty have conditions of one sort or another. The idea of a CCT is that an incentive is provided for parents in poor families to keep their children in school (and often with a healthcare incentive as well). Transfers are made under the condition that the children of the recipient family demonstrate adequate school attendance and healthcare in some versions. Plainly, the promotion benefits of these programs rest crucially on assuring that the transfers go to poor families, on the presumption that the children of the non-poor will already be in school. Thus, targeting has been instrumentally important to both the protection and promotion benefits. The promotion benefits also depend on designing the conditions such that the required level of schooling would not be attained in the absence of the program. Early influential examples of these programs in developing countries were Mexico's *PROGRESA* program (now called *Oportunidades*) and *Bolsa Escola* in Brazil. In the case of Brazil, a series of CCTs were targeted to poor families

---

[70] Recall from the discussion of figure 7.21, panel (b), that two-thirds of the data are in the region in which the absolute gap in schooling attainments between rich and poor tends to fall as the mean rises.

[71] See Gillie (1996).

[72] Similarly, the EITC in the United States gives different age cutoffs for full-time students.

and eventually consolidated (and extended to include conditions on child healthcare) under *Bolsa Família*, which grew to cover 11 million families, or about one-quarter of the population—rising to about 60% of the poorest decile in terms of income net of transfers.[73] The average transfer payment is about 5% of pre-transfer income. The poorest families receive a transfer even if they have no children. The targeting of poor families uses a PMT, based on readily observed covariates of poverty (including location). Another early example was FFE in Bangladesh for which the transfers were made in kind but also conditional on school attendance. Bolivia's CCT, *Bono Juancito Pinto*, introduced in 2006, is an example of a universal (untargeted) transfer program, for which every child enrolled in public school is eligible, irrespective of family income.

Over thirty developing countries now have CCT programs and the number is growing. And other countries have formally similar policies not called CCTs; for example, in attempting to assure that poverty does not constrain schooling, since 2002 China has had a *"two exemptions, one subsidy"* policy for students from poor rural families; the exemptions are for tuition fees and textbooks and the subsidy is for living costs.

A CCT is essentially a price subsidy on the schooling and healthcare of children. Because the transfer is tied to the stipulated conditions it makes satisfying those conditions cheaper than it would have been otherwise. Box 10.6 discusses the economic incentives generated by a CCT in greater detail. Critics of the use of such conditions argue that they are paternalistic; poor families will know better how to spend the transfer. Supporters question that assumption. Some well-off people are, it seems, more generous toward poor people if the latter are obliged to do something that is likely to get their children out of poverty in the future.

Box 10.6 Incentive Effects on Parental Choices

How will a CCT affect the choices made by recipients? The CCT provides a transfer to parents conditional on sending their children to school. Parents are free to determine how their children's time is allocated between schooling, labor, and leisure. In making that choice, let us assume that parents have preferences over the household's current consumption, the child's school attendance, and the child's leisure. It is assumed that those preferences can be represented by a utility function with smooth convex indifference curves (similarly to box 1.4).

In addition to the transfer payment and income from child labor, the household obtains an income from other sources of course. Parents maximize utility subject to both the budget constraint and the time constraint.

In this model, the price of schooling facing parents is the difference between the wage rate (w) for child labor and benefit level (b) received from the CCT. With no other constraints on time allocation, the parents' choice equates the MRS between consumption and schooling with this school price $w–b$, and it equates the MRS between consumption and leisure with the price of leisure, w. Doing so

continued

---

[73] See Fiszbein and Schady (2010, fig. 3.1).

Box 10.6 (Continued)

generates a set of derived demand functions for their children's schooling and leisure and (hence) their supply of labor to the market.

The effect of an increase in the stipend reveals how time allocation varies with the price of schooling. Consider how an increase in the benefit level on the CCT will affect child labor. There are three components to this effect. First, there will be a pure substitution effect toward schooling which has become cheaper (holding utility constant). Second, there will be an income effect on demand for schooling and children's leisure, which will also reduce child labor. However, that is not all. There is a utility-compensated cross-effect of the price of schooling on demand for children's leisure, or the effect of the price of leisure on schooling. The sign of this effect is ambiguous. It will be positive if schooling and leisure are (utility-compensated) substitutes. A sufficient condition for the CCT incentive to reduce child labor is that schooling and leisure are complements.

Further reading: For more on the theory and evidence (for Bangladesh's FFE program), see Ravallion and Wodon (2000a). The researchers found that FFE increased schooling by far more than it reduced child labor. Substitution effects helped protect current incomes from the higher school attendance induced by the program.

If the sole concern was with current income gains to poor households, then a policy-maker would not impose schooling requirements, which entail a cost to poor families by incentivizing them to withdraw children or teenagers from the labor force, thus reducing the (net) income gain to poor people. (There is still a current income gain, but less than it could be.) The costs include, of course, the forgone earnings of children and teenagers, but there are other costs too, such as the time of (typically) the mother in complying with the conditions. Based on what we see empirically, it is reasonable to assume that the poorer the parents the less likely the children will be in school at any given age. Thus, the cost of fulfilling the conditions of the CCT will be higher for poorer families. The fact that such costs are incurred does not mean that the CCT is a bad idea, but it does point to the importance of a comprehensive treatment of the costs and benefits.

Given these observations, it is clear that we need a good argument to justify a CCT over an unconditional transfer. Advocates see these programs as a means of breaking the poverty trap stemming from the economic gradient in human development, whereby poorer families cannot invest as much in their children and so those children are more likely to grow up poor. CCTs strive to strike a new balance between protection and promotion, premised on the presumption that poor families cannot strike the socially optimal balance on their own. The incentive effect on labor supply of the program (often seen as an adverse outcome of transfers) is now judged to be a benefit—to the extent that a well-targeted transfer allows poor families to keep the kids in school, rather than sending them to work.

Concerns about distribution *within* households are also found in the motivations given for such programs; the program's conditions entail that relatively more of the

(omit)

gains accrue to children. Here the argument made by defenders of CCTs (and other policies, such as compulsory schooling) is that children often lose out in solving the intra-family bargaining problem that decides how long they stay in school rather than work. The CCT incentive rebalances the problem in favor of women and children, especially girls.

The presumption that poor parents are not making the right choices for their families is one of the most contentious aspects of these schemes, and it would be fair to say that this aspect has not been well defended by proponents of CCT's. There is an echo here of old ideas that blame poverty on the behavior of poor men and women (as discussed in chapter 1). In this case, advocates of CCTs argue that poverty persists across generations because poor parents do not keep their children in school long enough or seek public healthcare. This can be debated. Poor parents may well be better informed than policymakers about the choices they face in life.

Some of the arguments made for CCTs are less compelling than others. Defenders of CCTs have sometimes argued that credit-market failures (whereby poor parents cannot borrow to finance their children's schooling) justify that incentive. However, this still requires that we do not think that parents are making the right choices; otherwise, the best way to relieve the borrowing constraint would be to make the transfer unconditional, since that will assure the largest income gain to the liquidity-constrained parents.

It has been argued that CCTs reduce child labor. Teenagers stay in school longer, delaying their entry into the workforce. For younger children, it is less clear. One study showed that, under standard economic assumptions, a tuition subsidy will increase schooling but has theoretically ambiguous effects on the supply of child labor.[74] Empirically, the study found little effect of a tuition subsidy on child labor in Bangladesh (box 10.6).

Another economic argument for a CCT emerges when we consider the role played by prevailing social norms in schooling and healthcare choices by parents. A CCT has the potential to nudge the economy out of the bad equilibrium in which very few girls are sent to school. (See box 9.2 for further discussion.) The incentive works initially at the individual level, but it yields a collective gain given that the non-pecuniary cost facing girls will fall as a consequence. Depending on how that cost varies with the initial school enrollment rate and the size of the incentive effect, a sufficiently large transfer conditional on girls' schooling may well be able to change local social norms, putting a community with low school attendance by girls onto a path toward universal enrollment. By implication there will also be spillover effects from those receiving the transfer to others, pointing to a source of bias in standard impact evaluations. Such a spillover effect has been described in the context of Mexico's *PROGRESA*.[75] The program appears to have changed local social norms related to women's use of health services; naturally this effect included the control group that had not actually received the program directly.

What is the evidence on the benefits of CCTs? There is evidence from impact evaluations that these schemes bring non-negligible benefits to poor households,

[74] See Ravallion and Wodon (2000a).
[75] See Avitabile (2012).

in terms of both current incomes and future incomes, through higher investments in child schooling and healthcare.[76] The conditions change behavior. In the United Kingdom, means tested grants paid to secondary students have been found to be very effective in reducing the incidence of school drop outs from poor families.[77] The various evaluations of Mexico's *PROGRESA/Oportunidades* program have been positive.[78] There is evidence that the incentive created by the conditions in *PROGRESA* enhanced the impact on schooling.[79] There is also evidence of general equilibrium effects on children's wages, which rose in program villages relative to the controls.[80]

While this has clearly been the most researched CCT program, there is now a body of evidence for other programs and diverse settings. One study found sizable reduction in school dropout rates of adolescent girls due to the conditions in a transfer program in Malawi.[81] A study for Burkina Faso found that the conditionality mattered more in encouraging the school enrollment of children who were initially less likely to go to school, including girls—children who are less likely to receive investments from their parents.[82] Another study found that a CCT program in Indonesia, *Jaring Pengamanan Sosial*, had greatest average impact at the lower secondary school level where children are most susceptible to dropping out.[83]

There is also evidence that CCT's can help reduce the long-term costs of crises and idiosyncratic shocks stemming from their impacts on schooling. Studying Mexico's *PROGRESA/Oportunidades* program, one study found evidence that the program helped protect the school enrollment of poor children, although parents still asked their children to help supplement family income at such times by working as well as staying at school.[84] A study of a CCT in Colombia found that the program helped poor families cope with the permanent departure of the father, which would otherwise curtail children's schooling, with implications for future poverty in addition to the loss of current income.[85]

Most evaluations have focused on the short-term impacts of CCTs. Are the gains in schooling sustained after the removal of the transfers? A study of the tuition-subsidy component of a poor-area program in rural southwest China found that the impact on

[76] Fiszbein and Schady (2010) provide a comprehensive review. Also see the discussion in Das et al. (2005).

[77] See Dearden et al. (2009).

[78] See the survey in Fiszbein and Schady (2010).

[79] See de Brauw and Hoddinott (2011) on Mexico's *PROGRESA*. The authors exploit the fact that some participants did not receive the forms necessary for monitoring school attendance, illustrating how we can sometimes learn from administrative errors.

[80] See Attanasio et al. (2012).

[81] See Baird, McIntosh and Ozler (2011). Impact was assessed relative to unconditional transfers, as well as a control group receiving no transfers. There was also a gain in school test performance attributable to the conditions. However, interestingly, the unconditional transfers were more effective in delaying marriage and pregnancy (relative to both the CCT and control group). The authors offer an explanation in terms of the total income gains to school dropouts receiving the unconditional transfers.

[82] See Akresh et al. (2013).

[83] See Cameron (2002).

[84] See de Janvry et al. (2006),

[85] See Fitzsimons and Mesnard (2014).

school enrollment vanished once the incentive had been removed.[86] The gain during the incentivized period was not diminished, however, implying a longer term gain in schooling. Another study found that the half-grade gain in schooling attributed to a CCT in Nicaragua persisted ten years later.[87] The same study also found gains in the math and language test scores of the young adults surveyed due to the earlier program. As noted in chapter 5, the same program was also found to improve the cognitive outcomes of children through better nutrition, and these gains also persisted two years after the program.

The design features of CCTs have also been critically assessed. A series of papers on *PROGRESA* revealed that a budget-neutral switch of the enrollment subsidy from primary to secondary school would have delivered a net gain in school attainments, by increasing the proportion of children who continue on to secondary school.[88] While *PROGRESA* had an impact on schooling, it could have had a larger impact. However, it should be recalled that this type of program has two objectives: promotion by increasing schooling (reducing future poverty) and protection by reducing current poverty, through the targeted transfers. To the extent that refocusing the subsidies on secondary schooling would reduce the impact on current income poverty (by increasing the forgone income from children's employment), the case for this change in the program's design would need further analysis.

Early Childhood Development

Poverty in the first few years of life can have lasting consequences for health and learning abilities, with implications for labor earnings later in life. In Chapter 7 we heard about research findings suggesting that poverty is associated with worse health and schooling outcomes. While these statistical associations do not imply causality, numerous psychosocial causal pathways have been identified from poverty in childhood to both current health status and health as an adult.[89] This is one way poverty perpetuates across generations.

There have been a number of efforts to break this link through Early Childhood Development (ECD) programs. Impact evaluations have also pointed to high returns to these programs.[90] The experimental *Perry Preschool Program* in the United States in the 1960s provided schooling and home visits to children aged three to four years from poor families. The benefits included higher adult earnings and reduced crime, and the benefit-cost ratio (even without putting higher weight on the pro-poor distribution of the gains) was estimated to be over eight to one.[91] *Head Start* (also starting in the United States' 1960s *War on Poverty*) was a similar national pre-school program, which

---

[86] See Chen et al. (2009).

[87] See Barham et al. (2013).

[88] See Todd and Wolpin (2006), de Janvry and Sadoulet (2006), and Attanasio et al. (2012).

[89] See Evans et al. (2012) for a survey of this literature. Also see the discussion in Haushofer and Fehr (2014).

[90] Useful reviews of the evidence and policy experiences can be found in Horton et al. (2008) and Walker (2011) (who focuses on the under-three age group).

[91] See Heckman (2006).

targeted a package of education, health, and nutrition services to poor families; the program continues at the time of writing and, as of 2005, some 22 million pre-school children had participated. *Head Start* has also been found to generate sizable long-term gains in schooling, earnings, and reduced crime.[92] The aggregate benefits from *Head Start* also appear likely to outweigh the cost, even without distributional weights.[93] Also in the US, the *Infant Health and Development Program* randomly assigned high-quality child care to low-birth-weight under-3 children. The program was able to raise the test performance of children from low-income families to about the same level as for high-income parents.[94] The literature on pre-school and other early childhood interventions targeted to poor families also points to complementarities with support for more standard school-age programs.

There is also evidence of long-term gains in adult health from ECD. The *Carolina Abecedarian Project* found that those children from poor families in the 1970s who had been randomly assigned to receive the program subsequently performed better in the standard school years.[95] A follow-up study in their adult years (mid-thirties) also found that the participants had significantly lower incidence of standard indicators of the risk of cardiovascular and metabolic diseases.[96] There was both pre-school (under five) and school age (under eight) components of the original study, but the pre-school component had the stronger effects on adult health.

The studies to date are encouraging on the scope for ECD as part of antipoverty policy. Granted, the sample sizes have been fairly small, some of the original sample inevitably drops out and this may well be a selective process that can bias the results, and there are also the danger that with the multiple outcomes being studied one will find at least one significant impact. One careful assessment of the statistical veracity of the main randomized evaluations of ECD interventions in the United States concluded that there were significant long-term impacts for girls, although the signs of long-term impacts were less convincing for boys.[97] One study did a number of tests and corrections for such problems (the small samples, the possibility of selective attrition, and the dangers of testing multiple hypotheses as if there was only one) and still found significant longer term health gains from ECD.[98]

There is also evidence of long-term gains from ECD interventions in developing countries. Mothers and their children in a district of rural Bangladesh received family planning and intensive early childhood healthcare in the 1980s. On comparing recipients with an observationally similar comparison group, the previously treated children had significantly higher cognitive functioning scores by ages 8–14.[99] A study for Guatemala followed up about 1,500 people who had joined a controlled trial program for nutritional supplementation in childhood, some twenty or more years

[92] See Garces et al. (2002).
[93] See Ludwig and Phillips (2007).
[94] See Duncan and Sojourner (2013).
[95] See Campbell and Ramey (1994).
[96] See Campbell et al. (2014).
[97] See Anderson (2008).
[98] See Campbell et al. (2014).
[99] See Barham (2012).

earlier.[100] Reduced stunting in the first few years was found to yield sizable longer term consumption gains and lower poverty rates in adulthood. These gains came with more schooling, better test scores, and higher adult wages. Allowing for costs, the results suggest quite high benefit-to-cost ratios for early childhood nutrition programs in poor countries.[101] Even without taking account of the likely pro-poor distribution of the benefits, public investments in early childhood nutrition supplementation—specifically in the first 1,000 days of life—can make economic sense.

In the light of the many positive findings on ECD, it is striking that very few CCTs in developing countries have yet applied conditions on behaviors relevant to ECD.[102] Such conditions could include pre-school attendance and/or visits to health clinics to obtain lessons on, for example, talking to children, feeding, and nutrition supplementation. Examples will surely emerge in due course, given the mounting body of evidence on the role of handicaps at early childhood in perpetuating poverty.

In one of the few evaluations to date of a pre-school program in a poor country, Bouguen et al. (2014) randomized pre-school construction in Cambodia, and followed up various outcome measures for both treatment and controls. Participating children saw only modest and statistically insignificant gains from improved access to pre-schools relative to the control group, and there was even evidence of an adverse impact on early childhood cognition tests. The main lessons drawn by the authors concerned program implementation and addressing demand-side constraints in ECD interventions in poor countries.

The balance of policy effort between children under three and over three remains an issue. It is easier to reach the latter group with pre-schools, and this has been the emphasis of many of the policies in place so far. While it is harder to reach the younger group, the benefits from doing so appear also to be larger, given that this is known to be a critical period for nutrition and brain development through interaction and stimulation. The available evidence and experience suggests that parenting education using home visits at high frequency (every two weeks say) can help, although this is costly.[103] Counseling mothers at clinics may well be more feasible although we do not appear to know much yet about its efficacy. There is much current interest in learning more about how effective ECD interventions might be devised for developing countries.

A Caveat on Service Quality

We have seen various examples in this section of policies that have aimed to create stronger incentives on the demand side for poor parents to invest in the human development of their children. Yet the quality of schooling and healthcare is a widespread

---

[100] See Maluccio et al. (2009) and Hoddinott et al. (2011). Also see the reviews of the evidence for other countries in Hoddinott, Behrman et al. (2013), Horton and Hoddinott (2014) and Behrman and Urzua (2013). The latter paper points to knowledge gaps relevant to assessing the costs and benefits of ECD interventions in developing countries.

[101] See Hoddinott, Alderman et al. (2013).

[102] The only example I know of is a World Bank–supported CCT-nutrition program in Yemen, approved by the Bank in 2014 and soon to be implemented at the time of writing.

[103] Walker (2011) reviews the evidence.

concern.[104] If the services are of poor quality, then the stronger incentive on the demand side may come to nothing. The success of these interventions may well require complementary efforts on the supply-side, through more effective (public or private) service delivery. This is not just about building and equipping facilities, though that is clearly important. There must also be adequate incentives for the performance of service providers (teachers and healthcare workers), with feedback to users on that performance. For example, parents should know how well their children are doing at school, not just that they are present.

The life-threatening dangers of encouraging greater use of public health facilities by poor people when service quality is inadequate were illustrated in the Indian state of Chhattisgarh, where twelve women died in 2014 after receiving tubal ligations. These operations and institutional deliveries were centrally encouraged as a matter of family planning policy in India. But the facilities were of uneven quality often with overworked staff. Nor was the evaluative evidence on the benefits as supportive as advocates had claimed.[105]

Equity issues also arise in efforts to improve service performance. A case in point is the idea of a *voucher program*, whereby parents receive a voucher for each school-age child which is redeemed by the school that the parents choose to send their child to. This directly links the income of each school to at least one aspect of performance: its enrollment rate. However, there are believed to be externalities in schooling—whereby children from richer families bring advantages to other students and staff—schools may become more socioeconomically segmented, with children from poorer families tending to go to different schools than those from better off families.[106] There is a risk that poor children end up with lower quality schooling.

10.4 Other Targeted Policies
Workfare

As was noted in chapter 1, policy efforts to make relief contingent on willingness to work have a long history. Incentives have always played a key role in such policies. The type of work that people are willing to do has long been seen as an indicator of poverty.[107] Thus, imposing a work requirement on welfare recipients offers a means of creating incentives in a program to assure that non-poor people are deterred. In the absence of the work requirement, the non-poor will masquerade as poor to receive benefits. (Recall the discussion of incentives in redistributive policy in box 10.2.)

The workhouses that emerged in Europe the sixteenth century famously used this device as a means of getting around the information and incentive problems of targeting (chapter 1). The design features only encourage those truly in need of help

[104] World Bank (2004b) reviews the evidence and discusses incentives for service delivery.

[105] See the comments in Das and Hammer (2014).

[106] As discussed by Gauri and Vawda (2004).

[107] Early examples include Young's (1792) travelogue from rural France in the later eighteenth century; a number of times he identifies the fact that women were willing to do menial labor in the fields as an indication of their poverty.

to turn to the workhouse and encourage them to drop out of it when public relief is no longer needed, given better options in the rest of the economy. The attraction of this approach is that it elegantly solves the information problem of targeting. However, it does so by imposing costs on participants, notably the forgone earnings and the welfare costs of stigma and subjugation (as Oliver Twist experienced). A truly utilitarian-welfarist assessment relative to untargeted transfers would clearly be ambiguous without further evidence.

England's workhouses of the nineteenth century clearly went too far in imposing costs on participants to assure self-targeting. The costs came to be widely seen as objectionable (chapter 1). But the idea of self-targeting had lasting influence. The workhouses are an example of a class of direct interventions often called today "workfare schemes"—schemes that impose work requirements on welfare recipients as a means of assuring incentive compatibility. Though not involving workhouses, this idea was embodied in the Famine Codes introduced in British India around 1880, and the idea has continued to play an important role to this day in the subcontinent.[108] Such schemes have helped in responding to, and preventing, famines including in sub-Saharan Africa.[109] Workfare was also a key element of the New Deal introduced by US President Roosevelt in 1933 in response to the Great Depression.

An important class of workfare schemes has aimed to guarantee employment to anyone who wants it at a pre-determined (typically low) wage rate. *Employment Guarantee Schemes* (EGSs) have been popular in South Asia, notably in India where the Maharashtra EGS, which started in 1973, was long considered a model. In 2005, the central government implemented a national version, the NREGS scheme we have heard about already. This promises one hundred days of work per year per household to those willing to do unskilled manual labor at the statutory minimum wage notified for the program. The work requirement is (more or less explicitly) seen as a means of assuring that the program is reaching India's rural poor.[110] These schemes can be interpreted as attempts to enforce a minimum wage rate in situations in which there is no other means of legal enforcement (chapter 9). In an EGS, anyone who wants work can (in theory) get it, provided they are willing to do unskilled manual labor at the statutory minimum wage rate.

A difference between an EGS and minimum wage legislation is that an EGS aims to provide comprehensive *insurance* for the able-bodied poor, in that anyone who needs work can get it, at least on paper. Eligibility is open to all, so that a farmer who would not need the scheme in normal times can turn to it in a drought (say). This was explicit from the outset of the idea of an EGS (as it developed in Maharashtra in the early 1970s). Whether this insurance function is served in practice is another matter. There is evidence of considerable rationing on India's national EGS, which clearly reduces the insurance benefits.[111] The rationing tends to be greater in poorer states of India,

---

[108] See Drèze (1990a).

[109] See Drèze (1990b).

[110] Dutta et al. (2014) provides an assessment. Also see Jha et al. (2012), Gaiha (1997), Imbert and Papp (2011).

[111] See Dutta et al. (2012).

which may well reflect weaker administrative capabilities for implementing a complex program such as an EGS.

Workfare schemes illustrate well the point that even a well-targeted transfer scheme can be dominated by untargeted transfers when one takes account of all the costs involved, such as income forgone or other costs in complying with the conditionalities imposed in more sophisticated transfer schemes. The evidence suggests that in both the Maharashtra EGS and the new national scheme an untargeted basic income scheme (a BIG) would have been more cost-effective in transferring money to poor people.[112]

Workfare schemes have typically been seen as short-term palliatives—a form of social insurance. In principle, a workfare scheme can also directly serve promotional goals. One way is by generating assets that could change the wealth distribution, or shift the production function, which could also allow people to break out of a poverty trap (chapter 8). In practice, asset creation has not been given much weight in these schemes in South Asia, although it seems to have higher weight elsewhere, including in Latin America (such as Argentina's *Trabajar Program*).

Another way that workfare programs have tried to better serve the promotional aim of antipoverty policies is by tying benefits to efforts to enhance human capital through training. Unemployed youth have been a special focal group for such efforts in a number of countries. Welfare reforms in many countries since the early 1990s have also aimed to make transfers conditional on investments in human capital, and to incentivize private employment search and take-up.[113] This form of workfare does not actually provide employment, as in the public-works form of workfare. Training and encouragements for private sector employment using wage subsidies have also been used to encourage the transition from public employment on workfare schemes to private employment.

Training and Wage-Subsidy Schemes

There is some evidence that low-wage workers tend to receive less training on-the-job, and invest less in skill enhancement by other means.[114] This has motivated interest in public programs that aim to provide training targeted to low-skilled workers. Efforts have also been made to subsidize the employment of such workers, such that they can find more high-paid work in the future, or simply get off the unemployment or workfare rolls into regular work. These are often called "active labor market programs."

There is evidence that such interventions can help in the transition to regular work. But the results appear to have varied greatly according to the setting and the method used to assess impact, defying generalizations.[115] While such policies have been less

---

[112] See Ravallion and Datt (1995) and Murgai et al. (2015).

[113] Hemerijck (2014) provides an overview of such reforms in Europe.

[114] Evidence on this point for the United Kingdom can be found in Booth and Bryan (2007), who also refer to other studies.

[115] An overview of the arguments for and against wage subsidies can be found in Katz (1996), Bell et al. (1999), and Blundell (2001). Impact assessments can be found in Burtless (1985), Woodbury

common in poor countries, they are getting more attention as those countries develop, and especially so with the rising concerns about youth unemployment, especially in the cities.

One of the difficulties faced in assessing this class of interventions is in obtaining reliable estimates of impact using non-experimental methods (recalling the discussion in chapter 6). One study found large biases in non-experimental methods when compared to a randomized evaluation of a US training program.[116] On the same data set, a follow-up study found that propensity-score matching achieved a good approximation (box 6.1).[117] Yet another study (again using the same data set), questioned this finding, arguing that the results are sensitive to choices made in sample selection and model specification.[118]

While generalizations about this class of programs can be hazardous, a closer look at one specific example can illustrate some key points. The example is the *Proempleo* scheme in Argentina, introduced around 2000. This was motivated by concerns about welfare dependency in "company towns" that had seen sharp reductions in employment due to retrenchments by the principal employer. The main form of welfare assistance provided to such towns was temporary work, at a relatively low wage, oriented to social infrastructure or community services. In some towns, a heavy dependence on such workfare programs emerged in the wake of privatizations and subsequent sharp contractions in local employment; an unusually higher take-up rate for workfare programs was being observed in these towns even five years later. Workfare participants may well need assistance in getting regular employment in the private sector.

Wage subsidies and/or training programs have seemed obvious responses. *Proempleo* provided both intensive training in skills identified as relevant to local labor demand and a sizable wage subsidy which was paid to the employer on registering any qualifying worker who had been given a private sector job. An evaluation of the pilot program used randomly assigned vouchers for the wage subsidy and training across (typically poor) people currently in a workfare program and tracked their subsequent success in getting regular work.[119] A randomized control group identified the counterfactual (chapter 6). The results indicated that the training component had an impact but only for those workers with a reasonable level of prior schooling. There was also a significant impact of the wage-subsidy voucher on employment. But when cross-checks were made against central administrative data, supplemented by interviews with the hiring firms, it was found that there was very low take-up of the wage subsidy by firms. The scheme was highly cost-effective; the government saved 5% of its workfare wage bill for an outlay on subsidies that represented only 10% of that saving.

---

and Spiegelman (1987), Dubin and Rivers (1993), and Galasso et al. (2004). The theory and evidence on training programs are reviewed by Heckman et al. (1999), and empirical studies include Lalonde (1986), Heckman et al. (1997), Dehejia and Wahba (1999), Smith and Todd (2001), and Galasso et al. (2004).

[116] See Lalonde (1986).

[117] See Dehejia and Wahba (1999).

[118] See Smith and Todd (2001).

[119] See Galasso et al. (2004).

However, the cross-checks against these other data revealed that *Proempleo* did not work the way its designers had intended. The bulk of the gain in employment for participants was not through higher demand for their labor induced by the wage subsidy. Rather the impact arose from supply-side effects; the voucher appears to have had credential value to workers—it acted like a "letter of introduction" that few people had (and how it was allocated was a secret locally). This finding could not be revealed by the RCT, but required supplementary qualitative data. The extra insight derived from the qualitative work also carried implications for subsequent scaling up, which put emphasis on providing better information for poor workers about how to get a job rather than providing wage subsidies.

Land-Based Targeting and Land Reforms

In rural economies, landholding has often played a role as an indicator of poverty for the purposes of targeting transfers in some form. Of course, if "poverty" is defined by landlessness, or having little land, such targeting has the potential for a large reduction in poverty. However, when a broader welfare metric is used based on consumption or income the case becomes less clear. There are naturally limitations to such targeting given that landholding is not a perfect correlate of income poverty. For example, while it makes sense to target assistance in rural Bangladesh toward households owning little or no land, one should not expect a large impact on consumption poverty. This was indicated by simulations done in the 1990s: even with complete control over the distribution of income across (but not within) six landholding classes in rural Bangladesh, the maximum attainable reduction in the aggregate severity of poverty (using the squared poverty gap index discussed in chapter 2) is no more than one could obtain by an untargeted lump-sum transfer to all households of about 3%–5% of mean income.[120] Various factors will detract from even that seemingly modest impact. For example, plausible restrictions on the government's redistributive powers would further diminish the gains to the poor. There may be potential for combining land-contingent targeting with other types of targeting. For example, there are poor households even among those with relatively large landholdings in Bangladesh. If these households can be identified with reasonable precision by other indicators, such as region of residence, then greater poverty alleviation would be feasible in practice.

The above discussion is a purely static assessment. It has also been argued that redistributive land reforms bring dynamic efficiency gains favoring poor people. The classic argument is based on the inverse relationship typically found between the productivity of land and farm size.[121] Family farms tend to use labor more efficiently because they face lower costs of monitoring effort and lower search and transaction costs. Redistributing land from large holdings to small ones will then generate a gain in aggregate productivity—enhancing both efficiency and equity. The efficiency gains

---

[120] See Ravallion and Sen (1994).

[121] Early evidence for this inverse relationship was provided by Berry and Cline (1979); for a recent review of the extensive literature broadly supporting the existence of this inverse relationship, see Lipton (2009).

may not materialize in practice in the presence of other market or governmental failures that restrict the access of smallholders to credit and new technologies.[122] The policy lesson here is to develop a package of interventions supporting smallholders.[123]

As noted in chapter 8, large-scale redistributive land reforms have been identified as a key factor in some of the success stories in poverty reduction, notably Taiwan. In the case of mainland China and Vietnam, it has also been argued that the relatively equitable distribution of land that could be attained as a result of agrarian reforms was important to the substantial growth in food output and fall in rural poverty (chapter 8).

There are a number of reasons why we have not seen more redistributive land reforms. The political power of the large landholding class has often been a factor given limited commitment (chapter 9).[124] Another reason is the widely held but generally false belief that large commercial farms are more efficient—the rejection of "the idea that small, ill-clothed and uneducated farmers can be more efficient than large, modern, well-dressed and well-educated ones."[125] And large landholders and their political representatives have undoubtedly encouraged such beliefs.

Microfinance for Poor People

As we have seen, credit market failures have been identified as a cause of poverty and a reason why it can be costly to overall economic performance. On top of long-standing moral arguments, transfers to poor people can be interpreted as a means of relieving the constraints stemming from such market failures. There is another option, namely policies that aim to make financial institutions for saving and borrowing work better for poor men and women, who cannot meet the collateral requirements. Such policies can matter for protection, by facilitating income and consumption smoothing. However, the new theories on inequality and development reviewed in chapter 8 also point to a motivation for such policies as a means of promotion, premised on the idea that it is the inequality in access to credit that matters to subsequent growth prospects in a credit-constrained economy.

Microfinance programs aiming to support small-scale credit and savings transactions by poor people have attracted much interest since the idea emerged in the late 1970s, and there are now many examples in the developing world. The instruments that emerged tend to be better suited to supporting small non-farm business development, rather than farming. This is because repayments start as soon as the loan is received, whereas a farmer must wait until after the harvest when credit is taken for agricultural inputs.

The classic argument for this class of interventions is about promotion, namely that relaxing borrowing constraints facing poor people allows them to invest and so giving them new freedom, including to eventually escape poverty by their own means.

---

[122] This point is made by Binswanger et al. (1995).

[123] On complementary policies for supporting smallholder agriculture, see IFAD (2011, ch. 5).

[124] As discussed by Alain de Janvry (1981) in the case of Latin America. For further discussion of land reforms, see Binswanger et al. (1995), Fields (2001, ch. 10), and Lipton (2009).

[125] Berry (2011, 642), in a review of Lipton (2009).

Credit and savings are also potentially important instruments for protection, by allowing poor households to more effectively smooth their consumption in the face of income fluctuations.

Much of the early (and ongoing) enthusiasm for microfinance was really little more than advocacy, with weak conceptual and empirical foundations. In recent times there has been a rise in popular concern in the media (in South Asia especially) about over-borrowing by poor people once given new access to microfinance as well as high interest rates charged by many "for profit" lenders to poor people. Much of this concern also appears to stem from anecdotes, and the debate has also become politicized. Positive average impacts do not, of course, mean that there are no losers among recipients. This is probably true of all antipoverty policies but it is especially so in the case of credit-based interventions. Risk is not eliminated, shocks do occur and mistakes are made, such as due to faulty expectations. There will be both gainers and losers.

The earliest and still most famous example of this class of policies is Bangladesh's group-based lending scheme, *Grameen Bank* (GB). GB has made a conscious effort to reach the poor both through their eligibility criteria and their branch location decisions, which (in contrast to traditional banks) have favored areas where there are unexploited opportunities for poor people to switch to non-farm activities.[126] Research on GB has indicated that the scheme has helped in both protection and promotion; in the former case by facilitating consumption smoothing and in the latter by helping to build the physical and human assets of poor people.[127] This was found in research by Mark Pitt and Shahidur Khandker who relied on the design features of GB for identifying its impact, notably that it is targeted to the landless, for identifying impacts.[128] Given that access to GB raises the returns to being landless, the returns to having land will be higher in villages that do not have access to GB credit. Thus, comparing the returns to having land between villages that are eligible for GB and those not (with controls for other observable differences) reveals the impact of access to GB credit. Put another way, the study measured impact by the mean gain among households who are landless from living in a village that is eligible for GB, less the corresponding gain among those with land. The results indicate a generally positive impact on measures relevant to both protection and promotion. This was confirmed in a subsequent study using survey data on 3,000 households spanning twenty years.[129] The success of GB has led to a proliferation of microfinance schemes in Bangladesh, with over five hundred providers at the time of writing, and the idea has spread to many other countries. Women have often been favored by these schemes.

Even careful observational studies require identifying assumptions that can be questioned, and there has been a debate in the literature about the robustness of past findings on the impacts of GB.[130] This is a type of policy intervention for which it will inevitably be hard to convince everyone of the validity of the identifying assumptions

---

[126] See Ravallion and Wodon (2000b).

[127] An early contribution to knowledge about GB was made by Hossain (1988).

[128] See Pitt and Khandker (1998).

[129] See by Khandker and Samad (2014).

[130] See Morduch (1999), Roodman and Morduch (2014), and Duvendack and Palmer-Jones (2012). Also see the detailed rejoinder in Pitt and Khandker (2012).

given the likelihood of unobservable factors jointly influencing take-up and impacts. Experimental evaluations relying on randomized assignment have offered the hope of more robust results and there have been some interesting examples. A study of the impacts of opening new micro-finance bank branches in the slums of Hyderabad India found that overall borrowing, business start-ups, and spending on consumer durables (but not non-durables) increased in the areas that were randomly assigned the new branches relative to the control areas.[131] However, the study did not find evidence of positive impacts on health, education, or women's self-efficacy. A recent review of lessons from such randomized evaluations concluded that there was "a consistent pattern of mostly positive but not transformative effects."[132] The review pointed to positive effects on access to credit—which is consistent with the presumption that such access was constrained in the first place. Relaxing such a binding constraint on choice must bring welfare gains. Whether they will be evident in current consumption or income and (hence) current poverty is another matter, and here the evidence is mixed.

Heterogeneity is evident in the evaluations to date. This was the focus of a recent experimental evaluation of access to micro-credit by working-age women in Mexico (under the *Compartamos Banco* scheme).[133] The authors found positive average impacts in a number of dimensions. There was heterogeneity in the impacts, but they found little evidence of significant losses, including among poor borrowers. More research on the benefits and costs of microfinance schemes can be expected.

We have seen a huge shift in thinking about this class of policies over the last two hundred years; in the days when poor men and women were routinely blamed for their poverty, giving them a loan would not have made much sense. Of course, identifying credit-market failures as one cause of poverty does not imply that credit for the poor will solve the problem. But well-designed programs have a role, as a complement to policies for both protection and promotion.

Poor Area Development Programs

Almost all countries (at all levels of development) have their well-recognized "poor areas," in which the incidence of absolute poverty is unusually high by national standards. We would hope, and under certain conditions expect, that the growth process will help these poor areas catch up. This process appears often to have been slow, and geographic divergence has sometimes been evident. This has led to antipoverty policies focused on lagging poor areas. "Poverty maps" are widely used in such geographic targeting (chapter 5).

The existence of lagging poor areas has led to a great many examples of poor area development projects—one of the oldest forms of development assistance, though under various headings (including "Integrated Rural Development Projects" and "Community Driven Development"). Extra resources are channeled to the targeted poor areas for infrastructure and services and developing (farm and non-farm) enterprises. Emphasis is often given to local citizen participation in deciding what is

[131] See Banerjee et al. (2009).
[132] See Banerjee et al. (2014).
[133] See Angelucci, Karlan, and Zinman (2013).

done, although a survey of the available evaluative research found somewhat mixed success given the scope for capture by local elites.[134] It is widely agreed that poor areas are typically characterized by low capital to labor ratios, but there is less agreement on whether it is better to augment local capital—investing in lagging poor areas—or provide support for out migration. Geographic externalities clearly play an important role, but a still poorly understood role for lack of convincing empirical research.

In the case of China, there is evidence of pervasive geographic externalities, whereby households living in poor areas have lower growth prospects than seemingly identical households living in well-off areas.[135] This suggests that there is scope for poor-area development in assuring longer term promotion from poverty, as well as protection. However, here too the evidence is mixed on the success of the policies found in practice.[136]

The main concerns about the incentive effects of poor-area programs relate to the responses of local governments to external aid and to migration. Box 10.7 discusses how spillover effects can be generated by local government responses to external aid.

For example, one study demonstrated that local government spending allocations changed in response to efforts by higher levels of government to target poor villages in rural China, dampening the targeting outcomes.[137] On migration, it appears to be a widely accepted assumption that there is limited intra-rural mobility in developing countries, sometimes reflecting institutional and policy impediments (such as local administrative powers for land reallocation as in China). It is not clear how confident we can still be in making that assumption. Box 10.8 discusses this example further.

---

*Box 10.7 **Spillover Effects through Local Public Spending Choices**

A theoretical model of the local public spending response to external aid can help inform an assessment of the likely spillover effects. There are two types of villages, indexed $j = A, N$ for Aid recipient and Non-recipient. Let G_j denote the local government's spending on its own poor-area development programs in villages of type j. Total spending is $G = G_A + G_N$. (I treat the two groups as having equal size but this does not change the main result as long as the group sizes are fixed.) The external aid provides extra spending in the amount AID in the type-A villages, so that total spending on poor-area programs in the project villages is $G_A + AID$.

The local government has a preference ordering over its spending allocation across villages and its spending on all other activities, denoted Z. The preference ordering is represented by the welfare function:

$$W(G_A + AID, G_N, Z).$$

---

[134] See Mansuri and Rao (2012).

[135] See Jalan and Ravallion (2002) and Ravallion (2005a).

[136] For example, contrast the findings of Jalan and Ravallion (1998b) with Chen et al. (2009) on poor area programs in China.

[137] See Chen et al. (2009).

This function is strictly increasing in all three elements, and to trace out smooth convex iso-welfare contours (the government's "indifference curves"). (It simplifies the analytics if we also assume that the function is additively separable between its components, though this can be weakened.) The local government maximizes W subject to its local (exogenous) revenue constraint, which creates an upper bound on $G + Z$.

Under these assumptions one finds that the external aid will displace local government spending in the project villages, increase spending in the comparison villages, but decrease total local government spending across both sets of villages. The implication for an evaluation is plain: Comparing outcome changes over time between SWP and (matched) non-SWP villages in the same counties will underestimate the project's true impact.

Further reading: See Chen et al. (2009).

Box 10.8 The Southwest China Poverty Reduction Project

In 1986, the Government of China designated about 15% of the country's 2,200 counties as "poor counties," which would receive extra assistance, mainly in the form of credit for development projects. Past research has suggested that the designated poor counties are in fact poor (by a range of defensible criteria) and that they have seen higher growth rates than one would have otherwise expected (Jalan and Ravallion 1998b; Park et al. 2002). The gains have not been sufficient to reverse the underlying tendency for growth divergence (whereby poorer counties tend to have lower growth rates) and there is evidence that the impacts on economic growth may have declined in the 1990s (Park et al. 2002). Within these designated poor counties, geographic pockets of extreme poverty have persisted to the present day, mainly in upland areas.

The Southwest China Poverty Reduction Project (SWP) was introduced in 1995 with the aim of reversing the fortunes of selected poor villages in the designated poor counties of Guangxi, Guizhou, and Yunnan. About one-quarter of the villages were selected for the SWP (1,800 out of 7,600 villages). The aim was to choose relatively poor villages within these counties, with selection based on objective criteria, although not formulaic. The program emphasized community participation in multi-sectoral interventions (including farming, animal husbandry, infrastructure, and social services). The selection was done by the county government's project office in consultation with provincial and central authorities and the World Bank.

Chen et al. (2009) evaluated the poverty impacts of this ambitious project, up to ten years after it began and four years after disbursements ended. Data were collected on 2,000 households in project and non-project areas, spanning ten years. A double-difference estimator of the program's impact (on top of

continued

Box 10.8 **(Continued)**

pre-existing governmental programs) revealed sizable short-term income gains that were mostly saved. Only small and statistically insignificant gains to mean consumption emerged in the longer term—though in rough accord with the average gain to permanent income. The main results are robust to corrections for various sources of selection bias, including village targeting and interference due to spillover effects generated by the response of local governments to the external aid.

The study also found evidence of significant spillover effects from the treatment villages to the comparison villages. The main way this happened was through the behavior of local governments, which diverted some of their own spending from the treated villages to other villages in response to the project. (This is a perfectly rational response of the local governments, and is to be expected.) Correcting for this spillover effect increased the impact estimates, but did not alter the main conclusions of the study.

The main finding was that the use of community-based beneficiary selection greatly reduced the overall impact, given that the educated poor were under-covered. The study's findings point to a potentially serious trade-off facing such community-based programs. The desirability of more participatory processes of local beneficiary selection may well come at a large cost to overall impacts, including on poverty. To assure larger impacts one would need to override this process by dictating the types of households that should be targeted, based on the likely benefits to them. It is unclear if this is feasible.

Further reading: Chen et al. (2009).

The balance between policy efforts to invest in poor areas versus encouraging exit from those areas has long been debated. In principle the low capital-to-labor ratios (K/L) in poor areas can be dealt with by either increasing the K or reducing the L. Some countries have combined poor area programs with restrictions on migration (such as in China where poor-area programs exist side by side with the *hukou* system that we heard about in chapter 8). This is suggestive of the left hand of government policy trying to undo the damage created by the right hand. There is evidence from the United States of significant benefits over the longer term (ten to fifteen years) in terms of health and subjective welfare from voucher policies that encourage outmigration from poor areas to less poor areas.[138] Children in the take-up families also benefit later through better schooling and higher earnings.[139]

There is still much we do not know about the impacts of poor-area development efforts, especially over the longer term, and the trade-offs faced against policy options,

---

[138] For a review of the evidence on one such program of the US government, *Moving to Opportunity*, see Ludwig et al. (2012). The vouchers were randomly assigned in the baseline (chapter 6).

[139] See Chetty et al. (2015). These benefits were confined to children under thirteen years at the time of moving.

including assisted migration. While local infrastructure development is clearly crucial to fighting poverty, it has not attracted the degree of attention in evaluative research that we have seen in social policies. Here an important factor is the extent to which "development impact" is challenged by donors and citizens. Impact is too often taken for granted with infrastructure. By contrast, the "softer" social policies have had to work hard to justify themselves, and evaluative research has served an important role. If the presumption of impact is routinely challenged by donors, aid organizations, and citizens, then we will see stronger incentives for learning about impact and fewer knowledge gaps.

Conclusions

PAST PROGRESS AND FUTURE CHALLENGES

The last two hundred years have witnessed a transition in the literature and policy debates between two radically different views of poverty. Early on, there was little reason to think that poor people had the potential to be anything other than poor; poverty would inevitably persist. Prominent thinkers even argued that poverty was necessary for economic advancement, since without it, who would farm the land, work the factories, and staff the armies? Avoiding hunger was the necessary incentive for doing work.

This way of thinking still left a role for policy in providing a degree of protection from shocks, which helped assure social stability in the wake of crises. The protection motive for antipoverty policy goes back well over two thousand years in both Western and Eastern thought. While the need for social protection was well understood in principle among the elites, their support tended to fade in normal times, and often needed to be re-established in new crises. However, mass poverty was largely taken for granted. Beyond short-term palliatives to address shocks, there was little or no perceived scope for public effort to permanently reduce poverty. Promotional antipoverty policies made little sense to those in power.

In the second, modern, view, poverty is not only seen as a social ill that can be avoided through public action, but doing so is seen as perfectly consistent with a robust growing economy. Indeed, the right antipoverty policies are expected to contribute to that growth by removing material constraints on the freedom of individuals to pursue their own economic interests. Granted, the commitment to fighting poverty is not universal today. Some observers still point to behaviors of poor people as causes of their poverty. Distributional struggles continue everywhere. Advocates of antipoverty policies are often frustrated by the setbacks, and there is still much to be done. However, the progress that has been made in both thinking and action is undeniable. For example, it would seem unlikely that anything more than a small minority of people today would accept how the founder of the modern police force Patrick Colquhoun (1806, 7) wrote about poverty over two hundred years ago:

> Poverty . . . is a most necessary and indispensable ingredient in society, without which nations and communities could not exist in a state of civilization. It is the lot of man—it is the source of wealth, since without poverty there would be no labour, and without labour there could be no riches, no refinement, no comfort, and no benefit to those who may be possessed of wealth.

Recognizing such a marked transition in mainstream thinking over two hundred years makes one more optimistic that the idea of eliminating poverty can be more than a dream.

Two key historical steps in the transition in thinking about poverty can be identified, dubbed here the First and Second Poverty Enlightenments, and each spanning a period of only twenty or so years. The First Poverty Enlightenment, near the end of the eighteenth century, saw the emergence of a new respect for poor people, as people— no longer the "shadows in a painting" or merely serving some purely instrumental role as the means of production. Instead, the economy came to be seen as a tool for promoting human welfare, including that of poor people. This was an important insight of Adam Smith. The Second Poverty Enlightenment, in the 1960s and 1970s, came with the strongest case yet for comprehensive antipoverty policies. Poverty came to be widely seen as a severe constraint, possibly the most important constraint, on freedom and personal self-fulfillment, and on aggregate economic growth. A consensus emerged that poverty was unacceptable, though with continuing debates on what to do about it.

While the foundation for this change was laid in the First Poverty Enlightenment— notably in seeing all human beings as morally equal, with legitimate desires for freedom and self-fulfillment—it was really only by the time of the Second Poverty Enlightenment that it came to be understood that freedom and self-fulfillment required that people were not constrained by material deprivations. Poverty was no longer seen as some inevitable, even natural, condition, but as something that could and should be eliminated. The state came to be given a prominent role in helping to assure that all individuals have access to the essential material conditions for their own personal fulfillment, arguably the most important requirement for equity, but also the key to breaking out of poverty traps. Antipoverty policy came to be seen as a matter of both promotion and protection. Along with rising real wages and (hence) savings by poor people, public education systems, sound health systems, and reasonably well functioning financial markets were deemed to be crucial elements for the next generation to escape poverty, for good.

The policy changes were rarely easy; indeed, they typically only emerged out of much debate and even conflict. The 1960s and 1970s was an unusual period in the extent of support that emerged for pro-poor policies. Opposition resurfaced in the 1980s. But progressive changes in thinking and policy survived.

Prevailing "mental models" for explaining poverty also changed. The notion that poverty is due to the bad behaviors of poor men and women is long-standing and is still heard today. However, a rival model has become dominant, emphasizing instead the external economic, social and political constraints facing poor people. The constraints sometimes stemmed from undemocratic political institutions that did little more than preserve the advantages of powerful elites. But even with reasonably open political institutions, there can be severe economic constraints. These include poverty traps, such as when threshold effects entail that small gains in wealth or productivity bring no lasting gain, or group memberships have causal effects on living standards. Or the constraints reflect more normal dynamics of poverty reduction, whereby imperfect or incomplete markets, uncorrected by governments, create inequitable access to productive or financial inputs and technologies, with consequently slow progress for poor people. To come full circle, the literature in economic psychology has also suggested that the behaviors that have often been identified as causes of poverty (such as myopia) may in fact be its effects.

The evolution in thinking came with an increasing respect for the constrained choices made by poor people. Policymakers became somewhat more sensitive to and respectful of those choices, and focused more on expanding options in life rather than constraining them. Nonetheless, paternalism remains common. While it can be readily granted that people make mistakes, well-intentioned policymakers presume too often that they are better informed about what poor families need than are those families themselves. A similar point holds for how aid donors often treat aid recipients.

Progress against Poverty

Roughly one billion people in the world are living in poverty as judged by the frugal standards of how "poverty" is defined in the world's poorest countries. As best can be determined from the data available, roughly the same number of people in the world lived in extreme poverty two hundred years ago. The big difference is that the one billion accounted for more than four out of five people in the world in the early nineteenth century, while today they account for less than one in five.

There is no denying that we have seen huge progress against absolute poverty in the world over the last two hundred years. The pace of progress accelerated after the middle of the twentieth century, and it accelerated again from the turn of the present century.

However, we have also seen a number of more sobering features of how the distribution of income is evolving. Despite the economic growth and expansion of more progressive social policies that we have seen in the developing world, the consumption floor—the lower bound to typical levels of living—does not appear to have been lifted much over the last thirty years and has stayed close to a level of about one half of the (already frugal) $1.25 a day line used to measure the incidence of extreme poverty globally. In this sense, the poorest have been left behind. While far fewer people live near the floor, the 400 million or so who live within a meager $0.20 of that floor remain extremely vulnerable.

It should also be recognized that much less progress is evident if one allows for growing relative deprivation and the rising costs of social inclusion. We are seeing rising numbers of relatively poor people in the world, alongside falling numbers of absolutely poor. These are two sides of the same coin; success against extreme absolute poverty has come hand in hand with upward pressure on the incidence of relative poverty.

Policies have helped by both supporting the expansion of economic opportunities and in helping to assure that poor people are able to benefit from those opportunities. The pessimism of two hundred years ago about the scope for pro-poor economic growth started to fade by the late nineteenth century and gave way to cautious optimism by the mid-twentieth century. The evidence suggests that economic growth typically comes with falling measures of absolute poverty. Even though the floor has proved to be rather "sticky," the levels of living of most poor people tend to improve with overall economic expansion in market economies. There are exceptions—highly inequitable growth processes can bring little or no gain to poor people—but they are the exceptions. In some settings, the growth unleashed by periods of pro-market reform has brought impressive absolute gains to poor people over a sustained period, such as China since the late 1970s. In other settings, the gains to poor people from growth-promoting reforms have been more muted. But as a rule gains have come.

That does not mean that growth in market economies is typically equitable by any measure. Rising relative inequality in growing economies has been about as common as falling inequality, and rising absolute inequality is the norm in growing economies. Even without rising inequality, high initial inequalities in various dimensions can greatly dull the gains to poor people from growth, and diminish the scope for reform and growth. China started its pro-market reform process with huge distributional advantages; the relatively low levels of inequality in command over agricultural land and in human capital facilitated both growth and poverty reduction. India, by contrast, did not have such advantages at the time its reforms began, and thus progress against poverty was slower.

The social costs of adjustment in a changing economy can often be high and the economic benefits can be quite unevenly distributed. Technological advances have sometimes created poverty by putting people out of work, although much technological progress has done more to increase the aggregate demand for labor than to reduce it. Antipoverty policies can play an important positive role in protection from economic and agro-climatic shocks. While this protection role for antipoverty policy goes back two thousand years or more, success has been uneven.

The big change in policy thinking over the last two hundred years has been the emergence of promotional policies. There are many examples, but the set of policies that have focused on human development must be put top of the list. This includes mass schooling and better nutrition and healthcare, especially for children. Children growing up in poorer families tend to suffer greater human development gaps, with lasting consequences for their adult lives. Successful public efforts to promote human development have been poverty reducing over the longer term.

There are both demand- and supply-sides to this change. New technologies lead to demands for new skills, which affordable schooling and healthcare help provide. When education expansion comes in step with the rising demand for skills the growth process tends to be more equitable. A smarter workforce also needs to be healthy, and much progress has been made in providing better health and nutrition for all. Governments are doing better in supporting promotional policies. Granted, there is still a long way to go, but progress has been made, and we now know a lot more about what needs to be done, drawing on global experience.

The history of thought on antipoverty policies provides examples of both successes and failures. At times, influential writings have misguided efforts for fighting poverty. At times, the enthusiasm for action has been out-of-step with the capacity for implementation and enforcement. Successful policies respect local constraints on the information available and administrative capabilities. There is a lasting lesson on the importance of tailoring intervention to the realities of the setting. Tapping local information can help identify the need for help and in responding. We have seen greater use of participatory, community-based (governmental and non-governmental), institutions for income support and/or service provision. However, these should not be seen as substitutes for sound public administration, which will still be needed in guiding and monitoring local institutions.

Knowledge has played an important role. New data and research influence public thinking and policymaking, and teach us about the efficacy of policy responses. This feeds back—in time but with varying lags—to create better policies. Of course, politics often gets in the way of pro-poor reforms that threaten those in power. Protracted debates and sometimes even open conflicts have been needed to assure better policies. Popular writings and other media have supported this struggle by transforming knowledge into public awareness and sometimes shame. Success of the (often painful and protracted) struggles for empowerment came roughly hand in hand with better informed policy debates and (ultimately) better policies, including better institutions.

Technology and knowledge are not independent, but interact. Here political voice can play an important role. Technological progress creates immediate opportunities for some, and promises the hope of a better future for others. But that is unlikely to be sufficient to assure that the opportunities are widely shared; indeed, the most plausible prior based on history must be that new opportunities will initially be captured by those most advantaged to do so, and that others will be left behind for some period. Well-informed political action is often needed to assure that poor people can benefit from technical progress and other sources of new opportunities, such as through external trade openness.

There must also be the expressed public demand for action to promote more equal opportunities. This is fueled by complementary changes in the aspirations of poor people. Poor parents need to have a realistic hope that their children can be anything but poor. Low aspirations reflect and rationalize lack of opportunity. This appears to have changed appreciably in today's rich world by the turn of the twentieth century, with more hope that those born poor had some decent chance of escaping poverty through their own efforts, and the sacrifices made by their parents. Public support congruent with these aspirations and efforts came to be demanded by citizens, and a degree of support came in time.

Changing aspirations of poor parents reflect both knowledge about new opportunities and new efficacy in seizing those opportunities. In the history of the successful transitions out of extreme poverty made in today's rich world, many people came to protest, join community or religious groups, labor and civil-rights movements, or political coalitions of one sort or another to lobby for governmental action. They often met staunch resistance and a great many brave people sacrificed their liberty and even their lives in those struggles over centuries. Successful promotion policies took time to evolve and were invariably mediated by politics. However, in due course, a self-reinforcing cycle emerged in the successful countries to help assure a sustained and (over time) more rapid escape from absolute poverty. Success in implementing partial antipoverty policies often fostered success in securing broader coverage and implementing new initiatives. Progress could be slow and the cycle has been broken at times. The history of thinking and action on poverty provides ample illustrations of the fragility of the progress that has been seen. Each Poverty Enlightenment was followed by a backlash in thinking and policymaking. But progress was made.

Over time and across countries, one tends to see more attention to direct interventions against poverty when there is less poverty. The balance between protection and promotion has also evolved over time. While the change has not been the same everywhere, or always in the same direction, it is clear that over some two hundred years we have seen greater efforts at promotion, and this has both fueled and been fueled by declining numbers living in extreme poverty. Many of the relatively new policies discussed in this book combine protection with promotion.

Explaining the Transition in Thinking

Why have we seen this transition toward more promotional policies? It is plausible that the political economy of antipoverty policy changes with the level of poverty. One can think of two equilibria. When the incidence of poverty is persistently very high, the wealth distribution implies a high cost to the non-poor of getting people out of a low-level trap (including the necessary infrastructure investments). Nor are the benefits obvious to the elites in an economy in which few economic opportunities appear to be available to children from poor families beyond those available to their parents. Thus, it may be accepted that the only realistic future prospect for the children of laboring (and hence poor) parents is to be laboring and poor as well. Schooling will be seen as socially wasteful. There may also be concerns among the ruling elites that mass education will (in due course) undermine the authority of the regime—that the poor would become frustrated with their lot in life and rebel. If pressed, the elites could well have imagined the theoretical possibility of a big push lifting the entire distribution in a beneficial way. But far more modest reforms were all that could be seriously contemplated. Working-class children would be born poor and stay poor. Limited protection from shocks becomes the main focus, as in England's Poor Laws and India's famine relief policies.

In this context, there may be little or no support among those in power for reducing poverty through direct interventions—including escaping from poverty traps. A trickle down process of poverty reduction through economic growth may then be the only feasible route, although high levels of poverty will make this a slow process.

We can see something like this pattern today, on comparing different regions of the developing world. In sub-Saharan Africa and South Asia, where poverty is greatest, direct interventions are bringing less benefit to the poor. There are some efforts, and some successes, but with very limited coverage of the poor population, and often with social protection as the primary goal, not promotion. This is not too surprising. Very poor countries have little capacity for redistribution as a means of eliminating poverty. In some cases, the simple arithmetic suggests that there are too few rich people to support this strategy, even before considering incentive effects and administrative constraints. The challenge of redistribution is magnified further by the fact that a large share of economic activity tends to be informal (and hence beyond the administrative reach of tax authorities) in poorer countries, entailing a lower effective tax base for financing redistribution. It is a cruel irony that in settings where the extent of absolute poverty is high we also tend to find lower economic and administrative capacities for fighting poverty through direct interventions. In poorer places it is just harder to fight poverty this way.

By contrast, in the second equilibrium, at sufficiently low levels of poverty, a wider range of more active policies for both promotion and protection become feasible. The political economy switches. Moving from the first equilibrium to the second is not easy, however, given that poverty and inequality also impede overall growth prospects.

These are tendencies not inevitabilities. Implementation of effective policies also depends on prevailing social preferences and institutions. Some poor countries and provinces within countries have demonstrated an ability to deliver comprehensive antipoverty policies. Elsewhere, however, inequalities, hierarchical social orders, and social divisions make it harder to attain consensus for effective antipoverty policies. Inequalities of political voice have not helped. It has been argued in political science that the extent to which the political system concentrates power influences the interests served by the chosen policies. By this view—dating back to at least Plato's *The Republic*—democracy leads to more socially representative and (hence) egalitarian policies.

It is tempting to argue that the transition to a more comprehensive agenda for antipoverty policies—combining promotion with protection—was the result of the switch to electoral democracy from the undemocratic political systems that were the norm globally until the end of the nineteenth century. Broad suffrage (for men) tended to precede mass schooling among the industrialized countries. The standard characterization of development in Western Europe postulates a linear path from the development of democratic political institutions to more pro-poor redistributive and growth-promoting policies. By this view, electoral democracy was the reason why we saw the emergence of promotional antipoverty policies.

However, there is clearly more to the story. Three points can be noted. First, democracy does not have an especially good reputation for favoring longer term investments, such as promotional antipoverty policies. This was another of Plato's concerns—that, while democracy in poor places may favor poor people, it is quite myopic about the interests it served. Apprehensions about democracy encouraging deficit financing of popular short-term programs echo this concern. Nor do the concerns about the scope for the capture of the democratic political process by rich elites sit well with any view that the process is automatically pro-poor.

Second, one can easily point to undemocratic states for which promotional antipoverty policies are far more prominent than effective protection policies (China is a good example), and democratic states where the imbalance goes in the other direction (e.g., India). Empirically, it is quite hard to maintain a "one-size-fits-all" model of a linear development path from democracy to more equitable growth.

Third, electoral democracy did not suddenly appear in Western Europe and North America, but it was the outcome of a long struggle by disadvantaged groups (including poor people) to secure basic rights for all. More inclusive political reforms were as much an effect as a cause of economic change. It was well over one hundred years between the emergence of popular protest movements for suffrage in England and their success in assuring a legal right to vote for all men (literally just men initially). That success was built on a foundation of legal institutions that could serve to protect individual rights, buttressed by important changes in philosophical and economic thought. Legal statutes were rarely sufficient, however, and struggles for genuine suffrage in rich countries continued well into the twentieth century. (In the United States, enforcing voting legal rights at local level was a key motivator of the civil rights movement in the 1960s.) Today's rich countries clearly did not follow a linear path from democracy to development. More plausibly, the struggle for democracy came side-by-side with the struggle for promotional policies, such as mass schooling.

This is not to deny the importance of the political voice of poor people in the domains of economic life that matter to them. But voice is the key, not electoral democracy *per se*. Poor people in non-democratic states can still have effective political voice in the affairs that matter; yet elsewhere poor people can find themselves effectively disempowered in a country with a robust electoral democracy nationally.

The time taken by the struggles for both suffrage and promotional policies depended on a number of other factors, which had an independent role in the transition in thinking and policy related to poverty. Knowledge about the living conditions of poor people has repeatedly played a shaming role in stimulating public action. The preferences of donors and taxpayers have also played a role; at least some of the non-poor are happy to be more generous when they know that the recipients are being compelled to do something to help themselves escape poverty in the future, thus allowing a coalition to form in favor of certain promotional policies (such as conditional cash transfers).

Technical progress was undoubtedly stifled to some degree by persistent poverty and inequality. But technical progress eventually happened, and it often generated greater demand for more skilled labor, which generated political demands for better working-class schooling. The expansion in production possibilities also helped directly in avoiding wealth poverty traps. Such changes in the economy came with new demands on the state. A more mobile and skilled labor force was essential for the modern capitalist economy, and this put pressures on the state to take on functions for both promotion and protection. And the initial successes of promotional policies would have helped create a virtuous cycle by reducing the fiscal burden of the types of policies needed to assure that mass promotion is politically feasible.

Knowledge Challenges

History teaches us that new knowledge and public awareness can at times tilt the balance of political forces to foster pro-poor reforms. Ideas and data have mattered. So it is fitting to discuss here the key challenges ahead in assuring that knowledge about poverty and antipoverty policies continues to improve.

Monitoring performance against poverty poses a number of data challenges. While there has been huge progress in collecting primary household survey data, many problems remain. There are persistent lags and uneven coverage. There are also continuing concerns about the comparability of the surveys over time and across countries, although there has been too little research on whether these concerns are really justified, and what types of differences between surveys matter most.

Despite the gains in knowledge, there is still much we do not know and there are new challenges threatening even past gains. A set of agreed international protocols for surveys (similar to the System of National Accounts) is long overdue. For example, while best practices can be identified by researchers, there is no commonly agreed set of standards for defining how a consumption or income aggregate should be formed at the household level. Conventional household surveys are also demanding and selective compliance with the randomized assignments of those to be interviewed appears to be an increasing problem. There are concerns about underreporting and biased samples. The rich are especially difficult to interview, and this task does not seem to be getting any easier. The technologies for doing surveys in the field are advancing and may well help.

New sources of data are also helping. While subjective data—essentially asking people whether they feel poor—have traditionally been shunned by economists, this is changing. New insights are emerging but also new puzzles. For example, subjective data often point to more significant scale economies in consumption than is typically assumed in practice by economists, with potentially important implications for some aspects of our knowledge about poverty, notably its demographics. But there are continuing uncertainties about whether the economies of scale suggested by subjective data are real welfare effects or psychological biases in such data, whereby intrinsically happier people tend to have larger families. Some of the claims found in the (large) literature on the determinants of average happiness are of questionable veracity.

Advances in analytic methods have expanded the range of the types of data that can be used in studying poverty and inequality. Different types of surveys, census and administrative data sets are being brought into the picture and are sometimes linked in innovative ways that improve knowledge. Supplementary data from income tax records have helped improve knowledge about the overall distribution of income (especially top incomes in rich countries). Surveys specializing on demographic and health factors have provided useful insights into non-income aspects of welfare, including intra-household inequalities. Imputation and small-area estimation methods have allowed us to learn more from short surveys of large samples. There will undoubtedly be further innovations of this sort.

Other types of data relevant to poverty measurement are facing new challenges, including price data, for which surveying practices and analytic methods are of uneven quality and worryingly variable over time. We still know very little about sub-national spatial price differentials, which are significant in many developing countries. Neither ignoring these differences nor relying on shortcut methods based on expenditure data alone are adequate responses. The weak integration of macro and micro data is another concern that warrants more attention. We need a better understanding of the discrepancies often found between survey-based consumption aggregates and those implied by the national accounts.

Poverty can now be seen as a global problem, but we still do not study it that way. Two worlds co-exist with very different approaches to measurement and even different databases. We need a truly global concept of poverty that recognizes that there are both absolute and relative dimensions and also unifies them in a consistent framework. We still do not have a globally relevant micro-data archive for research on poverty and inequality. There have been some important initiatives but they have been segmented—one or two databases have emerged that are good for work on rich countries but of limited use elsewhere, and similarly there are some good initiatives for low and middle-income countries.

It has long been recognized that even an excellent measure of command over commodities is an incomplete basis for assessing welfare. Multi-purpose integrated surveys and more specialized surveys (often on larger samples) have helped expand assessments to embrace other "non-income" dimensions. Recognizing that poverty is multidimensional and that we are genuinely interested in the joint distribution across multiple dimensions does not imply we need to add up the multiple dimensions into arbitrarily weighted composites collapsed into a single dimension. This is artificial knowledge that should not persuade someone who looks closely at how the mashup was formed.

We also face many knowledge challenges in learning about policy. Public and private efforts to fight poverty get more and more attention, which is a good thing. There is, however, a serious risk that our knowledge is becoming skewed toward a subset of the interventions that matter, and even then to a subset of the real-world circumstances in which those policies can be applied. The attractions to researchers of doing randomized control trials are considerable, and should not be dismissed as being purely of interest to researchers. However, randomized control trials are only one of the tools we need going forward. They will not answer all of the questions policymakers ask about the interventions that are studied this way, and they will answer almost none of the questions being asked about the many other relevant interventions that cannot be studied this way. Informing antipoverty policy going forward will probably require a more coordinated and holistic approach to identifying and responding to pressing knowledge gaps.

Two Paths Going Forward

The progress of the developing world against poverty has been uneven across countries and over time. However, since 2000, the developing world has been reducing the extreme poverty rate at slightly more than one percentage point per year—over three times the long-term annual rate for the world as a whole over the last two hundred years. If this progress can be maintained, then the developing world will eliminate at least the most extreme forms of absolute poverty in a much shorter timespan than did today's rich world. We should not, however, presume that the developing world's new pace of progress against poverty will automatically be sustained. That will require good policies and a measure of good luck.

There are two distinct paths going forward. The low-case, "pessimistic" trajectory entails that the developing world outside China regresses back to the relatively slow progress of the 1980s and 1990s. On this path, it would take another fifty years or more to lift one billion people out of poverty. This would surely be judged a poor performance. By contrast, an "optimistic path" would be to maintain the higher growth rate for the developing world as a whole seen since 2000 without a rise in overall inequality. If that could be achieved, then we can be reasonably confident of lifting that one billion people out of extreme poverty by sometime around 2030.

What are the principle challenges in assuring that the second path is followed? Among the list of threats one can identify to attaining that goal, inequality stands out as a major concern today. Rising inequality can mean that growth largely by-passes poor people. This has been happening in some countries of the rich world, including the United States. Experience among developing countries has been varied. Inequality falls about as often as it rises in growing developing countries, although absolute poverty measures tend to fall with growth. High-inequality countries have a harder time reducing poverty in that they typically need higher growth rates than low-inequality countries to attain the same pace of progress against poverty and their high inequality often makes that growth even harder to attain.

In thinking about the implications for policy, it is important to unpack inequality— to identify the specific dimensions most relevant to progress against poverty. Inequalities in access to good quality schooling and healthcare stand out in many developing countries today. In many rural economies, inequalities in access to land (including insecurity of rights over land) also remain an impediment to pro-poor growth. Gender inequalities stand out everywhere, though not just in terms of command over material goods.

More pro-poor policies call for better quality public institutions and services that are inclusive of the needs of poor people. With the required political will, there is much that can be done to improve health and education services in poor places and in making legal systems more inclusive. These are high priorities for antipoverty policy everywhere. There is also an important supportive role for redistribution and insurance using state-contingent transfers, ideally financed primarily by domestic taxation. And that role is unlikely to be temporary; all countries need a permanent safety net. In thinking about the (many) options, policymakers in developing countries should be more open to the idea of only broadly targeted and largely unconditional transfers (as distinct from finely targeted conditional transfers). Improving tax systems in poor countries to expand the revenue for domestic antipoverty policies must also be a high priority.

External development assistance should continue to play a role. This is ethically compelling in its own right but also as compensation for the costs rich countries impose on poor ones (such as through past contributions to the stock of greenhouse gases and the past injustices of colonial exploitation and trade restrictions). Aid has two important roles. First there will be emergency aid—short-term assistance to deal with crises. There will be concerns about moral hazard, which have to be taken seriously, but wealthier countries should be called upon to help poor countries deal with agro-climatic and other shocks. Second, development assistance should help foster the conditions for sustainable poverty reduction in the longer term, including institutional development and building better public administrations (such as for domestic resource mobilization). It must be acknowledged, however, that the record of development aid has been uneven, and not always well-considered in the light of what we have learned about the economics of poverty. For example, a common view among aid donors is that they need to incentivize better policies—to use a carrot and stick approach, rewarding good efforts and punishing bad ones. This is a risky strategy and may well push fragile states into a poor-institutions trap.

Market failures are an important reason why inequality matters to progress against poverty. Credit market failures have been a prominent concern. The policy responses entail some combination of efforts to make markets and institutions work better for poor people and efforts to compensate for market failures through other means, including redistribution. Inequality can also undermine the potential for making such policies happen. Those who benefit from their ability to capture new opportunities will often resist reforms that try to assure broader access to those opportunities, also given that poor people on their own have little current capacity to compensate the non-poor losers from pro-poor reforms. History is full of examples. English industrialists in the nineteenth century lobbied against compulsory schooling and against bans on child labor, and helped stall those reforms for a long period. Indian industrialists in the post-Independence decades lobbied for trade protection that diminished the scope for poverty reduction through labor-absorbing export-led manufacturing growth. Powerful landholders in both these countries (and elsewhere) effectively undermined the potential for land reforms and other redistributive policies. And in many countries, insiders in urban formal-sector labor markets (on both sides of the market) act to effectively restrict competition from outsiders.

"Inequality" is not a single idea, but takes many forms, and can be seen very differently by different people. This fact creates much debate—though sometimes this seems like a debate between ships passing in the dead of night, not seeing or understanding each other's perspective. The differences in how inequality is perceived can also stall pro-poor economic policies. A good example is the reaction that some people (understandably) have to rising absolute inequality. The once widely held "stylized fact" of development that higher relative inequality is the unavoidable "price" for growth and (hence) poverty reduction has been overturned in the light of new theories and evidence. Poor growing economies can and have avoided rising relative inequality, but they will have a much harder time avoiding rising absolute inequality—a rising absolute gap between the rich and the poor. And many citizens view inequality in absolute rather than relative terms. They are justified in taking that view; the concept of (relative) inequality held by most economists derives from an axiom that need not be accepted, and (indeed) appears to be rejected by many people. Those who view inequality as absolute and value it independently of poverty will see a trade-off between poverty and inequality. Ameliorating concerns about rising absolute inequality will almost certainly entail less progress against poverty.

Pro-poor policy reforms can also be stalled by another fear: horizontal inequality. Arthur Pigou (1949), one of the founders of public finance, called this "a sense of being unfairly treated . . . in itself an evil." Characterizations of the distributional impacts of policy reforms typically only consider the vertical redistributions involved—the differences in average impacts between rich and poor, say. Yet the political responses that can stall reform or create large social costs are in part horizontal in nature— between people at similar levels of living pre-reform. It can be deceptive to simply average across these horizontal differences. Some reforms also combine large losses (say) for a relatively small number of people with small gains to a large number. Citizens and policymakers are very likely to care about such differences. Better knowledge about horizontal impacts can also inform the design of social protection policies that anticipate what types of households lose.

Urban poverty is another challenge. The urbanization of poverty—whereby poverty rates fall more slowly in urban areas than in rural areas—is to be expected in almost any developing country that is successful in reducing poverty overall. Urban economies create new opportunities that poor people in rural areas have often sought out to improve their lives. Distorted urban labor markets can readily create excessive urbanization, as can the lack of effective public efforts to promote agriculture and rural development; indeed, many developing countries have gone even further in (explicitly or otherwise) taxing the rural economy to support the urban economy. Removing long-standing policy biases in both taxation and public spending remains a high priority for pro-poor growth. No less misguided are restrictions on migration and urban policies that undersupply services to poor urban residents, including rural migrants. Poor people are often trapped as the victims of policies that simultaneously repress agriculture while making life difficult for rural migrants. Development policymaking needs to be more neutral to these two sectors of economic activity. That will probably still entail an urbanization of poverty, but that should not be a cause for alarm as long as poverty is falling overall.

The sustainability of poverty-reduction efforts poses a further set of challenges in assuring that we can reach the optimistic path. We do not want to reach the poverty-reduction target only to fall back in subsequent years. On an encouraging note, research has suggested that lower initial levels of absolute poverty at a given mean consumption foster higher subsequent rates of growth in average living standards in developing countries and help to ensure that economic growth itself is poverty reducing. Thus, a "virtuous cycle" can be anticipated that would help to ensure the sustainability of the reduction in poverty.

Even the optimistic path will still leave another one billion or more people in the world who live above the frugal poverty lines typical of the poorest countries but are still poor by the standards of the countries they live in. Such relative poverty is still poverty. Welfare concerns about relative deprivation and costs of social inclusion demand higher real poverty lines as average incomes grow (though not as a constant proportion of average income). This type of poverty can also be eliminated, but it will almost certainly require much stronger redistributive efforts than we have seen to date in most countries. The policies are available. The bigger challenges ahead are in assuring the political will and administrative capabilities to implement and enforce sound antipoverty policies, and in adapting them to differing circumstances and evolving knowledge about their efficacy.

REFERENCES

Abel-Smith, Brian, and Peter Townsend. 1966. *The Poor and the Poorest: A New Analysis of the Ministry of Labour's Family Expenditure Surveys of 1953–54 and 1960.* London: Bell.

Abernethy, Simon. 2013. "Deceptive data? The New Survey of London Life and Labour 1928–31." Working Paper 16. Cambridge: Department of Economic and Social History, University of Cambridge, England.

Abler, David, and Vasant Sukhatme. 2006. "The 'Efficient but Poor' Hypothesis." *Review of Agricultural Economics* 28(3): 338–343.

Acemoglu, Daron. 2009. *Introduction to Economic Growth.* Princeton, NJ: Princeton University Press.

Acemoglu, Daron, Simon Johnson, and James Robinson. 2001. "The Colonial Origins of Comparative Development: An Empirical Investigation." *American Economic Review* 91(5): 1369–1401.

Acemoglu, Daron, Simon Johnson, and James Robinson. 2005. "Institutions as a Fundamental Cause of Long-Run Growth." In Philippe Aghion and Steven N. Durlauf (eds.), *Handbook of Economic Growth*, vol. 1A. Amsterdam: Elsevier.

Acemoglu, Daron, and Jörn-Steffen Pischke. 2003. "Minimum Wages and On-the-Job Training." *Research in Labor Economics* 22: 159–202.

Acemoglu, Daron, and James Robinson. 2000. "Political Losers as Barriers to Economic Development." *American Economic Review Papers and Proceedings* 90(2): 126–130.

Acemoglu, Daron, and James Robinson. 2006. *Economic Origins of Dictatorship and Democracy.* Cambridge: Cambridge University Press.

Acemoglu, Daron, and James Robinson. 2012. *Why Nations Fail. The Origins of Power, Prosperity and Poverty.* New York: Crown Business.

Acemoglu, Daron, and Fabrizio Zilibotti. 1997. "Was Prometheus Unbound by Chance?" *Journal of Political Economy* 105(4): 709–751.

Ackerson, Leland, and S. V. Subramanian. 2008. "State Gender Inequality, Socioeconomic Status and Intimate Partner Violence (IPV) in India: A Multilevel Analysis." *Australian Journal of Social Issues* 43(1): 81–102.

Addison, Tony, and Lionel Demery. 1985. "Macroeconomic Stabilization, Income Distribution and Poverty: A Preliminary Survey." Overseas Development Institute Working Paper 15. London: ODI.

Adelman, Irma, and Cynthia Taft Morris. 1973. *Economic Growth and Social Equity in Developing Countries.* Stanford, CA: Stanford University Press.

Agee, James, and Walker Evans. (1941) 2000. *Let Us Now Praise Famous Men: The American Classic, in Words and Pictures, of Three Tenant Families in the Deep South.* Boston, MA: Houghton Mifflin.

Aghion, Philippe, and Patrick Bolton. 1997. "A Theory of Trickle-Down Growth and Development." *Review of Economic Studies* 64: 151–172.

Aghion, Philippe, Eve Caroli, and Cecilia Garcia-Penalosa. 1999. "Inequality and Economic Growth: The Perspectives of the New Growth Theories." *Journal of Economic Literature* 37(4): 1615–1660.

Aghion, Philippe, and Peter Howitt. 1998. *Endogenous Growth Theory*. Cambridge, MA: MIT Press.

Ahluwalia, Montek S. 1976. "Inequality, Poverty and Development." *Journal of Development Economics* 3: 307–342.

Ahluwalia, Montek S. 2002. "Economic Reforms in India: A Decade of Gradualism." *Journal of Economic Perspectives* 16(3): 67–88.

Ahluwalia, Montek S., Nicholas G. Carter, and Hollis B. Chenery. 1979. "Growth and Poverty in Developing Countries." *Journal of Development Economics* 6: 299–341.

Ahmed, Akhter, Ruth Vargas Hill, Lisa C. Smith, Doris M. Wiesmann, and Tim Frankenberger. 2007. *The World's Most Deprived*. Washington DC: International Food Policy Research Institute.

Ainsworth, Martha, and Jacques van der Gaag. 1988. "Guidelines for Adapting the LSMS Living Standards Questionnaires to Local Conditions." Living Standards Measurement Study Working Paper 34. Washington, DC: World Bank.

Aizer, Anna, and Janet Currie. 2014. "The Intergenerational Transmission of Inequality: Maternal Disadvantage and Health at Birth." *Science* 344: 856–861.

Aizer, Anna, Shari Eli, Joseph Ferrie, and Adriana Lleras-Muney. 2014. "The Long Term Impacts of Cash Transfers to Poor Families." NBER Working Paper 20103. Cambridge, MA: NBER.

Ajwad, Mohamed Ihsan. 2006. "Coverage, Incidence and Adequacy of Safety Net Programs in India." Background paper for *Social Protection for a Changing India*. Washington, DC: World Bank.

Akerlof, George. 1970. "The Market for Lemons: Quality Uncertainty and the Market Mechanism." *Quarterly Journal of Economics* 84: 485–500.

Akerlof, George, and William Dickens. 1982. "The Economic Consequences of Cognitive Dissonance." *American Economic Review* 72(3): 307–319.

Akresh, Richard, Damien de Walque, and Harounan Kazianga. 2013. "Cash Transfers and Child Schooling: Evidence from a Randomized Evaluation of the Role of Conditionality." Policy Research Working Paper 6340. Washington, DC: World Bank.

Alam, M. Shahid. 2006. "Global Disparities since 1800: Trends and Regional Patterns." *Journal of World Systems Research* 12(2): 37–59.

Alatas, Vivi, Abhijit Banerjee, Rema Hanna, Benjamin A. Olken, and Julia Tobias. 2012. "Targeting the Poor: Evidence from a Field Experiment in Indonesia." *American Economic Review* 102(4): 1206–1240.

Albelda, Randy, Nancy Folbre, and the Center for Popular Economics. 1996. *The War on the Poor. A Defense Manual*. New York: New Press.

Albrecht, James, Lucas Navarro, and Susan Vroman. 2009. "The Effects of Labour Market Policies in an Economy with an Informal Sector." *Economic Journal* 119: 1105–1129.

Alderman, Harold. 2002. "Do Local Officials Know Something We Don't? Decentralization of Targeted Transfers in Albania." *Journal of Public Economics* 83: 375–404.

Alderman, Harold, John Hoddinott, and Bill Kinsey. 2006. "Long-Term Consequences of Early Childhood Malnutrition." *Oxford Economic Papers* 58(3): 450–474.

Alderman, Harold, and Ruslan Yemtsov. 2014. "How can Safety Nets Contribute to Economic Growth?" *World Bank Economic Review* 28: 1–20.

Alesina, Alberto, and Dani Rodrik. 1994. "Distributive Politics and Economic Growth." *Quarterly Journal of Economics* 108: 465–490.

Alik Lagrange, Arthur, and Martin Ravallion. 2015. "Policy Inconsistent Evaluation: A Case Study for a Large Workfare Program." NBER Working Paper 21041, National Bureau of Economic Research, Cambridge, Massachusetts.

Alkire, Sabina. 2002. *Valuing Freedoms*. Oxford: Oxford University Press.

Alkire, Sabina, and James Foster. 2011. "Counting and Multidimensional Poverty Measurement." *Journal of Public Economics* 95(7–8): 476–487.

Alkire, Sabina, and Maria Emma Santos. 2010. "Acute Multidimensional Poverty: A New Index for Developing Countries." Oxford Poverty and Human Development Initiative, Working Paper 38. Oxford: University of Oxford.

Allen, Robert. 2007. "Pessimism Preserved: Real Wages in the British Industrial Revolution." Department of Economics, Working Paper 314. Oxford: University of Oxford.

Allen, Robert. 2009. "Engels' Pause: Technical Change, Capital Accumulation, and Inequality in the British Industrial Revolution." *Explorations in Economic History* 46: 418–435.

Allen, Robert. 2013. "Poverty Lines in History, Theory, and Current International Practice." Mimeo. Oxford: Nuffield College, University of Oxford.

Almås, Ingrid. 2012. "International Income Inequality: Measuring PPP Bias by Estimating Engel Curves for Food." *American Economic Review* 102(2): 1093–1117.

Altonji, Joseph, Todd E. Elder, and Christopher R. Taber. 2005. "Selection on Observed and Unobserved Variables: Assessing the Effectiveness of Catholic Schools." *Journal of Political Economy* 113(1): 151–183.

Alvaredo, Facundo, Anthony B. Atkinson, Thomas Piketty, and Emmanuel Saez. 2014. "The World Top Incomes Database." http://topincomes.parisschoolofeconomics.eu/#Database: Paris: School of Economics.

Amiel, Yoram, and Frank Cowell. 1992. "Measurement of Income Inequality: Experimental Test by Questionnaire." *Journal of Public Economics* 47: 3–26.

Amiel, Yoram, and Frank Cowell. 1999. *Thinking about Inequality: Personal Judgment and Income Distributions.* Cambridge, MA: Cambridge University Press.

Anand, Sudhir. 1983. *Inequality and Poverty in Malaysia.* Oxford: Oxford University Press.

Anand, Sudhir, and Ravi Kanbur. 1993. "The Kuznets Process and the Inequality-Development Relationship." *Journal of Development Economics* 40: 25–52.

Anand, Sudhir, and Martin Ravallion. 1993. "Human Development in Poor Countries: On the Role of Private Incomes and Public Services." *Journal of Economic Perspectives* 7(Winter): 133–150.

Anderson, Kym, and Alan Winters. 2008. "The Challenge of Reducing International Trade and Migration Barriers." Policy Research Working Paper 4598. Washington, DC: World Bank.

Anderson, Michael. 2008. "Multiple Inference and Gender Differences in the Effects of Early Intervention: A Reevaluation of the Abecedarian, Perry Preschool, and Early Training Projects." *Journal of the American Statistical Association* 103: 1481–1495.

Anderson, Siwan, and Debraj Ray. 2010. "Missing Women: Age and Disease." *Review of Economic Studies* 77(4): 1262–1300.

Angelucci, Manuela, Dean Karlan, and Jonathan Zinman. 2013. "Win Some Lose Some? Evidence from a Randomized Microcredit Program Placement Experiment by Compartamos Banco." Mimeo.

Appleton, Simon. 1996. "Women-Headed Households and Household Welfare: An Empirical Deconstruction for Uganda." *World Development* 24(12): 1811–1827.

Apps, Patricia F., and Elizabeth J. Savage. 1989. "Labour Supply, Welfare Rankings and the Measurement of Inequality." *Journal of Public Economics* 39: 335–364.

Ardington, Cally, Anne Case, and Victoria Hosegood. 2009. "Labor Supply Responses to Large Social Transfers: Longitudinal Evidence from South Africa." *American Economic Journal: Applied Economics* 1(1): 22–48.

Aristotle. 350 B.C. a. *Nicomachean Ethics.* Book 7. Translated by W. D. Ross.

Aristotle. 350 B.C. b. *Politics.* Book 2. Translated by Benjamin Jowett. http://classics.mit.edu/Aristotle/politics.2.two.html.

Arndt, Channing, Sam Jones, and Finn Tarp. 2014. "What is the Aggregate Economic Rate of Return to Foreign Aid?" WIDER Working Paper 2014/089. (*World Bank Economic Review*, forthcoming.)

Arneson, Richard. 1989. "Equality and Equal Opportunity for Welfare." *Philosophical Studies* 56(1): 77–93.

Arneson, Richard. 2005. "Distributive Justice and Basic Capability Equality: 'Good Enough' Is Not Good Enough." Mimeo. San Diego: University of California–San Diego.

Arnott, Richard. 1995. "Time for Revisionism on Rent Control?" *Journal of Economic Perspectives* 9(1): 99–120.

Arnott, Richard, and M. Igarashi. 2000. "Rent Control, Mismatch Costs and Search Efficiency." *Regional Science and Urban Economics* 30: 249–288.

Arrow, Kenneth. 1951. *Social Choice and Individual Values.* New York: John Wiley.

Arrow, Kenneth. 1962. "The Economic Implications of Learning by Doing." *Review of Economic Studies* 29: 155–173.

Arrow, Kenneth. 1973. "Some Ordinalist-Utilitarian Notes on Rawls's Theory of Justice." *Journal of Philosophy* 70: 245–263.

Arrow, Kenneth, and Frank Hahn. 1971. *General Competitive Analysis*. San Francisco: Holden-Day.

Artz, Frederick B. 1934. *Reaction and Revolution: 1814–1834*. New York: Harper and Row.

Ashenfelter, Orley, Angus Deaton, and Gary Solon. 1986. "Collecting Panel Data in Developing Countries: Does it Make Sense?" Living Standards Measurement Study Working Paper No. 23. Washington, DC: World Bank.

Asian Development Bank. 2014. *Key Indicators for Asia and the Pacific 2014*. Manila: Asian Development Bank.

Atkinson, Anthony B. 1970. "On the Measurement of Inequality." *Journal of Economic Theory* 2: 244–263.

Atkinson, Anthony B. 1975. *The Economics of Inequality*. Oxford: Oxford University Press.

Atkinson, Anthony B. 1987. "On the Measurement of Poverty." *Econometrica* 55: 749–764.

Atkinson, Anthony B. 1989. *Poverty and Social Security*. New York: Harvester Wheatsheaf.

Atkinson, Anthony B. 1991. "Comparing Poverty Rates Internationally: Lessons from Recent Studies in Developed Countries." *World Bank Economic Review* 5(1): 3–21.

Atkinson, Anthony B. 1992. "Measuring Poverty and Differences in Family Composition." *Economica* 59: 1–16.

Atkinson, Anthony B. 1995. *Public Economics in Action: The Basic Income/Flat Tax Proposal*. Oxford: Oxford University Press.

Atkinson, Anthony B. 1998. *Poverty in Europe*. Oxford: Blackwell Press.

Atkinson, Anthony B., and Francois Bourguignon. 1982. "The Comparison of Multi-Dimensional Distributions of Economic Status." *Review of Economic Studies* 49: 183–201.

Atkinson, Anthony B., and Francois Bourguignon. 1987. "Income Distribution and Differences in Needs." In George R. Feiwel (ed.), *Arrow and the Foundations of the Theory of Economic Policy*. London: Macmillan Press.

Atkinson, Anthony B., and Francois Bourguignon. 1989. "The Design of Direct Taxation and Family Benefits." *Journal of Public Economics* 41: 3–29.

Atkinson, Anthony B., and Francois Bourguignon. 2001. "Poverty and Inclusion from a World Perspective." In Joseph Stiglitz and Pierre-Alain Muet (eds.), *Governance: Equity and Global Markets*. Oxford: Oxford University Press.

Atkinson, Anthony B., Thomas Piketty, and Emmanuel Saez. 2011. "Top Incomes in the Long Run of History." *Journal of Economic Literature* 49(1): 3–71.

Atkinson, Anthony B., and Joseph E. Stiglitz. 1980. *Lectures on Public Economics*. London: McGraw Hill Book Company.

Atkinson, Anthony B., and Holly Sutherland. 1989. "Analysis of a Partial Basic Income Scheme." In A. B. Atkinson (ed.), *Poverty and Social Security*. Hemel Hempstead, Hertfordshire: Harvester Wheatsheaf.

Attanasio, Orazio, Costas Meghir, and Ana Santiago. 2012. "Education Choices in Mexico: Using a Structural Model and a Randomized Experiment to Evaluate PROGRESA." *Review of Economic Studies* 79(1): 37–66.

Autor, David. 2014. "Skills, Education, and the Rise of Earnings Inequality among the Other 99 Percent." *Science* 344: 843–851.

Avitabile, Ciro. 2012. "Spillover Effects in Healthcare Programs: Evidence on Social Norms and Information Sharing." IDB Working Paper Series No. IDB-WP-380. Washington, DC: Inter-American Development Bank.

Aykroyd, Wallace R. 1974. *The Conquest of Famine*. London: Chatto and Windus.

Azam, Jean-Paul, and Jean-Jacques Laffont. 2003. "Contracting for Aid," *Journal of Development Economics* 70: 25–58.

Azariadis, Costas. 1996. "The Economics of Poverty Traps. Part One: Complete Markets." *Journal of Economic Growth* 1: 449–486.

Azariadis, Costas. 2006. "The Theory of Poverty Traps: What Have we Learned?" In Samuel Bowles, Steven Durlauf, and Karla Hoff (eds.), *Poverty Traps*. Princeton, NJ: Princeton University Press.

Bago d'Uva, T., E. Van Doorslaer, M. Lindeboom, and O. O'Donnell. 2008. "Does Reporting Heterogeneity Bias the Measurement of Health Disparities?" *Health Economics* 17(3): 351–375.

Baird, Sarah, Jed Friedman, and Norbert Schady. 2011. "Aggregate Income Shocks and Infant Mortality in the Developing World." *Review of Economics and Statistics* 93(3): 847–856.

Baird, Sarah, Craig McIntosh, and Berk Ozler. 2011. "Cash or Condition? Evidence from a Cash Transfer Experiment." *Quarterly Journal of Economics* 126(4): 1709–1753.

Bairoch, Paul. 1981. "The Main Trends in National Economic Disparities since the Industrial Revolution." In P. Bairoch and M. Levy-Leboyer (eds.), *Disparities in Economic Development since the Industrial Revolution*. New York: St. Martin's Press.

Bandiera, Oriana, Robin Burgess, Selim Gulesci, Imran Rasul, Munshi Sulaiman. 2013. "Can Entrepreneurship Programs Transform the Economic Lives of the Poor?" Discussion Paper EOPP 043, London School of Economics and Political Science, London.

Bandyopadhyay, Sanghamitra. 2004. "Twin Peaks: Distribution Dynamics of Economic Growth across Indian States." In Anthony Shorrocks and Rolph Van Der Hoeven (eds.), *Growth, Inequality and Poverty*. Oxford: Oxford University Press.

Banerjee, Abhijit. 2007. *Making Aid Work*. Cambridge, MA: MIT Press.

Banerjee, Abhijit, Rukmini Banerji, Esther Duflo, Rachel Glennerster, and Stuti Khemani. 2010. "Pitfalls of Participatory Programs: Evidence from a Randomized Evaluation in Education in India." *American Economic Journal: Economic Policy* 2(1): 1–30.

Banerjee, Abhijit, and Esther Duflo. 2003. "Inequality and Growth: What Can the Data Say?" *Journal of Economic Growth* 8(3): 267–299.

Banerjee, Abhijit, and Esther Duflo. 2008. "What Is Middle Class about the Middle Classes around the World?" *Journal of Economic Perspectives* 22(2): 3–28.

Banerjee, Abhijit, Esther Duflo, Rachel Glennerster, and Cynthia Kinnan. 2009. "The Miracle of Microfinance? Evidence from a Randomized Evaluation." BREAD Working Paper No. 278, BREAD.

Banerjee, Abhijit, Esther Duflo, Nathanael Goldberg, Dean Karlan, Robert Osei, William Parienté, Jeremy Shapiro, Bram Thuysbaert, and Christopher Udry, 2015, "A Multifaceted Program Causes Lasting Progress for The Very Poor: Evidence From Six Countries," *Science* 348: 773–789.

Banerjee, Abhijit, and Lakshmi Iyer. 2005. "History, Institutions and Economic Performance: The Legacy of Colonial Land Tenure Systems in India." *American Economic Review* 95(4): 1190–1213.

Banerjee, Abhijit, Dean Karlan, and Jonathan Zinman. 2014. "Six Randomized Evaluations of Microcredit: Introduction and Further Steps." *American Economic Journal: Applied Economics* 7(1): 1–21.

Banerjee, Abhijit, and Andrew Newman. 1994. "Poverty, Incentives and Development." *American Economic Review Papers and Proceedings* 84(2): 211–215.

Banerjee, Abhijit, and Thomas Piketty. 2005. "Top Indian Incomes, 1922–2000." *World Bank Economic Review* 19(1): 1–20.

Bangasser, Paul. 2000. "The ILO and the Informal Sector: An Institutional History." Employment Paper 2000/9. Geneva: International Labour Organization.

Bannock, Graham, R. E. Baxter, and Ray Rees. 1972. *The Penguin Dictionary of Economics*. Harmondsworth: Penguin.

Barder, Owen. 2013. "Is Aid a Waste of Money? Global Development: Views from the Center." Washington, DC: Center for Global Development.

Bardhan, Pranab. 1984a. *Land, Labor and Rural Poverty: Essays in Development Economics*. New York: Columbia University Press.

Bardhan, Pranab. 1984b, *The Political Economy of Development in India*. Oxford: Basil Blackwell.

Bardhan, Pranab. 2011. "Challenges for a Minimum Social Democracy in India." *Economic and Political Weekly* 46(10): 39–43.

Bardhan, Pranab, Samuel Bowles, and Herbert Gintis. 2000. "Wealth Inequality, Wealth Constraints and Economic Performance." In A. B. Atkinson and F. Bourguignon (eds.), *Handbook of Income Distribution*, vol. 1. Amsterdam: North-Holland.

Bardhan, Pranab, and Dilip Mookherjee. 2006. "Pro-Poor Targeting and Accountability of Local Governments in West Bengal." *Journal of Development Economics* 79(2): 303–327.

Bargain, Olivier, Olivier Donni, and Prudence Kwenda. 2014. "Intrahousehold Distribution and Poverty: Evidence from Côte d'Ivoire." *Journal of Development Economics* 107: 262–276.

Barham, Tania. 2012. "Enhancing Cognitive Functioning: Medium-Term Effects of a Health and Family Planning Program in Matlab," *American Economic Journal: Applied Economics*, 4(1): 245–73.

Barham, Tania, Karen Macours, and John Maluccio. 2013. "More Schooling and More Learning? Effects of a Three-Year Conditional Cash Transfer Program in Nicaragua after 10 Years." IDB Working Paper IDB-WP-432. Washington, DC: Inter-American Development Bank.

Barrett, Christopher, P. Marenya, J. McPeak, B. Minten, F. Murithi, W. Oluoch-Kosura, F. Place, J. Randrianarisoa, J. Rasambainarivo, and J. Wangila. 2006. "Welfare Dynamics in Rural Kenya and Madagascar." *Journal of Development Studies* 42(2): 178–199.

Barrientos, Armando. 2013. *Social Assistance in Developing Countries*. Cambridge: Cambridge University Press.

Barro, Robert. 2000. "Inequality and Growth in a Panel of Countries." *Journal of Economic Growth* 5(1): 5–32.

Barro, Robert, and Xavier Sala-i-Martin. 1992. "Convergence." *Journal of Political Economy* 100(2): 223–251.

Barro, Robert, and Xavier Sala-i-Martin. 1995. *Economic Growth*. New York: McGraw Hill.

Barros, Ricardo Paes de, Mirela de Carvalho, Samuel Franco, and Rosane Mendonça. 2006. "Determinantes Imediatos da Queda da Desigualdade de Renda Brasileira." In Ricardo Paes de Barros, Miguel Foguel, and Gabriel Ulyssea (eds.), *Desigualdade de Renda no Brasil: Uma analise da queda recente*. Rio de Janeiro: IPEA.

Barros, Ricardo Paes de, F. Ferreira, J. Molinas Vega, and J. Saavedra Chanduvi. 2009. *Measuring Inequality of Opportunities in Latin America and the Caribbean*. Washington, DC: World Bank.

Barrows, R., and M. Roth. 1990. "Land Tenure and Investment in African Agriculture: Theory and Evidence." *Journal of Modern African Studies* 28(2): 265–297.

Basu, Kaushik. 1999. "Child Labor: Cause, Consequence and Cure, with Remarks on International Labor Standards." *Journal of Economic Literature* 37: 1083–1119.

Basu, Kaushik. 2003. "Globalization and the Politics of International Finance: The Stiglitz Verdict." *Journal of Economic Literature* 41: 885–899.

Basu, Kaushik. 2011. *Beyond the Invisible Hand: Groundwork for a New Economics*. Princeton, NJ: Princeton University Press.

Basu, Kaushik. 2014. "Randomization, Causality and the Role of Reasoned Intuition." *Oxford Development Studies* 42(4): 455–472.

Basu, Sanjay, Jason Andrews, Sandeep Kishore, Rajesh Panjabi, and David Stuckler. 2012. "Comparative Performance of Private and Public Healthcare Systems in Low- and Middle-Income Countries: A Systematic Review." *PLOS Medicine* 9(6): 1–14.

Batana, Yele, Maurizio Bussolo, and John Cockburn. 2013. "Global Extreme Poverty Rates for Children, Adults and the Elderly." *Economics Letters* 120(3): 405–407.

Bates, Robert. 1981. *Markets and States in Tropical Africa*. Berkeley: University of California Press.

Bator, Francis M. 1958. "The Anatomy of Market Failure." *Quarterly Journal of Economics* 72(3): 351–379.

Bauer, Peter T. 1971. *Dissent on Development*. London: Weidenfeld and Nicolson.

Baulch, Robert, and Neil McCulloch. 2000. "Tracking Pro-poor Growth." ID21 insights No. 31. Brighton, Sussex: Institute of Development Studies.

Baumol, William. 1983. "Marx and the Iron Law of Wages." *American Economic Review, Papers and Proceedings* 73(2): 303–308.

Bazen, Stephen. 2007. "The Impact of Minimum Wages on the Distribution of Earnings and Employment in the USA." In J. Micklewright and S. Jenkins (eds.), *Inequality and Poverty Re-Examined*. Oxford: Oxford University Press.

Beaman, Lori, Dean Karlan, Bram Thuysbaert, and Christopher Udry. 2014. "Self-Selection into Credit Markets: Evidence from Agriculture in Mali." NBER Working Paper 20387.

Beaton, George H. 1983. "Energy in Human Nutrition: Perspectives and Problems." *Nutrition Reviews* 41: 325–340.

Beaudoin, Steven. 2006. *Poverty in World History.* New York: Routledge.

Beaumarchais, Pierre. (1778) 2007. *La Folle Journée ou Le Mariage de Figaro.* Paris: Nathan.

Beck, Thorsten, Asli Demirguc-Kunt, and Ross Levine. 2007. "Finance, Inequality and the Poor." *Journal of Economic Growth* 12: 27–49.

Beck, Thorsten, Ross Levine, and Norman Loayza. 2000. "Finance and the Sources of Growth." *Journal of Financial Economics* 58: 261–300.

Becker, Gary. (1964) 1993. *Human Capital: A Theoretical and Empirical Analysis, with Special Reference to Education.* 3rd ed. Chicago: University of Chicago Press.

Becker, Gary, and N. Tomes. 1979. "An Equilibrium Theory of the Distribution of Income and Intergenerational Mobility." *Journal of Political Economy* 87: 1153–1189.

Beckert, Sven. 2014. *The Empire of Cotton. A Global History.* New York: Alfred Knopf.

Beegle, Kathleen, Kristen Himelein, and Martin Ravallion. 2012. "Frame-of-Reference Bias in Subjective Welfare." *Journal of Economic Behavior and Organization* 81: 556–570.

Behrman, Jere. 1990. "The Action of Human Resources and Poverty on One Another: What We Have Yet to Learn." Working Paper 74, Living Standards Measurement Study, Poverty Analysis and Policy Division. Washington, DC: World Bank.

Behrman, Jere, and Anil Deolalikar. 1987. "Will Developing Country Nutrition Improve with Income? A Case Study for Rural South India," *Journal of Political Economy* 95: 108–138.

Behrman, Jere, Yingmei Cheng, and Petra Todd. 2004. "Evaluating Preschool Programs When Length of Exposure to the Program Varies: A Nonparametric Approach." *Review of Economics and Statistics* 86(1): 108–132.

Behrman, Jere and Sergio Urzua. 2013. "Economic Perspectives on Some Important Dimensions of Early Childhood Development in Developing Countries." In Pia Rebello Britto, Patrice L. Engle, and Charles M. Super (eds.) *Handbook of Early Childhood Development Research and Its Impact on Global Policy*, Oxford: Oxford University Press.

Bell, Brian, Richard Blundell, and John Van Reenen. 1999. "Getting the Unemployed Back to Work: The Role of Targeted Wage Subsidies." *International Tax and Public Finance* 6(3): 339–360.

Ben-David, Dan. 1998. "Convergence Clubs and Subsistence Economies," *Journal of Development Economics* 55(1): 155–171.

Bénabou, Roland. 1993. "Workings of a City: Location, Education and Production." *Quarterly Journal of Economics* 108: 619–652.

Bénabou, Roland. 1996. "Inequality and Growth." In Ben Bernanke and Julio Rotemberg (eds.), *National Bureau of Economic Research Macroeconomics Annual.* Cambridge, MA: MIT Press.

Bénabou, Roland. 2013. "Groupthink: Collective Delusions in Organizations and Markets." *Review of Economic Studies* 80: 429–462.

Bénabou, Roland, and Jean Tirole. 2006. "Belief in a Just World and Redistributive Politics." *Quarterly Journal of Economics* 121: 699–746.

Ben-Shalom, Yonatan, Robert Moffitt, and John Karl Scholz. 2012. "An Assessment of the Effectiveness of Antipoverty Programs in the United States." In Philip Jefferson (ed.), *The Oxford Handbook of the Economics of Poverty.* Oxford: Oxford University Press.

Benton, D. 2010. "The Influence of Dietary Status on the Cognitive Performance of Children." *Molecular Nutrition and Food Research* 54(4): 457–470.

Berg, Andrew, Jonathan D. Ostry, and Jeromin Zettelmeyer. 2012. "What Makes Growth Sustained?" *Journal of Development Economics* 98: 149–166.

Bergh, Andreas, and Therese Nilsson. 2014. "Is Globalization Reducing Absolute Poverty?" *World Development* 62: 42–61.

Bernheim, B. Douglas, and Michael Whinston. 2008. *Microeconomics.* New York: McGraw-Hill.

Berry, Albert. 2011. "The Case for Redistributive Land Reform in Developing Countries." *Development and Change* 42(2): 637–648.

Berry, Albert, and William Cline. 1979. *Agrarian Structure and Productivity in Developing Countries.* Baltimore, MD: Johns Hopkins University Press.

Bertola, Giuseppe. 2000. "Macroeconomics of Distribution and Growth." In A. B. Atkinson and F. Bourguignon (eds.), *Handbook of Income Distribution.* Amsterdam: North-Holland.

Bertrand, Marianne, Simeon Djankov, Rema Hanna, and Sendhil Mullainathan. 2007. "Obtaining a Driver's License in India: An Experimental Approach to Studying Corruption." *Quarterly Journal of Economics* 122(4): 1639–1676.

Bertrand, Marianne, and Sendhil Mullainathan. 2001. "Do People Mean What They Say? Implications for Subjective Survey Data." *American Economic Review* 91(2): 67–72.

Bertrand, Marianne, Sendhil Mullainathan, and Douglas Miller. 2003. "Public Policies and Extended Families: Evidence from Pensions in South Africa." *World Bank Economic Review* 17(1): 27–50.

Besley, Timothy. 1995a. "Property Rights and Investment Incentives: Theory and Evidence from Ghana." *Journal of Political Economy* 103(5): 903–937.

Besley, Timothy. 1995b. "Savings, Credit and Insurance." In Jere Behrman and T. N. Srinivasan (eds.), *Handbook of Development Economics*, vol. 3. Amsterdam: North-Holland.

Besley, Timothy, and Robin Burgess. 2003. "The Political Economy of Government Responsiveness: Theory and Evidence from India." *Quarterly Journal of Economics* 117(4): 1415–1451.

Besley, Timothy, and Ravi Kanbur. 1988. "Food Subsidies and Poverty Reduction." *Economic Journal* 98: 701–719.

Besley, Timothy, and Ravi Kanbur. 1993. "Principles of Targeting." In Michael Lipton and Jacques van der Gaag (eds.), *Including the Poor*. Washington, DC: Johns Hopkins University Press for the World Bank.

Besley, Timothy, and Torsten Persson. 2010. "State Capacity, Conflict, and Development," *Econometrica* 78(1): 1–34.

Besley, Timothy, and Torsten Persson. 2011. *Pillars of Prosperity: The Political Economy of Development Clusters*. Princeton, NJ: Princeton University Press.

Bethlehem, Jelke. 2009. *Applied Survey Methods: A Statistical Perspective*. New York: Wiley.

Beveridge, William. 1942. *Social Insurance and Allied Services*. London: His Majesty's Stationary Office.

Bhagwati, Jagdish. 1993. *India in Transition: Freeing the Economy*. Oxford: Clarendon Press.

Bhalla, Surjit. 2002. *Imagine There's No Country: Poverty, Inequality and Growth in the Era of Globalization*. Washington, DC: Institute for International Economics (Peterson Institute).

Bhargava, Alok. 1999. "Modeling the Effects of Nutritional and Socioeconomic Factors on the Growth and Morbidity of Kenyan School Children." *American Journal of Human Biology* 11: 317–326.

Bhargava, Alok, 2008, *Food, Economics, and Health*. Oxford: Oxford University Press.

Bhargava, Alok, and Martin Ravallion. 1993. "Is Household Consumption a Martingale? Tests for Rural South India." *Review of Economics and Statistics* 75: 500–504.

Bhutta, Zulfiqar A., Jai K. Das, Neff Walker, Arjumand Rizvi, Harry Campbell, Igor Rudan, and Robert E. Black. 2013. "Interventions to Address Deaths from Childhood Pneumonia and Diarrhoea Equitably: What Works and at What Cost?" *Lancet* 381: 1417–1429.

Bibi, Sami, and Jean-Yves Duclos. 2007. "Equity and Policy Effectiveness with Imperfect Targeting." *Journal of Development Economics* 83(1): 109–140.

Bidani, Benu, and Martin Ravallion. 1993. "A New Regional Poverty Profile for Indonesia." *Bulletin of Indonesian Economic Studies* 29: 37–68.

Bidani, Benu, and Martin Ravallion. 1997. "Decomposing Social Indicators Using Distributional Data." *Journal of Econometrics* 77(1): 125–140.

Bingley, Paul, and Ian Walker. 1997. "The Labour Supply, Unemployment and Participation of Lone Mothers in In-Work Transfer Programmes." *Economic Journal* 107: 1375–1390.

Binmore, Ken. 2007. *Playing for Real: A Text on Game Theory*. Oxford: Oxford University Press.

Binswanger, Hans, Klaus Deininger, and Gershon Feder. 1995. "Power, Distortions, Revolt and Reform in Agricultural and Land Relations." In Jere Behrman and T. N. Srinivasan (eds.), *Handbook of Development Economics*, vol. 3. Amsterdam: North Holland.

Birdsall, Nancy, Carol Graham, and Stefano Pettinato. 2000. "Stuck in the Tunnel: Is Globalization Muddling the Middle Class." Center on Social and Economic Dynamics, Working Paper 14. Washington, DC: Brookings Institution.

Birdsall, Nancy, and Juan Luis Londono. 1997. "Asset Inequality Matters: An Assessment of the World Bank's Approach to Poverty Reduction." *American Economic Review, Papers and Proceedings* 87(2): 32–37.

Birdsall, Nancy, D. Ross, and R. Sabot. 1995. "Inequality and Growth Reconsidered: Lessons from East Asia." *World Bank Economic Review* 9(3): 477–508.

Bishop, John, S. Chakraborti, and Paul D. Thistle. 1989. "Asymptotically Distribution-Free Statistical Inference for Generalized Lorenz Curves." *Review of Economics and Statistics* 71: 725–727.

Bishop, John, and Feijun Luo. 2006. "Economic Transition and Subjective Poverty in Urban China," *Review of Income and Wealth* 52(4): 625–641.

Bishop, John, Feijun Luo, and Xi Pan. 2006. "Economic Transition and Subjective Poverty in Urban China." *Review of Income and Wealth* 52(4): 625–641.

Black, John, Nigar Hashimzade and Gareth Myles. 2012. *A Dictionary of Economics*. Oxford: Oxford University Press.

Blackorby, Charles, and Donald Donaldson. 1980. "Ethical Indices for the Measurement of Poverty." *Econometrica* 48: 1053–1060.

Blackorby, Charles, and Donald Donaldson. 1984. "Social Criteria for Evaluating Population Change." *Journal of Public Economics* 25: 13–33.

Blackorby, Charles, and Donald Donaldson. 1987. "Welfare Ratios and Distributionally Sensitive Cost-Benefit Analysis." *Journal of Public Economics* 34: 265–290.

Blanchard, Olivier, and Lawrence Summers. 1986. "Hysteresis and the European Unemployment Problem." In Stanley Fischer (ed.) *NBER Macro Annual*. Cambridge, MA: MIT Press.

Blank, Rebecca M. 1995. "Unwed Mothers Need Role Models Not Roll Backs." *Wall Street Journal*, March 7, A18.

Blank, Rebecca M. 2008. "How to Improve Poverty Measurement in the United States." *Journal of Policy Analysis and Management* 27(2): 233–254.

Blattman, Christopher, and Edward Miguel. 2009. "Civil Wars." *Journal of Economic Literature* 48: 3–57.

Blau, Francine, and Lawrence Khan. 2007. "Changes in the Labor Supply Behavior of Married Women: 1980–2000." *Journal of Labor Economics* 25: 393–438.

Blaug, Mark. 1962. *Economic Theory in Retrospect*. London: Heinemann Books.

Blinder, Alan. 1973. "Wage Discrimination: Reduced Form and Structural Estimates." *Journal of Human Resources* 8: 436–455.

Bliss, Christopher. 1975. *Capital Theory and the Distribution of Income*. Amsterdam: North- Holland.

Bliss, Christopher, and Nicholas Stern. 1978. "Productivity, Wages and Nutrition." *Journal of Development Economics* 5: 331–362 and 363–398.

Bliss, Christopher, and Nicholas Stern. 1982. *Palanpur: The Economy of an Indian Village*. Oxford: Clarendon Press.

Block, Fred, and Margaret Somers. 2003. "In the Shadow of Speenhamland: Social Policy and the Old Poor Law." *Politics & Society* 31: 283–323.

Block, Steven A., William A. Masters, and Priya Bhagowalia. 2012. "Does Child Undernutrition Persist Despite Poverty Reduction in Developing Countries? Quantile Regression Results." *Journal of Development Studies* 48(12): 1699–1715.

Bloom, David, David Canning, and Günther Fink. 2008. "Urbanization and the Wealth of Nations." *Science* 319: 772–775.

Bluedorn, John, Rupa Duttagupta, Jaime Guajardo, and Nkunde Mwase. 2013. "The Growth Comeback in Developing Economies: A New Hope or Back to the Future?" IMF Working Paper 13/132. Washington, DC: IMF.

Blume, Larry, and Steven Durlauf, eds. 2008. *The New Palgrave Dictionary of Economics*. 2nd edn. London: Palgrave Macmillan.

Blundell, Richard. 2001. "Welfare to Work: Which Policies Work and Why?" Keynes Lectures in Economics, University College of London and Institute of Fiscal Studies.

Boadway, Robin. 1998. "The Mirrlees Approach to the Theory of Economic Policy." *International Tax and Public Finance* 5: 67–81.

Bond, Timothy, and Kevin Lang. 2014. "The Sad Truth about Happiness Scales." Mimeo, Boston University.

Boo, Katherine. 2012. *Behind the Beautiful Forevers*. New York: Random House.

Boone, Catherine. 2014. *Property and Political Order: Land Rights and the Structure of Politics in Africa.* Cambridge: Cambridge University Press.

Boone, Peter. 1996. "Politics and the Effectiveness of Foreign Aid." *European Economic Review* 40: 289–329.

Boone, Ryan, Covarrubias, Katia, Benjamin Davis, and Paul Winters. 2013. "Cash Transfer Programs and Agricultural Production: The Case of Malawi." *Agricultural Economics* 44(3): 365–378.

Booth, Alison, and Mark Bryan. 2007. "Training, Minimum Wages and the Distribution of Earnings." In J. Micklewright and S. Jenkins (eds.), *Inequality and Poverty Re-Examined.* Oxford: Oxford University Press.

Booth, Anne, and R. M. Sundrum. 1984. *Labour Absorption in Agriculture.* Delhi: Oxford University Press.

Booth, Charles. 1903. *Life and Labour of the People of London.* Vol. 5, *Industry.* Second Series. London: Macmillan and Co.

Borjas, George. 1995. "Ethnicity, Neighborhoods, and Human-Capital Externalities." *American Economic Review* 85: 365–390.

Bortz, Abe. 1970 (approximate date). "Mother's Aid." Social Welfare History Project. http://www.socialwelfarehistory.com/programs/mothers-aid/.

Boserup, Esther. 1981. *Population and Technological Change: A Study of Long-Run Trends.* Chicago: University of Chicago Press.

Boserup, Esther. 1985. "The Impact of Scarcity and Plenty on Development." In Robert Rotberg and Theodore Rab (eds.), *Hunger and History.* Cambridge: Cambridge University Press.

Bouguen, Adrien, Deon Filmer, Karen Macours, and Sophie Naudeau. 2014. "Preschools and Early Childhood Development in a Second Best World: Evidence from a Scaled-Up Experiment in Cambodia." Discussion Paper 10170. London: Center for Economic Policy Research.

Bouis, Howarth E., and Lawrence Haddad. 1992. "Are Estimates of Calorie-Income Elasticities too High? A Recalibration of the Plausible Range." *Journal of Development Economics* 39: 333–364.

Bourguignon, Francois. 1979. "Decomposable Income Inequality Measures." *Econometrica* 47: 901–920.

Bourguignon, Francois. 1989. "Family Size and Social Utility: Income Distribution Dominance Criteria." *Journal of Econometrics* 42: 67–80.

Bourguignon, Francois. 2003. "The Growth Elasticity of Poverty Reduction: Explaining Heterogeneity across Countries and Time Periods." In T. Eicher and S. Turnovsky (eds.), *Inequality and Growth: Theory and Policy Implications.* Cambridge, MA: MIT Press.

Bourguignon, Francois. 2014. "Reflections on the 'Equity and Development' World Development Report Ten Years Later." Mimeo, Paris School of Economics, Paris, France.

Bourguignon, Francois, and Satya Chakravarty. 2003. "The Measurement of Multidimensional Poverty." *Journal of Economic Inequality* 1: 25–49.

Bourguignon, Francois, and Francisco Ferreira. 2003. "Ex-ante Evaluation of Policy Reforms Using Behavioural Models." In Francois Bourguignon. and Luiz Pereira da Silva (eds.), *The Impact of Economic Policies on Poverty and Income Distribution.* New York: Oxford University Press.

Bourguignon, Francois, Francisco Ferreira, and Phillippe Leite. 2003. "Conditional Cash Transfers, Schooling, and Child Labor: Microsimulating Brazil's Bolsa Escola Program." *World Bank Economic Review* 17(2): 229–254.

Bourguignon, Francois, Francisco Ferreira, and Marta Menéndez. 2007. "Inequality of Opportunity in Brazil." *Review of Income Wealth* 53(4): 585–618.

Bourguignon, Francois, and Gary Fields. 1990. "Poverty Measures and Anti-Poverty Policy." *Recherches Economiques de Louvain* 56: 409–428.

Bourguignon, Francois, Victoria Levin, and David Rosenblatt. 2009. "International Redistribution of Income." *World Development* 37(1): 1–10.

Bourguignon, Francois, and Christian Morrisson. 1990. "Income Distribution, Development and Foreign Trade." *European Economic Review* 34: 1113–1132.

Bourguignon, Francois, and Christian Morrisson. 2002. "Inequality among World Citizens: 1820–1992." *American Economic Review* 92(4): 727–744.

Bourguignon, Francois, and Luiz Pereira Da Silva. 2003. "Introduction." In Francois Bourguignon Francois and Luiz Pereira Da Silva (eds.), *The Impact of Economic Policies on Poverty and Income Distribution: Evaluation Techniques and Tools*. New York: Oxford University Press.

Bowles, Samuel, Steven Durlauf, and Karla Hoff. 2006. "Introduction." In Samuel Bowles, Steven Durlauf, and Karla Hoff (eds.), *Poverty Traps*. Princeton, NJ: Princeton University Press.

Bowles, Samuel, and Herbert Gintis. 1976. *Schooling in Capitalist America: Educational Reform and the Contradictions of Economic Life*. New York: Basic Books.

Bowley, Arthur L. 1915. *The Nature and Purpose of the Measurement of Social Phenomena*. London: P. S. King and Sons.

Box, George E. P., William G. Hunter, and J. Stuart Hunter. 1978. *Statistics for Experimenters: An Introduction to Design, Data Analysis, and Model Building*. New York: John Wiley and Sons.

Boyce, James K. 2015. "Letter from Delhi Part 1: Air Pollution as Environmental Injustice," *Triple Crisis*, July 20.

Boyce, James K., and Léonce Ndikumana. 2001. "Is Africa a Net Creditor? New Estimates of Capital Flight from Severely Indebted Sub-Saharan Africa Countries, 1970–1996." *Journal of Development Studies* 38(2): 27–56.

Boyer, George. 2002. "English Poor Laws." *EH.Net Encyclopedia*. Edited by Robert Whaples.

Bragg, Rick. 1997. *All Over But the Shoutin.'* New York: Vintage Books.

Brandt, Loren, and Thomas Rawski. 2008. "China's Great Economic Transformation." In Loren Brandt and Thomas Rawski (eds.), *China's Great Economic Transformation*. Cambridge: Cambridge University Press.

Brauw, Alan de, and John Hoddinott. 2011. "Must Conditional Cash Transfer Programs be Conditioned to be Effective? The Impact of Conditioning Transfers on School Enrollment in Mexico," *Journal of Development Economics* 96 (2011) 359–370.

Bresciani, Fabrizio, Gerson Feder, Daniel Gilligan, Hanan Jacoby, Tongroj Onchan, and Jaime Quizon. 2002. "Weathering the Storm: The Impact of the East Asian Crisis on Farm Households in Indonesia and Thailand." *World Bank Research Observer* 17(1): 1–20.

Brinton, Crane. 1934. *A Decade of Revolution 1789–1799*. New York: Harper and Row.

Broad, Robin, and John Cavanagh. 2009. *Development Redefined: How the Market Met its Match*. Boulder, CO: Paradigm.

Brooke, Michael Z. 1998. *Le Play: Engineer and Social Scientist*. New Brunswick, New Jersey: Transaction Publishers.

Brownell, Kelly, and Katherine Horgen. 2004. *Food Fight*. New York: McGraw-Hill.

Browning, Martin. 1992. "Children and Household Economic Behavior." *Journal of Economic Literature* 30: 1434–1475.

Bruno, Michael, Martin Ravallion, and Lyn Squire. 1998. "Equity and Growth in Developing Countries: Old and New Perspectives on the Policy Issues." In Vito Tanzi and Ke-young Chu (eds.), *Income Distribution and High-Quality Growth*. Cambridge, MA: MIT Press.

Bryman, Alan. 2012. *Social Research Methods*. 4th edn. Oxford: Oxford University Press.

Bulow, Jeremy, and Larry Summers. 1986. "A Theory of Dual Labor Markets with Application to Industrial Policy, Discrimination and Keynesian Unemployment." *Journal of Labor Economics* 4(3): 376–414.

Burnside, Craig, and David Dollar. 2000. "Aid, Policies, and Growth." *American Economic Review* 90(4): 847–868.

Burtless, Gary. 1985. "Are Targeted Wage Subsidies Harmful? Evidence from a Wage Voucher Experiment." *Industrial and Labor Relations Review* 39: 105–115.

Bussolo, Maurizio, Rafale De Hoyos, and Denis Medvedev. 2008. "Is the Developing World Catching Up? Global Convergence and National Rising Dispersion." Policy Research Working Paper 4733. Washington, DC: World Bank.

Buvinic, Mayra, and G. Rao Gupta. 1997. "Female-Headed Households and Female-Maintained Families: Are they Worth Targeting to Reduce Poverty in Developing Countries?" *Economic Development and Cultural Change* 45(2): 259–280.

Buzby, Jean C., Hodan F. Wells, and Jeffrey Hyman. 2014. "The Estimated Amount, Value, and Calories of Postharvest Food Losses at the Retail and Consumer Levels in the United States,"

Economic Information Bulletin Number 121, Economic Research Service, United States Department of Agriculture.

Califano, Joseph A., Jr. 1999. "What Was Really Great about the Great Society: The Truth behind the Conservative Myths." *Washington Monthly*, October.

Cameron, Lisa. 2002. "Did Social Safety Net Scholarships Reduce Drop-Out Rates during the Indonesian Economic Crisis?" Policy Research Working Paper 2800. Washington, DC: World Bank.

Cammett, Ann. 2014. "Deadbeat Dads and Welfare Queens: How Metaphor Shapes Poverty Law." *Boston College Journal of Law and Social Justice* 34(2): 233–265.

Campbell, Frances, Gabriella Conti, James Heckman, Seong Hyeok Moon, Rodrigo Pinto, Elizabeth Pungello, and Yi Pan. 2014. "Early Childhood Investments Substantially Boost Adult Health." *Science* 343: 1478–1485.

Campbell, Frances, and Craig Ramey. 1994. "Effects of Early Intervention on Intellectual and Academic Achievement: A Follow-Up Study of Children from Low-Income Families." *Child Development* 65: 684–698.

Cantril, Hadley. 1965. *The Pattern of Human Concerns*. New Brunswick, NJ: Rutgers University Press.

Cappelen, Alexander, Shachar Kariv, Erik Ø. Sørensen, and Bertil Tungodden. 2014. "Is There a Development Gap in Rationality?" Working Paper, Norwegian School of Economics, Bergen, Norway.

Cappelen, Alexander, Ottar Mæstad, and Bertil Tungodden. 2010. "Demand for Childhood Vaccination—Insights from Behavioral Economics." *Forum for Development Studies* 37(3): 349–364.

Card, David, and Alan Krueger. 1995. *Myth and Measurement: The New Economics of the Minimum Wage*. Princeton, NJ: Princeton University Press.

Card, David, and Alan Krueger. 2000. "Minimum Wages and Employment: A Case Study of the Fast-Food Industry in New Jersey and Pennsylvania: Reply." *American Economic Review* 90: 1397–1420.

Carletto, Gero, and A. Zezza. 2006. "Being Poor, Feeling Poorer: Combining Objective and Subjective Measures of Welfare in Albania." *Journal of Development Studies* 42(5): 739–760.

Carter, Michael, and Christopher Barrett. 2006. "The Economics of Poverty Traps and Persistent Poverty: An Asset-Based Approach." *Journal of Development Studies* 42(2): 178–199.

Case, Anne, Darren Lubotsky, and Christina Paxson. 2002. "Economic Status and Health in Childhood: The Origins of the Gradient." *American Economic Review* 92(5): 1308–1334.

Case, Karl, Ray Fair, and Sharon Oster. 2012. *Principles of Microeconomics*. 10th edn. Boston: Prentice-Hall.

Chakravarty, S. R., and W. Eichhorn. 1994. "Measurement of Income Inequality: Observed versus True Data." In W. Eichhorn (ed.), *Models and Measurement of Welfare and Inequality*. Heidelberg: Springer-Verlag.

Chakravarty, Sukhamoy. 1987. *Development Planning: The Indian Experience*. Delhi: Oxford University Press.

Chant, Sylvia. 1997. *Women-Headed Households: Diversity and Dynamics in the Developing World*. Houndmills, Basingstoke, UK: Palgrave Macmillan.

Chant, Sylvia. 2008. "The 'Feminization of Poverty' and the 'Feminization' of Anti-Poverty Programs: Room for Revision?" *Journal of Development Studies* 44(2): 165–197.

Chaudhuri, Shubham, and Martin Ravallion. 1994. "How Well do Static Welfare Indicators Identify the Chronically Poor?" *Journal of Public Economics* 53: 367–394.

Chaudhuri, Shubham, and Martin Ravallion. 2006. "Partially Awakened Giants: Uneven Growth in China and India." In L. Alan Winters and Shahid Yusuf (eds.), *Dancing with Giants: China, India, and the Global Economy*. Washington, DC: World Bank.

Chen, Alice, Emily Oster, and Heidi Williams. 2015. "Why is Infant Mortality Higher in the U.S. than in Europe?" NBER Working Paper No. 20525.

Chen, Shaohua, Ren Mu, and Martin Ravallion. 2009. "Are There Lasting Impacts of Aid to Poor Areas? Evidence from Rural China." *Journal of Public Economics* 93: 512–528.

Chen, Shaohua, and Martin Ravallion. 1996. "Data in Transition: Assessing Rural Living Standards in Southern China." *China Economic Review* 7(1): 23–55.

Chen, Shaohua, and Martin Ravallion. 2001. "How Did the World's Poor Fare in the 1990s?" *Review of Income and Wealth* 47(3): 283–300.

Chen, Shaohua, and Martin Ravallion. 2004a. "Household Welfare Impacts of WTO Accession in China." *World Bank Economic Review* 18(1): 29–58.

Chen, Shaohua, and Martin Ravallion. 2004b. "How Have the World's Poorest Fared since the Early 1980s?" *World Bank Research Observer* 19(2): 141–170.

Chen, Shaohua, and Martin Ravallion. 2010a. "The Developing World Is Poorer than We Thought, but No Less Successful in the Fight against Poverty." *Quarterly Journal of Economics* 125(4): 1577–1625.

Chen, Shaohua, and Martin Ravallion. 2010b. "China Is Poorer than We Thought, but No Less Successful in the Fight Against Poverty." In Sudhir Anand, Paul Segal, and Joseph Stiglitz (eds.), *Debates on the Measurement of Poverty*. Oxford: Oxford University Press.

Chen, Shaohua, and Martin Ravallion. 2013. "More Relatively Poor People in a Less Absolutely Poor World." *Review of Income and Wealth* 59(1): 1–28.

Chenery, Hollis. 1977. Forward to David Morawetz, *Twenty-Five Years of Economic Development*. Washington, DC: World Bank.

Chenery, Hollis, Montek S. Ahluwalia, Clive Bell, John Duloy, and Richard Jolly. 1974. *Redistribution with Growth*. Oxford: Oxford University Press.

Chenery, Hollis, and A. Strout. 1966. "Foreign Assistance and Economic Development." *American Economic Review* 56: 679–733.

Chesher, Andrew, and C. Schluter. 2002. "Welfare Measurement and Measurement Error." *Review of Economic Studies* 69: 357–378.

Chetty, Raj, Nathaniel Hendren, Patrick Kline, Emmanuel Saez and Nicholas Turner. 2014. "Is the United States Still a Land of Opportunity? Recent Trends in Intergenerational Mobility." NBER Working Paper 19844.

Chetty, Raj, Nathaniel Hendren, and Lawrence Katz. 2015. "The Effects of Exposure to Better Neighborhoods on Children: New Evidence from the Moving to Opportunity Experiment," NBER Working Paper 21156.

Chong, Alberto, and Mark Gradstein. 2007. "Inequality and Institutions." *Review of Economics and Statistics* 89(3): 454–465.

Chong, Alberto, Rafeal La Porta, Florencia Lopez-de-Silanes, and Andrei Shleifer. 2014. "Letter Grading Government Efficiency." *Journal of the European Economic Association* 12(2): 277–299.

Christiaensen, Luc, Peter Lanjouw, J. Luoto, and David Stifel. 2012. "Small Area Estimation-Based Prediction Methods to Track Poverty: Validation and Applications." *Journal of Economic Inequality* 10(2): 267–297.

Chung, Kimberly. 2000. "Qualitative Data Collection Techniques." In Margaret Grosh and Paul Glewwwe (eds.), *Designing Household Survey Questionnaires for Developing Countries*. Washington, DC: World Bank.

Cinnirella, Francesco. 2008. "Optimists or Pessimists? A Reconsideration of Nutritional Status in Britain, 1740–1865." *European Review of Economic History* 12: 325–354.

Citro, Constance, and Robert Michael (eds.), 1995. *Measuring Poverty: A New Approach*. Washington, DC: National Academy Press.

Clague, Christopher, Philip Keefer, Stephen Knack, and Mancur Olson. 1997. "Democracy, Autocracy and the Institutions Supportive of Economic Growth." In Christopher Clague (ed.), *Institutions and Economic Development*. Baltimore, MD: Johns Hopkins University Press.

Clark, Andrew, and Andrew Oswald. 1994. "Unhappiness and Unemployment." *Economic Journal* 104: 648–659.

Clark, Andrew, and Andrew Oswald. 1996. "Satisfaction and Comparison Income." *Journal of Public Economics* 61: 359–381.

Clark, Andrew, Paul Frijters, and Michael Shields. 2008. "Relative Income, Happiness and Utility: An Explanation for the Easterlin Paradox and Other Puzzles." *Journal of Economic Literature* 46(1): 95–144.

Clark, Colin. (1940) 1957. *The Conditions of Economic Progress.* 3rd edn. London: Macmillan.

Clark, Gregory. 2005. "The Condition of the Working Class in England 1209–2004." *Journal of Political Economy* 113: 1307–1340.

Clarke, George R. G. 1995. "More Evidence on Income Distribution and Growth." *Journal of Development Economics* 47: 403–428.

Clemens, Michael, Steven Radelet, Rikhil Bhavnani, and Samuel Bazzi. 2011. "Counting Chickens When They Hatch: Timing and the Effects of Aid on Growth." *Economic Journal* 122: 590–617.

Cline, William. 1975. "Distribution and Development: A Survey of the Literature," *Journal of Development Economics* 1: 359–400.

Coady, David, Margaret Grosh, and John Hoddinott. 2004a. "Targeting Outcomes Redux." *World Bank Research Observer* 19(1): 61–86.

Coady, David, Margaret Grosh, and John Hoddinott. 2004b. *Targeting Transfers in Developing Countries: Review of Lessons and Experience.* Washington, DC: World Bank.

Coale, Ainsley. 1991. "Excess Female Mortality and the Balance of the Sexes in the Population: An Estimate of the Number of 'Missing Females.'" *Population and Development Review* 17(3): 517–523.

Cockburn, John, Jean-Yves Duclos, and Agnès Zabsonré. 2014. "Is Global Social Welfare Increasing? A Critical-Level Enquiry." *Journal of Public Economics* 118: 151–162.

Cogneau, Denis. 2012. "The Political Dimension of Inequality during Economic Development." *Région et Développement* 35: 11–35.

Cohen, Gerald. 1989. "On the Currency of Egalitarian Justice." *Ethics* 99(4): 906–944.

Cohen, Jessica, Pascaline Dupas, and Simone Schaner. 2015. "Price Subsidies, Diagnostic Tests, and Targeting of Malaria Treatment." *American Economic Review* 105(2): 609–45.

Cohen, Joshua. 1989. "Democratic Equality." *Ethics* 99(4): 727–751.

Collier, Paul, and David Dollar. 2002. "Aid Allocation and Poverty Reduction." *European* Economic Review 46(8): 1475–1500.

Collier, Paul, V. Elliott, Havard Hegre, Anke Hoeffler, Marta Reynal-Querol, and Nicholas Sambanis. 2003. *Breaking the Conflict Trap: Civil War and Development Policy.* Vol. 1. Washington, DC: World Bank.

Colquhoun, Patrick. 1806. *Treatise on Indigence.* London: Hatchard.

Congressional Budget Office. 2012. *The Distribution of Household Income and Federal Taxes, 2008 and 2009.* Washington, DC: Congressional Budget Office, Congress of the United States.

Conti, G., and S. Pudney. 2011. "Survey Design and the Analysis of Satisfaction." *Review of Economics and Statistics* 93(3): 1087–1093.

Cooper, Russell. 1999. *Coordination Games.* Cambridge: Cambridge University Press.

Coppola, Frances. 2014. "An Experiment with Basic Income." Pieria Blog Post. http://www.pieria.co.uk/articles/an_experiment_with_basic_income.

Cornia, Giovanni, Richard Jolly, and Francis Stewart, eds. 1987. *Adjustment with a Human Face: Protecting the Vulnerable and Promoting Growth.* Oxford: Oxford University Press.

Cornia, Giovanni, and Frances Stewart. 1995. "Two Errors of Targeting." In Dominique van de Walle and Kimberly Nead (eds.), *Public Spending and the Poor.* Washington DC: Johns Hopkins University Press for the World Bank.

Cortés, Hernán, and Anthony Pagden. 1986. *Letters from Mexico.* New Haven, CT: Yale University Press.

Coulter, Fiona, Frank Cowell, and Stephen Jenkins. 1992. "Equivalence Scale Relativities and the Extent of Inequality and Poverty." *Economic Journal* 102: 1067–1082.

Covarrubias, Katia, Benjamin Davis, and Paul Winters. 2013. "From Protection to Production: Productive Impacts of the Malawi Social Cash Transfer Scheme." Mimeo, FAO and American University.

Cowell, Frank. 1977. *Measuring Inequality.* Oxford: Philip Allan.

Cowell, Frank. 2000. "Measurement of Inequality." In A. B. Atkinson and F. Bourguignon (eds.), *Handbook of Income Distribution.* Amsterdam: North-Holland.

Cowell, Frank, and M. Victoria-Feser. 1996. "Robustness of Inequality Measures." *Econometrica* 64: 77–101.

Crowther, Margaret. 1981. *The Workhouse System 1834–1929: The History of an English Social Institution*. London: Batsford Academic and Educational.

Cunha, Flavio, and James Heckman. 2007. "The Technology of Skill Formation." *American Economic Review, Papers and Proceedings* 97(2): 31–47.

Cunha, Jesse. 2014. "Testing Paternalism: Cash versus In-kind Transfers in Rural Mexico." *American Economic Journal: Applied Economics* 6(2): 195–230.

Cunningham, Hugh. 1990. "The Employment and Unemployment of Children in England c.1680–1851." *Past and Present* 126: 115–150.

Currie, Janet. 2001. "Early Childhood Development Programs." *Journal of Economic Perspectives* 15(2): 213–238.

Currie, Janet. 2011. "Inequality at Birth: Some Causes and Consequences." *American Economic Review* 101(3): 1–22.

Currie, Janet. 2012. "Antipoverty Programs for Poor Children and Families." In Philip N. Jefferson (ed.), *The Oxford Handbook of the Economics of Poverty*. Oxford: Oxford University Press.

Currie, Janet, Stefano Della Vigna, Enrico Moretti, and Vikram Pathania. 2010. "The Effect of Fast Food Restaurants on Obesity and Weight Gain." *American Economic Journal: Economic Policy* 2: 32–63.

Cutler, David, Edward Glaeser, and Jesse Shapiro. 2003. "Why Have Americans Become More Obese?" *Journal of Economic Perspectives* 17(3): 93–118.

Cutler, David, and Grant Miller. 2005. "The Role of Public Health Improvements in Health Advances: The 20th Century United States." *Demography* 42(1): 1–22.

Dalton, Hugh. 1920. "The Measurement of the Inequality of Incomes." *Economic Journal* 30(9): 348–361.

Dandekar, V. M., and N. Rath. 1971. *Poverty in India*. Pune: Indian School of Political Economy.

Dang, Hai-Anh H., and Peter Lanjouw. 2014. "Welfare Dynamics Measurement: Two Definitions of a Vulnerability Line and Their Applications." Policy Research Working Paper 6944. Washington, DC: World Bank.

Daniel, Wayne W. 1990. *Applied Nonparametric Statistics*. Boston: PWS-KENT Publishing Company.

Darity, William, Jr., and A. H. Goldsmith. 1996. "Social Psychology, Unemployment and Macroeconomics." *Journal of Economic Perspectives* 10: 121–140.

Das, Jishnu, Quy-Toan Do, and Berk Ozler. 2005. "A Welfare Analysis of Conditional Cash Transfer Schemes." *World Bank Research Observer* 20(1): 57–80.

Das, Jishnu, and Jeffrey Hammer. 2014. "Are Institutional Births Institutionalizing Deaths?" Future Development Blog. World Bank.

Das, Mitali, and Pape N'Diaye. 2013. "Chronicle of a Decline Foretold: Has China Reached the Lewis Turning Point?" IMF Staff Working Paper 13/26.

Dasgupta, Partha. 1993. *An Inquiry into Well-Being and Destitution*. Oxford: Oxford University Press.

Dasgupta, Partha. 1997. "Poverty Traps." In David M. Kreps and Kenneth F. Wallis (eds.), *Advances in Economics and Econometrics: Theory and Applications*. Cambridge: Cambridge University Press.

Dasgupta, Partha. 2011. "Personal Histories and Poverty Traps." Annual World Bank Conference on Development Economics. Washington, DC: World Bank.

Dasgupta, Partha, and Geoffrey Heal. 1979. *Economic Theory and Exhaustible Resources*. Cambridge: Cambridge University Press.

Dasgupta, Partha, and Debraj Ray. 1986. "Inequality as a Determinant of Malnutrition and Unemployment." *Economic Journal* 96: 1011–1034.

Dasgupta, Partha, and Debraj Ray. 1990. "Adapting to Undernutrition. The Clinical Evidence and its Implications." In Jean Dréze and Amartya Sen (eds.), *The Political Economy of Hunger*. Oxford: Oxford University Press.

Dasgupta, Susmita, Mainul Huq, M. Khaliquzzaman, Kiran Pandey and David Wheeler. 2006. "Who Suffers from Indoor Air Pollution? Evidence from Bangladesh," *Health Policy and Planning* 21(6): 444–458.

Datt, Gaurav, and Martin Ravallion. 1992. "Growth and Redistribution Components of Changes in Poverty Measures: A Decomposition with Applications to Brazil and India in the 1980s." *Journal of Development Economics* 38: 275–295.

Datt, Gaurav, and Martin Ravallion. 1994. "Transfer Benefits from Public-Works Employment." *Economic Journal* 104: 1346–1369.

Datt, Gaurav, and Martin Ravallion. 1998a. "Farm Productivity and Rural Poverty in India." *Journal of Development Studies* 34(4): 62–85.

Datt, Gaurav, and Martin Ravallion. 1998b. "Why Have Some Indian States Done Better than Others at Reducing Rural Poverty?" *Economica* 65: 17–38.

Datt, Gaurav, and Martin Ravallion. 2002. "Has India's Post-Reform Economic Growth Left the Poor Behind." *Journal of Economic Perspectives* 16(3): 89–108.

Datt, Gaurav, and Martin Ravallion. 2011. "Has India's Economic Growth Become More Pro-Poor in the Wake of Economic Reforms?" *World Bank Economic Review* 25(2): 157–189.

Davala, Sarath, Renana Jhabvala, Soumya Mehta, and Guy Standing. 2015. *Basic Income: A Transformative Policy for India*. London and New Delhi: Bloomsbury Academic.

Davis, Donald, and Prachi Mishra. 2007. "Stolper-Samuelson is Dead: And Other Crimes of Both Theory and Data." In Ann Harrison (ed.), *Globalization and Poverty*. Chicago: University of Chicago Press.

Dawson, Miles Menander. 1915. *The Ethics of Confucius*. http://sacred-texts.com.

Day, Richard H. 1992. "Complex Economic Dynamics: Obvious in History, Generic in Theory, Elusive in Data." *Journal of Applied Econometrics* 7: S9–S23.

Dearden, Lorraine, Carl Emmerson, Christine Frayne, and Costas Meghir. 2009. "Conditional Cash Transfers and School Dropout Rates." *Journal of Human Resources* 44(4): 827–857.

Deaton, Angus. 1992. *Understanding Consumption*. Oxford: Oxford University Press.

Deaton, Angus. 1997. *The Analysis of Household Surveys: A Microeconometric Approach to Development Policy*. Washington, DC: Johns Hopkins University Press for the World Bank.

Deaton, Angus. 2006. "The Great Escape: A Review of Robert Fogel's *The Escape from Hunger and Premature Death, 1700–2100*." *Journal of Economic Literature* 44: 106–114.

Deaton, Angus. 2013. *The Great Escape: Health, Wealth, and the Origins of Inequality*. Princeton, NJ: Princeton University Press.

Deaton, Angus, and Alan Heston. 2010. "Understanding PPPs and PPP-Based National Accounts." *American Economic Journal: Macroeconomics* 2(4): 1–35.

Deaton, Angus, and John Muellbauer. 1980. *Economics and Consumer Behavior*. Cambridge: Cambridge University Press.

Deaton, Angus, and Salman Zaidi. 2002. "Guidelines for Constructing Consumption Aggregates for Welfare Analysis." Living Standards Measurement Study Working Paper 1135. Washington, DC: World Bank.

De Borger, Bruno. 1989. "Estimating the Welfare Implications of In-Kind Government Programs." *Journal of Public Economics* 38: 215–226.

Decancq, Koen, Andreas Peichl, and Philippe Van Kerm. 2015. "Assortative Mating, Joint Labor Supply and Spouses Earnings Correlation: Which do Matter for Long-Term Trends in US Household Earnings Inequality?" Paper Presented at the 6th ECINEQ conference, Luxembourg.

De Donder, Philippe, and Jean Hindriks. 1998. "The Political Economy of Targeting." *Public Choice* 95: 177–200.

Dehejia, Rajeev H., and Sadek Wahba. 1999. "Causal Effects in Non-Experimental Studies: Re-Evaluating the Evaluation of Training Programs." *Journal of the American Statistical Association* 94: 1053–1062.

Deininger, Klaus. 2003. *Land Policies for Growth and Poverty Reduction*. Washington, DC: World Bank.

Deininger, Klaus, and Pedro Olinto. 2000. "Asset Distribution, Inequality and Growth." Policy Research Working Paper 2375. Washington, DC: World Bank.

Deininger, Klaus, and Lyn Squire. 1996. "A New Data Set Measuring Income Inequality." *World Bank Economic Review* 10: 565–591.

Deininger, Klaus, and Lyn Squire. 1998. "New Ways of Looking at Old Issues: Inequality and Growth." *Journal of Development Economics* 57(2): 259–287.

De Janvry, Alain. 1981. *The Agrarian Question and Reformism in Latin America*. Baltimore, MD: Johns Hopkins University Press.

De Janvry, Alain, Frederico Finan, and Elisabeth Sadoulet. 2011. "Local Electoral Incentives and Decentralized Program Performance." *Review of Economics and Statistics* 94(3): 672–685.

De Janvry, Alain, Frederico Finan, Elisabeth Sadoulet, and Renos Vakis. 2006. "Can Conditional Cash Transfer Programs Serve as Safety Nets in Keeping Children at School and from Working When Exposed to Shocks?" *Journal of Development Economics* 79: 349–373.

De Janvry, Alain, and Elisabeth Sadoulet. 2006. "Making Conditional Cash Transfer Programs More Efficient: Designing for Maximum Effect of the Conditionality." *World Bank Economic Review* 20(1): 1–29.

De Janvry, Alain, Elisabeth Sadoulet, and Benjamin Davis. 2001. "Cash Transfer Programs with Income Multipliers: Procampo in Mexico." *World Development* 29(6): 1043–1056.

De Mandeville, Bernard. (1732) 1957. "An Essay on Charity and Charity Schools." In the *Fable of the Bees: or, Private Vices, Publick Benefits*. 6th edn. Oxford: Oxford University Press.

Demery, Lionel. 2003. "Analyzing the Incidence of Public Spending." In Francois Bourguignon and Luiz Pereira Da Silva (eds.), *The Impact of Economic Policies on Poverty and Income Distribution: Evaluation Techniques and Tools*. New York: Oxford University Press.

Deming, W. E. 1953. "On a Probability Mechanism to Attain an Economic Balance between the Resultant Error of Response and the Bias of Nonresponse." *Journal of the American Statistical Association* 48: 743–772.

Demombynes, Gabriel, and Berk Ozler. 2005. "Crime and Local Inequality in South Africa." *Journal of Development Economics* 76(2): 265–292.

de Montesquieu, Charles. (1748) 1914. *The Spirit of Laws*. Translated by Thomas Nugent. London: G. Bell and Sons.

Department of Health and Human Services (DHHS). 2008. "Appendix A: Program Data." Washington, DC: Department of Health and Human Services, US Government.

Dercon, Stefan, and Pramila Krishnan. 2000. "In Sickness and in Health: Risk Sharing within Households in Rural Ethiopia." *Journal of Political Economy* 108(4): 688–727.

Dercon, Stefan, and Ingo Outes. 2013. "The Road to Perdition: Rainfall Shocks, Poverty Traps and Destitution in Semi-Arid India." Mimeo, Oxford University.

Desai, Meghnad, and Anup Shah. 1988. "An Econometric Approach to the Measurement of Poverty." *Oxford Economic Papers* 40: 505–522.

de Tocqueville, Alexis. (1835) 2005. *Memoir on Pauperism: Does Public Charity Produce an Idle and Dependent Class of Society?* New York: Cosimo Classics.

Devarajan, Shanta. 2011. "Africa's Statistical Tragedy." *Africa Can End Poverty Blog*, World Bank, posted 6 October, 2011.

De Vos, Klaas, and Thesia Garner. 1991. "An Evaluation of Subjective Poverty Definitions: Comparing Results from the U.S. and the Netherlands." *Review of Income and Wealth* 37(3): 267–285.

De Vreyer, Philippe, Sylvie Lambert, Abla Safir, and Momar B. Sylla. 2008. "Pauvreté et Structure Familiale, Pourquoi une Nouvelle Enquête?" *Stateco* 102: 261–275.

de Waal, Frans. 2009. *The Age of Empathy: Nature's Lessons for a Kinder Society*. New York: Three Rivers Press.

de Walque, Damien. 2004. "How Does the Impact of an HIV/AIDS Information Campaign Vary with Educational Attainment? Evidence from Rural Uganda." Policy Research Working Paper 3289. Washington, DC: World Bank.

Dickens, Charles. (1838) 2003. *Oliver Twist*. London: Penguin.

Dickerson, Sally, and Margaret Kemeny. 2004. "Acute Stressors and Cortisol Responses: A Theoretical Integration and Synthesis of Laboratory Research." *Psychological Bulletin* 130(3): 355–391.

Diener, Ed, Eunkook Suh, Richard E. Lucas, and Heifi L. Smith. 1999. "Subjective Well-Being: Three Decades of Progress." *Psychological Bulletin* 125: 276–302.

Diewert, W. E. 1976. "Exact and Superlative Index Numbers." *Journal of Econometrics* 4: 115–145.

Diewert, W. E. 1980. "The Economic Theory of Index Numbers: A Survey." In Angus Deaton (ed.), *Essays in the Theory and Measurement of Consumer Behaviour*. Cambridge: Cambridge University Press.

Dinardo John, Nicole Fortin, and Thomas Lemieux. 1996. "Labor Market Institutions and the Distribution of Wages 1973–92." *Econometrica* 64: 610–643.

Di Tella, Rafael, Sebastian Galiani, and Ernesto Schargrodsky. 2010. "Reality versus Propaganda in the Formation of Beliefs about Privatization." *Journal of Public Economics* 96: 553–567.

Di Tella, Rafael, and R. MacCulloch. 2006. "Some Uses of Happiness Data in Economics." *Journal of Economic Perspectives* 20(1): 25–46.

Dixit, Avinash, and Sandmo, Agnar. 1977. "Some Simplified Formulae for Optimal Income Taxation." *Scandinavian Journal of Economics* 79: 417–423.

Djankov, Simeon, Rafael La Porta, Florencio Lopez-de-Silanes, and Andrei Shleifer. 2002. "The Regulation of Entry." *Quarterly Journal of Economics* 117(1): 1–37.

Do, Quy-Toan, Andrew Levchenko, and Martin Ravallion. 2014. "Copying with Food Price Volatility: Trade Insulation as Social Protection." In Jean-Paul Chavas, David Hummels, and Brian Wright (eds.), *The Economics of Food Price Volatility*. Chicago: University of Chicago Press.

Doepke, Matthias, and Fabrizio Zilibotti. 2005. "Social Class and the Spirit of Capitalism." *Journal of the European Economic Association* 3(2–3): 516–524.

Doeringer, Peter, and Michael Piore. 1971. *Internal Labor Markets and Manpower Analysis*. New York: Sharpe.

Dolan, Paul, Tessa Peasgood, and Mathew White. 2008. "Do We Really Know What Makes Us Happy? A Review of the Economic Literature on the Factors Associated with Subjective Well-Being." *Journal of Economic Psychology* 29: 94–122.

Dollar, David, Tatjana Kleineberg, and Aart Kraay. 2013. "Growth Still Is Good for the Poor." Policy Research Working Paper 6568. World Bank.

Dollar, David, and Aart Kraay. 2002. "Growth *Is* Good for the Poor." *Journal of Economic Growth* 7(3): 195–225.

Dollar, David, and Aart Kraay. 2004. "Trade, Growth and Poverty." *Economic Journal* 114(493): F22–F49.

Domar, Evsey. 1946. "Capital Expansion, Rate of Growth and Employment." *Econometrica* 14: 137–147.

Doron, Abraham. 1990. "Definition and Measurement of Poverty—The Unsolved Issue." *Social Security: Journal of Welfare and Social Security Studies*, Special English Edition, 2: 27–50.

Doucouliagos, Hristos, and Martin Paldam. 2008. "Aid Effectiveness on Growth: A Meta Study." *European Journal of Political Economy* 24: 1–24.

Drèze, Jean. 1990a. "Famine Prevention in Africa: Some Experiences and Lessons." In Jean Drèze and Amartya Sen (eds.), *The Political Economy of Hunger*, vol. 2. Oxford: Oxford University Press.

Drèze, Jean. 1990b. "Famine Prevention in India." In Jean Drèze and Amartya Sen (eds.), *The Political Economy of Hunger*, vol. 2. Oxford: Oxford University Press.

Drèze, Jean, and Amartya Sen. 1989. *Hunger and Public Action*. Oxford: Oxford University Press.

Drèze, Jean, and Amartya Sen. 1995. *India: Economic Development and Social Opportunity*. Delhi: Oxford University Press.

Drèze, Jean, and Amartya Sen. 2013. *An Uncertain Glory: India and its Contradictions*. London: Penguin Allen Lane.

Drèze, Jean, and P. V. Srinivasan. 1997. "Widowhood and Poverty in Rural India: Some Inferences from Household Survey Data." *Journal of Development Economics* 54: 217–234.

Drèze, Jean, and Nicholas Stern. 1987. "The Theory of Cost-Benefit Analysis." In Alan Auerbach and Martin Feldstein (eds.), *Handbook of Public Economics*. Amsterdam: North-Holland.

Dube, Arindrajit, T. William Lester, and Michael Reich. 2010. "Minimum Wage Effects across State Borders: Estimates Using Contiguous Counties." *Review of Economics and Statistics* 92(4): 945–964.

Dubin, Jeffrey A., and Douglas Rivers. 1993. "Experimental Estimates of the Impact of Wage Subsidies." *Journal of Econometrics* 56(1/2): 219–242.

Duclos, Jean-Yves, and Abdelkrim Araar. 2006. *Poverty and Equity: Measurement, Policy and Estimation with DAD*. Boston: Kluwer Academic Publishers.

Duclos, Jean-Yves, and Magda Mercader-Prats. 1999. "Household Needs and Poverty: With Application to Spain and the U.K." *Review of Income and Wealth* 45(1): 77–98.

Duesenberry, James S. 1949. *Income, Saving and the Theory of Consumer Behavior*. Cambridge, MA: Harvard University Press.

Duflo, Esther. 2006. "Poor but Rational?" In Abhijit Banerjee, Roland Bénabou, and Dilip Mookherjee (eds.), *Understanding Poverty*. Oxford: Oxford University Press.

Duflo, Esther, Michael Greenstone and Rema Hana. 2008. "Indoor Air Pollution, Health and Economic Well-Being," *Surveys and Perspectives Integrating Environment and Society* 1(1): 7–16.

Duflo, Esther, Michael Kremer, and Jonathan Robinson. 2008. "How High Are the Rates of Return to Fertilizer? Evidence from Field Experiments in Kenya." *American Economic Review, Papers and Proceedings* 98(2): 482–488.

Duncan, Greg, and Aaron Sojourner. 2013. "Can Intensive Early Childhood Intervention Programs Eliminate Income-Based Cognitive and Achievement Gaps?" *Journal of Human Resources* 48(4): 945–968.

Duncan, Otis, David Featherman, and Beverly Duncan. 1972. *Socioeconomic Background and Achievement*. New York: Seminar Press.

Dupas, Pascaline. 2014. "Getting Essential Health Products to Their End Users: Subsidize, but How Much?" *Science* 345: 1279–1281.

Durlauf, Steven. 2006. "Groups, Social Influences, and Inequality." In Samuel Bowles, Steven Durlauf, and Karla Hoff (eds.), *Poverty Traps*. Princeton, NJ: Princeton University Press.

Durr, Robert H. 1993. "What Moves Policy Sentiment?" *American Political Science Review* 87(1): 158–170.

Dutta, Puja, Rinku Murgai, Martin Ravallion, and Dominique van de Walle. 2012. "Does India's Employment Guarantee Scheme Guarantee Employment?" *Economic and Political Weekly* 48 (April 21): 55–64.

Dutta, Puja, Rinku Murgai, Martin Ravallion, and Dominique van de Walle. 2014. *Right-to-Work? Assessing India's Employment Guarantee Scheme in Bihar*. Washington DC: World Bank.

Duvendack, Maren, and Richard Palmer-Jones. 2012. "High Noon for Microfinance Impact Evaluations: Re-investigating the Evidence from Bangladesh." *Journal of Development Studies* 48(12): 1864–1880.

Easterlin, Richard A. 1974. "Does Economic Growth Improve the Human Lot? Some Empirical Evidence." In P. A. David and W. R. Melvin (eds.), *Nations and Households in Economic Growth*. Palo Alto, CA: Stanford University Press.

Easterlin, Richard A. 1995. "Will Raising the Incomes of all Increase the Happiness of all?" *Journal of Economic Behavior and Organization* 27: 35–47.

Easterly, William. 2001. "The Middle Class Consensus and Economic Development." *Journal of Economic Growth* 6(4): 317–335.

Easterly, William. 2006. *The White Man's Burden: Why the West's Efforts to Aid the Rest Have Done So Much Ill and So Little Good*. Oxford: Oxford University Press.

Easterly, William, and Stanley Fischer. 2001. "Inflation and the Poor." *Journal of Money, Credit and Banking* 33(2): 160–178.

Easterly, William, Ross Levine, and David Roodman. 2004. "Aid, Policies, and Growth: Comment." *American Economic Review* 94(3): 774–780.

Easton, Brian. 2002. "Beware the Median." *Social Policy Research Center Newsletter* 82: 6–7.

Eastwood, Robert, and Michael Lipton. 1999. "The Impact of Changes in Human Fertility on Poverty." *Journal of Development Studies* 36(1): 1–30.

Eastwood, Robert, and Michael Lipton. 2001. "Demographic Transition and Poverty: Effects via Economic Growth, Distribution and Conversion." In Nancy Birdsall, Allen Kelley, and Steven Sinding (eds.), *Population Matters*. Oxford: Oxford University Press.

Economist. 2013. "Still Lying After All These Years." *The Economist*, December 21.

Economist. 2014a. "The Big Fight." *The Economist*, May 10, 81.

Economist. 2014b. "The Big Mac Index." *The Economist*, January 25–31, 63.

Economist. 2014c. "What's Gone Wrong with Democracy?" *The Economist*, March 1, 47–52.

Economist. 2014d. "An On-Off Relationship." *The Economist*, December 13, 77.

Economist. 2015. "The Great Sprawl of China." *The Economist*, January 24.

Eden, Frederick Morton. 1797. *The State of the Poor*. London: J. Davis.

Edwards, Sebastian. 1997. "Trade Policy, Growth and Income Distribution." *American Economic Review, Papers and Proceedings* 87(2): 205–210.

Ehrlich, Isaac. 1973. "Participation in Illegitimate Activities: A Theoretical and Empirical Analysis." *Journal of Political Economy* 81: 521–565.

Elbers, Chris, Jean Lanjouw, and Peter Lanjouw. 2003. "Micro–Level Estimation of Poverty and Inequality." *Econometrica* 71(1): 355–364.

El-Gamal, Mahmoud. 1994. "A Dynamic Migration Model with Uncertainty." *Journal of Economic Dynamics and Control* 18(3–4): 511–538.

Ellwood, David, and Lawrence Summers. 1986. "Poverty in America: Is Welfare the Answer or the Problem?" In Sheldon Danziger and Daniel Weinberg (eds.), *Fighting Poverty: What Works and What Doesn't.* Cambridge, MA: Harvard University Press.

Elwell, Craig, and Linda Levine. 2013. "Inflation and the Real Minimum Wage: A Fact Sheet." Congressional Research Service 7–5700, US Congress.

Emran, M. Shahe, Virginia Robano, and Stephen C. Smith. 2014. "Assessing the Frontiers of Ultrapoverty Reduction: Evidence from Challenging the Frontiers of Poverty Reduction/ Targeting the Ultra-poor, an Innovative Program in Bangladesh," *Economic Development and Cultural Change* 62: 339–380.

Engel, Ernst. 1857. "Die Productions- und Consumtionsverhältnisse des Königreichs Sachsen." *Zeitschrift des statistischen Bureaus des Königlich Sächsischen Ministeriums des Inneren* 8–9: 28–29.

Engels, Friedrich. (1845) 1993. *The Condition of the Working Class in England.* Oxford: Oxford University Press.

Engerman, Stanley L., and Kenneth Sokoloff. 2006. "Colonialism, Inequality and Long-Run Paths of Development." In Abhijit Banerjee, Roland Bénabou, and Dilip Mookherjee (eds.), *Understanding Poverty.* Oxford: Oxford University Press.

Ensminger, Jean. 1997. "Changing Property Rights: Reconciling Formal and Informal Rights to Land in Africa." In John Drobak and John V.C. Nye (eds.), *The Frontiers of the New Institutional Economics.* San Diego, CA: Academic Press.

Ermisch, John, Markus Jäntti, and Timothy Smeeding. 2012. "Socioeconomic Gradients in Childrens' Outcomes." In John Ermisch, Markus Jäntti, and Timothy Smeeding (eds.), *From Parents to Children: The Intergenerational Transmission of Advantage.* New York: Russell Sage Foundation.

Eswaran, Mukesh, and Ashok Kotwal. 1994. *Why Poverty Persists in India.* Delhi: Oxford University Press.

Eurostat. 2005. "Income Poverty and Social Exclusion in the EU25." *Statistics in Focus 03 2005.* Luxembourg: Office of Official Publications of the European Communities.

Evans, Gary, Edith Chen, Gregory Miller, and Teresa Seeman. 2012. "How Poverty Gets Under the Skin: A Lifetime Perspective." In Valerie Mahomet and Rosalind King (eds.) *The Oxford Handbook of Poverty and Child Development.* Oxford: Oxford University Press.

Fafchamps, Marcel and Forhad Shipli. 2009. "Isolation and Subjective Welfare: Evidence from South Asia." *Economic Development and Cultural Change* 57(4): 641–683.

Fajnzylber, Pablo, Daniel Lederman, and Norman Loayza. 2002. "What Causes Violent Crime?" *European Economic Review* 46(7): 1323–1357.

Fan, Elliott. 2010. "Who Benefits from Public Old Age Pensions? Evidence from a Targeted Program." *Economic Development and Cultural Change* 58(2): 297–322.

Fan, Shenggen. 1991. "Effects of Technological Change and Institutional Reform on Growth in Chinese Agriculture." *American Journal of Agricultural Economics* 7: 266–275.

Feder, Gershon, and Raymond Noronha. 1987. "Land Rights Systems and Agricultural Development in sub-Saharan Africa." *World Bank Research Observer* 2(2): 143–169.

Fehr, Ernst, and Urs Fischbacher. 2002. "Why Social Preferences Matter: The Impact of Non-Selfish Motives on Competition, Cooperation and Incentives." *Economic Journal* 112: C1–C33.

Fei, John C. H., and Gustav Ranis. 1964. *Development of the Labor Surplus Economy.* Homewood, IL: Irwin.

Fei, John C. H., Gustav Ranis, and Shirley Kuo. 1979. *Growth with Equity: The Taiwan Case.* New York: Oxford University Press for the World Bank.

Feinstein, Charles H. 1998. "Pessimism Perpetuated: Real Wages and the Standard of Living in Britain during and after the Industrial Revolution." *Journal of Economic History* 58: 625–658.

Fernald, Anne, Virginia Marchman, and Adriana Weisleder. 2013. "SES Differences in Language Processing Skill and Vocabulary Are Evident at 18 Months." *Development Science* 16(2): 234–248.

Fernandez, C., E. Ley, and M. F. J. Steel. 2001. "Model Uncertainty in Cross-Country Growth Regressions." *Journal of Applied Econometrics* 16(5): 563–576.

Fernandez, Raquel, and Richard Rogerson. 1997. "Keeping People Out: Income Distribution, Zoning, and the Quality of Public Education." *International Economic Review* 38(1): 23–42.

Ferreira, Francisco, and Jèrèmie Gignoux. 2011. "The Measurement of Inequality of Opportunity: Theory and an Application to Latin America." *Review of Income and Wealth* 57(4): 622–657.

Ferreira, Francisco, Phillippe Leite, and Julie Litchfield. 2008. "The Rise and Fall of Brazilian Inequality: 1981–2004." *Macroeconomic Dynamics* 12: 199–230.

Ferreira Francisco, Phillippe Leite, and Martin Ravallion. 2010. "Poverty Reduction without Economic Growth? Explaining Brazil's Poverty Dynamics 1985–2004." *Journal of Development Economics* 93: 20–36.

Ferreira, Francisco, and Martin Ravallion. 2009. "Poverty and Inequality: The Global Context." In Wiemer Salverda, Brian Nolan and Tim Smeeding (eds.), *The Oxford Handbook of Economic Inequality*. Oxford: Oxford University Press.

Ferreira, Francisco, and Norbert Schady. 2008. "Aggregate Economic Shocks, Child Schooling and Child Health." Policy Research Working Paper 4701. Washington, DC: World Bank.

Ferrer-i-Carbonell, A. 2005. "Income and Well-Being: An Empirical Analysis of the Comparison Income Effect." *Journal of Public Economics* 89: 997–1019.

Ferrer-i-Carbonell, Ada, and Bernard Van Praag. 2001. "Poverty in Russia." *Journal of Happiness Studies* 2: 147–172.

Festinger, Leon. 1957. *A Theory Of Cognitive Dissonance*. Evanston, IL: Row Peterson.

Feyzioglu, T., V. Swaroop, and M. Zhu. 1998. "A Panel Data Analysis of the Fungibility of Foreign Aid." *World Bank Economic Review* 12(1): 29–58.

Fields, Gary S. 1975. "Rural–Urban Migration, Urban Unemployment and Underemployment and Job Search Activity in LDCs." *Journal of Development Economics* 2(2): 165–188.

Fields, Gary S. 1977. "Who Benefits from Economic Development? A Reexamination of Brazilian Growth in the 1960's." *American Economic Review* 67(4): 570–582.

Fields, Gary S. 1980. *Poverty, Inequality and Development*. Cambridge: Cambridge University Press.

Fields, Gary S. 1987. "Public Policy and the Labor Market in Developing Countries." In David Newbery and Nicholas Stern (eds.), *The Theory of Taxation for Developing Countries*. Washington, DC: Oxford University Press for the World Bank.

Fields, Gary S. 2001. *Distribution and Development*. New York: Russell Sage Foundation.

Fifield, Anna. 2013. "Starved of Healthy Options." *Financial Times*, June 14, 9.

Filmer, Deon. 2007. "If You Build It, Will They Come? School Availability and School Enrolment in 21 Poor Countries." *Journal of Development Studies* 43(5): 901–928.

Filmer, Deon. 2014. "Education Attainment and Enrollment around the World: An International Database." http://econ.worldbank.org/projects/edattain.

Filmer, Deon, and Lant Pritchett. 1999. "The Effect of Household Wealth on Education Attainment: Evidence from 35 Countries." *Population and Development Review* 25(1): 85–120.

Filmer, Deon, and Kinnon Scott. 2012. "Assessing Asset Indices." *Demography* 49(1): 359–392.

Fischer Walker, Christa, Igor Rudan, Li Liu, Harish Nair, Evropi Theodoratou, Zulfiqar Bhutta, Katherine L. O'Brien, Harry Campbell, and Robert E. Black. 2013. "Global Burden of Childhood Diarrhoea and Pneumonia." *Lancet* 381: 1405–1416.

Fisher, Gordon. 1992. "The Development and History of the Poverty Thresholds." *Social Security Bulletin* 55(4): 3–14.

Fisher, Ronald A. 1935. *The Design of Experiments*. Edinburgh: Oliver and Boyd.

Fishlow, Albert. 1972. "Brazilian Size Distribution of Income." *American Economic Review Papers and Proceedings* 62: 391–402.

Fishlow, Albert, and Catherine Gwin. 1994. "Overview: Lessons from the East Asian Experience." In Albert Fishlow, Catherine Gwin, Stephan Haggard, Dani Rodrik, and Robert Wade (eds.),

Miracle or Design? Lessons from the East Asian Experience. Washington, DC: Overseas Development Council.

Fiszbein, Ariel, and Norbert Schady. 2010. *Conditional Cash Transfers for Attacking Present and Future Poverty*. Washington, DC: World Bank.

Fitzsimons, Emla, and Alice Mesnard. 2014. "Can Conditional Cash Transfers Compensate for a Father's Absence?" *World Bank Economic Review* 28(3): 467–491.

Fleischacker, Samuel. 2004. *A Short History of Distributive Justice*. Cambridge, MA: Harvard University Press.

Fleurbaey, Marc. 2008. *Fairness, Responsibility and Welfare*. Oxford: Oxford University Press.

Fleurbaey, Marc. 2009. "Beyond GDP: The Quest for a Measure of Social Welfare." *Journal of Economic Literature* 47(4): 1029–1075. Fleurbaey, Marc, and François Maniquet. 2011. *A Theory of Fairness and Social Welfare*, Cambridge: Cambridge University Press.

Fogel, Robert W. 2004. *The Escape from Hunger and Premature Death, 1700–2100*. Cambridge: Cambridge University Press.

Fogel, Robert W., Stanley Engerman, Roderick Floud, Gerald Friedman, Robert Mango, Kenneth Sokoloff, Richard Steckel, James Trussell, Georgia Villaflor, and Kenneth Watchter. 1983. "Secular Change in American and British Stature and Nutrition." In Robert Rotberg and Theodore Rabb (eds.), *Hunger in History*. Cambridge: Cambridge University Press.

Foner, Eric. 1988. *Reconstruction: America's Unfinished Revolution 1863–1877*. New York: Harper & Row.

Food and Agricultural Organization (FAO). 2001. *Human Energy Requirements. Report of a Joint FAO/WHO/UNU Expert Consultation*. FAO Food and Nutrition Technical Report 1. Rome: Food and Agricultural Organization.

Food and Drug Administration. 2010. *Adaptive Design Clinical Trials for Drugs and Biologics*. Washington, DC: Food and Drug Administration, US Government.

Forbes, Kristin J. 2000. "A Reassessment of the Relationship between Inequality and Growth." *American Economic Review* 90(4): 869–887.

Foster, Andrew, and Naresh Kumar. 2011. "Health Effects of Air Quality Regulations in Delhi, India," *Atmospheric Environment* 45(9): 1675–1683.

Foster, James. 1984. "On Economic Poverty: A Survey of Aggregate Measures." *Advances in Econometrics* 3: 215–251.

Foster, James. 1998. "Absolute versus Relative Poverty." *American Economic Review* 88(2): 335–341.

Foster, James, Joel Greer, and Erik Thorbecke. 1984. "A Class of Decomposable Poverty Measures." *Econometrica* 52: 761–765.

Foster, James, and Amartya Sen. 1997. "On Economic Inequality after a Quarter Century." Annexe to Revised Version of Sen's *On Economic Inequality*, Oxford University Press.

Foster, James, Suman Seth, Michael Lokshin, and Zurab Sajaia. 2013. *A Unified Approach to Measuring Poverty and Inequality*. Washington, DC: World Bank.

Foster, James, and A. F. Shorrocks. 1988a. "Poverty Orderings." *Econometrica* 56: 173–177.

Foster, James, and A. F. Shorrocks. 1988b. "Poverty Orderings and Welfare Dominance." In W. Gaertner and P. K. Pattanaik (eds.), *Distributive Justice and Inequality*. Berlin: Springer-Verlag.

Foster, James, and A. F. Shorrocks. 1991. "Subgroup Consistent Poverty Indices." *Econometrica* 59: 687–709.

Fowler, Simon. 2007. *The Workhouse: The People, the Places, the Life Behind Doors*. Kew, Surrey: The National Archives.

Fox, Liana, Irwin Garfinkel, Neeraj Kaushal, Jane Waldfogel, and Christopher Wimer. 2013. "Waging War on Poverty: Historical Trends in Poverty Using the Supplemental Poverty Measure." Paper presented at the Association for Public Policy and Management (APPAM) Conference, Washington, DC, November 8.

Frank, Robert H. 1985. *Choosing the Right Pond: Human Behavior and the Quest for Status*. New York: Oxford University Press.

Frank, Robert H. 1997. "The Frame of Reference as a Public Good." *Economic Journal* 107: 1832–1847.

Frankel, Marvin. 1962. "The Production Function in Allocation and Growth: A Synthesis." *American Economic Review* 52: 995–1022.

Frankena, Mark. 1975. "Alternative Models of Rent Control." *Urban Studies* 12: 303–308.

Freedman, Benjamin. 1987. "Equipoise and the Ethics of Clinical Research." *New England Journal of Medicine* 317(3): 141–145.

Freedman, David. 2010. "Why Scientific Studies are so often Wrong: The Streetlight Effect." *Discover*, July–August.

Freiman, Christopher. 2012. "Why Poverty Matters Most: Towards a Humanitarian Theory of Social Justice." *Utilitas* 24(1): 26–40.

Frey, Bruno, and Stutzer, Alois. 2002. "What Can Economists Learn from Happiness Research?" *Journal of Economic Literature* 40: 402–435.

Friedman, Howard. 2013. "Causal Inference and the Millennium Development Goals (MDGs): Assessing Whether There was an Acceleration in MDG Development Indicators Following the MDG Declaration." Mimeo, Columbia University, School of International and Public Affairs.

Friedman, Jed. 2014a. "Quantifying the Hawthorne Effect." Development Impact Blog, World Bank.

Friedman, Jed. 2014b. "A Taxonomy of Behavioral Responses to Evaluation." Development Impact Blog, World Bank.

Friedman, Jed, and James Levinsohn. 2002. "The Distributional Impact of Indonesia's Financial Crisis on Household Welfare." *World Bank Economic Review* 16(3): 397–424.

Friedman, Jed, and Jennifer Sturdy. 2011. "The Influence of Economic Crisis on Early Childhood Development: A Review of Pathways and Measured Impact." In Harold Alderman (ed.), *No Small Matter*. Washington, DC: World Bank.

Friedman, Milton. 1957. *A Theory of the Consumption Function*. Princeton, NJ: Princeton University Press.

Friedman, Milton. 1962. *Capital and Freedom*. Chicago: University of Chicago Press.

Fuchs, Victor. 1967. "Redefining Poverty and Redistributing Income." *Public Interest* 8: 88–95.

Furnham, A., and Argyle, M. 1998. *The Psychology of Money*. London: Routledge.

Furniss, Edgar. 1920. *The Position of the Laborer in a System of Nationalism: A Study in the Labor Theories of the Later English Mercantilists*. Boston and New York: Houghton Mifflin.

Gaiha, Raghav. 1997. "Rural Public Works and the Poor: The Case of the Employment Guarantee Scheme in India." In S. Polachek (ed.), *Research in Labour Economics*. Greenwich CT: JAI Press.

Galasso, Emanuela, and Martin Ravallion. 2005. "Decentralized Targeting of an Antipoverty Program." *Journal of Public Economics* 85: 705–727.

Galasso, Emanuela, Martin Ravallion, and Agustin Salvia. 2004. "Assisting the Transition from Workfare to Work: Argentina's *Proempleo* Experiment." *Industrial and Labor Relations Review* 57(5): 128–142.

Galbraith, John Kenneth. 1958. *The Affluent Society*. Boston: Mariner Books.

Galiani, Sebastian, Stephen Knack, Lixin Colin Xu, and Ben Zou. 2014. "The Effect of Aid on Growth: Evidence from a Quasi-Experiment." Policy Research Working Paper 6825. Washington, DC: World Bank.

Gallup, John Luke. 2012. "The World Convergence of Income Distribution." Mimeo, Portland State University.

Galor, Oded, and Joseph Zeira. 1993. "Income Distribution and Macroeconomics." *Review of Economic Studies* 60(1): 35–52.

Gandhi, Mahatma. 1958. *The Last Phase*. Vol. 2. Ahmedabad: Navajivan Publishing House.

Gans, Herbert. 1995. *The War Against the Poor*. New York: Basic Books.

Garces, Eliana, Duncan Thomas, and Janet Currie. 2002. "Longer Term Effects of Head Start." *American Economic Review* 92(4): 999–1012.

Garenne, Michel. 2011. "Trends in Nutritional Status of Adult Women in sub-Saharan Africa." DHS Comparative Reports 27. Washington, DC: USAID.

Garroway, C., and de Laiglesia, J. R. 2012. "On the Relevance of Relative Poverty for Developing Countries." OECD Development Centre Working Paper 314. Paris: OECD.

Gastwirth, J. L. 1971. "A General Definition of the Lorenz Curve." *Econometrica* 39: 1037–1039.

Gates, Bill, and Melinda Gates. 2014. "Three Myths on the World's Poor." *Wall Street Journal*, January 17.

Gauri, Varun, and Ayesha Vawda. 2004. "Vouchers for Basic Education in Developing Economies: An Accountability Perspective." *World Bank Research Observer* 19(2): 259–280.

Gelb, Alan, and Sneha Raghavan. 2014. "Rolling Out the Aadhaar." Center for Global Development Blog Post.

Gelbach, Jonah, and Lant Pritchett. 2000. "Indicator Targeting in a Political Economy: Leakier Can Be Better." *Journal of Policy Reform* 4: 113–145.

Geremek, Bronislaw. 1994. *Poverty: A History*. Oxford: Blackwell.

Gertler, Paul, and Jacques van der Gaag. 1990. *The Willingness to Pay for Medical Care*. Baltimore, MD: Johns Hopkins University Press for the World Bank.

Ghatak, Maitreesh, and Neville Nien-Huei Jiang. 2002. "A Simple Model of Inequality, Occupational Choice, and Development." *Journal of Development Economics* 69(1): 205–226.

Gibson, John, Geua Boe-Gibson, Halahingano Rohorua, and David McKenzie. 2014. "Efficient Remittance Services for Development in the Pacific." *Asia-Pacific Development Journal* 14(2): 55–74.

Gibson, John, Trinh Le, and Bonggeun Kim. 2014. "Prices, Engel Curves and Time-Space Deflation: Impacts on Poverty and Inequality in Vietnam." Mimeo, University of Waikato, New Zealand.

Giles, Chris. 2014. "Piketty Findings Undercut by Errors." *Financial Times*, May 23.

Gillie, Alan. 1996. "The Origin of the Poverty Line." *Economic History Review* 49(4): 715–730.

Ginsburgh, Victor, and Michael Keyzer. 1997. *The Structure of Applied General Equilibrium Models*. Cambridge, MA: MIT Press.

Giving USA. 2014. The Annual Report on Philanthropy for the Year 2013. Giving USA.

Glazerman, Steven, Dan Levy, and David Myers. 2003. "Non-Experimental versus Experimental Estimates of Earnings Impacts." *Annals of the American Academy of Political and Social Sciences* 589: 63–93.

Glewwe, Paul. 2012. "How Much of Observed Economic Mobility is Measurement Error? IV Methods to Reduce Measurement Error Bias, with an Application to Vietnam." *World Bank Economic Review* 26(2): 236–264.

Glewwe, Paul, and Hanan Jacoby. 1995. "An Economic Analysis of Delayed Primary School Enrollment in a Low Income Country: The Role of Early Childhood Nutrition." *Review of Economics and Statistics* 77(1): 156–169.

Goldberg, Jessica. 2014. "The R-Word Is Not Dirty." Blog Post, Center for Global Development, Washington, DC.

Goldin, Claudia, and Lawrence F. Katz. 2008. *The Race between Education and Technology*. Cambridge, MA: Harvard University Press.

Goldstein, Markus. 2014. "Cash Transfers: Beyond Protection to Productive Impacts." Development Impact Blog, World Bank, February 12.

Golson, Kevin. 2006. "Chronology of Poverty." In Mehmet Odekon (ed.), *Encyclopedia of World Poverty*, vol. 1. London: Sage.

Gordon, David. 1972. *Theories of Poverty and Underemployment*. Lexington, MA: Heath and Company.

Gordon, Roger, and Wei Li. 2009. "Tax Structures in Developing Countries: Many Puzzles and a Possible Explanation." *Journal of Public Economics* 93(7–8): 855–866.

Gramlich, Edward. 1976. "Impact of Minimum Wages on Other Wages, Employment and Family Incomes." In Arthur Okun and George Perry (eds.), *Brookings Papers on Economic* Activity. Washington, DC: Brookings Institution.Green, Duncan. 2010. "Are Women Really 70% of the World's Poor? How Do We Know?" From Poverty to Power. Oxfam Blog, February 3.

Green, Duncan. 2012. "Why 'Why Nations Fail' Fails (Mostly): Review of Acemoglu and Robinson—2012's Big Development Book," People, Spaces, Deliberation, World Bank Blog, December 12.

Greenberg, Jon. 2014. "Carly Fiorina: 70% of World's Poor Are Women." *PunditFact* Blog, January 15.

Greenstone, Michael, Adam Looney, Jeremy Patashnik, and Muxin Yu. 2013. "Thirteen Economic Facts about Social Mobility and the Role of Education." Policy Memo, Hamilton Project, Brookings, Washington, DC.

Greer, J., and Erik Thorbecke. 1986a. "Food Poverty and Consumption Patterns in Kenya." Geneva: International Labor Office.

Greer, J., and Erik Thorbecke. 1986b. "A Methodology for Measuring Food Poverty Applied to Kenya." *Journal of Development Economics* 24: 59–74.

Griffin, Emma. 2013. *Liberty's Dawn: A People's History of the Industrial Revolution.* New Haven, CT: Yale University Press.

Griffin, Keith, and John Enos. 1970. "Foreign Assistance: Objectives and Consequences." *Economic Development and Cultural Change* 18(3): 313–327.

Grootaert, Christiaan. 1986. "Measuring and Analyzing Levels of Living in Developing Countries: An Annotated Questionnaire." Living Standards Measurement Study Working Paper No. 24. Washington, DC: World Bank.

Grosh, Margaret. 1994. *Administering Targeted Social Programs in Latin America: From Platitudes to Practice.* Washington, DC: World Bank.

Grosh, Margaret. 1995. "Toward Quantifying the Trade-Off: Administrative Costs and Incidence in Targeted Programs in Latin America." In Dominique van de Walle and Kimberly Nead (eds.), *Public Spending and the Poor.* Baltimore, MD: Johns Hopkins University Press for the World Bank.

Grosh, Margaret, Carlo del Ninno, Emil Tesliuc, and Azedine Ouerghi. 2008. *For Protection and Promotion: The Design and Implementation of Effective Safety Nets.* Washington, DC: World Bank.

Grosh, Margaret, and Paul Glewwe. 2000. *Designing Household Survey Questionnaires for Developing Countries: Lessons from 15 Years of the Living Standards Measurement Study.* 3 vols. Washington, DC: World Bank.

Groves, Robert E. 2006. "Nonresponse Rates and Nonresponse Bias in Household Surveys," *Public Opinion Quarterly* 70: 646–675.

Groves, Robert E., and Mick P. Couper. 1998. *Nonresponse in Household Interview Surveys.* New York: John Wiley and Sons.

Gustafsson Bjo, Li Shi, and Hiroshi Sato. 2004. "Can a Subjective Poverty Line be Applied to China? Assessing Poverty among Urban Residents in 1999." *Journal of International Development* 16: 1089–1107.

Gutiérrez, Catalina, and Ryuichi Tanaka. 2009. "Inequality and Education Decisions in Developing Countries." *Journal of Economic Inequality* 7: 55–81.

Gwatkin, Davidson. 2000. "Poverty and Inequalities in Health within Developing Countries: Filling the Information Gap." In David Leon and Gill Walt (eds.), *Poverty, Inequality and Health: An International Perspective.* Oxford: Oxford University Press.

Gwatkin, Davidson, Michel Guilot, and Patrick Heuveline. 1999. "The Burden of Disease among the Global Poor." *Lancet* 354: 586–589.

Gwatkin, Davidson, Shea Rutstein, Kiersten Johnson, R. Pande, and Adam Wagstaff. 2000. *Socioeconomic Differences in Health, Nutrition and Population (Country Reports).* Washington, DC: World Bank.

Gwatkin, Davidson, Shea Rutstein, Kiersten Johnson, Eldaw Suliman, Adam Wagstaff, and Agbessi Amouzou. 2007. *Socioeconomic Differences in Health, Nutrition and Population within Developing Countries.* Washington, DC: World Bank.

Hacker, Jacob S., and Paul Pierson. 2010. "Winner-Take-All Politics: Public Policy, Political Organization, and the Precipitous Rise of Top Incomes in the United States." *Politics and Society* 38(2) 152–204.

Haddad, Lawrence, and Ravi Kanbur. 1990. "How Serious is the Neglect of Intra-Household Inequality?" *Economic Journal* 100: 866–881.

Hagenaars, Aldi J. M. 1987. "A Class of Poverty Indices." *International Economic Review* 28: 583–607.

Hagenaars, Aldi J. M., and Klaas de Vos. 1988. "The Definition and Measurement of Poverty." *Journal of Human Resources* 23: 211–221.

Hagenaars, Aldi J. M., and Bernard M. S. van Praag. 1985. "A Synthesis of Poverty Line Definitions." *Review of Income and Wealth* 31: 139–154.

Haggblade, Steven, Peter Hazell, and J. Brown. 1989. "Farm-Nonfarm Linkages in Rural sub-Saharan Africa." *World Development* 17(8): 1173–1201.

Halter, Daniel, Manuel Oechslin, and Josef Zweimüller. 2014. "Inequality and Growth: The Neglected Time Dimension," *Journal of Economic Growth* 19: 81–104.

Hamilton, Bob, and John Whalley. 1984. "Efficiency and Distributional Implications of Global Restrictions on Labour Mobility." *Journal of Development Economics* 14: 61–75.

Hammer, Jeffrey, and Dean Spears. 2013. "Village Sanitation and Children's Human Capital: Evidence from a Randomized Experiment by the Maharashtra Government." Policy Research Working Paper 6580. Washington, DC: World Bank.

Hammond, Peter. 1976. "Equity, Arrow's Conditions and Rawls' Difference Principle," *Econometrica* 44: 793–804.

Handa, Sudhanshu, Michael Park, Robert Osei Darko, Isaac Osei-Akoto, Benjamin Davis, and Silvio Daidone. 2013. *Livelihood Empowerment Against Poverty Program Impact Evaluation*. Chapel Hill: University of North Carolina.

Hansen, Henrik, and Finn Tarp. 2001. "Aid and Growth Regressions." *Journal of Development Economics* 64: 547–570.

Harrington, Michael. 1962. *The Other America: Poverty in the United States*. New York: Macmillan.

Harris, John, and Michael Todaro. 1970. "Migration, Unemployment and Development: A Two Sector Analysis." *American Economic Review* 40: 126–142.

Harrison, Ann, and Andrés Rodríguez-Clare. 2010. "Trade, Foreign Investment, and Industrial Policy for Developing Countries." In Dani Rodrik and Mark Rosenzweig (eds.) *Handbook of Development Economics*, vol. 5. Amsterdam: North Holland.

Harrison, Elizabeth, and Christian Seidl. 1994. "Perceptional Inequality and Preferential Judgment: An Empirical Examination of Distributional Axioms." *Public Choice* 79: 61–81.

Harrison, Ross. 1987. "Jeremy Bentham." In John Eatwell, Murray Milgate, and Peter Newman (eds.), *The Invisible Hand*. New York: W. W. Norton.

Harrod, Roy. 1939. "An Essay in Dynamic Theory." *Economic Journal* 49: 14–33.

Harsanyi, John. 1975. "Can the Maximin Principle Serve as a Basis for Morality? A Critique of John Rawls's Theory." *American Political Science Review* 69(2): 594–606.

Hartmann, Betsy. 1987. *Reproductive Rights and Wrongs: The Global Politics of Population Control and Contraceptive Choice*. New York: Harper and Row.

Hartmann, Betsy, and James Boyce. 1983. *A Quiet Violence: View from a Bangladesh Village*. London: Zed Press.

Hartwell, Ronald Max. 1961. "The Rising Standard of Living in England, 1800–1850." *Economic History Review* 13: 397–416.

Hartwell, Ronald Max. 1972. "Consequences of the Industrial Revolution in England for the Poor." In Ronald Max Hartwell (ed.), *The Long Debate on Poverty*. London: Institute of Economic Affairs.

Hassett, Kevin. 2014. "Remarks on Thomas Piketty's Capital in the Twenty-First Century." American Enterprise Institute. http://www.aei.org/speech/economics/remarks-on-thomas-pikettys-capital-in-the-twenty-first-century/.

Haugen, Gary, and Victor Boutros. 2014. *The Locust Effect*. Oxford and New York: Oxford University Press.

Haughton, Jonathan, and Shahidur Khandker. 2009. *The Handbook on Poverty and Inequality*. Washington, DC: World Bank.

Hauk, William R., and Romain Wacziarg. 2009. "A Monte Carlo Study of Growth Regressions." *Journal of Economic Growth* 14: 103–147.

Haushofer, Johannes, and Ernst Fehr. 2014. "On the Psychology of Poverty." *Science* 344: 862–867.

Hausmann, Ricardo, Dani Rodrik, and A. Velasco. 2008. "Growth Diagnostics." In J. Stiglitz and N. Serra (eds.), *The Washington Consensus Reconsidered: Towards a New Global Governance*. New York: Oxford University Press.

Hayek, Friedrich. (1944) 1994. *The Road to Serfdom*. Fiftieth Anniversary edn. Chicago: University of Chicago Press.

Hazan, Moshe, and Binyamin Berdugo. 2002. "Child Labour, Fertility, and Economic Growth." *Economic Journal* 112: 810–828.

Hazell, Peter, and Steven Haggblade. 1993. "Farm-Nonfarm Growth Linkages and the Welfare of the Poor." In M. Lipton and J. van der Gaag (eds.), *Including the Poor*. Washington, DC, World Bank.

Heckman, James. 2006. "Skill Formation and the Economics of Investing in Disadvantaged Children." *Science* 30: 1900–1902.

Heckman, James. 2008. "Schools, Skills and Synapses." Institute for the Study of Labor (IZA) Working Paper 3515.

Heckman, James, Hidehiko Ichimura, Jeffrey Smith, and Petra Todd. 1998. "Characterizing Selection Bias using Experimental Data." *Econometrica* 66(5): 1017–1098.

Heckman, James, Hidehiko Ichimura, and Petra Todd. 1997. "Matching as an Econometric Evaluation Estimator: Evidence from Evaluating a Job Training Program." *Review of Economic Studies* 64(4): 605–654.

Heckman, James, Robert LaLonde, and Jeffrey Smith. 1999. "The Economics and Econometrics of Active Labor Market Programs." In O. Ashenfelter and D. Card (eds.), *Handbook of Labor Economics*, vol. 3A. Amsterdam: North-Holland.

Heckman, James, Lance Lochner, and Christopher Taber. 1998. "General Equilibrium Treatment Effects." *American Economic Review Papers and Proceedings* 88: 381–386.

Heckman, James, Lance Lochner, and Petra Todd. 2003. "Fifty Years of Mincer Earnings Regressions." NBER Working Paper 9732.

Heckman, James, and Jeffrey Smith. 1995. "Assessing the Case for Social Experiments." *Journal of Economic Perspectives* 9(2): 85–110.

Heckman, James, and Christopher Taber. 2008. "Roy Model." In Steven N. Durlauf and Lawrence E. Blume (eds.), *The New Palgrave Dictionary of Economics*. 2nd edn. London: Palgrave Macmillan.

Heckman, James, and Junjian Yi. 2014. "Human Capital, Economic Growth and Inequality in China." In Shenggen Fan, Ravi Kanbur, Shang-jin Wei, and Xiaobo Zhang (eds.), *Oxford Companion to the Economics of China*. Oxford: Oxford University Press.

Heclo, Hugh. 1986. "The Political Foundations of Antipoverty Policy." In Sheldon Danziger and Daniel Weinberg (eds.), *Fighting Poverty: What Works and What Doesn't*. Cambridge, MA: Harvard University Press.

Hemerijck, Anton. 2014. "The Reform Capacities of European Welfare States." In Bea Cantillon and Frank Vandenbroucke (eds.), *Reconciling Work and Poverty Reduction: How Successful Are European Welfare States?* Oxford: Oxford University Press.

Hentschel, Jesko. 1999. "Contextuality and Data Collection Methods: A Framework and Application to Health Service Utilisation." *Journal of Development Studies* 35: 64–94.

Hertel, T., ed. 1997. *Global Trade Analysis: Modeling and Applications*. Cambridge: Cambridge University Press.

Hertel-Fernandez, Alexander, and Jeffrey B. Wenger. 2013. "Taking Up Social Benefits: A Cautionary Tale from an Unemployment Insurance Survey Experiment." http://ssrn.com/abstract=2341885 or http://dx.doi.org/10.2139/ssrn.2341885.

Herzer, Dierk, and Sebastian Vollmer. 2012. "Inequality and Growth: Evidence from Panel Cointegration." *Journal of Economic Inequality* 10: 489–503.

Hicks, John. 1939. *Value and Capital*. Oxford: Clarendon Press.

Hill, Anne, and Elizabeth King. 1998. "Women's Education in Developing Countries: An Overview." In Anne Hill and Elizabeth King (eds.), *Women's Education in Developing Countries: Barriers, Befits and Policies*. Washington, DC: World Bank.

Hill, Christopher. 1972. *The World Turned Upside Down: Radical Ideas During the English Revolution*. London: Maurice Temple Smith.

Himmelfarb, Gertrude. 1984a. *The Idea of Poverty: England in the Early Industrial Age*. London: Faber and Faber.

Himmelfarb, Gertrude. 1984b. "The Idea of Poverty." *History Today* 34(4).

Hindle, Steve. 2004. *On the Parish? The Micro-Politics of Poor Relief in Rural England 1550–1750*. Oxford: Oxford University Press.

Hindriks, Jean, and Gareth Myles. 2006. *Intermediate Public Economics*. Cambridge, MA: MIT Press.

Hirschman, Albert. 1958. *The Strategy of Economic Development*. New Haven, CT: Yale University Press.

Hirway, Indira, and Piet Terhal. 1994. *Towards Employment Guarantee in India: Indian and International Experience in Rural Public Works Programmes*. New Delhi: Sage Publications.

Hnatkovska, Viktoria, and Amartya Lahiri. 2013. "Structural Transformation and the Rural–Urban Divide." Mimeo, University of British Columbia.

Hoddinott, John, Harold Alderman, Jere Behrman, Laurance Haddad, and Susan Horton. 2013. "The Economic Rationale for Investing in Stunting." *Maternal and Child Nutrition* 9(S2): 69–82.

Hoddinott, John, Jere Behrman, John Maluccio, Paul Melgar, Agnes Quisumbing, Manuel Ramirez-Zea, Aryeh D. Stein, Kathryn Yount, and Reynaldo Martorell. 2013. "Adult Consequences of Growth Failure in Early Childhood." *American Journal of Clinical Nutrition*, November: 1–9.

Hoddinott, John, Gussh Berhane, Daniel Gilligan, Neha Kumar, and Alemayehu Seyoum Taffesse. 2012. "The Impact of Ethiopia's Productive Safety Net Programme and Related Transfers on Agricultural Productivity." *Journal of African Economies* 21(5): 761–786.

Hoddinott, John, John Maluccio, Jere Behrman, Reynaldo Martorell, Paul Melgar, Agnes Quisumbing, Manuel Ramirez-Zea, Aryeh D. Stein, and Kathryn Yount. 2011. "The Consequences of Early Childhood Growth Failure over the Life Course." Discussion Paper 1073. Washington, DC: International Food Policy Research Institute.

Hoff, Karla. 1996. "Market Failures and the Distribution of Wealth: A Perspective from the Economics of Information." *Politics and Society* 24(4): 411–432.

Hoff, Karla, and Arijit Sen. 2006. "The Kin System as a Poverty Trap." In Samuel Bowles, Steven Durlauf, and Karla Hoff (eds.), *Poverty Traps*. Princeton, NJ: Princeton University Press.

Hogan, Margaret C., Kyle J. Foreman, Mohsen Naghavi, Stephanie Y. Ahn, Mengru Wang, Susanna M. Makela, Alan D. Lopez, Rafael Lozano, and Christopher J. L. Murray. 2010. "Maternal Mortality for 181 Countries, 1980–2008: A Systematic Analysis of Progress towards Millennium Development Goal 5." *The Lancet* 375(9726): 1609–1623.

Holden, Stein T., Klaus Deininger, and Hosaena Hagos Ghebru. 2009. "Impacts of Low-Cost Land Certification on Investment and Productivity." *American Journal of Agricultural Economics* 91(2): 359–373.

Holland, Paul. 1986. "Statistics and Causal Inference." *Journal of the American Statistical Association* 81: 945–960.

Holmlund, Bertil. 2014. "What do Labor Market Institutions Do?" *Labor Economics* 30: 62–69.

Holt, Stephen D., and Jennifer L. Romich. 2007. "Marginal Tax Rates Facing Low- and Moderate-Income Workers Who Participate in Means-Tested Transfer Programs." *National Tax Journal* 60(2): 253–276.

Holtz-Eakin, D., W. Newey, and H. Rosen. 1988. "Estimating Vector Autoregressions with Panel Data." *Econometrica* 56: 1371–1395.

Horrell, Sara, and Pramila Krishnan. 2007. "Poverty and Productivity in Female-Headed Households in Zimbabwe." *Journal of Development Studies* 43(8): 1351–1380.

Horton, Susan, Harold Alderman, and J. A. Rivera. 2008. "The Challenge of Hunger and Malnutrition." Copenhagen Consensus 2008 Challenge Paper. Copenhagen: Copenhagen Consensus Center.

Horton, Susan, and Hohn Hoddinott. 2014. "Benefits and Costs of the Food and Nutrition Targets for the Post-2015 Development Agenda." Working Paper. Copenhagen: Copenhagen Consensus Center.

Hossain, Mahabub. 1988. "Credit for Alleviation of Rural Poverty: The Grameen Bank in Bangladesh." IFPRI Research Report 65. Washington, DC: International Food Policy Research Institute.

Houthakker, H. S. 1957. "An International Comparison of Household Expenditure Patterns, Commemorating the Centenary of Engel's Law." *Econometrica* 25(4): 532–551.

Howe, Irving. 1993. Introduction to Michael Harrington's *The Other America*. New York: Touchstone.

Howes, Stephen, and Jean Lanjouw. 1997. "Poverty Comparisons and Household Survey Design." Living Standards Measurement Study Working Paper 129. Washington, DC: World Bank.

Howes, Stephen, and Peter Lanjouw. 1991. "Regional Variations in Living Standards in Urban China." Working Paper 17. London: Development Economics Research Programme, London School of Economics.

Hoxby, Caroline, and Sarah Turner. 2013. "Expanding College Opportunities." *Education Next* 14(4). http://educationnext.org/expanding-college-opportunities/.

Hoynes, Hilary. 1997. "Does Welfare Play Any Role in Female Headship Decisions?" *Journal of Public Economics* 65: 89–117.

Hume, David. 1739. *A Treatise of Human Nature*. Web edition published by eBooks@Adelaide.

Humphrey, Jean. 2009. "Child Undernutrition, Tropical Enteropathy, Toilets and Handwashing." *The Lancet* 374: 1032–1035.

Hunter, Robert. 1904. *Poverty*. London: MacMillan Company.

Huppi, Monika, and Martin Ravallion. 1991. "The Sectoral Structure of Poverty during an Adjustment Period: Evidence for Indonesia in the Mid-1980s." *World Development* 19: 1653–1678.

Hurt, L. S., C. Ronsmans, and S. Saha. 2004. "Effects of Education and Socioeconomic Factors on Middle Age Mortality in Rural Bangladesh." *Journal of Epidemiology and Community Health* 58: 315–320.

Ianchovichina, Elena, and Will Martin. 2004. "Impacts of China's Accession to the WTO." *World Bank Economic Review* 18(1): 3–28.

Iarossi, Giuseppe. 2006. *The Power of Survey Design*. Washington, DC: World Bank.

Iceland, John. 2003. "Why Poverty Remains High: The Role of Income Growth, Economic Inequality, and Changes in Family Structure, 1949–1999." *Demography* 40(3): 499–519.

Iceland, John. 2013. *Poverty in America: A Handbook*. 3rd edn. Berkeley: University of California Press.

Imbert, Clement, and John Papp. 2011. "Estimating Leakages in India's Employment Guarantee." In Reetika Khera (ed.), *The Battle for Employment Guarantee*. New Delhi: Oxford University Press.

Imrohoroglu, Ayse, Antonio Merlo, and Peter Rupert. 2006. "Understanding the Determinants of Crime." *Journal of Economics and Finance* 30: 270–283.

International Forum on Globalization. 2001. *Does Globalization Help the Poor? A Special Report*. San Francisco, CA: International Forum on Globalization.

International Fund for Agricultural Development. 2011. *Rural Poverty Report*. Rome: IFAD.

International Labour Office. 1972. *Employment, Incomes and Equity: A Strategy for Increasing Productive Employment in Kenya*. Geneva: International Labour Office.

International Labour Office. 1976. *Employment, Growth and Basic Needs: A One-World Problem*. Geneva: International Labour Office.

Isenman, Paul. 1980. "Basic Needs: The Case of Sri Lanka." *World Development* 8(3): 237–258.

Ishikawa, S. 1978. *Labour Absorption in Asian Agriculture: An Issues Paper*. Bangkok: International Labour Organization. Reprinted in Ishikawa 1981.

Ishikawa, S. 1981. *Essays on Technology, Employment and Institutions in Economic Development: Comparative Asian Experience*. Tokyo: Kinokuniya Company.

Ivanic, Maros, William Martin, and Hassan Zaman. 2011. "Estimating the Short-Term Poverty Impacts of the 2010–11 Surge in Food Prices." Policy Research Working Paper 5633. Washington, DC: World Bank.

Jack, William. 2008. "Conditioning Aid on Social Expenditures," *Economics and Politics* 20: 125–140.

Jack, William, Adam Ray, and Tavneet Suri. 2013. "Transaction Networks: Evidence from Mobile Money in Kenya." *American Economic Review Papers and Proceedings* 103(3): 356–361.

Jacoby, Hanan. 2013. "Food Prices, Wages, and Welfare in Rural India." Policy Research Working Paper 6412. Washington, DC: World Bank.

Jacoby, Hanan, and Bart Minten. 2007. "Is Land Titling in Sub-Saharan Africa Cost-Effective? Evidence from Madagascar." *World Bank Economic Review* 21(3): 461–485.

Jalan, Jyotsna, and Martin Ravallion. 1998a. "Transient Poverty in Post-Reform Rural China." *Journal of Comparative Economics* 26: 338–357.

Jalan, Jyotsna, and Martin Ravallion. 1998b. "Are There Dynamic Gains from a Poor-Area Development Program?" *Journal of Public Economics* 67(1): 65–86.

Jalan, Jyotsna, and Martin Ravallion. 1999. "Are the Poor Less Well Insured? Evidence on Vulnerability to Income Risk in Rural China." *Journal of Development Economics* 58(1): 61–82.

Jalan, Jyotsna, and Martin Ravallion. 2002. "Geographic Poverty Traps? A Micro Model of Consumption Growth in Rural China." *Journal of Applied Econometrics* 17(4): 329–346.

Jalan, Jyotsna, and Martin Ravallion. 2003. "Does Piped Water Reduce Diarrhea for Children in Rural India?" *Journal of Econometrics* 112: 153–173.

Jalan, Jyotsna, and Martin Ravallion. 2004. "Household Income Dynamics in Rural China." In Stefan Dercon (ed.), *Insurance Against Poverty*. Oxford: Oxford University Press.

Janis, Irving. 1972. *Victims of Groupthink: Psychological Studies of Policy Decisions and Fiascoes*. Boston, MA: Houghton Mifflin Company.

Jargowsky, P. A. 1997. *Poverty and Place: Ghettos, Barrios and the American City*. New York: Russell Sage.

Jayarajah, Carl, William Branson, and Binayak Sen. 1996. *Social Dimensions of Adjustment: World Bank Experience 1980–93*. Washington, DC: Operations Evaluation Department, World Bank.

Jazairy, Idriss, Mohiuddin Alamgir, and Theresa Panuccio. 1992. *The State of World Rural Poverty: An Inquiry into its Causes and Consequences*. New York: New York University Press.

Jejeebhoy, Shireen. 1998. "Wife Beating in Rural India: A Husband's Right? Evidence from Survey Data." *Economic and Political Weekly* 33(5): 11–17.

Jensen, Robert. 2007. "The Digital Provide: Information (Technology), Market Performance, and Welfare in the South Indian Fisheries Sector." *Quarterly Journal of Economics* 122(3): 879–924.

Jerven, Morten. 2013. *Poor Numbers. How We Are Misled by African Development Statistics and What to Do about It*. Ithaca, NY: Cornell University Press.

Jha, Raghbendra, Raghav Gaiha, and Manoj K. Pandey. 2012. "Net Transfer Benefits under India's Rural Employment Guarantee Scheme." *Journal of Policy Modeling* 34(2): 296–311.

Johnson, David, and Timothy Smeeding. 2012. "A Consumer's Guide to Interpreting Various US Poverty Measures." Fast Focus 14, Institute for Research on Poverty, University of Wisconsin.

Johnson, Steven. 2007. *The Ghost Map: The Story of London's Most Terrifying Epidemic and How It Changed Science, Cities and the Modern World*. New York: Riverhead, Penguin.

Jones, Charles. 1995. "R&D-Based Models of Economic Growth." *Journal of Political Economy* 103: 759–784.

Jones, Gareth Stedman. 2004. *An End to Poverty? A Historical Debate*. New York: Columbia University Press.

Jones, Ronald, and José Scheinkman. 1977. "The Relevance of the Two-Sector Production Model in Trade Theory." *Journal of Political Economy* 85: 909–935.

Jorgenson, Dale. 1961. "Development of the Dual Economy." *Economic Journal* 71: 309–334.

Jorgenson, Dale, and Daniel T. Slesnick. 1984. "Aggregate Consumer Behavior and the Measurement of Inequality." *Review of Economic Studies* 60: 369–392.

Jorgenson, Dale, and Daniel T. Slesnick. 1989. "Redistributional Policy and the Measurement of Poverty." In Daniel J. Slottje (ed.), *Research on Economic Inequality* Greenwich, CT: JAI Press.

Judge, Timothy, Joseph J. Martocchio, and Carl Thoresen. 1997. "Five-Factor Model of Personality and Employee Absence." *Journal of Applied Psychology* 82(5): 745–755.

Just, David, and Hope Michelson. 2007. "Wealth as Welfare: Are Wealth Thresholds behind Persistent Poverty?" *Applied Economic Perspectives and Policy* 29(3): 419–426.

Jütte, Robert. 1994. *Poverty and Deviance in Early Modern Europe*. Cambridge: Cambridge University Press.

Kakwani, Nanak. 1980a. *Income Inequality and Poverty: Methods of Estimation and Policy Applications*. Oxford: Oxford University Press.

Kakwani, Nanak. 1980b. "On a Class of Poverty Measures." *Econometrica* 48: 437–446.

Kakwani, Nanak. 1986. *Analyzing Redistribution Policies: A Study Using Australian Data*. Cambridge: Cambridge University Press.

Kakwani, Nanak. 1989. "On Measuring Undernutrition." *Oxford Economic Papers* 41: 528–552.

Kakwani, Nanak. 1990. "Testing for the Significance of Poverty Differences with Application to Cote d'Ivoire." Living Standards Measurement Study Working Paper No. 62. Washington, DC: World Bank.

Kakwani, Nanak. 1993. "Poverty and Economic Growth with Application to Côte D'Ivoire." *Review of Income and Wealth* 39: 121–139.

Kakwani, Nanak, and E. Pernia. 2000. "What Is Pro-Poor Growth?" *Asian Development Review* 18(1): 1–16.

Kaldor, Nicholas. 1955. "Alternative Theories of Distribution." *Review of Economic Studies* 23(2): 94–100.

Kalecki, Michael. 1942. "A Theory of Profits." *Economic Journal* 52: 258–267.

Kanbur, Ravi. 1987a. "Measurement and Alleviation of Poverty." *IMF Staff Papers* 36: 60–85.

Kanbur, Ravi. 1987b. "Structural Adjustment, Macroeconomic Adjustment and Poverty: A Methodology for Analysis." *World Development* 15: 1515–1526.

Kanbur, Ravi. 2006. "The Policy Significance of Inequality Decompositions." *Journal of Economic Inequality* 4: 367–374.

Kanbur, Ravi, Michael Keen, and Matti Tuomala. 1994. "Labor Supply and Targeting in Poverty Alleviation Programs." *World Bank Economic Review* 8(2): 191–211.

Kanbur, Ravi, and Diganta Mukerjee. 2007. "Premature Mortality and Poverty Measurement." *Bulletin of Economic Research* 59(4): 339–359.

Kanbur, Ravi, and Matti Tuomala. 2011. "Charitable Conservatism, Poverty Radicalism and Inequality Aversion." *Journal of Economic Inequality* 9: 417–431.

Kanbur Ravi, and Adam Wagstaff. 2015. "How Useful Is Inequality of Opportunity as a Policy Construct?" In Kaushik Basu and Joseph Stiglitz (eds). *Proceedings from IEA Jordan Roundtable on Shared Prosperity*. London: Palgrave McMillan.

Kant, Immanuel. 1785. *Fundamental Principles of the Metaphysic of Morals*. Edited by Thomas Kingsmill Abbott. 10th edn. Project Gutenberg.

Kaplow, Louis. 2008. *The Theory of Taxation and Public Economics*. Princeton, NJ: Princeton University Press.

Kapteyn, Arie, Peter Kooreman, and Rob Willemse. 1988. "Some Methodological Issues in the Implementation of Subjective Poverty Definitions." *Journal of Human Resources* 23: 222–242.

Kapteyn, Arie, James Smith, and Arthur Van Soest. 2008. "Comparing Life Satisfaction." Working Paper WR-623, Rand Corporation.

Katz, Lawrence F. 1996. "Wage Subsidies for the Disadvantaged." NBER Working Paper 5679. Cambridge, MA: NBER.

Katz, Michael B. 1986. *In the Shadow of the Poorhouse: A Social History of Welfare in America*. New York: Basic Books.

Katz, Michael B. 1987. *The Undeserving Poor: From the War on Poverty to the War on Welfare*. New York: Pantheon Books.

Katz, Michael B. 1993. *The "Underclass" Debate: Views from History*. Princeton, NJ: Princeton University Press.

Kaufmann, Bruce. 2010. "Institutional Economics and the Minimum Wage: Broadening the Theoretical and Policy Debate." *Industrial and Labor Relations Review* 63(3): 427–453.

Kaufmann, Daniel, and Aart Kraay. 2002. "Growth without Governance." *Economía* 3(1): 169–215.

Kaufmann, Daniel, Aart Kraay, and Massimo Mastruzzi. 2004. "Governance Matters III: Governance Indicators for 1996, 1998, 2000, and 2002." *World Bank Economic Review* 18(2): 253–287.

Kautilya. n.d. *Arthashastra*. Translated by R. Shamasastry. Bangalore: Government Press.

Keefer, Philip, and Stuti Khemani. 2005. "Democracy, Public Expenditures, and the Poor: Understanding Political Incentives for Providing Public Services." *World Bank Research Observer* 20(1): 1–28.

Keefer, Philip, and Stephen Knack. 2002. "Polarization, Politics and Property Rights: Links between Inequality and Growth." *Public Choice* 111: 127–154.

Kelley, Allen, and Robert Schmidt. 1995. "Aggregate Population and Economic Growth Correlations: The Role of the Components of Demographic Change." *Demography* 32(4): 543–555.

Kelley, Allen, and Robert Schmidt. 2001. "Economic and Demographic Change: A Synthesis of Models, Findings and Perspectives." In Nancy Birdsall, Allen Kelley, and Steven Sinding (eds.), *Population Matters*. Oxford: Oxford University Press.

Kelly, Morgan, and Cormac Ó Gráda. 2010. "Living Standards and Mortality since the Middle Ages." Working Paper 201026. Dublin: School of Economics, University College Dublin.

Kenny, Charles, and Andy Sumner. 2011. "More Money or More Development: What Have the MDGs Achieved?" Working Paper 278. Washington, DC: Center for Global Development.

Keyes, Ralph. 2006. *The Quote Verifier: Who Said What, Where and When.* New York: St. Martin's Press.

Keynes, John Maynard. 1936. *The General Theory of Employment, Interest and Money.* London: Macmillan Press.

Keysers, Christian. 2011. *Empathic Brain: How the Discovery of Mirror Neurons Changes our Understanding of Human Nature.* Amsterdam: Social Brain Press.

Khandker, Shahidur, and Hussain Samad. 2014. "Dynamic Effects of Microcredit in Bangladesh." Policy Research Working Paper 6821. Washington, DC: World Bank.

Kilic, Talip, and Thomas Sohnesen. 2014. "Same Question but Different Answer: Experimental Evidence on Questionnaire Design's Impact on Poverty Measured by Proxies." Policy Research Working Paper 7182. Washington, DC: World Bank.

Killingsworth, Mark. 1983. *Labor Supply.* Cambridge: Cambridge University Press.

Kilpatrick, R. W. 1973. "The Income Elasticity of the Poverty Line." *Review of Economics and Statistics* 55: 327–332.

Kim, Young-Chul, and Glenn Loury. 2014. "Social Externalities, Overlap and the Poverty Trap." *Journal of Economic Inequality* 12(4): 535–554.

King, Elizabeth, and Jere Behrman. 2009. "Timing and Duration of Exposure in Evaluation of Social Programs." *World Bank Research Observer* 24(1): 55–82.

King, Gary, C. Murray, J. Salomon, and A. Tandon. 2004. "Enhancing the Validity and Cross-Cultural Comparability of Measurement in Survey Research." *American Political Science Review* 98(1): 191–207.

King, Gary, and J. Wand. 2007. "Comparing Incomparable Survey Responses: Evaluating and Selecting Anchoring Vignettes." *Political Analysis* 15(1): 46–66.

King, Mervyn A. 1983. "Welfare Analysis of Tax Reforms Using Household Level Data." *Journal of Public Economics* 21: 183–214.

Kingdon, Geeta, and John Knight. 2006. "Subjective Well-Being Poverty vs. Income Poverty and Capabilities Poverty?" *Journal of Development Studies* 42(7): 1199–1224.

Kingdon, Geeta, and John Knight. 2007. "Community Comparisons and Subjective Well-Being in a Divided Society." *Journal of Economic Behavior and Organization* 64: 69–90.

Kinsey, Bill. 2013. "The Excluded Generations: Questioning a Leading Poverty Indicator." Paper presented at the UNU-WIDER conference "Inclusive Growth in Africa: Measurement, Causes, and Consequences."

Kish, Leslie. 1965. *Survey Sampling.* New York: John Wiley.

Klasen, Stephan. 1996. "Nutrition, Health and Mortality in sub-Saharan Africa: Is there a Gender Bias?" *Journal of Development Studies* 32(6): 913–933.

Klasen, Stephan, and Sebastian Vollmer. 2013. "Missing Women: Age and Disease: A Correction." Mimeo, University of Göttingen and Harvard School of Public Health.

Klebaner, Benjamin J. 1964. "Poverty and Its Relief in American Thought, 1815–61." *Social Service Review* 38(4): 382–399.

Knack, Stephen, and Philip Keefer. 1995. "Institutions and Economic Performance: Cross-Country Tests Using Alternative Institutional Measures." *Economics and Politics* 7: 202–227.

Knight, John. 1976. "Devaluation and Income Distribution in Less-Developed Countries." *Oxford Economic Papers* 38: 161–178.

Knight, John. 2013. "Inequality in China: An Overview." Policy Research Working Paper 6482. Washington, DC: World Bank.

Knight, John, and R. Gunatilak. 2010. "The Rural–Urban Divide in China: Income but Not Happiness?" *Journal of Development Studies* 46(3): 506–534.

Knight, John, and R. Gunatilak. 2012. "Income, Aspirations and the Hedonic Treadmill in a Poor Society." *Journal of Economic Behavior and Organization* 82(1): 67–81.

Knight, John, Deng Quheng, and Li Shi. 2011. "The Puzzle of Migrant Labor Shortage and Rural Labor Surplus in China." *China Economic Review* 22: 585–600.

Knowles, Stephen. 2005. "Inequality and Economic Growth: The Empirical Relationship Reconsidered in the Light of Comparable Data." *Journal of Development Studies* 41(1): 135–159.

Knudsen, Eric, James Heckman, Judy Cameron, and Jack Shonkoff. 2006. "Economic, Neurobiological, and Behavioral Perspectives on Building America's Future Workforce." *Proceedings of the National Academy of Sciences* 103(27): 10155–10162.

Kolm, Serge-Christophe. 1976. "Unequal inequalities. I." *Journal of Economic Theory* 12(3): 416–442.

Kolm, Serge-Christophe. 1998. *Modern Theories of Justice*. Cambridge, MA: MIT Press.

Korinek, Anton, Johan Mistiaen, and Martin Ravallion. 2006. "Survey Nonresponse and the Distribution of Income." *Journal of Economic Inequality* 4(2): 33–55.

Korinek, Anton, Johan Mistiaen, and Martin Ravallion. 2007. "An Econometric Method of Correcting for Unit Nonresponse Bias in Surveys." *Journal of Econometrics* 136: 213–235.

Kormendi, Roger, and Philip Meguire. 1985. "Macroeconomic Determinants of Growth: Cross-Country Evidence." *Journal of Monetary Economics* 16(2): 141–163.

Korpe, Poonum, and William Petri. 2012. "Environmental Enteropathy: Critical Implications of a Poorly Understood Condition." *Trends in Molecular Medicine* 18(6): 328–336.

Kozel, Valerie, and Barbara Parker. 2000. "Integrated Approaches to Poverty Assessment in India." In Michael Bamberger (ed.), *Integrating Quantitative and Qualitative Research in Development Projects*. Washington, DC: World Bank.

Kraay, Aart. 2006. "When is Growth Pro-Poor? Evidence from a Panel of Countries." *Journal of Development Economics* 80: 198–227.

Kraay, Aart, and Claudio Raddatz. 2007. "Poverty Traps, Aid and Growth." *Journal of Development Economics* 82(2): 315–347.

Kremer, Michael, and Edward Miguel. 2007. "The Illusion of Sustainability." *Quarterly Journal of Economics* 122(3): 1007–1065.

Kristensen, N., and E. Johansson. 2008. "New Evidence on Cross-Country Differences in Job Satisfaction Using Vignettes." *Labor Economics* 15(1): 96–117.

Krusell, Per, and Tony Smith. 2014. "Is Piketty's 'Second Law of Capitalism' Fundamental?" Mimeo.

Kunz-Ebrect, Sabine, Clemens Kirschbaum, Michael Marmot, and Andrew Steptoe. 2004. "Differences in Cortisol Awakening Response on Work Days and Weekends in Woman and Men from the Whitehall II Cohort." *Psychoneuroendocrinology* 29(4): 516–528.

Kuznets, Simon. 1933. "National Income." *Encyclopedia of the Social Science*, vol. 11. London: Macmillan and Co.

Kuznets, Simon. 1946. *National Product Since 1869*. New York: National Bureau of Economic Research.

Kuznets, Simon. 1955. "Economic Growth and Income Inequality." *American Economic Review* 45: 1–28.

Lakdawalla, Darius, Tomas Philipson, and Jay Bhattacharya. 2005. "Welfare-Enhancing Technological Change and the Growth of Obesity." *American Economic Review Papers and Proceedings* 95(2): 253–257.

Lakner, Christoph, and Branko Milanovic. 2013. "Global Income Distribution: From the Fall of the Berlin Wall to the Great Recession." Policy Research Working Paper 6719. Washington, DC: World Bank.

Lal, Deepak. 2000. *The Poverty of Development Economics*. Cambridge, Mass.: MIT Press.

Lalonde, Robert. 1986. "Evaluating the Econometric Evaluations of Training Programs." *American Economic Review* 76: 604–620.

Lambert, Peter J. 2001. *The Distribution and Redistribution of Income*. 3rd edn. Manchester: Manchester University Press.

Lambert, Sylvie, Martin Ravallion, and Dominique van de Walle. 2010. "A Micro-Decomposition Analysis of Aggregate Human Development Outcomes." *Oxford Bulletin of Economics and Statistics* 72(2): 119–145.

Lambert, Sylvie, Martin Ravallion, and Dominique van de Walle. 2014. "Intergenerational Mobility and Interpersonal Inequality in an African Economy." *Journal of Development Economics* 110: 327–344.

Lambert, Sylvie, and Pauline Rossi. 2014. "Sons as Widowhood Insurance: Evidence from Senegal." CREST Working Paper 2014–2004, Paris.

References

Lampietti, Julian, and Linda Stalker. 2000. "Consumption Expenditure and Female Poverty: A Review of the Evidence." Policy Research Report on Gender and Development Working Paper Series No. 11. Washington, DC: World Bank.

Landauer, Carl. 1959. *European Socialism: A History of Ideas and Movements from the Industrial Revolution to Hitler's Seizure of Power*. Berkeley: University of California Press.

Lanjouw, Jean, and Peter Lanjouw. 2001. "How to Compare Apples and Oranges: Poverty Measurement Based on Different Definitions Of Consumption." *Review of Income and Wealth* 47(1): 25–42.

Lanjouw, Peter, and Martin Ravallion. 1995. "Poverty and Household Size." *Economic Journal* 105: 1415–1435.

Lanjouw, Peter, and Martin Ravallion. 1999. "Benefit Incidence and the Timing of Program Capture." *World Bank Economic Review* 13(2): 257–274.

Lanjouw, Peter, and Nicholas Stern. 1991. "Poverty in Palanpur." *World Bank Economic Review* 5: 23–56.

Lanjouw, Peter, and Nicholas Stern. 1998. *Economic Development in Palanpur over Five Decades*. Oxford: Clarendon Press.

Lazear, Edward, and Robert Michael. 1980. "Family Size and the Distribution of Real Per Capita Income." *American Economic Review* 70: 91–107.

Lee, David. 1999. "Wage Inequality during the 1980s: Rising Dispersion or Falling Minimum Wages?" *Quarterly Journal of Economics* 114(3): 977–1023.

Lee, Donghoon. 2005. "An Estimable Dynamic General Equilibrium Model of Work, Schooling, and Occupational Choice." *International Economic Review* 46(1): 1–34.

Lee, Myoung-jae. 2005. *Micro-Econometrics for Policy, Program and Treatment Effects*. Oxford: Oxford University Press.

Leibenstein, Harvey. 1957. *Economic Backwardness and Economic Growth*. New York: Wiley.

Lemieux, Thomas, and Kevin Milligan. 2008. "Incentive Effects of Social Assistance: A Regression Discontinuity Approach." *Journal of Econometrics* 142(2): 807–828.

Leovy, Jill. 2014. *Ghettoside. A True Story of Murder in America*. New York: Spiegal and Grau.

Lepenies, Philipp H. 2014. "Of Goats and Dogs: Joseph Townsend and the Idealisation of Markets—A Decisive Episode in the History of Economics." *Cambridge Journal of Economics* 38: 447–457.

Leslie, Jacques. 2014. "Dams Aren't Worth the Cost." *International New York Times*, August 23–24, 8.

Levin, Michael. 1997. "Natural Subordination, Aristotle On." *Philosophy* 72: 241–257.

Levine, Ross, and David Renelt. 1992. "A Sensitivity Analysis of Cross-Country Growth Regressions." *American Economic Review* 82: 942–963.

Levine, Ruth, What Works Working Group, and Molly Kinder. 2004. *Millions Saved: Proven Successes in Global Health*. Washington, DC: Center for Global Development.

Levitt, Steven, and John List. 2011. "Was There Really a Hawthorne Effect at the Hawthorne Plant? An Analysis of the Original Illumination Experiments." *American Economic Journal: Applied Economics* 3(1): 224–238.

Levy, Paul S., and Stanley Lemeshow. 1991. *Sampling of Populations: Methods and Applications*. New York: John Wiley and Sons.

Lewis, Arthur. 1954. "Economic Development with Unlimited Supplies of Labor." *Manchester School of Economic and Social Studies* 22: 139–191.

Lewis, Arthur. 1976. "Development and Distribution." In A. Caincross and M. Puri (eds.), *Employment, Income Distribution and Development Strategy*. London: Macmillan.

Li, Chenyang. 2012. "Equality and Inequality in Confucianism." *Dao* 11(3): 295–313.

Li, Hongyi, Lyn Squire, and Heng-fu Zou. 1998. "Explaining International and Intertemporal Variations in Income Inequality." *Economic Journal* 108: 26–43.

Li, Hongyi, and Heng-fu Zou. 1998. "Income Inequality is not Harmful to Growth: Theory and Evidence." *Review of Development Economics* 2(3): 318–334.

Lichter, Daniel T., and Rukamalie Jayakody. 2002. "Welfare Reform: How Do We Measure Success?" *Annual Review of Sociology* 28: 117–141.

Lim, Janus. 2012. "The Emerging Pattern of Global Investment." Prospects for Development Blog, World Bank. http://blogs.worldbank.org/prospects/the-emerging-pattern-of-global-investment.

Lin, Justin Yifu. 1992. "Rural Reforms and Agricultural Growth in China." *American Economic Review* 82: 34–51.

Lin, Justin Yifu. 2012. *New Structural Economics: A Framework for Rethinking Development and Policy.* Washington, DC: World Bank.

Lin, Justin Yifu, and P. Liu. 2008. "Economic Development Strategy, Openness and Rural Poverty." In M. Nissanke and E. Thorbecke (eds.), *Globalization and the Poor in Asia: Can Shared Growth be Sustained.* London: Palgrave Macmillan.

Lindert, Peter H. 2000. "Three Centuries of Inequality in Britain and America." In A. B. Atkinson and F. Bourguignon (eds.), *Handbook of Income Distribution*, vol. 1. Amsterdam: North-Holland.

Lindert, Peter H. 2004. *Growing Public.* Vol. 1, *The Story: Social Spending and Economic Growth since the Eighteenth Century.* Cambridge: Cambridge University Press.

Lindert, Peter H. 2013. "Private Welfare and the Welfare State." In Larry Neal and Jeffrey Williamson (eds.), *The Cambridge History of Capitalism.* Cambridge: Cambridge University Press.

Lindgren, Mattias. 2015. "The Elusive Quest for the Subsistence Line. How Much Does the Cost Of Survival Vary Between Populations?" Comparative Institutional Analysis Working Paper 2015:1, Lund University, Sweden.

Lipton, Michael. 1968. "Urban Bias and Rural Planning: Strategy for Agriculture." In Paul Streeten and Michael Lipton (eds.), *The Crisis in Indian Planning.* Oxford: Oxford University Press.

Lipton, Michael. 1977. *Why Poor People Stay Poor: Urban Bias and World Development.* London: Temple Smith.

Lipton, Michael. 1983. "Poverty, Undernutrition, and Hunger." World Bank Staff Working Paper 597. Washington, DC: World Bank.

Lipton, Michael. 1988. "The Poor and the Poorest: Some Interim Findings." World Bank Discussion Paper 25. Washington, DC: World Bank.

Lipton, Michael. 2009. *Land Reform in Developing Countries: Property Rights and Property Wrongs.* New York: Routledge.

Lipton, Michael, and Richard Longhurst. 1989. *New Seeds and Poor People.* Baltimore, MD: Johns Hopkins University Press.

Lipton, Michael, and Martin Ravallion. 1995. "Poverty and Policy." In Jere Behrman and T. N. Srinivasan (eds.), *Handbook of Development Economics*, vol. 3. Amsterdam: North-Holland.

Lipton, Michael, and Jacques van der Gaag. 1992. "Poverty: A Research and Policy Framework." In Michael Lipton and Jacques van der Gaag (eds.), *Including the Poor.* Washington DC: Johns Hopkins University Press for the World Bank.

Little, Ian. 1982. *Economic Development: Theory, Policy and International Relations.* New York: Basic Books.

Little, R. J. A. and D. B. Rubin. 1987. *Statistical Analysis with Missing Data.* New York: Wiley.

Lokshin, Michael, and Martin Ravallion. 2000. "Welfare Impacts of Russia's 1998 Financial Crisis and the Response of the Public Safety Net." *Economics of Transition* 8(2): 269–295.

Lokshin, Michael, and Martin Ravallion. 2004. "Household Income Dynamics in Two Transition Economies." *Studies in Nonlinear Dynamics and Econometrics* 8(3).

Lokshin, Michael, and Martin Ravallion. 2005. "Rich *and* Powerful? Subjective Power and Welfare in Russia." *Journal of Economic Behavior and Organization* 56(2): 141–195.

Lokshin, Michael, Nithin Umapathi and Stefano Paternostro. 2006. "Robustness of Subjective Welfare Analysis in a Poor Developing Country: Madagascar 2001," *Journal of Development Studies* 42(4): 559–591.

Lopez, Humberto, and Luis Servén. 2006. "A Normal Relationship? Poverty, Growth and Inequality." Policy Research Working Paper 3814. Washington, DC: World Bank.

Lopez, Humberto, and Luis Servén. 2009. "Too Poor to Grow." Policy Research Working Paper 5012. Washington, DC: World Bank.

Lopez-Calva, Luis F., and Eduardo Ortiz-Juarez. 2014. "A Vulnerability Approach to the Definition of the Middle Class." *Journal of Economic Inequality* 12: 23–47.

Loury, Glenn. 1981. "Intergenerational Transfers and the Distribution of Earnings." *Econometrica* 49: 843–867.

Lovejoy, Paul. 1989. "The Impact of The Atlantic Slave Trade on Africa: A Review of the Literature," *Journal of African History* 30: 365–394.

Lucas, Robert. 1988. "On the Mechanics of Economic Development." *Journal of Monetary Economics* 22(1): 3–42.

Ludwig, Jens, Greg Duncan, Lisa Gennetian, Lawrence Katz, Ronald Kessler, Jeffrey Kling, and Lisa Sanbonmatsu. 2012. "Neighborhood Effects on the Long-Term Well-Being of Low-Income Adults." *Science* 337: 1505–1510.

Ludwig, Jens, and Deborah A. Phillips. 2007. "The Benefits and Costs of Head Start." NBER Working Paper 12973.

Lundberg, Mattias, and Lyn Squire. 2003. "The Simultaneous Evolution of Growth and Inequality." *Economic Journal* 113: 326–344.

Lustig, Nora. 2000. "Crises and the Poor: Socially Responsible Macroeconomics." *Economia* 1(1): 1–19.

Lustig, Nora, Carola Pessino, and John Scott. 2014. "The Impact of Taxes and Social Spending on Inequality and Poverty in Argentina, Bolivia, Brazil, Mexico, Peru and Uruguay: Introduction to the Special Issue." *Public Finance Review* 42(3): 287–303.

Luttmer, E. 2005. "Neighbors as Negatives: Relative Earnings and Well-Being." *Quarterly Journal of Economics* 120(3): 963–1002.

Maag, Elaine, Eugene C. Steuerle, Ritadhi Chakravarti, and Caleb Quakenbush. 2012. "How Marginal Tax Rates Affect Families at Various Levels of Poverty." *National Tax Journal* 65(4): 759–782.

MacGregor, David H. 1910. "The Poverty Figures." *Economic Journal* 20: 569–572.

Mackenbach, Johan, Anton Kunst, Adrienne Cavelaars, Feikje Groenhof, and Jose Guerts. 1997. "Socioeconomic Inequalities in Morbidity and Mortality in Western Europe." *Lancet* 349: 1655–1659.

Macours, Karen, Norbert Schady, and Renos Vakis. 2012. "Cash Transfers, Behavioral Changes and Cognitive Development in Early Childhood: Evidence from a Randomized Experiment." *American Economic Journal: Applied Economics* 4(2): 247–273.

Maddison, Angus. 1995. *Monitoring the World Economy*. Paris: OECD.

Maddison, Angus. 2005. *The World Economy*. Paris: Development Center, OECD.

Mahalanobis, Prasanta Chandra. 1953. "Some Observations on the Process of Growth." *Sankhya* 12: 307–312.

Mahalanobis, Prasanta Chandra. 1963. *The Approach of Operational Research to Planning in India*. New York: Asia Publishing House.

Maloney, William. 2004. "Informality Revisited." *World Development* 32(7): 1159–1178.

Malthus, Thomas Robert. 1806. *An Essay on the Principle of Population*. 1890 edn. London: Ward, Lock and Co.

Maluccio, John, John Hoddinott, Jere R. Behrman, Reynaldo Martorell, Agnes Quisumbing, and Aryeh D. Stein. 2009. "The Impact of Improving Nutrition during Early Childhood on Education among Guatemalan Adults." *Economic Journal* 119: 734–763.

Mangahas, M. 1995. "Self-Rated Poverty in the Philippines." *International Journal of Public Opinion Research* 7(1): 40–55.

Mani, Anandi, Sendhil Mullainathan, Eldar Shafir, and Jiaying Zhao. 2013. "Poverty Impedes Cognitive Function." *Science* 341: 976–980.

Mansuri, Ghazala, and Vijayendra Rao. 2012. *Localizing Development: Does Participation Work?* Washington, DC: World Bank.

Markandaya, Kamala. 1955. *Nectar in a Sieve*. New York: John Day Company.

Manski, Charles. 1990. "Nonparametric Bounds on Treatment Effects." *American Economic Review Papers and Proceedings* 80: 319–323.

Marmot, Michael, George Smith, Stephen Stansfeld, Chandra Patel, Fiona North, J. Head, Ian White, Eric Brunner, and Amanda Feeny. 1991. "Health Inequalities among British Civil Servants: The Whitehall II Study." *Lancet* 337: 1387–1393.

Marsh, Catherine. 1985. "Back on the Bandwagon: The Effect of Opinion Polls on Public Opinion." *British Journal of Political Science* 15(1): 51–74.

Marshall, Alfred. (1890) 1920. *Principles of Economics*. 8th edn. London: Macmillan.

Marshall, Alfred. 1907. "Some Possibilities of Economic Chivalry." *Economic Journal* 17(65): 7–29.

Marshall, Dorothy. (1926) 2006. *The English Poor in the Eighteenth Century: A Study in Social and Administrative History from 1662 to 1782*. Oxford: Routledge.

Martin, Will, and Kym Anderson. 2012. "Export Restrictions and Price Insulation during Commodity Price Booms." *American Journal of Agricultural Economics* 94(2): 422–427.

Marx, Ive, Brian Nolan, and Javier Olivera. 2014. "The Welfare State and Anti-Poverty Policy in Rich Countries." IZA Discussion Paper No. 8154.

Marx, Karl. (1867) 1966. *Capital.* Vol. 1. Moscow: Progress Publishers.

Marx, Karl, and Friedrich Engels. (1848) 1969. *Manifesto of the Communist Party.* Moscow: Progress Publishers.

Mayhew, Henry. 2008. *London Labour and the London Poor.* London: Wordsworth Classics (reprinting a selection of newspaper articles from the 1840s).

McElroy, Marjorie B. 1990. "The Empirical Content of Nash-Bargained Household Behavior." *Journal of Human Resources* 25: 559–583.

McKenzie, David. 2013. "How Should We Understand 'Clinical Equipoise' When Doing RCTs in Development?" Development Impact Blog, World Bank.

McKenzie, David, John Gibson, and Steven Sillman. 2010. "How Important is Selection? Experimental vs. Non-Experimental Measures of the Income Gains from Migration." *Journal of the European Economic Association* 8(4): 913–945.

McKenzie, David, and Hillel Rapoport. 2010. "Self-Selection Patterns in Mexico–U.S. Migration Networks." *Review of Economics and Statistics* 92(4): 811–821.

McKenzie, David, and Christopher Woodruff. 2006. "Do Entry Costs Provide an Empirical Basis for Poverty Traps? Evidence from Mexican Microenterprises." *Economic Development and Cultural Change* 55(1): 3–42.

McLaren, Lindsay. 2007. "Socioeconomic Status and Obesity." *Epidemiologic Reviews* 29: 29–48.

McNamara, Robert S. 1973. "Address to the Board of Governors," World Bank Group, Nairobi, Kenya, September 24.

Meade, James. 1972. "Poverty in the Welfare State." *Oxford Economic Papers* 24: 289–326.

Meessen, Bruno, Wim Van Damme, Christine Tashobya, and Abdelmajid Tibouti. 2006. "Poverty and User Fees for Public Health Care in Low-Income Countries: Lessons from Uganda and Cambodia." *Lancet* 368(9554): 2253–2257.

Mehlum, Halvar, Karl Moene, and Ragnar Torvik. 2003. "Predator or Prey? Parasitic Enterprises in Economic Development." *European Economic Review* 47: 275–294.

Mehrotra, Santosh, and Richard Jolly, eds. 1997. *Development with a Human Face: Experiences in Social Achievement and Economic Growth.* Oxford: Clarendon Press.

Mellor, John. 1976. *The New Economics of Growth: A Strategy for India and the Developing World.* Ithaca, NY: Cornell University Press.

Mencher, Samuel. 1967. *Poor Law to Poverty Program: Economic Security Policy in Britain and the United States.* Pittsburgh: University of Pittsburgh Press.

Mesnard, Alice, and Martin Ravallion. 2006. "The Wealth Effect on New Business Startups in a Developing Economy." *Economica* 73: 367–392.

Meyer, Bruce D., and James Sullivan. 2012. "Consumption and Income Poverty in the United States." In Philip N. Jefferson (ed.), *The Oxford Handbook of the Economics of Poverty.* Oxford: Oxford University Press.

Michel, Jean-Baptiste, Yuan Kui Shen, Aviva P. Aiden, Adrian Veres, Matthew K. Gray, The Google Books Team, Joseph P. Pickett, Dale Hoiberg, Dan Clancy, Peter Norvig, Jon Orwant, Steven Pinker, Martin A. Nowak, and Erez Lieberman Aiden. 2010. "Quantitative Analysis of Culture Using Millions of Digitized Books." *Science,* December 16: 176–182.

Michielse, H. C. M., and Robert van Krieken. 1990. "Policing the Poor: J. L. Vives and the Sixteenth-Century Origins of Modern Social Administration." *Social Service Review* 64(1): 1–21.

Milanovic, Branko. 2005a. "Can We Discern the Effect of Globalization on Income Distribution?" *World Bank Economic Review* 19(1): 21–44.

Milanovic, Branko. 2005b. *Worlds Apart: Measuring International and Global Inequality.* Princeton, NJ: Princeton University Press.

Milanovic, Branko. 2008. "Qat Expenditures in Yemen and Djibouti: An Empirical Analysis." *Journal of African Economies* 17(5): 661–687.

Milanovic, Branko, and Shlomo Yitzhaki. 2002. "Decomposing World Income Distribution: Does the World Have a Middle Class?" *Review of Income and Wealth* 48(2): 155–178.

Milazzo, Annamaria. 2013. "Son Preference, Fertility and Family Structure: Evidence on Reproductive Behavior among Nigerian Women." Working Paper. Washington, DC: World Bank.

Milazzo, Annamaria, and Dominique van de Walle. 2015. "Women Left Behind? Poverty and Headship in Africa," Policy Research Working Paper 7331, Washington, DC: World Bank.

Mill, John Stuart. (1848) 1965. *Principles of Political Economy*. New York: A. M. Kelly.

Mill, John Stuart. (1859) 2002. *On Liberty*. Toronto: Dover Thrift Edition.

Miller, Herman. 1964. "Measurements for Alternative Concepts of Poverty." Paper presented at the 124th meeting of the American Statistical Association, Chicago, Illinois.

Mincer, Jacob. 1958. "Investment in Human Capital and Personal Income Distribution." *Journal of Political Economy* 66(4): 281–302.

Ministry of Labor and Social Development (MLSD). 2000. *Prozhitochnui Minimum v Rosiiskoi Federacii* (The Subsistence Minimum in Russian Federation). Moscow: MLSD.

Mirrlees, James. 1971. "An Exploration in the Theory of Optimum Income Taxation." *Review of Economic Studies* 38: 175–208.

Mirrlees, James. 1975. "A Pure Theory Of Underdeveloped Economies." In L. G. Reynolds (ed.), *Agriculture in Development Theory*. New Haven, CT: Yale University Press.

Mirrlees, James. 1976. "Optimal Tax Theory: A Synthesis." *Journal of Public Economics* 6: 327–358.

Mirrlees, James. 2014. "Some Interesting Taxes and Subsidies." Lecture at the Lindau Nobel Laureate Meetings. http://www.mediatheque.lindau-nobel.org/videos/33973/james-mirrlees.

Mishan, Ezra J. (1967) 1993. *The Cost of Economic Growth*. Rev. edn. Westport, C T: Praeger.

Mishan, Ezra J. 1982. *Introduction to Normative Economics*. Oxford: Oxford University Press.

Moehler, Devra. 2010. "Democracy, Governance, and Randomized Development Assistance." *The ANNALS of the American Academy of Political and Social Science* 628: 130–146.

Moehling, Carolyn M. 1999. "State Child Labor Laws and the Decline of Child Labor." *Explorations in Economic History* 36(1): 72–106.

Moffitt, Robert. 1992. "Incentive Effects of the US Welfare System: A Review." *Journal of Economic Literature* 30(1): 1–61.

Moffitt, Robert. 2002. "Welfare Programs and Labor Supply." In A. Auerbach and M. Feldstein (eds.), *Handbook of Public Economics*, vol. 4. Amsterdam: North-Holland.

Moffitt, Robert. 2006. "Forecasting the Effects of Scaling Up Social Programs: An Economics Perspective." In Barbara Schneider and Sarah-Kathryn McDonald (eds.), *Scale-Up in Education: Ideas in Principle*. Place: Rowman and Littlefield.

Moffitt, Robert. 2015. "The Deserving Poor, the Family, and the U.S. Welfare System," *Demography* 52: 729–749.

Montagu, Askley. 1971. "Forward." In Joseph Townsend, *A Dissertation on the Poor Laws by a Well-Wisher to Mankind*. Berkeley and Los Angeles: University of California Press.

Montalvo, Jose, and Martin Ravallion. 2010. "The Pattern of Growth and Poverty Reduction in China." *Journal of Comparative Economics* 38: 2–16.

Morduch, Johnathan. 1998. "Poverty, Economic Growth and Average Exit Time." *Economics Letters* 59(3): 385–390.

Morduch, Johnathan. 1999. "The Role of Subsidies in Microfinance: Evidence from the Grameen Bank." *Journal of Development Economics* 60: 229–248.

Morelli, Salvatore, Timothy Smeeding, and Jeffrey Thompson. 2014. "Post-1970 Trends in within-Country Inequality and Poverty." In Anthony B. Atkinson and Francois Bourguignon (eds.), *Handbook of Income Distribution*, vol. 2. Amsterdam: Elsevier Science.

Morgan, Mary. 1990. *The History of Econometric Ideas*. Cambridge: Cambridge University Press.

Morgan, Mary. 2012. *The World in the Model: How Economists Work and Think*. Cambridge: Cambridge University Press.

Morris, Cynthia Taft, and Irma Adelman. 1988. *Comparative Patterns of Economic Development 1850–1914*. Baltimore, MD: Johns Hopkins University Press.

Mortensen, Dale, and Christopher Pissarides. 1994. "Job Creation and Job Destruction in the Theory of Unemployment." *Review of Economic Studies* 61: 397–415.

Moses, Jonathon, and Bjørn Letnes. 2004. "The Economic Costs to International Labor Restrictions: Revisiting the Empirical Discussion." *World Development* 32(10): 1609–1626.

Moss, Todd, Gunilla Pettersson, and Nicolas Van de Walle. 2006. "An Aid-Institutions Paradox? A Review Essay on Aid Dependency and State Building in Sub-Saharan Africa." Working Paper No. 74. Washington, DC: Center for Global Development.

Mossakowski, Krysia N. 2009. "The Influence of Past Unemployment Duration on Symptoms of Depression among Young Women and Men in the United States." *American Journal of Public Health* 99(10): 1826–1832.

Moyo, Dambisa. 2009. *Dead Aid: Why Aid Is Not Working and How There Is a Better Way for Africa.* New York: Farrar, Strauss and Giroux.

Muhutdinova, Raissa. 2006. "Feminization of Poverty." In Mehmet Odekon (ed.), *Encyclopedia of World Poverty*, vol. 1. London: Sage.

Muller, Jerry Z. 1993. *Adam Smith in his Time and Ours: Designing a Decent Society.* Princeton, NJ: Princeton University Press.

Mulligan, Casey. 2014. "The Economics of Randomized Experiments." *Economix Blog, New York Times*, March 5.

Murgai, Rinku, and Martin Ravallion. 2005. "Is a Guaranteed Living Wage a Good Antipoverty Policy?" Policy Research Working Paper 3460. Washington, DC: World Bank.

Murgai, Rinku, Martin Ravallion, and Dominique van de Walle. 2015. "Is Workfare Cost-Effective against Poverty in a Poor Labor-Surplus Economy?" *World Bank Economic Review*, forthcoming.

Murphy, Kevin, Andrei Schleifer, and Robert Vishny. 1989. "Industrialization and the Big Push." *Journal of Political Economy* 97(5): 1003–1026.

Murray, Charles A. 1984. *Losing Ground: American Social Policy 1950–1980.* New York: Basic Books.

Musgrave, Richard. 1985. "A Brief History of Fiscal Doctrine." In A. J. Auerbach and M. Feldstein (eds.), *Handbook of Public Economics*, vol. 1. Amsterdam: North-Holland.

Muth, Richard. 1969. *Cities and Housing.* Chicago: University of Chicago Press.

Myrdal, Gunnar. 1988. "International Inequality and Foreign Aid in Retrospect." In G. Meier and D. Seers (eds.), *Pioneers in Development.* New York: Oxford University Press.

Nadeau, Richard, Edouard Cloutier, and J. H. Guay. 1993. "New Evidence about the Existence of a Bandwagon Effect in the Opinion Formation Process." *International Political Science Review* 14(2): 203–213.

Narayan, Deepa, and Patti Petesch. 2002. *Voices of the Poor: From Many Lands.* New York and Oxford: Oxford University Press.

Naschold, Felix. 2013. "Welfare Dynamics in Pakistan and Ethiopia—Does the Estimation Method Matter?" *Journal of Development Studies* 49(7): 936–954.

Nash, John. 1951. "Noncooperative Games." *Annals of Mathematics* 54: 289–295.

Nath, Shiv K. 1969. *A Reappraisal of Welfare Economics.* London: Routledge and Kegan Paul.

Naudeau, Sophie, Sebastian Martinez, Patrick Premand, and Deon Filmer. 2011. "Cognitive Development among Young Children in Low-Income Countries." In Harold Alderman (ed.), *No Small Matter.* Washington, DC: World Bank.

Ndikumana, Léonce, and James K. Boyce. 2011. *Africa's Odious Debts: How Foreign Loans and Capital Flight Bleb a Continent.* London: Zed Books.

Nelson, Julie. 1988. "Household Economies of Scale in Consumption: Theory and Evidence." *Econometrica* 56: 1301–1314.

Nelson, Richard. 1956. "A Theory of the Low-Level Equilibrium Trap in Underdeveloped Economies." *American Economic Review* 46(5): 894–908.

Newbery, David. 1990. "Ramsey Model." In John Eatwell, Murray Milgate, and Peter Newman (eds.), *Capital Theory.* New York: W. W. Norton.

Newbery, David, and Nicholas H. Stern, eds. 1987. *The Theory of Taxation for Developing Countries.* Oxford: Oxford University Press.

Newmark, David, and William Wascher. 2000. "Minimum Wages and Employment: A Case Study of the Fast-Food Industry in New Jersey and Pennsylvania: Comment." *American Economic Review* 90: 1362–1396.

Ng, K. 1981. "Welfarism: A Defence Against Sen's Attack." *Economic Journal* 91: 527–530.

Ng, Marie, et al. 2014. "Global, Regional and National Prevalence of Overweight and Obesity in Children and Adults During 1980–2013: A Systematic Analysis for the Global Burden of Disease Study 2013." *Lancet* 384: 766–781.

Nicholson, J. L. 1976. "Appraisal of Different Methods of Estimating Equivalence Scales and their Results." *Review of Income and Wealth* 22: 1–11.

Nolan, Brian. 2007. *A Comparative Perspective on the Development of Poverty and Exclusion in European Societies.* Bonn: International Policy Analysis.

Nolan, Brian, Tereas Munzi, and Tim Smeeding. 2005. "Two Views of Irish Poverty Trends." Background Paper to Human Development Report 2005. New York: UNDP.

North, Douglas. 1990. *Institutions, Institutional Change and Economic Performance.* New York: Cambridge University Press.

North, Douglas, and Robert Thomas. 1973. *The Rise of the Western World: A New Economic History.* Cambridge: Cambridge University Press.

Nozick, Robert. 1974. *Anarchy, State and Utopia.* New York: Basic Books.

Nunn, Nathan. 2007. "Historical Legacies: A Model Linking Africa's Past to its Current Underdevelopment." *Journal of Development Economics* 83(1): 157–175.

Oaxaca, Ronald L. 1973. "Male–Female Wage Differentials in Urban Labor Markets." *International Economic Review* 14: 693–709.

O'Connor, Alice. 2002. *Poverty Knowledge: Social Science, Social Policy, and the Poor in Twentieth-Century U.S. History.* Princeton, NJ: Princeton University Press.

OECD. 1997. *Making Work Pay: Taxation, Benefits, Employment and Unemployment.* Paris: OECD.

OECD. 2013. *Measuring OECD Responses to Illicit Financial Flows from Developing Countries.* Paris: Organization for Economic Cooperation and Development.

Ogden, Cynthia L., Margaret D. Carroll, Brian K. Kit, and Katherine M. Flegal. 2012. "Prevalence of Obesity in the United States, 2009–2010." NCHS Data Brief No. 82.

Ogden, Cynthia L., Molly M. Lamb, Margaret D. Carroll, and Katherine M. Flegal. 2010. "Obesity and Socioeconomic Status in Adults: United States, 2005–2008." NCHS Data Brief No. 50.

Olinto, Pedro, Kathleen Beegle, Carlos Sobrado, and Hiroki Uematsu. 2013. "The State of the Poor: Where are the Poor, Where is Extreme Poverty Harder to End, and What is the Current Profile of the World's Poor?" Economic Premise No. 125, Washington, DC: World Bank.

Organization for Economic Co-Operation and Development (OECD). 2008. *Growing Unequal? Income Distribution and Poverty in OECD Countries.* Paris: OECD.

O'Rourke, Kevin, and Jeffrey Williamson. 1997. *Globalization and History: The Evolution of the Nineteenth Century Atlantic Economy.* Cambridge, MA: MIT Press.

Orshansky, Mollie. 1965. "Counting the Poor: Another Look at the Poverty Profile." *Social Security Bulletin* 28: 3–29.

O'Shaughnessy, Terry. 2011. "Hysteresis in Unemployment." *Oxford Review of Economic Policy* 27(2): 312–337.

Osmani, Siddiqur R. 1982. *Economic Inequality and Group Welfare.* Oxford: Oxford University Press.

Osmani, Siddiqur R. 1987. "Controversies in Nutrition and their Implications for the Economics of Food." WIDER Working Paper 16. Helsinki: World Institute for Development Economics Research.

Ostrom, Elinor. 1990. *Governing the Commons: The Evolution of Institutions for Collective Action.* New York: Cambridge University Press.

Ostry, Jonathan D., Andrew Berg, and Charalambos G. Tsangarides. 2014. "Redistribution, Inequality and Growth." IMF Discussion Note SDN/14/02.

Oswald, Andrew. 1997. "Happiness and Economic Performance." *Economic Journal* 107: 1815–1831.

Over, Mead. 1975. "An Example of the Simultaneous-Equation Problem: A Note on Foreign Assistance: Objectives and Consequences." *Economic Development and Cultural Change* 23(4): 751–756.

Pack, Howard, and Janet Pack. 1990. "Is Foreign Aid Fungible? The Case of Indonesia." *Economic Journal* 100: 188–194.

Pack, Howard, and Kamal Saggi. 2006. "The Case for Industrial Policy: A Critical Survey." Policy Research Working Paper 3839. Washington, DC: World Bank.

Paine, Thomas. (1797) 2004. *Agrarian Justice*. Edition published with *Common Sense* by Penguin.

Palmer, Tom. 2012. "Poverty, Morality and Liberty." In Tom Palmer (ed.), *After the Welfare State*. Ottawa, IL: Jameson Books.

Pandey, Priyanka, Sangeeta Goyal, and Venkatesh Sundararaman. 2009. "Community Participation in Public Schools: Impacts of Information Campaigns in Three Indian States." *Education Economics* 13(3): 355–375.

Papadimitriou, Dimitri, Michalis Nikiforos, and Gennaro Zezza. 2014. *Is Rising Inequality a Hindrance to the US Economic Recovery? Strategic Analysis*. Annandale-on-Hudson, NY: Levy Economics Institute of Bard College.

Papanek, Gustav. 1978. "Economic Growth, Income Distribution and the Political Process in Less Developed Countries." In Z. Griliches, W. Krelle, H. J. Krupp, and O. Kyn (eds.), *Income Distribution and Economic Inequality*. New York: Campus Verlag and John Wiley.

Pappas, Gregory, Susan Queen, Wilbur Hadden, and Gail Fisher. 1993. "The Increasing Disparity in Mortality between Socioeconomic Groups in the United States, 1960 and 1986." *New England Journal of Medicine* 329(2): 103–109.

Pareto, Vilfredo. (1906) 1971. *Manual of Political Economy*. Translation by Augustus Kelley. Oxford: Oxford University Press.

Parfit, Derek. 1984. *Reasons and Persons*. Oxford: Oxford University Press.

Park, Albert, Sangui Wang, and Guobao Wu. 2002. "Regional Poverty Targeting in China." *Journal of Public Economics* 86(1): 123–153.

Pashardes, Panos. 1991. "Contemporaneous and Intertemporal Child Costs: Equivalent Expenditure vs. Equivalent Income Scales." *Journal of Public Economics* 45: 191–213.

Pattanayak, Subhrendu K., Jui-Chen Yang, Katherine L Dickinson, Christine Poulos, Sumeet R. Patil, Ranjan K. Mallick, Jonathan L. Blitstein, and Purujit Praharaj. 2009. "Shame or Subsidy Revisited: Social Mobilization for Sanitation in Orissa, India." *Bulletin of the World Health Organization* 87: 580–587.

Paul, Satya. 1989, "A Model of Constructing the Poverty Line," *Journal of Development Economics* 30: 129–44.

Pearson, Karl. 1896. "Mathematical Contributions to the Theory of Evolution. III. Regression, Heredity and Panmixia." *Philosophical Transactions of the Royal Society of London* 187: 253–318.

Perotti, Roberto. 1996. "Growth, Income Distribution and Democracy: What the Data Say." *Journal of Economic Growth* 1(2): 149–187.

Persson, Torsten, and Guido Tabellini. 1994. "Is Inequality Harmful for Growth?" *American Economic Review* 84: 600–621.

Petrou, Stavos, and Emil Kupek. 2010. "Poverty and Childhood Undernutrition in Developing Countries: A Multi-National Cohort Study." *Social Science and Medicine* 71: 1366–1373.

Petty, Sir William. (1662) 1899. *A Treatise of Taxes and Contributions*. Reprinted in *The Economic Writings of Sir William Petty*. Vol. 1. Edited by C. H. Hull. Cambridge: University Press.

Philipson, T. 1997. "Data Markets and the Production of Surveys." *Review of Economic Studies* 64: 47–72.

Phillips, Meredith. 2011. "Parenting, Time Use, and Disparities in Academic Outcomes." In Greg Duncan and Richard J. Murnane, *Whither Opportunity? Rising Inequality, Schools, and Children's Life Chances*. New York: Russel Sage.

Pigou, Arthur. (1920) 1971. *The Economics of Welfare*. 4th edn. London: Macmillan.

Pigou, Arthur. 1949. *A Study in Public Finance*. 3rd edn. London: Macmillan.

Piketty, Thomas. 1997. "The Dynamics of the Wealth Distribution and the Interest Rate with Credit Rationing." *Review of Economic Studies* 64: 173–189.

Piketty, Thomas. 2006. "The Kuznets Curve: Yesterday and Tomorrow." In Abhijit Banerjee, Roland Bénabou, and Dilip Mookherjee (eds.), *Understanding Poverty*. Oxford: Oxford University Press.

Piketty, Thomas. 2014. *Capital in the Twenty-First Century*. Cambridge, MA: Harvard University Press.

Piketty, Thomas, and Emmanuel Saez. 2003. "Income Inequality in the United States, 1913–1998." *Quarterly Journal of Economics* 118: 1–39.

Pischke, Jörn-Steffen. 2004. "Labor Market Institutions, Wages, and Investment," NBER Working Paper 10735. Cambridge, MA: National Bureau of Economic Research.

Pissarides, Christopher. 2000. *Equilibrium Unemployment Theory*. 2nd edn. Cambridge, MA: MIT Press.

Pitt, Mark. 1983. "Food Preferences and Nutrition in Rural Bangladesh." *Review of Economics and Statistics* 65: 105–114.

Pitt, Mark, and Shahidur Khandker. 1998. "The Impact of Group-Based Credit Programs on Poor Households in Bangladesh: Does the Gender of Participants Matter?" *Journal of Political Economy* 106: 958–996.

Pitt, Mark, and Shahidur Khandker. 2012. "Replicating Replication Due Diligence in Roodman and Morduch's Replication of Pitt and Khandker (1998)." Policy Research Working Paper 6273. Washington, DC: World Bank.

Pitt, Mark, Mark Rosenzweig, and Donna Gibbons. 1995. "The Determinants and Consequences of the Placement of Government Programs in Indonesia." In D. van de Walle and K. Nead (eds.), *Public Spending and the Poor: Theory and Evidence*. Baltimore, MD: Johns Hopkins University Press.

Piven, Frances Fox, and Richard Cloward. 1979. *Poor People's Movements: Why they Succeed and How They Fail*. New York: Vintage Books.

Piven, Frances Fox, and Richard Cloward. 1993. *Regulating the Poor: The Functions of Public Welfare*. Updated edn. New York: Vintage Books.

Pogge, Thomas W. 1989. *Realizing Rawls*. Ithaca, NY: Cornell University Press.

Pollak. Robert. 1991. "Welfare Comparisons and Situation Comparisons." *Journal of Econometrics* 50: 31–48.

Pollak, Robert, and Terence Wales. 1979. "Welfare Comparison and Equivalence Scale." *American Economic Review* 69: 216–221.

Porter, Eduardo. 2013. "Public Schools Still Favor Rich." *Kansas City Star*, November 12.

Posel, D., and Rogan, M. 2013. "Measured as Poor *Versus* Feeling Poor: Comparing Objective and Subjective Poverty Rates in South Africa." Paper prepared for the UNU-WIDER Conference, Helsinki, Finland.

Pradhan, Menno, and Martin Ravallion. 2000. "Measuring Poverty Using Qualitative Perceptions of Consumption Adequacy." *Review of Economics and Statistics* 82(3): 462–471.

Pradhan, Menno, and Martin Ravallion. 2003. "Who Wants Safer Streets? Explaining Concern for Public Safety in Brazil" *Journal of Economic Psychology* 24(1): 17–33.

Pressman, Steven. 2007. "The Decline of the Middle Class: An International Perspective." *Journal of Economic Issues* 41(1): 181–199.

Preston, Samuel. 1975. "The Changing Relationship between Mortality and Level of Economic Development." *Population Studies* 29: 231–248.

Pritchard, Bill, Anu Rammohan, Madhurshree Sekher, S. Parasuraman, and Chetan Choithani. 2014. *Feeding India: Livelihoods, Entitlements and Capabilities*. London: Routledge.

Pritchett, Lant. 1997. "Divergence, Big Time." *Journal of Economic Perspectives* 11(3): 3–17.

Pritchett, Lant, and Charles Kenny. 2013. "Promoting Millennium Development Ideals: The Risks of Defining Development Down." Working Paper 338. Washington, DC: Center for Global Development.

Pritchett, Lant, and Lawrence Summers. 2014. "Asiaphoria Meets Regression to the Mean." NBER Working Paper 20573.

Probe Team. 1999. *Public Report on Basic Education in India*. New Delhi: Oxford University Press.

Probe Team. 2011. *Probe Revisited*. New Delhi: Oxford University Press.

Proceedings of the Old Bailey. 2012. *London, 1760–1815*. Website, London. http://www.oldbaileyonline.org/static/London-lifelate18th.jsp

Pyatt, Graham, and Michael Ward, eds. 1997. *Identifying the Poor*. Amsterdam: IOS Press and the International Statistical Institute.

Quisumbing, Agnes, Lawrence Haddad, and C. Pena. 2001. "Are Women Overrepresented among the Poor? An Analysis of Poverty in Ten Developing Countries." *Journal of Development Economics* 66(1): 225–269.

Radelet, Steven. 2015. *The Great Surge: The Unprecedented Economic and Political Transformation of Developing Countries around the World*. New York: Simon & Schuster.

Rajan, Raghuram. 2009a. "Rent Preservation and the Persistence of Underdevelopment." *American Economic Journal: Macroeconomics* 1(1): 178–218.

Rajan, Raghuram. 2009b. "Saving Growth from Unequal Influence." In Santiago Levy and Michael Walton (eds.), *No Growth without Equity? Inequality, Interests and Competition in Mexico*. Washington, DC: World Bank.

Rajan, Raghuram, and Arvind Subramanian. 2007. "Does Aid Affect Governance?" *American Economic Review* 97(2): 322–327.

Rajan, Raghuram, and Arvind Subramanian. 2008. "Aid and Growth: What Does the Cross-Country Evidence Really Show?" *Review of Economics and Statistics* 90(4): 643–665.

Ramsey, Frank. 1928. "A Mathematical Theory of Saving." *Economic Journal* 38: 543–549.

Ranis, Gustav. 2004. "Arthur Lewis's Contribution to Development Thinking and Policy." *The Manchester School* 72: 712–723.

Ranis, Gustav, and John Fei. 1961. "A Theory of Economic Development." *American Economic Review* 51: 533–565.

Rank, Mark Robert. 1994. *Living on the Edge: The Realities of Welfare in Ameri*ca. New York: Columbia University Press.

Rank, Mark Robert. 2005. *One Nation, Underprivileged: Why American Poverty Affects Us All*. New York: Oxford University Press.

Rank, Mark Robert, and Thomas Hirschl. 2002. "Welfare Use as a Life Course Event: Toward a New Understanding of the U.S. Safety Net." *Social Work* 47(3): 237–248.

Rao, Vijayendra. 1997. "Can Economics Mediate the Relationship between Anthropology and Demography?" *Population and Development Review* 23: 833–838.

Rao, Vijayendra. 2001. "Poverty and Public Celebrations in Rural India." *Annals of the American Academy of Political and Social Science* 573(1): 85–104.

Ravallion, Martin. 1984. "How Much Is a Transfer Payment Worth?" *Oxford Economic Papers* 36: 478–489.

Ravallion, Martin. 1986. "On Expectations Formation When Future Welfare Is Contemplated." *Kyklos* 39: 401–441.

Ravallion, Martin. 1987a. *Markets and Famines*. Oxford: Oxford University Press.

Ravallion, Martin. 1987b. "Trade and Stabilization: Another Look at British India's Controversial Food Grain Exports." *Explorations in Economic History* 24: 354–370.

Ravallion, Martin. 1988a. "Expected Poverty under Risk-Induced Welfare Variability." *Economic Journal* 98: 1171–1182.

Ravallion, Martin. 1988b. "Inpres and Inequality: A Distributional Perspective on the Centre's Regional Disbursements." *Bulletin of Indonesian Economic Studies* 24: 53–72.

Ravallion, Martin. 1990a. "Income Effects on Undernutrition." *Economic Development and Cultural Change* 38: 490–515.

Ravallion, Martin. 1990b. "Rural Welfare Effects of Food Price Changes under Induced Wage Responses: Theory and Evidence for Bangladesh." *Oxford Economic Papers* 42: 574–585.

Ravallion, Martin. 1991. "Reaching the Rural Poor through Public Employment: Arguments, Experience and Lessons from South Asia." *World Bank Research Observer* 6: 153–175.

Ravallion, Martin. 1992a. "Does Undernutrition Respond to Incomes and Prices: Dominance Tests for Indonesia." *World Bank Economic Review* 6: 109–124.

Ravallion, Martin. 1994a. "Measuring Social Welfare With and Without Poverty Lines." *American Economic Review* 84(2): 359–365.

Ravallion, Martin. 1994b. *Poverty Comparisons*. Chur, Switzerland: Harwood Academic Press.

Ravallion, Martin. 1994c. "Book Review: The State of World Rural Poverty: An Inquiry into its Causes and Consequences." *Journal of Economic Literature* 32: 1276–1278.

Ravallion, Martin. 1995. "Growth and Poverty: Evidence for Developing Countries in the 1980s." *Economics Letters* 48: 411–417.

Ravallion, Martin. 1997a. "Can High Inequality Developing Countries Escape Absolute Poverty?" *Economics Letters* 56: 51–57.

Ravallion, Martin. 1997b. "Famines and Economics." *Journal of Economic Literature* 35(3): 1205–1242.

Ravallion, Martin. 1998a. "Does Aggregation Hide the Harmful Effects of Inequality on Growth?" *Economics Letters* 61(1): 73–77.

Ravallion, Martin. 1998b. "Poor Areas." In David Giles and Aman Ullah (eds.), *Handbook of Applied Economic Statistics*. New York: Marcel Dekkar.

Ravallion, Martin. 1999a. "Are Poorer States Worse at Targeting their Poor?" *Economics Letters* 65: 373–377.

Ravallion, Martin. 1999b. "Is More Targeting Consistent with Less Spending?" *International Tax and Public Finance* 6: 411–419.

Ravallion, Martin. 2000. "Monitoring Targeting Performance When Decentralized Allocations to the Poor Are Unobserved." *World Bank Economic Review* 14(2): 331–345.

Ravallion, Martin. 2001a. "The Mystery of the Vanishing Benefits: An Introduction to Impact Evaluation." *World Bank Economic Review* 15(1): 115–140.

Ravallion, Martin. 2001b. "Growth, Inequality and Poverty: Looking Beyond Averages." *World Development* 29(11): 1803–1815.

Ravallion, Martin. 2003a. "The Debate on Globalization, Poverty and Inequality: Why Measurement Matters." *International Affairs* 79(4): 739–754.

Ravallion, Martin. 2003b. "Inequality Convergence." *Economics Letters* 80: 351–356.

Ravallion, Martin. 2004. "Competing Concepts of Inequality in the Globalization Debate." In Susan Collins and Carol Graham (eds.), *Brookings Trade Forum 2004*. Washington, DC: Brookings Institution.

Ravallion, Martin. 2005a. "Externalities in Rural Development: Evidence for China." In Ravi Kanbur and Tony Venables (eds.), *Spatial Inequality and Development*. Oxford: Oxford University Press.

Ravallion, Martin. 2005b. "On the Contribution of Demographic Change to Aggregate Poverty Measures for the Developing World." Policy Research Working Paper 3580. Washington, DC: World Bank.

Ravallion, Martin. 2005c. "A Poverty-Inequality Trade-Off?" *Journal of Economic Inequality* 3(2): 169–182.

Ravallion, Martin. 2006. "Looking Beyond Averages in the Trade and Poverty Debate." *World Development* 34(8): 1374–1392.

Ravallion, Martin. 2007. "Inequality *is* Bad for the Poor." In J. Micklewright and S. Jenkins (eds.), *Inequality and Poverty Re-Examined*. Oxford: Oxford University Press.

Ravallion, Martin. 2008a. "Evaluating Anti-Poverty Programs." In Paul Schultz and John Strauss (eds.), *Handbook of Development Economics*, vol. 4. Amsterdam: North-Holland.

Ravallion, Martin. 2008b. "Miss-Targeted, or Miss-Measured?" *Economics Letters* 100: 9–12.

Ravallion, Martin. 2008c. "On the Welfarist Rationale for Relative Poverty Lines." In Kaushik Basu and Ravi Kanbur (eds.), *The Oxford Handbook of Arguments for a Better World: Essays in Honor of Amartya Sen*, vol. 1, *Ethics, Welfare and Measurement*. Oxford: Oxford University Press.

Ravallion, Martin. 2009a. "Are There Lessons for Africa from China's Success Against Poverty?" *World Development* 37(2): 303–313.

Ravallion, Martin. 2009b. "Decentralizing Eligibility for a Federal Antipoverty Program: A Case Study for China." *World Bank Economic Review* 23(1): 1–30.

Ravallion, Martin. 2009c. "Evaluation in the Practice of Development." *World Bank Research Observer* 24(1): 29–54.

Ravallion, Martin. 2009d. "How Relevant is Targeting to the Success of the Antipoverty Program?" *World Bank Research Observer* 24(3): 205–231.

Ravallion, Martin. 2010a. "The Developing World's Bulging (but Vulnerable) Middle Class." *World Development* 38(4): 445–454.

Ravallion, Martin. 2010b. "Do Poorer Countries Have Less Capacity for Redistribution?" *Journal of Globalization and Development* 1(2): 1–29.

Ravallion, Martin. 2010c. "Understanding PPPs and PPP-Based National Accounts: A Comment." *American Economic Journal: Macroeconomics* 2(4): 46–52.

Ravallion, Martin. 2010d. "A Reply to Reddy and Pogge." In Sudhir Anand, Paul Segal, and Joseph Stiglitz (eds.), *Debates on the Measurement of Poverty*. Oxford: Oxford University Press.

Ravallion, Martin. 2011a. "A Comparative Perspective on Poverty Reduction in Brazil, China and India." *World Bank Research Observer* 26(1): 71–104.

Ravallion, Martin. 2011b. "On Multidimensional Indices of Poverty." *Journal of Economic Inequality* 9(2): 235–248.

Ravallion, Martin. 2011c. "The Two Poverty Enlightenments: Historical Insights from Digitized Books Spanning Three Centuries." *Poverty and Public Policy* 3(2): 1–45.

Ravallion, Martin. 2012a. "Mashup Indices of Development." *World Bank Research Observer* 27(1): 1–32.

Ravallion, Martin. 2012b. "Poverty Lines across the World." In Philip N. Jefferson (ed.), *The Oxford Handbook of the Economics of Poverty*. Oxford: Oxford University Press.

Ravallion, Martin. 2012c. "Troubling Tradeoffs in the Human Development Index." *Journal of Development Economics* 99: 201–209.

Ravallion, Martin. 2012d. "Why Don't We See Poverty Convergence?" *American Economic Review* 102(1): 504–523.

Ravallion, Martin. 2013. "How Long Will It Take To Lift One Billion People Out Of Poverty?" *World Bank Research Observer* 28(2): 139–158.

Ravallion, Martin. 2014a. "The Idea of Antipoverty Policy." In A. B. Atkinson and F. Bourguignon (eds.), *Handbook of Income Distribution*, vol. 2. Amsterdam: North Holland.

Ravallion, Martin. 2014b. "Poverty in the Rich World When It Was Not Nearly So Rich." Blog Post, Center for Global Development, Washington, DC. http://international.cgdev.org/blog/poverty-rich-world-when-it-was-not-nearly-so-rich.

Ravallion, Martin. 2014c. "The Luxembourg Income Study." ECINEQ Working Paper 332, Society for the Study of Economic Inequality.

Ravallion, Martin. 2014d. "Income Inequality in the Developing World." *Science* 344: 851–855.

Ravallion, Martin. 2014e. "Poor, or Just Feeling Poor? On Using Subjective Data in Measuring Poverty." In Andrew Clark and Claudia Senik (eds.), *Happiness and Economic Growth: Lessons from Developing Countries*. Oxford: Oxford University Press.

Ravallion, Martin. 2014f. "Are the World's Poorest being Left Behind?" NBER Working Paper 20791.

Ravallion, Martin. 2014g. "An Exploration of the International Comparison Program's New Global Economic Landscape." NBER Working Paper 20338.

Ravallion, Martin. 2014h. "An Emerging New Form of Social Protection in 21st Century China." In Shenggen Fan, Ravi Kanbur, Shang-jin Wei, and Xiaobo Zhang (eds.), *Oxford Companion to the Economics of China*. Oxford: Oxford University Press.

Ravallion, Martin. 2015a. "Inequality when Effort Matters," NBER Working Paper 21394, National Bureau of Economic Research, Cambridge, Massachusetts.

Ravallion, Martin. 2015b. "On Testing the Scale Sensitivity of Poverty Measures." *Economics Letters*, in press.

Ravallion, Martin, and Benu Bidani. 1994. "How Robust Is a Poverty Profile?" *World Bank Economic Review* 8: 75–102.

Ravallion, Martin, and Kalvin Chao. 1989. "Targeted Policies for Poverty Alleviation under Imperfect Information: Algorithms and Applications." *Journal of Policy Modeling* 11(2): 213–224.

Ravallion, Martin, and Shubham Chaudhuri. 1997. "Risk and Insurance in Village India: A Comment." *Econometrica* 65: 171–184.

Ravallion, Martin, and Shaohua Chen. 1997. "What Can New Survey Data Tell Us about Recent Changes in Poverty and Distribution?" *World Bank Economic Review* 11(2): 357–382.

Ravallion, Martin, and Shaohua Chen. 2003. "Measuring Pro-Poor Growth." *Economics Letters* 78(1): 93–99.

Ravallion, Martin, and Shaohua Chen. 2007. "China's (Uneven) Progress Against Poverty." *Journal of Development Economics* 82(1): 1–42.

Ravallion, Martin, and Shaohua Chen. 2009. "The Impact of the Global Financial Crisis on the World's Poorest." VOX, Portal of the Centre for Economic Policy Research, April 30.

Ravallion, Martin, and Shaohua Chen. 2011. "Weakly Relative Poverty." *Review of Economics and Statistics* 93(4): 1251–1261.

Ravallion, Martin, and Shaohua Chen. 2013a. "Benefit Incidence with Incentive Effects, Measurement Errors and Latent Heterogeneity." Policy Research Working Paper 6573. Washington, DC: World Bank.

Ravallion, Martin, and Shaohua Chen. 2013b. "A Proposal for Truly Global Poverty Measures." *Global Policy* 4(3): 258–265.

Ravallion, Martin, and Shaohua Chen. 2015. "Rising Food Prices in Poor Countries: A New Clue to those Puzzling PPP Revisions." Center for Global Development Blog Post.

Ravallion, Martin, Shaohua Chen, and Prem Sangraula. 2007. "New Evidence on the Urbanization of Global Poverty." *Population and Development Review* 33(4): 667–702.

Ravallion, Martin, Shaohua Chen, and Prem Sangraula. 2009. "Dollar a Day Revisited." *World Bank Economic Review* 23(2): 163–184.

Ravallion, Martin, and Gaurav Datt. 1995. "Is Targeting Through a Work Requirement Efficient? Some Evidence for Rural India." In Dominique de Walle and Kimberly Nead (eds.), *Public Spending and the Poor: Theory and Evidence*. Baltimore, MD: Johns Hopkins University Press.

Ravallion, Martin, and Gaurav Datt. 1996. "How Important to India's Poor is the Sectoral Composition of Economic Growth?" *World Bank Economic Review* 10: 1–26.

Ravallion, Martin, and Gaurav Datt. 2002. "Why Has Economic Growth Been More Pro-Poor in Some States of India than Others?" *Journal of Development Economics* 68: 381–400.

Ravallion, Martin, Gaurav Datt, and Dominique van de Walle. 1991. "Quantifying Absolute Poverty in the Developing World." *Review of Income and Wealth* 37: 345–361.

Ravallion, Martin, Madhur Gautam, and Dominique van de Walle. 1995. "Testing a Social Safety Net." *Journal of Public Economics* 57(2): 175–199.

Ravallion, Martin, Kristen Himelein, and Kathleen Beegle. 2015. "Can Subjective Questions on Economic Welfare be Trusted? Evidence for Three Developing Countries." *Economic Development and Cultural Change*, forthcoming.

Ravallion, Martin, and Monika Huppi. 1991. "Measuring Changes in Poverty: A Methodological Case Study of Indonesia during an Adjustment Period." *World Bank Economic Review* 5: 57–84.

Ravallion, Martin, and Michael Lokshin. 2000. "Who Wants to Redistribute? The Tunnel Effect in 1990s Russia" *Journal of Public Economics* 76(1): 87–104.

Ravallion, Martin, and Michael Lokshin. 2001. "Identifying Welfare Effects from Subjective Questions." *Economica* 6 8(271): 335–357.

Ravallion, Martin, and Michael Lokshin. 2002. "Self-Rated Economic Welfare in Russia." *European Economic Review* 46(8): 1453–1473.

Ravallion, Martin, and Michael Lokshin. 2006. "Testing Poverty Lines." *Review of Income and Wealth* 52(3): 399–421.

Ravallion, Martin, and Michael Lokshin. 2007. "Lasting Impacts of Indonesia's Financial Crisis." *Economic Development and Cultural Change* 56(1): 27–56.

Ravallion, Martin, and Michael Lokshin. 2008. "Winners and Losers from Trade Reform in Morocco." In Francois Bourguignon, Luiz Pereira da Silva, and Maurizio Bussolo (eds.), *The Impact of Economic Policies on Poverty and Income Distribution: Advanced Evaluation Techniques and Tools*. Oxford: Oxford University Press.

Ravallion, Martin, and Michael Lokshin. 2010. "Who Cares About Relative Deprivation?" *Journal of Economic Behavior and Organization* 73(2): 171–185.

Ravallion, Martin, and Binayak Sen. 1994. "Impacts on Rural Poverty of Land-Based Targeting: Further Results for Bangladesh." *World Development* 22: 823–838.

Ravallion, Martin, and Binayak Sen. 1996. "When Method Matters: Monitoring Poverty in Bangladesh." *Economic Development and Cultural Change* 44: 761–792.

Ravallion, Martin, and Dominique van de Walle. 1991a. "The Impact on Poverty of Food Pricing Reforms: A Welfare Analysis for Indonesia." *Journal of Policy Modeling* 13: 281–299.

Ravallion, Martin, and Dominique van de Walle. 1991b. "Urban–Rural Cost of Living Differentials in a Developing Economy." *Journal of Urban Economics* 29: 113–127.

Ravallion, Martin, and Dominique van de Walle. 2008. *Land in Transition: Reform and Poverty in Rural Vietnam*. Washington DC: Palgrave Macmillan.

Ravallion, Martin, Dominique van de Walle, and Madhur Gaurtam. 1995. "Testing a Social Safety Net." *Journal of Public Economics* 57(2): 175–199.

Ravallion, Martin, and Quentin Wodon. 1999. "Poor Areas, or Just Poor People?" *Journal of Regional Science* 39(4): 689–711.

Ravallion, Martin, and Quentin Wodon. 2000a. "Does Child Labor Displace Schooling? Evidence on Behavioral Responses to an Enrolment Subsidy." *Economic Journal* 110: 158–176.

Ravallion, Martin, and Quentin Wodon. 2000b. "Banking on the Poor? Branch Location and Non-Farm Rural Development in Bangladesh." *Review of Development Economics* 4(2): 121–139.

Raventós, Daniel. 2007. *Basic Income: The Material Conditions of Freedom*. London: Pluto Press.

Rawlings, Laura. 2000. "Evaluating Nicaragua's School-Based Management Reform." In Michael Bamberger (ed.), *Integrating Quantitative and Qualitative Research in Development Projects*. Washington, DC: World Bank.

Rawls, John. 1967. "Distributive Justice." In P. Laslett and W. G. Runciman (eds.), *Philosophy, Politics and Society*, Series III, Oxford: Basil Blackwell.

Rawls, John. 1971. *A Theory of Justice*. Cambridge, MA: Harvard University Press.

Rawls, John. 1999. *The Law of Peoples*. Cambridge, MA: Harvard University Press.

Ray, Debraj. 1998. *Development Economics*. Princeton, NJ: Princeton University Press.

Ray, Debraj. 2014. "Nit-Piketty: A Comment on Thomas Piketty's *Capital in the Twenty First Century*." Chhota Pegs Blog.

Reader, Soran. 2006. "Does a Basic Needs Approach Need Capabilities?" *Journal of Political Philosophy* 14: 337–350.

Reddy, Sanjay, and Thomas W. Pogge. 2010. "How *Not* to Count the Poor." In Sudhir Anand, Paul Segal, and Joseph Stiglitz (eds.), *Debates on the Measurement of Poverty*. Oxford: Oxford University Press.

Reich, Robert. 2014. "Back to School and Widening Inequality." http://robertreich.org/post/95749319170.

Reinikka, Ritva, and Jakob Svensson. 2005. "Fighting Corruption to Improve Schooling: Evidence from a Newspaper Campaign in Uganda." *Journal of the European Economic Association* 3(2/3): 259–267. Papers and Proceedings of the Nineteenth Annual Congress of the European Economic Association.

Reis, Elisa, and Mick Moore. 2005. "Elites, Perceptions and Poverties." In Elisha Reis and Mick Moore (eds.), *Elite Perceptions of Poverty and Inequality*. London: Zed Books.

Reynolds, Lloyd G., ed. 1975. *Agriculture in Development Theory*. New Haven, CT: Yale University Press.

Rhys-Williams, Juliet. 1943. *Something to Look Forward To*. London: MacDonald.

Ricardo, David. 1817. *Principles of Political Economy and Taxation*. London: Everyman Edition, 1911.

Riffault, Hélène. 1991. "How Poverty is Perceived." In Karlheinz Reif and Ronald Inglehart (eds.), *Eurobarometer: The Dynamics of European Public Opinion*. London: Macmillan Press.

Riis, Jacob. (1890) 2011. *How the Other Half Lives: Studies among the Tenements of New York*. Boston: Bedford/St. Martins.

Rist, Gilbert. 1997. *The History of Development*. London: Zed Books.

Rist, Gilbert. 2008. *The History of Development*. 3rd edn. London: Zed Books.

Robbins, Lionel. 1935. *An Essay on the Nature and Significance of Economic Science*. London: Macmillan.

Robinson, James. 2010. "The Political Economy of Redistributive Policies." In Luis Felipe López-Calva and Nora Lustig (eds.), *Declining Inequality in Latin America: A Decade of Progress?* Washington, DC: Brookings.

Robinson, Sherman. 1976. "A Note on the U-Hypothesis Relating Income Inequality and Economic Development." *American Economic Review* 66: 437–440.

Roche, Daniel. 1987. *The People of Paris: An Essay in Popular Culture in the Eighteenth Century*. Berkeley: University of California Press.

Rodgers, John L., and Joan R. Rodgers. 1993. "Chronic Poverty in the United States." *Journal of Human Resources* 28(1): 25–54.

Rodriguez, Francisco, and Dani Rodrik. 2001. "Trade Policy and Economic Growth: A Skeptic's Guide to the Cross-National Evidence." In *NBER Macroeconomic Annual 2000*. Cambridge, MA: MIT Press.

Rodrik, Dani. 1994. "King Kong Meets Godzilla: The World Bank and *The East Asian Miracle*." In Albert Fishlow, Catherine Gwin, Stephan Haggard, Dani Rodrik, and Robert Wade (eds.), *Miracle or Design? Lessons from the East Asian Experience*. Washington, DC: Overseas Development Council.

Rodrik, Dani. 2004. "Industrial Policy for the Twenty-First Century." Kennedy School of Government Working Paper RWP04-047. Cambridge, MA: Harvard University.

Roemer, John. 1996. *Theories of Distributive Justice*. Cambridge, MA: Harvard University Press.

Roemer, John. 1998. *Equality of Opportunity*. Cambridge, MA: Harvard University Press.

Roemer, John. 2014. "Economic Development as Opportunity Equalization." *World Bank Economic Review* 28(2): 189–209.

Rogot, E., P. D. Sorlie, N. J. Johnson, and C. Schmitt. 1992. *A Mortality Study of 1.3 Million Persons*. Bethesda, MD: National Institutes of Health.

Rogowski, Ronald. 1989. *Commerce and Coalitions: How Trade Affects Domestic Political Alignments*. Princeton, NJ: Princeton University Press.

Rojas, Mariano. 2007. "A Subjective Well-being Equivalence Scale for Mexico: Estimation and Poverty and Income-distribution Implications," *Oxford Development Studies* 35(3): 273–293.

Romer, Paul. 1986. "Increasing Returns and Long Run Growth." *Journal of Political Economy* 94(5): 1002–1037.

Romer, Paul. 1990. "Endogenous Technological Change." *Journal of Political Economy* 98(5): S71–S102.

Romer, Paul. 1998. *Equality of Opportunity*. Cambridge, MA: Harvard University Press.

Roodman, David, and Jonathan Morduch. 2014. "The Impact of Microcredit on the Poor in Bangladesh: Revisiting the Evidence." *Journal of Development Studies* 50: 583–604.

Roosevelt, Franklin D. 1937. "Second Inaugural Address." http://www.bartleby.com/124/pres50.html.

Rose, Elaina. 1999. "Consumption Smoothing and Excess Female Mortality in Rural India." *Review of Economics and Statistics* 81(1): 41–49.

Rosenbaum, Paul, and Donald Rubin. 1983. "The Central Role of the Propensity Score in Observational Studies for Causal Effects." *Biometrika* 70: 41–55.

Rosenberg, Nathan. 1963. "Mandeville and Laissez-Faire." *Journal of the History of Ideas* 24(2): 183–196.

Rosenhouse, Sandra. 1990. "Identifying the Poor: Is 'Headship' a Useful Concept?" Living Standards Measurement Study Working Paper No. 58. Washington, DC: World Bank.

Rosenstein-Rodan, Paul. 1943. "Problems of Industrialization of Eastern and Southeastern Europe." *Economic Journal* 53: 202–211.

Rosenzweig, Mark. 1988. "Labor Markets in Developing countries." In H. Chenery and T. N. Srinivasan (eds.), *Handbook of Development Economics*, vol. 1. Amsterdam: North Holland.

Rosenzweig, Mark. 2010. "Global Wage Inequality and the International Flow of Migrants." In Ravi Kanbur and Michael Spence (eds.), *Equity and Growth in a Globalizing World*. Washington, DC: World Bank.

Rothenbacher, Franz. 2002. *The European Population 1850–1945*. Basingstoke, UK: Palgrave.

Rothschild, Emma. 2001. *Economic Sentiments: Adam Smith, Condorcet, and the Enlightenment*. Cambridge, MA: Harvard University Press.

Rothschild, Michael, and Joseph E. Stiglitz. 1976. "Equilibrium in Competitive Insurance Markets: An Essay on the Economics of Imperfect Information." *Quarterly Journal of Economics* 90(4): 629–650.

Rothstein, Richard. 2012. "Public Housing: Government-Sponsored Segregation." *American Prospect*, October 11.

Rousseau, Jean-Jacques. 1754. *Discourse on the Origin of Inequality, A Discourse on a Subject Proposed by the Academy of Dijon: What Is the Origin of Inequality among Men, and Is It Authorised by Natural Law?* Indianapolis: Hackett Press.

Rowntree, Benjamin Seebohm. 1902. *Poverty: A Study of Town Life*. London: Macmillan.

Roy, A. D. 1951. "Some Thoughts on the Distribution of Earnings." *Oxford Economic Papers* 3: 135–146.

Royal Swedish Academy of Sciences. 2010. "Markets with Search Frictions." Background Paper on the Sveriges Riksbank Prize in Economic Sciences. Stockholm: Royal Swedish Academy of Sciences.

Rubin, Donald B. 1974. "Estimating Causal Effects of Treatments in Randomized and Nonrandomized Studies." *Journal of Education Psychology* 66: 688–701.

Runciman, W. G. 1966. *Relative Deprivation and Social Justice*. London: Routledge and Kegan Paul.

Sachs, Jeffrey. 2005a. *The End of Poverty: Economic Possibilities for Our Time*. New York: Penguin Books.

Sachs, Jeffrey. 2005b. *Investing in Development: A Practical Plan to Achieve the Millennium Development Goals*. New York: Millennium Project, United Nations.

Sachs, Jeffrey. 2012. "Government, Geography, and Growth : The True Drivers of Economic Development," *Foreign Affairs* 91(5): 142–150.

Sadoulet, Elisabeth, and Alain de Janvry. 1995. *Quantitative Development Policy Analysis*. Baltimore, MD: Johns Hopkins University Press.

Saez, Emmanuel. 2006. "Redistribution Toward Low Incomes in Rich Countries." In A. Banerjee, R. Benabou, and D. Mookherjee (eds.), *Understanding Poverty*. Oxford: Oxford University Press.

Sah, Raaj, and Joseph E. Stiglitz. 1992. *Peasant versus City-Dwellers: Taxation and the Burden of Economic Development*. Oxford: Oxford University Press.

Sahn, David, and Harold Alderman. 1995. "Incentive Effects on Labor Supply of Sri Lanka's Rice Subsidy." In Dominique van de Walle and Kimberly Nead (eds.), *Public Spending and the Poor*. Baltimore: Johns Hopkins University Press.

Sahn, David, Paul Dorosh, and Stephen Younger. 1997. *Structural Adjustment Reconsidered: Economic Policy and Poverty in Africa*. Cambridge: Cambridge University Press.

Sahn, David, and Stephen Younger. 2003. "Estimating the Incidence of Indirect Taxes in Developing Countries." In Francois Bourguignon Francois and Luiz Pereira Da Silva (eds.), *The Impact of Economic Policies on Poverty and Income Distribution: Evaluation Techniques and Tools*. New York: Oxford University Press.

Sahota, Gian S. 1990. *Poverty Theory and Policy: A Study of Panama*. Baltimore: Johns Hopkins University Press.

Saint-Paul, Gilles. 2011. *The Tyranny of Utility: Behavioral Social Science and the Rise of Paternalism*. Princeton, NJ: Princeton University Press.

Sala-I-Martin, Xavier. 2006. "The World Distribution of Income: Falling Poverty and... Convergence. Period." *Quarterly Journal of Economics* 121(2): 351–397.

Sala-I-Martin, Xavier, Gernot Doppelhofer, and Ronald Miller. 2004. "Determinants of Long-Term Growth: A Bayesian Averaging of Classical Estimates (BACE) Approach." *American Economic Review* 94(4): 813–836.

Salgado, Jesus F. 1997. "The Five Factor Model of Personality and Job Performance in the European Community." *Journal of Applied Psychology* 82(1): 30–43.

Salvatore, Dominick. 2009. *Microeconomics: Theory and Applications*. New York: Oxford University Press.

Samuelson, Paul. 1938. "A Note on the Pure Theory of Consumer Behaviour." *Economica* 5: 61–71.

Sandmo, Agnar. 2014. "The Principal Problem in Political Economy: Income Distribution in the History of Economic Thought." In *Handbook of Income Distribution*, vol. 2, edited by Anthony B. Atkinson and Francois Bourguignon. Amsterdam: Elsevier Science.

Sawhill, Isabel V. 1988. "Poverty in the U.S.: Why Is It So Persistent?" *Journal of Economic Literature* 26: 1073–1119.

Scammell, Geoffrey. 1989. *The First Imperial Age: European Overseas Expansion 1500–1715*. New York: Routledge.

Scarf, Herbert, and Terje Hansen. 1973. *The Computation of Economic Equilibria*. New Haven, CT: Yale University Press.

Schady, Norbert, Jere Behrman, Maria Caridad Araujo, Rodrigo Azuero, Raquel Bernal, David Bravo, Florencia Lopez-Boo, Karen Macours, Daniela Marshall, Christina Paxson, and Renos Vakis. 2014. "Wealth Gradients in Early Childhood Cognitive Development in Five Latin American Countries." Policy Research Working Paper 6779. Washington, DC: World Bank.

Schelling, Thomas. 1960. *The Strategy of Conflict*. Cambridge, MA: Harvard University Press.

Scherer, Frederic. 1965. "Invention and Innovation in the Watt-Boulton Steam-Engine Venture." *Technology and Culture* 6(2): 165–187.

Schiff, Maurice, and Alberto Valdes. 1992. *The Plundering of Agriculture in Developing Countries*. Washington DC: World Bank.

Schmitt, John. 2013. "Why Does the Minimum Wage Have No Discernible Effect on Employment?" Washington, DC: Center for Economic and Policy Research.

Schultz, Theodore W. 1961. "Investment in Human Capital." *American Economic Review* 51: 1–17.

Schultz, Theodore W. 1964. *Transforming Traditional Agriculture*. New Haven, CT: Yale University Press.

Schultz, Theodore W. 1965. "Investing in Poor People: An Economist's View." *American Economic Review* 55: 510–520.

Schultz, Theodore W. 1981. *Investing in People: The Economics of Population Quality*. Berkeley and Los Angeles: University of California Press.

Schultz, T. Paul. 1990. "Testing the Neoclassical Model of Family Labor Supply and Fertility." *Journal of Human Resources* 25: 599–634.

Schultz, T. Paul. 2006. "Fertility and Income." In A. Banerjee, R. Benabou, and D. Mookherjee (eds.), *Understanding Poverty*. Oxford: Oxford University Press.

Schulz, Laura. 2010. "The Dutch Hunger Winter and the Developmental Origins of Health and Disease." *Proceedings of the National Academy of Science* 107: 16757–16758.

Scitovsky, Tibor. 1978. *The Joyless Economy*. Oxford: Oxford University Press.

Scott, Kinnon, and Diane Steele. 2004. "Measuring Welfare in Developing Countries: Living Standards Measurement Study Surveys." In UN Statistical Division, *Surveys in Developing and Transition Countries*.

Seers, Dudley. 1963. "The Limitations of the Special Case." *Bulletin of the Oxford Institute of Economics and Statistics* 25(2): 77–98.

Seers, Dudley. 1969. "The Meaning of Development." *International Development Review* 11(4): 3–4.

Seidenfeld, David, Sudhanshu Handa, and Gelson Tembo. 2013. *Social Cash Transfer Scheme: 24-Month Impact Report for the Child Grant Programme*. Washington, DC: American Institutes for Research.

Sen, Abhijit and Himanshu. 2004. "Poverty and Inequality in India 2: Widening Disparities during the 1990s." *Economic and Political Weekly* 39 (September 25): 4361–4375.

Sen, Amartya. 1970. *Collective Choice and Social Welfare*. San Francisco, CA: Holden Day.

Sen, Amartya. 1973. *On Economic Inequality*. Oxford: Clarendon Press.

Sen, Amartya. 1976a. "Poverty: An Ordinal Approach to Measurement." *Econometrica* 46: 437–446.

Sen, Amartya. 1976b. "Real National Income," *Review of Economic Studies* 43(1): 19–39.

Sen, Amartya. 1979. "Personal Utilities and Public Judgments: Or What's Wrong with Welfare Economics?" *Economic Journal* 89: 537–558.

Sen, Amartya. 1980. "Equality of What?" In S. McMurrin (ed.), *Tanner Lectures on Human Values*. Cambridge: Cambridge University Press.

Sen, Amartya. 1981a. *Poverty and Famines: An Essay on Entitlement and Deprivation*. Oxford: Oxford University Press.

Sen, Amartya. 1981b. "Public Action and the Quality of Life in Developing Countries." *Oxford Bulletin of Economics and Statistics* 43(4): 287–319.

Sen, Amartya. 1983. "Poor, Relatively Speaking." *Oxford Economic Papers* 35(2): 153–169.

Sen, Amartya. 1985a. *Commodities and Capabilities*. Amsterdam: North-Holland.

Sen, Amartya. 1985b. "A Sociological Approach to the Measurement of Poverty: A Reply to Professor Peter Townsend." *Oxford Economic Papers* 37: 669–676.

Sen, Amartya. 1987. *The Standard of Living*. Cambridge: Cambridge University Press.

Sen, Amartya. 1990. "More than 100 Million Women Are Missing." *New York Review of Books* 37(20).

Sen, Amartya. 1992. *Inequality Reexamined*. Oxford: Oxford University Press.

Sen, Amartya. 1993. "Life Expectancy and Inequality: Some Conceptual Issues." In Pranab Bardhan, Mrinal Datta-Chaudhuri, and T. N. Krishnan (eds.), *Development and Change: Essays in Honour of K. N. Raj*. Bombay: Oxford University Press.

Sen, Amartya. 1999. *Development as Freedom*. New York: Alfred Knopf.

Sen, Amartya. 2000. "Social Justice and the Distribution of Income." In Anthony B. Atkinson and Francois Bourguignon (eds.), *Handbook of Income Distribution*, vol. 1. Amsterdam: Elsevier Science.

Sen, Amartya. 2001. "Globalization, Inequality and Global Protest." *Development* 45(2): 11–16.

Senik, Claudia. 2004. "When Information Dominates Comparison: Learning from Russian Subjective Panel Data." *Journal of Public Economics* 88: 2099–2123.

Shaffer, Paul. 2013. "Ten Years of 'Q-Squared': Implications for Understanding and Explaining Poverty." *World Development* 45: 269–285.

Shantz, Jeff. 2006. "Pro-Poor Growth." In Mehmet Odekon (ed.), *Encyclopedia of World Poverty*, vol. 1. London: Sage.

Shapiro, Carl, and Joseph Stiglitz. 1984. "Involuntary Unemployment as a Worker Discipline Device." *American Economic Review* 74(3): 433–444.

Shields, Liam. 2012. "The Prospects for Sufficientarianism." *Utilitas* 24(1): 101–117.

Shipler, David. 2005. *The Working Poor: Invisible in Americ*a. New York: Vintage.

Shorrocks, Anthony F. 1983. "Ranking Income Distributions." *Economica* 50: 3–17.

Shorrocks, Anthony F. 1995. "Revisiting the Sen Poverty Index." *Econometrica* 63(5): 1225–1230.

Short, Kathleen. 2011. "The Research Supplemental Poverty Measure: 2010." Current Population Reports P60-241, US Census Bureau.

Short, Kathleen. 2013. "The Research Supplemental Poverty Measure: 2012." Current Population Reports P60-247, US Census Bureau.

Shukla, Rajesh. 2008. "The Great Indian Middle Class." New Delhi: National Council of Applied Economic Research.

Silver, Hilary. 1994. "Social Exclusion and Social Solidarity: Three Paradigms." *International Labour Review* 133(5–6): 531–578.

Singer, Peter. 2010. *The Life You Can Save: How to Do Your Part to End World Poverty.* New York: Random House.

Skoufias, Emmanuel, and Vincenzo Di Maro. 2008. "Conditional Cash Transfers, Adult Work Incentives, and Poverty." *Journal of Development Studies* 44(7): 935–960.

Slesnick, Daniel. 1993. "Gaining Ground: Poverty in the Postwar United States." *Journal of Political Economy* 101(1): 1–38.

Slesnick, Daniel. 2001. *Consumption and Social Welfare.* Cambridge: Cambridge University Press.

Small, Mario Luis, David J. Harding, and Michèle Lamont. 2010. "Reconsidering Culture and Poverty." *Annals of the American Academy of Political and Social Science* 629: 6–29.

Smeeding, Timothy, Michael O'Higgins, and Lee Rainwater, eds. 1990. *Poverty, Inequality and Income Distribution in Comparative Perspective: The Luxembourg Income Study (LIS).* Washington, DC: The Urban Institute.

Smeeding, Timothy, Lee Rainwater, Martin Rein, Richard Hauser, and Gaston Schaber. 1985. "Income Poverty in Seven Countries: Initial Estimates from the LIS Database." In Timothy Smeeding et al. (eds.), *Poverty, Inequality and Income Distribution in Comparative Perspective: The Luxembourg Income Study (LIS).* Washington, DC: The Urban Institute.

Smil, Vaclav. 2011. "Nitrogen Cycle and World Food Production." *World Agriculture* 2: 9–13.

Smith, Adam. 1759. *The Theory of Moral Sentiments.* London: A. Millar.

Smith, Adam. 1776. *An Inquiry into the Nature and Causes of the Wealth of Nations.* Electronic Classic edn. Pittsburgh: Pennsylvania State University.

Smith, Jeffrey, and Petra Todd. 2001. "Reconciling Conflicting Evidence on the Performance of Propensity-Score Matching Methods." *American Economic Review* 91(2): 112–118.

Smith, Richard M. 2011. "Social Security as a Development Institution? The Relative Efficacy of Poor Relief Provisions under the English Old Poor Law." In C. A. Bayly, M. Woolcock, S. Szreter, and V. Rao (eds.), *History, Historians and Development Policy: A Necessary Dialogue.* Manchester: Manchester University Press.

Soares, Fabio Veras, Sergei Soares, Marcelo Medeiros and Rafael Guerreiro Osório. 2006. "Cash Transfer Programmes in Brazil: Impacts on Inequality and Poverty," Working Paper 21, International Poverty Center, United Nations Development Programme, Brazil.

Solar, Peter M. 1995. "Poor Relief and English Economic Development before the Industrial Revolution." *Economic History Review* 48: 1–22.

Solon, Gary, Steven Haider, and Jeffrey Wooldridge. 2013. "What Are We Weighting For?" NBER Working Paper 18859.

Solow, Robert. 1956. "A Contribution to the Theory of Economic Growth." *Quarterly Journal of Economics* 70(1): 65–94.

Sorlie, Paul D., Eric Backlund, and Jacob Keller. 1995. "US Mortality by Economic, Demographic and Social Characteristics: The National Longitudinal Mortality Study." *American Journal of Public Health* 85(7): 949–956.

Spears, Dean. 2013. "How Much International Variation in Child Height Can Sanitation Explain?" Policy Research Working Paper No. 6351, World Bank, Washington DC.

Spicker, Paul. 2007. *The Idea of Poverty*. Bristol, UK: Policy Press.

Sridharan, E. 2004. "The Growth and Sectoral Composition of India's Middle Class: Its Impact on the Politics of Economic Liberalization." *India Review* 3(4): 405–428.

Standing, Guy, and Michael Samson, eds. 2003. *A Basic Income Grant for South Africa*. Cape Town: University of Cape Town Press.

Stanton, Jeffrey. 2001. "Galton, Pearson, and the Peas: A Brief History of Linear Regression for Statistics Instructors." *Journal of Statistics Education* 9(3): 1–16.

Stein, A. D., W. Wang, R. Martorell, S. A. Norris, L. Adair, I. Bas, H. S. Sachdev, S. K. Bhargava, C. H. D. Fall, D. Gigante, and C. Victora. 2010. "Consortium on Health Orientated Research in Transitional Societies Group, Growth Patterns in Early Childhood and Final Attained Stature: Data from Five Birth Cohorts from Low and Middle-Income Countries." *American Journal of Human Biology* 22 (3): 353–359.

Steinberg, Stephen. 2011. "Poor Reason: Culture Still Doesn't Explain Poverty." *Boston Review*, January 13.

Stephens, W. B. 1998. *Education in Britain 1750–1914*. London: Macmillan.

Stern, Nicholas. 1989. "The Economics of Development: A Survey." *Economic Journal* 99: 597–685.

Stevenson, Betsey, and Justin Wolfers. 2008. "Economic Growth and Subjective Well-Being: Reassessing the Easterlin Paradox." *Brookings Papers on Economic Activity*, 1–87.

Stewart, Frances J. 1985. *Planning to Meet Basic Needs*. London: Macmillan.

Stifel, David, and Harold Alderman. 2005. "Targeting at the Margin: The 'Glass of Milk' Subsidy Programme in Peru." *Journal of Development Studies* 41(5): 839–864.

Stiglitz, Joseph E. 1969. "Distribution of Income and Wealth among Individuals." *Econometrica* 37(3): 382–397.

Stiglitz, Joseph E. 1974. "Incentives and Risk Sharing in Sharecropping." *Review of Economic Studies* 41: 219–255.

Stiglitz, Joseph E. 1976. "The Efficiency Wage Hypothesis, Surplus Labour and the Distribution of Income in L.D.Cs." *Oxford Economic Papers* 28: 185–207.

Stiglitz, Joseph E. 2012. *The Price of Inequality*. New York: W. W. Norton & Co.

Stiglitz, Joseph E. 2014. "Distribution of Income and Wealth among Individuals: Theoretical Perspectives." Paper presented at the IEA-World Bank Plenary and Roundtable Shared Prosperity and Growth, the Dead Sea, Jordan.

Stolper, Wolfgang, and Paul Samuelson. 1941. "Protection and Real Wages." *Review of Economic Studies* 9(1): 58–73.

Stone, Richard. 1997. *Some British Empiricists in the Social Sciences 1650–1900*. Cambridge: Cambridge University Press.

Strauss, John, and Duncan Thomas. 1998. "Health, Nutrition and Economic Development." *Journal of Economic Literature* 36(2): 766–817.

Streeten, Paul, Shahid Javed Burki, Mahbub ul Haq, Norman Hicks, and Frances Stewart. 1981. *First Things First: Meeting Basic Needs in Developing Countries*. New York: Oxford University Press.

Strömberg, David. 2004. "Radio's Impact on New Deal Spending." *Quarterly Journal of Economics* 119(1): 189–221.

Subramanian, Shankar, and Angus Deaton. 1996. "The Demand for Food and Calories." *Journal of Political Economy* 104(1): 133–162.

Sundquist, James L. 1968. *Politics and Power: The Eisenhower, Kennedy and Johnson Years*. Washington, DC: Brookings.

Swamy, Anand. 1997. "A Simple Test of the Nutrition-based Efficiency Wage Model." *Journal of Development Economics* 53: 85–98.

Swan, Trevor. 1956. "Economic Growth and Capital Accumulation." *Economic Record* 32(2): 334–361.

Swartz, Jonas, Danielle Braxton, and Anthony J. Viera. 2011. "Calorie Menu Labeling on Quick-Service Restaurant Menus: An Updated Systematic Review of the Literature." *International Journal of Behavioral Nutrition and Physical Activity* 8: 135.

Syrquin, Moshe. 1988. "Patterns of Structural Change." In H. Chenery and T. N. Srinivasan (eds.), *Handbook of Development Economics*, vol. 1. Amsterdam: Elsevier.

Székely, Miguel, Nora Lustig, Martin Cumpa, and José Antonio Mejía. 2004. "Do We Know How Much Poverty There Is?" *Oxford Development Studies* 32(4): 523–558.

Taddesse, Mekonnen, and Abebe Shimeles. 2005. "Perceptions of Welfare and Poverty: Analysis of the Qualitative Responses of Urban Households." In Arne Bigsten, Abebe Shimeles, and Bereket Kebede (eds.), *Poverty, Income Distribution and Labour Markets in Ethiopia*. Uppsala, Sweden: Nordic Africa Institute.

Tanaka, Shinsuke. 2014. "Does Abolishing User Fees Lead to Improved Health Status? Evidence from Post-Apartheid South Africa." *American Economic Journal: Economic Policy* 6(3): 282–312.

Tashakkori, Abbas, and Charles Teddlie. 1998. *Mixed Methodologies: Combining Qualitative and Quantitative Approaches*. London: Sage Publications.

Temple, Jonathan. 2010. "Aid and Conditionality." In *Handbook of Development Economics*, vol. 5. Amsterdam: North-Holland.

Thane, Pat. 2000. *Old Age in English History*. Oxford: Oxford University Press.

Theil, Henri. 1967. *Economics and Information Theory*. Amsterdam: North-Holland.

Theodossiou, I. 1998. "The Effects of Low-Pay and Unemployment on Psychological Wellbeing: A Logistic Regression Approach." *Journal of Health Economics* 17: 85–104.

Thistle, Paul D. 1989. "Ranking Distributions with Generalized Lorenz Curves." *Southern Economic Journal* 56: 1–12.

Thomas, Duncan. 1990. "Intrahousehold Resource Allocation: An Inferential Approach." *Journal of Human Resources* 25(4): 635–664.

Thon, Dominique. 1979. "On Measuring Poverty." *Review of Income and Wealth* 25: 429–440.

Thorner, Daniel. 1967. "Social and Economic Studies of Dr Mann." *Economic and Political Weekly* 2(13): 612–645.

Thurow, Lester. 1987. "A Surge in Inequality." *Scientific American* 256: 30–37.

Timmer, C. Peter. 1981. "Is Their Curvature in the Slutsky Matrix?" *Review of Economics and Statistics* 63(3): 395–402.

Timmer, C. Peter, and Harold Alderman. 1979. "Estimating Consumption Parameters for Food Policy Analysis." *American Journal of Agricultural Economics* 61: 982–987.

Tinbergen, Jan. 1975. *Income Distribution: Analyses and Policies*. Amsterdam: North-Holland.

Tjaden, Patricia, and Nancy Thoennes. 2000. *Full Report of the Prevalence, Incidence and Consequences of Violence Against Women: Findings from the National Violence Against Women Survey*. Washington, DC: National Institute of Justice, Office of Justice Programs, US Department of Justice.

Tjernström, Emilia, Patricia Toledo, and Michael Carter. 2013. "Identifying the Impact Dynamics of a Small-Farmer Development Scheme in Nicaragua." *American Journal of Agricultural Economics* 95(5): 1359–1365.

Todd, Petra, and Kenneth Wolpin. 2006. "Assessing the Impact of a School Subsidy Program in Mexico Using Experimental Data to Validate a Dynamic Behavioral Model of Child Schooling." *American Economic Review* 96(5): 1384–1417.

Townsend, Joseph. (1786) 1971. *A Dissertation on the Poor Laws by a Well-Wisher to Mankind*. Berkeley and Los Angeles: University of California Press.

Townsend, Peter. 1979. *Poverty in the United Kingdom: A Survey of Household Resources and Standards of Living*. Harmondsworth, UK: Penguin Books.

Townsend, Peter. 1985. "A Sociological Approach to the Measurement of Poverty: A Rejoinder to Professor Amartya Sen." *Oxford Economic Papers* 37(4): 659–668.

Townsend, Robert. 1994. "Risk and Insurance in Village India." *Econometrica* 62(3): 539–592.

Tsui, Kai-Yuen. 2002. "Multidimensional Poverty Indices." *Social Choice and Welfare* 19: 69–93.

Tucker, Rufus S. 1975. "Real Wages of Artisans in London, 1729–1935." In Arthur J. Taylor (ed.), *The Standard of Living in the Industrial Revolution*. London: Methuen.

Turner, Bengt, and Stephen Malpezzi. 2003. "A Review of Empirical Evidence on the Costs and Benefits of Rent Control." *Swedish Economic Policy Review* 10: 11–56.

Turnor, Charles. 1818. *Thoughts on the Present State of the Poor; With Hints for Improving their Condition.* London: W. Jeffery.

Ullmer, James. 2004. "The Macroeconomic Thought of Sir William Petty." *Journal of the History of Economic Thought* 26(3): 401–413.

United Nations. 2010. *The World's Women 2010.* New York: Department of Economic and Social Affairs, United Nations.

United Nations. 2011. *The Millennium Development Goals Report.* New York: United Nations Secretariat.

United Nations Development Programme (UNDP). 1990. *Human Development Report.* New York: Oxford University Press for the UNDP.

United Nations. 1995. *Human Development Report.* New York: Oxford University Press for the UNDP.

United Nations. 2005. *Human Development Report.* New York: Oxford University Press for the UNDP.

United Nations. 2010. *Human Development Report.* New York: Oxford University Press for the UNDP.

United Nations, Habitat. 2003. *The Challenge of Slums: Global Report on Human Settlements.* Nairobi: UN Habitat.

United Nations, National Household Survey Capability Programme. 1989. *Household Income and Expenditure Surveys: A Technical Study.* New York: UN Department of Technical Co-Operation for Development and Statistical Office.

Unruh John, and Rhodri Williams, eds. 2013. *Land and Post-Conflict Peacebuilding.* New York: Earthscan.

Vakil, C. N., and Brahmanand. 1956. *Planning for an Expanding Economy.* Bombay: Vora and Company.

van de Stadt, Huib, Arie Kaptyn, and Sara van de Geer. 1985. "The Relativity of Utility: Evidence from Panel Data." *Review of Economics and Statistics* 67: 179–187.

van de Walle, Dominique. 1985. "Population Growth and Poverty: Another Look at the Indian Time Series Data." *Journal of Development Studies* 21: 429–439.

van de Walle, Dominique. 1998a. "Assessing the Welfare Impacts of Public Spending." *World Development* 26(3): 365–379.

van de Walle, Dominique. 1998b. "Targeting Revisited." *World Bank Research Observer* 13(2): 231–248.

van de Walle, Dominique. 2013. "Lasting Welfare Effects of Widowhood in Mali." *World Development* 51: 1–19.

van de Walle, Dominique, and Dileni Gunewardena. 2001. "Sources of Ethnic Inequality in Vietnam." *Journal of Development Economics* 65: 177–207.

van de Walle, Dominique, and Ren Mu. 2007. "Fungibility and the Flypaper Effect of Project Aid: Micro-evidence for Vietnam." *Journal of Development Economics* 84: 667–685.

van de Walle, Nicolas. 2001. *African Economies and the Politics of Permanent Crisis 1979–1999.* Cambridge: Cambridge University Press.

van der Gaag, Jacques, and Eugene Smolensky. 1982. "True Household Equivalence Scales and Characteristics of the Poor in the United States." *Review of Income and Wealth* 28: 17–28.

Van Horn Melton, James. 1988. *Absolutism and the Eighteenth Century Origins of Compulsory Schooling in Prussia and Austria.* Cambridge: Cambridge University Press.

Van Parijs, Philippe. 1992. "Basic Income Capitalism." *Ethics* 102(3): 465–484.

Van Parijs, Philippe. 1995. *Real Freedom for All: What (if anything) Can Justify Capitalism?* Oxford: Oxford University Press.

Van Praag, Bernard. 1968. *Individual Welfare Functions and Consumer Behavior.* Amsterdam: North-Holland.

Van Praag, Bernard, and Michael R. Baye. 1990. "The Poverty Concept When Prices Are Income-Dependent." *Journal of Econometrics* 43: 153–166.

Van Praag, Bernard, Aldi Hagenaars, and W. Van Eck. 1983. "The Influence of Classification and Observation Errors on the Measurement of Income Inequality." *Econometrica* 51: 1093–1108.

Varian, Hal R. 1978. *Microeconomic Analysis*. New York: W. W. Norton.

Varian, Hal R. 2014. *Intermediate Microeconomics: A Modern Approach*. New York: W. W. Norton.

Vartia, Y. O. 1983. "Efficient Methods of Measuring Welfare Changes and Compensated Income in Terms of Ordinary Demand Functions." *Econometrica* 51: 79–98.

Venables, Anthony. 2008. "Perspectives on Reducing Barriers to Trade and Migration: Conditional Gains and Complex Obstacles." Perspective Paper. Copenhagen: Copenhagen Consensus Center.

Ver Ploeg, Michele, Vince Breneman, Tracey Farrigan, Karen Hamrick, David Hopkins, Phillip Kaufman, Biing-Hwan Lin, Mark Nord, Travis A. Smith, Ryan Williams, Kelly Kinnison, Carol Olander, Anita Singh, and Elizabeth Tuckermanty. 2009. "Access to Affordable and Nutritious Food—Measuring and Understanding Food Deserts and Their Consequences: Report to Congress." U.S. Department of Agriculture, Economic Research Service, Administrative Publication No. AP–036.

Villasenor, J., and B. C. Arnold. 1989. "Elliptical Lorenz Curves." *Journal of Econometrics* 40: 327–338.

Vincent, David. 2000. *The Rise of Mass Literacy: Reading and Writing in Modern Europe*. Oxford: Blackwell.

Viner, Jacob. 1953. "The Economics of Development." reprinted in A. N. Agarwala and S. P. Singh (eds.), *The Economics of Underdevelopment*. Oxford: Oxford University Press.

Vinovskis, Maris. 1992. "Schooling and Poor Children in 19th-Century America." *American Behavioral Scientist* 35(3): 313–331.

Visaria, Pravin. 1969. *The Sex Ratio of the Population of India*. Census of India, 1961. Vol. 1. Monograph No. 10. New Delhi: Government of India.

Visaria, Pravin. 1980. "Poverty and Living Standards in Asia: An Overview of the Main Results of Selected Household Surveys." Living Standards Measurement Study Working Paper No. 2. Washington, DC: World Bank.

Vives, Juan Luis. (1526) 1999. *On Assistance to the Poor*. Translation by Alice Tobriner. New York: Renaissance Society of America.

Voitchovsky, Sarah. 2005. "Does the Profile of Income Inequality Matter for Economic Growth?" *Journal of Economic Growth* 10: 273–296.

Voitchovsky, Sarah. 2009. "Inequality and Economic Growth." In Wiemer Salverda, Brian Nolan, and Tim Smeeding (eds.), *The Oxford Handbook of Economic Inequality*. Oxford: Oxford University Press.

Wacziarg, Romain, and Karen Horn Welch. 2008. "Trade Liberalization and Growth: New Evidence." *World Bank Economic Review* 22(2): 187–231.

Waddington, H., B. Snilstveit, H. White, and L. Fewtrell. 2009. *Water, Sanitation and Hygiene Interventions to Combat Childhood Diarrhoea in Developing Countries*. New Delhi: International Initiative for Impact Evaluation.

Wagstaff, Adam. 2000. "Socioeconomic Inequalities in Child Mortality: Comparisons across Nine Developing Countries." *Bulletin of the World Health Organization* 78(1): 19–29.

Wagstaff, Adam. 2003. "Child Health on a Dollar a Day: Some Tentative Cross-Country Comparisons." *Social Science and Medicine* 57(9): 1529–1538.

Wagstaff, Adam, Caryn Bredenkamp, and Leander Buisman. 2014. "Progress Toward the Health MDGs: Are the Poor Being Left Behind?" Policy Research Working Paper 6894. Washington, DC: World Bank.

Wald, Abraham. 1951. "On Some Systems of Equations in Mathematical Economics." *Econometrica* 19: 368–403.

Walker, Susan. 2011. "Promoting Equity through Early Child Development Interventions for Children from Birth through Three Years of Age." In Harold Alderman (ed.), *No Small Matter*. Washington, DC: World Bank.

Walker, Susan, T. D. Wachs, J. M. Gardner, B. Lozoff, G. A. Wasserman, E. Pollitt, and J. A. Carter. 2007. "Child Development: Risk Factors for Adverse Outcomes in Developing Countries." *Lancet* 369 (9556): 145–157.

Walker, Thomas, and James G. Ryan. 1990. *Village and Household Economies in India's Semi-Arid Tropics*. Baltimore, MD: Johns Hopkins University Press.

Wallerstein, Immanuel. 1971. "The State and Social Transformation." *Politics and Society* 1: 359–364.

Walras, Léon. 1874. Éléments D'économie Politique Pure, ou Théorie de la Richesse Sociale (Elements of Pure Economics, or the Theory of Social Wealth). London: Routledge.

Wang, Claire, Klim McPherson, Tim Marsh, Steven Gortmaker, and Martin Brown. 2011. "Health and Economic Burden of the Projected Obesity Trends in the USA and the UK." *Lancet* 378(9793): 815–825.

Watkins, Kevin. 2013. "Leaving No-one Behind: An Equity Agenda for the Post-2015 Goals." London: Overseas Development Institute.

Watkins, Susan, and Etienne van de Walle. 1985. "Nutrition, Mortality and Population Size: Malthus' Court of Last Resort." In Robert Rotberg and Theodore Rab (eds.), *Hunger and History*. Cambridge: Cambridge University Press.

Watts, Harold W. 1968. "An Economic Definition of Poverty." In Daniel P. Moynihan (ed.), *On Understanding Poverty*. New York: Basic Books.

Webb, Robert K. 1974. *Modern England from the 18th Century to the Present*. New York: Dodd, Mead and Company.

Webb, Sidney, and Beatrice Webb. 1927. *English Poor Law History*. London: Longmans Green.

Weil, David. 2005. *Economic Growth*. Boston: Addison-Wesley.

Weiner, Myron. 1991. *The Child and the State in India*. Princeton, NJ: Princeton University Press.

Wells, Thomas. 2010. "Adam Smith's Real Views on Slavery: A Reply to Marvin Brown." *Real Economics Review* 53.

Wicksell, Knut. (1901) 1934. *Lectures on Political Economy*. London: Routledge and Kegan Paul.

Widerquist, Karl. 2013. *Independence, Propertylessness, and Basic Income: A Theory of Freedom as the Power to Say No*. New York: Palgrave Macmillan.

Wiggins, David. 1987. *Needs, Values, Truth: Essays in the Philosophy of Value*. Oxford: Blackwell.

Wilkinson, R. G. 1996. *Unhealthy Societies: The Afflictions of Inequality*. London: Routledge.

Williamson, Jeffrey. 1965. "Regional Inequality and the Process of National Development: A Description of the Patterns." *Economic Development and Cultural Change* 13: 3–45.

Williamson, Jeffrey. 1985. *Did British Capitalism Breed Inequality?* London: Routledge.

Williamson, Jeffrey. 1998. "Globalization and the Labor Market: Using History to Inform Policy." In Philippe Aghion and Jeffrey Williamson (eds.), *Growth, Inequality and Globalization*. Cambridge: Cambridge University Press.

Williamson, Jeffrey. 2001. "Demographic Change, Economic Growth and Inequality." In Nancy Birdsall, Allen Kelley, and Steven Sinding (eds.), *Population Matters*. Oxford: Oxford University Press.

Williamson, John. 1989. "What Washington Means by Policy Reform." In John Williamson (ed.), *Latin American Readjustment: How Much has Happened*. Washington, DC: Institute for International Economics.

Wilson, William Julius. 1987. *The Truly Disadvantaged: The Inner City, the Underclass and the Truly Disadvantaged*. Chicago: Chicago University Press.

Winkelmann, L., and Winkelmann, R. 1998. "Why Are the Unemployed So Unhappy: Evidence from Panel Data." *Economica* 65: 1–15.

Winters, L. Alan, Neil McCulloch, and Andrew McKay. 2004. "Trade Liberalization and Poverty: The Evidence So Far." *Journal of Economic Literature* 42(March): 72–115.

Witt, Robert, Alan Clarke, and Nigel Fielding. 1999. "Crime and Economic Activity: A Panel Data Approach." *British Journal of Criminology* 39(3): 391–400.

Wodon, Quentin. 1997. "Food Energy Intake and Cost of Basic Needs: Measuring Poverty in Bangladesh." *Journal of Development Studies* 34: 66–101.

Wolf, Martin. 2014. "Why Inequality Is Such a Drag on Economies." *Financial Times*, September 30.

Woodbury, Stephen, and Robert Spiegelman. 1987. "Bonuses to Workers and Employers to Reduce Unemployment." *American Economic Review* 77: 513–530.

Woodham-Smith, Cecil. 1962. *The Great Hunger: Ireland 1845–9*. London: Hamilton.

Wooldridge, Jeffrey. 2002. *Econometric Analysis of Cross Section and Panel Data*. Cambridge, Mass.: MIT Press.

Wooldridge, Jeffrey. 2013. *Introductory Econometrics: A Modern Approach*. 5th edn. Mason: South-Western Learning.

World Bank. 1980. *World Development Report: Poverty and Human Development*. New York: Oxford University Press.

World Bank. 1985. *World Development Report*. New York: Oxford University Press.

World Bank. 1986. *Poverty and Hunger: Issues and Options for Food Security in Developing Countries*. Washington, DC: World Bank.

World Bank. 1990a. *The World Bank Annual Report 1990*. Washington, DC: World Bank.

World Bank. 1990b. *World Development Report: Poverty*. Oxford: Oxford University Press.

World Bank. 1993. *The East Asian Miracle: Economic Growth and Public Policy*. New York: Oxford University Press.

World Bank. 1994. *Adjustment in Africa*. New York: Oxford University Press.

World Bank. 1997. *India: Achievements and Challenges in Reducing Poverty*. Report No. 16483-IN. Washington, DC: World Bank.

World Bank. 2001a. *World Development Report: Attacking Poverty*. New York: Oxford University Press.

World Bank. 2001b. *Engendering Development*. New York: Oxford University Press.

World Bank. 2004a. *World Development Indicators*. Washington, DC: World Bank.

World Bank. 2004b. *World Development Report: Making Services Work for the Poor*. New York: Oxford University Press.

World Bank. 2006. *World Development Report: Equity and Development*. New York: Oxford University Press.

World Bank. 2007a. *Global Economic Prospects 2007: Confronting Challenges of the Coming Globalization*. Washington DC: Oxford University Press for the World Bank.

World Bank. 2007b. *World Development Report: Agriculture for Development*. Washington, DC: World Bank.

World Bank. 2008a. *Comparisons of New 2005 PPPs with Previous Estimates*. Revised Appendix G. Washington, DC: World Bank.

World Bank. 2008b. *Global Purchasing Power Parities and Real Expenditures 2005, International Comparison Program*. Washington, DC: World Bank.

World Bank. 2009. *World Development Report: Reshaping Economic Geography*. Washington, DC: World Bank.

World Bank. 2011. *World Development Report: Gender Equality and Development*. Washington, DC: World Bank.

World Bank. 2013. *World Development Indicators*. Washington, DC: World Bank.

World Bank. 2014a. *The State of Social Safety Nets 2014*. Washington, DC: World Bank.

World Bank. 2014b. *A Measured Approach to Ending Poverty and Boosting Shared Prosperity: Concepts, Data and Twin Goals*. Washington, DC: World Bank.

World Health Organization. 1985. "Energy and Protein Requirements." WHO Technical Report Series 724. Geneva: World Health Organization.

World Health Organization. 2002. *World Report on Violence and Health*. Geneva: World Health Organization.

World Health Organization. 2013a. *Ending Preventable Child Deaths from Pneumonia and Diarrhoea by 2025: The Integrated Global Action Plan for Pneumonia and Diarrhoea (GAPPD)*. Geneva: World Health Organization.

World Health Organization. 2013b. *Global and Regional Estimates of Violence Against Women: Prevalence and Health Effects of Intimate Partner Violence and Non-Partner Sexual Violence*. Geneva: World Health Organization.

Wrigley, E. Anthony, R. S. Davies, J. E. Oeppen, and Roger Schofield. 1997. *English Population History from Family Reconstitution 1580–1837*. Cambridge: Cambridge University Press.

Wrigley, E. Anthony, and Roger Schofield. 1981. *The Population History of England 1541–1871: A Reconstruction*. Cambridge: Cambridge University Press.

Yoshida, Nobuo, Hiroki Uematsu, and Carlos E. Sobrado. 2014. "Is Extreme Poverty Going to End? An Analytical Framework to Evaluate Progress in Ending Extreme Poverty." Policy Research Report 6740. Washington, DC: World Bank.

Young, Allyn. 1917. "Do the Statistics of the Concentration of Wealth in the United States Mean what they are Commonly Assumed to Mean?" *American Statistical Association New Series* 117: 471–484.

Young, Alwyn. 2013. "Inequality, the Urban–Rural Gap, and Migration." *Quarterly Journal of Economics* 128(4): 1727–1785.

Young, Arthur. 1792. *Travels During the Years 1787, 1788 and 1789*. London: Bury St Edmunds.

Young Lives Project. 2009. "Duy's story: A Profile from Young Lives in Vietnam." Young Lives Project. Oxford: Department of International Development, University of Oxford.

Zheng, Buhong. 1993. "Axiomatic Characterization of the Watts Index." *Economics Letters* 42: 81–86.

Zwane, Alix Peterson, and Michael Kremer. 2007. "What Works in Fighting Diarrheal Diseases in Developing Countries? A Critical Review." *World Bank Research Observer* 22(1): 1–24.

inequality measures (*continued*)
  translational invariance, 229
  within-country, 226
inequality of opportunity (INOP), 37, 39b–40b,
    141–142, 142b–143b, 270–271, 596
inequality of outcomes, 39b–40b
inequality, on growth
  macro evidence, 454–458
  vs. poverty, 454–458
  pro-poor, evidence, 445–447, 446f
  rising, 434
Infant Health and Development Program, 578
infant mortality, 350–351
  China, 463
  India, 475
  macroeconomic shocks, 450, 450b
  U.S., 365
inflation rates, high, 449
informal sector, 117–118
  on targeting mechanism, 551
  urban, 393
information, 502
  asymmetric, 87
  incentives and, 550–558 (*see also* incentives,
    information and)
  public information campaign, 362–363, 499–503
information campaign, 499–500
initial distribution of agricultural landholdings, on
    growth, 447
initial distribution of income
  in credit-constrained economy, 415b–416b
  on growth and subsequent distribution, 413
  inequality, on future wealth, 415b–416b, 416f
initial distribution of wealth
  on growth, 456
  on growth, inequality, 455–456
  on growth, long-run, 421
  persistence, 87
  on poverty reduction, 435
in-kind transfers, 96, 569
innovation error term, 300b
insider-outsider labor market model, 417
Institute for Research on Poverty, 96
institutions. *see also* International Financial
    Institutions (IFIs); poor institutions trap;
    specific types
  aid, policies, and, 529–546 (*see also* aid, policies,
    and institutions)
  coercive labor, 419
  definition, 408
  on distribution, 41
  good, 539–543, 540f
  growth and distributional change, 408
  inequality, 41, 418
  inequality, causality, 419
  persistently poor, 543–546, 544f
  poor, 539–543, 540f, 541f
  poor institutions trap, 543–546, 544f

poverty and inequality from, 41
  pro-market, 409–410
instrumental variable (IV), 296b, 298, 302b–303b
instrumental variables estimators, 301–304
instrumental variables methods, 296b–297b
insular poverty, 94
insurance
  employment guarantee scheme, 581
  poor, 156b–157b
  social, 34, 53, 64
Integrated Rural Development Projects, 587
intent-to-treat (ITT), 292
interaction effect (I), 252b, 306
inter-country inequality, 318f, 319
interest rate. *see also* rate of interest or correlation
    coefficient (r)
  credit-constrained economy, 415b
  marginal product of capital *vs.*, 394
internal validity, 292
internal validity threats, 292–295
  behavioral responses to evaluation, 294–295
  causal impact, 292
  endogenous interventions, 292–294
  intent-to-treat, 292
  missing data, 292
  misspecification of impact dynamics, 294
  spillover effects, 294
International Bank for Reconstruction and
    Development, 114
International Comparison Program (ICP), 123, 319b
  methodological differences in rounds of,
    320b–321b
  urban bias of, in China PPP, 336b–337b
International Financial Institutions (IFIs), 532
  social protection, 533
  structural adjustment programs, 533
  Washington Consensus, 470, 532–534, 532b,
    536–537
International Food Policy Research Institute survey,
    Philippines, 146–147
International Forum on Globalization, 511
International Income Distribution Database (I2D2),
    352
International Labour Organization, 118
International Monetary Fund (IMF), 114
interpersonal distribution, 84–85
inter-temporal consumption
  behavior, 78b–79b
  choice, Permanent Income Hypothesis, 155b
intimate partner violence, 376–378
intra-cluster correlation, 145b
intrasectoral effects, 253, 254b
invariance
  replication, 231b
  scale, 231b
inverted-U hypothesis, 396–397, 396b–397b
investment. *see also* institutions; *specific types*
  capital-output ratio, 410
  consumption floor, 239

The cover art is an early 19th century etching of a workhouse in London. For centuries, workhouses were an important element of antipoverty policy in England and elsewhere. To receive help, able-bodied people were often obliged to be confined to a workhouse. This was rationalized by economic arguments about incentives and cost-effectiveness. Critics argued that the policy treated innocent people like criminals. The workhouse policy discouraged many people, including some in real need, from seeking help.